Nineteenth-Century
Literature Criticism

Guide to Gale Literary Criticism Series

When you need to review criticism of literary works, these are the Gale series to use:

If the author's death date is: **You should turn to:**

After Dec. 31, 1959   ***CONTEMPORARY LITERARY CRITICISM***
(or author is still living)
                                         for example: Jorge Luis Borges, Anthony Burgess,
                                                  William Faulkner, Mary Gordon,
                                                    Ernest Hemingway, Iris Murdoch

1900 through 1959   ***TWENTIETH-CENTURY LITERARY CRITICISM***

for example: Willa Cather, F. Scott Fitzgerald,
Henry James, Mark Twain, Virginia Woolf

1800 through 1899   ***NINETEENTH-CENTURY LITERATURE CRITICISM***

for example: Fedor Dostoevski, George Sand,
Gerard Manley Hopkins, Emily Dickinson

1400 through 1799   ***LITERATURE CRITICISM FROM 1400 TO 1800***
(excluding Shakespeare)

for example: Anne Bradstreet, Pierre Corneille,
Daniel Defoe, Alexander Pope,
Jonathan Swift, Phillis Wheatley

SHAKESPEAREAN CRITICISM

Shakespeare's plays and poetry

Gale also publishes related criticism series:

CONTEMPORARY ISSUES CRITICISM

Presents criticism on contemporary authors writing
on current issues. Topics covered include the social
sciences, philosophy, economics, natural science, law,
and related areas.

CHILDREN'S LITERATURE REVIEW

Covers authors of all eras. Presents criticism on
authors and author/illustrators who write for the
preschool to junior-high audience.

ISSN 0732-1864

R

Volume 7

Nineteenth-Century Literature Criticism

Excerpts from Criticism of the
Works of Novelists, Poets, Playwrights,
Short Story Writers, Philosophers, and Other
Creative Writers Who Died between 1800
and 1899, from the First Published Critical
Appraisals to Current Evaluations

**Laurie Lanzen Harris
Sheila Fitzgerald**
Editor

Emily B. Tennyson
Associate Editors

 *Gale Research Inc.* · DETROIT · LONDON

STAFF

Laurie Lanzen Harris, Sheila Fitzgerald, *Editors*

Emily B. Tennyson, *Associate Editor*

Cherie D. Abbey, *Senior Assistant Editor*

Melissa Reiff Hug, Jelena Obradovic Kronick, Jeanne M. Lesinski, Patricia Askie Mackmiller,
Janet S. Mullane, Gail Ann Schulte, *Assistant Editors*

Sharon K. Hall, Phyllis Carmel Mendelson, Anna C. Wallbillich, *Contributing Editors*

Lizbeth A. Purdy, *Production Supervisor*
Denise Michlewicz, *Assistant Production Coordinator*
Eric Berger, Paula J. DiSante, Amy Marcaccio, *Editorial Assistants*

Karen Rae Forsyth, *Research Coordinator*
Jeannine Schiffman Davidson, *Assistant Research Coordinator*
Victoria B. Cariappa, Robert J. Hill, Harry Kronick, James A. MacEachern,
Rebecca Nicholaides, Leslie Kyle Schell, Valerie J. Webster, *Research Assistants*

Linda Marcella Pugliese, *Manuscript Coordinator*
Donna D. Craft, *Assistant Manuscript Coordinator*
Colleen M. Crane, Maureen A. Puhl, Rosetta Irene Simms, *Manuscript Assistants*

L. Elizabeth Hardin, *Permissions Supervisor*
Janice M. Mach, *Permissions Coordinator*
Filomena Sgambati, *Permissions Associate*
Patricia A. Seefelt, *Assistant Permissions Coordinator, Illustrations*
Mary M. Matuz, Susan D. Nobles, *Senior Permissions Assistants*
Margaret A. Chamberlain, Josephine M. Keene, *Permissions Assistants*
H. Diane Cooper, Dorothy J. Fowler, Kathy Grell, Virgie T. Leavens,
Yolanda Parker, Diana M. Platzke, Mabel C. Schoening, *Permissions Clerks*
Margaret Mary Missar, Audrey B. Wharton, *Photo Research*

Frederick G. Ruffner, *Publisher*
James M. Ethridge, *Executive Vice President/Editorial*
Dedria Bryfonski, *Editorial Director*
Christine Nasso, *Director, Literature Division*
Laurie Lanzen Harris, *Senior Editor, Literary Criticism Series*

Library of Congress Catalog Card Number 81-6943
ISBN 0-8103-5807-7
ISSN 0732-1864

Printed in the United States of America.

Published simultaneously in the United Kingdom
by Gale Research International Limited
(An affiliated company of Gale Research Inc.)

Contents

Preface

The nineteenth century was a time of tremendous growth in human endeavor: in science, in social history, and particularly in literature. The era saw the development of the novel, witnessed radical changes from classicism to romanticism to realism, and contained intellectual and artistic ideas that continue to inspire authors of our own century. The importance of the writers of the nineteenth century is twofold, for they provide insight into their own time as well as into the universal nature of human experience.

The literary criticism of an era can also give us insight into the moral and intellectual atmosphere of the past, for the criteria by which a work of art is judged reflect current philosophical and social attitudes. Literary criticism takes many forms: the traditional essay, the book or play review, even the parodic poem. Criticism can also be of several types: normative, descriptive, interpretive, textual, appreciative, generic. Collectively, the range of critical response helps us to understand a work of art, an author, an era.

The Scope of the Work

The success of Gale's two current literary series, *Contemporary Literary Criticism (CLC)* and *Twentieth-Century Literary Criticism (TCLC),* which excerpt criticism of creative writing from the twentieth century, suggested an equivalent need among students and teachers of literature of the nineteenth century. Moreover, since the critical analysis of this literature spans almost two hundred years, a vast amount of critical material confronts the student.

Nineteenth-Century Literature Criticism (NCLC) presents significant passages from published criticism on authors who died between 1800 and 1900. The author list for each volume of *NCLC* is carefully compiled to represent a variety of genres and nationalities and to cover authors who are currently regarded as the most important writers of this era as well as those whose contribution to literature and literary history is significant. The truly great writers are rare, and in the intervals between them lesser but genuine artists, as well as writers who enjoyed immense popularity in their own time and in their own countries, are important to the study of nineteenth-century literature. The length of each author's entry is intended to reflect the amount of critical attention the author has received from critics writing in English and from foreign critics in translation. Articles and books that have not been translated into English are excluded. Each author entry represents a historical overview of the critical response to the author's work: early criticism is presented to indicate initial responses, later selections represent any rise or decline in the author's literary reputation. We have also attempted to identify and include excerpts from the seminal essays on each author, and to include recent critical comment providing modern perspectives on the writer. Thus, *NCLC* is designed to serve as an introduction for the student of nineteenth-century literature to the authors of that period and to the most significant commentators on these authors.

NCLC entries are intended to be definitive overviews. In order to devote more attention to each writer, approximately twenty authors are included in each 600-page volume compared with about sixty-five authors in a *CLC* volume of similar size. Because of the great quantity of critical material available on many authors, and because of the resurgence of criticism generated by events such as an author's centennial or anniversary celebration, the republication of an author's works, or publication of a newly translated work or volume of letters, an author may appear more than once. Beginning with Volume 7, one or two author entries in each volume of *NCLC* will be devoted to single works by major authors who have appeared previously in the series. Only those individual works that have been the subject of extensive criticism and are widely studied in literature courses will be selected for this in-depth treatment. Fedor Dostoevski's *Crime and Punishment* is the subject of such an entry in *NCLC,* Volume 7.

The Organization of the Book

An author section consists of the following elements: author heading, biographical and critical introduction, principal works, excerpts of criticism (each followed by a bibliographical citation), and an additional bibliography for further reading.

- The *author heading* consists of the author's full name, followed by birth and death dates. The unbracketed portion of the name denotes the form under which the author most commonly wrote. If an author wrote consistently under a pseudonym, the pseudonym will be listed in the author heading and the real name given in parentheses on the first line of the biographical and critical introduction. Also located at the beginning of the biographical and critical introduction are any name variations under which an author wrote, including transliterated forms for authors whose languages use nonroman alphabets. Uncertainty as to a birth or death date is indicated by a question mark.

- A *portrait* of the author is included when available. Beginning with Volume 7, many entries will also feature illustrations, including manuscript pages, letters, book illustrations, and representations of important people, places, and events in an author's life.

- The *biographical and critical introduction* contains background information that elucidates the author's creative output. When applicable, biographical and critical introductions are followed by references to additional entries on the author in past volumes of *NCLC* and in other literary reference series published by Gale Research Company. These include *Dictionary of Literary Biography, Children's Literature Review,* and *Something about the Author.*

- The list of *principal works* is chronological by date of first book publication and identifies genres. In those instances where the first publication was in other than the English language, the title and date of the first English-language edition are given in brackets. Unless otherwise indicated, dramas are dated by the first performance, rather than first publication.

- *Criticism* is arranged chronologically in each author section to provide a perspective on any changes in critical evaluation over the years. In the text of each author entry, titles by the author are printed in boldface type. This allows the reader to ascertain without difficulty the works being discussed. For purposes of easier identification, the critic's name and the publication date of the essay are given at the beginning of each piece of criticism. Unsigned criticism is preceded by the title of the journal in which it appeared. For an anonymous essay later attributed to a critic, the critic's name appears in brackets at the beginning of the excerpt and in the bibliographical citation.

- Important critical essays are prefaced with *explanatory notes* as an additional aid to students using *NCLC.* The explanatory notes provide several types of useful information, including: the reputation of the critic, the importance of a work of criticism, the specific approach of the critic (biographical, psychoanalytic, structuralist, etc.), and the growth of critical controversy or changes in critical trends regarding an author's work. In many cases, these notes include cross-references to related criticism in the author's entry or in the additional bibliography.

- A complete *bibliographical citation* designed to facilitate the location of the original essay or book follows each piece of criticism. An asterisk (*) at the end of the citation indicates that the essay is on more than one author.

- The *additional bibliography* appearing at the end of each author section suggests further reading on the author. In some cases it includes essays for which the editors could not obtain reprint rights. An asterisk (*) at the end of a citation indicates that the essay is on more than one author.

An appendix lists the sources from which material in the volume is reprinted. It does not, however, list every book or periodical consulted for the volume.

Cumulative Indexes

NCLC also includes a cumulative index to authors listing all the authors who have appeared in *Contemporary Literary Criticism, Twentieth-Century Literary Criticism, Nineteenth-Century Literature Criticism,* and *Literature Criticism from 1400 to 1800,* along with cross-references to the Gale series *Children's Literature Review, Authors in the News, Contemporary Authors, Contemporary Authors Autobiography Series, Dictionary of Literary Biography, Something about the Author,* and *Yesterday's Authors of Books for Children.* Users will welcome this cumulated author index as a useful tool for locating an author within the various series. The index, which lists birth and death dates when available, will be particularly valuable for those authors who are identified with a certain period but whose death date causes them to be placed in another, or for those authors whose careers span two periods. For example, Fedor Dostoevski is found in *NCLC,* yet Leo Tolstoy, another major nineteenth-century Russian novelist, is found in *TCLC.*

NCLC also includes a cumulative nationality index to authors. Authors are listed alphabetically by nationality, followed by the volume numbers in which they appear.

A cumulative index to critics is another useful feature of *NCLC.* Under each critic's name are listed the authors on whom the critic has written and the volume and page where the criticism appears.

Acknowledgments

No work of this scope can be accomplished without the cooperation of many people. The editors especially wish to thank the copyright holders of the excerpts included in this volume, the permissions managers of the book and magazine publishing companies for assisting us in securing reprint rights, and the staffs of the Detroit Public Library, University of Michigan Library, and Wayne State University Library for making their resources available to us. We are also grateful to Jeri Yaryan for her assistance with copyright research and Norma J. Merry for her editorial assistance.

Suggestions Are Welcome

The editors welcome the comments and suggestions of readers to expand the coverage and enhance the usefulness of the series.

Authors to Appear in Future Volumes

About, Edmond Francois 1828-1885
Aguilo I. Fuster, Maria 1825-1897
Ainsworth, William Harrison 1805-1882
Aksakov, Konstantin 1817-1860
Aleardi, Aleadro 1812-1878
Alecsandri, Vasile 1821-1890
Alencar, Jose 1829-1877
Alfieri, Vittorio 1749-1803
Alger, Horatio 1834-1899
Allingham, William 1824-1889
Almquist, Carl Jonas Love 1793-1866
Alorne, Leonor de Almeida 1750-1839
Alsop, Richard 1761-1815
Altimirano, Ignacio Manuel 1834-1893
Alvarenga, Manuel Inacio da Silva
  1749-1814
Alvares de Azevedo, Manuel Antonio
  1831-1852
Anzengruber, Ludwig 1839-1889
Arany, Janos 1817-1882
Arene, Paul 1843-1893
Aribau, Bonaventura Carlos 1798-1862
Arjona de Cubas, Manuel Maria de
  1771-1820
Arnault, Antoine Vincent 1766-1834
Arneth, Alfred von 1819-1897
Arnim, Bettina von 1785-1859
Arnold, Thomas 1795-1842
Arriaza y Superviela, Juan Bautista
  1770-1837
Asbjornsen, Peter Christian 1812-1885
Ascasubi, Hilario 1807-1875
Atterbom, Per Daniel Amadeus
  1790-1855
Aubanel, Theodore 1829-1886
Auerbach, Berthold 1812-1882
Augier, Guillaume V.E. 1820-1889
Azeglio, Massimo D' 1798-1866
Azevedo, Guilherme de 1839-1882
Bagehot, Walter 1826-1877
Bakin (pseud. of Takizawa Okikani)
  1767-1848
Bakunin, Mikhail Aleksandrovich
  1814-1876
Banville, Theodore de 1823-1891
Baratynski, Jewgenij Abramovich
  1800-1844
Barnes, William 1801-1886
Batyushkov, Konstantin 1778-1855
Beattie, James 1735-1803
Beckford, William 1760-1844
Becquer, Gustavo Adolfo 1836-1870
Bentham, Jeremy 1748-1832
Beranger, Jean-Pierre de 1780-1857
Berchet, Giovanni 1783-1851
Berzsenyi, Daniel 1776-1836
Black, William 1841-1898
Blair, Hugh 1718-1800
Blake, William 1757-1827

Blicher, Steen Steensen 1782-1848
Bocage, Manuel Maria Barbosa du
  1765-1805
Boratynsky, Yevgeny 1800-1844
Borel, Petrus 1809-1859
Boreman, Yokutiel 1825-1890
Borne, Ludwig 1786-1837
Borrow, George 1803-1881
Botev, Hristo 1778-1842
Bremer, Fredrika 1801-1865
Brinckman, John 1814-1870
Bronte, Emily 1812-1848
Brown, Charles Brockden 1777-1810
Browning, Robert 1812-1889
Buchner, Georg 1813-1837
Burney, Fanney 1752-1840
Campbell, James Edwin 1867-1895
Campbell, Thomas 1777-1844
Carlyle, Thomas 1795-1881
Castelo Branco, Camilo 1825-1890
Castro Alves, Antonio de 1847-1871
Channing, William Ellery 1780-1842
Chatterje, Bankin Chanda 1838-1894
Chivers, Thomas Holly 1807?-1858
Clare, John 1793-1864
Claudius, Matthais 1740-1815
Clough, Arthur Hugh 1819-1861
Cobbett, William 1762-1835
Colenso, John William 1814-1883
Coleridge, Hartley 1796-1849
Coleridge, Samuel T. 1772-1834
Collett, Camilla 1813-1895
Comte, Auguste 1798-1857
Conrad, Robert T. 1810-1858
Conscience, Hendrik 1812-1883
Cooke, Philip Pendleton 1816-1850
Corbiere, Edouard 1845-1875
Cowper, William 1731-1800
Crabbe, George 1754-1832
Crawford, Isabella Valancy 1850-1886
Cruz E Sousa, Joao da 1861-1898
Desbordes-Valmore, Marceline
  1786-1859
Deschamps, Emile 1791-1871
Deus, Joao de 1830-1896
Dickinson, Emily 1830-1886
Dinis, Julio 1839-1871
Dinsmoor, Robert 1757-1836
Dumas, Alexandre (pere) 1802-1870
Dumas, Alexandre (fils) 1824-1895
Du Maurier, George 1834-1896
Dwight, Timothy 1752-1817
Echeverria, Esteban 1805-1851
Eden, Emily 1797-1869
Eichendorff, Joseph von 1788-1857
Eminescy, Mihai 1850-1889
Engels, Friedrich 1820-1895
Espronceda, Jose 1808-1842
Ettinger, Solomon 1799-1855

Euchel, Issac 1756-1804
Ferguson, Samuel 1810-1886
Fernandez de Lizardi, Jose Joaquin
  1776-1827
Fernandez de Moratin, Leandro
  1760-1828
Fet, Afanasy 1820-1892
Feuillet, Octave 1821-1890
Fitzgerald, Edward 1809-1883
Fontane, Theodor 1819-1898
Forster, John 1812-1876
Foscolo, Ugo 1778-1827
Frederic, Harold 1856-1898
Freiligrath, Hermann Ferdinand
  1810-1876
Freytag, Gustav 1816-1895
Gaboriau, Emile 1835-1873
Ganivet, Angel 1865-1898
Garrett, Almeida 1799-1854
Garshin, Vsevolod Mikhaylovich
  1855-1888
Gezelle, Guido 1830-1899
Ghalib, Asadullah Khan 1797-1869
Godwin, William 1756-1836
Goldschmidt, Meir Aron 1819-1887
Goncalves Dias, Antonio 1823-1864
Griboyedov, Aleksander Sergeyevich
  1795-1829
Grigor'yev, Appolon Aleksandrovich
  1822-1864
Groth, Klaus 1819-1899
Grun, Anastasius (pseud. of Anton
  Alexander Graf von Auersperg)
  1806-1876
Guerrazzi, Francesco Domenico
  1804-1873
Gutierrez Najera, Manuel 1859-1895
Gutzkow, Karl Ferdinand 1811-1878
Ha-Kohen, Shalom 1772-1845
Halleck, Fitz-Greene 1790-1867
Harris, George Washington 1814-1869
Hayne, Paul Hamilton 1830-1886
Hazlitt, William 1778-1830
Hebbel, Christian Friedrich 1813-1863
Hebel, Johann Peter 1760-1826
Hegel, Georg Wilhelm Friedrich
  1770-1831
Heiberg, Johann Ludvig 1813-1863
Herculano, Alexandre 1810-1866
Herder, Johann Gottfried 1744-1803
Hernandez, Jose 1834-1886
Hertz, Henrik 1798-1870
Herwegh, Georg 1817-1875
Herzen, Alexander Ivanovich 1812-1870
Hoffman, Charles Fenno 1806-1884
Holderlin, Friedrich 1770-1843
Holmes, Oliver Wendell 1809-1894
Hood, Thomas 1799-1845
Hooper, Johnson Jones 1815-1863

Hopkins, Gerard Manley 1844-1889
Horton, George Moses 1798-1880
Howitt, William 1792-1879
Hughes, Thomas 1822-1896
Imlay, Gilbert 1754?-1828?
Irwin, Thomas Caulfield 1823-1892
Issacs, Jorge 1837-1895
Jacobsen, Jens Peter 1847-1885
Jippensha, Ikku 1765-1831
Kant, Immanuel 1724-1804
Karr, Jean Baptiste Alphonse 1808-1890
Keats, John 1795-1821
Keble, John 1792-1866
Khomyakov, Alexey S. 1804-1860
Kierkegaard, Soren 1813-1855
Kinglake, Alexander W. 1809-1891
Kingsley, Charles 1819-1875
Kivi, Alexis 1834-1872
Klopstock, Friedrich Gottlieb 1724-1803
Koltsov, Alexey Vasilyevich 1809-1842
Kotzebue, August von 1761-1819
Krasicki, Ignacy 1735-1801
Kraszewski, Josef Ignacy 1812-1887
Kreutzwald, Friedrich Reinhold
    1803-1882
Krochmal, Nahman 1785-1840
Krudener, Valeria Barbara Julia de
    Wietinghoff 1766-1824
Lamartine, Alphonse 1790-1869
Lamb, Charles 1775-1834
Lampman, Archibald 1861-1899
Landon, Letitia Elizabeth 1802-1838
Landor, Walter Savage 1775-1864
Larra y Sanchez de Castro, Mariano
    1809-1837
Lautreamont (pseud. of Isodore Ducasse)
    1846-1870
Lebensohn, Micah Joseph 1828-1852
Leconte de Lisle, Charles-Marie-Rene
    1818-1894
Le Fanu, Joseph Sheridan 1814-1873
Lenau, Nikolaus 1802-1850
Leontyev, Konstantin 1831-1891
Leopardi, Giacoma 1798-1837
Leskov, Nikolai 1831-1895
Lever, Charles James 1806-1872
Levisohn, Solomon 1789-1822
Lewes, George Henry 1817-1878
Lewis, Matthew Gregory 1775-1810
Leyden, John 1775-1811
Lobensohn, Micah Gregory 1775-1810
Longstreet, Augustus Baldwin 1790-1870
Lopez de Ayola y Herrera, Adelardo
    1819-1871
Lover, Samuel 1797-1868
Luzzato, Samuel David 1800-1865
Macedo, Joaquim Manuel de 1820-1882
Macha, Karel Hynek 1810-1836
Mackenzie, Henry 1745-1831
Malmon, Solomon 1754-1800
Mangan, James Clarence 1803-1849
Manzoni, Alessandro 1785-1873
Mapu, Abraham 1808-1868
Marii, Jose 1853-1895

Markovic, Svetozar 1846-1875
Martinez de la Rosa, Francisco
    1787-1862
Mathews, Cornelius 1817-1889
McCulloch, Thomas 1776-1843
Merriman, Brian 1747-1805
Meyer, Conrad Ferdinand 1825-1898
Montgomery, James 1771-1854
Moodie, Susanna 1803-1885
Morike, Eduard 1804-1875
Morton, Sarah Wentworth 1759-1846
Muller, Friedrich 1749-1825
Murger, Henri 1822-1861
Nekrasov, Nikolai 1821-1877
Neruda, Jan 1834-1891
Nestroy, Johann 1801-1862
Newman, John Henry 1801-1890
Niccolini, Giambattista 1782-1861
Nievo, Ippolito 1831-1861
Nodier, Charles 1780-1844
Novalis (pseud. of Friedrich von
    Hardenberg) 1772-1801
Obradovic, Dositej 1742-1811
Oehlenschlager, Adam 1779-1850
Oliphant, Margaret 1828-1897
O'Neddy, Philothee (pseud. of
    Theophile Dondey) 1811-1875
O'Shaughnessy, Arthur William
    Edgar 1844-1881
Ostrovsky, Alexander 1823-1886
Paine, Thomas 1737-1809
Parkman, Francis 1823-1893
Patmore, Coventry Kersey Dighton
    1823-1896
Peacock, Thomas Love 1785-1866
Perk, Jacques 1859-1881
Pisemsky, Alexey F. 1820-1881
Pompeia, Raul D'Avila 1863-1895
Popovic, Jovan Sterija 1806-1856
Praed, Winthrop Mackworth 1802-1839
Prati, Giovanni 1814-1884
Preseren, France 1800-1849
Pringle, Thomas 1789-1834
Procter, Adelaide Ann 1825-1864
Procter, Bryan Waller 1787-1874
Pye, Henry James 1745-1813
Quental, Antero Tarquinio de 1842-1891
Quinet, Edgar 1803-1875
Quintana, Manuel Jose 1772-1857
Radishchev, Aleksander 1749-1802
Raftery, Anthony 1784-1835
Raimund, Ferdinand 1790-1836
Reid, Mayne 1818-1883
Renan, Ernest 1823-1892
Reuter, Fritz 1810-1874
Rogers, Samuel 1763-1855
Ruckert, Friedrich 1788-1866
Runeberg, Johan 1804-1877
Rydberg, Viktor 1828-1895
Saavedra y Ramirez de Boquedano,
    Angel de 1791-1865
Sacher-Mosoch, Leopold von 1836-1895
Saltykov-Shchedrin, Mikhail 1826-1892
Satanov, Isaac 1732-1805

Schiller, Friedrich von 1759-1805
Schlegel, August 1767-1845
Schlegel, Karl 1772-1829
Scott, Sir Walter 1771-1832
Scribe, Augustin Eugene 1791-1861
Sedgwick, Catherine Maria 1789-1867
Senoa, August 1838-1881
Shelley, Mary W. 1797-1851
Shelley, Percy Bysshe 1792-1822
Shulman, Kalman 1819-1899
Sigourney, Lydia Howard Huntley
    1791-1856
Silva, Jose Asuncion 1865-1896
Slaveykov, Petko 1828-1895
Slowacki, Juliusz 1809-1848
Smith, Richard Penn 1799-1854
Smolenskin, Peretz 1842-1885
Southey, Robert 1774-1843
Stagnelius, Erik Johan 1793-1823
Staring, Antonie Christiaan
    Wynand 1767-1840
Stendhal (pseud. of Henri Beyle)
    1783-1842
Stifter, Adalbert 1805-1868
Stone, John Augustus 1801-1834
Taine, Hippolyte 1828-1893
Taunay, Alfredo d'Ecragnole 1843-1899
Taylor, Bayard 1825-1878
Tennyson, Alfred, Lord 1809-1892
Terry, Lucy (Lucy Terry Prince)
    1730-1821
Thompson, Daniel Pierce 1795-1868
Thompson, Samuel 1766-1816
Thomson, James 1834-1882
Tiedge, Christoph August 1752-1841
Timrod, Henry 1828-1867
Tommaseo, Nicolo 1802-1874
Tompa, Mihaly 1817-1888
Topelius, Zachris 1818-1898
Turgenev, Ivan 1818-1883
Tyutchev, Fedor I. 1803-1873
Uhland, Ludvig 1787-1862
Valaoritis, Aristotelis 1824-1879
Valles, Jules 1832-1885
Verde, Cesario 1855-1886
Very, Jones 1813-1880
Villaverde, Cirilio 1812-1894
Vinje, Aasmund Olavsson 1818-1870
Vorosmarty, Mihaly 1800-1855
Wagner, Richard 1813-1883
Warren, Mercy Otis 1728-1814
Weisse, Christian Felix 1726-1804
Welhaven, Johan S. 1807-1873
Werner, Zacharius 1768-1823
Wescott, Edward Noyes 1846-1898
Wessely, Nattali Herz 1725-1805
Whitman, Sarah Helen 1803-1878
Whittier, John Greenleaf 1807-1892
Wieland, Christoph Martin 1733-1813
Woolson, Constance Fenimore
    1840-1894
Wordsworth, William 1770-1850
Zhukovsky, Vasily 1783-1852

Hans Christian Andersen

1805-1875

(Also wrote under pseudonym of Villiam Christian Walter). Danish fairy tale writer, poet, short story writer, novelist, travel sketch writer, autobiographer, and dramatist.

Andersen is known as one of the most distinguished writers of fairy tales in literary history. His enduring legacy includes tales such as ''Thumbelina,'' ''The Princess and the Pea,'' and ''The Ugly Duckling,'' which combine folklore with aspects of Andersen's own life. Before Andersen published his stories, fairy tales had been part of the oral tradition of literature passed through generations and recorded in writing only for historical interest. Andersen revitalized and expanded the genre by simplifying the structure and employing conversational language suitable for children. Although Andersen intended the fairy tales for an older audience, he created a blend of wit and whimsy that both young and old readers found appealing. While the fairy tales in the original Danish form are often praised for their moral sophistication, critics note that translations do not aptly capture the subtleties of Andersen's language. Andersen, who wished for greater success as a dramatist than as a children's author, wrote a number of dramas and novels; none of these works, however, was as popular as his fairy tales. He called his children's works ''bagatelles'' and said of himself: ''My goal was to be a poet for all ages and children [alone] could not represent me.''

Andersen was born in Odense, Denmark to a poor shoemaker and his superstitious and uneducated wife. Andersen's father, a religious man who had hoped for a more fulfilling career, encouraged his young son to aspire to a better life. He inspired his son with tales from Danish folklore, as well as with stories about the glamour and opportunities available in a future with the theater or opera. The elder Andersen built his son a puppet theater and encouraged the boy's vivid imagination. Instead of playing with other children, Andersen wrote puppet dramas and designed costumes for his characters. Andersen's mother and paternal grandmother, however, did not approve of the boy's passion for the theater and wanted him to apprentice in a lucrative trade.

In 1819, following his father's death and several attempts at apprentice work, Andersen migrated to Copenhagen where he sought a career in drama and opera. As a young boy without references, Andersen was denied admittance to the Royal Theater and was also rejected by Copenhagen's opera company. However, Jonas Collin, a director of the Royal Theater, was impressed by the youth and felt that he showed promise as a writer. Collin took Andersen into his home, sent him to grammar school, and supported him until he passed the entrance exams to the University of Copenhagen. Andersen remained closely connected with the Collin family and never saw his own family again. Collin became the father-figure Andersen had lost; he was Andersen's confidant, critic, and friend.

Andersen's initial works were inspired by William Shakespeare and Sir Walter Scott; his pseudonym at that time, Villiam Christian Walter, was adopted in homage to the two writers. Although his first works were virtually ignored, in 1829 Andersen won recognition for *Fodreise fra Holmens Canal til*

østpynten af amager, the chronicle of an imaginary journey through Copenhagen. He traveled to Germany in 1831 and composed several poems and travel sketches, but real success came after his migration to Italy in 1833. There, in 1835, Andersen's first successful novel, a disguised autobiography entitled *Improvisatoren (The Improvisatore; or, Life in Italy),* was published and met with encouraging response. Though Andersen wrote many other travel accounts, most notably *I Sverrig (Pictures of Sweden)* and *I Spanien (In Spain),* he achieved little recognition in that genre.

During his stay in Italy, Andersen began his *Eventyr, fortalte for børn (Fairy Tales Told for Children),* the first of four sections that would later be recognized as his most significant work. Included in this initial volume were three adapted tales, ''The Tinderbox,'' ''Little Claus and Big Claus,'' and ''The Princess and the Pea,'' as well as an original story, ''Little Ida's Flowers.'' Although Andersen intended the fairy tales for adults as well as children, he amended the title to ''tales for children'' after critics faulted the simplistic dialogue and style of the stories.

Andersen divided the original tales into two distinct classes: *eventyr* and *historier.* The *eventyr* are stories in which a supernatural element contributes to the fairy tale's outcome; the *historier* are those stories that do not employ a supernatural element. Of all his 168 stories, Andersen's autobiographical sketches are considered to be the most enduring. "The Little Mermaid," "The Nightingale," and "The Steadfast Tin Soldier" reflect Andersen's own unrequited love affairs. "The Ugly Duckling," the story of a homely cygnet who becomes the most beautiful of all swans, is the best loved and most popular of Andersen's autobiographical stories. While some of the fairy tales end happily, many of the stories conclude with a tragic note, often with the death of the main character. These tales, too, indicate the hardships Andersen knew as a child and depict his childlike perception of death as a reward for a difficult life. Many critics have faulted the tragic note in stories designed for children, but Andersen also reflected an optimistic approach to otherwise distressing situations. During his lifetime, Andersen was unpopular in Denmark; his popularity increased however, outside of his native country, and he traveled extensively throughout Germany, Holland, and England. It was not until his health began to fail that Denmark acknowledged him as its national author. He died in Copenhagen in 1875.

In general, Andersen's works have been consistently well received. George Brandes, one of the first prominent critics to recognize Andersen's literary significance, especially commended Andersen's use of conversational language, which distinguished the author from other children's writers. Later, Danish critics such as Elias Bredsdorff and Erik Haugaard praised the uncluttered structure of the tales. Some twentieth-century commentators have considered Andersen's works too disturbing for small children. Despite the objections of several critics, Andersen's fairy tales are still popular today and remain the enduring favorites of children and adults.

(See also *Children's Literature Review,* Vol. 6 and *Yesterday's Authors of Books for Children,* Vol. 1.)

PRINCIPAL WORKS

Ungdoms-Forsøg [as Villiam Christian Walter]   (novel)   1822

Fodreise fra Holmens Canal til østpynten af amager   (travel essay)   1829

Eventyr, fortalte for børn. 2 vols.   (fairy tales)   1835-42
   [*Fairy Tales Told for Children,* 1845]

Improvisatoren   (novel)   1835
   [*The Improvisatore; or, Life in Italy,* 1845]

Kun en spillemand   (novel)   1837
   [*Only a Fiddler,* 1845]

De to baronesser   (novel)   1838
   [*The Two Baronesses,* 1848]

Billedbog uden billeder   (short stories)   1840
   [*Picture Book without Pictures,* 1847]

En digters bazar   (poetry, short stories, and travel essays) 1842
   [*A Poet's Bazaar,* 1846]

Das marchen meine lebens ohne dichtung   (autobiography) 1847
   [*The True Story of My Life,* 1847; also published as *The True Story of My Life* (abridged edition) in *Masterworks of Autobiographies: Digests of Ten Great Classics,* 1946]

I Sverrig   (sketches)   1852
   [*Pictures of Sweden,* 1852]

At voere eller ikker voere   (novel)   1857
   [*To Be or Not To Be,* 1857]

I Spanien   (travel essays)   1863
   [*In Spain,* 1864]

Lykke-Peer   (novel)   1870
   [*Lucky Peer,* 1871]

Samlede voerker. 15 vols.   (fairy tales, short stories, travel essays, novels, and poetry)   1876-80

Eventyr og historier. 5 vols.   (short stories)   1894-1900

Levnedsbog   (autobiography)   1927

The Complete Andersen. 6 vols.   (fairy tales and short stories)   1942-48

Hans Christian Andersen's Fairy Tales   (fairy tales)   1950

THE ATHENAEUM   (essay date 1845)

[*In an early review of* The Improvisatore *the critic finds the novel to be a charming tale with distinctive scenes of Italy.*]

The charm and character of pictures like [those in **'The Improvisatore'**] are sure, we think, to make themselves felt: they have detained us, at all events, so long on the threshold of the story, that we may not attempt to unfold the mysteries of poetry and passion which its inner chambers (so to say) reveal. . . . A poet himself, Andersen has conceived the Poet's nature nobly, as one the gifts whereof should encourage their owner to resist, not to yield—to aspire rather than indulge. How far the spirituality with which he has invested the character be human—above all, how far Italian—we will not pretend to decide. But it gives the tale a charm, and a health and a beauty without impairing, in the slightest degree, the glow, the fervour, and the music of its scenes. We can but further add, that there is a fine discrimination of touch, which other rhapsodists about Italy, less intimately penetrated with its spirit than our author, have failed to acquire. The melancholy solemnity of Rome is admirably distinguished from the fascinating voluptuousness of Naples and the fantastic romance of Venice. In short, it is long since we have met with a novel which has so pleased us; and though something of the spell may lie in individual sympathies, we still expect that **'The Improvisatore'** will speak with welcome music alike to travelled and untravelled—to the former recalling delicious visions, to the latter conjuring up phantoms almost vivid enough to stand in the stead of recollections. We are by no means sure that we here take our last leave of the book. (p. 237)

   A review of "The Improvisatore; or, Life in Italy," in The Athenaeum, *No. 906, March 8, 1845, pp. 235-37.*

[WILLIAM HENRY SMITH]   (essay date 1847)

[*Smith examines the strengths and weaknesses of Andersen's novels and discusses the autobiographical elements of these works.*]

If our readers, we say, have fallen upon [**"The Improvisatore"**], and other novels of Andersen, they have probably passed them by as things belonging to the literary *season:* they have been struck with some passages of vivid description, with touches of genuine feelings, with traits of characters which, though imperfectly delineated, bore the impress of truth; but they have pronounced them, on a whole, to be unfashioned things, but half made up, constructed with no skill, informed by no clear spirit of thought, and betraying a most undisciplined taste.

Such, at least, was the impression their first perusal left upon our mind. Notwithstanding the glimpses of natural feeling and of truthful portraiture which caught our eye, they were so evidently deficient in some of the high qualities which ought to distinguish a writer, and so defaced by abortive attempts at fine writing, that they hardly appeared deserving of a very critical examination, or a very careful study. But now there has lately come into our hands the autobiography of Hans Christian Andersen, **"The True Story of my Life,"** and this has revealed to us so curious an instance of intellectual cultivation, or rather of genius exerting itself without any cultivation at all, and has reflected back so strong a light, so vivid and so explanatory, on all his works, that what we formerly read with a very mitigated admiration, with more of censure than of praise, has been invested with quite a novel and peculiar interest. Moreover, certain tales for children have also fallen into our hands, some of which are admirable. We prophesy them a immortality in the nursery—which is not the worst immortality a man can win—and doubt not but that they have already been read by children, or told to children, in every language of Europe. Altogether Andersen, his character and his works, have thus appeared to us a subject worthy of some attention. (p. 388)

When Andersen writes *for* childhood or *of* childhood, he is singularly felicitous—fanciful, tender, and true to nature. This alone were sufficient to separate him from the crown of common writers. For the rest of his works, if you will look at them kindly, and with a friendly scrutiny, you will find many a natural sentiment vividly reflected. But traces of the higher operations of the intellect, of deep or subtle thought, of analytic power, of ratiocination of any kind, there is absolutely none. If, therefore, his injudicious admirers should insist, without any reference to his origin or culture, on extolling his writings as works submitted, without apology or excuse, to the mature judgment and formed taste—they can only peril the reputation they seek to magnify. They will expose to ridicule and contempt one who, if you allow him a place apart by himself, becomes a subject of kindly and curious regard. If they insist upon his introduction, unprotected by the peculiar circumstances which environ him—we do not say amongst the literary magnates of his time, but even in the broad host of highly cultivated minds, we lose sight of him, or we follow him with something very much like a smile of derision. (p. 389)

Those who have read **"The Improvisatore,"** the most ambitious of the works of Andersen, and by far the most meritorious of his novels, will . . . [recognize the autobiographical] materials of which it has been constructed. His own early career, and his travels into Italy, have been woven together in the story of Antonio. So far from censuring him—as some of his Copenhagen critics appear to have done—for describing himself and the scenes he beheld, we are only surprised when we read **"The True Story of my Life,"** that he has not been able to employ in a still more striking manner, the experience of his singular career. But, as we have already observed, he betrays no habit or power of mental analysis; he has not that introspection which, in the phrase of our poet Daniel, "raises a man above himself," so that Andersen could contemplate Andersen, and combine the impartial scrutiny of a spectator with the thorough knowledge which self can only have of self. So far from censuring him for the frequent use he makes of the materials which his own life and travels afforded him, we could wish that he had never attempted to employ any other. Throughout his novels, whenever he departs from these, he is either common place or extravagant,—or both together, which in our

days, is very possible. If he imitates other writers, it is always their worst manner that he contrives to seize; if he adopts the worn-out resources of preceding novelists, it is always (and in this he may be doing good service) to render them still more palpably absurd and ridiculous then they were before. He has dreams in plenty—his heroes are always dreaming; he has fevered descriptions of the over-excited imagination—a very favourite resource of modern novelists; he has his moral enigmas; and of course he has a witch (Fulvia) who tells fortunes and reads futurity, and reads it correctly, let philosophy or common sense say what it will. His Fulvia affords his readers one gratification; they find her fairly hanged at the end of the book. (pp. 398-99)

"Only a Fiddler" proceeds, in part, on the same plan as **"The Impovisatore."** Here, too, the author has drawn from his own early experience; here, too, we have a poor lad of genius, who will "go through an immense deal of adversity and then become famous;" here too we have the little ugly duck, who, however, was born in a swan's egg. The commencement of the novel is pretty where it treats of the childhood of the hero; but Christian (such is his name) does not win upon our sympathy, and still less upon our respect. We are led to suspect that Christian Andersen himself is naturally deficient in certain elements of character, or he would have better upheld the dignity of his namesake, whom he has clearly no desire to lower in esteem. With an egregious passion for distinction, a great vanity, in short, we are afraid that he himself (judging from some passages in his Autobiography) hardly possesses a proper degree of pride, or the due feeling of self-respect. The Christian in the novel is the butt and laughing-stock of a proud, wilful young beauty of the name of Naomi; yet does he forsake the love of a sweet girl Lucie, to be the beaten spaniel of this Naomi. He has so little spirit as to take her money and her contempt at the same time.

This self-willed and beautiful Naomi is a well-imagined character, but imperfectly developed. Indeed the whole novel may be described as a jumble of ill-connected scenes, and of half-drawn characters. We have some sad imitations of the worst models of our current literature. Here is a Norwegian godfather, the blurred likeness of some Parisian murderer. Here are dreams and visions, and plenty of delirium. He has caught the tricks, perhaps, from some of our English novelists, of infusing into

Illustration from "Thumbelina," one of the most enduring of Andersen's fairy tales. By Gordon Browne, 1895.

the persons of his drama all sorts of distorted imaginations, by way of describing the situation he has placed them in. (p. 403)

"O. T." commenses in a more lively style . . . but soon becomes in fact the dullest and most wearisome of the three. During a portion of this novel he seems to have taken for his model of narrative the "Wilhelm Meister" of Goethe; but the calm domestic manner which is tolerable in the clear-sighted man, who we know can rise nobly from it when he pleases, accords ill enough with the bewildered, most displeasing, and half intelligible story which Andersen has here to relate. (p. 405)

> [*William Henry Smith*], *"Works of Hans Christian Andersen,"* in Blackwood's Edinburgh Magazine, *Vol. LXII, No. CCCLXXXIV, October, 1847, pp. 387-406.*

THE DUBLIN UNIVERSITY MAGAZINE (essay date 1855)

[In Andersen's **"The Improvisatore"**] his temperament found vent, and we are presented with a book which, for rich and brilliant word-painting, has not its equal in the whole range of literature. Italy in body and soul is evoked, and passes before our vision as clearly, as truthfully, as captivatingly, as though we literally were amid and beheld the scenes and people depicted. . . . The fervid glow pervading this book is indescribable. It is a perfect treasury of enthusiasm—of prose-poetry—of exquisite sensibility—of luxuriant imagination—of unchecked delight in all around. . . .

[Andersen's **"Eventyr,"** or **"Fairy Tales,"**] have from the first met with universal favour. They have appeared under different titles in many languages, and the author yet continues the series from time to time. He, in fact, is quite unrivalled for power in rivetting the attention of children by his fascinating little stories. He himself says that "children are most amused with new expressions, and being spoken to in an unusual manner." This, however, would by no means explain satisfactorily the secret of his power of charming them. We rather would attribute it to the soul of goodness that shines in such a transparent manner through all that he writes. Children are acute critics in these matters. They can intuitively distinguish between tinsel and pure gold—between simulated sensibility and goodness, and the genuine thing. Then his style is so genial, so winning; his words are so happily chosen, that every sentence is a picture instinct with life. Yes, Andersen is the prince of fairy lore and story-telling, in the estimation of children of every growth. (p. 609)

In 1837 appeared his celebrated novel of **"Only a Fiddler"**—a powerful, but, to us individually, a painfully interesting work, which we cannot take up and glance over without feeling very sad, and almost regretful that Andersen gave it to the world. Nevertheless this work is perhaps the most popular with his countrymen of any that has proceeded from his pen. . . .

Like all Andersen's fictions, [**"Only a Fiddler"**] can hardly be said to have a plot, although it is by no means devoid of artistic construction and development. Its chief characters are drawn so strongly and so clearly, that they stand forth like portraits on which the sunlight falls. The pictures presented of Danish country life and customs are vividly drawn, and faithful as though produced by the daguerreotype. Andersen, in fact, is throughout the book reproducing the scenery and recollections of his own early life. The father of the hero is just Andersen's own father—the terrible early struggles of the gifted but unhappy Fiddler are those of Andersen himself in his own

individuality. He says that he wrote it after much thought, and certainly it is full of splendid passages, and vigorous from first to last. Andersen's novels are comparatively so little known and understood in England, that, perhaps, we should only weary the reader were we to analyse them at any length; but we may be permitted to express our opinion, that they are well deserving of careful perusal by all who appreciate artistic delineation of character, and exquisitely truthful and vivid pictures of nature. (p. 610)

[**"A Poet's Bazaar"**] is a spirited, enthusiastic work, and seems to mark the era in which the author's style became permanently fixed and determined, for he has never swerved from it since. It is totally different from all ordinary books of travel—giving little or no information of a practical character, and entirely ignoring the every-day scenes and lions. It is a gallery hung with pictures, each separate and complete in itself, yet each a link of a chain, looped up with graceful negligence. Many of these pictures—for such they truly are—teem with vivid fancies, and are brilliant specimens of what is called word-painting. A more consummate master of words than Andersen, and one who knows how to use them with more felicitous effect, does not exist. The subject chosen by him to exercise the witcheries of his genius upon is of little consequence; for whether he writes a chapter about the Alps, or about *his old boots* (which he actually has done in the **"Bazaar"**), we are almost equally carried away with him at his potent will and pleasure. Yes, he is a great enchanter! (pp. 611-12)

Andersen does not possess a sufficient combination of powers to enable him to produce any work of epical compass; he is by no means Shakspearian in genius. His most ambitious poem, **"Ashauerus,"** to produce which he had read and studied intensely, sufficiently evinces this. In dramatic talent also he falls immeasurably short of his countryman, Oehlenschlaeger, and appears to advantage only in such humorous trifles as **"Ole Luck-Oin"** (*Ole Shut-Eye*). But his short lyrics, written on the inspiration of the moment, and founded on incidents drawn chiefly from every-day life, may be pronounced masterly of their kind.

Again, in his prose writings we are not called on to admire any very comprehensive grasp of intellect, no profound and subtle philosophical acumen; nothing at all exciting in incident nor enthralling in interest; no attempt whatever to command attention by startling disquisitions or brilliant declamation; nothing at all indicative at a first glance of something far beyond ordinary story-telling. Perhaps the reader, who for the first time in his life holds a volume by Andersen in his hand, may hastily turn over its pages with a perplexed and disappointed air; but let him fairly commence a quiet perusal, and he will quickly cease to marvel at the reputation the writer has acquired, and will find himself unable to resist the charm thrown over the most homely and apparently unattractive subject by the very peculiar genius of the gentle Dane. He will first admire the astonishingly affluent imagery, the genial, playful fancy, and unaffected poetical powers of the author; and next he will irresistibly be drawn to love him for his pure, healthy morality, warm-heartedness, and deep feeling of appreciation for all that is good and ennobling. Moreover, he will recognise a literally unrivalled power of word-painting, a prodigious effluence of felicitous phrases and expressions, and a mode of treating all subjects as fascinating as it is original and indescribable. All these qualities combined render him one of the most delightful companions for a quiet hour, when the heart is disposed to commune with a kindred spirit, that we could name in the whole range of literature. His beautiful fairy-tales charm the child; his sweet and truly exquisite poetic fancies gratify all who derive pleasure from the sparkling freaks of a most vivid, yet tender imagination; and the melodious utterances in which he embodies his more serious and solemn thoughts and reflections at once delight and instruct the thoughtful and mature reader.

If we might venture to attempt an allegory, we should not compare Andersen's writings to a broad, deep, majestic stream, itself the recipient of a hundred minor streams in its steady course to the ocean; yet less should we compare them to an impetuous mountain torrent, leaping franticly from crag to crag, foaming, and roaring, and vexing the still air with its rolling mists, until it loses itself in the black waters of some sullen lake, deeply imbedded amid frowning rocks; but we would rather compare them to a pellucid stream, gently flowing adown a verdant hill-side, reflecting every sunbeam, singing a pleasant under-song throughout its fanciful course, and ever and anon breaking up in sparkling dimples, or joyously bubbling around some water-worn stone. (pp. 617-18)

[Andersen] is undoubtedly an enthusiast of his kind, and he sings whatever his own heart prompts, without hesitation or reserve. He undeniably is original to a remarkable degree, but there is no affectation whatever in that originality, and it always evinces itself within the bounds of good taste. One thing may be said alike of the man and his writings—both personally and in them he evinces a sort of restlessness. His mind is so full of fancies, so overflowing with quaint and novel ideas, that it seems incapable of settling down for any length of time to work out a great subject in the calm, persistent manner its importance would demand. His pen appears ever eager to dash off one theme, only to fly to another, and treat it so in turn. He is incapable of deliberately sitting down to a task which will chain him to its thorough development for a lengthened period, and call into calm and continuous exertion his best and highest powers. Thus we see, in all his largest works, that he presents us with a gallery of most delightful *cabinet* pictures, which do not illustrate in unbroken order any given subject or leading idea, but are, so to speak, quite separate and independent of each other, and possess little more connexion and relation than that which arises from bearing a certain family likeness—a certain and unmistakable imprint of having been produced by the same master-hand. Even in his most elaborate novels, we plainly see that it costs him the greatest effort to keep strictly to his subject; in fact, he does not and cannot do so, but presents all in an episodical form. Again, his books of travel are *not* books of travel in the common acceptation of the word: they are rather reminiscences of all sorts of things, scenes, and ideas of a poetical and attractive nature; but all are dressed up in such a charming garb, that no one can quarrel with the author for his wayward fancies, and peculiar mode of conveying his ideas and recollections of foreign lands. As to anything in the shape of dry detail, of mere facts and figures, he shuns it with horror. And the man himself is quite as discursive, restless, and fanciful as his pen. He is a real *Wandernde Vogel*—a wandering bird, and as essentially migratory in his habits as are the storks, which he so delights to introduce in every book he has written. (pp. 618-19)

[Andersen] is an author whom of all others we should carry with us as a companion in our light, cheerful rambles through the fields, and by the river's bank, or the shell-strewn seashore, or in the open sunny glades of the forest, where birds are flitting to and fro, and the cooing of the stock-dove and the hum of animated nature fills the air. We should then enjoy the beauties of the landscape, the odour of the flowers, the twittering of the birds, the rustling of the long green grass, and the murmuring of the bubbling rivulet, with increased intensity, for *he* would teach us how to find hitherto hidden charms in all around, and would stand forth an eloquent interpreter between us and nature. . . .

We are inclined to reckon ["**Pictures of Sweden**"] as the most delightful book he ever wrote, always excepting his own autobiography. Like the "**Poet's Bazaar**," it is not a regular book of travels, but a number of episodical chapters, scarcely connected together; and yet, as we happen to know, Andersen was excessively fastidious in their arrangement, with a view to consecutive reading—though why he was so we do not clearly perceive, for several of the chapters have no more connexion with Sweden than with China. There are also some passages scarcely worthy of Andersen; but, taking it altogether, it is an embodiment of all his excellencies of style and tone, and some parts are of transcendent beauty. (p. 619)

We cannot name any book whatever that, in our opinion, contains such brilliant examples of a great writer's mastery over the art of "word-painting" as the "**Pictures of Sweden.**" It is the bouquet of all the author's works. Imagination, fancy, humour, deep insight into the springs of human affections, are all blended together so as to form a genial, radiant, fascinating book, which it is impossible to read without loving the gentle, large-hearted author, even if you knew no more of him than that book reveals. (pp. 619-20)

As the touch of Midas transmutes all things into gold, so does that of Andersen all things into poesy. He takes a stalk of flax, a tree, a flower, or even a solitary blade of grass growing in a barren, thirsty soil, and endows it with eloquent language, with melodious utterance of charming thoughts; and yet we cannot smile, and say, this is a childish conceit, for we feel and know that a profound moral truth or wise counsel is symbolised in the beautifully-worded allegory. There is a *purpose* in the most seemingly fanciful and fantastic of his conceptions—another meaning than what prominently meets the eye, and the youngest of his readers is aware of this. No living author has so perseveringly and successfully laboured to show us that the elements of the richest poetry, and a soul of goodness, dwell in every thing that surrounds us, as Andersen. He invests the most common productions in nature, and the meanest and most familiar domestic objects, with a halo of poesy, and we glow with pleasure, and wonder that we never appreciated the real loveliness and spiritual symbolism of all created things, till he, the magician, unveiled all before us, and bade us rejoice and thank God for the innumerable gifts and blessings that fill the earth for our use and delight! Say, do we not owe a deep dept of gratitude to the man who, with resistless eloquence, and in all sincerity of purpose, strives to enable us to better appreciate all visible things—strives, with yearning heart and soul, to induce us to love God and one another better than we do—strives to purify us, to gladden and ennoble us by gentlest, sweetest teachings—strives to eschew the evil, and to search out only the good, and true, and beautiful, in nature and in man—strives to impart to us all a portion of his own genial faith and sensibility, so that we may become happy even as he is himself? Say, what does this man deserve of his fellows? He is a poet, a true poet, and a great poet, and he would have us all be poets also, for he knows there are the elements of poetry inherent in every man, although unto very few is given the faculty to adequately express what they feel. He would have us all participate in that exquisite enjoyment of the works of creation which is the poet's birthright—a birthright that kings can neither give nor take away. He would have us live somewhat more after the fashion that the Almighty designed, when He bade man replenish the earth with his kind. Say, then, reader, hath this man—this prescient poet—lived altogether in vain in his generation, and shall his name perish with his body on earth? We trow not.

Andersen writes not as philosophers write; he does not group facts and figures, and make scientific deductions therefrom; but he has, nevertheless, hymned the power and glory of scientific skill (as exemplified in the steam-engine) in a recent work, in a way that proves he may yet become the Poet of Science, *par excellence,* even as he is already the Poet of Nature. (pp. 621-22)

Andersen's strength lies in his vivid imagination, his sweet quaint fancy, his impassioned feeling, his keen perception of the beautiful, his loving heart, and his fascinating gift of writing a species of prose-poetry in a style of unapproachable eloquence. The heart of man is his empire; our best aspirations and affections are the strings of the harp whereon he plays with such masterly skill. His own heart is the source of his inspiration—and to appeal to and move the hearts of others is his object. Poetry is as natural to him as the odour to the rose; and it is ever uttered in melodious and happily chosen words. (p. 622)

Andersen's mind is stored with picturesque legends, and he is exceedingly well read in the old *sagas,* and in the chronicles of his country. These he occasionally introduces and details, after his own fashion, in his writings, with such a vivid, startling effect, that we have often wished he would undertake a history, or a consecutive series of annals of Scandinavia in the remote ages. He could depict the ancient Vikings—their warriors and skalds, their battlings and their feastings, their life in the field and in the hall, so that they would almost seem to us to be bodily resuscitated, and their era returned again, in the great cycle of change. What he is capable of doing in this style may easily be seen by referring to some of the historical chapters in the **"Pictures of Sweden."** There is no mysticism, no obscurity, in what Andersen writes; whatever the subject, all is clear: all can be understood by the merest child, for each sentence is rendered luminous by the light of genius. (pp. 622-23)

"Hans Christian Andersen, His Life and Writings," in The Dublin University Magazine, *Vol. XLV, No. CCLXIX, May, 1855, pp. 605-23.*

HANS CHRISTIAN ANDERSEN   (essay date 1855)

[*In his autobiography,* The Story of My Life, *Andersen discusses his own perceptions of his writings. He says that he wrote as children might speak, and his style reflects spoken, rather than written, language. However, Andersen adds that his works were written to entertain adults as well as children. In fact, Andersen states that the fairy tales were called tales for children solely to explain their simple style and to avert unfavorable criticism. Parts of the work excerpted below were originally published in Danish as Andersen's* Mit Livs Eventyr *in 1855.*]

In the volume which I first published, [**"Eventyr, fortalte for børn"**], I had . . . related old stories, which I had heard as a child. The tone in which they still sounded in my ears seemed a very natural one to me, but I knew very well that the learned critics would censure the style of talk, so, to quiet them I called

them **"Wonder Stories told for Children,"** although my intention was that they should be for both young and old. (pp. 203-04)

I had written my narrative down upon paper exactly in the language, and with the expressions in which I had myself related them, by word of mouth, to the little ones, and I had arrived at the conviction that people of different ages were equally amused with them. The children made themselves merry for the most part over what might be called the actors; older people, on the contrary, were interested in the deeper meaning. The stories furnished reading for children and grown people; and that assuredly is a difficult task for those who will write children's stories. They met with open doors and open hearts in Denmark; everybody read them. I now removed the words, "told for children," from my title, and published three volumes of **"New Stories,"** all of which were of my own invention, and were received in my own country with the greatest favor. I could not wish it greater; I felt a real anxiety in consequence, a fear of not being able to justify afterward such an honorable award of praise.

A refreshing sunshine streamed into my heart; I felt courage and joy, and was filled with a living desire of still more and more developing my powers in this direction,—of studying more thoroughly this class of writing, and of observing still more attentively the rich wells of nature out of which I must create it. If attention be paid to the order in which my stories are written, it certainly will be seen that there is in them a gradual progression, a clearer working out of the idea, a greater discretion in the use of agency, and, if I may so speak, a more healthy tone and a more natural freshness may be perceived.

As one step by step toils up a steep hill, I had at home climbed upward, and now beheld myself recognized and honored; appointed a distinct place in the literature of any country. This recognition and kindness at home atoned for all the hard words that the critics had spoken. Within me was clear sunshine; there came a sense of rest, a feeling that all, even the bitter in my life, had been needful for my development and my fortune. (pp. 204-05)

Hans Christian Andersen, in his The Story of My Life, *Houghton Mifflin Company, 1871?, 569 p.*

ELIZABETH BARRETT BROWNING   (poem date 1861)

[*A leading poet in Victorian England, Browning is best known for her cycle of love poetry,* Sonnets from the Portuguese. *The following poem, written in 1861, was inspired by Andersen, who visited the Browning family during his travels in Italy.*]

'Now give us lands where the olives grow,'
   Cried the North to the South,
'Where the sun with a golden mouth can blow
Blue bubbles of grapes down a vineyard row!'
   Cried the North to the South.

'Now give us men from the sunless plain,'
   Cried the South to the North,
'By need of work in the snow and the rain,
Made strong, and brave by familiar pain!'
   Cried the South to the North.

'Give lucider hills and intenser seas,'
   Said the North to the South,

'Since ever by symbols and bright degrees
Art, childlike, climbs to the dear Lord's knees,'
    Said the North to the South.

'Give strenuous souls for belief and prayer,'
    Said the South to the North,
'That stand in the dark on the lowest stair,
While affirming of God, 'He is certainly there,''
    Said the South to the North.

'Yet oh, for the skies that are softer and higher!'
    Sighed the North to the South;
'For the flowers that blaze, and the trees that aspire,
And the insects made of a song or a fire!'
    Sighed the North to the South.

'And oh, for a seer to discern the same!'
    Sighed the South to the North;
'For a poet's tongue of baptismal flame,
To call the tree or the flower by its name!'
    Sighed the South to the North.

The North sent therefore a man of men
    As a grace to the South;
And thus to Rome came Andersen.
—'Alas, but must you take him again?'
    Said the South to the North.

(pp.195-97)

*Elizabeth Barrett Browning, "The North and the South
(The Last Poem)," in her* Last Poems, *James Miller,
1863, pp. 195-97.*

THE ATHENAEUM (essay date 1864)

[*Comparing Andersen's travel book on Spain with his work on
Italy, the reviewer notes that* In Spain *lacks the "felicity of observation and touch" that characterizes the Italian sketches.*]

Writing books of travel becomes a craft like everything else,
one into which something of study and super-subtlety is apt to
enter as years go on, and the freshness of life and spirit fades
away. There is no repeating the first sight of the sea—the first
Alp—the first awe of the Coliseum—the first entry into
Venice. . . .

We have been insensibly thrown back among these truisms by
reading Herr Andersen's Spanish experiences [in his book **'In
Spain'**], as compared with the Italian pictures in that delicious
book **'The Improvisatore.'** It may not be his fault so much as
Time's (or ours) that we fancy more effort in this than in that
record of strange sights in strange places. Certainly, too, Spain
requires more preparation than Italy. The latter land, with its
wonders, has been a cradle-word with most of us. Spain (though
the country holds those who know it with a spell not to be
outdone in strength,—though it is full of matchless surprises,
making a Northern feel, as in Toledo, Cordova, Seville, Gran-
ada, Elche, that the East and the South have come together to
prepare shows royal and peculiar in their munificence) has been
less talked of—less thought of. It might be asserted, without
much chance of error, that with ninety out of a hundred tourists
the list of preparatory expectations on the strength of which
they cross the Pyrenees is made up of a bull-fight, Don Quixote,
some notion of an *olla podrida,* and a gipsy dance with cas-
tanets. Such, of course, cannot have been altogether Herr Andersen's case; yet, somehow, we do not feel that his heart is
in his subject as it was in his Italian books. . . . Nevertheless,

the book has its pictures,—some bright and minutely touched.
(p. 769)

It may belong to the "hour on the clock" that Herr Andersen
shows himself somewhat more querulous in regard to the inconveniences of Spanish travel than he used to do. The recollection of these things—the suffocating dust—the parching
glare—the poor wayside food—the shrieks and grunts of the
mule-drivers—how feebly do they figure as compared with an
evening at the Escurial, or any of the views from the platform
on which Toledo is perched,—or the wealth of unfamiliar treasure which the lover of painting will find in the Madrid Gallery,
or the fragrant gardens of the Generalife! Then, too, Herr
Andersen, handed about as he was from Dane to Dane, seems
hardly to have sufficiently appreciated a marking feature of
Spanish travel, which at least has registered itself with pleasant
distinctness on our memory—the courtesy, clear of sycophancy
or rapacity, which every traveller willing to be pleased will
find among the common people. A hundred instances of this
rise up without prompting as we write,—memories entirely
apart from any French, or German, or Italian experiences. But
enough: since what has been said will convey our impression
that Herr Andersen has not "hit off" Spain with his usual
felicity of observation and touch. (p. 770)

A review of "In Spain," in The Athenaeum, *No.
1910, June 4, 1864, pp. 769-70.*

THE ATHENAEUM (essay date 1864)

Herr Andersen, king of the minnows or little folk, is well
known in England: his writings are loved by thousands of tiny
people, whose laughter rings and whose tears flow at every
true magician's bidding. He is the Santa Claus of the singers.
Himself unseen, he sweeps quietly down the chimneys of our
English home, puts bonnie dreams into the little golden heads
asleep, and freshens the cheek with his healthy kiss. Well may
the worthy citizens of Copenhagen cry "God bless Hans Christian Andersen," and watch him with a gratitude which paternal
and maternal love has spiritualized into religion. To full-grown
readers . . . Andersen is but a pigmy—the writer of infinites-
imal *pretty* things, the warbler of dulcet tweedledum and twee-
dledee; but this is a mistaken view. Intellectually speaking, he
is not a giant. . . . But better be monarch of Lilliputians than
hewer of wood and drawer of water to the Titans. As a writer
for children, Andersen is positively without an equal. His successes in that direction are, however, too well known to need
more than passing mention here. Rather let us turn to his
"Samlede Digte," a collection of lyric poems, dedicated to his
friend, Oehlenschläger. Here all sorts of innocent subjects are
nicely treated, to the delight of the homely Danish public. . . .

It is one of those trifles . . . in which Danish literature abounds—
a gossamer which, though light as air, shows how the wind
blows. The Danish poets like this sort of trifling, and are
encouraged so to do by the public at large. With all its puerilities, it is healthy—healthier, perhaps, then all the cold Ger-
manisms of would-be Goethes. Danish humour, we fancy, is
fairly represented by the light touches of Hans Andersen. It is
a humour which delights in detail and practical joking, and
which ever avoids the sin of Scottish "wut"—that of plunging
into what Sydney Smith called the "abstract." Thus, its points
are unmistakable. Nothing resembles Danish humour so much
as the right way of telling a story to children. There must be
no wandering, no prevaricating; everything must be clear, concise, realizable; and the smile on the face must cast a sunshine

and tenderness that pervades them, the perfect yet not over-subtle dramatic insight, the democratic sympathy with all things in adverse and humble circumstances, and their exquisite freshness of invention that characterise them most, and set them on so lofty a height above the best of other modern stories for children. The style in which they are composed is one never before used in writing; it is the lax, irregular, direct language of children that Andersen uses, and it is instructive to notice how admirably he has gone over his earlier writings and weeded out every phrase that savours of pedantry or contains a word that a child cannot learn to understand. . . .

In character, Andersen was one of the most blameless of human creatures. A certain irritability of manner that almost amounted to petulance in his earlier days, and which doubtless arose from the sufferings of his childhood, became mellowed as years went on into something like the sensitive and pathetic sweetness of a dumb animal. There was something in his whole appearance that claimed for him immunity from the rough ways of the world, a childlike trustfulness, a tremulous and confiding affectionateness that appealed directly to the sympathy of those around. (p. 169)

> *Edmund W. Gosse, "Hans Christian Andersen," in* The Academy, *n.s. Vol. VIII, No. 171, August 14, 1875, pp. 168-69.*

From Andersen's "The Little Mermaid." This illustration depicts the rescue of the prince who has fallen into the ocean. The mermaid relinquishes her immortality for the love of the prince. By Gordon Browne, 1895?

over all. In fact, the good Danes seem to like to be treated like children: they really enjoy their literary sugar-plums, and praise the confectioner. They are simple, gentle, fresh, hearty, yet stubborn withal, and they never forget their school days. (p. 456)

> *A review of "Danske Romanzer, hundrede og ti" and "Nordens Guder," in* The Athenaeum, *No. 1928, October 8, 1864, pp. 455-57.**

EDMUND W. GOSSE   (essay date 1875)

[*A distinguished English literary historian, critic, and biographer, Gosse wrote extensively on seventeenth- and eighteenth-century English literature. He is also credited with introducing the works of Norwegian dramatist Henrik Ibsen and other Scandinavian writers to English readers. In the following essay on Andersen's fairy tales, Gosse praises Andersen's natural style and his "extraordinary genius."*]

Among all his multitudinous writings, it is of course [Andersen's] so-called Fairy Tales, his *Eventyr,* that show most distinctly his extraordinary genius. No modern poet's work has been so widely disseminated throughout the world as these stories of Andersen's. . . . It is the simple earnestness, humour

GEORG BRANDES   (essay date 1883)

[*Brandes, a Danish literary critic and biographer, was the principal leader of the intellectual movement that helped to bring an end to Scandinavian cultural isolation. He believed that literature reflects the spirit and the problems of its time, and that it must be understood within its social and aesthetic context. Brandes's major critical work,* Hovedstremninger i det 19de Aarhundredes Litteratur *(Main Currents in Nineteenth-Century Literature), won him admiration for his ability to view literary movements within the broader context of all of European literature. Brandes is considered the first prominent scholar to write extensively on Andersen. The following discussion initially appeared in Danish in Brandes's* Det moderne gjennembruds maend *(Creative Spirits in the Nineteenth Century), which was first published in 1883. Considered one of the most significant examples of Andersen scholarship, the essay indicates Brandes's favorable appraisal of Andersen's works. In particular, Brandes praises Andersen's ability to depict animals in a human light and to write as a child might speak.*]

[In Andersen's stories we find that the] construction, the position of the words in individual sentences, the entire arrangement, is at variance with the simplest rules of syntax. "This is not the way people write." That is true; but it is the way they speak. To grown people? No, but to children; and why should it not be proper to commit the words to writing in the same order in which they are spoken to children? In such a case the usual form is simply exchanged for another; not the rules of abstract written language, but the power of comprehension of the child is here the determining factor; there is method in this disorder, as there is method in the grammatical blunder of the child when it makes use of a regular imperfect for an irregular verb. . . . [Andersen] has the bold intention to employ oral speech in a printed work, he will not write but speak, and he will gladly write as a school-child writes, if he can thus avoid speaking as a book speaks. (p. 2)

Happy, indeed, is Andersen! What author has such a public as he?. . . His stories are numbered among the books which we have deciphered syllable by syllable, and which we still read to-day. There are some among them whose letters even now, seem to us larger, whose words appear to have more value than all others, because we first made their acquaintance letter by letter and word by word. (p. 4)

The starting-point for this art is the child's play that makes everything out of everything; in conformity with this, the sportive mood of the artist transforms playthings into natural creations, into supernatural beings, into heroes, and, *vice versa,* uses everything natural and everything supernatural—heroes, sprites, and fairies—for playthings, that is to say, for artistic means which through each artistic combination are remodelled and freshly stamped. The nerve and sinew of the art is the imagination of the child, which invests everything with a soul, and endows everything with personality; thus, a piece of household furniture is as readily animated with life as a plant, a flower as well as a bird or a cat, and the animal in the same manner as the doll, the portrait, the cloud, the sunbeam, the wind, and the seasons. . . . This is the way a child dreams, and this is the way a poet depicts to us the dream of a child. The soul of this poetry, however, is neither the dream nor the play; it is a peculiar, ever-childlike, yet at the same time a more than childlike faculty, not only for putting one thing in the place of another (thus, for making constant exchange, or for causing one thing to live in another, thus for animating all things), but also a faculty for being swiftly and readily reminded by one thing of another, for regaining one thing in another, for generalizing, for moulding an image into a symbol, for exalting a dream into a myth, and through an artistic process, for transforming single fictitious traits into a focus for the whole of life. . . . A form that for any one else would be a circuitous route to the goal, a hindrance and a disguise, becomes for Andersen a mask behind which alone he feels truly free, truly happy and secure. His child-like genius, like the well-known child forms of antiquity, plays with the mask, elicits laughter, awakens delight and terror. Thus the nursery story's mode of expression, which with all its frankness is masked, becomes the natural, indeed, the classic cadence of his voice, that but very rarely becomes overstrained or out of tune. The only disturbing occurrence is that now and then a draught of whey is obtained instead of the pure milk of the nursery story, that the tone occasionally becomes too sentimental and sickly sweet (**"Poor John," "The Poor Bird," "Poor Thumbling"**), which, however, is rarely the case in materials taken from folk-lore tales, as **"The Tinder-Box," "Little Claus and Big Claus,"** etc., where the naïve joviality, freshness, and roughness of the narrative, which announces crimes and murders without the slightest sympathetic or tearful phrase, stand Andersen in good stead, and invest his figures with increased sturdiness. Less classic, on the other hand, is the tone of the lyric effusions interwoven with some of the nursery stories, in which the poet, in a stirring, pathetic prose gives a bird's-eye view of some great period of history (**"The Thorny Path of Honor," "The Swan's Nest"**). In these stories there seems to me to be a certain wild flight of fancy, a certain forced inspiration in the prevailing tone, wholly disproportionate to the not very significant thought of the contents; for thought and diction are like a pair of lovers. Thought may be somewhat larger, somewhat loftier, than diction, even as the man is taller than the woman; in the opposite case there is something unlovely in the relation. With the few exceptions just indicated, the narrative style of Andersen's nursery stories is a model of its kind. (pp. 5-8)

Now what is there in plants, in animals, in the child, so attractive to Andersen? He loves the child because his affec-

tionate heart draws him to the little ones, the weak and helpless ones to whom it is allowable to speak with compassion, with tender sympathy, and because when he devotes such sentiments to a hero,—as in **"Only a Fiddler,"** —he is derided for it. . . . but when he dedicates them to a child, he finds the natural resting-place for his mood. It is owing to his genuine democratic feeling for the lowly and neglected that Andersen, himself a child of the people, continually introduces into his nursery stories (as Dickens, in his novels), forms from the poorer classes of society, "simple folk," yet endowed with the true nobility of the soul. . . . The poor are as defenseless as the child. Furthermore, Andersen loves the child, because he is able to portray it, not so much in the direct psychologic way of the romance,—he is by no means a direct psychologist,—as indirectly, by transporting himself with a bound into the child's world, and he acts as though no other course were possible. . . . He seldom introduces the child into his nursery stories as taking part in the action and conversation. He does it most frequently in the charming little collection **"A Picture-Book without Pictures"** where more than anywhere else he permits the child to speak with the entire simplicity of its nature. In such brief, naïve child-utterances as those cited in it there is much pleasure and entertainment. . . . Yet his child forms are comparatively rare. The most noteworthy ones are little Hjalmar, little Tuk, Kay and Gerda, the unhappy, vain Karen in **"The Red Shoes,"** a dismal but well-written story, the little girl with the matches and the little girl in **"A Great Sorrow,"** finally Ib and Christine, the children in **"Under the Willow-Tree."** Besides these real children there are some ideal ones, the little fairy-like Thumbling and the little wild robber-maiden, undoubtedly Andersen's freshest child creation, the masterly portrayal of whose wild nature forms a most felicitous contrast to the many good, fair-haired and tame children of fiction. (pp. 23-5)

An author like Andersen, who has so great a repugnance to beholding what is cruel and coarse in its nakedness, who is so deeply impressed by anything of the kind that he dare not relate it, but recoils a hundred times in his works from some wanton or outrageous deed with the maidenly expression, "We cannot bear to think of it!" Such an author feels content and at home in a world where everything that appears like egotism, violence, coarseness, vileness, and persecution, can only be called so in a figurative way. It is highly characteristic that almost all the animals which appear in Andersen's nursery stories are tame domestic animals. This is, in the first place, a sympton of the same gentle and idyllic tendency which results in making almost all Andersen's children so well-behaved. It is, furthermore, a proof of his fidelity to nature, in consequence of which he is so reluctant to describe anything, with which he is not thoroughly familiar. It is finally an interesting phenomenon with reference to the use he makes of the animals, for domestic animals are no longer the pure product of nature; they remind us, through ideal association, of much that is human; and, moreover, through long intercourse with humanity and long education they have acquired something human, which in a high degree supports and furthers the effort to personify them. These cats and hens, these ducks and turkeys, these storks and swans, these mice and that unmentionable insect "with maiden's blood in its body," offer many props to the nursery story. They hold direct intercourse with human beings; all that they lack is articulate speech, and there are human beings with articulate speech who are unworthy of it, and do not deserve their speech. Let us, therefore, give the animals the power of speech, and harbor them in our midst.

On the almost exclusive limitation to the domestic animal, a double characteristic of this nursery story depends. First of all, the significant result that Andersen's animals, whatever else they may be, are never beastly, never brutal. Their sole faults are that they are stupid, shallow, and old-fogyish. Andersen does not depict the animal in the human being, but the human in the animal. In the second place, there is a certain freshness of tone about them, a certain fulness of feeling, certain strong and bold, enthusiastic, and vigorous outbursts which are never found in the quarters of the domestic animal. Many beautiful, many humorous and entertaining things are spoken of in these stories, but a companion piece to the fable of the wolf and the dog—the wolf who observed the traces of the chain on the neck of the dog and preferred his own freedom to the protection afforded the house dog—will not be found in them. The wild nightingale, in whom poetry is personified, is a tame and loyal bird. "I have seen tears in the Emperor's eyes; that is the real treasure to me," it says. "An emperor's tears have a peculiar power!" Take even the swan, that noble, royal bird in the masterly story, **"The Ugly Duckling,"** which for the sake of its cat and its hen alone cannot be sufficiently admired,—how does it end? Alas! as a domestic animal. This is one of the points where it becomes difficult to pardon the great author. (pp. 26-7)

Andersen prefers the bird to the four-footed animal. More birds than mammals find place with him; for the bird is gentler than the four-footed beast, is nearer to the plant. The nightingale is his emblem, the swan his ideal, the stork his declared favorite. It is natural that the stork, that remarkable bird which brings children into the world,—the stork, that droll, long-legged, wandering, beloved, yearningly expected and joyfully greeted bird, should become his idolized symbol and frontispiece.

Yet plants are preferred by him to birds. Of all organic beings, plants are those which appear most frequently in the nursery story. For in the vegetable world alone are peace and harmony found to reign. Plants, too, resemble a child, but a child who is perpetually asleep. There is no unrest in this domain, no action, no sorrow, and no care. Here life is a calm, regular growth, and death but a painless fading away. Here the easily excited, lively poetic sympathy suffers less than anywhere else. Here there is nothing to jar and assail the delicate nerves of the poet. Here he is at home; here he paints his Arabian Nights' Entertainments beneath a burdock leaf. Every grade of emotion may be experienced in the realm of plants,—melancholy at the sight of the felled trunk, fulness of strength at the sight of the swelling buds, anxiety at the fragrance of the strong jasmine. Many thoughts may flit through our brain as we follow the history of the development of the flax, or the brief honor of the fir-tree on Christmas evening; but we feel as absolutely free as though we were dealing with comedy, for the image is so fleeting that it vanishes the moment we attempt to render it permanent. Sympathy and agitation gently touch our minds, but they do not ruffle us, they neither rouse nor oppress us. A poem about a plant sets free twofold the sympathy to which it lays claim; once because we know that the poem is pure fiction, and again because we know the plant to be merely a symbol. Nowhere has the poet with greater delicacy invested plants with speech than in **"The Fir-Tree," "Little Ida's Flowers,"** and in **"The Snow Queen."** (pp. 28-9)

Yet a step farther, and the fancy of the poet appropriates all inanimate objects, colonizes and annexes everything, large and small, an old house and an old clothes-press (**"The Shepherdess and the Chimney Sweep"**), the top and the ball, the darning needle and the false collar, and the great dough men with bitter almonds for their hearts. After it has grasped the physiognomy of the inanimate, his fancy identifies itself with the formless all, sails with the moon across the sky, whistles and tells stories like the wind, looks on the snow, on sleep, night, death, and the dream as persons.

The determining element in this poetic mind was, then, sympathy with all that is childlike, and, through the representation of such deep-seated, elementary, and constant spiritual conditions as those of the child, the productions of this imagination are raised above the waves of time, spread beyond the boundaries of their native land and become the common property of the divers classes of society. (pp. 29-30)

The most marked trait in Andersen's mode of viewing life, is that which gives the ascendency to the heart, and this trait is genuinely Danish. Full of feeling itself, this method of contemplation takes every opportunity to exalt the beauty and significance of the emotions. It overleaps the will (the whole destiny of the Flax, in the story of its life, comes from without), does combat with the critique of the pure reason as with something pernicious, the work of the Devil, the witch's mirror, replaces pedantic science with the most admirable and witty side-thrusts (**"The Bell," "A Leaf From the Sky"**), describes the senses as a tempter, or passes them over as unmentionable things, pursues and denounces hardheartedness, glorifies and commends goodness of heart, violently dethrones coarseness and narrowness, exalts innocence and decorum, and thus "puts everything in its right place." The key-note of its earnestness is the ethic-religious feeling coupled with the hatred felt by geniality for narrowness, and its humorous satire is capricious, calm, in thorough harmony with the idyllic spirit of the poet. (pp. 33-4)

Andersen writes a grotesque, irregular prose, full of harmless mannerisms, and whose poetry is a luxuriant, gushing, rapturous conceit. It is this fantastic element which makes Andersen so foreign to the French people whose rather gray poetry wholly lacks the bright-hued floral splendor found among the Northern people and attaining its highest beauty in Shakespeare's "Midsummer Night's Dream," a splendor which may be detected throughout Andersen's nursery stories, and which imparts to them their finest perfume. And as the fantastic caprice of this element is Norse-Danish, its idyllic key-note is purely Danish. No wonder that the earliest and most original of these nursery stories were written during the reign of Frederick VI. and bear the stamp of his day. We recognize this monarch in all the fatherly, patriarchal old kings represented in them; we find the spirit of the age in the complete lack of social, to say nothing of political satire, that we detect in them. (pp. 34-5)

The romance is a species of poetic creation which demands of the mind that would accomplish anything remarkable in it, not only imagination and sentiment, but the keen understanding, and the cool, calm power of observation of the man of the world; that is the reason why it is not altogether suited to Andersen, although it is not wholly remote from his talent. In the entire scenery, the background of nature, the picturesque effect of the costumes, he is successful; but where psychological insight is concerned, traces of his weakness may be detected. He will take part for and against his characters; his men are not manly enough, his women not sufficiently feminine. I know no poet whose mind is more devoid of sexual distinctions, whose talent is less of a nature to betray a defined sex, than

Title page to an 1895 English-language edition of Andersen's fairy tales. By Gordon Browne, 1895.

Andersen's. Therefore his strength lies in portraying children, in whom the conscious sense of sex is not yet prominent. The whole secret lies in the fact that he is exclusively what he is,— not a man of learning, not a thinker, not a standard bearer, not a champion, as many of our great writers have been, but simply a poet. A poet is a man who is at the same time a woman. Andersen sees most forcibly in man and in woman that which is elementary, that which is common to humanity, rather than that which is peculiar and interesting. I have not forgotten how well he has described the deep feeling of a mother in **"The Story of a Mother,"** or how tenderly he has told the story of the spiritual life of a woman in **"The Little Sea-Maid."** I simply recognize the fact that what he has represented is not the complicated spiritual conditions of life and of romance, but the element of life; he rings changes on single, pure tones, which amid the confused harmonies and disharmonies of life, appear neither so pure nor so distinct as in his books. Upon entering into the service of the nursery story all sentiments undergo a process of simplification, purification, and transformation. The character of man is farthest removed from the comprehension of the poet of childhood, and I can only recall a single passage in his stories in which a delicate psychological characteristic of a feminine soul may be encountered, and even this appears so innocently that we feel inclined to ask if it did not write itself. (pp. 36-7)

[The] drama is still farther removed from the genius of Andersen than the romance, and that his lack of capacity for the dramatic style increases with mathematical exactness in the same ratio as each variety of dramatic art is removed from the nursery story, and consequently from his gifts. He naturally succeeds best with the nursery-story comedy; although, to be sure, it possesses little more of comedy than the name. It is a mixed species, and if it were put to the test of the Spanish story, it would be recognized as a bastard. In the comedy of special situations he is happy with respect to the poetic execution of single scenes (**"The King's Dream"**), but singularly unfortunate in the execution of the idea as a whole (**"The Pearl of Good Fortune"**). The comedy proper is not poorly suited to his gifts. . . . In stories of this kind character delineation comes easier to him than in the grave drama, for in them he walks directly in the footsteps of Holberg, so strikingly does his talent accord in a single direction with that of this early Northern dramatist. (p. 38)

In his descriptions of travel very naturally a large number of his best qualities come to light. Like his favorite, the migratory bird, he is in his element when he travels. He observes with the eye of a painter, and he describes like an enthusiast. Yet even here two faults are apparent: one is that his lyric tendency at times runs away with him, so that he chants a hymn of praise instead of giving a description, or exaggerates instead of painting . . . ; the other, that the underlying, personal, egotistical element of his nature, giving evidence that his innermost personality lacks reserve, occasionally obtrudes itself in a most disturbing manner.

The latter tendency characterizes with especially marked force the style of his autobiography. The criticism that can with justice be made on his **"Story of My Life"** is not so much that the author is throughout occupied with his own private affairs (for that is quite natural in such a work); it is that his personality is scarcely ever occupied with anything greater than itself, is never absorbed in an idea, is never entirely free from the ego. The revolution of 1848 in this book affects us as though we heard some one sneeze; we are astonished to be reminded by the sound that there is a world outside of the author. (pp. 39-40)

Thus the nursery story remains his sole individual creation, and for it he requires no patent, since no one is likely to rob him of it. . . . Andersen's nursery story has its individual character, and his theories are comprised in the law it obeys, whose boundaries it may not overstep without bringing to light a monster. Everything in the world has its law, even that species of poetry which transcends the laws of nature. (pp. 40-1)

The form of fancy and the method of narration in the nursery story admit the treatment of the most heterogeneous materials in the most varied tones. Within its province may be found sublime narratives, as **"The Bell"**; profound and wise stories, as **"The Shadow"**; fantastically bizarre, as **"The Elfin Mound"**; merry, almost wanton ones, as **"The Swineherd,"** or **"The Leap Frog"**; humorous ones, as **"The Princess on the Pea,"** **"Good Humor," "The False Collar," "The Lovers"**; also stories with a tinge of melancholy, as **"The Constant Tin Soldier"**; deeply pathetic poetic creations, as **"The Story of a Mother"**; oppressively dismal, as **"The Red Shoes"**; touching fancies, as **"The Little Sea-Maid"**; and those of mingled dignity and playfulness, as **"The Snow Queen."** Here we encounter an anecdote like **"A Great Sorrow,"** which resembles a smile through tears, and an inspiration like **"The Muse of the Coming Age,"** in which we feel the pinion strokes of history, the heart-throbs and pulse-beats of the active, stirring life of the present, as violent as in a fever, and yet as healthy as in a happy moment of enthusiastic inspiration. In short, we find everything that lies between the epigram and the hymn.

Is there, then, a boundary line which limits the nursery story, a law which binds it? If so, where does it lie?. . . The nursery story, which unites unbridled freedom of invention with the restraint its central idea impresses upon it, must steer between two rocks: between the luxuriance of style that lacks ideas, and dry allegory; it must strike the medium course between too great fulness and too great meagreness. This, Andersen most frequently succeeds in doing, and yet not always. Those of his stories that are based on materials derived from folk-lore, as **"The Flying Trunk,"** or those that may be classed with the fairy-tale proper, as **"Thumbling,"** do not attract grown people as they do children, because the story in such instances conceals no thought. In his **"Garden of Paradise"** everything preceding the entrance to the garden is masterly, but the Fairy of Paradise herself seems to me to be invested with little, if any, beauty or charm. (pp. 41-3)

The first duty of the nursery story is to be poetic, its second to preserve the marvellous element. Therefore, it is first of all necessary that the order of the legendary world be sacred to it. What in the language of legendary lore is regarded as a fixed rule, must be respected by the nursery story, however unimportant it may be in relation to the laws and rules of the real world. Thus it is quite inappropriate for the nursery story, as in Andersen's **"The Dryad,"** to part its heroine from her tree, to let her make a symbolic journey to Paris, to go to the "bal Mabille," etc., for it is not more impossible for all the kings of the earth to place the smallest leaf on a nettle than it is for legendary lore to tear a dryad away from its tree. But in the second place, it lies in the nature of the nursery story form that its outline can frame nothing that, in order to obtain its poetic rights, requires a profound psychological description, an earnest development, such as would be adapted either to the nature of the drama or the romance. (pp. 44-5)

[Andersen] has the genuine gift for creating supernatural beings, in modern times so rare. How deeply symbolical and how natural it is, for instance, that the little sea-maid, when her fish-tail shrivelled up and became "the prettiest pair of white feet a little girl could have," should feel as though she were treading on pointed needles and sharp knives at every step she took! How many poor women tread on sharp knives at every step they take, in order to be near him whom they love, and are yet far from being the most unhappy of women! (p. 47)

> Georg Brandes, "Hans Christian Andersen," in his Creative Spirits of the Nineteenth Century, translated by Rasmus B. Anderson, Thomas Y. Crowell Company, 1923, pp. 1-53.

THE SPECTATOR   (essay date 1892)

[Hans Christian Andersen's Correspondence] is a selection from the Danish edition of **Andersen's Correspondence,** which contains upwards of eight hundred letters. His vanity led him to cherish every line, important or trivial, written or in print, that touched upon his career; but English readers, who already know Andersen through his Autobiography and in his works, will probably find enough in the letters chosen . . . [in this volume] to satisfy their curiosity. . . .

His letters show what we knew already, his delight in travel, his ardent love of Nature, and the eye for colour which he had in common with Scott, whose poetry as well as prose were dear to him throughout life. Feeling rather than intellect, a keen sense of enjoyment, and a disposition ready to discern whatever is loveable and beautiful, are among the characteristics of a correspondence wholly devoid of humour or originality of thought. Always there is the expression of delight and gratitude. His impressions of his "beloved Italy" afford slight indications of what he expressed afterwards more forcibly in **The Improvisatore.** . . .

The freshness of the correspondence is its special attraction. If the reader is sometimes inclined to smile at Andersen's egotism and simplicity, he will not esteem the man the less. (p. 205)

> "Hans Andersen's Correspondence," in The Spectator, Vol. 68, No. 3319, February 6, 1892, pp. 205-06.

HORACE E. SCUDDER   (essay date 1894)

[Scudder is considered Andersen's first American champion. As the editor of Riverside Monthly Magazine for Young People, Scudder negotiated a contract between Andersen and Hurd and Houghton, Riverside's publishers. Although Andersen's popularity had soared in America, before Scudder's intervention he had never received payment for any of his American publications. Although Scudder and Andersen never met personally, they corresponded for a number of years. Scudder translated many of Andersen's tales, as well as an edition of his autobiography, The Story of My Life. In the following essay, originally published in 1894 in Scudder's Childhood in Literature and Art, Scudder discusses Andersen's contribution to children's literature. According to Scudder, Andersen was not only childlike; he was "the first child who made a real contribution to literature." Scudder defines Andersen's work as "literature in which conceptions of childhood are embodied, and as literature which feeds and stimulates the imagination of children."]

It is Andersen himself who has made the most unique contribution not only to the literature which children read, but to that which is illustrative of childhood. He attained his eminence sheerly by the exhibition of a power which resulted from his information by the spirit of childhood. He was not only an interpreter of childhood; he was the first child who made a real contribution to literature. The work by which he is best known is nothing more nor less than an artistic creation of precisely the order which is common among children. (p. 50)

Hans Christian Andersen should have come forward as master in a new order of stories, which may be regarded as the true literary successor to the old order of fairy tales, answering the demands of a spirit which rejects the pale ghost of the scientific or moral or jocular or pedantic fairy tale. Andersen, indeed, has invented fairy tales purely such, and has given form and enduring substance to traditional stories current in Scandinavia; but it is not upon such work that his real fame rests, and it is certain that while he will be mentioned in the biographical dictionaries as the writer of novels, poems, romances, dramas, sketches of travel, and an autobiography, he will be known and read as the author of certain short stories, of which the charm at first glance seems to be in the sudden discovery of life and humor in what are ordinarily regarded as inanimate objects, or what are somewhat compassionately called dumb animals. When we have read and studied the stories further, and perceived their ingenuity and wit and humane philosophy, we can after all give no better account of their charm than just this, that they disclose the possible or fancied parallel to human life carried on by what our senses tell us has no life, or our reason assures us has no rational power.

The life which Andersen sets before us is in fact a dramatic representation upon an imaginary stage, with puppets that are not pulled by strings, but have their own muscular and nervous economy. The life which he displays is not a travesty of human life, it is human life repeated in miniature under conditions which give a charming and unexpected variety. By some transmigration, souls have passed into tin-soldiers, balls, tops, beetles, honey, pigs, coins, shoes, leap-frogs, matches, and even such attenuated individualities as darning-needles; and when, informing these apparently dead or stupid bodies, they begin to make manifestations, it is always in perfect consistency with the ordinary conditions of the bodies they occupy, though the several objects become by this endowment of souls suddenly expanded in their capacity. Perhaps in nothing is Andersen's delicacy of artistic feeling better shown than in the manner in which he deals with his animated creations when they are brought into direct relations with human beings. The absurdity which the bald understanding perceives is dexterously suppressed by a reduction of all the factors to one common term. For example, in his story of **"The Leap-Frog,"** he tells how a flea, a grasshopper and a leap-frog once wanted to see which could jump highest, and invited the whole world "and everybody else besides who chose to come," to see the performance. The king promised to give his daughter to the one who jumped the highest, for it was stale fun when there was no prize to jump for. The flea and the grasshopper came forward in turn and put in their claims; the leap-frog also appeared, but was silent. The flea jumped so high that nobody could see where he went to, so they all asserted that he had not jumped at all; the grasshopper jumped in the king's face, and was set down as an ill-mannered thing; the leap-frog, after reflection, leaped into the lap of the princess, and thereupon the king said, "There is nothing above my daughter; therefore to bound up to her is the highest jump that can be made: but for this, one must possess understanding, and the leap-frog has shown that he has understanding. He is brave and intellectual." "And so," the story declares, "he won the princess." The barren absurdity of a leap-frog marrying a princess is perhaps the first thing that strikes the impartial reader of this abstract, and there is very likely something offensive to him in the notion; but in the story itself this absurdity is so delightfully veiled by the succession of happy turns in the characterization of the three jumpers, as well as of the old king, the house-dog, and the old councilor "who had had three orders given him to make him hold his tongue," that the final impression upon the mind is that of a harmonizing of all the characters, and the king, princess, and councilor can scarcely be distinguished in kind from the flea, grasshopper, leap-frog, and house-dog. After that, the marriage of the leap-frog and princess is quite a matter of course.

The use of speaking animals in story was no discovery of Andersen's, and yet in the distinction between his wonder-story and the well-known fable lies an explanation of the charm which attaches to his work. The end of every fable is *haec fabula docet*, and it was for this palpable end that the fable was created. The lion, the fox, the mouse, the dog, are in a very limited way true to the accepted nature of the animals which they represent, and their intercourse with each other is governed by the ordinary rules of animal life but the actions and words are distinctly illustrative of some morality. The fable is an animated proverb. The animals are made to act and speak in accordance with some intended lesson, and have this for the reason of their being. The lesson is first; the characters, created afterward, are, for purposes of the teacher, disguised as animals; very little of the animal appears, but very much of the lesson. The art which invented the fable was a modest hand-maid to morality. In Andersen's stories, however, the spring is not in the didactic but in the imaginative. He sees the beetle in the imperial stable stretching out his thin legs to be shod with golden shoes like the emperor's favorite horse, and the personality of the beetle determines the movement of the story thoughout; egotism, pride at being proud, jealousy, and unbounded self-conceit are the furniture of this beetle's soul, and his adventures one by one disclose his character. Is there a lesson in all this? Precisely as there is a lesson in any picture of human life where the same traits are sketched. The beetle, after all his adventures, some of them ignominious but none expelling his self-conceit, finds himself again in the emperor's stable, having solved the problem why the emperor's horse had golden shoes. "They were given to the horse on my account," he says, and adds, "the world is not so bad after all, but one must know how to take things as they come." There is in this and other of Andersen's stories a singular shrewdness, as of a very keen observer of life, singular because at first blush the author seems to be a sentimentalist. The satires, like **"The Emperor's New Clothes"** and **"The Swiftest Runners,"** mark this characteristic of shrewd observation very cleverly. Perhaps, after all, we are stating most simply the distinction between his story and the fable when we say that humor is a prominent element in the one and absent in the other; and to say that there is humor is to say that there is real life.

It is frequently said that Andersen's stories accomplish their purpose of amusing children by being childish, yet it is impossible for a mature person to read them without detecting repeatedly the marks of experience. There is a subtle undercurrent of wisdom that has nothing to do with childishness, and the child who is entertained returns to the same story afterward to find a deeper significance than it was possible for him to apprehend at the first reading. The forms and the incident are in consonance with childish experience, but the spirit which moves through the story comes from a mind that has seen and felt the analogue of the story in some broader or coarser form. The story of **"The Ugly Duckling"** is an inimitable presentation of Andersen's own tearful and finally triumphant life; yet no child who reads the story has its sympathy for a moment withdrawn from the duckling and transferred to a human being. Andersen's nice sense of artistic limitations saves him from making the older thought obtrude itself upon the notice of children, and his power of placing himself at the same angle of vision with children is remarkably shown in one instance, where, in **"Little Klaus and Big Klaus,"** death is treated as a mere incident in the story, a surprise but not a terror.

The naïveté which is so conspicuous an element in Andersen's stories was an expression of his own singularly artless nature. He was a child all his life; his was a condition of almost arrested development. He was obedient to the demands of his spiritual nature, and these led him into a fresh field of fancy and imagination. (pp. 53-5)

The result has been a surprise in literature and a genuine addition to literary forms. It is possible to follow in his steps, now that he has shown us the way, but it is no less evident that the success which he attained was due not merely to his happy discovery of a latent property, but to the nice feeling and strict obedience to laws of art with which he made use of his discovery. Andersen's genius enabled him to see the soul in a darning-needle, and he perceived also the limitations of the life he was to portray, so that while he was often on the edge of absurdity he did not lose his balance. Especially is it to be noted that these stories, which we regard as giving an opportunity for invention when the series of old-fashioned fairy tales had been closed, show clearly the coming in of that temper in novel-writing which is eager to describe things as they are. Within the narrow limits of his miniature story, Andersen moves us by the same impulse as the modern novelist who depends for his material upon what he has actually seen and heard, and for his inspiration upon the power to penetrate the heart of things; so that the old fairy tale finds its successor in this new realistic wonder-story, just as the old romance gives place to the new novel. In both, as in the corresponding development of poetry and painting, is found a deeper sense of life and a finer perception of the intrinsic value of common forms.

This, then, may be taken as the peculiar contribution of Andersen: that he, appearing at a time when childhood had been laid open to view as a real and indestructible part of human life, was the interpreter to the world of that creative power which is significant of childhood. The child spoke through him, and disclosed some secrets of life; childhood in men heard the speech, and recognized it as an echo of their own half-forgotten voices. The literature of this kind which he produced has become a distinct and new form. It already has its imitations, and people are said to write in the vein of Andersen. Such work, and Andersen's in particular, presents itself to us under two aspects: as literature in which conceptions of childhood are embodied, and as literature which feeds and stimulates the imagination of children. (p. 56)

> Horace E. Scudder, "Of Classics and Golden Ages: Hans Christian Andersen," in Children and Literature: Views and Reviews, edited by Virginia Haviland, The Bodley Head Ltd., 1974, pp. 50-6.

R. NISBET BAIN   (essay date 1895)

[Bain's Hans Christian Andersen, from which the following excerpt is taken, was the first English-language biography of Andersen. Published ten years before the first full-length Danish study on Andersen appeared, the biography brought Andersen's English-speaking audience their first glimpse of the renowned author.]

The very limitations of [Andersen's] fancy, its excessive delicacy, flightiness, and instability, its trick of perpetually hovering around a thousand objects without fastening on any, its superficiality, which made him but an indifferent dramatist, and not much more than second-rate novelist, were in their proper element among the ever-shifting phantasmagoria of fairyland. He had, too, a child's imagination, which personifies and vivifies everything, whether it be a plant, a flower, a bird, a cat, a doll, or clouds, sunbeams, winds, and the seasons of the year. The determining quality of Andersen's art, therefore, was sympathy with the childlike in the widest sense—with children first of all, and then with everything that most nearly resembles children; with animals, for instance, who may be regarded as children who are never anything but children; and with plants, who are also like children, but children who are always sleeping. Nay, even his defects, mental and moral, that sensitive shrinking from all that is disgusting or distressing, that disinclination to look the uglier facts of life fairly in the face, defects that are responsible for so much of the indefi-

niteness and mawkish sentiment of his novels and plays, do but lend an additional charm to his fairy tales, and make them suitable above all others for children. What is mawkishness elsewhere here becomes simply sweetness. Hence it is that all, or nearly all, the children in his fairy tales are good children, and all the animals friendly domestic animals, who may sometimes be stupid and snobbish, but are never savage or brutal. Finally—and here we hit upon the real secret of Andersen's unique art as a teller of fairy tales—he possessed the rare gift of fashioning, or rather evoking supernatural beings of every sort and kind, elves, gnomes, nixies, trolls, dryads and mermaids, who are always true to the characters he gives them. It is impossible not to believe in Andersen's fantastic creations; he had as keen an eye for the oddities of the elfin race as Dickens had for the oddities of human nature. . . . Andersen also drew largely from the common stock, and such little masterpieces as **"The Tinder Box"** and **"The Wild Swans"** are living instances of the inimitable skill with which he could transform a good old story into a new one, and even improve it in the process; but he is at his best when he is original—he never wrote anything finer than **"The Shadow"** or **"The Little Mermaid."** (pp. 140-42)

> R. Nisbet Bain, in his Hans Christian Andersen: A Biography, Dodd, Mead and Company, 1895, 461 p.

SHIRLEY KNAPTON   (essay date 1903)

[Andersen] was unencumbered by any machinery of retributive justice. . . . He did not, for example, think godmothers were the only philanthropists, and if he indulged a national affection and wrote a great deal about storks, it was because he loved storks himself. . . . There is a more or less justifiable prejudice in the world in favour of tales that end up "and they were married and lived happily ever after." The subject of this article, though untinged by the gloomy melancholy which pervades at this latter-day, was given, even in ["**Andersen's Fairy Tales**"], to set it somewhat at defiance, and several of his tales end in a minor key. His principal novel, **"Kun en Spillemand"** (**"The Fiddler"**), notably does, yet the impression it leaves on the mind is not a dreary one, for, it must be remembered, a performance in the minor key of life is not necessarily dismal: it sometimes stirs us to tears of genuine relief. He certainly liked a happy ending, if he could contrive it without violating any human law, for he was not one of those who love tragedy, with all the stops pulled out, for its own sake—just as village people love a funeral; nor had he any of that fierce joy in making us wretched, displayed by some modern novelists, whose one idea seems to be to leave their heroines out in the drifting rain or their heroes buried under the Southern Cross; but he was an artist, and, as such, set telling the truth, as he conceived it, high above any other aim, and he told it unrelentingly, even when it did not include a marriage or a blare of trumpets. Yet I do not think this fact contradicts the assertion that the teaching he tried to instil was largely connected with the doctrine of cheerfulness. But he was a pitiful man, therefore he was not blatantly cheerful. He did not tell those to whom the gods had been unkind that they had probably got as much as they deserved, and ought to be as ready as anybody to sing the Nunc Dimittis from the bottom of their hearts. He knew there were plenty of stony-hearted people in the world carrying about that message, and he had no desire to swell their ranks. . . . He recognised that life was inevitably and eternally a battle, and perceived that nothing was to be gained by an attempt to inculcate the joie de vivre [joy of living] either by insisting on it or by presenting human nature and human possibilities under rosy aspects, such as they have never exhibited since the world was evolved from chaos. What he tried to do was this—to show that, after all, a great deal of sweet went with the bitter; that life, being but an April day, would have showers as well as sunshine; that it was to our advantage to endure such in as philosophic a spirit as we could; and that, if the worst came to the worst, to look on the best side of things was to exercise a manly virtue. (pp. 123-24)

There was an element of spontaneity about all that he wrote, and his treatment was so natural that his writings, especially his short tales and sketches, often touch the high-water mark of art and read artlessly. He wrote of things just as it seemed to him they would have occurred, always bearing in mind that it is the unexpected that is inclined to happen. However, it must be confessed he did not see Nature as the majority of people do. . . . He had, in common with the poet Burns, a fine gift for the small things of life—no incident was too slight to be reckoned with, no detail minute enough to escape his mental vision. His mind had no shut windows. He was readily touched by small pathoses, small joys, and small weaknesses. **"The Picture-Book without Pictures"** (almost his top notch) illustrates this quality of mind better than anything else that he wrote. It is the Doxology of the Small. . . . Hans Christian Andersen was not, in a learned sense, a philosopher, but there is a great deal of shrewd philosophy, such as the world at large can appreciate, in what he wrote, and he is probably the only writer of fiction who has done ample justice to this *power of association*. He recognised in it a subtle and deep-seated faculty to which the beginning of many results in after life might be traced. He was of the opinion that a man's whole future fortune might turn on a game he played as a child. Such a fine appreciation of small things—such an aptitude for detail—would be a very dangerous possession for a man of letters did it not run in double harness with a capacity for nice discrimination. Fortunately in Andersen's case it did. He never fell into the fallacy of supposing that, because the important happenings of life are often externally trivial, therefore all externally trivial happenings are important. His eye was true with regard to salient points, and his tales are never overburdened. Some of them—the shorter fairy-tales, in particular—are plain to bareness. But they grip. Moreover, it must be remembered he was a master of style. He could, in a few happy words, clutch a new truth from a commonplace, and he had an inexhaustible fund of simile and metaphor, of which he made free use, but which never led him into the error of tediousness. There is nothing final to be said about his style: it eludes hard-and-fast definition. Perhaps the best adjective to apply to it is "happy." He had the good fortune to think some very happy thoughts about men and things, and the almost better fortune to express some very ordinary ones happily. For example, when he described people in love for the first time as seeing the world through a *prismatic glass*, so that, for them, for the time being, "seven-coloured Hope" rested on each of life's hard corners and sharply-defined limitations, he was only giving expression to the old truth that at such a period of existence we are all liable to look at things through rose-coloured spectacles; but he was not only expressing it in a new and therefore arresting manner, but was also making use of a figure of speech which surely hails from a higher region of fancy. The *prismatic glass* certainly appeals to a finer and more imaginative faculty of mind than the *rose-coloured spectacles*, and is perhaps for that reason less likely to be popular. (pp. 124-26)

In these days of prolific Christmas literature for children, we are well accustomed to the animation of the inanimate; when

Illustration from Andersen's "The Emperor's New Clothes." Historical Pictures Service, Chicago. By Hans Tegner.

Andersen wrote talking was not considered part of a darning-needle's mission. His undertaking was a dangerous one, with more than the usual number of possibilities of straying into the by-ways of bathos. With less genius some of his stories might have drifted into sheer nonsense (as many of his disciples have demonstrated in treating similar themes), but he was a man of genius, and he was not afraid. He succeeded signally. (pp. 126-27)

Shirley Knapton, "Hans Andersen: An Appreciation," in The Bookman, London, Vol. 25, No. 147, December, 1903, pp. 121-28.

GILBERT K. CHESTERTON   (essay date 1916)

[*Remembered primarily for his detective stories, Chesterton was also an eminent English man of letters of the early twentieth century. His essays are characterized by their humor, frequent use of paradox, and rambling style. In his commentary on Andersen, Chesterton praises his rendering of inanimate objects and adds that Andersen's sensitive depictions of everyday life are appropriate for fairy tale settings.*]

[English] children owe to Hans Andersen more than to any of their own writers, that essential educational emotion which feels that domesticity is not dull but rather fantastic; that sense of the fairyland of furniture, and the travel and adventure of the farmyard. His treatment of inanimate things as animate was not a cold and awkward allegory: it was a true sense of a dumb divinity in things that are. Through him a child did feel that the chair he sat on was something like a wooden horse. Through him children and the happier kind of men did feel themselves covered by a roof as by the folded wings of some vast domestic fowl; and feel common doors like great mouths that opened to utter welcome. In the story of **"The Fir Tree"** he transplanted to England a living bush that can still blossom into candles. And in his tale of **"The Tin Soldier"** he uttered the true defence of romantic militarism against the prigs who would forbid it even as a toy for the nursery. He suggested, in the true tradition of the folk-tales, that the dignity of the fighter is not in his largeness but rather in his smallness, in his stiff loyalty and heroic helplessness in the hands of larger and lower things. (pp. 107-08)

> Gilbert K. Chesterton, *"Hamlet and the Danes,"* in
> his The Crimes of England, *John Lane Company,*
> 1916, pp. 95-112.*

E. V. LUCAS   (essay date 1920)

[It is] by his fairy tales that Hans Andersen lives and will ever live. There he stands alone, supreme. As a whole, there is nothing like them. One man of genius or another has now and then done something a little in this or that Hans Andersen manner. Heine here and there in the "Reisebilder"; Lamb in "The Child Angel" and perhaps "Dream Children"; and one sees affinities to him occasionally in Sir James Barrie's work (the swallows in "The Little White Bird," for example, build under the eaves to hear the stories which are told to the children in the house, while in Hans Andersen's **"Thumbelina"** the swallows live under the poet's eaves in order to tell stories to him); but Hans Andersen remains one of the most unique and fascinating minds in all literature. Nominally just entertainment for children, these **"Eventyr og Historier"** are a profound study of the human heart and a ''criticism of life'' beyond most poetry. And all the while they are stories for children too; for though Hans Andersen addresses both audiences, he never, save in a very few of the slighter satirical apologues, such as **"The Collar"** and **"Soup from a Sausage Skewer,"** loses the younger. He had this double appeal in mind when, on a statue being raised in his honour at Copenhagen just before his death, showing him in the act of telling a tale to a cluster of children, he protested that it was not representative enough.

I would apply to Hans Andersen rather than to Scott the term "The Wizard of the North"; because whereas Scott took men and women as he found them, the other, with a touch of his wand, rendered inhuman things—furniture, toys, flowers, poultry—instinct with humanity. He knew actually how everything would behave; he knew how a piece of coal talked, and how a nightingale. He did not merely give speech to a pair of scissors, he gave character too. This was one of his greatest triumphs. He discerned instantly the relative social positions of moles and mice, bulls and cocks, tin soldiers and china shepherdesses. He peopled a new world, and, having done so, he made every incident in it dramatic and unforgettable. He brought to his task of amusing and awakening children gifts of humour and irony, fancy and charm, the delicacy of which will probably never be surpassed. He brought also an April blend of tears and smiles, and a very tender sympathy with all that is beautiful and all that is oppressed. He did not preach, or, if he did, he so quickly rectified the lapse with a laugh or

a quip that one forgets the indiscretion; but he believed that only the good are happy, and he wanted happiness to be universal. Hence to read his tales is an education in optimism and benevolence. (pp. 39-41)

> E. V. Lucas, *"The True Wizard of the North,"* in
> his Adventures and Enthusiasms, *George H. Doran*
> *Company, 1920, pp. 30-41.*

ROBERT LYND   (essay date 1922)

[*In the following essay, first published in 1922, Lynd considers Andersen's narrative technique to be his greatest merit as a children's author. Lynd concludes that "there was nothing else like* [*Andersen's tales*] *in the fairy-tale literature of the nineteenth century."*]

[Hans Andersen] was in many respects more nearly akin to the writers of tracts and moral tales than to the folklorists. He was a teller of fairy-tales. But he domesticated the fairy-tale and gave it a townsman's home. In his hands it was no longer a courtier, as it had been in the time of Louis XIV, or a wanderer among cottages, as it has been at all times. There was never a teller of fairy-tales to whom kings and queens mattered less. He could make use of royal families in the most charming way, as in those little satires, **'The Princess and the Pea'** and **'The Emperor's New Clothes.'** But his imagination hankered after the lives of children such as he himself had been. He loved the poor, the ill-treated, and the miserable, and to illuminate their lives with all sorts of fancies. His miracles happen preferably to those who live in poor men's houses. His cinder-girl seldom marries a prince: if she marries at all, it is usually some honest fellow who will have to work for his living. In Hans Andersen, however, it is the exception rather than the rule to marry and live happily ever afterwards. The best that even Hans the cripple [in Andersen's fable **"The Cripple"**] has to look forward to is being a schoolmaster. There was never an author who took fewer pains to give happy endings to his stories. (p. 82)

[Even] in his fairy-tales Hans Andersen has always appealed to men and women as strongly as to children. We hear occasionally of children who cannot be reconciled to him because of his incurable habit of pathos. A child can read a fairy-tale like 'The Sleeping Beauty' as if it were playing among toys, but it cannot read **'The Marsh King's Daughter'** without enacting in its own soul the pathetic adventures of the frog-girl; it cannot read **'The Snow Queen'** without enduring all the sorrows of Gerda as she travels in search of her lost friend; it cannot read **'The Little Mermaid'** without feeling as if the knives were piercing its feet just as the mermaid felt when she got her wish to become a human being so that she might possess a soul. . . . Hans Andersen is surely the least gay of all writers for children. He does not invent exquisite confectionery for the nursery such as Charles Perrault, having heard a nurse telling the stories to his little son, gave the world in 'Cinderella' and 'Bluebeard.' To read stories like these is to enter into a game of make-believe, no more to be taken seriously than a charade. The Chinese lanterns of a happy ending seem to illuminate them all the way through. But Hans Andersen does not invite you to a charade. He invites you to put yourself in the place of the little match-girl who is frozen to death in the snow on New Year's Eve after burning her matches and pretending that she is enjoying all the delights of Christmas. He is more like a child's Dickens than a successor of the ladies and gentlemen who wrote fairy-tales in the age of Louis XIV and Louis XV. He is like Dickens, indeed, not only in his genius for compassion, but in his abounding inventiveness, his grotesque detail, and his humour. He is never so recklessly cheerful as Dickens with the cheerfulness that suggests eating and drinking. He makes us smile rather than laugh aloud with his comedy. (pp. 85-7)

But Hans Andersen was too urgent a moralist to be content to write stories so immorally amusing as this. He was as anxious as a preacher or a parent or Dickens to see children Christians of sorts, and he used the fairy-tale continually as a means of teaching and warning them. . . . His stories as a whole are an imaginative representation of [a] gospel—a gospel that so easily becomes mush and platitude in ordinary hands. But Andersen's genius as a narrator, as a grotesque inventor of incident and comic detail, saves his gospel from commonness. He may write a parable about a darning-needle, but he succeeds in making his darning-needle alive, like a dog or a schoolboy. He endows everything he sees—china shepherdesses, tin soldiers, mice and flowers—with the similitude of life, action and conversation. He can make the inhabitants of one's mantelpiece capable of epic adventures, and has a greater sense of possibilities in a pair of tongs or a door-knocker than most of us have in men and women. He is a creator of a thousand fancies. He loves imagining elves no higher than a mouse's knee, and mice going on their travels leaning on sausage-skewers as pilgrims' staves, and little Thumbelina, whose cradle was 'a neat polished walnut-shell . . . blue violet-leaves were her mattresses, with a rose-leaf for a coverlet.' His fancy never becomes lyrical or sweeps us off our feet, like Shakespeare's in *A Midsummer Night's Dream.* But there was nothing else like it in the fairy-tale literature of the nineteenth century. (pp. 87-9)

> *Robert Lynd, "More or Less Ancient: Hans Andersen," in his* Books and Authors, *Jonathan Cape, 1929, pp. 81-9.*

PADRAIC COLUM (essay date 1932)

[*An Irish poet, dramatist, editor, and critic, Colum was one of the major writers of the Irish Literary Renaissance. In his discussion of Andersen, Colum praises the wisdom and insight of Andersen's tales.*]

It is not always easy to make up a story, and he who would make up one that will be remembered for generations has to do more than arrange properties and play up the arch and the whimsical; he has to create a living, a personal way of writing. When we read, even in a translation in which little care has been taken to bring out a special rhythm, **"The Wind's Story"**— the story about Waldemar Daa and his daughters—we know that Hans Christian Andersen has a living and a personal style; we move with the element he writes of, we hear its soughing, we feel the spaces it has gone over. . . .

The world he belonged to is far away from the world of the fanciful writers who make up a story by arranging properties he has left. (p. 125)

It should have been less difficult . . . to make up such stories as Andersen told, for the people he came from had in those days a life of their own; they had their stories, songs, and music, their hereditary occupations and costumes. (p. 128)

[Andersen, who shaped] stories for children first of all, had humour, poetry, knowledge of the world, a clear sense of form. He is a great writer because he has created a world that we can move in and live in. . . . Andersen's stories have in them

a heroism that transcends the military virtue—they have the sort of heroism that one finds in the lives of the saints—indeed the story of the Little Mermaid and the Princess who wove shirts for her swan-brothers out of churchyard nettles remind one of stories about the saints. What heroic virtue was in this man who made out of his memories stories which have such humour, such poetry, such keen and kindly observation! In his own life he must have seemed something of the fool—but a fool that Shakespeare might quote from—the fool in King Lear. (pp. 131-32)

> *Padraic Colum, "It's Not Always Easy to Make Up a Story," in his* A Half Day's Ride; or, Estates in Corsica, *The Macmillan Company, 1932, pp. 124-34.*

NESCA A. ROBB (essay date 1948)

[*Robb analyzes the contrasting elements found in Andersen's tales. She finds that his fairy tale world "holds no rose-coloured image of human nature, but shows it with all its too-familiar burden of weaknesses and sins."*]

[In Andersen's *Tales* there] are stories like **The Little Mermaid** or **The Wild Swans** or **The Garden of the World** that move in an air of dream remote from ordinary life. Others, such as **Ib and Little Christine** or **Under the Willow** are episodes of common life, only faintly touched with dream. There are besides plays of pure fantasy like **The Constant Tin Soldier** and **Thumbelina;** series of bedtime stories like **What the Moon Saw;** and pageants of Danish history such as **Holger Danske** or **Little Tuk.** Each, from the most elaborately wrought story to the slightest anecdote has its own individual atmosphere. Each is a little cosmos with its own vivid background, its own spiritual climate. The people and places in **The Storks** are as fully realised in their way as are those in **The Ice Maiden,** and as impossible to confuse with those of any other story. The more one reads, the more one marvels at that rich variety, so sealed as the work of a single imagination. In the same way Andersen contrives to be at once universal and local, for, if he is Everychild, in the way that Shakespeare is Everyman, he expresses much of that universal life through folk-lore and scenes and memories homely and personal. . . . (pp. 122-23)

Andersen kept through life the child's pleasure in descriptive detail that appeals vividly to eye, or ear, or, even, tongue. How good, for instance used one's favourite dishes to taste when served to Cinderella and her Prince at the ball by some obliging story-teller! Andersen offers many such imaginary banquets, recapturing with them all the joys of anticipatory gazing at the party sweetmeats, and, here and there, sounding, even through such childish longings, a note of tragedy. The roast goose, stuffed with apples and prunes, that comes waddling towards the Little Match Girl is the mind's release into an illusion of pleasure from a body too starved and wretched for further endurance. It has the brightness not of sound imagination but of fevered dream. So with all the details of Andersen's world. They are true to life, yet more vivid than our ordinary perceptions of it. Each lovely thing seems as new as its first prototype in Eden, a small overflowing focus of beauty and power. A sense of strange life clings even to inanimate objects. (p. 124)

[Andersen] brings back the freshness of long, inviolate, days when all experience, happy or sad, had a pristine character of wonder. It is a quality which, as the records of childhood show, makes outward things appear as but accidents of a human state which is always and everywhere fundamentally the same. . . . The *Tales* swarm with figures we all know and have ourselves at times impersonated; children at play and at school, children care-free and secure, children, sometimes, prematurely aged by poverty and trouble. One sees them learning or omitting to learn their lessons, running errands with varying degrees of willingness, running wild in the country, hanging about on the fringe of every excitement in the town, playing statues with or without their nightshirts on, inserting odd petitions into their prayers, eating, sleeping, teasing, being naughty. Andersen nowhere explicitly says so, but it is obvious that some of his urchins blow their noses on their sleeves, and rejoice to go unwashed, and that all can on occasion be infernal nuisances. Yet they live always with zest, and often highly and passionately. (pp. 124-25)

Not often can the adult mind renew within itself the lost content that was for ever quiveringly expectant of a further joy just out of reach; rarely too, outside dream or madness, does it know such darkness as can overwhelm an unhappy child. That all things pass is one of the hard lessons of maturity, but also one of its consolations. To the child his sorrows, whether born of his own imaginings or of outward circumstances, are not only painful, but final and inescapable. Life, in Hans Andersen's vision, is seen at a certain remove, as a child sees it, but there is no blinking of its realities. Its harsher aspects have the heightening of nightmare, just as its happier ones have the heightening of dream. It holds a full measure of mental and physical pain, of disaster and death—death too, that does not merely remove undesirables, as it commonly does in fairytales, but that snatches with the ruthlessness of actual fact the young, the beloved and the triumphant. At the very moment when one expects to read "they lived happily ever after," Rudy is claimed by the Ice Maiden, and Helga forgets her prince in the ecstasy that rives her soul from her body. (pp. 125-26)

This fairy-tale world holds no rose-coloured image of human nature, but shows it with all its too-familiar burden of weaknesses and sins. Pride, greed, envy, hypocrisy, selfishness and treachery are all active in it. We see great gifts, and affection, and happiness, cast aside so that their possessors may clutch at false treasures and lose the substance for the shadow. There is cruelty, from the sheer dull indifference of man towards man, to the active delight in giving pain that seizes Kay when the splinter flies into his eye. There is the helplessness of love, even at its last limit of sacrifice and agony, before the fate that crushes the beloved. Finally, there is the spirit's capacity for self-torture, a revelation of the dark places where it may wander, a prey to remorse or shame or false pride, shapes which, as in the tales of Karen and Inger, haunt the very borderlands of insanity. If one were to catalogue the sorrows of Hans Andersen's stories they would leave the impression of a world far more closely akin to that of Shakespeare's tragedies than to that of the average book for "little people." What is more, the same "little people" often return to this chequered scene with more zest than they do to the smoother paths laid out for them. These vicissitudes touch them nearly. To stories of danger and tribulation and, above all, of heroism, they respond with an eager sense of the value of the struggle. Because their own trails call for courage, they see in the overcoming of others of which as yet they have no direct knowledge, something that commands their sympathy and stirs their emulation. Deeper and more silent, but more universal, than the desire to be a success, is the desire to be a hero. (p. 126)

There is in all the *Tales* an atmosphere at once romantically adventurous and passionately local. It brings back hours spent

in exploring, on foot or perhaps in an old boat, some few hundred yards of glen or seashore, that were transformed for us into undiscovered lands and oceans. Since then perhaps, those distant places have been visited, known, even loved, but it is to that glen and seashore that the enchantment of other days will cling for ever. (p. 128)

All Andersen's descriptions are . . . significant, with a beauty or a terror that shines through the material objects, whether he speaks of an actual scene or of some dream landscape yet more vivid—the home of the Sea King, the city where the Ice Maiden holds her victims, the house by the river with its cherry trees and flowers and coloured windows where Gerda stayed with the friendly witch. Fairyland wears the colours of mortal earth washed in the dews of immortality, just as the earth is never quite devoid of the magic of fairyland. The glimpses of our world seen by the Little Mermaid's sisters when they first rise to the surface, have the very quality of strangeness and wonder that dwellers in "the wave's intenser day" might find in them. The North Wind's tale of the Polar seas is savage as a Norse Saga, but realistic too in its gruesomeness. (pp. 128-29)

In fact there is no firm dividing line between earth and faery; natural and supernatural are for ever melting into one another. The fairy world impinges on human life continually, flowing into it through innumerable channels, joined to it by a thousand fine filaments. There is, for instance, the queer secret life that may enter into inanimate objects, and possess anything from a porcelain figure to a darning needle. Then there are the animals, aloof, yet friendly, loyal, yet faintly patronising. They are well-informed about the doings of the fairies, and watch human affairs with a tolerant eye, though they are generally ready to help mankind if the need arises. They are very few disagreeable or unfriendly beasts in the *Tales*. For the most part indeed they compare very favourably with human beings. (p. 129)

Andersen's own snatches of animal talk suggest a vivid memory of those conversations; they have just the touch of condescension, the bland amusement at men's antics that one often surprises behind the steady gaze of one's silent fellow-creatures. Yet almost without exception they are faithful and loving, with an instinctive wisdom that links them not only with the fairy world, but with something yet greater. Within their limits they see clearly; they cannot enter fully into the truth, but they cannot pervert it as men do. . . . They hold, like man, a place between fairy-land and heaven, and possess enough of our nature to let Andersen poke delicate fun at human foibles through such creations as the Stork Parents in *The Marsh King's Daughter* or the farmyard animals in *The Ugly Duckling*. (pp. 129-30)

[In the *Tales* there] is room for the beautiful and the repulsive, the quaint and the awful, but not for the meretricious. The fairy world is essentially serious and its interventions in human life, whether they bring delight or, as sometimes, horror are not to be lightly dismissed. It is no mere playground, but has its dark elements as real and unavoidable as the pain of daily life. Andersen here holds fast as ever to the truth of the child's experience. Modern children's books may have banished imaginative terrors from their pages, but one doubts if they have fled from their readers' hidden thoughts. (pp. 130-31)

There is a matter-of-factness, not to say a certain happy murderousness, about the very young. They may be at home in heaven, but their feet are also often planted on earth in ways positively disconcerting to their elders. They are unrelenting judges too, whether of the villain in the story or the misfit in the schoolroom; and have little use for games whether of Arthurian knights, or redskins, or plain modern gangsters, that do not leave a field as full of corpses as Traddles's slate was of skeletons. This open, cut-and-thrust bloodshed, however, is in the main a social activity; one usually enjoys it in parties. If Andersen finds little place for it in his world, he misses nothing of the child's shuddering wooing of more subtle fears. . . . In creating *that* atmosphere of beguiling dread Andersen has few rivals. (p. 131)

There are, however, moments in which the nightmare element passes beyond all tolerable bounds and the pursuer becomes the pursued. Has anyone ever really *enjoyed The Red Shoes?* or *The Story of a Mother,* so heavy with the pain, more terror than sympathy, with which one watched the half-comprehended troubles of one's elders? Its physical horrors of the piercing thorns and the eyes wept away, were overshadowed by such icy supernatural gloom as the final reconciliation could scarcely soften; it was like one's first taste of the fear of death.

Worse still is the grim tale of Inger—"**The Girl who trod on the loaf**"—a vision of Hell more appalling than the cruder fire and brimstone of popular report. It is an Inferno less majestic than Dante's, but there is more than a suggestion in its dreariness of that eternal misery without hope. . . . (pp. 131-32)

[That] is the voice of nightmare with a vengeance, and one all but wakes up screaming. Whether or not children should read such things may be debated; but few can doubt that they are capable from their own imaginations of conjuring up mental torments hardly less fearful, though with the reticence of their kind they can rarely be brought to speak of them and indeed lack words to describe them if they would. Perhaps, in childhood and maturity alike, such things are a necessary counterpart of imaginative bliss; and the glories of the fairy world could never shine so brightly if they had no foil of darkness. There could be no such dewy freshness, no such divine sense of liberty on the shores of Purgatory if the fiery bondage of the Inferno had not been passed. So, by contrast with their supernatural shadows, the *Tales* are flooded with a blaze of supernatural light. They shine and overflow with images of joy, that often

Illustration from the fairy tale "The Flying Trunk." This depiction was taken from an early English-language edition of Andersen's works. By Gordon Browne, 1895?

burgeon from the very heart of misery, like sudden sunshine from stormy skies. . . . Just as the nightingale banishes death by its song, so beauty and delight are never far off even from the miasma of horror, and may ever at a touch dispel it, leaving its prisoners free. The pyre where Elise was to have died becomes a hedge of roses; the Little Mermaid leaps to destruction and is caught up into the dazzling life of the children of the air. The last we see of Inger, her ordeal past, is a sea-swallow that flies straight into the sun. Yet the delight of common life and fairy life alike has always in it some quality of anticipation. Always just out of sight there must be one joy more, perfect and satisfying beyond the rest, which sooner or later must be won; and it is easy for the child's mind to link that joy with what it has heard or read of heaven; and with a symbolism old as humanity to imagine its abiding place somewhere in the shining deeps of the sky. (pp. 132-33)

Most fairy tales are moral, but there can be few so uniformly and explicitly devout. Their piety can at times revive for us something of the innocent smugness of early church-goings—the new shoes, slightly squeaky, the threepenny bit thrust into the palm of unaccustomed gloves, the unction of joining in when one knew the hymn, and the satisfied feeling that God must be very pleased with one's efforts. None the less its background of Puritan devoutness gives a special, sober beauty to Andersen's world of childhood. (p. 133)

It is a faith that imposes its own dignity on its followers. Its outward expression may be austere and spare, but as with the northern landscape, that very austerity may reveal depths of serene tenderness to the eye that loves it. Andersen's peasants have lived in such close contact with the words of Scripture that these have become part of the texture of life, a continuous quiet rhythm to which thought and speech and action are, even unconsciously, attuned. It is as natural for him as it was for Bunyan, that an old country woman should spend her small leisure in reading the Bible, and should find there wisdom and strength that raise the commonplace of her existence to the heroic. For the sense of immediate contact with the word of God—of direct, personal speech of the Creator with His creature—lends to the creature the dignity of a being honoured by such a confidence, and gives to his every action a value far greater than appears to the careless observer. . . .

Deep-rooted in his religion is the sense that our concerns, however apparently trivial, are never small in reality, but belong as surely as the processes of nature to a whole, every atom of which is significant. It is "with the sun" that our daily stage of duty is completed; the world of faith gives meaning to the world of everyday. (p. 134)

All this, one may well say, is what no child would analyse. That is true; yet where the world of faith has been so presented to its consciousness the child may, without analysing the mystery, possess it and in great measure live by it. Andersen's vision of childhood is so penetrating because it recognises continually this underlying seriousness. It sees that along with its ignorances and faults and light fantasies the small heart may inarticulately harbour the passion of the lover or the poet, the strength of martyr or mystic. (p. 135)

However complex a man's development, however numerous his activities, he lives essentially in three things; in human relationships, in imagination, and in his relation to whatever final reality there may be. Because the child is less cumbered than his elders with superficial cares, this fundamental life of the spirit shines out in him unclouded. It is the miracle of Hans

Andersen's art that he is able to reveal it in terms of the child's own private imagery, and to hold his attention both with the magic of the tales and with the sense of a full sympathy discovered and established, while giving to the adult a sequence of parables inexhaustibly rich.

Yet even as one sets down any interpretations of Andersen's fables it takes on an arbitrary look, as do all analyses of living thought and feeling. By thus dividing and simplifying one may make one's perception of the truth more precise, and still be conscious that the whole eludes definition. Andersen's allegories, and even his individual figures, have about them something of the complexity of life; they change as one looks at them. Each is many things in one. The Ice Maiden, for instance, is first a beautiful and sinister spirit, queen of the wild powers of the mountains who, as she looks down from her eyrie on the human life of the valleys, appears as the embodiment of all that in nature seems hostile to man; but when she meets Rudy and steals his bethrothal ring, she becomes a minister of moral evil. In Danish folk lore she stands for death, and she brings death indeed to body and soul. Finally she is a part of Rudy's own being, for the kiss she gave him in his childhood has left something of herself in him, which all his life she struggles to reclaim. She is a principle of death within him, and though she is worsted in the struggle for his soul she triumphs inevitably over his mortal body. (pp. 135-36)

For the adult, as a rule, it is only in some moment of supreme tension—Rudy's meeting with the Ice Maiden on the Mountain, or his lightening perception on the island that ''If it were now to die It were to be most happy''—that life takes on this quality of imaginative depth. For the most part we see our surroundings in the flat. But to the child, or to the poet, all life is significant because even its trivialities are suffused with the lights of enchantment.

Thus it is that Andersen can restore a lost world to us in all its concrete richness, with its joys and wonders and sorrows, its very sights and sounds and smells. . . . To be as a little child is certainly not, for him, to be irrational or gullible, immune from suffering or out of touch with reality. It is rather to accept life humbly and spontaneously in its completeness, and to be, to the fullest of one's capacity, a whole human being. Childhood is not a time of undiluted happiness. The everyday world, for all its exhilarating novelty, is often hard; and even the shining realm of the imagination and the secret places of the heart offer experiences that may be still more agonising. Yet the child, while he remains a child in spirit, preserves a certain integrity in the midst of this strangely ordered life. (pp. 136-37)

Of all the contrasts in Hans Andersen there is none more persistent than the antithesis of truth and falsehood, reality and unreality. Genuineness is a passion with him. Again and again he returns to the strange perversity that afflicts men in their dealings with life, the blindness that makes them spurn the real and prefer the illusory. It is the condemnation of the Princess in *The Swineherd,* for instance, that she has made just such a choice.

''I have learned to despise you,'' says the Prince as they stand out in the storm. ''You have refused an honourable prince. You could not appreciate a rose or a nightingale, but you could stoop to kiss a swineherd for a toy.'' (pp. 138-39)

[For many of Andersen's characters] disaster comes through rejecting the truth that is in them, with its possibilities of fulfilment, in order to snatch at a specious good that flatters their vanity or their desires. So too, it is again and again through a child, or through one who has kept the single eye of childhood, that the balance is redressed. The little kitchen-maid and the poor fishermen are not deceived by the artificial nightingale, and know the real one whom the courtiers have never heard. A child brings the whole people back to reality when its more sophisticated elders have hoodwinked themselves into believing in the imposture of the Emperor's New Clothes. (p. 139)

Life, as Andersen well knows, does not deal out prizes and punishments with the obvious justice of some moral tales. His sinners—Inger and Kay, Karen and Christine—suffer terrible things, but so do Ib and Canute, Gerda and Elise, the Ugly Duckling and the Little Mermaid. It is not in outward circumstances that we must look for the true state of things. People may suffer through their own faults or through those of others, or simply through apparently casual happenings; but it is not what befalls them that matters, but the way in which they meet their fate. All evil, all suffering seems at first sight destructive. Man's true victory lies in making even these things into sources of strength. As an artist Andersen knew that it could be done. He had put his beliefs to the test of his own experience, and he writes with insight of the special perils and delights of the imaginative life. It is a life in which all men have, or should have, a part. Not for nothing does the fairy world mingle so intricately with the world of everyday and lay its spell even on the most commonplace objects and events. For imagination is not mere fantasy, though that is included in it; rather it is a mode of love, the understanding that sees things in their true significance. It can rise to the triumphant vision of the poet, but it includes also the miracles of memory and knowledge. (p. 140)

Andersen draws faithfully the painful growth through childhood and adolescence of one who finds himself inept for the life of his circle. Outwardly unattractive, inwardly ill at ease because the world seems to have no place for him, he has not enough self-knowledge to realise what he wants, or why life bears upon him so hardly. The talent that is to be his strength is as yet only a dumb torment to him. He can neither make himself socially pleasing nor economically profitable—neither purr nor lay eggs—and so he receives, very naturally, the treatment proper to so wretched a creature, from the dismayed scoldings of his foster parent to the kicks of the farm girl. He is scared and shot at, starved and frozen, but he accepts and endures, driven on by something within him that he himself does not understand. So all the time he is growing, though he himself is unaware of it, and when at last he sails trembling into the company of his peers, he is greeted by the watching children as the most beautiful of all. Suffering has fostered his swan nature and brought it to maturity. The outcast years have given him a grace that even those who have lived all their lives in the garden have not achieved.

Loyalty to his vocation may cost the artist dear, yet be the only way of ultimate happiness. So the lover, whose lot is more common than the artist's, must guard the integrity of his special gift through all vicissitudes. Love in its many manifestations holds a place in the *Tales* only a little below religious devotion. Often it appears as the love of man and woman: in *The Ice Maiden,* for instance, or *Under the Willow* or *Ib and Little Christine.* But we see it also as maternal love in *The Story of a Mother* or *The Marsh King's Daughter;* as filial love in *The Fellow Traveller;* as sisterly devotion in *The Wild Swans;* as pure compassion in *The Girl Who Trod on the Loaf.*

Often these loves have a tragic history. "They lived happily ever after" is by no means their inevitable end. Many are boken by death; and those that reach a happy consummation in this life do so only through pain and sacrifice. Yet to the true of heart throughout the *Tales* love is a destiny which they cannot escape and would not if they could. . . . It may be necessary to forgo the satisfaction of love; and it is like the severing of a limb. The sacrifice is made, and the maker goes through life maimed. But to cast love out would be like the removing of a vital organ; it would be to cast out life. Circumstances may make it pure pain to the heart that holds it; and like all pain mental or bodily, it may either embitter the sufferer and cut him off from other men, or become a means by which he enters more fully into life through his very infirmity. (pp. 143-44)

In all moments of extreme tension men cry instinctively for death. It is natural that the wretched should look to it as a release from their pain; it is a strange, yet often proven fact, that the soul in its moods of sovereign happiness should thus desire extinction. To Andersen that yearning is the response, conscious or unconscious, of the restless infinity in man to the stable infinity that surrounds him. The poet or the lover at the height of his individual rapture so breaks free of himself that he catches sight of eternity. For an instant he is made whole and perfect, and his eyes are opened to wholeness and perfection. He becomes again the child whose more abundant life thrills with the expectation of bliss not yet attained; but now he knows that it is only through death that he can embrace what he desires. (pp. 146-47)

Nesca A. Robb, "Hans Andersen," in her Four in Exile, *Hutchinson & Co. (Publishers) Ltd., 1948, pp. 120-53.*

PAUL V. RUBOW (essay date 1955)

The idea in Andersen's stories is emphasized by small, intimate observations on the visible world, or by those happenings—apparently insignificant in themselves, but none the less important—which the poet chances to encounter on his way. When his thoughts seek the causes and the consequences of all this, the result is a story, a wonderful tale where the writer's thoughts reach their greatest heights.

Andersen makes use of supernatural elements with the greatest prudence, and all the more so because he makes himself independent of the contents of the ancient folk-tales and legends. In *The Traveling Companion* and *The Wild Swans* traces are still to be found of the magic symbolism which was so beloved of the ancient story-tellers. . . . Compare with this the stories Andersen wrote later in his life, for instance *The Story of a Mother.* Even if the Night, the lake and the thorn-bush, all of which can speak, are personifications unknown in real life, a mother's love such as he depicts it for us is one of the greatest and most wonderful natural forces for those who know it. Or think of the conclusion which Andersen liked best and which we see in *The Little Match-Seller* and *A Story from the Dunes.* The movement of death is immediately preceded by a great feeling of ecstasy and relief which raises us above earthly suffering and is accompanied by an impression of the greatness and inexorability of Nature. After this the story continues on a less elevated plane, and we hear the simple conversation of people discussing the misfortune. And finally the poet stresses the fact—not without a certain sense of pride—that he alone has been initiated into what has just taken place. It should be noted that he has kept the supernatural element until the last

moment, when Man and Nature make their supreme effort. (pp. 116-18)

[We] must take into account the poet's profound faith in Providence and in his own genius; most often, at least in his days of prosperity, this rich and happy soul feels no need to distinguish between a loving God who guides everything to a happy conclusion, and his own Fortune, his "Star."

Then we must also remember [another] principal idea. . . . The old Romantic school does indeed possess the same type of character, but it presents it to us in its own way:—the elected genius is favoured by Chance: it is by accident that the orange falls into Aladdin's turban. Andersen's heroes, on the other hand, deserve their success. True it is that the poet has thought of himself, but it is without pride: he knew he had a mission to carry out.

He felt that he himself was one of the elect and, . . . capable of reading the great book of Nature. This awareness of a vocation or of his being destined to carry out a mission is found for instance in his first tale *The Galoshes of Fortune.* Andersen was not so presumptuous as not to believe that every human being has a calling in this world, be it large or small.

But Andersen has added [yet another] idea to this, an idea which is of the greatest interest for us, since it is this which determines the action in his stories: life is hard in his works. (pp. 118-19)

[Andersen] shouts at us from every page of his writings the realistic philosophy which he had so painfully acquired: "We must pass through many hard trails." Without this thought he would never have become the rejuvenator of the folk-tale. . . .

It lasted some time before Andersen learned to write in this tiny genre [of fairytales or folk stories], fine and polished as it is; at first his talents were so rough and unpolished that he was only able to produce incoherent works which were more or less devoid of idea or form.

It is especially in his interesting but badly constructed novels that he has continually presented us with his material in a rough form. It is the struggle for life he describes for us in his books. *Only a Fiddler* is typical: it describes the man who is crushed beneath the weight of life. It is a book without an idea. As far as the argument is concerned—that all material difficulties ought to be removed from the life of the unfortunate genius—it is no more than a philanthropic project worthy of being dealt with in a brochure and not in a novel. But it is a book full of life and reality. (p. 120)

On a vertical plane his works are full of impartial descriptions of all stations in life. We must turn to Balzac to find such a perfect depiction of so many types of people in so many different social strata: the galley-slave in his prison, the little girl dying of cold out in the street, the night-watchman, the minor official, the young soldier, the priest, the artist, the scholar, noble and middle-class societies.

And on the horizontal plane he has painted all parts of the Denmark of his age. We find Funen, the island of his birth, in stories such as *The Travelling Companion* and *The Buck-Wheat;* Copenhagen, for instance in *The Galoshes of Fortune,* and Zealand in the large number of tales he wrote during his stays at the mansions of the aristocracy (*The Wind Tells of Valdemar Daae; The Happy Family*); then there is Jutland, which he discovered in 1830—after Blicher to be sure—and which after 1850 became the province of which he was most

From a 1900 Danish-language collection of Andersen's works. This illustration is taken from one of Andersen's most widely-known fairy tales, ''The Ugly Duckling.'' By Hans Tegner, 1900.

fond. He loved the heath and the ceaseless wind in these regions.

It is remarkable that the very Danish poet who more than anyone else has had to suffer the reproach of vanity and of being absorbed in preoccupation with himself possesses an awareness of the beauties of nature to a far higher degree than any of his contemporaries. . . . Think of his flowers; they are not like the lilies, the roses, the fig-trees of the folk-tale; they are a complete flora, and the poet knows the secret of each flower, both the humble blossom and the magnificent flower. Remember the little girl in *The Snow Queen* who reveals the thoughts of the flowers. And it is with the same intimate knowledge we see him depict all the seasons and each month, all of them with their own peculiar characteristics. (pp. 123-24)

[Andersen's] tales can be classified under two headings.

In the tales belonging to the first group he limits himself to reproducing—and in a language closely related to that of the people—the tales he has learned from tradition. They are *The Tinder Box, The Princess on the Pea, The Swineherd, The Emperor's New Clothes* (after a Spanish tale), *Simple Simon,* and in the same style, *What Daddy Does Is Always Right.* (p. 126)

The other group consists of serious stories: *The Little Mermaid, The Travelling Companion, The Rose Elf, The Snow Queen, The Red Shoes, The Story of a Mother,* etc. Here the poet takes all the liberties with his models that he wishes, and often he works prompted only by his own imagination, and in his own style which, in an ingenious manner, combines wit and sentiment, pathos and satire, picturesqueness and rationalism. (pp. 126-27)

It was [Andersen's] intention to create in the mould of the ancient folk-tales a new and universal genre which was to absorb all other literary genres. In his novels he often discussed

artistic questions, and in one of the later ones he gives his views on the literature of the future. According to him it must be *brief, lucid and rich,* and these expressions are often to be found again in his correspondence. It was his ambition to write his own tales according to this formula. It is not, however, only the tales which he rejuvenates or continues. He takes the formal elements from the other genres in order to remould the subjects into fairy tales; so we discover the comical epic in *The Staunch Tin Soldier,* and the galant comedy in *The Shepherdess and the Chimney-Sweep.* In this manner his works have become a sort of transportable world literature.

And so his tales became the same for the 19th century, and perhaps for the 20th century as well, as the novels of Voltaire were for the 18th century. The most profound of them closely resemble Voltaire's as far as the pattern is concerned; they are short tales containing a great idea. We could give them all double titles, just as Voltaire did beforehand: *The Story of a Mother, or the Closed Book of Destiny; The Fir Tree, or Ambition; The little Match-Seller, or Charity.* These titles would perhaps be less fitting for Andersen's tales, because in them the idea is very often understood. . . . (p. 128)

Andersen made his debut as a quite young man, but for the first ten years of his career his works lacked a character of their own. We can say that they have one from 1835.

We find the first typical trait of Andersen in tales like *The Galoshes of Fortune,* for instance in the prelude. It is written in the easy, pleasant style of the Heiberg school, only with a natural magic and with an elasticity which that literary group could never have commanded. The beginning will perhaps be remembered: it is a little comedy, a glance at the Copenhagen society of the day; but a sudden change of scene brings us into fairyland, and Andersen's pen does not tremble or lose anything of its elegance when it has to talk of the Fairy of Sadness and of the assistant of the lady in waiting of Fortune. The goddess who inspired Andersen at that time seems to us to be like a young lady from Copenhagen who is both lively and witty.

The second characteristic appears in the tragic tales such as **The Story of a Mother** and in amusing stories such as **It is Quite True.** There is no one else it reminds us of. In future he will produce great and robust art in a small compass. Sentimental digressions and the satirical pieces of mischief from his first period have disappeared. He did not feel the lack of a tenth Muse, the Muse of the Fairy Tale, for it appears he was inspired by Melpomene and Thalia when, at a mature age, he was pondering over his most successful works. But this striking characteristic, pronounced as it is, is not his last.

The third characteristic of Andersen is quite astonishing. From eighteen-fifty-odd we see him in the guise of a bard inspired by divine powers. Just like Ossian on his heaths he gives the elements and nature the gift of reason in his works. Now he is the *Skald* who has sung the most original work in our literature, **The Wind Tells of Valdemar Daae and His Daughters;** and then there is his most sublime poetic work, **The Old Oak Tree's Last Thoughts,** in the face of which, it is true, we cannot help thinking of Goethe's words that Providence does not allow trees to grow right up to the sky. The tree stretches so much towards heaven that at last it breaks, but it is with a crash that is worth hearing. (pp. 129-30)

He had the intelligence of primitive men, the faculty of creating new conceptions rather than of using those which are within the reach of everyone. He had the impressionable feelings of primitive men; he saw, tasted and felt everything: after Oehlenschläger's verse Andersen's stories are the most "felt" works in the whole of our literature; he has himself experienced and reproduced everything in them: light, colour, movements are described with a sureness of touch which only nature can give to a man. (p. 131)

Andersen's greatness consisted in the manner in which he accepted his extraordinary faculties as a gift from Heaven, and in the sublime fact that he felt at one with his vocation as a poet. He knew his own worth, and while we now know that he sacrificed everything for the sake of his missions, his contemporaries scarcely saw anything but vanity in this characteristic of his. (p. 134)

Two fundamental traits in his spiritual life he has in common with other great representatives of art and poetry. One is his unflinching confidence in the guardian angel of his genius, and the conviction that this genius would never leave him. The other is his apprenticeship to Nature, for he never ceased to observe her and to venerate her. This is how the great man is best represented: listening to his genius, and respectfully taking notice of Nature. These two powers never opposed one another; they formed a perpetual alliance, and what is promised by the one is kept by the other. (p. 135)

> *Paul V. Rubow, "Idea and Form in Hans Christian Andersen's Fairy Tales," in* A Book on the Danish Writer, Hans Christian Andersen: His Life and Work, *edited by Svend Dahl and H. G. Topsøe-Jensen, translated by W. Glyn Jones, Det Berlingske Bogtrykkeri, 1955, pp. 97-135.*

FREDRIK BÖÖK   (essay date 1955)

[*The following excerpt is taken from the first work to appear in English translation by this noted Swedish critic. The English version is based on the revised edition of Böök's biography of Andersen, which first appeared in Swedish as* H. C. Andersen: En levnadsteckning *in 1955. Here, Böök discusses Andersen's religious beliefs as the basis of his optimism.*]

No one denies that Hans Christian Andersen was a brilliant artist; but if we wish to take him and his fairy tales seriously, we must ask what sort of wisdom it is he preaches.

At first glance it seems to be anything but deep. Life is a beautiful fairy tale, and there is a loving God Who arranges everything for the best. Andersen takes the practical proof of this teaching from his own life story; the hopeful dream was realized as if through a miracle.

This is the basic type of all his fairy tales: that they treat of fortune's chosen darling. It can scarcely have escaped the author that not all the children of men maintain a magical alliance with the Almighty: on the contrary, some of them lead an unhappy life, in want and poverty, frustrated and betrayed in their fondest desires. Andersen does not close his eyes to any of these unfortunates, and he has a consolation for them, for the little match girl frozen to death, for the withered cripple in the cellar beside a metropolitan street: the joys of Heaven, bliss in the arms of God. Even the little mermaid, apparently excluded, will reach this goal by a detour. Thus the books always balance; we all become favorites like the ugly duckling, although some of us do not attain happiness save through that second sandman, the one who is called "Death." (pp. 208-09)

Religion, a firm belief in an eternal bliss, is thus the foundation of the fairy tales and their optimism. However, Andersen was by no means an orthodox Christian. He resembled the picture he had given of his poor father, a seeker, a brooder, a doubter. Now and then he glorified the faith, the mystery of Christ, and the authority of the Bible, but it was more an expression of his longing than of his conviction. . . . Andersen had also lost the faith of his childhood, and he was also an idealist, a believer in the spirit. He never abandoned his belief in a personal God. He fought eagerly against the doctrine of hell and eternal punishment; and he had every conceivable difficulty in holding fast to his belief in the immortality of the soul—in other words, he had to fight hard to maintain the very basis of both his own existence and that of the fairy tales. (pp. 209-10)

[Andersen] distinguished himself from the vast majority of his Romantic fellow poets by never believing in the "good old days"—the great teller of fairy tales had no patience for that fairy tale. . . . [Andersen] needed neither ingenious philosophical arguments nor learned historical comparisons in order to become conscious of these reactionary sophistries. Like all other genuinely poor people, he had made the necessary studies in his own self and his relatives; he knew the truth about the good old days at first hand, just as he knew the poetry of the stagecoach. Conservative panegyrics about the happiness and harmony of the past, about the healthy satisfaction of the spirit which more than outweighs its concomitant, an apparent poverty of the flesh, have stemmed, of course—directly or indirectly, consciously or unconsciously—from those privileged circles standing to profit by the idyl. If one allows members of the proletariat (or anyone else who has come to grips with the good old days) to bear witness, then the story has a different flavor. However well things went for H. C. Andersen, he was never ashamed of his origins; he never went back on his childhood memories or his family's experiences.

Thus there is no doubt at all where Andersen's deepest sympathies lie: with the unpropertied, the oppressed, and the cowed, with the people—the withered cripple in a back street, the beggar girl, the drunken laundress and her boy in his broken-billed cap. To be sure, he did not demand reforms or pose problems or incite to revolution; but although he stayed quite clear of politics, his fairy tales perhaps exerted a psychological influence nonetheless, an influence which then extended itself into the sphere of action: they had a chastening, a softening, a disturbing effect upon their readers. (pp. 215-17)

Fredrik Böök, in his Hans Christian Andersen: A Biography, *translated by George C. Schoolfield, University of Oklahoma Press, 1962, 260 p.*

ELIAS LIEBERMAN (poem date 1957)

[*The following poem was written by Lieberman in conjunction with a commemorative statue of Andersen which was erected in New York's Central Park in 1957.*]

> To bright-eyed children row on row
> Enraptured by your fancies you
> Are all the magic they need know
>
> To make a story wonder-true.
> A kitchen pan begins to talk
> At dead of night when work is through;
>
> The stars peep in and see brooms walk.
> Your barnyard animals discourse
> On puzzling ways of grown-up folk
>
> And vain, deluded Emperors
> May be reminded by a child
> That flattery begets remorse.
>
> In tales you tell, when winds blow wild,
> The falling snowflakes gently patch
> The cracking roof against the cold
>
> Where heaven is a lighted match.

Elias Lieberman, "Story-Teller's Memorial," in The American Scandinavian Review, *Vol. XLV, No. 1, March, 1957, p. 54.*

BETTINA HÜRLIMANN (essay date 1959)

[*The following essay was first published in German in 1959 as* Europäische kinderbucher in drei jahrhunderten. *Hürlimann assesses Andersen's position in literature as a pivotal figure between Romanticism and the age of technology. She cites Andersen as the first fairy tale writer to incorporate a tragic ending in his tales, suggesting that the tragedy serves the important purpose of "introducing children to literature."*]

Everything in Andersen has a soul of its own and is correspondingly capable of appealing to the reader's imagination. Only seldom are children moved to tears over Grimm's fairy tales, and then only when something particularly sad or horrible is taking place. The fairy tales always remain to a certain extent independent of the reader's experience, tales simply of what goes on in fairyland and thus impossible for ourselves. But with Andersen it is completely different. It is true that he adopts elements from old tales, but what happens to them then? What happens to the little mermaid, for instance, who to begin with is an actual figure from Nordic legend? In order to be near her beloved prince she barters her tail for a pair of human legs, but after that a great change takes place. In spite of her goodness and her obvious faery characteristics, the little princess from the sea must suffer monstrous agonies. Her happiness is paid for with pain, human happiness with human pain. With her we must walk on a thousand knives and our buried feelings are stirred up from depths far removed from those of the folk-tale, whose world of feeling is unsophisticated, and follows accepted rules among which the so-called happy and just ending to stories is one.

For the first time in fairy stories Andersen admits the tragic ending. The little tin-soldier melts in the stove, the little match-girl freezes to death in the street, and the lovelorn little mermaid vanishes in foam at the end of her life as a mortal. Nor is the effect of these tragic conclusions, which stem from Andersen's own experience of life, in any way mitigated by the superb poetry of their telling. The effect they have on a sensitive child is enormous. Thus when people talk about the dangerous influence of fairy tales on children (and people, especially in the fields of education and psychology, often do, thinking mostly of the rather horrific witches and stepmothers that are found in Grimm) it is necessary to affirm that such plainly wicked characters are common to all folk-tales and never emerge triumphant anyway. They cause a much less profound emotional disturbance in a child than the 'pure tragedy' of *The little mermaid,* to take one of the most prominent examples. Basically, however, both forms of fairy tale serve the purpose of introducing children to literature, representing as they do all the elements which will be met with later on in life in novels, in poetry, and on the stage. (pp. 49-50)

[Another] important aspect of Andersen's tales is the fantasy in their poetic association with nature and with the cosmos, above all the moon, which finds its most beautiful expression in *The picture-book without pictures.* Andersen here places himself in the tradition of the great Romantics, except that his attitude to nature is free from their brand of mysticism, being on the contrary full of intelligence and wit. (This, of course, applies less to the kind of story which has been prevalent since classical times and which, by allowing animals speech and free-will, more or less robs them of their real nature.)

In Andersen animals remain animals and plants plants, each peculiar to itself. If he allows the storks to speak then they have to speak Egyptian and they remain storks living on rooftops and spending eight months of the year beside the Nile. . . . But Andersen could get the subject for a story from such everyday things as a drop of water, which he observed through the recently perfected microscope, or a family of snails, simply by revealing the marvel of their real nature. In *Five peas from one pod,* for instance, a pea lodges in the crack in some roof-tiles outside a little girl's bedroom window. It germinates, grows, and blossoms, and saves the life of a child whom everyone expected to die. In other words, a small, accepted process of nature is seen in the light of its own mystery and turned into a fairy tale.

Simply by looking at the openings of these tales one can see how the countryside, the seas, and the rivers are made to become backcloths or even performers. Winds and tempests, the sun, the moon and the stars, elves, water-sprites, and mermen all push the action along, and often Death will come too. For Andersen was no escapist taking refuge in nature. He stood centrally between the age of Romanticism and the age of Technology. The one gave him his profundity, bearing him forward and enriching him, the other he greeted with enthusiasm. (pp. 50-1)

Bettina Hürlimann, "'The Ugly Duckling'," in her Three Centuries of Children's Books in Europe, *edited and translated by Brian W. Alderson, The World Publishing Company, 1968, pp. 42-52.*

ERIK HAUGAARD (essay date 1973)

[*Haugaard, a poet and author of children's books, published an English translation of Andersen's collected fairy tales in 1974. Haugaard was preeminent among Andersen's translators as the first to render the tales in a colloquial prose style. The following essay was originally presented as a lecture to the Library of Congress on March 5, 1973.*]

A great writer is part of his native land, as if his name stood for something we could point to, like a mountain or a lake. This is the proof of our acceptance of his immortality. I could as little imagine a Denmark in which Hans Christian Andersen did not exist as I could believe that the island of Fyn or Odense, Andersen's birthplace, could vanish. . . .

[Andersen] wrote a clear, unassuming prose that he was much criticized for in his own times but that we in the 20th century admire. Andersen never used dialect. Everyone from kings to darning needles speaks an educated Danish, for he never patronized his characters. Their tragedies were real to him, and he made them real to us. He considered neither the fairytale nor the folktale unworthy of becoming literature. And when he tampered with his source material, which he almost always did, it was never to make it more folksy or quaint but to add that dimension which he hoped would give it the dignity of a work of art. (p. 5)

All artists are fascinated by their own kind; they cannot escape this preoccupation, at least the artists of the last two centuries have not been able to. Andersen is no exception to this rule. He wrote innumerable stories about the poet. Some of the finest of them are almost unknown: "**The Gardener and His Master**," "**Psyche**," "**In the Duckyard**," "**The Bronze Pig**." The most famous is that lovely fairytale to which Andersen gave the title "**The Nightingale**," and I do think it is a little misleading to call it "**The Emperor's Nightingale**" when one of the points of the story is that the little bird belongs to no one. (p. 7)

We have a tendency to think too much in terms of economics, and the life of the poor we imagine as one long chain of miseries. But in reality there is such a thing as a rich little poor boy, and I think that this was exactly what Andersen must have been. He was seldom scolded and never hit. He was given all the time he wanted to dream, and he had the whole town to play in. . . .

Although the confines of Andersen's Christianity were vague, and within them was to be found the deist worship of nature, which he himself loved so passionately, Andersen believed in divine justice and a merciful God. He thought that man's redemption was always possible but only through personal suffering, as he shows us in "**The Red Shoes**" and in two lesser known but also very lovely stories, "**The Girl Who Stepped on Bread**" and "**Ann Lisbeth**." (p. 9)

What distinguishes the fairytale world from the other world of fiction? First of all, the most obvious: its universality. The same plots appear again and again; it is only the physical environment that is changed; for the fairytale is so simple, so sparsely told, that the more refined and complex aspects of society cannot be included. A king is a king; a pauper, a pauper; and a rich merchant, a rich merchant: archetypes all and as such recognizable. Its philosophy is simple and pragmatic, learned from hard knocks rather than intellectual pursuits. This unbookishness makes the reader secure: this is a friend telling him a story. No one questions that it is better to be born a rich man's son than a pauper's; and if one is so unfortunate as to be born poor, then it is advisable to try to marry a princess. People are divided into good and bad, but this very division means that these qualities exist and are recognizable. Women are often shrewish and mean, men brutal and hard; but love is possible and so is happiness—even ever after.

"Once upon a time" is no time, just as east of the sun and west of the moon, or the end of the world, is no place. In reality, however, it means "at all times, in all places." It is a declaration, announcing that what you are now going to hear is the truth—both in time and space. And we must, to a certain extent, all agree or we would not love the fairytale so much.

Lost as we are in our own particular problems, locked in a world all too unique, we draw comfort from the fairytale world, finding in its simplicity, if not solutions to our private troubles, then at least a momentary respite from them. For the purpose of the fairytale is to let out a little truth in a world of lies. It is a safety valve and a necessary one. (p. 16)

> *Erik Haugaard, in his* Portrait of a Poet: Hans Christian Andersen and His Fairytales, *Library of Congress, 1973, 17 p.*

GERALD WEALES (essay date 1974)

Andersen's strain of conventional piety, his sentimentality (Maurice Sendak once called it "sentiment," but to me it is schmaltz), his morality in a nutshell, his understandable preoccupation with his own country—all these make it difficult for me to take Andersen in bulk. Still, there are many pleasures.

He is often funny, frequently in a parenthetic throwaway or a surprise turn of phrase. "**The Shadow**" is not only Andersen's best treatment of his recurrent appearance-substance theme, but a fine story by any standards, and "**In the Duckyard**" is a marvelously sardonic treatment of the destructive do-gooder. One of my favorite tales is "**How to Cook Soup Upon a Sausage Pin**," but since the titular phrase means "to make a lot out of nothing," I may have over-responded after having crept through too many sketches that were no more than simple conceits. It is possible, of course, that Andersen provides a kind of Rorschach. If that is the case, the publication of [*The Complete Fairy Tales and Stories*] provides every reader with the opportunity to make up his own Andersen anthology, sweet or sour.

> *Gerald Weales, in a review of "The Complete Fairy Tales and Stories," in* The New York Times Book Review, *April 28, 1974, p. 8.*

WILLIAM MISHLER (essay date 1978)

[*In the following essay Mishler provides a Freudian interpretation of "The Steadfast Tin Soldier." Mishler states that Andersen implemented a style of romance that resembles the Freudian concept of wish-fulfillment.*]

The story [of "**The Steadfast Tin Soldier**"] is of a one-legged tin soldier who falls in love with a ballerina doll, is propelled upon a series of adventures which culminate in his being swallowed by, then rescued from, a fish; and who finally, once back home, is united with the dancer in a fiery death in the

One of the most elaborate illustrations to appear in early Andersen collections. This drawing depicts the popular "The Steadfast Tin Soldier." By Hans Tegner, 1900.

stove, a death which reveals his heroic excellence and her vanity.

It is true that it is a story which exhibits in miniaturized form what Northrop Frye would call "the complete form of romance," i.e., "the successful quest (which has) three main stages: the stage of the perilous journey and the preliminary minor adventures; the crucial struggle, usually some kind of battle in which either the hero or his foe, or both, must die; and the exaltation of the hero." What seems less likely, however, is that we respond to the story simply because it is a good parody of the heroic mode. Parody it is, but it is not a simple one. Andersen has modified romance not only by casting it in a miniature frame; he has dislocated something at its principle and source.

Romance, Frye suggests with much good evidence, is a literary form very close to dream and wish-fulfillment. Typically, it stages a struggle between a Hero and an Enemy, and in the victory of the former over the latter, the forces of life, order, renewal are shown to triumph over those of death and sterility. . . . (p. 390)

Applying Frye's account of romance to Andersen's story, we quickly perceive the essential difference between the two. The soldier has an enemy in the black troll in the tobacco jar, but

whether their discord has anything to do with the agency of events is deliberately left unclear. . . . The opposing force which ought to be of such strength as to allow the hero to define himself against it is undercut and made merely hypothetical.

Correspondingly, the hero's will is diminished as the motor of the plot. Things do not happen because he wants them to, but for some other, unexplained reason. Hazy causality, in fact, is one of the story's principle features, providing it with a point of mystery which has intrigued many of its readers. The soldier moves through all the positions of the heroic paradigm (trip to the underworld, etc.) seemingly without wanting to.

Why?

Some readers have said that it is because the soldier is made of tin. Their argument is that once Andersen had chosen to write about a tin soldier, poetic decorum demanded that he respect the fact that metal dolls cannot move. (p. 391)

Attractive as such a view is—it shows us the artist as game player who wins by scrupulously following the rules which, with apparent nonchalance, he has set himself—it nevertheless disregards an important passage in the story which clearly shows us that the toys are not bound by the inertness of their substance. . . . (pp. 391-92)

The passage makes clear that at night the toys can act just like people. Now if all the toys but the soldier and the dancer do not move, then the reason must be found not in the materials of which they are composed but rather in the supposition that they do not want to, or are emotionally unable to. Their rigidity is not physical but psychical.

As for the ballerina, we learn at the end of the story (and in this she resembles numerous heroines in Andersen's other stories) that her immobility is the expression of her narcissism; she is a prisoner of a pervasive sense of her own loveliness. The fire at the end of the story proves that her life was vanity. . . .

While the soldier, we remember, melted into "et lille Tin-hjerte," [a little tin heart] showing that in life and in death he incarnated a lofty Eros. Not entirely after the fact—for something in Andersen's tone has alerted us—we begin to recognize how the soldier's love and his steadfastness are related. They are linked by way of an absence, a blanking out, of erotic desire. (p. 392)

Not only does the soldier, in effect, forbid himself the dancer with the very breath with which he appropriates her, he also mimes his reluctance by *lying down* behind the tobacco jar, home of the repressive troll, in order to see her better: seeing will keep her at a distance. Thus at the outset of the story, in the arrangement of figures upon the table we have a concrete rebus for the repressive force which will deflect the story away from romance. If we remember Frye's description of romance as a literary form close to wish-fulfillment, in Andersen's story we find the wish in the process of being repressed.

The romantic quest is at a basic level an erotic one; this is why Andersen's story has an odd feel to it—like a clock in which the mainspring is not missing, for the mechanism works, but a clock working in spite of itself. Stifled desire on the part of the soldier accounts for several significant peculiarities of the text; it tells us why, on the formal level, causality has given way to a mere temporal linking of events, and why, on the level of plot, the otherwise essential enmity between the hero and the enemy is here of such a nebulous character. Often in Andersen, as in the later writings of Freud, the forces of life and death are not clearly at odds. **"The Steadfast Tin Soldier"** is informed by a great hesitation as to whether the real danger lies in the direction of the ballerina or of the troll. (Of course it stems from neither.) In mutely gazing upon the ballerina while all the other toys are playing and dancing, the soldier bears witness to the doubleness of the force which is carrying him—into a vital embrace in his lover's arms which perhaps (and ultimately, of course) is fatal.

He yields nevertheless. That is to say, he is carried. His unrecognized and unavowed desire becomes a nebulous external force which animates a series of apparently unrelated incidents which, however, after the fact are seen to have traced an unswerving line leading to the conjunction of erotic love with death—an equivalency which the reader can now recognize was implicit at the start as the alienating curve upon which the story shaped itself.

The irony of Andersen's method consists, then, in presenting the soldier's stalemate as a kind of victory. The completed design of the story suggests to the reader that steadfastness is another name for fear, or the result of fear. On the level of plot, it is an attitude which allows the soldier to move without moving; on the formal level, it allows the story to come to its conclusion without resolving its central conflict. Indeed, the story enacts a nonresolution, it dramatizes an impasse. (pp. 392-93)

Whatever his resistance, the tin soldier is carried toward the furnace. The account of his fate, however, does not appal us, not even when we become aware of the fear which informs it. Perhaps this is thanks to the voice of the narrator, Andersen's justly famous "spoken" style. The wilfulness of the voice proclaims its freedom, and the freedom of the voice strikes a richly appropriate balance with the unrelentingness of the subject matter. The reader comes away grateful, not so much for the charm of this miniaturized world, as for the reassurance of a voice in control of itself as it speaks its inevitable fate. (p. 394)

> William Mishler, "H. C. Andersen's 'Tin Soldier' in a Freudian Perspective," in Scandinavian Studies, Vol. 50, No. 4, Autumn, 1978, pp. 389-95.

ADDITIONAL BIBLIOGRAPHY

Andersen, Hans Christian. *The Complete Andersen: All of the 168 Stories by Hans Christian Andersen*. Edited and translated by Jean Hersholt. 6 vols. New York: Heritage Press, 1942.
> A valuable collection of Andersen's fairy tales. Hersholt provides the reader with detailed notes and an extensive chronological bibliography.

Auden, W. H. "Grimm and Andersen." In his *Forewords and Afterwords*, pp. 198-208. New York: Random House, 1973.*
> Argues that fairy tales are an essential part of childhood and maintains that a fairy tale should never be considered a reflection of the real world. Auden discusses the differences between the fairy tales of the Brothers Grimm and Andersen's fairy tales; he concludes that Andersen's style is immortal and impossible to duplicate.

Bennett, James O'Donnell. "Hans Andersen's Fairy Tales." In his *Much Loved Books: Best Sellers of the Ages*, pp. 291-96. New York: Boni and Liveright, 1927.

> A charming account of the similarities between Andersen's personal life and his fairy tale "The Ugly Duckling."

Bredsdorff, Elias. "Hans Andersen and Scotland." *Blackwood's Edinburgh Review* (April 1955): 297-312.
> Chronicles Andersen's extensive travels through Scotland and discusses Sir Walter Scott's influence upon Andersen. Bredsdorff is considered by many to be the foremost contemporary Andersen scholar.

————. *Hans Christian Andersen: The Story of His Life and Dissolution*. Anglistica, edited by Torsten Dahl, Kemp Malone, and Geoffrey Tillotson, Vol. VII. Copenhagen: Rosenkilde and Bagger, 1956, 140 p.*
> Traces the stormy friendship of Charles Dickens and Andersen through an analysis of their correspondence. Bredsdorff argues that the relationship has been both misinterpreted and misrepresented and presents his own explanation for the dissolution of their friendship.

Bredsdorff, Elias. *Hans Christian Andersen: The Story of His Life and Work, 1805-75*. New York: Charles Scribner's Sons, 1975, 376 p.
> An authoritative, well-organized biography that also discusses Andersen's stories. Bredsdorff organizes Andersen's stories into seven groups: 1) fairy tales possessing a supernatural element, 2) tales in which magic is involved within a natural setting, 3) tales in which animals are main characters, 4) tales in which the main characters are plants and/or trees, 5) tales in which inanimate objects become animate, 6) "realistic" tales in fantastic settings, and 7) realistic stories set in the real world. He illustrates the significance of each of these groups and provides examples from the tales themselves. Bredsdorff also discusses the inconsistencies found in English translations of Andersen's works, concluding that the best English translators of the tales are R. P. Keigwin, Reginald Spink, L. W. Kingsland, and Jean Hersholt.

De la Mare, Walter. "Hans Christian Andersen." In his *Pleasures and Speculations*, pp. 14-23. London: Faber and Faber, 1940.
> Discusses the difficulties involved in translating Andersen's fairy tales. De la Mare emphasizes the imperfections of Andersen's Danish, which make literal translation of the fairy tales impossible.

Grønbech, Bo. *Hans Christian Andersen*. Boston: Twayne Publishers, 1980, 170 p.
> An extensive study that combines a biographical sketch of Andersen with short commentaries on a number of his works.

Hazard, Paul. "Superiority of the North over the South." In his *Books, Children, & Men*, 3d ed., translated by Marguerite Mitchell, pp. 77-110. Boston: Horn Book, 1947.*
> Praises Andersen's ability to represent "the very soul of beings and of things." Hazard maintains that Andersen's tales reflect the true meaning of life.

Hersholt, Jean, and Westergaard, Waldemar, eds. *The Andersen-Scudder Letters*. Berkeley and Los Angeles: University of California Press, 1949, 181 p.
> A compilation of Andersen's correspondence with his American editor, Horace E. Scudder.

Mayer, Hans. "Alternatives in the Nineteenth Century: Life in Conformity, Hans Christian Andersen." In his *Outsiders: A Study in Life and Letters*, translated by Denis M. Sweet, pp. 191-99. Cambridge, Mass.: MIT Press, 1982.
> Asserts that Andersen lived a "double life." According to Mayer, Andersen led an existence of total conformity, as Andersen himself asserted in *The Story of My Life*. However, Mayer also proposes that Andersen was in reality a timid homosexual. This view receives little support from other sources.

Mudrick, Marvin. "The Ugly Duck." In his *Books Are Not Life but then What Is?*, pp. 87-97. New York: Oxford University Press, 1979.
> Challenges the views of other critics who favorably compare Andersen to Dickens (see R. Nisbet Bain, 1895 and Robert Lynd, 1922) and asserts that Andersen's best work "reads like the worst

of Dickens.'' Mudrick admits that Andersen possesses talent as a storyteller, but says that much of the author's original work is overly sentimental ''Victorian trash.''

''Hans Christian Andersen: The Story of His Life and His Fairy Tales.'' *The New York Times,* Pictorial Supplement (2 April 1905): 1-4.
    An entertaining biographical account commemorating the hundredth anniversary of Andersen's birth, including excerpts from his fairy tales.

Spink, Reginald. *Hans Christian Andersen and His World.* London: Thames and Hudson, 1972, 128 p.
    An excellent biographical source. Spink consulted numerous Andersen scholars in the compilation of this biography. He provides the reader with a pictorial glimpse of Andersen, including caricatures, reproductions of title pages, and various other illustrations.

Stirling, Monica. *The Wild Swan: The Life and Times of Hans Christian Andersen.* New York: Harcourt, Brace & World, 1965, 383 p.
    A well-written, authoritative biography.

Toksvig, Signe. *The Life of Hans Christian Andersen.* New York: Harcourt, Brace and Co., 1934, 289 p.
    A personal approach to Andersen. Toksvig's biography emphasizes Andersen's emotional growth throughout his career.

Hugh Henry Brackenridge

1748-1816

American novelist, dramatist, poet, essayist, short story writer, and journalist.

Brackenridge's best known work, *Modern Chivalry: Containing the Adventures of Captain John Farrago and Teague O'Regan, His Servant,* is considered by many critics to be one of the best American novels produced in the eighteenth century. As the first novel to successfully incorporate frontier subjects, local color, and colloquial language, *Modern Chivalry* is now acknowledged as a neglected comic masterpiece. In addition, the novel paved the way for the growth of frontier literature as a genre and for the work of such later writers as James Fenimore Cooper and Mark Twain. Brackenridge's deft use of satire, raucous plots, and vivid characterization, as well as his Neoclassical prose style, have earned him a distinguished place among eighteenth-century American novelists.

Born in Scotland, the son of farmers who emigrated to America in 1753, Brackenridge grew up in Pennsylvania. The family endured many hardships of pioneer life, including the constant threat of Indian attacks, incidents that Brackenridge described in his later works. Since his family was poor, Brackenridge had to be resourceful in his efforts to gain an education. He bartered goods in exchange for schooling while working on his family's farm, taught school in Maryland from 1763 to 1768, and worked his way through Princeton College. While a student at Princeton, Brackenridge met Philip Freneau and James Madison, and the three friends founded the Whig Society, a student group active in political debating. He and Freneau collaborated on "The Rising Glory of America," a patriotic poem, and on *Father Bombo's Pilgrimage to Mecca,* a comic novel about the travel adventures of a priest. Brackenridge's courses at Princeton immersed him in the study of classical literature, eighteenth-century English novelists such as Tobias Smollett, Henry Fielding, Samuel Butler, Laurence Sterne, and Jonathan Swift, and European authors such as François Rabelais and Miguel de Cervantes, all of whom influenced his later works.

In 1772, Brackenridge became master of an academy in Maryland, where, according to critics, his two dramas, *The Battle of Bunkers-Hill* and *The Death of General Montgomery in Storming the City of Quebec,* were first performed. In 1774, Brackenridge earned a master's degree in theology from Princeton and composed his "Poem on Divine Revelation" in honor of his commencement. After graduating, Brackenridge, a Whig and ardent patriot, served as chaplain in George Washington's army during the Revolutionary War, composing *Six Political Discourses Founded on the Scriptures,* a series of sermons intended to improve troop morale. After the war, Brackenridge abandoned the ministry and became a lawyer, settling in Pittsburgh in 1781. His interest in politics grew: he served as a member of the State Assembly of Pennsylvania, became a prominent voice in the Republican (now Democratic) party, and established the politically strident *United States Magazine* and *The Pittsburgh Gazette.* While trying to mediate between rebels and officials during the 1794 Whiskey Rebellion, Brackenridge was accused of treason but was acquitted by Alexander Hamilton. The episode left Brackenridge disillusioned and de-moralized; *Incidents of the Insurrection in the Western Parts of Pennsylvania in the Year 1794* is a fictionalized autobiographical account of that crisis. Several years later Brackenridge again entered politics and was appointed a judge of the Supreme Court of Pennsylvania. In his remaining years he wrote legal studies, which he published in his *Law Miscellanies.* Though often considered an eccentric and controversial figure, Brackenridge enjoyed much respect as an author and statesman.

Brackenridge's earliest works, *Father Bombo's Pilgrimage to Mecca, A Poem on the Rising Glory of America,* and *A Poem on Divine Revelation,* anticipate his later style and themes. Informed by his satire and humor, the poems testify to Brackenridge's faith in progress and to his patriotism. The two blank verse dramas, *The Battle of Bunkers-Hill* and *The Death of General Montgomery in Storming the City of Quebec,* attest to his ability to write in a formal, Neoclassical manner and also display Brackenridge's patriotic fervor. The two dramas are written in Hudibrastic verse, a form based on Samuel Butler's satiric poem *Hudibras,* which emphasizes humor, burlesque, and mock heroic elements. Though some of Brackenridge's later works, such as the so-called Scottish poems (collected in *Gazette Publications*) and the second part of *Modern Chivalry,* appear more lyrical and sentimental, his work is generally characterized by realistic treatment and subject matter. Brackenridge was also one of the first American writers to use native themes, local color, and colloquial speech in his works. His short story "The Cave of Vanhest" holds an important place in American literature as the first story set against the realistic background of the American Revolution. Similarly, "The Trial of Mamachtaga" was an unusual story in its time because it sympathetically depicted American Indians.

Modern Chivalry, Brackenridge's most famous work, originated as a poem, "The Modern Chevalier," and later evolved into a novel. Brackenridge published the work serially between 1792 and 1797, issued Part II in 1804-05, and then revised the entire piece in 1816. *Modern Chivalry* combines the various aspects of Brackenridge's style and many of his interests. Loosely episodic in structure, the novel relates the adventures of Captain Farrago and his servant Teague O'Regan, with sections interspersed in which the narrator makes didactic comments on the action. The structure, characters, and narrative are based in part on Cervantes's *Don Quixote* and reflect the European picaresque tradition. Critics have commented that the plot is digressive, but add that Brackenridge's slapstick humor and witty satire hold the reader's attention. Neoclassical both in form and content, the novel is influenced by the satiric style of Jonathan Swift. Part II of the novel is generally considered less effective and more subdued than its predecessor. Primarily a didactic work, *Modern Chivalry* was intended to point out the dangers of a fledgling democracy and to reaffirm the true potential of this form of government. As a believer in the values of the Enlightenment, Brackenridge focused on reason and balance as the necessary guides in a sound democracy and attacked the demagoguery and human weakness that he saw around him. His satire, though sharp, is not vindictive or bitter, but some critics consider his humor too intellectual to have had wide influence. However, *Modern Chivalry* was an extremely popular work, containing racy plot elements, earthy western humor, and language so frank that certain sections were censored for the 1819 edition.

Most critical studies of Brackenridge's works examine the nature and purpose of his satire. One early review of *Modern Chivalry* praised its "whimsical and ludicrous" tone, but ignored Brackenridge's serious didactic intent. Later reviewers realized that there were "sound political maxims embodied in the jokes." All of Brackenridge's critics have agreed that his satire is essentially good-natured and that his desire to educate American citizens about democracy is praiseworthy. Yet his effectiveness as a satirist has been questioned by some. Ernest Brennecke, Jr. commented that Brackenridge's satiric style "lacks the polish, the concentration, the detached sharpness and wit" of his models, Swift and Cervantes. Some critics fault Brackenridge for attempting to accommodate his satiric style to a general audience. Most commentators, however, praise Brackenridge's use of humor and artistry in the service of instructive satire. While earlier critics assumed that Brackenridge's views were always equivalent to those of the narrator, recent critics focus on Brackenridge's conscious manipulation of point of view, indicating artistry not noted by earlier commentators.

Alexander Cowie has called Brackenridge "the first distinguished American novelist to make substantial use of political satire." Criticism of his work, however, indicates that Brackenridge's contribution to American literature encompasses more. *Modern Chivalry* opened up the western frontier as a subject for other American writers and confirmed the value of exploring native themes and subjects. The patriotic spirit evident in each of Brackenridge's works makes them not only literary, but social documents as well.

(See also *Dictionary of Literary Biography*, Vol. 11: *American Humorists, 1800-1950*.)

PRINCIPAL WORKS

A Poem on the Rising Glory of America [with Philip
    Freneau] (poetry) 1772
The Battle of Bunkers-Hill (drama) 1772?
*The Death of General Montgomery in Storming the City of
    Quebec* (drama) 1772?
A Poem on Divine Revelation (poetry) 1774
Six Political Discourses Founded on the Scriptures
    (sermons) 1778
"The Cave of Vanhest" (short story) 1779; published in
    journal *The United States Magazine*
*Modern Chivalry: Containing the Adventures of Captain
    John Farrago and Teague O'Regan, His Servant*. 4
    vols. (novel) 1792-97, 1816
*Incidents of the Insurrection in the Western Parts of
    Pennsylvania in the Year 1794* (novel) 1795
*Modern Chivalry: Containing the Adventures of a Captain,
    Etc., Part II* (novel) 1804-05, 1816
Gazette Publications (essays, poetry, and letters) 1806
**"The Trial of Mamachtaga" (short story) 1808;
    published in *A Selection of Some of the Most Interesting
    Narratives of Outrages Committed by the Indians in
    Their Wars with the White People*
Law Miscellanies (essays) 1814

****Father Bombo's Pilgrimage to Mecca* [with Philip
    Freneau] (novel) 1975

*This work includes the poem "The Modern Chevalier."

**This work was written in 1785.

***This work was written in 1770.

THE UNIVERSAL ASYLUM AND COLUMBIAN MAGAZINE
(essay date 1792)

Mr. [Brackenridge] pursuing the plan of his first volume [of *Modern Chivalry*], continues, in this, his satires upon various descriptions of men. His remarks are occasionally whimsical and ludicrous, but have seldom the appearance of ill nature. He seems to have been, for the most part, in a laughing humour, when he wrote; and we believe few persons will peruse the work, without also experiencing risible emotions.

We are sorry to observe, that the captain's travels are not very remarkable for variety. Some favourite scenes, which were exhibited in the first volume, are again brought forward, with little variation, in this. Peter Pindar is not more desirous of ridiculing, again and again, kings and royal academicians, than our author appears disposed to satirize popular elections, the American Philosophical Society, ignorance in the clergy, and Indian treaties, &c. Not satisfied with the strictures upon these several subjects, in his first volume, he has again attacked them in this. Several new characters, however, are brought into view; and amidst much light reading, new and valuable observations frequently occur. Mr. B. affects to write merely for the sake of style, but no person, who has perused the work, can for a moment, look upon this pretension in a serious light. (pp. 115-16)

> *A review of "Modern Chivalry: Containing the Adventures of Captain John Farrago, and Teague O'Regan, His Servant," in* The Universal Asylum and Columbian Magazine, *Vol. 11, August, 1792, pp. 115-17.*

THE SOUTHERN LITERARY MESSENGER   (essay date 1842)

[*The following review of* Modern Chivalry *is notable because the critic introduces the ideas that Brackenridge's purpose was to "indoctrinate the people" and that his work was influenced by Samuel Butler's* Hudibras *and Miguel de Cervantes's* Don Quixote. *Both of these comments are frequently repeated by later critics of Brackenridge's work.*]

[Brackenridge's object in writing *Modern Chivalry*] was to write something that would indoctrinate the people themselves on the subject of government, and correct those errors into which their almost boundless state of freedom would be apt to lead them. Dry dissertations, like those of Montesquieu and others, would do for the learned, but would not be read by one in ten thousand of the people. He, at first, thought of a form like Butler's *Hudibras*—but concluding that this would not be so likely to be read as prose, he determined to try the plan of Cervantes in his *Don Quixotte*. His hero, Capt. Farrago, is however no madman, but simply an eccentric. He found it difficult to supply the place of Sancho, and had recourse to a Milesian Irishman of the lower order, of the Thady or Paddy-from-Cork species. The character is certainly not so successful as that of Sancho; but there is much humor in it; and it answered his purpose better than any he could find of American original. His Scotchman, Duncan Ferguson, is better sustained, and more natural. *Modern Chivalry* is a profound philosophical and political work, under the guise of pleasantry. It is wonderful what a variety of topics is touched, in the most compendious way, and admirably adapted to form the people to the true principles of a democratic republic. (pp. 18-19)

> *"Biographical Notice of H. H. Brackenridge, Late of the Supreme Court of Pennsylvania," in* The Southern Literary Messenger, *Vol. VIII, No. 1, January, 1842, pp. 1-19.*

THE LITERARY WORLD   (essay date 1847)

[Brackenridge's *Modern Chivalry* is] a book of cleverness on an old model; but, if the truth, must be confessed, occasionally tedious and rarely shaking the diaphragm. Yet there are good hits in *Modern Chivalry,* as there are in . . . [Tabitha Tenney's] *Female Quixotism.* The fare is not so abundant as at the glorious entertainment of Camacho's wedding [in *Don Quixotte*], when Sancho ladled out the pullets; but that is not to be expected. An Irish bog-trotter in the wilds of America is not in a situation, like his Spanish original, to gather up a harvest of humor, which had been ripening among his countrymen for centuries. . . .

The Captain of course is the representative of Don Quixotte, a clear-headed man, whose independent way of looking at things from living out of the world, has gained him the credit of eccentricity. He is withal a practical wag, setting out with his Irish servant in search of adventures. The gist of his observations and experiences lies in this, that the duties and responsibilities of a new state of society have been thrust upon a race of men so suddenly, that, unused to their new democratic privileges, they are very much in the way of abusing them. (p. 250)

[Teague's adventures,] with every other chapter a semi-satirical essay on the duties of governor and governed, make up the first portion of the *Modern Chivalry.* The opinions expressed are those of a canny Scotchman, and the main purpose of the satire, to rebuke misplaced inefficiency in office, is very commendable. (p. 251)

> *A review of "Modern Chivalry," in* The Literary World, *Vol. I, No. 11, April 17, 1847, pp. 250-51.*

GRAHAM'S MAGAZINE   (essay date 1847)

The style [of *Modern Chivalry*] is clear and familiar, the humor such as touches the risibilities, and the strokes of satire sometimes peculiarly happy. Though the author formed himself on the model of [Henry] Fielding, the allusions and subject matter are essentially American. The illustrations by Darley are excellent. Like all true humorists the author makes his pleasantries the vehicle of knowledge and wisdom. He has sound political maxims embodied in jokes, and curious bits of learning swimming on the surface of his humor.

> *A review of "Modern Chivalry; or, The Adventures of Captain Farrago and Teague O'Regan," in* Graham's Magazine, *Vol. XXX, No. 6, June, 1847, p. 380.*

HENRY ADAMS   (essay date 1889)

[*Adams was an American autobiographer, historian, essayist, and novelist whose work is less pertinent to the history of literature than it is to the history of ideas. In the latter context, Adams embodies for many a particularly modern viewpoint, one which sees the world becoming less stable and coherent than it once was and which predicts that this trend will continue, never to be arrested. Adams developed this doctrine most thoroughly in his best-known work,* The Education of Henry Adams.]

[Backenridge] showed genuine and original qualities. American humor was not then so marked as it afterward became, and good-nature was rarer; but H. H. Brackenridge set an example of both in a book ["*Modern Chivalry*"] once universally popular throughout the South and West. A sort of prose "Hudibras," it had the merit of leaving no sting, for this satire on democracy was written by a democrat and published in the most democratic community of America. . . . "*Modern Chivalry*" was not only written in good last-century English, none too refined for its subject, but was more thoroughly American than any book yet published, or to be published until . . . [A. B. Longstreet's] "Georgia Scenes" of forty years later. Never known, even by title, in Europe, and little enjoyed in the seaboard States, where bog-trotters and weavers had no such prominence, Judge Brackenridge's book filled the place of Don Quixote on the banks of the Ohio and along the Mississippi. (pp. 124-25)

> *Henry Adams, "Intellect of the Middle States," in his* History of the United States of America during the First Administration of Thomas Jefferson, *Vol. I, Charles Scribner's Sons, 1889, pp. 108-30.**

MOSES COIT TYLER   (essay date 1897)

[*Though this essay was composed in 1897, it was first published in 1957.*]

Hugh Henry Brackenridge demands and deserves our notice on account of two dramatic poems produced by him soon after the opening of the physical conflict of the Revolution, and having in themselves a striking distinctness of method and of purpose. Like every other writer of this period, he seems to have been deeply stirred by the significance of the military events of the first year of that conflict—the year 1775—their pathos, their tragic horror, and their prodigious messages both of warning and of good-cheer. From all these events he selects two, each as the subject of a serious dramatic poem,—the one being the first real clash between American and Briton as displayed on the seventeenth of June, upon a height in full view from Boston; the other being the death of the high-minded American leader, General Montgomery, in his baffled attempt at the capture of Quebec. Both of these dramas are wrought out with strict attention to the classic unities of time, place, and action; and both are intended merely as dramatic poems to be read, not at all as plays to be acted.

The chief purpose of the earlier poem—"**The Battle of Bunker's Hill**"—. . . was one exactly fitted to the need of the hour in which it sprang into life: it was to inspire Americans with military confidence by setting forth, in opposition to the old taunts of cowardice and incapacity, the remarkable fighting qualities—the almost unrivaled military effectiveness—exhibited by their brethren in that battle. This is the controlling idea of the poem; and while it is indicated from the very beginning of the action, the full development of it is delayed till near the end, when it is accomplished with striking effect in the form of spontaneous admissions from the lips of the victorious British officers then commenting on the battle they had just won at so great a cost. Finally, the lesson of military confidence which the poem is meant to teach, has an added impressiveness from the fact that the poet, while recognizing the physical conditions on which military success depends, gives great prominence, also, to the moral conditions of such success. Thus, the object for which a man fights, is sure to tell on his success in fighting. (pp. 210-11)

[To] the end of the poem, the scene shifts in quick succession from one side of the fight to the other; and at every stage of its progress comes out in deeper colors the contrast in moral significance between the objects of the two armies. This effect reaches its culmination in a noble scene wherein the very defeat of the Americans is consecrated by the blood of their chieftain, Warren. This leader—a hero of the antique mold, one of Plutarch's men—having received his death wound, falls upon his right knee, and "covering his breast with his right hand, and supporting himself with his firelock in his left," spends his fast-ebbing strength in this appeal to his comrades. . . . (pp. 215-16)

[In **"The Death of General Montgomery at the Siege of Quebec,"** the] chief purpose was to stimulate American military ardor by stimulating American hatred of the enemy; and this it sought to accomplish through a presentation of their detestable character, especially their sordidness, perfidy, and cruelty. Thus, in the two poems, the argument is made complete: first, that we have the ability to fight the British; and, secondly, that we have every possible motive for fighting them—since they are monsters of greed, treachery, and inhumanity. (pp. 218-19)

[As a chaplain in Washington's army,] he composed for [the troops] the **"Six Political Discourses Founded on the Scripture,"** which, in 1778, were given forth in print to all who cared to read them; the range and method of which may partly be guessed from their titles: **"The Bloody Vestiges of Tyranny," "The Nature and Artifice of Toryism," "The Fate of Tyranny and Toryism," "The Agency of Heaven in the Cause of Liberty," "The Blasphemy of Gasconade and Self-Dependence in a Certain General," "The Great Wrath of the Tyrant and the Cause of It."** These discourses do indeed announce themselves as **"Founded on the Scripture."** It may be so; but it is chiefly to Old Testament Scripture that the reference must be meant, and particularly to those portions of it which recite the slaughter of the Canaanites by Joshua, the pitiless deed of Jael the wife of Heber, the imprecations of the Psalmist David, the fierce valor and terribleness of the Maccabees.

Thus, the first discourse, entitled **"The Bloody Vestiges of Tyranny,"** was written and spoken just after the rout and slaughter of our men at the battle of Brandywine, and is a weird rhythmic chant of rage and patriotic hate and vengeance. (pp. 299-300)

> *Moses Coit Tyler, "The Dramatic Literature of the Revolution" and "Pulpit-Champions of the American Revolution," in his* The Literary History of the American Revolution, 1763-1783: 1776-1783, Vol. II, *Frederick Ungar Publishing Co., 1957, pp. 188-227, 278-316.**

LILLIE DEMING LOSHE   (essay date 1907)

[The] satirical form of didacticism, which gave rise to the large family of eighteenth century Quixotes, is represented in America by Hugh Henry Brackenridge's *Modern Chivalry:* containing the *Adventures of Captain John Farrago and Teague O'Regan his Servant.* This story, which displays more ability than any other American tales before those of Charles Brockden Brown, describes the travels of a thoughtful man whose ideas of life have been derived entirely from books. He is accompanied by an ignorant Irish servant, half-fool, half-knave, who by constantly getting into difficulties affords a text for satirical moralizings by his master.

In the earlier portions the satirical note is more sustained, and the adventures follow a fixed plan. At each stage of their journey the Captain and his servant fall in with some foolish assemblage, now of scientists seeking recruits for their society, now of citizens about to elect a representative, and the like. Each foolish group finds something to admire in the foolish and vain Teague O'Regan, and offers him membership or office. To prevent his acceptance the Captain is obliged to invent ridiculous objections, and then follows a chapter of reflections by the author, suggested by the previous adventure. This order, however, is gradually abandoned toward the end of the first part of the story, and is not resumed in the second. (pp. 22-3)

The second part of the story, added later, is devoted to the description of a new settlement founded by the Captain and his friends, the governmental problems which arise being mere pretexts for long chapters setting forth Brackenridge's political beliefs. The relief given by comic adventure and satiric reflection to the educational intention of the first part is often lacking here, and there is no real plot.

At his best Brackenridge shows great satiric power, and a vigor and clearness of style unusual in that day of somewhat tawdry elegance in fiction. Although he took the form of his narrative from [Miguel de] Cervantes, he is nearer [Samuel] Butler in spirit. Indeed it was his original intention to put his story into Butler's jolting couplets, and a beginning was actually made, but he finally abandoned the idea and adopted the prose form for his narrative. (p. 23)

> *Lillie Deming Loshe, "The Didactic and the Sentimental," in her* The Early American Novel, *Columbia University Press, 1907, pp. 1-28.**

CARL VAN DOREN   (essay date 1921)

As a description of manners in the early days of the Republic [Hugh Henry Brackenridge's book *Modern Chivalry*] is unapproached by any other. Races, elections, rural conjurors, village "philosophers" or pseudo-scientists, inns, duels and challenges, treaties with Indians, the Society of the Cincinnati, hedge parsons, brothels, colleges, Congress, Quakers, lawyers, theaters, law courts, Presidential levees, dancing masters, excise officers, tar and feathers, insurrections—all these are displayed in the first part of the book with obvious verisimilitude and unflagging spirit. Much of the action of this part is furnished by the doings of Teague, a grotesque and witless Sancho Panza, whose impudent ambition survives the most ludicrous and painful misadventures. Brackenridge regards him as typical of the political upstarts of the period, and his triumphs as an accusation properly to be brought against the public which followed such sorry leaders. In Part II Captain Farrago, after a brief hiatus spent on his farm, resumes his travels, which at first do not take him beyond the limits of the nearest village, with its newspaper, academy, lunatic asylum, and fair, but which eventually bring him to a settlement in the back country of which he becomes governor. The remainder of the book, ostensibly a chronicle of the new settlement, is practically a burlesque of the history of civilization in America. The settlers war with the Indians and make a constitution. They legislate like madmen, under the guidance of a visionary from Washington who holds that beasts should have the vote as well as men, and actually persuades his fellows to commission a monkey clerk and admit a hound to the bar. Brackenridge aimed his satire primarily at doctrinaires and demagogues, but he whipped as well almost all the current follies and affectations, revising his book from time to time to keep pace with new absurdities. For half a century *Modern Chivalry* was widely popular, and nowhere more so than along the very frontier which it satirized and which read it as more or less a true history. It was among the earliest books printed west of the Alleghanies. (pp. 5-6)

> Carl Van Doren, "The Beginnings of Fiction," in his The American Novel, *The Macmillan Company,* 1921, pp. 1-23.*

ERNEST BRENNECKE, JR. (essay date 1926)

Although it was not at first recognized as a contribution to literary art—a fortune shared by many another picaresque work—and although it has scarcely ever been even mentioned in histories of American letters, [*Modern Chivalry*] went through edition after edition in its own day. In many ways it may be considered as a direct product of the War of Independence, of the struggle over the adoption of the United States Constitution, and of the Western or Whiskey Insurrection of 1794, for it mirrors in striking fashion much of the chaos and violence and many of the stirring ideals of its epoch. As it further contains many a hilarious episode of roguery, it is included in the present series of narratives as one of the earliest American essays in the picaresque manner. Both as rousing entertainment and as a unique social document, it distinctly merits its twentieth-century resurrection.

Those early days of the American Republic poured a peculiarly rich variety of fertilizer into the soil which was to nurture realistic stories of rascality and quixotic adventure. Such stories thrive with great difficulty under conditions of drawn-out refinement and delicate culture. Their inspiration and subject matter are found in low life, or among the socially and morally oblique elements of politer circles; Teague O'Regan, Huckleberry Finn and the outcasts of Poker Flat spring out of Vagabondia. And the American States, towards the end of the eighteenth century, teemed with the varieties of people and conditions which tempt the hand of the picaresque raconteur. Against a rude and tragic background of bitter primitive struggle, of hardship and bloodshed, of volatile radical thought and iron reaction, there passed an endless display of comic human detail which could be recorded with high spirits, with humor and raciness, with satire and irony. It was one of the roughneck stages in our still very incomplete progress towards something like a civilization.

This may partially account for the uncompromising directness, the occasional bluster, the heavy-handedness and the rather crude slapstick qualities in *Modern Chivalry.* With all its balanced judicial sentiment, its irony and soundness of sense, it lacks the polish, the concentration, the detached sharpness and wit that distinguish the ingenuous old Spanish tale of Lazarillo the beggar. But it must be remembered that *Lazarillo* had behind it centuries of polite romance, which its author used as

his point of departure. Our American author was too close to the turmoil of a wilderness in the pangs of social childbirth to be influenced by the finer overtones of his literary models. They supplied him with a convenient structural formula, it is true, but they could not modify the muscular vitality of his execution.

His formula was that of the peripatetic narrative; his immediate model was *Don Quixote,* the structure of which is episodic rather than cumulative or broadly dramatic. His wandering protagonist, Captain Farrago, is simple-minded to the point of eccentricity, like the gullible Don, but he is not driven insane by a fixed idea. His philosophy, again like the Spanish knight's, is drawn chiefly from books—but from good books—and when it is confronted with actually existent foolishness or crookedness, it provides the author with a heavy, blunt instrument for satirical use. The rascally clown, the bog-trotting Milesian Teague, whose resemblance to Sancho Panza is still more superficial, supplies the rogue-elements: his attempted seduction of the barmaid in the eighth chapter is typically picaresque. The exhibition of the tarred and feathered Hibernian as a curious monster in the Second Part recalls a similar episode in *Lazarillo;* and again the parallel is more interesting in its contrasts than in its similarities. For O'Regan's function is not mere entertainment; his idiotic ambitions and his consequent scrapes serve to point-up the unique didactic motive which distinguishes *Modern Chivalry* from other tales of the same genre. Its mingling of a propaganda-objective with its pure diversion does not too perceptibly diminish its value as intelligent amusement. Its exposures of dishonest practices of the turf and of politics, of the excesses of unripe, untempered democracy, of female partiality towards uncouthness, of the vagaries of so-called natural philosophers, of the stupid elevation of inferiors to high offices—all are legitimate sport, and many of them still retain their educational value today. (pp. vii-ix)

> Ernest Brennecke, Jr., in an introduction to Modern Chivalry: Containing the Adventures of Captain Farrago and Teague O'Regan *by Hugh Henry Brackenridge, Greenberg, Publisher, 1926, pp. vii-xiii.*

VERNON LOUIS PARRINGTON (essay date 1927)

[*An American historian, biographer, and critic, Parrington is best known for his unfinished literary history of the United States,* Main Currents in American Thought. *Though modern scholars now disagree with many of his conclusions, they view Parrington's work as a significant first attempt at fashioning an intellectual history of America based on a broad interpretive thesis. Written from the point of view of a Jeffersonian liberal,* Main Currents in American Thought *has proven a widely influential work in American criticism. Parrington praises Brackenridge's independent thinking, his refusal to "howl with the pack," and his tendency toward realism. He concludes that the historical value of* Modern Chivalry *rivals its literary value because the work embodies Brackenridge's belief in democratic ideals and his criticism of the perversions of that ideal.*]

In taking leave of [a] disturbant time when new social theories were bringing confusion to weak understandings, one cannot do better than to dip into [*Modern Chivalry,*] the wittiest and most readable sketch produced by that vigorous generation, as well as one of the sanest. . . . [Brackenridge] wrote for his own amusement and tried his hand at various kinds of polite literature, producing a masque, a poetic drama on Bunker Hill, prose essays, some sermons, and turned at last to satire. For this he was admirably equipped; he possessed a keen, well-balanced mind, a prose style delightfully colloquial and a wit pleasantly caustic.

Brackenridge is a refreshing person to come upon after one is satiated with the heroic. A free-lance critic, independent in thought and act, he was no vociferous party or class advocate given to enlisting God on his side. Federalist and Republican alike might lose their heads and indulge in unseemly clamor, but Brackenridge with good Scotch judgment refused to howl with the pack. A stout and unrepentant democrat, he was no visionary to shut his eyes to unpleasant facts lest they disturb his faith. As he considered the turbulent confusions of an America in rough process of democratization, he saw the evils as clearly as the hope, and it amused him to satirize those evils after the manner of Don Quixote. *Modern Chivalry* has proved somewhat of a puzzle to later critics who have not cleared their minds of the old cobwebs of Federalist criticism. Thus a literary historian has suggested that it is "a half-hidden satire on democracy" and he inclines to number it among the literary ram's horns that were blown against the walls of the democratic Jericho. But such an interpretation certainly misses the point. Brackenridge had become a thorough Westerner with a fresh point of view. Among the stump fields of his Pennsylvania circuit he was equally removed from the cynicism of Hamilton and the romanticism of Barlow. He saw all about him a rough and tumble democracy, living a vigorous and capable if not lovely life. As a democrat he accepted the fact of political equality and approved of it; the thing was there and needed no justification or defense. Some of its ways were foolish, many of its purposes were shortsighted; it amused him therefore to sharpen his pen against certain of its absurdities and essay the remedial effects of unembittered laughter. He was a realist concerned with realities.

Modern Chivalry is our first backcountry book. It is redolent of stump-lands and their rude leveling ways, and for years it was immensely popular along the western frontier. It is a satire aimed primarily at backwoods shortcomings, but with an eye that kept turning towards the older settlements to scrutinize their equal shortcomings. Its main theme is concerned with certain weaknesses of popular sovereignty already unpleasantly evident as a result of the extension of suffrage; and in particular with the unseemly office-hunting zeal of coonskin candidates. The preposterous spectacle of a pushing fellow with no qualifications setting himself up for high office was to become more frequent with the later rise of Jacksonian democracy; but already there was abundant justification for the satire of Brackenridge. The records of the time are loud in criticism of the demagoguery that resulted from the sudden shift of leadership in consequence of the social upheaval following the Revolutionary War. The old leaders of the aristocratic tradition had fled or had fallen into disfavor, and new men, too often of small capacity and less breeding, had pushed into the seats of authority. With the triumph of Jefferson this transfer of power went forward briskly to the scandal of all aristocrats. The lust of office spread like the plague, and demagogues caught the popular ear, none too nice to distinguish between sense and fustian. Irving brushed against the democratic weakness in his brief venture into politics, and vented his spleen in *Rip Van Winkle*. It is this which Brackenridge deals with primarily in *Modern Chivalry*. . . . The general leveling of offices, he pointed out, was not democracy, but the abuse and ruin of democracy. America was engaged in a great and noble experiment; the success of that experiment depended upon an honest and in-

telligent electorate; it must not be brought to failure by demagogues through the incapacity of the voter. (pp. 390-92)

A reasonable and intelligent democracy, holding steadily to the purpose of the common good, was his cherished ideal. He was not a political philosopher interested in general principles. His purpose was to satirize manners, not to speculate on causes; and in the days of triumphant republicanism the most conspicuous target was offered by the tousled head of the demagogue, "the courtier of democracy." (p. 392)

One may do a worse service to democracy than to point out its faults. Brackenridge was no truckler either to King George or to his neighbors. Living in the midst of a coonskin democracy, he refused to believe that there was any particular virtue in coonskin. It is not the cap but what is under it that signifies. He was a vigorous individualist, a confirmed democrat, a friend of all honest liberalisms, a man who honored his own counsels and went his own way. We could better spare more pretentious books from the library of our early literature than these clever satires that preserve for us some of the homely ways of a time when American institutions were still in the making. (p. 395)

Vernon Louis Parrington, "The War of Belles Lettres," in his The Colonial Mind: 1620-1800, *Harcourt Brace and Company, 1927, pp. 357-95.**

CLAUDE MILTON NEWLIN   (essay date 1932)

[*Newlin's* The Life and Writings of Hugh Henry Brackenridge *is considered the authoritative biography of the author. He documents Brackenridge's personal life, his political activities, and his literary endeavors. In the excerpt below, Newlin focuses on what he perceives as a discrepancy between form and content in Brackenridge's work. He argues that although Brackenridge's writings are stylistically weak and encumbered with didacticism, they form "vigorous expressions of American patriotic feeling."*]

Brackenridge's great passion was for learning and literature. He longed for fame in these pursuits, but he did not have sufficient talent to produce the great works of which he dreamed, nor did the communities in which he lived after the Revolution provide a social background suitable to the encouragement of literary production.

His writings are not completely satisfying if judged only from the literary point of view. His serious verse does not show a mastery of poetic form. It was, of course, written in his early years, but there is no reason to believe that he would ever have achieved a high degree of competence in poetic composition. His later Hudibrastic verse is too carelessly written even for that type, and is often obscure. His prose, at its best, is more satisfactory than his verse. It often has a colloquial ease not found in most American prose of the period. It is frequently careless, however, and sometimes lacks clearness. The lack of a national literary tradition and criticism no doubt accounts for these defects. Evidently Brackenridge did not often feel compelled to do his best. It is not only in the smaller units of phrase and sentence that his work is imperfect. None of his prose works are well organized. Even in *Modern Chivalry,* he seemed more eager to deliver his opinion on all topics of interest to him than to compose a unified narrative.

To yield its full value, his work must be considered historically. From the literary point of view, it is interesting to observe that he borrowed literary forms from Milton, Dryden, Swift, Butler, Addison, and Burns for the treatment of American political and social life. Although he wrote under the influence of great

English models, he did not produce vapid provincial imitations of them.

His work is to be judged, then, by its content, historically considered. From this point of view his early writings appear as vigorous expressions of American patriotic feeling during the Revolution. His journalistic writings are sources of interesting data for the study of the frontier and of legal history. But **Modern Chivalry** is the book on which his reputation must rest. Certainly it deserves a high place among minor American classics. . . . Studied in its evolution and in relation to its background, it not only throws light on the beginnings of American democracy, but it also stands as a permanently valid commentary on persistent problems. It shows Brackenridge to have been steadfast in his allegiance to a thoroughly rational ideal. When the frontier democrats talked, acted, and voted foolishly, they became the butt of his satire. When the Federalists appeared to be serving the "moneyed interests," they were the objects of his criticism. Then again, when his own Republican party absorbed too much French and Irish radicalism, he directed his satire toward its follies. In a turbulent and critical period, in a crude environment, Brackenridge's vigorous good sense found authentic democracy in Plutarch and Thucydides rather than in Tom Paine and [William] Godwin. This fact no doubt partially accounts for his lack of success on the frontier where democracy was a state of feeling rather than a conviction of intellect. (pp. 305-06)

Considering his temperament and the disappointments of his career, it is certainly greatly to his credit that his satire was so good natured, so lacking in fundamental cynicism. He had, in fact, the true philosopher's touchstone: he was able to laugh at himself as well as at others, and, ultimately, to face with equanimity the realization of the modest character of his own abilities. Perhaps no greater praise can be spoken of any man of talent than that he has been able to face this knowledge without bitterness. (p. 307)

> *Claude Milton Newlin, in his* The Life and Writings of Hugh Henry Brackenridge, *Princeton University Press, 1932, 328 p.*

ARTHUR HOBSON QUINN (essay date 1943)

[*Though this essay was composed in 1943, it was first published in 1951.*]

In **The Battle of Bunkers Hill,** published in 1776 in Philadelphia, the sentiment of love of country is well and not theatrically displayed. The drama is carried on through conversation, first between the American leaders, Warren, Putnam, and Gardiner. There is no satire here; it is the expression of one great quality, that of courage. As Gardiner says:

> The free born spirit of immortal sire[s]
> Is stranger to ignoble deeds, and shuns
> The name of cowardice. But well thy mind,
> Sage, and matur'd by long experience, weighs
> The perilous attempt, to storm the town,
> And rescue thence, the suff'ring citizens.
> For but one pass to that peninsula,
> On which the city stands, on all sides barr'd,
> And here what numbers can supply the rage,
> Of the all devouring, deep mouth'd cannon, plac'd,

> On many a strong redoubt; While on each side,
> The ships of war, moor'd, in the winding bay,
> Can sweep ten thousand from the level beach,
> And render all access impregnable.

Even when we turn to the British side, and witness the deliberations of Gage, Howe, Burgoyne, Clinton, and Lord Pigot, the tone is serious. The British are represented as not very anxious to fight. General Howe speaks of the friendships which his brother, Lord Howe, had made during the French and Indian War with the very colonists he is now sent to attack. There is no doubt that Brackenridge represented Howe's sentiments correctly, and he gained in dramatic effectiveness by having the very enemy contribute to establish the motive of the drama, the courage and ability of the American troops.

The verse of Brackenridge is flexible and dignified, and the speeches of Warren and Gardiner as they lead their men to the attack reveal the spirit of the "times that try men's souls." . . . (pp. 50-1)

The Death of General Montgomery was written in 1777, and by that time Brackenridge had become a chaplain in the Army. He showed his confidence, at a dark time in our history, by stating in the introduction that he believed the publication of the drama might be more helpful to the colonial cause than "hereafter when the foe is entirely repulsed and the danger over." The play opens with the explanation of the plan of operation by General Montgomery, to Arnold, in which there is quite an exact description of the circumstances of that brave but ill-starred attack, on a snowy night, upon the fortress of Quebec. There runs through several of the speeches the note of impending disaster, well expressed in the words of Captain Cheeseman, of the New York militia:

> The hour is dreary, and all Nature dark;
> But yet, Macpherson, there is something more;
> In melancholy, and a mind o'ercast:
> In this presentiment of some sad change,
> This throb of heart, that bodes fatality,
> And is not cowardice, but God himself,
> That in the knowledge, of the future ill,
> Doth touch the mind, with apprehension strange,
> And feeling sensible of its approach.

Montgomery's death is only indicated in the speech of Aaron Burr, an eloquent tribute to the dead leader and his companions. Brackenridge departs from his cherished unities to bring in the ghost of General Wolfe, who reproaches the King and Parliament in good round fashion. The play continues with Arnold's attack, in which it is interesting to note that the Pennsylvania militia carried a flag representing

> With thirteen streaks of ivory and blue
> The extended provinces.

The play ends with a note of bitterness toward General Carleton, the British commander. This is the more remarkable since Carleton was a noteworthy exception to the general rule and seems to have treated the American prisoners with real consideration.

Brackenridge's dramas are better than the other Revolutionary plays from the point of structure and expression, even if they have not the vigor of action of Leacock's one effort [*The Fall of British Tyranny; or, American Liberty Triumphant*] or the sharp satire of Mrs. [Mercy Otis] Warren's plays. It is interesting that he chose defeats for his celebration, but they were defeats that were greater than victories, for they revealed the triumph of character. (pp. 52-3)

Arthur Hobson Quinn, "The Drama of the Revolution," in his A History of the American Drama: From the Beginning to the Civil War, *second edition, Appleton-Century-Crofts, Inc., 1951, pp. 33-60.* *

ALEXANDER COWIE   (essay date 1948)

[*A noted authority on American fiction, Cowie is also an esteemed historian, biographer, and critic. His* The Rise of the American Novel *and* American Writers Today *are studies that trace the evolution of the American novel by studying the artistic development of the novelists themselves. In his criticism, Cowie disavowed the practice of relegating works and their authors to social and political schools. Instead, he emphasized the combined effects of economic, religious, and political factors prevalent in the writer's life during the production of a single novel. Here, Cowie places Brackenridge "among the finest prose stylists, whether English or American, of the eighteenth century," yet he qualifies his judgment by adding that he is "not really a great novelist." Analyzing Brackenridge's satirical technique in* Modern Chivalry, *Cowie comments on the author's attitudes toward education, law, government, writing, and humor. Finally, Cowie deems Brackenridge "at once an American and an exile," thereby diverging from the critical opinions of Henry Adams (1889) and Vernon Louis Parrington (1927) who stress Brackenridge's strong sense of identity with America.*]

Hugh Henry Brackenridge, author of **Modern Chivalry,** belongs among the finest prose stylists, whether English or American, of the eighteenth century. The term novel must be stretched considerably to accommodate **Modern Chivalry,** a bulky, episodic, almost plotless book. Yet the history of fiction clearly shows that whereas a good plot may be the bait which first attracts readers to a novel, in the long run it is by no means the most important element of fiction. Such an inference is suggested by the solid reputations of such loose-jointed stories as [William Thackeray's] *Vanity Fair,* [Charles Dickens's] *Pickwick Papers,* [Samuel Butler's] *The Way of All Flesh,* and many other novels. Of the things that weigh more heavily—characterization, setting, and a certain richness of texture betokening the author's understanding of life—Brackenridge had a goodly share. And he possessed abundantly the crowning glory of the novelist, namely, mastery of his medium, a perfect sense for the words which will obey the thought of the writer and gratify the ear of the reader. Not a really great novelist, Brackenridge is nevertheless a far more important writer than one would guess from the brief and cool entries accorded him by most historians of literature. He was the first distinguished American novelist to make substantial use of picaresque technique and of political satire. (p. 43)

Conscious of the integrity of his own motives, Brackenridge was embittered by his experience of public life; and his greatest work, **Modern Chivalry,** was begun as in some measure a retaliation against political enemies. Yet no partisan skulduggery could kill his love for democratic government, and no disillusionment could rob him of either his sense of humor or his artistry. Begun in rancor, **Modern Chivalry** developed into a brilliant but objective inquiry into the political principles and the actual conditions of the young republic. It is not, however, a treatise on government but an episodic narrative of the adventures of Captain Farrago and Teague O'Regan, whose peregrinations provide the basis of a panoramic view of American frontier life in Pennsylvania.

Brackenridge's first impulse had been to write a Hudibrastic poem on the theme of young democracy, and he actually composed a long narrative poem which he called **The Modern Chevalier.** Yet he was not really at home in verse forms and he presently adopted a prose vehicle. (pp. 44-5)

[In **Modern Chivalry** there] are prolonged passages of satire on legislation, the practice of law, the ministry, the press, higher education, duelling, scientific research, political chicanery, etc. The author's method is to show Teague in a ludicrously incongruous situation and then to pass on to general reflections of serious import regarding government or society. (p. 47)

Employing episode, conference, and reflection . . . , Brackenridge delivers a series of ironical commentaries on the abuses of democratic government and on various social institutions. A certain sameness of approach and even of material marks the first three volumes of Part One. The fourth (and last) volume of Part One, however, grew out of one specific experience of the author, namely, the Whiskey Insurrection of 1794. Brackenridge's own plight during this disturbing uprising was a painful one, which he recorded directly in his **Incidents of the Insurrection.** . . . In 1797 he incorporated some of the same facts in a fourth volume of **Modern Chivalry.** True to his satirical plan, however, he arranges that Teague shall play the leading role. (p. 48)

[In the second part of **Modern Chivalry,** the] action is even more deliberate than in Part One. Teague continues to aspire toward positions unsuitable to him, but new materials are also introduced. The impetus toward the first volume of Part Two . . . was Brackenridge's desire to express his scorn of the cheap journalists of the stripe of Peter Porcupine (the pen-name of William Cobbett) who had vilified Brackenridge's name on the occasion of his re-entrance into Pennsylvania politics in 1799-1800. (p. 49)

In this part of the work he also showed his deepening despair of the populace on account of its attitude toward education. When public zeal for equalitarianism leads to the proposal that a college be burned down because "all learning is a nuisance," the Captain comments on the proposal with what for him is unusual bitterness, suggesting that the mob eject the professors but save the college building—for use as a hospital when the abolition of "learning and law" shall have reduced society to chaos and "trial by battle." Similarly he is more caustic than usual in his protest against a man's being regarded as a poor candidate for office merely because he is educated. With fierce indignation at this perversion of the idea of democracy Brackenridge makes his point by means of irony, causing the candidate to protest [that he is no scholar]. . . . (p. 50)

The principal innovation in Part Two, however, is concerned with the common law, the judiciary, and the Constitution. . . . In general Brackenridge, himself a lawyer and a judge, defended the *status quo.* To the charge that our common law was unsuitable because it was derived in large part from English law, he replied that in reality the common law is ours for we "derive it from a common source with the inhabitants of Britain . . . Abolish the common law? why not abolish the art of medicine, because it has been cultivated in Great Britain? . . . Why not make war upon the apothecaries, because they sell English drugs?" Undoubtedly a democrat and an "American," Brackenridge thus ventured to express opinions which could not be popular with proponents of a strong nationalism. Similarly he defended the judiciary at a time when radical thinkers were leading "an attack that was practically nationwide in its scope.'' . . . Brackenridge was himself by no means a reactionary; yet with his usual desire to find the wise mean between extremes he was moved to write in a vein of caution against too great zeal for reform. . . . Brackenridge deprecates both revolution and reform movements for their own sakes. Clearly his main concern is to counsel government by the intelligent and the trained. So much is implied, in connection with the controversy over the judiciary, by having the dauntless Teague made a judge.

In the last installment of Part Two Brackenridge analyzes yet another aspect of republican government, namely, the qualifications for voting—a subject which arises in connection with the move to revise the Constitution. It is his opinion that the property qualification for voting is utterly wrong. His Swift-like method of exposing the absurdity of such an institution is to develop a bizarre account of a community in which animals are represented as voting and otherwise carrying out the functions of ordinary citizens. Then he answers his objectors:

> The preceding painting may be considered as extravagant; and exceeding all probability; the voting of beasts. But is it a new thing in the history of government that the right of suffrage should be made to depend upon property? No man shall be entitled to a vote unless he is worth so much, say some of the constitutions. In this case is it not his property that votes? If this property consists in cattle, can it be said that his cattle do not vote. Ergo, a cow or a horse, in some communities have the privilege of a vote in the enacting laws.

In the last section, the fictional thread becomes even more tenuous than before. The author pronounces opinions on a great variety of subjects including war in general, the War of 1812 in particular, but always he sticks to his general position as observer of the commonwealth. A ''visionary philosopher'' is the mouthpiece of the author in much of this portion of the narrative. Teague, however, remains available for further mock-heroics, and in this section he becomes a popular military hero and almost reaches the rank of general. Thus to the last he serves as an embodiment of the author's conviction that private ambition is the ''poison weed'' of a republic. What a republic needs, the author finally avers, is ''less eminence'' and ''more goodness.''

Modern Chivalry is a book of such bulk and diversity that its outward appearance is one of disorder, almost anarchy. No principle of plot construction controls it, and the pretense of fiction becomes extremely shadowy toward the end. Brackenridge recognized as much, saying frankly on one occasion: ''the fact is, that I mean this tale of a Captain travelling, but as a vehicle to my way of thinking on some subjects.'' Chapters and episodes appear to exist of and for themselves as independent units. Opinions expressed in one chapter are found to be in apparent conflict with those expressed elsewhere. Thus at different times the author ridicules the farcical procedure of courts of justice and he defends the judiciary; he praises Jefferson's political principles and he pours obloquy on specific acts of Jefferson; he blows hot and blows cold on the subject of the French Revolution; he supports the Federalist creed of centralization and he resists Hamiltonian political maneuvers; he argues the need of reform (as of Indian treaties), but decries professional reformers; he at times seems to despair of popular sovereignty and at other times seems confident of the basic intelligence of the masses. *Modern Chivalry* is full of apparent

inconsistencies. Yet examined as a whole the book is seen to contain a fairly coherent centre of thought which exercises sovereignty over its diverse parts. It is governed by the principle of balance or proportion. Brackenridge believed in the Greek maxim, nothing too much. The romantic democracy of Joel Barlow and of the youthful Charles Brockden Brown could never appeal to the level-headed Brackenridge. He feared excess of any sort. An enlightened democracy he believed to be the best form of government. (pp. 51-3)

Modern Chivalry is often called a ''satire on democracy.'' The term is partially appropriate, for the book gives more space to the condemnation and ridicule of popular errors than to the indictment of patrician arrogance. In fact the author himself said that the ''great moral of this book is the evil of men seeking office for which they are not qualified.'' Yet the term does not do justice to Brackenridge's political position. Had he lived in the days of the Puritan theocracy in Massachusetts, Brackenridge would undoubtedly have given proportionately more space to attacking the aristocratic political theories of Governor Winthrop and his associates. In Pennsylvania during the infancy of the nation a different emphasis seemed necessary. To be a self-appointed guardian of republican principles was a thankless task: Brackenridge alienated men and constituencies on both sides. Not that he was a fiercely aggressive man in an argument: like Franklin (whom he admired) he generally tried to ''dominate his adversary by doubts.'' He employed the Socratic method instead of the doctrinaire. The Captain's (that is, Brackenridge's) ''reflections'' following the most outrageous conduct are always couched in the most temperate terms. His tolerance and breadth of observation prevented his joining heart and soul with any party. Life would have been easier for him if he could have accommodated himself permanently within the folds of one party. But he was constitutionally unable to commit himself to any platform which forbade freedom of inquiry. He had more wisdom for his country than for himself. (pp. 54-5)

Brackenridge as a writer has not yet received the full measure of praise to which he is entitled. Indeed, it is probable that comparatively few readers have explored fully the vast domain of *Modern Chivalry*, Brackenridge's only work of fiction. To the casual reader, moreover, its very real defects are at once apparent. The book is as unorganized as the weather. Clear and precise in smaller units—the sentence, the paragraph, and even the chapter—it becomes jumbled and unpredictable in the longer sequences. It is also repetitious—a fact to be accounted for partly by the intermittent nature of its composition. Brackenridge recognized this defect, saying in the last volume of the book that ''if [he] were to go over the same ground again, [he] would make one word do where two were used.'' The average novel-reader must be disappointed in its lack of a good plot. Characterization is excellent so far as typical human conduct is concerned, but individuals tend to be absorbed into generalizations. Readers seeking thrills of the sort that are crowded into the sentimental and Gothic novel must certainly have been disappointed. Emotions tend to be understated or ironically expressed, or generalized out of all capacity to agitate the pulse of the popular reader. Consequently although Brackenridge repeatedly said that he aimed to make his book agreeable to ''Tom, Dick, and Harry, in the woods,'' rather than to ''delegated authorities,'' it is doubtful if he reached his ''democratic'' objective. For first and last *Modern Chivalry* is a book for the intelligentsia. It is the fruit of one of the ripest minds of the century. It is an aristocrat among books. Brackenridge's convictions embraced the welfare of the commoner, but his art could not stoop to the level of mass appeal, try as he would. (pp. 55-6)

[Humor] was what he quarried in greatest quantity from the past. Humor gleams from almost every page of **Modern Chivalry**. Sometimes a crude picaresque jest explodes upon the page, but Brackenridge's more characteristic humor is quiet, quizzical, reflective—perhaps quieter than that of his predecessors but no less pervasive. His wit is often incisive but it is not generally destructive, for finally it is subservient to his larger purpose of examining the bearings on which America's comparatively new machinery of government rested. Nevertheless Brackenridge's humor was often misunderstood. Like Fielding and Sterne he valued humor as a sanative or corrective agency, a device to cure one of the spleen, a rectifier of the mind. Yet he found to his sorrow that his ironical method was often beyond the intelligence of the persons it was intended to please. (p. 58)

Brackenridge was an American—and more than an American. . . . His **Modern Chivalry** reports backwoods life in America in general terms—not with the intimacy implied by many critics who iterate accurately but misleadingly, Parrington's observation that **Modern Chivalry** was our "first backcountry book." **Modern Chivalry** is our first picaresque novel, but its roots are only partly American. Captain Farrago is partly American—but, being a literary creation, somewhat less American than Brackenridge himself. American character was difficult to define in the early days of the republic. Indeed Brackenridge went so far as to say that "the American has in fact, yet, no character; neither the clown, nor the gentleman." As for Brackenridge the writer, he was a mixture. He addressed himself to contemporary problems and he knew the smell of political warfare. But when he was in his study, it is fair to suppose, he was a lonely and often dispirited soul. Like Miniver Cheevy, he sighed for an earlier era. A vast and varied literary tradition lay behind him, but he was consigned to an outpost of the youngest nation of all. He craved more literary companionship than was available in the border village of Pittsburgh. His British heritage beckoned to him: "How often have I sighed for the garrets of London . . ." Such a writer was not of the stuff of nationalism; he was at once an American and an exile. (pp. 58-9)

Alexander Cowie, "Early Satire and Realism," in his The Rise of the American Novel, *American Book Company, 1948, pp. 38-68.**

JACOB BLANCK (essay date 1953)

The Death of General Montgomery was something more than a dramatic composition: it was also a glorification of the Revolution and its soldiers and, at the same time, a gory bit of anti-British propaganda. It is quite beside the immediate point whether Brackenridge assumed the role of propagandist consciously or otherwise, although I believe he did so wittingly and with the highest motives. What does concern us here . . . is that in this one piece we have both an early native American play and a fair example of war propaganda. Brackenridge's genius in this last falls far short of the master who first presented the picture of Belgian babies bayoneted to barn doors; but given time he might have risen to the heights. An excellent sample of Brackenridge's touch occurs at pages 10-11 of **The Death:**

> . . . brethren, did I say? O God!
> Are we the offspring of that cruel foe,
> Who late, at Montreal, with symbol dire,
> Did call, the Savages, to taste of blood,

> Life-warm, and streaming, from the bullock slain,
> And with fell language, told it was the blood,
> Of a Bostonian, made the sacrament?
> At this, the Hell-hounds, with infernal gust,
> To the snuff'd wind, held up, their blood-stain'd
>   mouths,
> And fill'd, with howlings, the adjacent hills.

> • • • • •

>   . . . Savages inspir'd,
> With horrid passion, of inhuman war,
> By these our butchers butchers of the ox
> First slain, symbolical, in place of us.
> For, while the blood, ran streaming, from the
>   wound,
> The Indian warrior, tasted it, and sware,
> By that fell Demon, whom he hates and prays,
> That thus the blood of each Bostonian shed,
> Should slake his appetite . . .

A long footnote to the tenth line quoted above then retails the account, reported to the Continental Congress by General Schuyler, of General Carleton's invitation to the Indians convened at Montreal to partake of a Bostonian under the symbolism of a roasted ox, a fitting example 'of the diabolical spirit of tyranny,' couched in language 'which only the imagination of an arbitrary and cruel Englishman, could in our age have conceived.' Precisely, or even approximately, how many Brackenridge thus persuaded to take up arms is a problem the bibliographer, with propriety, may be excused from attacking. (pp. 357-58)

Jacob Blanck, "Brackenridge's 'Death of General Montgomery' (1777)," in Harvard Library Bulletin, *Vol. VII, No. 3, Autumn, 1953, pp. 357-61.*

LEWIS LEARY (essay date 1965)

[*Leary terms* Modern Chivalry *"a distinctively American book," with Captain Farrago as "a good-natured caricature of the Jeffersonian agrarian ideal." Unlike most earlier critics who equated Brackenridge's opinions with those of the narrator of* Modern Chivalry, *Leary warns that Brackenridge's narrative persona is a "wily and unreliable witness" whose views are not necessarily Brackenridge's own. Leary also praises Brackenridge's skill in handling characterization and incident in* Modern Chivalry, *extols his frankness in language, and briefly discusses his influence on later American literature.*]

Like **Don Quixote,** Sterne's **Tristram Shandy,** and Fielding's **Tom Jones,** all of which must often have been in Brackenridge's mind as he wrote, **Modern Chivalry** is a tale of adventuring, episodic and repetitive—what is generally known, perhaps with not too much discrimination, as a picaresque novel. But whatever its European antecedents, it is distinctively an American book, not just because of its homespun, native characters and its often slapstick, broad humor which links it casually to Irving's "Legend of Sleepy Hollow" (1820), to Augustus B. Longstreet's **Georgia Scenes** (1835), and to Seba Smith's accounts of the escapades of Jack Downing; but also because it is a narrative of journeying and questing, like **The Adventures of Huckleberry Finn** or, at farther remove, **Moby Dick**—another of those tales, loosely strung, which it seems might go on and on, without plotted ending. There is no central story to **Modern Chivalry,** except the journeying and the adventures met on the way: it contains one elastically adaptable situation, and a single theme. Like Cooper's **Home As Found** (1838) and H. L.

Mencken's bellicose jocosities a century later, it stands firm on its premise that democracy as practiced in America is a good thing (''beyond all question,'' said Brackenridge, ''the freest government''); but that it is subject to amazing malfunctionings when tinkered with by bumbling, ignorant, or conscienceless men.

It is not necessary to study Brackenridge's biography nor to follow his public career as politician and occasional writer in newspapers of his time to understand that he was a loyal American democrat who thought his own thoughts, unencumbered by what other people supposed that he should think, for **Modern Chivalry** makes that plain. A Jeffersonian Democrat who was rewarded with a judgeship for his contributions to politics, he recognized the shortcomings of his own party as candidly as he did those of the opposition. The enemy was not narrowly political; it was human greed and human stupidity, and man's failure to recognize the place which his talents have prepared for him.

Captain Farrago is a good-natured caricature of the Jeffersonian agrarian ideal—a small farmer, well-read and well-mannered, who had patriotically enlisted for the defense of his country (stumbling his way through the army with a commission which he was not always sure that he knew how to use), and who then returned to cultivate his lands and observe his countrymen, quick to correct and admonish. If his first thought was always of himself, his comfort and his persistent concern that, by whatever means, he must keep his servant with him, to curry his horse and shine his boots, the Captain is nonetheless an honest republican, whose second and longer thoughts are deviously humane and generous. That he rides while his servant walks, that he sips wine in the parlor while Teague eats in the kitchen or pigs it in the stable with the hostlers, that Farrago is a gentleman and the bog-trotter certainly is not—these things are intentional and subtle commentaries on democracy in Brackenridge's time, which even small stretching of imagination can make apply to other times as well.

Only the most matter-of-fact reader will accept verbatim everything which Brackenridge has to say, even in those chapters **"Containing Observations"** or **"Containing Reflections,"** in which he seems to step aside from the narrative, as Fielding did in *Tom Jones,* to comment in his own voice. He is a wily and unreliable witness, whether talking of his purpose in writing; the books which have influenced him—and what an impressive listing it is: Rabelais, Le Sage, Cervantes, Swift, and all the rest; the plainness of his style; or his attitudes toward the American Philosophical Society, the American Indian, or the aristocratic Order of the Cincinnati. As a humorist, he can stand aside, recognizing that serious advocates for any single aspect of a question are likely to appear ridiculous, but also that his own mediating attitudes are often ridiculous. The sensible man, he seems to say, will recognize that intelligent, informed, disinterested reasoning is necessary for the solution of every problem—whether it is concerned with dueling or voting or meddling with servant girls; but that even so rational a man as Captain Farrago or the narrator himself is finally caught up in the inevitable, human, lovable, laughable trap of self-interest.

To find ridiculous only what Brackenridge seems repetitively to attack is to lose much of the finer flavor of his satire. Physicians, lawyers, clergymen, army veterans, strong-armed and strong-voiced politicians; makers of treaties with underprivileged people, mob violence, and lovesickness all come under his bantering double-edged observations. Most people,

by and large, are foolish. Brackenridge, to be sure, is serious about the dangers of popular suffrage; he manifestly distrusts the Indian and says some scurrilous things about the Negro—though many readers will agree with his quizzical logic which explains that, of course, Eve was black; he cared little for the Order of the Cincinnati, and spoke of that tediously at length in bad verse which he cannily pretends was someone else's, but he indubitably would not have liked later democratic veterans' groups either. Whatever historians may say of his attitudes as being representative, either of the best thought or of the most ill-considered judgments of his time, most readers will not pause long over them, nor worry much about them, but will accept Brackenridge's ''playful satire,'' not in the manner of ''weak brethren, who might be offended,'' but for ''the pleasure that a little mirth gives.''

For it is not Brackenridge's ideas which can give continuing life to **Modern Chivalry,** nor even his assurance that ''the people are a sovereign, and greatly despotic; but, in the main, just'': these only reserve it a place on the historian's shelf as a quaint and curious volume, valuable in explaining how strangely people sometimes used to think, one more testimony to be added to other books which do the same thing as well. It is the episodes, humorous and humane, and the lively, plain-spoken words which Brackenridge finds for talking about them, which can certify the book as still alive. Sometimes they will produce only the kind of thoughtless guffaw which slapstick usually elicits; but at another time, they coax a quiet smile. Some readers, when presented with Teague befeathered and caged, will recall Melville's later presentation in *Israel Potter* of a manacled Ethan Allen who was also made the sport of curious, well-meaning people, or, fiction submitting to fact, Ezra Pound caged on the parade ground at Pisa. Brackenridge's language, particularly in the early versions, before he cleaned it up for respectable presentation in the revised posthumous edition of 1819, is simple, direct, colloquial, and sometimes coarse. He calls a hussy a hussy, speaks with natural familiarity of bodily functions, and does not feel that he needs to use dashes or asterisks when it is necessary to have a character described as a son of a bitch. Many years would pass, and much public and private censorship, before everyday speech was more faithfully recorded, or the activities of ordinary people presented with such unblushing candor. If incidents of a similar kind seem too often repeated, Brackenridge has an explanation for that also: ''as the human mind can not be reached all at once, . . . I give . . . here a little, there a little,'' wishing not to glut the appetite.

Not all of **Modern Chivalry** will please all palates. Some of it is riotously vulgar, its humor too broad, its dialect exaggerated. Some of its stories will be dismissed as old chestnuts, often cracked open before. Brackenridge's straight-faced suggestions about what to do to the Indians or about Negroes or Irishmen may seem bluntly inhumane, offensive to readers of strong opinion. Many will find the book uneven, with too many pages devoted to too little matter or to chattering irrelevancies. Others will inevitably regard it as a quaint artifact, revelatory of idiosyncrasies among their forebears and proof of their own advance. Many more, however, may accept it for what it is— perhaps, as Brackenridge said of it, ''a book without thought, or the smallest degree of sense''; certainly not as a testimony to man's tragic plight, but as a stalwart but stumbling ancestor of other American books which have dared the sacrilegious, comic view that man is queer and crotchety and that he strays often from the path of righteousness, but that he is about the best that can be had or enjoyed or scolded. Teague O'Regan had less good sense than Huckleberry Finn, and fewer moments of grace—unlike Huck, he yearned to be "civilized," and all at once; but as much as Huck, he was his own worst enemy and, as an observer and commentator or as a person to be observed and commented on, he is every reader's good friend. Captain Farrago never did cut him down completely; not even Brackenridge could laugh him off the stage. He was sturdy, sometimes honest, and not always bright; but he prevailed. We recall that he eventually did become an ambassador—and to the Court of St. James. What followed after that, we are not told. (pp. 15-19)

> *Lewis Leary, in an introduction to* Modern Chivalry: Containing the Adventures of Captain John Farrago and Teague O'Regan, His Servant *by Hugh Henry Brackenridge, edited by Lewis Leary, College and University Press, Publishers, 1965, pp. 7-19.*

WILLIAM L. NANCE   (essay date 1967)

[*Nance focuses on Brackenridge's use of satire in* Modern Chivalry. *In his examination of burlesque and verbal irony as technique in the work, Nance argues that Brackenridge chose to write satirically because it* "gave him the detachment necessary to avoid simple abuse or didacticism." *Though he feels that* Modern Chivalry *lacks unity and that Brackenridge's technique is heavily derivative of European models, Nance contends that Brackenridge ultimately succeeded in his desire to* "express his deeply felt convictions." *For similar views on Brackenridge's polemical intent, see essays by Lillie Deming Loshe (1907), Ernest J. Brennecke, Jr. (1926), and Vernon Louis Parrington (1927).*]

Like the Liberty Bell, Hugh Henry Brackenridge's sprawling **Modern Chivalry** is a flawed but proud relic of early America. After granting its importance as a forebear of the American novel, a panoramic view of the early republic, and an intelligent treatise on practical democracy, an age of formalistic criticism has found little to say in its favor. Judged in its own right as an example of prose fiction or even as a unified work of exposition it is undeniably faulty; quite possibly its greatest value is its historical and political content. Nevertheless, **Modern Chivalry** continues to attract and hold readers by its principal artistic asset, its satire. Satire was Brackenridge's medium, responsible for whatever the book contains of value as fiction. In view of the truism that the use of satire is one of the first signs of intellectual and artistic maturity, an examination of this element should make clearer just how conscious a literary artist Brackenridge was, and how successful.

In one respect at least, that of purpose, **Modern Chivalry** is all of a piece. Brackenridge states his aim frequently and clearly. It is to expose certain abuses in the new democracy, especially misguided ambition in candidates for public office and folly in the voters who elect unqualified men. (p. 381)

Once Brackenridge decided upon the aim of his novel, his next step was a selection of the means to employ. Late in the book Brackenridge states emphatically, "It is only by *reason, or by ridicule, that what is excessive in the exercise of the right, and erroneous in the deductions of the mistaken, can be corrected*" (. . . italics his). The choice of satire was a good one for several reasons. Most important, irony was congenial to Brackenridge both by education and by the nature of his mind. The satiric approach, insofar as he used it, gave him the detachment necessary to avoid simple abuse or didacticism. Furthermore, as a man trained in law and active in public life, he was aware of the social effectiveness of satire, so well illustrated by the familiar analogy recorded by David Worcester [in his *The Art*

of Satire]: "The cumbrous machinery of law is the guardian of the flock. Where the task is too subtle or intricate for the heavy-footed shepherd, the nimble sheep-dog comes into his own." Brackenridge's satiric propensity had been strengthened by a lifetime of reading. . . . It is primarily the satiric passages which give **Modern Chivalry** its tone, and in this respect the novel is, like dozens of contemporary works, quite close to Hudibrastic low burlesque.

Satire is highly rhetorical, making use of many forms of persuasion, two general varieties of which—burlesque and irony—are especially evident in **Modern Chivalry**. Let us first consider burlesque. The choice is not completely arbitrary, as there is some basis for it both in the nature of the two forms and in Brackenridge's use of them. David Worcester seems to be at least generally correct in finding the natural order of development to be invective-satire, low burlesque, high burlesque, irony. Of the two elements, burlesque and irony, the latter is much the more important and more protean, appearing sometimes as a characteristic of one's whole view of life. In **Modern Chivalry** it is more pervasive than burlesque, and plays an important part in the burlesque itself, as the following discussion will attempt to show. (pp. 382-84)

Modern Chivalry, especially in Part II, can be considered a long, rambling treatise with burlesque episodes. Since, however, most of the episodes are given simple continuity by the characters of Captain Farrago and Teague, and since at least in the early part of the book the fictional passages predominate, it qualifies to some extent as a novel of a semipicaresque variety, as does *Don Quixote*, on which its structure is loosely patterned. It likewise borrows picaresque elements from Butler, as well as Lucian and Swift. [E. V. Knox in his *Mechanism of Satire*] observes that the picaresque rogue is a convenient medium, lending himself to satire which is usually "more laughter than homily," for "many satires are more playful and fantastic than didactic." **Modern Chivalry** seems to lack this quality of predominant humor to about the extent that it fails of being fully a picaresque novel. One of its weaknesses in this latter respect is the author's custom of following most of the episodes with a chapter of comment. Precedent for this has been found in Swift's *Tale of a Tub* and also in Fielding; and Brackenridge himself, in a digression in which he discusses his digressions, refers to both these authors. . . . (p. 384)

The characters of burlesque are to some extent caricatures, and the sharpness with which they are presented, both through direct description and through their words and actions, is one of the measures of the success of the work. Brackenridge gives practically no concrete description of his characters. Teague is the central agent in the burlesque, the fulcrum of the satire directed against incompetent office-seekers and foolish voters. One of the strongest elements in his portrayal is his dialect, of which the following is a random sample: "God love your shoul, my dear cratur, but you are de beauty of de world. Sleeping or waking, I could take you to my heart and ate you wid de very love o'd' my shoul dat I have for you. De look o'd' dur face, like de sun or de moon, run trugh me, and burn up like a coul o'd de fire: dat I am shick and fainting to take du in my arms, my dear cratur." . . . This is caricature and, for its time, no negligible achievement. There is little direct description of Teague, except for the bare essentials of his origin, mind, character, and state of life. The partially successful presentation of him that is achieved is almost wholly through his speech and his escapades. Other characters are portrayed almost wholly in terms of their speech or thought processes. (p. 385)

Action remains, however, the most important measure of the success of burlesque. *Modern Chivalry* contains several episodes of considerable humor. Some of the best are associated with the Captain's campaign to educate Teague in the fine points of social intercourse. The narrative style is admittedly weak and the action is often halted by long speeches. Much more harmful, even almost disastrous to the burlesque effect, are the Captain's reasoned exhortations to Teague in the midst of the action and the long explanatory passages and chapters. This is in direct violation of the laws of burlesque, depriving the reader as it does of intellectual participation in the satiric action. One short example of the deadening effect of such lapses from the burlesque tone is the following. A fake "Indian treaty maker" is giving the Captain a sharply ironic burlesque account of his practices—but then comes the plodding commentary (in this instance placed in the mouths of both characters) to drive the lesson home.

> How the devil, said the Captain, do you get speeches made, and interpret them so as to pass for truth. That is an easy matter, said the other; Indian speeches are nearly all alike. You have only to talk of burying hatchets under large trees, kindling fires, brightening chains; with a demand, at the latter end, of blankets for the backside, and rum to get drunk with.
>
> I much doubt, said the Captain, whether treaties that are carried on in earnest are of any great use. Of none at all, said the other; especially as the practice of giving goods prevails; because this is an inducement to a fresh war. This being the case, it can be no harm to make a farce of the whole matter; or rather a profit of it; by such means as I propose to you, and have pursued myself. . . .
>
> (pp. 386-87)

If the literary stature of *Modern Chivalry* rested solely upon its success as a burlesque, it would stand considerably below its present modest position. This, however, is not the case. Much of the book is vivified by another technique which contributes to the burlesque effect and gives comic value and satiric sharpness to many other passages—the technique, namely, of irony. Brackenridge's irony has necessarily entered into the discussion of his burlesque, but it is deserving of a more careful examination. (p. 387)

Brackenridge shows skilful management of verbal irony . . . ; indeed, it seems to be a characteristic of his mind, though at times in *Modern Chivalry* he drops it in favor of frank and directly rational discourse. Yet rationality and satire are closely related and one is not surprised to find them together. Although Brackenridge admittedly lapses artistically in his long departures from irony, much of the book gains in ironic force by the reader's need for constant alertness to know just when the author is serious and when he is not. For example, irony and candor or literal meaning are cleverly mingled in the following passage:

> The company of horses is by no means favorable to good taste and genius. The rubbing and currying them, but little enlarges the faculties, or improves the mind; and even riding, by which a man is carried swiftly through the air, though it contributes to health, yet stores the mind with few or no ideas; and as men naturally consim-

ilate with their company, so it is observable that your jockeys are a class of people not far removed from the sagacity of a good horse. . . .

Usually, as in this instance, the irony lies in exaggeration, but it may also take the form of understatement, as in the following highly Swiftian lines on dueling: "It is no uncommon thing to have an arm broken or a splinter struck off the nose or an eye shot out; but as in that case, the ball mostly passes through the brain, and the man being dead at any rate, the loss of sight is not greatly felt." . . . (p. 388)

Verbal irony, if skilfully articulated with burlesque, can become irony of manner—a sustained pose on the part of the author. While Brackenridge's use of even simple verbal irony is far from consistent, his burlesque narrator nevertheless sometimes approaches an ironic stance. This is achieved principally in his numerous protestations of complete innocence of satiric intent. In the postscript to the second volume he announces that public officials may rejoice that he writes "harmless nonsense, rather than strictures on their conduct," and farther on he takes a different, but equally ironic, tack: "Having given the preceding history, and put my name to it, there is no man that knows me, will doubt of the truth of it." . . . But these strokes are light, denoting only brief veerings from verbal irony in the direction of irony of manner. Furthermore, so far does consistency break down that in the latter portion of the book Brackenridge speaks openly of his satiric purpose.

This examination has been an attempt not to conceal the artistic weaknesses of *Modern Chivalry* but to make more evident its artistic strength. Brackenridge's technique is almost completely derived from the great masters of satire, and if his work fails to equal theirs, still it is not entirely unworthy of such predecessors. The burlesque comes only in imperfect chunks, but it furnishes some delightful moments and must have been effective satire in its day. The irony is often crude and irregular and sometimes breaks down completely, but it heightens the burlesque, provides many passages of undeniable humor and satiric force, and succeeds to some extent in buttressing the structural disunity of the novel with unity of tone. The strength of Brackenridge's ironic instinct, coupled with his balanced rationality, while failing to unify his rambling book, at least preserves him from the human and artistic pitfall of raw invective, while permitting him to express his deeply felt convictions with force. Confronted with the abuses of a nascent democracy and holding his humanistic standards firmly in view, he exposes evil, exaggerates it by burlesque, probes it with irony, and forces the flattered reader to join him in condemning it. In fairness we should judge Brackenridge in the light of his purpose. If, as seems probable, he set out not primarily to write a novel but rather to defend true democracy in a long, forceful, illustrated lecture to his countrymen, he succeeded in no small degree. (pp. 388-89)

> *William L. Nance, "Satiric Elements in Brackenridge's 'Modern Chivalry'," in* Texas Studies in Literature and Language, *Vol. IX, No. 3, Autumn, 1967, pp. 381-89.*

DANIEL MARDER (essay date 1967)

[Beginning with the premise that Brackenridge's "life and works have an esthetic appeal and a significance not fully realized," Marder examines Brackenridge's work "in terms of art and history." Marder avoids purely literary criticism of Brackenridge's works, however, because it would deemphasize his "typically

utilitarian intent." He especially stresses Brackenridge's use of local color and realism as aspects of his style that prefigure later developments in American literature. Brackenridge's satire, Marder claims, ridicules the failures of democracy and asserts his ideal of a "cultured democracy." Marder interprets Brackenridge's tone in Modern Chivalry *as "uncongenial" and feels that sentiment is continually checked by realism in the novel.]*

Brackenridge never satirized with Swift's bitterness nor with Butler's malignity. In his adaption of Cervantes' picaresque form for **Modern Chivalry** he rendered an aspect of the American society in its essence, as Cervantes rendered an aspect of the Spanish national character. Brackenridge's satire was intended not only to ridicule but also to assert. Consequently, this work differs from its English models in openly stating ideals and in displaying evils. His assertions tend to dilute the moral indignation. . . . The satire of Brackenridge is, at core, moral instruction. . . . Brackenridge, a lone satirist on the frontier, had old-world literature but no fellows to sustain his feelings. Thus, he could not depend on the group to perceive his positive meanings. To be effective, he had to teach the moral that was being abused. As a result, the bite of his satire weakened. (p. 80)

Only in his first story, the picaresque **"Father Bombo's Pilgrimage,"** does Brackenridge attempt metaphorical representation in the style of the master [Swift]. Ludicrous as it may be, this first groping towards the Swiftean manner displays a robust, boisterous humor that is always on the verge of breaking through the author's control, and thus it imparts the feeling of the baroque. This feeling emerges from much of his later prose, most obviously from **Modern Chivalry.**

Although his hopes of a cultured democracy—a nation of educated gentlemen—dimmed through the personal defeats of his life, nothing could extinguish them. **"Father Bombo's Pilgrimage"** emits sparks of these abiding hopes. It reveals that even before his celebration of **"The Rising Glory of America,"** Brackenridge was absorbed with problems of maintaining cultural values in a democracy and with the relations of these values to democratic success. With wit and learning, Bombo extricates himself from one difficulty after another. Most significant is the fact that all the human barriers share the traits of ignorance and superstition. (pp. 81-2)

"Father Bombo's Pilgrimage" anticipates the theme of all the author's satire. Ignorance and freedom of choice continually confront and thwart Bombo, and they become the most outstanding qualities of Teague O'Regan in **Modern Chivalry.** In fact, Teague, the generic term for the ignorant Irish immigrant, first appears in **"Father Bombo's Pilgrimage."** The story also foreshadows elements of his style—the use of dialect, low-level language, exaggeration, and commonplace detail—which became major characteristics in American Western humor. (pp. 82-3)

The novel form allowed Brackenridge to round Teague into the first developed character in American fiction and to place him in a real world. The Hudibrastic prototype of **Modern Chivalry** [Brackenridge's poem, **"The Modern Chevalier,"**] was formed in an abstract region of the author's political thought; but Teague's picaresque adventures carry the reader through the real country from the Western frontier to Philadelphia and back again.

Although the picaresque structure is borrowed from Cervantes' *Don Quixote,* the representations and mood of **Modern Chivalry** are original, arising from the impact of frontier life upon the

mind of a trained classicist. The satirical mood approaches the geniality of Horace rather than the severity of Juvenal. (p. 86)

The satirical representations of actual events in **Modern Chivalry** serve as exaggerated examples or anecdotes from which morals, ideals, or lessons can be induced. **Modern Chivalry** is structured to emphasize the positive assertions made by the author or his spokesman, Captain Farrago. Its narrative action is subordinated to its expository lessons in democracy. Brackenridge states that this structure is an imitation of nature: "It is so in nature; and why should it not be so represented in the image of her works[?] We have the sage and the fool interspersed in society, and the fool gives occasion for the wise man to make his reflections. So in our book." The fiction of **Modern Chivalry,** then, is but an emphatic technique to introduce unmasked lessons. An excellent storyteller, Brackenridge employed exaggerated narrative illustration as the point of departure in many of his journalistic essays. **Modern Chivalry** can be viewed as a continuing collection of such essays unified through the consistent use of two central characters. (p. 90)

Modern Chivalry can hardly be considered a novel even in the didactic or picaresque sense because the episodes fail to create a cumulative effect. . . . Its theme is not developed but repeated or applied in a variety of situations. Although Teague O'Regan and Captain Farrago are given enough roundness to appear real, they are not developed, changed, or revealed through the action; and the other characters are caricatures simply used to illustrate social habits, abuses, and absurdities. The events proceed to no outcome. (pp. 90-1)

Although the light of **Modern Chivalry** is exaggerated, it reveals the substance of early democratic life as well as its problems. Through the exaggeration the reader discerns the reality of the cultured, the ignorant, the rich, and the poor in their daily lives and common places. He sees the statesmen, philosophers, ecclesiastics, Philadelphia belles, frontier gamecocks. He is thrust into the economic and political conditions and experiences the stupidity of the electors, the hypocrisy of the demagogues. He hears a meaningless speech in Congress, witnesses a trial by a jury of ignoramuses, listens to radical political reformers, observes the misuse of Indian appropriations, and battles with the blackguard journalists. He endures the snobbishness and artificiality of the East—and the Western resentment of law, learning, and anything associated with the East. (p. 91)

The characteristics associated with the term "local color"— scenery, custom and mood of a place, moral contrast, exaggerated story and characters, local dialect, provincial nomenclature, adoption of colorful nicknames, vigilante committees, reformers, bungling of justice, farcical legal machinery and electioneering, gamblers and self-righteous ministers, foreigners and queer and cultured Easterners, treacherous Indians and the white man's manipulation of them—these are the elements that flavor Brackenridge's prose satires.

Like the later local colorists, Brackenridge wrote within an atmosphere of rough humor, incongruity, and exaggeration. Like them, he burlesqued his boisterous settings without the painstaking patience and restraint necessary for developing concise form. In no way did his prose contribute to the development of the American novel and short story as art forms. . . . (pp. 91-2)

Whether or not Brackenridge directly influenced the Western tall story, his satire is in the same vein. The adventures of Teague O'Regan are actually tall stories. Without the moralizing intervention of Captain Farrago, they would seem as anecdotal as Twain's "Notorious Jumping Frog of Calaveras County." (p. 92)

The frequent bitterness in Twain, however, is seldom found in Brackenridge's satire. Twain begins his fiction without any hope for a rising glory of America. If the reader can view the corrupt politicians in *The Gilded Age* as later Teague O'Regans who have more nearly realized their ambitions, he can attribute Twain's caustic tone to the hopelessness of political ideals in his own day, that is, to the defeat of all Brackenridge's democratic instruction.

Teague O'Regan is as innocent as Huck Finn, but his ambitious acts are potentially harmful to society. A fundamental difference between these rogues is their social orientation. Brackenridge employs his rogue to point the reader toward social reform; Twain concentrates on the rogue as an innocent individual faithful to himself in a society that frequently opposes him. Twain ignores concepts of reform or social change. *Huckleberry Finn* emphasizes what is; *Modern Chivalry* emphasizes what ought to be. (p. 93)

The tone of Brackenridge's satire, however, can never be taken as congenial. It has little in common with the satire of Washington Irving, who attacked neither individuals nor groups and who sought no direct social progress. Aimed at social change, Brackenridge's satire cannot afford relaxation and therefore cannot acquire Irving's congenial tone. Brackenridge, under constant attack from political enemies, could not indulge in the luxury of self-parody or of kindness toward the demagogues at whom his satire was aimed. The absurdities of American life amused Irving but they threatened Brackenridge. . . .

Modern Chivalry is touched frequently with sentiment. However, sentiment seldom occupies the focal point of his work, and it is never idealized as in the standard novels of seduction in his time. (p. 94)

The sentiment of Brackenridge is usually checked by one quality that the sensibility writers seldom displayed, an abiding realism. (p. 95)

Conscientiously, Brackenridge worked to keep his style from intruding upon the sense. . . . If *Modern Chivalry* appears to ramble, it is by design. . . . In spite of digressions in his own work, the loose organization guides the reader to the point, which usually is approached inductively and often ironically. (pp. 95-6)

Today Brackenridge is recognized chiefly for *Modern Chivalry*. But, in his middle years on the frontier, he wrote two remarkable narratives that should prove of equal worth. They too foreshadow local-color qualities, but they deviate from all his other modes. **"The Trial of Mamachtaga"** and *The Incidents of the Insurrection* are not satirical; neither are they oratorical or reflective. Both are distinguished by an objective observation of scene, character, and action, and by a selection and an arrangement of these observations to produce climax. They are true accounts which bring to mind the fiction at the end of the nineteenth century that one calls realism. (p. 99)

["**The Trial of Mamachtaga**"] tells of an Indian brought to justice for killing a white man. In spite of his loathing for the American Indian, Brackenridge was intrigued with this savage, whose name stood for trees blown in a tempest and who was rejected even by his own tribe. His intrigue allowed him to penetrate beyond predetermined notions of the American native as a noble savage or as a savage beast. A real portrait of the

Indian character emerges, perhaps for the first time in American literature. (p. 101)

Actually, Brackenridge offered no philosophy about Indians as individuals. His arguments against Indian rights to the soil were political rationalizations. He saw the Indian as an individual only when his curiosity was aroused by events on the frontier, and then he wrote from observation which was rare, if not unique, in either late eighteenth- or early nineteenth-century treatment of Indians. In **"The Trial of Mamachtaga"** Brackenridge treats the Indian neither from an idealistic nor from a shocked point of view, but from a realistic one. Brackenridge tries to see the events as the Indian sees them. Consequently, the reader perceives in the respectable white men who try the Indian a fundamental lack of humane sentiment. They reveal themselves as utterly incapable of understanding the Indian or appreciating his culture. (p. 103)

With the economy of modern short fiction, this little-known story produces a single effect and does so through an objective approach. The intended effect is never stated but is revealed through sharp selection of environmental details, actions, and characterizing elements; and the effect is wrought ironically from the point of view of a major character. Through Attorney Brackenridge, the reader recognizes in the savage some fundamental requirements for civilized individuals; and in the civilized white men, a fundamental savageness when acting en masse. The obvious lessons for democratic conduct are never obtrusive.

The story is rare for its time because the author ignored rather justifiable prejudices against the Indians and rather steadfast "morals" concerning the punishment of murderers. It compels sympathy for the Indian, though he is ugly by most ordinary standards. It investigates character, both of the social violator and of the society violated. (p. 105)

[Since almost all] remarks pertaining to [*Incidents of the Insurrection*] are historical, they ignore the psychological revelation of character under mob pressures and the evocative depiction of events, their causes, and the narrator's motives in guiding them. Instead, the comments invariably point to incriminating evidence of the author's guilt in the [Whiskey Insurrection of 1794]. (p. 107)

Questions of Brackenridge's guilt fade, however, when the reader becomes absorbed in the literary effects of Brackenridge's narrative. Perhaps the digressions and intruding pleas of innocence have distracted readers from the psychological intensity as the narrator attempts to moderate the rebellious action that he cannot prevent. The tension increases throughout the lawyer's efforts at the risk of his life to outwit the mob by reasoned appeals to desires and egos. Perhaps the reader not anticipating literary experience overlooks the unfolding characterization of the insurrection leaders and the narrator's subtle manipulation of them. Most important, such a reader may fail to orient himself with the focal point of the book, the actions and reactions of the individual under the intense stress of social upheaval. He may also fail to appreciate the delicate treatment of the main character's internal conflict between his sympathies for the insurgents and his duties as a patriot. For want of editorial pruning, this dramatic and realistic narrative has been neglected. (pp. 107-08)

The narrative is, precisely, a picture rather than an explanation or an apology, in spite of the author's first intentions; but it is far more than a picture of a people. It is the story of conflict between a torn people and a person who attempts to repair the rupture, and the story is presented with artistic awareness. Many of the events, re-arranged in time, are offered at the most pertinent point, as they impinge on the narrator's thought and action. (p. 108)

The playfulness that disturbs the tonal unity in most of Brackenridge's work is completely avoided. He uses humor as a persuasive instrument. At the Mingo Creek meeting he arouses laughter when the members of the Jacobin society threaten violence. Aimed at diverting action, the humor is painfully pulled forth; and it enhances rather than disrupts the tone and the tension. His life is at stake at every meeting and in every mass action. And his position becomes more dangerous as the events proceed.

Brackenridge sympathetically portrays the leaders of both sides. Most of them seem to share his predicament of being drawn into the events reluctantly. (pp. 108-09)

When the narrative elements are disassociated from the rest, they combine into a story of an idealistic yet ambitious man— a man caught in the complexities and dangers of social upheaval which lead him to a view of the base self beneath his ideals and ambitions, a view that is but a momentary glimpse. It passes with the dangers that unveil it. On a more obvious level, the narrative elements combine into a story of the individual's will exerted upon social forces in tumult. On the level of the author's overt intention, the narrative elements are but explanations of a man's conduct in the frontier turmoil known as the Whiskey Rebellion. (p. 112)

Incidents of the Insurrection combines the characteristics of Brackenridge's early and late writings. Under intense stress, the narrator calls upon his classical knowledge and thought habits to guide him. On occasion, he sees his material in terms of heroic similes: "when a scud of wind takes the standing corn of the farmer, and on the field bows the stalks to the earth, so languished my brother at the bar." And in the midst of terror he cannot resist the touch of satire: "Hearing that I had been considered as a leader of the insurgents, I thought I must endeavor to support the appearance, as I would be a good deal looked at." However, the light strains of satire never disturb the serious mood. They are matched with strains of sensibility. . . . As in *Modern Chivalry,* sentiment is again checked by an abiding realism. (pp. 113-14)

A number of poems preserved in *Gazette Publications* illustrate a dimension of feeling unsuspected in the public life of Brackenridge. Two of them, written about 1790, are totally out of tone with the austere satire of the first volume of *Modern Chivalry* that he was composing at the time. One is an elegy occasioned by the death of his friend, the wife of Doctor Nathanial Bedford of Pittsburgh. From its opening stanza, the control of rhythm and sound is surprising:

> Whether the spirit doth survive
> The body and doth live
> In the Elysium of the Greeks
> Or heaven of which the Christian speaks,
> I know not; but, if there be
> Such immortality to thee or me,
> Fair shade, this thing call'd death
> And the mere stopping of breath,
> Not being to oblivion brought,
> Is a light matter in the scale of thought,
> And not the proper subject of a tear.

The treatment is not realistic, but sentiment is checked by the author's strong sense of Greek and Roman culture. Ancient motifs of fate and fortitude, for example, are woven with those of sensibility—purity and innocence:

> For pure as Innocence and Love
> She felt the will of Jove,
> With proper forbearance complied
> And like the unstain'd lily dropp'd her head and died.

(p. 119)

The first of several pieces composed in Scottish dialect, ["**St. Andrew's Anniversary**" is a] reaction, almost a recoil, from the embroilments of the frontier village. It is a nostalgic vehicle returning the poet to his roots where his limitations became most evident. . . . (p. 120)

Six years after "**St. Andrew's Anniversary,**" Brackenridge again employed the Scottish dialect to compose a series of poems in response to those of David Bruce, who ran a country store near Pittsburgh. These poems [known as his Scottish poems] stem from a base of real experience. Unlike the clumsy Hudibrastics, they reflect through the senses rather than the intellect; and, unlike his early fiction and other poetry, they pull at experience stored in the subconscious. His own youth and the Scottish folkways replace the abstraction of beautiful life experienced in dreams, and affection for his past tends to replace social criticism. The sensibility is combined with a humor which has deepened through the suffering endured in the Whiskey Rebellion. This humor, which emerges in various scenes of *Incidents,* dominates the Scottish poems. (pp. 120-21)

There is little satire in these poems. The humor is warmed by wistful reflections upon the sights, sounds, and activities of the Scotsmen on the frontier, and by reminiscence of earlier traditions. They sound none of the gay, celebrative notes of [Robert] Burns. They comprise no effort to establish a revival of Scottish folk poetry on this side of the Atlantic as the songs of Burns had done in his homeland. Although Brackenridge owned a collection of Scottish poetry and songs, as did Burns, he was out of the milieu and could not immerse his senses in the actual sounds of the vernacular as Burns could. Brackenridge's Scottish verse, therefore, would lack the naturalness and spontaneity of Burns, even if Brackenridge had possessed equal musical genius. Where Burns could directly represent, Brackenridge could only reminisce. (p. 122)

Under the influence of Burns . . . , the verse took a natural turn. Rhythm, sound, and sense coalesce. Although he did not achieve the lyrical qualities of Burns, [Brackenridge's] language was no longer fettered by mock-heroic mechanisms. Like those of his countryman, these Scottish verses are autobiographical and concerned with rural domesticity. The satire is slight; he aims no hard blows at specific objects. In place of conscious efforts to achieve the eloquence of classical and Augustine poets, the tendency is lyrical, expressing less wisdom derived from life than the experience of life itself.

Whatever is good about the second part of *Modern Chivalry* owes its value to the happy concurrence of the material with the author's pervading mood: it is good whenever the material contains the stuff of sensibility. Brackenridge knew his satirical powers had evaporated; indeed, he lamented this fact in later pages and also admitted the loss of desire to outfit his strictures with appropriate dress. Unfortunately, he found no unifying device to substitute for the narrative of the first part of *Modern Chivalry.* Even more unfortunate, he did not recognize the literary legitimacy of his mood. Consequently, he was enticed by his mood into the kind of reflections found in the Scottish poetry and then, forcibly disciplining himself, turned about and continued his endlessly redundant lessons to grown-ups. (pp. 123-24)

The mood in Brackenridge's ["**Epistle to Sir Walter Scott**"] is regret that the beautiful American wilderness has no Scott to immortalize it; and, though he will try, he has not the genius:

> Here by Ohio's stream my pen
> Gives image to a sort of strain
> Which feeling prompts but Genius none,
> So gifted to a native son.
> My gift is only to admire;
> In madness I attempt the lyre,
> At hearing this celestial sound
> From Scotia's hills and distant bound
> Of this I dream and when awake,
> I read the Lady of the Lake.

A poetic experience emerges from the very clumsiness of the non-poet who desperately seeks to fulfill the poetic need. The impulse is to mirror nature for individual pleasure and exaltation, not social utility, the only purpose his society seems to recognize in living:

> Inglorious I must bend my head,
> And think of something else than fame,
> Though in my bosom burns the flame
> That in a happier age and clime
> Might have attempted lofty ryme.

To the end Brackenridge clung to the "**Rising Glory.**" (pp. 128-29)

In mood, thought, and manner most American literature produced before 1800 resembles the products of England; and perhaps that is why Emerson and others would not recognize it as American. (p. 139)

At least one distinctive break with English literature, however, does not parallel the drawn lines of our history. One literary man of the eighteenth century—a trained classicist—ventured West in the last days of the Revolutionary War. His work reflects the mood and thought of the American frontier decades before attention is focused on movements West and on the literary attitudes summarized as romanticism. Brackenridge's best work, completed before 1800, is clearly out of phase with the usual view of America's literary development. His narratives, short fiction, poetry, and essays fuse into a portrait of new country far from English dominance. At the center of the portrait is the antipathy of the frontiersman to Eastern influences and propositions such as the new Federal Constitution. By showing democracy at work in the new land, Brackenridge not only brings into focus the disunity of national ideals, but he also renders the image of an American cultural pioneer planting seeds of education, art, communication, and a sense of political idealism on the frontier; and of suffering personal defeat in return.

When the literary spotlight finally turned west, it shone upon a farther West, one beyond the early American frontier. Rendering the incubation of the American spirit as it was evolving out of English tradition and into Jacksonian democracy, the work of Brackenridge represents a most vital transition in American literary history. Perhaps the meaning of this transition is stated most cogently in Emerson's often quoted as-

sessment: "Europe extends to the Alleghenies, America lies beyond." (p. 140)

> *Daniel Marder, in his* Hugh Henry Brackenridge, *Twayne Publishers, Inc., 1967, 159 p.*

ROBERT HEMENWAY (essay date 1968)

[*Hemenway suggests that Brackenridge's depiction of an irrational world in* Modern Chivalry *stems from his fears of the subversion of Neoclassical ideals such as decorum, subordination, and proportion. According to Hemenway, Brackenridge worried that the new wave of Romantic sentiment "constituted a threat to the orderly process of living and the reasonable functioning of democratic government." In satirizing a nonrational world in* Modern Chivalry, *Brackenridge was able to register his bewilderment at the failure of Neoclassicism, but unable "to affirm his faith in a reasoned, ordered system of human government."*]

Hugh Henry Brackenridge has been said to represent "more completely and more vitally than any other [writer of his period] the classical and eighteenth century ideals of sanity and moderation." Born in Scotland in 1748, Brackenridge lived and wrote by eighteenth century ideals; the rambling, often unreadable ***Modern Chivalry*** frequently sounds like a Joshua Reynolds discourse: "The great secret of preserving respect, is the cultivating and shewing to the best advantage the powers that we possess, and not going beyond them. Everything in its element is good, and in their proper sphere all natures and capacities are excellent." Such a statement of the Neo-classical doctrines of proportion and subordination makes clear why the book has been called the "most complete . . . expression of the neo-classical spirit in the new nation."

Yet ***Modern Chivalry*** . . . , has too often been misread as a treatise of Neo-classic principles; the novel also confirms the existence of a Romantic attack upon Neo-classic rationalism, an attack which, surprisingly, almost always succeeds within the rhetorical pattern of the novel. Instead of writing a novel in praise of those eighteenth century ideals which he considered essential to a successful democracy, Brackenridge composed a Swiftian satire in which he despairs of a triumph for reason and common sense. Although it has been claimed that there is "no principle of plot construction" controlling ***Modern Chivalry,*** a very clear principle becomes manifest, and it is not necessarily a principle supporting the "ideal of sanity." The book's consistent narrative sequence is: (1) the humorous description of an absurd, irrational proposal, (2) an appeal to reason in argument against that irrational proposal, (3) the failure of reason to change men's minds or to ridicule the situation, (4) a capitulation to irrationality through a new mode of unreasoned argument which (5) does change men's minds, and ironically, defeats the absurd proposal, and (6) a chapter of authorial commentary discussing the folly of the previous sequence. Paradoxically, it is only by forgetting to be reasonable that Brackenridge's advocate of reason, Captain Farrago, is able to effect change. Although obviously Brackenridge did not intend it, ***Modern Chivalry*** documents the efficacy of *non-reason* in dealing with a world where the unexplainable, irrational act can be successfully proposed. The novel argues, despairingly, that the democratic process usually supports the non-rational solution to political problems. While Brackenridge's despair is never absolute, since he continues to find solace in the ideals of democratic theory, ***Modern Chivalry*** serves more to prove his bewilderment when confronted by a seemingly insane world than to affirm his faith in a reasoned, ordered system of human government. (pp. 92-3)

Captain Farrago, a man ''of good natural sense,'' . . . begins a journey across the countryside accompanied by his servant, the Irish bog-trotter, Teague Oregan; the Captain's purpose is ''to see how things were going on here and there and to observe human nature.'' . . . From his very first encounter, what Captain Farrago discovers ''going on'' is irrational: he is unable to convince a group of country jockeys that the common plough horse serving as his mount ''can scarce go beyond a trot.'' . . . They insist, since a horse race is about to commence, ''that the horse was what they called a bite and that under the appearance of leanness and stiffness there was concealed some hidden quality of swiftness uncommon.'' . . . This disturbing evidence of absurdity, of people refusing to recognize the truth when it stands in front of them, is quickly confirmed by a series of episodes which the Captain can only interpret as arising from a world gone mad. (p. 93)

Brackenridge establishes in these first volumes a narrative strategy for his novel, and the famous episode in which Teague is proposed as a candidate for the legislature illustrates the pattern well. Coming upon a number of people meeting to elect a state legislator, the Captain is appalled to find they prefer an ignorant weaver over a man of education. . . . Concerned for ''the order of things,'' he argues for the Neo-classical principle of subordination by telling the weaver: ''You are not furnished with those common place ideas with which even very ignorant men can pass for knowing something. There is nothing makes a man so ridiculous as to attempt what is above his sphere.'' . . . To the Captain, the reasonableness of his discourse has been self-evident: ''It is unnecessary to enlarge on this subject; for you must all be convinced of the truth and propriety of what I say.'' . . . But the people are *not* convinced; indeed, they remain so unconvinced that before the Captain realizes the danger, the fickle public with an alarming ''disposition to what is new and ignoble'' has proposed Teague as a candidate. . . . Describing what will happen when Teague takes his office, the Captain foregoes the reasonable argument, capitulates to the same sort of public irrationality that could propose Teague as a candidate, and tells his servant:

> When a man becomes of a public body, he is like a racoon, or other beast that climbs upon the fork of a tree; the boys pushing at him with pitch-forks, or throwing stones or shooting at him with an arrow, the dogs barking in the mean time . . . For I would not for a thousand guineas, though I have not the half of it to spare, that the breed of the Oregans should come to this; bringing on them a worse stain than stealing sheep; to which they are addicted. . . .

The Captain has not become irrational himself, of course, but sarcastic; his conclusions, however, are irrational, and these conclusions are accepted *as rational* by Teague, the public's representative. (pp. 94-5)

The narrative pattern in this episode is clear: confronted with an absurd proposal, the Captain appeals to reason and common sense; this appeal fails and he resorts to irrational arguments (state office is a worse stain than sheep stealing), and, ironically, is effective. The narrator's ''reflections'' make it especially obvious, of course, that this pattern operates within the structure of satire, and that Brackenridge deplores such a nonsensical world. But the irrational world is consistently revealed as the *dominant* world in *Modern Chivalry,* and through the rest of the novel it is only by irrational appeals that Captain

Farrago is able to keep Teague from positions he is unsuited for. (p. 95)

Even if this rhetorical pattern affirming a pervasive irrationality were not so obvious in *Modern Chivalry,* additional evidence proves that the irrational is the book's major concern. Time after time, the world is referred to as a madhouse, inhabited by madmen; the Captain asks the electorate, ''What can be the madness that possesses you?'' . . . A preacher, observing the operations of popular democracy, cries out ''Oh; monstrous! The folly, the fury, the madness of the populace!'' . . . ; a group of peace officers tell the Captain, ''A madness prevails at present . . . When the people get a thing into their heads, the best way is to let them go on. They will come to themselves by and by.'' . . . (p. 96)

Clearly, Brackenridge is saying that often the excesses of popular democratic government are insane, that the people are seldom coaxed out of their madness by voices of common sense. Indeed, the novel's repository of common sense is not primarily Captain Farrago, who constantly capitulates to the irrational method, but the ''implied narrator'' of the many chapters labeled **''Concerning Reflections,''** or **''Concerning Observations.''** Always a voice of reason, this figure usually feels compelled to comment on irrational scenes, and his commentary, surprisingly free of irony or satire, presents the rational, orderly solution to each episode; it is this figure who offers Neo-classical principles, and he is never a part of the fictional narrative, perhaps because he speaks for Brackenridge himself.

Modern Chivalry is a novel in which fiction argues for one kind of truth—the Captain never succeeds on rational terms, and at book's end has given up and permitted Teague to become a judge—and authorial commentary suggests another. Intended to plead for the desirable, Neo-classical ideal of a stable, coherent existence, Brackenridge's novel exposes an irrational world, a world where a bog-trotter can be a statesman, philosopher and judge, all through the consent of the rabble. Brackenridge seriously attacks the pretensions of the uneducated masses, and he interprets those pretensions in terms of a changing world view. *Modern Chivalry* illustrates the apparent failure of Neo-classical rationalism to check uninhibited, unreasonable democratic individualism. This undesirable individualism, lampooned and yet confirmed as the dominant voice of the new America, is primarily a Romantic individualism; while Wordsworth was asserting the inherent dignity of Cumberland peasants, Brackenridge was assailing American egalitarians who held that Pennsylvania frontiersmen were capable of enlightened legislation. Brackenridge felt that he was exposing an irrational world, but he really only confronted, and despaired of, that nineteenth century Romantic world which was confounding Western civilization in his time. His countrymen had begun to define themselves differently toward a whole set of supposedly inviolable principles inherited from English Neo-classicism: decorum, subordination, rationality, proportion; Brackenridge felt strongly that such redefinition constituted a threat to the orderly processes of living and the reasonable functioning of democratic government. (pp. 96-7)

> *Robert Hemenway, ''Fiction in the Age of Jefferson: The Early American Novel As Intellectual Document,'' in* Midcontinent American Studies Journal, *Vol. 9, No. 1, Spring, 1968, pp. 91-102.**

WENDY MARTIN   (essay date 1971)

[*Martin posits the view that ''Brackenridge is the first American novelist to focus on the theme of the alienated artist in a democ-*

racy '' and discusses Farrago in Modern Chivalry *as ''the first . . . in a long list of solitary figures'' to appear in American literature. In her analysis she focuses on the characters's self-definition in a world of multiple values and multiple points of view. Martin connects the novel's philosophical and psychological underpinnings to its structure and form and ultimately praises Brackenridge for his ability to convey ''the private vision of the artist.'']*

In addition to providing extensive commentary on the political differences of the Jeffersonians and Hamiltonians, [**Modern Chivalry**] attempted to establish an apolitical value system for the new democracy which was based on philosophical reflection rather than existing social precedence. Brackenridge's concern with independent thinking in **Modern Chivalry** foreshadows the themes of artistic isolation, subjectivity, and alienation which preoccupy many nineteenth- and twentieth-century American novelists.

Brackenridge is the first American novelist to focus on the theme of the alienated artist in a democracy. The problem of artistic self-definition in a society which denies the value of art can be better understood in the context of the efforts of Captain Farrago, the protagonist of **Modern Chivalry,** to survive the levelling influence of the mob and to counteract the confused values of the new democracy. Farrago, unable to accept the emphasis on profit and the materialistic definition of success in post-Revolutionary America, becomes a pioneer on the psychological frontier, and he is the first fictional protagonist in a long list of solitary figures who appear in later novels. (p. 241)

In part, the tradition of the solitary, introspective author stems from the Puritan habit of self-scrutiny in an effort to detect sin and discern God's message. . . . Puritan introspection is reflected in Brackenridge's insistence that ''the man of real genius will never walk in the beaten track, because his object is what is new and uncommon''. . . . Brackenridge warns his readers, however, that ''it requires great courage to bear testimony against an error in the judgment of the multitude'' . . . and that ''the man is a hero, who can withstand unjust opinion. It requires more courage, than to fight duels''. . . . As a result of having to develop the habit of psychological self-reliance as an adaptive response to social rejection, Brackenridge's protagonist Captain Farrago learns that he must develop a sense of self that does not depend on community approval, social ritual or categories. . . . Because Farrago realizes that social labels do not reflect his individuality, his sense of self is not dependent on social approbation but rather on an awareness of his own uniqueness and conviction of the validity of his personal moral code. Although Brackenridge counsels intellectual and social independence, he realizes that some men prefer to be enslaved rather than to experience the uncertainty that accompanies freedom from social rituals. . . . (pp. 242-43)

This habit of psychological self-reliance creates a sensitivity to the difference between the individual's perceptions and social forms which pre-structure these perceptions. It is this preoccupation with subjective truth and the consequent sense of isolation which many critics maintain characterizes the American novel; however, no critic discusses these characteristics as being the special problems of the novelist in a democracy. (p. 243)

As Brackenridge observes the disparity between his version of reality and social versions, he becomes aware of the subjective nature of his experience and the relativity of his point of view—an awareness which is reflected in both the narrative technique and form of **Modern Chivalry.** The narrator of the novel is a

detached observer who evaluates and discourses at length on the significance of the adventures of the philosopher and profiteer on the road; he is intellectually superior to Captain Farrago, who is depicted as being virtuous but often naive: ''John Farrago, a man of about fifty-three years of age, of good natural sense, and considerable reading; but in some things whimsical, owing perhaps to his greater knowledge of books than that of the world''. . . . The narrator, more knowledgeable and worldly than Farrago, often assumes a protective role toward the quixotic philosopher, and since his ego is not directly affected by the events of the journey, he is freer to reflect at length on the significance of Farrago's experiences. The narrator elucidates the meaning of Farrago's travels, which, in part, can be seen as a secular extension of the Puritan journey in which the voyager must endure trials from within and without: since the narrator is once removed from the action of the novel, like the Puritan preacher, he is able to play the role of penetrating social critic who provides deeper insights into the significance of the social drama in which Farrago and Teague are actors. At the same time, the perspective of the novel serves to heighten the reader's awareness of the subjective nature of reality as it becomes clear that the narrator, Farrago, and O'Reagan are each focusing on somewhat different worlds—the narrator is concerned with human values which transcend sociocultural variables, Farrago with virtue in a democratic political system, and Teague with profit in a capitalistic economy and status in an upwardly mobile society.

The literary significance of the frontier is also clarified when evaluated in terms of the possibilities it offers for self-definition by freeing the individual from confining social roles. Brackenridge embodies the frontier ideals of getting back to essentials and psychological self-reliance in the character of the Marquis de Marnessie, a French emigrant who rids himself of a title—a comfortable social category—and returns to a more basic life-style. . . . [The] frontier by freeing the individual from the elaborate social and economic patterns of the city or town enables him to get closer to the core of human experience.

Brackenridge's preoccupation with human values which transcend pragmatic imperatives and which are concerned with subjective experience rather than excessively stylized social interaction or entrepreneurial activities, explains why in **Modern Chivalry** there is no description of physical environment—landscape or buildings—or financial transactions and why there are almost no details of clothing or material goods. Instead, the novel concentrates on the narrator's response to the experiences of the social philosopher and the profiteer as they explore life in the new nation. . . . [The] divergence in world-views of Farrago, the philosopher, and Teague, the profiteer, is reinforced by the economic structure of capitalism. Max Weber and Emile Durkheim argue that the division of labor creates multiple realities often resulting in social dislocation of the individual, which is experienced as solitude or anomie depending on the degree of alienation, and while the existence of multiple realities helps the con man to conceal his trickery, it causes the American writer to feel all the more alienated.

In addition to the tensions created by a democratic social structure and a capitalistic economic system, the distinction between matter and mind, subject and object, which separates the knower from the known, manifests itself in the eighteenth century in Lockean associationism, an approach to perception based on the conviction that reason is simply an arranger of experience—that there are no a priori principles for structuring experience. . . . Thus, experience becomes process, knowledge and reality subjective states of mind. The loose structure of *Modern Chivalry* reflects this shift from experience as product to experience as process, and the open form of the novel captures the fluidity of associative subjective experience. . . . The novel does not conclude with a scene which resolves all of the tensions in the plot; instead it ends as it began, with Teague still successfully conning the public and Farrago still wandering around the countryside—hence, the conclusion creates no artificial break with reality but presents life as an unbroken process. (pp. 244-48)

While the entrepreneur perceives his world in terms of profit and losses, the independent thinker is free to explore many versions of reality because he is not bound by pragmatic imperatives. As *Modern Chivalry* progresses, Brackenridge develops a growing sense of cultural relativity: the first two books of *Modern Chivalry* concentrate on the detection of Teague's plots and the training of Teague to be president; the subsequent books not only survey the new democracy in an attempt to determine national values, but also reveal a contempt for ethnocentricity which limits the horizon of the new nation to the profit motive. (p. 248)

Madness, a major theme in *Modern Chivalry,* is often seen as sanity in a society where profit takes precedence over knowledge, an inversion of values which is reflected in the mad philosopher's lament: "Oh! the inconsistency of human life and manners. I am shut up here as a mad man, in a mad place, and yet it appears to me that I am the only rational being amongst men, because I know that I am mad, and acknowledge it, and they do not know that they are mad, or acknowledge it". . . . The madman asks the question that reveals he has more wisdom than those who judge him: "But how can one rebut the imputation of madness; how disprove insanity? The highest excellence of understanding, and madness, like the two ends of a right line, turned to a circle, are said to come together". . . . (p. 249)

Just as the creative efforts of the poet or the painter shape primordial energy giving rise to the tradition of artist as maker, legal and educational systems channel this undifferentiated energy in order to make civilization possible; thus, Brackenridge subscribes to the classical conviction that institutions enable men to be human. Denying the Rousseauian doctrine of spontaneity which asserts that institutions are repressive and hostile to man's true nature, Brackenridge insists that the "spontaneous overflow of emotions" is not self-expression but destructive mobism and that political and educational institutions convert primitive energy into culture. Brackenridge is a conscious mythmaker: he knows that a "self" can exist only in civilization and that all legal and moral codes such as Christianity are designed for this purpose; "All the rules of morality are but maxims of prudence. They all lead to self-preservation". . . . (p. 255)

Although Brackenridge knows that "there is no perfection in any human institution" . . . and therefore refuses to subscribe to popular utopian theories of exponential growth in man's capacity to solve his problems, "Time and chance happeneth to all men" . . . , he insists that reason and moderation enable man to resist his destructive potential and to realize his creative capacity. In spite of the fact that he maintains that the institutions of law, education, and art will enable men to be more fully human by establishing agreed-upon reality, he respects the necessity of the independent thinker in the new democracy to explore his subjective reality as an adaptive response to a society which denies his worth. Thus, *Modern Chivalry* chron-

icles the *private vision* of the artist as well as narrating the adventures of the rogue and the rational man. (p. 256)

> *Wendy Martin, "On the Road with the Philosopher and the Profiteer: A Study of Hugh Henry Brackenridge's 'Modern Chivalry'," in Eighteenth-Century Studies, Vol. 4, No. 3, Spring, 1971, pp. 241-56.*

WENDY MARTIN   (essay date 1973)

[*Asserting that "Modern Chivalry is the first American novel in which a confidence man appears," Martin explores Brackenridge's censure of the con man in the novel. She also links Brackenridge's exposure of the tactics of this figure with his own position as an alienated artist in the new republic, deducing that "it is especially painful for an artist to live in a society which accepts the false identity of the con man while denying the worth of the artist as an individual."*]

Modern Chivalry reflects the tensions created by shifting political, social, and economic realities of late-eighteenth-century and early-nineteenth-century America, but in addition to revealing the problems of a culture in flux, it also represents an effort to establish values which transcend the limitations of a nation committed to industrial growth and social mobility.

Because Brackenridge's vision of the democratic state is not limited to such nearsighted economic and political interests as taxes and votes, he attempts to teach his readers standards of conduct such as the classical virtues of judgment, fortitude, and self-denial . . . which will withstand the erosion of time and circumstance. . . . Captain Farrago, the modern chevalier and true democrat, dedicates himself to exposing the false gods of profit and property, and the satire of *Modern Chivalry* attempts to solve the problems of ambition and self-interest which threaten to undermine the young democracy.

Theoretically, individuals in a democracy have an equal opportunity to gain status because they are not locked into fixed categories in a hierarchical system based on ancestry or inherited wealth; but since the shift from a stratified to linear social structure was still occurring in the late-eighteenth and early-nineteenth centuries, clear-cut standards for "evaluating status" had not yet evolved. Hoping to counteract the confusion created by the shift from religious to secular values, Brackenridge warns the readers of *Modern Chivalry* that democracy by its very nature invites roguery by encouraging the belief that all men have the right to be president. He also points out that the confusion created by a social system based on upward mobility but which has no defined standards to evaluate performance is aggravated by an economic system which rewards profiteering in any form. (pp. 179-80)

Modern Chivalry is the first American novel in which a confidence man appears, and his appearance coincides not only with the confusion created by a political and social system in flux, but also with the emergence of a world-view which no longer sees politics as an embodiment of God's will, but as an instrument for controlling men. The eighteenth century is characterized by the belief that it is possible to legislate social harmony, and the conviction that man's impulses can be curbed and controlled by a political program gives rise to the concept of the politician as a manipulator of the masses. Accompanying the shift from the concept of statesman as God's agent to that of the politician as manipulator of men, the con man emerges as the politician par excellence. The con man actively shapes the world in which he operates and the very fact that he manipulates his world at will reveals that he spurns the alliance of statecraft with soulcraft; the con man knows that social control depends more on the skillful use of awe and shame than it does on discerning God's will, and he uses this knowledge for self-aggrandizement at the expense of those who are less worldly or less selfish.

Modern Chivalry criticizes the schemes of con men and profiteers in post-Revolutionary America; and Farrago, the modern chevalier, exposes Teague's efforts to con people into believing that he is a senator, Greek scholar, philosopher, clergyman, and Indian treatymaker. Farrago is the rational man or philosopher who is more concerned with community welfare than individual profit; disturbed by Teague's efforts to play roles he is not qualified for, his criticism of Teague's exploits is intended to teach his audience that common sense and moderation can counteract the rampant opportunism fostered by the myth of equality. . . . (pp. 181-82)

In spite of the fact that Brackenridge denounces scoundrels like Teague O'Regan for taking advantage of the public confidence, he realizes that in the absence of a well-defined social order, status in a democracy is often determined in a more informal manner—by a general social acceptance of an individual's performance rather than his inheritance of a predetermined social location. The con man takes advantage of this informal method of determining status by carefully staging his performance, giving special attention to details such as costumes, setting, and props—thus, the con man is a master of the art of illusion. Farrago, refusing to accept the appearance of capability, insists on performance rather than props; he will not allow clothing to substitute for competence—periwigs and gavels do not make a judge, knowledge of the law and impartial decisions do. As we have seen, the modern chevalier is dedicated to piercing the veil of illusion created by rogues like Teague; and often the captain, as the man of sense and reason, performs the function of distinguishing appearance from reality. For example, in the case of the two men who both claim to be preachers, Farrago decides that the one who sermonizes best rather than the one who wears clerical vestments is legitimate: "Gentlemen," said the Captain, "there is a text in your own Scripture, which, I think, might enable you to decide: It is this, 'by their fruits ye shall know them.' Let the two men preach and the best sermon take the purse; or laying aside the figure, let him that expounds the scripture best, be adjudged the clergyman". . . . (pp. 184-85)

Although Brackenridge demands performance rather than props, his satire on the con man is double-edged because he realizes that people by their very nature are actors—that the word *person,* in its first meaning, means mask. . . .

Just as the actor must first learn his script, the postures and mannerisms appropriate to the role, so the individual in society must master the behavior traits appropriate to his social identity. . . .

The confidence man has an instinctive knowledge of the fact that social behavior requires dramatic skills by giving a polished performance; therefore Brackenridge hopes to eliminate some of the dramatic opportunities open to the con man by preventing proliferation of meaningless symbols, rituals, and ceremonies which do not contribute to competence but which assist the confidence man in his performance. (p. 186)

Insisting that "almost all unnecessary ceremony is displeasing to a man of sense" . . . , Brackenridge undercuts false rituals by burlesquing them, or by using mock heroic techniques which

reduce human affairs to the level of barnyard activities: he suggests that treaty negotiations with Indians be extended to bears and wolves: "If our traders go amongst wolves in consequence of a treaty, I wish they could check themselves in the introduction of spirituous liquors. A drunk wolf, or bear, would be a dangerous animal" . . . ; property requirements for voting privileges might be fulfilled by cattle: "Not that a brute beast is not entitled to a vote, or be voted for; but this is an *English bull.* No English bull can vote" . . . ; lions and bears be given official government posts: "if pards and bears are to be admitted to appear, or officiate in any department or representative capacity, it ought to be at the bar, where noise may be better tolerated, and growling may pass for ability." . . . Like Swift, who accepts neither the view that man is hopelessly depraved like the Yahoos, *animal, inplume bipes* [two-legged animal without feathers], nor totally rational like the Houyhnhms, *animal rationis* [rational animal], but *animal rationis capax*—capable of reason—Brackenridge is frequently angered by the wilful refusal to exercise rational potential. (p. 187)

Ironically, the very fluidity of democratic social structure which allows the con man to perpetuate his schemes through the art of illusion causes the satirist to pay a double price for his art because the society which is taken in by the con man's trickery often invalidates the contribution of the artist. It is especially painful for an artist to live in a society which accepts the false identity of the con man while denying the worth of the artist as an individual. (p. 188)

Brackenridge clearly understood that the price of writing satire is that ironically, society may deny the satirist's worth as an individual, just as the satirist denies the validity of the performance of the con man or the values of the mob. Nevertheless, Brackenridge, by ridiculing the excesses of the new democracy and by encouraging his readers to develop reflective habits and humane values, not only defends the new nation against rogues like Teague O'Regan but upholds the rational principles of the social philosopher and also articulates the vision of the artist. (p. 190)

> *Wendy Martin, "The Rogue and the Rational Man: Hugh Henry Brackenridge's Study of a Con Man in 'Modern Chivalry','" in* Early American Literature, *Vol. VIII, No. 2, Fall, 1973, pp. 179-92.*

MICHAEL DAVITT BELL   (essay date 1975)

[*Bell discusses the importance of* Father Bombo's Pilgrimage to Mecca *in terms of the political climate at Princeton during the time that Brackenridge and Philip Freneau attended college there. In addition, Bell analyses Brackenridge's use of the motif of orientalism and his handling of humor and the theme of moral incoherence in the novel. He echoes the comments of Lewis Leary (1965) regarding the influence of Brackenridge's work on later trends in American literature and argues that Brackenridge and Freneau's characterizations anticipate the motif of the anti-hero in later American literature. In his conclusion Bell states that, though* Father Bombo's Pilgrimage to Mecca *is "hardly a neglected masterpiece," it is important as "quite plausibly the 'first American novel'."*]

While the late 1760's and early 1770's were . . . a time for insecurity, for the questioning of traditional roles and patterns of belief, this was also a period of great excitement, in part political. From 1765 on, undergraduates at the College of New Jersey, in Princeton regularly registered their objections to the repressive actions of the British Parliament. Their patriotism was supported by President Witherspoon, who would later sign the *Declaration of Independence* and serve in the Continental Congress. (p. xvii)

[The] excitement agitating undergraduate life in Princeton in 1770 was also more generally literary, as the apparently enormous volume of writings exchanged in the 1770-71 paper war [between the Whig and the Tory clubs] would suggest. Literature, like politics, provided an outlet for the frustrations and uncertainties of undergraduates in a period of transition; and the study of literature lay at the core of their formal curriculum. This is the excitement that animates *Father Bombo's Pilgrimage* written by Hugh Henry Brackenridge and Philip Freneau. The chapters set at Nassau Hall—Book I, Chapter 2; and Book I, Chapter 4 (consisting of the interpolated story of "Aliborah the Skipper")—are centrally concerned with the uses and misuses of literature, especially poetry. And throughout the novel one finds burlesques of the literary forms most familiar to late-eighteenth-century undergraduates: the formal debate, which Witherspoon had instituted at the college (Book II, Chapter 3), the sermon (II, 4), the topical essay (III, 2: on "Luxury"), the Latin Epitaph (in the Conclusion) and, most notably, Freneau's various pastiches of lachrymose verse. Also, as the chapter-epigraphs from Homer and Virgil suggest, the novel as a whole was at least partially intended as an American (or Princetonian) mock-epic. (pp. xviii-xix)

[*Father Bombo's Pilgrimage* was written] at a time when it was still permissible . . . to hope that the pursuit of letters might provide a sense of purpose or stability generally lacking at Princeton in the 1760's and '70's. In this light the book is especially fascinating for the almost manic abandon with which it burlesques the literary traditions its authors most admired, and the literary forms with which they would soon become identified—the picaresque novel and the lyric poem. It is, for the most part, an indulgence, an extravagance, a sport. (p. xxii)

[The] newly discovered first book [of *Father Bombo's Pilgrimage*] would seem to be virtually a *roman à clef*. Many of its incidents are apparently thinly-fictionalized accounts, from the Whig point of view, of incidents in the paper war and many of its characters correspond to actual members of the two societies, although most of these specific references remain obscure to the modern reader. In this light the immediate object of the novel is identical with that of the poetic "Satires Against the Tories" and the other, lost documents of the literary battle: to defame by any means, fair if necessary but foul wherever possible, the principal champions of the rival society. (p. xxiii)

[Whatever] the specific identities of its characters, *Father Bombo's Pilgrimage* was initially inspired by the beginnings of the paper war between the Whig and Cliosophic [Tory] Societies. But it was more generally inspired by the literary excitement which lay behind the formation of these societies. With the formal college curriculum dominated by the classics the societies provided a forum for the discussion of modern literature, and their libraries made many works of this literature available to members. The influence of this reading is clear throughout *Father Bombo's Pilgrimage*. Lewis Leary finds in Book III "something of Don Quixote and a little of Lemuel Gulliver." In addition to Cervantes and Swift one might cite, as influences on the novel, Rabelais, Smollett, Sterne and Fielding. Bombo's combination of pugnacity and professed erudition particularly recalls Fielding's Parson Adams, in *Joseph Andrews*. But the most obvious debt of the young American authors is revealed in the basic plot of their novel; for in sending their hero to Mecca, dressed in the supposed costume of a "devout mus-

selman," they were clearly drawing on the vogue of oriental and pseudo-oriental fiction that swept England following the translation of the *Arabian Nights* between 1704 and 1712. (pp. xxvii-xxviii)

Yet *Father Bombo's Pilgrimage* does not conform at all closely to any of these modes current in English oriental fiction. It is clearly not a moral allegory on the model of [Samuel Johnson's] *Rasselas*. And while Fred Lewis Pattee could write of Bombo's adventures in Book III that they "read like chapters from the 'Arabian Nights,'" even here the similarity is not very deep. Bombo does not reach Arabia itself until the final chapter, where his adventures are described in an extremely perfunctory manner. The climactic visit to Mecca occupies only two pages. Most of Bombo's "oriental" adventures actually take place in a very non-exotic America—an America to which Bombo tries, without much success, to attribute the romance of Arabia.

In fact the novel's veneer of orientalism is quite thin, being mainly a matter of costumes and names. Bombo wears a turban, carries a copy of the Koran (or "Alcoran"), calls inns "Caravanseries" and encounters characters with such pseudo-Arabian names as Nadir Gaw, Aliborah, or Solyman Houli Hhan (although the latter has an unsettling Irish ring to it). One might compare Bombo to the visiting foreigner of the oriental satire tradition, viewing Western customs through an outsider's eye. But Bombo's "oriental" perspective (like the "oriental" setting through which he moves) is bogus. And the contrast between East and West, between Bombo's exotic mission and the mundane world in which he travels, is by and large not satirical but simply humorous. The placing of an Arabian barber in Princeton, or of a turban on Bombo's head, is a joke, a juxtaposition of incongruous elements; but the joke has no discernable satirical import beyond general mockery—of the Cliosophians, of the American setting, of the tradition of oriental romance. All of this is to say that *Father Bombo's Pilgrimage* is less a satire than a burlesque, an effort to "make fun" of everything within the authors' purview.

The novel's humor is distinguished by a kind of vigorous aimlessness, an air of exuberant excess masking a profound uncertainty of general attitude. Literary clichés are mocked throughout, but the book has no language of its own. While drawing on a host of sources, it does so only superficially, and always in the form of burlesque. Its mockery of institutions and behavior is not supported by any norm, any imagined set of alternative values. Its world is one, finally, of relativity, in which *everything* becomes the object of mockery and parody. One curious result of this universal air of mockery is that Father Bombo himself, who begins as an object of ironic satire, becomes by the end almost a genuine hero—at least the sort of hero suited to a world which seems to *require* mendacity, buffoonery, self-absorption and physical durability for survival. For there is, in this world, no ultimate standard of literary or moral authority. All standards and values are fair game for the authors' humor.

The absence of value in *Father Bombo*—what one might call, less charitably, its moral and aesthetic incoherence, its pervasive air of adolescence—no doubt owes much to the immaturity and inexperience of its authors. One cannot expect too much of the "first American novel." But the very faults of the book provide much of its historical interest. It is the product, after all, of a period of rapid transition and uncertainty in American culture—qualities particularly crucial to the experience of undergraduates at the College of New Jersey. Old traditions of authority—personal, literary and political—were being profoundly challenged. New sources of legitimacy had not yet been tested. It is small wonder that such a climate should produce a work like **Father Bombo's Pilgrimage.** In its most adolescent qualities it seems most indicative of its milieu and moment.

These same qualities forge the most significant link between **Father Bombo** and the subsequent development of American literature. Humor has lain behind many of the works of our major writers, and it has often been characterized by generalized mockery, uncertainty of value and near or total moral incoherence. One thinks of some of the works of Mark Twain—particularly *A Connecticut Yankee,* in which satirical impulses war continually with moral confusion and the impulse to the joke, however grotesque or inappropriate. Even closer to Freneau and Brackenridge is the humor of the young Washington Irving (especially in *Salmagundi*) in which, as William Hedges has written, attempts at satire are accompanied by "no sure sense of authority." Lacking such a sense, and unable otherwise to find coherence in its world, as Hedges writes, "*Salmagundi* pushes the tendency of self-mockery to the point of explicitly defying its readers to make sense of the contents." This is not to imply that **Father Bombo's Pilgrimage** is by any standard on the same aesthetic level as the works of Irving or Twain; it most assuredly is not. Yet it suggests, nevertheless, some of the directions in which American fiction would go following the Revolution. And its protagonist suggests the effect humor and social instability would have on our perception of the American character. Bombo may be based, strictly speaking, on Joshua Hart or some other Cliosophian; and he may occasionally resemble Don Quixote . . . or Parson Adams. But one finds in him, as well, fascinating hints of such later American anti-heroes as Ichabod Crane . . . or even Huckleberry Finn.

Father Bombo's Pilgrimage to Mecca is hardly a neglected masterpiece. In most respects it falls short of the minimal standards of "good" fiction. . . . Yet the book is fascinating for several reasons. It *is* quite plausibly the "first American novel." Its authors became, later, important American writers. It gives a sense of the fictional models and modes to which young Americans turned before the ascendency of Sentimental and Gothic influence in the works of William Hill Brown, Susannah Haswell Rowson, Charles Brockden Brown and their contemporaries—or before the later domestication of historical romance by James Fenimore Cooper and the many American adulators of Sir Walter Scott. It suggests some of the directions American humor would take in the next century. And it is especially fascinating as a document of an aspect of American culture for which few such documents exist—namely, the intellectual history of that generation of college students who later comprised the political and cultural elite of the new nation. (pp. xxix-xxxii)

> *Michael Davitt Bell, in an introduction to* Father Bombo's Pilgrimage to Mecca: 1770 *by Hugh Henry Brackenridge and Philip Freneau, edited by Michael Davitt Bell, Princeton University Library, 1975, pp. ix-xxxii.**

WILLIAM W. HOFFA (essay date 1980)

[*Developing Lewis Leary's concept of the nature of the narrative voice in* Modern Chivalry *(see excerpt above, 1965), Hoffa analyzes Brackenridge's narrative strategy in the novel. He concludes that Brackenridge uses irony in an inconsistent way which forces the reader to be vigilant about the narrator's credibility. Hoffa*

terms Modern Chivalry *a "highly conscious work of comic art" because of the subtlety and complexity of Brackenridge's instructive technique. His remarks about "linguistic precariousness" in the novel also recall the interpretation of William L. Nance (1967) on verbal irony in* Modern Chivalry.]

Because of its weak and thin characterization, its open-ended, episodic movement which offers no satisfying dramatic resolution, and its general essayistic tone, our interest in [**Modern Chivalry**] is necessarily limited to the historical and biographical correspondences which have been shown to exist between Brackenridge's own career as a Pennsylvania lawyer, editor, and Jeffersonian democrat and the social and political events taking place in America during the decades immediately following the Revolution and the establishment of the high constitutional principles of the new Republic. Thus, most discussions of **Modern Chivalry** readily convert the picaresque adventures on the rocky American road of the patrician Captain Farrago and his unruly and ambitious Irish servant, Teague O'Regan, into a kind of autobiographical commentary or into slightly dramatized social and political history. In short, its documentary value is seen to be far superior to its dramatic value; Brackenridge's rhetorical manner and philosophical musings far superior to his artistry.

However, judged not against the mostly later conventions and values of the literary genre of the "novel"—especially to the degree that this includes notions of psychological and social realism or even mythic "romance"—**Modern Chivalry** may be seen . . . as a primary American contribution to that loosely generic body of European works which are encyclopedic in scope, engagingly shifty in tone and perspective, and exasperatingly digressive in manner, works such as Erasmus's *Praise of Folly,* Rabelais' *Gargantua and Pantagruel,* Butler's *Hudibras,* Burton's *Anatomy of Melancholy,* Cervantes's *Don Quixote,* Sterne's *Tristram Shandy,* and Swift's *Tale of a Tub.*

In common with most of these multiformed and multitoned books, Brackenridge's **Modern Chivalry** has at its center a complexly "comic" vision of man's warring allegiances to "apollonian" order and "dionysian" disorder. It contains within itself, in conscious artistic suspension, both the moral earnestness of social and political satire, with its dimensions of ethical and social high seriousness, *and* the gay and witty irreverence and irony of burlesque, parody, and nonsense. Brackenridge's Enlightenment skepticism, which caused him to see mankind as likely to be "weak and visionary," is balanced by the implicit norms of common sense, which he assumed would allow his readers a basis for judging the excesses depicted in the narrative. Above all, Brackenridge seems interested in the viability and stability of social institutions as a civilized check against perennial human folly.

But while Brackenridge's concern with the "democratic" basis of America's new systems of governance stemmed from his career as a lawyer and his backing of the new Constitution, his underlying concern in **Modern Chivalry** is less with law than with language. Indeed, though much of the novel concerns the misuses and abuses of the legal system and of many other social institutions, fundamental to them all he posits the matter of language as the common sense basis of all social discourse and, less obviously so, individual freedom. Brackenridge is less interested in the much debated stylistic question of "American English" than in the possibility that the democratic impulse might usher in an atmosphere of such linguistic license and illusory liberation that skillful and unprincipled manipulators of words will be able to invent and control not just the illusions but the reality of the weak and visionary "many." *Modern Chivalry*, then, dramatizes a vision of linguistic precariousness, emblematic of the shaky foundations of the whole American enterprise. On the one extreme Brackenridge satirizes the ultimate foolishness of those who assume that there is a fixed, natural, logical correspondence between *words* and the *world;* between linguistic symbols and social realities. His book makes fun of those who are gullible enough to be taken in by the linguistic manipulations of clever and unprincipled, fast-talking rogues. On the other, it suggests that while language cannot, by its nature, be "fixed" in rigid rules and forms, its vitality and validity depend upon social consensus governed by common sense and alerted skepticism. Though Brackenridge informs his reader in his Introduction that his central concern in *Modern Chivalry* will be the relation between "style" and "sense," between "language" and "knowledge," the classical indirection of his fictional voice has here and throughout the following eight hundred pages been generally misunderstood. These emphases can be demonstrated in a brief examination of the actions of his minor characters, the interactions of his two central figures, and, most clearly, in the conflicting poses and postures of his narrator.

At the lowest and least ambiguous level, the level of simple satire, *Modern Chivalry* presents us with a motley collection of often stock, two-dimensional characters who attempt to draw Teague O'Regan and Captain John Farrago into miscellaneous schemes, devices, deceptions, ploys, fantasies, and delusions. The "rogues," interestingly, seem drawn not only from the common people, but from the professions of medicine, law, diplomacy, journalism, and the military, or from the realms of commerce or politics; whereas, the "fools" are generally misguided scientists, philosophers, educators, and lovers—as well as the uneducated, recent immigrants, Indians, blacks, and the shiftless poor. Farrago and Teague are set upon by both rogues and fools, and their "adventures" involve more than anything else their ability to penetrate the false language of these many figures. In the case of the physicians, lawyers, evangelists, office seekers, and others, this is a matter of their cutting through layers upon layers of gobbledygook, jargon, cant, and rarified doubletalk to the cunning selfishness and aggrandizement which lie beneath such linguistic subterfuge. The "fools" they meet are of two types: those who are taken in by the linguistic allusions of the rogues, and those who spin their own blinding fantasies. They share a weakness for impractical or sentimental abstractions which exist at a laughable distance from physical, political, economic, or social realities. Their language is inflated, illogical, nonsensical, and their efforts ineffectual.

Increasingly, *Modern Chivalry* seems concerned with mankind's surrender of its humanity to the herdish instincts of the Mob and the tyranny of the demagogue. Beside the threat of the mob, the delusions of individual rogues and fools seem nearly petty and insignificant. For, acting as a mob, mankind is seen by Brackenridge as simultaneously foolish and roguish. Mobs are shown to be not only mulish, intractable, insensitive, and amoral—especially when presented with ideas which they do not want to consider—but also unpredictable, capricious, and violent. Law, learning, moral decency, sincere religion, and property are all attacked at one time or another by the Mob in *Modern Chivalry*. Buildings are burned and torn down, legal justice is overturned; people are hanged, harried, and chased out of town. While Farrago and other "rational" spokesmen occasionally temper and "cool" down the "enthusiasm" of the Mob, its mood and actions prove nearly irrepressible. Its loud and mindless shout easily drowns out with superior volume the separate voices of "designing men," misguided idealists, and philosophers alike.

The Cervantean interplay of *Modern Chivalry*'s two central characters, Farrago and Teague, also turns on the axis of linguistic foolishness and roguishness. While Farrago is, as he is usually seen to be, a man whose opinions and actions express "good sense," he is also at times a snob, a bigot, a pedant, and a coward—these mixed qualities being signalled even by his name, which means in Latin, "a mishmash of grain." Much of what he says contains sound principles and rational counsel, but he also is guilty of hyperbolic, ineffectual, loaded, deceitful, and misleading language, especially in his "advice" to Teague and to the others to whom he feels himself superior (which includes nearly everyone he meets on his mock chivalric quest). Many of his lectures to Teague, for instance, condescendingly seek not to assist and instruct Teague out of his foolish aspirations as much as to befuddle and frighten him. (pp. 289-92)

But Farrago's assessment of himself is also frequently misguided. His many lectures to various assemblages of the American citizenry are frequently so arch and pompous in tone, manner, and presumption that he succeeds only in making a fool of himself. While he tries to be witty and to parade his superior erudition or experience, his auditors often react with understandably mute incomprehension, disdain, and even anger and violence. On the other hand, in some situations which require tact and delicacy, Farrago is too blunt—as when he proposes to Miss Fog by telling her, "You are a young lady of great beauty, great sense, and fortune still greater than either". . . . In another instance, his intended expression of sympathy for a seduced and abandoned maiden is so gratuitous, moralistic, and stilted, that it only increases her misery and drives her into a further and irreversible depression. As these and innumerable other examples spread throughout the novel suggest, to see Farrago as Brackenridge's "spokesman," is to miss the subtleties and ironies of his characterization.

Moreover, whereas the voice of Farrago reveals the confusions of his mind, and the artfulness of his creator's irony, Teague is a figure who lacks a voice of his own—his stock Irish dialect is indeed borrowed by his creator from stage burlesque. He is continually berated by Farrago (for his own ends, mostly) and laughed at for his general clownish and cloddish rascality. . . . Few if any of the masks we see him temporarily assume, for instance, come into being from his own initiative. He is, in fact, a remarkably passive rogue, for he is gullible and he is desperate in his futile attempts to become a philosopher, Indian chief, candidate, journalist, courtier, civil servant, clerk, travel writer, preacher, university lecturer, orator, judge, military officer, or any of the other selves he assumes. Indeed, Teague is a dupe, to a large degree, of the lofty rhetoric of the American Constitution and all its official and unofficial promotional literature. He seems naively to believe he can put his background behind him and become whatever he aspires to become. On the other hand, there are instances scattered throughout the narrative, in which Teague's sensible and earthy realism functions to deflate Farrago's misguided notions and grandiloquent linguistic posturing. Whereas Farrago often wanders aimlessly in a maze of mere rhetoric, mistaking language for knowledge of the ways of the world, Teague's actions speak louder and more forcefully of his fundamental will to succeed than the Irish brogue of his words.

A good portion of the "adventures" of Farrago and Teague are not "dramatized" to any great degree; we do not *see* them occur, but rather *hear about* them occurring or having occurred. For every page of drama there are three or four pages of recapitulation or commentary, some of which is indeed, in the omniscient manner of Fielding, actually portioned off into chapters called **"Containing Observations"** or **"Containing Reflections,"** but much of which is not. . . . While Brackenridge's voice is occasionally seen to be diverted into humorous over- or understatement, his purpose is judged to be to heighten our perception of the follies of those he is attacking.

But while it is generally true that the narrative voice which dominates *Modern Chivalry* assumes the characteristics of detached, expansive omniscience, interpreting and judging the immediate and broader social political, philosophical significance of the adventures of Farrago and Teague, its ultimate seriousness is continually, though unpredictably, undercut by degrees of doubt, self-consciousness, ludicrousness, and even nonsense. This is to say that the roguishness and foolishness which are dramatized in the schemes and illusions of the minor characters and in the word play of the major characters of the novel is ironically but purposefully present in the *narration* as well. (pp. 293-94)

[Brackenridge's narration] is sometimes straight but sometimes ironic; it speaks with at least two voices, the one, like Fielding's; the other like Sterne's or Swift's. In the former case, it comments sagely on the adventures of Farrago and Teague and the lessons to be drawn from these adventures. Thus, for instance, after Farrago has resisted the temptation to race his old nag against some hostlers and their trim horses, the narrator says:

> The first reflection which arises, is, the good sense of the Captain; who was unwilling to impose his horse for a racer; not being qualified for the course. Because, as an old lean beast, attempting a trot, he was respectable enough; but going out of his nature and affecting speed, he would have been contemptible. The great secret of preserving respect, is the cultivating and shewing to the best advantage the powers that we possess, and the not going beyond them. Everything in its element is good, and in their proper sphere all natures and capacities are excellent. This though might be turned into a thousand different shapes, and cloathed with various expressions; but after all, it comes to the old proverb at last *Ne sutor ultra crepidam,* Let the cobler stick to his last; a sentiment we are about more to illustrate in the sequel of his work. . . .

In the latter, it comments ironically on the perhaps foolish and futile task of writing those adventures and in particular on the crucial but vacillating relation between "style" and "sense." From the opening pages onward, the teasing ironic voice is heard:

> It has been a question for sometime past, what would be the best means to fix the English language. . . . Some have thought of Dictionaries, others of Institutes, for that purpose. Swift, I think it was, who proposed in his letters to the Earl of Oxford, the forming of an academy of learned men, in order by their observations

and rules, to settle the true spellings, accentuation, and pronunciations, as well as the proper words, and the purest, most simple, and perfect phraseology of language. . . .

[Brackenridge's purpose in *Modern Chivalry*] is to caution his readers to use their own vigilance, skepticism, and common sense so as to avoid having the semantic wool, which the narration spins, pulled over their own eyes. Further instances of this ironic voice, alternate in mood from pure whimsy to dilettantism, from the mock-heroic to presumed weariness and cynicism. (pp. 295-96)

While this ironic voice is pervasive throughout the book, counterpointing both the narrative action and the serious commentary, Brackenridge, of course, in true comic fashion, does not signal when he is shifting to it from his more serious voice. Thus the reader is forced constantly to remain alert, skeptical, attentive, so as not to mistake serious comment for facetious *esprit,* or frivolous comment for autobiographical or philosophical seriousness. Indeed, Brackenridge asks his readers to be aware that the pose of omniscience or sincerity is often yet another device of the rogue and that the avoidance of foolishness involves the constant vigilance of common sense.

In conclusion, *Modern Chivalry* is a book which is concerned not merely with American democracy as a political process but with the state and health of language as the most important social institution in that process. Using the devices, techniques, and themes of comedy and proceeding from the comic assumption that all men are likely, sooner or later, in whatever position of apparent wisdom or virtue, to reveal their roguish and foolish sides, Brackenridge presents us with a gallery of rogues and fools which extends from the most obvious instances in his minor characters; to the less obvious, in his two "heroes"; and finally to the least obvious in the "narrator," whose omniscience is only apparently his own. As such the book demands to be read not merely as a serious commentary on the social and political foibles of an early era in American history, but also as a highly conscious work of comic art with its own complex view of the timelessness of human folly. Its enormous length and breadth is an enduring testament both to Brackenridge's documentary grasp of the many roots and branches of life in the new democracy, and to his artistic awareness that the American soil was fertile ground for the growth of a vision both democratic and comic. (p. 299)

William W. Hoffa, "The Language of Rogues and Fools in Brackenridge's 'Modern Chivalry'," in Studies in the Novel, *Vol. XII, No. 4, Winter, 1980, pp. 289-300.*

ADDITIONAL BIBLIOGRAPHY

Andrews, J. Cutler. "The Pittsburgh Gazette—A Pioneer Newspaper." *Western Pennsylvania Historical Magazine* 15, No. 4 (November 1932): 293-307.*

    A brief history of *The Pittsburgh Gazette,* the newspaper on which Brackenridge served as editor. Cutler states that "the files of the paper constitute a significant social document."

Buell, Lawrence. Review of *Father Bombo's Pilgrimage to Mecca,* by Hugh Henry Brackenridge and Philip Freneau. *New England Quarterly* XLIX, No. 2 (June 1976): 332-34.*

    Brief commentary on *Father Bombo's Pilgrimage to Mecca.* Buell judges the novel to be "utterly devoid of merit" as a literary contribution. However, Buell adds that it is notable for its insight into the literary development of Brackenridge and Philip Freneau, and because it anticipates several elements that became important in later American literature.

Cobbett, William. "Miscellaneous Anecdotes of Various Dates: Brackenridge." In his *Porcupine's Works, Vol. IX*, pp. 381-88. London: Cobbett and Morgan, 1801.

An amusing collection of anecdotes about the "mad circuit" of Judge Brackenridge, recounted by a foremost English critic of the American contemporary scene. Cobbett reveals Brackenridge's personal eccentricities in vivid detail.

Cowie, Alexander. "The Beginnings of Fiction and Drama." In *Literary History of the United States: History*, 4th ed., edited by Robert E. Spiller, Willard Thorp, Thomas H. Johnson, Henry Seidel Canby, Richard M. Ludwig, and William M. Gibson, pp. 177-91. New York: Macmillan Publishing Co.; London: Collier Macmillan Publishers, 1974.

A short critical appraisal of *Modern Chivalry*. Cowie calls Brackenridge "a deliberate craftsman " and adds that *Modern Chivalry* may be included among the "more important achievements in the last decade of the eighteenth century" in American literature.

Dos Passos, John. "On the White Porch of the Republic: *Modern Chivalry*." In his *The Ground We Stand On: Some Examples from the History of a Political Creed*, pp. 381-401. New York: Harcourt, Brace and Co., 1941.

A largely biographical account, with emphasis on Brackenridge's role in the Whiskey Rebellion of 1794. Dos Passos calls *Modern Chivalry* the book "that made fun of everything and everybody."

Haims, Lynn. "Of Indians and Irishmen: A Note on Brackenridge's Use of Sources for Satire in *Modern Chivalry*." *Early American Literature* X, No. 1 (Spring 1975): 88-92.

Argues that Brackenridge's negative attitude toward Indians and the Irish is reflected and parodied in *Modern Chivalry*, especially in the characterization of Teague O'Regan.

Harkey, Joseph H. "The *Don Quixote* of the Frontier: Brackenridge's *Modern Chivalry*." *Early American Literature* VIII, No. 2 (Fall 1973): 193-203.*

Discusses similarities and differences between Miguel de Cervantes's *Don Quixote* and Brackenridge's *Modern Chivalry*.

Haviland, Thomas P. "The Miltonic Quality of Brackenridge's 'Poem on Divine Revelation'." *PMLA* LVI, No. 2 (June 1941): 588-92.*

A close study of Brackenridge's "Poem on Divine Revelation." Haviland detects several echoes and devices which attest to Brackenridge's poetic debt to John Milton.

Heiser, M. F. "The Decline of Neoclassicism, 1801-1848." In *Transitions in American Literary History*, edited by Harry Hayden Clark, pp. 91-160. 1954. Reprint. New York: Octagon Books, 1967.*

Proclaims *Modern Chivalry* "the most complete . . . expression of the Neoclassical spirit in the new nation." Further, Heiser contends that *Modern Chivalry* satirizes one of the causes of the decline of Neoclassicism in the United States—"the violation of the rational balance of society by an unenlightened and uneducated populace."

Holliday, Carl. "The Humor of the Republic: Hugh Brackenridge." In his *The Wit and Humor of Colonial Days (1607-1800)*, pp. 272-88. Philadelphia: J. B. Lippincott Co., 1912.

Describes *Modern Chivalry* as "rough," "manly," and a necessary comic antidote to the problems of democracy and the new republic. "If you are a believer in the infallibility of Democracy," Holliday writes, "read this book, and your faith will be considerably shaken."

Marder, Daniel. Introduction to *Incidents of the Insurrection*, by Hugh Henry Brackenridge, edited by Daniel Marder, pp. 7-21. New Haven: College & University Press, 1972.

Terms *Incidents of the Insurrection* "at once a suspenseful drama of individual versus mob psychology, a realistic portrait of social movement, and a story of individual sensibility." Marder adds that Brackenridge's realistic use of character, action, and frontier speech is especially well done in this work.

McDowell, Tremaine. "Sensibility in the Eighteenth-Century American Novel." *Studies in Philology* XXIV, No. 3 (July 1927): 383-402.*

Discusses the sentimental novel in America. McDowell states that sentimental literature was a blight on the literary development of the new nation. Except for *Modern Chivalry*, which burlesques sentimental novel traits, "the triumph of the feeling soul" was predominant in eighteenth-century American literature, according to McDowell.

Newlin, Claude M. Introduction to *Modern Chivalry*, by Hugh Henry Brackenridge, edited by Claude M. Newlin, pp. ix-xl. American Fiction Series, edited by Harry Hayden Clark. New York: American Book Co., 1937.

A brief general introduction to Brackenridge's life, political and literary ideas, and the origin and development of *Modern Chivalry*.

Petter, Henri. "Satirical and Polemical Fiction." In his *The Early American Novel*, pp. 87-167. Columbus: Ohio State University Press, 1971.

An analysis of Brackenridge's political ideas as they are revealed in *Modern Chivalry*. Petter ventures that the structure of the novel "might be interpreted as expressing the author's aristocratic prejudices," for Brackenridge focuses on "the human shortcomings which could endanger the realization of the democratic plan."

Quinn, Arthur Hobson. "The Foundations of American Fiction." In his *American Fiction: An Historical and Critical Survey*, pp. 3-24. New York: D. Appleton-Century Co., 1936.*

A brief critique of *Modern Chivalry*. Quinn emphasizes Brackenridge's use of satire in the novel and concludes that he "left few institutions of his day untouched by his shrewd and penetrating insight into pretence and hypocrisy."

Schultz, Lucille M. "Uncovering the Significance of the Animal Imagery in *Modern Chivalry*: An Application of Scottish Common Sense Realism." *Early American Literature* XIV, No. 3 (Winter 1979-80): 306-11.

Examines the philosophical implications of Scottish common sense realism and their influence on Brackenridge's *Modern Chivalry*. Schultz maintains that Brackenridge came to accept the notion that the Teague O'Regans could be disruptive to democracy, but adds that he also believed that people of common sense could "negotiate a successful democracy."

Smeall, J.F.S. "The Evidence that Hugh Brackenridge Wrote 'The Cornwalliad'." *PMLA* LXXX, No. 5 (December 1965): 542-48.

Presents textual, editorial, and biographical proof for the view that Brackenridge was the author of "The Cornwalliad," an anonymous verse satire printed in *The United States Magazine* in 1779.

————. "The Respective Roles of Hugh Brackenridge and Philip Freneau in Composing 'The Rising Glory of America'." *Bibliographical Society of America* 67 (July 1973): 263-81.*

A highly technical analysis in which Smeall strives to identify which sections of "The Rising Glory of America" were written by Brackenridge and which by Philip Freneau.

Whittle, Amberys R. "*Modern Chivalry*: The Frontier as Crucible." *Early American Literature* VI, No. 3 (Winter 1972): 263-70.

Argues that *Modern Chivalry* "is fundamentally an examination of basic human nature in an ideal situation, the American frontier." Moreover, the scope of the satire, according to Whittle, "approaches that of Swift in being all-pervasive."

Fedor Mikhailovich Dostoevski

1821-1881

(Also transliterated as Feodor, Fyodor; also Mikhaylovich; also Dostoyevsky, Dostoievsky, Dostoevskii, Dostoevsky, Dostoïewsky, Dostoiefski, Dostoïevski, Dostoyévskiiy, Dostoieffski) Russian novelist, short story writer, and journalist.

The following entry presents criticism of Dostoevski's novel *Prestuplenye i nakazanye (Crime and Punishment)*. For a complete discussion of Dostoevski's career, see *NCLC*, Vol. 2.

Crime and Punishment is considered one of Dostoevski's masterpieces and one of the most outstanding novels in modern literature. Through the story of Raskolnikov, an impoverished student who commits murder for what he considers to be moral principles, Dostoevski probes the psychological, religious, and moral ramifications of crime and its effect on the human soul. Raskolnikov is presented as the embodiment of spiritual nihilism, who in his attempt to transcend moral codes, tries to become a "superman," or "extraordinary man." *Crime and Punishment* is Dostoevski's first novel concerned with a theme that was to dominate his later works, that of redemption through suffering.

Dostoevski was born into a strict family in Moscow. He was sent away to school at an early age, and though his school years were lonely, they afforded Dostoevski a release from the stern regime of his father's household. In his solitude he developed an interest in literature and spent most of his time reading. At his father's insistence, Dostoevski attended engineering school, but he chose to pursue a literary career. His first novel, *Bednye lyudi (Poor Folk),* a naturalistic tale with a message of social awareness, was acclaimed by Vissarion Belinski, the foremost literary critic of the day. From the time of his first success, however, Dostoevski was plagued with financial problems that were intensified by a compulsive gambling habit.

Commentators have often noted the biographical nature of *Crime and Punishment*; perhaps the experience exerting the strongest influence on the novel was Dostoevski's imprisonment in Siberia from 1845 to 1859. As a member of a young group of intellectuals, the Petrashevski circle, Dostoevski was arrested and found guilty of subversion. Although he was initially condemned to death, his sentence was later commuted to hard labor in Siberia. Dostoevski's life as a prisoner, which he documented in his 1862 novel *Zapiski iz myortvogo doma (The House of the Dead),* instilled in him a compassion for the Russian lower classes and an insight into the issues of crime and guilt. Furthermore, his intense study of the New Testament, the only book prisoners were allowed to read, also influenced Dostoevski's thought and is perhaps responsible for the strong religious and moral basis of *Crime and Punishment* and of his later works as well. Most critics agree that the plot of *Crime and Punishment* mirrors Dostoevski's own troubled life at the time of the novel's composition. Sonia Marmeladov, the "angel of mercy" who saves Raskolnikov, is thought by many to represent Anna Snitkina, who became Dostoevski's second wife. With her support, Dostoevski, like Raskolnikov, overcame many of his personal problems and experienced a physical and spiritual rejuvenation.

Most critics believe that much of the material of *Crime and Punishment,* particularly the portrait of the downtrodden Marmeladov family, was originally intended for a novel that was to have been titled *The Drunkards.* In June, 1865, Dostoevski wrote to his publisher outlining the novel, which he described as a tale of "drunkenness, particularly pictures of families, the bringing up of children in such surroundings. . . ." When another publisher offered Dostoevski a contract for *The Drunkards,* he took his advance payment and traveled to Wiesbaden, Germany, where he quickly lost all his earnings at roulette. In order to earn his passage back to Russia, he was forced to sell his belongings at local pawnshops. Critics conjecture that a German pawnbroker inspired Dostoevski's portrait of Alyosha Ivanovna, the cold-hearted usurer of *Crime and Punishment,* and that from his experiences in Germany Dostoevski conceived the novel's plot. When he returned to Russia, Dostoevski submitted a detailed synopsis of *Crime and Punishment* to M. N. Katkov, the publisher of the prominent journal *Russky Vestnik,* describing the proposed work as "the psychological *compte-rendu* [report] of a crime." Katkov accepted the sketch, and Dostoevski composed the first chapters of his novel. In his earlier works of fiction, Dostoevski had consistently employed first-person narrative, and his diaries show that he initially intended to continue in this manner by telling the story of *Crime and Punishment* from Raskolnikov's perspective.

However, he abandoned this approach, and after attempting a diary format, finally wrote *Crime and Punishment* in the third person.

Crime and Punishment is the story of Rodion Raskolnikov, a young, impoverished law student. He decides to commit murder or, in his eyes, rid society of a worthless person as an experiment to see if he can circumvent social restrictions. Raskolnikov also wants to release his devoted mother and sister from the financial burden of supporting him; largely, however, he wishes to prove that he is an extraordinary individual, entitled to break accepted moral codes without suffering moral or societal repercussions. After Raskolnikov carries out his plan and kills a miserly pawnbroker and her sister, he is soon possessed by guilt and confesses to his crime. Subsequently, he is convicted and sentenced to prison in Siberia, where his humanitarian instincts are developed through suffering.

Crime and Punishment secured Dostoevski's reputation as one of Russia's greatest novelists, though critical interpretations of the work initially varied. The early Radical critics of Russia, including Belinski and Nikolay Dobrolyubov, believed that the purpose of literature was to truthfully depict reality, and so they praised the vivid portraits of lower-class life that Dostoevski presented in *Crime and Punishment*. They disapproved, however, of the fantastic and mystical elements which Dostoevski utilized in this novel. The most outspoken of these critics, Dmitri Pisarev (see *NCLC*, Vol. 2), read the work as a novel of social realism and argued that Raskolnikov's crime was motivated by hunger and financial need rather than by any philosophical principle. However, several of Dostoevski's contemporaries, most notably N. Strakhov, acknowledged *Crime and Punishment*'s nihilistic overtones and contended that Raskolnikov did murder for philosophical rather than financial reasons.

Crime and Punishment came to the attention of the English-speaking public in 1886 when the French critic E. M. De Vogüé recommended Dostoevski and *Crime and Punishment* as an antidote to the influence of French Naturalist authors Émile Zola and Théophile Gautier. De Vogüé praised *Crime and Punishment*, stating that he was both horrified and awed by the novel. Subsequent critics concurred that Dostoevski's realism was overwhelming. Lafcadio Hearn (see *NCLC*, Vol. 2), for example, sounded a recurrent note when he stated that the reader "actually *becomes* Raskolnikov."

Critical interpretations during the twentieth century have tended to be more specific in their approach to the novel. Among the most important concerns in the twentieth-century criticism of *Crime and Punishment* are Raskolnikov's redemption through suffering, as well as the exact nature of his redemption. Critics also frequently discuss Raskolnikov's character, the motive of his crime, and the structure of the novel.

The theme of redemption through suffering was initiated by Dostoevski himself in his letter to Katkov, where he indicated that this was to be a major thrust of the novel. He describes Raskolnikov's crime and adds that "he ends by feeling *compelled* to inform against himself. Compelled—although he may perish in the galleys—yet he will link himself to humanity again." Two early commentators on the book, Robert Louis Stevenson and William Dean Howells, noted that the presentation of such a theme establishes a message of self-renewal and hope. Later, J. Middleton Murry argued that Raskolnikov's redemption is insignificant because Raskolnikov is too weak to undergo a spiritual conversion of any consequence. Numerous critics have turned their attention to the nature of Raskolnikov's redemption. Nicholas Berdyaev argued for a purely Christian reading, maintaining that, to Dostoevski, there is no salvation without faith in Jesus Christ. Vyacheslav Ivanov contended that Raskolnikov's suffering is his sole link to humanity and added that only in suffering is one reunited with society; thus Raskolnikov is redeemed only by confessing and atoning for his crime. An influential interpretation of Raskolnikov's spiritual renewal was offered by Konstantin Mochulsky, who proposed that in denying Christ, Raskolnikov becomes a slave to destiny.

Commentators are divided in their conception of the character of Raskolnikov. Two interpretations recur: that of Raskolnikov as the "extraordinary man" and that of Raskolnikov and his "doubles": characters whose emotions and actions mirror those of the central character. At the turn of the century, critics such as Berdyaev interpreted Raskolnikov as a would-be "superman" whose inability to supercede moral laws indicated his, and humanity's, need for God, thus sounding a note that reappears throughout the criticism. Terming Raskolnikov "a Hamlet who dreams of becoming Napoleon," Janko Lavrin attributed Raskolnikov's failure to his inability to assess the motive behind his own crime. In a similar vein, Mochulsky interpreted Raskolnikov as an aspiring demi-God who would never be able to escape fate.

The motif of the double, which appears throughout Dostoevski's work beginning with his novel *Dvoynik (The Double)*, figures prominently in *Crime and Punishment*, and critics in the twentieth century note its importance. Murry detailed the parallel actions of Raskolnikov and Svidrigailov and argued that Dostoevski constructed the novel so that Svidrigailov, by reflecting Raskolnikov, becomes the central character of *Crime and Punishment*. Similarly, R. P. Blackmur simply termed Svidrigailov "Raskolnikov's other self." Ernest J. Simmons briefly examined the similarity of *Crime and Punishment*'s minor characters to Raskolnikov, while Edward Wasiolek drew a more detailed conclusion, contending that Marmeladov, Sonia, and Svidrigailov are all doubles of Raskolnikov. To Wasiolek, Marmeladov represents Raskolnikov's debasement, Sonia reflects his pious, spiritual side, and Svidrigailov mirrors his destructive impulses. Nicholas M. Chirkov agreed that Raskolnikov and Svidrigailov are reflections of one another, but also proposed that Svidrigailov's acceptance and acquiescence in the world is meant to parallel Raskolnikov's struggle with society.

Numerous critics have attempted to analyze Raskolnikov's motive for the murder. Both Lavrin and F. I. Evnin argued that Raskolnikov was unsure of his motive and consequently oscillated between his idealistic desires and moral values. According to Maurice Beebe, Raskolnikov has three motives, each represented by a different aspect of his personality. While Philip Rahv stated that Dostoevski's refusal to identify a single motive is the source of the book's greatness, Joseph Frank maintained that the power of *Crime and Punishment* lies in Raskolnikov's progression from one explanation of the crime to another. In another interpretation, Michael Holquist proposed that Raskolnikov's search to discover his motive is really a search for his own identity, or what the critic termed "authentic self."

Recently, contemporary critics such as Robert Louis Jackson have focused on the issue of Raskolnikov's moral concerns, and interpretations of the novel continue to vary. While *Crime and Punishment* has inspired a broad spectrum of thematic readings, critics unanimously praise the depth and range of

Dostoevski's artistic vision and his ability to probe complex philosophical questions. For its brilliant prose and spiritual insight, *Crime and Punishment* endures as one of world literature's finest achievements.

FEDOR DOSTOEVSKY   (letter date 1865)

[*Dostoevski wrote the following letter to M. N. Katkov, the editor and publisher of the review* Russky Vestnik, *asking him to publish* Crime and Punishment. *The early outline of the novel was altered radically when Dostoevski wrote his first draft, for while he states, in the letter that Raskolnikov is motivated by the desire to help his mother and save his sister from a disastrous marriage, Dostoevski's final version indicates that Raskolnikov commits murder for more complex and philosophical reasons.*]

[*Crime and Punishment*] is a psychological account of a crime. The action is contemporary, taking place this year. A young student, a member of the lower middle class, expelled from the university—through lightmindedness, through the instability of his conceptions, through living in extreme poverty, through having succumbed to the influence of certain strange "incomplete" ideas, which are floating in the air—makes up his mind to get out of his unfortunate position at one bound. He decides to murder a certain old woman, a money-lender, who is the widow of a Government clerk. The old woman is stupid, deaf, ill and miserly, charges Jew's interest, is spiteful and worries the life out of her younger sister who is slaving for her. "She is good for nothing," "what does she live for?" "is she of any use to anyone?" etc., etc. These questions haunt the young man. He decides to murder her and to rob her, in order to benefit his mother who lives somewhere in the provinces and to save his sister—who is engaged as companion in the family of a country squire—from the amorous advances of the head of that family, advances that threaten her with ruin, and in order that he himself may complete his studies at the University, go abroad and then remain throughout his life honest, firm, undaunted in fulfilling "the humanitarian notion of his duty towards mankind"—through which of course the crime will be "blotted out," if indeed it could be called a crime—that act perpetrated on the old, deaf, stupid malicious and sick woman, who herself does not know what she lives for on earth, and who may die in a month.

In spite of the fact that similar crimes are attended with terrible difficulty, that is, they nearly always leave obvious traces and clues, and allow a good deal to chance which nearly always betrays the malefactor, yet this young man by the merest chance manages to achieve his object quickly and successfully.

He spends nearly a month after that until the final catastrophe. There are no suspicions against him nor could there be any. Here then the whole psychological process of the crime is unfolding itself. Insoluble questions arise before the murderer, unsuspected and unexpected feelings torment his heart. The divine truth, the law of this world prevails against him and he ends by feeling *compelled* to inform against himself. Compelled—although he may perish in the galleys—yet he will link himself to humanity again. The feeling of disconnection and of isolation from mankind, which he had realised immediately on committing the crime, torments him to death. The law of truth and human nature prevail against him and the murderer

by conviction decides to pay the penalty in order to expiate his deed. Yet I find it difficult to explain my idea fully.

In my short novel there is apart from that an allusion to the idea that legal punishment inflicted for a crime deters the criminal much less than the lawgivers think, partly because *he himself morally demands it.*

I have seen this even in the crudest cases. But I want to show it in the case of an educated man, a man of the new generation, so that my idea shall be seen more clearly and palpably. (pp. 43-7)

> *Fedor Dostoevsky, in a letter to M. N. Katkov in September-October, 1865, in his* New Dostoevsky Letters, *translated by S. S. Koteliansky, Haskell House Publishers Ltd., 1974, pp. 42-51.*

N. STRAKHOV   (essay date 1867)

[*A friend of Dostoevski, Strakhov was a noted Russian literary critic. The following excerpt originally appeared in 1867 in Strakhov's two-part review in* Otechestvennye zapiski, *a prominent Russian journal. Strakhov interprets* Crime and Punishment *as a nihilistic novel in which Dostoevski intended to depict the struggle of "life and theory" and the victory of faith. While Strakhov believes that Raskolnikov killed for his beliefs rather than money, he maintains that it was the crime itself that reinforced Raskolnikov's reverence for life.*]

Nihilist men and women have been represented in our novels and stories for a long time. . . . What did Dostoevsky do? He took on a very much deeper and more difficult task than that of ridiculing the ugliness of empty and anemic natures. His Raskolnikov may suffer from youthful depression and egoism, but he represents a man gifted with a strong mind and warm heart. He is not a phrase-monger devoid of blood and nerves; he is a real man. . . .

For the first time, an unhappy nihilist, a nihilist suffering in a deeply human way, is depicted before us. . . . The author took nihilism in its extreme form, at the point beyond which there is no further place to go. . . . The task of the novel is to show how life and theory fight each other in man's heart, to show that struggle in the form in which it reaches its highest degree, and to show that victory was won by life. . . .

It is odd to argue that Raskolnikov is not insane. In the novel itself there are characters close to Raskolnikov who watch his torments and do not understand the sources of the strange behavior to which his inner torments lead him and who begin to suspect that he may be losing his mind. But then the mystery is solved. Something immeasurably less probable is revealed: he is not an insane man, but a criminal. (p. 485)

Raskolnikov is hardly at all described by the author speaking in his own person, but rather he is everywhere *shown* to be a man endowed with a clear mind, firm character, and noble heart. He is such in all his actions except for the crime. Thus he is regarded by the other characters, above whom he towers in every way possible. . . . Even the horrible thing done by Raskolnikov indicates to people who know him closely the power of his mind, albeit a perverted mind which has lost its way. . . . The author clearly wants to represent a strong soul, a man full of life, not one who is demented and weak. The secret of the author's intention is particularly clearly revealed in the words which he put in Svidrigaylov's mouth when he explains her brother's conduct to Raskolnikov's sister: "Russian people are broad people." The author wants to depict the broad Russian nature, that is, a living nature, little inclined to walk the beaten, worn path of Russian life, capable of living and feeling in various ways. (pp. 485-86)

The very essence of the crime of Raskolnikov is that it is a murder for a principle. It was not the three thousand rubles that attracted Raskolnikov. Strange as it may be to say so, it is true that if he could have obtained that sum by stealing, cheating at cards, or by some other petty fraud, he hardly would have decided to do it. He was attracted by the killing of a principle, by permitting himself that which is most forbidden. A theorist, he did not know that in killing a principle, he was at the same time making an attempt at the very life of his own soul. (p. 486)

The general theme of Dostoevsky's novel is the extremely deep perversion of the moral sense and the subsequent return of the soul to truly human feelings and concepts. (p. 487)

> *N. Strakhov, in an extract from "The Nihilists and Raskolnikov's New Idea," translated by George Gibian, in "Crime and Punishment" by Feodor Dostoevsky: A Norton Critical Edition, the Coulson Translation, Backgrounds and Sources, Essays in Criticism, edited by George Gibian, revised edition, W. W. Norton & Company, Inc., 1975, pp. 485-87.*

THE ATHENAEUM (essay date 1886)

Dostoieffsky is one of the most remarkable of modern writers, and [**'Crime and Punishment'**] is one of the most moving of modern novels. It is the story of a murder and of the punishment which dogs the murderer; and its effect is unique in fiction. It is realism, but such realism as M. Zola and his followers do not dream of. The reader knows the personages—strange, grotesque, terrible personages they are—more intimately than if he had been years with them in the flesh. He is constrained to live their lives, to suffer their tortures, to scheme and resist with them, exult with them, weep and laugh and despair with them; he breathes the very breath of their nostrils, and with the madness that comes upon them he is afflicted even as they. This sounds extravagant praise, no doubt; but only to those who have not read the volume. To those who have, we are sure that it will appear rather under the mark than otherwise. Every one has read the pages in which Dickens has dealt with the murder of Montague Tigg and the agony of Jonas Chuzzlewit [in 'Martin Chuzzlewit']. The effect of [**'Crime and Punishment'**] is more poignant and devouring; and it is some six hundred pages long. To analyze such a work in detail is manifestly impossible. Every incident—and there are many—is worthy of comment; every character—and there is at least a dozen—would furnish the matter of a long discourse. All we can do in this place is to remark upon the strange completeness of the book as a work of art; to describe, however imperfectly and inadequately, the extraordinary nature of its peculiar quality and the incomparable potency of its peculiar effect; and to note that, in spite of its sordid subject and the sense of grinding misery which informs it throughout, its teaching is in the main ennobling and good. It is absolutely nonpolitical; and, if we accept it as a true picture—and apparently we have no choice—it is the best and fullest explanation of Nihilism in existence. (pp. 99-100)

> *A review of "Le Crime et le Châtiment" ("Crime and Punishment"), in The Athenaeum, No. 3038, January 16, 1886, pp. 99-100.*

ROBERT LOUIS STEVENSON (letter date 1886)

[*A famed Scottish novelist and essayist, Stevenson wrote some of the nineteenth century's most beloved novels, including* Treasure Island, Doctor Jekyll and Mr. Hyde, *and* Kidnapped. *His novels are considered classics for their fast-paced action, strong plots, and well-drawn characters. In the following letter, Stevenson expresses his admiration for* Crime and Punishment.]

[**Crime and Punishment**] is easily the greatest book I have read in ten years. . . . Many find it dull: Henry James could not finish it: all I can say is, it nearly finished me. It was like having an illness. James did not care for it because the character of Raskolnikoff was not objective; and at that I divined a great gulf between us, and, on further reflection, the existence of a certain impotence in many minds of to-day, which prevents them from living *in* a book or a character, and keeps them standing afar off, spectators of a puppet show. To such I suppose the book may seem empty in the centre; to the others it is a room, a house of life, into which they themselves enter, and are tortured and purified. The Juge d'Instruction [Porfiry Petrovich] I thought a wonderful, weird, touching, ingenious creation: the drunken father, and Sonia, and the student friend, and the uncircumscribed, protoplasmic humanity of Raskolnikoff, all upon a level that filled me with wonder: the execution also, superb in places. Another has been translated—[**Injury and Insult**]. It is even more incoherent than [**Crime and Punishment**], but breathes much of the same lovely goodness. . . . Dostoieffsky is a devil of a swell, to be sure. (p. 323)

> *Robert Louis Stevenson, in a letter to John Addington Symonds in Spring, 1886, in his* The Letters of Robert Louis Stevenson: 1880-1887, Alps and Highlands—Hyères—Bournemouth, Vol. II, *edited by Sidney Colvin, revised edition, Charles Scribner's Sons, 1911, pp. 322-25.*

WILLIAM WALLACE (essay date 1886)

Absurdly bepraised, extravagant, incoherent, and even tedious, though *Crime and Punishment* is, it is not devoid of literary force. It is described as a Russian "realistic" novel, presumably because the heroine is one of the saints of the pavement who have recently become fashionable. But M. Fedor Dostoieffsky does not, to do him justice, search the gutter for his characters. Raskolnikoff, the St. Petersburg student-hero of this story, who finds his guardian angel in Sounia, a poor girl whom the poverty of her family and the drunkenness of her father have driven into the streets, is not bad in the ordinary sense of the word. He is only mad and poor, and given to what he calls psychology. . . . Besides Raskolnikoff and Sounia, the chief characters in *Crime and Punishment* are his mother, his sister, and her three lovers—Razoumikhin, a fellow-student, Looskhin, a low-minded official, and Svidrigaïloff, a wild sensualist. These three last, especially Razoumikhin, who is a sort of Russian George Warrington [from William Makepeace Thackeray's novel *The History of Pendennis*], are ably drawn. There are many passionate scenes in *Crime and Punishment;* one of them, between Svidrigaïloff and Raskolnikoff's sister, in which the latter fires at her lover with a revolver, is sketched with great, and, indeed, revolting, power. Nor is *Crime and Punishment* devoid of humour, or of almost Juvenalian satire, upon the present condition of society in Russia. But before M. Dostoieffsky can become a successful novelist of the realistic, or of any other, order, he must learn the art of condensation.

William Wallace, in a review of "Crime and Punishment," in The Academy, n.s. Vol. 29, No. 730, May 1, 1886, p. 306.

THE WESTMINSTER REVIEW　(essay date 1886)

"**Crime and Punishment**" is the English name of a so-called "Russian realistic novel." . . . The first title is accurately descriptive, but we do not see how it can be called "realistic." To us it seems rather to be phantasmagoric. Hardly one of the characters acts or speaks like a sane person. If it is a realistic presentation of Russian life and character, human nature in Russia must be strangely unlike human nature everywhere else. Not but what there are many natural touches scattered here and there throughout the story; but there is a general want of intelligible relation between action and motive, and an imperfect adaptation of means to ends, noticeable in a greater or less degree in every personage put on the scene; and this gives to the whole book a strange air of unreality, even to the verge of incoherency. It is not like real life either in Russia or anywhere else; it is like a wild, feverish dream. Nevertheless it is powerful, and not without a certain weird fascination.

A review of "Crime and Punishment," in The Westminster Review, n.s. Vol. LXX, No. 1, July, 1886, p. 298.

[WILLIAM DEAN HOWELLS]　(essay date 1886)

[*Howells was the chief progenitor of American realism and one of the most influential American critics during the late nineteenth century. Here, Howells provides one of the first American reviews of* Crime and Punishment. *He stresses that while Dostoevski graphically depicts sin in the novel, he also presents the "hope, the relief, that human sympathy gives." Therefore, unlike most early critics, who found* Crime and Punishment *to be pessimistic, Howells states that the novel is hopeful.*]

The readers of Tourguéneff and of Tolstoï must now add Dostoïevsky to their list if they wish to understand the reasons for the supremacy of the Russians in modern fiction; and we think they must put him beside these two, and not below either, in moral and artistic qualities. . . . [In *Crime and Punishment*] the author studies the effect of murder in the assassin, who is brought to confession and repentance by a hapless creature whom poverty has forced to a life of shame. Yet there is nothing of the maudlin glamour of heroism thrown about this pair; Raskolnikoff is the only man who has not been merely brutal to Sonia, and she divines his misery through her gratitude; this done, her one thought, her only hope, is not to help him hide his crime, but to help him own it to the law and to expiate it. She sees that there is no escape for him but this, and her inspiration is not superior to her; it is not from her mind, but from her soul, primitively good and incorrupt, amidst the hideous facts of her life, which, by-the-way, are in nowise brought forward or exploited in the story. Raskolnikoff is not her lover; he becomes so only when his expiation has begun; and the reader is scarcely allowed to see beyond the first breaking down of his egotistic self-justification in the Siberian prison. He has done the murder for which he suffers upon a theory, if not a principle: the theory that the greatest heroes and even benefactors of the race have not hesitated at crime when it would advance their extraordinary purposes or promote their development. . . . [It] cannot properly be said that Raskolnikoff feels regret or even remorse for his crime until he has confessed it. Till then his terrible secret, which all the accidents and

endeavors of the world seem conspiring to tear from him, forms his torment, and almost this alone. His repentance and his redemption begin with his penalty. The truth is a very old one, but what makes this book so wonderful is the power with which it is set forth. The story is not merely an accumulation of incident upon incident, a collection of significant anecdotes, as it might be in the hands of an inferior artist, but a mounting drama, to the catastrophe of which all the facts and characters tend, not mechanically or intentionally, but in the natural and providential way; it is only in the latter half of the story that you suspect a temptation in the author to intensify and to operate. At moments the stress of the story is almost intolerable. . . . (pp. 639-40)

The arrival of [Raskolnikoff's] mother and sister in the midst of his wretchedness, to be the loving and trusting witnesses of suffering of which they cannot understand the cause, is merely one of the episodes of the book which penetrate the soul by their reality, by their unsparing yet compassionate truth. But the impressive scenes abound so that it is hard to name one without having seemed to leave a finer one unmentioned. Perhaps there is nothing of higher and nobler strain than that series of passages in which the Judge of Instruction, softened and humanized by the familiarity with crime which hardens so many, tries to bring Raskolnikoff to confess for his own sake the murder which the Judge is sure he committed. . . .

[*Crime and Punishment* depicts] a lurid chapter of human life certainly, but the light of truth is in it; and in the ghastliest picture which it presents there is the hope, the relief, that human sympathy gives, and everywhere there is recognition of the fact that behind the supreme law is the supreme love, and only there. It is therefore by no means a desperate book, nor a wholly depressing book. It is not only clearly indicates the consequences of sin, but it attempts to define their bounds, the limits at which they seem to cease. Raskolnikoff suffers, but we reach the point at which he begins not to suffer. He makes others suffer, but we see where the suffering which his guilt inflicts must naturally end. It leaves him at the outset of a new life, the life of a man who has submitted to punishment, and has thereby won the privilege to repent. It is the reverse of a pessimistic book. (p. 640)

[William Dean Howells], in a review of "Crime and Punishment," in Harper's New Monthly Magazine, Vol. LXXIII, No. CCCCXXXVI, September, 1886, pp. 639-42.

GEORG BRANDES　(essay date 1889)

[*Brandes, a Danish literary critic and biographer, was the principal leader of the intellectual movement which helped to bring an end to Scandinavian cultural isolation. He believed that literature reflects the spirit and problems of its time and that it must be understood within its social, historical, and aesthetic context. Brandes's major critical work,* Main Currents in Nineteenth-Century Literature, *won him admiration for his ability to view literary movements within the broader context of all of European literature. Brandes states that in* Crime and Punishment *Dostoevski intended to create an accurate picture of Russia, specifically its political climate, although politics are never directly discussed. Brandes asserts that Raskolnikov committed murder to discover whether he could supercede moral codes. The critic concludes that Raskolnikov is unsure of his action and hence unable to finally assess what he has done.*]

[In *Crime and Punishment*] Dostoyevski has plainly intended to give a picture of the times. . . . The author evidently has political ferments in view, although he takes care not to say a single word directly about politics. There is undoubtedly contained in it an allusion to the murder of the Tsar. (p. 251)

Even if it is not a political crime which Dostoyevski has represented, it is a crime which has this in common with the political, that it is not mean, was not committed for the vulgar, low object of procuring for the perpetrator greater personal profit, but was in a certain degree unselfish, and, what is most important above all, it was committed by a person who at the moment of the crime does not harbor a doubt as to his right. In the mean time, if we compare the men and women whom in recent years we have seen sentenced in Russia for intent to commit murder, and not less those who have been executed as accessories to the assassination of the Tsar with this homicide, then the contrast is striking. Those persons were not in any way ruined by the spiritual consequences of their deed; they had as conspirators in and after the moment of the murder been in full accord with their inmost being; their conviction continued to be unshaken and unmoved to the last. If they had escaped detection, in all probability they would have lived to the end of their lives without any other than peaceful and proud thoughts about their attempts at the murder of a being whose extermination they regarded as a good deed, nay, as a duty. Raskolnikof, on the other hand, is destroyed by the consequences of the murder.

Like the political criminals, he started from a certain fixed principle, which, it is true, is not mentioned in the book, but which, nevertheless, lies at the foundation of his way of proceeding, that the end justifies the means.

This principle, which simplicity has misunderstood and Jesuitism has misused, is exactly and literally sound. The word "justifies" indicates that a good, valuable end is meant. He has a good valuable end who would maintain or produce results of real value. (p. 252)

[Dostoyevski] does not particularly deny the justice of Raskolnikof's reasoning, but shows that he is confused as to his end, uncertain if it is really good or not. In desperation he says to Sonya, a month after the deed, that he has continually been uncertain. When he examines himself he finds that in fact he has not committed murder to support his mother nor to become a benefactor of mankind, but in order to find out if he like the others was a "louse," not a man, that is, if he was in a position to overstep the barriers or not. He is uncertain about his end and uncertain about his inward authority to pursue this indefinite end, which, according to his own theory, only the elect are at liberty to use all means to attain. (pp. 253-54)

[We] very often in reading Dostoyevski have a feeling that the characters which he has created are more profound than the author himself. He was not capable of understanding the scope of his own work.

If we should now study the subordinate characters . . . , we shall find that they, almost without exception, ten in number as they are, stand on a level with the hero by the force and truth with which they are drawn, and that all stand in some relation to him. There is no superfluous person in the book. Among the most admirably conceived characters are the examining magistrate Porfyrius, a legal genius, and the landed proprietor Svidrigaïlof, a very complex nature, a voluptuary, who is in love with Raskolnikof's sister, and who pursues her. He is a man of intellect, has an excellent head, and, although he has one or more unrepented murders on his conscience, he possesses both courage and sense of honor in his way. As the

murderer from selfishness, by numerous details in regard to his way of acting and thinking, he forms a contrast to the hero of the book, who writhes under Svidrigaïlof's contention that they have one certain characteristic in common.

Dostoyevski's delineation of character here is of the first rank; it is profound, and bold. Nevertheless, after the manner of Dickens, it leaves almost the whole of the relations between the sexes, if not untouched, yet undescribed. In this domain, however, the poet does not escape the paradoxical; thus the morally irreproachable fallen woman reminds us more of an antithesis in human form by Victor Hugo than of a real person.

His aversion to describing the natural sensual life is all the more impressive since here, as in most of the author's other books, he dwells on unnatural, turbid appetites. We notice Svidrigaïlof's hideous passion for young girls. (pp. 254-55)

It is evident that Dostoyevski's fancy frequently turned on such unnatural inclinations, just because, according to his train of reasoning, there is no room left for a sound sensuousness. His inclination to describe bodily sufferings, the dwelling greatly on cruelties, are suggestive of unnatural desires. (pp. 255-56)

Thus much is clear at all events, that with Dostoyevski's gifts there was a perverse nervousness.

However high the delineation of character stands in **"Crime and Punishment,"** the book suffers from the imperfections of the narrative style. The portions in dialogue are immeasurably the best. As soon as the author himself begins to talk, art ceases. . . .

Though an author of such a high rank, [Dostoyevski] was an artist of a low rank. He allowed all his writings to be printed as they ran off from his pen, without revision of any kind whatever, to say nothing of recasting them. He did not trouble himself to give them the highest possible degree of perfection by condensation or pruning, but only worked as a journalist works, and is therefore universally too prolix. (p. 256)

Georg Brandes, "Dostoyevski," *in his* Impressions of Russia, *translated by Samuel C. Eastman, 1889. Reprint by Thomas Y. Crowell Co., Inc., 1966, pp. 236-63.*

K. WALISZEWSKI (essay date 1900)

[*Waliszewski's assessment of* Crime and Punishment, *first published in 1900 in his* Littérature russe, *was considered biased and unduly harsh by many critics; some even believe that Waliszewski intentionally misinterpreted Dostoevski's work. The critic states that Raskolnikov finds his incarceration in Siberia to be just and accepts his punishment without complaint. Further, Waliszewski questions Dostoevski's moral vision in the novel.*]

[Dostoevski] did not believe in his own martyrdom, just as he had no belief in the infamy of the common thieves and murderers who were his companions in durance. This confusion arose in his mind naturally, as the result of a general tendency which leads his fellow-countrymen to place the moral law and the political law on one and the same conventional level, and to ascribe the same relative value to each. In their eyes, infractions of either of these laws possess the same character, are of equal importance, and may be paid for by a system of forfeits, just as in a round game. Once the forfeit is paid, the individual is clear, and neither crime nor dishonour remains. This feature [appears] in *Crime and Punishment.* Note the behaviour of the examining magistrate once he is convinced that

Raskolnikov is really guilty of the crime—a murder followed by robbery—which has just been committed. Afterwards, as before, he gives the assassin his hand, and treats him as his friend. . . . No writer in any other country would dream of assimilating the social position of a natural child with that of the legitimate child of a father sentenced to banishment for theft. . . . The idea that crime is not a fault, but a misfortune, and the idea of the sovereign power of expiation, are the basis of this method of thought and feeling. They pervade the whole of Dostoïevski's work, and his residence in the convict prison only defined them more clearly in his mind, and drove him to adopt their extreme though logical consequences. The common-law prisoners whom he met never dreamt, on their side, of giving him the benefit of a superior position from the moral point of view. He had broken one law, and they had broken another. In their eyes it was all the same thing. This fact made a deep impression upon Dostoïevski. His imagination was romantic, his power of feeling was very keen, and he possessed no ground-work of philosophic education. He was very easily affected by the moral atmosphere of the place. It was full of floating ideas, religious and mystic, drawn from the common basis of Russian life in the popular classes. These influenced the author, and through them he entered into communion with the simple souls of a certain number of criminals resigned to their fate. The man who had refused to make his confession on the scaffold, reads a Bible with his fellow-prisoners—a Bible given them by the wife of a Decembrist whom they had met on their road into exile, the only book permitted within the prison walls. He ends by not only submitting to his fate, but acknowledging his guilt. This is the second false note in the book.

By an error of interpretation which indicates the danger of the cryptographic artifices forced on the literature of the country, the passages which express this sentiment have been taken by certain critics to partake of the nature of a *protest*. The mistake is evident. Dostoïevski sympathises, that is clear, with his fellow-prisoners of every kind. He has a sincere admiration for the strength and brute energy of some of these wretches, and endeavours to justify it by dwelling on the qualities of goodness and generosity which he has discovered under their rough exterior. But this is a mere echo of the Romantic school and the humanitarian leanings of the West. Apart from it, the book is all submission. It presents the feelings of a man who not only uncomplainingly accepts a punishment which is at all events out of proportion to his offence, but who acknowledges its justice and equity. And the whole of Dostoïevski's subsequent attitude proves the fact. Not only did he never pose as a martyr, but he avoided all allusion to his painful past, like a man who regarded it as nothing but a stain, which had been wiped out and redeemed. (pp. 339-41)

[Dostoïevski devoured Victor Hugo's *Les Misérables*,] and memories of it are evident in *Crime and Punishment*. (p. 342)

Raskolnikov, the student who claims the right to murder and steal by virtue of his ill-applied scientific theories, is not a figure the invention of which can be claimed by the Russian novelist. It is probable that before or after reading the works of Victor Hugo, Dostoïevski had perused those of Bulwer Lytton. Eugène Aram, the English novelist's hero [from his book of the same name], is a criminal of a very different order, and of a superior species. When he commits his crime, he not only thinks, like Raskolnikov, of a rapid means of attaining fortune, but also, and more nobly, of a great and solemn sacrifice to science, of which he feels himself to be the high-priest. Like

Raskolnikov, he draws no benefit from his booty. Like him, too, he hides it, and like him, he is pursued, not by remorse, but by regret;—haunted by the painful thought that men now have the advantage over him, and that he no longer stands above their curiosity and their spite,—tortured by his consciousness of the total change in his relations with the world. In both cases, the subject and the story, save for the voluntary expiation at the close, appear identical in their essential lines. This feature stands apart. Yet, properly speaking, it does not belong to Dostoïevski. . . . [Some students] have looked on Raskolnikov as a political criminal, disguised after the same fashion as Dostoïevski himself may have been, in his *Memories of the House of the Dead*. But this version appears to me to arise out of another error. A few days before the book appeared, a crime almost identical with that related in it, and committed under the apparent influence of Nihilist teaching, though without any mixture of the political element, took place at St. Petersburg. These doctrines . . . are, in fact, general in their scope. They contain the germs of every order of criminal attempt, whether public or private; and Dostoïevski's great merit lies in the fact that he has demonstrated the likelihood that the development of this germ in one solitary intelligence may foster a social malady. In the domain of social psychology and pathology, the great novelist owes nothing to anybody; and his powers in this direction suffice to compensate for such imperfections as I shall have to indicate in his work.

The "first cause" in this book, psychologically speaking, is that individualism which the Slavophil School has chosen to erect into a principle of the national life;—an unbounded selfishness, in other words, which, when crossed by circumstances, takes refuge in violent and monstrous reaction. And indeed, Raskolnikov . . . is so full of contradictions, some of them grossly improbable, that one is almost driven to inquire whether the author has not intended to depict a condition of madness. We see this selfish being spending his last coins to bury Marméladov, a drunkard picked up in the street, whom he had seen for the first time in his life only a few hours previously. From this point of view Eugène Aram has more psychological consistency, and a great deal more moral dignity. Raskolnikov is nothing but a poor half-crazed creature, soft in temperament, confused in intellect, who carries about a big idea, in a head that is too small to hold it. He becomes aware of this after he has committed his crime, when he is haunted by hallucinations and wild terrors, which convince him that his pretension to rank as a man of power was nothing but a dream. Then the ruling idea which has lured him to murder and to theft gives place to another,—that of confessing his crime. And even here his courage and frankness fail him; he cannot run a straight course, and, after wandering round and round the police station, he carries his confession to Sonia.

This figure of Sonia is a very ordinary Russian type, and strangely chosen for the purpose of teaching Raskolnikov the virtue of expiation. She is a woman of the town, chaste in mind though not in deed, and is redeemed by one really original feature, her absolute humility. . . . Sonia is like an angel who rolls in the gutter every night, and whitens her wings each morning by perusing the Holy Gospels. We may just as well fancy that a coal-heaver could straighten the back bowed by the weight of countless sacks of charcoal by practising Swedish gymnastics!

The author's power of evocation, and his gift for analysing feeling, and the impressions which produce it, are very great, and the effects of terror and compassion he obtains cannot be denied. Yet, whether from the artistic or from the scientific point of view (since some of his admirers insist on this last), his method is open to numerous objections. It consists in re-producing, or very nearly, the conditions of ordinary life whereby we gain acquaintance with a particular character. Therefore, without taking the trouble of telling us who Raskolnikov is, and in what his qualities consist, the story relates a thousand little incidents out of which the personal individuality of the hero is gradually evolved. And as these incidents do not nec-essarily present themselves, in real life, in any logical se-quence, beginning with the most instructive of the series, the novelist does not attempt to follow any such course. As early as on the second page of the book, we learn that Raskolnikov is making up his mind to murder an old woman who lends out money, and it is only at the close of the volume that we become aware of the additional fact that he has published a review article, in which he has endeavoured to set forth a theory justifying this hideous design.

Apart from the weariness and the mental effort involved in this method, the picture it produces is naturally somewhat confused. It has another fault, which is shared by the majority of Russian novelists. Their art resembles the architectural style affected by the builder of the church of St. Basil, at Moscow. The visitor to this church is astonished to see five or six edifices interlaced one with the other. There are at last as many distinct stories in *Crime and Punishment,* all connected by a barely perceptible thread. . . . This is the method of the *feuilletonist* [serial writer], who writes copy at his utmost speed. Even in the present day, the line so clearly drawn in France between the artistic novel and that other—the sole object of whose existence is to attract and keep up the number of general sub-scribers to widely circulated newspapers—cannot be said to exist in Slav countries. Dostoïevski, who was always short of money, and always behind with his copy, looked about at last for a shorthand writer, to help him to expedite matters. . . . His urgent desire to keep up constant communication with the public, and his ambition to preserve his influence over it, drove him into a feverish productiveness which wore down his talent and his life. These drawbacks are evident in *Crime and Pun-ishment.* (pp. 342-47)

> K. Waliszewski, ''The Preachers—Dostoïevski and Tolstoï,'' in his A History of Russian Literature, 1900. Reprint by D. Appleton and Company, 1910, pp. 330-402.*

FRANCIS HACKETT   (essay date 1911)

[*This essay originally appeared on June 30, 1911, in* The Chicago Evening Post.]

In the great Russian novels there is a naïve, an extraordinarily fresh personal impression of life. Not only do the Russians conceive specific impressions with the clarity of children, but they have the gift of placing a true value on their emotions. The moment does indeed pass when they stand on the threshold, tremulous and eager, lips parted, cheeks flushed, heart beating high. But whether life leaves them reverent or bitter, deeply humble or sadly ironical, it has given them treasured and in-eradicable memories. And not only do the great interpreters of Russian life seem to evaluate their experience according to the dreams and expectations of youth, but they never appear to be drained of their human sympathies. (p. 178)

In *Crime and Punishment* the horizontal partitions of society are pulled out, as well as the vertical, and we observe with

Dostoevsky the fate of a man, wretchedly poor, who contem-plates, commits and expiates the crime of murder. In writing of Raskolnikov, Dostoevsky has a singularly different manner from Tolstoy. Tolstoy has been called crazy, but there never was a writer who had such a clear, such a reasonable view of people. He delights to show us his hero as he wakes in the morning in bed, and to depict each move as the hero bathes and shaves and puts on one garment after another, and to tell us exactly how much toast and how much coffee he took for breakfast, and how he read the morning paper, and agreed or disagreed with the editorials, one by one. By such details of daily life, familiar to every man and interesting for the most personal reasons, Tolstoy gets our confidence. We know these things to be true. We have felt them and seen them, and we marvel at the insight of this man who interprets us to ourselves. When it comes to the less familiar events, we are already persuaded of Tolstoy's immense good sense and wisdom (which certainly exists) and he has taken the best way to overwhelm us by his conclusions. Nothing at all of this large, paternal, almost omniscient feeling is communicated by Dostoevsky. Dostoevsky does not surround his story with the atmosphere of familiarity and common sense. . . . On the contrary, his novel is bathed in sepulchral blackness, and his murderer moves about the stage in a single intense spot of light. There is no familiarity about the scene, but an exceptional set of circum-stances, presented with an uncanny sense of their morbidity. Each definition of Raskolnikov's state of mind insists upon his fever and his monomania. It is actually a clinic—a clinic, however, of such extraordinary realism that it is very nearly insupportable.

It is the convention among Anglo-Saxons to desist when a situation becomes too intense, and to convert the tale of horror into palpable fiction—a game at horror. There is no game about *Crime and Punishment.* The pool of blood into which Raskol-nikov accidentally steps after he has murdered the old money-lender is the most real thing one can conceive. One does not see that blood. But one feels Raskolnikov's ever present sense of it. One feels his terror lest he step in it, or get blood on his clothes. One realizes his chilled frenzy as he washes his hands, and his renewed horror as he discovers that the blood has got on his boots. It is not grewsome exactly. It is simply real. . . . It is ''only a book'' of course. But it is a book that obsesses its reader night and day. The crime of Raskolnikov stains one's own conscience. Unbearably does Dostoevsky keep up the suspense and agony, and it is only after passing through the worst vicissitudes of a guilty criminal that a partial and scru-pulously honest relief is granted.

Had Raskolnikov had any moral justification for his crime, or been a defenseless victim of society, this book would have few elements of horror. But Raskolnikov is an ''intellectual.'' His crime is the outcome of a monomania. Although a destitute student, anxious to help the mother and sister he loves, the motives of his crime are utterly insufficient to support it. It is morbidity, diseased intellectualism, which makes the plan pos-sible. And the thing that gives the book its peculiar hold on the imagination is the shocking lucidity of Raskolnikov. If he were remorseful, the centre of one's interests would be his moral fate. But for the first 400 pages one lives with the man in the midst of exterior circumstances. It is agony over his possible detection that is exciting. (pp. 179-81)

If the interest of Raskolnikov's situation were confined to its dangers, *Crime and Punishment* would be essentially melo-drama. Where Dostoevsky converts it from melodrama is in the sympathy with which he depicts the murderer's environment. There is a curious quality in Dostoevsky's recital. It has at times the fitful, outrageous character of a dream. But when the situation is brought into focus, and Dostoevsky escapes his Dickens-like tendency to draw grotesques and freaks (increased so much by his dwelling on neurasthenic and hallucinatory factors), he induces the reader to share his exalted sympathy for misfortune and wretchedness. During the period when Raskolnikov is brooding over his plan, he wanders into a filthy saloon, where he is joined by a fatuous drunkard. Into Raskolnikov's ears the drunkard pours all his woes. It is the kind of story almost everyone has heard, but Dostoevsky gives it a new human significance. To his raucous tenement home Raskolnikov accompanies the drunkard, and there he meets the consumptive Catherine Ivanovna, whose blows but increase the humility of the drunken husband. . . . Catherine Ivanovna is a portrait full of wry humor, and Sonia, from under whose hat appeared "a poor little wan and frightened countenance," is a character beautifully and sublimely conceived. It is she who has taken the yellow ticket at the behest of Catherine Ivanovna, and it is to her that Raskolnikov eventually unburdens his soul. Were the irony, the fantastic humor, of these slums less clearly perceived, the pathos of Sonia could not deeply touch us. But Dostoevsky has no brief for the miserable. And it is characteristic that when he makes Raskolnikov empty his pockets for the drunkard's home he lets it be considered by one a noble impulse, and by another a pathological sympathy, an aberration. (pp. 181-82)

The fact that *Crime and Punishment* has a moral for those animalculae who are endued only with intellect and will is one of its unexpected disclosures. Not till half the book is read is the Superman idea introduced. But the moral of *Crime and Punishment* would be nothing if it were not a novel at once fascinating and horrifying. That horror could so fascinate, or fascination be so horrible, is one of the wonders of the written word.

To conclude everything as to Dostoevsky from this one novel would be fatuous, but it is at least possible to recognize a master, one of the few great interpreters of man. On the borderland Dostoevsky stands, the borderland between sanity and insanity, between poverty and crime, between student life and the underworld. There, where men and women flash from one side to the other in the phantasmagoria of passion and necessity, Dostoevsky watches with intensity and yet with consummate patience. He has no illusions and no useless pity. He attempts no easy pathos. The Crime, at which so many sympathies halt and hearts begin to harden, Dostoevsky accepts without protest. It is the Punishment that awakens his soul, and as the flame of the inner life rises and falls, one can feel the heart of Dostoevsky beat quicker, believing as he does in the forces that heal as well as wound. (pp. 184-85)

Francis Hackett, "'Crime and Punishment'," in his Horizons: A Book of Criticism, *B. W. Huebsch, 1918, pp. 178-85.*

J. MIDDLETON MURRY (essay date 1916)

[*A noted English twentieth-century critic and journalist, Murry is renowned as a scholar of Russian literature. In the following excerpt from Murry's* Fyodor Dostoevsky: A Critical Study, *Murry states that in* Crime and Punishment *Dostoevski finally confronted the moral dilemma that had plagued him all his life. In Svidrigailov, Murry maintains, Dostoevski particularly manifested his doubts about God. According to Murry, Svidrigailov embodies*

Dostoevski's exploration of the nature of evil, because Raskolnikov's will is too weak to strive for complete omnipotence. For further discussions of the relationship between Raskolnikov and Svidrigailov, see excerpts below by Jacques Madaule (1938), R. P. Blackmur (1943), and Nicholas M. Chirkov (1945-49)].

Crime and Punishment is the first of Dostoevsky's great books. It is the first in which he dared really to state the doubt which tortured him. Hitherto he had been on the side of the law. (p. 102)

Hitherto he had been content to state a simple antagonism, and to pronounce himself without reserve upon the side of the good. No doubt for those who read even *The Insulted and Injured* with clairvoyant eyes, he did protest too much. To them it may have seemed that he knew rather too much about the enemy, more than could be learned by a simple soldier in the cause of the simple good. (pp. 102-03)

But if there were any uneasy at the intimacy of Dostoevsky's knowledge of the dark power, they seem to have held their peace. Apparently the Russian world was well content with the new champion of the old morality. But if they were content, Dostoevsky himself was not. He could not suffer that his expression should so far run short of his knowledge. He must follow out his thought in the language of his imagination—and who knows how much actual experience went to the making of that imagination—wherever it would lead him, for he too was possessed with a devil that drove him to his own fulfilment. (p. 103)

A Dostoevsky can paint the moral in the imperishable stuff of humanity, he can show the very pulses of the heart which drives the murderer to the stool of repentance. By his art they can have the inexpressible consolation of watching the sinner in his self-created agony, of seeing his lips move and hearing the words come "softly and brokenly, but distinctly," from his lips:—

> It was I killed the old pawnbroker woman and her sister Lizaveta with an axe and robbed them.

That is enough. The Law is vindicated out of the inevitable workings of the human heart. Even though its officers may fail, conscience flings a wider net than theirs, into which the enemies of society are safely gathered. So can the citizens sleep quietly in their beds.

But Dostoevsky, though he deceived them, did not deceive himself. He knew that in Raskolnikov he had chosen a weak vessel, but one in whom, though the flesh was weak the spirit was willing. Not even Raskolnikov will confess himself repentant of his crime with his own lips. (p. 106)

[Later,] his logic is forgotten and his will bent . . . but neither the logic is recanted nor the will denied. There is no hint of repentance, and no more than the doubtful promise of his acceptance of Sonia's beliefs. "Can her convictions not be mine now? her feelings, her aspirations at least. . . ." That gradual diminuendo, upon which the book closes, is of most dubious omen for the future. Perhaps Raskolnikov did wholly forget his old determination and his reasoning: but to forget is not to repent. Repentance demands an ever-present memory of the sin. The most we can hope for Raskolnikov is that he should be too happy in the present to remember the past, for, if he should remember, the old problem would face him still.

But, long before Raskolnikov had reached the security of calm, Dostoevsky had turned away from him. Raskolnikov was for Dostoevsky, as he was for himself, merely the victim of his unsuccess and of his weakness. He was not even an unsuccessful criminal, but an unsuccessful philanthropist. . . . Did not Raskolnikov choose out with infinite precaution "a louse," a vile insect that preyed upon mankind, and guarded a treasure of gold within its den that might be of bountiful service in the cause of the Good? In so doing did he do more than that which the very Law he defied may soon by its own ordinance accomplish? He rid, by murder, society of a pest. . . . It is in vain that he cries out:—

> I wanted to murder without casuistry, to murder for my own sake, for myself alone! I didn't want to lie about it even to myself. It wasn't to help my mother I did the murder—that's nonsense—I didn't do the murder to gain wealth and power and become the benefactor of mankind. Nonsense!

But it is not nonsense. The very stones cry out, not that this was the only cause, but that it for him was a necessary consequence of his act. Only in the magniloquence of his own conceit, only in the intoxication of his own vision of himself as a Napoleon, could he dare to deny it. It is true that the motive was deeper than this, that he murdered because "he wanted to have the daring." But that was his fevered dream. He had already chosen the lesser part when he began to search for "a louse" for his victim. He had dreamed of a will which should trample all things under foot, for the sake of its own pure assertion; but he knew that this was for him only a dream, he knew that even should he find the courage to kill the usurer, he would have proved nothing to himself. (pp. 108-10)

The magnificently triumphant will of which he had dreamed, had in the first moment of his conception of his plan, been degraded into a cowardly shivering caricature of itself, a little feeble thing that could not for one second stand alone but must lean upon Right. In the underworld Raskolnikov had dreamed of committing crime for its own sake; in the waking world he was one of the thousands who do evil that good may come. (p. 111)

Raskolnikov had done no crime. He had done no more than to transgress the Laws which are human institutions; like a timid child, who holds his nurse's hand, he invokes the Good of All for a sanction to his beneficent destruction. No wonder he does not repent, when he has done no sin. What defeats him is the never slumbering consciousness that he is at the mercy of the law. He surrenders to the dead weight of an enemy, not to any Right. Right is on his side, and that not merely his own right—that is a power he had not the courage to invoke—but a right which any clear-seeing man might recognise, and society itself at no far point in the future ratify.

And because he had done no crime, his punishment is beside the mark. Dostoevsky knew that the fate of a Raskolnikov is a baby-problem. Evil, at this phase, has not yet begun to be. . . . If the killing of "a louse" be crime, then crime is only a name, a convention as the laws by which it is defined are a convention. This was not the thing Raskolnikov had dreamed of attempting when he muttered: "I want to attempt a thing *like that*." Crime, as Raskolnikov knew, was crime for it own sake, the naked working of the evil will. . . . His loving friends will tell him that he cannot do evil because his nature is good. It may be so, but Raskolnikov, who sees clearly, suspects that it is because his will is weak.

But what of the man whose will is strong? Dostoevsky knew that the problem was here, and towards the end of *Crime and*

Punishment he turns away from Raskolnikov, whom he has weighed in the balances and found wanting, to Svidrigailov. Svidrigailov is the real hero of the book. Raskolnikov himself acknowledges it, and makes way for him when, in spite of his horror of Svidrigailov, he cannot deny that there is something in common between them. The potentialities of Raskolnikov are made real in Svidrigailov; the dialectic of the student has been carried to its last conclusion in the person of the man. (pp. 111-13)

[Svidrigailov] is Raskolnikov grown old, but one who with advancing years has abated nothing of his resolution, that his will should compass all things. He has stood alone with the power which is in him, which is the will to know life to the uttermost, and by that will to triumph over life. He has passed beyond good and evil. He has willed that his will should be omnipotent. Nothing shall be forbidden him. He has taken his stand against the whole of life to wrest its secret from it. Svidrigailov is real, real even beyond reality, and he is also Raskolnikov's dream. To be a Svidrigailov and not a mere Napoleon—that was the vision which had haunted the murderer. But Svidrigailov does no murder before the law, for he knows that this is no question for him, nor will he deceive himself by having even the faint semblance of a right upon his side. He is his own right; another right can only take away from him and blunt the barb of his question.

And the question is this: Which shall prevail, the I, the self, which I know, or some power which I know not? Shall I be forced to recognise any will beyond my own? Though Svidrigailov appears chiefly to be a manifestation of the will to evil in act, he is far more than this. He appears to us first as evil, because the deliberate working of evil is portentous to our minds. Because he does evil things, he is a monster of depravity. Yet this monster does good with the same even hand; he spares Raskolnikov's sister, Dounia, whom he desires, when she is at his mercy; he cares for Sonia and the orphaned children of the Marmeladovs; he makes over a fortune to the girl bride whom he does not marry. In him both good and evil may be found side by side, yet he is neither a good man with evil impulses nor an evil man with reactions to the good. For all the appearance of contradiction, we feel that he is not divided against himself but one; and the secret of his singleness is his single will. This he has measured against life and the laws of life. He has done evil, not because he desired it, but because he desired to be beyond it. In the process of his complete assertion, every letter upon the working of the will to be free must be broken, simply because it is a fetter. The things which he knew to be evil he has done simply because an instinct within him recoiled from the evil: therefore that instinct must be crushed. He, like Raskolnikov, had "wanted to have the daring," and he had found it in himself. (pp. 114-16)

[We] must understand Svidrigailov at all costs. He may be a monster, conjured out of the darkness, but he too is human, too human. Watch him when he has enticed Dounia, whom he loves with a passion of desire, into the solitary room, intending—to do her violence?—he does not know. But the gleam of the beast began to shine in his eyes, that light in them which months before "had frightened Dounia, and had grown stronger and stronger and more unguarded till it was hateful to her." To defend herself from the horror of this she draws a pistol and shoots at him. The first shot goes wide; he does not move. The second shot misses fire. (p. 117)

Twice she fires at him. He does not move. His will remains to him, even though the desire to use it is gone from him. The third time she drops the pistol. Something then remains, one last gleam of hope is fired within him, and he asks in a fever of despairing passion if she loves him, or will ever love him. That hope too is destroyed. He is alone; he has crossed the bounds of all human experience, in his desire to find whether the burden of Life rests on his will alone, or whether there is something beyond, and he has found nothing. Now one thing remains. Death is untried. He tries it, for it lies in his destiny that he should will all things, and will that he should not be.

But to will his own annihilation is easier than to be assured of victory. A Svidrigailov is not deceived by mortal death. (pp. 119-20)

[Death is] the one last issue, which, being untried, must be tried. Yet is it the most hopeless of all. The silence in which the great question echoes here, may there give back an echo of laughter, of vulgar, sordid, malignant laughter.

But a will which by willing its own omnipotence has nothing left to will, is a living death. (p. 121)

"Is there Crime? Is there Punishment?" Not in the person of Raskolnikov does Dostoevsky ask these questions, but in that of Svidrigailov. Therefore Raskolnikov's repentance and regeneration is no reply, nor is the foolishly repeated panacea of "Purification by Suffering." Suffering may have been enough for Raskolnikov, though Dostoevsky leaves the proof of that to another story, which he never wrote. It would not have interested him enough to write. In Dostoevsky's eyes Raskolnikov could never have been more than an incomplete Svidrigailov, and once he had found in himself the courage and the genius to grapple with the imagination of Svidrigailov, Raskolnikov was no more than a puppet to him.

In truth those parts of *Crime and Punishment* which closely concern the regeneration of Raskolnikov, the history of Sonia Marmeladov and her family, of Luzhin and Razumihin, are in the last resort unessential. They are hardly more than the scaffolding which supports the living idea. The Marmeladovs represent the existence of suffering in the world; they are as it were the embodiment of the fact of pain. By this awful fact Dostoevsky had been fascinated ever since his eyes had been opened on the world, and pain is the incessant undertone of all his work. By nakedly presenting pain continually in his work, Dostoevsky established the foundations of his created characters. He himself had looked upon pain. . . . Perhaps because his hold on the physical being of life was weak, or because the fires of his spirit burnt his body away, he was never for one moment content merely to be. "I have been all my life tormented by God," he writes, and all his life he attempted with all his strength to answer the question: "Is there a God?" Champion after champion he sent forth on to the bloody field, to contend with life, as he himself contended, even unto death.

Of these champions Svidrigailov was the first. He is as it were the symbol of Dostoevsky's passionate denial of God, when he had looked on pain. To deny God is to assert one's own divinity. Therefore Dostoevsky conceived a Man who should have the courage of his own divinity, who denying a will beyond his own, should be brave enough to assert his own will to the uttermost. The frame of Svidrigailov is an unshakable dialectic. If there is a Will beyond my own it must be an evil Will because Pain exists, therefore, I must will evil to be in harmony with it. If there is no Will beyond my own, then I must completely assert my own will, until it is fully free of all check beyond itself. Therefore I must will evil. This man's

bones Dostoevsky fashioned thus out of his own reason, and from his imagination clothed him in flesh and blood. He placed him in life to contend with it, and the end of Svidrigailov was death by his own hand. Svidrigailov found no answer, and he brought none back to Dostoevsky: perhaps Dostoevsky expected none, for he knew that his creature was predestined to die. Svidrigailov was a scapegoat sent from his creator's soul.

Yet that the individual will incarnate should be destroyed in this life was no answer to Dostoevsky's question: for he asked, how shall a man, who has a heart to feel pain and a brain to think and a will to act upon it, live? . . . Raskolnikov was recreant and weak. He had the mind, but the will had failed him. But perhaps that way lay salvation—not, indeed, in the weakness and the failure of the will, but in its complete assertion still. Only let the will be asserted after the pattern of the one perfect man, and be turned not to the final affirmation of the self, but to its utter annihilation. Let a man be created who shall be completely passive, who shall suffer all things in himself, and thereby be not less wholly man than a Svidrigailov.

Of this counter-creation it may be said that Sonia Marmeladov contains the promise. But for all her pathos, Sonia hardly exists. She is certainly not real, as Raskolnikov and Svidrigailov are real, and, in comparison with Dostoevsky's later women, she is no more than a lay-figure. (pp. 122-25)

Sonia is indeed a part of Dostoevsky's story, but in comparison with the idea which he desired to realise, the story in which Sonia has her part is of but little importance. A story of some kind is necessary to the novelist, and Dostoevsky needed one to work upon, since he used the novel form; but in a deeper sense, Dostoevsky was not a novelist at all. The novelist accepts life and takes for granted the great process of becoming, of evolution and growth. His mind is as it were bathed in the sense of time and succession. Dostoevsky did not accept life; in him there is no sense of evolution and slow growth. . . . As Dostoevsky's art developed and his thought went deeper and ranged farther, we must be prepared to discern in them more and more clearly symbolic figures. They are real, indeed, and they are human, but their reality and humanity no more belongs to the actual world. They have not lived before the book, and they do not live after it. They have no physical being.

Ultimately they are the creations not of a man who desired to be, but of a spirit which sought to know. They are the imaginations of a God-tormented mind, not the easy overflow and spontaneous reduplication of a rich and generous nature. Principalities and powers strive together in this imagined world, and the men and women are all in some sort possessed, and because they are possessed are no longer men and women. Therefore they are not to be understood or criticised as real, save in the sense that the extreme possibility of the actual is its ultimate reality. Before *Crime and Punishment* Dostoevsky is a novelist in the old and familiar sense. With *Crime and Punishment* he leaves the material world, never to return to it. The bonds that united him to it had been at all times slender as gossamer, and weak as the frail body which kept his spirit on the earth; but now he had revealed himself for what he was, a soul possessed with the agony to know. (pp. 126-28)

J. Middleton Murry, in his Fyodor Dostoevsky: A Critical Study, *Martin Secker, 1916, 263 p.*

NICHOLAS BERDYAEV (essay date 1923)

[*Berdyaev was a Russian Christian philosopher and scholar, and his* Dostoievsky: An Interpretation, *first published in 1923 as*

Mirosozercanie Dostoevskago, is one of the most influential studies of the author. According to Berdyaev, Dostoevski's message in Crime and Punishment *is simply that we, as humans, cannot violate moral laws. Berdyaev perceives Raskolnikov as a "maniac possessed by vicious delusions," and maintains that Dostoevski used Raskolnikov to explore the fallacy of the notion of the "superman." According to Berdyaev, the message of* Crime and Punishment *is that one must acknowledge the higher will of God. This interpretation is supported by Janko Lavrin (1947) and Konstantin Mochulsky (1947).*]

To speak of wrongdoing raises the question of what is allowable. Everything? It is a question that always troubled Dostoievsky, and he was always putting it in one form or another: it is behind **Crime and Punishment**. . . . Free man is faced with this dilemma: Are there moral norms and limits in my nature or may I venture to do anything? When freedom has generated into self-will it recognizes nothing as sacred or forbidden, for if there be no god but man then everything is allowable and man can try himself out at will. At the same time he lets himself get obsessed by some fixed idea, and under its tyranny freedom soon begins to disappear—a process that Dostoievsky has set out with all his power. It was the case with Raskolnikov. He does not give the impression of a free man at all but of a maniac possessed by vicious delusions; there is no sign of that moral independence that goes with self-purification and self-liberation. Raskolnikov's fixed idea is to experiment with the uttermost limits of his own nature and that of mankind in general. He regarded himself as belonging to the pick of the world, one of those remarkable people whose mission is to confer benefits on humanity at large. He believed nothing to be impossible, and was anxious to prove it in himself. Dostoievsky simplified Raskolnikov's theorem by reducing it to the terms of an elementary question: Has a very unusual man, who is called to the service of his fellows, the right to kill a specimen of the lowest sort of human creature, who is only a source of evil to others, a repulsive and aged usuress, with the sole object of contributing to the future good of mankind? In **Crime and Punishment** he set out most forcefully that such a thing is forbidden us and that the man who does it is spiritually lost.

All things are *not* allowable because, as immanent experience proves, human nature is created in the image of God and every man has an absolute value in himself and as such. The spiritual nature of man forbids the arbitrary killing of the least and most harmful of men: it means the loss of one's essential humanity and the dissolution of personality; it is a crime that no "idea" or "higher end" can justify. Our neighbour is more precious than an abstract notion, any human life and person is worth more here and now than some future bettering of society. That is the Christian conception, and it is Dostoievsky's. Even if he believes himself a Napoleon, or a god, the man who infringes the limits of that human nature which is made in the divine likeness falls crashing down: he discovers that he is not a superman but a weak, abject, unreliable creature—as did Raskolnikov. . . . [He had learned] that it is easy to kill a man but that spiritual and not physical energy is expended in the doing of it. Nothing "great" or "marvellous," no world-wide echo, followed the murder, only a nothingness that overwhelmed the murderer. The divine law asserted itself, and Raskolnikov fell beneath its power. (pp. 95-8)

Raskolnikov was a divided, riven being, from whom freedom was already alienated by his inner unhealthiness, whereas the truly great are integral and jealous for their own unity. Dostoievsky showed the folly of claiming to be a superman, a lying idea that is the death of man: this claim and all its cognate

aspirations sooner or later collapse into a state of pitiable weakness and futility which is no longer human, and against it the true nature of religious and moral consciousness stands out with everlasting majesty. The sin and the powerlessness of man in his pretension to almightiness are revealed in sorrow and anguish; the tortured conscience of Raskolnikov is a witness not only to his transgression but also to his weakness.

The case of Raskolnikov illustrates the crisis of Humanism, what its morality leads to, the suicide of man by self-affirmation; it is played out, as the emergence of a visionary superman with a "higher" morality proves. There is no humanitarianism left in Raskolnikov, who is cruel and without pity for his neighbour: concrete, living, suffering men must be sacrificed to the idea of a superman. But Dostoievsky taught the religion of love for one's neighbour, and he denounced the falsity of this disinterestedness in favour of some far-away end out of sight and reach of mankind: there *is* a "far-away" principle, it is God—and he tells us to love our neighbour. (pp. 98-9)

Dostoievsky studied the results of man's obsession by his own deification under several forms, individual and collective. One consequence is that there is an end to compassion, there is no more mercy. Compassion is a ray of the truth by which Christianity enlightened the world, and a renunciation of this truth completely changes one's attitude towards one's fellows. In the name of his Magnificence the Superman, in the name of the future happiness of some far-away humanity, in the name of the world-revolution, in the name of unlimited freedom for one or unlimited equality for all, for any or all of these reasons it is henceforth lawful to torture and to kill a man or any number of men, to transform all being into a means in the service of some exalted object or grand ideal. Everything is allowable when it is a question of the unbounded freedom of the superman (extreme individualism), or of the unbounded equality of all (extreme collectivism). Self-will arrogates to itself the right to decide the value of a human life and to dispose of it. The control of life and the judgment of mankind do not belong to God; man, as the depository of the "idea of the superman," takes them upon himself and his judgments are pitiless, impious and inhuman at the same time. Raskolnikov is one of the individuals possessed by this fallacious notion in whom Dostoievsky examined the progress of self-will: Raskolnikov answered the question whether or no he had the right to kill a human being in furtherance of his "idea" solely by reference to his own arbitrary will. But the answering of such a question does not belong to man but to God, who is the unique "higher idea." And he who does not bow before that higher will destroys his neighbour and destroys himself. That is the meaning of **Crime and Punishment**. (pp. 99-101)

Nicholas Berdyaev, in his Dostoievsky: An Interpretation, *translated by Donald Attwater, Meridian Books, 1957, 227 p.*

JACQUES MADAULE (essay date 1938)

[*Madaule provides an assessment of Raskolnikov's spiritual and intellectual degradation. Madaule describes the nature of this debasement and examines Sonia and Svidrigailov as characters who represent salvation and damnation to Raskolnikov. Similarly, J. Middleton Murry (1923), R. P. Blackmur (1943), and Nicholas M. Chirkov (1945-49) discuss the antithetical relationship of Raskolnikov and Svidrigailov. Madaule's essay was first published in 1938 in his* Le Christianisme de Dostoïevsky.]

Dostoevski as a young man. Courtesy of Ardis Publishers.

Raskolnikov is typical of . . . intellectuals who have been led astray, who have not lost all their conscience nor all their generosity, but who think that the old morality is out of date and that a superior man is not always obliged to obey the injunctions to the letter. He gives himself over to an experiment. The murder of an old usurer who appears to have done nothing but evil in her life, who is not useful to anybody and hateful to everybody: do we not have here an obstacle that we have the right to overturn? Is not murder an act that we have the right to dare? It will be noted that however poor he is it is not his poverty that drives him to crime. He had many other ways of getting along, such as throwing himself wholeheartedly into work or having recourse to the generosity of his friend Razumikhin. But the murder is a ''model'' act—one of those acts which one must commit to be sure of escaping the limits of ordinary humanity. In Raskolnikov's situation Napoleon would not have hesitated, he thinks.

One must be fairly sturdy to carry out such a heinous crime. Raskolnikov puts himself to the test. Not only his own future, but perhaps that of all humanity depends on its results. With evil one can do good. We have rejected the vulgar notions of good and evil, anyway. There is no such thing as evil in itself, just as there is no absolute good. The morality of the strong cannot be that of the weak. Now just here the crime overwhelms Raskolnikov, and that is the whole tragedy: because other than rational values are involved in crime. We are not masters of life. Vainly do we calculate everything down to the last detail: along comes the unexpected to confound us. He had to kill not only the old pawnbroker, but Lizaveta as well, a simple and innocent creature. Raskolnikov no longer had a choice.

And now comes the punishment. It is not penal servitude, of which we barely get a glimpse and where the criminal will find in suffering the source of his own resurrection. Neither is it remorse, in the sense that one ordinarily gives to this term. Rather, it seems to me, it is the sudden collapse of a whole mental universe. Raskolnikov finds himself in that immense crowd of the insulted and injured who never cease to be present for Dostoevsky. They are the limbs of the suffering Christ; the unbearable reproach abides in them. In his dream of glory the young student had forgotten them. They flow back towards him, as soon as the crime is committed, and envelop him in their destiny. (pp. 43-4)

In the abyss into which he sank of his own will, Raskolnikov can be reached only by somebody who partakes to some degree of his own degradation; and it is Sonia who suspects the crime and who forces the confession. There is also, of course, Porfiry Petrovich, the examining magistrate, who shares the Western culture of Raskolnikov, and who plays with him as a cat with a mouse. But Porfiry Petrovich would not have sufficed. Raskolnikov would still have been able victoriously to escape his rigorous deductions had it not been for the mortal weakness into which he is plunged by his contact with Sonia. It is here that we take the measure of the whole depth of Dostoevsky's ''realism.'' No sooner does one wish to penetrate to the depth of truth of things than one perceives that they exist on several planes. There is the juridical and rational plane where Porfiry Petrovich operates. He investigates the motives of the crime; he understands the mechanics of it and, at times, he enjoys it as an enlightened connoisseur. But nothing in him is capable of forcing the confession which is indispensable in the absence of material evidence. This confession must be spontaneous, must come from the depths of freedom, that is to say, in the final analysis, from the place out of which the crime itself emerged.

Here is where Sonia comes in: she is completely incapable of analyzing the motives for the act, but she senses the fault because she is aware of the unhappiness. For her Raskolnikov is nothing else than a being infinitely more miserable than she is herself. She does not condemn him, because we do not have the right to judge our fellow man. (p. 44)

Raskolnikov, reduced here to the level of the most humble and despised, is forced to accept his own salvation from Sonia, and to receive in exchange a suffering that he has not chosen. This defeat of a man which can only change into victory through a confession of weakness appears before us in infinitely more atrocious form in the person of Svidrigailov. He is one of those astounding characters in Dostoevsky who are human only in appearance. (p. 45)

Svidrigailov is situated, in *Crime and Punishment,* at the edge of the drama. He plays there, without doubt, an important ''supporting'' role, but this role could have been taken by somebody else; moreover, it was not necessary to stress this character so strongly had Dostoevsky not had another purpose beyond telling the story of Raskolnikov. . . . Raskolnikov marks a moment of the fall; a moment where, whatever be the crime, the possibility of a redemptive punishment still remains. With Svidrigailov we touch the bottom of the abyss, we penetrate into a kind of earthly hell. (pp. 45-6)

[The] causes of Svidrigailov's damnation remain obscure. Nevertheless, we know his history well enough to understand that he has deliberately chosen evil. . . . He who does not choose good, necessarily chooses evil. Now what is evil if not suffering inflicted gratuitously, and as though out of pleasure, on an innocent creature?

Such is absolute evil. Although he had committed a double murder, and one of his victims, at least, was precisely such an innocent creature, yet Raskolnikov has not committed the absolute evil. The notion of the distinction between good and evil remains alive in him even when he contemplated his crime. He believed in a double morality: a broad one for superior beings and a narrow one for the generality of men. . . . In order to understand what is happening . . . one must analyze Russian boredom, such, in any case, as it appeared to Dostoevsky.

This boredom, for absentee landlords and the poorly educated like Svidrigailov . . . may be explained by purely natural and, to some extent, sociological motives. . . . (p. 46)

This boredom is man's affirmation of his own solitude, that irremediable solitude in which man finds himself when he sets his face against God and thereby communion with other men; it is a metaphysical boredom. There is little doubt that Dostoevsky was himself the victim of that kind of boredom. He was born at a time when the spirit realized that nothing matters—not even, indeed, the satisfaction of those instincts which seem innate to it. One yawns, and does any old thing; but what one does then is always evil. A sick soul continually calls for a stronger and stronger wine. This wine can only be that of suffering. There is no error more naive than to believe that man seeks happiness. He convinces himself that he does; but, in reality, happiness which results from the permanent absence of real suffering (for the happiness at issue here is a purely negative one) is boring. The soul no longer seems to live, and this state resembles death—but one in which time would continue to flow with an inexpressible slowness; a death whose victim would be continually witnessing his own nothingness. How, then, does one feel oneself alive if not by making others suffer for it? And there is no suffering more exquisite for man than that which he brings about through his own cruelty. For man, if he is not naturally good, is capable of feeling pity. We know that Schopenhauer wanted to found morality on this natural pity. No heart can fail to be secretly touched by the impotent moans of the oppressed. This state is a suffering which is accompanied by a pleasure and pity for ourselves. The road which leads from a somewhat facile sentimentality to a more perverse cruelty is a road quickly traversed. (p. 47)

Do not think, moreover, that the perverse man exercises this cruelty solely on others. He exercises it first with a voluptuous refinement on himself. Svidrigailov began by degrading himself in his country solitude, and he drew from this degradation as much sorrow as pleasure. . . . Dissatisfied with himself, incapable through his own weakness of the effort which would be necessary to control himself, he has long abandoned himself, like an exhausted dog flowing with the current. But he suffers from it, and that is why he exhibits his own humiliation, so as to redouble his suffering and draw from it a more exquisite delight. This strange face which looks at him with horror is not that of an unknown person whom he has drawn into a cabaret by chance: it is his own. He watches himself suffer. . . . And it is the same when Svidrigailov faces Raskolnikov.

These degraded beings, after all, however stupid they be in other respects (and Dostoevsky often indulgently stresses their great stupidity), are always endowed with a formidable lucidity. They choose with perfect aim their witnesses or their victims. Raskolnikov, laden with his crime, in some kind of automatic way, creates around him complementary characters. Svidrigailov is no less necessary than Sonia, when one looks at the drama on this level. They are both drawn by the same smell of murder, the one an angel of light, and the other an angel of darkness. They take their positions around the criminal in order to mark his place exactly. A soul to save and a soul to lose. Or rather, they are the salvation and the damnation which are simultaneously offered to Raskolnikov, so that he might make the decisive choice in full knowledge of the case. Svidrigailov has no more need than Sonia herself to hear the confession of the crime in order to know who Raskolnikov is. It is striking that these are the two privileged witnesses to that confession. Nothing better demonstrates the true theatre of the Dostoevsky novel which opens on the abyss above and the abyss below, that of the heavens and that of hell. (p. 48)

Jacques Madaule, "Raskolnikov," translated by Robert Louis Jackson, in Twentieth Century Interpretations of "Crime and Punishment": A Collection of Critical Essays, *edited by Robert Louis Jackson, Prentice-Hall, Inc., 1974, pp. 41-8.*

GEORGY CHULKOV   (essay date 1939)

[*Chulkov was a Russian Symbolist poet and critic. The following excerpt is drawn from his* Kak rabotal Dostoevsky, *first published in 1939. Here, Chulkov briefly assesses* Crime and Punishment *in relation to Dostoevski's other works and contends that* Crime and Punishment *reflects the social consciousness of Dostoevski's earlier works and also originates a new cycle concerned with "revaluation of values." Chulkov praises Dostoevski's narrative technique, which he characterizes as "scenic and theatrical."*]

What place does *Crime and Punishment* oocupy among the works of Dostoevsky? On one hand, this novel completes the cycle of social motifs going from *The Poor Folk* through *The Insulted and Injured* and *The Notes from the House of the Dead*. The theme of the Marmeladovs is the same familiar theme of people ruined by poverty, of their impotent effort at passive protest. But on the other hand, the theme of Raskolnikov and Svidrigaylov moves into the foreground, partly prepared for by *Notes from the Underground*. This is the beginning of a new narrative cycle, where the theme of "revaluation of values" is the basis of the artist's intention. Raskolnikov will naturally be followed by other moral rebels not content with the passive protest of the "insulted and injured." (p. 487)

The composition of *Crime and Punishment* . . . differs from the composition of other novels through the unity and goal-orientation of the action. The novel about Raskolnikov does not have that complexity of material which is so characteristic of *The Possessed,* for example, or *The Raw Youth.* The interest of the story does not lose thereby, since all the properties of a "criminal novel" are present in *Crime and Punishment*—lively interest in the outcome of events—but Dostoevsky concentrated all his artistic dialectic on one basic theme. Sonya Marmeladova is necessary to him only as an antithesis to the murderer-for-an-idea. The social background (the poverty of the Marmeladovs and of Raskolnikov's own family) is essential for the clarification of material conditions of the crime, whereas the character itself of the crime becomes intelligible only in the conditions of a bourgeois society torn apart by contradictions, which Dostoevsky knew how to depict with the highest artistry. True, the novel has one other theme—that of Svidrigaylov and Dunya. Some commentators even consider Svidrigaylov and not Raskolnikov to be the chief hero of the novel.

But this view can hardly be argued convincingly, if only because Svidrigaylov does not appear until the fifth part of the novel and plays an important role only in the last, sixth part. That is of course a formal observation, but even substantively, Svidrigaylov is needed in the composition of the novel as the crooked mirror to Raskolnikov himself, and Svidrigaylov's ideas caricature his ideas. (p. 489)

All of Raskolnikov's tragedy lies in the fact that his extreme individualism leads him to a murder for an idea, and murder convinces him that through crime, man loses all the threads which tie him to humanity. The idea of "humanity" of course is refracted in a peculiar manner in Dostoevsky's thought, but in analyzing his books, if we are not to be formalists, we must find the central idea which guided him in writing his works. This idea consists in this: no moral prohibitions will help man to enter into a real communication with other people, with humanity, with the whole world, nor will they save him from individualism, in the last analysis a suicidal individualism, if he does not find in life some kind of *point d'appui*, some kind of ultimate incarnation of living reality, expressing in itself all the perfection of possible harmony. Dostoevsky saw that reality in the myth of Christ. For him, Christ was not an abstract mythology, it was a real truth, and he used it as a criterion of good and evil. (p. 490)

Wherein lies the uniqueness of Dostoevsky's novel? It consists in a whole number of original artistic devices. . . . He dramatized the narrative form of the novel. If in other writers we find such a theatricalization from time to time as an exception in their narrative experiments, in Dostoevsky on the contrary this artistic device remains basic. His novels are in their essence tragedies, and therefore all their elements of narration are scenic and theatrical.

Raskolnikov's dialogues with Porfiry, Svidrigaylov, Sonya, and other characters are dramatic to the highest degree. Each reply, though it may seem unexpected, seems to conform to the scene and arouses keen interest. All of Dostoevsky's dialogues are ideological and psychological duels, and the reader, as if he were a spectator, follows with tense excitement the rapier thrusts of the duelists. Dostoevsky's novels are always catastrophic. Expectation of catastrophe also calls forth a purely theatrical pathos. All these devices would be a very bad means of affecting the reader if all of them were not conditioned by inner inevitability. The secret of those devices lies in the author's high art with which he preserves the organic unity of his intention. Therefore there is no room in his novels for mechanical effects.

The landscape, settings, the outside appearance of heroes in Dostoevsky's novels are like theatrical stage directions. That is why descriptive elements are either absent in his novels or very laconic. Sometimes, of course, the descriptions, without losing the nature of a stage direction, develop into rather long protocol-like accounts. This device makes it possible for Dostoevsky to give the reader an impression of confidence in the accuracy of the facts. This device, which at first sight seems "naturalistic" because of its bareness, achieves the author's aim of convincing the reader of the authenticity of the account. Such a hyperbolic "naturalism" is theatrical and decorative in its essence and naturally has nothing in common with vulgar naturalism. (p. 491)

Dostoevsky's novels are filled with the sharpest contradictions and the most daring irrational symbols. Almost all writers placed some central idea or complex of ideas at the center of their large works, but no one besides Dostoevsky used ideas as artistic material. This is the exceptional peculiarity of Dostoevsky's work. His artistic or rather poetic "I" was always the center of a tremendous number of ideas not abstracted from reality and linked to it inseparably. These idea-feelings, these idea-forces, actually *operate*, under specific social conditions. They arise, enter into battles, develop, diminish, find their rival-ideas, and win or die defeated. The acting personages of his novels do not merely represent certain characters or express social types; they are bearers of living ideas. Ideas in Dostoevsky's novels are, so to speak, living creatures. (pp. 492-93)

> *Georgy Chulkov, "Dostoevsky's Technique of Writing," translated by George Gibian, in "Crime and Punishment" by Feodor Dostoevsky: A Norton Critical Edition, the Coulson Translation, Backgrounds and Sources, Essays in Criticism, edited by George Gibian, revised edition, W. W. Norton & Company, Inc., 1975, pp. 487-93.*

ERNEST J. SIMMONS (essay date 1940)

[*Simmons is a famed American biographer and Russian scholar. His study* Dostoevski: The Making of a Novelist *is one of the foremost discussions of Dostoevski's life and writings. In the following excerpt, Simmons focuses on the secondary characters of* Crime and Punishment *and pays special attention to Sonia Marmeladova, whom he considers to be a definitive example of Dostoevski's "Meek" characters because she is selfless, submissive, and suffering. Simmons briefly assesses her relationship with Raskolnikov and praises Dostoevski's artistry in depicting the nuances of their relationship. Though Simmons criticizes Dostoevski's overuse of coincidence and telescoping of time in the novel, he concludes that, on the whole,* Crime and Punishment *has few serious artistic flaws. Nicholas M. Chirkov (1945-49) also discusses the minor characters and the use of coincidence in* Crime and Punishment. *Several critics, in contrast to Simmons, have praised Dostoevski's treatment of time in the novel; among them are Konstantin Mochulsky (1947), F. I. Evnin (1948), and Philip Rahv (1960). Michael Holquist (1977) offers an analysis of the temporal structure of* Crime and Punishment.]

[Perhaps the most striking and memorable of the secondary characters in *Crime and Punishment*] is Sonya Marmeladova. She is first mentioned in the novel by her father in his remarkable confession to Raskolnikov in the tavern. This favourite indirect method of introducing a character is employed most effectively here. The father's description of how his daughter was forced to become a prostitute makes an immediate impression which creates eager suspense until the actual appearance of Sonya on the scene. The horror of her position is only intensified by its profoundly despairing effect on her human derelict of a father. In his description of this tragic incident in Sonya's life there is an unusually clear anticipation of her whole nature. She is an outstanding representative of Dostoevsky's Meek characters and one of the most noteworthy of all his female creations.

In one of [his] notebooks, Dostoevsky jotted down a few brief characterizing phrases which are elaborated in the complete portrait of the novel: "Sonya is always meek and has no humour at all; she is always grave and quiet." The father describes her as "a gentle creature with a soft little voice, fair hair and such a pale, thin little face." . . . She is utterly unequal to the struggle with life. (p. 159)

Dostoevsky's feminine characters of the Meek type are all of lowly origin, as though he were convinced that their special attributes would seem natural and plausible only among women close to the soil or crushed by poverty. Complete passivity exists in them to an equal degree, and they accept humbly and uncomplainingly everything that fate sends their way. The humility and submissiveness of Sonya, however, contain a more poignant and extreme quality because of her dishonourable calling, for she is the only prostitute among the Meek characters. This is why she experiences such horror when Raskolnikov declares that she is as honourable as his mother and sister. (p. 160)

The relationship between Sonya and Raskolnikov is of the utmost importance, for upon it turns the ultimate fate of both. His intellectual pride forces him to hate everything she represents. In his amazing categories of humanity, Sonya would occupy the lowest place among those despised ''ordinary people'' who are born to be submissive. On the other hand, Sonya also appeals to all the finer instincts of his nature. The submissive aspects of his own dual personality lead him to see in this prostitute an embodiment of Christian love and the very image of chastity. (p. 161)

For artistic reasons Dostoevsky deliberately mutes every outward show of love between Sonya and Raskolnikov. In the hero's case a confession of love would have amounted to an act of submission foreign to the dominant pride of his nature. His authoritarian theory of greatness has no place for love; he can neither give nor receive it. . . .

With Sonya, certainly, any active expression of love would have been contrary to the characteristic emotional features of her type. All the passive and submissive traits of the Meek characters are most clearly evinced in their relations with the opposite sex. One hesitates to call this relationship love, since the sex element is virtually negligible. The Meek woman in love is utterly devoid of passion. In love, as in nearly everything else, she is destined to play the role of the sufferer. (p. 162)

From the point of view of the novelist's art, the material for the characterization of Sonya would seem to have nothing more viable in it than the stuff of a picture of ''still life.'' It is a tribute to Dostoevsky's genius that he was able to breathe the breath of real life into this exceptional figure. If she reminds one at times of an allegorical personification of some abstract virtue in a medieval morality play, she transcends her allegorical significance by the sheer force of the novelist's art. Perhaps it would be better to say that Sonya is a kind of living universal symbol of crushed and suffering humanity that bears within itself the undying seed of joyous resurrection.

The other members of the family have nothing in common with Sonya, emotionally or spiritually, unless it be her father. Marmeladov has something of Sonya's deep religious feeling, of her conviction that God will receive the lowliest sinner if only he be contrite and humble of heart. Marmeladov is a unique creation. He takes his place, although a lesser one, among that memorable company of exaggerated, off-centre heroes of world literature to which belong Don Quixote, Parson Adams, Uncle Toby, and Micawber [from, respectively, *Don Quixote* by Miguel de Cervantes, *Joseph Andrews* by Henry Fielding, *Tristram Shandy* by Laurence Sterne, and *David Copperfield* by Charles Dickens]. This may appear to be an ill-assorted group, but like all these famous figures, Marmeladov strikes us as comical, even ridiculous, and at the same time the ridiculous in him is never far removed from an abiding pathos that makes us pity while we smile. (pp. 163-64)

Nothing could be more effective as a piece of characterization than Marmeladov's own revelation of his nature to Raskolnikov

in the tavern. Beneath the verbiage, pomposity, and unintentional humour of this inimitable confession is revealed the soul of a man who has experienced every feeling of degradation in an unequal, hopeless struggle to preserve his human dignity. Nowhere else in his fiction is Dostoevsky's intense sympathy for the poor and downtrodden more feelingly expressed than in his treatment of Marmeladov and his family. (p. 164)

The mysterious Svidrigailov, no less than Valkovsky in *The Insulted and Injured,* gives one the eerie feeling of coming to grips with a human phantom. The identification suggests itself naturally enough, for Svidrigailov belongs to the same type of Self-Willed characters. So obvious is their similarity that it scarcely requires any pointing out. The shamelessly frank confession of Svidrigailov to Raskolnikov in the tavern is almost an exact duplication of Valkovsky's confession to Ivan Petrovich in the tavern. The setting, thoughts, criminal adventures, frank admission of immorality, and even some of the turns of expression are repeated in the scene in *Crime and Punishment.* Svidrigailov is especially addicted to Valkovsky's dominating passion—women. Debauching young girls, which runs so strangely through Dostoevsky's fiction, is a particular feature of Svidrigailov's immoral nature. (pp. 164-65)

There is no uncertainty about the ultimate fate of Svidrigailov. For the entirely Self-Willed type, whose rational or instinctive actions represent a criminal force directed against society, there can be only one solution—death. (pp. 165-66)

If Dostoevsky has scorn for any of the characters in the novel, it is for Luzhin, the would-be suitor of Raskolnikov's sister. One gathers from the notes that Dostoevsky originally intended Luzhin to be more complex and his actions more extensive than they actually are in the novel. (p. 166)

The traits of Luzhin's nature were precisely those which Dostoevsky despised in real life—the cautious, reasoned, calculating, middle-of-the-road bourgeois attitude, bourgeois hypocritical respectability, and a petty sense of self-importance. Luzhin has nothing of the largeness, generosity, intense passion, or impulsiveness which Dostoevsky admired in real men and women as well as in his imaginary creations. (pp. 166-67)

However small their roles may be, it is surprising how well Dostoevsky individualizes [the minor characters of *Crime and Punishment*] with a few strokes. Raskolnikov's mother is ineffably human. Her cares, joys, and sorrows over her erring son, whose strange behaviour she cannot possibly understand, reflect a natural maternal exaggeration. The long letter she writes to Raskolnikov to tell of the proposed marriage of Dunya shows all the love and self-sacrifice for a son and daughter who have left her far behind in everything but affection.

The police inspector, Porfiri, is endowed with Dostoevsky's own powerful dialectical method. He bears little resemblance to the scientific sleuth of the modern detective story, but he is no less real for that. What he may lack in scientific technique he compensates by possessing a deep sense of human values which is never devoid of a sympathetic understanding of his victim. Not only was Dostoevsky intensely interested in criminal psychology, but he sought special knowledge in crime detection and legal procedure. This expert information is revealed in the police inspector's handling of Raskolnikov's case. . . . In Porfiri's subtle psychologizing one perceives Dostoevsky's mind at work. In fact, through the police inspector he seems to be projecting his own opinions on Raskolnikov's crime and his moral need for punishment.

On the whole, the faults of *Crime and Punishment* as a work of art are not very serious. Critics have censured the melodramatic element, but the unusual fact, in this novel of crime, is that the melodrama is rarely overdone. The murder of the old pawnbroker and Lizaveta is one of the best pieces of expository narrative in literature. This scene cannot be called melodrama. It is so intensely imagined that the author appears to be describing a vividly realized experience of his own. The cold logic of events is never sacrificed to extra-melodramatic effects. If anything, Dostoevsky consistently underwrites this unforgettable account of crime. He is not always so successful in other scenes, however, where the action crackles with horrific effects. For example, there is more melodramatic exaggeration than artistic measure in the scene in the locked room where Dunya shoots from close range at the imperturbable Svidrigailov and manages to miss him.

Coincidence is an ever-present trap for weary novelists, and in this respect Dostoevsky nodded rather frequently in *Crime and Punishment*. It is perhaps the principal artistic blemish in the work. Coincidence, of course, may be justifiable in a novel, for it is a legitimate part of the pattern of reality. In real life, however, coincidental happenings do not violate the laws of probability, and in fiction our credibility is forfeited if coincidence is overworked. Dostoevsky certainly carries the matter too far in *Crime and Punishment*. Svidrigailov is allowed to pass Sonya precisely at the moment when she asks Raskolnikov an important question. Svidrigailov overhears the reply which significantly affects the action. Lebezyatnikov bumps into Raskolnikov on the crowded city streets just when he is looking for him. Indeed, such opportune meetings in the busy city occur frequently and create the impression that Dostoevsky took the easiest way out when it was necessary to get his characters together. Following this line of least resistance, he often ignored the time-sequence. . . . On occasions the action is so telescoped that time indeed does not seem to exist. And this compressed action and time-sequence literally force him to group his characters in a most improbable manner: Luzhin lives in the same house as the Marmeladovs, and Svidrigailov hires quarters in Sonya's house. The restricted stage, which recalls the misdirected application of the unities in some bad imitations of classical drama, results in forced situations and unbelievable coincidences.

Apart from these faults, however, there is little else to quarrel with in *Crime and Punishment* as a work of art. Dostoevsky's powerful dialectic admirably satisfies the realistic demands of the reader, for the author rarely fails to present, with equal persuasiveness, both sides of the intellectual, moral, and spiritual contradictions which evolve out of his hero. Although Dostoevsky may seem at times to sympathize with Raskolnikov's unique theory of murder, this fact does not interfere with his convincing presentation of the negative side. In the struggle between good and evil that goes on in the mind of Raskolnikov, Dostoevsky does not hesitate in the end to take a positive stand on the side of the good. This does not mean that he projected, in a didactic manner, his personal moral or ethical discrimination into a work of art. He clearly recognizes that the moral and artistic spheres are quite distinct from each other, for he never confuses his own morality, which is primarily concerned with the way men behave in the real world, with the morality of art which is not, or should not be, conditioned by the personal factors of ordinary life. (pp. 168-70)

> *Ernest J. Simmons, in his* Dostoevsky: The Making
> of a Novelist, *Vintage Books, 1940, 396 p.*

R. P. BLACKMUR   (essay date 1943)

[*Blackmur, an American critic, poet, and editor, is regarded as a significant contributor to the New Criticism movement. In the following excerpt, he analyzes the impact that* Crime and Punishment *has on the reader, and discusses the "tearing down of order" as a key concept in the novel. In addition, Blackmur discusses Svidrigailov, Sonia, and Porfiry as foils of Raskolnikov.*]

Crime and Punishment has upon most readers an impact as immediate and obvious and full as the news of murder next door; one *almost* participates in the crime, and the trivial details become obsessively important. It has besides a secondary impact, by which, as one feels it, one discovers that one has been permanently involved in the nature of the crime: one has somehow contributed to the clarification of the true residual nature of crime in general through having contributed to the enactment of this crime in particular. It is the feeling of this impact that leads us to say our powers of attention have been exhausted. But there is a third and gradual impact, which comes not only at the end but almost from the beginning to the end, creating in us new and inexhaustible powers of attention. This is the impact of what Dostoevsky meant by punishment. The three impacts are united by the art of the novelist, and they are felt simultaneously. It is only that we are not aware at the time of the triple significance, and must, when it does transpire, rebuild it analytically. Thus we may come to estimate what it is that we know—what it is that has been clarified in the history of Raskolnikov which we had known all along in ourselves without being aware of it: we estimate our own guilt.

A crime is above all an act against the institutions of human law, custom, or religion; and there is a sense in which any act may be understood as criminal, for if the institution cannot be found against which it is committed, then it may be called an anarchic act—against some institution that has not yet come to exist, but which will exist because of the crime. (pp. 7-8)

How easy it is to believe that [Raskolnikov] this young, handsome, proud, and sensitive boy might be drawn *first of all* to the possibility of murder as the way out of an intolerable situation. It is the situation of poverty, debt, starvation, shabbiness, sickness, loneliness; for Raskolnikov has reached such a stage of privation that even thought has become a luxury—a kind of luxurious hallucinated hysteria; an extremity in which only the rashest dream seems a normal activity. It is the situation of the sponge, too, for Raskolnikov has come to depend on his mother and sister for help they cannot afford to give, for help they can give only by prostituting themselves in marriage and servile relationships. The sponge who is aware that he is a sponge is in an awkward situation; the pride of his awareness deprives him of the use of the exactions he makes; and that is how it is with Raskolnikov, as he lies in his attic committing symbolic murder. (pp. 8-9)

What is fully imagined as necessary has goodness and freedom at the very heart of its horror, a sentiment which may be interpreted in different ways, having to do either with the tearing down of order or with the envelopment of disorder, or, finally, with the balancing of several disorders so as to form an order. At the level of immediate impact, Raskolnikov's story is concerned with the tearing down of order; that is the melodrama which carries us along and exhausts our attention. . . . Dostoevsky never fails of the primary task of the novelist; if his story seems for the moment to have been left behind, it is only that in reality it has got ahead of us, and when we catch up we see how much has been done without our noticing it. The story of the Crime is blended with the clarification of the

Punishment; the actor creates the role which expresses the nature and significance of his deed; Raskolnikov, in the end, becomes the product of his crime, but still depends on it to command our attention.

That is how Dostoevsky envelopes the disorder consequent upon Raskolnikov's attempt at the destruction of order. With the third possibility, whereby the imagination not only envelops disorder—our substantial chaos—in a created personality, but proceeds to balance the sense of several disorders—the tensions of chaos—against each other so as to form a new order; with this possibility Dostoevsky has little to do. (pp. 9-10)

[It] becomes evident that the act of life itself is the Crime, and that to submit, by faith, to the suffering of life at the expense of the act is to achieve salvation—or, if you like a less theological phrase, it is to achieve integration or wholeness of personality. It is only dramatically true that the greater the sin the greater the salvation, and it is only arbitrarily true that any one act is sinful more than another act or than all acts. (p. 11)

Raskolnikov is balanced . . . against the other characters in this novel, and . . . the other characters and their stories make something with Raskolnikov which is quite different from anything found in them as types, though there would be no product of their whole conflict if there was not a great deal that was living within each type, from Razumihin to Porfiry to Svidrigailov to Sonia, and all the rest. (p. 19)

Svidrigailov is a foil for the whole story. He comes before the crime, in a way induces the crime to come into being, is the first to perceive the crime, and in a way *finishes* the crime without (since he does not have Raskolnikov's luck in finding Sonia) reaching the punishment. He *is* Raskolnikov in simpler perspective, he is Raskolnikov's other self, a mirror of being into which Raskolnikov never quite dares to look. He is the mystery of Raskolnikov's other self. The sense of him is symbolic, as it always is with mystery. (p. 25)

Svidrigailov envelops the disorder brought about by Raskolnikov's crime by imaging a kind of order which we cannot reach but which is always about to overwhelm us. He is a symbol of the mystery of the abyss, and it is a great witness to the depth of Dostoevsky's imagination that he is able to create in the flesh, with eyes too blue and flesh too youthful, such figures at will.

It is no less a test of Dostoevsky's skill—not his depth but his skill—that he is able to employ the one remaining major character in the book without, as it were, creating him at all. I mean, of course, that thirty-five year old roly-poly of the disengaged intellect called Porfiry, that man whose life, as he insists to Raskolnikov, is already finished, who has no other life to live, and nothing to do with what remains to him but probe and prance intellectually. Porfiry is so much a victim of moral fatigue that he is beneath every level of being but that of intellectual buffoonery. He represents order; he understands desire, ambition, all forms of conduct, but he knows nothing of the sources and ends of conduct, except that he can catch at them, in the midst of the game of the drowning man which he plays so long and so skilfully, like so many straws that only just elude his dancing fingers. But he is unreal, except as an agency of the plot, something to make the wheels go round; he is a fancy of the pursuing intellect whom Raskolnikov must have invented had he not turned up of his own accord. As Svidrigailov and Sonia between them represent the under-part, and the conflict in the under-part, of Raskolnikov's secret self, so Porfiry represents the maximum possible perfection of the artificial, intellectual self under whose ministrations Raskolnikov *reasons* himself into committing his crime, and who therefore is the appropriate instrument for driving him to the point of confessing it. (pp. 26-7)

R. P. Blackmur, '''Crime and Punishment': A Study of Dostoevsky's Novel,'' in The Chimera, *Vol. I, No. 3, Winter, 1943, pp. 7-29.*

JANKO LAVRIN (essay date 1947)

[*A twentieth-century critic, Lavrin is best known as a literary historian. In his writings on Russian novelists and poets, Lavrin used a ''psycho-critical'' method which takes into account the artist's personality and social milieu as well as the aesthetic value of the artist's work. In the following excerpt, Lavrin stresses that weakness, not strength, motivated Raskolnikov's crime. Lavrin contends that Raskolnikov's torment immediately following the murder was aesthetic rather than moral, and that through his crime he succeeded only in disgusting himself.*]

What transpires even from the early chapters of [*Crime and Punishment*] is the fact that Raskolnikov himself is not entirely sure as to the chief motive of his crime. He . . . is a split personality, divided all the time between the most contradictory impulses and actions. (p. 76)

Raskolnikov is an inflated egotist: a would-be 'superman' who wants to assert his personality by overstepping the values of good and evil and thus prove to himself that he is an exception, a law-giver, a new Napoleon. With such an ambition in his mind, he chooses murder as his expedient—that is, the very crime through which one human being can assert a maximum of self-will and power over another human being. But Raskolnikov happens to be also a new variety of the brooding 'underworld-man'. He is a Hamlet, who dreams of becoming Napoleon and is not quite sure as yet whether he is entitled to cherish such ambitions or not. It was not his strength, but his lack of strength, or rather his doubt of it, that drove him to the crime. He wanted to prove to himself that he was able to 'take the daring'—to send the old moral values flying, and bravely face the principle of 'all things are lawful'.

The curious point about it was that his logic did not raise any objections. 'Since there is anyway no God, the new man may well become man-God, and promoted to his new position, he may lightheartedly overstep all the barriers of the old morality, of the old slave-man, if necessary.' . . . Yet in spite of the sanction on the part of his logic, he was troubled and hesitating. Thus after his hideous symbolic dream, in which drunken peasants had beaten to death an old horse, Raskolnikov awoke in horror at the mere idea of his criminal design. Once again he began to doubt whether he could accomplish it at all. (pp. 77-8)

Dostoevsky unfolds [the second act of Raskolnikov's drama, after the crime,] with uncanny intuition. To begin with, he shows that Raskolnikov's reaction to the crime was not one of remorse, but a vague half-conscious mood which gradually undermined him from underneath as it were. (p. 78)

[What] now oppressed him was not the crime itself, but the mean and loathsome way in which it had happened. (p. 79)

Raskolnikov's torment was not one of moral remorse. His loathing of himself and of his deed was above all aesthetic. . . . While his theoretical reason was beyond good and evil, he was yet compelled to stop on this side of it, without knowing exactly why. The only thing he was aware of was his weakness and self-disgust. . . .

Had he murdered the old woman only for money and had he failed, his stake would have been trifling in comparison with this sudden crumbling down of all his 'independent volition'. Having asserted his self-will in such a revolting manner at the expense of another person's life, Raskolnikov was now unable either to remain on this side of good and evil (since he did not believe in its validity), or to go beyond it. He was thus thrown into a spiritual vacuum which he was unable to bear by his very nature. (p. 80)

He needed faith, a value and a 'principle', in order to be able to live at all. It was for the sake of a principle (the 'suprahuman' beyond good and evil) that he had undertaken his crime. But in killing the old woman, he killed also the principle itself as far as he was concerned. (p. 81)

> *Janko Lavrin, in his* Dostoevsky: A Study, *The Macmillan Company, 1947, 161 p.*

KONSTANTIN MOCHULSKY   (essay date 1947)

[*A contemporary Soviet critic, Mochulsky is considered the foremost scholar of Dostoevski, and his* Dostoevsky: His Life and Work, *first published in Russian in 1947, is regarded as the definitive study of the author's life and work. In the following excerpt, Mochulsky analyzes* Crime and Punishment *as a recasting of ancient tragedy in the form of the contemporary novel. Mochulsky asserts that while Raskolnikov does succeed in becoming a "strong individual" and transgressing moral laws, he fails to escape from fate. Thus, Mochulsky contends, his story is a new embodiment of the myth of Prometheus's revolt and the tragic hero's destruction in the course of his struggle with fate. According to Mochulsky, however, as a Christian writer Dostoevski deepens the metaphysical significance of the myth by asserting that Raskolnikov gives himself up to destiny by denying God. For in Dostoevski's view, the critic asserts, one who does not seek freedom in Christ, which is the only true freedom, is enslaved by destiny. Nicholas Berdyaev (1923) also focuses on the Christian elements of* Crime and Punishment.]

Crime and Punishment is a tragedy in five acts with a prologue and an epilogue. The *prologue* (the first part) depicts the preparation and perpetration of the crime. The hero is enveloped in mystery. The impoverished student is afraid of his landlady; we find him in a state of illness that "resembles hypochondria." He goes to a money-lender to pawn his silver watch, and talks about a certain "venture." "I want to undertake a *venture* of those proportions, and yet at the same time I am frightened by nonsense such as this! . . . Am I really capable of *it*?" The word "murder" is not spoken. "My God!" Raskolnikov cries out as he is leaving the money-lender's apartment, "how disgusting *this* all is! . . . Is it really possible that *such an appalling thing* could have entered my mind! . . . Above all it's filthy, obscene, vile, vile!" This "unseemly dream," which for a whole month has filled his being as he sat deliberating in his corner, now provokes within him spasms of revulsion. And so on the very first pages of the novel we find the hero in a state of intense conflict. . . . The dreamer [in Raskolnikov] abhors his own practical inability; the romantic is aesthetically repulsed by the "vileness" of murder. This dichotomy within the hero's consciousness is the beginning of his self-knowledge. Two motifs are struck in the tavern scene with Marmeladov, the endlessness of human sorrow and the inefficacy of sacrifice (Sonya). His mother's letter presses the hero to face some decision. His own sister is preparing to sacrifice herself, having sold her life to the contemptible businessman Luzhin. She is stepping out onto Sonya's road. . . . And this sacrifice is being made for him. Can he accept it?

And if he refuses to accept it, what then awaits him? Poverty, hunger, destruction?

"Or should one renounce life completely," he says, "and docilely accept one's fate as is, once and for all, and stifle everything in oneself having renounced any *right to act, to live and to love*?" The dilemma is posed in its most acute form. Christian morality preaches humility and sacrifice, but Raskolnikov has lost his faith. He is an atheistic humanist, for him the old norms of truth and justice have become lies. He is convinced that humility and sacrifice ultimately lead only to ruin. And what does one do—accept this destruction? Is it possible that man has no *right to life*? (pp. 300-01)

His mother's letter is the turning point in the hero's fate. Up until now he had been lying on his sofa resolving abstract questions; now life itself demands that he take immediate action. The dreamer is caught unawares. . . . A new level of consciousness has been reached: the idea is beginning to take on substance. Nonetheless, the hero cannot reformulate his entire being in one stroke. Reason embraces the new "idea," but "nature" continues to live within the framework of the old moral order. Little by little the abstract dream seizes possession of his consciousness. "Nature" struggles with it in desperation, is horrified, strives not to believe, pretends that it does not know it. In order to weaken its resistance, the author introduces the motif of sickness. The hero's pathological condition is repeatedly underlined: after the murder he lies for four days in a state of nervous delirium and this illness perdures through the end of the novel. Thus by his very example Raskolnikov proves the reasonableness of his theory. Did he not maintain in an article entitled *About Crime* that "the act of committing a crime is always accompanied by sickness"? Only illness can ultimately succeed in demolishing the disillusioned romantic's "nature," in overcoming the aesthete's revulsion when faced with the "vileness" of murder. In the end "nature" declares open warfare upon the "unseemly dream." All of Raskolnikov's compassion, all his anguish and horror when confronted with world evil find expression in his nightmare about the horse. . . . This nightmare that brought him back to childhood, resurrects his childhood faith, and the atheist turns and appeals to God. He had grown up in a religious family. "Remember, my precious," his mother writes him, "how when you were a child, when your father was still alive, you used to mouth your prayers at my knees, and how we were all happy then." "Nature" rejects the poison that is in its system—the thought of crime. Raskolnikov exalts in his deliverance: "Freedom! Freedom! He was now free from that spell, from that sorcery, the fascination, from the temptation." But this victory on the side of good does not perdure for long. The idea has already penetrated his subconscious, and after this final outburst of rebellion it becomes his driving force, his *destiny*. The hero no longer exercises control over his life; he is drawn forward. (pp. 301-02)

The *first act of the tragedy* (the second part) portrays the crime's immediate effects upon the criminal's soul. It deals a terrible spiritual blow to Raskolnikov. He comes down with a nervous attack and fever. He is close to madness and wants to kill himself. . . . He is summoned to the police bureau because of a debt that he has not paid his landlady. He concludes that his crime has been discovered and prepares to throw himself on his knees and confess everything. In the office his nerves fail and he falls into a faint. This is a fatal moment in his destiny: the murderer attracts the attention of the clerk Zametov and this latter tells the prosecuting magistrate Porfiry Petrovich about the strange student. The counteraction against Raskolnikov is set in motion as a result of this fainting spell; this serves to fasten the first thread of the net in which the magistrate eventually envelops him. The criminal is betrayed by "nature."

In the storm of feelings and sensations that have engulfed the murderer, one begins to predominate. "A dismal sensation of acutely painful, infinite *solitude and alienation* became consciously apparent in his soul." He awaited the punishment with which the pangs of conscience would afflict him; there was none. There was, however, something else: a mystical awareness of his estrangement from the human family. The murderer has stepped beyond something more than the moral law: *the very basis of the spiritual world itself.* After he has buried the stolen articles under a stone, he suddenly asks himself a question: "If in fact this whole thing was done with a purpose and not just frivolously, if you really had a definite and set *design,* then why didn't you look and see how much money there was?" The humanist-dreamer has suffered defeat. He displayed his utter helplessness in action; he grew frightened, committed blunders, lost his head. If in fact he had killed the old woman in order to rob her, then why is he not interested in the stolen goods? Or the deed was perpetrated "frivolously," and the humanistic motivation served only as a pretext. This *crisis* within his conscience is underlined by his illness and loss of memory which lasts over a period of three days. When the hero finally comes to himself, the old man, the sensitive "friend of humanity," has already died in him. . . . Thus a new consciousness is born—the consciousness of a strong personality, fiendishly proud and solitary. His fear, his faintheartedness, the sickness have passed. The hero senses a terrible energy that has been aroused within him; he feels that they are suspicious of him, that they are following him, and with ravishing flee he throws himself into the battle. (pp. 303-04)

The *second act* (part three) relates the course of the strong individual's struggle. The author intensifies our new impression of the hero by means of various indirect characterizations. Razumikhin remarks about his comrade: "I know Rodion: morose, somber, *haughty and proud.* . . . Sometimes . . . cold and *insensible* to the point of being inhuman. Really, it's just as if there were *two* opposing characters in him which alternately replace one another. . . . *He sets a terribly high value upon himself,* and not completely without reason. . . . *He doesn't love anyone,* and never will." . . . Raskolnikov's "second character" is revealed to us as being diametrically opposed to the first. (pp. 304-05)

During the course of his first meeting with the prosecuting magistrate, he expounds his theory of "exceptional people." "The exceptional man has the right . . . that is, not a legally established right, but he himself has the right to permit his conscience to step over . . . certain obstacles." Razumikhin perceives the terrible essence of this theory: "What's original in these ideas," he says, "is that ultimately you are allowing a man to shed blood in accord with the design of his conscience. . . . Why, this license to shed blood according to your conscience . . . it's, it's, in my opinion, more terrible than an official authorization to shed blood, a legal one." What is terrible is that Raskolnikov's theory does not merely negate Christian morality, it goes further; it sets another, an antiChristian code of morality in its stead. The "strong individual" is not without conscience: he has *his own conscience which authorizes the shedding of blood.* The proud demon is sad in his lonely grandeur. "It seems to me," Raskolnikov says, "truly great people experience an immense sadness while on earth." The whole tragedy of man-godhood is expressed in these few words.

And suddenly the hero founders; after this first encounter Raskolnikov undergoes an utter humiliation. An artisan comes to him, and in a "quiet, but clear and distinct voice" says: "murderer." . . . This crisis culminates in a terrible dream. Raskolnikov takes up an ax and strikes the old woman across her skull, but she inclines her head forward and "breaks out in a quiet, hardly audible laugh." (pp. 305-06)

The *third act* of the tragedy (part four) carries Raskolnikov's struggle to its ultimate climax. The hero has apparently triumphed, but his victory is only veiled defeat. He awakes from his terrible dream; there standing before him is Svidrigailov, the man who has wronged his sister. Raskolnikov is tragically divided: there are "two opposing characters" within him. The "strong individual" convulsively struggles against the humanist, torturously frees himself from "principles" and "ideals." Svidrigailov is exactly the same as Raskolnikov, but he has already succeeded in completely "curing himself" of all moral prejudices. He is the embodiment of one possible resolution of the hero's fate. There exists a metaphysical similitude between them. (p. 306)

Raskolnikov has abolished the old morality, and yet he still clings to beauty, honor and all the rest of humanistic rubbish. Svidrigailov is more consistent: good and evil are merely relative concepts; everything is permitted—all things are one and the same. What is left is universal boredom and vulgar banality. And he is bored. . . . Svidrigailov's boredom is not psychological, but rather metaphysical. The ultimates merge together; good and evil are indistinguishable—a deformed infinity, indifference, absurdity. Svidrigailov is not a simple villain: generously he lets Dunya go, he contributes money, helps the Marmeladovs. He tests his freedom in evil and finds that it has no limit. (p. 307)

[Svidrigailov] is placed next to Raskolnikov to serve as his dark and somber double. He is born of the hero's nightmare; he emerges out of his dream. The hero asks Razumikhin: "You actually saw him—saw him clearly? Hm . . . in that case. But then you know, it struck me . . . it all seemed to me that perhaps this was just a fantasy. . . ." In exactly the same way after his nightmare [in Dostoevsky's *The Brothers Karamazov*], Ivan Karamazov asks Alyosha if he has seen his visitor. Svidrigailov is Raskolnikov's "devil."

This meeting with his double marks a new stage in the hero's consciousness. Being convinced of his defeat ("Not a Napoleon, but a louse") he begins to lose his sense of reality. He lives in a state of delirium, is no longer capable of distinguishing dream from reality (Svidrigailov's appearance). Precipitously the action moves on to its denouement.

In opposition to this scene with Svidrigailov stands the scene with Sonya; the evil angel is counterbalanced by the good angel, the "bathhouse with its spiders" by the resurrection of Lazarus. Svidrigailov showed Raskolnikov that the demonic way leads only to the boredom of nonbeing. Sonya points out another way and discloses the image of Him who said: "I am the way." The murderer can be saved only by a *miracle,* and Sonya passionately prays for a miracle. As in the case of the conversation with Svidrigailov, the dialogue with Sonya proceeds to soar to metaphysical heights. Sonya answers the hero's arguments about the absurdity of sacrifice, the futility of compassion, and the inevitability of ruin and destruction, *by her faith in a miracle.* "'God, God will not permit anything so awful.' 'But it is possible that this God doesn't even exist,' Raskolnikov answered with a certain malicious pleasure." Suddenly he asks Sonya to read to him from the Gospels "about Lazarus." She believes that "even he, he—though he is blinded and does not believe—now he too will hear, he too will believe, yes, yes, immediately, now." The reading is over. Raskolnikov has received an answer to his mute question: "What is it she's waiting for, a miracle? Yes, it must be. *But really isn't this a sign of insanity?*" The miracle did not take place. The murderer's faith was not restored, and he only concluded that Sonya was mad: she actually believes in the resurrection of a corpse that has been dead for four days!

He calls Sonya "a great sinner"; she is as guilty of damning her soul as he. "You have ruined a life . . . your own (it's the very same thing)."

These terrible five words in parentheses (*it's the very same thing*) are filled with malice and a fiendish lie. To lay down one's life for one's friends is *the very same thing* as destroying the life of one's neighbor! In horror Sonya asks: "And what—and what should one do?" "What should one do?" answers the demon, "*Wreck and demolish* what one has to, once and for all, that's what; and then take the suffering upon yourself. What? You don't understand? You'll understand later. *Freedom and power*, but mainly, power! Over every trembling creature and over the whole anthill!" The reading of the Gospel occasions an outburst of diabolic pride. Ruin and destruction are set in opposition to the Resurrection ("wreck and demolish what one has to"); love of power stands and defies humility; the figure of the man-god opposes the images of the God-man. (pp. 307-08)

The *fourth act* (part five) marks a slowing in the action before the culmination of the catastrophe. Its major section is devoted to the scene in which the characters gather for Marmeladov's funeral dinner. In the course of this second meeting with Sonya, the strong individual arrives at the final stage of his self-knowledge. With scorn he rejects as "rubbish" the idea that the crime was committed out of humanistic motivations. "Nonsense! I simply committed murder! *I committed murder for myself, for myself alone,*" Raskolnikov declares. He performed an experiment; he was resolving the enigma of his own personality. "I had to *find out*, and find out quickly whether I was merely a louse just like everybody else, or whether I was a *man*. Would I be able to step beyond, or not? Was I a trembling creature, or did I possess the right?" He nurtures the greatest possible contempt for the human "herd." This "trembling creature" must be made to submit to the iron rod. . . . Raskolnikov continues the revolt begun by the man from underground ("and hadn't we better send all this good sense flying . . . to hell") and prepares the way for the Grand Inquisitor's despotism. A morality of force leads to a philosophy of violence. The superman is revealed as the Prince of this world—the Antichrist. (p. 309)

The *fifth act* (the sixth part) presents the catastrophe. The author depicts the parallel ruin of the two "strong individuals"—Raskolnikov and Svidrigailov. The murderer has a premonition of his end: he is in a state of semidelirium, wanders about the streets without purpose, sits down in a tavern, then falls asleep somewhere in the bushes. . . . "The lack of air in all this congestion began to suffocate him." Porfiry Petrovich's arrival resolves this tension. The magistrate analyzes the whole "psy-chological process of the crime" and gives him an historic definition. . . .

After the "strong personality" has been defeated, it is then exposed. Svidrigailov follows in Porfiry Petrovich's place. The latter has pointed out Raskolnikov's theoretical mistake ("a bookish dream"); the former discloses his moral hypocrisy. (p. 310)

Svidrigailov, Raskolnikov's double, laughs at him, just as Ivan Karamazov's double, the devil, amuses himself with him. They both embody a strong individual's doubt in himself. Now the hero is faced with only two possibilities: either to shoot himself or give himself up. He does not have enough strength of will to commit suicide, and so he surrenders to the authorities. This is not a sign of penitence but of pusillanimity: for him punishment is an "unnecessary shame" and "senseless suffering." (p. 311)

Raskolnikov's tragedy ends with an *epilogue*. The criminal has now spent a year and a half in penal servitude. Sonya has followed him to Siberia, but nonetheless he "tortures her by his contemptuous and rude manner." Has he changed? No, he is the same—solitary, morose, proud. "He examined himself thoroughly and severely and his obdurate conscience could find no particularly terrible fault in his past, except perhaps a simple *blunder* which might have happened to anyone. . . . *He did not repent of his crime.*"

"'Well, why is it that my act seems so unseemly to them?' he used to say to himself, 'Because it was evil? What does the word "evil" mean? *My conscience is at peace.*'" In the words "My conscience is at peace," the final truth about Raskolnikov is suddenly revealed. He is in fact superman. He has not been defeated; it is he who has conquered. He wanted to try out his strength and found that there were no limits to it. He wanted "to transgress" and he transgressed. He wanted to show that the moral law had no relevance for him, that he stood beyond the confines of good and evil, and now—his conscience is at peace. He has not been ruined because "his rupture with mankind has proved a source of torment" for him—oh no, he loves his proud solitude; or because "his nerves did not hold out," "nature surrendered"—all that is nonsense. His strength would have been sufficient. . . . It is only while serving his sentence that he comes to understand the reason for his downfall. "He was ashamed precisely because he, Raskolnikov, had come to his ruin so blindly, desperately, onerously, and stupidly, *through some decree of blind fate.*" This last feature crowns his majestic image. None of his adversaries is worthy of the strong individual; he has but one single enemy—fate. *Raskolnikov has been brought to destruction like a tragic hero in battle with blind Destiny.* . . . The novel ends with a vague anticipation of the hero's "renewal." It is promised, but it is not shown. We know Raskolnikov too well to believe this "pious lie."

Crime and Punishment resuscitates the art of ancient tragedy in the form of a contemporary novel. Raskolnikov's story is a new embodiment of the myth of Prometheus' revolt and the tragic hero's destruction in the course of his struggle with Fate. But Dostoevsky, the great Christian writer, adds an infinitely more profound dimension to the metaphysical significance of the myth. It is to the Russian people themselves that the author consigns the role of passing final judgment upon the "strong individual." On one occasion "everyone at once fell upon him with fury. 'You're an atheist! You don't believe in God!' they shouted at him. 'We must kill you!'"

This judgment, as it is expressed by the people, conveys the *religious idea* of the novel. Raskolnikov's "heart has grown troubled"; he has stopped believing in God. For Dostoevsky, atheism reverts invariably to the deification of man. If there is no God, then I myself am God. The "strong individual" sought to free himself from God—and he has succeeded. His freedom proved to be infinite. But in this infinity ruin awaited him. Freedom from God shows itself as sheer demonism; renunciation of Christ, as *slavery to Fate*. After having traced the course of atheistic freedom, the author leads us to the religious basis of his world-outlook: *there is no freedom other than freedom in Christ; he who does not believe in Christ stands subject to the power of Destiny.* (pp. 311-13)

> *Konstantin Mochulsky, in his* Dostoevsky: His Life and Work, *translated by Michael A. Minihan, Princeton University Press, 1967, 687 p.*

F. I. EVNIN   (essay date 1948)

[*Evnin is a Soviet scholar well known for his writings on Dostoevski. The following excerpt first appeared in* Tvorchestvo F.M. Dostoevskogo *in 1948. Evnin discusses what he considers the "perfect" construction of* Crime and Punishment, *focusing on the way that the outer action of the novel reflects the inner struggle of Raskolnikov as he oscillates between the "polar extremes which coexist in him." Leonid P. Grossman (1959) joins Evnin in praising the construction of* Crime and Punishment; *Ernest J. Simmons (1940), in contrast, cites the novel's plot structure and treatment of time as its chief flaws. For an additional discussion of the structure of* Crime and Punishment, *see Konstantin Mochulsky (1947).*]

Crime and Punishment is the best constructed of Dostoevsky's later novels. The individual lines of action of the novel are unified by the socio-philosophical problem; the various sides of the problem ("the ideas") of Raskolnikov and the various means of its resolution are embodied in these lines of action. "Existence in a yard of space," which serves as the taking-off point for Raskolnikov's whole theory, is written all over the misfortunes of the Marmeladov family, on whose undeserved human suffering Raskolnikov tormentedly meditates. The plot of Svidrigaylov demonstrates that he who was able to transgress the taboos of morality (Raskolnikov was not able) is not a "superman" but a half-man, unworthy of life and rejecting it. In opposition to this, the plot of Sonia Marmeladov must, according to the author's plan, point out the true solution of Raskolnikov's "problem": selfless love of people and service to them. The central plot, that of Raskolnikov, is summoned forth to discredit directly his misanthropic "theory." Finally, the episodes connected with Luzhin discredit this "theory" indirectly by means of directing it towards an ordinary, everyday level. The unscrupulous, bourgeois Luzhin puts into practice in trifles the very same idea of the right to commit crime. One could say that the novel tells not one crime, but several, and their corresponding punishments: the unsuccessful attempt of the would-be "Napoleon" to step over blood; the monstrous, bestial crimes of the cynic Svidrigaylov, who is forced to execute the death sentence upon himself; the self-sacrificing crime of Sonia; Luzhin's revolting, everyday swindling crimes.

Thus the central problem of the novel subordinates to itself all the lines and links of a broadly branched-out subject.

The novel's perfect composition is also the result of the presence of a single core subject, a center. The chief incident (in which the "idea" of the main hero finds expression), the mur-der of the money-lender, ties the work into a unified whole. As far as plot alone goes, all the chief peripeteias of *Crime and Punishment* either prepare for this incident or are a result of it, in one way or another being interrelated with it. (Almost all of the characters are involved in the struggle brought forth by the murder and in the search for its perpetrator.) (pp. 656-57)

A peculiar dynamism of plot development in *Crime and Punishment* (which sets it so far apart from the novels of Turgenev and Goncharov) is immediately brought to our attention. The plot of the novel is reminiscent of a kaleidoscope: it is some sort of a whirlwind of events uninterruptedly piling up one on top of the other. But each one individually and all of them together are fully motivated both by the inner logic of the emotions of the characters and by the external connection of everything that is occurring. Dostoevsky knows how to find ever new "pushes," to put into action ever new springs of action, and he does not weaken the tension of the action for a minute.

After the murder is committed and the loose ends are tied up, nothing, it would seem, could lead to the unmasking of the criminal. It would seem that the action ought to slow down. But an "accidental" call to the police station (already prepared for several chapters before "Praskovia Ivanovna wants to complain to the police about you"), and then an "accidental" talk with Zametov and the "accidental" appearance of the criminal at the apartment of the murdered woman (both naturally resulting from his emotional state) create a chain of circumstantial evidence and draw Raskolnikov into a struggle with the investigators.

On the other hand, a series of dramatic episodes arises in connection with the arrival of the mother and sister (also fully motivated by the entire chain of events). The encounters of the hero with Luzhin, Sonia, and Svidrigaylov also serve as a powerful impetus to the action. As a result, a turmoil of events fills the novel right up to the epilogue.

The exceptional dynamism of the plot is particularly evidenced by the fact that the incidents of the novel are extremely concentrated in time. According to the interesting calculations of A. G. Tseitlin, the entire complex kaleidoscope of events which are directly related in *Crime and Punishment* is placed within 9½ days. At that, the events of the first part of the novel are confined to 2½ days, of the second part in two, and of the fifth and sixth in one day. (pp. 657-58)

The tenseness and dynamism of the plot also find expression in another manner: in the unexpected, sharp turns of the action, in the masterful "backward moves," which suddenly alter the entire situation. Let us recall, for instance, the story of Raskolnikov's rescue after the murder of the money-lender. Maximally intense situations succeed one another as if on the blade of a knife. Each thematic peripeteia cancels out the previous one. Dostoevsky keeps opening the way to escape for the murderer but then convinces the reader that the capture of the criminal is inevitable. (pp. 658-59)

[Turnabouts] in action—completely credible, having none of the fantastic in them—are one of the manifestations of Dostoevsky's inventiveness in the plot. The alternation of contrasting situations is the law of development of the plot in *Crime and Punishment*. . . .

The fog of mystery which enwraps Raskolnikov also adds to the excitement of the novel and sharpness of plot. He is immediately presented to the reader as an "enigmatic hero." In the first chapter his "trial run" is described. Trial of what? One can only guess at this in the beginning. Even after it becomes clear that the matter concerns the proposed murder of an old woman and the murder itself is committed, his motives remain insufficiently clear to the reader. (p. 659)

In order to introduce Raskolnikov as a mysterious stranger Dostoevsky does not give any exposition in *Crime and Punishment,* nor does he inform the reader of his hero's past. Only step by step, parallel to the development of the plot, do the most important parts of his past become known (his relations with his family, with his friends; the episode with the bride; the episode of the article). It is noteworthy that two incidents from Raskolnikov's past which are essential to the understanding of his character (aid to his sick friend; saving the children during a fire) are found out by the reader only in the epilogue. Raskolnikov's inner struggle (the scene in the tavern, the talk between the student and officer) is related to the reader as late as possible: directly before the recounting of the old woman's murder.

However, in order for the aura of mystery really to surround Raskolnikov, it was not enough to keep silent concerning his "past": a particular tone and manner in the narration of his "present," engulfed by the novel's plot, was necessary. Dostoevsky therefore used a suitable narrative method in *Crime and Punishment. . . .* When he speaks in the person of the author he fulfills, as a rule, only a "protocol-informational" function: he tells of incidents, but does not completely reveal their inner meanings; he fixes emotions, actions, thoughts, the hero's internal monologues, but never fully explains them. Nothing is more alien to Dostoevsky than the role of an all-evaluating and all-explaining author. . . . (pp. 659-60)

The exceptional dynamism, "plottedness," of the novel is in the first place conditioned by the exceptional dynamism of the main hero. *Crime and Punishment* is almost wholly the story of Raskolnikov's violent oscillations. But the peculiar dynamism of Raskolnikov . . . is deeply original and distinctive.

The novels of Dostoevsky, as a rule, do not tell of changes in the hero, but of his incessant, more and more intense oscillations between the same polar extremes which coexist in him—which are the result of his "idea-emotion." (pp. 660-61)

[Raskolnikov's] entire progression in the novel is an uninterrupted, tortured "change of phases" of his internal struggle.

At the beginning of the novel, the reader finds Raskolnikov in a state of uncertainty. As is made known later, he has been tortured by the thought of murdering the money-lender for a month and a half, but is incapable of coming to a decision. The first link of the plot, the "trial run," leads to the rejection of the planned crime (". . . no, this is nonsense, this is absurd . . ."). But already the second link—the meeting of Marmeladov and the visit to the Marmeladovs'—signals a reversal in motion in the direction of the "idea." Raskolnikov again relives that inner process which had formerly brought him to the thought of killing the old woman. What he sees and hears at the Marmeladov's as it were confirms the correctness of his theory (the amorality of existing relationships by which people live at the expense of the "sufferings of Sonias"; the right of the strong to "transgress" moral taboos).

The third peripeteia—(Raskolnikov's receiving the letter from his mother)—increases the tension and brings him face to face with decision ("whatever happens, I must decide . . ."). He feels responsible for the fact that his sister's fate will be partly similar to Sonia's, because Dunia is marrying a man whom she does not love in order to help Raskolnikov ("Sonechka, Sonechka Marmeladova, the eternal Sonia, since the world began! . . . And what are you doing now? You take from them.").

The fourth peripeteia (meeting the drunken girl on the boulevard) forces Raskolnikov to make a decision. In his mind he sees his sister in her place. However, after this there is a last convulsive repulsion away from the evil undertaking. The fifth peripeteia (the dream about the horse being beaten) cancels the decision made. It is as if Raskolnikov casts off a spell. But it is the turn of the sixth, decisive peripeteia—the accidental encounter with Lizaveta on Haymarket Square. This puts an end to the oscillations and forces Raskolnikov to take up the axe.

This ends the first round of the internal struggle. It is followed by the second, in which the instinct of self-preservation struggles with the instinctive urge of the criminal to cast off from himself the heavy burden—to make a confession. Intercourse with people close to him becomes impossible for the murderer. Further, the same inner collision leads to the waverings of the hero between Sonia Marmeladova (the epitome of his "good half") and Svidrigaylov (the epitome of his "evil half"). The inner waverings of the hero are accompanied by an external struggle, until finally he confesses to the crime committed. (pp. 661-62)

Thus the "changes of phases" of Raskolnikov's inner struggle passes through the entire novel. The collision resulting from the hero's "idea" is revealed through the principle of dramatic build-up—ever increasing in depth, sharpness, and width.

The repetition of inner action sometimes calls forth the repetition of more or less analogous plot situations or scenes. With each one of these subsequent situations, however, comes a deepening and dramatic sharpening of the former situation (Raskolnikov's two talks with Sonia, his two talks with Svidrigaylov). On this point, the poetics of Dostoevsky's novel are linked with the poetics of drama. In the plot of a drama, the repetition of more or less analogous situations with an increased depth of the conflict is an important, frequently used artistic technique.

In spite of the repetitive actions and scenes, Dostoevsky actually does not repeat himself in his novel. Through the prism of the same internal collision, Dostoevsky knows how to refract newer and newer depths of the human soul—the most varied and complex feelings, experiences, and emotions. (pp. 662-63)

A wonderful artistic technique in Dostoevsky's hands is the contrasting "Rembrandt" light in which he shows the squalid rooms of the capital's poor and their faces distorted by suffering.

This is an important element of the background against which Dostoevsky exhibits his tragic heroes. This sort of light—the light of a candle stub in a room, the light of a gas lamp in the street at night—as though impotently struggling with the darkness, unable to dispel it, is the light that shades the terrible world in which the author's characters live. . . . It is not accidental that Raskolnikov's confession of the murder of the old woman to Razumikhin takes place in a dark corridor by a lamp. The lamp casts reflections on the "painfully distorted face" of the criminal. (p. 663)

F. I. Evnin, "Plot Structure and Raskolnikov's Oscillations," translated by Natalie Bienstock, in "Crime and Punishment" by Feodor Dostoevsky: A Norton Critical Edition, the Coulson Translation, Backgrounds and Sources, Essays in Criticism, *edited by George Gibian, revised edition, W. W. Norton & Company, Inc., 1975, pp. 656-64.*

NICHOLAS M. CHIRKOV   (essay date 1945-49)

[*A respected Russian scholar, Chirkov wrote extensively on Dostoevski. The following, composed between 1945 and 1949, is drawn from his* O stile Dostoevskogo. *Like Georg Brandes (1889), Chirkov regards* Crime and Punishment *in part as a portrait of Russian society; he specifically assesses it as a novel about the destructive aspects of Russian capitalism during the 1860s. Chirkov also examines the historical perspective in* Crime and Punishment *and discusses the book's minor characters. Like J. Middleton Murry (1923), Jacques Madaule (1938), and R. P. Blackmur (1943), Chirkov touches upon Svidrigailov and his antithetical relationship to Raskolnikov.*]

Crime and Punishment is first of all a novel about Russian capitalism, its manifestations and effects at the beginning of the post-reform period. But in what form or shape does capitalism present itself to the reader? An atmosphere of general trafficking and exploitation is immediately noticeable in those first forays of Raskolnikov onto the streets of the city. We do not see capitalist production in its organizing role at that stage of capitalism. There is nothing to indicate the progressive significance of capitalism for the historical moment which Dostoevsky describes. Capitalism in *Crime and Punishment* is shown exclusively in its destructive aspects.

Two characters are particularly important for an understanding of the essence of capitalism in this novel: the old pawnbroker, Aliona Ivanovna, and Peter Petrovich Luzhin, Dunia Raskolnikov's fiancé. Both figures are portrayed in their extreme deformity. The moral deformity of the wizened old lady, the "louse," is reflected in her outer appearance. In our first view of Luzhin, in Raskolnikov's "ship's cabin," Dostoevsky accents the decorous, proper bridegroom his strikingly modish dress, his sleek, manufactured appearance. His propriety, however, conceals an experienced "wheeler-dealer," a swindler capable of every kind of vileness (see, for example, the scene at Marmeladov's funeral gathering).

Dostoevsky uses Luzhin as the spokesman for the "philosophy of the age"—the philosophy of the "whole coat," of extreme utilitarianism and of the complete justification of the existing social order. One notes Luzhin's smug social optimism. (pp. 49-50)

The figures of the old pawnbroker and Luzhin are not only significant for Dostoevsky in themselves. More important is how Dostoevsky as author relates to these characters—the emotional tone of his artistic presentation. This tone is one of constant aversion and, with respect to Luzhin, of outright sarcasm. Dostoevsky does not simply describe his characters, but constantly polemicizes with them.

The capitalist ethos is further expressed in the atmosphere of acquisitiveness, speculation and profiteering which encompasses even the minor townfolk in *Crime and Punishment*. The novel is thronged with a multitude of rapacious petty traffickers: street hawkers, proprietors of taverns and "establishments," where liquor is consumed on the premises and sold "to take out," and peddlars in the Haymarket with rags, rubbish, and all kinds of junk. Hopeless and utter poverty exists inseparably from this petty thievery and profiteering. Rag-pick-

ers and "industrialists" appear side by side throughout the novel. Raskolnikov himself at the beginning of the novel is described as a "ragamuffin and a rag-picker." Inseparable from poverty, finally, is prostitution.

Crime and Punishment picks up and carries on the motif of prostitution, which had been introduced earlier in *Notes from the Underground*. In his development of this motif Doestoevsky employs the stylistic devices of emotional and thematic repetition or echo. At every stage of the novel, Raskolnikov experiences certain recurring impressions: especially striking are those created by Marmeladov's story of Sonia's plight and by the letter Raskolnikov receives from his mother, which describes Dunia's predicament, its possible outcome. Raskolnikov cannot fail to link the fates of Sonia and Dunia. (p. 50)

The theme of prostitution in *Crime and Punishment* is treated quite differently [however] from the way it is in *Notes from the Underground*—on an immeasureably broader scale and in its entire social context. Dostoevsky shows how the debasement of women and children is indigenous to the whole environment of rapacious exploitation, profiteering and speculation which forms the setting of his novel. The prostitution of young girls contains something both fascinating and fatal, forming one of the basic leitmotifs of *Crime and Punishment*. Prostitution, shown in the novel to be inseparable from the essence of capitalism, at the same time is shown to involve the desecration of a primevally pure, childlike image in man, not only in the children depicted in the novel but in all men. This image of the child in man emerges with special clarity in the person of Sonia Marmeladov.

Essential, also, for the treatment of prostitution in *Crime and Punishment* is the notion of the absence of a clear-cut, real boundary between innocence and vice. The recurrent motif just described, with its strong emotional resonances—the comparisons between Sonia and Dunia, and between the drunken girl whom Raskolnikov meets on the Konnogvardeysky Boulevard and the "dame aux camélias" in Svidrigailov's dream—have one thematic orientation: they link in a common chain what the language of moral categories calls "virtue" and "vice." A kind of tragic necessity is revealed in this contiguity, interaction, and merging of "virtue" and "vice," of childlike innocence and extreme degradation. . . .

Dostoevsky emphasizes the striking contradictions in the social life of St. Petersburg. Two kinds of impressions, mutually complementary and contradictory, occur as leitmotifs throughout the entire novel. The first is linked with the feeling of extreme confinement, with the lack of space or the need for air. . . . The novel is studded with images of confinement, stuffiness, and crowds. People, as though obeying some irresistible command, press as closely as possible to each other. They even press together while gathering around filth. . . . But an acute sense of alienation from one another accompanies this irresistible impulse of the people in the city to crowd together, even in filth and ugliness. The extreme inner solitude of the individual contrasts sharply with the physical proximity of men to one another.

A fundamental problem in all of Dostoevsky's works, touched upon with special clarity in *Notes from the House of the Dead*, occupies a central place in *Crime and Punishment:* the antinomy of the social and anti-social in man. The murder which Raskolnikov commits is a consistent, logically inevitable act, emerging from the laws of the society in which he lives.

The moral atmosphere of Petersburg in *Crime and Punishment* is one of universal frustration, spite, and derision. Each group and each clique reacts to the misfortunes or failures of the individual man with spiteful, malicious laughter. (pp. 51-2)

Dostoevsky characteristically asserts in *Crime and Punishment* that antisocial feeling is deeply instinctive in man. In describing Marmeladov's death Dostoevsky reports only his observations on the reactions of the people present, but as novelist he generalizes with respect to what he observes: "One by one the tenants crowded back to the doorway, with that strange inner feeling of satisfaction that may always be observed in the course of a sudden accident, even in those who are closest to the victim, and from which no living man is exempt, however sincere his sympathy and compassion." . . .

The story of Raskolnikov's crime is the story of the maximum intensification of both social and antisocial feeling in the soul of a man. Dostoevsky emphasizes Raskolnikov's heightened social consciousness in a number of places. He is portrayed as extremely sensitive to the fate of others and to the fate of those close to him, his sister and his mother; but his sensitivity extends beyond his family. . . .

Raskolnikov possesses moral awareness in the deepest sense and represents the highest moral potential in man. . . . His sensitivity to the sufferings of others, his acute reaction to such social evils as prostitution, in a word, his heightened social consciousness are among the strongest factors leading Raskolnikov to crime. Indeed we may say that Raskolnikov's intense moral feeling and awareness—what might be called his moral maximalism—is one of the essential preconditions of his crime. But most remarkable in the novel is the fact that this depth of moral feeling and awareness is closely related to his isolation and estrangement from other men. . . .

Dostoevsky describes the process of Raskolnikov's growing feelings of alienation, which lead him in the end to a spiritual impasse. The conflicts which Raskolnikov experiences are agonizing: his antisocial feelings are forced to their maximum intensity at the same time that he feels the evils of society as if they were wounds in his own body. Dostoevsky takes care to map the development of this complex intellectual and emotional condition from every angle. (p. 53)

How does Raskolnikov's isolation begin? Where do the roots of his antisocial feeling lie? Is it in his personality? Yes, indisputably; but not only in his personality. To a great extent his emotional state stems from his response to the impressions he receives from the social environment around him, from objective reality. *Crime and Punishment* responds to the questions of the sources of Raskolnikov's behavior in many ways and with a number of situations, the main idea of which may be formulated in the phrase: tragic necessity. In conversation with Dunia, Raskolnikov says: "You'll reach a certain point, and if you can't go beyond it, you'll be unhappy. If you do go beyond it, though, you might even be more unhappy." Raskolnikov here is referring to himself. He recognizes the inevitable necessity of the act he has committed.

And in fact, all the most important stages Raskolnikov passes through in the novel are shown in the light of their inescapable necessity. Above all, Raskolnikov is faced with the inevitability of his conclusions on the full moral permissibility of murder, with the logical irrefutability of these conclusions, and of his idea of the "justice" of the murder of the old woman. A number of important encounters and coincidences drive Raskolnikov directly to the murder. Moreover, the theme of prostitution, which occurs, as we have noted, throughout the entire novel, is indissolubly linked with Raskolnikov's "crime."

Raskolnikov's apprehension and interpretation of prostitution is the most important point in the formation and fulfillment of his plan. According to his logic, prostitution, and in particular Sonia's plight, serves as complete justification for the murder which he has committed. (p. 55)

Throughout the entire novel Raskolnikov is tormented by recurrent images of beating—violent beating and beating to death. These images haunt him. First, before his murder of the old woman, he dreams of a peasant beating a horse to death. Then, after the murder, he has a new dream: this time the police lieutenant, Ilya Petrovich, is beating Raskolnikov's landlady half to death. Finally, Raskolnikov relives in a dream his murder of the old woman. All of Raskolnikov's experiences, thoughts, and feelings seem to point to the fact that the supreme law of the universe and its highest imperative is murder. He commits a "murder of principle," as if obeying some kind of absolute command. Raskolnikov learns completely by accident from Lizaveta's conversation with a merchant in the Haymarket that the old woman will be alone the next day at seven o'clock in the evening; he has a superstitious reaction: "as if some kind of predetermined law in fact were operating here."

In describing how Raskolnikov carries out his plan for murder, Dostoevsky repeatedly and persistently stresses two points: on the one hand, there is Raskolnikov's desperate inner resistance to what he is doing; and on the other—the automatism inherent in his actions. These two points are psychologically inseparable from one another. (pp. 55-6)

The process by which Raskolnikov is exposed as the murderer and, more important, the process of Raskolnikov's own exposure of himself occur with the same force of necessity that drives him to commit the murder in the first place. Dostoevsky stresses clear parallels between the "crime" and the "punishment," between Raskolnikov's preparation for the murder and his own exposure of himself. After he has committed the murder, we see a sharp dichotomy between his thoughts and his actions. On the one hand, right up to the epilogue Raskolnikov's statements and avowals testify to the fact that he does not renounce his ideas, his theory, and his logical conclusions. On the other hand, something stronger than consciousness and will—a kind of instinct—drives him on toward self-revelation. (pp. 56-7)

A perspective is introduced in *Crime and Punishment*, a point of view, which imparts a historical dimension to the action. . . . Raskolnikov's theory and practice are illumined not only in the context of capitalism in Russia and in Petersburg in the sixties, but also in the context of that broad historical perspective which constitutes the particular background for the crime.

This historical perspective makes itself clearly felt for the first time in Raskolnikov's article "On Crime," which is a topic of discussion at Porfiry Petrovich's apartment. Raskolnikov illustrates his division of people into "ordinary" and "extraordinary" with such examples as Lycurgus, Solon, Mohammed, and Napoleon, who "were all criminals, to a man. Even if only because they violated the old law in giving a new one—law handed down by their fathers and considered sacred by society . . . these benefactors and architects of our humanity have been for the most part especially fierce at shedding blood." (pp. 57-8)

Figures from world history occur not only in the pages of Raskolnikov's article; they repeatedly crop up in his thoughts and his monologues and, in their own way, form one of the basic leitmotifs of the novel. The images of Napoleon and Mohammed come again to Raskolnikov's mind when he returns to his room after his encounter with the artisan who looks him in the eyes and utters solemnly: ''Murderer!'' . . .

In one respect, this historical perspective imparts a tragic intensity to Raskolnikov's design: because of it, his theory in his own mind receives philosophical substantiation and takes on the aspect of historical necessity. In another respect, however, when compared with the poverty of Raskolnikov's action, this perspective has an obviously ironical ring. A completely new interpretation arises as a result of the comparison of the lives of such historical figures as Lycurgus, Mohammed and Napoleon with the murder of an insignificant old pawnbroker woman. . . . Raskolnikov's entire fate in the novel is seen in the context of passionate self-affirmation, and affirmation of his ''idea''—the justification of murder by conscience. It is at the same time seen in the context of a no less sweeping self-negation. Raskolnikov's ironical view of his ''undertaking'' is one of the instances of this self-negation. (p. 58)

Particularly important for an understanding of the entire ideological conception of *Crime and Punishment* is the antithesis of Raskolnikov and Svidrigailov. The life and fate of Raskolnikov are characterized by a ''nonacceptance of the world,'' a principled battle against the world order; the life and fate of Svidrigailov, by an overacceptance, by a complete acquiescence to everything, good and evil, a kind of principled nonresistance to existence in all its aspects. . . .

Svidrigailov in every aspect is a ''man of the past.'' His whole life, reflecting the process of the degradation of the nobility, destines Svidrigailov for a knowledge of people on the most diverse levels of the social ladder, down to the most abjectly poverty-stricken dregs of the city. And thus Svidrigailov, with all his depravity, is bathed in an atmosphere of peculiar wisdom. Concerned with the affair of the ''brutal and, so to speak, fantastic murder,'' guilty of the rape of a young girl, guilty of the suicide of his servant, Filipp, evidently responsible for the death of his wife, Marfa Petrovna, Svidrigailov can, from a distance, sense in Raskolnikov his own kind of man, that they are birds of a feather, ''berries from the same tree.'' He instinctively detects Raskolnikov's ''crime,'' sets himself up as his shadow, and uncovers his secret. Svidrigailov's amoralism is sharply delineated; to possess Dunia he would do anything. His consistent amoralism is in contrast to Raskolnikov's frenzied moralism. (p. 60)

Svidrigailov, however, is capable of completely understanding not only Raskolnikov but also Sonia and the other characters. . . . Svidrigailov is capable of infinite awareness, with a capacity to combine in his thoughts and actions the most extreme contradictions. Svidrigailov, a man who in the past seduced a young girl, causing her to commit suicide, in his own words ''loves children.'' He contemplates suicide and relentlessly, inflamed with passion, pursues Dunia yet at the same time intends to marry another. He has a young fiancée; he makes her sit on his lap and brings her to tears with his unceremonious caresses. This same Svidrigailov, however, enters most intimately into the fate of the Marmeladov family, contributes to the support of its orphaned children, sincerely helps Sonia, refuses marriage, and provides for the future of his young fiancée. (pp. 60-1)

Svidrigailov has still one more important trait which is later characteristic of the true Dostoevskian hero (Myshkin, Aliosha). Svidrigailov declares to Dunia: ''You know, in general, how I think; I make it a rule to condemn absolutely nobody.'' He does not even condemn Raskolnikov. He allows everything and judges nothing. . . . [Svidrigailov] possesses an unlimited capacity for vice, an absolute nonresistance, and even submission, to evil, and at the same time a capacity for the highest moral order, with a limitless ability to seek out the good. He is a man, he says, and nothing human is foreign to him. He is allowed the whole range of human experiences, feelings, and actions.

Svidrigailov is a character with deep social and historical significance. ''Russians, in general,'' he says to Dunia during their last meeting, ''are people of a certain breadth. They are broad like their land, and they are exceptionally strongly drawn to the fantastic and the disorderly. But the trouble consists in being broad without any special genius. . . . As you know, Avdotia Romanovna, we don't have any especially sacred traditions in our educated society; it's as if somebody patched something together the best he could out of books, one way or another, or extracted it out of the ancient chronicles.'' (p. 62)

Svidrigailov provides a clear illustration of how the ''educated class,'' as Dostoevsky conceives it, is lacking in social-historical foundations. Svidrigailov is cut off from any deep social-historical roots. By the whole stamp of his personality he has little in common with the landowning nobility, yet at the same time he has no links whatever with the popular masses. He moves in a social vacuum. Svidrigailov serves to illustrate Dostoevsky's idea that the ''educated class'' has been alienated from the people since the time of the reforms of Peter I, and that the rapid surge of capitalism into Russian life after 1861 revealed this alienation in all its depth. The ''multiplicity of feelings'' in Svidrigailov, his capacity for everything, both good and evil, is at the same time his total indifference to everything, his complete spiritual emptiness, his irremediable melancholy and apathy (because of which he is even ready, he says, to fly off with Berg in a balloon), his absolute skepticism and nihilism—all these, after the last strong emotional attraction (Dunia) is lost to him—lead Svidrigailov inevitably to suicide. (pp. 62-3)

The antithesis of Raskolnikov and the police inspector, Porfiry Petrovich, is of great significance to the ideological conception of *Crime and Punishment*. Like Svidrigailov, Porfiry Petrovich is depicted as a man of exceptional awareness and intuition. In his role as investigator, the inspector immediately hits the mark in exposing Raskolnikov as the murderer. But Porfiry Petrovich is more than a clever and astute investigator. He is also shown to be a man with a deep knowledge of life. He not only immediately surmises that Raskolnikov is the murderer but also discerns Raskolnikov's personality and perceives his private thoughts and impulses. (p. 63)

When Raskolnikov meets the prostitutes at the entrance of the tavern in the Haymarket and his thoughts turn to the meaning of life (''constructing one's whole life on a square yard of space for a thousand years, through all eternity''), he cries out: ''It would still be better to live like that than die at the moment. To live and to live and to live and to live! No matter how you live, if only to live! How true that is! God, how true! What a scoundrel man is! And he's a scoundrel who calls him a scoundrel for that,'' he added a minute later. . . . Porfiry Petrovich has a different conception of this power of life: ''I know it's hard to believe,'' he says to Lizaveta's murderer, ''but give yourself up to life directly, without sophistry; don't puzzle over it. Don't worry. It will carry you straight to shore and set you on your feet. What shore? How should I know! I only believe you still have a lot for which to live.'' (p. 64)

The theme of Sonia is not only that of self-condemnation, but especially that of infinite self-renunciation, a willingness for the sake of her relatives and for others to accept utter disgrace and the most extreme humiliation—the selling of her body—and to sharing with a murderer his life's path. The meeting of Raskolnikov and Sonia is as much an ideological key to the novel as are Porfiry Petrovich's last words to Raskolnikov. Dostoevsky's emphasis on comparing the fates of Raskolnikov and Sonia has been noted time and again. . . .

Indeed there is the deepest consonance in the fates of these two, and in this consonance lies the ultimate meaning of the novel. Raskolnikov resorts to murder because of his extreme sensitivity to the suffering of others and above all to the suffering of his relatives. Sonia, because of the same sensitivity, becomes a prostitute. But Raskolnikov is driven to murder through extreme self-assertion; Sonia, to prostitution through extreme self-negation. (p. 65)

Sonia, moreover, possesses still another important trait—one that constitutes the transition to the image of the character, Mikolka. In the epilogue Dostoevsky mentions that the prisoners did not like Raskolnikov and were once even ready to kill him. They didn't like him because of his excessive pride and the distance he maintained from them, even in prison. By way of contrast, Sonia is extremely well-liked by everyone. "Sofia Semyonovna, ma'am, you're our tender, aching mother!" So spoke these coarse, branded convicts to this tiny, skinny creature.

The thematic line to the earth and to the people originates in Sonia; it is here that we find the keystone of Dostoevsky's world view. To Dostoevsky the idea of the earth is inseparable from the idea of the people and the motherland. The earth, the people, and the motherland are for him an indissoluble ideological complex. (p. 66)

Contact with the earth and repentance before it signify for Dostoevsky a return to a whole and integrated life. The order for atonement of guilt before the earth originates from Sonia, and it is Sonia, too, who in prison preserves a vital link with the masses. Raskolnikov's rebirth is effected not only through repentance before the earth but also through the restoration of an organic link with the people as a result of his acceptance of Sonia's "truth."

Lastly, the relationship of Raskolnikov and Mikolka is very important for an understanding of the meaning of the novel. The house painter Mikolka is not a secondary figure, but a character of tremendous symbolic significance. How is he depicted? (pp. 66-7)

Porfiry Petrovich in his last meeting with Raskolnikov describes Mikolka to him in this way:

First he's immature, still a child; and not that he's a coward, but sensitive, a kind of artist type. Yes, really. You mustn't laugh at me for explaining him like that. He is innocent and completely impressionable. He has feelings; he is a fantast. He can sing and dance, and they say he can tell stories so people gather from all around to listen. And he'll go to school and he'll laugh himself silly because somebody

somehow crooked a finger at him; and he'll drink himself senseless, not because he's a drunkard, but just every now and then, when people buy him drinks; he's like a child still. . . .

Mikolka is always presented to the reader in this way—in bursts of revelry and mirth. Mikolka is life itself in its untouched, fresh, pure, almost childlike form, life with its turbulent, varied, creative possibilities. Dostoevsky's idea consists in the fact that Mikolka, a grown man and at the same time a child, a Russian country lad capable of limitless merriment and daring, conceals a capacity for limitless self-abnegation and deeds of great heroism. (p. 67)

Nicholas M. Chirkov, "A Great Philosophical Novel," translated by Cerylle A. Fritts, in Twentieth Century Interpretations of "Crime and Punishment": A Collection of Critical Essays, *edited by Robert Louis Jackson, Prentice-Hall, Inc., 1974, pp. 49-70.*

MAURICE BEEBE (essay date 1955)

[*Beebe proposes that Raskolnikov is a character divided into three parts, with the intellectual, sensual, and spiritual sides of his personality in conflict. According to Beebe, each of these represents a different motive for Raskolnikov's crime and he contends that they are, respectively, his desire to administer justice, or "to play God," his need to prove himself as an "extraordinary man," and his will to suffer. Beebe further notes that each of these is embodied by a double: Luzhin represents the intellect, Svidrigailov the senses, and Sonia the spirit. For additional discussions of the various aspects of Raskolnikov's personality and Dostoevski's use of doubles, see J. Middleton Murry (1923), Jacques Madaule (1938), R. P. Blackmur (1943), Nicholas M. Chirkov (1945-49), and Edward Wasiolek (1964). Among other critics who discuss Raskolnikov's motives are Philip Rahv (1960), Joseph Frank (1966), and Michael Holquist (1977).*]

Crime and Punishment meets the test of unity in fiction: all the parts contribute to the whole, and the parts may be fully understood only when the whole is known. . . .

[The] ending is artistically and psychologically inevitable because the basic motive of regeneration is the same as the underlying motive for the crime. The spiritual principle of the novel, represented in part by Sonia, is equated with the passive will-to-suffering that impelled Raskolnikov to punish himself by murdering Alyona Ivanovna and her sister. Without the Epilogue much that precedes would seem confused and contradictory.

Theme and technique overlap. One of the ways in which Dostoevsky unifies his novel is through [his] technique of "doubles." The dual nature of his heroes is, of course, a commonplace of criticism. Because his protagonists are usually split personalities, the psychological and philosophical drama in a Dostoevsky novel is expressed in terms of a conflict between opposite poles of sensibility and intelligence, spirit and mind, passiveness and aggressiveness, self-sacrifice and self-assertion, God-man and Man-god, or, sometimes, "good" and "bad." . . . [The] struggle within Raskolnikov becomes physical, external action as he wavers between Svidrigailov, epitome of self-willed evil, and Sonia, epitome of self-sacrifice and spiritual goodness.

When we apply this thesis of doubles to the novel, we meet difficulties. The doubles are themselves complex personalities. (pp. 151-52)

Dostoevski during his imprisonment in Siberia. This photograph was taken shortly before his release. Courtesy of Ardis Publishers.

Perhaps the ambiguity results from a failure to recognize that man is not split into two parts, but divided into three: Mind, Body, and Spirit. The conflict in the tripartite Raskolnikov is a struggle between the intellectual, sensual, and spiritual parts of his nature. Each of these three parts corresponds to a reason or motive for his crime, and for each part, each motive, there is a separate alter ego: Luzhin, who stands for the intellect; Svidrigailov, who represents the senses; and Sonia, who is a symbol of spirit. . . .

[Within] Raskolnikov there are three motives which during the course of the narrative rise to the surface of his consciousness and become reasons for his crime. The first of these, his wish to rob and murder the old pawnbroker that he may administer justice by distributing her ill-gotten riches to the more deserving poor or, more probably, that he may finance the education that is to make him a benefactor of mankind, is *motive* only in that it is rooted in Raskolnikov's dominating characteristic, the egoistic pride that makes him want to play God. Pride combined with intelligence and unencumbered with spiritual or ethical feeling leads to the doctrine of expedient self-interest, which is the intellectual justification of the crime. Because this motive supplies the idea for the crime, it becomes a reason almost immediately—and almost as immediately it is repudiated as the real cause. (p. 152)

The final dismissal of "thinking" in the last few pages of the novel should come as no surprise, for throughout the book the intelligence is presented as essentially an evil power. (p. 153)

To refuse to give away half a coat is one thing; to steal a coat is another. But as long as man is not alone, self-interest begins

in the passive refusal to help others and leads almost inevitably to the aggressive use of others. Luzhin thinks of Dounia as a potential business and social asset, of sex solely in terms of possession. . . . The most unfeeling, cold-blooded, and self-willed crime in the novel is not Raskolnikov's murder of the old pawnbroker nor Svidrigailov's attempted seduction of Dounia, but Luzhin's false accusation of Sonia on the day of her father's funeral. In fact, if we look for the real symbolic antithesis of Sonia, we are much more likely to find it in Luzhin, the enemy who attempts to use her for his own selfish interests, than in Svidrigailov, the benefactor who makes a disinterested offering before her. (pp. 153-54)

Raskolnikov's first reason, his rational one, is dismissed even before Luzhin appears to make it look ridiculous. . . .

Raskolnikov's second motive also appears to him first in the form of a rational theory: his much-discussed notion of the "extraordinary" man who, above good and evil, may transgress any law that stands in the way of his uttering a "new word." . . .

Raskolnikov commits a murder not that he may *be* an "extraordinary" man but that he may *see* if he is one. (p. 154)

The real motive behind this second reason is suggested when Raskolnikov admits to himself that he knew *before the murder* that he would be shaken and horrified by it, that he would be unable to withstand the test. . . . He has, in a sense, committed a murder for the thrill of it, because of his fascination with the horror of the very idea; and the murder is, in part, an act of aggressive lust.

This motive is revealed symbolically in Raskolnikov's dream of the horse beaten by drunken peasants. (pp. 154-55)

The introvert Raskolnikov is, however, more masochistic than sadistic. The passive will-to-suffering is stronger within him than the aggressive will to make others suffer. Dostoevsky does little more than suggest the sadistic side of Raskolnikov in order that he may place more emphasis on the will-to-suffering which is finally revealed as the basic, underlying motive of his crime. The greatest advantage of Dostoevsky's technique of alter egos is that it permits him to write with greater economy and clarity than would otherwise be possible. Once he has established the link between the hero and his symbolic "double" or "triple," he can show both sides at once. Thus Svidrigailov not only stands for the sensualist in Raskolnikov but also represents the outer-directed form of the sensuality which in Raskolnikov is primarily inner-directed. . . .

Svidrigailov is usually described as self-willed. He is self-willed in the sense that he recognizes no spiritual force outside of himself—even the ghosts that plague him rise, he insists, from his own illness—but if *self-willed* implies that he controls his existence, then the designation is a misleading one. He is the victim of instincts within himself that he has not summoned into existence, but which are simply there. When he finally appears in person, he seems to have difficulty living up to the reputation that has preceded him, and he proves as capable of doing good as proficient in doing evil. (p. 155)

Although Svidrigailov appears to be a victim of the lust within him, he tries to rationalize his sensuality. . . . Because he has seen no evidence of anything else more noble or permanent than this natural instinct, his only purpose in life is to seek out new thrills.

Svidrigailov's view rests, of course, upon an unfavorable impression of human nature. And nothing ever happens to him that would disprove his theory that man is a brute. It is significant that all of his victims appear to be willing and that he, when the chance arises, is incapable of rape. . . .

The third and most important of Raskolnikov's three motives is his will to suffer. . . .

Only if we recognize this masochistic motive in Raskolnikov can we understand much of his conduct both before and after the murder. *Motive,* "a continuing and developing process," determines Raskolnikov's actions after the *reasons* are rejected. The absence of remorse may be explained not only by his sense of the chain of fate that led to the murder but also by his overwhelming conviction that he is the principal victim of his crime. (p. 156)

[This] sense of alienation is not the product of his obsession with the idea of murder, but something that appears to be deeply rooted in his nature. It revealed itself long before he thought of the murder. We know very little of his childhood, but the dream-episode of the beaten horse tells us that he was extremely sensitive, and we may conjecture that perhaps from that moment—or some such moment—he began to withdraw, denying in himself what he held in common with the human brutes. . . .

[The] alienation is cause as well as temporary result of the crime. When, after the murder, he tells Sonia, "Did I murder the old woman? I murdered myself, not her!" . . . , he means, I take it, that he has destroyed his separateness. For a time, his action has seemed to alienate him more than ever from his fellow men, but by the end of the novel he has identified his particular suffering with the suffering that is the natural lot of humanity: making this discovery, he joins society. What, intellectually rationalized, was to have proven his superiority and right to detachment from lesser men only reveals to him what he has in common with mankind. (p. 157)

As long as Raskolnikov seeks in suffering a masochistic pleasure demanded by his particular psychological make-up, his aloneness, the second motive remains dominant; when he recognizes in suffering a force greater than himself outside of himself, his motivation becomes spiritual and, in time, a conscious reason by which to live. . . .

Raskolnikov never repented of his crime because he did not hold himself responsible for the murder. . . . Man must suffer, he decides, because man, his intellect a delusion and its power demonic, trapped by his instinctive brutality and the conspiracy of his victims, does not will his destiny. . . . The revelation that comes to Raskolnikov through love and humility "in prison, *in freedom*" . . . , is inevitable because it is the obverse side, the *pro,* of the will-to-suffering, the *contra,* that has been throughout the entire novel his primary motivation. (p. 158)

Maurice Beebe, "The Three Motives of Raskolnikov: A Reinterpretation of 'Crime and Punishment'," *in* College English, *Vol. 17, No. 3, December, 1955, pp. 151-58.*

GEORGE GIBIAN   (essay date 1955)

[*A noted American scholar and translator, Gibian translated a number of Russian studies on Dostoevski into English. He asserts that traditional symbolism is an important element in the structure of* Crime and Punishment *and an important means by which Dostoevski presents his ideas. Gibian discusses water, vegetation, sun,*

air, the resurrection of Lazarus and Christ, and the earth as the outstanding symbolic imagery in the novel.]

In *Crime and Punishment* the reader, as well as Raskolnikov, must struggle to draw his own conclusions from a work which mirrors the refractory and contradictory materials of life itself, with their admixture of the absurd, repulsive, and grotesque. The oblique presentation of ideas was Dostoevsky's favorite technique. . . . (p. 981)

Traditional symbolism, that is, symbolism which draws on images established by the Christian tradition and on those common in Russian non-Christian, possibly pre-Christian and pagan, folk thought and expression, is an important element in the structure of *Crime and Punishment*. The outstanding strands of symbolic imagery in the novel are those of water, vegetation, sun and air, the resurrection of Lazarus and Christ, and the earth.

Water is to Dostoevsky a symbol of rebirth and regeneration. It is regarded as such by the positive characters, for whom it is an accompaniment and an indication of the life-giving forces in the world. By the same token, the significance of water may be the opposite to negative characters. Water holds the terror of death for the corrupt Svidrigaylov, who confirms his depravity by thinking: "Never in my life could I stand water, not even on a landscape painting." . . . Water, instead of being an instrument of life, becomes for him a hateful, avenging menace during the last hours of his life. (pp. 981-82)

When Raskolnikov is under the sway of rationalism and corrupting ways of thinking, this also is indicated by Dostoevsky by attributing to him negative reactions to water similar to those of Svidrigaylov. In Raskolnikov, however, the battle is not definitely lost. A conflict still rages between his former self—which did have contact with other people and understood the beauty of the river, the cathedral (representing the traditional, religious, and emotional forces), and water—and the new, rationalistic self, which is responsible for the murder and for his inner desiccation. (p. 983)

There is still left in Raskolnikov an instinctive reaction to water (and to beauty) as an instrument of life, although this receptivity, which had been full-blown and characteristic of him in his childhood, is now in his student days overlaid by the utilitarian and rationalistic theories. (In contrast to Svidrigaylov, who feels clearly and unequivocally depressed by the contemplation of beauty.) But Raskolnikov also realizes that his trends of thought have banished him, like Cain, from the brotherhood of men and clouded his right and ability to enjoy beauty and the beneficent influences of life symbolized by water; hence his perplexity and conflict. (pp. 983-84)

A cogent expression of the dominant significance of water to Raskolnikov is available in his dream of the oasis: "He kept day-dreaming, and his day-dreams were all so strange: mostly he imagined himself to be somewhere in Africa, in Egypt, in some sort of oasis. The caravan is resting, the camels are lying down peacefully; palms are growing in a circle all around; they are all having their meal, but he is drinking water all the time, straight from a little stream that flowed babbling close by. And it is so cool, and the wonderful, blue, cold water is running over stones of many colors and over such clean sand, which here and there glittered like gold." . . . (pp. 984-85)

The stream here represents Raskolnikov's desire to be saved from his criminal plan. He is attracted by the possibility of a restful, serene life (expressed here, as frequently elsewhere in the novel, by the cluster of images of water, vegetation, and restfulness) which would be very different from the horrible existence (represented in the first dream by the beating of the mare) into which, Raskolnikov subconsciously realizes, his life will develop if he perseveres in his determination to kill the pawnbroker.

The dream is the last attempt by his subconscious to hold out to him a way of life opposite to that to which his reason and will have committed him. It is a desperate and unheeded call which he scornfully rejects as a sign of a passing disease. Symbolism of water is the language used to express the conflict; Raskolnikov's reaction to water is a gauge of his inner state.

Related to the many references to the river and rain, and often closely associated with them, are two other groups of symbolic imagery: that of vegetation (shrubbery, leaves, bushes, flowers, and greenness in general) and that of the sun (and the related images of light and air).

In contrast to the dusty, hot, stifling, and crowded city, a fitting setting for Raskolnikov's oppressive and murderous thoughts, we find, for example, "the greenness and the freshness" of the Petersburg islands. Before the murder, Raskolnikov walked over to them and "the greenness and the freshness at first pleased his tired eyes, used to the dust of the city, to the lime, and the huge, enclosing, confining houses. Here there were no bad smells, no oppressive heat, no taverns. . . . The flowers particularly attracted his attention." . . . He made his way "into some bushes, lay down on the grass and fell asleep at once," and had the dream of the mare and Nikolka. The natural surroundings reawakened in him the feelings of his youth, through which he came close to avoiding his crime and to finding regeneration without having to pass through the cycle of crime and punishment. It is significant that it was in that particular setting that the dream foreshadowing the murder came to him, with the mare standing for the pawnbroker and all the victimized women of the novel, and with Raskolnikov—this time not a tormentor and criminal, but a child-bystander—sympathizing with the victim and wishing to save her.

By the same token, vegetation exercised the opposite effect on Svidrigaylov: it repelled him. In the inn on the night of his suicide, when he heard the leaves in the garden under his window, he thought, "How I hate the noise of trees at night in a storm and in darkness." . . . The forces symbolic of new life, vegetation as well as rain, either became hateful to him or were perverted by him to serve his destructive purposes, just as he had abused all the relationships of his life: in marriage giving hate instead of love, in presents to his fiancée aiming at causing embarrassment and shock instead of pleasure, and in his relations with his servant domineering and bullying instead of guiding.

Svidrigaylov's perversion of instruments of life is manifested in his dream of the fourteen-year-old girl whom he had driven to suicide—significantly, to suicide by drowning. He first dreams of a profusion of flowers. . . . The flowers suggest the last outburst of his craving for life which is doomed to end in failure; the luxuriant vegetation already contains something sickly and artificially exuberant and unnatural, and turns out to be a setting for the opposite of life—death; and the death is one which Svidrigaylov himself had brought about through a violation of the girl. (pp. 985-86)

Similarly to water and vegetation, sunshine, light in general, and air are positive values, whereas darkness and lack of air are dangerous and deadening. The beauty of the cathedral flooded by sunlight ought to be felt and admired: "The cupola of the cathedral . . . glittered in the sunshine, and in the clear air every ornament on it could be plainly distinguished." . . . During the service of the dead at the Marmeladovs', an occasion which helps to stir Raskolnikov's conscience and brings him closer to the beneficent influence of Sonya, "The room was full of sunshine; the incense rose in clouds; the priest read, 'Give unto her, O Lord, eternal peace'." . . . Sunshine is again associated with beauty, calm, and religion. The sun is a symbol of those forces of life which combat deadly theory. (p. 988)

When we turn to specifically Christian symbolism in *Crime and Punishment,* we find the outstanding images to be those of New Jerusalem, Christ's passion, and Lazarus. (p. 989)

The confession of Raskolnikov is described in terms reminiscent of Christ's passion on the road to Golgotha: he goes on "his sorrowful way." . . . When Raskolnikov reads in his mother's letter of Dunya's having walked up and down in her room and prayed before the Kazan Virgin, he associates her planned self-sacrifice in marrying Luzhin with the biblical prototype of self-assumed suffering for the sake of others: "Ascent to Golgotha is certainly pretty difficult" . . . , he says to himself. When Raskolnikov accepts Lizaveta's cypress cross from Sonya, he shows his recognition of the significance of his taking it—the implied resolve to seek a new life though accepting suffering and punishment—by saying to Sonya, "This is the symbol of my taking up the cross." . . .

One of the central Christian myths alluded to in the novel is the story of Lazarus. It is the biblical passage dealing with Lazarus that Raskolnikov asks Sonya to read to him. The raising of Lazarus from the dead is to Dostoevsky the best *exemplum* [example] of a human being resurrected to a new life, the road to Golgotha the best expression of the dark road of sorrow, and Christ himself the grand type of voluntary suffering. "I am the Resurrection and the Life" is the refrain in this book of a man who lost his life and found it again.

The traditional emphasis of the Eastern Church is on Resurrection—of the Western, on the Passion. In *Crime and Punishment* both sides are represented: the Eastern in its promise of Raskolnikov's rebirth, the Western in the stress on his suffering. Perhaps at least part of the universality of the appeal of the novel and of its success in the West may be due to the fact that it combines the two religious tendencies. (p. 990)

Christian symbolism is underlined by the pagan and universal symbolism of the earth. Sonya persuades Raskolnikov not only to confess and wear the cross, but also to kiss the earth at the crossroads—a distinctly Russian and pre-Christian acknowledgment of the earth as the common mother of all men. The earth is the source of fertility and the sanction for all family and community ties. . . . In bowing to the earth and kissing it, Raskolnikov is performing a symbolic and non-rational act; the rationalist is marking the beginning of his change into a complete, organic, living human being, rejoining all other men in the community. By his crime and ideas, he had separated himself from his friends, family, and nation, in one word, he had cut himself off from Mother Earth. By the gesture of kissing the earth, he is reestablishing all his ties. (pp. 991-92)

When Raskolnikov kisses the earth at the crossroads, the meeting place of men, a bystander sarcastically suggests that he may be saying goodby to his "children and his country" and leaving on a pilgrimage to Jerusalem. There is deep irony in the mocking words. Raskolnikov is indeed saying goodby—to Petersburg, for he will be sent to Siberia. At the same time he is taking farewell of his false ideal of the New Jerusalem. In another sense, he *is* now about to embark on a search for a new ideal, another New Jerusalem—and in this sense he will be a pilgrim, seeking personal regeneration which is to replace his earlier social-rationalistic ideal. Thus at the turning point of the novel, there is a fusing of the Christian symbolism of taking up the cross and New Jerusalem with the primeval symbolism of Gaea, Mother Earth. (p. 992)

The epilogue [to *Crime and Punishment*] has been called unprepared for, weak, and disjointed. These strictures are natural if we pay attention exclusively to "rational" aspects of the book and look for connections between the epilogue and the body of the novel only in the realms of outward plot and explicit statement. It is true that the regeneration of Raskolnikov is not presented as fully or as dramatically as the events leading to its inception; yet its beginning and its future course are indicated sufficiently by other means. The frequent undervaluation of the epilogue may be symptomatic of the lack of attention to Dostoevsky's communication through the symbolic pattern of the novel.

If we approach the epilogue with the various preparatory strands of images clearly in our minds, what do we find? Raskolnikov is in a Siberian city on the banks of "a broad, deserted river," a reprise of water imagery. He has relapsed into isolation from his fellow men; he is sunk into apathy and gloom: "He looked at his fellow-prisoners, and was surprised at them: how they all loved life! . . . What terrible agonies and tortures some of them had endured—the tramps, for instance. Did a ray of sunshine or the primeval forest mean so much to them? Or some cold spring in some far-away, lonely spot which the tramp had marked three years before and which he longed to see again as he might long to see his mistress, dreamed of it constantly, and the green grass around it, and the bird singing in the bush?" . . . Here . . . we see the state of the soul of the unregenerate Raskolnikov, the Lazarus before the rebirth, expressed by Dostoevsky through the symbolic imagery to which the novel has made us accustomed—water and vegetation. The love for life (which Raskolnikov does not yet comprehend) is represented by a spring with green grass and bushes around it.

When the regeneration of Raskolnikov begins, it is expressed in a manner still more closely linked to previously introduced imagery. His dream of the plague condemns Raskolnikov's own rationalism. It shows people obsessed by reason and will losing contact with the soil. . . . The dream is an expression of a new way of looking at reason and will—a way diametrically opposed to Raskolnikov's previous exaltation of those two faculties and rejection of all else. This dream of the plague, coming immediately before the start of the hero's regeneration, may also be another reminiscence of the Book of Revelation with its last seven plagues coming just before the millennium and the establishment of the New Jerusalem.

The epilogue then goes on to emphasize that it is the second week after Easter—the feast of Christ's passion, death, and resurrection; and that it is warm, bright spring—the season of the revival of dead nature, again a coupling of Christian and non-Christian symbolism of rebirth. . . . (pp. 992-93)

The crucial final scene . . . takes place on "a bright and warm day," and "on the bank of the river." . . . The river which Raskolnikov sees now is no longer a possible means for committing suicide nor a sight inducing melancholy; it is the river of life. Calm countryside opens up before Raskolnikov across the river, where he sees nomads' tents on a steppe flooded with sunlight. They seem to be men of the age of Abraham and his flocks, truly free and living people, not living dead as Raskolnikov had been. Now he can identify himself with these nomads, although he has only one thing in common with them, the most important thing of all—humanity. A short time before, he had been cut off from his fellow-prisoners and all mankind, even those who ought to have been very close to him, his friends and family. (pp. 993-94)

Then appears Sonya, and with her arrival comes the moment when Raskolnikov is suffused with love for his guide and savior. Sonya plays in the novel a part comparable to that performed by Beatrice and Lucia taken jointly in [Dante Alighieri's] *Divine Comedy.* . . . Sonya sees that all exists in God; she knows, and helps Raskolnikov to recognize, what it means to anticipate the millennium by living in rapt love for all creation here, in this world.

It was Sonya who had brought Raskolnikov the message of Lazarus and his resurrection; she had given him the cypress cross and urged him to kiss the earth at the crossroads. On the evening of the day when, by the bank of the river and in the presence of Sonya, Raskolnikov's regeneration had begun, the New Testament lies under his pillow as a reminder of the Christian prototype of resurrection which had been stressed earlier in the novel. Against the background of all the important symbols of the book, Easter, spring, Abraham's flocks, the earth of Siberia, the river, the dream, and Sonya, the drama within Raskolnikov's mind assumes its expressive outward form. (pp. 994-95)

George Gibian, "Traditional Symbolism in 'Crime and Punishment'," in PMLA, *70, Vol. LXX, No. 5, December, 1955, pp. 979-96.*

ALBERTO MORAVIA   (essay date 1956)

[*Moravia, a noted Italian novelist and critic, is considered the leader of the Neorealist school of writing in Italy. Here, he discusses the Marxist overtones of* Crime and Punishment *and describes the differences between the philosophies of Marxism and those expressed in the novel. Moravia defines Raskolnikov as a prototype of the Marxist people's commisar because of his indignance at the "social injustice and abject misery of Czarist Russia." Ultimately, however, Moravia argues, Raskolnikov deviates from Marxist thought because of the firm Christian grounding of his beliefs.*]

[*Crime and Punishment*] will for a long time remain an indispensable key to understanding what has happened in Russia and Europe during the last fifty years. Who is Raskolnikov? He is the intellectual before the advent of Marxism, indignant against the social injustice and abject misery of Czarist Russia, and resolved to carry out a demonstrative, symbolic action against these conditions. Raskolnikov had not read Marx and he admired Napoleon, the model for the entire 19th century of the superman; yet it is symptomatic that, contrary to the Stendhalian Julian Sorel [of Stendhal's novel *The Red and the Black*], another admirer of Napoleon, Raskolnikov does not dream of greatness, but rather of justice. And further, that his hate centres on a usurer, that is, on the extreme instance, according to the Marxist formula, of the exploitation of man by man. (p. 5)

Although he had not read Marx and regarded himself as a superman beyond good and evil, Raskolnikov was already, in embryo, a people's commissar; and, in fact, the first people's commissars came out of that same class of the intelligentsia to which Raskolnikov belonged, and possessed his identical ideas—the same thirst for social justice, the same terrible ideological consistency, the same inflexibility in action. And Raskolnikov's dilemma is the very same one that confronts the people's commissars and Stalin: "Is it right for the good of humanity to kill the old usurer (read: liquidate the bourgeoisie)?" So why should the Communists have such an aversion to Dostoevsky?

The reason is quite simple. Raskolnikov's hatred of the usurer has a Christian origin. In reality, this hate is the hate of the medieval Christian for commerce and profit-making, the irreconcilability of the Bible's teachings with banking and interest rates. This hate, this irreconcilability placed banking and commerce for centuries in the hands of the Jews until the day when the Christian peoples of Europe (and first among them the Italians) realised that they could be bankers or merchants and at the same time upright folk fearful of God, at peace with themselves and their religion. But Raskolnikov belonged, as did the people's commissars and Stalin, to a medieval country where banking and commerce were controlled by restricted racial and social groups, a backward peasant country attached to a still primitive and mystical Christianity. Thus for Raskolnikov banking and commerce are usury and the European and Russian bourgeoisie which practises usury becomes the old usurer; one must therefore kill the old usurer, that is, liquidate the bourgeoisie.

But at this point the until-then united roads of Dostoevsky and Marxism divide and branch off. The Marxists, who are not Christians, say: "Let us eliminate the usurers and go forward. After the death of the usurer we shall inaugurate a new society without classes and without usury. The creation of this society fully justifies the murder of the usurer." On the other hand Dostoevsky, who has remained a Christian, after having led us step by step through all the stages of a crime that he had doubtlessly meditated, fondled, and approved a thousand times in his heart, suddenly, with an unexpected *volteface* [change of plans], puts Raskolnikov in the wrong, that is, the Marxists and Stalin, and declares: "No, it is not right to kill, even if it be for the good of mankind. Christ has said: You must not kill." And in fact Raskolnikov repents, and reads the Bible together with Sonia. Dostoevsky swathes the end of his novel in a mystical aura: "But here begins a new story, the story of the gradual rebirth of a man, the story of his gradual regeneration, of his gradual passing from one world to another, of his advance towards a new and hitherto unknown reality." The Marxists, however, would have ended it thus: "But here begins the revolution."

This divergence between Dostoevsky and Marxism is the result of different evaluations of what constitutes evil. For the Marxists evil is the usurer, that is, the bourgeoisie; Dostoevsky, however, after having at first accepted this thesis, rejects it and comes to the Christian conclusion that the evil is not so much the usurer as the means adopted by Raskolnikov to eliminate the usurer, namely, violence. In the novel this evil as seen by Dostoevsky is not only represented by the violent death of the usurer, but also and above all by that of the innocent and pious Lizabeta, the usurer's sister, whom Raskolnikov murders so as to get rid of a witness to his crime. In short, for the Marxists evil does not really exist, since it is solely a matter of a social evil which can be eliminated by the revolution. But for Dostoevsky evil exists as an individual fact, in each man's heart, and expresses itself precisely in the violent means used by the revolution. With their historic and social

justifications the Marxists can wash clean even the blackest of consciences. Dostoevsky rejects this sort of cleansing and affirms the ineradicable existence of evil. (pp. 5-6)

Alberto Moravia, "The Marx-Dostoevsky Duel and Other Russian Notes," in Encounter, *Vol. VII, No. 5, November, 1956, pp. 3-12.**

RUTH MORTIMER   (essay date 1956)

[*Mortimer discusses the significance of the four dreams presented in* Crime and Punishment.]

[In *Crime and Punishment,* there] are four fully told dreams which concern the chief character, Raskolnikov. Each of these dreams leads into the next, illustrating both the significance of the dream in the complex psychology of a character like Raskolnikov and the use of the dream for dramatic atmosphere. In creating these dreams, Dostoevski has repeated events or reshaped ideas in terms of the unconscious of the character who is dreaming. Thus the succession of dreams forms a psychic pattern of motivation as valid as the course of external episodes.

The novel, as all its readers know, is centered around Raskolnikov's theory of the self-willed criminal, the extraordinary man, the Napoleon, who has a right to transgress the laws of ordinary men in order to carry out an idea. The test of this theory, the proof that Raskolnikov himself is one of these extraordinary men, is to be the murder of an old pawnbroker, and the novel opens with an experimental visit to the old woman's flat. The first four scenes of the book [the visit to the pawnbroker's flat; the meeting with Marmeladov; the letter from Raskolnikov's mother; the encounter with the drunken girl] form the substance of the first dream. (p. 108)

The four . . . scenes are associated in Raskolnikov's mind by the conscious theme, the state of poverty and degradation into which he has fallen. He counts his money, reckoning the kopecks given to the Marmeladovs, to the servant Nastasya for his mother's letter, and to the policemen, all taken from the amount which the old pawnbroker had just given him in exchange for his father's watch. Thus are they linked by purely mechanical means. That they have another, an implicit, connection is evident from the mode of their convergence and translation into the dream of the beaten horse.

This dream in outline moves swiftly. Raskolnikov as a child is accompanying his father to a requiem service for his grandmother and a visit to the grave of his brother. The road to the church runs past a tavern, and there the child is frightened by the rough sport of a group of drunken peasants. Outside the tavern stands a heavy cart with a mare, "a thin little sorrel beast," in the shafts. Mikolka, the owner of the cart, calls to his friends to get in, so that the mare can pull them all. When he finds that the horse cannot move the heavy load, he and his comrades beat her to death before the eyes of the child Raskolnikov. Not until the mare has been brutally killed with whips and crowbars before the grief-stricken child, does Raskolnikov awaken from this violent nightmare.

From the desperate confusion of his adult life, Raskolnikov has returned in this dream to his childhood, to the town of his birth, in order to find again the same security of that time so recently recalled to him by his mother's letter. The letter closed with the words, "Remember . . . when your father was living . . . how happy we all were in those days." This last sentence had taken hold of Raskolnikov; but the unconscious attempt to relive a moment of that innocent happiness fails, and the childhood experience in the dream evolves as one of intense fear and suffering, from which even his father cannot shield him. The preliminary details of the country landscape—the "grey and heavy day," the town "on a level flat as bare as the hand," the corpse, "a dark blur on the very edge of the horizon," the black dust of the winding road—all create an atmosphere of oppression and foreboding. The grotesque meeting with Marmeladov in the tavern is directly responsible for the dream setting.

Raskolnikov's contemplation of the act of murder means that he has renounced both family ties and early religious training. The dream is a return to both. Raskolnikov is now with his father, whose protection he has lost. In this loss he must feel an additional sense of his own responsibility toward his mother and his sister Dounia. Dounia and his father have a definite symbolic association with the murder. It is the ring which his sister had given him which he takes to the pawnbroker's on his first visit, and it is his father's silver watch which he uses as the excuse for his experimental visit to complete his preparations for the murder. (pp. 108-09)

In a sense, the struggling mare, so ridiculously unsuited to her heavy load, symbolizes a whole class of "sacrificial" women, of whom Raskolnikov's mother is one; but a more specific examination of the details of this part of the dream shows how closely Raskolnikov's meeting with the drunken girl and the stout sensualist on K——— Boulevard parallels this scene. At the time he compared the obvious plight of the unknown girl with that of Sonia, "the eternal victim," and of Dounia, at one moment at the mercies of Svidrigailov, at another selling herself to Luzhin as his fiancée. Identified in the dream with the mare, helpless under the primitive passion of her tormentor, these women are translated by Raskolnikov into animals for hire. . . . In the prolonged struggle of the mare is dramatized the senseless suffering and the strange endurance under that suffering of women like Sonia.

Because of the conflict in Raskolnikov's mind, the figures in this dream have a double significance. Behind Mikolka's act of violence lies the larger design of Raskolnikov's intended murder of the old woman. In this context, Mikolka is Raskolnikov himself, and the mare, his victim. Mikolka, warm-blooded, violent, is the opposite of Raskolnikov, the cold theorist; but the act of murder is the same. The peasant's reckless shout, "I feel as if I could kill her," is a direct statement of Raskolnikov's thought displaced into this situation. He hates his victim as Raskolnikov hates the old woman. As he brandishes the axe over the mare, he stands as Raskolnikov has imagined himself standing, administering the blows which receive their strength only from an elemental fury, not from reasoned theories. The cry, "You are not a Christian," repeatedly rises from the crowd; and throughout his preparations for the murder, Raskolnikov has tortured himself with that same accusation. In the death of the mare Raskolnikov sees the blood of the old woman. Had he examined his theory further, he would have seen that the old woman, once murdered, would be as useless to him as the dead mare to Mikolka, that his aid, little as it might be, would come from the living and not from the dead. (pp. 109-10)

In order to commit murder, Raskolnikov must stop believing both in the power of life and in the horror of violent death. The death scene of the mare is prolonged for two reasons: to define the character of the murderer and to imply the existence of a life-force in the animal which will resist the brutal attack almost to the breaking point of the murderer himself. Extended

to the human personality, this resistance may be involuntary. Raskolnikov is a witness, later in the novel, to an unsuccessful suicide attempt, the second failure on the part of a strange and hopeless woman. Or the life-force may be based on spiritual conviction. Sonia, even in despair, will not listen to Raskolnikov's suggestion of suicide as the way out of her responsibilities. Raskolnikov himself cannot take his own life, even in his delirium after the murder. Directly after the murder, he cannot believe in the ease of his own crime; he interrupts his hasty search of the old woman's rooms to make sure she is not still alive.

We have in this dream a tragic comparison of the adult Raskolnikov with the child. One suggestion may be traced back from a statement toward the end of the novel, in the description of a requiem service for Marmeladov's wife, Katerina Ivanovna: "From his childhood the thought of death and the presence of death had something oppressive and mysteriously awful." At the time of the dream, Raskolnikov's waking thoughts revolved around death, the violent death he would inflict upon the old woman. The dream concerns two forms of death, contrasting the ritual of the church service, the solemn peace of the graveyard, with the horrible death of the mare. In the child there is respect even for those whom he does not know; in the mature Raskolnikov the outward isolation and indifference to humanity are frightening. As a child, he loved the church, the ikons, the old priest; as a murderer, he hurriedly drops the old woman's crosses on the body of his victim.

Yet the terror which Raskolnikov experiences as a child over the death struggles of the helpless mare predicts his loss of control over the act of murder. The early emotions aroused in the dream are still within him. The basic feelings of pity and compassion, natural to the child, must still exist in Raskolnikov if he can suffer them so acutely in a dream. . . . The dream serves as a warning to him, a warning which he partially realizes as he shudders at the recollection but which is yet powerless against the fixation of his theories. He still believes in his motive for the murder, but, unconsciously, he searches for an argument which will invalidate that motive. He is not to be released until he recognizes that there are no rational answers to his questions. In the first moments after the dream, moments of supposed freedom from the obsession of the murder, he prays, "Lord, show me my path—I renounce that accursed . . . dream of mine." But the prayer is an empty prayer, and the word "dream" means not the theory of the murder as Raskolnikov intended it to mean but a fatal renunciation of the child of the beaten-horse dream.

The second dream, which follows the actual murder, has as its direct stimulus a summons to the police office, a coincidence involving not the expected accusation of murder, but only a charge of nonpayment of an I.O.U. to his landlady. The latent content of the dream is the act of murder. In this dream Raskolnikov starts up in terror at the sound of screams, blows, and curses coming from somewhere outside his room. In a moment he recognizes that the screams are those of his landlady and that her assailant is Ilya Petrovich, the "Explosive Lieutenant" of the police office scene. There is here a return of the fear Raskolnikov had had on facing that official in the police office, a subjective continuation of the beaten-horse dream and also a reflection of the sordid surroundings of his present lodgings, in which such an incident was not unlikely to occur. There is, more significantly, an adaptation of the murder, in which the hot-tempered official takes the place of Raskolnikov himself. (pp. 110-11)

This dream is imaginatively closer to his emotional experience of the crime than is the actual murder scene. There is no conclusion to the last part of this dream and intentionally no sense of Raskolnikov's awakening from it. His terror of revelation and his relief when he is loosed from the trap unharmed, begun in the police office scene, occur periodically throughout the remainder of the novel in a definite series of tensions and releases—with his questioning by Porfiry Petrovitch, his mock confession to the head clerk, Zametov, his fear of the evidence of an unknown informer—of which this dream is only a foreshadowing.

During the fever which follows the dream of Ilya Petrovitch and the landlady, the murder is so far repressed by Raskolnikov that he is aware only that he has forgotten something which he ought to remember. The indirect character of the dream—he is neither a witness to the action nor a participant in it, in spite of his emotional identification—defines this defensive state of mind before its manifestation in his illness. For Raskolnikov, the interval between the second and third dreams, longer than that between the first two, is one of alternate moods of terror and extreme lucidity. (p. 112)

The third dream is . . . an attempt to relive the murder, and its outline is closely drawn from the two specific scenes, the actual murder scene and Raskolnikov's compulsive return to the flat after it. The immediate stimulus is the accusation from the "man in the long coat," a stranger met on the street, who suddenly turns on Raskolnikov with the words "You are a murderer." Raskolnikov unconsciously reproduces the scene of his crime in a dream in order to place this stranger there, to discover what evidence he might have for his sinister charge. The confusion of this direct dream-return to the murder throws an interesting light upon Raskolnikov's changing attitude toward his act. His uncertainty at the beginning of the dream indicates a clear break in the motivation of the crime. Throughout the first part of the dream, Raskolnikov is not moving of his own accord but is following the stranger to the scene of the murder, attributing to him complete responsibility for the action, as though this dream figure were again a projection of his act, as in the first two dreams. Once Raskolnikov is in the house and on the staircase, however, the stranger, though still leading him, is not seen, and the details begin to draw on other threads of thought.

It is the disappearance of the stranger from the dream at this point which proves that here he is not fundamentally a projection of the murderer but actually Raskolnikov's conscience, stating the accusation and bringing him finally, of his own volition, to re-experience the murder. This dream is concentrated upon Raskolnikov himself performing the act of violence, whereas, in the preceding dreams, the murder was so far repressed that the furious peasant, Mikolka, and Ilya Petrovitch were the assailants. This repression was caused by an unconscious refusal to admit his own crime. The murder dream implies an extremely intricate psychic motivation: at the moment when Raskolnikov is able to recognize his act sufficiently to reproduce it as his own, the final impression is of failure. Here he finds himself incapable of murder, from a purely physical standpoint. Under the blows of the axe, the old woman sits as though made of wood and only laughs at his vicious attempt. The fact, here reduced to its simplest terms, is, in actuality, the growing realization that psychologically Raskolnikov cannot endure the effects of the murder.

Once again the essential dream image has a dual meaning. The old woman, sitting bent double so that Raskolnikov cannot see her face, is not presented in the dream as anything more than a victim. (pp. 112-13)

The final dream is objectified in several respects. It is not told directly in the novel but is remembered by Raskolnikov as a dream he had had while in the prison hospital in Siberia. Nor did he himself take any active part in it; he seems rather to have observed its progress. Thus it does not involve specific conscious experience and cannot be subjected to the same type of analysis as the preceding dreams. Its purpose is, in a sense, to present the thesis of the novel in slightly different terms. The entire dream is an allegory, with a fairly uncomplicated symbolism. Representing the final stage in Raskolnikov's renunciation of his theory, this dream is indicative also of a new attitude toward life. Raskolnikov has begun, unconsciously, to fit himself into society once more, to think again in terms of humanity. He visualizes the dangers of the extreme relativism which his theory required, dangers not only to society but also to the man of will.

This idea is translated in the final dream into a plague, a disease brought on by an attack of microbes "endowed with intelligence and will." The mad victims of these attacks believe themselves intellectually infallible and in complete possession of the truth. They cannot understand one another, and they can form no standards of judgment. . . . Only a few, a chosen people, will be saved from annihilation, and these will live "to found a new race" and "to renew the earth." The choice of words in the recollection of this dream is important. Here are brought together some of the key concepts of the novel and of Dostoevski's work in general: "the condemned," "the chosen," "intelligence," "will," "the sufferers," "truth."

In a discussion of crime, early in the novel, Dostoevski writes of Raskolnikov: "It was his conviction that [an] eclipse of reason and failure of will power attacked a man like a disease." In the dream his idea is reversed so that "intelligence and will" are the diseases of humanity. Raskolnikov's theory required the division of mankind into material and superior persons, those who merely existed and those with the will to act. The dream dictates a division also, but the chosen people are not the rationalists, the frustrated victims of the plague, but the quiet people like Sonia. (pp. 113-14)

The central theme of these four dreams is that of violence. Psychologically, each of them effects for Raskolnikov a catharsis, in a vivid manifestation of the dominant idea from both his conscious and his unconscious thought, a terrifying release of primitive forces. Before each such release, he is in a state of disease and delirium and close to complete loss of control. There is a constant attempt to shift responsibility, as though he believed himself incapable of such imaginings. Unconsciously, however, he is grasping seemingly isolated threads in these dreams: the sympathy of the child in the dream of the beaten horse, the awareness of the "crowd" in the second dream, the projected mockery of his efforts in the murder dream, the treachery of free will in the dream of the plague. Touching him at first indirectly, these images approach conscious realization until, in the final dream, Raskolnikov himself recognizes the means for his spiritual regeneration. The awakening from the last dream is literally an awakening from the "dream" of the murder. (p. 114)

Ruth Mortimer, "Dostoevski and the Dream," in Modern Philology, *Vol. LIV, No. 2, November, 1956, pp. 106-16.*

VYACHESLAV IVANOV (essay date 1957)

[*Ivanov is recognized as a leading member of the Russian Symbolist movement. This essay was written in the 1920s and published in English in 1957. In the following excerpt from his philosophical study of Dostoevski and his work,* Freedom and the Tragic Life: A Study in Dostoevsky, *Ivanov discusses Dostoevski's philosophy as manifested in* Crime and Punishment. *The critic analyzes Raskolnikov's self-incarceration, which the critic considers to be part of the crime process. Sonia urges Raskolnikov to rejoin humanity and Ivanov argues that Raskolnikov's confession and subsequent "salvation through atonement" advances Dostoevski's idea that one achieves redemption through suffering because in suffering one is joined to all humanity. According to Ivanov, Dostoevski believed that every crime is a sin of the society that allowed it to happen; therefore, everyone is guilty of every crime that is committed. This discovery, Ivanov states, culminates in Dostoevski's realization that "all humanity is—one man."*]

Crime and Punishment was Dostoevsky's first great revelation to the world, and the main pillar of his subsequent philosophy of life. It was a revelation of the mystic guilt incurred by the personality that shuts itself up in solitude, and for this reason drops out of the comprehensive unity of mankind, and thus also out of the sphere of influence of moral law. A formula had been found for negative self-determination by the individual: the name for it was—isolation. Raskolnikov's incarceration within himself, which was a result of the supreme decision of his free will (a will cut off from the universal whole), finds its final expression in the crime he commits. The sequence is not from crime to self-incarceration, but the converse: for from the latter arises the attempt to ensure the strength and autarky of the solitary personality—an attempt which, on the plane of external events, expresses itself as a crime.

It seemed to Dostoevsky that no symbolic action was expressive enough to convey a sense of the strange and almost incomprehensible—because so anomalous—spiritual condition of one who, like Cain, rejects God and man, shunning and fleeing all that lives. When Raskolnikov, after accepting the kindly gift that had been offered to him in error, later flung the small silver coin into the Neva, he knew that by this action he was severing the last bond between himself and mankind. Within the framework of the story we do not meet the rebel repentant of the murder he has committed, but merely one who refuses to endure the isolation which, under the mad illusion that it was a gauge of spiritual grandeur, he has voluntarily brought upon himself.

Worth noting is the dual character, deliberately emphasized by the author, of Raskolnikov's actions. On the one hand, all the circumstances, even the most trivial, array themselves in such a fashion that each separately and all collectively impel, adjure and force him to commit the deed that is apparently so contrary to his nature: a deed that results from some strange prompting from without, and is thereupon immediately regarded by Raskolnikov as an inexorable destiny. All his hesitation, all attempts to resist, are annulled by chance incidents, and conduce inevitably to the fatal step; as if his whole life were a torrent that with all its force surges irresistibly towards the huge precipice close ahead. On the other hand, Raskolnikov's whole environment appears to be in some sort a product of his imagination; and he who by chance puts the thought of murdering the old woman into his mind only gives utterance to something hidden and dormant within him. Raskolnikov himself creates this world of his. He is a magician of self-incarceration, and conjures up at will his miraculously created world of madness. He is also, however, the prisoner of his own phantom. He is

saved by Sonia, who asks only one thing of her beloved: that he should acknowledge the reality of man and mankind outside of himself, and should solemnly declare his acceptance of this new and, to him, strange faith by an act of confession before all the people. (pp. 78-80)

The announcement of salvation through atonement—of the manner in which the personality discovers itself anew in God, by overcoming its illusory autarky of isolation—finds its climax in the Apotheosis and the cult of the Passion. In suffering man is truly united to all humanity. Be it even on the thief's cross, he experiences the mystery of contact with Christ. The sacramental significance, and thus the justification, of suffering resides in the fact that the victim, without knowing that he does so, suffers not only for himself, but also for others; that he not only himself experiences salvation through suffering, but also, whether he knows it or not, is saving others.

Even "the human louse"—as Raskolnikov calls the old female moneylender—atones through her suffering for some part of humanity's common sin. But he is none the less an evil-doer, that madman who conceives himself to be an instrument of the justice that he cannot comprehend: he does not alleviate, but only adds to the world's sorrow. The murder of the old woman becomes, in a manner unforeseen by Raskolnikov, also the murder of the simple, innocent Elizaveta. She who brings salvation to the murderer, the teacher of repentance, the meek-hearted Sonia, who becomes a prostitute in order to save her parents, brothers and sisters from starvation, is also a victim for the sins of others. In contrast to Elizaveta, however, Sonia is at the same time herself a great sinner; for, albeit to save others, she deliberately and overweeningly takes upon herself not only suffering, but also the curse of another's deed, by making it her own. In the sinner who expiates his sin by suffering, there is an antinomy of curse and salvation—unless it happens that love has not been extinguished within him; unless, like Svidrigalov, he has not become incapable of loving. (pp. 81-2)

The act of suffering finds a recognition appropriate to its dignity in Raskolnikov's prostration of himself before Sonia, and in the obeisance made by Father Zosima before Dimitri [in **The Brothers Karamazov**]. This respect for suffering is the reason, according to Dostoevsky, why the Russian people adopt an attitude of deferential compassion towards "the unfortunate", as Russians call the criminal who is paying a just penalty.

The new theories of the irresponsibility of the criminal are to Dostoevsky objects of loathing: for they take from man his freedom and nobility, his divine dignity. No, the criminal must, and wants to, accept retribution for the act that expresses the metaphysical self-determination of his free will. It is unjust to deny to the criminal the responsibility that raises him above the beasts, and also to deny him the punishment that purifies him and gives him new being. Only the death-penalty, which forcibly curtails his Calvary of expiation, is to be condemned, since it is both hateful to God and also inhuman.

Nevertheless, every crime is not only a sin of the criminal, but also a sin of the community and of society: nobody has a right to say that he has no share in the guilt of the guilty. This opinion of Dostoevsky has its roots in the deepest and oldest strata of the national soul. (pp. 82-3)

Raskolnikov dreams of a pitiful old nag that is being tortured to death by a jeering, wild and drunken mob. Who bears the guilt of this disgusting act of cruelty? Obviously not only the wildly excited owner of the unfortunate animal, who is swaggeringly eager to amuse the company, but also every individual of those who in sheer wantonness add to a load that is already beyond the animal's strength.

Which, then, of the characters in the novel resembles this obscure victim? Sonia alone? No, also her father and mother—and Elisaveta. And not only they: also the murdered old moneylender, and above all the murderer himself, who has been condemned, or has condemned himself, to accomplish that which the collective will demanded.

Already in *Crime and Punishment* Dostoevsky discovers, to his horror, the truth which he later on expresses as a dogma: the truth of the guilt of all men, for all men and for everything. This dreadful discovery opens before him still another abyss, both terrifying and illumining: he begins to apprehend that all humanity is—one man. (pp. 84-5)

> *Vyacheslav Ivanov, in his* Freedom and the Tragic Life: A Study in Dostoevsky, *edited by S. Konovalov, translated by Norman Cameron, Noonday Press, 1957, 166 p.*

LEONID P. GROSSMAN   (essay date 1959)

[Grossman is one of Russia's most prominent Dostoevski critics. His major works on Dostoevski were published before World War II; these were later censored by the Soviet regime because Grossman had delineated Western literary trends and artistic elements in Dostoevski's writing. In the following essay, originally published in 1959 in Tvorchestvo F.M. Dostoevskogo, *Grossman characterizes* Crime and Punishment *as primarily a social novel with strong philosophical and psychological overtones. He admires Dostoevski's vivid portrayal of St. Petersburg and observes that the "widely developed background of a capitalistic capital determines . . . the character of the conflicts and drama" of the novel. Like F. I. Evnin (1948), Grossman praises the construction of* Crime and Punishment, *asserting that all the action of the novel is "connected to the center and circumscribed by a single circle." In addition, Grossman discusses Dostoevski's skillful use of both visual description and speech patterns to bring his characters to life. For additional commentary on the structure of* Crime and Punishment, *see Ernest J. Simmons (1940) and Konstantin Mochulsky (1947).]*

Crime and Punishment firmly establishes Dostoevsky's characteristic form. This is his first philosophical novel on a criminal basis. It is also at the same time a typical psychological novel, partly even a psychopathological one, with rather noticeable traces of the police novel-feuilleton and the "black" or morbid-adventure novel of the English school (Dostoevsky was captivated by examples of all these genres in his youth). But it is, above all . . . a social novel, which places in the thick of action and under dialectic fire the large, painful themes of the contemporary political moment in all the intensity of the battle of ideas and social forces. (p. 650)

Crime and Punishment is first of all a novel of a big city in the nineteenth century. A widely developed background of a capitalistic capital determines here the character of the conflicts and dramas. Saloons, taverns, houses of prostitution, slum hotels, police stations, the attic of a student and the apartment of a money-lender, streets, alleys, courtyards and back yards, Haymarket Square and the "canal"—all of this produces the criminal scheme of Raskolnikov and marks the stages of his complex inner struggle.

Depicting this specifically Petersburgian "landscape and genre," in the tradition of the early "Natural School," Dostoevsky makes concrete the abstract idea of his composition. With inimitable talent and striking sharpness, he etches the urban struggles which he unfolds with that living palpability which evokes in the reader the feeling of full life and irresistible authenticity.

The principle of how to present this "account of a certain crime" was not immediately found. Dostoevsky had jotted down three basic forms for his novel: (1) narrative in the first person or a confession of the hero himself, (2) the ordinary form of narration from the author's point of view, and (3) a mixed form ("the narration ends and the diary begins"). The first form (*i.e.,* the "I-narrative") in turn presumed two versions: recollection of an old crime (eight years ago) and the testimony during the trial. (pp. 650-51)

[The] principle of narration in the author's person worked out in the process of [Dostoevsky's] artistic searchings, a narration which as much as possible stays with the main hero, gave to *Crime and Punishment* that tightness, unity, and concentration of action which make this novel in terms of composition the best of Dostoevsky's works. The relating of events almost always from the subjective position of the main hero (a vestige, in the final version, of the original first-person narration) transforms the entire novel into a peculiar internal monologue of Raskolnikov, which gives the whole history of his crime an exception wholeness, tenseness, and fascination.

The concentration of a big novel on one topic which extends throughout all its action is accomplished here by Dostoevsky with rare mastery and persistence. Everything is connected to the center and circumscribed by a single circle. From the very first paragraphs of the novel the reader learns that a murder is being planned. For the duration of six chapters he is entirely in the grip of ideological motives for the crime and the material methods of its preparation. Immediately after the murder, Dostoevsky presents Raskolnikov's inner struggle, complicated most by its psychological drama—his plan, his theory, his conscience, as well as his outer struggle with authority in the person of the strongest of opponents, Porfiry Petrovich, and partly in the person of the police clerk Zametov. All who surround him are pulled into the murderer's drama. (p. 652)

The drama's line of development is interrupted nowhere. It is not broken by side episodes. Everything serves a single action, shading and deepening it. The tragedy of the Marmeladov family is the strongest argument for Raskolnikov's theory and action, as is the Svidrigaylov motif in his sister's fate arising out of his mother's letter, which rapidly receives a full and deep development in the novel. Svidrigaylov's character does not function at all as an independent, parenthetical episode. He illuminates Raskolnikov's fate and personality marvellously.

The portraiture in the novel is distinguished by an exceptional compression and expressiveness. The heroes' exteriors are shown with a particular concentrated expression, recalling later famous portrayals, for example Stavrogin or Grushenka [in *The Possessed* and *The Brothers Karamazov*], but not yet requiring large canvases and a background of deep perspective.

In *Crime and Punishment* Dostoevsky is, according to Pushkin's favorite epithet, a "fast" painter. A few immediate strokes take the place of the usual pages of broad descriptions. In the six lines of the old woman's portrait there is a forceful concentration of typical features, giving an image of such amazing lifelikeness that much of what is unexpected in Raskolnikov's deed is made clear to the reader by this externally repulsive appearance of the revolting money-lender: "This was a tiny, dried up little old lady of about sixty with sharp and evil little eyes, with a small sharp nose and a bare head. Her light, slightly grey hair was greasily smeared with oil. Around her skinny, long neck, which looked like a chicken leg, was wrapped some sort of flannel rag and on her shoulders, in spite of the heat, there dangled a mussed and yellowed fur jacket.'' (p. 653)

Dostoevsky's philosophical novel gives a rich collection of Petersburg types, resembling the albums or ''panorama'' of the outstanding illustrators of the period of the 1840's-60's. In the sharp, synthesizing images of *Crime and Punishment,* which are so characteristic and lifelike, even in spite of the occasional presence of a grotesque style (''he linked up with these little clerks for the very reason that both of them had crooked noses: the nose of one was crooked to the right, and the other's to the left''), Dostoevsky appears as an original and piercing draughtsman from nature. . . .

The persons are characterized not only by their external appearances, but also by their speech peculiarities. [One critic] correctly notes the stylistic ''office jargon'' of Luzhin, the ironic carelessness of Svidrigaylov, and the ecstatic ornamentality of Razumikhin. It is also not difficult to catch the sarcastic businesslike way of talking of the legal scholar Porfiry and the affected politeness of Marmeladov's civil servant's speech, lavishly supported with Church Slavisms for the expressive painting of the shattering story of his falls and sufferings. In addition to their diction, the ''verbal gestures'' and the intonational systems of the heroes are apparent in the novel with ineffaceable variety. (p. 654)

In *Crime and Punishment* the internal drama is in a peculiar manner carried out into the crowded streets and squares of Petersburg. The action is constantly transferred out of narrow and low rooms into the noise of the capital's streets. It is in the street that Sonia sacrifices herself, it is here that Marmeladov falls dead, Katerina Ivanovna bleeds to death on the pavement, Svidrigaylov shoots himself on the avenue before a watch-tower, Raskolnikov attempts to confess publicly on Haymarket Square. Many-storied houses, narrow alleyways, dusty squares and hump-backed bridges—the entire structure of a big city of the mid-century looms as a heavy and merciless hulk above the dreamer of limitless rights and possibilities of the lone intellect. Petersburg is inseparable from the personal drama of Raskolnikov: it is that fabric upon which his cruel dialectic draws its designs. The Czar's capital sucks him into its saloons, police stations, taverns, hotels. Over this scum and foam of life with its drunkards, debauchers of minors, prostitutes, usurers, detectives, tuberculosis, venereal diseases, murderers, madmen, there looms, with the strict design of its architectural lines, the city of famous architects and sculptors, luxuriantly sprawling its ''magnificent panorama'' and hopelessly breathing out a ''spirit deaf and dumb.''

In view of the complexity of the inner scheme, the unity and fullness of its basic tone of narration is amazing. It is as if it absorbs all the intonations and shadings of the individual scenes and images (such varied motifs as those of Sonia, Svidrigaylov, Raskolnikov, Marmeladov, and the old woman) in order to merge them into one whole. The constant returning to these dominating and alternating themes imparts to the novel the symphonic sound of contemporary Petersburg, merging the enormity of its many voices, its weeping, its screams, into the unified, powerful whole of Raskolnikov's tragedy. (pp. 655-56)

> *Leonid P. Grossman, ''The Construction of the Novel,'' translated by Natalie Bienstock, in ''Crime*

and Punishment'' by Feodor Dostoevsky: A Norton Critical Edition, the Coulson Translation, Backgrounds and Sources, Essays in Criticism, *edited by George Gibian, revised edition, W. W. Norton & Company, Inc., 1975, pp. 650-56.*

PHILIP RAHV   (essay date 1960)

[*Essentially a social and historical critic, Rahv came to the forefront of American literary criticism during the 1930s when he helped found the left-wing periodical* Partisan Review. *In all his critical work, he focuses on the social, cultural, and intellectual milieu which influences art and is in turn influenced by it. Rahv maintains that in* Crime and Punishment *Dostoevski intentionally withholds information about Raskolnikov's motive for his crime from the reader. According to Rahv, Dostoevsky is the first novelist to manifest uncertainty in a character, a trait which Rahv considers to be the novel's greatest strength. This contention is disputed by Joseph Frank (1966). For other views on Raskolnikov's motive, see Maurice Beebe (1955) and Michael Holquist (1977).*]

[Is *Crime and Punishment*] the type of narrative nowadays called a psycho-thriller? Yes, in a sense it is, being above all, in its author's own words, the psychological account of a crime. The crime is murder. But in itself this is in no way exceptional, for the very same crime occurs in nearly all of Dostoevsky's novels. Proust once suggested grouping them together under a single comprehensive title: The Story of a Crime.

Where this novel differs, however, from the works following it is in the totality of its concentration on that obsessive theme. Virtually everything in the story turns on Raskolnikov's murder of the old pawnbroker and her sister Lizaveta, and it is this concentration which makes the novel so fine an example of artistic economy and structural cohesion. Free of distractions of theme and idea, and with no confusing excess of over-ingenuity in the manipulation of the plot, such as vitiates the design of *A Raw Youth* and reduces the impact of *The Idiot, Crime and Punishment* is the one novel of Dostoevsky's in which his powerful appeal to our intellectual interests is most directly and naturally linked to the action.

The superiority of this work in point of structure has been repeatedly remarked upon, but what has not been sufficiently noted is its extraordinary narrative pace. Consider the movement of Part I, for instance. In this comparatively short section . . . , we get to know the protagonist fairly well, to know the conditions of crushing poverty and isolation under which he lives and the complex origins of his ''loathsome scheme.'' . . . (pp. 393-94)

[In the] first section of seven chapters a huge quantity of experience is qualitatively organized, with the requisite information concerning the hero's background driven into place through a consummate use of the novelistic device of foreshortening, and with the swift narrative tempo serving precisely as the prime means of controlling and rendering credible the wild queerness of what has been recounted. For this wild queerness cannot be made to yield to explanation or extrinsic analysis. To gain our consent—to enlist, that is, our poetic faith—the author must either dramatize or perish, and for full success he must proceed with the dramatic representation at a pace producing an effect of virtual instantaneousness. To have secured this effect is a triumph of Dostoevsky's creative method—a triumph because the instantaneous is a quality of Being rather than of mind and not open to question. As the vain efforts of so many philosophers have demonstrated, Being is irreducible to the categories of explanation or interpretation.

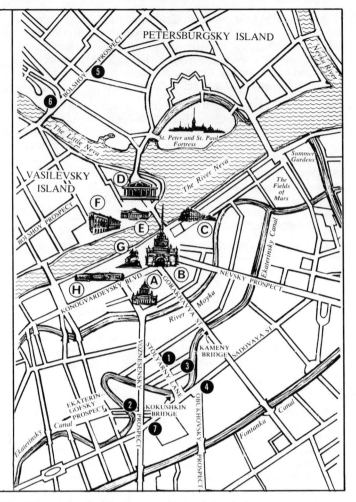

The St. Petersburg of Crime and Punishment

Places important in *Crime and Punishment*

1   Raskolnikov's room (No. 9, Srednaya Meshchanskaya Street).
2   The pawnbroker's room.
3   Sonya's room.
4   Haymarket Square (where Raskolnikov bows and kisses the earth).
5   Place of Svidrigaylov's suicide.
6   Tuchkov Bridge.
7   Yusupov Gardens.

Important Petersburg Locations

A   St. Isaac's Cathedral.
B   The Admiralty Building.
C   The Winter Palace and the Ermitage (Tsar's Palaces).
D   The Bourse (Stock Exchange).
E   Academy of Sciences.
F   Leningrad University.
G   Falconnet's statue to Peter the Great.
H   The Senate.

General Note

Petersburg was built early in the eighteenth century by Peter the Great, close to the Gulf of Finald, in a marshy region around the river Neva, which flows westward to the sea. A system of canals and small rivers drained the location of Petersburg; the city continued (and continues to this day) to have the character of a city criss-crossed by rivers and canals, with many bridges.

The area around the Haymarket, where Sonya and Raskolnikov lived, was a slummy section. Most of the locations which Dostoevsky had in mind have been identified; artists have painted the houses and even the doorways important in the novel. For the identification of houses referred to in *Crime and Punishment*, the editor is indebted to an unpublished radio script prepared, for Leningrad Radio, by Dostoevsky's grandson, Andrey Fyodorovich Dostoevsky, who is a specialist in the study of the Petersburg backgrounds of Dostoevsky's writings, and to *Literaturnye pamyatnye mesta Leningrada* (Leningrad, 1959), a book edited by A. M. Dokusov, which discusses Leningrad places important in literature.

On the map, it is possible to trace exactly Raskolnikov's various walks (his three trips from his room to the pawnbroker's, as well as his usual route to the university, with a view of the city from the bridge), Sonya's route from Raskolnikov's room to her own, and Svidrigaylov's last journey before his suicide.

The observant reader will note that "Kameny Bridge" (p. 1 in our text of the novel) ought to read "Kokushkin Bridge." (Dostoevsky's text used only the initial, "K—— Bridge." Somewhere along the line, an editor substituted "Kameny"—erroneously, as the map makes clear, since Dostoevsky's text shows that Raskolnikov must have turned towards Kokushkin Bridge on his way to Alena Ivanovna.)

A map of St. Petersburg at the time of Crime and Punishment. *Locales significant to the novel are cited. Reproduced from* Crime and Punishment, *by Feodor Dostoevski, A Norton Critical Edition, edited by George Gibian. Copyright © 1975, 1964 by W.W. Norton & Company, Inc. By permission of W.W. Norton & Company, Inc.*

The artistic economy, force and tempo of Part I is sustained throughout the novel. (The epilogue, in which hope and belief play havoc with the imaginative logic of the work, is something else again.) There is no wasted detail in it, none that can be shown to be functionally inoperative in advancing the action and our insight into its human agents. And it is important to observe that the attaining of this fullness and intensity of representation is conditional upon Dostoevsky's capacity to subdue the time element of the story to his creative purpose. Readers not deliberately attentive to the time-lapse of the action are surprised to learn that its entire span is only two weeks and that of Part I only three days. Actually, there is no real lapse of time in the story because we are virtually unaware of it apart from the tension of the rendered experience. Instead of time lapsing there is the concrete flow of duration contracting and expanding with the rhythm of the dramatic movement.

Least of all is it a chronological frame that time provides in this novel. As the Russian critic K. Mochulsky has so aptly remarked [see excerpt above, 1947], its time is purely psychological, a function of human consciousness. . . . Truly, Dostoevsky succeeds here in converting time into a kind of progress of Raskolnikov's mental state, which is not actually a state but a process of incessant change eating into the future

and expanding with the duration it accumulates, like a snowball growing larger as it rolls upon itself. . . . (pp. 394-95)

This effect is partly accomplished by the exclusion from Raskolnikov's consciousness of everything not directly pertaining to his immediate situation. From beginning to end he is in a state of crisis from which there is no diversion or escape either in memory or fantasy. The import of what he thinks, feels, and remembers is strictly functional to the present. Thus he thinks of his mother, who is involved in the action, with distinct alternations of feelings, while his dead father hardly exists for him. He belongs to the past, and so far as Raskolnikov is concerned the past is empty of affect. The one time he evokes his father's figure is in the anguished dream of the beating to death of the little mare, and his appearance in that dream is singularly passive, manifestly carrying with it no charge of emotion. This dream, enacting a tragic catharsis, is introduced with calculated ambiguity. Is the dreamer actually remembering an episode of his childhood or is he imagining the memory? . . . [The] mare stands above all for Raskolnikov himself, and in embracing her bleeding head in a frenzy of compassion it is himself he is embracing, bewailing, consoling. He is present in the dream not only as the little boy witnessing an act of intolerable brutality but as at once its perpetrator and victim too. The dream's imagery is entirely prospective in that it points ahead, anticipating the murder Raskolnikov is plotting even while exposing it as an act of self-murder. Its latent thought-content is a warning that in killing the pawnbroker he would be killing himself too, and it is indeed in this light that he understands his deed afterwards when, in confessing to Sonia, he cries out: "Did I murder the old woman? I murdered myself, not her! I crushed myself once and for all, forever." (pp. 395-96)

Yet, for all his living in the present, Raskolnikov wills and acts with his whole past back of him; and it is for a very good reason that we are not permitted to gain a privileged understanding of his past in the sense of entering a series of his mental states anterior to the action. By denying us such intimacy the author effectively prevents us from rationalizing the mystery of the crime and its motive—the mystery which is never really solved but toward the solution of which everything in the novel converges. Now the study of Dostoevsky's manuscripts has shown that he was himself disturbed no end by the indefiniteness and uncertainty of Raskolnikov's motive, and he wrote a note reminding himself that he must once and for all clear up the uncertainty and isolate the "real" motive in order "to destroy," as he put it, "the indefiniteness and explain the murder this way or that way." . . . Fortunately he was able to forget this injunction as the novel progressed. For his basic idea of his hero's motivation is such as to identify it with the totality of his consciousness, and to have changed that conception to a more conventional one would have led to the withering of that fine insight; and what that insight comes to, in the last analysis, is that human consciousness is inexhaustible and incalculable. It cannot be condensed into something so limited and specific as a motive. The consciousness is ever obliging in generating a sufficiency of reasons, but it is necessary to distinguish between reasons and motives. Not that motives have no existence; they exist, to be sure, but only on the empirical plane, materializing in the actual practice of living, primarily in the commitment of action. Existentially speaking, the acting man can be efficient and self-assured only insofar as his consciousness is non-reflective. Raskolnikov, however, is above all a man of reflection, and his crime is frequently described in the book as a "theoretical" one, "theoretical" not only in the sense of its being inspired by a theory but also in the sense that theory, that is to say abstraction, is of its very essence: no wonder he carries out the murder in the manner of a sleep-walker or of a man falling down a precipice. The textual evidence shows that what his crime mainly lacks is empirical content, and that is what some critics had in mind, I think, in defining it as a pure experiment in self-cognition. Thus it can be said of this murderer that he produces a corpse but no real motive. His consciousness, time and again recoiling upon itself in a sickening manner, consumes motives as fast as it produces them.

Crime and Punishment may be characterized as a psycho-thriller with prodigious complications. It is misleading, however, to speak of it as a detective story, as is so often done. It is nothing of the sort, since from the outset we know not only the murderer's identity but are also made to enter into some of his innermost secrets. True, the story is almost entirely given over to detection—not of the criminal, though, but of his motive. Inevitably it turns out that there is not one but a whole cluster of motives . . . , and if the criminal himself is in his own fashion constrained to take part in the work of detection it is because he is soon lost in the maze of his own motivation. Never quite certain as to what it was exactly that induced him

to commit murder, he must continually spy on himself in a desperate effort to penetrate his own psychology and attain the self-knowledge he needs if he is to assume responsibility for his absurd and hideous act. And this idea of him as the criminal in search of his own motive is precisely what is so new and original in the figure of Raskolnikov.

His knowing and not knowing is in a sense the worst of his ordeal. He is aware of several motives that keep eluding him as his thought shifts among them, and there are times when they all seem equally unreal to him. To sustain himself in the terrible isolation of his guilt he must be in complete possession of a single incontrovertible motive representing his deepest self, his own rock-bottom truth. (pp. 397-99)

Dostoevsky is the first novelist to have fully accepted and dramatized the principle of uncertainty or indeterminacy in the presentation of character. In terms of novelistic technique this principle manifests itself as a kind of hyperbolic suspense— suspense no longer generated merely by the traditional means and devices of fiction, though these are skilfully brought into play, but as it were by the very structure of human reality. To take this hyperbolic suspense as a literary invention pure and simple is to fail in comprehending it; it originates rather in Dostoevsky's acute awareness (self-awareness at bottom) of the problematical nature of the modern personality and of its tortuous efforts to stem the disintegration threatening it. Thus Raskolnikov, like Stavrogin and other protagonists of Dostoevsky's, is represented throughout under the aspect of modernity (the examining magistrate Porfiry Petrovitch sees him very specifically as "a modern case") understood as spiritual and mental self-division and self-contradiction. It is in this light that the search for the true cause of the crime becomes ultimately intelligible, the search that gives the novel at once its form and meaning, taking us where no psycho-thriller before or after ***Crime and Punishment*** has ever taken us, into a realm where only the sharpest psychological perception will see us through and into another realm still where our response to ideas is impetuously solicited: ideas bearing on crime and its relation to psychic illness on the one hand and to power and genius on the other; ideas about two kinds of human beings, ordinary and extraordinary, with the former serving as mere material for the latter who arrogate to themselves the right "to overstep the line" and remove moral obstacles at will; ideas concerning the supernal value of suffering and the promise of deliverance in Christ.

The principal characters (Raskolnikov, Svidrigailov and others) are the carriers of these ideas, and if we are not to sever the unity of thought and action, theory and practice, prevailing in the Dostoevskyean world, it is necessary to take their ideas for what they are, without reducing them, with the purely psychological critics, to a species of "interesting" rationalization, or, with the formalistic critics, to mere "fictive matter" drawn fortuitously from the intellectual sphere. That we must first of all regard the ideas as dramatic motivation goes without saying; but that should not deter us from also accepting them as given on the level of thought. "I killed not an old woman but a principle," declares Raskolnikov. What is that principle and why does he want to kill it? The answer to such questions has been much simplified or, worse, still, credulously taken for granted.

From the Christian standpoint Raskolnikov is easily enough perceived to be a kind of Lazarus whom Sonia strives to raise from the dead. Yet if he comes forth from the tomb it is only after experiencing the ecstasy and terror of having touched for one moment the secret springs of freedom and power. "What, then, is to be done?" asks Sonia. This is indeed the fateful question which reverberates throughout the whole of Russian literature and to which all the leaders of Russian thought, from Chaadayev to Lenin, sought to provide an answer. Raskolnikov, too, accepts the challenge. "Break what must be broken," he replies, "once and for all, and take the suffering on oneself. . . . Freedom and power! Over all trembling creation and all the antheap! . . . That is the goal, remember that!" No wonder that though apparently renouncing that goal in yielding to Sonia's entreaties that he save himself through penance and submission, nevertheless remains essentially unrepentant to the end. At the very least it can be said that he remains so deeply divided in his mind as to give himself up more because of confusion and despair than because of any real change of heart. About his regeneration we are told only in the epilogue, when at long last the pale sickly faces of the murderer and the saintly prostitute become "bright with the dawn of a new future." But this happy Siberian aftermath is the beginning of something altogether new and different. As the author observes in the last paragraph of the text, it "might be the subject of a new story but our present story is ended." We, as critical readers, cannot overmuch concern ourselves with such estimations of ultimate reconcilement and salvation. Our proper concern is with the present story, with the story as written. (pp. 400-03)

Philip Rahv, "Dostoevsky in 'Crime and Punishment'," in Partisan Review, *Vol. XXVII, No. 3, Summer, 1960, pp. 393-425.*

KONRAD ONASCH (essay date 1961)

[*This essay originally appeared in German in Onasch's* Dostojewski als Verführer, *which was published in 1961. The critic here discusses the juxtaposition of "true religiosity and organized religion" in the scene depicting Marmeladov's death.*]

One sentence in Dostoevsky's "symbol of faith" credo describes Sonia's [religious] position exactly: "Even if somebody proved to me that Christ was outside the truth, and it *really* was true that the truth was outside Christ, then I would rather remain with Christ than with the truth." By "truth" here Dostoevsky undoubtedly had in mind Christian dogma. It is possible, then, for Sonia, as in Schleiermacher's theology of "feeling" and "consciousness" to stand with Christ as the embodiment of all that is good and noble in man, quite apart from the truth and teachings of the church. . . .

It is well known that church and dogma play no role in Dostoevsky's work, though a few scenes in *Notes from the House of the Dead* may have some relevance to them. In *Crime and Punishment,* however, we are confronted directly with a moving encounter between the pious soul and the church—from which, despite her participation in its rituals, she is nonetheless inwardly emancipated. The scene is that of the dying Marmeladov. . . .

The death of the ecstatic drunkard Marmeladov is described in chapter 7, Part II of *Crime and Punishment.* He has been run down by a horse and carriage. Raskolnikov carries him into his wretched flat. Dostoevsky depicts his death with consummate artistry. . . . Marmeladov's death is marked by unusual agitation and unseemliness: the room is crowded with curiosity-seekers, cigarettes dangling perpetually from their lips; with police officials; with a continual bustling in and out; with the whimpering of Marmeladov's children and the frightful wheezing, dry cough of his wife. All the indescribable misery of

phantasmagoric Petersburg seems to have been concentrated in this room. . . . After the confession and extreme unction a conversation takes place between the priest and an embittered Katerina Ivanovna who is completely upset and distraught. Dostoevsky's characterization of the priest is entirely devoid of irony. He is, indeed, perhaps the only real person in this fantastic throng of human spectres. A cleric who has grown gray in service, he is only doing his duty. He says what he has probably said countless times in these circumstances: "God is merciful, look to the Almighty for help." Katerina Ivanovna reacts bitterly, though, when the priest bids her forgive her dying husband. "'Eh, Father! Those are words, just words! Forgive! . . . What's this talk about forgiveness! As it is, I have forgiven!' A deep and terrible coughing fit interrupted her words. She coughed up into her handkerchief and thrust it at the priest to show him as she clutched her chest with the other hand. The handkerchief was covered with blood. The priest bowed his head and said nothing." At this very moment, in fact, when Katerina Ivanovna with the children against the background of the crowd has knelt for the confession, a quiet power enters—*the* opponent of an organized, hierarchical church which rules dogma, souls and lands: . . . just *how* this power makes its appearance is breath-taking:

> Then timidly and inaudibly a girl squeezed through the crowd. Strange indeed was her sudden appearance in that room, in the middle of beggary, rags, death and desperation. She, too, was in rags. She was cheaply dressed, but tricked out gutter-fashion, according to the rules and taste of that special world whose shameful purpose was all too apparent. Sonia paused on the landing, right on the threshold. She did not cross the threshold, though, and looked like some lost soul, oblivious of everything, it seemed, unconscious of her fourth-hand gaudy silk dress with its long absurd train and the immense crinoline that filled the entire doorway, so inappropriate here, and her bright-colored shoes, and the parasol she scarcely needed at night, but which she took with her, and her foolish round straw hat with the bright red feather on top. From under this hat, which was cocked at a rakish angle, gazed a thin, pale, frightened little face, with parted lips and eyes immobile in terror. Sonia was a small, thin girl of about eighteen, fairly pretty, blonde, with remarkable blue eyes.

Once again we encounter the "grotesque." It is not necessary to realize at once that the bright red feather on Sonia's hat recalls the red feather on Mephistopheles' hat in order to grasp the daring alienating effect of this strange juxtaposition. Marmeladov breathes his last in the arms of this alienated girl, this religious soul. Katerina Ivanovna, who cannot forgive her husband, speaks almost (or perhaps even consciously) in defiance of Christ's last words on the cross: "He's got his!" I know of no other scene in nineteenth-century literature in which true religiosity and organized religion are more vividly set off against each other than here; but its genius will only reveal itself to one who has first thoroughly grasped and analyzed the elaborate contrasts and intricate style of the grotesque—this intermingling of eros and religion. (pp. 106-08)

Konrad Onasch, "The Death of Marmeladov," translated by Robert Louis Jackson, in Twentieth Century Interpretations of "Crime and Punishment":

A Collection of Critical Essays, *edited by Robert Louis Jackson, Prentice-Hall, Inc., 1974, pp. 106-08.*

EDWARD WASIOLEK (essay date 1964)

[*Wasiolek is a contemporary American scholar of Russian literature, and his* Dostoevsky: The Major Fiction *is considered an important study of Dostoevski's life and writings. In the following excerpt, Wasiolek analyzes Dostoevski's use of Gothic character types, sentimental situations, and the double in* Crime and Punishment. *In addition to citing Sonia and Svidrigailov as doubles of Raskolnikov, Wasiolek draws a parallel between Raskolnikov and Marmeladov. Wasiolek states that* Crime and Punishment *signals the introduction of the theme of crime in Dostoevski's work, and he concludes with an extensive discussion of the opposition of divine and human logic in Raskolnikov. For further commentary on Dostoevski's use of the double, see J. Middleton Murry (1923), Jacques Madaule (1938), R. P. Blackmur (1943), Nicholas M. Chirkov (1945-49), and Maurice Beebe (1955).*]

There is in *Crime and Punishment* a little of everything that Dostoevsky had experimented with in the forties and the early sixties: character types, Gothic elements, sentimental situations, social elements. . . . But under the pressure of the dialectic that is brought to maturity in the [*Notes from the Underground*], many of the elements are transformed. (p. 60)

Svidrigaylov and Alyona Ivanovna are not far removed from the conventional villains of the gothic novel, yet both are raised to profound moral significance. Svidrigaylov has flaxen hair, pale blue eyes, red lips, and a masklike face; he carouses in the dens of the city, seduces young girls, and mysterious crimes are reported about him. He embodies all the artifice and melodrama of the gothic villain, but he is also something more. As Raskolnikov's double and as the bronze man who can commit crimes without feeling any pangs of conscience, the terror and mystery which was artifice and melodrama become, at least in part, the terror and mystery of the will and the moral nature of man.

Alyona Ivanovna has sharp evil eyes, a pointed nose, hair smoothed with grease, a flannel rag wrapped around a neck that looks like a chicken leg. She is not just a victim, but the kind of victim Raskolnikov needs. For him, she represents the heart of the corrupt society against which he revolts. Her image is almost mythic: a kind of female Minotaur devouring the prey of society until a white knight is able to destroy her. She is "gothic," yet she is real, and she is real because she answers to one of the deceptive motivations Raskolnikov gives himself: the killing of evil to do good. (p. 61)

The Marmeladov subplot is almost a paradigm of the sentimental situation, which had already influenced many of Dostoevsky's early works, especially *The Insulted and the Injured*. . . . But in *Crime and Punishment* the sentimental situation takes on a new significance; it becomes a tool of moral perception.

Consider the scene in which Marmeladov and Raskolnikov return to Marmeladov's apartment: Katerina, her arms clutching her breast, is walking back and forth, consumptively coughing; she is breathing unevenly, her eyes are flashing unnaturally as if from fever; her lips are parched, and the reflection of a dying candle flickers on her consumptive, pale, sickly face. In the corner a seven-year-old boy is trembling and crying from a recent beating, and his nine-year-old sister with a torn shirt and arms as thin as matchsticks tries to comfort him. Her eyes

follow with fear the nervous walking of her mother. A third child, a six-year-old, is asleep on the floor. And on the threshold, kneeling down and ready to accept his punishment, is Marmeladov. The scene is classically sentimental and repeats situations Dostoevsky has used before: weeping children, a sick wife, joblessness, a daughter in prostitution, a husband who from weakness has been reduced to stealing money from his family and to drinking from the gains of his daughter's prostitution. But something has changed! Katerina, for instance, refuses to close the door of the adjoining apartment from which billows tobacco smoke; she insists on leaving the door open to the staircase from which the smells pour in; and she refuses to open windows, even though the room is very stuffy. She *wants* to irritate her coughing and feels satisfaction in coughing up her blood. She has apparently just beaten the little boy, whose misery has driven her to desperation. It is clear that she is intentionally irritating her misery, and seeking to exaggerate it. The same is even more true of Marmeladov. At the tavern where we first meet him, he is described as a drunk with a bloated greenish face, puffed eyelids, hysterical eyes, and ruffled hair. He holds his head with his hand, the table is sticky with liquor, his clothes are awry, the buttons barely hanging on and wisps of hay sticking to them after five nights on a hay barge. He has been, in his own words, reduced to destitution by drink and misfortune. . . . [This] is what Dostoevsky had called "self-interested suffering" in *The Insulted and the Injured*.

The conventional sentimental scene in which circumstances *bring* an unfortunate individual to misery and destitution is transformed into one in which the individual *looks* for his misery and destitution, and derives some strange satisfaction from displaying it and even exaggerating it. *Marmeladov has, clearly, chosen his destitution.* Five days before his confession to Raskolnikov, when the solution to all his difficulties was entirely in his hands, he was at the peak of happiness; his wife, delighted with his job, was calling him darling and protector; suddenly he throws it all over, steals the last kopeks from his children's mouths, spends it all on drink, sells his uniform, and ends up taking kopeks earned by his daughter from her prostitution. Why does he do this? Marmeladov himself gives us a hint when he says: "I am a dirty swine; but she is a lady! I may be a beast, but my dear wife, Katerina Ivanovna, is a highly educated lady and an officer's daughter. Granted, I am a scoundrel; but she, sir, is an educated lady of noble heart and sentiments. And yet—oh, if only she'd take pity on me!" She is a lady, and he is a beast—he insists on it—but it is because he is a beast and she is a lady that he cannot help dragging both her and himself down. He cannot live up to her high feelings and sublime pride. . . . When he realizes that he will never match the dream of her past life, he begins to drink and to pursue the opposite. . . . If he cannot participate in her life, he will make her participate in his life. . . . What he wants is to be accepted as a person, not as someone who couldn't live up to her former husband. And it is by his lowness that he attempts, and succeeds, to turn [Katerina Ivanovna's] attention to him.

Marmeladov is Raskolnikov's double. Like Raskolnikov, he has been swept out of society; he has nowhere to go and is, or feels, persecuted by society. This is obviously one of the reasons Raskolnikov feels sympathy for him and is interested in him. More important, Marmeladov repeats the basic psychology of Raskolnikov. In his desire for self-worth he hurts himself and those he loves. Unable to command the respect and admiration of his wife through good acts (hard work, position, sobriety), he forces her attention through bad acts (theft, drunkenness, and destitution). The pleasure he gets out of having his hair pulled is analogous to the pleasure Raskolnikov gets in having society punish him for his wrongdoing.

If much of Dostoevsky's old material is welded into new tools of perception and interpretation, the most important theme of **Crime and Punishment** is new. This is the sudden emergence of ''crime'' as the dominant theme of the novel and of almost all the works that follow. (pp. 61-4)

Crime becomes Dostoevsky's great theme, not because he had a dark, secret sympathy for crime, but because it expresses and dramatizes so beautifully the metaphysic of freedom that had taken form in the **Notes**. Crime becomes precisely the theme that permits him to wed drama and metaphysic so masterfully. Why? What is the criminal for Dostoevsky? He is someone who has broken a law and thus put himself outside of society. Every society draws a narrow circle of what is permitted, and every human being carries within him the impulses and dreams of acts that pass the pale of the permitted. Crime is this ''might be'' which the forces of law, convention, and tradition hold at bay. It lies in the undefined regions beyond the clear line that society has drawn about us. In those regions man's nature is unrealized, undefined, and undared. Society, like individual man, is for Dostoevsky an arbitrary power, constructed by arbitrary wills for purposes of self-protection. What is ''lawful'' is arbitrary; and what is unlawful, *crime,* is arbitrary. The criminal merely opposes his arbitrary will against the arbitrary will of society. He transgresses no sacred canon; he merely dares what the timid and unfree dare not do. It is only when one is free of the domination of society's will that one is free to exercise one's will. A free act is necessarily a ''criminal'' act, in the special sense of being beyond what is permitted by law and custom. It is in this sense that all of Dostoevsky's great heroes are criminals; all of them step outside the circle of the permitted into the undefined region of the unpermitted. (p. 65)

Dostoevsky sees the opposed impulses in Raskolnikov's nature as the signs of two kinds of ''logic'' that are basic to the human condition. They correspond to the two poles of his moral dialectic. There is God, and there is the self. Each has roots in the real impulses of men. There is no bridge between these two natures, and man is poised in fearful anxiety with every choice between them. Raskolnikov carries these twin impulses throughout the novel; and in the second half of the novel, he confronts them objectified in the persons of Sonia and Svidrigaylov. His choice between these impulses is dramatized as a choice between Sonia and Svidrigaylov. The skill with which Dostoevsky expresses this choice in structure, incident, and detail is commensurate with the refinement of his dialectic.

Sonia and Svidrigaylov are doubles of Raskolnikov in that they embody in a fully developed manner the two impulses he carries within him. The first half of the novel is structured by Raskolnikov's visits to Alyona Ivanovna; the second half of the novel by his visits to Sonia and Svidrigaylov. Sonia, the symbol of true rebirth in faith, balances antithetically the image of the murdered Alyona Ivanovna, the symbol of false rebirth. Raskolnikov now visits Sonia instead of Alyona, and instead of death, there is birth in the reading of the story of Lazarus. If the murder is the central point of the testing of the rational principle, the confession becomes the central point of the testing of Raskolnikov's rebirth. Appropriately, since these two scenes balance each other, there is a rehearsal for the confession as there was for the murder scene. To be sure, Raskolnikov

attempts to corrupt Sonia, and his listening to her reading of Lazarus and his confession do not come from compassion and repentance. But Sonia remains uncorrupted, and the mysterious attraction Raskolnikov feels for her is already a sign of Raskolnikov's acceptance of what she represents.

In going to see Svidrigaylov, Raskolnikov goes toward the destructive idea that had ruled his life in the first half; he goes to meet the ultimate consequences of the idea. Everything about this line of action is characterized by limitation and futile circularity. Raskolnikov and Svidrigaylov hunt each other out to learn from the other ''something new,'' but when they meet— significantly near Haymarket Square, where Raskolnikov's idea grew into decision to act—they are like mirrors reflecting each other's dead idea. Sonia had offered Raskolnikov a new word; Svidrigaylov, the old word, only in grimmer, more naked terms than he had known it. Between the two Raskolnikov wavers, coming to a decision only with the death of one part of himself, only after Svidrigaylov—the objective correlative of the part— has acted out his play of self-destruction. (pp. 80-2)

Raskolnikov carries within him the antithetic poles of Dostoevsky's dialectic: human logic and divine logic. There can be no compromise between them. The English word ''crime'' is exclusively legalistic in connotation and corresponds to the ''human logic''; but the Russian word for crime, *prestuplenie,* carries meanings which point both to human and divine logic. *Prestuplenie* means literally ''overstepping,'' and is in form parallel to the English word ''transgression,'' although this word no more than ''crime'' is adequate to translate *prestuplenie* because of its Biblical connotations. But *prestuplenie* contains both poles of Dostoevsky's dialectic, for the line of the permitted which one ''oversteps'' may be drawn both by human or by divine logic.

Because the two impulses of self and God battle within him to the very end, Raskolnikov's confession is at once a sign of his self-will and his acceptance of God. He confesses because he will no longer be pursued, and it is only by his confession that he can provoke the punishment and hence the image of society he wants; yet he is simultaneously being moved toward the kind of punishment that Sonia wants him to accept. The battle between the two principles continues to the very end. Dostoevsky resolves the conflict by legislating Raskolnikov's conversion. The conversion is motivated, as indeed suicide or a new crime is motivated, in Raskolnikov's character. Dostoevsky does not really have grounds for ending the conflict, and it would have been much better, I believe, to have ended the novel with Raskolnikov's confession. The confession itself is at once . . . a self-interested and a selfless act. This is to say that the confession would have dramatized at the very end of the novel the fury of the conflict, and the effort of the will to penetrate and corrupt even the holiest of gestures.

But Dostoevsky was not yet ready to grant so much to his antagonists. He had dramatized masterfully the strength and power of the self, and his very skill had increased the probability of the self's domination of Raskolnikov. But he had also discerned the springs of another ''nature'' in Raskolnikov's compassion, and he had set this against the powerful and cunning self-interest of Raskolnikov's nature. For the moment Dostoevsky settles the issue by nudging Raskolnikov into God's camp. But Dostoevsky will not be satisfied with his own solution, and again and again he will grant more and more to his antagonists, so as to test his belief that man can be reborn into selflessness. (pp. 83-4)

Edward Wasiolek, in his Dostoevsky: The Major Fiction, *1964. Reprint by The M.I.T. Press, 1971, 255 p.*

JOSEPH FRANK   (essay date 1966)

[*Frank is a noted contemporary American scholar. In the following essay, he asserts that Dostoevski wrote chiefly ideological novels and that any "realist" traits of his works do not derive from a depiction of the normal range of social experience; rather, their sources include the doctrines of the Russian radical intelligentsia which Dostoevski would then recreate to their most extreme consequences. In addition to discussing the contemporary philosophies that influenced* Crime and Punishment, *Frank examines the duality of the impetus behind Raskolnikov's crime and explores the techniques by which Dostoevski reveals his motivation. For additional discussions of Raskolnikov's motive, see Maurice Beebe (1955), Philip Rahv (1960), and Michael Holquist (1977).*]

If Dostoevsky has one claim to fame, it is certainly as a great *ideological* novelist—perhaps not the greatest, for that would involve comparisons with Sterne and Cervantes, but at least the greatest in the 19th century. And if his status as such is so generally accepted, it must be because his creative imagination was stimulated primarily by the problems of his society and his time rather than by his personal problems and private dilemmas. Or, to put the point the other way round, he was always able to project these private dilemmas in terms that linked up with the sharp conflict of attitudes and values occurring in the Russia of his time.

This is the reason why psychology in Dostoevsky's novels, vivid and unforgettable though it may be, is invariably only an instrument or tool used for a thematic purpose that is ultimately moral-ethical and ideological in import—ideological in the sense that all moral values are connected in Dostoevsky's sensibility with the future destiny of Russian life and culture. More particularly, he saw all moral and ethical issues in the light of the inner psychological problems posed for the Russian intelligentsia by the necessity of assimilating (and living by) alien Western European ideas. . . . We cannot take even the first step towards understanding his major aim as a novelist, if we do not realise that he wished to portray the *new* types and modalities of this perennial Russian inner struggle springing up all around him in the turbulent and evolving Russia of the 1860s and 1870s.

It is from this point of view that we must take very seriously Dostoevsky's claim to "realism" for his novels—a claim which, in my opinion, is entirely justified. But let us be clear about the nature of this "realism" and the nature of Dostoevsky's imagination. He knew very well that he was not a "realist" in the sense of getting the normal, middle range of private and social experience on the page. This was why he spoke of his bent for "fantastic realism"; but what he meant by this term was something very clear and very specific. He meant that the process of his creation would invariably start from some doctrine that he found prevalent among the Russian radical intelligentsia. It was there in black-and-white in the magazines or novels everybody was reading, and in this sense was perfectly "real"—particularly since Dostoevsky believed in the reality of ideas. But then he would take this doctrine and imagine its most extreme consequences *if* it were really to be put into practice and carried through in all its implications; and this was where his psychological gifts came in to aid him in dramatising the "fantasy" of this idea relentlessly translated into life.

Dostoevsky was perfectly well aware that the extremism he depicted in such a character as Raskolnikov was not at all the way in which the vast majority of the radical intelligentsia would hold the doctrines in question, or the way in which it would affect their lives. . . . I think the best way to define Dostoevsky's particular uniqueness as a novelist is to call him a writer whose imagination naturally inclined to the *conte philosophique* [philosophical tale], but who, happening to be born in the century of the realistic novel, possessed enough psychological genius to give his characters verisimilitude and to fuse one *genre* with the other. (pp. 30-1)

If Dostoevsky invariably began with some doctrine of the Russian radical intelligentsia, what was his starting-point in [*Crime and Punishment*]? . . . Ordinarily, this novel is linked with [Dostoevsky's] prison-term in Siberia, first because of his use of this setting in the Epilogue, and secondly because this period was supposed to have focused his attention on the problem of crime and the psychology of the criminal. None of this needs to be denied; but if this were the whole story, it is impossible not to wonder why Dostoevsky did not write **Crime and Punishment** when he came out of imprisonment and wrote so many other things instead. The truth is that the novel as we know it could not have been conceived before 1865 because the situation of Russian culture that Dostoevsky could imagine as Raskolnikov had not existed before that time.

If we look at Russian culture in the early and mid-1860s—and this means, for our purposes, the doctrines of the radical intelligentsia—we can easily spot the "reality" that is incarnated in Raskolnikov. In the first place, all the radical intelligentsia were convinced that the theories of English Utilitarianism solved all the problems of ethics and personal conduct. (p. 31)

It is by no means accidental that we find Raskolnikov's crime planned on the basis of a Utilitarian calculus; this was the very essence of the matter for Dostoevsky. And we see too that . . . Raskolnikov believes that his reason can overcome the most fundamental and deeply rooted human feelings. . . .

Ordinary criminals, Raskolnikov had theorised, rob and steal out of need or viciousness; and they break down at the moment of the crime, leaving all sorts of clues scattered about, because they inwardly accept the justice and validity of the law they are breaking. The irrational forces of their conscience interfere with the rational lucidity of their action. But, he was convinced, nothing of the kind would happen to him because he knew that his so-called crime was not a crime. Reason had persuaded him that the amount of harm his crime would do was far outweighed by the amount of good it would allow him to accomplish. Hence his irrational conscience would not trouble and distort his reason, and he would not lose control of his nerves and make blunders.

This is one way in which the very conception of Raskolnikov springs from the ideology of the Russian radicals in the mid-1860s, and shapes the basic psychological conflict in the book between reason and the irrational. But another essential ideological component is derived from the evolution of Russian left-wing ideas between 1860 and 1865. In this period, for various reasons, we find a shift from the ideals of Utopian Socialism, with its semi-religious glorification of the people, to that of an embittered élitism, which stressed the right of a superior individual to act independently for the welfare of humanity.

The most important event in Russian culture between 1863 and 1865 was a public quarrel between two groups of radicals—the old Utopian Socialists, and the new Nihilists. (p. 32)

[Dostoevsky's aim in *Crime and Punishment*] was to portray the inescapable contradictions in this radical ideology of Russian Nihilism. To do so, he adopted his usual procedure (in his mature work) of imagining its ''strange, incomplete ideas'' put into practice by an idealistic young man whose character traits embody its various conflicting aspects. Now Dostoevsky knew very well that the emotional impulses inspiring the average Russian radical were generous and self-sacrificing. They were moved by love, sympathy, altruism, the desire to aid, heal and comfort suffering—whatever they might believe about the hard-headedness of their ''rational egoism.'' The underlying foundation of their moral nature was Christian and Russian (for Dostoevsky the two were the same), and in total disharmony with the superimposed Western ideas they had assimilated, and on whose basis they believed they were acting. Hence over and over again in Dostoevsky's major works we find him dramatising the inner conflict of a member of the Russian intelligentsia torn between his innate feelings and his conscious ideas, between the irrational (which, by the way, is never Freudian in Dostoevsky but always moral as in Shakespeare) and the amorality of reason in one form or another.

In *Crime and Punishment,* Dostoevsky set himself the task of portraying this conflict in the form of a self-awakening, the gradual discovery by Raskolnikov *himself* of the unholy mixture of incompatibles in his ideology. This is why Raskolnikov seems to have one motive for his crime at the beginning of the book and another towards the end, when he makes his famous confession to Sonia. Many critics have pointed to this deeming duality of motive as a weakness in the novel, an artistic failure on Dostoevsky's part to project his character unifiedly. On the other hand, Philip Rahv [see excerpt above, 1960] quite recently has maintained that this is precisely what makes the book great—that in failing to provide a clear and single motive Dostoevsky reveals ''the problematical nature of the modern personality,'' or the startling fact ''that human consciousness is inexhaustible and incalculable.''

Both these views, however, are equally and egregiously wrong. The whole point of the book lies precisely in the process by which Raskolnikov moves from one explanation of the crime to another, and in so doing discovers the truth about the nature of the deed he committed. (pp. 33-4)

Why, for example, does Dostoevsky begin his narrative just a day before the actual commission of the crime, and convey Raskolnikov's *conscious* motivation in a series of flashbacks? One reason, of course, is to obtain the brilliant effect of dramatic irony at the close of Part I. For the entire process of reasoning that leads to Raskolnikov's theory of the altruistic Utilitarian crime is only explained in detail in the tavern-scene, where Raskolnikov hears his very own theory discussed by another student and a young officer; and this scene is the last important one just before the crime is committed. (It may be well, incidentally, to recall that when the officer doubts the possibility of anyone committing such a crime, the student retorts that, if this were so, ''there would never have been a single great man.'' The ''great man'' component of Raskolnikov's theory is thus there from the very first, and is not unexpectedly tacked on later.) Temporally, the tavern-scene and the murder itself are at the very opposite ends of a single time-sequence; but they are telescoped together deftly by Dostoevsky's narrative technique—and for a very important purpose. And if we grasp the thematic significance of Dostoevsky's dramatic irony here, I think it will give us a model to illuminate the whole vexed question of Raskolnikov's motivation.

The purpose of Dostoevsky's juxtaposition and telescoping of the time-sequence is obviously to undermine Raskolnikov's *conscious* motivation for the reader. The hypnotic hysteria in which he kills the old pawnbroker could not reveal more clearly, in an objective, dramatic fashion, that Raskolnikov's crime is not being committed according to his altruistic, Utilitarian theory. Whatever Raskolnikov may have believed about himself, he is now acting in the grip of other forces and not on the basis of the theory, which is still fresh in our minds because we have met it only a page or two before. Dostoevsky's technique is thus intended to force the reader, if he is at all attentive, to pose to himself the question of what Raskolnikov's *true* motive can possibly be.

Now I believe that the entire construction of the first part of the book is intended to give an answer to this question in the same objective, dramatic fashion. Part I consists of two alternating sequences of episodes. In one sequence, composed largely of flashbacks, we learn about Raskolnikov's past, his desperate family situation, and all the circumstances pushing him towards the crime. All these scenes build up the altruistic side of his character, and reinforce our sense of his essential goodness, humanity, and sympathy for suffering. It is this aspect of his nature which forever distinguishes him from a real criminal, and that makes him think of expiating his crime—if one can really call it a crime—by future services to humanity. But then we also see him in *action* in this part, in the series of episodes with Marmeladov and his family, and with the young girl on the boulevard. And in these scenes we notice a very significant dialectic occurring, which undermines the foundations of his altruistic, Utilitarian theory in exactly the same way as the later dramatic irony; this latter is, indeed, only the final crescendo of this whole masterly sequence.

In each of these episodes, Raskolnikov at first responds purely instinctively to the spectacle of human misery and suffering, and he spontaneously rushes to help and to succour. But at a certain point, a total transformation of his personality occurs from one moment to the next. Suddenly he withdraws, becomes indifferent and contemptuous, and instead of pitying mankind he begins to hate it for being weak and contemptible. In each case, this change of feeling is indicated to be the result of the application of a Utilitarian calculus. For example, he is starving and yet leaves all his money at the Marmeladovs; but as he walks out he begins to laugh at himself scornfully for this gesture. Why? Because, he thinks, ''after all they have Sonia and I need it myself.'' This leads him into reflections on how despicable human beings are because they can become accustomed to anything—like living off the income of a prostitute daughter. (pp. 34-5)

Each step, then, in the *backward* process of revealing Raskolnikov's conscious, altruistic motive for the contemplated crime is accompanied by another episode moving *forward* in time that undercuts it, and that reveals the *true* effect of his ideas on his feelings. In each case the reader can see clearly that when Raskolnikov acts under the influence of his Utilitarian ideas, he unleashes in himself a cold and pitiless egomaniac who hates humanity although he continues to believe that he loves it. . . .

In Part II, Dostoevsky begins to close the gap that exists between the reader's awareness of Raskolnikov and Raskolnikov's awareness of himself. For in Part II, as he begins to recover from his illness, Raskolnikov starts to ponder all the anomalies of the crime and to realise that he no longer knows *why* it was committed. At this point he is confronted with his old article *"On Crime,"* which reveals to what extent egomania had always been an inseparable part of the Utilitarian love of humanity. Dostoevsky withholds the full development of this motif, though he had carefully foreshadowed it earlier, until it becomes relevant both to answer Raskolnikov's own questions about his crime and to crystallise and define the reader's earlier impressions. The experience of the crime, however, has not shown Raskolnikov that the feelings which inspired his altruistic love of humanity cannot co-exist in the same sensibility with those necessary to be a Napoleon, a Solon, or a Lycurgus. For the true great man, possessed by his sense of mission, cannot have any thoughts to spare for the suffering humanity on whom he tramples for their own future happiness.

Once Raskolnikov's original theory breaks apart in this way, he is then confronted with the choice between non-Utilitarian Christian love and self-sacrifice in Sonia or total amorality leading to self-destruction in Svidrigailov. The construction of the latter half of the book thus clearly reflects its purpose, which was to persuade Dostoevsky's readers among the radical intelligentsia that they had to choose between a doctrine of love and a doctrine of power. (p. 35)

> Joseph Frank, *"The World of Raskolnikov,"* in Encounter, *Vol. XXVI, No. 1, June, 1966, pp. 30-5.*

YURY F. KARYAKIN (essay date 1971)

[*In the following, first published in 1971 as "O filosofskoeti-cheskoj problematike romana 'Prestuplenie i nakazanie'" in* Dostoevskij i ego vremja, *Karyakin discusses the function of the epilogue of* Crime and Punishment. *The critic contends that the epilogue is a necessary finale to the novel, because only in this section does Raskolnikov face the ultimate consequences of his crime, and only here does he open himself to the boundless love of Sonia and his family which allows him to begin to repent. For additional discussions of the epilogue, see Konstantin Mochulsky (1947) and Michael Holquist (1977).*]

In *Crime and Punishment,* after Porfiry finally "catches" Raskolnikov and he confesses to the murder, many readers and critics, losing interest in the novel, give the epilogue only a perfunctory reading. After all, they think, everything is clear without it: the crime has been exposed, punishment has followed. What more is necessary?

But the crime and punishment of which Dostoevsky wrote is something else again. He looked at the criminal and civil code from a philosophical point of view. He examined legal questions and even the "detective story" features of the novel in the context of his own world outlook. Without the epilogue we should have a distorted view of *Crime and Punishment;* it is not only a formal conclusion, but a necessary finale where the main knots are disentangled or sundered (though new ones, still to be loosened, are formed here too).

Only in the epilogue does Raskolnikov reap the ultimate consequences of his crime—there is nothing beyond: the death of his mother, his rejection even by the convict community and, in his nightmare, doomsday. *Crime and Punishment* is not only a novel about the murder of an old woman, a moneylender, but a nvoel about matricide, about the moral suicide of a criminal and about the potential self-destruction of humanity.

Only in the epilogue does Raskolnikov become convinced of the boundless love and faith of those close to him and ready to sacrifice themselves for him—his mother, Sonia, his sister, Razumikhin. *Crime and Punishment,* then, is a novel not only

about the extremes of evil the criminal inflicts on others, but also about people's unlimited goodness, a goodness which can save the criminal.

Only in the epilogue does Raskolnikov recognize the full depths of his crime and find in himself forces to correct the wrong direction of his strivings. *Crime and Punishment* is not a detective novel about the pursuit, capture, confession and legal punishment of a criminal, but a philosophical, psychological novel about the difficulties of repentance and how to overcome them. . . .

It is essential to note that until the epilogue itself Raskolnikov will only confess to the murder, but not repent of it. (pp. 94-5)

In Svidrigailov and Luzhin, whom he hates, Raskolnikov recognizes himself but is afraid to admit the image. They are his doubles, negative doubles, so to speak, who embody all that is bad in him. He looks into them as into a mirror and is ready to cut them down. He is drawn to them and repelled by them. He would like to regard them as caricatures of himself but gradually, though reluctantly, comes to realize that his own "cursed dream" is grotesque and terrible. . . . Still another double of Raskolnikov is Porfiry. Despite all his splendid and well-aimed shots at Raskolnikov, the reader barely masters his dislike of him. . . .

At the outset, neither Luzhin nor Svidrigailov nor Porfiry can influence Raskolnikov—quite the contrary; but all the same they help lay the groundwork for that crisis in prison when he will recall his terrible dreams. This crisis, though, is prepared by others as well. In order that a man not merely acknowledge, but also repent of his crime and expiate it, he needs positive help. (p. 95)

Raskolnikov's repentance would have been impossible had it not been for other "positive" doubles near him, for other "mirrors" into which he could look to discover all that was good and human in himself. Without people who loved him for the things really worth loving in him, Raskolnikov might just have gone mad or, like Svidrigailov, have killed himself.

The first among these people is Raskolnikov's mother. . . . She is one of the main heroes of the novel. True, only a very few pages are given over to her (the reading of the mother's letter, three meetings with her, his thoughts about her in the epilogue). But her main importance lies in the fact that *Crime and Punishment* is among other things a novel about matricide: it is just because of her son's crime that the mother falls spiritually ill and dies. (pp. 95-6)

Razumikhin also influences Raskolnikov positively and is himself attracted to the Raskolnikov who is on the side of life. This "busybody," as he is sometimes called, is not so limited or unimportant a character as one might suppose. In some respects he is superior to Raskolnikov, for he understands with his mind and heart that one cannot violate the living life; he understands that love for humanity divorced from tangible help to real people is deception and self-deception. (pp. 96-7)

For the sake of his "dream" Raskolnikov wants to stifle his conscience, crush everything human in himself; but he is unable to do so. Thus, he comes out in defense of a girl pursued by some fop who reminds him of Svidrigailov, then suddenly reflects: "Why the hell did I have to butt in! Is it my business to help? Suppose they swallow each other alive, what's it to me?" Again, he is prepared finally to carry out the crime, but his whole nature protests against its "logic," protests even unconsciously, as in the dream in which, as a boy, he watches as drunken people beat a horse to death. (p. 97)

The irreconcilable nature of the contradiction appears at the very beginning when Raskolnikov speaks of his "cursed dream." The dream is tempting, attractive, but nonetheless cursed." . . . The contradiction, seemingly is insoluble: he must either view the dream as not cursed, or renounce it altogether. . . . When Raskolnikov yields to base impulses he maliciously laughs (though not without self-laceration) at his own magnanimity—it is just Schilleresque rhetoric, he thinks; and he vows not to yield to it in the future. But when (at first only briefly) he nonetheless yields to positive impulses he also acts accordingly, with passion and again with self-laceration, and wants to renounce his "cursed dream."

No matter whether he is providing a theoretical groundwork for the crime, or carrying it out, or seeking to rationalize it, he is nonetheless at the same time violating his true nature, compelling himself to act in contradiction to it. But when he gives embodiment to those "gestures" (of which Razumikhin speaks) he acts naturally, organically, and expands with affirmative, not somber exaltation. There is, was, and will be born in him a dream, not a "cursed" one, but one which even his mother would bless. (pp. 98-9)

If there is no conscience, all is permissible, all evil is permissible. If there is conscience, all is also permissible, and all good is permissible: this, it appears, is the logic of Dostoevsky. It is a long time before this logic wins over Raskolnikov. . . .

Raskolnikov repents after his painful anxiety over the fate of his mother, after he recognizes that she had fallen ill and died because of him. . . . He repents after Sonia follows him to prison, after he had scornfully turned away from her, all the while that she was patiently bearing everything and awaiting the "moment." He repents after he becomes aware of that fearful and impassable gulf that lies between him and the other convicts. (p. 100)

Raskolnikov repents only after his long illness, after recalling his nightmares. . . . Raskolnikov recoils from his "cursed dream" only when he discovers its final consequences on a world scale. Self-will (not freedom) of the individual becomes the condition for the self-will of all. The "dream" leads to doomsday. (pp. 100-01)

The novel concludes with the idea that an even more difficult period lies ahead for Raskolnikov—a period of expiation. "That is the beginning of a new story, though; the story of a man's gradual renewal, the story of his gradual regeneration, of his gradual transition from one world to another, of his acquaintance with a new reality of which he had previously been completely ignorant." Dostoevsky repeats the word "gradually" three times, emphasizes the difficulty Raskolnikov will face in remaking himself. The last paragraph of the novel concludes with the words: "That would make the subject of a new story; our present story is ended." Here we have, in essence, a courageous confession of a major defeat of Dostoevsky as a Christian ideologist, a defeat which turns out to be a major victory for Dostoevsky the artist. (pp. 101-02)

> *Yury F. Karyakin, "Toward Regeneration," translated by Robert Louis Jackson, in* Twentieth Century Interpretations of "Crime and Punishment": A Collection of Critical Essays, *edited by Robert Louis Jackson, Prentice-Hall, Inc., 1974, pp. 94-102.*

MICHAEL HOLQUIST   (essay date 1977)

[*Holquist proposes that* Crime and Punishment *is composed of two sections, each of which is guided by a different "clock," or temporal structure: a detective story, which forms the body of the novel, and a wisdom tale, which is contained in the epilogue. According to Holquist, Raskolnikov functions as detective as well as criminal in the former, since he pursues his own motives for the crime in order to discover an identity, or what Holquist terms his "authentic self." Holquist ascribes to Raskolnikov a historical motive for his crime and considers Raskolnikov's crime as the test of his ability to institute historical change. Discovering that he is unable to ground his identity in secular history, Raskolnikov, in Holquist's view, seeks his place instead in the narrative of the wisdom tale of the epilogue. For additional discussions of Raskolnikov's motive, see Maurice Beebe (1955), Philip Rahv (1960), and Joseph Frank (1966).*]

E. M. Forster once said [in his *Aspects of the Novel*] that "in a novel there is always a clock," by which he meant, of course, that just as clocks organize time outside of texts, so does plot within them. (p. 77)

[The] plot of *Crime and Punishment* is arranged around two moments, each of which is privileged in a different way, and each of which results in a different sequence. The first is the moment of Raskolnikov's crime that occurs in Book One, and the sequence of punishment that flows from it in the following five books. The second is the moment of Raskolnikov's conversion in the epilogue, and the sequence of the "new story" with which the novel ends. The first has the formal properties of a detective story, the second of a wisdom tale.

The two clocks of a detective story are represented by two characters, the criminal and the detective. Now to the list of oppositions that is usually invoked to capture the duality of a typical Dostoevskian character (sinner-saint, proud-humiliated, etc.), we must in the case of Raskolnikov add another: he is both hunter and hunted. (pp. 87-8)

He is the criminal, so much is obvious. But he is also victim: on the way to commit the murder he compares himself to a man on his way to execution . . . ; and as he confesses to Sonya later . . . , "I killed myself, not the old woman." What he means by this is that the man who murdered the pawnbroker *in that act* got rid of the self Raskolnikov conceived himself to be before the act of murder. Raskolnikov's identity is felt by him not to be continuous with itself before and after the crime: after discovering that the role of murderer made his old self a victim, in the first book, Raskolnikov is forced to take up a new role, that of detective of his old self's motive, in order to create a new identity, a new life for himself. If he can understand *why* his old self committed the crime he will know the self whodunit; and insofar as he understands whodunit, he will know who he is.

The crime itself is performed in a fog of uncertainty; everything happens by chance. Raskolnikov acts as if in a delirium; he is constantly surprised to find himself in this or that place, holding the axe, running away. His dream-like state is dramatized by the narrator's subtle but insistent emphasis on the cut-off between Raskolnikov's hallucinatory uncertainties and the precise chronology of all his movements, which are charted from moment to moment. . . . (pp. 88-9)

The confusion of the crime itself is contrasted in the rest of the novel with Raskolnikov's acute attempts to analyze it. He isolates three different motives, each of which becomes the iconic attribute of a self who is presented as a suspect, only to be cleared in favor of one of the other motive-defined selves.

In chapter iv of book v he reviews them all for Sonya. The first is robbery. . . . But he quickly dismisses this; he admits he buried the purse he stole without even looking into it. . . . (pp. 89-90)

The second motive is one that is much more deeply explored in the novel: "I wanted to make myself a Napoleon, and that is why I killed her. . . ." Earlier . . . we learn that Raskolnikov's old, pre-murder self had written an article; in it Raskolnikov "developed the idea that all the . . . law-givers and regulators of human society, beginning with the most ancient, and going on to Lycurgus, Solon, Mahomet, Napoleon and so on, were without exception transgressors, by the very fact that in making a new law they *ipso facto* broke an old one, handed down from their fathers and held sacred by society." . . . While such ideas have obvious parallels in Nietzsche's essay on "The Uses and Abuses of History," Philip Rahv was surely right to point to the greater fruitfulness of a comparison with Hegel's conception of the world historical individual: "Dostoevsky gives us a parody-version of Hegel's theory of two types of men [the superior hero and the inferior mass he is to lead] by abstracting [the theory] from its historical logic" [see excerpt above]. Raskolnikov's conception of the murder as a world-historical act is absurd, as he becomes painfully aware. He does so under the shadow of yet another brutalized aspect of Hegel's philosophy of history, an aspect often expressed in Schiller's line, *Weltgeschichte ist Weltgericht*, "world history is the world court." That is, Raskolnikov not only advances as his most programmatically complete reason for *committing* the murder a motive derived from Hegel; he also *judges* his act by appealing to a debased Hegelian principle of interpretation: what succeeds is correct, what fails is wrong. (p. 90)

Raskolnikov committed the murder as in a trance, it is like a dream he must interpret. . . . Raskolnikov, dreamer and analyst, turns for the ground of his interpretation to history: the causes can be known only in their effects. There is nothing higher than history; there is no transcendent, so the truth can be known only retrospectively, in events, as a judgment of historical trial by combat. The shape of events will explain them. As Hegel said, "It was for a while the fashion to admire God's wisdom in animals, plants, and individual lives. If it is conceded that Providence manifests itself in such objects and materials, why not also in world history? . . . Our intellectual striving aims at recognizing that what eternal wisdom *intended,* it has actually *accomplished.* . . ."

Raskolnikov's historicism is important to any understanding not only of his own motives, the thematics of the novel if you will, but also to its morphology. Since Raskolnikov uses historical method in his search for self, he inevitably acts like a detective interpreting "the traces left by earlier events in terms of the same laws and principles as apply in the present. Since all that is real is rational, and all that is rational real, in Hegel's oft-misunderstood formulation, reason will suffice unto a solution. It is reason that tells Raskolnikov he has failed in his intention to transcend morality; therefore at the end of the novel he turns himself in—he has finally discovered that he is no more than a criminal. The true self has been found, and like the detective story whose temporality it shares, the novel thus can close.

But of course there is still the epilogue. In it, as Raskolnikov finds a new conception of time and selfhood, we discover that his Hegelian motive and its consequences are a false solution. Already in the novel proper Raskolnikov had hinted at a reason for his crime other than robbery or a secularized messianism.

The murder was simply an extreme situation he sought to exploit in order to find out who he really *was;* as he says—in one of those terrifying Dostoevskian immediacies—"I longed to kill without casuistry, to kill for my own benefit and for that alone! I would not lie about it even to myself! I did not commit murder in order to use the profits and power gained to make myself a benefactor to humanity. Rubbish! I simply murdered; I murdered for myself, for myself alone . . . it was only to *test myself* . . .". . . . But of course—given his historical bias—he can only conclude he failed the test. . . . Raskolnikov had sought to give himself definitive knowledge of his self in the murder; it was an attempt to create a . . . moment that would insure the validity of all his other moments. Among his other dualities, he thus has taken on the roles of both Christ and Lazarus, seeking to gain a new identity by his *own* actions, to bestow a new life through his own mediation. But instead of raising a new self, his old identity is executed in the murder. (pp. 91-3)

[In the novel's] last three pages, however, he is granted another moment, another sequence, as he becomes a character in the wisdom tale with which the epilogue concludes.

It is Easter, time for rebirth. Raskolnikov has just come out of the hospital, where, in his illness, he has had one of those great Dostoevskian programmatic dreams that recapitulates in symbols the meaning of his novelistic actions. He sits by the bank of "the wide, solitary river. From the high bank a broad landscape was revealed. From the other bank far away, was faintly borne the sound of singing. There in the immensity of the steppe . . . it seemed as though . . . *time had stood still,* and the age of Abraham and his flocks was still the present" [emphasis added]. Sonya appears and "how it happened he himself did not know, but suddenly he seemed to be seized and cast at her feet . . . *now at last the moment had come*" [emphasis added]. What has happened here, of course, is that Raskolnikov has undergone a conversion experience. . . . (pp. 93-4)

But in order to be reborn, the old self must die. We are here touching on the main theme of *Crime and Punishment*. . . . [Raskolnikov's] mystical suppression of self, the death of his old identity ("Love had raised [him] from the dead"), is just as decisive as was the death of an even earlier self, the one that died in the act of murder. Raskolnikov is a completely different person as the epilogue closes. . . . (p. 95)

The whole novel is an account of Raskolnikov's various attempts to forge an identity for himself with which he can live. From the very beginning of the novel he has sought a means to justify his existence or, in the language of the text, to find a faith. . . . All Raskolnikov's actions—his article on new law givers (who found a new faith), the murder itself, and his attempts to understand it—are probes toward a moment that will give lasting meaning to the rest of his life. (p. 96)

[Raskolnikov] attempts to ground his identity . . . in historical narratives. The six parts of the novel tell how Raskolnikov, who feels he is existentially out of place in the historical context of nineteenth-century Russian society, tries to create a *new* historical sequence. . . . But he discovers that he is not a world historical individual; he is not a character in *that kind* of a history. It is only in the epilogue that he discovers the kind of narrative that is properly his own to live: it is not a secular history to which he belongs, but a wisdom tale. (pp. 96-7)

Thematically *Crime and Punishment* is the account of Raskolnikov's search for a story that will endow his life with validity. He first seeks such a narrative structure in a theory of history that is recognizably Hegelian and unquestionably secular. He kills in order to test whether he is, or is not, an instrument of historical change: since there is nothing higher than history itself, you can know its judgments only after having acted. Having committed the murder, he discovers he is in fact not a character in the drama of historicism. In order, then, to establish a continuity in his identities, to reassemble the shattered "I" destroyed in the outcome of the crime, he seeks the existential glue of another kind of story. But since historicism is the source of the murder—and of the confusion following upon it until Raskolnikov turns himself in—this part of the narrative is told in a way that employs many of the features of a detective story. . . . (pp. 98-9)

Since an authentic self is the object of Raskolnikov's various attempts to explain why he committed the murder (if he understands *why*-dunit, he'll know *who*-dunit), it is clear that his first public confession—which ends the novel proper—is an unsatisfactory solution. A self-construction has *not* [resulted from the confession]. . . . Raskolnikov exhausts the detective story formula without achieving its benefit—a complete resolution of the mystery that sets the story going. If we invoke the metaphor with which we began, the two clocks of the plot fail to synchronize. (p. 99)

Raskolnikov has failed to find a self in the detective story into which his attempt to enter historical narrative has devolved; but another plot is vouchsafed to him, . . . in the epilogue's last pages—another time is broached. The last pages of the novel are not only *about* another time; they are told in a different time: the movement from the dream to the final word of the text is constituted in a manner that sets it off from the body of the novel insofar as it tells of years in sentences, while in the body of the text minutes are told in pages. (p. 100)

[If] there is a disjunction between the temporal structure of the novel proper and its epilogue, does this mean—as many readers have felt—that there is a break in the unity of *Crime and Punishment*? The suggestion of this chapter has been, rather, that there is a bond between the parts, a bond that derives from the direction of time in the two story types that define the novel, on the one hand, and the epilogue, on the other. The detective story properties shaping Raskolnikov's search for identity in the novel tend toward a conclusion that will resolve all the mysteries.

But it does not, because in the course of his investigation Raskolnikov has, in his obsessive honesty, raised the question of evil, and, as H. R. Niebuhr has said [in "The Truth in Myths"], "the mystery of good and evil in human life and in the world cannot be completely comprehended as stated in perfectly logical terms." What the theologian here states is the ancient message of the wisdom tale: "Knowest thou the ordinance of heaven? Canst thou set the dominion thereof in the earth?" The movement of the epilogue is analogous to the wisdom tale in that it points back to the inadequacy of answers that precede its concluding insistence on *another* realm, *another* time: the "correct" answer is not a solution, but the reminder of another and greater mystery. Thus the historical movement of the novel is a necessary step toward the debunking of its assumptions in the epilogue. The underground man, who never found a plot, is therefore condemned to a dreary life of "bad infinity," and endless succession of empty moments. Thus the formal conclusion of the Dostoevskian plot that contains him is a note from the editor who says "the 'notes' of this paradoxalist do not end here. . . ." Whereas *Crime and*

Punishment may conclude with a "new tale"—Raskolnikov has found a role for himself in the detective-story-become-wisdom-tale that defines the Dostoevskian plot containing him. (pp. 100-01)

> *Michael Holquist, in his* Dostoevsky and the Novel, *Princeton University Press, 1977, 202 p.*

ROBERT LOUIS JACKSON   (essay date 1981)

[*Jackson examines the philosophical pro and contra that engages Raskolnikov in part one of* Crime and Punishment. *In exploring the issue of Raskolnikov's moral concerns, Jackson discusses Raskolnikov's "dialectic of consciousness," which involves the character's conflicting feelings of sympathy and disgust with humankind and his struggle with the question of whether humanity is morally viable or irredeemably evil. Jackson also analyzes the elements of Raskolnikov's mare dream, which he views as a psychological metaphor for Raskolnikov's own crime and also as a revelation of Raskolnikov's philosophy. Ruth Mortimer (1956) also discusses the mare dream in her discussion of the significance of the four dreams presented in* Crime and Punishment.]

The burden of part one of *Crime and Punishment* is the dialectic of consciousness in Raskolnikov. This dialectic propels him to crime and, in so doing, uncovers for the reader the motives that lead him to crime, motives deeply rooted in his character and in his efforts to come to terms with the necessities of his existence. (p. 189)

Part one begins with Raskolnikov's test visit to the old pawnbroker and ends with the visit in which he murders the old lady and, incidentally, her sister Lizaveta. The murder itself is also, in a deeper sense, a test or experiment set up to determine whether he has the right to transgress. He starts out in a state of indecision or irresolution and ends with a decisive action—murder—an apparent resolution of his initial indecision. But does the murder really constitute a resolution of Raskolnikov's dialectic? Does he really "decide" to murder the pawnbroker? Or does not chance, rather, serve to mask his failure to decide with his whole being? Is he master or slave here?

The final line of part one alone suggests the answer: "Bits and fragments of some kind of thoughts swarmed about in his head, but he was unable to get hold of a single one of them, he could not concentrate upon a single one of them in spite of all his efforts." Raskolnikov's dialectic of consciousness continues to be dramatized in his thoughts, actions, and relationships after the murder (parts two-six). It is only in the epilogue (chap. 2) that this dialectic is dissolved—not resolved—on a new, developing plane of consciousness. Raskolnikov's inability to focus his thoughts on anything, his inability consciously to resolve anything after his reconciliation with Sonya in the epilogue ("he was simply feeling") constitutes a qualitatively different state of consciousness from the chaos of mind he experienced right after the murder. These two moments of consciousness are in almost symmetrical opposition. The movement or shift from one to the other constitutes the movement in Raskolnikov's consciousness from hate (unfreedom) to love (freedom).

The movement from test to test, from rehearsal to experimental crime, from theory to practice, is marked by a constant struggle and debate on all levels of Raskolnikov's consciousness. Each episode—the meeting with Marmeladov and his family, Raskolnikov's reading of his mother's letter with its account of family affairs, his encounter with the drunken and bedraggled girl and the policeman, and his dream of the beating of the mare—is marked by a double movement: sympathy and disgust, attraction and recoil. Each episode attests to what has been called Raskolnikov's "moral maximalism." Yet each also attests to a deepening skepticism and despair on the part of Raskolnikov, a tragic tension toward crime in both a psychological and a philosophical sense.

The immediate issues of this pro and contra are nothing more or less than injustice and human suffering and the question of how a person shall respond to them. But the deeper evolving question—on which turns Raskolnikov's ultimate response to this injustice and suffering—is a judgment of mankind: is man a morally viable creature or simply and irredeemably bad? Do man and the world make sense? Raskolnikov's murder of the old pawnbroker is the final expression of the movement of his dialectic toward a tragic judgment of man and society. The ideological concomitant of his paralysis of moral will (the scenes following his chance encounter on the street with Lizaveta) is a rationalistic humanism that is unable to come to terms with evil in human existence. Lacking larger spiritual dimensions, this ideology ends by postulating incoherence and chaos in man and his environment and, in turn, in a universe in which man is a victim of fate. (pp. 189-91)

If Marmeladov's "confession," which opens chapter two, accents the central redemptive note in *Crime and Punishment,* the final lines of the chapter stress antithetical notes of despair and damnation. The sight of human degradation [experienced by the Marmeladov family] so overwhelms Raskolnikov that fundamental doubts about man and human nature are called forth in him. Stunned that people can live in this way, that indignity, vulgarity, and discord can become an accepted part of man's life, Raskolnikov explodes: "Man can get used to anything—the scoundrel!" (p. 191)

The motif of adaptation is heard throughout Dostoevsky's works. . . . It attests, from one point of view, to human endurance, the will to survive. Yet from another view, it expresses a deeply tragic idea, implying that man will yield feebly to suffering, oppression, injustice, unfreedom, in short, to triumphant evil. Man in this conception is man as the Grand Inquisitor [in Dostoevsky's novel *The Brothers Karamazov*] finds him: weak and vile. Such adaptation arouses only contempt in the rebellious Raskolnikov.

Raskolnikov's rebellion implies a positive standard or norm of human behavior, morality, life. Merely to speak of man as a scoundrel for adapting to evil is to posit another ideal, to affirm by implication that man ought not to yield weakly to degradation and evil. But the thought that occurs to Raskolnikov at this point is one that links him directly with the Grand Inquisitor. We may paraphrase it as follows: what if all this vile adaptation to evil is not a deviation from a norm; that is, what if villainy pure and simple is . . . the human condition? . . .

Raskolnikov's intense moral concerns provide evidence that man is not a scoundrel and predator by nature. And it is the idea of adaptation as testimony to man's endurance and will to live that is ultimately accepted by Raskolnikov. Thus, Raskolnikov, after an encounter with prostitutes on the streets, declares that it would be better to live an eternity on a "square yard of space" than to die. . . . (p. 192)

Svidrigailov, the character who comes closest to an embodiment of the principle that all is permissible, also poses the question that Raskolnikov is deliberating, though more dis-

passionately and cynically. Defending himself against the charges that he persecuted Dunya in his home, he observes:

> Now let's just assume, now, that I, too, am a man, *et nihil humanum* [and nothing human] . . . in a word, that I am capable of being attracted and falling in love (which, of course, doesn't happen according to our own will), then everything can be explained in the most natural way. The whole question is: am I a monster or am I myself a victim? Well, and what if I am a victim?

Barely concealed in Svidrigailov's jocular question is the issue of human nature. The underlying ethical and philosophical import of his question—"Am I a monster or am I myself a victim?"—is clear: does a consideration of his acts—man's acts ("Just assume, now, that I, too, am a man")—fall under the rubric of ethics or the laws of nature? Are we really responsible for our behavior? Are the morally pejorative epithets "monster" or "scoundrel" really in order? Are we not simply creatures of nature?

Svidrigailov, we note, likes to appeal to natural tendencies. Very much like the Marquis de Sade's alter egos Clement (*Justine,* 1791) or Dolmance (*La philosophie dans le boudoir,* 1795), he appeals to nature as a reason for disposing entirely of moral categories or judgment. "In this debauchery, at least, there is something constant, based even on nature, and not subject to fantasy," Svidrigailov remarks in his last conversation with Raskolnikov. Indeed, Svidrigailov's conception of man would appear to be wholly biological—"Now I pin all my hope on anatomy alone, by God!"—a point of view that certainly undercuts any concept of personal responsibility.

The concept *homo sum, et nihil humanum a me alienum puto* ("I am a man and nothing human is alien to me") was for Dostoevsky a profoundly moral concept, implying the obligation squarely to confront human reality. . . . To be a man, in [Svidrigailov's] view, is to be open to all that is in nature, that is, to nature in himself; it is to be in the power of nature (if not to *be* nature) and therefore not to be responsible. But his hope for salvation through Dunya and his final suicide are evidence that his confidence in anatomy has its cracks and fissures. In the final analysis, then, even for Svidrigailov (though infinitely more so for Raskolnikov), the question, "monster or victim?"—is he morally responsible or free to commit all vilenesses?—is a fateful question. Posing this question, in Dostoevsky's view, distinguishes man, even the Svidrigailovs, from Sade's natural man.

The problem of human nature raised by Raskolnikov and Svidrigailov, and lived out in their life dramas, is expressed directly by Ivan Karamazov [in *The Brothers Karamazov*]. Apropos of his belief that man is incapable of Christian love, Ivan observes: "The real issue is whether all this comes about because of bad elements in people's character or simply because that is their nature." Raskolnikov's pessimistic conjecture at the conclusion of chapter two (and, even more, the evidence of his dream in chapter five) can be compared with Ivan's bitter judgment of man in his famous rebellion. It can be described as the opening, and dominant motif, in a prelude to murder. The whole of *Crime and Punishment* is an effort to refute this judgment of man, to provide an answer, through Raskolnikov himself, to this tragic conjecture. The action in part one, however, is moved by the almost syllogistic logic of Raskolnikov's pessimistic supposition.

Chapter two of part one contains the extreme moral and philosophical polarities of the novel: affirmation of both the principle of love, compassion, and freedom (which will ultimately embrace Raskolnikov through Sonya) and the principle of hate, the pessimistic view of man as a scoundrel by nature, the projection of the idea that all is permissible. The events of this chapter bring Raskolnikov full circle from compassion to nihilistic rage. (pp. 193-95)

Here is our first contact with the matrix of Raskolnikov's "theoretical" crime, with the responses that will find explicit formulation in Raskolnikov's article ["On Crime"] and arguments. . . . Here we see how the raw material of social and psychological experience begins to generalize into a social and philosophical point of view—and ultimately, into those ideas of Raskolnikov's that will tragically act back again upon life and experience.

The same cyclical pattern we have noted in chapter two dominates chapter three. The chapter opens on a subtle note that disputes the depressing and abstract conjectures of Raskolnikov. (p. 195)

Raskolnikov's basic skepticism about man and human nature emerges in his reflections on his mother, his sister Dunya, and their critical situation. He comprehends the sacrifice his mother and sister make for him as an ascent to Golgotha but in bitterness casts them among the innocents, those "Schilleresque 'beautiful souls'" who wave the truth away, who would rather not admit the vile truth about man. (p. 196)

Raskolnikov's powerful impulses to good and his high potential for self-sacrifice are short-circuited by a sense of overwhelming injustice and evil, of absurd imbalance in the scales of good and evil. In the face of the world's misery, the rapacious Svidrigailovs and Luzhins, the pitiful and loathesome spectacle of man-adapting, Raskolnikov rebels: "I don't want your sacrifice, Dunya, I don't want it, mother dear! It shall not be as long as I live, it shall not, shall not! I won't accept it!"

Dostoevsky uses the word "anguish" to express Raskolnikov's state of mind here. His rebellion, indeed, looks back on the revolt of the Underground Man [in *Notes from the Underground*] and forward to Ivan Karamazov's rebellion against divine harmony (if it be based on the innocent suffering of children). Deeply responsive to human suffering, Ivan, in his indignation, returns to God his "ticket" to future harmony. Yet this same humanitarian revolt, with its despair in a meaningful universe, leads him unconsciously to sanction the murder of his father. This same ethical paradox lies at the root of Raskolnikov's crime. Starting out with love and compassion for the "eternal" Sonya and for Dunya and his mother, Raskolnikov ends up with a rejection of love and sacrifice and with a rage at evil—a rage that itself becomes disfigured and evil. This rage, ethically motivated in its origins, deforms Raskolnikov and accentuates in him the elements of sick pride and self-will. (p. 197)

Raskolnikov's dream [of the beating and killing of the mare], echoing earlier incidents, situations, and emotional experience, is a psychological metaphor in which we can distinguish the conflicting responses of Raskolnikov to his projected crime: his deep psychological complicity in, and yet moral recoil before, the crime. What has received less attention, however, is the way in which the underlying philosophical pro and contra is revealed in the separate elements of the dream (pastoral church and cemetery episode, tumultuous tavern, and mare-beating scene); how the scene of the beating itself, this picture

of Russian man and reality, raises the central and grave question of part one: what is the nature of man? . . .

The opening recollection in Raskolnikov's dream, though darkened by an atmosphere of impending evil, embodies Dostoevsky's pure aesthetic-religious ideal. Sacred form, harmony, and reverence define the boy's first memory of the tranquil open landscape, the stone church with its green cupola, the icons, the simple rituals, the cemetery, and, finally, the tombs of his grandmother and younger brother, with their clear promise of resurrection. "He loved this church" and its atmosphere. In Raskolnikov's purified and almost completely submerged memory of sacred form, spirituality, and beauty, there lies the seed of Raskolnikov's own moral and spiritual renewal. But the path to the church and cemetery—to resurrection—goes by the tavern on the edge of town. Here he encounters the crowd of drunken, brawling peasants with their "drunken, fearsome distorted faces" and their "shapeless and hoarse singing." Here everything is desecration and deformation. The faces of the people in Raskolnikov's nightmare tell the tale: this is a demonized universe. (p. 198)

[The] fractured character of Raskolnikov's moral consciousness is revealed in this dream. The boy identifies with the suffering mare, with the victim, as Raskolnikov does initially in his various encounters in part one. He is in anguish to the point of hysteria. He cries and screams and at the end puts his arm around the mare's "dead, bloodstained muzzle, and kisses her, kisses her on the eyes, on the mouth." But, as in Raskolnikov's waking hours, anguish turns into rage, and the boy "suddenly leaps up and in a frenzy rushes at Mikolka with his little fists."

Mikolka is clearly the oppressor, the embodiment of the principle of self-will. He could easily stand in for types like the pawnbroker, Luzhin, or Svidrigailov—all vicious people exploiting and degrading innocent people like Dunya, Lizaveta, or Sonya, quiet timid creatures with gentle eyes like those of the mare. It is against these vicious people that Raskolnikov revolts. But in his revolt, he is himself transformed into a monstrous, shapeless Mikolka. He himself becomes the alien oppressor, exalted by a new morality that crushes the guilty and innocent alike. In the image of the child, Raskolnikov recoils from the horror that Raskolnikov the man contemplates. But in the image of Mikolka, Raskolnikov prefigures his own role as murderer. Raskolnikov's dream has often been described as revealing the last efforts of his moral conscience to resist the crime. And this is true. The dream is a battle; but it is a battle that is lost. On the philosophical plane, as a statement on man, the dream is the tragic finale to the pro and contra of part one, the final smashing of barriers. (pp. 200-01)

Robert Louis Jackson, in his The Art of Dostoevsky: Deliriums and Nocturnes, *Princeton University Press, 1981, 379 p.*

ADDITIONAL BIBLIOGRAPHY

Beach, Joseph Warren. "Philosophy: Dostoevski." In his *The Twentieth Century Novel: Studies in Technique*, pp. 94-102. New York: D. Appleton-Century Co., 1932.
    A philosophical analysis of *Crime and Punishment*. Beach studies Raskolnikov's spiritual isolation following the murders and his resultant religious regeneration.

Beebe, Maurice, and Newton, Christopher. "Dostoevsky in English: A Selected Checklist of Criticism and Translations." *Modern Fiction Studies* IV, No. 3 (Autumn 1958): 271-91.

A bibliography of English-language criticism on Dostoevski through 1958. The authors have devoted a special section to studies on and existing translations of *Crime and Punishment*.

Beyer, Thomas R., Jr. "Dostoevsky's *Crime and Punishment*." *Explicator* 41, No. 1 (Fall 1982): 33-6.

A study of Raskolnikov's unplanned "other" murder, the murder of the pawnbroker's sister, Lizaveta. Beyer proposes that her murder, rather than the murder of Alyosha Ivanovna, the pawnbroker, is responsible for Raskolnikov's guilt. According to Beyer, Raskolnikov does not regret the murder of Alyosha Ivanovna, whom he refers to later as a "useless, vile, pernicious louse." Lizaveta, Beyer contends, was a harmless individual whose death illustrated to Raskolnikov that he could not control his life.

Blodgett, Harriet. "Dostoyevsky's *Crime and Punishment*." *Explicator* 40, No. 1 (Fall 1981): 35-7.

A study of hat imagery in *Crime and Punishment*.

Dauner, Louise. "Raskolnikov in Search of a Soul." *Modern Fiction Studies* 4, No. 3 (Autumn 1958): 199-210.

Traces Raskolnikov's spiritual evolution and regeneration.

Deneau, Daniel P. "Dostoevsky's *Crime and Punishment*." *Explicator* 40, No. 3 (Spring 1982): 36-8.

An analysis of Porfiry Petrovich as a reflection of Raskolnikov's personal torment following Alyosha Ivanovna's murder.

Fanger, Donald. "Apogee: *Crime and Punishment*." In his *Dostoevsky and Romantic Realism: A Study of Dostoevsky in Relation to Balzac, Dickens, and Gogol*, pp. 184-213. Cambridge: Harvard University Press, 1965.

A consideration of *Crime and Punishment* as both a metaphysical thriller and a social novel.

Fueloep-Miller, René. "Dostoevsky's Literary Reputation." *The Russian Review* 10, No. 1 (January 1951): 46-54.

A collection of brief responses to *Crime and Punishment* by Dostoevski's literary contemporaries, including Friedrich Nietzsche, Sigmund Freud, and Maxim Gorky.

Jackson, Robert Louis, ed. *Twentieth Century Interpretations of "Crime and Punishment": A Collection of Critical Essays*. Englewood Cliffs, N.J.: Prentice-Hall, 1974, 122 p.

In-depth studies by a number of prominent twentieth-century critics analyzing various aspects of *Crime and Punishment*. Among the scholars represented are Vadim Kozhinov and Aron Steinberg.

Jones, Malcolm V. "*Crime and Punishment*: Transgression and Transcendence." In his *Dostoyevsky: The Novel of Discord*, pp. 67-89. New York: Harper & Row, Barnes & Noble, 1976.

Relates *Crime and Punishment* historically to the social and ideological problems of its era in Russia.

Laing, R. D. "The Counterpoint of Experience." In his *Self and Others*, pp. 39-52. New York: Random House, Pantheon Books, 1969.*

A Freudian interpretation of Raskolnikov's dreams.

Peace, Richard. "The Ethical Reappraisal: *Crime and Punishment*." In his *Dostoyevsky: An Examination of the Major Novels*, pp. 19-33. Cambridge: Cambridge at the University Press, 1971.

Considers *Crime and Punishment* to be a reflection of Dostoevski's tumultuous personal life at the time of the novel's composition. *Crime and Punishment*, Peace believes, mirrors Dostoevski's own spiritual crisis and subsequent rebirth.

Powys, John Cowper. "*Crime and Punishment*." In his *Dostoievsky*, pp. 88-94. London: John Lane The Bodley Head, 1946.

A brief biographical study of Dostoevski at the time that he wrote *Crime and Punishment*. According to Powys, Dostoevski's own difficulties provided the novel's greatest inspiration.

Reeve, F. D. "*Crime and Punishment* (Dostoevsky)." In his *The Russian Novel*, pp. 159-204. New York: McGraw-Hill Book Co., 1966.*

A discussion of *Crime and Punishment* as a historical novel. Reeve likens *Crime and Punishment* to Honoré de Balzac's *Père Goriot;* he contends that both works indicate that one's self-awareness increases through personal guilt.

Snodgrass, W. D. "Crime for Punishment: The Tenor of Part One." *The Hudson Review* XIII, No. 2 (Summer 1960): 202-53.

An analysis of the first section of *Crime and Punishment*, which foreshadows Raskolnikov's murder. Snodgrass disputes critics who believe that *Crime and Punishment* "aimed only to show remorse after crime." According to Snodgrass, the murder is, in fact, the novel's climax.

Squires, Paul Chatham. "Dostoevsky's 'Raskolnikov': The Criminalistic Protest." *The Journal of Criminal Law and Criminology* XXVIII, No. 4 (November-December 1937): 478-94.

A character analysis of Raskolnikov. Squires defines Raskolnikov as "the very essence of Dostoevsky himself, . . . the revelation of the novelist's secret being."

Wasiolek, Edward, ed. *"Crime and Punishment" and the Critics*. Belmont, Calif.: Wadsworth Publishing Co., 1961, 166 p.

A representative collection of criticism on *Crime and Punishment* that reflects the work's critical reception up to 1961. Included are translations of essays by such seminal critics as D. I. Pisarev and E. M. De Vogüé.

Yarmolinsky, Avrahm. "A Russian Tragedy." In his *Dostoevsky: His Life and Art*, 2d ed., pp. 205-16. New Jersey: S. G. Phillips, 1965.

A study of the circumstances surrounding Dostoevski's composition of *Crime and Punishment*. Yarmolinsky adds a brief character analysis of Raskolnikov and discusses his motive for murder. According to Yarmolinsky, Raskolnikov committed murder simply to test himself morally.

Zander, L. A. *Dostoevsky*. Translated by Natalie Duddington. London: SCM Press, 1948, 140 p.

Discusses the concept of ultimate good in Dostoevski's work. Zander analyzes characters that he considers to be the embodiment of goodness, including Sonia Marmeladova of *Crime and Punishment*. However, Zander adds that universal harmony, rather than individual perfection, was Dostoevski's goal.

Frederick Douglass

1817?-1895

(Born Frederick Augustus Washington Bailey) American lecturer, autobiographer, editor, essayist, and novella writer.

Douglass is considered one of the most distinguished black writers in nineteenth-century American literature. Born into slavery, he escaped in 1838 and subsequently devoted his considerable rhetorical skills to the abolitionist movement. Expounding the theme of racial equality in stirring, invective-charged orations and newspaper editorials in the 1840s, 50s, and 60s, he was recognized by his peers as an outstanding orator and the foremost black abolitionist of his era. Douglass's current reputation as a powerful and effective prose writer is based primarily on his 1845 autobiography *Narrative of the Life of Frederick Douglass, an American Slave, Written by Himself*. Regarded as one of the most compelling antislavery documents produced by a fugitive slave, the *Narrative* is also valued as an eloquent argument for human rights. As such, it has transcended its immediate historical milieu and is now regarded as a landmark in American autobiography.

The son of a black slave and an unidentified white man, Douglass was separated from his mother in his infancy. Nurtured by his maternal grandmother on the Tuckahoe, Maryland estate of his master, Captain Aaron Anthony, he enjoyed a relatively happy childhood until he was pressed into service on the plantation of Anthony's employer, Colonel Edward Lloyd. There Douglass endured the rigors of slavery. In 1825, a significant change occurred in Douglass's life when he was transferred to the Baltimore household of Hugh Auld, who inadvertently provided Douglass with his first critical insight into the slavery system. In an incident that Douglass described as a "revelation," he overheard Auld rebuke his wife for teaching the boy the rudiments of reading. Deducing that ignorance perpetuated subjugation, Douglass undertook reading as an avenue to freedom. His secret efforts to educate himself—aided by *Webster's Spelling Book* and the random instruction of white playmates—were fruitful: obtaining a copy of *The Columbian Orator,* a popular collection of writings on democratic themes, he avidly studied the speeches of Richard Brinsley Sheridan, Charles James Fox, and other advocates of liberty. Douglass grew restive as his desire for freedom increased, and he was eventually sent to be disciplined, or "broken," by Edward Covey. When he refused to submit to Covey's beatings and instead challenged him in a violent confrontation, Douglass overcame an important psychological barrier to freedom. In 1838, he realized his long-cherished goal by escaping to New York.

Once free, Douglass quickly became a prominent figure in the abolitionist movement. In 1841, he delivered his first public address—a moving extemporaneous speech at an antislavery meeting in Nantucket, Massachusetts—and was invited by William Lloyd Garrison and other abolitionist leaders to work as a lecturer for the Massachusetts Antislavery Society. Sharing the podium with such renowned orators as Garrison and Wendell Phillips, he served successfully in that capacity for four years. By 1845, Douglass's eloquent and cogent oratory had led many to doubt that he was indeed a former slave. When urged by supporters to authenticate his experiences, he responded with a detailed account of his slave life, the *Narrative*

of the Life of Frederick Douglass, which was an immediate popular success. Liable to capture under the fugitive slave laws, Douglass fled the United States in late 1845 and traveled to Great Britain, where he was honored by the great reformers of the day. Returning to the United States in 1847, he received sufficient funds to purchase his freedom and establish *The North Star,* a weekly abolitionist newspaper.

During the 1850s and early 1860s, Douglass continued his activities as a journalist, abolitionist speaker, and autobiographer. After splitting with Garrison over the issue of disunion, he aligned himself with Gerrit Smith's conservative Liberty Party and marked the change by rechristening his periodical *Frederick Douglass' Paper.* By the outbreak of the Civil War, Douglass had emerged as a nationally-recognized spokesman for black Americans and, in 1863, he advised President Abraham Lincoln on the use and treatment of black soldiers in the Union Army. Douglass then founded *The New National Era,* a short-lived newspaper, and delivered numerous addresses on the lyceum lecture circuit, but his last years were chiefly devoted to political and diplomatic assignments. When he revised his final autobiographical work, the *Life and Times of Frederick Douglass, Written by Himself,* he was able to record numerous political honors, including presidential assignments as assistant secretary to the Santo Domingo Commission, marshal of the District of Columbia, and United States minister resident and consul-general to the Republic of Haiti. Douglass died at his home in Anacostia Heights, D.C., in 1895.

In his speeches on abolition, Douglass frequently drew on his first-hand experience of slavery to evoke pathos in his audience. He is most often noted, however, for his skillful use of scorn and irony in denouncing the slave system and its abettors. One of the stock addresses in his abolitionist repertoire was a "slaveholder's sermon" in which he sarcastically mimicked a pro-slavery minister's travesty of the biblical injunction to "do unto others as you would have them do unto you." His most famous speech, an address delivered on 5 July 1852 in Rochester, N.Y., commonly referred to as the "Fourth of July Oration," is a heavily ironic reflection on the significance of Independence Day for slaves. Douglass was described by a contemporary critic as being "particularly obnoxious to . . . those in general who mix up character and color, man and his skin—to all, in short, who have little hearts and muddy heads," and he is occasionally criticized for indiscriminate severity and humorlessness. In general, however, his polemical techniques are praised as commendable attributes of reformist oratory. Douglass's postbellum orations are regarded as more intellectual—and by many critics as less artistic—than his abolitionist addresses. In J. Saunders Redding's words, he had become a "finished public speaker" by the 1880s, "more concerned with intellectual than emotional responses."

A similar estimate has been made of Douglass's powers as an autobiographer. Critics generally agree that, in retelling and updating his life history in *My Bondage and My Freedom* and the *Life and Times of Frederick Douglass,* Douglass provided a classic American story of struggle and achievement but failed to recapture the artistic vitality of the *Narrative.* Valued by historians as a detailed, credible account of slave life, the *Narrative* is widely acclaimed as an artfully compressed yet extraordinarily expressive story of self-discovery and self-liberation. Recording his personal reactions to bondage in such simply-written yet moving passages as his apostrophe to the vessels sailing free on the Chesapeake Bay and his account of his confrontation with Edward Covey, Douglass distinguished himself from most other slave narrators.

Appealing variously to the political, sociological, and aesthetic interests of successive generations of critics, Douglass has maintained an enviable reputation as an orator and prose writer. Douglass's contemporaries, who were influenced by Garrison and other abolitionist sympathizers, viewed him primarily as a talented antislavery agitator whose manifest abilities as an orator and writer refuted the idea of black inferiority. This view persisted until the 1930s, when both Vernon Loggins and J. Saunders Redding called attention to the "intrinsic merit" of Douglass's writing and acknowledged him to be the most important figure in nineteenth-century black American literature. In the 1940s and 50s, Alain Locke and Benjamin Quarles respectively pointed to the *Life and Times of Frederick Douglass* and the *Narrative* as classic works which symbolize the black role of protest, struggle, and aspiration in American life. Led by Albert E. Stone, Robert B. Stepto, and Houston A. Baker, Jr., Douglass's critics have become far more exacting in recent years, for they have analyzed—and usually praised—the specific narrative strategies that Douglass employed in the *Narrative* to establish a distinctly individual black identity. Stepto's recent examination of Douglass's long-neglected novella, *The Heroic Slave,* testifies to the growing recognition of Douglass's narrative skills.

Distinguished by praise and diversity, the history of critical response to Douglass's works may be taken as an indication of their abiding interest. As G. Thomas Couser has observed, Douglass was a remarkable man who lived in an exceptionally tumultuous period in American history. By recording the drama of his life and times in lucid prose, he provided works which will most likely continue to attract the notice of future generations of American literary critics and historians.

(See also *Something about the Author,* Vol. 29, and *Dictionary of Literary Biography,* Vol. 1: *The American Renaissance in New England.*)

PRINCIPAL WORKS

Narrative of the Life of Frederick Douglass, an American Slave, Written by Himself (autobiography) 1845
Oration, Delivered in Corinthian Hall, Rochester, by Frederick Douglass, July 5th, 1852 (speech) 1852
The Heroic Slave (novella) 1853; published in *Autographs for Freedom*
The Claims of the Negro Ethnologically Considered (speech) 1854
My Bondage and My Freedom (autobiography) 1855
Men of Color, to Arms! (essay) 1863
"What the Black Man Wants" (speech) 1865; published in *The Equality of All Men before the Law Claimed and Defended in Speeches by Hon. William D. Kelley, Wendell Phillips, and Frederick Douglass*
John Brown (speech) 1881
Life and Times of Frederick Douglass, Written by Himself (autobiography) 1881; also published as *Life and Times of Frederick Douglass, Written by Himself* [revised edition], 1892
The Life and Writings of Frederick Douglass. 5 vols. (letters, speeches, and essays) 1950-75
The Frederick Douglass Papers. 2 vols. (speeches and debates) 1979-82

NATHANIEL PEABODY ROGERS (essay date 1841)

[*Rogers's laudatory account of one of Douglass's early abolitionist addresses originally appeared on 5 December 1841 in the* Herald of Freedom. *Testifying to his commanding physical presence and exceptional oratorical ability, Rogers treats Douglass as a living challenge to slavery and the notion of black inferiority.*]

The fugitive Douglass was up when we entered. This is an extraordinary man. He was cut out for a hero. In a rising for Liberty, he would have been a Toussaint or a Hamilton. He has the "heart to conceive, the head to contrive, and the hand to execute." A commanding person—over six feet, we should say, in height, and of most manly proportions. His head would strike a phrenologist amid a sea of them in Exeter Hall, and his voice would ring like a trumpet in the field. Let the South congratulate herself that he is a *fugitive.* It would not have been safe for her if he had remained about the plantations a year or two longer. . . . As a speaker he has few equals. It is not declamation—but oratory, power of debate. He watches the tide of discussion with the eye of the veteran, and dashes into it at once with all the tact of the forum or the bar. He has wit, argument, sarcasm, pathos—all that first-rate men show in their master efforts. His voice is highly melodious and rich, and his enunciation quite elegant, and yet he has been but two or three years out of the house of bondage. We noticed that he had strikingly improved, since we heard him at Dover in September. We say thus much of him, for he is esteemed by our multitude as of an inferior race. We should like to see him before any New England legislature or bar, and let him feel the freedom of the anti-slavery meeting, and see what would become of his inferiority. Yet he is a *thing,* in American estimate. He is the chattel of some pale-faced tyrant. How his owner would cower and shiver to hear him thunder in an antislavery hall! How he would shrink away, with his infernal whip, from his flaming eye when kindled with anti-slavery emotion! And the brotherhood of thieves, . . . we wish a hecatomb or two of the proudest and flintiest of them, were obliged to hear him thunder for human liberty, and lay the enslavement of his people at their doors. They would tremble like Belshazzar. (pp. 99-100)

> *Nathaniel Peabody Rogers, in an extract from* "*'Magnificent Orator',*" *in* Frederick Douglass, *edited by Benjamin Quarles, Prentice-Hall, Inc., 1968, pp. 99-100.*

WILLIAM LLOYD GARRISON   (essay date 1845)

[*Garrison was a nationally recognized leader in the abolitionist movement and a key figure in Douglass's rise to public prominence. The first person to publicly acknowledge Douglass's speaking abilities, Garrison subsequently advised him early in his career as an antislavery agent and promoted his speeches and writings in his influential abolitionist newspaper,* The Liberator. *In the following essay, which was originally published as the preface to the 1845 edition of the* Narrative of the Life of Frederick Douglass, *he records his passionate reaction to Douglass's first public address, praises his influence and skill as a public speaker, and recommends the* Narrative *as an authentic and unexaggerated account of slave life. For a discussion of Garrison's preface as an authenticating device for the* Narrative, *see Albert E. Stone (1973) and Robert B. Stepto (1979).*]

In the month of August, 1841, I attended an anti-slavery convention in Nantucket, at which it was my happiness to become acquainted with Frederick Douglass, the writer of the following *Narrative.* He was a stranger to nearly every member of that body; but, having recently made his escape from the southern prison-house of bondage, and feeling his curiosity excited to ascertain the principles and measures of the abolitionists, . . . he was induced to give his attendance, on the occasion alluded to. . . . (p. 3)

Fortunate, most fortunate occurrence!—fortunate for the millions of his manacled brethren, yet panting for deliverance from their awful thraldom!—fortunate for the cause of negro emancipation, and of universal liberty!—fortunate for the land of his birth, which he has already done so much to save and bless! . . . [Fortunate] for himself, as it at once brought him into the field of public usefulness, "gave the world assurance of a MAN," quickened the slumbering energies of his soul, and consecrated him to the great work of breaking the rod of the oppressor, and letting the oppressed go free!

I shall never forget [Douglass's first speech at an anti-slavery convention in Nantucket in 1841]—the extraordinary emotion it excited in my own mind—the powerful impression it created upon a crowded auditory, completely taken by surprise. . . . I think I never hated slavery so intensely as at that moment; certainly, my perception of the enormous outrage which is inflicted by it, on the godlike nature of its victims, was rendered far more clear than ever. There stood one, in physical proportion and stature commanding and exact—in intellect richly endowed—in natural eloquence a prodigy—in soul manifestly "created but a little lower than the angels"—yet a slave, ay, a fugitive slave,—trembling for his safety, hardly daring to believe that on the American soil, a single white person could be found who would befriend him at all hazards, for the love of God and humanity! Capable of high attainments as an intellectual and moral being—needing nothing but a comparatively small amount of cultivation to make him an ornament to society and a blessing to his race—by the law of the land, by the voice of the people, by the terms of the slave code, he was only a piece of property, a beast of burden, a chattel personal, nevertheless! (pp. 4-5)

As soon as he had taken his seat, filled with hope and admiration, I rose, and declared that Patrick Henry, of revolutionary fame, never made a speech more eloquent in the cause of liberty, than the one we had just listened to from the lips of that hunted fugitive. So I believed at that time—such is my belief now. (p. 5)

As a public speaker, [Douglass] excels in pathos, wit, comparison, imitation, strength of reasoning, and fluency of language. There is in him that union of head and heart, which is indispensable to an enlightenment of the heads and a winning of the hearts of others. May his strength continue to be equal to his day! May he continue to "grow in grace, and in the knowledge of God," that he may be increasingly serviceable in the cause of bleeding humanity, whether at home or abroad! (p. 7)

Mr. Douglass has very properly chosen to write his [*Narrative of the Life of Frederick Douglass*], in his own style, and according to the best of his ability, rather than to employ some one else. It is, therefore, entirely his own production; and, considering how long and dark was the career he had to run as a slave,—how few have been his opportunities to improve his mind since he broke his iron fetters,—it is, in my judgment, highly creditable to his head and heart. He who can peruse it without a tearful eye, a heaving breast, an afflicted spirit,—without being filled with an unutterable abhorrence of slavery and all its abettors, and animated with a determination to seek the immediate overthrow of that execrable system,—without trembling for the fate of this country in the hands of a righteous God . . .—must have a flinty heart, and be qualified to act the part of a trafficker "in slaves and the souls of men." I am confident that it is essentially true in all its statements; that nothing has been set down in malice, nothing exaggerated, nothing drawn from the imagination; that it comes short of the reality, rather than overstates a single fact in regard to SLAVERY AS IT IS. The experience of Frederick Douglass, as a slave, was not a peculiar one: his lot was not especially a hard one. . . . Many have suffered incomparably more, while very few on the plantations have suffered less, than himself. Yet how deplorable was his situation! what terrible chastisements were inflicted upon his person! what still more shocking outrages were perpetrated upon his mind! with all his noble powers and sublime aspirations, how like a brute was he treated, even by those professing to have the same mind in them that was in Christ Jesus! (pp. 9-10)

This *Narrative* contains many affecting incidents, many passages of great eloquence and power; but I think the most thrilling one of them all is the description Douglass gives of his feelings, as he stood soliloquizing respecting his fate, and the chances of his one day being a freeman, on the banks of the Chesapeake Bay—viewing the receding vessels as they flew with their white wings before the breeze, and apostrophizing them as animated by the living spirit of freedom. Who can read that passage, and be insensible to its pathos and sublimity? Compressed into it is a whole Alexandrian library of thought, feeling, and sentiment—all that can, all that need be urged, in the form of expostulation, entreaty, rebuke, against that crime of crimes,—making man the property of his fellow-man! (p. 11)

So profoundly ignorant of the nature of slavery are many persons, that they are stubbornly incredulous whenever they read or listen to any recital of the cruelties which are daily inflicted on its victims. . . . Such will try to discredit the shocking tales of slaveholding cruelty which are recorded in this truthful *Narrative;* but they will labor in vain. Mr. Douglass has frankly disclosed the place of his birth, the names of those who claimed ownership in his body and soul, and the names also of those who committed the crimes which he has alleged against them. His statements, therefore, may easily be disproved, if they are untrue. (pp. 11-13)

The effect of a religious profession on the conduct of southern masters is vividly described in the following *Narrative,* and shown to be any thing but salutary. In the nature of the case, it must be in the highest degree pernicious. The testimony of Mr. Douglass, on this point, is sustained by a cloud of witnesses, whose veracity is unimpeachable. "A slaveholder's profession of Christianity is a palpable imposture. He is a felon of the highest grade. He is a manstealer. It is of no importance what you put in the other scale."

Reader! are you with the man-stealers in sympathy and purpose, or on the side of their down-trodden victims? If with the former, then are you the foe of God and man. If with the latter, what are you prepared to do and dare in their behalf? Be faithful, be vigilant, be untiring in your efforts to break every yoke, and let the oppressed go free. Come what may—cost what it may—inscribe on the banner which you unfurl to the breeze, as your religious and political motto—"No Compromise with Slavery! No Union with Slaveholders!" (pp. 14-15)

> *William Lloyd Garrison, in a preface to* Narrative of the Life of Frederick Douglass, an American Slave *by Frederick Douglass, edited by Benjamin Quarles, Cambridge, Mass.: Belknap Press, 1969, pp. 3-15.*

WENDELL PHILLIPS   (letter date 1845)

[*Like Douglass, Phillips was a renowned nineteenth-century reformist orator. Both men were associated with William Lloyd Garrison in the 1840s, and they frequently appeared together at antislavery meetings. In the letter excerpted below, Phillips discusses the soon-to-be published* Narrative *and expresses his gratitude to Douglass for recording his sense of the spiritual degradation of slavery, which Phillips regards as the most compelling argument for abolition. His letter was first published in the 1845 edition of the* Narrative; *for a discussion of the letter as an authenticating device for the book, see Albert E. Stone (1973) and Robert B. Stepto (1979).*]

You remember the old fable of "The Man and the Lion," where the lion complained that he should not be so misrepresented "when the lions wrote history."

I am glad the time has come when the "lions write history." We have been left long enough to gather the character of slavery from the involuntary evidence of the masters. . . . [A man

must be disposed] to hate slavery for other reasons than because it starves men and whips women,—before he is ready to lay the first stone of his anti-slavery life.

I was glad to learn, in your [*Narrative of the Life of Frederick Douglass*], how early the most neglected of God's children waken to a sense of their rights, and of the injustice done them. Experience is a keen teacher; and long before you had mastered your A B C, or knew where the "white sails" of the Chesapeake were bound, you began, I see, to gauge the wretchedness of the slave, not by his hunger and want, not by his lashes and toil, but by the cruel and blighting death which gathers over his soul.

In connection with this, there is one circumstance which makes your recollections peculiarly valuable, and renders your early insight the more remarkable. You come from that part of the country where we are told slavery appears with its fairest features. Let us hear, then, what it is at its best estate—gaze on its bright side, if it has one; and then imagination may task her powers to add dark lines to the picture, as she travels southward to that (for the colored man) Valley of the Shadow of Death, where the Mississippi sweeps along. (pp. 17-18)

Every one who has heard you speak has felt, and, I am confident, every one who reads your book will feel, persuaded that you give them a fair specimen of the whole truth. No one-sided portrait,—no wholesale complaints,—but strict justice done, whenever individual kindliness has neutralized, for a moment the deadly system with which it was strangely allied. (pp. 18-19)

In reading your life, no one can say that we have unfairly picked out some rare specimens of cruelty. We know that the bitter drops, which even you have drained from the cup, are no incidental aggravations, no individual ills, but such as must mingle always and necessarily in the lot of every slave. They are the essential ingredients, not the occasional results, of the system.

After all, I shall read your book with trembling for you. . . . They say the fathers, in 1776, signed the Declaration of Independence with the halter about their necks. You, too, publish your declaration of freedom with danger compassing you around. In all the broad lands which the Constitution of the United States overshadows, there is no single spot,—however narrow or desolate,—where a fugitive slave can plant himself and say, "I am safe." The whole armory of Northern Law has no shield for you. I am free to say that, in your place, I should throw the MS. into the fire.

You, perhaps, may tell your story in safety, endeared as you are to so many warm hearts by rare gifts, and a still rarer devotion of them to the service of others. (pp. 19-20)

Yet it is sad to think, that these very throbbing hearts which welcome your story, and form your best safeguard in telling it, are all beating contrary to the "statute in such case made and provided." Go on, my dear friend, till you, and those who, like you, have been saved, so as by fire, from the dark prison-house, shall stereotype these free, illegal pulses into statutes; and New England, cutting loose from a blood-stained Union, shall glory in being the house of refuge for the oppressed;— till we no longer merely "*hide* the outcast," or make a merit of standing idly by while he is hunted in our midst; but, consecrating anew the soil of the Pilgrims as an asylum for the oppressed, proclaim our *welcome* to the slave so loudly, that the tones shall reach every hut in the Carolinas, and make the broken-hearted bondman leap up at the thought of old Massachusetts.

God speed the day!

(pp. 20-1)

Wendell Phillips, in a letter to Frederick Douglass on April 22, 1845 in Narrative of the Life of Frederick Douglass, an American Slave *by Frederick Douglass, edited by Benjamin Quarles, Cambridge, Mass.: Belknap Press, 1960, pp. 17-21.*

[REV. SAMUEL HANSON COX]   (essay date 1846)

[Cox's comments, which were originally published in a letter to the New York Evangelist *in 1846, refer to Douglass's 7 August 1846 address before the World's Temperance Convention in London, England. In his address, Douglass reminded the convention that, by virtue of their bondage, slaves were effectively excluded from American temperance societies, and that black freedmen were barred from them by racial prejudice. Cox, who was a member of the American delegation, here charges Douglass with opportunism, indiscriminate severity, and condescension. John Herbert Nelson (1926) also criticizes Douglass for being "grossly unfair."]*

[The convention delegates] advocated the same cause, showed a glorious union of thought and feeling, and the effect was constantly being raised—the moral scene was superb and glorious—when Frederick Douglass, the colored Abolitionist, agitator and ultraist, came to the platform and so spoke *á la mode* [according to the fashion] as to ruin the influence almost of all that preceded! (p. 108)

What a perversion, an abuse, an iniquity against the law of reciprocal righteousness, to call thousands together and get them, some certain ones, to seem conspicuous and devoted for one sole and grand object, and then all at once, with obliquity, open an avalanche on them for some imputed evil or monstrosity, for which, whatever be the wound or injury inflicted, they were both too fatigued and hurried with surprise, and too straitened for time, to be properly prepared. I say it is a streak of meanness; it is abominable. On this occasion Mr. Douglass allowed himself to denounce America and all its temperance societies together as a grinding community of the enemies of his people; said evil with no alloy of good concerning the whole of us; was perfectly indiscriminate in his severities; talked of the American delegates and to them as if he had been our schoolmaster, and we his docile and devoted pupils; and launched his revengeful missiles at our country without one palliative word, and as if not a Christian or a true anti-slavery man lived in the whole United States. (p. 109)

[Rev. Samuel Hanson Cox], in an extract from an account of Frederick Douglass's address at the World's Temperance Convention at Covent Garden on August 7, 1846, in Frederick Douglass *by Booker T. Washington, Haskell House Publishers Ltd., 1968, pp. 108-09.*

THE LIBERATOR   (essay date 1848)

[Many of Douglass's essays and numerous accounts of his speeches were published in The Liberator, *a major abolitionist newspaper which was founded and edited by William Lloyd Garrison. Until Douglass broke with Garrison in the early 1850s,* The Liberator *treated him favorably, as the two following excerpts indicate.]*

Four numbers of [Mr. Douglass's newspaper *North Star*] have been issued, and they are sufficient to indicate what will be its character, and the probability of its success. They have appeared with commendable punctuality, and exhibited no lack on the score of editorial tact or talent. The facility with which Mr. Douglass has adapted himself to his new and responsible situation is another proof of his genius, and worthy special praise. His editorial articles are exceedingly well written; and the typographical, orthographical and grammatical accuracy with which the *Star* is printed surpasses that of any other paper ever published by a colored man. . . . Success to our friends, even beyond their most sanguine anticipations, or the warmest wishers of their coadjutors! . . .

"Douglass's 'North Star'," in The Liberator, *Vol. XVIII, No. 4, January 28, 1848, p. 15.*

THE LIBERATOR   (essay date 1849)

Frederick Douglass addressed the people of this city last Thursday evening, upon the subject of American Slavery. We listened to him for the first time, and with a gratification seldom felt. From the reputation of the man, as an able and eloquent champion to the rights of the African race, we were led to expect much: we were not disappointed. . . .

He is a swarthy Ajax, and with ponderous mace he springs into the midst of his white oppressors, and crushes them at every blow. With an air of scorn he hurls his bolts on every hand. He feels his wrongs, and his heart is in every blow.

Douglass is a master of every weapon. His powers of ridicule are great. Wo to the man or the church whose hypocricy passes in review!

His address was confined to the subject of the prejudice against color. It was sometimes very severe, especially upon the churches while proclaiming that of one flesh and blood God made all nations, and called upon Ethiopia to partake of free salvation of a God who is no respecter of persons, and yet rear around the communion of common Savior a black and white table! . . .

We wonder not that Douglass is severe. We applaud him for his boldness. We like to see a man stand erect and plead for himself, for his race and for truth, though blood drip from his blade. Our own shoulders may bleed, but we admire a fearless arm.

Douglass is logical. His review of Clay's letter upon Emancipation was close, severe, and annihilating. Not one who heard it could say otherwise.

Douglass is a strong man.

"Frederick Douglass" (originally appeared in Cayuga Chief), in The Liberator, *Vol. XIX, No. 16, April 20, 1849, p. 62.*

WILLIAM G. ALLEN   (essay date 1852)

[Allen's remarks were originally presented as part of an address delivered before the Dialexian Society of New York Central College on 22 June 1852.]

In versatility of oratorical power, I know of no one who can begin to approach the celebrated Frederick Douglass. He, in very deed, sways a magic wand. In the ability to imitate, he stands almost alone and unapproachable; and there is no actor living, whether he be tragedian or comedian, who would not give the world for such a face as his. His ["**Slaveholder's Sermon**"] is a master-piece in its line. When he rises to speak, there is a slight hesitancy in his manner, which disappears as he warms up to his subject. He works with the power of a mighty intellect, and in the vast audiences which he never fails to assemble, touches chords in the inner chambers thereof which vibrate music now sweet, now sad, now lightsome, now solemn, now startling, now grand, now majestic, now sublime. He has a voice of terrific power, of great compass and under most admirable control. Douglass is not only great in oratory, tongue-wise, but, considering his circumstances in early life, still more marvellous in composition pen-wise. He has no fear of man; is no abstractionist; he has a first-rate philosophy of reform; believes the boy would never have learned how to swim if he had not gone into the water; and is, consequently, particularly obnoxious to tavern-keepers and steamboat captains, and those in general who mix up character and color, man and his skin—and to all, in short, who have little hearts and muddy heads. He is the pride of the colored man, and the terror of slaveholders and their abettors. Long may he live—an honor to his age, his race, his country and the world.

> *William G. Allen, "Orators and Oratory," in* The Liberator, *Vol. XXII, No. 44, October 29, 1852, p. 176.*

FREDERICK DOUGLASS   (letter date 1855)

[*In the letter excerpted below, Douglass explains his reasons for writing* My Bondage and My Freedom, *his second autobiographical work. The letter is directed to the book's editor.*]

In my letters and speeches, I have generally aimed to discuss the question of Slavery in the light of fundamental principles, and upon facts, notorious and open to all; making, I trust, no more of the fact of my own former enslavement, than circumstances seemed absolutely to require. I have never placed my opposition to slavery on a basis so narrow as my own enslavement, but rather upon the indestructible and unchangeable laws of human nature, every one of which is perpetually and flagrantly violated by the slave system. I have also felt that it was best for those having histories worth the writing—or supposed to be so—to commit such work to hands other than their own. To write of one's self, in such a manner as not to incur the imputation of weakness, vanity, and egotism, is a work within the ability of but few; and I have little reason to believe that I belong to that fortunate few.

These considerations caused me to hesitate, when first you kindly urged me to prepare for publication a full account of my life as a slave, and my life as a freeman.

Nevertheless, I see, with you, many reasons for regarding my autobiography as exceptional in its character, and as being, in some sense, naturally beyond the reach of those reproaches which honorable and sensitive minds dislike to incur. It is not to illustrate any heroic achievements of a man, but to vindicate a just and beneficent principle, in its application to the whole human family, by letting in the light of truth upon a system, esteemed by some as a blessing, and by others as a curse and a crime. I agree with you, that this system is now at the bar of public opinion—not only of this country, but of the whole civilized world—for judgment. Its friends have made for it the usual plea—"not guilty;" the case must, therefore, proceed. Any facts, either from slaves, slaveholders, or by-standers, calculated to enlighten the public mind, by revealing the true nature, character, and tendency of the slave system, are in order, and can scarcely be innocently withheld.

I see, too, that there are special reasons why I should write my own biography, in preference to employing another to do it. Not only is slavery on trial, but unfortunately, the enslaved people are also on trial. It is alleged, that they are, naturally, inferior; that they are *so low* in the scale of humanity, and so utterly stupid, that they are unconscious of their wrongs, and do not apprehend their rights. Looking, then, at your request, from this stand-point, and wishing everything of which you think me capable to go to the benefit of my afflicted people, I part with my doubts and hesitation, and proceed to furnish you the desired manuscript. . . . (pp. vi-vii)

> *Frederick Douglass, in a letter to an unidentified recipient on July 2, 1855, in his* My Bondage and My Freedom, *Dover Publications, Inc., 1969, pp. v-viii.*

JAMES M'CUNE SMITH   (essay date 1855)

[*Smith was a respected nineteenth-century spokesman for the black race. A medical doctor by profession, he is reputed to have been the "leading Negro in reformist movements and civic affairs" in New York City during Douglass's lifetime. Smith repeats the opinion of previous critics that Douglass's accomplishments argue for the safety and justice of emancipation, but he also anticipates later critics such as Vernon Loggins (1931) and J. Saunders Redding (1939) who regard Douglass's autobiography as a classic American story of struggle and achievement.*]

[Probably] not less than one hundred newspaper enterprises have been started in the United States, by free colored men, born free, and some of them of liberal education and fair talents for this work; but, one after another, they have fallen through. . . . It had almost been given up, as an impracticable thing, to maintain a colored newspaper, when Mr. Douglass, with fewest early advantages of all his competitors, essayed, and has proved the thing perfectly practicable, and, moreover, of great public benefit. [*Frederick Douglass' Paper*], in addition to its power in holding up the hands of those to whom it is especially devoted, also affords irrefutable evidence of the justice, safety and practicability of Immediate Emancipation; it further proves the immense loss which slavery inflicts on the land while it dooms such energies as his to the hereditary degradation of slavery. (pp. xxiv-xxv)

As a successful editor, in our land, [Mr. Douglass occupies the highest position in society]. Our editors rule the land, and he is one of them. As an orator and thinker, his position is equally high, in the opinion of his countrymen. . . . During the past winter—1854-5—very frequent mention of Frederick Douglass was made . . . in the daily papers; his name glided as often—this week from Chicago, next week from Boston—over the lightning wires, as the name of any other man, of whatever note. To no man did the people more widely nor more earnestly say, *"Tell me thy thought!"* And, somehow or other, revolution seemed to follow in his wake. His were not . . . [mere words of eloquence], that delight the ear and then pass away. No! they were *work*-able, *do*-able words, that brought forth fruits in the revolution in Illinois, and in the passage of the franchise resolutions by the Assembly of New York.

And the secret of his power, what is it? He is a Representative American man—a type of his countrymen. . . . Frederick Douglass passed through every gradation of rank comprised in our national make-up, and bears upon his person and upon his soul every thing that is American. And he has not only full sympathy with every thing American; his proclivity or bent, to active toil and visible progress, are in the strictly national direction, delighting to outstrip "all creation." (pp. xxv-xxvi)

When unexcited, his mental processes are probably slow, but singularly clear in perception, and wide in vision, the unfailing memory bringing up all the facts in their every aspect; incongruities he lays hold of incontinently, and holds up on the edge of his keen and telling wit. But this wit never descends to frivolity; it is rigidly in the keeping of his truthful common sense, and always used in illustration or proof of some point which could not so readily be reached any other way. "Beware of a Yankee when he is feeding," is a shaft that strikes home in a matter never so laid bare by satire before. "The Garrisonian views of disunion, if carried to a successful issue, would only place the people of the north in the same relation to American slavery which they now bear to the slavery of Cuba or the Brazils," is a statement, in a few words, which contains the result and the evidence of an argument which might cover pages, but could not carry stronger conviction, nor be stated in less pregnable form. (p. xxvi)

"The man who is right is a majority," is an aphorism struck out by Mr. Douglass in that great gathering of the friends of freedom, at Pittsburgh, in 1852, where he towered among the highest, because, with abilities inferior to none, and moved more deeply than any, there was neither policy nor party to trammel the outpourings of his soul. Thus we find, opposed to all the disadvantages which a black man in the United States labors and struggles under, is this one vantage ground—when the chance comes, and the audience where he may have a say, he stands forth the freest, most deeply moved and most earnest of all men.

It has been said of Mr. Douglass, that his descriptive and declamatory powers, admitted to be of the very highest order, take precedence of his logical force. Whilst the schools might have trained him to the exhibition of the formulas of deductive logic, nature and circumstances forced him into the exercise of the higher faculties required by induction. The first ninety pages of this ["**My Bondage and My Freedom**"], afford specimens of observing, comparing, and careful classifying, of such superior character, that it is difficult to believe them the results of a child's thinking. . . . (p. xxvii)

To such a mind [as Mr. Douglass's] the ordinary processes of logical deduction are like proving that two and two make four. Mastering the intermediate steps by an intuitive glance, . . . it goes down to the deeper relation of things, and brings out what may seem, to some, mere statements, but which are new and brilliant generalizations, each resting on a broad and stable basis. . . . [In] his **"Lecture on the Anti-Slavery Movement,"** delivered before the Rochester Ladies' Anti-Slavery Society, Mr. Douglass presents a mass of thought, which, without any showy display of logic on his part, requires an exercise of the reasoning faculties of the reader to keep pace with him. And his **"Claims of the Negro Ethnologically Considered,"** is full of new and fresh thoughts on the dawning science of race-history.

If, as has been stated, his intellection is slow, when unexcited, it is most prompt and rapid when he is thoroughly aroused. Memory, logic, wit, sarcasm, invective, pathos and bold imagery of rare structural beauty, well up as from a copious fountain, yet each in its proper place, and contributing to form a whole, grand in itself, yet complete in the minutest propor-

tions. It is most difficult to hedge him in a corner, for his positions are taken so deliberately, that it is rare to find a point in them undefended aforethought. (pp. xxvii-xxviii)

The most remarkable mental phenomenon in Mr. Douglass, is his style in writing and speaking. (p. xxviii)

The style of Mr. Douglass in writing, is to me an intellectual puzzle. The strength, affluence and terseness may easily be accounted for, because the style of a man is the man; but how are we to account for that rare polish in his style of writing, which, most critically examined, seems the result of careful early culture among the best classics of our language. . . . But Frederick Douglass was still calking the seams of Baltimore clippers, and had only written a "pass," at the age when Miller's style was already formed.

I asked William Whipper, of Pennsylvania, . . . whether he thought Mr. Douglass's power inherited from the Negroid, or from what is called the Caucasian side of his make-up? After some reflection, he frankly answered, "I must admit, although sorry to do so, that the Caucasian predominates." At that time, I almost agreed with him; but, facts narrated in the first part of ["**My Bondage and My Freedom**"], throw a different light on this interesting question. (p. xxix)

[The facts that Mr. Douglass relates regarding his mother and grandmother] show that for his energy, perseverance, eloquence, invective, sagacity, and wide sympathy, he is indebted to his negro blood. The very marvel of his style would seem to be a development of that other marvel,—how his mother learned to read. The versatility of talent which he wields, in common with Dumas, Ira Aldridge, and Miss Greenfield, would seem to be the result of the grafting of the Anglo-Saxon on good, original, negro stock. If the friends of "Caucasus" choose to claim, for that region, what remains after this analysis—to wit: combination—they are welcome to it. (pp. xxx-xxxi)

The son of a self-emancipated bond-woman, I feel joy in introducing to you my brother, who has rent his own bonds, and who, in his every relation—as a public man, as a husband and as a father—is such as does honor to the land which gave him birth. I shall place ["**My Bondage and My Freedom**"] in the hands of the only child spared me, bidding him to strive and emulate its noble example. You may do likewise. It is an American book, for Americans, in the fullest sense of the idea. It shows that the worst of our institutions, in its worst aspect, cannot keep down energy, truthfulness, and earnest struggle for the right. It proves the justice and practicability of Immediate Emancipation. It shows that any man in our land, "no matter in what battle his liberty may have been cloven down, . . . no matter what complexion an Indian or an African sun may have burned upon him," not only may "stand forth redeemed and disenthralled," but may also stand up a candidate for the highest suffrage of a great people—the tribute of their honest, hearty admiration. (p. xxxi)

James M'Cune Smith, in an introduction to My Bondage and My Freedom *by Frederick Douglass, Miller, Orton & Mulligan, 1855, pp. xvii-xxxi.*

DAVID W. BARTLETT (essay date 1855)

Mr. Douglass is a powerful writer, but we confess that we think he erred in attempting to maintain a weekly journal. We do not mean that [*Frederick Douglass' Paper*] is not an excellent, and often an eloquent one, but nature intended Douglass for an orator—not to be an editor. As an orator, he has few superiors in this or any other country, and it seems to us that he cannot do full justice to himself as an orator while attempting to edit a newspaper. (p. 63)

To those foolish people who contend that the African race is essentially a brute race, and far inferior to any other existing, we commend Frederick Douglass. He is perfectly competent to defend his race, and is *himself* an argument that cannot be refuted, in favor of the capability of the negro race for the highest degree of refinement and intellectuality. The more such men his race can produce, the sooner the day of its freedom will come. (p. 71)

> *David W. Bartlett, ''Frederick Douglass,'' in his* Modern Agitators; or, Pen Portraits of Living American Reformers, *Miller, Orton & Mulligan, 1855, pp. 55-72.*

WILLIAM WELLS BROWN (essay date 1874)

[*Brown was the first black American novelist and playwright, as well as one of the most significant of the early black historians. He also published a valuable historical work, the* Narrative of William W. Brown, a Fugitive Slave, Written by Himself, *and supported the abolitionist cause as an antislavery lecturer. In* The Rising Son; or, The Antecedents and Advancement of the Colored Race, *excerpted below, Brown emphasizes the importance of Douglass's publishing and editorial efforts, which he regards as Douglass's most significant contribution to the advancement of the black race.*]

[The **''Narrative of the Life of Frederick Douglass, An American Slave''**] gave a new impetus to the black man's literature. All other stories of fugitive slaves faded away before the beautifully-written, highly-descriptive, and thrilling memoir of Frederick Douglass. Other narratives had only brought before the public a few heart-rending scenes connected with the person described. But Mr. Douglass, in his book, brought not only his old master's farm and its occupants before the reader, but the entire country around him, including Baltimore and its shipyard. (p. 436)

As a speaker, Frederick Douglass has had more imitators than almost any other American, save, perhaps, Wendell Phillips. Unlike most great speakers, he is a superior writer also. Some of his articles, in point of ability, will rank with anything ever written for the American press. He has taken lessons from the best of teachers, amid the homeliest realities of life; hence the perpetual freshness of his delineations, which are never overcoloured, never strained, never aiming at difficult or impossible effects, but which always read like living transcripts of experience.

Mr. Douglass has obtained a position in the front rank as a lyceum lecturer. His later addresses from manuscripts, however, do not, in our opinion, come up to his extemporaneous efforts.

But Frederick Douglass's abilities as an editor and publisher have done more for the freedom and elevation of his race than all his platform appeals. Previous to the year 1848, the colored people of the United States had no literature. . . . Newspapers, magazines, and books published in those days by colored men, were received with great allowance by the whites, who had always regarded the negro as an uneducated, inferior race, and who were considered out of their proper sphere when meddling with literature.

The commencement of the publication of the ''North Star'' was the beginning of a new era in the black man's literature. Mr. Douglass's well-earned fame gave his paper at once a place with the first journals in the country; and he drew around him a corps of contributors and correspondents from Europe, as well as all parts of America and the West Indies, that made its columns rich with the current news of the world. (pp. 438-39)

[**''My Bondage and My Freedom''**], besides giving a fresh impulse to anti-slavery literature, showed upon its pages the untiring industry of the ripe scholar. . . .

Of all his labors, however, we regard Mr. Douglass's efforts as publisher and editor as most useful to his race. For sixteen years, against much opposition, single-handed and alone, he demonstrated the fact that the American colored man was equal to the white in conducting a useful and popular journal. (p. 440)

> *William Wells Brown, ''Representative Men and Women,'' in his* The Rising Son; or, The Antecedents and Advancement of the Colored Race, *A. G. Brown & Co., Publishers, 1874, pp. 418-552.**

JOHN EDWARD BRUCE (letter date 1889)

[*Although he was generally revered by his contemporaries, Douglass had his detractors. One of his most outspoken critics in the 1880s was the black newspaper editor and journalist John Edward Bruce. On 11 May and 8 June 1889—apparently in reaction to remarks that Douglass had made in a speech commemorating the twenty-seventh anniversary of the abolition of slavery in the District of Columbia—he published the following comments in letters to the editor of the* Cleveland Gazette.]

Mr. Frederick Douglass, in a speech delivered [in Washington D.C.] on the 16th of April last, took occasion to advise the colored people of the United States against encouraging race pride, arguing that a solid black minority would tend to array the white people against us—intimating that we would come nearer to the solution of the problem by assimilating with the whites, etc., etc. This is Mr. Douglass' advice to the Negro. It is bad advice; it is one of Mr. Douglass' dreams, which he nor his posterity will hardly live to see realized. Mr. Douglass evidently wants to get away from the Negro race, and from the criticism I have heard quite recently of him, he will not meet with any armed resistance in his flight. (p. 118)

[Mr. Douglass] owes much of his popularity to the colored fool editors around the country whose little patent inside and outside sheets have made him something less than a god, by keeping his name continually in their columns, and in endeavoring to convince ordinary mortals that when God created Frederick Douglass, He finished His work with the exception of the sun, moon and stars to reflect their rays upon him as he walked up and down the land. Mr. Douglass has courted their attention; he has coquetted with their editors, correspondents and reporters; he has used them to the extent of his ability; he has commended them as indispensable auxiliaries in the work of lifting the race to a higher plane in the social and intellectual world. And now that he sees or imagines that they can no longer be used, the question of their utility as helps in the solution of the Negro problem is disposed of by him with a slur and a contemptuous fling at their ''youthful imperfections.'' . . . Socrates said, ''He is unjust who does not return deserved thanks for any benefit, whether the giver be friend or foe.'' Noble words, these, and fitly spoken. Mr. Douglass may not be able to discover at this time any thing in colored journalism worthy of his support and encouragement. His own failures as a journalist and publisher may have doubtless embittered him somewhat, but all colored journals are not failures. Many of them manage to exist without the yearly subscription of Frederick Douglass some way or another. (pp. 118-19)

> John Edward Bruce, "Somewhat Less than a God,"
> in Frederick Douglass, edited by Benjamin Quarles,
> Prentice-Hall, Inc., 1968, pp. 118-20.

GEORGE L. RUFFIN (essay date 1892)

Douglass' fame will rest mainly, no doubt, upon his oratory. His powers in this direction are very great, and, in some respects, unparalleled by our living speakers. His oratory is his own, and apparently formed after the model of no single person. . . . If his oratory must be classified, it should be placed somewhere between the Fox and Henry Clay schools. Like Clay, Douglass' greatest effect is upon his immediate hearers, those who see him and feel his presence, and, like Clay, a good part of his oratorical fame will be tradition. The most striking feature of Douglass' oratory is his fire, not the quick and flashy kind, but the steady and intense kind. Years ago, on the anti-slavery platform, in some sudden and unbidden outburst of passion and indignation, he has been known to awe-inspire his listeners as though Ætna were there.

If oratory consists of the power to move men by spoken words, Douglass is a complete orator. He can make men laugh or cry, at his will. He has power of statement, logic, withering denunciation, pathos, humor, and inimitable wit. . . . Douglass is brim full of humor, at times, of the dryest kind. It is of a quiet kind. You can see it coming a long way off in a peculiar twitch of his mouth. It increases and broadens gradually until it becomes irresistible and all-pervading with his audience. (pp. 20-1)

His writings, if anything, are more meritorious than his speaking. . . . He is a forcible and thoughtful writer. His style is pure and graceful, and he has great felicity of expression. His written productions, in finish, compare favorably with the written productions of our most cultivated writers. His style comes partly, no doubt, from his long and constant practice, but the true source is his clear mind, which is well stored by a close acquaintance with the best authors. His range of reading has been wide and extensive. He has been a hard student. In every sense of the word, he is a self-made man. By dint of hard study he has educated himself, and to-day it may be said he has a well-trained intellect. (p. 21)

> George L. Ruffin, in an introduction to Life and
> Times of Frederick Douglass by Frederick Douglass,
> revised edition, De Wolfe, Fiske & Co., 1892, pp.
> 17-24.

JAMES M. GREGORY (essay date 1893)

[The following remarks were originally published in the 1893 edition of Gregory's Frederick Douglass: The Orator.]

By whatever standard judged Mr. Douglass will take high rank as orator and writer. . . . He belongs to that class of orators of which Fox of England and Henry and Clay in our own country are the most illustrious representatives. His style, however, is peculiarly his own.

Cicero says, "The best orator is he that so speaks as to instruct, to delight, and to move the mind of his hearers." Mr. Douglass

is a striking example of this definition. Few men equal him in his power over an audience. He possesses wit and pathos, two qualities which characterized Cicero and which, in the opinion of the rhetorician Quintilian, gave the Roman orator great advantage over Demosthenes. . . . The humor of Mr. Douglass is much like that of Mr. Joseph Jefferson, the great actor, who never makes an effort to be funny, but his humor is of the quiet, suppressed type. Like Mr. Jefferson, now he excites those emotions which cause tears, and now he stirs up those which produce laughter. (pp. 89-90)

The power of simple statement is one of the chief characteristics of Mr. Douglass' style of speaking, and in this respect he resembles Fox, the great British statesman, who, above all his countrymen, was distinguished on account of plainness, and, as I may express it, homeliness of thought which gave him great power in persuading and moving his audience.

Mr. Douglass' influence in public speaking is due largely to the fact that he touches the hearts of his hearers—that he impresses them with the belief of his sincerity and earnestness. His heart is in what he says. (p. 91)

Mr. Douglass, as an extemporaneous speaker, was much more impressive than he has been since he began to write out his speeches and deliver them from manuscript. . . . By not being confined to his manuscript, he caught the inspiration of his audience. This inspiration, so essential to true eloquence in the orator, can never be secured by the essayist, however finished and perfect he may be.

While Mr. Douglass may have lost much of his eloquence in using manuscript, yet some important advantages have resulted from this practice. He was led to investigate more extensively the subjects on which he wrote, and to take more time for preparation; and thus made his speeches more complete. Formerly, many of his best extemporaneous efforts were never fully reported, and consequently much that he said has been lost. His later lectures and speeches have been preserved in manuscript form, and when published together, as they will be one day, will prove a valuable contribution to literature.

Some of his best lectures are **"The Mission of the War," "The Sources of Danger to the Republic," "Self-made Men," "Recollections of the Antislavery Contest," "William the Silent," "Santo Domingo," "The National Capital, Abraham Lincoln," "John Brown."**

The discourses of Mr. Douglass when reviewed, will bear the test of criticism, and will be found to contain the requisites of a correct and finished style. His language is pure, his words are choice, and in accordance with the best usage. His sentences are constructed in the English idiom, and have the elements of strength because preference is given in their formation to short Anglo-Saxon words, rather than to those derived from Latin and Greek. So carefully is the rule of propriety observed by him that one would think he had thoroughly mastered the principles of grammar and rhetoric under the most competent instructors. From the discrimination he uses in the selection of words to express the idea he wishes to convey, we conclude he must have been for many years a diligent student of the dictionary. His writings are remarkably free from obscurity and affectation, which Macaulay regards as "the two greatest faults in style," and they may, therefore, be taken as models of perspicuity, so essential to one who would become eminent as an essayist. This excellence to which we allude, is due, no doubt, to the fact that he first forms clear and distinct conceptions of the truth he wishes to illustrate, and then making use of simple language to express the ideas arranged in his mind in logical order, writes freely as if under inspiration. Since he has followed the practice of writing his speeches his style has become more argumentative and massive, similar to that of Webster and Burke. In all he says, like these great masters, whom none have surpassed, there is so much beauty of expression, elegance of diction, dignity of thought, and elevation of moral feeling that the most happy and lasting effect is produced upon the mind of the reader. (pp. 93-5)

> *James M. Gregory, in his* Frederick Douglass: The Orator, *Afro-Am Press, 1969, 309 p.*

PAUL LAURENCE DUNBAR   (poem date 1896)

[*Dunbar was a late-nineteenth and early-twentieth century black American poet renowned for his skillful use of dialect, humor, and folkways. Befriended by Douglass early in his career, he published the following eulogistic ode to him in 1896 in his* Lyrics of Lowly Life.]

A hush is over all the teeming lists,
    And there is pause, a breath-space in the strife;
A spirit brave has passed beyond the mists
    And vapors that obscure the sun of life.
And Ethiopia, with bosom torn,
Laments the passing of her noblest born.

She weeps for him a mother's burning tears—
    She loved him with a mother's deepest love.
He was her champion thro' direful years,
    And held her weal all other ends above.
When Bondage held her bleeding in the dust,
He raised her up and whispered, "Hope and Trust."

For her his voice, a fearless clarion, rung
    That broke in warning on the ears of men;
For her the strong bow of his power he strung,
    And sent his arrows to the very den
Where grim Oppression held his bloody place
And gloated o'er the mis'ries of a race.

And he was no soft-tongued apologist;
    He spoke straightforward, fearlessly uncowed;
The sunlight of his truth dispelled the mist,
    And set in bold relief each dark-hued cloud;
To sin and crime he gave their proper hue,
And hurled at evil what was evil's due.

Through good and ill report he cleaved his way
    Right onward, with his face set toward the heights,
Nor feared to face the foeman's dread array,—
    The lash of scorn, the sting of petty spites.
He dared the lightning in the lightning's track,
And answered thunder with his thunder back.

When men maligned him, and their torrent wrath
    In furious imprecations o'er him broke,
He kept his counsel as he kept his path;
    'T was for his race, not for himself, he spoke.
He knew the import of his Master's call,
And felt himself too mighty to be small.

No miser in the good he held was he,—
    His kindness followed his horizon's rim.
His heart, his talents, and his hands were free
    To all who truly needed aught of him.
Where poverty and ignorance were rife,
He gave his bounty as he gave his life.

The place and cause that first aroused his might
    Still proved its power until his latest day.
In Freedom's lists and for the aid of Right
    Still in the foremost rank he waged the fray;
Wrong lived; his occupation was not gone.
He died in action with his armor on!

We weep for him, but we have touched his hand,
    And felt the magic of his presence nigh,
The current that he sent throughout the land,
    The kindling spirit of his battle-cry.
O'er all that holds us we shall triumph yet,
And place our banner where his hopes were set!

Oh, Douglass, thou hast passed beyond the shore,
    But still thy voice is ringing o'er the gale!
Thou 'st taught thy race how high her hopes may soar,
    And bade her seek the heights, nor faint, nor fail.
She will not fail, she heeds thy stirring cry,
She knows thy guardian spirit will be nigh,
And, rising from beneath the chast'ning rod,
She stretches out her bleeding hands to God!

(pp. 8-11)

> *Paul Laurence Dunbar, "Frederick Douglass," in his* Lyrics of Lowly Life, *The Gregg Press, 1968, pp. 8-11.*

JOHN HERBERT NELSON   (essay date 1926)

[*Nelson characterizes the* Narrative *as an exaggerated and bitter account of slave life and ascribes Douglass's rancor to the influence of his "white blood." His comments reflect his belief that the typical black slave was "happy-go-lucky" and "ignorant." Nelson's* The Negro Character in American Literature, *from which the following essay is excerpted, is a revision of a dissertation originally submitted at Cornell University in September 1923.*]

[Just] as the most restrained accounts [of the lives of slaves], the fairest in tone, were from pure-blooded Africans, so the bitterest, the most overdrawn ones came from mulattoes or men of more white blood still. Typical of this class [were] Frederick Douglass [and William Wells Brown]. . . . Douglass's well written narrative, grossly unfair to Southern life and people, is yet highly meaningful in showing how an intelligent man—a man whose mental constitution was Anglo-Saxon, whose will was the white man's also—how such a man reacted to being classed as another man's property. Brown was likewise more white than negro, but his narrative is fairer in tone, less impassioned, less bitter; in his capacity as plantation waiter, house servant, henchman of a slave trader, he saw more of slavery, but suffered less from its cruelty than Douglass. (p. 64)

> *John Herbert Nelson, "The Heroic Fugitive," in his* The Negro Character in American Literature, *Department of Journalism Press, 1926, pp. 60-8.**

VERNON LOGGINS   (essay date 1931)

[*Loggins was one of the first literary critics to recognize the artistic merit of Douglass's work. His survey of Douglass's career in* The Negro Author: His Development in America to 1900, *excerpted below, is distinguished by his appreciation of Douglass's compression of language in the* Narrative *and* My Bondage and My Freedom *and by his discussion of the structure of Douglass's "John Brown" oration. Loggins's book was originally published in 1931.*]

NARRATIVE

OF THE

LIFE

OF

FREDERICK DOUGLASS,

AN

AMERICAN SLAVE.

WRITTEN BY HIMSELF.

BOSTON:

PUBLISHED AT THE ANTI-SLAVERY OFFICE,

No. 25 CORNHILL.

1846.

Title page of Douglass's Narrative. *Historical Pictures Service, Chicago.*

The earliest [published writings of Frederick Douglass] are open letters, printed usually in the abolition journals. In the issue of the *Liberator* for November 18, 1842, appeared the first, an overstrained and crudely written expression of Douglass' feelings in regard to the case of George Latimer, whose imprisonment in Boston as a fugitive slave claimed in Norfolk, Virginia, was then stirring the abolition North. The letter is concluded with an appropriate apology:

> I can't write to much advantage, having never had a day's schooling in my life, nor have I ever ventured to give publicity to any of my scribbling before; nor would I now, but for my peculiar circumstances.

Although this original effort shows little promise, three years later Douglass' letters became what might be called a regular feature of the antislavery press. . . . The [style] of these communications . . . shows a constant improvement. . . . (p. 137)

In addition to the open letters, a number of his orations were printed in the antislavery press. But the most important production of his period of apprenticeship was the *Narrative of the Life of Frederick Douglass*. . . . (p. 139)

Among the American makers of autobiography, Frederick Douglass is unique. Probably no other American, not excepting Benjamin Franklin, lived a life marked with such contrasts. . . . The intellectual and moral growth which Douglass

attained, in spite of the long years which he spent as a slave and in spite of the lifetime of struggle which he experienced because of prejudice against his color, makes him a most remarkable figure among the celebrated Americans. And modern Europe has no match for him, simply because modern Europe has never known such violent racial discrimination as was practiced against the blacks in America throughout the period when Douglass lived. He recognized the drama in his career, and recorded it at appropriate times in four autobiographical works.

The first, *Narrative of the Life of Frederick Douglass,* follows in general the plan of the conventional slave autobiography. . . . Its main difference is that it is immeasurably better than any previous narrative which we can without doubt ascribe wholly to Negro authorship. (pp. 139-40)

There is still interest in Douglass' *Narrative,* even considered apart from the fact that he, a fugitive, only seven years out of the degradation of slavery, produced it. . . . From the store of his memories of his intimate contact with slavery he selected details for his *Narrative* which at one moment provoke laughter and at the next, pity. They are always clear and concrete, and from them we build up a unified picture of Douglass' life from his infancy to the year in which he became an antislavery agent. Nothing argues more strongly for the precociousness of his mind than the detached perspective with which he looks back upon his wretched past even though removed from it by a very brief lapse of time.

The style of the *Narrative* is childlike in its simplicity. But it is marked with two effects, no doubt brought about unconsciously, which many writers labor vainly to obtain. One is evident in the following passage, illustrative of the manner in which a weight of feeling is compressed into very few sentences:

> I never saw my mother, to know her as such, more than four or five times in my life and each of these times was very short in duration, and at night. She was hired by a Mr. Stewart, who lived about twelve miles from my home. She made her journeys to see me in the night, travelling the whole distance on foot, after the performance of her day's work. She was a field hand, and a whipping is the penalty of not being in the field at sunrise, unless a slave has special permission from his or her master to the contrary.

An equally difficult stylistic accomplishment is seen in the gracefulness with which Douglass mingles argument with incident. His sole purpose in writing his autobiography was to produce antislavery propaganda. Unlike the great majority of abolition writers, however, he possessed the ability to bring out his sermon without destroying his story. (pp. 141-42)

Douglass' second autobiographical work, *My Bondage and My Freedom,* appeared in 1855, near the middle of the period of his maturity as an author, which we might say extended from 1848 to the close of the Civil War. Almost four times the length of the *Narrative,* it reveals in more respects than in size that it is the work of the mature Douglass. The introductions by Garrison and Phillips which served the *Narrative* [see excerpts above, 1845] give way to an introduction by a member of Douglass' own race, James McCune Smith [see excerpt above, 1855]. The dedication is to Gerrit Smith, who . . . had replaced Garrison as Douglass' idol among the Abolitionists. . . . That his position as a free man could not be disputed when he wrote *My Bondage and My Freedom* was of great advantage to him. The book brings out in elaborate detail the story of his life as a slave, including minute descriptions of customs on a great Maryland plantation. What he did not dare say in the *Narrative* he now says with boldness. The book is in every sense a surer and bigger work than the earlier autobiography. While the style shows the same simplicity and compression, it is more accurate. If there is more argument, there is also more human interest, especially humor. (pp. 143-44)

In his autobiographical accounts as in everything else he wrote, Douglass seems to be speaking from the platform. His genius lay in his passion for meeting an antagonistic public with the spoken word. All of his writing is in the spirit of spontaneous and racy and stirring oratory. (p. 145)

Douglass' supremacy as a platform speaker was established by the time he returned from his first trip to Great Britain. There were few questions that arose in regard to his race during the succeeding eighteen years upon which we do not have a printed speech from him. (p. 146)

As representative as any speech which we have from him is *John Brown*. . . . (p. 148)

Avoiding the apology with which he was wont to begin so many of his early speeches, Douglass gets into his subject with a sustained periodic sentence, such as the fashions of nineteenth-century oratory freely permitted:

> Not to fan the flame of sectional animosity now happily in the process of rapid and I hope permanent extinction; not to revive and keep alive a sense of shame and remorse for a great national crime, which has brought its own punishment in the loss of treasure, tears, and blood; not to recount the long list of wrongs inflicted on my race during more than two hundred years of merciless bondage; nor yet to draw, from the labyrinth of far-off centuries, incidents and achievements wherewith to arouse your passions, and enkindle your enthusiasm, but to pay a just debt long due, to vindicate in some degree a great historical character, of your own time and country, one with whom I was myself well acquainted, and whose friendship and confidence it was my good fortune to share, and to give you such recollections, impressions, and facts, as I can, of a grand, brave, and good old man, and especially to promote a better understanding of the raid on Harper's Ferry, of which he was the chief, is the object of this address.

Then follows a skillfully constructed summary, scarcely more than a page in length, of the events leading up to Brown's execution. The main theme is brought out in a few flash-like sentences.

> There is, in the world's government, a force which has in all ages been recognized, sometimes as Nemesis, sometimes as the judgment of God, and sometimes as retributive justice; but under whatever name, all history asserts the wisdom and beneficence of its chastisements, and men become reconciled to the agents through

whom it operates, and have extolled them as heroes, benefactors, and demi-gods. . . . That startling cry of alarm on the banks of the Potomac was but the answering back of the avenging angel to the midnight invasions of Christian slave-traders on the sleeping hamlets of Africa. The history of the African slave-trade furnishes many illustrations far more cruel and bloody.

The body of the speech, in which the central idea is frequently repeated, is devoted to an account of Douglass' various meetings with Brown. There is a picturesque recital of the last conference between the two, held in a deserted stone quarry near Chambersburgh, Pennsylvania, just twelve days before the raid. There are occasional touches of humor, such as the reference to those who accused Douglass of being an accomplice of Brown—

> Governor Henry A. Wise was manifestly of that opinion. He was at the pains of having Mr. Buchanan send his Marshals to Rochester to invite me to accompany them to Virginia. Fortunately I left town several hours before their arrival.

After a tribute to Shields Green, the loyal fugitive slave executed with Brown, Douglass begins the peroration. He makes of it a restatement of his main theme. The Civil War, of which John Brown is named the first great hero, is proclaimed as the retributive justice which divine right had visited upon the slaveholder.

In spite of the flimsiness of the philosophy on which Douglass based the idea of the speech, and in spite of his faithfulness in following the standards of old-fashioned oratory, held in debasement by the taste of today, he produced in *John Brown* an oration that still stirs. Even in print, it seems warm and passionate. Fired by emotion, the message moves in a rhythm in which there is no hint of halt or hesitation. But Douglass in his maturity never allowed feeling to run away with him. The admirable structure of *John Brown* is an evidence of the exactness of his sense of logical symmetry. Each phrase, however sonorous it may be, has a definite and practical meaning. And *John Brown* is only one of a great number of orations of excellence which Douglass delivered and printed after 1847. . . . In the oratory of Frederick Douglass, American Negro literature aside from its folk song has reached perhaps its highest plane. And the significance of his speeches lies in their intrinsic merit, not in the fact that they were created by a Negro who for the first twenty-one years of his life was a slave. (pp. 148-50)

The *North Star,* except for contributions concerning Douglass himself, such as his manumission papers and the series of letters to Thomas Auld, his master when he was in slavery, was a general abolition paper. It contained little to identify it as a publication controlled and edited by a Negro. . . . (p. 152)

It was perhaps less a Negro journal when the name was changed to *Frederick Douglass' Paper.* The new title was adopted at the time Douglass became a publicly confessed convert to the abolition theories of Gerrit Smith. . . . What had been begun as just another antislavery paper was . . . turned into a political organ. . . . Although it bore Douglass' name, and although he was the chief contributor as well as the editor, the discussion of Negro affairs found place only when not crowded out by Presidential messages, speeches in Congress, reports of party caucuses and conventions, Douglass' answers to the political enemies who were attacking him right and left, and his apparently endless defenses of the Constitution as an antislavery document. But however embroiled in politics it became, Douglass' paper remained the champion of the people of color. He went into politics as a Negro fighting sincerely for the welfare of his race; and the turn of events in the Civil War proved that in renouncing Garrison's radical doctrine of disunion he showed himself a more practical, farsighted, and useful fighter. (pp. 152-53)

After the Civil War, Douglass had no paper of his own in which to record his numerous speeches and communications to the public, except for the years from 1869 to 1872, when he conducted and edited at Washington the *New National Era,* a Negro weekly. But his final period of authorship was none the less productive. . . . Many of his later orations, like *John Brown,* were printed as pamphlets. In 1881 appeared his third autobiographical work, the *Life and Times of Frederick Douglass.* The fourth and final autobiographical account came in 1892, the *Life and Times* enlarged by more than a hundred pages. In either edition, the story related is a strange one, peculiarly American. A man who has been a United States Marshal, a Recorder of Deeds, a Minister to Hayti, looks over his dramatic past, back into the desperate years which he spent in servitude in Maryland. Occasional passages reveal the oratorical Douglass still brimming with emotion. An example is the tribute to Theodore Parker, introduced into a brief description of a visit to the graves of Parker and Elizabeth Barrett Browning in Florence. . . . But the *Life and Times* is the work of an aging man. One finds in it verbosity and tediousness, not the compression which makes the earlier autobiographies very readable. (pp. 154-56)

Most of the work which [Douglass] produced in his prime, including his autobiographies, was evidently rushed through the press. There is at least one notable exception, **"The Heroic Slave,"** an account of Madison Washington's mutiny, which appeared in 1853 in *Autographs for Freedom,* an annual remarkable for its artistic typography. To see Douglass' writing in such decent dress, when the great mass of it is in timeworn newspapers or cheaply printed pamphlets, makes one feel that justice has not been done to the greatest of American Negroes, the most important figure in American Negro literature before 1900. Douglass' extant writings are worth preservation in a complete and scholarly edition. (p. 156)

> *Vernon Loggins, "Writings of the Leading Negro Antislavery Agents: 1840-1865," in his* The Negro Author: His Development in America to 1900, *Kennikat Press, Inc., 1964, pp. 127-75.**

BENJAMIN BRAWLEY   (essay date 1937)

Douglass was essentially an orator, not a debater, and was at his best in exposing the evils of slavery. He was not a man of great faith, and sometimes, as when he opposed the Negro exodus from the South in 1879, did not fully fathom the yearning of his people. After all, it was not the work of his later years that made him great, but that of his young manhood, when he had a story to tell, and when none who heard him could fail to be moved. In him the cause of freedom found a voice, a voice that spoke for thousands; and greater than anything he might say was himself, the supreme exhibit from the house of bondage. He had irony and he could be harsh, but he had little humor and could not be witty. (pp. 63-4)

Perhaps the greatest speech of Douglass was that which he delivered at Rochester July 5, 1852. With withering scorn he asked, "What to the slave is the Fourth of July?" In a superb passage he showed his aptness in quoting the Bible and likening the sorrows of his people to those of the children of Israel.

> By the waters of Babylon, there we sat down. Yea! we wept when we remembered Zion. We hanged our harps upon the willows in the midst thereof, for there they that carried us away captive required of us a song; and they who wasted us required of us mirth, saying, Sing us one of the songs of Zion. How can we sing the Lord's song in a strange land? If I forget thee, O Jerusalem, let my right hand forget her cunning. If I do not remember thee, let my tongue cleave to the roof of my mouth.

An address not more powerful but of more abiding significance was **"What the Black Man Wants,"** delivered in 1865, at a time of hesitation, to the Massachusetts Anti-Slavery Society. As the objectives of the war had been realized, and as Negro soldiers had assisted in the fight, Douglass could not understand how some people, even in New England, seemed disposed to give the black man a special status rather than the full measure of American citizenship. (pp. 64-5)

[Douglass's] speeches were generally well organized. At certain moments, in the dignity of his manner, he suggests the English humanitarian, John Bright; but he made more use of invective and scorn than Bright did. In the sharpness of his irony he recalls Wendell Phillips, but, eloquent though he was, he could hardly surpass that speaker in the liquid quality of his utterance; no one in the world could. Perhaps he is closest to the Irish orator, Daniel O'Connell; but his instrument had not as many keys as that of O'Connell, nor did he equal that speaker in human appeal. His effects were those of earnestness and massiveness; he aroused the respect and admiration if not always the affectionate regard of his hearers. All told, he gave to the western world a new sense of the Negro's possibilities. (pp. 65-6)

> *Benjamin Brawley, "Frederick Douglass As an Orator," in his* Negro Builders and Heroes, *The University of North Carolina Press, 1937, pp. 61-6.*

J. SAUNDERS REDDING   (essay date 1939)

> [*Like Vernon Loggins (1931), Redding calls attention to the artistic qualities of Douglass's works and accords him an important place in American literature. While Loggins, Henry Dan Piper (1977), and other critics fault the verbose style of the* Life and Times of Frederick Douglass, *Redding praises the "lucid simplicity" of the first edition of the book and regards it as Douglass's best work. This essay was first published in 1939.*]

The 1845 autobiography, *Narrative of the Life of Frederick Douglass,* came at a time when the writing of slave narratives, real or fictitious, was popular propaganda, but Douglass's book is in many ways too remarkable to be dismissed as mere hack writing. . . . In utter contrast to the tortured style of most of the slave biographies, Douglass's style is calm and modest. Even in this first book his sense of discrimination in the selection of details is fine and sure. The certainty of the book's emotional power is due in part to the stringent simplicity of style and in part to the ingenuous revelation of the author's character. (p. 32)

The same dignity with which [Douglass's letters to the press] answered malicious attacks or set forth his arguments marked his speeches. Indeed, reading his letters now, one feels that they were written for speech, that Douglass made no difference between the written and the spoken word. (p. 33)

The speeches [that Douglass] made between 1849 and 1860 were never equaled in logic, in emotional force, or in simple clarity. His peculiarly stony denunciation, the calm bitterness of his irony, and his frequent use of the simple and emotional language of the Bible make the speeches of this period memorable examples of the oratorical art. (pp. 33-4)

In 1855 the autobiographical *My Bondage and My Freedom* was published. His style, still without tricks, proves surer. Considerably longer than his first book, its length is amply justified by its matter. Though the first part follows in general the simple plan of the *Narrative*, he acquaints us more intimately with slavery and expresses his more mature thoughts on the problems which he faced. It is evident, especially when he writes of his English trip, that his knowledge of men had grown. Equally evident in the logic and sincerity of his arguments is the growth of his knowledge of issues. . . . *My Bondage and My Freedom* is the high mark of the second stage of Douglass's career. Indeed, though for many years after 1865 he was active as both speaker and writer, and though his thoughts steadily matured, he did not exceed the emotional pitch of this second period. As his intellectual vigor increased (and became, it may be said, a little warped by the overdevelopment of his capacity for irony), his emotional and artistic powers fell off. By the 1880's he was not an orator speaking with a spontaneous overflow of emotion: he was a finished public speaker, more concerned with intellectual than emotional responses. (p. 35)

[*Life and Times of Frederick Douglass*] was published in 1881. Its interest comes authentically from the man's life and thought. It has been called properly the most American of American life stories. Unconsciously, with no fanfare of self-satisfaction, the story develops the dramatic theme from bondage to the council tables of a great nation. It is written with the same lucid simplicity that marks all of Douglass's best work, but there is still the lack of differentiation between speaker and writer. *Life and Times* is his best book. (pp. 36-7)

[The larger edition of *Life and Times,* issued in 1892,] is slow and repetitious. [Douglass's] powers had waned, but he was still aware that all was not finished. He had mellowed with only slight decay; grown into acceptance without resignation. To the last, he wrote as he spoke. (p. 37)

The literary work of Douglass is first important as examples of a type and period of American literature. Many of his speeches rank with the best of all times. . . . That at least two of his books, *My Bondage and My Freedom* and the first *Life and Times,* have not been recognized for what they are is attributable more to neglect than to the judgment of honest inquiry. Certainly no American biographies rank above them in the literary qualities of simplicity, interest, and compression of style. They delineate from an exceptional point of view a period in the history of the United States than which no other is more fraught with drama and sociological significance. By any standard his work ranks high.

That he was easily the most important figure in American Negro literature at the time of his death goes without saying. He was the very core of the For Freedom group, fitting his art more nearly to his purposes than any of the others—and suffering less intrinsically for doing it. Without him the For Freedom group would be destitute of true greatness, Negro literature would be poorer, and American literary fields of oratory and

autobiography would be lacking a figure in whom they might justly claim pride. (pp. 37-8)

J. Saunders Redding, "Let Freedom Ring: Charles Remond, William W. Brown, Frederick Douglass, Frances Ellen Watkins, James Madison Bell," in his To Make a Poet Black, *McGrath Publishing Company, 1968, pp. 19-48.**

ALAIN LOCKE   (essay date 1941)

[*During the 1920s, 30s, and 40s, Locke wrote and edited several works exploring black society and art in the United States; he is best known as the editor of* The New Negro: An Interpretation, *a famous anthology in which he introduced the "New Negro" writers of the Harlem Renaissance. In the excerpt below, Locke promotes the* Life and Times of Frederick Douglass *as "the classic of American Negro biography" and reaffirms the relevance of Douglass's life and thought. His comments, which were originally published in a foreword to the 1941 edition of the* Life and Times, *are in large measure a response to Booker T. Washington's implicit repudiation of Douglass's relevance in his* Frederick Douglass *(see Additional Bibliography).*]

In the lengthening perspective of the Negro's history in America the career and character of Frederick Douglass take on more and more the stature and significance of the epical. For in terms of the race experience his was, beyond doubt, the symbolic career, typical, on the one hand, of the common lot, but on the other, inspiringly representative of outstanding achievement. Its basic pattern is that of the chattel slave become freeman, with the heroic accent, however, of self-emancipation and successful participation in the struggle for group freedom. Superimposed is the dramatic design of a personal history of achievement against odds, in the course of which the hero becomes both an acknowledged minority leader and spokesman and a general American publicist and statesman. Both chance and history conspired toward this, as he himself acknowledges, modestly enough, in his autobiography, but no one can come away from the reading of it except with the conviction that in mind and character he was, in large part, author of his own destiny. This heroic cast makes the story of Fred Douglass an imperishable part of the Negro epic, and should make his *Life and Times* . . . the classic of American Negro biography.

Another narrative of outstanding individual achievement and group service, however,—Booker Washington's *Up From Slavery,* has long held pre-eminence in popular attention and favor. Its author, himself a biographer of Frederick Douglass [see Additional Bibliography], gives an apt clue to at least one important reason for this. . . . Washington speaks of the Douglass career as falling "almost wholly within the first period of the struggle in which the race problem has involved the people of this country,—the period of revolution and liberation." "That period is now closed," he goes on to say, "we are at present in the period of construction and readjustment." So different did it seem, then, to Washington in 1906 that he could regret "that many of the animosities engendered by the conflicts and controversies of half a century ago still survive to confuse the councils of those who are seeking to live in the present and future rather than in the past" and express the hope that nothing in Douglass's life narrative should "serve to revive or keep alive the bitterness of those controversies of which it gives the history." In so saying Washington does more than reveal the dominant philosophy of his own program of conciliation and compromise; he reflects the dominant psychology of a whole American generation of materialism and reaction which dimmed, along with Douglass and other crisis heroes, the glory and fervor of much early American idealism.

That period, in its turn, is closed or closing. . . . A chronicle of the initial struggles for freedom and social justice is . . . particularly pertinent again in our present decade of crisis and social reconstruction. Without undue belittlement, then, of Booker Washington in his time and place of limited vision and circumscribed action, it is only fair and right to measure Douglass, with his militant courage and unequivocal values, against the yardstick, not of a reactionary generation, but of all times. It is thus evident why in the intervening years Douglass has grown in stature and significance, and why he promises to become a paramount hero for Negro youth of today.

This can happen most sanely and effectively if today we read or re-read Douglass's career in his own crisp and graphic words, lest he be minimized or maximized by the biographers. There is most truth and best service in a realistic rather than a romanticized Frederick Douglass. For he was no paragon, without flaw or contradiction, even though, on the whole the consistent champion of human rights and the ardent, ever-loyal advocate of the Negro's cause. His life was full of paradoxes, and on several issues he can be quoted against himself. In the course of events, for example, the man who "unsold himself from slavery" accepted, for expediency at the hands of philanthropic Anti-Slavery friends, the purchase price of his legal freedom; he could whip his overseer and defy, physically and morally, the slaveholder and yet forgive and benefact his old master. . . . [In] 1850, he declared uncompromisingly for pacifism and peaceful Abolition, but in 1862 pleaded with Lincoln to enlist Negro troops and when the order finally came, sent in his two sons and started out himself as a recruiting agent. More contradictions of this sort could be cited, none more illustrative than the dilemma of intermarriage, which he had to face late in life before the bar of divided public opinion after a long and happy first marriage to his devoted wife, Anna Murray Douglass, a free Negro woman who had befriended him while he was still a slave in Baltimore and who aided him to escape from slavery. Said he to friends, in skillful but incisive self-justification, "In my first marriage I paid a compliment to my mother's race; in my second, to my father's." Whoever reads the full story will doubtless grant him in all cases the tribute of sincerity and courage, and in most instances, too, the vindication of the higher consistency. (pp. 169-72)

Douglass's long and close identification with the Anti-Slavery cause, by which he is generally known, obscures his many-sided public life and service. Perhaps his surest claim to greatness came from his ability to generalize the issues of the Negro cause and see them as basic principles of human freedom, everywhere and in every instance. We see him accordingly taking sides with land and labor reforms in England and Ireland when there on a two-year Anti-Slavery campaign. Similarly he became one of the first public advocates of woman's rights and suffrage. . . . His advocacy of Civil Rights legislation and of free public education . . . showed him far in advance of any narrowly racialist view or stand. (p. 172)

Indeed, objectives which later seem to have become rivals and incompatibles in the hands of leaders of lesser calibre were, in the conception of Douglass, allies in the common-sense strategy of a common cause. In this respect, he seems, particularly as we read his pithy prose so different from the polished and often florid periods of his orations, a sort of Negro edition of Ben Franklin, reacting to the issues of his time with truly profound and unbiased sanity. It is unusual for a campaigning advocate of causes and a professional orator to be so sane.

Witness his shrewd realistic comment that flanks, in his autobiography, his impassioned editorial *Men of Color, to Arms!:*—showing him to be by no means the dupe of his own rhetoric,—"When at last the truth began to dawn upon the administration that the Negro might be made useful to loyalty as well as to treason, to the Union as well as to the Confederacy, it then considered in what way it could employ him, which would in the least shock and offend the popular prejudice against him."

Much of his writing has upon it the timeless stamp of the sage. "No people," he says, "to whom liberty is given, can hold it as firmly and wear it as grandly as those who wrench their liberty from the iron hand of the tyrant." . . . "Neither we, nor any other people, will ever be respected till we respect ourselves, and we will never respect ourselves till we have the means to live respectably." . . . "My hope for the future of my race is further supported by the rapid decline of an emotional, shouting, and thoughtless religion. Scarcely in any direction can there be found a less favorable field for mind or morals than where such a religion prevails." Obviously there is much in Douglass, both of word and deed, which is vital and relevant to this present generation and to our world of today. Racially and nationally we still need the effective re-enforcement of his career and personality. Youth, in its time of stress and testing crisis, needs and can benefit by the inspiring example of a crusading and uncompromising equalitarian. (pp. 172-73)

> *Alain Locke, in an extract from "The Enduring Douglass," in* Frederick Douglass, *edited by Benjamin Quarles, Prentice-Hall, Inc., 1968, pp. 169-73.*

ROBERT E. HAYDEN (poem date 1947)

[*The black experience in America is a prominent theme in the work of Robert Hayden, an award-winning American poet. Originally published in* The Atlantic Monthly *in February 1947, his "Frederick Douglass," which follows, testifies to the continuing appeal of Douglass's life and message.*]

When it is finally ours, this freedom, this liberty, this beautiful
and terrible thing, needful to man as air,
usable as the earth; when it belongs at last to our children,
when it is truly instinct, brain-matter, diastole, systole,
reflex action; when it is finally won; when it is more
than the gaudy mumbo-jumbo of politicians:
this man, this Douglass, this former slave, this Negro
beaten to his knees, exiled, visioning a world
where none is lonely, none hunted, alien,
this man, superb in love and logic, this man
shall be remembered—oh, not with statues' rhetoric,
not with legends and poems and wreaths of bronze alone,
but with the lives grown out of his life, the lives
fleshing his dream of the needful, beautiful thing.

(pp. 173-74)

> *Robert E. Hayden, in an extract from "The Enduring Douglass," in* Frederick Douglass, *edited by Benjamin Quarles, Prentice-Hall, Inc., 1968, pp. 173-74.*

BENJAMIN QUARLES (essay date 1959)

[*Quarles, who wrote the standard study of Douglass's life* [*see Additional Bibliography*], *is regarded as a leading Douglass scholar among American historians. In the following excerpt, he discusses the qualities which made the* Narrative *an effective vehicle of social reform. This essay was written in 1959.*]

[*Narrative of the Life of Frederick Douglass*] is absorbing in its sensitive descriptions of persons and places; even an unsympathetic reader must be stirred by its vividness if he is unmoved by its passion. It is not easy to make real people come to life, and the *Narrative* is too brief and episodic to develop any character in the round. But it presents a series of sharply etched portraits, and in slave-breaker Edward Covey we have one of the more believable prototypes of Simon Legree.

Contributing to the literary effectiveness of the *Narrative* is its pathos. Douglass scorned pity, but his pages are evocative of sympathy, as he meant them to be. Deeply affecting is the paragraph on his nearest of kin, creating its mood with the opening sentence: "I never saw my mother, to know her as such, more than four or five times in my life; and each of these times was very short in duration, and at night."

Perhaps the most striking quality of the *Narrative* is Douglass' ability to mingle incident with argument. He writes as a partisan, but his indignation is always under control. One of the most moving passages in the book is that in which he tells about the slaves who were selected to go to the home plantation to get the monthly food allowance for the slaves on their farm. Douglass describes the manner in which these black journeyers sang on the way, and tells us what those "rude and incoherent" songs really meant. He concludes,

> If any one wishes to be impressed with the soul-killing effects of slavery, let him go to Colonel Lloyd's plantation, and, on allowance-day, place himself in the deep pine woods, and there let him, in silence, analyze the sounds that shall pass through the chambers of his soul,—and if he is not thus impressed, it will only be because "there is no flesh in his obdurate heart."

Aside from its literary merit, Douglass' autobiography was in many respects symbolic of the Negro's role in American life. Its central theme is struggle. The *Narrative* is a clear and passionate utterance both of the Negro's protest and of his aspiration. The book was written, as Douglass states in the closing sentence, in the hope that it would do something toward "hastening the glad day of deliverance to the millions of my brethren in bonds."

The *Narrative* marked its author as the personification not only of struggle but of performance. "I can't write to much advantage, having never had a day's schooling in my life," stated Douglass in 1842. . . . Yet three years later this unschooled person had penned his autobiography. Such an achievement furnished an object lesson; it hinted at the infinite potentialities of man in whatever station of life, suggesting powers to be elicited. (pp. xvii-xviii)

A product of its age, the *Narrative* is an American book in theme, in tone, and in spirit. Pre-Civil-War America was characterized by reformist movements—woman's rights, peace, temperance, prison improvements, among others. In the front rank of these programs for human betterment stood the abolitionist cause. During the middle decades of the nineteenth century, antislavery sentiment was widespread in the Western world, but in the United States more distinctively than anywhere else the abolitionists took the role of championing civil liberties. Thus they identified themselves with the great American tradition of freedom, which they proposed to translate into a universal American birthright. (pp. xix-xx)

Naturally the *Narrative* was a bitter indictment of slavery. The abolitionists did not think much of the technique of friendly persuasion; it was not light that was needed, said Douglass on one occasion, but fire. The Garrison-Phillips wing did not subscribe to a policy of soft words, and Douglass' volume indicated that he had not been a slow learner. (p. xx)

Similarly the *Narrative* recognizes no claim other than that of the slave. To Douglass the problems of social adjustment if the slaves were freed were nothing, the property rights of the masters were nothing, states' rights were nothing. He simply refused to discuss these matters. As he viewed it, his function was to shake people out of their lethargy and goad them into action, not to discover reasons for sitting on the fence. . . .

[The *Narrative* is distinguished by] its credibility. The book is soundly buttressed with specific data on persons and places, not a single one of them fictitious. (p. xxi)

While Douglass' facts, by and large, can be trusted, can the same be said for his points of view? Did he tend to overstate his case? It must be admitted that Douglass was not charitable to the slave-owning class, and that he did not do justice to master Thomas Auld's good intentions. Let it be said, too, that if slavery had a sunny side, it will not be found in the pages of the *Narrative*. It may also be argued that the bondage that Douglass knew in Maryland was relatively benign. For a slave, Douglass' "lot was not especially a hard one," as Garrison pointed out in his Preface [see excerpt above, 1845].

Slavery differed from place to place and elicited differing responses (surface responses particularly) from different slaves. Hence Douglass' treatment of slavery in the *Narrative* may be almost as much the revelation of a personality as it is the description of an institution. But, as the *Narrative* strongly testifies, slavery was not to be measured by the question whether the black workers on Colonel Lloyd's plantation were better off or worse off than the laboring poor of other places; slavery was to be measured by its blighting effect on the human spirit.

It is always easy to stir up sympathy for people in bondage, and perhaps Douglass seemed to protest too much in making slavery out as a "soul-killing" institution. But the first-hand evidence he submitted and the moving prose in which he couched his findings and observations combine to make his *Narrative* one of the most arresting autobiographical statements in the entire catalogue of American reform. (pp. xxiii-xxiv)

> *Benjamin Quarles, "Introduction," in* Narrative of the Life and Times of Frederick Douglass, an American Slave *by Frederick Douglass, edited by Benjamin Quarles, Cambridge, Mass.: Belknap Press, 1960, pp. vii-xxiv.*

KENNETH REXROTH (essay date 1968)

[*Rexroth was a prolific mid-twentieth-century poet, critic, essayist, translator, and playwright. Associated with the San Francisco Renaissance and the Beat poets, he was generally acknowledged to be one of America's major poets during his lifetime. In the excerpt below, Rexroth maintains that Douglass's* Narrative *meets the criteria that modern, "radical" critics have established for a classic of black literature. His definition of a classic of black*] *literature as a work which can "transcend racial conflict and exist in the fully human. Its terms would be self-sufficient, self-determining and black" is important, for it outlines the critical concerns of such later critics as Robert B. Stepto (1979) and Houston A. Baker, Jr. (1980). Rexroth's comments were originally published in December 1968 in the* Saturday Review.]

[Those] earliest works of black Americans are of greatest value when their subject is not simply escape from slavery, but the achievement of true freedom. This is the essence of the program of the radical exponents of black culture today. They point out most correctly that as long as black literature concerns itself with racial conflict in terms that appeal primarily to a white audience it is not a free literature. A classic of black literature would transcend racial conflict and exist in a realm of the fully human. Its terms would be self-sufficient, self-determining and black. (p. 108)

Frederick Douglass was born free. His servile status was a juridical delusion of his owner. His race, his existence as a Negro, was the "custom of the country." It was also his deliberate choice. . . . Although his adult life was spent almost entirely with white people, Frederick Douglass chose to think as a black man. This in itself was no small accomplishment. It is more difficult to avoid becoming an assimilado than, for Douglass at least, to escape from slavery.

The most remarkable thing about Frederick Douglass' story of his childhood and youth, the thing that gives the narrative its simple and yet overwhelming power, is his total inability to think with servility. Aristotle said that it was impossible for a slave to be the subject of tragedy because a slave had no will of his own and could not determine his own conduct. Aristotle probably meant this as a permanent, indelible condition conferred by servile status. . . . Aristotle's is a false assumption. It does not apply to Douglass. He does not escape from slavery, he does not revolt against it, he simply walks away from it, as soon as he gets a chance, as from an absurdity which has nothing to do with him.

We accept the preconditions of Frederick Douglass' life far too easily. We forget how extraordinary it is to witness the growth and ultimate victory of a truly autonomous man in such a situation. The details are amazing enough, his struggle to obtain an education, to learn a trade, his adventures with cruel, or kind, or indifferent owners. Most amazing is the indestructible total humanity of one whom society called a thing, a chattel to be bought and sold. (pp. 108-09)

[Douglass's] writing is colored by the oratorical rhetoric of the first half of the nineteenth century, yet this has singularly little effect upon the present cogency of his style. We find similar rhetoric on the part of white men unreadable today. Douglass' is as effective as ever. It's not just that he is in fact simpler and more direct than his white contemporaries. It is that his rhetoric is true. He believes and means what he says. He is not trying to seduce the reader with the false promises of a flowery style. A hard, true rhetoric is not rhetoric in the pejorative sense. So today his autobiography is completely meaningful. . . .

One of the great values of Frederick Douglass to us is that he makes it abundantly clear that not all white people, even in the slave states, partook of the collective guilt of mastership. Most of his early education was due to the sister-in-law of one of his owners, Mrs. Thomas Auld. The Aulds later took him back from an owner who had imprisoned him for "suspicion of planning an escape," and apprenticed him to a ship caulker,

and thus gave him a trade which enabled him at last to get away. (p. 110)

The autobiography of Frederick Douglass is a "Great Book," a classic—not because it is the story of a Negro escaped from slavery, but because it is the story of a human being who always knew he was free and who devoted his life to helping men realize freedom. (p. 111)

> *Kenneth Rexroth, "Frederick Douglass," in his* The Elastic Retort: Essays in Literature and Ideas, *The Continuum Publishing Company, 1973, pp. 108-11.*

ALBERT E. STONE (essay date 1973)

[*Stone perceived that writing the* Narrative *was, for Douglass, an act of creative self-presentation. In the following excerpt, he approaches Douglass as an "artificer of the self" and closely examines the various narrative and rhetorical strategies that he uses in the* Narrative *to re-create his own identity.*]

Douglass's identification of self begins with the title and prefaces [of his *Narrative*], which establish conditions of the autobiographical contract between black writer and white audience. *Narrative of the Life of Frederick Douglass, An American Slave, Written by Himself* has a directness later replaced by the more figurative title, *My Bondage and My Freedom,* in the 1855 version and then in 1892 by the final, historical *Life and Times of Frederick Douglass.* Probably the most meaningful part of the title to the reader of 1845 was *Written by Himself.* The phrase reverberates with *An American Slave* to suggest the poles of Douglass's experience—his past as dependent slave, his present as independent author. (p. 198)

Whereas Douglass's title asserts the identity and responsibility of its black author, the first pages of the *Narrative* are devoted to guarantees by white sponsors. The Preface and Introduction by William Lloyd Garrison and Wendell Phillips [see excerpts above, 1845] are double assurances by two of abolitionism's greatest names of the book's authenticity. Virtually every nineteenth-century slave narrative carried such seals of white approval. Indeed, the practice has persisted long after Emancipation, as Dorothy Canfield Fisher's introduction to [Richard Wright's] *Black Boy* (1945) and M. S. Handler's to *The Autobiography of Malcolm X* (1965) both attest. (p. 199)

What immediately distinguishes the *Narrative* from most other slave accounts is Douglass's skill in using the introductions for his own purposes, so that what is elsewhere an extraneous essay becomes part of a unified form. The first advantage, of course, is a dramatic presentation of himself by another, thus dealing at once with the reader's possible imputation of vanity. . . . [As Garrison praises Douglass, the introduction is] turned into a speech and the personal subject largely lost in oratorical emotion. Though briefer, Wendell Phillips, too, falls into similar pulpit language and righteous regional feeling. These fulsome outpourings are deftly counterpointed by Douglass's own style and language throughout the *Narrative.* His final paragraph brings the reader back full circle to Garrisons's opening one [describing Douglass's speech at the 1841 Nantucket antislavery convention], but the Nantucket event is now re-created with the quiet authority of his own and not the white man's voice:

> I had not long been a reader of the "Liberator," before I got a pretty correct idea of the principles, measures and spirit of the antislavery reform. I took right hold of the cause. . . . I

seldom had much to say at the meetings, because what I wanted to say was said so much better by others. But, while attending an anti-slavery convention at Nantucket, on the 11th of August, 1841, I felt strongly moved to speak, and was at the same time much urged to do so by Mr. William C. Coffin, a gentleman who had heard me speak in the colored people's meeting at New Bedford. It was a severe cross, and I took it up reluctantly. The truth was, I felt myself a slave, and the idea of speaking to white people weighed me down. I spoke but a few moments, when I felt a degree of freedom, and said what I desired with considerable ease. From that time until now, I have been engaged in pleading the cause of my brethren—with what success, and with what devotion, I leave those acquainted with my labors to decide. . . .

Here the whole movement of the autobiography is succinctly recapitulated—the desire for freedom but the sense of being a slave, speaking out as the symbolic act of self-definition, Douglass's quiet pride in his public identity. Though the Appendix apparently undercuts the symmetry of this ending, this afterthought on religious hypocrisy also asserts his independence of official white institutions. Thus the original contrast is maintained throughout: while the white men Garrison and Phillips, argue a cause and point to this extraordinary black man as proof, Douglass's own account creates the image of a man, and this act of identity authenticates the cause of abolition.

The process from first to last is the creation of an *historical* self. "I was born in Tuckahoe, near Hillsborough, and about twelve miles from Easton, in Talbot County, Maryland." . . . So begins his story, which ends on an equally matter-of-fact note: "I subscribe myself, FREDERICK DOUGLASS. Lynn, Mass., April 28, 1845." . . . Both statements sound flatly conventional but carry a special meaning. Under slavery, man possesses no such historic identity as name, date, place of birth or residence usually provide. Douglass has *achieved* these hallmarks of historicity, has attached himself to time, place, society. Therefore he shows no wish to escape from history. As soon as memory provides them, and it is safe to do so, he gives names, dates, titles, places—all the usual evidence of existence which many slaves are denied. Yet Douglass never loses himself in memoir, as do many slave narrators, by making his account merely factual or typical. To be sure, the *Narrative* records many experiences and emotions shared by other fugitive slaves, but these are stamped with Douglass's own imagination.

This individual vision develops gradually, but can be seen even in the first primal scene, the flogging of Aunt Hester. . . . Douglass terms his initiation "the blood-stained gate, the entrance to the hell of slavery, through which I was about to pass," . . .—apt imagery for the violent emotions of master, slave woman, and the terrified child in the closet. The metaphor of "the blood-stained gate" is typical of Douglass's language. Traditionally Christian on one level, it also communicates more private and inchoate feelings about birth, sexuality, violence, dark mothers and white fathers. . . . [His later experiences] continue his personal history in terms also representative. However, Douglass prefers the personal and seldom goes out of his way to dramatize situations which his readers are expecting but which are not actually part of his own remembered past. When he does refer to the sufferings of other slaves, these are

carefully identified. The result is a narrative with less violence but more authority than many works in this genre.

The gradual enlargement of perspective in the *Narrative* is made natural and appropriate by Douglass's autobiographical point of view. He does not limit himself to the growing child's impressions but, like Benjamin Franklin (with whom, Alain Locke has noted, he has several parallels [see excerpt above, 1941]), writes both as experiencing boy and experienced adult. This double vision is managed with considerable skill throughout the book. On the opening page he contrasts himself as a young slave whose only birthday is an animal's—"planting-time, harvest-time, cherry-time, spring-time, or fall-time" . . .—with the grown writer whose present identity shares the anonymity and ignorance of slavery. "The nearest estimate I can give makes me now between twenty-seven and twenty-eight years of age. I come to this, from hearing my master say, some time during 1835, I was about seventeen years old." . . . Like Malcolm X and Claude Brown, Douglass is a very youthful autobiographer, with a young man's vivid memories instead of an older writer's diaries or reminiscences as resources. (pp. 199-202)

Still more striking is the memorable description of the slaves' songs he remembers hearing on the road to the Great House Farm. He writes first from his present perspective. "I have often been utterly astonished, since I came to the north, to find persons who could speak of the singing, among slaves, as evidence of their contentment and happiness," . . . he remarks. Then he recaptures his past emotion: "those wild notes always depressed my spirit, and filled me with ineffable sadness." Finally he returns to the present to drive home his point: "I did not, when a slave, understand the deep meaning of those rude and apparently incoherent songs. I was myself within the circle; so that I neither saw nor heard as those without might see and hear." . . . His message is clear, but more complex than with most slave narrators. Neither the slaves themselves nor a sympathetic outsider—like, say, the sympathetic English actress Fanny Kemble who could not fathom the significance of the slave singing on her Georgia plantation—is in a position to tell the truth about this music. Only by being *black* and *becoming* free has Douglass earned the rank and right of interpreter. It is a message whose precision Stephen Crane would have understood. (p. 203)

Among later episodes which express this writer's evolving identity, the crucial ones are his learning to read and write. Expression is at the core of selfhood for Frederick Douglass. (p. 204)

[In the *Narrative*] one may see the ultimate effect on the young boy of discovering how the aspirations and realities of his slave's life could find adequate expression. (p. 206)

But to reach this point he needed to write. This decisive step towards his present identity as a free black man occurred under circumstances which are recollected in detail:

> The idea as to how I might learn to write was suggested to me by being in Durgin and Bailey's ship-yard, and frequently seeing the ship carpenters, after hewing, and getting a piece of timber ready for use, write on the timber the name of that part of the ship for which it was intended. . . .

Specific details like these have a deceptive simplicity. Learning to write in a ship-yard bearing in part his own name is both an historical and a symbolic event. In recording an actual occurrence, one which connects the twelve-year-old boy to the present writer in Lynn, he continues a pattern of event and image linked together to articulate his autobiographical identity. For Douglass's association of learning to read and write with ships and ship-yards is not accidental. It recalls earlier and later moments when boy and man are seen in terms of ships, shipbuilding, and sailing across the water. . . . [One such] moment is the famous apostrophe to the ships on the Chesapeake:

> Those beautiful vessels, robed in purest white, so delightful to the eye of free-men, were to me so many shrouded ghosts, to terrify and torment me with thoughts of my wretched condition. . . . I would pour out my soul's complaint, in my rude way, with an apostrophe to the moving multitude of ships:—
>
> You are loosed from your moorings, and are free; I am fast in my chains, and am a slave! . . . You are freedom's swift-winged angels, that fly round the world; I am confined in bands of iron! . . .

Beneath this awkward rhetoric are some powerful personal associations linking ships and sails not simply to freedom, adventure, and literacy, but also the color white and the word "angel" with Mrs. Hugh Auld, his white preceptress who started him on the voyage to a free self and then betrayed him. In less emotional language, Douglass records another event in this complex when he describes his last act of self-assertion as a Maryland slave—his fight in Gardner's ship-yard with the white apprentices. In his memory and imagination Douglass identifies freedom with both learning from and fighting with whites; both relationships are often associated with ships or their construction. Thus though we do not learn so in the *Narrative,* but only later in *Life and Times,* it is fitting that this young plantation slave escaped to the North disguised as a sailor. . . . Here manifestly is a rich mixture of persons, places, sights, acts, and emotions which have combined in the autobiographer's memory to become what James Olney would call a "metaphor of self." Douglass's deepest impulses towards freedom, personal identity, and self-expression are fused and represented in these memories and images of ships and the sea. Therefore it is wholly appropriate that the final act by which selfhood is confirmed in the *Narrative* is speaking at the meeting on the island of Nantucket. Far more so than animal imagery, I believe, this pattern is central to Frederick Douglass's first autobiography for it connects and defines all stages of his personal history. "The following of such thematic designs through one's life," writes Vladimir Nabokov in *Speak, Memory,* "should be, I think, the true purpose of autobiography."

These literary strategies of self-presentation . . . set Douglass's *Narrative* apart from other artful accounts by ex-slaves like Henry Bibb, Solomon Northup, and Harriet Jacobs. But one must not forget that autobiography depends upon memory as much as on imagination. All remembered events do not fit readily into neat structural or imagistic patterns, no matter how many emotional needs are satisfied by trying to make them do so. Furthermore, one should not lose sight of Douglass's polemical purposes or the expectations of his readers. These readers, some of them unsophisticated and many suspicious of too much artistry, would be won over more immediately by a *story* than by a *point of view* or a *pattern of imagery.* Hence Douglass's emphasis upon exciting narrative, hence his climax in

the gripping fight with Edward Covey. This event, he tells us, was the turning-point of his life. It occupies the same central place in the *Narrative.* (pp. 206-08)

The fight between the sixteen-year-old boy and the white farmer occurs in Chapter X—nearly at the end of the *Narrative.* In content, this chapter is a microcosm of the whole *Narrative.* The events described cover exactly a year . . . and thus possess some of the symbolic unity of [Henry David Thoreau's] *Walden.* In becoming the clumsy field hand sent out with the equally clumsy oxen, Douglass is thrust back into the animal's place, easily brutalized there by Covey's whip. But like the oxen he, too, kicks over the lines, will not finally be broken to the yoke. . . . After the fight, which lasts two hours, his transformation is sudden and complete:

> It rekindled the few embers of freedom, and revived within me a sense of my own manhood. . . . It was a glorious resurrection, from the tomb of slavery, to the heaven of freedom. My long-crushed spirit rose, cowardice departed, bold defiance took its place; and I now resolve that, however long I might remain a slave in form, the day had passed forever when I could be a slave in fact. . . .

The remainder of the chapter completes in narrative terms the rebirth here announced. From Covey's hell he moves to the comparative heaven of Mr. Freeland's. . . . However, a slave's life even under a "good" master cannot be heavenly, as the brutal disruption of his Sabbath school and the betrayal by a fellow slave of his attempted escape both prove. Nonetheless, he affirms, "my tendency was upward." . . . The chapter closes with the young slave back in Baltimore and earning a good wage, which his master appropriates. (pp. 208-09)

As in narrative form and content, so in style is Chapter X representative of the whole work. It exhibits his two voices with characteristic clarity. The dominant one is the unassuming prose narrator who can set a scene, describe an action, or portray a person with forceful economy. This, for instance, is Edward Covey:

> Mr. Covey's *forte* consisted in his power to deceive. His life was devoted to planning and perpetrating the grossest deceptions. Every thing he possessed in the shape of learning or religion, he made conform to his disposition to deceive. He seemed to think himself equal to deceiving the Almighty. He would make a short prayer in the morning, and a long prayer at night; and, strange as it may seem, few men would at times appear more devotional than he. The exercise of his family devotions were always commenced with singing; and, as he was a very poor singer himself, the duty of raising the hymn generally came upon me. He would read his hymn, and nod at me to commence. I would at times do so; at others, I would not. . . .

Such a description characterizes both the individual and an institution—here the "religion of the south." Thus the balanced antiphonal structure of many of Douglass's sentences is wholly appropriate. A sentence like "The longest days were too short for him, and the shortest nights too long for him" . . . reveals Covey as slave-driver and also as self-driven Southern Protestant, and does so in rhythms strongly reminiscent of the Old Testament, particularly the Psalms. Once attuned to this cadence, the reader recalls how many of the work's aptest aphorisms obey this pattern. "What he most dreaded, that I most desired. What he most loved, that I most hated," . . . describes Hugh Auld's opposition to his learning to read. "I was ignorant of his temper and disposition; he was equally so of mine," . . . is another comment which also reveals the psychological inspiration for this balanced style. The ex-slave sees himself from the start on equal and opposite terms with the white world of slavery. The shape as well as the content of his sentences expresses this equality and energetic opposition. Hence the formal fitness of the ***Narrative***'s key sentence: "You have seen how a man was made a slave; you shall see how a slave was made a man." Douglass's story rests and rocks upon that semi-colon.

Douglass has, of course, another voice—the rich periods of the pulpit and platform, which sound so inflated and indulgent to modern ears. However, Alain Locke has warned that Douglass was "by no means the dupe of his own rhetoric." Like his fellow abolitionists, he knew that readers as well as conventioneers expected large doses of sentiment and pathos. In Chapter X the only instance of this style is the apostrophe to the sailboats. An earlier, lengthier one, which reads almost like a parody of John Pendleton Kennedy's *Swallow Barn*, is the bathetic description . . . of his grandmother and her solitary cabin. Both passages, despite their fitness for other purposes, sound out of pitch with other parts of the ***Narrative*** written to more telling emotional effect in Douglass's quieter style. (pp. 209-10)

[Charles Nichols maintains that when American hearts were moved against slavery] it was chiefly in a sentimental fashion. Settled convictions about the inferiority of the Negro . . . were, it appears, seldom changed. If this is true—and questions of the impact of propaganda art on public opinion and behavior are exceedingly difficult to measure—a small but significant factor may be the development towards sentimentality and extreme bathos in the slave narratives published after 1849. The later autobiographies of Douglass himself are, if not representative, at least indicative of a general loss of emotional force and economy. ***My Bondage and My Freedom*** and the ***Life and Times*** are not only greatly expanded accounts of a long, distinguished career but are also much looser in style, structure, and imaginative power. . . . [For example,] what was originally an organic pattern of meaningful events and images evoking ships and the sea as metaphors of Douglass's self becomes in later versions mere literary allusions, as in the following: "My poor weather-beaten bark now reached smoother water and gentler breezes. My stormy life at Covey's had been of service to me. The things that would have seemed very hard had I gone directly to Mr. Freeland's from the home of Master Thomas, were now 'trifles light as air.'" (p. 212)

[In general, Douglass] was unable to sustain a sharp sense of his own voice and identity through a long historical narrative. After reading the ***Narrative*** and then turning to ***Life and Times,*** one has difficulty agreeing with Rayford Logan in calling the later autobiography a "classic" [see Additional Bibliography]. This reader records a different impression—of the imaginative unity and superior force of the young man's self and story. Reading all three versions of this remarkable life makes one recognize afresh the difficulties of dealing with the long sweep of a public and private history. Douglass is no more to be criticized for writing more than one (and more than one kind of) personal history than are W.E.B. Du Bois or Mark Twain or Gertrude Stein. But if ***Life and Times of Frederick Douglass***

shows some of the strains of multiple autobiography, the ***Narrative*** should remind us how hard it is to repeat an early success. But then many of the most compelling black autobiographies have been the work of the young—*Black Boy, The Autobiography of Malcolm X, Manchild in the Promised Land, I Know Why the Caged Bird Sings* [written, respectively, by Richard Wright, Malcolm X, Claude Brown, and Maya Angelou]. Their precursor is the ***Narrative of the Life of Frederick Douglass, An American Slave, Written by Himself.*** It is the first native American autobiography to create a black identity in a style and form adequate to the pressures of historic black experience. (p. 213)

> Albert E. Stone, "Identity and Art in Frederick Douglass's 'Narrative',"" in CLA Journal, Vol. XVII, No. 2, December, 1973, pp. 192-213.

HENRY DAN PIPER (essay date 1977)

[*In the following excerpt, Piper refers to* My Bondage and My Freedom *(1855);* Life and Times of Frederick Douglass *(1881); and* Life and Times of Frederick Douglass, *revised edition, (1892) as subsequent "versions" of Douglass's 1845* Narrative. *These works are "versions" of the* Narrative *in the restricted sense that, in each book, Douglass revised his earlier account of his life as a slave; he also expanded his autobiography in* My Bondage and My Freedom *and the two editions of the* Life and Times *to include recent events in his career.*]

By all odds the most eloquent and most moving account of [Frederick Douglass's] life is to be found in the . . . 1845

Frederick Douglass in 1855, the year in which My Bondage and My Freedom *was first published. The Granger Collection, New York.*

Narrative. The three subsequent and better-known versions (which actually do not vary a great deal in style) are markedly inferior so far as literary values are concerned. (p. 183)

One simple, straightforward way of demonstrating the literary superiority of the 1845 *Narrative* over later versions is to compare parallel passages. In the earliest version Douglass's first twenty-six years of life are covered in a narrative of around 40,000 words. His account of the same twenty-six-year period in the 1855 and later versions is almost three times as long. It is marred by a long-winded verbosity that compares unfavorably with the concise, sharply focussed and swift paced earlier narrative. . . .

Here, for example, is a typical passage as it was originally published in 1845, together with the 1892 version:

> My master and myself had quite a number of differences. He found me unsuitable for his purpose. My city life, he said, had had a very pernicious effect upon me. It had almost ruined me for every good purpose, and fitted me for every thing bad. One of my greatest faults was that of letting his horse run away, and go down to his father-in-law's farm, which was about five miles from St. Michael's. I would then have to go after it. My reason for this kind of carelessness, or carefulness, was, that I could always get something to eat when I went there. Master William Hamilton, my master's father-in-law, always gave his slaves enough to eat. I never left there hungry, no matter how great the need of my speedy return. Master Thomas at length said he would stand it no longer. I had lived with him nine months, during which time he had given me a number of severe whippings, all to no good purpose. He resolved to put me out, as he said, to be broken; and, for this purpose, he let me for one year to a man named Edward Covey. . . . [1845 *Narrative*]
>
> (p. 184)

The many differences springing up between Master Thomas and myself, owing to the clear perception I had of his character, and the boldness with which I defended myself against his capricious complaints, led him to declare that I was unsuited to his wants; that my city life had affected me perniciously; that in fact it had almost ruined me for every good purpose, and had fitted me for everything bad. One of my greatest faults, or offences, was that of letting his horse get away and go down to the farm which belonged to his father-in-law. The animal had a liking for that farm with which I fully sympathized. Whenever I let it out it would go dashing down the road to Mr. Hamilton's, as if going on a grand frolic. My horse gone, of course I must go after it. The explanation of our mutual attachment to the place is the same—the horse found good pasturage, and I found there plenty of bread. Mr. Hamilton had his faults, but starving his slaves was not one of them. He gave food in abundance and of excellent quality. In Mr. Hamilton's cook—Aunt Mary—I found a generous and considerate friend. She never allowed me to go there with-

out giving me bread enough to make good the deficiencies of a day or two. Master Thomas at last resolved to endure my behavior no longer; he could keep neither me nor his horse, we liked so well to be at his father-in-law's farm. I had lived with him nearly nine months and he had given me a number of severe whippings, without any visible improvement in my character or conduct, and now he was resolved to put me out, as he said, *"to be broken."*
There was, in the Bay-side, very near the camp-ground where my master received his religious impressions, a man named Edward Covey, who enjoyed the reputation of being a first rate hand at breaking young Negroes. . . . [1892 *Life and Times*]

(pp. 185-86)

Comparing these two passages, it is easy to see that the literary power of the earlier one is due to two important factors: shorter sentences, and lively, concrete monosyllables rather than the more heavy-footed, abstract polysyllables of the later version. In the 1845 *Narrative* the average number of words per sentence, based on random counts of selected passages, is around 18 words, compared to an average of at least 30 words for the later versions. Similarly, the average number of polysyllabic words per sentence (i.e., those with two or more syllables, and excluding proper names) runs around 1.2 for the 1845 *Narrative* compared with 2.3 in the 1855 and later versions.

What prompted Douglass to so inflate and muddy his admirable narrative style in his later revisions? One answer is suggested by his mentor, William Lloyd Garrison. . . . (p. 186)

[Douglass tells us that] he began subscribing to [Garrison's] *Liberator* and reading it regularly "with such feelings as it would be quite idle for me to attempt to describe. The paper became my meat and my drink. My soul was set all on fire. Its sympathy for my brethren in bonds—its scathing denunciation of slaveholders—its faithful exposures of slavery—and its powerful attacks upon the upholders of the institution—sent a thrill of joy through my soul, such as I had never felt before!" . . .

Yet Garrison, the highly-cultivated Harvard intellectual, wrote a very different literary style from that of Douglass. The average number of words per sentence in Garrison's moving "Preface" to the 1845 *Narrative* [see excerpt above, 1845] is 28, compared to Douglass's 18. Moreover, the average number of polysyllables per sentence in the Garrison selection is 3.0 compared to Douglass's 1.2.

Random samplings from the writings of other eminent Victorian contemporaries of Douglass reveal the prevalence of a similar long-winded verbosity of style. Take, for instance, the distinguished abolitionist and friend of Garrison's, Wendell Phillips. Garrison published Phillips' congratulatory letter to Douglass next to Garrison's own "Preface" at the front of the 1845 *Narrative* [see excerpt above, 1845]. Phillips' letter averages around 28.1 words to the sentence, almost exactly that of the Garrison Preface! (p. 187)

The lesson is clear. As Douglass, the former slave who laboriously taught himself to read and write English, rose higher up the ladder of Victorian success he abandoned the simple, straightforward language of the streets and adopted instead (perhaps unconsciously) the long-winded rhetoric of the power establishment. . . . No one would censor Douglass the man for following this path. It was undoubtedly a necessary step in his attempt as a newspaper man to reach the widest and most influential American public. ''When in Rome. . . .'' But nonetheless the lesson is clear. Douglass, the escaped slave, wrote far more powerfully and eloquently when he simply ''told it the way it was,'' in his own way, than when he adopted the over-upholstered prose of the New England establishment.

In the process, Douglass abandoned the ordinary speech of the common man that has remained at the heart of the American language since it first sought its independence from the Old World—the speech of Benjamin Franklin, Abraham Lincoln, Mark Twain's *Huckleberry Finn,* and Ernest Hemingway. It is no coincidence that the average number of words per sentence in Douglass's *Narrative* is almost exactly the same as the average from a random sampling of Ernest Hemingway's first important book of short stories, *In Our Time.* Or that both are almost identical with the average in an essay, ''Advice to a Young Tradesman,'' by that influential newspaper editor, Benjamin Franklin, back in 1748. Abraham Lincoln's short and pithy ''Notes for a Law Lecture'' written for his fellow members of the bar, averages almost the same—17.4. (p. 188)

One of the challenges we have faced as the first modern democratic society of any size has been the creation of an indigenous written prose style readily grasped and understood by the common man yet capable of conveying the most complex and subtle feelings and moral ideas. Hemingway claimed that this all started with *Huckleberry Finn.* . . . But the origins of that style lie deeper in our national past—in the simple prose of Franklin and Lincoln. And to that literary tradition, as we have seen here, we must now add Frederick Douglass's 1845 *Narrative.* (p. 189)

> *Henry Dan Piper, ''The Place of Frederick Douglass's 'Narrative of the Life of an American Slave' in the Development of a Native American Prose Style,'' in* The Journal of Afro-American Issues, *Vol. V, No. 2, Spring, 1977, pp. 183-91.*

G. THOMAS COUSER   (essay date 1979)

[*Couser argues that Douglass uses the structure of the religious conversion narrative to organize and focus the* Narrative. *He thus joins Albert E. Stone (1973) and Robert B. Stepto (1979) in supporting the view that the* Narrative *shows Douglass to be a skillful, self-conscious narrator.*]

[The *Narrative of the Life of Frederick Douglass*] reveals the impact on the slave narrative of most of the acknowledged literary influences—the Bible, [John Bunyan's] *Pilgrim's Progress,* abolitionist oratory, and sermon rhetoric. But more significant than these literary influences were several experiential ones—Douglass's experience of slavery, of the anti-slavery movement, and of religious conversion. The relevance of the first two is obvious enough. (p. 51)

How Douglass's conversion is relevant to the *Narrative* is less obvious, for it is never mentioned in the text. Nevertheless, it plays an important role, for Douglass employs the structure of the conversion narrative to organize and focus his autobiography. (p. 52)

[Central] to his narrative [is] an analogy between the process of conversion and that of liberation.

According to this analogy, slavery is equivalent to a state of sin or existence in Hell, freedom to grace or Heaven, and escape or liberation to salvation or conversion. While the analogy itself

may not have been original with Douglass, the consistency of its application in the narrative suggests that it was a conscious narrative and rhetorical strategy. It is the development of this analogy, I think, that structures and controls the narrative, giving it a classic shape unique among slave narratives. Like other American autobiographers in the nineteenth century, . . . Douglass exploits the patterns of spiritual autobiography for prophetic purposes; for throughout the book, he writes not merely as an autobiographer concerned with his own experience but also as a prophet commenting upon American history from a supramundane viewpoint. However, Douglass's strategy is a double-edged sword, for he manages at once to use Christian values to condemn the institution of slavery and to use his knowledge of slavery to criticize some of the preaching and practice of nominal Christians. As a prophet, he calls not only for the abolition of slavery but also for the purification of American Christianity.

The implications of Douglass's conversion analogy provide an ironic commentary at every point on the doctrines of Southern Methodism. . . . For example, Douglass portrays himself as having been born innocent into a sinful condition; instead of revealing man to be innately sinful, Douglass exposes slavery as inherently evil. When he calls the experience of witnessing the whipping of his aunt ''the bloodstained gate, the entrance to the hell of slavery, through which I was about to pass,'' he makes explicit part of his analogy. But the implications the metaphor holds for the slave differ from those it holds for the master. The sin of slavery is most obviously the master's, as is evident from his cruelty. But just as it is evil to be a master, it is also a sin to be a slave, if the slave accepts his condition as proper and accepts fallen Christians as his true superiors. (pp. 53-4)

Douglass's penetrating perception of the slave's moral dilemma is expressed in his discussion of a garden kept by his first owner, Colonel Lloyd. Abounding in fruit, the garden is described as a land of worldly paradise from which slaves are excluded. In one respect it serves as a metaphor for the plantation system; it stands for all the goods, comforts, and pleasures denied to the slaves. Naturally, and justifiably, they seek access to it. The colonel's response is to tar the fence around it and to interpret tar on a slave's clothing as evidence of sin. According to Douglass, the plan succeeded because the slaves realized ''the impossibility of touching *tar* without being defiled.'' . . . The implication here is that the slaves are morally superior to their masters, who feel that they can participate without guilt in a sinful social system. By the very fact of its exclusiveness, the garden becomes a place of corruption rather than of Edenic innocence. But the sin inherent in its existence is complicated by the temptation the system offers the disadvantaged slaves. There is little danger of their committing the sin of the master—the exploitation of others; rather, the temptation is to submit to mastery by another. Colonel Lloyd is a powerful but not an omnipotent master; rather, he is a false god—irrational, unjust, vengeful, and dishonest. To maintain his integrity—to be saved—the slave must look beyond his master's authority and resist the lure of white values. (p. 54)

Douglass's condition was somewhat mitigated by his belief in his eventual deliverance from slavery. . . . The first confirmation of his sense of election, and hence the first use in the narrative of the providential framework, comes with his transfer from the plantation to Baltimore. There is, however, a certain irony in his sense of divine favoritism, for the real benefits of his selection become evident only as the apparent advantages are revealed to be illusory. . . . It is, ironically, through the revocation of certain privileges that Douglass comes to understand the means of his enslavement. Thus, in being denied instruction in literacy, he learns a more significant lesson about "the white man's power to enslave the black." . . . The idea that slavery depends on the ignorance of the enslaved is "a new and special revelation, explaining dark and mysterious things." . . . (p. 55)

The essence of his new insight is that his proper goals for himself are inevitably the opposite of his master's: "What he most dreaded, that I most desired. What he most loved, that I most hated. That which to him was a great evil, to be carefully shunned was to me a great good, to be diligently sought." . . . Similarly, his valuation of himself must differ from his master's. Since his sinful condition is his master's creation, Douglass's salvation lies in committing what are sins in his master's eyes. Hence he undertakes a course of self-improvement, bribing poor white boys to teach him to read. Newly aware of his master's vision, values, purposes, and methods, Douglass begins to equip himself to subvert them. Implicit and instrumental in the quest for self-mastery is a sense of loyalty to a higher master; Douglass must betray his white master to be faithful to himself and to God.

Once he has been exposed to the gospel of freedom—the arguments against slavery—as set forth in "The Columbian Orator," Douglass's condition is analogous to that of the convert in the stage of conviction. He is aware of his sin, but helpless to avoid it, aware of grace but unable to possess it. Thus, he says of his reading: "It had given me a view of my wretched condition without the remedy. It opened my eyes to the horrible pit, but to no ladder upon which to get out." . . . (pp. 55-6)

Douglass's spiritual progress enters its climactic phase when . . . he is put out to be broken as a field hand by a man named Covey. The narrative veers toward allegory here, for Covey, a notorious slave-breaker, is characterized in fairly explicit terms as a satanic figure: "He had the faculty of making us feel that he was ever-present with us. . . . He always aimed at taking us by surprise. Such was his cunning that we used to call him, among ourselves, 'the snake'." . . . Covey's role is to tempt (actually, to threaten) Douglass into slavish behavior and attitudes that betray not only his humanity but his divine potential. Just as the convert's heart is broken before it is made new, Douglass's spirit is broken before it is regenerated. The nadir of the narrative comes when, during his first six months with Covey, he goes through a stage analogous to the stage of humiliation: "I was broken in body, soul, and spirit. . . . The dark night of slavery closed in upon me; and behold a man transformed into a brute!" . . .

Not Douglass's flight from the South but a fight between him and Covey completes the conversion analogy. . . . Retrospectively, [Douglass] portrays this battle, in which he gave more punishment than he received, as a crisis conversion: "This battle . . . was the turning-point in my career as a slave. . . . It was a glorious resurrection from the tomb of slavery, to the heaven of freedom. My long-crushed spirit rose, cowardice departed, bold defiance took its place; and I now resolved that, however long I might remain a slave in form, the day had passed when I could be a slave in fact." . . . (p. 56)

The source of freedom, then, is not dependence on one's legal master or faith in superstition but reliance on one's self. The slave must not only invert his master's values, he must finally act out his resistance to his master's intentions. . . . [Douglass's] implicit "theology," then, rejects not only superstition and slaveholding but also the otherworldly Christianity of slaves who would wait passively for the Lord to deliver them.

Throughout the narrative, Douglass's prophetic motive impels him to generalize from his own experience and to shift back and forth between the narrative of events and the analysis of a social system. He not only participates in the communal "rites" inherent in the slave and fugitive experience, he often gives explicit interpretations of such rituals. At this point in the narrative, as if to explain why his crisis experience was not more common, Douglass explains the ulterior purpose of granting holidays to the slaves at Christmas time. According to Douglass, these holidays function as "safety-valves" which carry off the "spirit of insurrection." . . . Released from work and encouraged to use their leisure for dissipation, slaves understandably become disgusted with what they take to be freedom. However, Douglass points out that those who mistake license for liberty are, in effect, obstructing their own liberation and participating in a kind of idolatrous rite.

Douglass's treatment of his escape represents a striking and significant deviation from the conventional pattern of the slave narrative. Often, the story of the escape provides the climax of the fugitive narrative. . . . However, Douglass entirely omits this anticipated episode from his book. He makes the strategic reasons for this omission explicit. He does not wish, by divulging details of his escape, to endanger those who have helped him, nor does he want, by alerting slaveholders to his method, to hinder future attempts at flight. Thus, Douglass's annotated omission reminds the reader that flight from slavery, which provides the readers of most slave narratives with easy wish-fulfillment, is still a matter of life and death for fugitives. Furthermore, his assertion that he is not "at liberty" to tell all of his tale suggests that the full realization of his freedom depends on the emancipation of all slaves. Finally, the omission of the conventional climax emphasizes his use of the conversion analogy. The fight with Covey—the crisis of liberation-as-conversion—remains the structural and symbolic center of the book; the achievement of freedom in mind and soul replaces bodily flight to Northern states [as] the crucial event of his life.

Sidonie Smith has observed that there is a double pattern inherent in the slave narrative—that of the fugitive's break *away* from an oppressive community and that of his entry *into* a community which would permit his self-realization. The conclusion of Douglass's narrative shows that the pattern remained, for him, existentially and historically incomplete. Two episodes in particular qualify the affirmation of the ending. According to the logic of his analogy, the North, the land of freedom, ought to be described as a kind of paradise. But the fugitive slave can no more find absolute security than the convert can, and, on his arrival, Douglass finds New York a forbidding and anxiety-producing place. So long as the sin of slavery exists, the fugitive is threatened with capture, and his freedom remains tentative.

A similar lesson is suggested by Douglass's account of his induction into the abolitionist movement with which the narrative concludes. His career as a professional abolitionist commenced when he rose to speak of his bondage at an antislavery convention on Nantucket in 1841: "It was a severe cross, and I took it up reluctantly. The truth was, I felt myself a slave, and the idea of speaking to white people weighed me down. I spoke but a few moments, when I felt a degree of freedom, and said what I desired with considerable ease. From that time until now, I have been pleading the cause of my brethren. . . ." Again, Douglass recognized the incompleteness of his transition from slavery to freedom, but he accepted responsibility for completing the process, in two ways. First, while his reluctance to express himself before a white audience betrayed a vestige of the slave mentality, his decision to do so reenacted and reinforced his liberation from the community that fostered that sense of his inferiority. . . . Second, having failed to *discover* a free community into which he and his brothers could enter in a new relationship, Douglass here began the task of *creating* one.

The significance of the conclusion, then, refers us back to the importance of the conversion analogy. For if, as John L. Thomas has said, "the American abolitionists constituted a religion," then Douglass's narrative records not only his conversion to the faith but also his ordination as a minister. When he wrote the book, he was one of Garrison's most prominent and precious converts, and Garrison's "Preface" reinforces one's sense that the use of the conversion analogy was deliberate [see excerpt above, 1845]. In it, he used the terms borrowed from revival preaching to describe the response desired in the reader: "He who can peruse [this book] without a tearful eye, a heaving breast, an afflicted spirit,—without being filled with an unutterable abhorrence of slavery and all its abettors . . . without trembling for the fate of this country in the hands of a righteous God . . . must have a flinty heart and be qualified to act the part of a trafficker in slaves and the souls of men." . . . Garrison suggested, then, that the narrative was calculated to awaken the reader from his spiritual lethargy, to alert him to his implication in the sin of slavery, to melt his heart, and to convert him to the abolitionist cause.

Douglass's remarks in the appendix further characterize the impulse behind the narrative. Having emphasized at every opportunity the cruelty of his churchgoing masters, Douglass felt impelled to point out that he was not an opponent of Christianity: "What I have said respecting and against religion I mean strictly to apply to the slaveholding religion of this land, and with no possible reference to Christianity proper; for, between the Christianity of this land and the Christianity of Christ, I recognize the widest possible difference—so wide that to receive the one as good, pure, and holy is of necessity to reject the other as bad, corrupt, and wicked." . . . Douglass did not identify slaveholding religion with Southern Christianity, however. Far from intending to reassure his Northern readers, he wished to show that their Christianity was nominal, and hence hypocritical, if it did not include the belief that slavery was a sin. If the reader found himself included in the indictment of slaveholding religion, Douglass invited him to come out of his corrupt institution into the abolitionist church—out of a slave community into a free one. Thus, like most conversion narratives, Douglass's *Narrative* was written not only to record the author's conversion but to precipitate or confirm that of the reader. (pp. 57-60)

The benefits of modeling his slave narrative on the conversion narrative were many. Although Douglass's "theology" might have offended some conservative Christians, the religious language and providential apparatus of the narrative encouraged them to read it as an enactment of God's plot for Douglass. Moreover, the radical implications of Douglass's theology would have been acceptable to the religious groups most influential in the antislavery crusade—Quakers and evangelical Arminians. These Christians would have been comfortable with Douglass's belief in the divine potential of the individual, with his

implication that the individual could, with divine inspiration and assistance, achieve his own regeneration, and with his sense that conversion needed to be followed by reform activity. Indeed, like the theology of Charles G. Finney, Douglass's had perfectionist implications, for following his original "conversion," he experienced greater and greater degrees of freedom, as he explored its existential and political implications.

Douglass's analogy had the further advantage (for his rhetorical purposes) that it presented something with which his audience was not directly familiar—the experience of slavery—in terms of something with which they were presumably familiar. Without violating the integrity of his experience as a black slave, Douglass managed to cast it in a form accessible to his predominantly Northern white audience. His adaptation of a well-known narrative formula to his materials encouraged the reader to expand his sphere of moral concern to include the issue of slavery. As a strategy for organizing a slave narrative, the use of the conversion analogy had a certain elegance, for it employed one of the premises of radical abolitionism—that slavery was a sin—as the foundation of the structural framework of the book. By means of this gesture, the narrative achieved in its form the convergence between religion and reform it tried to bring about in life; Douglass created a historical as well as a literary model.

Finally, for Douglass, the conversion-liberation analogy must have seemed an appropriate way of giving his experience coherence and shape. While it sacrificed some factual detail and complexity, it was an apt metaphor for his life. It offered him, then, a way of expressing the significance of his experience in a convenient, symbolic shorthand which gave his life the resonance of a myth and the power of prophecy. (pp. 60-1)

> G. Thomas Couser, "Frederick Douglass: Abolitionism and Prophecy," in his American Autobiography: The Prophetic Mode, *University of Massachusetts Press, 1979, pp. 51-61.*

ROBERT B. STEPTO (essay date 1979)

[*As part of his study of the development of Afro-American narrative forms in* From Behind the Veil, *excerpted below, Stepto explores the extent to which white authority figures "controlled" slave narratives through appended documents which served to validate the narrators' texts. According to Stepto, Douglass assumed authorial control over his* Narrative *by adroitly integrating these documents with his text and validating or "authenticating" his own story within the* Narrative *proper.*]

[Frederick Douglass's **Narrative of the Life of Frederick Douglass, an American Slave, Written by Himself**] is an integrated narrative of a very special order. . . . [Its] new and major thrust is the creation of . . . [an] energy which binds the supporting texts to the tale, while at the same time removing them from participation in the narrative's rhetorical and authenticating strategies. Douglass's tale dominates the narrative because it alone authenticates the narrative.

The introductory texts to the tale are two in number: a "Preface" by William Lloyd Garrison . . . and a "Letter from Wendell Phillips, Esq." [see excerpts above, 1845]. . . . In theory, each of these introductory documents should be classic guarantees written almost exclusively for a white reading public, concerned primarily and ritualistically with the white validation of a newfound black voice, and removed from the tale in such ways that the guarantee and tale vie silently and surreptitiously for control of the narrative as a whole. But these entries are not fashioned that way. To be sure, Garrison offers a conventional guarantee when he writes, "Mr. Douglass has very properly chosen to write his own *Narrative* in his own style, and according to the best of his ability, rather than to employ some one else. It is, therefore, entirely his own production; and . . . it is, in my judgment, highly creditable to his head and heart." And Phillips, while addressing Douglass, most certainly offers a guarantee to "another" audience as well:

> Every one who has heard you speak has felt, and, I am confident, every one who read your book will feel, persuaded that you give them a fair specimen of the whole truth. No one-sided portrait,—no wholesale complaints,—but strict justice done, whenever individual kindliness has neutralized, for a moment, the deadly system with which it was strangely allied.

But these passages dominate neither the tone nor the substance of their respective texts.

Garrison is far more interested in writing history (specifically, that of the 1841 Nantucket Anti-Slavery Convention, and the launching of Douglass's career as a lecture agent for various antislavery societies) and recording his own place in it. . . . His "Preface" ends, not with a reference to Douglass or his tale, but with an apostrophe very much like one he would use to exhort and arouse an antislavery assembly. With [his closing] cry Garrison hardly guarantees Douglass's tale, but enters and reenacts his own abolitionist career instead. . . . (pp. 17-18)

In the light of [his] closure . . . we might be tempted to see Garrison's "Preface" at war with Douglass's tale for authorial control of the narrative as a whole. Certainly there is a tension, but that tension is stunted by Garrison's enthusiasm for Douglass's tale. Garrison writes:

> This *Narrative* contains many affecting incidents, many *passages* of great eloquence and power; but I think the most thrilling one of them all is the *description* Douglass gives of his feelings, as he stood soliloquizing respecting his fate, and the chances of his one day being a free man. . . . Who can read that *passage,* and be insensible to its pathos and sublimity? [Italics added.]

Here Garrison does, probably subconsciously, an unusual and extraordinary thing—he . . . not only directs the reader to the tale, but also acknowledges the tale's singular rhetorical power. . . . He fashions his own apostrophe, but finally he remains a member of Douglass's audience far more than he assumes the posture of a competing or superior voice. In this way Garrison's "Preface" stands outside Douglass's tale but is steadfastly bound to it.

Such is the case for Wendell Phillips's "Letter" as well. As I have indicated, it contains passages which seem addressed to credulous readers in need of a "visible" authority's guarantee, but by and large the "Letter" is directed to Frederick Douglass alone. . . . [And] it becomes clear that [Phillips] both addresses Douglass and writes in response to the tale. These features, plus Phillips's specific references to how Douglass acquired his "A B C" and learned "where the 'white sails' of the Chesapeake were bound," serve to integrate Phillips's "Letter" into Douglass's tale.

Above all, we must understand in what terms the "Letter" is a cultural and linguistic event. Like the Garrison document, it presents its author as a member of Douglass's audience; but the act of letter-writing, of correspondence, implies a moral and linguistic parity between a white guarantor and black author which we haven't seen before [in slave narratives]—and which we do not always see in American literary history *after* 1845. The tone and posture initiated in Garrison's "Preface" are completed and confirmed in Phillips's "Letter"; while these documents are integrated into Douglass's tale, they remain segregated outside the tale in the all-important sense that they yield Douglass sufficient narrative and rhetorical space in which to render personal history in—and as—a literary form.

What marks Douglass's narration and control of his tale is his extraordinary ability to pursue several types of writing with ease and with a degree of simultaneity. The principal types of writing we discover in the tale are: syncretic phrasing, introspective analysis, internalized documentation, and participant observation. Of course, each of these types has its accompanying authorial posture, the result being that even the telling of the tale (as distinct from the content of the tale) yields a portrait of a complex individual marvelously facile with the tones, shapes, and dimensions of his voice.

Douglass's syncretic phrasing is often discussed; the passage most widely quoted is probably, "My feet have been so cracked with the frost, that the pen with which I am writing might be laid in the gashes." The remarkable clarity of this language needs no commentary, but what one admires as well is Douglass's ability to conjoin past and present, and to do so with images that not only stand for different periods in his personal history but also, in their fusion, speak of his evolution from slavery to freedom. The pen, symbolizing the quest for literacy fulfilled, actually measures the wounds of the past, and this measuring process becomes a metaphor in and of itself for the artful composition of travail transcended. . . . Of course, this is effective writing—far more effective than what is found in the average slave narrative. But my point is that Douglass seems to fashion [such] passages for both his readership and himself. Each example of his increasing facility and wit with language charts his ever-shortening path to literacy; thus, in their way, Douglass's syncretic phrases reveal his emerging comprehension of freedom and literacy, and are another introspective tool by which he may mark the progress of his personal history.

But the celebrated passages of introspective analysis are even more pithy and direct. In these, Douglass fashions language as finely honed and balanced as an aphorism or Popean couplet, and thereby orders his personal history with neat, distinct, and credible moments of transition. When Mr. Auld forbids Mrs. Auld from teaching Douglass the alphabet, for example, Douglass relates, "From that moment, I understood the pathway from slavery to freedom. . . . Whilst I was saddened by the thought of losing the aid of my kind mistress, I was gladdened by the invaluable instruction which, by the merest accident, I gained from my master." The clarity of Douglass's revelation is as unmistakable as it was remarkable. As rhetoric, the passage is successful because its nearly extravagant beginning is finally rendered quite acceptable by the masterly balance and internal rhyming of "saddened" and "gladdened," which is persuasive because it is pleasant and because it offers the illusion of a reasoned conclusion.

Balance is an important feature to two other equally celebrated passages which open and close Douglass's telling of his relations with Mr. Covey. . . . At the beginning of the episode, in which Douglass finally fights back and draws Covey's blood, he writes: "You have seen how a man was made a slave; you shall see how a slave was made a man." And at the end of the episode, to bring matters linguistically as well as narratively full circle, Douglass declares: "I now resolved that, however long I might remain a slave in form, the day has passed forever when I could be a slave in fact. I did not hesitate to let it be known of me, that the white man who expected to succeed in whipping, must also succeed in killing me."

The sheer poetry of these statements is not lost on us, nor is the reason why the poetry was created in the first place. One might suppose that in another age Douglass's determination and rage would take a more effusive expression, but I cannot imagine that to be the case. In the first place, his linguistic model is obviously scriptural; and in the second, his goal, as Albert Stone has argued, is the presentation of a *"historical self,"* not the record of temporary hysteria [see excerpt above, 1973]. (pp. 18-21)

[This latter point] is one of the prime distinctions between Solomon Northup and Frederick Douglass—one which ultimately persuades me that Douglass is about the business of discovering how personal history may be transformed into autobiography, while Northrup is not. Both narratives contain episodes in which the author finally stands up to and soundly beats his overseer, but while Douglass performs this task and reflects upon its place in his history, Northup resorts to effusion:

> As I stood there, feelings of unutterable agony overwhelmed me. I was conscious that I had subjected myself to unimaginable punishment. The reaction that followed my extreme ebullition of anger produced the most painful sensations of regret. An unfriended, helpless slave— what could I *do,* what could I *say,* to justify, in the remotest manner, the heinous act I had committed . . . I tried to pray . . . but emotion choked my utterance, and I could only bow my head upon my hands and weep.

Passages such as these may finally link certain slave narratives with the popular sentimental literary forms of the nineteenth century, but Douglass's passages of introspective analysis create fresh space for themselves in the American literary canon.

Internal documentation in Douglass's tale is unusual in that, instead of reproducing letters and other documents written by white guarantors within the tale or transforming guarantees into characters, Douglass internalizes documents which, like the syncretic and introspective passages, order his personal history. Again a comparison of Douglass and Northup is useful, because while both authors present documents having only a secondary function in the authenticating process, their goals . . . seem quite different.

Northup, for example, documents slave songs in [the text of his tale]. . . . His discussion of the songs within the tale is one dimensional, by which I mean it merely reflects his limited comprehension and appreciation of the songs at a given moment in his life. Rather than establishing Northup within the slave community, remarks like "those unmeaning songs, composed rather for [their] adaptation to a certain tune or measure, than for the purpose of expressing any distinct idea" or "equally nonsensical, but full of melody" serve only to reinforce his displacement as a participant-observer. One might have assumed that Northup (who was, after all, kidnapped into slavery partly because of his musicianship) found music a bond be-

tween him and his enslaved brethren, and in passages such as these would relinquish or soften his objective posture. But apparently the demands of audience and authentication precluded such a shift.

In contrast, Douglass's discussion of slave songs begins with phrases such as "wild songs" and "unmeaning jargon" but concludes, quite typically for him, with a study of how he grew to "hear" the songs and how that hearing affords yet another illumination of his path from slavery to freedom:

> I did not, when a slave, understand the deep meaning of those rude and apparently incoherent songs. I was myself within the circle; so that I neither saw nor heard as those without might see and hear. They told a tale of woe which was then altogether beyond my feeble comprehension. . . . Every tone was a testimony against slavery, and a prayer to God for deliverance from chains. The hearing of those wild notes always depressed my spirit, and filled me with ineffable sadness. I have frequently found myself in tears while hearing them. The mere recurrence to those songs, even now, afflicts me; and while I am writing these lines, an expression of feeling has already found its way down my cheek.

The tears of the past and present interflow. Douglass not only documents his saga of enslavement but also, with typical recourse to syncretic phrasing and introspective analysis, advances his presentation of self. (pp. 21-3)

All of the types of narrative discourse discussed thus far reveal features of Douglass's particular posture as a participant-observer narrator. . . . But the syncretic phrases, introspective studies, and internalized documents only exhibit Douglass as a teller and doer, and part of the great effect of his tale depends upon what he does *not* tell, what he refuses to reenact in print. . . . [In his tale, Douglass] never divulges a detail of his escape to New York. (That information is given ten years later, in ***My Bondage and My Freedom*** and other statements.) This marvelously rhetorical omission or silence both sophisticates and authenticates his posture as a participant-observer narrator. When a narrator wrests this kind of preeminent authorial control from the ancillary voices in the narrative, we may say that he controls the presentation of his personal history, and that his tale is becoming autobiographical. (pp. 24-5)

[Important], I think, is Douglass's final image of a slave shedding his last fetter and becoming a man by first finding his voice and then, as surely as light follows dawn, speaking "with considerable ease." In one brilliant stroke, the quest for freedom and literacy, implied from the start even by the narrative's title, is resolutely consummated. (pp. 25-6)

[The final text of the narrative, the Appendix, is] a discourse by Douglass on *his* view of Christianity and Christian practice, as opposed to what he exposed in his tale to be the bankrupt, immoral faith of slaveholders. As rhetorical strategy, the discourse is effective because it lends weight and substance to what passes for a conventional complaint of slave narrators, and because Douglass's exhibition of faith can only enhance his already considerable posture as an articulate hero. But more specifically, the discourse is most efficacious because at its heart lies a vitriolic poem written by a northern Methodist minister that Douglass introduces by writing: "I conclude these remarks by copying the following portrait of the religion of the south, (which is, by communion and fellowship, the religion of the north,) which I soberly affirm is 'true to life,' and without caricature or the slightest exaggeration.'' The poem is strong and imbued with considerable irony, but what we must appreciate here is the effect of the white Northerner's poem conjoined with Douglass's *authentication* of the poem. The tables are clearly reversed: Douglass has not only controlled his personal history, but also fulfilled the prophecy suggested by his implicit authentication of Garrison's ''Preface'' by explicitly authenticating what is conventionally a white Northerner's validating text. Douglass's narrative thus offers what is unquestionably our best portrait in Afro-American letters of the requisite act of assuming authorial control. (p. 26)

> Robert B. Stepto, ''I Rose and Found My Voice: Narration, Authentication, and Authorial Control in Four Slave Narratives,'' in his From Behind the Veil: A Study of Afro-American Narrative, *University of Illinois Press, 1979, pp. 3-31.**

HOUSTON A. BAKER, JR. (essay date 1980)

[*According to Baker, Douglass and other early black autobiographers faced the daunting task of representing their unique identity as black persons in literary forms that were oriented toward white cultural values. Noting the conventional values and style of the* Narrative, *he maintains that Douglass never represented his ''authentic self'' in his autobiographies and moved instead to a ''public version of the self—one molded by the values of white America.''*]

[Much of *The Narrative of the Life of Frederick Douglass*] counterpoints the assumption of the white world that the slave is a brute against the slave's expanding awareness of language and its capacity to carry him toward new dimensions of experience. . . .

For [Douglass], language brings the possibility of freedom but renders slavery intolerable. It gives rise to his decision to escape as soon as his age and the opportunity are appropriate. (pp. 34-5)

When clarified and understood through language, the deathly, terrifying nothingness around [Douglass] reveals the grounds of being. Freedom, the ability to choose one's own direction, makes life beautiful and pure. Only the man free from bondage has a chance to obtain the farthest reaches of humanity. From what appears a blank and awesome backdrop, Douglass wrests significance. His subsequent progression through the roles of educated leader, freeman, abolitionist, and autobiographer marks his firm sense of being.

But while it is the fact that the ships are loosed from their moorings that intrigues the narrator [in his famous passage describing the ships on Chesapeake Bay], he also drives home their whiteness and places them in a Christian context. Here certain added difficulties for the black autobiographer reveal themselves. The acquisition of language, which leads to being, has ramifications that have been best stated by the West Indian novelist George Lamming, drawing on the relationship between Prospero and Caliban in [Shakespeare's] The Tempest:

> Prospero has given Caliban Language; and with it an unstated history of consequences, an unknown history of future intentions. This gift of language meant not English, in particular, but speech and concept as a way, a method, a necessary avenue towards areas of the self which

could not be reached in any other way. It is in this way, entirely Prospero's enterprise, which makes Caliban aware of possibilities. Therefore, all of Caliban's future—for future is the very name for possibilities—must derive from Prospero's experiment, which is also his risk.

Mr. Auld had seen that ''learning'' could lead to the restiveness of his slave. Neither he nor his representer, however, seem to understand that it might be possible to imprison the slave even more thoroughly in the way described by Lamming. The angelic Mrs. Auld, however, in accord with the evangelical codes of her era, has given Douglass the rudiments of a system that leads to intriguing restrictions. True, the slave can arrive at a sense of being only through language. But it is also true that, in Douglass's case, a conception of the preeminent form of being is conditioned by white, Christian standards. (pp. 35-6)

In recovering the details of his past, . . . [Douglass] shows a progression from baffled and isolated existent to Christian abolitionist lecturer and writer. The self in the autobiographical moment (the present, the time in which the work is composed), however, seems unaware of the limitations that have accompanied this progress. . . . One can realize one's humanity through ''speech and concept,'' but one cannot distinguish the uniqueness of the self if the ''avenue towards areas of the self'' excludes rigorously individualizing definitions of a human, black identity.

Douglass grasps language in a Promethean act of will, but he leaves unexamined its potentially devastating effects. One reflection of his uncritical acceptance of the perspective made available by literacy is the *Narrative* itself, which was written at the urging of white abolitionists who had become the fugitive slave's employers. The work was written to prove that the narrator had indeed been a slave. And while autobiographical conventions forced him to portray as accurately as possible the existentiality of his original condition, the light of abolitionism is always implicitly present, guiding the narrator into calm, Christian, and publicly accessible harbors. The issue here is not simply one of intentionality (how the author wished his utterances to be taken). It is, rather, one that combines Douglass's understandable desire to keep his job with more complex considerations governing ''privacy'' as a philosophical concept.

Language, like other social institutions, is public; it is one of the surest means we have of communicating with the ''other,'' the world outside ourselves. Moreover, since language seems to provide the principal way in which we conceptualize and convey anything (thoughts, feelings, sensations, and so forth), it is possible that no easily describable ''private'' domain exists. By adopting language as his instrument for extracting meaning from nothingness, being from existence, Douglass becomes a public figure.

He is comforted, but also restricted, by the system he adopts. The results are shown in the hierarchy of preferences that, finally, constitute value in the *Narrative*. The results are additionally demonstrated by those instances in the *Narrative* where the work's style is indistinguishable from that of the sentimental-romantic oratory and creative writing that marked the American nineteenth century. Had there been a separate, written black language available, Douglass might have fared better. What is seminal to this discussion, however, is that the nature of the autobiographer's situation seemed to force him to move to a public version of the self—one molded by the values of white America. (pp. 38-9)

[The slave narrator must] accomplish the almost unthinkable . . . task of transmuting an authentic, unwritten self—a self that exists outside the conventional literary discourse structures of a white reading public—into a literary representation. The simplest, and perhaps the most effective, way of proceeding is for the narrator to represent his "authentic" self as a figure embodying the public virtues and values esteemed by his intended audience. Once he has seized the public medium, the slave narrator can construct a public message, or massage, calculated to win approval for himself and (provided he has one) his cause. In the white abolitionist William Lloyd Garrison's preface to Douglass's *Narrative,* for example, the slave narrator is elaborately praised for his seemingly godlike movement "into the field of public usefulness" [see excerpt above, 1845]. . . . Obviously, a talented, heroic, and richly endowed figure such as Garrison describes [in the preface] was of inestimable "public usefulness" to the abolitionist crusade. (pp. 39-42)

The issue that such an "autobiographical" act raises for the literary analyst is that of authenticity. Where, for example, in Douglass's *Narrative* does a prototypical black American self reside? What are the distinctive narrative elements that combine to form a representation of this self? . . . [It] seems that such elements would be located in those episodes and passages of the *Narrative* that chronicle the struggle for literacy. For once literacy has been achieved, the black self, even as represented in the *Narrative,* begins to distance itself from the domain of experience constituted by the oral-aural community of the slave quarters. . . . The voice of the unwritten self, once it is subjected to the linguistic codes, literary conventions, and audience expectations of a literate population, is perhaps never again the authentic voice of black American slavery. It is, rather, the voice of a self transformed by an autobiographical act into a sharer in the general public discourse about slavery.

How much of the lived (as opposed to the represented) slave experience is lost in this transformation depends upon the keenness of the narrator's skill in confronting both the freedom and the limitations resulting from his literacy in Prospero's tongue. By the conclusion of Douglass's *Narrative,* the represented self seems to have left the quarters almost entirely behind. The self that appears in the work's closing moments is that of a public spokesman, talking about slavery to a Nantucket convention of whites:

> while attending an anti-slavery convention at Nantucket, on the 11th of August, 1841, I felt strongly moved to speak, and was at the same time much urged to do so by Mr. William C. Coffin, a gentleman who had heard me speak in the colored people's meeting at New Bedford. It was a severe cross, and I took it up reluctantly. The truth was, I felt myself a slave, and the idea of speaking to white people weighed me down. I spoke but a few moments, when I felt a degree of freedom, and said what I desired with considerable ease. From that time until now, I have been engaged in pleading the cause of my brethren—with what success, and with what devotion, I leave to those acquainted with my labors to decide. . . .

The Christian imagery ("a severe cross"), strained reluctance to speak before whites, discovered ease of eloquence, and

public-spirited devotion to the cause of his brethren that appear in this passage are all in keeping with the image of the publicly useful and ideal fugitive captured in Garrison's preface. Immediately before telling the reader of his address to the Nantucket convention, Douglass notes that "he had not long been a reader of the 'Liberator' [Garrison's abolitionist newspaper]" before he got "a pretty correct idea of the principles, measures and spirit of the anti-slavery reform"; he adds that he "took right hold of the cause . . . and never felt happier than when in an anti-slavery meeting." . . . This suggests to me that the communication between Douglass and Garrison begins long before their face-to-face encounter at Nantucket, with the fugitive slave's culling from the white publisher's newspaper those virtues and values esteemed by abolitionist readers. The fugitive's voice is further refined by his attendance and speeches at the "colored people's meeting at New Bedford," and it finally achieves its emotionally stirring participation in the white world of public discourse at the 1841 Nantucket convention.

Of course, there are tangible reasons within the historical . . . domain for the image that Douglass projects. The feeling of larger goals shared with a white majority culture has always been present among blacks. . . . From at least the third decade of the nineteenth century this feeling of a common pursuit was reinforced by men like Garrison and Wendall Phillips, by constitutional amendments, civil rights legislation, and perennial assurances that the white man's dream is the black man's as well. Furthermore, what better support for this assumption of commonality could Douglass find than in his own palpable achievements in American society?

When he revised his original *Narrative* for the third time, therefore, in 1893, the work that resulted represented the conclusion of a process that began for Douglass at the home of Hugh Auld. *The Life and Times of Frederick Douglass Written by Himself* is public, rooted in the language of its time, and considerably less existential in tone than the 1845 *Narrative.* What we have is a verbose and somewhat hackneyed story of a life, written by a man of achievement. The white externality has been transformed into a world where sterling deeds by blacks are possible. Douglass describes his visit to the home of his former master who, forty years after the slave's escape, now rests on his deathbed:

> On reaching the house I was met by Mr. Wm. H. Buff, a son-in-law of Capt. Auld, and Mrs. Louisa Buff, his daughter, and was conducted to the bedroom of Capt. Auld. We addressed each other simultaneously, he called me "Marshal Douglass," and I, as I had always called him, "Captain Auld." Hearing myself called by him "Marshall Douglass," I instantly broke up the formal nature of the meeting by saying, "not *Marshal,* but Frederick to you as formerly." We shook hands cordially and in the act of doing so, he, having been long stricken with palsy, shed tears as men thus afflicted will do when excited by any deep emotion. The sight of him, the changes which time had wrought in him, his tremulous hands constantly in motion, and all the circumstances of his condition. affected me deeply, and for a time choked my voice and made me speechless.

A nearly tearful silence by the black "Marshal" (a term repeated three times in very brief space) of the District of Columbia as he gazes with sympathy on the body of his former master—this is a great distance, to be sure, from the aggressive young slave who appropriated language in order to do battle with the masters. (pp. 42-5)

> Houston A. Baker, Jr., *"Autobiographical Acts and the Voice of the Southern Slave," in his* The Journey Back: Issues in Black Literature and Criticism, *University of Chicago Press, 1980, pp. 27-52.*

ROBERT B. STEPTO   (essay date 1982)

[*Douglas published his only fictional work, a novella based on the 1841 revolt on board the slave ship* Creole, *in 1853. Entitled* The Heroic Slave, *the story was long neglected by Douglass's critics. Stepto's criticism of* The Heroic Slave *supports the view that Douglass was a sophisticated narrator.*]

"The Heroic Slave" is not an altogether extraordinary piece of work. I'm not about to argue that it should take a place beside, say, [Herman Melville's] *Benito Cereno* as a major short fiction of the day. Still, after dismissing the florid soliloquies which unfortunately besmirch this and too many other antislavery writings, we find that the novella is full of craft, especially of the sort which combines artfulness with a certain fabulistic usefulness. Appropriately enough, evidence of Douglass' craft is available in the novella's attention to both theme and character. In Part I of **"The Heroic Slave,"** we are told of the "double state" of Virginia and introduced not only to Madison Washington but also to Mr. Listwell, who figures as the model abolitionist in the story. The meticulous development of the Virginia theme and of the portrait of Mr. Listwell, much more than the portrayal of Washington as a hero, is the stuff of useful art-making in Douglass' novella. (p. 360)

[The first paragraph of the novella,] but especially its initial sentences, can be seen as significant revoicing of the conventional opening of a slave narrative. Slave narratives usually begin with the phrase "I was born." . . . In **"The Heroic Slave,"** however, Douglass transforms "I was born" into the broader assertion that in Virginia many heroes have been born. After that, he then works his way to the central point that a certain *one*—an unknown hero who lives now only in the chattel records and not the history books—has been born. Douglass knows the slave narrative convention, partly because he has used it himself; but more to the point, he seems to have an understanding of how to exploit its rhetorical usefulness in terms of proclaiming the existence and identity of an individual without merely employing it verbatim. This is clear evidence, I think, of a first step, albeit a small one, toward the creation of an Afro-American fiction based upon the conventions of the slave narratives. That Douglass himself was quite possibly thinking in these terms while writing is suggested by his persistent reference to the "chattel records" which must, in effect, be transformed by "the pen of genius" so that his hero's merits may be set forth—indeed, set free. If by this Douglass means that his hero's story must be liberated from the realm—the text—of brutal fact, and more, that texts must be created to compete with other texts, then it's safe to say that he brought to the creation of **"The Heroic Slave"** all the intentions, if not all the skills, of the self-conscious *writer*.

The other key feature of the paragraph pertains more directly to the novella's Virginia theme. . . . After declaring that his hero loved liberty as much as did Patrick Henry, and deserved it as much as Thomas Jefferson, Douglass refuses to name the third famous son of Virginia with whom his hero is to be compared. He speaks only of "he who led all the armies of the American colonies through the great war for freedom and independence." Of course, as any school boy or girl knows, the mystery man is Washington. And that is the answer—and point—to Douglass' funny-sad joke about the "double state" of Virginia as well: *his* mystery man is also a hero named Washington. Thus, Douglass advances his comparison of heroic statesmen and heroic chattel, and does so quite ingenuously by both naming and *not* naming them in such a way that we are led to discover that statesmen and slaves may share the same name and be heroes and Virginians alike. Rhetoric and meaning conjoin in a very sophisticated way in this passage, thus providing us with an indication of how seriously and ambitiously Douglass will take the task of composing the rest of the novella.

"The Heroic Slave" is divided into four parts, and in each Virginia becomes less and less of a setting (especially of a demographic or even historical sort) and more of a ritual ground . . . for symbolic encounters between slaves and abolitionists or Virginians and Virginians. For example, in Part I, the encounter between Mr. Listwell, our soon-to-be abolitionist, and Madison Washington, our soon-to-be fugitive slave, takes place in a magnificent Virginia forest. In accord with many familiar notions regarding the transformational powers of nature in its purest state, both men leave the sylvan glen determined and resolved to become an abolitionist and a free man respectively. Thus, the Virginia forest is established as a very particular space within the figurative geography of the novella. . . . (pp. 361-62)

Part II of **"The Heroic Slave"** takes place in Ohio. Listwell lives there and has the opportunity to aid an escaping slave who turns out to be none other than Madison Washington. This change in setting from Virginia to Ohio assists in the development of the Virginia theme chiefly because it gives Douglass the opportunity to stress the point that something truly happened to each man in that "sacred" forest, one happy result being that their paths did cross once again in the cause of freedom. . . . By the end of Part II, it becomes clear in the context of the emerging novella that Ohio, as a free state, is an increasingly symbolic state to be achieved through acts of fellowship initiated however indirectly before. (pp. 362-63)

Having portrayed Virginia's heaven—the forest replete with pathways to freedom—Douglass now offers Virginia's hell [in Part III]. As one might imagine, given Douglass' zeal for temperance and the abolition of slavery, hell is a tavern full of drunkards, knaves, and traders of human flesh. Hell's first circle is the yard adjacent to the tavern where slaves on their way to market are "stabled" while the soul-driver drinks a dram. Its second circle is the remaining fifteen miles to Richmond where a slave auction awaits. The third circle may be sale to a new Virginia master and a long walk to a new plantation, or it may be a horrific re-encounter with middle passage, in the form of a "cruise" aboard a Baltimore-built slaver bound for New Orleans. (p. 363)

The point to Part III is that while Washington has returned to Virginia, lost his wife in their escape attempt, and been re-enslaved, Listwell is also there and able to provide the means by which Washington may free himself—*and others*. The suggestion is that it is quite one thing to aid an escaping slave in Ohio and quite another to assist one in deepest, darkest Virginia. Listwell rises to the occasion and . . . slips Washington several files for the chains binding him. What Washington and the rest do once on board the *Creole* is, of course, a matter of historical record.

One might think that the fourth and last part of **"The Heroic Slave"** would be totally devoted to a vivid narration of swashbuckling valor aboard the high seas. This is not the case. The scene is once again Virginia; the time is set some time after the revolt on the *Creole;* the place is a "Marine Coffee-house" in Richmond; and the conversation is quite provocatively between two white Virginia sailors. . . . The conversation takes a sharp turn when . . . [Jack Williams, who had not shipped on the *Creole,*] makes it clear that, "For my part I feel ashamed to have the idea go abroad, that a ship load of slaves can't be safely taken from Richmond to New Orleans. I should like, merely to redeem the character of Virginia sailors, to take charge of a ship load of 'em to-morrow." . . . Tom Grant, who had been on the *Creole,* soon replies, "I dare say *here* what many men *feel,* but *dare not speak,* that this whole slave-trading business is a disgrace and scandal to Old Virginia." . . . The conversation goes on, and before it's done, Tom Grant has indeed told the story of the revolt led by Madison Washington. (pp. 363-64)

Thus, Douglass ends his novella by creating the dialogue between Virginians about the "state" of Virginia which was effectively prefigured in the novella's first paragraph. The duality or doubleness of Virginia (and indeed of America) first offered as an assertion and then in the form of a riddle now assumes a full-blown literary form. More to the point, perhaps, is the fact that Tom Grant . . . [has become something of an abolitionist] and, most certainly, something of a white Southern storyteller of a tale of black freedom. This particular aspect of Grant's transformation is in keeping with what happens to our white Northerner, Mr. Listwell. What we see here, then, is an expression within Douglass' narrative design of the signal idea that freedom for slaves can transform the South and the North and hence the nation.

This brings us to Mr. Listwell, whose creation is possibly *the* polemical and literary achievement of the novella. In many ways, his name is his story and his story his name. He is indeed a "Listwell" in that he *enlists* as an abolitionist and does *well* by the cause. . . . He is also a "Listwell" in that he *listens* well; he is, in the context of his relations with Madison Washington and in accord with the aesthetics of storytelling, a model storylistener and hence an agent, in many senses of the term, for the continuing performance of the story he and Washington increasingly share and "tell" together. Of course, Douglass' point is that both features of Listwell's "listing" are connected and, ideally, inextricably bound: one cannot be a good abolitionist without being a good listener, with the reverse often being true as well.

Douglass' elaborate presentation of these ideas begins in Part I of **"The Heroic Slave"** when Washington apostrophizes in the Virginia forest on his plight as an abject slave and unknowingly is *overheard* by Listwell. At the end of his speech, the storyteller slave vows to gain freedom and the storylistener white Northerner vows to become an abolitionist so that he might aid slaves such as the one he has just overheard. This is storytelling of a sort conducted at a distance. Both storyteller and storylistener are present, and closure of a kind occurs in that both performers resolve to embark on new journeys or careers. But, of course, the teller (slave) doesn't know yet that he has a listener (abolitionist, brother in the cause), and the listener doesn't know yet what role he will play in telling the story that has just begun. In this way, Douglass spins three primary narrative threads: one is the storyteller/slave's journey to freedom; another is the storylistener/abolitionist's journey to service; the third is the resolution or consummation of purposeful human brotherhood between slave and abolitionist, as it may be most particularly achieved through the communal aesthetic of storytelling.

In Part II, the three primary threads reappear in an advanced state. Washington has escaped and is indeed journeying to freedom; Listwell is now a confirmed abolitionist whose references to conversations with other abolitionists suggest that he is actively involved; and Washington and Listwell are indeed in the process of becoming brothers in the struggle, both because they befriend each other on a cold night and because, once settled before Listwell's fire, they engage for long hours in storytelling. Several features of their storytelling are worth remarking upon. One is that Washington, as the storyteller, actually tells two stories about his adventures in the Virginia forest, one about a thwarted escape attempt and the resulting limbo he enters while neither slave nor free, and the other about how he finally breaks out of limbo, reasserting his desire for freedom. The importance of this feature is that it occasions a repetition of the novella's "primary" forest episode which creates in turn a narrative rhythm which we commonly associate with oral storytelling. (pp. 364-66)

Another pertinent feature is that Listwell, as the storylistener, is both a good listener and, increasingly, a good prompter of Washington's stories. Early on, Listwell says, "But this was five years ago; where have you been since?" Washington replies, "I will try to tell you," and to be sure storytelling ensues. Other examples of this abound. In one notable instance, in response to Washington's explanation as to why he stole food while in flight, Listwell asserts, "And just there you were right. . . . I once had doubts on this point myself, but a conversation with Gerrit Smith . . . put an end to all my doubts on this point. But do not let me interrupt you." . . . Listwell interrupts, but his is what we might call a good interruption, for he *authenticates* the slave's rationale for stealing instead of questioning it. In this way, Listwell's remarks advance both story *and* cause, which is exactly what he's supposed to do now that he's an abolitionist.

Resolution of this episode takes the form of a letter from Washington to Listwell, written in Canada a few short days after both men have told stories into the night. It begins, "My dear Friend,—for such you truly are:—. . . Madison is out of the woods at last. . . ." The language here takes us back to the initial encounter in the Virginia forest between Washington and Listwell, back to a time when they weren't acquaintances, let alone friends—nor on their respective journeys to freedom and service. In examining the essential differences between Washington's apostrophe to no apparent listener and his warm letter to a dear friend, we are drawn to the fact that in each case, a simple voice cries out, but in the second instance a listener is not only addressed but remembered and hence recreated. The great effect is that a former slave's conventional token of freedom and literacy bound and found in Canada takes on certain indelible storytelling properties.

From this point on in **"The Heroic Slave"** little more needs to be established between Washington and Listwell, either as fugitive slave and abolitionist or as storyteller and listener, except the all important point that their bond is true and that Listwell will indeed come to Washington's aid in Virginia just as promptly as he did before in the North. In a sense their story is over, but in another respect it isn't: there remains the issue, endemic to both oral and written art, of how their story will live on with full flavor and purpose. On one hand, the story told by Washington and Listwell lives on in a direct, apparent way in the rebellion aboard the *Creole,* the resulting dialogue between the two Virginia sailors who debate the state of their State, and the transformation of one of the sailors, Tom Grant, into a teller of the story. On the other, the story lives on in another way which draws the seemingly distant narrator into the communal bonds of storytelling and the cause.

Late in the novella, in Part III, the narrator employs the phrase "Mr. Listwell says" and soon thereafter refers to Listwell as "our informant." These phrases suggest rather clearly that Listwell has told his shared tale to the narrator and that he has thus been a storyteller as well as a storylistener all along. The other point to be made is, of course, that the narrator has been at some earlier point a good storylistener, meaning in part that he can now tell a slave's tale well because he was willing to *hear* it before making it his own tale to tell. What's remarkable about this narrative strategy is how it serves Douglass' needs both as a novelist and as a black public figure under pressure. Here was a theory of narrative distilled from the relations between tellers and listeners in the black and white worlds Douglass knew best; here was an answer to all who cried, "Frederick, tell your story"—and then couldn't or wouldn't hear him. (pp. 366-68)

> *Robert B. Stepto, "Storytelling in Early Afro-American Fiction: Frederick Douglass' 'The Heroic Slave'," in* The Georgia Review, *Vol. XXXVI, No. 2, Summer, 1982, pp. 355-68.*

ADDITIONAL BIBLIOGRAPHY

Baker, Houston A., Jr. "Revolution and Reform: Walker, Douglass, and the Road to Freedom." In his *Long Black Song: Essays in Black American Literature and Culture,* pp. 58-83. Charlottesville: University Press of Virginia, 1972.*

   A discussion of Douglass's use of humor, verisimilitude, animal imagery and other narrative devices in the *Narrative of the Life of Frederick Douglass.*

Bontemps, Arna. *Free at Last: The Life of Frederick Douglass.* New York: Dodd, Mead & Co., 1971, 310 p.

   A popularized account of Douglass's life following his escape from slavery in 1838.

Chesnutt, Charles W. *Frederick Douglass.* 4th ed. The Beacon Biographies of Eminent Americans, edited by M. A. DeWolfe Howe. Boston: Small, Maynard & Co., 1899, 141 p.

   An early biography that focuses on Douglass's career as an abolitionist and civil rights advocate. Chesnutt is recognized as a pioneer in Afro-American fiction.

Foner, Philip S. *Frederick Douglass.* New York: Citadel Press, 1964, 444 p.

   A major biographical study. Although Foner is critical of Douglass's approach to certain issues affecting the economic welfare of blacks, he otherwise praises him as an uncompromising and effective agitator for the "full freedom" of his race.

Holland, Frederic May. *Frederick Douglass: The Colored Orator.* Rev. ed. 1895. Reprint. New York: Haskell House Publishers, 1969, 431 p.

   The first comprehensive Douglass biography. As part of his research for the volume, Holland interviewed Douglass at his home in Anacostia Heights, D.C.

Logan, Rayford W. Introduction to *Life and Times of Frederick Douglass,* by Frederick Douglass, pp. 15-24. New York: Collier Books, Macmillan Publishing Co., 1962.

   A biographical and critical essay on Douglass and his *Life and Times.* Logan, who describes the work as a "classic in American literature," challenges the view that the *Life and Times* reveals only the worst aspects of slavery.

Miller, Kelly. "Frederick Douglass." In his *Race Adjustment. The Everlasting Stain,* pp. 211-20. 1908; 1924. Reprint. New York: Arno Press and The New York Times, 1968.

   An appreciation honoring Douglass as the outstanding model of emulation of black Americans. Miller's essay appears in the *Race Adjustment* portion of this volume of reprints.

Quarles, Benjamin. *Frederick Douglass.* Washington, D.C.: Associated Publishers, 1948, 378 p.

   The standard biography.

Quarles, Benjamin. "Abolition's Different Drummer: Frederick Douglass." In *The Antislavery Vanguard: New Essays on the Abolitionists,* edited by Martin Duberman, pp. 123-34. Princeton: Princeton University Press, 1965.

   Examines the factors that contributed to Douglass's prominence as an abolitionist. According to Quarles, Douglass was distinguished by his oratorical skills, race, fundamental concern for human rights, and intransigent opposition to slavery.

Quarles, Benjamin. *"Narrative of the Life of Frederick Douglass."* In *Landmarks of American Writing,* edited by Hennig Cohen, pp. 90-100. New York: Basic Books, 1969.

   A general discussion of the qualities which give the *Narrative* its pre-eminent position among American slave narratives. Quarles here repeats many of the views expressed in his introduction to the 1960 edition of the *Narrative* (see excerpt above).

Stowe, Harriet Beecher. "Frederick Douglass." In her *Men of Our Times; or, Leading Patriots of the Day,* pp. 378-404. Hartford, Conn.: Hartford Publishing Co., 1868.

   A contemporary memoir by the author of *Uncle Tom's Cabin.* Founding her account on Douglass's *Narrative,* Stowe perceives and presents Douglass's personal history as "a comment on the slavery system which speaks for itself."

Takaki, Ronald T. "Not Afraid to Die: Frederick Douglass and Violence." In his *Violence in the Black Imagination: Essays and Documents,* edited by Herbert Hill, pp. 17-35. New York: G. P. Putnam's Sons, 1972.

   An examination of Douglass's attitude toward the use of violence in achieving black emancipation. Takaki interprets the slave rebellion in *The Heroic Slave* as an expression of Douglass's ultimate acceptance of violence as a means of black liberation.

Washington, Booker T. *Frederick Douglass.* 1907. Reprint. New York: Haskell House Publishers, 1968, 365 p.

   A biography that focuses primarily on Douglass's public life, interspersed with comments on social and political issues relevant to his career. In his preface, Washington implicitly disassociates himself from Douglass's militancy, stating: "Frederick Douglass's career falls almost wholly within the first period of the struggle in which [the race] problem has involved the people of this country,—the period of revolution and liberation. That period has now ended. . . . This book will have failed of its purpose just so far as anything here said shall serve to keep alive the bitterness of those controversies of which it gives the history. . . ."

Yellin, Jean Fagan. "William Wells Brown." In her *The Intricate Knot: Black Figures in American Literature, 1776-1863,* pp. 154-81. New York: New York University Press, 1972.*

   Includes an insightful critical description of Douglass's autobiographies.

Edmond (Louis Antoine Huot) de Goncourt

1822-1896

Jules (Alfred Huot) de Goncourt

1830-1870

French diarists, novelists, historians, biographers, critics, dramatists, and essayists.

The Goncourt brothers were literary innovators who are noted for their diverse contributions to the world of letters. As historians, they revitalized interest in the eighteenth century with intimate social histories based on seemingly trivial documents; as art critics and collectors, they were instrumental in introducing eighteenth-century Japanese art to France and in reviving interest in several eighteenth-century French painters; as novelists, they were realists whose careful methods of documentation and depiction of the lower classes influenced the development of literary Naturalism. In their best-known work, *Journal des Goncourt: Mémoires de la vie littéraire,* a diary that contains a detailed record of the literary society of Paris during the second half of the nineteenth century, the brothers proved themselves to be adept historians of their own age. Neurotic, hypochondriac, and suspicious, the Goncourts declared that ''sickness makes a man sensitive like a photographic plate,'' and they developed their own impressionistic style, *écriture artiste (artistic writing),* with which they attempted to reproduce the subtleties of their observations. The *écriture artiste,* which is marked by highly visual imagery, repetition, neologisms, word inversions, and an abundance of technical terms, reflects both the Goncourts' heightened sensitivity and their interest in painting. The Goncourts are considered especially remarkable for their ability to think and write as one, and their collaborations are praised by critics for their unity. Until Jules's death, all their literary productions, including the *Journal,* were joint efforts. They claimed that they were ''one soul placed in two bodies,'' and although Edmond continued to write for twenty-six years after the death of his brother, most critics believe that their careers cannot be separated.

The Goncourts were raised and educated in Paris. Their father, a military soldier who served Napoleon Bonaparte, died in 1834, and their mother died in 1848, leaving the brothers financially comfortable. Although different in temperament, the two shared, according to Edmond, ''absolutely the same ideas, the same sympathies and antipathies for people, the same intellectual optics.'' Neither married; in fact, critics often note their tendency toward misogyny. From an early age, they developed similar interests in literature, history, and art. Both were skilled watercolor artists and passionate collectors of objets d'art.

Initially the Goncourts intended to become painters. In 1849 they toured France and North Africa, making sketches and taking notes as they traveled. Edmond later remarked that it was their travel diary that induced them to pursue literature rather than art. In 1850, traveling through Switzerland, Belgium, and Normandy, the brothers collaborated on several one-act plays, none of which was ever performed or published.

When they returned to Paris they published their first novel, *En 18 ..,* and for a short time contributed reviews and articles to two newspapers, *L'Eclair* and *Le Paris. En 18 ..,* published on the day of Napoleon III's coup d'etat, received little attention. Its date of publication, December 2, 1851, is significant, however, because it marks the inauguration of the Goncourts' *Journal.*

Discouraged by the poor reception of *En 18 ..,* the Goncourts turned their attention to historical subjects of the eighteenth century, an era that attracted them by its elegance, grace, and charm. The brothers' enthusiasm for objets d'art and bibelots determined their novel approach to history. By examining apparently insignificant contemporary documents, such as handbills and dress patterns, in such works as *Histoire de la société française pendant la révolution, Les maîtresses de Louis XV (The Confidantes of a King: The Mistresses of Louis XV),* and *Histoire de Marie-Antoinette,* they acted on their theory that ''a period must be known by its dinner-menus, a courtly period must be sought out amid its fêtes and its attire.'' Some critics concur with W. Somerset Maugham in dismissing the Goncourts' social histories as "back-stairs gossip," but most praise their telling presentation of eighteenth-century manners and morals. In their most famous study of the eighteenth century, *L'art du dix-huitième siècle (French XVIII Century Painters),* which was originally published in twelve separate volumes between 1859 and 1870, the brothers celebrated several eighteenth-century French artists who had fallen into disfavor, most notably Jean Antoine Watteau, François Boucher, Jean Honoré Fragonard, and Jean Baptiste Chardin. Although the book is now recognized as a classic, many point out that, as art critics, the Goncourts remained curiously blind to the importance of the Impressionist painters who were their contemporaries, despite their own impressionistic literary style. In addition to awakening interest in eighteenth-century French painting, the Goncourts helped to secure the recognition of eighteenth-century Japanese art in France both by their art criticism and their extensive collection of Japanese paintings and embroideries.

The Goncourts' historical works were followed by several novels of contemporary life, each of which is a case history of a neurotic type that describes a particular aspect of nineteenth-century society. The brothers attributed their renewed interest in the novel to their work as historians. As they expressed it: "What is history based on? Documentation. And the documentation of the novel is life itself." With the depiction of "life itself . . . its entrails still warm, and its tripe still palpitating" as their goal, the Goncourts created their characters by means of minute observation and meticulous attention to detail, frequently modeling their subjects on friends and acquaintances whose behavior they had recorded in their *Journal. Madame Gervaisais,* for example, is an account of the conversion to Catholicism of the Goncourts' aunt, while the middle-class heroine of *Renée Mauperin* is patterned on a childhood friend. The Goncourts' most acclaimed novel, *Germinie Lacerteux,* recounts the double life of their own housekeeper who, they learned after her death, had been robbing them in order to finance her secret debauchery. The preface to this novel is a ringing proclamation in defense of the presentation of the lower classes in works of fiction. *Germinie Lacerteux* is often cited as the first realistic French novel with a working-class heroine, and many critics maintain that it served as the prototype for Émile Zola's naturalistic novels. While modern commentators regard the Goncourts' scientific methods as well as their portrayal of the lower classes as significant to the development of Naturalism, they also note that the Goncourts were not themselves Naturalists because they viewed reality as artists, rather than as objective reporters.

The Goncourts were admired by some of France's best-known writers and personalities, such as Charles Augustin Sainte-Beuve, Gustave Flaubert, Théophile Gautier, Joseph Ernest Renan, and Alphonse Daudet, but the critics and the public were hostile to all of their works. The *écriture artiste,* in particular, restricted the Goncourts' circle of readers and outraged contemporary critics who complained that the Goncourts had violated traditional conventions of the French language. In the twentieth century, the *écriture artiste* has been judged variously. While some critics share Lewis Galantière's opinion that the *écriture artiste* is "gibberish," others contend that it was influential, pointing out that many of the Goncourts' stylistic innovations have been incorporated into the French language. Still others argue that the Goncourts were too intent on reproducing the effects of painting by this impressionistic literary style.

Many commentators suggest that the Goncourts' innovative methods were inspired by their determination to achieve immortality. In order to ensure the recognition that had been denied the Goncourts in their lifetime, Edmond provided in his will for the establishment of a literary academy. Most critics agree, however, that the *Journal* is the best check against the obscurity they feared. Besides delineating the Goncourts' literary theories, the *Journal* contains sardonic portraits of their contemporaries, scandalous anecdotes, and records of the conversations of some of France's leading writers, including Sainte-Beuve, Flaubert, Gautier, and Renan, many of them reported verbatim from bimonthly dinners attended by prominent literary figures at the Magny restaurant in Paris. An expurgated version of the *Journal,* published in nine separate volumes during Edmond's lifetime, was met with angry protests from critics, who attacked the Goncourts for their indiscretion, and by friends and acquaintances, who believed they had been betrayed. It was not until 1959 that the entire text was made public. While modern critics acknowledge the Goncourts' frequent spitefulness, most praise the *Journal* as an indispensable chronicle of the literary and social history of the second half of the nineteenth century. According to Kenneth Rexroth, the *Journal* is a "case history of the style of an epoch." Some commentators, including Galantière and Robert Baldick, note that the Goncourts' documentary approach works to greater advantage in the *Journal,* where unity of construction is of little importance, than in their social histories and novels.

In 1868 Jules began to suffer the debilitating effects of syphillis, which he had contracted in 1850, and he died two years later. Devastated by the loss of his partner, Edmond vowed to abandon writing. His resolve to describe Jules's death in the *Journal,* however, compelled him to continue both the diary and his literary career, and he went on to publish four novels and several works of art criticism. With *Outamaro, Hokousaï,* and *La maison d'un artiste,* a book-length essay that meticulously describes the furnishings and art objects in his home, he resumed the brothers' effort to popularize eighteenth-century Japanese art. Of the novels that he wrote alone, *La fille Élisa (Elisa),* a tragic account of a prostitute who is imprisoned for murder, and *Les frères Zemganno (The Zemganno Brothers),* a story of a circus team that imaginatively reconstructs the creative relationship of Edmond and Jules, have been judged most favorably. Some critics assert that Edmond's solo works indicate that Jules was the greater stylist. Richard B. Grant and Baldick, for example, note that in Edmond's novels, the phrasing is clumsier and the dialogue less convincing than in the brothers' joint productions.

The Goncourts themselves declared that their greatest achievements were "the pursuit of truth in literature, the resurrection of eighteenth-century art, and the triumph of things Japanese." Critics avow, however, that their most impressive work is the *Journal,* which remains an invaluable account of contemporary development in art and literature.

PRINCIPAL WORKS

By Edmond de Goncourt and Jules de Goncourt:

En 18 .. (novel) 1851
Histoire de la société française pendant la révolution
    (history) 1854
Histoire de la société française pendant le directoire
    (history) 1855
Les actrices (biography) 1856

Histoire de Marie-Antoinette   (biography)   1858
Les hommes de lettres   (novel)   1860; also published as
    Charles Demailly, 1868
Les maîtresses de Louis XV   (history)   1860
    [*The Confidantes of a King: The Mistresses of Louis XV,*
    1907]
Soeur Philomène   (novel)   1861
    [*Sister Philomene,* 1890]
Germinie Lacerteux   (novel)   1864
    [*Germinie Lacerteux,* 1887]
Renée Mauperin   (novel)   1864
    [*Renée Mauperin,* 1887]
Henriette Maréchal   (drama)   1865
Idées et sensations   (journal and criticism)   1866
Manette Salomon   (novel)   1867
Madame Gervaisais   (novel)   1869
L'art du dix-huitième siècle   (biography and criticism)
    1875
    [*French XVIII Century Painters,* 1948]
Journal des Goncourt: Mémoires de la vie littéraire. 9 vols.
    (journal)   1887-96; also published as *Journal:*
    Mémoires de la vie littéraire. 22 vols. [enlarged
    edition], 1956-59
    [*The Goncourt Journals: 1851-1870* (partial translation),
    1937; also published as *Pages from the Goncourt*
    Journal (partial translation), 1962; *Paris under Siege,*
    1870-1871: From the Goncourt Journal (partial
    translation), 1969; and *Paris and the Arts, 1851-1896:*
    From the Goncourt Journal (partial translation), 1971]

BY EDMOND DE GONCOURT:

La fille Élisa   (novel)   1877
    [*Elisa,* 1959]
Les frères Zemganno   (novel)   1879
    [*The Zemganno Brothers,* 1879]
La maison d'un artiste   (essay)   1881
La Faustin   (novel)   1882
    [*La Faustin,* 1882]
Chérie   (novel)   1884
Outamaro   (biography and criticism)   1891
Hokousaï   (biography and criticism)   1896

HENRY JAMES   (essay date 1876)

[*James was an American-born English novelist, short story writer, critic, essayist, and playwright of the late nineteenth and early twentieth centuries who is considered one of the greatest novelists in the English language. Although best known for his novels, James is also admired as a lucid and insightful critic. His discussion of the Goncourts' works first appeared in his essay "The Minor French Novelists" which was published in* The Galaxy, *Vol. XXI, No. 2, February, 1876. James argues that the Goncourts are "extremely clever writers," rather than "men of genius," who are "worth attention because they are highly characteristic of contemporary French culture." He praises the Goncourts for their literary style and their powers of observation but contends that their works, particularly* Soeur Philomène (Sister Philomene), *exhibit "superficial unity." In addition, James condemns* Sister Philomene *for its "morally and physically unsavory" subject matter.*]

A critic has not spoken fully of Gustave Flaubert unless he has spoken also of MM. de Goncourt. These gentlemen, brothers, collaborators, and extremely clever writers, have certainly plenty of talent of their own, but it may fairly be suspected that without Flaubert's example they would not have used their talent in just the way they have done. If we have nothing in English like M. Flaubert, we are still further from having anything like Edmond and Jules de Goncourt. . . . Everything they have written exhibits a perfect superficial unity. . . . [They] produced a series of volumes at once solid and entertaining upon the French society of the last century and the early years of the present one. These volumes are a magazine of curious facts, and indicate a high relish for psychological research. In addition MM. de Goncourt are art students, and have published several elaborate monographs on painters. It has been very well said of them that the eighteenth century is their remotest antiquity; that for them the historical imagination ends there, after a long revel in sights of its goal. If time with these writers terminates at about 1730, space comes to a stop at the limits of Paris. They are the most Parisian thing I know. Other writers—Balzac, Sainte-Beuve, Edmond About—are intensely French; MM. de Goncourt are essentially Parisian. Their culture, their imagination, their inspiration, are all Parisian; a culture sensibly limited, but very exquisite of its kind; an imagination in the highest degree ingenious and, as the French say, *raffiné*—fed upon made dishes. Their inspiration is altogether artistic, and they are artists of the most consistent kind. Their writing novels strikes me as having been a very deliberate matter. Finding themselves in possession of a singularly perfect intellectual instrument—men of the study and of the drawing-room, with their measured and polished literary style, their acute observation of material things, their subtle Parisian imagination, their ingrained familiarity with questions of taste—they decided that in the novel of the most consummately modern type they could manifest themselves most completely. They inevitably went into "realism," but realism for them has been altogether a question of taste—a studio question, as it were. They also find the disagreeable particularly characteristic, and there is something ineffably odd in seeing these elegant erudites bring their highly complex and artificial method—the fruit of culture, and leisure, and luxury—to bear upon the crudities and maladies of life, and pick out choice morsels of available misery upon their gold pen-points. . . . With MM. de Goncourt [all] is a spectacle, a shaded picture, and the artist's mission is to reproduce its parts in a series of little miniatures of the highest possible finish. A novel, for them, is a succession of minute paintings on ivory, strung together like pearls on a necklace. Their first tale, indeed—**"Renée Mauperin,"** which is also their most agreeable—has more of the old-fashioned narrative quality. I use "agreeable" here in a purely relative sense. The book is an attempt to portray the young girl "of the period" in France—but the young girl of the period at her best, the young girl whose instincts are pure and elevated. It proposes to show us what *"l'éducation garconnière et artistique"* of the day makes of such a character. It does this in a very pretty fashion. I remember no French novel in which the consequences of allowing a young girl a moderate amount of liberty are more gracefully and naturally presented. (pp. 157-59)

MM. de Goncourt have possessed themselves of every literary secret; they have made a devout study of style. **"Soeur Philomène,"** as a piece of writing and of visual observation, is a masterpiece; refinement of observation, an unerring scent for the curious and morbid, can hardly go further. The book is worth reading, from beginning to end, for its exquisite art—

although the art is, to my mind, superficial, and the subject both morally and physically unsavory. It required great skill to interest us during a whole volume in the comings and goings of a simple and ignorant man, around the sickbeds of a roomful of paupers. The authors have "got up" their subject, as the phrase is, with extraordinary care; I do not know what their personal experience of hospital wards has been, but the reader might suppose that they had spent years in one. MM. de Goncourt are *dilettanti;* they are *raffinés* and they write for *raffinés;* but they are worth attention because they are highly characteristic of contemporary French culture. They are even more characteristic than some stronger writers; for they are not men of genius; they are the product of the atmosphere that surrounds them; their great talent is in great part the result of sympathy, and contact, and emulation. They represent the analysis of sensation raised to its highest powers, and that is apparently the most original thing that the younger French imaginative literature has achieved. But from them as from Gustave Flaubert the attentive reader receives an indefinable impression of perverted ingenuity and wasted power. The sense of the picturesque has somehow killed the spiritual sense; the moral side of the work is dry and thin. I can hardly explain it, but such a book as **"Soeur Philomène,"** with all its perfection of manner, gives me an impression of something I can find no other name for than cruelty. There are some things which should be sacred even to art, and art, when she is truly prosperous, is comfortably contented to let them alone. But when she begins to overhaul the baser forms of suffering and the meaner forms of vice, to turn over and turn again the thousand indecencies and impurities of life, she seems base and hungry, starving, desperate, and we think of her as one who has wasted her substance in riotous living. (p. 162)

> Henry James, "Minor French Novelists: The Goncourts, Etc," in his Literary Reviews and Essays: On American, English, and French Literature, *edited by Albert Mordell, Twayne Publishers, 1957, pp. 157-64.**

HENRY JAMES　(essay date 1877)

[*James's discussion of* Elisa, *which he considers inferior to the Goncourts' collaborative efforts, was first published as an unsigned review of* "La fille Elisa" *in* The Nation, *Vol. XXIV, No. 619, May 10, 1877. The essay echoes James's earlier commentary on* Sister Philomene *(see excerpt above, 1876). He praises Edmond de Goncourt for his careful methods of documentation but concludes that the subject of* Elisa *is "distasteful to healthy appetites."*]

The great success of Emile Zola's remarkable and repulsive novel, 'L'Assommoir,' . . . has been, if not equalled, at least emulated, by **'La Fille Elisa'** of Edmond Goncourt. . . . M. Edmond de Goncourt has gone into [his subject] in a more amateurish sort of way than his rival, who is thoroughly professional and business-like; and **'La Fille Elisa'** is very inferior in ability to [Zola's] history of Gervaise and Coupeau. It is equal, however, or perhaps even superior, in audacity. . . . **'La Fille Elisa'** is the first production upon the title page of which the name of one of the [Goncourt] brothers has stood alone; and, curiously enough, it offers some enlightenment . . . as to the mystery of French "collaboration." The book is feebler, thinner, less clever than its predecessors; it seems to prove that there are some talents that need to "collaborate," and that they are fully themselves only on this condition. . . . [The] preface is the best part of the work. M. de Goncourt

says, very justly, that it is an unwarrantable pretension on the part of certain critics to forbid the school of novelists to which he belongs—"la jeune école sérieuse" [the young serious school]—to write anything but what may be read by young ladies in railway trains. This is really what the prohibitory legislation amounts to. The author asserts that the young serious school, if not interfered with, stands ready to divest the novel of its traditional frivolity, and make it co-operate with history and scientific research in the task of enlightening and instructing mankind. As an example, M. de Goncourt devotes himself to showing up the horrors of the régime of silence in prisons. . . . His heroine, convicted of manslaughter, is imprisoned for life, and, being never allowed to speak, becomes after a certain number of years idiotic and dies of a sort of chronic stupor. This part of the book, the last third, dealing with her prison life, shows most ability, and has doubtless a certain value. The author has evidently "studied up" his subject. The preceding chapters, which describe minutely the career of the unfortunate Elisa as a street-walker of the lowest class, and include an account of the circumstances of her childhood—as daughter of a *sagefemme* [midwife] also of the lowest class—are not practically agreeable, however valid the theory upon which they have been composed. As we read them we wonder what is becoming of the French imagination, and we say that even readers who have flattered themselves that they knew the French mind tolerably well find that it has some surprisingly unpleasant corners. M. de Goncourt's theory is perfectly respectable; novelists are welcome to become as serious as they please; but are the mysteries of such a career as Elisa's the most serious thing in the list? M. de Goncourt's fault is not that he is serious or historical or scientific or instructive, but that he is intolerably unclean. The proof of the pudding is in the eating, and, in spite of its elevated intentions, **'La Fille Elisa'** must be profoundly distasteful to healthy appetites. (pp. 164-65)

> Henry James, "Edmond de Goncourt's 'La fille Elisa'," in his Literary Reviews and Essays: On American, English, and French Literature, *edited by Albert Mordell, Twayne Publishers, 1957, pp. 164-65.*

ELIE RECLUS　(essay date 1878)

[*Reclus declares that the Goncourts' literary skills progressively improved. He dismisses their social histories of the eighteenth century as "nothing but romance," but praises their novels for their historical value. In contrast to Henry James (1876, 1877), Reclus approves of the "crudity of detail" in the Goncourts' novels and notes that "in books destined to become monuments of contemporary history, accuracy is of far more importance than elegant prudery."*]

[*Les Idées et Sensations*] may be said to represent [all the writings of the Goncourts]; . . . it is composed of independent fragments, thrown together as if by chance, and treating of a multitude of subjects. It consists of the impressions of an artist intermingled with the conclusions of a thinker. It is a conglomeration of apothegms, a *pot-pourri* of reflections, some serious, others fantastic, when indeed they are not serious and fantastic at the same time. There is almost everything in this book; for the writers have thrown themselves entirely into it, and, almost unconsciously, have thereby given to the world a complete epitome of their intellectual and moral development. (p. 180)

The first productions signed Goncourt were a *Revue du Salon* . . . and a few light pages, *La Lorette, Les Actrices, Les Mystères du Théâtre, La Voiture de Masques,*—pages wherein fantasy entirely predominated over the observation which, at a later period, became so closely intertwined with it. . . .

The Goncourts were artists in history. They wrote books composed mainly of anecdotes, collected to justify whatever theories were advanced. They made a specialty of the second half of the eighteenth century, and studied minutely its art, its literature, and above all its manners and customs. They collected pamphlets, drawings, autographs, engravings, newspapers, neglected nothing, however trifling or obscure, which might revive the life of the time. It was their ambition to paint France exactly as it had existed,—in its customs, its characters, its national physiognomy, its true color, its life. It was a great ambition. We dare not say that it has been realized. (p. 181)

Enrolling themselves among the anti-revolutionists, they wrote a book [*Histoire de la Société Française pendant la Révolution*] containing a few fine effects of rhetoric, but no impartiality. Their so-called Social History is only a conglomeration of tittle-tattle, fibs, and gossiping stories, whose veracity is unchallenged if their wit passes muster and if they "produce a good effect in the scenery." This superficiality is not very surprising in young writers who were mingling dissertations upon the terrible duel between the Old World and the New with studies, not less serious, on the mysteries of the theatre and on the life of the lorette. But the real reason for this superficiality lies below the surface. The habit of trifling seems to confer the right to be unjust, to omit saying all that one knows, to evoke or to silence one's conscience. With this habit, also, it is much easier to be amusing, and wit is hard to impress into the service of equity and of laborious exactitude. The Goncourts did not lack erudition, but were entirely deficient in the philosophical capacity, the breadth of view, the warm breath of humanity, which make the true historian. They wished to prove something with [*Histoire de la Société Française pendant la Révolution*], and the thesis which they maintained, and which is still popular in fashionable circles at Paris, is the assertion that 1793 was an invasion of barbarians, an ebullition of bad passions, a paroxysm of fury and of stupidity. Intrenched behind their hedge of quotations, Edmond discharged his popgun of peas and Jules fired off his mortar of pins upon Robespierre, Danton, Saint Just, and Marat, and riddled the grand corpses with their petty projectiles. The Castor and Pollux of *bric-à-brac* set out to war upon the dead giants as if they were going to hunt mosquitoes, and after each well-aimed blow exclaimed with lively satisfaction, "Ah, well done! That monster will not raise his head again!" (pp. 181-82)

When [*Histoire de la Société Française pendant la Révolution*] appeared, all "respectable people" were regarding Napoleon III. as a revival of Napoleon I., as the saviour of society, as the predestined hero who should reassure the good and make the wicked tremble. Such enthusiasm was pardonable in dupes or in rogues, but inexplicable in the brothers Goncourt, assuredly neither the one nor the other, and who nevertheless consented to enlist on the side of the adventurer. Having completed their invective against the Revolution, the Goncourts proceeded naturally to a pleading in favor of its enemy, and wrote a second bad book,—the *History of Marie Antoinette*. Their heroine is represented as constantly a victim,—victim of the court, victim of the diplomatic policy, victim of the bigots, victim of slander and calumny, victim of the *bourgeoisie*, victim of the people, victim of feminine jealousies, victim of

human perversity. By an inexplicable fatality the entire world was leagued against her, and of a saint made a martyr. Our authors admire this royal saint without reserve,—admire her when she gets up and when she sits down; when she dances; when she walks; when she acts as a queen and when she poses as a milk-maid; when she rises and when she goes to bed. This admiration is not history, it is esoteric enthusiasm. Thanks to Messrs. Edmond and Jules, Marie Antoinette became at once the ideal of the fashionable Bonapartist world. . . . (pp. 182-83)

But the brothers Goncourt have turned their studies on the eighteenth century to better account than in their histories of Marie Antoinette and of French society during the Revolution. At the time they began to write, it was fashionable in France to speak with extreme disdain of the literature and art of the last century, for contempt is always facile to ignorance. But in rapid succession the brothers Goncourt published their *Portraits Intimes of the Eighteenth Century,* a biography of Sophie Arnaud, and studies on Watteau, the painter of their predilection. A reaction of public opinion set in; a taste revived for the subtle and delicate qualities of these eighteenth century artists, and to the Goncourts in great measure belongs the honor of the revival. (p. 183)

This bold campaign secured for the authors a merited reputation, and their intellectual horizon enlarged with their renown. They succeeded in so impregnating themselves with the art which they studied, in so saturating themselves with the literature, that their own sense of the beautiful developed, and with it the brilliant logic, the agreeable good sense, the light and delicate handling, characteristic of the eighteenth century. These conscientious studies, moreover, enabled the brothers better to understand the century in which they themselves were living. They learned to observe the *salons* and workshops of the world around them with the rigid exactitude of which they had acquired the habit in the retrospective observation of a former world. The success obtained by this method made them enthusiastic for it. (pp. 183-84)

It is in the patient and intelligent study of certain sides of contemporary social existence that the Goncourts have disclosed their real originality, and have developed into artists of intrinsic value. Hitherto they had written history which was nothing but romance; now they wrote romances which were in reality history. Hitherto they had modeled in clay, but henceforth they were destined to cast in bronze. . . .

Renée Mauperin was a great success. The world was taken by surprise, all the more because the authors were not unknown. But in them had not been suspected the new talents which were now exhibited,—the penetration of character, the living psychology, which determined at once the success of the book. This success was confirmed by the romances which followed. . . . We may pardon the *Marie Antoinette,* in consideration of *La Fille Elisa*. The truth, cold and severe, the healthy emotion, the advocacy of a justice superior to legality, which appear in their last work, may serve to redeem the tinsel, the gilding, the false elegancies, the vicious perfumes, of the pretended history of which the maids of honor at the Tuileries had such a high opinion. . . .

The Goncourts have been reproached for their frankness and for the minuteness with which they depict things which are coarse, unwholesome, or painful, not hesitating to use the plain name for the plain thing. For our part, we approve of the physiology which the Doctors Robin and Ouimus have taught them; we approve even of this crudity of detail, for, in books destined to become monuments of contemporary history, accuracy is of far more importance than elegant prudery. (p. 184)

The Goncourts are at the same time delicate and realistic; they know themselves to be refined. . . . They are sculptors who carve conscientiously after their model, and dissect their "subject" as expert anatomists. . . .

Our artists condemn [the] bourgeoisie as foolish and spiteful, as envious, vain, and timid. . . . The masses seem to them *canaille,* but as such more *distingué* than the bourgeoisie, which is vulgar. They are capable of frightful stupidities, of ignoble crimes, and sometimes of sublime virtues; they are personified by the authors in the features of Germaine Lacerteux [in *Germinie Lacerteux*]. More far-sighted than many of their fellows, the Goncourts see that the flood of democracy is rising, but they see it with keen regret. (p. 185)

The grand preoccupation of the Goncourts is, lest the European proletariat, by means of popular education, should become transformed into something resembling the American democracy,—a democracy rich, powerful, ambitious, but destitute of all feeling for art. . . .

In reality the authors dissect their subject with too lively curiosity to permit them to compassionate the sufferings which may have been borne before it was stretched on the marble table. And it is to this very curiosity, to this intense mental activity, that they owe the preservation of their mental health. For it must be admitted, the subjects to which our two writers devote themselves are not enlivening. A thousand times must their eyes be saddened at the contemplation of so many wounds, of so many ulcers, of the ignominies and perfidies,—the stratagems and the treasons, which abound in society, in business, in politics, in industry. Humanity is stupid and perverse, and they have not failed to perceive it. They accuse nature of cruelty, and we dare not affirm that they are altogether wrong. (p. 186)

The works of the Goncourts . . . will gain in value as they grow older, differing in this from many contemporary productions. They have solid qualities which deserve permanent fame, an artistic sincerity, a truthfulness, a manner of representation, which will render them precious in the eyes of future moralists and historians. Their agreeable water colors, their charming sketches, wherein they have caught the essence of contemporary French intellect and the features of Parisian physiognomy, will be one day studied by antiquaries with the same curious care which they have themselves expended upon the pictures of Fragonard or the pastels of Latour. Their exceptional merit consists in the happy alliance of a lively imagination with patient and conscientious work; of a witty and mercurial poetic faculty with an observation as delicate and precise as that of the physician and statistician; of exact drawing, brilliant color, elegant style, and a form often exquisite, united to a perfect command of technicalities. Passing with singular facility from graceful fancies to painful realities, they find on their rich palette colors at once for the diaphanous wings of the butterfly, and also for malignant pustules and cancers in suppuration. They transport themselves readily from the infirmary to the workshop of the painter or of the sculptor; they pass from the salon of the Princess Mathilde to the bedside of the outcast.

Doubtless there exists an obverse to these multiform talents. A severe critic will notice that these authors describe too much for the sake of the description; that they too often paint objects which have no other merit than to have been looked at by the artists; that they encroach deliberately upon the domain of painting, and exact from their pen what the brush alone is able to give; that they are sometimes over-refined, and perhaps affected; that occasionally they seem to be the dupes of their own paradoxes, and insist upon an apparent opposition of ideas which in reality is only a juggle of words; that the artistic effect becomes of too much importance to them, and the moral significance too little. Nevertheless, while we might often wish them to be other than they are, we must acknowledge that the Goncourts as Goncourts are a decided success. And in view of the steady progress manifested in the succession of their books, they deserve to be judged, above all, by their latest productions.

Finally, should we attempt to trace the intellectual paternity of the Goncourts, we should say that they proceed chiefly from Théophile Gautier, who was at once a realist and a man of fantasy. They are also assimilated in method to Watteau as a painter, and to Flaubert as an observer; they are impregnated with the doctrines of Taine, but most of all are they disciples of Gavarni. What Gavarni concentrates in an outline drawing, they develop in one or more pages, or they extend it even to a book. They explain Gavarni to us, and Gavarni explains them. Having traversed several schools, and having learned something of each, they in their turn have become masters, and have acquired a style peculiar to themselves. It is a style of a secondary sort. In order to rank among the first, they require more strongly accentuated qualities and defects than they possess. Such as it is their art is delicate rather than powerful, and perhaps the reader must be himself an artist to be able fully to appreciate it. And we seem to be able to trace in the productions of this art the various influences which have contributed to its development, as distinctly as we perceive in a smooth and polished agate the different silicious strata by which it has been successively constituted. These rose-tinted lines we have already seen in Boucher and in Watteau; these gray bands are from Flaubert; this lace-work in opaque red reveals Gautier; these amber-hued crystals are of Musset; and from Gavarni, this opal veined with sombre violet. All these concretions are united in a fine and hard cement, which has assumed the most brilliant polish. To such a curious union of lines curved and broken, of angular designs, of variegated colors in whimsical yet harmonious juxtaposition,—to this agate, this gem of subtle, unconscious workmanship, would we compare the brothers Goncourt. (pp. 187-88)

Elie Reclus, "Edmond and Jules Goncourt," in The Atlantic Monthly, *Vol. XLI, No. CCXLIV, February, 1878, pp. 180-88.*

ÉMILE ZOLA (essay date 1880)

[*Zola was a French novelist, short story writer, critic, essayist, dramatist, poet, and journalist of the nineteenth century who is considered by many to be the foremost disciple of the Goncourt brothers. Zola, however, favored an approach informed by the methods of scientific determinism and thus eschewed some of the elements of realism and the emphasis on style that characterizes the work of the Goncourts. Although Zola's scientific conception of literature is no longer popular, he served as Naturalism's most devoted spokesman and his* Les Rougon-Macquart, *a twenty-novel series, is considered the masterpiece of the French Naturalist movement. In the following excerpt, which first appeared in 1880 in Zola's* Le roman expérimental, *Zola classifies Edmond de Goncourt as a Naturalistic novelist and praises his preface to* The Zemganno Brothers *as a "manifesto" on Naturalism. In particular, he admires Goncourt for stressing that Naturalism does not confine itself to the depiction of the lower classes, as many of its critics contended. Zola argues that Naturalism is a "common method of observation and experiment" that is equally applicable to the "salon" and the "hovel." In advancing his argument, he cites* Renée Mauperin *and* Manette Salomon *as examples of Naturalistic literature that do not describe the lower classes. According to Zola,* The Zemganno Brothers *is further proof that Naturalism is a question of method; he maintains that the "poetic reality" of the novel exhibits the "great difference between the imagination of the story-tellers, who turned the facts topsy-turvy, and the imagination of the Naturalistic novelists, who set out from facts."*]

[The preface to **"Les Frères Zemganno"**], which has all the importance of a manifesto, is excellent. (p. 267)

The thesis maintained by the author is that the decisive triumph of the naturalistic formula will be complete when it shall have been applied to the study of the higher classes of society. He says as follows: "We can publish 'Assommoirs' [by Zola] and books like **'Germinie Lacerteux,'** and by them agitate, stir up, and excite one part of the public. Yes, but to my thinking the success of these books are only brilliant skirmishes by the advance guard, and the great battle which will determine the victory of realism and naturalism, and of analysis according to nature in literature, will not be fought on the ground that the authors of these two novels have chosen. The day in which the cruel analyses which my friend M. Zola and perhaps myself have brought to bear upon the picture of life in our lower classes shall be taken up by a writer of talent, and employed in the reproduction of fashionable men and women, placed amid surroundings of education and distinction—on that day only classicism and its following will be killed."

This could not be better put. . . . [Naturalism] does not confine itself to a choice of subjects; in the same manner that the savant applies his magnifying glass as much to the rose as to the nettle, the naturalistic novelist has for his field of observation the whole of society, from the *salon* to the hovel. Fools alone make naturalism the literature of the slums. M. Edmond de Goncourt expresses in an excellent manner this very fine thought, that for a certain prejudiced public, frivolous, unintelligent, if you wish, the naturalistic formula will never be accepted until this public shall perceive by examples that it is a question of formula, of a general method which is as applicable as well to duchesses as to *grisettes*. (pp. 267-68)

M. de Goncourt completes and explains his idea by adding that naturalism "has not in fact only the mission of describing what is low, what is repugnant, what is disgusting; it has come into this world to define in artistic expression that which is elevated, pretty, and noble, and, still more, to give to the world a picture of the doings and appearances of refined men and women and their rich and sumptuous surroundings; but it will do this in a consistent, vigorous, unconventional, and unimaginative study of beauty, a study such as the new school has just made these few years back of ugliness." (p. 268)

People affect to see but our brutalities, they pretend to be convinced that we shut ourselves up in the horrible; all this is a maneuver on the part of our enemies, made in very bad faith. We wish to depict the whole world, we mean to submit to our analysis beauty as well as ugliness. I will add that M. de Goncourt might have been a little less modest for us. Why should he leave it to be imagined we have only depicted ugliness? Why does he not show us carrying out the same work under all conditions, in all classes of society at the same time? Our adversaries alone play us this villainous trick of only speaking of our **"Germinie Lacerteux"** and our "Assommoirs," keeping silent about our other works. We must protest, we must show the general whole of our efforts. . . . [I] insist upon doing M. de Goncourt justice; I wish to show him writing **"Renée Mauperin"** after **"Germinie Lacerteux,"** touching the higher classes after the people, and writing a *chef-d'oeuvre* after a *chef-d'oeuvre*.

What an exquisite and deep study **"Renée Mauperin"** is! We are no longer in the midst of the roughness and savageness of the lowest class. We have gone up into the middle class, and the conditions become terribly complicated. I know very well that this is not yet the aristocracy, but it is, at any rate, "an environment of education and distinction." At this time the classes are so intermingled, the pure aristocracy hold so small a place in the social machinery, that the study of it is not very interesting. M. de Goncourt, when he asks for the aspects and profiles of refined people and costly things, evidently speaks of the Parisian world, so elegant, so modern, and so variegated. He has already presented one side of this Parisian world in the publication of **"Renée Mauperin."** . . . In that book will be found all that his great modesty asks from those writers of talent who are to come after him. Why, then, should he wish to remain the author of **"La Fille Elisa"** and **"Germinie Lacerteux,"** when he has written **"Renée Mauperin"** and **"Manette Salomon,"** that other *chef-d'oeuvre* of rare and vigorous charm?

It is true that M. de Goncourt has left one point in obscurity, which it is necessary clearly to establish. He demands "a well carried out study, rigorous, non-conventional, and non-imaginative, of beauty"; and further on he adds that human data alone make good books—"books which set mankind, as it truly is, standing squarely on its legs"—an opinion which I have defended for years past. There is the tool, the naturalistic formula, that we can apply to all conditions and to all characters. Then the worst of it is that we at once reach the human beast under the black broadcloth coat as well as under the blouse. Let us look at **"Germinie Lacerteux."** The analysis is cruel there, for it uncovers terrible sores. But carry the same analysis into a higher class, into educated and distinguished surroundings; if you tell everything, if you probe below the skin, if you expose man and woman in their nakedness, your analysis will be as cruel there as with the lower classes, for it will only mean a change of scene and many more hypocrisies. When M. de Goncourt shall desire to depict a Parisian drawing room and to tell the truth, he will certainly have some pretty descriptions to make of beautiful toilets, flowers, politenesses, refinements, with an infinite variety of shadings. Only if he undresses his characters, if he passes from the *salon* to the bedchamber, if he enters into the intimacy, into the private and hidden life of every day, he must dissect monstrosities so much more unpardonable from the fact that they have grown and been cultivated in a richer soil.

And besides, is not **"Renée Mauperin"** a proof of what I have just said? Is not the refined wickedness of that book much more disgusting than the instinctive and desperate dissoluteness of **"Germinie Lacerteux,"** this poor sick girl who was dying for want of love? Yet M. de Goncourt has surfeited us with delicate tints in **"Renée Mauperin."** The surroundings are luxurious; they smell good. The characters are respectable; they do not talk slang, and they are careful of all the proprieties.

It is necessary to state this plainly. Our analysis will always be cruel, because our analysis goes to the bottom of the human body. High and low we throw ourselves at the beast. Certainly there are veils more or less numerous, but when we have described them one after another, and when we have lifted up the last one, we see behind it more dirt than flowers. This is why our books are so black, so severe. We do not seek for what is repugnant—we find it; and if we try to hide it we must lie about it, or at least leave it incomplete. The day that M. de Goncourt conceives the notion of writing a novel on the fashionable world, wherein all will be pretty, or where there will be no bad odors, that day he will have to content himself with painting light Parisian pictures, sketches made on the surface, observations taken in the vestibule. If he goes down into the psychological and physiological study of characters, if he goes below the laces and jewels, well! he will write a novel which will poison the minds of delicate readers, and which they will look upon as frightful lies, for nothing seems less truthful than truth as soon as you search for it in the more elevated classes. (pp. 269-72)

[In the principal sentence in the preface] M. de Goncourt explains why he has written it, saying: "This preface aims to say to the young writers that the success of realism lies there [in depicting the higher classes] and only there, and no longer in the *canaille littéraire* [proletarian literature] as it is exhausted in our day, by their forerunners." I agree with him precisely, only I ask the right to comment upon the phrase as I understand it.

Evidently M. de Goncourt could not have meant that the study of the people was already an exhausted subject because he has written "**Germinie Lacerteux.**" That would be conceited and false. The field of observation cannot be exhausted by a single crop when it is as vast a field as that of the people. What! we have been given a "freedom of the city" as regards the people in the literary domain, and back of us, all at once, there is nothing more to say about it. We may have made mistakes, but in any case we have not seen everything.

Besides, M. de Goncourt speaks of the *canaille littéraire*. I do not understand this expression, and for my part I do not accept it. In my opinion "**Germinie Lacerteux**" is not of the order of *canaille littéraire;* it is a superb study of living, throbbing humanity. I would rather think, then, that by this expression of *canaille littéraire* M. de Goncourt intends to designate a certain mode of expression in which crude words are the invariable rule. (p. 273)

[There] are no exhausted subjects; . . . the literary methods alone are exhausted. M. de Goncourt rightly desires no pupils. But let him be reassured: he will have none; I mean by this that simple imitators die quickly, while the newcomers who bring a temperament of their own with them will soon break away from any fatal traditions. . . . We need no more masters, we want no more schools. What keeps us together is a common method of observation and experiment. (p. 274)

You can see M. de Goncourt [in "**Les Frères Zemganno**"] has not confined himself to a strictly exact analysis. As he says himself, he has used imagination in constructing a story out of a dream, mingled with a remembrance. Since the public demand imagination, here it is. Only just see what imagination can become in the hands of a naturalistic novelist when he takes the notion not to press too near the reality.

Evidently M. de Goncourt did not exercise this imagination as regards the facts. It is impossible to build up a more simple drama. . . . [When] M. de Goncourt speaks of imagination he does not mean by it what the critic does, the imagination of Alexander Dumas and Eugene Sue; he means a particular po-

etical arrangement, an individual fancy, made in the face of the truth, but based all the same on the truth.

Nothing could be more typical . . . than "**Les Frères Zemganno**" from this point of view. All the facts which are presented to us are facts strictly taken from reality. The author does not invent a plot; the most everyday history is sufficient to put his heroes forward; the secondary characters hardly mingle in the action at all; it is a matter of analysis that he desires, and not the symmetrical and opposed elements of a drama. Only when he has this matter for analysis before him, when he possesses the needed amount of human data, he gives the rein to his imagination, he builds upon these data the poem which pleases him. In a word, the work of the imagination is, in this case, not in the events nor in the characters, but in the way the analysis is turned into another path and the incidents and characters are made to symbolize a certain truth.

Thus it is evident that *Gianni* and *Nello* do nothing that circus athletes could not do. They are constructed according to exact data. But they are idealized; they represent a symbol. In their ordinary condition things would not happen with such refined sensations. We have here very delicate minds in very coarse bodies. M. de Goncourt has lifted these clowns out of the material atmosphere of violent exercises, to place them in one of exquisite nervous sensibility. Notice that I do not deny the reality of this story; roughs might have these adventures and feel these sensations, only roughs would feel them in a different way—more confusedly. In a word, in reading "**Les Frères Zemganno**" you immediately understand that the work does not ring with the exact truth; it rings with truth transformed by the imagination of the author.

What I have said of the two principal characters I could say of the less important ones. I could also say it of the surroundings. These people and these things have reality as their basis, but they are a little touched up later on: they enter into what M. de Goncourt has so happily called "a poetic reality." You must . . . make a great difference between the imagination of the story-tellers, who turned the facts topsy-turvy, and the imagination of the naturalistic novelists, who set out from facts. This is poetic reality, that is to say, reality taken and poetically treated subsequently.

Certainly we do not condemn such imagination as this. It is an inevitable escape, a flight from the bitterness of truth, a caprice of the writer, whom the truths torment which have fallen from him. (pp. 277-79)

[The] question of method dominates everything. When M. de Goncourt, when the other naturalistic writers add their fantasy to the truth, they still keep the analytical method, they prolong their observation beyond what is. It becomes a poem, but it still remains a logical work. They admit, besides, that their feet no longer rest on the earth; they do not pretend to give out their work as a truth. On the contrary, they warn the public of the exact moment when they enter upon the dream, which is, to say the least, an act of good faith. (p. 279)

[It] would be very easy to tell how this book was conceived by M. de Goncourt. He felt the need, at one moment of his life, of symbolizing the powerful tie which united his brother and himself at every hour of the day in an intimacy and joint work. Recoiling from an autobiography, looking simply for a frame for his memories, he said to himself that two gymnasts, two brothers, who risked their lives together, who had become united together as much through the body as through the mind, would actualize in a powerful and original manner the two beings, blended into a single whole, whose sentiments he wished to analyze. But, on the other side, from an easily explained feeling of delicacy, he recoiled before the brutal surroundings of a circus, before certain uglinesses and certain monstrosities belonging to the characters whom he had chosen. **"Les Frères Zemganno"** is, therefore, the result of a conception materialized and then idealized.

The result is a very touching book, startling in its strangeness. . . . [You] soon feel that you are not in a real world; but, under the caprice of a symbol, there is in it a throbbing humanity. . . . Human data are so touching here that they are felt even under the poetic veil which is thrown over them.

In his pure descriptions M. de Goncourt has retained his exact and fine touch. There is, in this connection, at the commencement of the book, a marvelous description: a landscape at the hour of twilight, with a little city in the distance whose lights twinkle on the horizon. I will also cite the description of the circus the night *Nello* broke his legs; the silence of the audience after the fall has a superb effect. (pp. 280-81)

["**Les Frères Zemganno**"] brings a new note into M. de Goncourt's work, and it will remain by its originality and its emotion. The author has written simpler and completer books, but he has put into this one all his tears, all his tenderness, and that often is sufficient to render a work immortal. (p. 281)

> *Émile Zola, "'Les frères Zemganno': The Preface,"* in his The Experimental Novel and Other Essays, *translated by Belle M. Sherman, Cassell Publishing Company, 1894, pp. 267-81.*

THE NATION   (essay date 1888)

The Goncourts really seemed to have had one heart and one brain; there is no sign which can help you to say, Here I recognize one and here the other. This mental and intellectual identification is all the more remarkable because these two brothers were not merely given to receiving and translating sensations: they had theories, they made plans, they were full of ambition, of hopes; they meant to create a literary school; they considered themselves as the true precursors of the naturalistic school.

Still, their dualism was a weakness, and it probably accounts for the failure of many of their hopes and ambitions. [Gustave Flaubert's] 'Madame Bovary' will be read when '**Germinie Lacerteux**,' '**Madame Gervaisais**,' '**Renée Mauperin**,' '**Manette Salomon**,' will be forgotten. I might say, without much injustice, that they are forgotten. Flaubert impressed his strong individuality on his work; the Goncourts had not the same creative force. They had a great sensibility, and received sensations as a mirror receives images. They were never able to give a dramatic form to their thoughts, to condense their observations in living types. They were witnesses rather than actors in the struggle of their own time, and though they pretended to be naturalists and impressionists, there is a curious want of reality in all their work. They always produce on me the effect of men who are just out of a dream. . . .

Their fine book entitled '**L'Art au XVIIIe. Siècle**' will keep a very honorable place among the art literature of our time.

Their familiarity with the painters and engravers who lived during the French Revolution gave them opportunities for studying the French society of that period and of the Directory. The pictures they drew of these extraordinary times are vivid and full of interest, as well as their studies on the actresses of the eighteenth century, on the Duchesse de Châteauroux and her sisters, on Mme. de Pompadour, on Mme. Du Barry, on Marie-Antoinette. . . .

The '**Journal**' shows us, so to speak, the gradual development of the Goncourts; it takes us into their society. Flaubert plays a very important part in it, as well as Gautier. (p. 27)

Renan comes in, in many places, as he was a member of the once famous Friday dinners which made some noise under the Second Empire. Some of these dinners are well described in their disorderly conversations. The student of the literature of France between 1850 and the present day will find many notes to take in this '**Journal.**' There are some parts which might well have been omitted, but the authors, I suppose, wished to give a proof of their perfect sincerity. The central figure of these littérateurs is the Princess Mathilde. The Goncourts worship her as the poets of the Pleiad celebrated the great ladies of their time. . . . (p. 28)

> *"Journal of the Brothers Goncourt," in* The Nation, *Vol. XLVI, No. 1176, January 12, 1888, pp. 27-8.*

HENRY JAMES   (essay date 1888)

> [*James regards Edmond de Goncourt's decision to publish the* Journal *as "madness" and he attacks the Goncourts for their undue license in recording their impressions of their contemporaries in the work. Despite these reservations, James concedes that if the* Journal *had not been published, "we should have been deprived of a very curious and entertaining book." James considers the Goncourts' talent to consist "in their feeling life as a theme for descriptive pictorial prose," but he criticizes them for persisting "in the effort to render impressions which the painter renders better, neglecting too much those which the painter cannot render." Nevertheless, James praises the Goncourts for the originality and modernity of their style.*]

[For] persons interested in questions of literature, of art, of form, in the general question of the observation of life for an artistic purpose, the appeal and solicitation of Edmond and Jules de Goncourt were not simple and soothing; their manner, their temper, their elaborate effort and conscious system suggested a quick solution of the problems that seemed to hum in our ears as we read, almost as little as their curious, uncomfortable style, with its multiplied touches and pictorial verbosity, evoked as a general thing an immediate vision of the objects to which it made such sacrifices of the synthetic and the rythmic. None the less, if one liked them well enough to persist, one ended by making terms with them. . . . The great characteristic of the way of the brothers de Goncourt was that it was extraordinarily "modern;" so illustrative of feelings that had not yet found intense expression in literature that it made at last the definite standpoint, the common ground and the clear light for taking one's view of them. They bristled (the word is their own) with responsible professions and took us further into the confidence of their varied sensibility than we always felt it important to penetrate; but the formula that expressed them remained well in sight—they were historians and observers who were painters; they composed biographies, they told stories, with the palette always on their thumb.

Now, however, all that is changed and the case is infinitely more complicated. . . . [The] *Journal* makes all the difference. The situation was comparatively manageable before, but now it strikes me as unprecedentedly embarrassing. M. Edmond de Goncourt has mixed up the cards in the most extraordinary way; he has transformed his position with a thoroughness of which I know no other example. Who can recall an instance of an artist having it in his power to modify to such a degree the critical perspective in which he stands and being so eager to use that power?

My question is an intimation that the modification is (to my sense) for the worse. . . . That MM. de Goncourt should have kept their *Journal* is a very interesting and remarkable fact . . . ; but it has an almost vulgarly usual air in comparison with the circumstance that one of them has proceeded to give the document to the light. The survivor of the distinguished pair has, I believe, held a part of it back, but that only adds to the judicious, responsible quality of the act. He has selected, and that indicates a plan and constitutes a presumption of sanity. There has been, so to speak, a method in M. Edmond de Goncourt's madness. I use the term madness because it seems to me that scarcely any other will cover the ground. How else should one express it when a man of talent defaces with his own hand not only the image of himself that public opinion has erected on the highway of literature but also the image of a loved and lost brother who can raise no protest and offer no explanation? If instead of publishing his *Journal* M. de Goncourt had burnt it up we should have been deprived of a very curious and entertaining book; but even with that consciousness we should have remembered that it would have been impertinent to expect him to do anything else. Barely conceivable to us would it have been had he withheld the copious record from the flames for the perusal of a posterity who would pass judgment on it when he himself should be dust. That would have been an act of high humility—the sacrifice of the finer part of one's reputation. . . . (pp. 501-02)

There is scarcely any account we can give of the motive of the act that does not make it almost less an occasion for complacency than the act itself. (I still refer, of course, to the publication, not to the composition, of the *Journal*. The composition, for nervous, irritated, exasperated characters, may have been a relief—though even in this light its operation appears to have been slow and imperfect. Indeed, it occurs to one that M. Edmond de Goncourt may have felt the whimsical impulse to expose the remedy as ineffectual—in a malady so aggravated as his own and that of his brother.) . . . If MM. de Goncourt were two almost furious *névrosés* [neurotics], if the infinite vibration of their nerves and the soreness of their sentient parts were the conditions on which they produced many interesting books, the fact was pathetic and the misfortune great but the legitimacy of the whole thing incontestable. . . . What passes our comprehension is the state of mind in which their weakness appears to them a source of glory, or even of dolorous general interest. It may be an inevitable thing or it may even for certain sorts of production be an indispensable thing to be a *névrosé*, but one is surely at a loss to conceive the circumstances in which it is a presentable thing. M. de Goncourt not only presents his own case and his brother's but insists upon it. . . . [M. de Goncourt] waves the banner of the infirmity that his *collaborateur* [collaborator] shared with him and invites all men to marvel at such a fine morbid case. (pp. 502-03)

The reason why it must always be asked in future with regard to any appreciation of these gentlemen, ''Was it formed before the *Journal* or after the *Journal*?'' is simply that this publication has obtruded into our sense of their literary performance the disturbance of a revelation of personal character. . . . [If] today we wish to judge the writings of the brothers de Goncourt freely, largely, historically, the feat is almost impossible. We

have to reckon with a prejudice—a prejudice of our own. . . . The difficult point to deal with as regards [the *Journal*] is that it is a journal of pretensions; for is it not a sound generalisation to say that when we speak of pretensions we always mean pretensions exaggerated? If the *Journal* records them it is in the novels that we look to see them justified. If the justification is imperfect that will not disgust us, for what does the disparity do more than help to characterise our authors? The importance of their being characterised depends largely on their talent . . . , and of a poverty of talent even the reader most struck with the unamiable way in which as diarists they for the most part use their powers will surely not accuse MM. de Goncourt. They express, they represent, they give the sense of life; it is not always the life that such and such a one of their readers will find most interesting, but that is his affair and not theirs. Theirs is to make their picture abound in the recognisable. This art they possess in an unmistakable way, and the *Journal* testifies to it still more than *Germinie Lacerteux* and *Manette Salomon;* infinitely more, I may add, than the novels published by M. Edmond de Goncourt since the death of his brother.

I do not pronounce for the moment either on the justice or the generosity of the portrait of Sainte-Beuve produced in the *Journal* by a thousand small touches, entries made from month to month and year to year and taking up so much place in the whole that the representation of that figure (with the Princess Mathilde, Gavarni, Théophile Gautier and Gustave Flaubert thrown in a little behind) may almost be said to be the purpose of the three volumes. What is incontestable is the intensity of the vision, the roundness of the conception and the way that the innumerable little parts of the image hang together. The Sainte-Beuve of MM. de Goncourt may not be the real Sainte-Beuve, but he is a wonderfully possible and consistent personage. He is observed with detestation but at least he is observed, and that does not happen every day. That is what we mean by talent—by having something fresh to contribute. (pp. 503-04)

What makes it important not to sacrifice the *Journal* . . . [is] the degree to which, for the indefatigable diarists, the things of literature and art are the great realities. . . . [Their talent] consists in their feeling life altogether as a theme for descriptive pictorial prose. Their simplicity in this respect is, so far as I know, unprecedented, for if we have encountered men of erudition and science as deeply buried in learning and physics we have never encountered a man of letters (our authors are really one in their duality) for whom his profession was so identical with his moral life. Their friend and countryman Flaubert gave himself up with as few reservations to his sentiment of *his* art . . . , but the Goncourts have over him exactly the superiority that the *Journal* gives them; it is a proof the more of their concentration, of their having thought of little else than what to write about and how to write it. . . . Their concentration comes in part doubtless from the fact that the power of two men was given to it, but that also would have counted in favour of expansion, of leakage. ''Collaboration'' is always a mystery, and that of MM. de Goncourt was probably close beyond any other; but we have seen it successful several times, so that the real wonder is not that in this case the two parties to it should have been able to work together, to divide the task without dividing the effect, but rather that nature should have struck off two copies of a rare original. . . . The relation borne by their feelings on the question of art and taste to their other feelings . . . , this peculiar proportion constitutes their originality. In whom was ever the group of ''other feelings'' proportionately so small? In whom else did the critical vibration (in respect to the things cared for, limited in number, and even very limited, I admit) represent so nearly the totality of emotion? The occasions left for MM. Goncourt to vibrate differently were so few that they need not be counted.

The subject of their critical unanimity is largely, or indeed predominantly, the part of life that is represented by painting and sculpture, but especially by painting and most of all by the French school of the last century. The manifestation of life that appeals to them most is that of Watteau and Lancret and Boucher and Fragonard; they are primarily critics of pictorial art (with sympathies restricted very much to a period) whose form of expression happens to be literary, but who are struck with things in the same way in which a painter is struck and attempt, allowing for the difference of the instrument, to reproduce them in the same way. The most general stricture to be made on their work is probably that they have not allowed enough for the difference of the instrument, have persisted in the effort to render impressions which the painter renders better, neglecting too much those which the painter cannot render. One of the labours of these gentlemen is in particular a monument of misapplied ingenuity. *Madame Gervaisais* is a picture of the visible, sketchable Rome of twenty-five years ago, in which we seem to hear the voice forced to sing in a register to which it does not belong, or rather . . . to attempt effects of sound that are essentially not vocal. The novelist competes with the painter and the painter with the novelist, in the treatment of the world's appearances; but what a happy tact each of them needs to keep his course straight, without poaching on the other's preserves! . . . [No] one probably has poached more than MM. de Goncourt. (pp. 505-07)

[The] manner in which our authors abound in their own sense and make us feel that they would not for the world do anything but what, exactly, they do, raises to my mind a great presumption in their favour. If literature is kept alive by certain persons having a passion for it, MM. de Goncourt have rendered real services. . . . [Their] *Journal,* for instance, is a great piece of work to point to as a proof of good faith. Wonderful are the courage, the patience, the industry of a vast deal of it; with the sense they give us of being constantly a fatigued, displeased, disappointed pair we as constantly applaud the resolution not to let it drop. . . . What strikes an English reader . . . is the small surface over which the career of MM. de Goncourt is distributed. It seems all to take place in a little ring, a coterie of a dozen people. Movement, exploration . . . , plays almost no part in it; the same persons, the same places, names and occasions perpetually recur; there is scarcely any change of scene or any enlargement of horizon. The authors rarely go into the country and when they do they hate it, for they find it *bête* [silly]. To the English mind that item probably describes them better than anything else. We end by having the sensation of a closed room, of a want of ventilation; we long to open a window or two and let in the air of the world. The *Journal* of MM. de Goncourt is mainly a chronicle of suffering, and to this circumstance they attribute many causes; but we, as readers, suspect at last that the real cause is for them too that from which we suffer—simply the want of air.

Though the surface of the life represented is, as I have said, small, it is large enough to contain a great deal of violent reaction; quite extraordinary is the number of subjects of animadversion that spring up under the feet of the diarists. . . . That is precisely the interesting point and the fact that arrests us, that the *Journal* being a copious memorandum of the artistic life, it is in so abnormally small a degree a picture of enjoyment. (pp. 507-08)

The aversion they entertained for [Saint-Beuve] . . . has brought them good luck; in this sense, I mean, that they have made a more living figure of him than of any name in their work. The taste of the whole evocation is, to my mind, and speaking crudely, atrocious; there is only one other case (the portrait of Madame de Païva) in which it is more difficult to imagine the justification of so great a licence. (p. 510)

This publication brings up afresh the whole matter of exposure . . . , and it will have rendered at least the service of fortifying the cause of delicacy. If the plan of MM. de Goncourt was to make Sainte-Beuve odious it has suffered this injury that we are really more disagreeably affected by the character of the attack. . . . [What] superior interest was served by the fabrication week by week of this elaborate record of an implacable animosity? To write down so religiously that you hate a person gives the queerest account of your own mind—and indeed there are strange lights thrown throughout these pages on that of MM. de Goncourt. (p. 511)

Mémoires de la Vie Littéraire is the sub-title of their *Journal;* but what sort of a life will posterity credit us with having led and for what sort of chroniclers will they take the two gentlemen who were assiduous attendants at the Diner Magny only to the end that they might smuggle in, as it were, the uninvited (that is you and me who read), and entertain them at the expense of their colleagues and fellow-members? The Diner Magny was a club, the club is a high expression of the civilization of our time. . . . "If this was the best society," our grandchildren may say, "what could have been the *procédés* [behavior] in that which was not so good?" (p. 512)

The demeanour of MM. de Goncourt, as diarists, in regard to Madame de Païva, to the Princess Mathilde Bonaparte, leaves us absolutely without a rule of translation. If it be correct according to the society in which they live we have only to learn the lesson that we have no equivalent for some of the ideas and standards of that society. . . . On what theory has M. Edmond de Goncourt handed over to publicity the whole record of his relations with the Princess Mathilde? . . . The liberty taken is immense and the idea of gallantry here has undergone a transmutation which lifts it quite out of measurement by any scale of ours. There is something so sacred in the life of a lady and something so profane in the attitude of the reporter. . . . [The] plea is surely idle that the brothers are accomplished reporters, to whom an enterprising newspaper would have found it worth while to pay a high salary for that cleverness, that intelligence. . . . The betrayal of the Princess is altogether beyond us. (pp. 513-14)

[Our] authors are, in a very particular degree, specialists, and the element in this autobiographic publication that fails to endear them to us is largely the result of a disastrous attempt, undertaken under the circumstances with a strangely good conscience, to be more general than nature intended them. Constituted in a remarkable manner for receiving impressions of the external and resolving them into pictures in which each touch looks fidgety but produces none the less its effect—for conveying the suggestion (in many cases, perhaps in most, the dreary or the invidious suggestion) of scenes, places, faces, figures, objects, they have not been able to deny themselves in the [*Journal*] the indulgence of a certain aspiration to the abstract, to reflections and ideas. In this direction they are not happy, not general and serene; they have a way of making large questions small, of thrusting in their petulance, of belittling even the religion of literature. . . . But when we meet them on their own ground, that of the perception of feature and expression, that of translation of the printed text of life, they are altogether admirable. It is mainly on this ground that we meet them in their novels, and the best pages of the *Journal* are those in which they return to it. There are very few of these in fact that do not contain some striking illustration of the way in which every combination of objects about them makes a picture for them, and a picture that proves something in regard to the life led in the midst of it. . . . The object, rare or common, has on every occasion the highest importance for them, when it is rare it gives them their deepest pleasure, but when it is common it represents and signifies, and it is ever the thing that characterises life most. (pp. 517-18)

The people for whom [the visible world] does not exist . . . are the people who are most antipathetic to them, and their vision of literature is as an affair in which such people have no part. Moreover, oddly enough, even as specialists they pay for their intensity by stopping short in certain directions; the country is a considerable part of the visible world, but their *Journal* is full of little expressions of annoyance and disgust with it. What they like is the things they can do something with, and they can do nothing with woods and fields, nothing with skies that are not the ceiling of crooked streets or the ''glimmering square'' of windows. However, we must of course take people for what they have and not for what they have not, and the good faith of the two brothers is immensely vivifying when they project it upon their own little plot. What an amount of it they have needed, we exclaim as we read, to sustain them in such an attempt as *Madame Gervaisais*—an attempt to trace the conversion of a spirit from scepticism to Catholicism through contact with the old marbles and frescoes, the various ecclesiastical bric-à-brac of Rome. Nothing could show less the expert, the habitual explorer of the soul, than the manner in which in this work the demonstration contents itself with being purely pictorial and the scanty, perfunctory nature of the psychological portion. (p. 518)

The weak element in *Madame Gervaisais* is that as the history of the supreme years of a distinguished mind we have to take it too much on trust; the strong element is that it expresses some of the aspects of the most interesting city in the world with an art altogether peculiar, an art which is too much, in places, an appeal to our patience but which says a hundred things to us about the Rome of our senses a hundred times better than we could have said them for ourselves. At the risk of seeming to attempt to make characterisation an affair of as many small touches as MM. de Goncourt themselves . . . , I must add that their success, even where it is great, is greatest for those readers who are submissive to description and even to enumeration. The process, I say, is an appeal to our patience, and . . . the image, the picture, is not immediate, as it is for instance with Guy de Maupassant; our painters believing in shades, dealing copiously in shades and attempting an exceedingly exact specification. They arrive at it, but it is above all on a second reading that we see that they arrive, so that they perhaps suffer a certain injustice from those who are unwilling to give more than a first. They select, but they see so much in things that even their selection contains a multitude of items. The *Journal*, none the less, is full of examples of clever directness of portraiture. (pp. 518-19)

A complete account of MM. de Goncourt would not close without some consideration of the whole question of, I will not say the legitimacy but the discretion of the attempt on the part of an artist whose vehicle is only collocations of words, to be extremely plastic, to do the same things and achieve the

same effects as the painter. . . . The value of the attempt I speak of will be differently measured according as people like to see as they read and according as in their particular case our authors will appear to have justified by success a style of which the connection is more direct with the brush than with the pen. My own idea would be that they have given this style unmistakable life. They have had an observation of their own, which is a great thing, and it has made them use language in a way of their own. They have attempted to say many a thing that was difficult and they have made some remarkable hits. . . . [The] general truth remains that if you wish to compete with the painter prose is a roundabout vehicle and it is simpler to adopt the painter's tools. To this MM. de Goncourt would doubtless have replied that the point where you should stop is a matter of appreciation, that you cannot tell what can be done with a language, in certain directions of ingenuity, till you have tried, and that they themselves have the merit of having tried and found out something. What they have found out, what they show us, is not certainly of the importance that all the irritation, all the envy and uncharitableness of their *Journal* would seem to announce for compositions brought forth in such throes; but the fact that they themselves make too much of their genius should not lead us to make too little. (pp. 519-20)

> *Henry James, in a review of ''The Journal of the Brothers de Goncourt,'' in* The Fortnightly Review, *n.s. Vol. XLIV, No. CCLXII, October 1, 1888, pp. 501-20.*

ANATOLE FRANCE   (essay date 1889)

[*France was a French novelist, short story and novella writer, essayist, critic, biographer, dramatist, and poet of the late nineteenth and early twentieth centuries. During his lifetime, he was widely recognized as his country's greatest author. In this highly commendatory essay, which was originally published in 1889 in France's* La vie littéraire, *Vol. I, France likens the Goncourts' dedication to their work to a spiritual commitment. He regards the* Journal *as the best evidence of the Goncourts' complete devotion to literature and hails the* écriture artiste *as ''a thing to be reverenced.''*]

[It is to be noted that the perfectly private **''Journal of the Goncourts''**] is at the same time perfectly literary. The two authors, who form but one, are so entirely devoted to their art, they are to such an extent its sacrifice and its victim, they have so entirely offered themselves to it, that their most secret thoughts belong to letters. They have taken pen and paper as one takes the veil and the scapular. Their life is a perpetual work of observation and expression. Everywhere they are in the workshop—I was going to say at the altar and in the cloister.

One is seized with respect for this persistent labour, which even sleep scarcely interrupted, for they observed and noted their very dreams. So, although day by day they put in writing what they saw and heard, one cannot suspect them for a single moment of frivolous curiosity and indiscretion. They neither heard nor saw except in art and for art. One would not, I think, easily find a second example of that perpetual tension of two intelligences. For one of them it was a torture. All their feelings, all their ideas, all their sensations have a book as their aim. They lived in order to write. In that, as in their talent, they are essentially of their age. (pp. 79-80)

Without distinguishing themselves by any external mark from the society in which they were born, without affectation, simply and resolutely, [the Goncourts] lived a particular, special life, made up of religious observances, of harsh privations, of painful practices, like those pious persons who, mingling with the crowd and dressed like it, yet observe the monastic rules of the congregation to which they are secretly affiliated. In this respect the **"Journal of the Goncourts"** is a unique document. . . . [When] one has read the **"Journal"** of the years from 1851 to 1861, one understands better how an excessive cultivation of the nervous organism, a constant tension of eye and brain, produced "that artistic writing" which M. Edmond de Goncourt justly recognises as his own, and that minute notation of sensations which is the most salient feature of the work of the two brothers. Their thought and their style, created in a special atmosphere, have not the gaiety of the open air and the easy joy of those forms which are ripened by the sun. But it is a rare thing, and it is a thing to be reverenced; for one of them died of finding it. The **"Journal"** explains to us how. (pp. 80-1)

> *Anatole France, "'The Journal of the Goncourts',"* in his On Life & Letters, *first series, translated by A. W. Evans, John Lane/The Bodley Head, 1924, pp. 72-81.*

FREDERICK WEDMORE   (essay date 1894)

The position of the De Goncourts in fiction and art-criticism is peculiar, and is due in some measure to the period of their birth. They saw the last of the romanticists; they were themselves among the very first of realists (I use the words for convenience, not granting all that the employment of such labels might suppose); [Edmond de Goncourt] has survived to find that, whatever be his personal success, realism, at least in the cruder forms of it, has come to be discredited and *démodé* [old-fashioned]. . . . In one of the later of Edmond de Goncourt's books, in *La Fille Elisa*—which our young ladies very discreetly tell us may be compared, in some respects, with [Émile Zola's] *Nana*—there is perceptible, I cannot help feeling, a certain dependence on the realism that is only ugly. Of poetic realism—the only realism that I care for, the realism that we may find in [Zola's] *L'Assommoir* and in the *Paye d'Amour,* though not, indeed, in *Nana*—there is in *La Fille Elisa* scarcely a trace. Yet of such higher realism Edmond and Jules de Goncourt were certainly not incapable: *Soeur Philomène* and *Renée Mauperin* witness to that.

In art-criticism, quite as much as in novel-writing, the De Goncourts have been "path-breakers." They have initiated methods, they have led fashions; and this notwithstanding (or shall I say perhaps because of?) their employment of a French scarcely more faultless than the French of the great Balzac; often just as much laboured over, and sometimes reaching, only with obvious difficulty, the *mot juste* [right word]—the epithet which is priceless, as long as it does not seem to have been paid for. But in art-criticism, alike when their style has been perfect and when their style has been charming, the De Goncourts have been on the side of sanity. They have been able to appreciate the relatively modern, the actually modern even, without extolling the ugly—without an unmixed eulogy of that strong characterisation which to some seems incompatible with the research of beauty. And from one very English affectation, the De Goncourts have not unnaturally been wholly free—they have never endeavoured to persuade themselves that salvation is to be found in, or culture proved by, a minute study of the Italian Primitive; they have never for a moment assumed, by the collections they have made, or by the articles and books they have written, that in reaching the fourteenth century we have gained the point with which is our most natural

concern. Too serious to be occupied wholly with the contemporary, too wise to be entrapped by the fads of the moment, they are without the prejudices of the academic and the mediaeval: they put in its right place the exquisite and brilliant art of Watteau and Latour, of Gainsborough and Moreau. (p. 504)

> *Frederick Wedmore, in a review of "Edmond and Jules de Goncourt: With Letters and Leaves from Their Journal," in* The Academy, *n.s. No. 1180, December 15, 1894, pp. 504-05.*

EDMOND DE GONCOURT   (journal date 1895)

[*In the following entry from the* Journal, *Edmond de Goncourt describes the history of the Goncourts' collaboration. According to Edmond, as their careers developed, Jules "took over more specifically the direction of style" while he assumed responsibility for the "overall plan and content" of their works. Later critical response supports Edmond's assessment of Jules as the more accomplished stylist; Robert Baldick (1960) and Richard B. Grant (1972) argue that in Edmond's individual efforts, the phrasing is clumsier and the dialogue is less convincing than in the brothers' joint productions.*]

I do not want to bring the Goncourt *Journal* to an end without giving the history of our collaboration, without relating its origins, describing its phases, and indicating in this work in common, year after year, now the predominance of the elder brother over the younger, now the predominance of the younger over the elder.

First of all, two absolutely different temperaments; my brother, a gay, exuberant, expansive nature; I, a melancholy, dreamy, introverted one, yet—what is odd—two minds receiving identical impressions from contact with the external world.

Now at the time when, having both done painting, we turned to literature, my brother, I must admit, was a more developed stylist, more the master of turns of phrase, in short, more of a writer than I, who, at that time, had scarcely any advantage over him other than being the better *seer* into things around us and into the essential nature of beings and things not yet brought into view which could become the material of literature, of novels, short stories, and plays.

There at the beginning of our careers, my brother was under the influence of Jules Janin, and I under that of Théophile Gautier; and one can detect in *En 18 ..* those two ill-matched inspirations which gave to our first book the character of a work produced by two voices, two pens. . . .

Biographies of art and historical works succeeded one another, written somewhat under my pressure and the natural predilection of my mind for the truth of the past and present—works to which I brought perhaps somewhat more than my brother. But as these works appeared one after the other there was a fusion, an amalgam of our two styles, which united in the creation of a single style, one that was very personal, very Goncourt.

In this brotherly rivalry over writing well it came about that my brother and I sought to rid ourselves of what we owed to our elders, my brother to reject the glitter of Janin's style, I the materiality of Gautier's. We were in search of a style which, while it would be altogether modern, would be masculine, concrete, concise, in its underlying Latinity coming close to the language of Tacitus, whom we were reading a great deal at that time. Above all we came to hold in horror the high coloring to which I had inclined too much, and we sought in the depiction of material things to spiritualize them by means of moral details. . . .

It gradually came about in the making of our volumes that my brother took over more specifically the direction of style and I the overall plan and content of the book. He came to feel a somewhat disdainful laziness about seeking, finding, inventing supportive data—even though he could imagine more striking details than I when he wanted to take the trouble. . . .

But while he turned over to me the workmanlike construction of the book, my brother remained passionate over style; and I have told, in a letter to Zola written shortly after his death, of the loving care he put into elaboration of form, the chiseling of phrase, the choice of words, of the way in which he would take up again passages which we had written in common and with which we had at first been satisfied, in order to rework them for hours, for half days, with an almost angry stubbornness, changing an epithet here, giving a more rhythmic cadence there, further along refashioning an expression, tiring and wearing out his brain in the pursuit of that perfection of style which is so difficult, sometimes impossible, for the French language when it comes to expression of modern sensations, and, after this labor, remaining for long moments worn out on a sofa, silent in the smoke of a cigar mixed with opium. (pp. 322-24)

> *Edmond de Goncourt, in a journal entry of December 26, 1895, in* Paris and the Arts, 1851-1896: From the Goncourt Journal *by Edmond de Goncourt and Jules de Goncourt, edited and translated by George J. Becker and Edith Philips, Cornell University Press, 1971, pp. 322-24.*

THE NATION   (essay date 1896)

I have read [the last volume of the **'Journal of Goncourt'** by Edmond de Goncourt] with as much interest as its predecessors; it seems like a conversation between clever people, free to say to each other what they think and all they think. The conversation, to be sure, in this case becomes a mere monologue; and the *moi* [me] (the hateful *moi*, to use Pascal's word) is too omnipotent, too startling. But, with all its defects, this **'Journal of Goncourt'** has the great merit of sincerity. You see in it as in a mirror the fluctuation of the thought of a man of imagination, who looks on the world's stage with some fastidiousness and with an independent mind. . . .

In the pages written on March 18, 1892, Goncourt, in a fit of melancholic dreaming, gives us many interesting details regarding his family. (p. 27)

[These] descriptions have a strange sensation of reality mixed with a sort of dreamy and poetical feeling. They have a minuteness which appears almost exaggerated, but the result is sometimes very powerful. Goncourt has pushed almost *ad absurdum* [to the absurd] the descriptive mania; he gives us, for instance, a description of his *Grenier* (the name he bestows on the rooms where he keeps his collections), and of the works of art of all sorts which he keeps in it; in this curious catalogue, you will find elaborate accounts of Japanese drawings, bronzes, vases, which are really astonishing, and are at the same time almost untranslatable. . . .

Goncourt's style becomes particularly picturesque when he speaks of Japanese art. . . .

On the whole, his **'Journal'** will be chiefly consulted for its detailed documents on the literary period which covers the end of the nineteenth century. It teems with small anecdotes and sayings which throw light on many writers and many artists. People will not care for all the endless details which Goncourt gives concerning the representations of his plays, of his difficulties with the managers of theatres, with the critics; he is morbidly sensitive on this subject, and can write page after page on it. It would have been better if he had left out a number of such pages, as well as certain anecdotes which are improper and disgustingly indecent. I can imagine an edition of the **'Journal'** in which the present nine volumes would be reduced to three or four. In this condensed state, I believe that it would gain much in value and have a more lasting interest. (p. 28)

> *"Goncourt's Last Volume," in* The Nation, *Vol. LXIII, No. 1619, July 9, 1896, pp. 27-8.*

THE SPECTATOR   (essay date 1896)

Being the legitimate heir of Balzac, [Edmond de Goncourt] was also a godfather of modern realism, and he stands sponsor, with Flaubert and Stendhal, for the industry of Zola and the graver indiscretions of Médan.

From the very first he cultivated the ambition of an innovator. Associated with his brother, he was determined upon the invention of a new literature. In their eyes romance was dead, imagination discredited, the street the only proper field of observation. It was their purpose to produce an impression of truth by a multiplicity of detail, and since, in their view, the elder Dumas had brought action into disrepute, they preferred a state of mind to a dramatic situation. . . .

But a new school of literature merges imperceptibly in the old, and **"Charles Demailly,"** the earliest challenge of the Goncourts, is little else than the small change of Balzac. It is written with a more scrupulous study of phrase than the author of the "Comédie Humaine" bestowed upon his creations. The hero is dissected with a patience which the creator of Lucien de Rubempré could only have despised. But in invention and in truth **"L'Homme de Lettres"** (under which name **"Charles Demailly"** made its appearance) fell hopelessly below its magnificent model, **"Illusions Perdues."** . . . Thereafter the Goncourts produced a series of romances, fresh sometimes in their material, and always in their alert and critical treatment. But their success was still a success of esteem, and even **"Germinie Lacerteux,"** their masterpiece of workmanship and construction, has gained only a tardy and grudging popularity. And yet this tragedy of a housemaid deserved a better fate, for not merely is it composed with an almost Greek simplicity, not merely is it written with unfailing tact and reticence, but it proved one of the most prolific examples (for good or evil) of modern literature. . . .

Edmond has acknowledged his brother the finer master of style, and has claimed for himself a more fertile imagination [see excerpt above, 1895]. But it would be pedantic to pretend that **"Les Frères Zemganno"** differs in style or method from **"Manette Salomon."** . . . [To Edmond] belongs whatever there may be of praise or blame. Indeed, it was part of his loyalty to work until the end as though Jules were still there to counsel or reprove; he wrote not merely as his judgment dictated, but as he believed he would have written in collaboration. Realism being his aim, he was foredoomed to disappointment, and he has related, somewhat sadly, that his most successful passages were his own invention. Yet he was always loyal to what he believed the duty of observation. When he wrote **"Les Frères Zemganno"** he haunted the country fairs of his province. To catch the local colour of **"La Faustin"** he attended rehearsals at the Odéon [Theatre], notebook in hand, though he had known the *coulisses* of the theatre for thirty years. And then Zola was certain that Athanassiadis, the old Greek of **"La Faustin,"** was sketched from life! And Athanassiadis is the one character of the book born in the author's brain! How could you prove more conclusively the fatuity of realism? When the masters of the craft deceive each other and themselves, is it not time to condemn an artifice, which was never completely sincere? . . .

[Edmond de Goncourt] was a disappointed man. He would have invented a new literature, and he felt dimly that there is safety only in tradition. (p. 110)

To reveal the pathos of his life would be an indiscretion, had he not recorded day after day his own unhappiness. When his novels are forgotten, when the theatres know no longer those dramas, which never should have been written, the **"Journal"** will be remembered as one of the amazing documents of the century. For in the pages of his **"Journal"** Edmond de Goncourt revealed not only the indiscretions of his friends, but his own miseries and disappointments. The book is both above and below criticism. At the beginning, when Jules held the pen, it was simple, candid, and invaluable. Even after Jules' death it contains the bones of history, and the description of Paris during the siege is the more moving, because it seems scarce deliberate. But as the years go by, Goncourt becomes more personal, less considerate of others, until at last the reader convicts himself of eavesdropping. In every preface you are told that the sole object of the **"Journal"** is truth; but with the deliberate carelessness of the realist its author accepts the merest gossip for gospel, and insults Swinburne (for example) on the tenth-hand authority of a youth who never saw the poet. In one aspect the book is a *chronique scandaleuse* [scandalous chronicle] of the period; in another it is a storehouse of inaccurate "tit-bits." "The Protestants of Glasgow," says Goncourt, "cover their birdcages with a cloth on Sundays, because on that day birds are not allowed to sing in Scotland." Now this astonishing jest is made in all simplicity of heart, for Goncourt was incapable of humour, and furthermore it is made by a man who proclaims publicly that the dominant ambition of his life is *la vérité absolue* [the absolute truth]. Thus also he discusses the notorious English novel, entitled "Sarah Grand;" thus also he tells you that, when one of his stories was appearing in *Gil Blas,* an admirer read it piece by piece through an opera-glass in the office window. Doubtless the mischievous were eager to deceive him and to see their deception in print, but his credulity was equal to the most shameless assault, and doubtless also he died believing that his popularity was immense in the Behring Straits, where they read **"Germinie Lacerteux"** by the light of a lamp fed by blubber.

None of his novels presents a stranger psychological problem than his career. An apostle of style, a master of epigram, a champion of correct observation, he composed, in the interest of truth, a **"Journal,"** which is a monument of inaccuracy. By his own confession, he betrays confidences, he reveals the grossness and stupidity of his friends. Nor does he for a moment spare himself; indeed, he is gibbeted on every page, a miracle of arrogance and self-consciousness. Yet he was a man of taste and erudition. His studies of the last century are unequalled in modern literature. He was a collector of genius, and he did more than any other to reveal Japan to Europe, not only in his ceaseless quest of prints, but in such masterpieces of biography as **"Hokusai"** and **"Outamaro."** Yet he composed the **"Journal,"** and one hopes, for the credit of intelligence, that posterity will pronounce him a better historian of the eighteenth than of

his own century. For, despite his protestation, Goncourt knew no realism save romance, and was even forced to invent the world wherein he lived. (pp. 110-11)

"Edmond de Goncourt," in The Spectator, *Vol. 77, No. 3552, July 25, 1896, pp. 110-11.*

ROBERT H. SHERARD   (essay date 1896)

[Edmond de Goncourt] had a unique position in literature, and was certainly recognised in France, among his brother littérateurs, as *the* master; yet he was dissatisfied and wanted more. What it was, one hardly knows. It is certain he felt very sore at having failed to win any great success as a dramatist, yet his *Germinie Lacerteux,* dull and ill constructed as it was, was very well received. He may have contrasted the smallness of his editions with the colossal sales of some of his contemporaries, and have vexed his soul thereat, yet he always used to . . . flatter himself that if his public was small it was at least select. And he must have known very well that the insincerity of his work could only appeal to a limited audience, such as overlook the *fond* [subject matter] when the *forme* is good, those, in one word, whom a literary *pose* interests. Now, as a novelist, the whole of De Goncourt's work was a literary pose. He had no sympathy whatever with the phases of life or the class of characters which he handled with such apparent gusto. As a matter of fact he denied, in his heart of hearts, the novel as a vehicle of thought, in which respect he was in direct opposition to Zola, and, as I think, most absolutely in the right. In Germany, for instance, when a man has anything to say, any truth to formulate, he expresses his thoughts directly in the form of essays. In England, and in France also, the novel . . . is used. De Goncourt really felt that the German method was the right one, but followed—another insincerity—the French fashion. Over and over again has he said and written that the day of the novel as a vehicle for thought or doctrine was over. . . . Yet it was by his novels that he hoped to convey his message to the world. (pp. 52-3)

What I liked less in him was the pleasure he seemed to take in listening to anything detrimental to any of his contemporaries, and the greater the man, the better was he pleased. A story of that sort would light up his eyes and suffuse his face with cheerfulness. Mental notes would be taken for his diary, in which everything of that description found a certain place. I do not think anything can excuse an artist for such conduct toward his *confrères,* as De Goncourt's toward many celebrated men, unless it be that there is always something feminine in the artistic temperament, and that to women a modicum of peevishness (not to call it spite) is allowed. The last volume of his diary particularly offends in this respect. . . . [There] are many things in his last *Journal* which will leave their sting for years. And what is worse, many old-standing friendships have been imperilled by these indiscretions.

I think it is a pity that De Goncourt did not write a book on gastronomy, à la mode de Brillat-Savarin. It was a subject in which he was particularly erudite, and I cannot remember ever to have met a finer connoisseur. Also when he talked of eating and drinking he was delightful to listen to, and the little gastronomical anecdotes and apothegms which one finds here and there in his diary are excellent and inspiriting matter. One is glad to think that he at least thoroughly enjoyed one pleasure in life. . . . (p. 53)

Robert H. Sherard, "The Late Edmond de Goncourt," in The Bookman, London, Vol. IV, No. 1, September, 1896, pp. 52-3.

YETTA BLAZE DE BURY (essay date 1896)

The Goncourts—this plural will remain necessary, since death itself did not sever one brother's talent from the other—were, first and above all, historians; this quality remained paramount even when they wrote novels. They were inspired by the curiosity of documents, we might call it restitutive curiosity, whether manifested in their historical or their psychological studies. Where Balzac created, they reconstituted. Germinie Lacerteux, Renée Mauperin, are human reconstitutions, much more than creations; in the order of historical restitutions the "pretty" attracted [the Goncourts], and conformably to the suggestion of their nervous temperament, they reconstituted Madame Dubarry and Madame de Pompadour's surroundings by means of picturesque flashes, as they reconstituted poor Germinie Lacerteux by means of traits and *chiaroscuro*. Their "style" . . . is pre-eminently a gift of the "painter," though it certainly betrays a nervous character. . . . [The brothers] may be called historians, because they possessed, both in history and the novel, curiosity of the restitutive order. We should be judging by appearances only if we were to consider such realistic books as *Germinie Lacerteux* and *Renée Mauperin* as contradictory to their historical work. Physiology, the anatomical side of human phenomena, was always a subject of preoccupation to them. Let us not, however, confound what is "contemporary" with what is "life"; though Germinie Lacerteux or Renée Mauperin are more properly "contemporary," they are to no greater extent life-studies than Madame Dubarry or Madame Pompadour. In the former, as in the latter, the consideration of the physiological contingents which affect the psychological ones, was paramount in the mind of our writers. In order to pass judgment on the Queens of the Left and Right, the two brothers made use of no other means, inductive or deductive, than those employed in studying and classing the hearts of the heroines in their novels. (pp. 333-34)

With regard to [their] dexterity of manipulation of the eighteenth century, there is no more interesting study than that of theirs on Honoré Fragonard; it is also one of the most convincing testimonies to the artistic and colour-loving nature of the Goncourts. We may remark, by the way, that some of Taine's qualities are found in their work, partly in the way they select and arrange the fragments of an art or of a personality. It is Taine, however, without his philosophy; for they lack general ideas, and linger more willingly over the dissection of an individual or a branch of art, than over the task of noticing, in a period, all that its contingent ideas has furnished, to such and such attitude of thought in the aggregate, during the years it encloses. (p. 334)

[*Les maîtresses de Louis XV*] was the beginning of the reconstitution of the eighteenth century, in which the brothers went from Queen Marie Antoinette to the portrait-painters of the day, and from them to the courtesans. These last particularly were placed before the modern readers' eyes, with all their detailed characteristics. The brothers had already at that period fixed their attention on one side of their subject, and were seeking for the "spirit" of the age they described, above all, in its manners and customs. (p. 335)

In the way the brothers Goncourt have treated history, there is more than one point in common with Taine, yet with this difference, shall I say again, that Taine does not content himself with arranging the human mosaic, what the English call the "cumulative" evidence. Taine concludes, he unites pieces of evidence into a whole which he comments on, and from which he draws conclusions. Taine is a philosopher, a deducer, a receiver of ideas, whereas the Goncourts are only observers, delicate pryers into the secret movements of a century.

They were lucky finders; engravings, libraries, newspapers brought them treasures. Now it is the *Mémoires de Sophie Arnoud,* now the *Mémoires du Marquis de Calvière* . . . ; another time it is a Watteau, one of the least written-about painters of his time. . . . With certain Marie Antoinette documents they have constructed an admirable and living figure. . . . [They] have revealed beneath the brilliant exterior of the Princess of Versailles, the mien of grandeur and nobility the woman will oppose to the blind fury of a maddened populace. . . . Neither Michelet nor Carlyle, nor yet Tacitus, has introduced impassibility into history; and when the model is, at once, the most attractive and the most unhappy of queens, and this model is painted by colourists so ardent as our authors, one need not be astonished at the enthusiasm of the tone.

The eighteenth century which, underneath its furbelows, powder, and patches, its frivolous artificial fripperies, its outrageous crinolines and head-dresses, was about to give birth to the picturesque naturalism of Rousseau and the impulsiveness of Diderot; the eighteenth century, more than any other period, was that of which the Goncourts could say, "A period must be known by its dinner-menus, a courtly period must be sought out amid its fêtes and its attire." Moreover, the two brothers, who handled the engraver's burin as they handled the pen, were peculiarly fitted to arrange and classify the indications of the future, in the descriptions of the present which they gave of the eighteenth century.

They were among the first to introduce the *living document,* and thus, in drawing up the indictment of a century, they call in the aid of all possible witnesses; none are unworthy or puerile in their eyes. In the France of the eighteenth century the Goncourts see the present equality-loving and democratic France in its slow elaboration as expressed by the claims of the Beaumarchais *Figaro,* that hybrid production of an epoch in which Voltaire is the last classical death-rattle, as Rousseau is the first breath of romanticism. One of the original ideas of the Goncourts was in particular to revive the vivid and sprightly art of Moreau, Fragonard, and Watteau, at a time when the French school of painting was living on the academicism of David and Ingres. It was by the "melancholy" of its gaiety that the Goncourts understood to what extent the eighteenth century was the ancestor of our own. (pp. 338-40)

[*Germinie Lacerteux* began] a new period of the novel. Hitherto medical science had dealt with the physiology of the bodies' ills, and philosophy had contented itself with the therapeutics of the minds' troubles. Thirty years before Robert Louis Stevenson the story of Germinie Lacerteux furnishes us with a case of moral and physical reduplication no less precise and verifiable than that of "Dr. Jekyll and Mr. Hyde"; moreover the study of the double life in Germinie, carried out by the brothers, is based on fact. . . . There is a taking into account of the "whole being" on the dissecting table, a noting of *all* the contingents, physiological and appetitive, generous and self-sacrificing, and an absolute separation of the movements, so that the two beings which exist in Germinie live separately. Each runs a different career. It is precisely the diversity in these two careers of Germinie and the non-confusion in her of the contradictory elements of her nature, which constitutes the curiosity and truth of this study of the Goncourts. It is the co-existence in this soul of morally morbid elements with others that are sound, the absence of contagion between the good and the bad, the inward flourishing together of poisonous plants and other perennial ones; it is the juxtaposition in the same ground of decomposition and vigour, of purulence and purity, which makes this study so singular and yet, we dare to say, so like truth. . . . *Germinie Lacerteux* is not a bad book, since it is a "humane" book, in which the heart is torn with pity in presence of so much inward misery. (pp. 344-46)

The *Journal* of the Goncourts, which is one of the most contemporary and sprightly fragments of their work . . . will always raise polemics. Has any one the right to cast abroad, for generations to come, conversation freely indulged in, among private friends? It is the Goncourts themselves who have given a reply to this question by establishing their accounts of the eighteenth century on notes, fragments, diaries, gossip, and indiscretions of all kinds, in which this century was so rich. Their historical work is built up out of the men and women whose portraits they have painted. And these portraits are the outcomes of the diverse *Journals* of the eighteenth century—that is their answer.

As long as their books are read there will be the joint work of the Goncourts to take into account; and it would be a barren task to separate, in what is left us of them, the two minds whose every intellectual movement was executed in married unity and harmony. (p. 347)

As for "glory," the centuries to come shall decide. The two brothers instigated, influenced, and guided the movement of a whole school of young writers, and that is saying a great deal without anything else! Glory is shy. It is her prerogative to give or withhold the kiss her lovers pray for. Her fancies are unanticipated and sometimes surprising to herself. Will Edmond de Goncourt be one of those temporary favourites? If so, in spite of the Goncourts' voluminous work it would be an exceptional piece of good fortune, more than an expected one! (p. 349)

Yetta Blaze de Bury, "Edmond de Goncourt," in The Fortnightly Review, *n.s. Vol. LX, No. CCCLVII, September, 1896, pp. 333-49.*

HENRI FRANTZ (essay date 1896)

[*Frantz's eulogistic essay presages the approach of Ernest Boyd (1922). He argues that Edmond de Goncourt has been erroneously categorized as a Realist because "he never accepted the license of extreme description allowed by the realistic novel." Nevertheless, according to Frantz, Goncourt was a "creator of truth because he was a creator of beauty."*]

[Edmond de Goncourt] seems to belong to those whose work shall know the rare and enviable fortune of an almost intact survival. . . . [His work] will impress by its faultless style, while it brings to bear upon the period a judgment at once absolute and true. But above all it will reveal to the gaze of the future, whatever that may be, one of those intelligences most enamoured of the divine, of imperishable beauty,—one of those existences which, like Flaubert, knew no loftier ideal, no more ardent passion. (p. 176)

In a higher degree than any other writer of his time he possessed delicate and refined tendencies, which persistently recurred in his work, influencing it and inspiring in him scorn of easy success and of the fame he cared so little to acquire. (p. 177)

The widespread fame of the de Goncourts really began with the novel **"Charles Demailly,"** their genius manifesting itself in these touching and vibrant pages. From that time every hour has been marked by creative activity sufficiently attested by the large number of works remaining to us. Whether it be in the history of the eighteenth century, which they have revived with marvellous brilliancy; in the novels in which they created a realism more vivid and actual than Zola's; in their notes of travel, or works on art;—their impeccable mastery as writers flashes forth everywhere victoriously, showing their continual anxiety to create the true and the beautiful. (p. 178)

The activity of this great thinker [Edmond de Goncourt] was both formidable and diversified. As an art critic, he was able to depict the artists and the society of the eighteenth century, entering with subtle intuition into the life of the woman of this epoch, reviving all the charm of the somewhat affected delicacy of atmosphere by which she was surrounded. Not satisfied with conjuring up in perfection both men and places, as in works like **"La Femme au 18ᵉ Siècle," "L'Amour au 18ᵉ Siècle," "Les Maîtresses de Louis XV,"** and **"L'Oeuvre de Watteau,"** he did more—he redoubled his qualifications as an observer and his scrupulous study of facts, with a solicitude for style and refinement carried at times to the extreme limit of sensibility. (pp. 178-79)

As a dramatic author Edmond de Goncourt moved a world of imagination and fact, but his genius—above all else that of an incomparable stylist—could not become acclimatized to the exigencies and requirements of the stage, and in this respect none of his plays met with success or held its own before the footlights. . . . [His] marvellous qualities of style and observation could not take the place of the scenic action wherein he failed. But if de Goncourt could not rise to the height of great dramatic talent, he has created an enduring work in romance, stamped with the seal of genius. . . . (p. 179)

Many critics have pronounced the word "realism" in connection with him, but it seems to me that it is to misunderstand the tendencies of de Goncourt's genius to associate him with a school with which he held nothing in common but the name. In the restricted sense of the word he was no more a realist than Flaubert; he never accepted the license of extreme description allowed by the realistic novel. He was none the less a creator of truth because he was a creator of beauty; and perhaps for the very reason that he was a creator of beauty no one has better understood, studied, or felt the different aspects of modern life. He desired to substitute for the romance, which transports us into the realms of fancy and interests us solely by the picturesqueness of its incidents, a novel real in its scrupulous reproduction of the spectacle of daily life reflected through the sensibilities of the writer. And his charm lies partly in the concise and temperate manner he employs to depict this same truth that others are wild to show us in an accumulation of facts, in a compilation of proofs. This charm consists in a fine power of portrayal, often in very few words, but with that perfection of style which reproduces the essential in a situation or landscape and is, in short, the appanage of the classical masters.

His procedure—if one may thus speak of so noble a method—consisted in the selection of a picturesque centre, and the placing in it of characters which are portraits and which move in a plot of anecdote and impressions rather than invention. (pp. 179-80)

In this life so filled by the activity of the novelist, historian, and critic,—a life that counted friendships as unique as they were rare,—place must be made for the daily labor de Goncourt imposed upon himself in the writing of his "**Journal.**" . . . In these pages, wherein the *I* of the writer frequently assumes so large a place that we are made to see every event only in the relation which it appears to have solely to him, he has written the literary history of his time, and more particularly of his own life and work. The "**Journal**" was to him not merely a daily exercise; it was, so to speak, the scales by which the virtuoso regulated his thoughts; but for us it will remain one of the most precious and complete of documents.

Unhappily one is grieved at times to find regrettable small-nesses in the man,—to see that the world existed *for* him only when it occupied itself *with* him. He shows therein a constant susceptibility, an irritability, I might almost say an egotism, which is astonishing in so great a mover of thought. He frequently manifests an incomprehensible severity toward writers of such unquestionable and undisputed merit as Flaubert or Maupassant. In [the] ninth and last volume of memoirs, whose frankness made him so many enemies, he went so far as to be unwilling to recognize in Guy de Maupassant aught else than the talent of "novelière," instead of the grand breadth of the writer which amazes one in each of his novels. Such trivialities must be pardoned, however, in a man irritated by the morti-fication and disappointment which, since the death of his brother, have overshadowed his literary career.

What appears clearly from his "**Journal,**" as from the general body of his work, is the impassioned worship he entertained for polite literature and the beautiful: herein lies the funda-mental trait which explains his talent and his life. Noble and admirable are those who bring into our age of utilitarianism and base thirst for money a little of the religion of a past era! This creed as an aim and object filled his life and became the serene conclusion of which his whole existence was the ex-ponent. (pp. 180-81)

Henri Frantz, "Edmond de Goncourt," in Forum, *Vol. XXII, October, 1896, pp. 176-81.*

JAMES FITZMAURICE-KELLY (essay date 1902)

[It] may be well to observe . . . that the creative work of the Goncourts is not to be condemned or praised *en bloc,* for the simple reason that it is not a spontaneous, uniform product, but the resultant of diverse forces varying in direction and intensity from time to time. . . . Beginning, under the influ-ence of Heine and Poe, with purely imaginative conceptions, they rebounded to the extremest point of realism before de-termining on the intermediate method of presenting realistic pictures in a poetic light. Pure imagination in the domain of contemporary fiction seemed to them defective, inasmuch as its processes are austerely logical, while life itself is compact of contradictions; and their first reaction from it was entirely natural. . . . (pp. xv-xvi)

The Goncourts did not—could not—pretend that they were the first to introduce truth into literature: they merely professed to have attained it by a different route. The innovation for which they claimed credit is a matter of method, of technique. Their deliberate purpose is to surprise us by the fidelity of their studies, to captivate and convince us by an accumulation of

exact minutiae: in a word, to prove that truth is more interesting than fiction. (p. xvi)

[If] the Goncourts had, as they believed, something new to say, it was inevitable that they should seek to invent a new manner of utterance. . . . [They] were exquisitely susceptible to every shade and tone of concrete objects, and the endeavour to convey their innumerable impressions taxed the resources of that French vocabulary on whose relative poverty they so often insist. . . . It was not given to them to realize their ambition—to write novels which should not contain a single bookish expression, plays which should reveal that hitherto undiscoverable quantity—colloquial speech, raised to the level of consummate art. The famous *écriture artiste* remained an unfulfilled ideal. The expression, first used in the preface to **Les Frères Zemganno,** merely foreshadows a possible devel-opment of style which shall come into being when realism or naturalism, ceasing to describe the ignoble, shall occupy itself with the attempt to render refinements, reticences, subtleties, and half-tones of a more elusive order. It is an aspiration, a counsel of perfection offered to a younger school by an artist in experiment, who declares the quest to be beyond his powers. It is nothing more. (pp. xix-xx)

[It] may safely be said that in the novels of the Goncourts the characters are less memorable, less interesting as individuals than as illustrations of an epoch or types of a given social sphere. Charles Demailly, Madame Gervaisais, Manette Sal-omon, Renée Mauperin, Soeur Philomène, are not so much dramatic creations as figures around which is constituted the life of a special *milieu.* . . . There are in the best work of the Goncourts astonishingly brilliant scenes; there is dialogue vi-vacious, witty, sparkling, to an extraordinary degree. And this dialogue, as in **Charles Demailly,** is not only supremely inter-esting, but intrinsically true to nature. It could not well be otherwise, for the speeches assigned to Masson, Lampérière, Remontville, Boisroger, and Montbaillard are, as often as not, verbatim reports of paradoxes and epigrams thrown off a few hours earlier by Théophile Gautier, Flaubert, Saint-Victor, Banville, and Villemessant. But these flights, true and well worth preserving as they are, fail to impress for the simple reason that they are mere exercises in bravura delivered by men much less concerned with life than with phrases, that they are allotted to subordinate characters, and that they rather serve to diminish than to increase the interest in the central figures. The Goncourts themselves are much less absorbed in life than in writing about it: just as landscapes reminded them of pic-tures, so did every other manifestation of existence present itself as a possible subject for artistic treatment. . . . [Each] character is studied after nature with a grim, revolting per-sistence. (pp. xx-xxii)

[Yet,] for all their care, their personages do not abide in the memory as living beings. We do not see them as individuals, but as types; and, strangely enough, the authors, despite the remarkable skill with which they materialize many of their impressions, are content to deliver their characters to us as so many illustrations of a species. . . . And the same types con-stantly reappear. The physician Monterone in **Madame Ger-vaisais** is simply an Italian version of Denoisel in **Renée Mau-perin;** the Abbé Blampoix has his counterpart in Father Giansanti; Honorine is Germinie, before the fall; Nachette and Gautruche might be brothers. The procedure, too, is almost invariable. The antecedents of each personage are given with abundant detail. We have minute information as to the family his-tory. . . . There is a frequent repetition of the same idea with scarcely any verbal change: *un dos d'amateur* in **Renée Mauperin** and *le dos du cocher* in **Germinie Lacerteux.** (pp. xxii-xxiv)

It is by no means an accident that the most frequent theme of the brothers is illness. . . . Emotion in less tragic circumstances they rarely convey; and when they attempt it they are prone to stumble into an unimpressive sentimentalism. Their strength lay in pure observation, not in the philosophic or psychological presentment of nature. For their fine powers to have full play, it was necessary that they should deal with things seen: in other words, that feeling should take a concrete shape. Once this condition is fulfilled, they can focus their own impressions and render them with unsurpassable skill. We shall find in them nothing epic, nothing inventive on a grand scale: the transfiguring, ennobling vision of the greatest creators was denied them. But they remain consummate masters in their own restricted province: delicate observers of externals, noting and remembering with unmatched exactitude every detail of gesture, attitude, intonation, and expression. The description of landscape—of the Bois de Vincennes in **Germinie Lacerteux,** the Forest of Fontainebleau in **Manette Salomon,** or of the Trastevere quarter in **Madame Gervaisais**—commonly affords them an occasion for a triumph; but the description of prolonged malady gives them a still greater opportunity. Nor is this due simply to the fact that they, who had never known what it was to enjoy a day of perfect health, spoke from an intimate knowledge of the subject. Each landscape preserves at least its abstract idiosyncrasy; illness is an essentially "typical" state in which individual characteristics diminish till they finally disappear. And it is especially in the portraiture of types, rather than of individuals, that the genius of the Goncourts excels. (pp. xxiv-xxv)

In their most candid moods they confessed that they were all brain and no heart, that they were without real affections; and their writings naturally suffer from this unsympathetic attitude. But when every deduction is made, it is impossible to deny their importance and significance. For they represent a distinct stage in an organized movement—the reaction against romanticism in the novel and lyrism in the theatre. And there is some basis for their bold assertion that they led the way in every other development of the modern French novel. They believed that they had founded the naturalistic school in **Germinie Lacerteux,** the psychological in **Madame Gervaisais,** the symbolic in **Les Frères Zemganno,** and the satanic in **La Faustin.** It is unnecessary to recognise all these claims in full: to discuss them at all, even if we deny them, is to admit that the Goncourts were men of striking intellectual force, of singular ambition, of exceptionally rich and diverse gifts amounting, at times, to unquestionable genius. If they were unsuccessful in their attempt to create an entire race of beings as real as any on the planet, their superlative talent produced, in the form of novels, invaluable studies of manners and customs, a brilliant series of monographs on the social history of the nineteenth century. And Daudet and M. Zola, and a dozen others whom it would be invidious to name, may be accounted as in some sort their literary descendants. (pp. xxvi-xxvii)

> *James Fitzmaurice-Kelly, "Edmond and Jules de Goncourt," in* Renée Mauperin *by Edmond de Goncourt and Jules de Goncourt, translated by Alys Hallard, Appleton & Company, 1902, pp. v-xxix.*

L. MARILLIER (essay date 1903)

[*In this laudatory essay, Marillier asserts that the Goncourts exerted a noteworthy influence on the development of art criticism, literary criticism, and language, as well as on the drama and the novel. Unlike Olin H. Moore (1916) and Lewis Galantière (1937), who argue that the characters in the Goncourts' novels are too clinically dissected to be realistic, Marillier maintains that the Goncourts' characters are depicted with a psychological accuracy that allows "us to penetrate into the secret places of the conscience." In contrast to Henry James (1888), Marillier applauds the Goncourts for their painterly style, and he states that this style enables readers to "understand the state of mind of the various characters" in the Goncourts' works.*]

[It strikes us] as singularly unjust, and at first sight inexplicable, that a master-work like [**"Men of Letters" (Charles Demailly)**] should have proved a failure, considering that the De Goncourts had put into it all that was best, most delicate, most incisive, most sparkling in the way of the thoughts they had turned over for ten years; a book in which descriptions of natural scenes, filled with tender and penetrating grace, alternate with scenes of literary life written with incomparable fire, dash, and vigor; a book in which the feminine mind has been analyzed with a pitiless clearsightedness that at times equals that of Balzac or Stendhal. (p. 334)

The Goncourts' first novel [**"En 18 .."**] had been forgotten, and deservedly so. . . . Barring a few pages in which their gift of style revealed itself, a style so original and so peculiar to them, and that vision of things that has the very color and motion of life, and which imparts such marked interest and piquancy even to the least note of theirs,—barring these two qualities, the book was unmistakably a youthful work in which the authors were seeking to ascertain the effect their prose would produce once it was set up in type and dressed in a yellow cover. (p. 335)

Every one of their novels caused a scandal, and, strange to say, in spite of the noise made about them, these novels failed to secure readers. This double ignoring of their talent was due to the same cause: their very originality that disconcerted the habits both of the critics and of the reading public. The novelty of their methods of composition and of style, the novelty of their conception itself of the novel scarcely attract any attention today. We admire their works, we enjoy their power and charm, we feel in them the free and spontaneous expression of the least conventional, the least factitious, and the most individual of talents, but there is nothing in them to shock our customary modes of thought, our usual way of looking at things. Perchance at times we are struck by a certain unfamiliarity in some chapter or some page, but the reason is that they contain peculiarities of style that are now obsolete, and ideas that strike us somewhat old fashioned and that indicate the date of publication of the work. The audacity of which the two brothers gave proof in the selection of their subjects, in the plot of their novels, the boldness of the opinions they have put into the mouths of their characters, the liberties they take with the conventions of every-day grammar, and the harmoniously balanced and constructed periods of academic speech, their use of inversions and neologisms, their habit of introducing into their style, which is always highly wrought and exceedingly literary, every carelessness of familiar conversation, technical terms drawn from the vocabulary of artists, and the slang of every business, whether reputable or not, their mode of writing itself, which is practically a means of transposing sensations of color into verbal images, all these things, it must be owned, appear to us the most natural possible, and it becomes necessary to make an effort in order not to deny the authors a portion at least of that innovating originality to which they are unquestionably entitled.

It is because we have ourselves adopted the best part, the most individual part of their style and their modes of thought that the novels of the Goncourts no longer startle any one nowadays, even when read for the first time. Most of our contemporary novelists are their disciples, unwittingly at times; and their imitators, whose name is legion, have, though they did not set out to do so, transformed the revolutionaries of yesterday into the classical writers of today.

Art criticism and literary criticism have felt their influence just as deeply as the novel, while it is possible to find marked proofs of it in nearly every column of the newspapers and table talk. But it is probably the stage that has most felt that influence of theirs. . . . (pp. 338-39)

Our historians have very often in recent years, and without being aware of it, adapted their works to the new taste the cultured public has exhibited for accurate and colored descriptions, for life-like and picturesque details, for unpublished documents, for narrations drawn from the memoirs of the people who witnessed or shared in events. It is now a recognized custom to greatly enlarge the number of illustrations in serious works and to draw from the best sources the images of life in the past that are to be placed before readers. And historians have contracted this habit . . . because they had to take into account the new exigencies of the public, and the share of the Goncourts in giving rise to these exigencies is larger than is generally believed.

Their very keen appreciation of French art in the reign of Louis XV and that of Louis XVI . . . contributed unmistakably to determine the profound transformation in the modern fashion of furnishing and decorating homes. True, fashion has changed once more . . . , but we have grown up in the artistic atmosphere created by the writings of the Goncourt brothers. (p. 339)

[The Goncourts'] mode of speech has unconsciously become our usual mode of speech, and by dint of repeating their paradoxes, which we are quite unaware of not having invented, they have ceased to be paradoxes for us.

It is not surprising, therefore, that we do not find in their works that piquancy and startling novelty which repelled the reading public of the Second Empire. . . . (p. 340)

At the time when the Goncourts were publishing their first novels, Flaubert was about the only writer who had managed to combine in himself the consummate learning and the calm reflection of a psychologist of the first rank with the marvelous gift of evoking the life-like aspect not of men alone but of the things in which they leave something of themselves, of the things which have made them what they are and a reflection of which still clings to their faces. These qualities are met with in the Goncourts, but multiplied, increased, and exaggerated, if I may say so; exaggerated to such a degree that the happy equilibrium which existed between them in the case of Flaubert, became impossible through their very excess. (p. 344)

[Flaubert's characters] are the product of his recollections and of the laborious effort of his thought, but no part of his heart beats within their bosoms. Thus it is that after reading his works one knows but little of the kind of man he was. . . . (p. 345)

Whoever, on the contrary, is somewhat familiar with the novels of the Goncourts, feels as though he had been intimate with them. . . .

In every turn of the phrase the men appear under the writers, and not dressed up either, but in their books exactly such as they are in their daily life. They are constantly on the stage by the side of their characters, often without desiring it, often, too, without being aware of it. They live the same exciting, nervous life, and weep over the same sorrows. . . . [The] reality in which they thus infused their souls was not reality harmonized, arranged, and managed with careful, intelligent thought of the effect to be produced, and with the consummate skill in composition that makes Flaubert the equal of the greatest orators and dramatists of every age; it was reality itself, throbbing and burning, with its incoherences, its peculiarities, and its contradictions.

There is no novelist who has more faithfully reproduced in his work what he has seen than the Goncourts have done. A methodical comparison of their novels and their "**Journal,**" is exceedingly instructive in this respect. Whole pages of the "**Journal,**" have been transferred to all the books they have produced and even to their dramas, without other change almost than corrections in the style. If it be not the world as it really is that is reflected in their works, it certainly is the world as they saw it. (pp. 345-46)

[They were] incapable of writing a novel in which there should be no figure of man or woman that did not attract attention by the beauty or the ugliness of its soul, by the complexity of its thoughts, the singularity of its attitude, capacity for suffering or loving, by fancifulness of imagination, in a word, by a strong and original personality manifesting itself in word and action. (pp. 346-47)

It appears to pain them if they have to separate themselves from their characters, and whenever circumstances allow of it, they come on the stage themselves, with so ill fitting a mask that the meanest observer cannot fail to recognize them. . . .

Occasionally the man, under his own name, and not the writer, intervenes directly in the action of the tale, as, for instance, Edmond de Goncourt in the last chapter of "**Eliza the Slut.**" The presence of the author of the novel in that silently tragical scene is both a blunder and artistically a mistake; it takes from the dolorous pages a part of the funereal sadness that wells up out of them, renders them the less sincere and less apparently true. (p. 347)

[It is not] their every throbbing and sickly sensitiveness that causes them to bend . . . over souls and that makes it difficult for them to part with the men and women to whom they have communicated the magic gift of life, it is also their ardent curiosity. It is not enough for them to describe attitudes, to narrate thoughts, to tell of actions, they must also understand them. It does not satisfy them to know what a man feels and wills if they do not know why he wills and feels as he does. Consequently they must penetrate into his most secret being in order to attempt to discover the hidden motives that give birth to the resolves, manifest to all, and to follow the many phases of the slow, inward labor that leads to resolutions and action.

They very often have recourse to physiology and medicine. . . . Themselves almost constantly ailing, their own perspicacity has been sharpened by the minute and painful observation of their physical troubles. Better than most novelists they have understood that very often one could translate into physiological terms and explain by the disorders of which our bodies are the seat, what cannot be explained by the action upon our consciences of external events and the innumerable sensations that penetrate into us through our eyes and our ears. They studied, with a care and an accuracy which many professional psychologists might envy, the part played by heredity, and of that social heredity, possibly no less powerful than biological heredity, which is called tradition. . . . (pp. 348-49)

[Explaining] a psychological phenomenon means determining the laws of its genesis and evolution, and this the Goncourts clearly understood. Hence there is not in their analyses that mechanical and artificial feeling that strikes one at times in Stendhal's analogous work. They enable us to penetrate into the secret places of the conscience and to witness the slow transformations by which, influenced in many ways, emotions, desires, and passions change one into another. Their masterpiece in this line is the story of the conversion of Mme. Gervaisais to Roman Catholicism, which forms one of the finest chapters in mystical psychology and which is at the same time one of the most profound every written. From these tendencies of their minds it is easy to deduce the uneven and stumbling aspect of their published novels: narrations, biographical notes, medical reflections, subtile and refined psychological analyses, scenes hot and throbbing with realism, cries of restrained pain, expositions of aesthetic, literary, or social doctrines; thoughts on passing events and public personages are mingled and confounded in them in an apparent disorder in which comicalities are cheek by jowl with grave dissertations, and sinister portrayals are placed side by side with the most delicate and exquisite accounts of feminine emotions.

Then the excessive side of their marvelous artistic qualities and the peculiar style consequent upon their restless and penetrating way of looking at things intensifies somewhat this impression. . . . (p. 349)

[Flaubert's] descriptions, however carefully finished, are the work of a literary man, and in his landscapes one does not feel the hand of the painter. Besides, these descriptions enter into his novels only because they serve as settings for his characters. . . . It is otherwise in the work of the Goncourts; anything and everything affords them opportunities for describing and painting. . . . They care little,—and for this much thanks,—whether the pictures they paint with such consummate understanding of the play of light, and in which they turn to account their thorough knowledge of the idiom of painters, are or are not linked to the action of the tale. If they had cared overmuch for this, we should have been heavy losers indeed. (p. 350)

The moment they feel an impression they endeavor to render it with as much accuracy, subtile lightness, vigor, and feeling as they can encompass with the imperfect instrument of writing, in which words with clear cut contours and frozen meaning, words that are heavy with innumerable remembrances, and call up, by tenuous and distant associations, a whole world of confused images, take the place of the colors on the painter's palette that docilely obey his will, colors that can express anything and will render only what the painter desires to express.

The overmastering spell of art fascinates them, and every object on which a human thought, whether graceful or vigorous, has left its mark, holds their attention in spite of them and compels them to do artistic work in their turn by describing it. . . . Nature does not affect them with quick emotion as do works that still bear the imprint of the human hand; indeed, nature appeals to them only when saturated with humanity and impregnated with history. (pp. 350-51)

Yet, though they do not care for nature, they see it with the eyes of painters, and there is not one of our novelists, Gautier, Hugo, Daudet, Zola, not even Loti himself, who has equaled them in the power of making us behold the slow flow of waters between the green fronds of plants, the silvery shimmer cast by the noonday sun upon the still surface of the streams, the robust grace of trees. . . . Every touch of color they put upon their canvas is right, and the words into which they transpose them allow them to be seen so plainly that while reading certain pages, one would swear the painting was growing of itself upon the margin of the book.

Their style is absolutely the best fitted to attain the end they seek. Their sole object is to make the reader see the men and the things of which they speak as clearly as if these were present, and to make him understand the state of mind of the various characters whose lives they are engaged in relating. Small, however, is the number of people for whom "the visible world" exists, and most difficult is it for any one not a psychologist to lay aside his own self and to feel, if but for a brief time, as others feel. It is repugnant to the best minds to admit into themselves the mystical notions of a woman like Madame Gervaisais, the carnal impulses of a Germinie, or to apply themselves to the quivering of leaves trembling in the breeze or the changing colors of a vail of mist that reflects the rosy light of morn. The reader's attention fails, and it must be compelled not to fail, hence that style will be the best that will manage to do this, and will do it without sacrificing any part of the analysis or of the description, which are the very "raison d'être" of the pages on which they figure. The problem the Goncourts had to solve, and which it may almost be said they did solve, was to render as delicately and accurately as possible the most subtile and fleeting color effects, to analyze with the utmost clearness and minuteness of which they were capable the inward motions of the mind, and to compel the reader, who cares in nowise for all this, to become absorbingly interested in it. They were bound, therefore, to cast aside whatever did not bear directly upon the end they desired to attain. They have not Théophile Gautier's unconscious certainty of language or the fluid ease of George Sand; they are not indifferent to form as was Lamartine, who cared only to move those who listened to his melodious song, yet style, the skilful and complicated structure of periods, the harmony and sonorousness of words, the harmony and cadence of phrases, does not greatly preoccupy them. It is not with them as with Flaubert, to whom these matters were of the supremest importance.

The Goncourts have not much musical sense, and their qualities as writers are the very antithesis of oratorical qualities; it is, indeed, difficult to read their works aloud. What is important in their view, is appropriateness of expression, intensity, and finish of rendering, and the use of novel turns that shall compel attention; anything else scarcely appeals to them; they do not mind incorrections or repetitions. For them the characteristic trait of a writer is the finding of an unusual epithet, by which must not be understood a curious word or a deliberate singularity, but the expression that brings out an unperceived characteristic in an object, an almost effaced trait in a figure, and which is the one and only expression that will do this. Genuine verbs, verbs that describe, abound in their speech, and from this point of view their vocabulary is incomparably rich. To describe by means of verbs is almost to describe the "becoming" of beings; it is describing the soul of them, while the epithet merely gives the external appearance, the contour and the color of them.

They were exceedingly fond of technical terms, of words drawn from the speech of the people, of local expressions, which give a clearer and fuller impression of an environment and brings out more strongly the individuality of the one who makes use of them.

Yet they do not waste time upon curiosities of style, to which Edmond de Goncourt objected as strongly as to the platitudes of academic speech; their sole object is to communicate to others the sensations they themselves experience when they come in contact with events, persons, and things. They seek for combinations of words that shall surprise the reader and awaken his attention. The order of their words is not the logical order, but as in English, as in ancient languages, very often, as in children's speech, it is the emotional order, yet the sentence, though filled with anacoluths and inversions, remains clear, precisely because of the psychologically accurate notation of all the shades of thought and passion. Further, it is not only the feelings that exist in the characters that their style is marked with, but also the feelings that animate the authors themselves. . . . [They] are led by a sort of natural affinity to give the place of honor in their novels to those characters whose wounded and easily moved souls makes them kin. And as they feel the sufferings and disappointments of their heroes as keenly as they do their own, there is no style more bewildering, more broken, more loose, more uneven than theirs; none which communicates more suddenly the very throbbing and quaking of life.

Yet in those very parts in which passion exhibits itself most freely, in which the dialogue is the most natural and at times the most brutal, there is never a trace of vulgarity or platitude. . . . (pp. 351-53)

The marvel is that a work of art, the unity of which, in spite of its wondrous diversity, is so evident, and the style of which is so homogeneous, should have resulted from the collaboration of two writers, of two minds. . . . (p. 353)

[Edmond de Goncourt] had a clearer and more personal feeling for reality, which was most curiously united in him with a marked liking for the vague and mysterious images that suggest to the mind what they cannot evoke. He was irresistibly attracted by the impenetrable unknown that throbs in the very heart of things, and that he did not yield to it is due to his brother's influence and to that of Théophile Gautier, which was marked in his case. After his brother's death, he allowed himself to follow the bent of his own imagination, and by the side of **"Eliza the Slut,"** that strong, cruel book, so masterly in its simplicity, . . . appeared novels woven out of dreams, such as **"The Zemganno Brothers"** and **"Faustina."** His favorite poets were Edgar Allan Poe and Heinrich Heine, and his soul, like Shelley's and Renan's, was full of sorrow and tenderness. But he was passionately fond of erudition and research, passionately fond of "human documents," of observations noted on the spot and put down in their brutal reality, and it was the patient study of the dapper and witty society of the eighteenth century, so fond of pretty things and so careless of the world beyond, the study, also, of the Paris of the Second Empire, thirsting for wealth, eager for enjoyment, and resolutely realistic, that made of him the great novelist and penetrating analyst we have known. (p. 354)

It was to the constant perusal of Janin's works that Jules owed his affected, spangled style, his fad of passing abruptly from one idea to another, his lack of sequence, his boyishness of thought, his dandyism, and his airy impertinence that at times

make the reading of the first works that he wrote in collaboration with his brother rather wearisome. . . . The affected and elaborate manner, the striving after witticisms in words, the glittering style, the fondness for bravura passages and sensational tirades which mark the articles published by the Goncourts in "l'Éclair" and "Paris" . . . lead one to think that it was Jules who, at that time, did most of the writing and that he made his brother adopt his own ways. A very good reason for this is that he was better endowed as a writer; he had a greater mastery of sentences; he knew better how to light upon an ingenious tone, a difficult expression, and he had the gift of dialogue rarely acquired by those who have it not naturally. (pp. 354-55)

They belonged to the very small company of those realists,— they are called realists at times,—who, though carried away by the observation of contemporary life, never forgot that the world was not made yesterday, and that nothing of what surrounds us is capable of being understood unless one knows accurately what the men who created the society in which we live, and who have transmitted to us the particular turn of mind, the instincts and tendencies which cause us to be what we are, what these men thought, felt, and did. The peculiar merit of the Goncourts lies in the fact that they studied the antecedents of the characters in their novels, not merely as naturalists, psychologists, and physicians, but as historians, just as they had studied **"The Mistresses of Louis XV"** or the great actresses of the eighteenth century.

The environment in which they had grown up was a family one, a normal and healthy environment. It is not with the eyes of Bohemia or of the frequenters of cosmopolite drawing rooms that they look upon the society of their day. . . . They lived in constant intercourse, in close intimacy with honest women who were relatives of theirs. . . . And it is this intercourse with their aunts, their cousins, and the friends of these ladies, along with their own remembrances, that explains how it is that, in spite of its audacity, their work has remained chaste. Nowhere in it is the lust of the flesh visible; they have depicted reality freely, but even in their boldest books, such as **"Germinie Lacerteux"** and **"Eliza the Slut,"** not a single erotic sentence is to be found. (pp. 356-57)

L. Marillier, "The Goncourts," translated by F. C. de Sumichrast, in The International Quarterly, *Vol. VII, No. II, June-September, 1903, pp. 334-58.*

JAMES HUNEKER (essay date 1905)

What *Henrietta Maréchal* accomplished despite its failure, was in the dialogue—modern, picturesque, and of the best style for the stage, because it set forth the particular turn of mind of each talker; and it was also the first attack on that stronghold of French dramatic tradition the monotonous semi-chanting of the conservatoire-taught actor. Here was an elastic, natural dialogue, charged with turns of phrases taken up from the sidewalk, neologisms, slang—in a word, lifelike talk as opposed to the old stilted verbiage. (pp. 312-13)

[Edmond] De Goncourt, who naturally ranks the drama below the novel as literature, upholds the conventions of the former. The drama is by its nature romantic and limited in scope. The monologues, asides, dénouements, sympathetic characters, and the rest must always endure. He does think, however, that reality may be brought nearer, and that literary language should give place to a style which will reveal the irregularity and abruptness of vital conversation. In this latter particular he has been a benefactor. Unnatural theatrical dialogue he slew with his supple, free, naturally coloured speech in *Henrietta Maréchal.* Stage talk should be, De Goncourt asserted, flowing and idiomatic—never bookish. (p. 315)

James Huneker, ''Princess Mathilde's Play,'' in his Iconoclasts, a Book of Dramatists: Ibsen, Strindberg, Becque, Hauptmann, Sudermann, Hervieu, Gorky, Duse and D'Annunzio, Maeterlinck and Bernard Shaw, *Charles Scribner's Sons, 1905, pp. 304-19.*

OLIN H. MOORE (essay date 1916)

[*Moore's study is an ''empirical investigation'' in which he attempts to determine the extent to which the Goncourts used the* Journal *in the composition of their novels. Moore finds that while the Goncourts' characters are ''founded upon a documentary basis,'' they are frequently composites, consisting of the ''exact'' attributes of several different persons whose behavior the Goncourts had recorded in the* Journal. *According to Moore, this technique renders the characters ''contrary to 'nature,' to 'history,' and to the medical science of which the Goncourts professed themselves disciples.''*]

[The] literary productions of the Goncourts give every evidence of a perfect accord with their theory that the novel should be a sort of up-to-date history, founded upon a documentary basis, and hence absolutely true to life.... [The] authors subject their fundamental principle to a very severe strain [by their habit of creating composite characters].... (p. 51)

[For example,] our authors added to Renée Mauperin a number of features not belonging to the original. Such is their usual plan of procedure, and in order to appreciate fully the significance of this fact, a moment's reflection is necessary. The proposition that one man partakes of the characteristics of many others is not to be gainsaid: it is an easy inference from the kinship of the human race. Yet the impossibility of *perfect* duplication anywhere in nature has been recognized from time immemorial.... Nevertheless, the Goncourts, with their photographic method, often attempt to attribute to ''A'' as it were the *exact* finger-print of ''X,'' the *exact* head of ''Y,'' and the *exact* temperament of ''Z.'' Their method would be less vulnerable if ''A's'' finger bore only an ordinary resemblance to that of ''X.'' The difficulty is that the Goncourts, by renouncing the principle of selection in art, are prone to insist upon an *absolute resemblance*—their notes frequently being thrust into their novels without alteration. Thus their characters, though possessing features, living in surroundings, and speaking a language precisely such as have been observed in real life, and jotted down with infinite pains upon the author's pads, are far from being truly realistic. They are contrary to ''nature,'' to ''history,'' and to the medical science of which the Goncourts professed themselves disciples. Many a romantic character of the early nineteenth century novel, though improbable, was at least possible, while the characters of the Goncourts would seem, if our reasoning is just, to be in many cases impossible. (pp. 58-9)

The Goncourts themselves have condemned in no uncertain terms not only a plot, but also every work of the imagination, with its too rigorous logic. Yet where they have attempted a plot, the Goncourts have generally proceeded with a mechanical method totally at variance with their own doctrine. Their desire seems to be to heap as many misfortunes upon their heroes and heroines as possible, the result, if not actually the cause, of their method of combining in one person the lives of several. Indeed, it is quite inconceivable that anybody in

real life could undergo quite the total number of tortures that they many times inflict upon the individuals in their stories. Often when they have brought a character to the point of exhaustion, he is allowed to escape miraculously for a time, only that his agony may be prolonged, and the horror of the inevitable tragedy increased. One is frequently reminded, for all the world, of that favorite deity of the classical drama, the *deus ex machinâ.* (p. 60)

[While] the art theories of the authors call for anachronisms and disarray here and there ..., they fall, whenever they are obliged to invent a plot, unconsciously into that very rigor of logic which they condemn. Such is particularly the case where they would narrate a series of misfortunes. We may be certain in advance that nothing which makes life worth living will be allowed to remain. (p. 62)

[The] theories of the Goncourts, if carried out completely, ought to mean no novel at all, but a biography pure and simple. ... The one production of the Goncourts which does not transgress their principle is the *Journal,* a more or less disconnected series of notes, trivial at times, but often interesting. The trouble is that the Goncourts have not been satisfied with the domain of the biographical sketch, and have attempted to construct works of fiction which should contain no element of the unreal. Struggling thus to continue two contradictory *genres,* they have felt obliged to weld together characters that were distinct in actual life, while those which remain comparatively intact are depicted in an environment not their own. The cumulative effect of their combinations of characters upon the exaggerations in their plots is a matter of importance that has been neglected by the critics. The total result of the defects in literary method ... and of the exclusive attention which the Goncourts gave to the abnormalities of human nature is a type of fiction which is far removed from the truly natural. (p. 64)

Olin H. Moore, ''The Literary Methods of the Goncourts,'' in PMLA, 24, n.s. Vol. XXIV, No. 1, March, 1916, pp. 43-64.

ARTHUR SYMONS (essay date 1916)

[*An English critic, poet, dramatist, short story writer, and editor, Symons initially gained notoriety as an English decadent of the 1890s and eventually established himself as one of the most important critics of the modern era. Symons's essay, which was first published in 1916 as ''The Goncourts'' in his* Figures of Several Centuries, *was drawn from his* The Symbolist Movement in Literature, *a work that provided his English contemporaries with an appropriate vocabulary with which to define their new aesthetic—one that communicated their concern with dreamlike states, imagination, and a reality that exists beyond the boundaries of the senses. Symons maintains that the Goncourts were ''psychologists'' who were interested primarily in the ''inner history'' of their characters. In agreement with James Fitzmaurice-Kelly (1902), Ernest Boyd (1922), and D. L. Murray (1926), Symons stresses that the Goncourts viewed reality as artists. He compares their manner of presentation to the ''method of the painter who accumulates detail on detail ... and then omits everything which is not an essential part of the* ensemble *which he sees.'' Symons adds that the* écriture artiste *is the ''most wonderful'' of all the Goncourts' inventions.*]

[Edmond de Goncourt once said to me], ''The thing is, to find a lorgnette'' (and he put up his hands to his eyes, adjusting them carefully) ''through which to see things. My brother and

I invented a lorgnette, and the young men have taken it from us.''

How true that is, and how significantly it states just what is most essential in the work of the Goncourts! It is a new way of seeing, literally a new way of seeing, which they have invented; and it is in the invention of this that they have invented [a] ''new language.'' . . . (p. 144)

It is difficult, in speaking of Edmond de Goncourt, to avoid attributing to him the whole credit of the work which has so long borne his name alone. That is an error which he himself would never have pardoned. *Mon frère et moi* [My brother and I] was the phrase constantly on his lips, and in his journal [see excerpt above, 1895], his prefaces, he has done full justice to the vivid and admirable qualities of that talent which, all the same, would seem to have been the lesser, the more subservient, of the two. Jules, I think, had a more active sense of life, a more generally human curiosity; for the novels of Edmond, written since his brother's death, have, in even that excessively specialised world of their common observation, a yet more specialised choice and direction. But Edmond, there is no doubt, was in the strictest sense the writer; and it is above all for the qualities of its writing that the work of the Goncourts will live. It has been largely concerned with truth—truth to the minute details of human character, sensation, and circumstance, and also of the document, the exact words, of the past; but this devotion to fact, to the curiosities of fact, has been united with an even more persistent devotion to the curiosities of expression. They have invented a new language: that was the old reproach against them; let it be their distinction. Like all writers of an elaborate carefulness, they have been accused of sacrificing both truth and beauty to deliberate eccentricity. Deliberate their style certainly was; eccentric it may, perhaps, sometimes have been; but deliberately eccentric, no. It was their belief that a writer should have a personal style, a style as peculiar to himself as his handwriting. . . . (pp. 145-46)

It may be asserted that the Goncourts are not merely men of genius, but are perhaps the typical men of letters of the close of our century. They have all the curiosities and the acquirements, the new weaknesses and the new powers, that belong to our age; and they sum up in themselves certain theories, aspirations, ways of looking at things, notions of literary duty and artistic conscience, which have only lately become at all actual, and some of which owe to them their very origin. . . . [Their] excursions in so many directions, with their audacities and their careful limitations, their bold novelty and their scrupulous exactitude in detail, are characteristic of what is the finest in the modern conception of culture and the modern ideal in art. . . . To be the bookworm and the magician; to give the actual documents, but not to set barren fact by barren fact; to find a soul and a voice in documents, to make them more living and more charming than the charm of life itself: that is what the Goncourts have done [in their studies of the eighteenth century]. And it is through this conception of history that they have found their way to that new conception of the novel which has revolutionised the entire art of fiction. (pp. 146-47)

The old notion of the novel was that it should be an entertaining record of incidents or adventures told for their own sake; a plain, straightforward narrative of facts, the aim being to produce as nearly as possible an effect of continuity, of nothing having been omitted. . . . That is not how the Goncourts apprehend life, or how they conceive it should be rendered. As in the study of history they seek mainly the *inédit* caring only to record that, so it is the *inédit* of life that they conceive to

be the main concern, the real ''inner history.'' And for them the *inédit* of life consists in the noting of the sensations; it is of the sensations that they have resolved to be the historians; not of action, nor of emotion, properly speaking, nor of moral conceptions, but of an inner life which is all made up of the perceptions of the senses. It is scarcely too paradoxical to say that they are psychologists for whom the soul does not exist. One thing, they know, exists: the sensation flashed through the brain, they image on the mental retina. Having found that, they bodily omit all the rest as of no importance, trusting to their instinct of selection, of retaining all that really matters. It is the painter's method, a selection made almost visually; the method of the painter who accumulates detail on detail, in his patient, many-sided observation of his subject, and then omits everything which is not an essential part of the *ensemble* which he sees. Thus the new conception of what the real truth of things consists in has brought with it, inevitably, an entirely new form, a breaking up of the plain, straightforward narrative into chapters, which are generally quite disconnected, and sometimes of less than a page in length. . . . No doubt the Goncourts, in their passion for the *inédit,* leave out certain things because they are obvious, even if they are obviously true and obviously important; that is the defect of their quality. To represent life by a series of moments, and to choose these moments for a certain subtlety and rarity in them, is to challenge grave perils. Nor are these the only perils which the Goncourts have constantly before them. There are others, essential to their natures, to their preferences. And, first of all, as we may see on every page of that miraculous ***Journal,*** which will remain, doubtless, the truest, deepest, most poignant piece of human history that they have ever written, they are sick men, seeing life through the medium of diseased nerves. . . . This unhealthy sensitiveness explains much, the singular merits as well as certain shortcomings or deviations, in their work. The Goncourts' vision of reality might almost be called an exaggerated sense of the truth of things; such a sense as diseased nerves inflict upon one, sharpening the acuteness of every sensation; or somewhat such a sense as one derives from haschisch, which simply intensifies, yet in a veiled and fragrant way, the charm or the disagreeableness of outward things, the notion of time, the notion of space. What the Goncourts paint is the subtler poetry of reality, its unusual aspects, and they evoke it, fleetingly, like Whistler; they do not render it in hard outline, like Flaubert, like Manet. . . . [Theirs] is a world which is extraordinarily real; but there is choice, there is curiosity, in the aspect of reality which it presents.

Compare the descriptions, which form so large a part of the work of the Goncourts, with those of Théophile Gautier, who may reasonably be said to have introduced the practice of eloquent writing about places, and also the exact description of them. Gautier describes miraculously, but it is, after all, the ordinary observation carried to perfection, or, rather, the ordinary pictorial observation. The Goncourts only tell you the things that Gautier leaves out; they find new, fantastic points of view, discover secrets in things, curiosities of beauty, often acute, distressing, in the aspects of quite ordinary places. They see things as an artist, an ultra-subtle artist of the impressionist kind, might see them; seeing them indeed always very consciously with a deliberate attempt upon them, in just that partial, selecting, creative way in which an artist looks at things for the purpose of painting a picture. In order to arrive at their effects, they shrink from no sacrifice, from no excess; slang, neologism, forced construction, archaism, barbarous epithet, nothing comes amiss to them, so long as it tends to render a sensation. Their unique care is that the phrase should live, should palpitate, should be alert, exactly expressive, super-subtle in expression; and they prefer indeed a certain perversity in their relations with language, which they would not have merely a passionate and sensuous thing, but complex with all the curiosities of a delicately depraved instinct. . . . [This is the Goncourts'] distinction; it is the most wonderful of all their inventions: in order to render new sensations, a new vision of things, they have invented a new language. (pp. 148-51)

*Arthur Symons, "Edmond and Jules de Goncourt"
in his* The Symbolist Movement in Literature, *E. P.
Dutton and Co., Inc., 1919, pp. 143-51.*

GEORGE SAINTSBURY   (essay date 1917)

[*Saintsbury was an English literary historian and critic of the late nineteenth and early twentieth centuries. A prolific writer, Saintsbury composed a number of histories of English and European literature as well as several critical works on individual authors, styles, and periods. In this derogatory essay, Saintsbury cites the Goncourts' novels as evidence of the inherent weaknesses of Naturalism. He argues that the "doctrine of rigid 'observation,' 'document,' 'experience,' and the like is bad in art," and maintains that a writer must have an aesthetic purpose. In opposition to James Fitzmaurice-Kelly (1902), Arthur Symons (1916), Ernest Boyd (1922), and D. L. Murray (1926), Saintsbury contends that the Goncourts were reporters, rather than artists, who "deliberately and habitually" depicted "repulsive" subjects devoid of any aesthetic attraction. Saintsbury finds that the Goncourts' literary style is further evidence of the flaws of Naturalism, commenting that the* écriture artiste "*appears to prove . . . that an unsound principle is not a certain means to secure sound practice.*"]

[The **Journal des Goncourt** is] saturated, larded, or whatever word of the kind be preferred, with observations on the taste, intellect, and general greatness of the MM. de Goncourt, and on the lamentable inferiority of other people, etc., etc. If it could be purged of its bad blood, the book would really deserve to rank, for substance, with Pepys' diary or with Walpole's letters. As it is, when it has become a little forgotten, the quarterly reviewers, or their representatives, of the twenty-first century will be able to make endless *réchauffés* of it. (pp. 461-62)

To analyse all [the Goncourts'] novels, or even one of them, at length, would be a process as unnecessary as it would be disagreeable. The "chronicles of wasted *grime*" may be left to themselves, not out of any mere finical or fastidious superiority, but simply because their own postulates and axioms make such analysis (if the word unfairness can be used in such a connection) unfair to them. For they claimed—and the justice, if not the value, of the claim must be allowed—to have rested their fashion of novel-writing upon two bases. The substance was to be provided by an elaborate observation and reproduction of the facts of actual life, not in the least transcendentalised, inspirited, or in any other way brought near Romance, but considered largely from the points of view which their friend Taine, writing earlier, used for his philosophical and historical work—that of the *milieu* or "environment," that of heredity, though they did not lay so much stress on this as Zola did—and the like. The treatment, on the other hand, was to be effected by the use of an intensely "personal" style. . . . (p. 462)

[Germinie Lacerteux] is as different as possible, not merely from the usual heroine, but from the *grisette* of the first half of the century and from the *demi-mondaine* of Dumas *fils,* and Daudet, and even Zola. She is not pretty; she is not fascinating in any way; she is neither good- nor ill-natured in any special fashion; she is not even ambitious of "bettering" herself or of having much pleasure, wealth, etc. If she goes to the bad it is in the most commonplace way and with the most unseductive seducer possible. Her progress and her end are, to borrow a later phrase and title metaphorically, merely a tale of the meanest streets; untouched and unconfirmed by the very slightest art; as destitute of any aesthetic attraction, or any evidence of artistic power, as the log-books of a common lodginghouse and a hospital ward could be. In *Chérie* there is nothing exactly improper; it is merely an elaborate study of a spoilt—at least petted—and unhealthy girl in the upper stages of society, who has at last the kindness—to herself, her relations, and the reader—to die. If [Edmond] de Goncourt had had the slightest particle of humour, of which there is no trace in any of his works, one might have taken this, like other things perhaps, as a slightly cryptic parody—of the *poitrinaire*-heroine [consumptive-heroine] mania of times a little earlier; but there is no hope of this. The subject was, in the sense attached to the word by these writers, "real"; it could be made useful for combined physiological and psychological detail; and, most important of all, it was more or less repulsive.

For this is what it really comes to in the Goncourts, in Zola, and in the rest, till Guy de Maupassant, not seldom dealing with the same material, sublimes it, and so robs it of its repulsiveness, by the force of true comic, tragic, or romantic art. Of course it is open to any one to say, "It may repel *you,* but it does not repel *me.*" But this is very cheap sophistry. . . . I have never given up the doctrine that *any* subject *may* be deprived of its repulsiveness by the treatment of it. But when you find a writer, or a set of writers, deliberately and habitually selecting subjects which are generally held to be repellent, and deliberately and habitually refusing or failing to pass them through the alembic in the manner suggested—then I think you are justified, not merely in condemning their taste, but in thinking not at all highly of their art. (pp. 463-64)

Dismissing, however, for a moment the question of mere taste, it should be evident that the doctrine of rigid "observation," "document," "experience," and the like is bad in art. Like so many . . . bad things, it is, of course, a corruption, by excess and defect both, of something good or at least true. It cannot be necessary . . . to admit or urge the importance of observation of actual life to the novelist. . . . [But] you must not confine your observation to Ugliness and exclude Beauty. . . . You are not a reporter; not a compiler of *dossiers;* not a photographer. You are an artist, and you must do something with your materials, add something of yourself to them, present something not vamped from parts of actual life itself, but reinforcing those parts with aesthetic re-creation and with the sense of "the whole." . . . I never find [this] in the Goncourts: and when I find it in the others it is because they have either never bowed the knee to, or have for the nonce discarded, the cult of the Naturalist, experimental, documentary idol, in itself and for itself.

"But," some one may say, "you have neglected one very important point to which you have yourself referred, and as to which you have just recommitted yourself. Did not [the Goncourts] 'add something,' a very considerable something, 'of their own'? How about their style?"

Certainly they prided themselves on this, and certainly they took a great deal of trouble about it. If any one likes the result, let him like it. It appears to me only to prove that an unsound principle is not a certain means to secure sound practice. Possibly, as Edmond boasted, this style is not the style *de tout le monde* [of all the world]. And *tout le monde* may congratulate itself on the fact. (pp. 465-66)

> George Saintsbury, "Naturalism—The Goncourts, Zola, and Maupassant," in his A History of the French Novel (to the Close of the 19th Century): From 1800 to 1900, Vol. II, *1917. Reprint by Russell & Russell, Inc., 1964, pp. 459-517 .*

ERNEST BOYD   (essay date 1922)

[*In contrast to George Saintsbury (1917), Boyd asserts that the Goncourts viewed reality "through [an] artistic vision, not through the eyes of a mere reporter." Like Henri Frantz (1896), Boyd distinguishes between the realism of the Goncourts and that of Émile Zola, stressing that the Goncourts' works do not exhibit "the endless piling up of detail" that characterizes Zola's novels.*]

When Zola's *L'Assommoir* was published the indebtedness of the new school to **Germinie Lacerteux** was apparent. . . . Zola, however, represented the Left, or radical, wing of realism, while Edmond and Jules de Goncourt stood for the Right, or aristocratic, section. As Naturalism developed it became increasingly an appeal to mass suggestion, and relied more and more upon mass effects, the endless piling up of detail, the ceaseless extension of the field of observation and documentation. With this phase of the movement the Goncourts had nothing in common.

They were essentially and primarily artists, and if they claimed for the novelist the right to transcribe reality, it was reality as seen through artistic vision, not through the eyes of a mere reporter. Life as the Goncourts saw it was far from the immense and crude reality of Zola. While they sought to reach the heart of things through a meticulous realisation of externals, Zola professed to be a scientist, a social anatomist, whose novels would have the precision and practical value of scientific studies. It did not take long to demonstrate that this conception of realism led through monotony and repetition to the inevitable assumption of a democratic mission. Zola ended as reformer and a Messiah with a panacea and a message for humanity. Oblivion was imminent. Edmond de Goncourt resolutely held aloof in those last novels, **La Faustin, Les Frères Zemganno** and **Chérie,** from the current practice of his disciples. And so his work and that of his brother—for to the end they remained indistinguishable—still survive with that of Flaubert, because they created works of art in which reality endures through the spirit of life breathed into them by imagination that embraces and transcends the exterior world. (pp. xv-xvi)

> Ernest Boyd, in an introduction to Germinie Lacerteux by Edmond de Goncourt and Jules de Goncourt, translated by Ernest Boyd, Knopf, 1922, pp. vii-xvi.

D. L. MURRAY   (essay date 1926)

[*Murray's essay was originally published as "The Art of the Goncourts" in The Times Literary Supplement, No. 998, March 3, 1921. Murray is one of several twentieth-century critics, including Olin H. Moore (1916), Frank Harris (1927), and Lewis Galantière (1937), who assert that the Goncourts failed to represent reality factually in their novels. According to Murray, the Goncourts had "no wish to photograph or record reality; they set themselves at once to turn it into a work of art." Murray argues that the Goncourts' descriptive passages frequently suggest paintings of objects rather than the objects themselves. In*]

addition, he maintains that the fragmented construction and excessive detail of the Goncourts' novels result in an "ultimate artificiality."]

The *bibelot* is the key to the aesthetic of the Goncourts; it fills their house and their heads and their books. They are more than curio-hunters and lovers of *bric-à-brac;* they can only be termed the slaves of the *bibelot.* . . . Rather than abstract ideas or ideals, it is concrete social usages that the trinkets of the *bibeloteur* recall to mind. . . . From a fan you may deduce, if you have the power, the whole series of **Les Actrices du XVIIIᵉ siècle,** from an aquarelle the upbringing of the little *bourgeoise* Renée Mauperin, and from the odour encrusted at the base of a thurible the Roman basilicas of **Madame Gervaisais.** This is a form of evocation that proceeds by sense— by visual or tactile suggestion—to the images of memory, without calling on the creative or logical faculties. . . . (p. 227)

Let us keep . . . [the] suggestible temperament of the *bibeloteur* as our clue to the genius of the Goncourts. We find, as it would lead us to expect, a predominance of the receptive mood in their work. . . . Not only the Goncourts themselves, but the creatures of their imagination lay themselves open . . . passively to the influences that environ them. . . . In the Goncourts themselves this waiting on the external stimulus was a symptom of inventive sterility. Their fiction was an elaboration of souvenirs, notes and readings. The **Journal** was but one main source among those that fed their novels; the minor tributaries will never perhaps be exhaustively mapped. Assuredly the Goncourts touched nothing that they did not magically transform, but they needed their block to work upon. Perhaps the poverty of their philosophical and religious ideas is accounted for by the fact that general ideas . . . are only to be acquired by speculative effort, and cannot be gained by a process of infiltration.

In dwelling . . . on the Goncourts' sensibility we must emphasize the extreme refinement and acuity of their perceptions. . . . To realize [the] daily martyrdom of their senses is to excuse much that seems at the first blush insolent in the judgments and preferences of the Goncourts. The truth is that their strained sensibility no longer responded to the objects of normal aesthetic perception. . . . They required to be touched on some chord not dulled by use. . . . [In] history they valued above all things *l'inédit,* the thrill of the undiscovered document. They suffer, too, from an inversion of *la folie des grandeurs* [megalomania]; they evade whenever possible the great events of history or contemporary affairs, the grand passions of love, the expressions in art of majesty and vigour. All this is to them as the glare of the sun in sore eyes, and they shrink in the same way in the fabrication of their books from large effects and designs of ample scope. They paint corners and glimpses of movement, where they can, in preference to broad scenes or crowd-pieces. Each book is a succession of tiny, disconnected chapters; each chapter is formed by the laying of one small stroke upon another, till the general effect is not that of life and movement, but that of a table piled with small objects of *virtu.*

We begin, perhaps, to discern at this point what the Goncourts meant by 'la recherche du vrai' ['the pursuit of truth'], and how far they may rightly be called Realists or fathers of Naturalism. They sought *le vrai* [the truth] in the sense that only by contact with the stuff of reality could they set their faculties in action; but this contact was never more than their point of departure. . . . [They] have as a rule no wish to photograph or record reality; they set themselves at once to turn it into a work of art. It is the marked peculiarity of their descriptive passages that they usually suggest a painting of the object rather than the object itself—a point in which they differ from Zola, Huysmans, and many later writers who show signs of their influence. (pp. 228-32)

The Goncourts have no deep impulse to realism, and with them 'la recherche du vrai' is, after all, but a variant of their pleasure in . . . a piece of Japanese lacquer. It is a means of acquiring sensations. How unscrupulously, when they choose, they heighten reality to serve their purposes! . . . Nature itself stiffens gradually under the eye of the Goncourts into a brocaded screen or an inlay of lapis lazuli. (pp. 237-38)

Perhaps the Goncourts could only have avoided this ultimate artificiality by possessing a larger measure than was theirs of human sympathy. . . . It is only from acute outside observation that they recount the sufferings of the servant girl Germinie Lacerteux and the prostitute Elisa: they are untouched themselves by the feelings of their characters. Indeed, these books, in which they make a resolute effort to quench their dilettantism and restrain their love of decoration, exhale through long passages a grey *ennui*. It is as though we were listening to the carefully formed sentences of an unusually intelligent police officer at an inquest. Had the Goncourts worked more from the interior of their personages and not so much from collected gossip and curiosity, they would have had less recourse to those romantic *coups de théâtre* [dramatic surprises]—Madame Gervaisais struck dead on the threshold of her audience with the Pope, the gruesome suicide of the young doctor in *Soeur Philomène*, the circus-rider's revenge in *Les Frères Zemganno*—which Edmond realized in the end to be mere machinery. But they had to work within their limitations. (pp. 238-39)

> *D. L. Murray, ''The Goncourt Brothers,'' in his* Scenes & Silhouettes, *Jonathan Cape, 1926, pp. 225-40.*

FRANK HARRIS   (essay date 1927)

[Striving] after realistic effects and photographic exactitude, like Daudet, Huysmans and Zola, was not the pitfall which trapped the realism of the Goncourts. Their method was even more faulty. In attempting to depict La Faustin, for example, they soon saw that it was useless to depict an ordinary bad woman: the result would be a mere photograph, and they were too artistic to be satisfied with such a poor result. They sought a type, therefore, and then attempted to depict her soul, and in order to do this they had to invent a special language extraordinarily sensitive and extraordinarily subtle and precise.

But to give the impression of reality, the style too must be commonplace, and here were the Goncourts manufacturing a new style to render ordinary life; the antinomy was too glaring. (pp. 231-32)

Accordingly the Goncourts are not memorable to us for any picture of real life which they have left us, for all their pictures of real persons are absurdly unreal, comically unlike any persons that we have ever known, or indeed any that we have ever seen. They show us an ordinary girl's face under a microscope, so to speak, which reveals the pores to us as abysses and transforms a pimple into a Vesuvius; by dint of painstaking exactitude they lose all likeness to reality. (pp. 232-33)

These men are too peculiar, too aristocratic by dint of refinement, to work as realists; they tried, indeed, to observe and

record what they saw, but, to use the great phrase of Turgeniev, they were never able to cut ''the umbilical cord which unites the artist to his work.'' Their best novels are pictures of their own artist nature and the artistic weakness of will. Charles Demailly is their portrait in the guise of an unfortunate man of letters; Coriolis, the painter, in **''Manette Salomon,''** is blood-brother to Demailly; they can only paint themselves with any success and their own weaknesses.

And the whole painting is that of a critic and not that of a creator; they tell you the qualities the man possessed, but they don't group together his powers and shortcomings round an *ego* of purpose and desire; they put too much of themselves into their creations, and so their men never live, much less cast a shadow. As workmen they are rather like Bernard Shaw, who poses frankly for Caesar, never realising that a man of such delicate humanitarianism and conscientious self-questioning would be incapable of Caesar's instantaneous decisions and inflexible resolution.

In fine, the de Goncourts were not creative artists, but critics and collectors, and the great public took no interest in their work, though from the very beginning they were hailed as equals by the Masters. This want of popular success, combined with a consciousness of extraordinary ability, makes the life and fate of the de Goncourts symbolic and significant. No great master is ever likely to be as successful in the day and hour as Zola or Daudet or de Maupassant. The de Goncourts realised perfectly that it was the small men who were popular in their lifetime, while the Rembrandts are scorned. . . . (pp. 234-36)

Were they really justified in thinking themselves more important than their famous contemporaries? Or was the popular verdict indeed a true verdict? In such a case one can only speak for oneself; to me the de Goncourts are infinitely more interesting than Daudet or Zola, or even Flaubert. I could not re-read a book of Daudet or Zola. . . . [But] again and again I dip into the **''Journal''** of the de Goncourts and read fifty pages of their great book on the French painters of the eighteenth century, while **''La Maison d'un Artiste''** is never far from my hand. They suffered and laboured, did good work, and got no thanks; the despised and rejected of men were the most important spiritual influence in France for the last half of the nineteenth century. (p. 237)

> *Frank Harris, ''The Brothers de Goncourt and Realism,'' in his* Latest Contemporary Portraits, *The Macaulay Company, 1927, pp. 231-38.*

ALBERT THIBAUDET   (essay date 1936)

[*A French critic of the early twentieth century, Thibaudet wrote extensively on nineteenth-century French writers. In the following excerpt, which first appeared in 1936 in Thibaudet's* Histoire de la littérature française de 1789 à nos jours, *Thibaudet ranks the Goncourts ''high in the history of style'' but considers the* écriture artiste *an inappropriate literary style for the novel. Nevertheless, he regards* Manette Salomon *and* The Zemganno Brothers *as two books that have been unjustly forgotten.*]

[The Goncourts were knickknack collectors of documents and] knickknack collectors of style. They did not create the documentarily written novel, since there was Champfleury, but they did create the artistically written novel—in other words, the celebrated artistic writing. They recounted, with some exaggeration, the tortures that they had suffered in establishing their style, and no one can challenge the incomparable task of creation that this studied style represents. Through their novels and the notes in their *Journal* in preparation for the novels, the Goncourts rank high in the history of style. Of good style? That is something else.

In any case, not of good novelistic style. This brush style, made of strokes that dazzle and that play their part without entering further into the line of a sentence than the chapters pretend to enter into a line of composition and a well-made book, made remarkable phenomena of their novels at the end of a half century. For today's public, as much as there is a style to be learned, there is a language to be learned, Goncourtese—and life is short. If it were essential to name two books that deserved to be rescued from oblivion, one would be *Manette Salomon,* the only respectable novel that has been written about the painter's life, which is still full of vigor, and the other would be *Les Frères Zemganno,* a novel that Edmond de Goncourt wrote alone, in memory of the collaboration, and that removes brotherly love and joint effort to the world of acrobats: it is new, ingenious, and, in its closing pages, filled with powerful feeling. (pp. 325-26)

> *Albert Thibaudet, "Realism," in his* French Literature from 1795 to Our Era, *translated by Charles Lam Markmann, Funk & Wagnalls, 1968, pp. 321-27.*

LEWIS GALANTIÈRE (essay date 1937)

[*Galantière argues that although the Goncourts were prolific, they were not fond of literary composition. Rather, he asserts, "what they loved was collecting objects and documents and recording their own feelings and observations." This, according to Galantière, accounts for the success of the* Journal. *Galantière prefers the Goncourts' studies of the eighteenth century to their novels, which he considers "dismal, airless," and "something of a trial." Like Olin H. Moore (1916), he finds that their clinically scrutinized fictional characters bear no resemblance to reality.*]

The Goncourts were by no means little men. They possessed a considerable culture. Their sensibility was infinitely exquisite and responsive. They were excited by the shapes and colours of the external world, and this excitation was, with the years, disciplined by an intensive and deliberate training in exact observation. Since they were at the same time remarkably intuitive, it was natural that they should not merely paint a man or draw a house front, but be impelled to divine a character and imagine a household.

Two influences pulled them in contrary directions. Their aristocratic and feminine refinement drew them to the admiration of prettiness rather than beauty, and *le joli* [the pretty] became one of their animating passions. Of that eighteenth century about which they wrote so much, they hated its intellectual ferment and loved only what in it was material—its fans, its porcelains, its paintings. Meanwhile, rising up from a long immersion in Balzac, they saw in the streets and the people of Paris a rich vein open to exploitation by someone who would deal realistically with *le vrai* [the truth] (as it was called), sparing none of its hideousness, describing item by item every rag, missing tooth, mephitic smell, squalid shame. (pp. viii-ix)

If we except such hors d'oeuvres as their few plays and occasional journalism, the thirty volumes, more or less, which the Goncourts produced up to the death of Jules . . . fall into two categories. On the one side we may place books about the things they loved—personages and society in the century pre-

ceding their own, and its painters and engravers. On the other side stand the novels they wrote about a world they loathed, a world that sickened them—the world of the impoverished, the defeated, the hysterical.

Their books on painting continue to enjoy some reputation, which will doubtless be greater when their subjects come again into fashion. I confess to a weakness for their writings on the eighteenth century. . . . [Though] the books are not history, but are rather a series of picture albums, they give off, nevertheless, a certain atmosphere. One can feel the moral texture of the century in the three volumes on the mistresses of Louis XV, in the anecdotes, witticisms and gestures collected in *La Femme au XVIIIᵉ siècle,* and in the bits which they strung together to make their books on society in the Revolution and under the Directory.

But the novels are another matter. Dismal, airless, written only for the sake of the "scientific, clinical observation" with which the authors fancied they were scrutinizing human beings who were to them so many monstrosities; shapeless, lopsided, filled with whole chunks of décor minutely described and scenes recounted in detail, all of no significance to the march of their story or the personality of their characters; written partly in a gibberish of which the poor dears were actually proud, perhaps because it cost them more effort than to write French; concentrated with nerve-racked anguish upon *the thing seen*—their novels are something of a trial. They elected these subjects, not because of a concern for social reform, not because they had themselves known these horrors and were bitterly moved to expose them, but because, first, these lovers of *le joli* were also men of a morbid inquisitiveness who were fascinated by the repellent; and second, it had not been done before and they felt themselves born to innovate.

And they were innovators. They were the progenitors of a whole brood of writers, among them Zola, Alphonse Daudet, the proletarian novelist Jules Vallès, the whole of the Académie Goncourt, who claimed them for ancestors. Charity nuns, domestic servants, prostitutes, artists' models, had indeed appeared in literature before; but they had never been the cause of literature, had never been the heroines of fiction, until the Goncourts wrote *Soeur Philomène, Germinie Lacerteux, Manette Salomon.* This was of itself enough to establish a school; and, bearing in mind the generosity and rebelliousness of youth, when we remember the novelty of the Goncourts' language, . . . it is easy to understand that younger writers followed them with enthusiasm. (pp. ix-x)

The judgment has more than once been pronounced that the *Journal des Goncourt* was their best book. Reasons for this judgment are not far to seek. Despite the loyalty, the scrupulous severity, with which they practised their profession, despite the fifty titles which, between them, they published in forty-five years of writing, it is not too extravagant to say that their passion was not literary composition. Except under the readily comprehensible impulsion of vanity, they could have been happy, probably, without publishing a single book. What they loved was collecting objects and documents and recording their own feelings and observations. I say "their own", and I mean not the observations and feelings of creatures of their imagination. There is a difference. The filling of their diaries, not the writing of their books, consoled them for their inability to accept life in a world they detested; and their collection of bric-a-brac, paintings and precious books, which became celebrated, was the other solace of their existence. In the circumstances, that they did plan, write and finish novel after novel of the kind they produced must seem to anyone who has known the torment of literary composition . . . a kind of moral heroism, a triumph of will. In this struggle lies the direct explanation of their many bouts of lassitude and enervation. (p. xi)

Freed from the tormenting thought of construction, of placing a scene, a person or a document deftly and tellingly within the framework of a larger composition, the Goncourts could indulge in the diaries their special taste for the instantaneous and exercise their particular genius for the anecdote or the portrait in miniature. . . . The presence of [prominent literary figures in the *Journal*], incidentally, has been too much stressed. It is worth remarking that quite apart from recording painstakingly their not invariably precious words, the Goncourts painted a whole world in their diaries. Town and country, café and theatre, drawing room and street scene, out front and backstage, . . . academician and bohemian—it is society under the Second Empire that is in this book, not merely a literary circle. (p. xii)

> *Lewis Galantière, in an introduction to* The Goncourt Journals: 1851-1870 *by Edmond de Goncourt and Jules de Goncourt, edited and translated by Lewis Galantière, 1937. Reprint by Doubleday, 1958, pp. vii-xii .*

ERICH AUERBACH   (essay date 1942-45)

[*Auerbach was a German critic and philologist of the first half of the twentieth century who published several studies on Italian, French, and Medieval Latin literature, as well as on methods of historical criticism. The following is drawn from Auerbach's most critically acclaimed work,* Mimesis: The Representation of Reality in Western Literature, *which was first published in 1942-45 as* Mimesis: Dargstellte Wirklichkeit in der abendländischen Literatur. *Auerbach's essay focuses on the preface to* Germinie Lacerteux. *He posits that the lower classes appealed to the Goncourts as a literary subject not because they were interested in social reform, but rather because they were aesthetically attracted to the "ugly and pathological." According to Auerbach, the Goncourts' "purely literary" instincts limited their powers of judgment and made their works seem "petty" in comparison with the works of Stendhal and Honoré de Balzac.*]

We live, say the Goncourts [in their preface to *Germinie Lacerteux*], in an age of universal suffrage, democracy, and liberalism. . . . Hence it is not just to exclude from literary treatment the so-called lower classes of the population, as is still being done, and to preserve in literature an aristocraticism of subject matter which is no longer in keeping with our social picture. It should be admitted, they argue, that no form of unhappiness is too low for literary treatment. . . . The novel, they insist, has grown in scope and significance. It is the serious, passionate, and living form of literary study and social inquiry . . . , through its analyses and psychological investigations it will become *l'Histoire morale contemporaine* [the contemporary moral history], it has taken over the methods and duties of science, hence it can also lay claim to the rights and freedoms of science. . . . [In the preface, the] work of the novelist is compared to scientific work, and it seems beyond doubt that here the Goncourts are thinking of the methods of experimental biology. We are here under the influence of the enthusiasm for science which marked the first decades of positivism, when all active intellects—insofar as they were consciously searching for new methods and values in accord with the times—strove to assimilate the experimental techniques of science. Here the Goncourts are in the extreme vanguard; it is, so to speak, their vocation to be in the extreme vanguard. (pp. 437-38)

[However] we may feel . . . about the way in which the Goncourts plead their cause there is no doubt that they were right, and the suit has long since been settled in their favor. . . . Realism had to embrace the whole reality of contemporary civilization, in which to be sure the bourgeoisie played a dominant role, but in which the masses were beginning to press threateningly ahead as they became ever more conscious of their own function and power. The common people in all its ramifications had to be taken into the subject matter of serious realism: the Goncourts were right, and they were to be borne out in it. The development of realistic art has proved it.

The first defenders of the rights of the fourth estate—politically as well as in literature—almost all belonged not to it but to the bourgeoisie. This is also true of the Goncourts, who, by the way, had little sympathy with political socialism. They were half-aristocratic upper bourgeois, not only by birth but also in their attitude and way of life, in their views, concerns, and instincts. In addition they were endowed with hypersensitive nerves; they dedicated their lives to a search for aesthetic sense impressions. They were, more completely and exclusively than anyone else, aesthetes and eclecticists of literature. To find them in the role of champions of the fourth estate, even though only of the fourth estate as a source of literary subject matter, is a surprise. What was it that connected them with the fourth estate? What did they know about its life, its problems, and reactions? And was it really nothing but a sense of social and aesthetic justice which induced them to dare this experiment? It is not difficult to answer these questions. It can be done simply on the basis of the Goncourts' bibliography. They wrote a considerable number of novels, almost all of them based on their own experience and observation. In these novels, in addition to the milieu of the lower classes, other milieux appear—the upper bourgeoisie, the underworld of the metropolis, various types of artistic circles; but whatever the milieu, the subjects treated are always strange and unusual, often pathological. In addition they wrote books on their travels, on contemporary artists, on women and art in the eighteenth century, and on Japanese art. Then there is that mirror of their life, the Diary. Their bibliography alone, then, reveals the principle of their choice of subject matter. They were collectors and depicters of sensory impressions, especially of sensory impressions valuable for their strangeness or novelty. They were professional discoverers or rediscoverers of aesthetic, and particularly of morbidly aesthetic, experiences suited to satisfy an exacting taste surfeited with the usual. It was from this point of view that the common people appealed to them as a literary subject. Edmond de Goncourt expressed this excellently in a diary entry of December 3, 1871: . . .

> [Why] choose these milieux? . . . [Perhaps] because I am a well-born man of letters, and because the people, the mob, if you will, has for me the attraction of unknown and undiscovered populations, something of the *exoticism* which travelers go to seek. . . .

As far as this impulse took them, they could understand the people. But no further. And that automatically excludes everything functionally essential, the people's work, its position within modern society, the political, social, and moral ferments which are alive in it and which point to the future. The very fact that *Germinie Lacerteux* is once again a novel about a maid, that is, about an appendage of the bourgeoisie, shows that the task of including the fourth estate in the subject matter of serious artistic representation is not centrally understood and approached. The thing that drew the Goncourts in the subject matter of *Germinie Lacerteux* was something quite different. It was the sensory fascination of the ugly, the repulsive, and the morbid. In this, to be sure, the Goncourts are not entirely original, for Baudelaire's *Fleurs du mal* had appeared as early as 1857. But they would seem to have been the first to import such motifs into the novel; and this was the fascination which the strange erotic adventures of an elderly maid-servant had for them. For it is a true story, of which they learned after the woman's death and from which they built up their novel. In an unexpected fashion the inclusion of the common people connected itself in them (and not only in them) with the need for sensory representation of the ugly, repulsive, and pathological—a need which went far beyond the factually requisite, the typical and representative. There was in it a radical and bitter protest against the forms of an idealizing and palliating elevated style, whether of classical or romantic origin, which despite its decline continued to govern the average taste of the public. . . . (pp. 439-40)

As soon as we examine the content [of *Germinie Lacerteux*] carefully, we recognize the driving force to be an aesthetic and not a social impulse. The subject treated is not one which concerns the center of the social structure; it is a strange and individual marginal phenomenon. For the Goncourts it is a matter of the aesthetic attraction of the ugly and pathological. By this I do not mean to deny the value of the courageous experiment the Goncourts undertook when they wrote and published *Germinie Lacerteux*. Their example helped to inspire and encourage others who did not stop with the purely aesthetic. (p. 445)

When we compare Stendhal's or even Balzac's world with the world of Flaubert or the two Goncourts, the latter seems strangely narrow and petty despite its wealth of impressions. Documents of the kind represented by Flaubert's correspondence and the Goncourt diary are indeed admirable in the purity and incorruptibility of their artistic ethics, the wealth of impressions elaborated in them, and their refinement of sensory culture. At the same time, however, we sense—because today we read with different eyes than we did only twenty or thirty years ago—something narrow, something oppressively close in these books. They are full of reality and intellect but poor in humor and inner poise. The purely literary, even on the highest level of artistic acumen and amid the greatest wealth of impressions, limits the power of judgment, reduces the wealth of life, and at times distorts the outlook upon the world of phenomena. And while the writers contemptuously avert their attention from the political and economic bustle, consistently value life only as literary subject matter, and remain arrogantly and bitterly aloof from its great practical problems, in order to achieve aesthetic isolation for their work, often at great and daily expense of effort, the practical world nevertheless besets them in a thousand petty ways. There is vexation with publishers and critics; hatred of the public, which is to be conquered despite the fact that there is no common basis of emotion and thought. Sometimes there are also financial worries, and almost always there are nervous hypertension and a morbid concern with health. But since on the whole they lead the lives of well-to-do bourgeois, since they are comfortably housed, eat exquisitely, and indulge every craving of refined sensuality, since their existence is never threatened by great upheavals and dangers, what finally emerges, despite all their intellectual culture and artistic incorruptibility, is a strangely petty total impression: that of an "upper bourgeois" egocentrically concerned over his aesthetic comfort, plagued by a thousand small vex-

ations, nervous, obsessed by a mania—only in this case the mania is called "literature." (pp. 446-47)

> Erich Auerbach, "'Germinie Lacerteux'," in his Mimesis: The Representation of Reality in Western Literature, *translated by Willard Trask, 1953. Reprint by Anchor Books, 1957, pp. 434-63.*

ROBIN IRONSIDE   (essay date 1948)

By the time the Goncourts' great work *L'Art au Dix-huitième Siècle* was in progress, there were available for consultation the invaluable contents of the Marcille, Walferdin and other collections devoted to the representation of the masters whom they were studying; Watteau's fan was already a coveted item . . . , and, seven years before Edmond de Goncourt, at the age of sixteen, acquired his first picture, a water-colour by Boucher, Turner had exhibited at the Royal Academy his tribute to Watteau's genius, the 'Watteau Painting' of 1831. Such scattered facts must impair the claim (on which, indeed, there is no absolute insistence in their book) that the Goncourts rediscovered the art of the eighteenth century. . . . The brothers neither rediscovered the eighteenth century, nor belonged to that rare class of collectors, if it exists, who are content to exercise and reluctant to propagate a quality of taste impervious to the most commanding variations of fashion. The triumph of *L'Art au Dix-huitième Siècle* was a triumph of vulgarization. (p. ix)

The Goncourts had absorbed the Romanticism of the thirties and abandoned themselves feverishly to the realism, the meticulous modernism, of the fifties. Both in their novels and in their life as men of letters, they revealed themselves as pursuing and sometimes guiding the intellectual currents of the age. Though they did not, as art critics, discover the eighteenth century, they did discover the terms on which the nineteenth might take the rococo period to its heart. They re-created its charms so that it became, as it were, part of the peculiar mythology of the *fin-de-siècle*, part of its special stock of imagery. That picture of the graces and liberties of the eighteenth century, of its masques and fountains, its ribbons and alcoves, which inspired so many writers and poets of the nineties, was largely of their fashioning. (p. x)

As given by the Goncourts, [the eighteenth century] glows with a special accent of reality. In their account of eighteenth-century art, its poetry grew out of their subtle analyses of individual works; it was a poetry perceived equally in the variation of a tone or the grace of a brush stroke, and in the elegance of a pose or a costume; they hailed its presence in the tiniest material detail of the work before them with an ecstasy that a woman might display over the minutiae of personal adornment. Their whole vision of the period was coloured by the potent sensuous impressions they received from its paintings, their delight in powder and satin being inextricably fused with their delight in crumbling impasto and filmy glazes. At the same time, they were zealous in the field of documentary research. As historians they sought the same detailed realism which they cultivated as novelists. . . . [They] spent a tireless energy upon the study of texts, and the information they accumulated was an additional impetus to the effervescence of their aesthetic perceptions. Their imaginative interpretation of the art of Watteau and his successors was founded upon the strength of the sensations it aroused in them and upon a studied intimacy with the available documents concerning it.

In their enthusiasm for their subject they exploited exhaustively both their sensations and their historical findings. It is an enthusiasm which lives in every chapter of their book and engulfs the repetitions, the superfluity of annotation with which the work might otherwise seem burdened. They were themselves passionate collectors and their criticism is the mirror not only of their delight in the beauties they expounded, but also of this passion for its possession, a passion . . . which burnt with that particular intensity reserved by less chaste individuals for their physical loves. The sense of enthusiastic excitement conveyed in their pages is the elixir, so to speak, whose attractive stimulations have ensured, and still ensure, the value of the book for posterity. The language in which it speaks, at once choice and diffuse, sometimes execrable, with its Latin affectations, its interminable apostrophes, its allusive rhetoric and abandoned use of technical terminology is the true utterance of its authors' sensuous, romantic but also botanizing approach. . . . *L'Art au Dix-huitième Siècle* is still the most compact corpus of information on the subject anywhere available. . . . (pp. x-xi)

> *Robin Ironside, in an introduction to* French XVIII Century Painters: Watteau, Boucher, Chardin, La Tour, Greuze, Fragonard *by Edmond de Goncourt and Jules de Goncourt, translated by Robin Ironside, Phaidon Publishers, Inc, 1948, pp. vii-xi.*

THE TIMES LITERARY SUPPLEMENT   (essay date 1949)

Naturally the Goncourts . . . were affected by modes of thought that flourished—and sometimes declined—in the course of their own lives. Like all notable *amateurs* of the arts they had their own individual, and sometimes eccentric, tastes. It is to their credit that [in *L'art du dix-huitième Siècle*] they never indulged in that kind of totalitarianism of judgment which can so easily become the bugbear of good, and even great, critics.

Their somewhat florid verbal reconstructions, for example, of Watteau's scenes are not greatly to contemporary taste, though they should be thought of as belonging to a time when copious illustration was not so generally available; Mr. Ironside [the translator] comments: "Though they did not, as art critics, discover the eighteenth century, they did discover the terms on which the nineteenth century might take the rococo period to its heart" [see excerpt above, 1948]. They did, indeed, do this—and to some purpose—for even to-day and in this country it would probably be true to say that the eighteenth century is still largely regarded through the Goncourts' spectacles. . . . At the same time, the good sense of what they have to say is on the whole much more remarkable than certain almost inevitable *longueurs*. They contrive in a relatively small space to convey to the reader's mind not only an idea of the sort of pictures that a specific artist painted, with his good and bad qualities, but also the character and career of the man himself. Their method of setting out information is sometimes a trifle confused but the final result is extraordinarily effective in the impression left on the mind. The painter and his work are treated as if they were living entities: not as if both had to be fitted into an aesthetic strait-waistcoat of the critic's devising.

> *"Moonlight and Candlelight," in* The Times Literary Supplement, *No. 2476, July 15, 1949, p. 458.*

MARTIN TURNELL   (essay date 1955)

[In this appreciative essay, Turnell argues that the Goncourts made a significant contribution to the literature of the nineteenth

century. *He regards their studies of the eighteenth century as "fresh and impartial" and calls the* Journal *"one of the indispensable source books for the literary history of their period." Turnell contends that the Goncourts' scientific methods as well as their depiction of the lower classes signalled the transition from Realism to Naturalism in the novel, but he stresses that the brothers were Realists, not Naturalists, because they subjected their vision of reality to artistic treatment. Later, Turnell reversed his assessment (see excerpt below, 1962).]*

[Edmund and Jules de Goncourt] were gifted, industrious and versatile, and made a specific contribution to nearly all those branches of writing at which they tried their hand. Their historical work represented a fresh and impartial approach to the French Revolution. Their study of eighteenth-century art is among the best art-criticism of the century, and they virtually rediscovered Watteau and Fragonard who had been unjustly neglected since the Romantic Movement. Their novels possess great merits and played an important part in the development of French fiction in the second half of the nineteenth century, while the *Journal* is one of the indispensable source books for the literary history of their period. . . . Comparison between the works written in collaboration and those produced by Edmond after his brother's death suggest that Jules was the writer, the creator of the highly individual style, the possessor of genuine insight into human nature, and that Edmond was the talented man of letters who planned and organized the books. (p. v)

Germinie Lacerteux is the finest as it is the most popular of the Goncourts' novels. Their aims are stated clearly in the Preface to the first edition which is a literary document of considerable historical importance. . . . [The virtues of the novel, they said,] were Art and Truth, but it must be informed by that religion which the eighteenth century revered under the name of *"Humanity"*. (p. vii)

The Realists were essentially artists, and the Goncourts knew precisely what they were doing when they made Art and Truth the cardinal values of the novel and gave the same weight to both. . . . The Goncourts' championship of "the lower classes", their insistence on scientific method, and their interest in sickness and squalor undoubtedly mark the transition from Realism to Naturalism and probably influenced Zola. . . . They were not, however, Naturalists. . . . For the Goncourts the equation was Art + Truth = the Novel. For practical purposes the first term disappears from the Naturalists' equation and we have Truth = Natural-and-Social History = the Novel. (pp. viii-ix)

The Goncourts were not good starters. In the opening chapters [of *Germinie Lacerteux*], which describe the early life of Mlle de Varandeuil [Germinie's mistress] the historians are much more in evidence than the novelists. Once these chapters are behind us, however, the book seems to develop of its own accord and moves with gathering momentum to its climax. The authors transformed their material as surely as Flaubert in *Madame Bovary* and projected their own tendency to nervous instability into their principal character. (pp. ix-x)

> *Martin Turnell, in an introduction to* Germinie *by Edmond de Goncourt and Jules de Goncourt, Grove Press, 1955, pp. v-x.*

W. SOMERSET MAUGHAM   (essay date 1958)

[Maugham was an English dramatist, short story writer, novelist, and critic who is considered a skilled satirist. One of the most

popular writers of the twentieth century, Maugham is best known for his autobiographical novel Of Human Bondage. *Maugham finds little to praise in the Goncourts' works. In addition to denouncing their habit of describing things "at dreary length," he regards the* Journal *as a "disappointing" book. Maugham also dismisses the Goncourts' histories of the eighteenth century as "backstairs gossip." According to Maugham, the Goncourts' greatest flaw is their overly repetitive literary style. Despite these reservations, Maugham admires the Goncourts' passionate devotion to art.*]

[The Goncourts] were, apparently, the first to write that bastard kind of history which is concerned with back-stairs gossip and which in our own day finds favour with the public. I cannot pretend that I have read all these books, but I have read some of them. I found them dull. The Goncourts seem to have had no sense of selection and you are told the same sort of facts over and over again. They went into intolerable detail. Their books would have been twice as good if they had been half as long. (p. 196)

The two brothers were industrious, but they had little imagination and no sense of form. They had conceived the idea that things are as important as people, and this led them to describe places, houses, furniture, objects of art, at dreary length. In *Manette Salomon,* their most readable novel, Coriolis, the painter, is never so vividly presented to the reader as the elaborately described studio in which he works. *Manette Salomon* is a picture of the way the painters of the time led their lives and, since the two brothers were always careful to document themselves, one may be sure that the picture was faithful. It is the story of a painter of talent who is destroyed by the Jewish model who is his mistress and whom he eventually marries; but before you come to this, you are asked to read a hundred and fifty pages relating the high jinks, the outings, the practical jokes of the art students of the day. I think the fault of the Goncourts as novelists was that they did not start a novel because they were absorbed by a theme and the characters which were needed to develop and expound it, but because its success would give them the literary status to which, they were firmly assured, they were by their talent and originality entitled. But though their novels were unsatisfactory, the Goncourts were intelligent and observant, and there are passages in them that in a book of sketches or brief essays would be very readable. They bore because they interrupt the flow of narrative. (pp. 197-98)

[What] the Goncourts chiefly set store by was the beauty and originality of their style. . . . [To] my mind their greatest defect was that they could never bring themselves to say a thing once and leave it at that, but repeated it in other words two, three or even four times. (p. 198)

Since they were [in their *Journal*] . . . careful to be exact, we may be pretty sure that their report of the talk [at the Magny dinners] . . . was faithful. It must be admitted that it is disappointing. It is true that when you are eating a good dinner and have drunk two or three glasses of wine, a commonplace uttered with assurance may look like an epigram, but when you see it in print it has sadly lost much of its lustre; and the fact is that you look in vain in these conversations for a clever repartee or a scintillating witticism. (p. 201)

The Goncourts claimed that with *Germinie Lacertaux* they had created the realistic novel and, moreover, had discovered the eighteenth century and Japanese art. "These," said Jules, "are the three great literary events of the second half of the nineteenth century, and we have led them, we, poor and obscure.

Well, when one has done that, it is really difficult not to be somebody in the future." Though there is exaggeration in this, there *is* a grain of truth.

They never doubted that they were men of outstanding talent. They were, indeed, preposterously self-satisfied. . . . The Goncourts were arrogant, vain and conceited, but it is only fair to admit that their passion for art, though often misguided, was genuine. They were disinterested and honest in a world in which corruption was rampant. (pp. 209-10)

> W. Somerset Maugham, "Three Journalists," in his Points of View, *Heinemann, 1958, 189-255.**

ROBERT BALDICK   (essay date 1960)

[*In* The Goncourts, *one of the major critical studies of the Goncourts' works, Baldick concentrates primarily on the novels. He asserts that the Goncourts were pioneers whose novels are distinguished by vivid description and frequent psychological analyses of the characters' degeneration. Baldick notes, however, that the Goncourts' novels are often marred by lengthy introductions, excessive dialogue, superficial documentation, and fragmented construction. He cites* Germinie Lacerteux *as the Goncourts' greatest novel, arguing that in this book they attained "that rare combination of subjectivity and objectivity, of involvement and detachment, which Flaubert achieved in* Madame Bovary.*" Baldick concludes his study with an assessment of the Goncourts' literary achievements. He lauds the* Journal *as their most impressive work and finds that in the* Journal, *their "merits are not, as in their novels, vitiated by their failings." In addition to praising the Goncourts for recognizing the appeal of Japanese art, Baldick contends that many of their stylistic innovations have been incorporated into the French language. Furthermore, he maintains that the importance of the Goncourts' studies of the eighteenth century "cannot be over-emphasized."*]

As art-critics the Goncourts showed little flair or discernment when judging their contemporaries, and although they were themselves the foremost literary Impressionists of the nineteenth century, Edmond remained curiously blind to the merits of the Impressionist painters; but their study of eighteenth-century French art [*L'art du dix-huitième siècle*] . . . was a brilliant pioneer work which is now generally recognized as a classic. Though not, as they claimed, the first to appreciate eighteenth-century art at its true value, they undoubtedly did more than anyone else to rescue Watteau, Fragonard, Boucher and Chardin from the discredit into which they had fallen. . . . [Their obsession for *objets d'art*] had an important influence on their work, for it not only formed their concept of history—witness their famous dictum that a historian cannot fully appreciate a period of which no dress pattern or dinner menu has survived—but also affected their descriptive style.

Closely linked with their artistic penchants was their neurotic sensibility. . . . [If] they had been healthy in mind and body, their work, with its distinctive sick-room flavour, its morbid atmosphere, its ailing characters and its nervous, tortured style, would never have been written. (pp. 8-9)

The only noteworthy features of [*En 18 ..*] are, firstly, the theme of maleficent woman, which was to be treated again with greater skill in such novels as *Charles Demailly* and *Manette Salomon,* and secondly, an inspired description of Bas-Meudon . . . which pointed the way to similar descriptions of sad suburban landscapes in *Renée Mauperin* and *Germinie Lacerteux.* (p. 16)

The most striking feature of **Charles Demailly** . . . is probably the account of the hero's growing insanity in the last part of the novel. This, the first of many studies of mental sickness which the neurotic brothers were to present in their works, is not the masterpiece of scientific realism it was once considered; for it has been discovered that the Goncourts drew heavily and carelessly on Esquirol's monumental treatise on the subject, not confining themselves to any particular study of insanity but taking snippets from one case-history after another. . . . Yet one cannot but be impressed by the subtle, sensitive rendering of certain impressions. (p. 21)

In both its defects—the excessive amount of dialogue, the faulty construction, the over-long introduction, the superficial documentation—and its merits—the visual descriptions, the study of the husband-wife relationship, the account of the hero's neurosis and madness—**Charles Demailly** foreshadows the Goncourts' subsequent novels. (pp. 21-2)

In construction [**Soeur Philomène**] sometimes recalls **Charles Demailly,** the rather tedious introductory account of the heroine's childhood and convent education matching the lengthy survey of the journalistic world in the earlier novel, and Barnier's final degeneration and suicide corresponding to Demailly's final degeneration and madness. But **Soeur Philomène** is a far shorter, simpler work than its predecessor, skilfully and solidly built around the central episode of Romaine's operation and death, and mercifully free of the innumerable characters and long descriptions which had burdened **Charles Demailly.**

The authors' documentation has likewise been used with greater skill and restraint. For their account of Soeur Philomène's convent education they drew on some letters given them by their housekeeper, Rose Malingre, and written to Rose's niece, an orphan in the care of the Sisters of Saint-Laurent, by a convent friend. These letters, reinforced by the idea, derived from *Madame Bovary*, that a convent education unfitted lower-class girls for their natural environment, enabled the Goncourts to characterize successfully their heroine's mystico-poetic sensibility, her repugnance for her social equals and her romantic love for the student Barnier. When they turned their attention from the convent to the hospital, the Goncourts displayed even greater restraint in the use of their material, for the very good reason that their documentation had been sketchier than ever. . . . The hospital atmosphere is rendered with remarkable success, every detail garnered in the ten hours being used to good advantage somewhere in the novel. True, the paucity of the authors' material has resulted in some odd effects: thus, although the story extends over several years, it always appears to be snowing or freezing, while Barnier's fellow students seem unsubstantial and Soeur Philomène's fellow sisters non-existent. But it can be argued that the perpetual winter intensifies the austere atmosphere, and that the isolation of Barnier and Soeur Philomène, as the Goncourts pointed out to Flaubert, concentrates the reader's attention on the couple and especially on the sister. Generally speaking, the skill with which the brothers adapted their meagre notes to the purposes of their story could scarcely be bettered. (pp. 24-5)

The first part of [**Renée Mauperin**] suffers, as do the first parts of so many Goncourt novels, from the over-detailed presentation of a milieu, in this case the world of the rich bourgeoisie. The characterization too is not entirely successful. For example, Denoisel, the fatherly friend, though an attractive figure, never quite comes to life; while Madame Bourjot's resignation when Henri deserts her for her daughter is remarkable,

not to say incredible. On the other hand some of the secondary characters are very well drawn, particularly the worldly Abbé Blampoix. . . . As for the brother and sister, Henri and Renée, their danger was to become mere types, rather as Edmond saw them some years later—the modern young man as the doctrinarians and parliamentary government have made him since the accession of King Louis-Philippe', and 'the modern girl as the artistic and mannish education of the past thirty years have made her'. In fact, however, both are skilfully depicted and both come to life. . . . [Renée] is certainly one of the most convincing girls in the nineteenth-century novel; and even when she begins the lengthy process of dying, she seems to do so with greater liveliness than, for instance, Balzac's moribund Ursule Mirouët [in his novel of the same name]. In this connexion, it is interesting to note how, yet again, the Goncourts have ended a novel with a description of degeneration, here the result, not of insanity or alcohol, but heart disease. It is delicately, convincingly done. . . . [But,] as in **Charles Demailly,** the Goncourts' method is anything but scientific. (pp. 28-9)

Germinie Lacerteux is yet another of those studies of degeneration and decline in which the Goncourts excelled and which formed the pattern for the realist and naturalist novels of the next two or three decades. The heroine's decline is plausibly motivated and skilfully described, every incident contributing to and accelerating her downfall, and there is only one major improbability in the book. That is that Mlle de Varandeuil . . . should display the same obtuse lack of interest in her housekeeper's illnesses as [the Goncourts had in their housekeeper's]. On the other hand it is hard to see how the Goncourts could have avoided this difficulty without making Germinie's employers mere men like themselves, a device they would have rejected as too crude and obvious.

As in **Soeur Philomène,** there are very few secondary characters in this novel. . . . But in the background we catch glimpses of dozens of ordinary Parisian working men and women, the very representation of whom was a bold innovation. . . . The Goncourts themselves were fully conscious of their originality and audacity in producing a book of this sort, as can be seen from the proud, almost pompous preface they wrote for the novel. (pp. 35-6)

The Goncourts' innovations in the field of social documentary may now seem of small account, especially in comparison with Zola's subsequent achievements. Set against such vast crowd-scenes as the magnificent description in *L'Assommoir* of the workers streaming through the Paris streets in the early morning, the Goncourts' thumbnail sketches of individual workers caught in characteristic attitudes appear slight indeed. The details the Goncourts furnish about the trades of Jupillon the glove-maker and Gautruche the house-painter [in **Germinie Lacerteux**] . . . pale into insignificance beside the accumulation of technicalities in any Zola novel. The slang which the Goncourts put into the mouths of their characters seems unremarkable when compared with the forceful and authentic-sounding language of Zola's workers. And the Goncourts' pictures of the streets and dance-halls of Paris are dwarfed by Zola's immense symbolic evocations of mines, markets and tenements.

Yet such comparisons are more than usually odious, for when they are made the Goncourts' pioneer work tends to be underrated, just as Zola's achievements tend to be overrated. Before **Germinie Lacerteux** the lower classes had rarely figured in the French novel, and then only to be travestied by such writers as Champfleury or Eugène Sue; and if in portraying them realistically for the first time the Goncourts used a more limited and individualistic technique than Zola, it was a no less valid or effective technique than their successor's. Their technical descriptions are adequate without being obtrusive, while the slang they put in their characters' mouths—slang taken from court reports, the popular Press, and above all from conversations overheard in the street by Jules's keen ears—is both more realistic and more apposite than Zola's slang, which was generally culled from dictionaries and used without much discrimination. As for their sad, bleak descriptions, perfectly adapted to the subject and mood of *Germinie Lacerteux,* they not only inaugurated the naturalistic cult of the seedy suburban landscape to which Zola among others adhered, but they have a haunting charm which survives to this day.

The book's chief merit and originality lies, however, not in its language or descriptions, but in the characterization of its heroine. From the medical point of view, this was both the boldest and the most successful attempt the Goncourts ever made to establish the case-history of a character in a novel. . . . [In] the description of Germinie's hysterical tendencies in the first half of the novel, the Goncourts . . . for once showed that they could use a medical source-book with skill and intelligence. Their account of their heroine's later degeneration owes less to medical treatises and more to their own psychological insight, which is shown to particular advantage in the pages describing the 'uterine frenzies' which drove her to pick men up in the streets. Attached to Germinie by their affection for her prototype and by their fellow-feeling for her neurotic sensitivity, yet at the same time separated from her by class and circumstance . . . they attained in this novel that rare combination of subjectivity and objectivity, of involvement and detachment, which Flaubert achieved in *Madame Bovary.* (pp. 37-9)

The central theme of *Manette Salomon*—the destruction of an artist's talent by a woman—is of course largely the same as that of *Charles Demailly,* as is the misogynistic moral that woman, with her base materialism, cannot appreciate man's aesthetic aspirations and must inevitably try to reduce the artist to her level. . . .

The importance of the thesis in *Manette Salomon* does not imply that the two principal characters are mere abstractions, born of the Goncourts' fear and hatred of woman: here again the brothers have followed their usual practice of painting from life. (p. 42)

[Using] friends and acquaintances as their models, the Goncourts succeeded in creating two extremely lifelike characters in Coriolis and Manette. . . . Unfortunately the Goncourts gave free rein here to their violent anti-semitism—a longstanding prejudice of theirs, to judge by the fact that the hero of *En 18 ..* had been revolted by the discovery that his love, like Manette, was not merely a model, but a Jewish model. Combining their hatred of woman with their hatred of the Jews they have made . . . Manette, the domineering shrew, a caricatural figure. . . . [It is] difficult to believe wholeheartedly in the transformation of Coriolis under Manette's influence, for the reader is simply told that Coriolis has lost his talent, instead of being shown him losing it as he was shown Charles Demailly losing his reason. Indeed, the only major character in the book who is consistently convincing is the Bohemian artist Anatole. . . . [Anatole's] pet monkey Vermillon . . . is a portrait of Koko, a monkey which Jules bought in 1854 and which died after falling from a fourth-floor window. Koko's death

had occurred too long ago to be remembered with any accuracy, so in order to describe Vermillon's death the brothers went to the Jardin des Plantes as soon as they heard that a monkey was dying, and watched the animal in its last agony. The result is a passage which, with its blend of controlled emotion and clinical realism, is perhaps the most effective and moving death-scene in any of the Goncourts' works. (pp. 43-5)

[Minor figures in *Manette Salomon*], together with the whole background and atmosphere of the artistic milieu, are brilliantly represented to the reader—far better, in fact, than the denizens and atmosphere of the world of letters in *Charles Demailly.* The Goncourts also reproduce faithfully the artistic theories and tendencies of the eighteen-forties and fifties, notably the question of open-air painting and the idea of treating contemporary subjects in a modern style. The twentieth-century reader, aware that these were the ideas which gave birth to Impressionism and that the new movement was gaining momentum while *Manette Salomon* was being written, may complain that the Goncourts' prognostications . . . were very wide of the mark. But to expect prophetic judgments from two critics writing in the middle of an artistic revolution and easily swayed by considerations of friendship or enmity would doubtless be asking too much. (p. 45)

[In *Madame Gervaisais,* the Goncourts] went about the bookish part of their heroine's conversion in a singularly inept fashion. . . . On the other hand, they treat the psychological and physiological aspects of Madame Gervaisais's conversion with a certain skill, though even here one has the impression that they are out of their depth and relying too much on their source-books. If Madame Gervaisais is not entirely a credible figure, most of the other characters in the novel, from the mystical Countess Lomanossov to the villainous Father Sibilla, are even less convincing. Indeed, the only completely successful piece of characterization in the book is to be seen in the pathetic figure of Pierre-Charles. The Goncourts' portrait of the dumb child admittedly owes something to one of their inevitable medical treatises . . . but their reading has been supplemented by a remarkable understanding of child behaviour and skilled observation of gesture and expression to create a character who, though silent, is more convincing than his loquacious elders.

One other aspect of the book must be mentioned, and that is the picture it gives of Rome. The city was, of course, bound to occupy a considerable place in the novel since it was intended to have a profound influence on Madame Gervaisais; and it cannot be denied that the Goncourts' descriptions of Rome are both impressive and less hackneyed than might have been expected. But even so, and even admitting the necessity for the inclusion of numerous descriptive passages, the fact remains that at times the novel is almost indistinguishable from a well-written guidebook. One is tempted to attribute this major defect, so much more serious than similar defects in the earlier novels, to Jules's failing health; and the temptation becomes stronger when one notices that the book is entirely lacking in those brilliant passages of dialogue which graced *Manette Salomon* and which were largely Jules's work. (pp. 50-1)

Though not to be compared with such novels as *Germinie Lacerteux, La Fille Élisa* is an impressive work, in which a sensational subject is handled with delicacy and skill. The form of the book is also remarkable, representing as it does the most ambitious and successful essay in composition in any Goncourt novel: in order to vary the tedium of the descriptions of brothel and prison life, Edmond has used a complex arrangement of flashbacks of the cinematic variety, moving back and forth between courtroom and brothel, childhood home and prison cell. On the other hand, the sudden introduction of the author himself into the last chapter of the book strikes a jarring note; the style, with its rather clumsy phrasing, seems heavier than that of the novels written by both brothers; while Edmond's inability to write convincing dialogue led him to ignore the overwhelming evidence of prostitutes' natural garrulity and make his brothel almost as silent as his prison. . . . [The] book can be seen as a record of the grief which Jules's death caused his brother, a less obvious but no less sincere memorial tribute than Edmond's next novel, *Les Frères Zemganno*. (p. 56)

[The] two brothers Gianni and Nello were portrayed with skill and sensitivity, Edmond giving of his best to this tribute to the years with Jules. . . . [No one, however,] could describe the bare-back rider, a lady rejoicing in the name of La Tompkins, as anything but improbable; for some reason best known to himself, Edmond chose to alienate even the most credulous reader by making this woman an American millionairess who worked in a circus for the love of the life. (pp. 59-60)

Unfortunately, [in *La Faustin*] just as in *Les Frères Zemganno* excellent social and psychological characterization was offset by the improbable figure of La Tompkins, so here a striking picture of theatre life and a sensitive study of an actress's personality are vitiated by the introduction of an unconvincing English aristocrat, one Lord Annandale. (pp. 60-1)

[*Chérie*] constituted an unorthodox attempt to depict the character of a French girl: unorthodox because Edmond had solicited the collaboration in his enterprise of all the women readers of *La Faustin* [in his preface to that work]. . . . The book which he wrote with the aid of the confessional documents furnished by anonymous readers or uninhibited friends is not as sensational as one might expect, partly because Edmond made no use of the more shocking confidences and partly because we have seen bolder psychological and physiological studies of girlhood since 1884; thus the account of the heroine's first experience of menstruation, which no doubt scandalized many contemporary readers, now raises only a smile at Edmond's selfconscious delicacy in treating the subject. There is no plot to the novel. . . . Though doubtless realistic, the sequence of loosely connected letters, impressions, diary entries, descriptions and psychological observations, unrelieved by the smallest incident or the slightest passion, is tedious in the extreme; while if Chérie occasionally comes to life, she nonetheless seems a pale, uninteresting figure in comparison with Renée Mauperin. (pp. 62-3)

The complete *Journal* is an impressive work and one of the great literary achievements of modern times. It is sometimes objected that it contains an excessive number of malicious and often scabrous anecdotes which the brothers, and Edmond in particular, did not trouble to verify; but it is difficult to see how they could have checked on the truth of these stories, which in any event are often amusing and always enlightening—about either their subjects or their authors. For on every page of the *Journal* the authors stand revealed with all their many qualities and their still more numerous defects, against a meticulously observed and brilliantly depicted background of the leading events and personalities of their age. Whether it is read as a monumental autobiography or as a history of social and literary life in Paris in the second half of the nineteenth century, the *Journal des Goncourt* is a document of outstanding interest and incomparable importance. (p. 68)

Their concept of style was fundamentally artistic and aristocratic, preferring the artificial to the natural, the exquisite to the crude. Their cult of the *bibelot* . . . and their admiration for modern Japanese art, with its miniature effects, had a marked influence on their visual sense, and hence on their works, which depended in great part on visual observation. Just as their novels are built up piecemeal, so their descriptive passages reveal a distaste for large-scale effects and an obsession with details which are both picturesque and significant.

The brothers had a highly developed sense of form, shown in countless descriptions from that of Manette Salomon's body to that of the monkey Vermillon's ear; but it was as nothing in comparison with their sense of colour. Like the Impressionist painters, they tried to reproduce in their works the actual colour of an object or a scene at a specific time of day and year and in specific conditions, without regard for the colour conventionally attributed to it. They also made every effort to communicate to the reader the exact quality of a colour, however strange or elaborate the image they found it necessary to employ—writing for instance of 'a cold, dirty yellow light which looked as if it had been filtered through old tulle curtains'. It was to colour too that these painterly writers turned when they wished to convey an otherwise indescribable impression, as in the phrase 'an olive heat'. But even so, there were moments when they despaired of rendering some particular shade in words, and their despair is occasionally revealed in the frantic repetition of the primary colour notation involved: 'that blue, the blue of sky and sea intermingled, a blue for which there exists no term or equivalent, a blue rather like a translucent turquoise'.

Their intense dissatisfaction with the inadequacies of French vocabulary and syntax led them increasingly to devise new constructions and new terms in an attempt both to capture the infinite complexities of modern life and to make a more profound and direct impression on the reader than could be achieved with the hackneyed words and phrases of everyday language. Instead of using conventional, long-winded approximations, they would often describe a sensation in an unexpectedly contracted phrase, thereby arresting the reader's attention and obtaining unusual cohesion between idea and expression. . . . As for the new words which they used, some were true neologisms, created to perform a function for which no existing term was considered suitable; but the majority were technical, professional or foreign terms which were unfamiliar to the French reader, and which the Goncourts employed for the dual reasons of realism and effectiveness—because they were both correct and picturesque. Foods such as 'Lithuanian varenikis and vatrousihkis in white cheese' or weapons such as 'yatagans, khandjars and flissats' may not lie within every reader's experience, but their names are respectively appetizing and alarming. (pp. 69-71)

[The Goncourts' *écriture artiste*] is now widely regarded as an outdated, affected literary idiom of interest only to linguistic historians. Yet few of the modern French writers who glibly condemn the *écriture artiste* realize that every day they use words and constructions introduced by the Goncourts but so completely integrated into the language that their origin has become obscured. This is a risk run by all stylistic innovators, and as innovators on a large scale the Goncourts have suffered more than most: their successes are adopted but not acknowledged, their failures noted and condemned.

If we are to do the brothers justice as stylists, we should remember the essential differences between them and the classical writers of French prose. The latter avoided technicalities since their ideal was the general, not the particular; they avoided the neologism since it prevented immediate understanding; they avoided the picturesque effect since it detracted from the uniformity of the work. Theirs was an abstract prose, where ideas were everything and pictorial values nothing, where words were analytical symbols and not the colourful literary equivalents of sensations. Where they amassed weighty clauses, the Goncourts employed delicate phrases, as brittle as the nerves of their creators. To the classical writers the sound of words was important; to the Goncourts vision mattered more. The classical authors were psychologists or orators; the Goncourts were artists. (pp. 71-2)

Though the most important artistic movement of the nineteenth century is now seen to have been Impressionism, not Japanism [as Jules de Goncourt declared] the recent revival of interest in Japanese art has shown that the Goncourts were not mistaken in their estimate of its appeal to modern Western tastes. Again, if they were not, as they liked to think, the first to rediscover Watteau and Fragonard, the importance of their work on both eighteenth-century art and eighteenth-century social history cannot be over-emphasized. And while they cannot be counted among the world's greatest novelists, Jules was undoubtedly right in claiming that '*Germinie Lacerteux* is the prototype-book which has served as a model for everything which has been done since under the name of realism or naturalism'.

This last judgment requires qualification: it would be misleading to suggest that the Goncourts' only achievement as novelists was to influence others. In many respects their novels are, as they had hoped and intended, 'the most historical novels of their era': anyone wishing to become acquainted with the external characteristics and psychological climate of a particular Parisian milieu in the second half of the last century could scarcely do better than read the relevant Goncourt novel. . . . The general reader will also find that the Goncourts' regard for realism was combined with considerable artistry. But unfortunately they suffered from the defects of their qualities. Their desire to paint truthful pictures of isolated scenes and characters led them to compose their works on a fragmentary pattern and make jigsaw puzzles of their novels. Their lofty conception of style led them to adopt a mannered form of expression which can at length become irritating. And finally their clinical objectivity is scarcely distinguishable from inhuman detachment: except in *Germinie Lacerteux* and *Les Frères Zemganno* they appear indeed as gentlemen of letters whose interest in their subjects is psychological, historical or aesthetic, but rarely human.

It seems strange to us today that apparently neither Jules nor Edmond ever realized that it was their *Journal* which would prove their best defence against the oblivion which both dreaded. For in the *Journal* the Goncourts' merits are not, as in their novels, vitiated by their failings. The work combines realistic observation with fragmentary presentation, purple passages with starkly simple vignettes, serenely objective entries with paragraphs of unexampled malevolence or warm sympathy; it is of equal interest to the historian, the stylist and the student of human nature. But if the Goncourt brothers misjudged the respective merits of their weapons in the struggle for survival, they have certainly survived: they are and will remain *somebody* in the history of literature. (pp. 73-5)

> *Robert Baldick, in his* The Goncourts, *Bowes & Bowes, 1960, 79 p.*

MARTIN TURNELL   (essay date 1962)

[*In a reversal of his previous assessment of the Goncourts (see excerpt above, 1955), Turnell dismisses the* Journal *as a "multi-*

volume nineteenth-century horror comic" and likens their social histories to gossip columns. Further, he considers their écriture artiste nothing more than a literary "gimmick." Turnell concedes, however, that the Goncourts' art criticism helped to revive interest in eighteenth-century painting, and he notes that their clinical scrutiny of disease and vice influenced the development of the novel.]

The brothers [Goncourt] did not possess either the intelligence, the moral qualities or the insight which go to the making of a great work. They were not writers of the same caliber or, indeed, in the same sense as Flaubert and Zola whom they so grievously maligned at one time or another. They were talented men of letters who were fanatically determined to win immortality at any price. The *Journal* is filled with lamentations over their lack of recognition, the severity of reviewers or the absence of congratulatory letters when a new novel comes out. In his later years Edmond actually refused to marry a girl who was much too good for him because he wished his fortune to be used to found a literary academy and the prize which was to confer an undeserved cachet on so many bad or indifferent novels.

One may feel that in the long run the Goncourts had little cause for complaint. They had a gift for choosing the subject or the literary form which allowed them to make the best use of their talents. The result is that their work has enjoyed a fame and has exercised an influence which were out of all proportion to its intrinsic merits. Their art criticism is not comparable to the best of Baudelaire or Fromentin, but their appreciations of minor masters like Watteau, Fragonard and Boucher led to a revival of interest in eighteenth-century painting. Their inborn taste for tittle-tattle and a flair for putting their hand on the right document made it possible for them to present social history from a new angle—one well-known to us today—the angle of the gossip columnist.

Neither were they genuine novelists. Their works of fiction are examples of the man-of-letters novel. Yet in a curious way a morbid preoccupation with mental and physical disease, their interest in case histories, a liking for the seamy side of working-class life and their theories of naturalism had a decisive influence on Zola and most of the late nineteenth-century French novelists. The *écriture artiste*, which was a form of literary Impressionism, also influenced Zola and Huysmans; but in the hands of its inventors it was never more than a gimmick, an interesting specimen for dissection in the philologist's laboratory.

Much has been written of the importance of the *Journal* as a source book for nineteenth-century literary history. It is rather a repository of discreditable anecdotes and spiteful judgments which one reads with a sort of horrified fascination. It offers a full-length portrait of two excessively unpleasant and highly neurotic characters who are obsessed with the macabre, with the grisly detail, and who cannot abide the successes of those who are supposed to be their friends. It also gives an extremely one-sided picture of literary society with its hair down. (p. 118)

The examples of literary conversion [in the *Journal*] are not impressive. The views of the brothers on religion, like those of other contemporary writers, are embarrassing in their ignorance and their shallowness. . . .

It is, however, their judgments on their contemporaries which leave the worst taste. We see [for example] Gautier "heavy of face, with all his features sagging, his lines thickening, a sleepy countenance, a mind drowned in a barrel of matter.'' . . .

The Goncourts set their sights high. Their aim was not merely to equal Saint-Simon: it was to surpass him. But they possessed neither the genius nor the fire power of the great duke. They had an eye for the graphic detail, as we can see from the glimpse of Gautier quoted above, but they never managed to penetrate beneath the surface. That is why their portraits, or what Edmond called ''speaking likenesses,'' transform the models into figures from a strip cartoon. For what we have here is not the memoirs of a latter-day Saint-Simon, but a kind of multi-volume nineteenth-century horror comic. (p. 119)

> *Martin Turnell, ''A Genius for Gossip: The Brothers Goncourt,'' in* Commonweal, *Vol. LXXVII, No. 5, October 26, 1962, pp. 117-19.*

PATRICK ANDERSON   (essay date 1970)

[In *Paris under Siege, 1870-1871: From the Goncourt Journal,* Edmond de Goncourt's] is the eye of a very superior journalist, part clinician, part aesthete. For all his inner suffering, he excels at the group picture which is irradiated by one or two carefully selected details. . . . Paris becomes a confused but flowing organism, often productive of ironically beautiful effects of light and colour, which he attempts to fix by the examination of a single cell: the gleam of a cannon, the cry of a cock, the smoke of a cooking fire in front of a tent, a shelled balcony hanging in mid-air, the yellow slabs of horse fat now substituted for butter, the shadows inside an old man's nostrils.

Naturalism expectedly—to borrow for a moment Tennyson's puritanism—stirs the slime. 'In the street you run into old streetwalkers . . . who rejoice at the prospect of caressing the wounded with sensual hands and picking up a little love among the amputations.' The invading Germans excrete through a hole made in the mouth of an ancestral portrait. Literary friends, although mentioned rarely, contribute some catty gossip. And then art gathers the material up again, distancing it uncomfortably far from the middle ground between anguished ego and objective composition where one could have hoped to see Edmond in action and positively involved—how rarely he talks to, let alone touches, anyone. (pp. 447-48)

Limited to one year of peculiarly messy crisis, [*Paris under Siege, 1870-1871: From the Goncourt Journal*] seems a gloss on Baudelaire, a prelude to [T. S. Eliot's] *The Waste Land.* But it is also shocking as the work of a *voyeur.* It lacks the two passions of politics and love. (p. 448)

> *Patrick Anderson, ''Private Eye,'' in* The Spectator, *Vol. 224, No. 7397, April 4, 1970, pp. 447-48.*

JEAN T. JOUGHIN   (essay date 1970)

[*Paris under Siege, 1870-1871: From the Goncourt Journal*] is a joy. It is a book for the reader to savour, for him to hold on his tongue as it were each of the rich evocations—of a scene, a mood, an episode, a bit of gossip—that crowd upon his consciousness as he follows Edmond de Goncourt in far-ranging promenades through a Paris twice besieged in the space of nine months. The section of the Goncourt *Journal* here presented is much more than a description of what life during the ''Terrible Year'' was like as seen by a remarkably perceptive and literate man; it is a primary document filled with insights

for the study of French letters and history. I believe that if anyone were limited to reading only a single book as background for the Third Republic, he could scarcely choose better than this.

Edmond de Goncourt was a quintessential snob, and his *Journal*—carried on alone after the death of his brother Jules in June 1870—is a deeply subjective work. Nevertheless, his entries for 1870-1871 contain a surprising amount of material revelatory of wider attitudes and values in his world, of ideas and feelings that were to have profound effects upon subsequent events in France. This is so because of his forthright pronouncements on what he was seeing, because of his candor about his own emotions and biases, and because of what he picked up to report. What, for example, is that yearning for ''audacity'' (this during the Franco-Prussian War), for the wild, reckless doing of the ''impossible'', if not an early version of belief in that fighting *juria franchesa* [rage for freedom] which figured importantly in General Staff plans on the eve of the First World War? And how well we see, in the attacks on ''military stupidity'' in 1870, the Army in defeat unwilling—as in 1940—to allow last-ditch civilian efforts at salvation. There are, too, in the *Journal* several passages anticipatory of the outlook—later termed fascist—that extolls the life-giving exhilaration, the sweet dangerousness to be found only in mortal combat.

The *Journal* reflects much about the deepening of class hatred and the vehement rejection of the republican idea by an important segment of society. In doing so, it underscores the enduring legacy of the Commune to France; and what it shows about these developments is hence far more significant than the random glimpses of things to come mentioned above. (pp. 620-21)

If the views of the elder Goncourt brother were to find echoes through subsequent decades, the same cannot be said for his style, for here he is unique. The power of the *Journal* for 1870-1871 derives not only from its sense of immediacy but first and foremost from its language. In every day's entry the imagery is exquisite. Goncourt was no mere diarist. He combined the temperament of an inveterate *flâneur* with the eye of an impressionist painter. . . .

Many books will see the light of day in connection with the hundredth anniversary of the Siege and of the Commune. I can only hope the others will be as graceful, as charming, and as enlightening as *Paris under Siege.* Once more the Goncourt *Journal* has demonstrated its unique merit. (p. 621)

> *Jean T. Joughin, in a review of ''Paris under Siege, 1870-1871: From the Goncourt Journal,'' in* The Modern Language Journal, *Vol. LIV, No. 8, December, 1970, pp. 620-21.*

RICHARD B. GRANT   (essay date 1972)

[*In his book-length study of the Goncourts, Grant argues that the brothers have been unjustly forgotten because they were ''too much ahead of their time,'' particularly in their approach to the novel. Grant maintains that En 18 .. and Charles Demailly are ''anatomies,'' or formless works of fiction in which ''both plot and milieu are subordinated to a basic theme.'' With* Sister Philomene, *he asserts, the Goncourts evolved beyond anatomy, choosing instead the novel form. Grant laments this transition, hypothesizing that ''had the Goncourts truly believed in writing what they wanted . . . , they might have been recognized in the twentieth century as the foremost anatomists of their age.'' Grant views the conflict between illusion and reality as the central theme of the Goncourts' novels and notes that "when the Goncourts get to the point of making the characters—and even the reader—doubt the nature of reality itself, they anticipated some of the literary preoccupations of the twentieth century."*]

[The novelistic elements of *En 18 ..*] are so feeble and so submerged that they almost do not exist. In point of fact, the Goncourts were experimenting with new departures in fiction and were reacting against the "typical" novel. Throughout their lives they rejected plot as an organizing principle of fiction, even when they found themselves obliged—by the very traditions of the fiction of their age—to use one. What is at work here is an attempt to organize fiction not along the usual lines of linear plot, but thematically. (p. 20)

En 18 .. has considerable coherence of composition provided that we do not try to view it as a novel. . . . Jules likened [the] work to that of Sterne. The juxtaposition is an excellent one. *Tristram Shandy . . .* of Laurence Sterne has the same "incoherent" structure to judge by novelistic standards, the same love of wit and digression, the same primacy given to ideas. (pp. 22-3)

To answer this question of a "formless" work of fiction that takes on form when one focuses on theme and idea, it is of value to consider this text as an example of a separate genre of fiction, one that Northrop Frye has called the anatomy [in his *The Anatomy of Criticism*]. Frye defines it as "not primarily concerned with the exploits of heroes" but as that which relies on the free play of intellectual fancy and on the kind of humorous observation that produces caricature. Further, "the intellectual structure built up from the story makes for violent dislocations in the customary logic of narrative." In this kind of writing, characterization seems to be "stylized rather than naturalistic, and presents people as mouthpieces of the ideas they represent," and in *En 18 ..* it is true that the characters are stylized to some extent, being subordinated to the thematic and intellectual thrust of the work. In summary, *En 18 ..* is a piece of fiction that presents a systematically pessimistic view of the nineteenth century. It claims that all morality, all idealisms are illusions. Secular humanism and the doctrine of progress are repudiated; society is labeled as false, politics as vanity; the family is meaningless; love, women, and marriage are a horrible trap; and man is weak before this grim world where people and objects appear good but are in reality evil. We have, then, in this trial effort of Jules and Edmond a fascinating, rather brief anatomy or dissection of their times, a work that should only secondarily be considered in the novelistic tradition. It has been unjustly neglected. (p. 23)

[*En 18 ..*] has a weakness, one that points to the unique feature of the two brothers' creative effort, namely their collaboration. In *En 18 ..* the technique was simple: Jules wrote some chapters, and Edmond wrote the others. At this time their styles were markedly different, and the difference is quite visible. Edmond wrote in the heavy descriptive style of Théophile Gautier, whereas Jules's style was sprightly, paradoxical, a perpetual display of fireworks. The two did not fit very well. But with practice, the brothers learned to write in closer harmony. (pp. 23-4)

As lovers of the past, they were horrified that the great works of the eighteenth century were being neglected, and [in *L'Art du dix-huitieme siècle*] they attacked with feeling the prejudice that reigned during the early part of the nineteenth century. (p. 26)

[One] of their principal purposes in doing art history was to remind France that a glorious heritage was being neglected. The Goncourts, themselves artists, spoke accurately and shrewdly at times about technique. For instance, they could observe how in a still life the dominant color tones were carried over with great subtlety from one center of interest to another. They could also comment on the sociological implications of an artist, considering Chardin, for example, the epitome of the bourgeoisie and the spokesman for his class. But the main desire of Jules and Edmond was less to interpret the past than to bring it to life. Operating on the reasonable assumption that the art of the previous century was almost unknown, they tried to transpose into words what was visible on canvas, to capture the tone as well as the image. . . . [The] charm of these evocations . . . , coupled with the serious study and technical competence of the two brothers, earned for them a genuine place in the history of art criticism. (pp. 26-7)

[In describing] unknown masterpieces of the past so that they could come alive through words, the brothers were in fact reinforcing tendencies already visible in their descriptive prose technique. . . . Hence in their fiction, details of a room, a person, and so on, almost seem to be descriptions of a painting. There is often a heavy emphasis on light and shadow, on detail of color, and on composition, and there are even explicit parallels to the styles of various painters. But the technique transposed to prose fiction is double-edged. If it captures nuance, it loses power and directness. Frequently a Goncourt descriptive seems to be made at one remove, becoming a description of a picture of a landscape, a room, or a person. (p. 27)

[As social historians, their] instincts drew them to private correspondence, memoirs, novels, brochures, and newspapers. . . . [*L'Histoire de la société française pendant la Révolution* reveals] weaknesses in their method. The Goncourts' disdain for progress and for the masses was reflected in their horror of the French Revolution. Because of this bias they neglected revolutionary newspapers, choosing other material that fit their thesis. Further, they treated all documentation as equally valuable, unwilling to see that their own favorite sources could be heavily biased. (p. 28)

What is the *Journal*? Can it be viewed as more than just a mine of information? Can we treat it as a work of art in itself? Kenneth Rexroth, for one, believed so [see Additional Bibliography]. . . . The *Journal* is indeed a fascinating document. . . . But it does not truly have the contrapuntal structure that Rexroth claims for it. The patterns of rise and fall seem really to take place at random, and the system of daily jottings often kept the material from being more artistically organized by the authors' imaginative processes. It remains a precious document of the age, but no more. (p. 30)

[The merits of the novel *Charles Demailly*] are numerous. It is unified and carefully elaborated on a thematic basis. The world of letters and of journalism is explored by people who knew it well and who convince us of the accuracy of their picture. The dialogue is very well handled, and while some novelists (such as Flaubert) caution against too much dialogue in fiction, any technique is successful if one can get away with it, and the Goncourts do. There are interesting innovations that vary the style, with some chapters in the form of letters, one as a diary, and one even as a play taken from a newspaper (a thinly veiled parody of [the characters] Charles and Marthe's life together). All this should spell success, but there is a serious flaw. While the Goncourts always claimed that art and style were their main concerns in writing, and while they insisted on the function of their work in exposing the evils of their day, they also wanted . . . to capture human reality, to give a sense of ''real'' human beings. Here they fail with both hero and heroine. (pp. 42-3)

Marthe is based on a real person, but what is true is not necessarily true to life. We are convinced when Marthe reveals her stupidity, but there is no explanation of her viciousness to her husband whom she loved when they were married. The idea that she carries her roles as villainess over from the theater does not solve the problem, for it is merely stated, not built up minutely through watching her in her professional life. As the action of the novel hangs on this point, the flaw is serious.

The hero too is unbelievable, although for different reasons. We have no idea of what he looks like, no idea of his early years. . . . Demailly floats in a vacuum. He has no past, no family to situate him; even the world of letters is shown often as apart from him. And time itself is a problem, for the novel is shattered into ninety-four chapters which present vignettes without continuity, a technique acceptable in an anatomy but awkward for a novel. Hence no organic growth seems feasible for the hero. Further, given the importance of the central theme, the hero tends to become a vehicle for the theme to a point where he becomes too abstract. . . . (p. 43)

The essential explanation for the sharp difference between [*Soeur Philomène*] and their previous efforts is that the new vogue for Realism had caught up with [the Goncourts]. (p. 44)

The Goncourts rejected the view that realism should be a flat imitation of reality . . . and held out for fine writing and unusual effects. But they did accept the principle that man was formed by his milieu and, in the positivistic tradition of Auguste Comte, believed that he could be studied with documented rigor. Later as the ''Realistic'' movement became ''Naturalistic'' they added to this importance of milieu an insistence on physiology and its impact on the nervous system, and hence on psychology—an idea already visible in their portrayal of women. Moreover, their training as historians led them further into the practice of documentation. . . . [In *Soeur Philomène*] the Goncourts provided a careful, lengthy development of the heroine in a sharp change from their previous works of fiction. They wished to show how the girl became a nurse on the basis of temperament and upbringing. [In] a convincing manner the Goncourts create a real girl, give a direction to her life, and prepare her for the facing of its reality. (pp. 45-6)

Despite defects, as a novel *Soeur Philomène* shows a marked improvement over the earlier efforts. The protagonist is provided with a credible past that convincingly shows how milieu and physiology can create character. The doctor is given some motivation for his self-destruction. The Goncourts had done something new; they had roused themselves out of their normal upper-class habitat and had made a conscious effort to examine a disagreeable aspect of human society, one which is often ignored, in a scientific manner. This kind of anlysis of the hospital world separated them from Balzac and justifies the label ''pre-Naturalistic'' for the novel. But in addition, it is a mark of the Goncourts' artistry that they united this method and this subject matter with their own vision of illusion and reality, here reduced to the ultimate terms of life and death. With *Soeur Philomène* the Goncourts showed that they had evolved beyond the anatomy and had learned to handle the novel proper as a genre. (p. 52)

The intricacies of the plot [of *Renée Mauperin*] show the Goncourts' desire to be more traditional in their fiction, conforming to what is expected of a novel, but even so, the narrative events are still secondary. . . . Sociological dissection and character analysis of the heroine are their main concern, and the real strength of the novel is that these two seemingly disparate elements are smoothly fused into a whole. (p. 56)

[An] aspect to the heroine that keeps us from believing in her human and social reality [is] her death from heart disease. With their growing awareness of things medical, the Goncourts believed and would have us believe that her death is medically credible. . . . Renée is healthy at the beginning of the novel, but the heart damage is supposed to be the result of the shock she receives when she realizes that she has caused her brother's death, and the Goncourts believed, as we do not, that emotion can cause *direct* and *immediate* physiological damage of this type in a healthy girl. . . . Further, once she falls ill, . . . her death is very decorative. One might even say that her death has a decided literary flavor (only slightly disguised by medical terminology) reminiscent of many another heroine dying of a broken heart. Once again the Goncourts have inadvertently flawed their novel, which is in many ways a superior creation. But even so, *Renée Mauperin* gave the Goncourts the chance to ponder class attitudes. (pp. 61-2)

In writing *Germinie Lacerteux*, they had to revise their previous practices. First of all, there was the heavy temptation to describe their protagonist simply as a *débauchée* hiding behind a hypocritical mask and thus deceiving her masters. This vision would have fit in neatly with the patterns of *En 18 ..* and *Charles Demailly* concerning illusion and reality. But both the more thoughtful exploration of personality that they had undertaken in *Soeur Philomène* and the years of close frequentation of [their housekeeper Rose, on whom Germinie is based] made this facile answer unacceptable, and so they tried to make sure to seek a more profound truth. . . .

Another change that they needed to make was in the concept of time. In their previous fictional works, especially the first two, the two brothers had presented life as a series of essentially discontinuous tableaux with the result that often the characters seemed a bit shallow, for they were not anchored in a developing historical tradition of a family or a society. But in the case of Rose, the continuity of her being was thrust on them by the fact that she had lived continuously with them over the years. Time was in this case inescapable and provided the skeleton for a good novelistic structure. . . . [In] the earlier efforts the action was paced into one explosive incident, but much of the rest of the work did not seem to be telling a story. In *Soeur Philomène* they started with continuously developing time when telling of the heroine's childhood, but the novel eventually disintegrated into vignettes and tableaux at the hospital. In *Germinie Lacerteux* time is maintained quite well throughout, permitting the exploration of the development of personality, the authors' chief aim. (p. 66)

[It] is unlikely that Zola's *L'Assommoir* would have been possible without *Germinie Lacerteux*. The novel is a great one, for it combines new views of personality with powerful social protest, in a milieu described to bring out the horrors that can surround the existence of a human being. (p. 72)

[In *Manette Salomon*, the] verdicts rendered on contemporary artists are decisive enough, but history has proved that as art critics the Goncourts sometimes failed to recognize true masters. . . . Into the context of this semiaccurate panorama of nineteenth-century art history the Goncourts try to fit their several fictional painters. Each exemplifies a given trend of the times and therefore is a type, but each is portrayed also as a human being struggling with the awesome difficulties of becoming an artist. . . . (pp. 87-8)

Coriolis comes to life as a person whenever we feel him straining to achieve the absolute through art. This quest for the ideal the Goncourts themselves felt keenly and they were able to transfer a sense of urgency, even of frenzy, to their fiction. (p. 91)

[When Manette, Coriolis's wife, becomes a mother the] novel rapidly becomes a vehicle for anti-Semitic diatribes. One by one, Manette alienates all of Coriolis' gentile friends and replaces them with Jewish relatives that are nothing but anti-Semitic caricatures. Coriolis, too weak to fight her successfully, tolerates these changes. Even his son is alienated and grows up a little monster. These pages with their crude bias are repellent to any sensitive reader, but they should not blind one to a deeper meaning. At first glance, it seems as if a noble mask (Art) is removed and that reality in the form of a greedy Jewess is revealed. However, the experience in multiple personality that the Goncourts encountered in the case of Rose leads them to try to express a different view. . . . Rather than a mask being torn off, there is clearly intended a real change of personality, although the reader may not be convinced of its truth because of the abruptness of the change and the unpleasant racism. Unpalatable as well is the implied condescending misogyny, for the Goncourts believed firmly that maternity was the only genuine emotion of which a woman was capable. (p. 93)

As for the structure of the novel, it is not unlike many of the earlier efforts in that it is composed of a large number (155) of chapters, each a tiny self-contained unit. This fragmentation leads to odd effects. . . . The Goncourts did not weave a unified tapestry. Their technique is rather more that of the mosaic, fragmented when seen close to, meaningful (in their successful works) when viewed from a greater distance. (p. 96)

[*Madame Gervaisais*] cannot be considered of first quality. . . . The attempt to provide [Madame Gervaisais] with an authentic past is frankly fraudulent. We are told that she is a philosopher, a painter, and has real talent, but never does the reader get any glimpse of her accomplishments. She has no permanent relationship with other adults that attach her to a milieu. Mindless, she floats disembodied through pages rich with description and barren of action. Further, her turning against her own child seems unconvincing and thereby weakens what is of value in the psychological study. The satire of the clergy is heavy, and in fact the sense of heaviness is pervasive, in part because there is so little dialogue. This absence of human give and take may be due only to the fact that she never has anyone to talk to but is more probably due to Jules's failing creative powers. (pp. 101-02)

La Fille Elisa impresses today's reader as being most visibly a novel of social protest. While it is true that out of fear of censorship, Edmond left unexplored the world of pimps and rich roués, his narrative still makes clear society's failures. Edmond and Jules may have been hostile to the *political* demands of the poor and had no love for their company, but they knew social injustice when they saw it and were outraged. (p. 117)

[The] structure is based on an alternation of present reality and flashbacks in a manner that at times becomes mechanical, and Elisa's fellow prostitutes are often just listed and do not participate in the development of the narrative or of the heroine's

psychology. . . . [The] Goncourts did not show individuals and society in their complex interaction, nor paint tableaux that had continuity in time, nor create secondary characters with a life of their own. The aristocratic Goncourts instinctively shied away from crowds and were never happier than when the action moved inside and unfolded behind closed doors. Progressive isolation seems the normal pattern for their fiction, whether in *Renée Mauperin, Germinie Lacerteux,* or *Madame Gervaisais,* with the consequence that the number of secondary characters is almost automatically reduced. This refusal to paint a broad literary canvas is at times a weakness in the Goncourts' fiction, but here it is fully justified. In a novel that examines the progressive dehumanization of an individual, detachment and increasing solitude are entirely appropriate. (p. 118)

[*Les Frères Zemganno*] is no mean achievement. Sociologically accurate in its description of a milieu, and believable . . . in its presentation of the psychology of circus performers, rich in its inner exploration of the love between two men, and in its wider exploration of the double-edged nature of Western man, it stands as the last great work of fiction to come from the Goncourts. . . . *Les Frères Zemganno* deserves to be better known. (p. 130)

[One] serious flaw in *La Faustin* is the "hero," Lord Annandale, who is a grotesque caricature of the English aristocrat. For instance, when inspecting a new Parisian home in which to live with his Juliette (La Faustin), he utters only two words on the whole inspection trip: "bird" and "bath." Edmond apparently saw these two subjects as the only things that could wrench an English lord out of total taciturnity. Equally unsatisfactory is the final *agonie sardonique* [sardonic agony] of a disease which, conveniently left unexplained, is far too literary a device to inspire belief. . . . Clearly its purpose was not medical but moral, suggesting, in the satanic appearance that the rictus gives to Lord Annandale's face, the evil of the British character. His coldness and his suppressed homosexuality . . . give an almost allegorical quality to the hero, and allegory is out of place in a novel that tries to re-create the reality of France in the mid-nineteenth century. . . . [The] deathbed scene reveals a complete failure on the part of Edmond to grasp the psychology of either a woman in love or a great actress, neither of whom would feel "compelled" to imitate the dying grimace of a beloved person. (pp. 135-36)

In spite of all Edmond's documentation, heightened sensitivities, and realistic energy, *Chérie* is a very anemic work. . . . Many of Edmond's most stubborn faults remain. He uses the same mechanical device to introduce secondary characters that he and Jules had used in *Charles Demailly:* a simple listing in one chapter of all of Chérie's friends; only at the end of the work do any of these other young women reappear in the narrative. As a result, Chérie floats detached from life despite Edmond's effort to integrate her into the Parisian scene in the 1860's. Another flaw is the absurd intellectual premise on which the "novel" (for lack of a better word) is constructed. . . . We are asked to believe that ovulation without fecundation in a Parisian woman of high-strung temperament often leads to madness and death, which is indeed Chérie's fate. . . . Finally, the "novel" lacks even a simple plot. . . . Actually, the fiction gives in chronological sequence a series of vignettes. . . . Many of the vignettes are successful, and yet many seem quite pointless, for not only do they fail to constitute a plot, they do not even fit in with the stated purpose of the biography, to wit, that modern society is destructive of women, who become so warped by the artificial life they lead that they cannot love, marry and procreate in natural rhythm. (pp. 137-39)

In the race for literary immortality, the Goncourts started with a heavy handicap, for it seems as if they almost deliberately set about to alienate their future judges, the literary critics of the twentieth century. They scorned women, Jews, the working class, the bourgeoisie, and foreigners, relying with vague trust on future artists and men of letters to keep their memory alive. . . . [These men] spent their lives in other people's drawing rooms, rushing home late each night to distill their nasty little remarks in a diary so venomous at times that even the complimentary entries offended people when it was published. Even a critic willing to be sympathetic has a hard time in warming up to them. (pp. 143-44)

The Goncourts often spoke of their interest in others, of their desire to penetrate beneath the surface of real or fictional beings, to explore the recesses of the human heart, but [some] critics are eager not to believe them. . . . [These critics fail] to take into account the sense of human compassion of which Jules and Edmond were at times capable. One should never forget the ringing prefaces to *Germinie Lacerteux* and *La Fille Elisa* in which they pleaded for an understanding of the working class and protested against unjust penal conditions. And on occasion in their *Journal*, in the midst of all the gossiping one can find a brief compassionate sketch of human suffering that they have observed. (p. 144)

As for the stylistic contribution of the Goncourts, it seems to have had no major influence on the development of the French language. Scholars have studied the lexical innovations that appear in the *Journal* and have showed the many neologisms and archaisms of their style. But in general these innovations have not lasted. . . . As for the "impressionistic style" that they developed to such an extent, we can say that while its excesses are only too visible, the technique did draw attention to the possibility of giving the language greater flexibility— such as using a noun for an adjective. Concerning the matter of Japanese art, it is certainly true that the Goncourts participated in the introduction of this vogue. . . . But Japanese art was little more than an extended fad, and if the Goncourts' only claim to immortality resided in the introduction of the East to French culture, they would already be forgotten. Even their rehabilitation of eighteenth-century French art, something they thought was unquestioned and unquestionable, has come under scrutiny. But while scholars have shown that the previous century had not been as neglected as the Goncourts claimed, they did play a role in its revival, and their *L'Art du dix-huitième siècle* is still used today by students of art history, a fact which suggests the importance and solidity of their work in this field. We must accord them a modest plus here. (pp. 145-46)

[Scholars] say, that as the authors of *Germinie Lacerteux,* [the Goncourts] created a prototype for an entirely new kind of literature. Here they are right. This novel led directly to Zola's *L'Assommoir* and through it to a whole generation of fiction dealing with the working class. Their influence was also strongly felt by Joris-Karl Huysmans. . . . Their physiological analysis of Germinie, already anticipated in *Soeur Philomène,* constituted a new and valid literary manner of exploring the human organism. Balzac had understood the importance of the milieu; the Goncourts, even more than Zola, contributed to our realization that our character owes much to our physiology.

But contributing to the establishment of an historical "school" does not constitute the only manner in which one may con-

tribute to the literature of a culture. The Goncourts were also trying to reform the novel itself. (p. 146)

What the Goncourts really wanted to write . . . was not a traditional story but a vast satire debunking all personal, artistic, and social sacred cows, to show the hypocrisy of their culture in its institutions and its values. . . . That the anatomy was a form natural to the Goncourts is visible in their first work of fiction, *En 18 . . ,* as well as in the myriad essays and digressions that appear in later novels. But the two brothers discovered that the public did not respond to plotless literature; it wanted the eternal patterns of romance. Had the Goncourts truly believed in writing what they wanted and had not tried to cater to public taste, they might have been recognized in the twentieth century as the anatomists of their age. But whether it was the powerful influence of the standard traditions of the novel, or whether it was their own vanity that wanted their books to sell, the Goncourts always felt obliged to create some plot, protesting against this necessity every step of the way. As a consequence, their novels sometimes seem to be caught halfway between two genres, failing to succeed completely in either. The plots are defective, and the analyses stop short of that total commitment and exuberance which marked the brilliance of Rabelais. *Charles Demailly, Madame Gervaisais,* and *Chérie* suffer the most from this indecisiveness, and we may call them solid failures, whose only value today is as documents that shed light on social customs of the day and on the artistic development of Jules and Edmond. The other works of fiction, despite some weaknesses, deserve a better reputation. . . . [The] Goncourts were trying to create a new type of fiction, not one in which the milieu supports and enriches the plot, but one in which the plot is broken up and fragmented with the results that both plot and milieu are subordinated to a basic theme. (pp. 146-47)

The Goncourts never had any belief in Progress, and hence had no disillusionment concerning the quest for the ideal. They had no illusions about the possibility of any viable restored monarchy. . . . But the illusions of society were not their only concern. They dealt with the same problem on the individual level, believing that the only "progress" was through time on the road to death. In showing the illusions of human desire they used varied and at times imaginative techniques. Descriptions of nature, dialogue, diaries, and direct essays all play their role. But perhaps the most striking device is the use of the theater, the mask, pantomime, which in one form or another is found in all their fiction. . . . When the Goncourts got to the point of making the characters—and even the reader—doubt the nature of reality itself, they anticipated some of the literary preoccupations of the twentieth century and, because of this timeliness, should be better known. Certainly, their three finest creations—*Germinie Lacerteux, La Fille Elisa,* and *Les Frères Zemganno*—owe much of their value to the Goncourts' concern with these matters.

That they are *not* better known is due not only to the arrogance of these two brothers, or to some genuine weakness in their fiction, but also to the fact that the Goncourts were perhaps too much ahead of their time. It was not until the disasters of the twentieth century had descended upon the Western world that Europeans and even Americans faced up to the emptiness of the nineteenth-century concept of progress. Modern writers like Pirandello, Beckett, Ionesco, and Genêt are forever dealing with the themes of illusion and reality. It is significant, incidentally, that these writers are playwrights. The stage, an arena of illusion in itself, is an excellent place to discuss these problems. Although not influenced by the Goncourts, whose power to shape future generations of writers had faded out, their work has continued and developed many of these techniques. If we reread the Goncourts with the realization of the centrality of this theme in their work, their novels will appear in a more favorable light.

In addition to dealing imaginatively with reality, in addition to leaving the *Journal* as a document of their age and to making modest contributions to the language and to the history of art, in addition to writing three very superior novels, they opened the realm of fiction to the working class. Because of these real successes, the Goncourts seem destined to have an enduring and respectable place in the history of French literature. (pp. 148-49)

Other writers of that day also turned their attention to the sufferings of the working classes, but they often let their sympathy for these victims of social exploitation lead them into idealizing them simply *because* they were victims. . . . The Goncourts scoffed at such sentimental idealism, preferring to paint a more human picture. They showed in *Germinie Lacerteux* and in *La Fille Elisa* the lower classes as true victims of social injustice but never assumed that victims were inherently virtuous. . . . If the keen ability, such as that possessed by the Goncourts, to see beyond a simplistic moral façade to the more baffling ethical and ontological complexities of human nature had been more widespread, the twentieth century might have avoided some of the deadly struggles caused by an oversimplified vision of man and ethics. Through their work, the Goncourts repudiated impossible dreams of perfection and also the complacent bourgeois illusions which claim that all is basically well. While their penetrating insight made them so pessimistic that they were incapable of action and reduced them to the role of eternal spectators, they should not be scorned. Mankind will always need to be reminded of the limits of human achievement. (pp. 149-50)

> *Richard B. Grant, in his* The Goncourt Brothers, *Twayne Publishers, 1972, 163 p.*

ADDITIONAL BIBLIOGRAPHY

Bascelli, Anthony L. "Flaubert and the Brothers Goncourt." *Nineteenth-Century French Studies* V, Nos. 3, 4 (Spring-Summer 1977): 277-95.*
    A study of the tenets of Naturalism based on the Goncourts' critical treatment of Gustave Flaubert in the *Journal.*

Belloc, M. A., and Shedlock, M. *Edmond and Jules de Goncourt: With Letters, and Leaves from their Journals.* 2 vols. New York: Dodd, Mead and Co., 1895.
    Detailed biography that relies heavily on the Goncourts' letters and journal entries.

Billy, Andre. *The Goncourt Brothers.* Translated by Margaret Shaw. London: Andre Deutsch, 1960, 352 p.
    The most comprehensive and illuminating biography of the Goncourts by a member of the Goncourt Academy. Billy's study provides background information on the Goncourts' works and insightful commentary on their personal relationships with some of France's leading writers. In addition, Billy describes "the extent, according to others and to themselves, of the Goncourts' influence in various . . . domains. . . ."

Cameron, Arnold Guyot. Introduction to *Selections from Edmond and Jules de Goncourt,* edited by Arnold Guyot Cameron, pp. 17-56. New York: American Book Co., 1898.
    Laudatory survey of the Goncourts' works written in a highly descriptive prose reminiscent of the *écriture artiste.*

Duncan, J. Ann. "Self and Others: The Pattern of Neurosis and Conflict in *Germinie Lacerteux." Forum for Modern Language Studies* XIII, No. 3 (July 1977): 204-18.
    Attempts to show that the originality of *Germinie Lacerteux* lies in its psychological analysis of the behavior of the central character, rather than in its "somewhat suspect fame as the first French novel with a proletarian heroine." In advancing her argument, Duncan discusses the novel's structure, vocabulary, and characterization.

James, David. "Gavarni and the Goncourts' *Henriette Maréchal." Modern Language Notes* LXII, No. 6 (June 1947): 405-09.*
    Asserts that the Goncourts viewed the theater as a "living fusion of the pictorial and the literary arts" and finds that their dramatic productions, especially *Henriette Maréchal,* were inspired by the lithographs of Paul Gavarni.

Jarman, Laura Martin. "The Goncourt Brothers: Modernists in Abnormal Psychology." *The University of New Mexico Bulletin* 6, No. 3 (15 April 1939): 5-52.
    A careful, thorough study of the Goncourts' interest in abnormal psychology. Jarman cites numerous examples from the Goncourts' novels to substantiate her claim that they adopted a positivistic, case-history approach to the delineation of the abnormal character. Jarman also discusses the Goncourts' techniques in presenting the abnormal character.

Matthews, J. H. "From Naturalism to the Absurd: Edmond de Goncourt and Albert Camus." *Symposium* XXII, No. 3 (Fall 1968): 241-55.*
    Complains that critics have failed to recognize the Goncourts' influence on Albert Camus and finds that a close analogy exists between the murder scenes in Camus's *L'étranger* and in *La fille Élisa.*

Michot-Dietrich, Hela. "Blindness to 'Goodness': The Critics' Chauvinism? An Analysis of Four Novels by Zola and the Goncourts." *Modern Fiction Studies* 21, No. 2 (Summer 1975): 215-22.*
    Argues that the female protagonists in *Germinie Lacerteux, La fille Elisa,* and Émile Zola's *L'assommoir* and *Nana* are victims of their own generosity and goodness, rather than of their desire for sexual love, as critics commonly believe. Michot-Dietrich believes that bourgeois chauvinism has blinded critics to the virtuous qualities of these poor, socially-outcast women.

Niess, Robert J. "Émile Zola and Edmond de Goncourt." *The American Society Legion of Honor Magazine,* XLI, No. 2 (1970): 85-105.*
    Investigates the tumultuous friendship of Edmond de Goncourt and Émile Zola.

Quennell, Peter. "The Goncourts." In his *Casanova in London,* pp. 25-33. New York: Stein and Day, 1971.
    Brief biographical and critical sketch that concentrates on the Goncourts' *Journal.*

Rexroth, Kenneth. "The Goncourt *Journal." Saturday Review* XLIX, No. 43 (22 October 1966): 75-6.
    Praises the *Journal* as a dramatic recreation of life in France during the second half of the nineteenth century. Rexroth explores the structure of the *Journal* which he describes as contrapuntal because "from what at first seems only a random diary a philosophy of history certainly emerges. . . ."

Routh, H. V. "Chapter XIX." In his *Towards the Twentieth Century: Essays in the Spiritual History of the Nineteenth,* pp. 294-300. New York: The Macmillan Co.; Cambridge: Cambridge University Press, 1937.
    Proposes that the Goncourts' novels are representative of neorealism, a form of literature devoted to scientific documentation of human behavior that developed in response to Darwinism. Routh argues that neo-realism fails because "a man of letters cannot record his impressions as if he were a man of science"

and he cites the Goncourts as the "best illustration of [the school's] disabilities."

Schier, Donald. "Voltaire and Diderot in the Goncourt *Journal*." *French Review* 39 (1965): 258-64.*

Asserts that the Goncourts' critical estimates of Voltaire and Diderot in the *Journal* are irrational and fragmentary. Schier complains that the Goncourts minimize Voltaire's talents as a writer by representing him as "a symbol of the past" and "a fomenter of the hated Revolution." Diderot's philosophical and scientific speculations are neglected, Schier maintains, in the Goncourts' effort to depict him as the "pure artist whose technical achievements introduced the future (i.e. themselves)."

Schwartz, William Leonard. "The Priority of the Goncourts' Discovery of Japanese Art." *PMLA* XLII, No. 3 (September 1927): 798-806.

Argues that the Goncourts did not, as Edmond de Goncourt claimed on several occasions, discover Japanese art. Schwartz does allow, however, that they were the first French writers to recognize its importance, and he notes that Edmond's use of similes based upon his knowledge of Japanese art influenced French prose writers, notably Joris-Karl Huysmans and Marcel Proust.

Ullmann, Stephen. "Word Order as a Device of Style: E. and J. de Goncourt, *Manette Salomon*." In his *Style in the French Novel*, pp. 167-73. New York: Barnes & Noble, 1964.

A detailed textual analysis of the Goncourts' use of inverted word order in *Manette Salomon*.

Wood, J. S. "A Problem of Influences: Taine and the Goncourt Brothers." In *Studies in French Language, Literature, and History Presented to R. L. Graeme Ritchie*, pp. 248-58. Cambridge: Cambridge at the University Press, 1949.*

Examines the literary climate in France during the period of the Goncourts' collaboration in an effort to arrive at a plausible explanation for the brothers' sudden decision to pursue Realism. Wood concludes that the Goncourts' enthusiasm for Hippolyte Taine's philosophic defense of scientific research in the study of human behavior influenced their literary approach.

Gerald Griffin

1803-1840

Irish novelist, short story writer, dramatist, poet, and essayist.

Griffin is remembered for his realistic depiction of peasant and middle-class life in Ireland during the eighteenth and nineteenth centuries. In his works Griffin primarily described the people and countryside of his native province of Munster, and his pictures of the fishermen, smugglers, peasants, and emerging middle class of southern Ireland are enhanced both by his command of the Anglo-Irish dialect and his knowledge of Irish folklore. Although he was most familiar with the peasantry and the middle class, in his masterpiece, *The Collegians,* Griffin successfully presented an entire social hierarchy. *The Collegians,* which is considered the most comprehensive and accurate delineation of provincial Irish society by an Irish novelist, has influenced a number of other writers. It was the basis for Dion Boucicault's popular melodrama, *The Colleen Bawn,* and Jules Benedict's opera *Lily of Killarney,* as well as the inspiration for Theodore Dreiser's novel *An American Tragedy.* A devout Roman Catholic, Griffin believed that literature was a valuable source of moral instruction, and his early stories combined didactic intentions with aesthetic considerations. After the publication of *The Collegians,* however, Griffin's propensity to moralize dominated his artistic concerns; he came to regard as evil "such works of the imagination as were founded upon deep and absorbing passion." Critics agree that Griffin's creative development climaxed with *The Collegians.* His later stories, though often praised for their vivid accounts of the political and economic chaos that plagued Irish society during the early part of the nineteenth century, are generally dismissed as overly didactic.

The ninth child in a middle-class family, Griffin was born in Limerick. When he was seven, his father, whose brewery business had suffered severe losses, moved the family to Fairy Lawn, on the banks of the Shannon River. Griffin's formal education was scattered; he received his instruction from local tutors and scholars in rural schools. Memories of these experiences are preserved in the schoolroom scene of *The Rivals,* which is praised for its comic effects. In 1820, Griffin's mother and father and several of his brothers and sisters emigrated to Pennsylvania. Griffin remained in Ireland, where he lived with his older brother, William, in the village of Adare. While still in his teens, Griffin wrote poems and plays and, for a short time, contributed articles to two Limerick newspapers, the *General Advertiser* and the *Limerick Evening Post.*

In 1823, encouraged by the success his friend John Banim had achieved in London as a dramatist, Griffin moved to England. However, his hopes of attaining popularity in the theater were quickly shattered. Griffin's plays were repeatedly rejected by the London theaters, and he lived in extreme poverty, producing anonymous hackwork for various London periodicals until, through Banim's influence, he was offered a regular position on *News of Literature and Fashion,* a widely read weekly magazine. While contributing to *News of Literature and Fashion,* Griffin wrote *Holland-Tide; or, Munster Popular Tales,* a critical and popular success for which he gained immediate recognition as a talented writer of colorful regional tales. Having earned, in his own words, "half a name" for himself in

London with *Holland-Tide,* Griffin returned to Ireland, where he began a second series of Irish stories, *Tales of the Munster Festivals.* This collection, which is even more well received than *Holland-Tide,* is consistently acclaimed by critics for its effective characterization.

Griffin ensured his reputation as an outstanding chronicler of Irish life and character with *The Collegians,* which is judged his finest achievement. Based on a famous murder case, *The Collegians* tells the story of the well-to-do Hardress Cregan, who marries a peasant girl and later hires his servant to drown her so that he may marry a woman of his own class. Primarily, *The Collegians* is admired for its masterly depiction of every strata of Irish society. While early critics declared that the work was distinguished by its dramatic power, some twentieth-century commentators, including Padraic Colum, maintain that Griffin's histrionic inclinations caused him to protract the novel's denouement, rendering it less effective. Recent critics frequently attribute the power of *The Collegians* to the psychological intensity with which Griffin portrayed the novel's two main characters, the brilliant but wicked Cregan and his dull but virtuous friend Kyrle Daly. Benedict Kiely and John Cronin contend that the intellectual discussions between Cregan and Daly reflect Griffin's attempts to resolve his own moral dilemmas.

The Collegians marked a turning point in Griffin's life and writing. After its publication he decided that morally corrupt characters such as Cregan had a detrimental influence on the public, and he resolved to direct his characters' feelings "in the line they ought to go in." Critics concur that this decision proved fatal to Griffin's career as a storyteller. Many commentators fault his later works, particularly the historical novels *The Invasion* and *The Duke of Monmouth*, for their stock characterization and didacticism. *The Rivals* and *Tracy's Ambition*, though considered artistically flawed, are singled out by modern critics for their attention to the concerns of the Irish peasantry following the Act of Union in 1800.

In 1838, convinced of the impossibility of writing morally perfect stories, Griffin burned most of his unpublished works and entered the Society of the Christian Brothers, a religious community of lay monks dedicated to the teaching of the poor. Before he completed his novitiate, however, he contracted typhus and died at a monastery in Cork in 1840. Griffin's tragedy in verse, *Gisippus*, was one of the few manuscripts that escaped destruction and was successfully produced at London's Drury Lane Theatre in 1842. Critics unanimously agree that this play, written when Griffin was only twenty, displays great artistic potential.

During his own lifetime, Griffin's fame rested on *Holland-Tide, Tales of the Munster Festivals, The Collegians,* and his lyrical poetry, which was scattered throughout his stories and later collected in *The Works of Gerald Griffin*. In the twentieth century critical attention has focused on *The Collegians*. It is frequently pointed out, however, that Griffin's talents were best suited to the short story. Critics note that his longer works are marred by digression and lack the unity of his shorter tales.

Nearly all the biographical information about Griffin is contained in *The Life of Gerald Griffin*, written by his brother Daniel. Since this portrait presents Griffin as a deeply religious man tormented by self-doubts, several of Griffin's critics have emphasized and, according to recent scholars, exaggerated Griffin's sufferings. Today Griffin is widely viewed as an author who wrote primarily in a moralistic vein for a didactic purpose: he believed that national unity in Ireland could be achieved if the peasantry received Christian instruction. With the exception of *The Collegians*, Griffin's works are largely ignored. Nevertheless, he remains a respected figure in Irish literature because, in the words of Cronin, "at his best he is a powerfully realistic depictor of the troubled Ireland of his time."

PRINCIPAL WORKS

Holland-Tide; or, Munster Popular Tales   (short stories) 1827

Tales of the Munster Festivals   (short stories)   1827

The Collegians   (novel)   1829

The Christian Physiologist: Tales Illustrative of the Five Senses   (short stories)   1830

The Rivals. Tracy's Ambition   (novels)   1830

The Invasion   (novel)   1832

Tales of My Neighborhood   (short stories)   1835

The Duke of Monmouth   (novel)   1836

Gisippus   (drama)   1842

*The Works of Gerald Griffin. 8 vols.   (novels, short stories, biography, and poetry)   1842-43

*This work also includes *The Life of Gerald Griffin* written by Daniel Griffin.

SIR WALTER SCOTT   (journal date 1828)

[*Scott was a Scottish novelist, poet, historian, biographer, and critic of the Romantic period who is best known for his historical novels, which were a great popular success. In the following excerpt, he describes* Tales of the Munster Festivals *as "admirable," but complains that the stories are flawed by their protracted crises. In faulting Griffin for his "impolitic" tendency to digress, Scott sounds a critical point that will be repeated throughout the criticism, particularly with regard to Griffin's longer stories.*]

[The ***Tales of the Munster Festivals***] are admirable. But they have one fault, that the crisis is in more cases than one protracted after a keen interest has been excited, to explain and to resume parts of the story which should have been told before. Scenes of mere amusement are often introduced betwixt the crisis of the plot and the final catastrophe. This is impolitic. But the scenes and characters are traced by a firm, bold, and true pencil, and my very criticism shows that [the] catastrophe is interesting,—otherwise who would care for its being interrupted? (pp. 505-06)

> *Sir Walter Scott, in a journal entry on March 13, 1828, in his* The Journal of Sir Walter Scott, *edited by John Guthrie Tait, revised edition, Oliver and Boyd, 1950, pp. 505-06.*

GERALD GRIFFIN   (conversation date 1829?)

[*In the following excerpt, which is drawn from a conversation between Griffin and his brother Daniel shortly before the publication of* The Collegians, *Griffin laments the impossibility of writing novels that are both morally and artistically perfect. Anticipating popular response to* The Collegians, *he confidently predicts that readers will prefer the wicked Hardress Cregan to the virtuous Kyrle Daly.*]

Isn't it extraordinary how impossible it seems to write a perfect novel; one which shall be read with deep interest, and yet be perfect as a moral work. One would wish to draw a good moral from [*The Collegians*], yet it seems impossible to keep people's feelings in the line they ought to go in. Look at [the] two characters of Kyrle Daly and Hardress Cregan, for example: Kyrle Daly, full of high principle, prudent, amiable, and affectionate; not wanting in spirit, nor free from passion; but keeping his passions under control; thoughtful, kind-hearted, and charitable; a character in every way deserving our esteem. Hardress Cregan, his mother's spoiled pet, nursed in the very lap of passion, and ruined by indulgence—not without good feelings, but for ever abusing them, having a full sense of justice and honour, but shrinking like a craven from their dictates; following pleasure headlong, and eventually led into crimes of the blackest dye, by the total absence of all self-control. Take Kyrle Daly's character in what way you will, it is infinitely preferable; yet I will venture to say, nine out of ten of those who read the book would prefer Hardress Cregan, just because he is a fellow of high metal, with a dash of talent about him. . . . [What] is the reason that integrity, generosity, honour, and every virtue . . . is so little appreciated? Kyrle Daly would be considered a mere milk-and-water character compared to Hardress [Cregan]. (pp. 228-29)

> *Gerald Griffin, in an extract from a conversation with Daniel Griffin in 1829? in* The Works of Gerald Griffin, Vol. 1 *by Daniel Griffin, second edition, D. & J. Sadlier & Co., 1857, pp. 228-29.*

DUBLIN REVIEW (essay date 1844)

The publication of the *Collegians* was . . . the culminating point in Griffin's career; and it were well for his fame if he had never published any of his later stories, which, though they abound with many beauties, yet fall very far short of the strong but sustained interest, the tender and natural truthfulness of this exquisite story. When Griffin first appeared as a writer of Irish tales, the interest of the subject had long been forestalled, and might almost be deemed exhausted. . . . [And] yet Griffin, without trenching a single inch on the province of any of his predecessors, made the subject so peculiarly his own, that he was at once installed in the very highest rank among the painters of the national character. He did not copy the flippant and caustic satire of Lady Morgan, nor the quiet and half-hidden moral, the ever-present, though unfelt, philosophy of Miss Edgeworth; nor Banim's stern and painfully graphic pictures of passion and crime; nor the exaggerated caricature and elaborate absurdity of Crofton Croker. It was perfectly plain, even in his earliest tales—in the comparatively trifling sketches of *Holland-tide*—that he had shaken himself clear of all foregone conclusions; that he thought and wrote from himself; that he described not what had been described by others, but what he had himself seen,—seen too with his own eyes, and independently of the description of any previous writer. (pp. 287-88)

Banim alone, among the writers of Irish fiction, can be considered a kindred spirit; and Banim,—though his works as a whole are more uniformly in good taste, and though, in depicting strong passion, especially of the darker hue, he is more successful,—yet has not produced anything half so touching, or so perfectly finished in all its parts, as Griffin's exquisite story of the *Collegians*. It is easy to observe, though it is not so easy to define exactly, many points of difference between them. A great deal of Banim's power, at least in the less impassioned scenes, lies in the ability with which he seizes the externals of a character—the look, the air, the dress, the bearing. Griffin's forte, on the contrary, lies below the surface. He always probes to the quick. He is thoroughly master of the character which he professes to describe, and, generally speaking, conveys his conception of it to the reader, less by his own description (though in this too he excelled), than by a happy art of making it develope itself. He takes but little pains to tell us what his personages thought and felt; for in truth it would be unnecessary; we see it in the developement of the story itself. For example, we know few characters in any author to which less of mere description is devoted, than that of Hardress Cregan in the *Collegians*. Yet we know no character of which the reader carries away a more distinct and vivid impression. Indeed few writers have excelled Griffin in dramatic power. There are many scenes in this same tale;—for instance, Mrs. Daly's wake, Hardress's meeting with Eily's father, the discovery of the dead body at the fox hunt, and the scene at the ball before the arrest,—which are not inferior in energy, and force of colouring, and life-like truth, and absorbing interest, to anything in the pages of Scott; nay, even of Shakspeare. Banim's characters, for the most part, are individuals. Griffin's—at least in the *Collegians*—are all representatives of a class, and interest us, not on account of their private peculiarities, but because they remind us of individuals whom we know in real life. We recognize an acquaintance in every page. Banim's humour—in which he is often far from happy—is of a broad and noisy kind. You see that he is doing his best to raise a laugh, and that, to encourage it, he himself sets the example. Griffin's is of a quiet and silent cast; as for example,

in Myles Murphy's appeal in behalf of his delinquent ponies, or Lowry Looby's attempt to discover the supposed sister of the little boatman. But it is not the less effective from the apparent absence of effort. He shakes your sides, and makes your cheeks ache, with laughter, while not a muscle is moved upon his own quiet, but yet waggish countenance. Above all, the great difference lies in the moral tone and tendency of their writings. Banim is often light, or even coarse. . . . Griffin never wrote a word or dropped an allusion, which would bring a blush to the most delicate cheek, or a twinge to the most tender conscience.

In all this, however, we are speaking principally of the *Collegians*. His attempt in the historical school of romance, was a signal failure. *The Duke of Monmouth* . . . is by many degrees below mediocrity. His Irish historical novel, *The Invasion*, however, though its success with the public was equally bad, is in every respect a more creditable performance. . . . To the character of a regular tale it makes no pretension; but it is intended to present a picture of the social condition of Ireland [during the eighth century]. Of romance there is but little in the plot; too little to relieve, for the ordinary novel reader, the learned and elaborate dissertations upon the laws, government, social usages, and civil and military institutions of the time, which are occasionally introduced. But for those who are really interested in the antiquities of their country, it has many attractions, and will well repay an attentive perusal. Even the story itself, though it is slight and inartificial, and though some of the characters are harsh and unpleasing, is not without many beauties. The character of the hero, Elim, is one of the most beautiful Griffin ever drew. His mother is a charming specimen of the high-born matron of the olden time; and Duach is a perfect impersonation of the traditional fidelity and devotedness of the Irish kerne. (pp. 290-92)

The prevailing tone of Griffin's poetry resembles that of his prose. Strong passion (except in his play of *Gisippus*), he seldom attempts to draw. He has few affinities with the Byron school. You look in vain in his pages for the blighted lives and seared affections, the gloomy passion and remorseful misanthropy, which form their staple material. He rather seems to have written for those happy times,

> Ere sorrow came, and sin had drawn
> 'Twixt man and heaven her curtain yet.

The leading characteristics of his muse are tenderness and feeling; we do not mean that mawkish tenderness which borrows both the thoughts and the language of sentimentality, but that which comes warm from the affections, which has real feeling for its basis, and finds its echo in every heart. His fancy, very seldom exuberant, is always rich and playful, though the images from which he delights to draw his illustrations, are often of the most melancholy cast; and the effect is heightened by his peculiarly correct and graceful diction, and the easy and natural flow of his versification.

These observations, however, apply chiefly to his shorter pieces; for in the others he is far from being so happy. The **"Fate of Cathleen"** appears altogether unworthy of him: it is at once, strange as it may seem, weak and exaggerated. And though the opening of **"Shanid Castle"** (which is in the Spenserian stanza), is extremely beautiful, the historical portion of the poem is sadly out of keeping with its magnificent commencement, which might take its place among the finest passages of [Byron's] *Childe Harold*. The longest of these pieces is **"Matt Hyland."** . . . It contains many exquisite passages . . . , but the effect of the whole is entirely destroyed by excessive amplification; and though the story is an interesting one, and has quite enough of romance to form the subject of a few verses, yet the case is very different when it is extended to six cantos. Like all ballad poetry, its great beauty is its simplicity; and this charm is entirely destroyed, when, with but little additional incident, it is diluted into half a volume of sentiment and mysticism. (pp. 300-01)

> *A review of "The Works of Gerald Griffin," in* Dublin Review, *Vol. XVI, No. XXXII, June, 1844, pp. 281-307.*

MARY RUSSELL MITFORD   (essay date 1852)

[Mitford was an English sketch writer, dramatist, poet, novelist, and critic whose legacy to English literature includes some of the nineteenth century's most endearing sketches of English country life. Here, Mitford favorably compares The Rivals *to* The Collegians *and attributes the former's unpopularity to the moral repugnance of the heroine's disinterment.]*

"**The Collegians,**" partly from the striking interest of the story, partly from a certain careless grace and freshness of narration, won immediate popularity. "**The Rivals,**" equally true to individual nature, and superior in constructive skill, was comparatively unsuccessful.

Perhaps the reason of this failure may be found in the principal incident, resembling in its main points that of Mr. Leigh Hunt's "Legend of Florence." The heroine, like Ginevra, is buried while in a trance, and recovered, not like the Italian wife, from the effects of natural causes, but by the half-crazy efforts of her lover, who violates the sanctity of the tomb that he may gaze once again in death upon the form he so loved while living. Now this catastrophe, although it may have occurred, and there is reason to believe has occurred in more instances than one, is yet, even in the Italian version, so improbable and so horrible, so utterly repugnant to human sympathy as to be, in spite of Mr. Hunt's success, of exceedingly dangerous and questionable use, whether in play or in story. Shakspeare, who always foresaw as by instinct, the objections of his audience, seems to have composed Juliet's famous speech before taking the sleeping draught, by way of forestalling their distate to the possible consequences of the act; and this horror is so much aggravated in the Irish tale by the circumstance of the closed coffin, that no power of conception or skill in execution could insure an extensive or a durable popularity to a work founded on such a basis. Therefore, and as I think for that reason only, "**The Rivals**" will never command the same full applause as "**The Collegians,**" which, however little talked of at this moment, is sure to retain a permanent station in Irish literature. . . . (pp. 465-66)

> *Mary Russell Mitford, "Irish Authors," in her* Recollections of a Literary Life; or, Books, Places, and People, *Harper & Brothers, Publishers, 1852, pp. 457-73.**

THE DUBLIN UNIVERSITY MAGAZINE   (essay date 1855)

The leading (perhaps the only important) defect in *Gisippus* lies in the utter insignificance of the heroine, and the total want of female interest. The language is highly poetical, the versification fervid, harmonious, and expressive; there is abundance of highly-wrought passion naturally depicted, and enough of incident, while the construction of the play is essentially dramatic. But the action centres too exclusively in one character. Fulvius is a good second, but Sophronia is reduced almost to a nonentity, particularly in the latter portion of the drama. This is a mistake in a young author which practice would have rectified, had the opportunity been afforded. Admitting the errors and crudities of inexperience, it would be difficult in the whole range of the English drama to produce so good a play from any other writer at the same period of youth. It is much to be regretted, that the mind which was capable of conceiving and completing *Gisippus* at the unripe age of twenty, did not meet at once with fostering encouragement in the line to which it was at first so strongly turned. (p. 565)

> *J.W.C., "The Dramatic Writers of Ireland: Richard Lalor Sheil—John Banim—Gerald Griffin," in* The Dublin University Magazine, *Vol. XLVI, No. CCLXXV, November, 1855, pp. 548-65.**

THE IRISH QUARTERLY REVIEW   (essay date 1855)

Gerald Griffin, possessing an intellect not indeed so towering or versatile as that of [Thomas] Davis, but one which closely resembled his in the character of his love songs, and in the same deep and tender method of expressing his love for his country, has done a great deal for the literature of Ireland. . . . [Griffin's Poetry has not] obtained anything like the degree of public approval and warm admiration to which it appears so admirably entitled. . . . It does not, however, require any very extraordinary power of divination to foresee the time when these beautiful ballads will emerge from the present gloom which envelopes them, and shine like some "bright particular star," in their own exalted sphere: when the sweet pathos, angelic tenderness, native richness of fancy, and delicious harmony which belong to them, will have interwoven themselves thoroughly in our minds, with all those glorious scenes, and dear traditions which they describe, and beautify; and when their general perusal will have given another incentive to our countrymen to.

> Be up and doing,
> With a heart for any fate;
> Still achieving, still pursuing,
> Learn to labour and to wait.

Tender pathos is evidently the chief characteristic of Griffin's Poetry: it permeates everything his muse has attempted, like a gentle rivulet flowing through velvet meads. Here it is that he resembles Davis so closely, and indeed it would be difficult to determine upon whose brow to place the crown in this particular. (pp. 709-10)

Who does not know that sweet song, "Gilli ma chree," which literally teems with unbounded devotion, melting love and shadowed melancholy? The English language does not possess a more exquisite composition of the kind. . . . ["**The Fate of Cathleen**" possesses] many claims upon our attention, from its simple grace, and eloquent narrative.

"**The Orange and Green,**" perfect as a ballad, and highly indicative of all those fascinating attributes which belonged to Griffin, is still more precious for the invaluable sentiment which it discloses; it may not be completely utopian to suppose that much of that acerbity which at present unfortunately exists between the members of both persuasions, might be gradually softened down, and ultimately swept away altogether, were our gifted literary men of every creed, to join in a crusade against the existence of such a cruel system, by inculcating lessons of good will, and elucidating them by such pleasant illustrations as those [in **"The Orange and Green."** . . .]

It were quite unnecessary to dwell for any time upon the beauty of that inimitable composition, **"The Sister of Charity."** Its touching simplicity, and numberless graces are so well known to the Irish reader, that its fame, at least, has been raised, we should trust upon an imperishable basis. The same may be said of that harmonious and sadly beautiful ballad, **"The Bridal of Malahide." "Shanid Castle,"** . . . written in the Spenserian metre, contains many bold and striking passages . . . : it is graphically bold, and powerfully handled, and well repays perusal. (p. 713)

There are so many lovely snatches of verse in [*The Poetical Works of Gerald Griffin, Esq.*], that we resemble those genii-conducted mortals in the Oriental fables, wandering through subterranean palaces, whose glistening treasures are so splendid and multiform, that it is impossible for the eye to fix on any one, as a superior object of admiration, without regretting the selection it has made, on account of the outstanding magnificence of those which it subsequently beholds. All that the character of this undertaking will permit us to accomplish, would be to exhort our readers to see and judge for themselves, assuring them on our sacred reputation as sagacious critics, that we are directing their footsteps towards delicious gardens, where their eye will never tire, nor their lip ever parch with thirst, where sweets abound which will not cloy the appetite, and colors of brilliant beauty gladden the sight, without aching it with its tawdry lustre, or flaming hues which ape the name of splendor. (pp. 713-14)

The harmony and divine sweetness of [the Italian dramatist, Metastasio], are fully equalled by our Irish Poet, and the heavenly benignity which pervades the dramas of the one, is no less assuredly the prominent quality in the ballads and narrative poems of the other. In almost all the other essentials for good poetry, Griffin is not deficient. In clarity, vigour, strength, and affluence of images, dramatic skill, fancy, copious and appropriate diction, he can almost compete with Campbell, Southey, or Rogers: he is as good a moralist as Cowper, as sweet a melodist as Moore, and his language taken "from the pure well of English undefiled," is as chaste as that of Goldsmith. What a contrast does not his beautiful poetry afford to the pantheistic absurdities, and extravagant apostrophes of Bailey, the woful inanities of Browning, the unintelligible puerilities of [Tennyson's] Maud! Would that one like him still lived to retard by the dignity of his presence amongst us, the unprecedented appearance of everything in poetry, which typifies mawkish sentiment, and undisguised folly. (pp. 714-15)

N.J.G., "A Quartet of Irish Poets," in The Irish Quarterly Review, *Vol. V, No. XX, December, 1855, pp. 697-731.**

J. V. H[UNTINGDON]   (essay date 1859)

[*In this sympathetic account of Griffin's life and career, Huntingdon delineates the strengths and weaknesses of Griffin's works. He portrays Griffin as a talented "Catholic man of letters" who is primarily remarkable for his "faithful, true, and loving picture" of Ireland's peasantry. Huntingdon is one of the first critics to express the opinion, often echoed by later critics, that Griffin's longer works abound in digressions and lack the unity of his shorter tales; he cites this defect as one of the reasons Griffin "just fell short of being the Irish Walter Scott." Huntingdon also attributes Griffin's failure to attain Scott's eminence as a national*]

novelist to Ireland's turbulent political situation. He ventures that Griffin would have achieved greater success "had he possessed a better subject for his canvas, in a nation liberated, disenthralled and united."]

Gerald Griffin is a writer who just fell short of being the Irish Walter Scott. If we ask what prevented him from equalling Scott as a national novelist, we shall perhaps find that it was, in the first place, the early age at which he embarked in a literary career; next, the poverty which, even without his enthusiasm, rendered this premature labor inevitable; and lastly, an original defect of that simple and comprehensive intuition which, when improved by experience and practice, becomes the gift of *judgment,* and crowns all the other gifts of artistic genius. Gerald Griffin possessed every other native faculty of the artist in an eminent degree: he did not absolutely want the crowning faculty of judgment, but it was not equally developed with the others, and probably was originally weak in comparison with the rest. Or rather, his intuition was not simple, comprehensive, and penetrating: he saw things in detail, observed carefully, and described with grace, with humor, and with graphic fidelity; but he did not see the whole at once with the eye of a master, and consequently he was rarely able to present either scene or landscape, or incident, or entire story, with that admirable character of unity which distinguishes the master's work.

This want of unity, of wholeness, of simplicity, and consequently of grandeur, is so conspicuous in Gerald Griffin, that it forms the most characteristic feature of his longer and more serious works. In the shorter tales we do not perceive the same fault. The same vigor of intuition, the same comprehensive grasp of mind, and the same degree of practised skill, are not required in order to impart the requisite unity to a short and simple story as to a long and elaborate fiction. Hence it is in short and simple tales that Gerald's genius unfolds itself. He has a fine eye for the dramatic morality of common life: he seizes the vicious principle, the sinful act on which turns the catastrophe of a peasant career, and develops it in all its modifications of passion and guilt, in all its providential consequences, with a power that is perfectly his own. He could not have unfolded the drama of a rebellion like that in [Scott's] *Waverley,* nor painted the passions and crimes of great nobles, nor the mighty heart of kings. (pp. 342-43)

There is another kind of grandeur in fiction which arises from the adequate representation of deeply tragic passions and incidents. Here again our Gerald shows that his power is not of the highest and most commanding order. He shrinks from handling this style of incident and pitch of passion. Ireland surely is full enough of violence, and Gerald Griffin has introduced many a scene of blood, but where is there one that can be compared to the slaughter of Morris by the wife of Rob Roy [in Scott's *Rob Roy*] . . .? In the **Duke of Monmouth** the main incident was a real event of the history, and one of the most profoundly tragic, as it really occurred, that fiction ever seized upon: but Griffin was afraid of it—he has softened it so that it loses at once its probability and its pathos, without losing its disgusting horror. We allude . . . to the fate of the heroine, whom the infamous Col. Kirk robbed of her innocence as the price of her brother's life, and then gave her brother's lifeless corpse in fulfilment of his equivocal promise. Gerald Griffin introduces a marriage celebrated by a mad clergyman and denied by Kirk, which alike confuses the plot and emasculates the horror. Hardress Cregan, in the **Collegians,** is a very feeble villain: he is, and he is *not*, a murderer. Scott would have made him a murderer pure and simple, and would have conducted him all simply and purely to the gallows. This want of artistic nerve was an effect of Gerald's pure, pious, and gentle character, in part; but also, in part, it indicates the absence of a certain clear and vigorous intuition. (pp. 343-44)

Gerald Griffin is evidently a Catholic novelist; not because he was individually a Catholic; not that he introduced any controversy, open or tacit and implied, into his stories; but simply because he described with unaffected truth a Catholic society, a society eminently interpenetrated with the sentiment of the supernatural, a society instinct with the spirit of faith, that of Catholic Ireland. The humblest peasant who believes the Catholic faith, is a more poetical personage than a Protestant king. The only thing that renders Griffin's Irish stories less poetical, more vulgar and commonplace, is the introduction of so many Protestant characters, especially of Protestant heroes and heroines—a capital mistake, for such people can have little interest in fiction, except as criminals, and as such it is neither fair nor expedient to represent them. (p. 345)

Gerald Griffin has the remarkable merit . . . of having described Irish society with the utmost fidelity. Irish vice and Irish crime are represented in his pages with all their native colors; if, indeed, he can be justly complained of in this respect, it is that he has not done sufficient justice to Irish virtue, which is owing perhaps to the fact that he was so good and pure himself. . . . To the good man, goodness is not sufficiently remarkable to strike his fancy; and he passes over traits of heroic virtue as common things, because they are his own familiar actions. . . . [Nothing] can be less exaggerated, less partial, than Gerald Griffin's representation of the Irish peasant, or indeed of any class of Irishmen that he undertakes to set before us . . . : there are some classes that he avoids introducing; he has neither peer nor priest in his stories, and the latter omission is not a little remarkable. Probably he felt the subject to be too sacred for a purely literary treatment, and he was too sincere a man of letters to attempt any other. (p. 346)

In estimating the literary genius of Griffin, there is a difficulty arising from his age, and another from his very limited experience of life. It is almost always a pity when a genius rushes early into print. . . . No doubt Gerald gained in point of facility, but he lost in point of concentration. He drew too early and too heavily on his genius, which can no more be done with impunity, than on the bodily health. (p. 348)

[How] much did the **Munster Festivals** lack of being an Irish Waverley? By being three stories instead of one, in the first place. By a most remarkable defect of interior unity in each separate tale, in the second place. Of these three, **Suil Dhuv** is far the finest, and yet it contains some very striking anomalies in composition. There is one heroine for the first part of the story, and another for the conclusion. The latter heroine is not even introduced until the closing scene—the *dénouement*—is ripe, and all the other actors are in motion to accomplish it. . . . (p. 351)

Gerald Griffin's tales abound in digressions; some one is always ready to tell a story, and capitally told it is. These episodes are often the most charming part of the work, to the unity of which they do not contribute. Some personage, too, is sure to be poetical, which affords Gerald an opportunity of interweaving one of his own agreeable songs; but they are always his own, and he takes no trouble whatever to render them characteristic of their supposed authors. This want of dramatic consistency in his characters occurs in more serious instances, as for example in **Tracy's Ambition,** the admirable plot of which

is ruined by it. Dalton, the villain of the story, describes Irish scenery with the graphic and poetic vein of Griffin himself, and lets fall sentiments in regard to the country, which belong to a philosophic philanthropist. There is nothing in which the *coup d'oeil* [stroke] of the master in fiction is more unequivocally displayed than in the avoidance of this fatal impropriety. Gerald Griffin wrote rapidly, and seldom or never corrected his work. . . . [But] the question is not did he revise and correct his work or not, but did it need correction and revision. The best writers probably fall into the same faults in the heat of composition; but a sound judgment points them out afterwards, and a patient industry removes them. That Gerald Griffin wrote [**Munster Festivals**] in four months, and completed [**Suil Dhuv**] in two, is a poor lesson for young writers, unless they are told that in consequence the series is full of serious faults, and that the plot of the tale is disjointed, its *dénouement* unskilful, and that in fine all the genius lavished on it has failed to produce a masterpiece. (pp. 351-52)

But if these are the defects of Gerald Griffin as a writer, and we think we have handled them with sufficient plainness, what are his merits? The first and most conspicuous is his delineation of Irish character; next, ranks his insight into human nature; then, his vivid apprehension of the supernatural; and among minor excellencies, his vivacious dialogue, his high descriptive power; and lastly, the beauty and purity of his English style.

The prose style of Gerald Griffin is very unequal; in many parts of his stories, it is exceedingly careless; and yet, though it cannot be compared with the uniform elegance of Irving, it often possesses a clear and simple beauty which can only be matched by the author of the *Sketch-Book*. Some passages in the **Collegians** and the **Invasion** can hardly be surpassed in this respect; and where the style does not attain to absolute beauty, or even falls short of absolute correctness, it is never disfigured by fustian, is always simple and of a crystalline clearness. The directness and simplicity of his narrative is one of the traits in which he most resembles Scott. There is a quiet consciousness of power in this unpretending manner of telling a story, which at once lifts Gerald Griffin above the crowd of novel writers to the dignity of a classic.

His powers of description are, upon the whole, very great; although the school in which he learned to describe, his own haste, and perhaps some of the defects to which we have before alluded, cause him to overload his descriptions with minute detail. In description, he belongs to the real school, not to the epic. Frequently, the first few lines of a descriptive passage in his novels set before you the scene with great vividness and beauty; but as he proceeds, he adds circumstance after circumstance, the whole becomes confused, and you end by getting no distinct image whatever. The most charming *pictures* in his tales are of the Shannon scenery. The finest single scene is, perhaps, the description of an Irish waterfall in the **Rivals**. The pencil of Church could hardly have done it better. (pp. 352-53)

Scott describes admirably landscapes, interiors, and persons, even to their costume. How vividly Meg Merrilies and Dominie Sampson [in Scott's *Guy Manning*] are set before us! There are glimpses in the works of our author of a faculty, which might easily have been matured into a similar power: take, for instance, the old Irish witch in **Card Drawing,** and Danny Mann in the **Collegians**. The portrait of Lilly Byrne in **Suil Dhuv** proves Gerald's taste in female beauty to have been exquisitely refined: altogether, we have so far the native elements which go to the making of a great novelist. Add the vivacity of his dialogue, which he considered the test of a story, and which is a great proof of a distinct and vigorous conception of individual character. (p. 354)

Those minor stories of Gerald's in which his genius reveals itself so unequivocally, are mostly imbued with the supernatural. How should an Irish tale be at all national without this element? To be original, by the way, is always (for a poet or novelist) to be national. The English taste of the period when Griffin wrote, was all for reality. . . . Yet, although he was strictly a London man of letters, writing for the great British public . . . , the ideal, the supernatural, and the miraculously Providential, pervade his happiest and most popular stories. He differs in this respect most remarkably from Carleton, Lever, and most of his gifted rivals and compatriots; and that is why we are inclined to take him, agreeably (we think) to the general verdict, as the most truly Irish of them all. The *Rock of the Candle* (a beautiful Irish superstition, woven into a perfectly national and patriotic tale), *Owney and Owney Napeak, The Story Teller at Fault, The Swans of Lir, The Brown Man, Phadrig's Dilemma,* and other stories, expressly founded on supernatural legends, show this characteristic and national tendency of his mind. (pp. 354-55)

[The *Duke of Monmouth* is an English historical novel] of a period so comparatively recent that the introduction of any distinct supernatural element would have been impossible: yet Gerald Griffin contrives to produce all the effect of a ghost rising to warn the heroine of the treachery of Kirke, and vanishing with a movement of silent lips that refuse to tell their tale of horror! We see at once that her brother, though yet living, is marked for the grave, and that the sacrifice she is about to make for him will be fruitless. In the romances of Hawthorne, who has been driven by the necessities of a New England *locale,* and by the tendencies of his own weird inspiration, to employ similar expedients, we find nothing more admirable.

The peculiar power which is here indicated is intimately allied to that profound and instinctive knowledge of the secret springs of human character, so necessary to the dramatist and the novel writer. . . . [Griffin] is often deficient in art, but never untrue to nature; or, if this appear rather too antithetical, we may certainly say that his analysis of character is penetrating and true, but that the construction of his narrative is careless and unskilful. (pp. 355-56)

Has any one described the Irish peasant upon the whole so well as Gerald Griffin? We think not. And the proof is that no other writer has rendered Irish character in the lower orders so poetical. We often shrink with disgust from the delineations of Carleton, but Gerald Griffin's Irishmen are never vulgar. It certainly must arise in part from the religious faith of Griffin that he is so successful in this respect, even when he is setting before us some unmitigated rascal. (pp. 357-58)

It is not at all implied in this eulogium of Gerald Griffin, that he has sacrificed truth to poetry in describing his countrymen. On the contrary, he has been fearfully candid. In *Tracy's Ambition* we have an Irishman of the middle class, more consistently mean than Thackeray ever painted, under the inspiration of his malice. Certainly the Irish witnesses in the *Collegians* are not flattered, yet it is impossible to be otherwise than fascinated, as well as amused, by their ingenious insincerity, and its perfect triumph over all the resources of the examining magistrate. Such wicked wretches as Suil Dhuv and his white-haired partner in crime—the palsied villain Rody, the cowardly

murderer [in *The Aylmers of Bally-Aylmer*], Fitz Maurice, Danny Mann, and his meaner master, and Black Yamon of the *Hand and Word,* are pretty specimens of Irish human nature as an enemy would wish to portray. Heaven save us from falling into the hands of such villains, outside of a book! (p. 358)

There is indeed less of sham sentimentality in the works of Gerald Griffin than in those of almost any other Irish novelist. Hence his pathos is genuine pathos, and when he gives the people credit for virtue you can heartily believe him. There is in this bold style of treatment a generous confidence in the strength of the Irish cause, which its advocates too often seem to lack. Gerald Griffin's nationality implied genuine sympathy for his countrymen, a deep-seated respect and veneration for his native land—its faith, its history, its essential character, and its holy and patriotic traditions. He had the noble courage, therefore, to paint Ireland as she is; and the fidelity of the portrait, while it makes his fame as an artist, possesses, in the eyes of the world, that beauty and dignity which must always attach to the true and unaffected picture of a Catholic people. Indeed, first of all in his hands, the Irish dialect of the English language and the peculiarities of Irish provincialism in accent, character, and mental traits become, like those of Scotland in the hands of Scott and Burns, invested with a halo of poetry. This is one of the attributes of poetry and romantic fiction, which show us how much every historic nation—every nation which aspires to respect itself and to love and cherish its own peculiarities—owes to its men of literary genius.

The novel of *The Invasion,* so far as we know, is the only Irish historical novel of the highest class ever attempted: it is admirably conceived, and though upon the whole the execution must be regarded as a failure, it gives us a higher idea of the author's latent powers than any other of his works, not excepting *Suil Dhuv* and *The Collegians.* (pp. 360-61)

Several of [Griffin's] songs possess that universal popularity which is the best test of excellence. . . . As a song-writer he belongs to the school of Moore, or perhaps we might say to the Irish school of which Moore is the best representative. Few have known so well how to interweave Irish words in English songs, with a pathetic effect, as in—

> The mie-na-mallah now is past,
> O wirra-sthru! O wirra-sthru!
> And I must leave my home at last,
> O wirra-sthru! O wirra sthru!
> I look into my father's eyes,
> I hear my mother's parting sighs,—
> Ah! fool to pine for other ties—
> O wirra-sthru! O wirra-sthru!

Or in **"My Mary of the curling hair,"** to the air "Shule a-gra," which words, and some more which we don't understand a syllable of, are mingled in very musically, in one of the sweetest love-songs poet ever penned. (p. 365)

["**Matt Hyland**"] is a ballad of very sweet and flowing versification, something diluted perhaps, the fruit hidden in that leafy luxuriance of words which characterizes Irish poetry. As a specimen of what Wordsworth calls "that dear production of our days, the metrical novel," it does great credit to Gerald Griffin. . . . *Gysippus* is a good acting play: it does not possess any remarkable poetic beauties, but its construction must be good, or it would not stand the test of performance. The main action is improbable, in attributing to Pagans a power of self-abnegation which flourishes only on soil fertilized with the blood of the Cross. Interior consistency is further violated by representing Gysippus, after a sacrifice which a Christian only could have made, as feeling all the desolation of a heathen. One must remember, in reading the play, that the author was only nineteen when he composed it. As a proof of his native capacity it is striking; as a work to be judged on its intrinsic merits, it cannot claim a very high rank. The fame of Griffin must rest ultimately on the *Collegians,* on *The Invasion,* which reveals even higher qualities, on the beautiful tales of Irish legendary and preternatural lore, in which he surpasses all his countrymen, and on a few of his songs—gems, as they doubtless are, of lyric grace and feeling. (p. 366)

We see in [Gerald Griffin] a Catholic man of letters, abounding in talent, adorned with singular and precocious gifts of genius, of irreproachable morals, of great industry, and who had the rare felicity of a new and unexplored field for his imagination in the history and the social features of his country. But that country possessed no distinct national organization apart from religion; her independence, her autonomy, she had either never enjoyed or had lost: it was a Catholic people with a Protestant government. Yet this young Irishman succeeded in a literary career, not by virtue of any support he derived from his own country, but in the great British world of letters, where he challenged comparison with such a name as Walter Scott. He succeeded without betraying either his faith or his race. He would have succeeded one can hardly guess how much better, had Ireland been a free and organized nation in the same sense as Scotland is. The success that he had was due to the faithful, true, and loving picture which he drew of a living but oppressed, disunited, and unorganized Catholic people; it would have been greater had he possessed a better subject for his canvas, in a nation liberated, disenthralled and united, and could he have commanded a more solid position than that of a London literary hack. It was the difficulties and necessities of this position which, in our point of view, ultimately drove him from literature; when, being a Catholic, he became, not a suicide or a misanthrope, but a Religious and (if you please) almost a saint. From the contemplation of such a career, we could not but turn thoughtfully to our own beloved country, and to the position and duties of its Catholic men of letters, or those who aspire to be such; and we think that the comparison is not at all discouraging. (pp. 371-72)

> *J. V. H[untingdon], in a review of "The Complete Works of Gerald Griffin," in* Brownson's Quarterly Review, *n.s. Vol. IV, No. III, July, 1859, pp. 342-72.*

THE CHRISTIAN EXAMINER   (essay date 1865)

Griffin was certainly a man of genius; a man having a certain inborn aptitude, which is not the result of education and industry. . . . [When] Griffin gave up literature, he was still young, so that Griffin was always a young author; and yet we might say that he was always a ripe one. From the first, he displayed a certain masculine vigor altogether different from the feebleness which sometimes characterizes the compositions of young writers, who afterwards become remarkable for their strength. . . . He had an inventive and bold imagination: to this his power and variety in the creation of character bear witness. He had great fulness of sensibility and fancy, as we observe in the picturesqueness of his style, and in his wealth of imagery. He delighted in outward nature, and is a fine describer of it; but, like Sir Walter Scott, he never describes for the sake of description, but always in connection with human interest and incident. He excels in the pathetic: but it

is in passion that he has most power; strong natural passion, and such as it is in those individuals in whom it is strongest and most natural,—individuals in the middle and lower ranks of life, especially in the middle and lower ranks of Irish life. It was in these ranks and in Irish life that Griffin found the spirit and the substance of his characters. He was a rapid and productive writer, and as much at home in criticising as in creating. He passionately loved music, and by instinct, taste, and knowledge, was an excellent critic of it, as he was also of literature. His genius, too, was of the most refined moral purity, without sermonizing or cant; and when we reflect that guilt and sin and passion, low characters, vulgar life, and broad humor, are so constantly the subjects with which it is concerned, this purity is no less remarkable than it is admirable. (pp. 357-58)

[Griffin's poems] are characterized by sweetness, feeling, and fancy. We regard Griffin's lyrics as his best poems, and his simple songs as his best lyrics. We think that, had he chosen to write *"Songs of Ireland"* and *"Songs for Ireland,"* though he might never have attained the indescribable refinement of Moore, his songs would have had in them more music of the heart, and more homely nationality. (p. 358)

As a poem, [**"Gisippus"**] has been much admired; and it deserves admiration. We admire it much ourselves for its generous and elevated sentiments, its dramatic style, with its absence of long and formal speeches, with its dialogue, sharp, natural, and rapid. We admire many of the situations and incidents as striking and pathetic; still, as a whole, we do not think that it reaches those depths and mysteries of life and passion, which it is the province of great tragedy to fathom and reveal. But, then, it is the tragedy of a boy; and who can tell what the boy might have become, had he devoted his manhood to compositions for the stage? As the fact stands, we have Gerald Griffin's fullest power in his prose fictions.

Gerald Griffin is a delightful story-teller. The merest matters of fact and the wildest legends are alike at his command; and he tells with the same ease and the same fascinating interest a story of ghosts, fairies, witchcraft, or a story of guilt, grief, passion. His stories are of great variety; but they are all characteristically Irish; and Ireland has no need to be ashamed of them. The *spirit* of them is national; but the genius in them is individual: Gerald Griffin's own mark is on them. Nor are they mere copies—as Crofton Croker's are—of fireside stories which the people used to tell among themselves. . . . (pp. 361-62)

As a dramatic tale of passion, we hardly know another which so quickly awakens interest, and which so intensely holds it to the end [as **"The Collegians"**]. This absorbing interest even the mechanical joinery of a playwright has not been able to weaken, in an adaptation of the story for the stage. The story has unity, action, movement; movement that like fate goes onward from the cheerful opening to the tragic close. The characters are numerous; and each, high or low, serious or comic, is a distinct individual. Hardress Cregan is very powerfully conceived, and the conception is carried out with consistency and force. High genius was required to make a man like Hardress Cregan, so inconsistent, preserve the unity of his character in the most contradictory of his inconsistencies. It was an extraordinary achievement to bring together in one individual qualities so opposite, and yet to make the union accordant with the facts of life and nature. . . . In this powerfully conceived character we see the havoc which passion, severed from the divine part of humanity, and moved by the sensual self, can work in the whole moral nature of an individual, and what misery and ruin it can bring on all that have any intimate relations with him. The utter wretchedness of Hardress Cregan's mind, as he approaches the crisis of his fate; his fitful, violent changes of mood and temper, amounting almost to paroxysms, especially in his later interviews with his mother and Ann Chute,—show how well the author, both in action and suffering, knew the elements of tragedy that lie within the human heart.

Danny Mann, the athletic hump-backed servant, is as tragic a character as his master, and as powerfully drawn. The author is true to nature and art also in his female characters. Ann Chute is a very brilliant creature; but Eily O'Connor rises into the very poetry of ideal girlhood: a sweeter, a more beautiful, a more lovable feminine character, rendered imperfect by the imprudence of the heart, it never entered into the imagination of the poet to conceive. This character, and many others in the story, give evidence that the author was as able a master of the affections as of the passions. The Daly Family, both in their joys and sorrows, might be placed beside the ''Primrose Family'' [in Oliver Goldsmith's ''The Vicar of Wakefield'']. They give occasion to very touching pictures of domestic life. The Cregan Family, however, consists of characters that are more individual, more striking, and more original. The comic characters are all very amusing in their humor, and very Irish. (pp. 365-66)

No one can fail to admire the skill by which so extraordinary a variety of materials as there is in [''The Collegians''] is fused into a complete whole, and how every scene, character, and description, incident, falls necessarily into the drama of the story,—falls into it in the right time and place, and contributes each a needful share to the plot and to the catastrophe.

Still we might make objections. . . . We might adduce instances of melodramatic exaggeration; but allowance must be made for Gerald Griffin's youth. We think that Ann Chute's saying to her lover a few days before she is to be married to him, ''What a dreadful death hanging must be!'' is an instance of this kind. Though ignorant that Hardress, at the moment, was in mortal fear of such a death, the saying is coarse from a lady, and rather weakens the force of tragic impression. . . . We object to the catastrophe. We cannot agree that Hardress should get off with transportation, and respectably die of consumption at the end of the passage, while Danny Mann, the less guilty culprit, is left for the gallows. . . . John Scanlan was hanged in fact, and so should his representative, Hardress Cregan, have been hanged in fiction: then poetical justice and practical justice would have corresponded. The real execution, moreover, of Scanlan, was attended with strange and melancholy circumstances, that made it solemnly dramatic; besides, the discrepancy between the fiction and the fact weakens the catastrophe and injures the illusion. (p. 367)

[We commend] the moral spirit of Gerald Griffin's writings. Our commendation is deserved, and with pleasure we declare it. How often has one to lament that he is compelled to admire grand intellectual power, which only lowers or disheartens him, darkens his spirit, or constrains his sympathies! A sure test, it has been often said, as to the good influence of a writer, is, that, when we lay aside his book, we feel better in ourselves, and think better of others: this test, we believe, Gerald Griffin can safely stand. (p. 368)

''Gerald Griffin,'' in The Christian Examiner n.s. Vol. XVI, No. III, Vol. LXXVII, May, 1865, pp. 346-68.

[J. G. McGEE] (essay date 1870)

[In his *Invasion, Duke of Monmouth,* and some minor stories, Griffin] travelled out of his favorite province with some degree of success. But even in his wanderings in Wicklow, Taunton dene, and the wilds of Northumbria, we are constantly catching glimpses of the Shannon and Killarney. The reason of this is obvious. He aimed to be a strict and minute copyist of nature; and nature to him was bounded by the lovely scenery of Munster and the people with whom he had been in daily intercourse for almost the whole of his short life. His power of observation, thus limited, became intensified, and what he lost in breadth of view and amplitude of knowledge, he gained in the distinctness and fidelity of his pictures. . . . For Gerald Griffin we may not, perhaps, claim the universality of those great Masters [Miguel de Cervantes Saavedra, Oliver Goldsmith, Honoré de Balzac, and Charles Dickens]; but in purity of expression, truthfulness to nature, and delicacy of moral perception he is the equal of any of them.

There are some persons conversant with Irish character who maintain that its essential element is neither gayety nor combativeness, but melancholy, and sustain their apparently singular theory by reference to the national music and poetry. Griffin's writings would afford an additional argument in favor of this position. His genius was decidedly tragic, his muse sad and retrospective. His pauses to give us a glimpse of fireside enjoyment appear to be more as tributes to old home memories, than as arising from any natural desire to linger over the recollections of such tranquil scenes; and his snatches of humor and merriment seem thrown in artistically, not so much to relieve the sombre shading of his picture as to give its most prominent figures greater depth and boldness. He also labored under the disadvantage of all tragic minds; for, though he never can be said to have ignored the ''eternal fitness of things'' in rewarding the good and punishing the wicked, we close many of his volumes with a feeling more akin to sorrow than rejoicing, and while admitting the righteousness of his judgments, we sigh to think how God's best gifts to man may be turned to his own destruction. . . . [Griffin's] moral heroes are good enough in their way, but their virtues are of too negative a character. Kyrle Daly, in the *Collegians,* and young Kingsly, in the *Duke of Monmouth,* have all the qualities we could desire in a friend or brother; but while we honor and respect them, a something akin to sympathy is clandestinely stealing out to the proud and wilful Hardress Cregan [in the *Collegians*], and even to the cool malignity of that unparalleled scoundrel, Colonel Kirke [in the *Duke of Monmouth*]. O'Haedha, in the *Invasion,* is an exception. He is *sui generis* [unique] in Griffin's pantheon, being not only a man of pure morality and well up in the lore of his times, but he is also a chieftain governing wisely and firmly, a man of war as well as of love and peace, strong in his affections and hatreds, living, moving, and breathing like one who has a subtle brain, warm blood, and a powerful arm to enforce his authority. He is decidedly not only Griffin's grandest conception, but will stand in favorable comparison with any we can recall in historical romance.

The *Collegians* is Gerald Griffin's best known and most popular novel; and, when we consider the early age of the author at the time it was written, and the circumstances amid which it was composed, we are equally surprised at his knowledge of the springs of human action, and at the excellences of the book, both as regards correctness of style and completeness of plot. Though the working of some of the strongest passions of our nature is portrayed in it—love, hatred, revenge, ambition—

there is nothing about them sensational or melodramatic; and though many different characters are introduced, and incidents necessarily occur in a short space of time, there is nothing hurried or disjointed, one character acting upon another and each event following and hinging on the one preceding so gracefully and naturally that the reader is borne along on an unbroken current, as it were, from cause to effect till he reaches the final catastrophe. (pp. 668-69)

The moral of the book, however, is its greatest merit. The character of Hardress Cregan is inimitably drawn. Young, gifted both in person and mind, with a disposition naturally inclined to good, but warped and misled by a fond, proud, worldly mother, and the example of a dissolute father and his associates; early left to his own guidance and the indulgence of his whims and fancies, he descends from the high position in which we find him at the opening chapter, through all the stages of crime— parental disobedience, ingratitude, deceit, debauchery, and finally murder. Through each step in guilt we can trace the cause of his ruin—moral cowardice, false pride, absence of self-control, alternating or uniting, but always with disastrous effect, until in the culminating scene, in which, torn by remorse and conscious guilt, he leaves his native shores a condemned felon and dies at sea, we feel that the punishment, no matter how severe, is but in strict accordance with our highest sense of retributive justice. Nor are the almost equally, though perhaps unconsciously, guilty parents forgotten. Like a just judge, Griffin not only punishes the actual perpetrator of crime, but metes out penalties to those whose duty it is to correct the excesses of youth, restrain their passions, and lead them by precept and example to the practice as well as the knowledge of good, and who neglect the sacred trust. (p. 670)

[We commend] the treatment of the humbler personages introduced [in the *Collegians*], equally free as they are from that stilted phraseology and broad caricature which too often disgrace Irish novels and so-called Irish plays. Poor Eily O'Connor, in all her simple innocence and ignorance of the world, is a beautiful creation. . . .

Altogether different in design and scope is the *Invasion,* a historical novel intended to describe the institutions, manners, and ways of life of the ancient Irish, and it is much to be regretted that it is so little read by the descendants of that peculiar people, especially by those who turn aside from the difficulties of nomenclature presented by the actual history of Ireland. With the same motive that actuated Scott to present the otherwise unattractive and obscure facts of the early history of Britain in the fascinating garb of romance, our author, always deeply imbued with love of country and reverence for the past, sought in this book to give a complete picture of the public, social, and religious life of his ancestors as it was known or supposed to exist in the eighth century. (p. 673)

[The] limited knowledge of the epoch which he proposed to illustrate, while it in some degree unfortunately lessens the authority of the novel in an antiquarian point of view, does not impair its harmony of design, or weaken the moral and intellectual beauty of its entire composition. . . . (p. 674)

[In the *Invasion*] we find grouped together, gracefully and artistically, the leading historical features of the period, the old superstitions and the beneficent fruits of the new faith, the faults and follies, virtues and graces of the christianized Celts, contrasted with the physical prowess and ferocious temperament of the hordes who were so soon to deluge with blood,

not only Erin, but the adjacent isles and the greater part of the coasts of Europe. (p. 675)

The *Duke of Monmouth* is also a historical novel, but more modern in its character and incidents. . . . The style is faultless, the prominent actors mostly taken from real life, though few are truthfully drawn. Still, we cannot but regret for the sake of poetical justice that Griffin chose this subject for a novel, from the fact that the truth of history compelled him to let the notorious Kirke, who figures so largely in his pages, go unwhipped of justice. . . .

[Notwithstanding this fault], the book is one that merits attention both as being the production of the author's more mature years and as furnishing us an insight into the modes of life, manner of living, and unreasonable preconceptions of politics and religion of the humbler classes of England at the period immediately preceding the downfall of the house of Stuart. (p. 676)

[There] is a feature in its composition which by some readers may be considered a grave defect. The interest which surrounds the heroine, Aquila Fullarton, from the very beginning of the tale deepens by degrees until it becomes painfully intense, and the scene between her and Kirke, wherein that monster perpetrates one of the greatest crimes known to humanity, and she in consequence loses her reason, though founded on well-authenticated facts, and described with all the delicacy of diction possible, is almost too horrible to receive mention. The necessarily gloomy pages of the story are occasionally enlivened by the introduction of two Irish characters—brothers— Morty and Shamus Delaney. . . . (p. 677)

Of Griffin's minor works . . . , the *Rivals, Barber of Bantry,* and *Shuil Dhuv* are decidedly the most entertaining. The latter particularly, though irregular in composition, is a story evincing great dramatic power and knowledge of the human heart. The dark-eyed hero, if such he may be called, who gives the title to the tale, stands out before us in all the enormity of his guilt as distinctly as if he had been an actual acquaintance, and we venture to say that there are few who have read the book but have experienced that feeling. In this story, also, Griffin departs from his usual custom of avoiding personal description of his female characters, and gives us an elaborate picture of his heroine, which, whether it be drawn from life or the creation of his own imagination, calls up before us an image of surpassing loveliness.

Griffin's other tales, such as the *Half-Sir, Card-Drawing,* and *Tracey's Ambition,* have all much merit, and though not so prolonged as those we have mentioned, exhibit in a greater or lesser degree the skilful hand and rich imagination of the author. The *Christian Physiologist,* comprising a series of beautiful tales intended to illustrate the use and abuse of the senses, is worthy a place near the writings of that friend of childhood, Canon Schmidt.

As a poet, Griffin is remarkable for the beauty of his delineations of natural scenery, his elevation of sentiment and purity of conception. His lyrics remind us of Moore, and are scarcely inferior to some of the best of that immortal bard's in feeling and choiceness of metaphor; but being somewhat deficient in rhythm, they have never found much favor in the drawing or concert-room, **"A Place in thy Memory, Dearest," "My Mary of the Curling Hair,"** and one or two others excepted. (p. 678)

We are not aware that [Griffin] ever attempted an epic or anything more extended than the beautiful ballad of **"Matt Hy-**

land'' . . . ; nor do we think his ambition ever soared to higher flights than songs and short descriptive poems. The most meritorious of these, or, at least, the one which has obtained the greatest popularity, is the **"Sister of Charity,"** written on the occasion of a dear friend becoming a religious; and, though several gifted pens have been employed on the same subject, we know of none who has embodied so true an appreciation of the self-denial and entire devotion which mark that order—the boast and glory of all womanhood. Several of his best pieces, indeed, are written in the same devotional spirit. . . .

[Enough] dramatic ability is displayed in [*Gisippus*] to make us regret that Griffin abandoned writing for the stage so early in life. We are inclined to imagine that a young man, scarcely twenty years of age, who was capable of managing so successfully a subject that required the highest powers of Boccaccio, could in his maturer years have effected even greater things. However, we must console ourselves with the reflection that what has been lost to the drama, we have gained in [Griffin's novels, short stories, and poems]; and as the drama is necessarily limited to the few, the world is also the gainer by the change. (p. 679)

[*J. G. McGee*], *"The Works of Gerald Griffin," in* Catholic World, *Vol. 11, No. 65, August, 1870, pp. 667-79.*

MRS. OLIPHANT   (essay date 1886)

[*Oliphant was a Scottish novelist, biographer, and critic of the nineteenth century who is chiefly remembered for her stories of Scottish life and her contributions to* Blackwood's Edinburgh Magazine. *In this appreciative essay, Oliphant hails Griffin as one of Ireland's most important nationalistic novelists. In addition, she maintains that Griffin's descriptions of the Irish peasantry and gentry in* The Collegians *are more "trenchant" and "individual" than those in the novels of Maria Edgeworth. Oliphant concludes by expressing surprise that* The Collegians, *which was written during a period of political upheaval in Ireland, is characterized by a tone of "easy lightheartedness" rather than bitterness.*]

The names of John Banim, Gerald Griffin, William Carleton, and Thomas Crofton Croker cannot, any of them, be placed in the first rank—but their works were more national, more worthy of being considered as elucidations of the life of their country and the character of their race than those of any previous writers, with the exception of Miss Edgeworth. . . . Gerald Griffin is perhaps the most noticeable of this band. . . . [The] story is the least satisfactory part of [*The Collegians*], and the sketches of life and character to be met with in the book are infinitely more worth the reader's while than the melodramatic fate of Eily O'Connor, and the despair and misery of her lover. Not even Miss Edgeworth's account of the successive squires of *Castle Rackrent* sets forth the wild groups of Irish gentry with so trenchant a touch as that with which Griffin represents his Cregans and Creaghs in their noisy carouses: and his peasants of all descriptions are full of humour and life—more individual and displaying a more intimate knowledge than those of Miss Edgeworth. . . . We naturally look in a work written before the repeal of the Catholic disabilities for some deep rankling of injured feeling, but the reader will find no trace of it in *The Collegians*. Griffin was a pious Catholic, and ended his life in a religious brotherhood; his sympathies were entirely with his race: but the picture he puts before us bears little trace either of a persecuted faith or an oppressed nationality. The tragic elements of his story are drawn,

as they might have been in a tale of the Scottish Highlands, from the exaggerated and unscrupulous devotion of a faithful servant to what in his warped and gloomy mind he thinks the interests of his master; and while we have a fine example of the astute and triumphant policy of a couple of the rudest peasants in baffling the united powers of magistrate and counsellors, it is in behalf of no political criminal, nor is any feud between landlord and tenant so much as hinted at. A good deal of this is no doubt due to the mind and tendencies of the writer and his pure and gentle genius—but something too must belong to the atmosphere of the time. . . . [Griffin] shows us no gloom upon the skies, no burning at the heart of his country. As we walk with him along the mountain paths every one we meet has a cheerful greeting, a genial jest, a song upon his lips—the country is gay, brighter than our fat English levels, the long-winded peasant-stories are full of a humorous contemplation both of earth and heaven. It is hard to realise that the easy lightheartedness which we meet with everywhere is the atmosphere of a country which not very long before had been rent by armed rebellion, and still more recently convulsed by a political struggle in which every element of national bitterness might have been expected to manifest itself. We have few materials for determining what is the poet's, the romancer's account of the country now—but if the daily records be trustworthy the picture would be a very different one in our own day. (pp. 226-27)

Mrs. Oliphant, "Literature in Ireland," in her The Literary History of England in the End of the Eighteenth and Beginning of the Nineteenth Century, Vol. III, *Macmillan and Co., 1886, pp. 209-35.**

W. B. YEATS   (essay date 1889)

[*Yeats was an Irish poet, playwright, essayist, and autobiographer of the late nineteenth and early twentieth centuries. Although he wrote distinguished works in several genres, it is as a poet that Yeats takes his place as a major figure in English literature. As a critic, he judged the works of others according to his own poetic values of sincerity, passion, and vital imagination. Yeats's introduction to* Representative Irish Tales, *from which the following is drawn, was first written in 1899. In Griffin's works, Yeats discerns the beginnings of an Irish middle-class literature. He dismisses the majority of Griffin's short stories as "filmy and bloodless" but considers a few of his tales to be "perfect." In a later essay in* The Bookman *in October, 1895, Yeats included* The Collegians *in his "List of Best Irish Books."*]

In Gerald Griffin, the most finished storyteller among Irish novelists, . . . I think I notice a new accent—not quite clear enough to be wholly distinct; the accent of people who have not the recklessness of the landowning class, nor the violent passions of the peasantry, nor the good frankness of either. The accent of those middle-class people who find Carleton rough and John Banim coarse, who when they write stories cloak all unpleasant matters, and moralise with ease, and have yet a sense of order and comeliness that may sometime give Ireland a new literature. Many things are at work to help them: the papers, read by the Irish at home and elsewhere, are in their hands. They are closer to the peasant than to the gentry, for they take all things Irish with conscience, with seriousness. Their main hindrances are a limited and diluted piety, a dread of nature and her abundance, a distrust of unsophisticated life. But for these, Griffin would never have turned aside from his art and left it for the monastery; nor would he have busied himself with anything so filmy and bloodless as the greater portion of his short stories. As it is, he has written a few perfect tales. (p. 31)

W. B. Yeats, in an introduction to his Representative Irish Tales, *edited by W. B. Yeats, Humanities Press, Inc., 1979, pp. 25-32.*

HORATIO SHEAFE KRANS (essay date 1903)

The Collegians, upon which alone [Gerald Griffin's] fame as a novelist now rests, represents all his gifts and graces. . . . No other novel has made so complete a synthesis of Irish society. No other novel has presented faithfully and effectively so many phases of Irish life. It presents life in the cabin; the well-ordered, prudent, busy, middle-class life (so seldom represented in Irish novels) of the prosperous middleman Daly and his happy family; and the life of the "big house" at Castle Chute. In fact most phases of Irish life, excepting the political and the highest social life, are introduced. And the typical happenings that make up the daily round are woven into the story—holiday merrymakings, marriages, births and deaths, wakes and funerals, hunts and races, dining, dancing, drinking, and duelling. The book has a wide range of characters to correspond with the broad pictures of Irish life. There are humble characters like the gentle heroine Eily, and at the other remove Fighting Poll Naughten—"a terrible 'oman she was, comin' again' a man with her stockin' off, an' a stone in the foot of it;" or characters like the genial Lowry Looby, and, contrasting with him, the dangerous humpback Danny Mann. There is the same variety among the characters of a higher social scale, at the one extreme Father Edward, the kind, charitable parish priest, and at the other groups of tumultuous, uproarious country gentlemen like Fireball Craigh, the notorious duellist, former Pinkindindie, and member of the Hell-Fire Club.

The Collegians is not merely the most comprehensive picture of Irish life. There is more art in the structure of the story than there is in any other [Irish novel]. . . . (pp. 304-05)

This story is enacted before an elaborate and detailed background, but neither the background, the high coloring of particular scenes, the variety of incidents, nor the crowd of characters is permitted to withdraw the attention from the leading persons, or to obscure the main movement of the story. The talent that made the author's *Gisippus* a success upon the London stage is felt all through the narrative. The scene in which the company of hunters, of whom the hero is one, comes upon the body of the murdered Eily, is a startling dramatic climax, and is only one of a number of such striking moments. Minor climaxes all through make the narrative admirably lively, and keep the interest tense. It was this dramatic quality in the novel that led to its dramatization in the popular play of [Dion Boucicault's] *The Colleen Bawn.* . . . (pp. 306-07)

[*The Collegians*] is enriched, too, by minor contributions in the author's best vein. There are bits of manners-painting done with delicacy or spirit as the case requires; there are love-scenes between arch maids and rustic gallants, done with the lightest touch and in the brightest, gayest moods; there are drinking-bouts and fights; there are tales of tricksy goblins and of ghosts, half comic, half horrible; and folk-tales in which the wanton Celtic fancy is ever flying off into new and delightfully unexpected vagaries and caprices.

The Collegians seems less commendable on the score of depth and truth of characterizaton, than in point of comprehensiveness of subject, art in construction, and excellence in the detail work of the composition. The minor characters live, but are not known intimately. Of the characters who play important rôles, all are lay-figures with the exception of the hero, Hardress Cregan, the humpback Danny, and Eily the heroine.

Hardress Cregan has not the elevation of character that belongs to the tragic hero. He has not the general nobility, the strong tides of feeling that make disaster tragically impressive. The true tragic note is not within the compass of the hero, and the novel on the whole is pathetic or melodramatic, not tragic. Hardress's passionate whim for Eily, blown away by the first adverse wind, is a slight thing. The love for Anne Chute that displaces his love for Eily is a fevered melodramatic emotion scarcely worth the name of passion, more smoke than flame for all the sound and fury with which it is voiced. And, what is quite fatal to the pretensions of a tragic hero, Hardress earns and gets the hearty contempt of the reader, which changes to something more like loathing when he breaks the heart of his bride with the brutal confession that he hates her and all her endearments, and when he hints to his servant the murderous plot against her life. So far as Hardress is concerned, the reader will agree with the author's remark upon his hero, made in a letter to his brother—"he deserves hanging as richly as any young man from this to himself."

If the hero of *The Collegians* is melodramatic and stagey, the character of Eily is presented with a simple truth of portraiture untouched by such faults. The scenes in the lonely cabin where Eily went after sacrificing her peace and the peace of her father's old age to her love for Hardress, and where she was to remain in hiding until he should be ready to claim her as his wife before the world, are scenes of the deepest and most appealing pathos. Eily, in her weakness and dependence, despite the passive courage to endure, is not of the heroic fibre that awakens admiration. But when, after Hardress's cruel confession that his love for her is dead and that he hates the ties that bind him, she stands like a helpless thing at bay, her sad case draws deep upon the pity and sympathy of the reader. That scene is a stroke of genius memorable as a poignantly felt and faithfully rendered situation.

Danny Mann, the humpback, led, by the faithful retainer's unquestioning devotion, to an atrocious crime, is also a real creation. The creative touch is felt in scenes like that where Danny, denounced as a villain by his master for the perpetration of the crime to which he was incited by him, throws off his doglike devotion, turns like a wolf upon his ungrateful master, and at the price of his own life gives him over to the mercy of the law.

The Collegians is undoubtedly the best Irish novel in its comprehensiveness and its structure, and in the minor embellishments carefully subordinated to the main theme; but the hero Hardress has the noise, the rant, and all the limitations of the melodramatic type of character. In point of characterization, this novel, representing Griffin at his best, cannot compare with the nobility, elevation, and full-pulsed humanity of Carleton's creations. (pp. 307-10)

Horatio Sheafe Krans, "Literary Estimate," in his Irish Life in Irish Fiction, *Columbia University Press, 1903, pp. 270-326.*

PADRAIC COLUM (essay date 1918)

[*An Irishman who contributed to the literature of the twentieth century as a poet, dramatist, editor, and critic, Colum is remem-*

bered for his efforts to champion the varied heritage of Irish literature. The following excerpt is drawn from Colum's introduction to The Collegians. *Subsequent critics such as Donald Davie and Thomas Flanagan (1953, 1959) share Colum's admiration for Griffin's masterly depiction of Irish society in* The Collegians, *while others, including John Cronin and Robert Davis (1978, 1980), echo Colum's opinion that the novel marks the climax of Griffin's creative development. Colum is one of the first twentieth-century critics to discuss Griffin's propensity for strong dramatic scenes. His contention that Griffin "possibly injured* The Collegians *by thinking of some of its scenes as being rendered by an actual performer" is disputed by Cronin.*]

In "**The Collegians**" love and murder may be treated conventionally, but the episodes depending upon these themes are made vivid, racy, and entertaining. We move through Munster and are shown Munster life and character in such variety that we feel for a while that the story has the spaciousness of the old national novels of England and Spain. Lowry Looby goes with his master "at a sling trot," telling stories and singing snatches of songs, and Myles-na-Coppaleen, in the drawing-room of the castle, shows the mountaineer's quickness of mind; Mihil O'Connor rides wildly with his faction, and the Munster gentlemen drink deep and come to the duel; the sinister Danny Mann is put beside the grotesque Lowry Looby and his evil idiom mixes with the other's mellow discourse; manners that have lapsed are mingled with manners that are familiar, and we hear of a lady riding to a gentleman's door with a whip in one hand and a brace of duelling pistols in the other; we listen to the old fox-hunter hillooing on his death-bed and watch the gentlemen exchanging shots in the dining-room; the peasantry live as they lived before the famine, poor, rack-rented, but merry-hearted and delighting in music and story, and the gentry gallop towards bankruptcy. "**The Collegians**" is the best of the Irish romantic novels. (p. ix)

Gerald Griffin liked to talk about his popular novel. He told his brother he wrote every passage as if it belonged to an actual drama. Certainly it has scenes that are vividly dramatic; one remembers the hunchback condemning his master while the firelight reddens the walls of the place where he is confined. . . . But [Griffin] possibly injured "**The Collegians**" by thinking of some of its scenes as being rendered by an actual performer. "What a deal I would give," he said, "to see Edmund Kean in that scene of Hardress Cregan, at the party, just before his arrest, while he is endeavouring to do politeness to the ladies, while the horrid, warning voice is in his ear." Now, as drama, this particular scene is very second rate, and Griffin was affected by it because the vision of Kean in the part made him think histrionically instead of dramatically. One cannot help imagining that the situation that should have marked the arrest of Hardress Cregan had already been passed. The young man, to effect the release of his confederate before they were both incriminated, had come into the stable where Danny Mann was confined. The hunchback escapes and Hardress Cregan stays behind to answer the sentry's challenge. But his consciousness is so strained that it lapses, and he becomes oblivious of the sentry, who thereupon breaks open the door. Hardress Cregan is now in the place of the man whose crime he had prompted, and his resolute attempt to stave off discovery has brought about his betrayal. His arrest then and there would have dramatic fitness. But the author is thinking about the wedding later on with "the horrid, warning voice" in Hardress Cregan's ear; his eye is fixed on the actor, and to make the part suit Edmund Kean the course of the narrative is strained. After Danny Mann's flight from the stable all is mechanical. The hunchback who informs on Hardress Cregan is not con-

sistent with the retainer of the earlier part of the story and the prisoner who sends a warning to the bridegroom is not consistent with the informer. (pp. x-xi)

The novel "**The Collegians**," and the poem "**Eileen a Ruin**" are the works that keep Gerald Griffin's name remembered. Some of the books written after "**The Collegians**"—"**The Invasion**," "**The Duke of Monmouth**," and "**The Christian Physiologist**," are difficult to read, and the other books, "**Hollantide**," "**Tales of the Munster Festivals**," "**Tales of the Juryroom**," have not the continuous interest of "**The Collegians**." Was he a one-novel author then and did his creative powers exhaust themselves with ["**The Collegians**"]? Those who know the facts of his life will not admit this. "**Hollantide**" was written when he was twenty-three, and "**Tales of the Munster Festivals**" before he was twenty-five. These two volumes would make a creditable introduction to a series of powerful novels—they are on the level, for instance, with Thomas Hardy's early books. With "**The Collegians**" the series seems to have been begun. Why was it not continued? Immediately [after] this story was published the writer's powers began to be checked by a conflict in his mind. He writes in a letter that he is being haunted by the thought that in working at literature "it might possibly be that he was mis-spending his time." Then a notion fatal to story-telling begins to possess him—that what he writes should convey a direct moral. . . . He denied that it was right for an author to put himself into the position of a particular character and endeavour to feel his passion for a moment. He came to regard as mischievous "such works of imagination as were founded upon deep and absorbing passion." Holding such views it is obvious that he could not tolerate, much less create, literary work that was in any way interesting. The literature that has interested mankind always deals with "deep and absorbing passions," even if it makes laughter out of their effects. Such literature has been created by those who have the will and the power to put themselves in the position of a particular character. . . . When [Griffin] became convinced that people's feelings should be kept "in the line they ought to go in" he was finished as a story-teller. It is because people's feelings cannot be bounded by the moralist that dramas and stories are possible. (pp. xv-xvii)

Padraic Colum, in an introduction to The Collegians *by Gerald Griffin, The Phoenix Publishing Company Limited, 1918, pp. ix-xxii.*

DONALD DAVIE (essay date 1953)

[*Davie argues that* The Collegians "*is far richer and articulated far more closely than is generally supposed*" *by critics who view it solely as "a gallery of peasant studies" in the style of Sir Walter Scott. He complains that critics who interpret* The Collegians *as an "Irish* Waverley" *ignore the novel's "firm and consistent moral discrimination." In particular, Davie faults Padraic Colum (1918) for his failure to recognize that* The Collegians *is "very deliberately didactic."*]

[In *The Collegians*,] the story of the low-born secret wife betrayed and murdered by her high-born husband is used by Griffin, as by Dreiser [in *An American Tragedy*], . . . to establish a whole social hierarchy in all its niceties of class-distinction. It is this that gives to Griffin's story of Munster society a sort of depth and density such as we find in [George Eliot's] *Middlemarch,* and makes it a novel of manners in Lionel Trilling's sense. . . . (p. 23)

The Collegians is intended for a historical novel, set back fifty years or so before the time at which it is written; and the very first chapter, a threnody on the decline of Garryowen, is bathed in an almost cloying nostalgia. This was a characteristic of nearly all the fiction of this period, English and Scottish as well as Irish. . . . And in Griffin this is so pervasive that we get a sort of nostalgia inside nostalgia. . . . This nostalgia is really irrelevant to the book, and indeed it disappears as soon as the story gets under way. A purist may object to it on these grounds. But at least it makes an insinuating introduction; and in any case . . . it is equally present in novelists for whom people make much greater claims than are ever made for Griffin.

According to Padraic Colum, in his Introduction to *The Collegians* [see excerpt above, 1918], Griffin lost interest in literature after that novel, and never again produced anything so good, because of his pietistic and didactic prejudices. This may well be. But Colum is too sure of himself on this issue:

> When he became convinced that people's feelings should be kept 'in the line they ought to go in' he was finished as a story-teller. It is because people's feelings cannot be bounded by the moralist that dramas and stories are possible.

This may serve as a general principle; but it cannot be applied without lots of qualifications—or what would become, for instance, of the doctrinaire but delightful stories of Miss Edgeworth? At any rate, it is impossible to see *The Collegians* for what it is, without realising that, in intention, it was very deliberately didactic.

The very title advertises as much. At first sight, the title is just capricious, for the story has nothing to do with academic life; but the point is that two of the characters [Kyrle Daly and Hardress Cregan] have been to the University, and the story is focussed on this pair to show what use they make of their education when they return to their provincial community. . . . Griffin is hardly fair to his readers, for it is not as if Daly and Cregan got equally close attention—Cregan is in the forefront of the action all the way, Daly hovers a great deal in the wings. But in other respects this is probably a fair assessment of how the book affected its earliest readers. For Cregan is the Romantic hero, the hero of Byron and the Brontës, where Daly (the prudent though impassioned) is the Augustan hero, the hero of Miss Austen and Miss Edgeworth; and in the 1820's it was probably true that nine-tenths of the reading-public were vowed to sympathy with the Romantic hero at whatever cost.

For the modern reader it is different. Not that we now cold-shoulder the Romantic hero: on the contrary, I suppose even to-day it is easier to like Mr. Rochester [in Charlotte Brontë's *Jane Eyre*] than Mr. D'Arcy [in Jane Austen's *Pride and Prejudice*]—other things being equal. But in *The Collegians* other things are *not* equal. There can be no question of our choosing between Daly and Cregan, or preferring one to the other. For Daly, whenever he appears, is truly "there", a presence embodied; and Cregan for the most part is a mouthing phantom. There is a fine Bronte-esque set-piece when he is first introduced, at the tiller of his boat in a storm on the Shannon estuary; and in chapter XIX there is a subtle analysis of his bashfulness in society, a trait which distinguishes him from the type and makes him grow for the moment into a third dimension. But his behaviour and his conversation are more usually like this:—

"I will!" said Hardress, setting his teeth, and rising with a look of forced resolution. "I know that it is merely a courting of ruin, a hastening and confirming of my own black destiny, and yet I will go seek her. . . . The way is torture, and the end is hell, and I know it, and I go! And there is one sweet spirit, one trembling, pitying angel, that waves me back with its pale, fair hands, and strives to frown in its kindness, and points that way to the hills! Mother! mother! the day may come when you will wish a burning brand had seared those lips athwart before they said—'Go to her!'"

"What do you mean?" said Mrs. Cregan, with some indignant surprise.

What, indeed! It is no wonder if we cannot take seriously a character that speaks such ridiculous fustian as this. Daly's conversation on the other hand, though no less stilted, is less tawdry because less vehement; and the stiltedness does not matter so much, because it is in character for him to be very deliberate and punctilious, like Mr. Knightley [in Austen's *Emma*] or Mr. D'Arcy. To modern taste, in fact, Daly, who might have been a prig or a lay-figure, is credible and engaging, where Cregan, on the whole, is neither. To some extent, therefore, Griffin's didactic intention is achieved. And since this intention is the elevation of the Augustan ideals of personal behaviour, it may well be asked in what sense *The Collegians* is a *"romantic"* novel at all.

It is so, of course, so long as it is taken to be an Irish "Waverley". . . . But it is part of my purpose to argue that the comparison with Scott is not the inevitable comparison; that *The Collegians* has other virtues than as a gallery of peasant studies; and in general that the book is far richer and articulated far more closely than is generally supposed.

The strongest argument for the comparison with Scott rests upon Griffin's style. In *The Collegians,* as in many of Scott's novels, there is a yawning gulf between the vitality of the peasant's brogue and the frigidity of the more genteel dialogue. In Griffin, indeed, the gulf is far wider than ever it is in Scott. And in the same way, the descriptive writing is more florid and turgid than Scott's. In fact, Griffin's style is sometimes so florid that it is ludicrous. . . . (pp. 25-8)

At other times . . . the writing recalls nothing so much as *The Young Visiters* [by the English children's novelist, Daisy Ashford]:—

> Light and laughter—mirth and music—plenteous fare and pleasant hearts to share it, were mingled in the dining-room on this occasion. . . . [Every] eye seemed lighted up, to contribute its portion of gaiety to the domestic jubilee. A cloud of vapour, thin and transparent as a Peri's sighs, arose from the dishes which adorned the table, and was dissipated in the air above.

(pp. 29-30)

This is babu's English, neither more nor less; and one can readily imagine the reader who asks indignantly whether the writer of such passages can be considered as anything but a joke, let alone mentioned in the same breath with Scott.

One answers this in a way by pointing to such vivid and unembarrassed prose as the description of Lowry Looby in Chapter

IV. But it is not just a question of balancing the good against the bad. For Griffin is a case that calls for special pleading, just as the babu does. What we have in both cases is an un-English mind trying to express itself in a language wholly foreign to its most intimate habits of thought and feeling. Whether Griffin was bred to speak Irish, I do not know and perhaps it does not matter. For a great deal of the earlier Anglo-Irish writing is of this "babu" type. In Chapter XXIII, Lowry Looby sings—

> And are you Aurora or the goddess Flora,
> 	Or Eutherpasia, or fair Venus bright,
> Or Helen fair, beyond compare,
> 	Whom Paris stole from the Grecian's sight?
> Thou fairest creature, how you've inslaved me!
> 	I'm intoxicated by Cupid's clue,
> Whose golden notes and infatuations
> 	Have deranged my ideas for you, Colleen rue.

And Poll Naughten rejoins:—

> Sir, I pray be aisy, and do not tease me
> 	With your false praises most jestingly;
> Your golden notes and insiniwayshuns
> 	Are vaunting speeches decaiving me.
> I am not Aurora, nor the goddess Flora,
> 	But a rural female to all men's view,
> Who's here condoling my situation,
> 	And my appellation is the Colleen rue. . . .

To the English reader these stanzas are comic, because they recall English comic verse; but even to him, if he is at all sensitive, it must soon become apparent these poems have a beauty and an interest not of the "Stuffed Owl" variety at all. "I'm intoxicated by Cupid's clue" is memorable, euphonious and haunting, even if it's nonsense.

Now this, I think, is true of some of Griffin's prose as of this folk-poetry. Hardress Cregan's pretentious rant is bad on any account, if only because we could imagine it written by an Englishman. But passages like that on the "portals of the Shannon", or that on the "domestic jubilee", with its "cloud of vapour, thin and transparent as a Peri's sighs'', could not have been written by an Englishman, and exhibit a native eloquence making sense and poetry out of a sort of artifice long grown faded and cumbrous in the land of its origin. (pp. 29-31)

The Collegians, then, is a novel with several grave faults; but it is a great deal richer, more various and more disciplined than is generally acknowledged. The genre-pictures of Irish life and character are as good as Scott and it contains elements (for instance, of firm and consistent moral discrimination) which are seldom to be found in Scott at all. Moreover, it is Irish through and through, down to the very fibres of style, in imagery, rhythm, and turn of phrase. It is surely not given the recognition it deserves. (p. 31)

> *Donald Davie, "Gerald Griffin's 'The Collegians',"
> in The Dublin Magazine, Vol. XXVIII, No. 2, April-
> June, 1953, pp. 23-31.*

THOMAS FLANAGAN   (essay date 1959)

[*The Irish Novelists: 1800-1850, from which the following excerpt is drawn, is considered an important critical study of early nineteenth-century Irish fiction. In his preface, Flanagan stresses that an examination of the social, political, and religious issues of Griffin's time is essential to an understanding of his fiction. His discussion of "The Aylmers of Bally-Aylmer" from Holland-Tide,*

"Suil Dhuv the Coiner" from Tales of the Munster Festivals, *and* The Collegians *focuses on Griffin's depiction of the "explosive, anarchic power which lay at the center of Irish life, unchecked by social forms." Flanagan maintains that "the law, or rather the absence of law, is at the center of every story which Griffin was to write." Thus, while he praises* The Collegians *as a comprehensive and accurate delineation of provincial Irish society, he contends that the novel derives its "richness of substance" from the way in which Griffin relates Hardress Cregan and his crime to the anarchic society that produced them both.*]

There is a kind of geography of the spirit in Griffin's representation of Ireland, and much of this he entrusted to the [Shannon] river. There is also in his work, as he came to have knowledge of himself and of his country, a sense of the conflicting traditions which went into his making—his father's Whiggish patriotism; his mother's responsiveness to Anglo-Irish culture, with all its tense adjustments; the Gaelic underworld . . . ; the time-haunted stones of abbeys, towers, and fortresses. (p. 210)

The law, or rather the absence of law, is at the center of every story which Griffin was to write. Most of his characters stand outside it in one sense or another, though they may recognize the need to placate or circumvent it. Law makes its first appearance in **"The Aylmers"** in the person of Mr. Hassett, the landowner and magistrate: . . .

> The music being hushed for a moment into delicious silence, and the open carriage drawn up, the school-master inflicted a harangue on the occupant, which was borne with gracious patience, and suitably acknowledged; after which, with tremendous yells, the crowd bounded on the carriage, emancipated the four-footed cattle, cashiered the postillion, and fastening two ropes on either side, hurried the vehicle across the rough and stony road. . . .
> As they hurried him along, amid terrific shouts, and bursts of wild laughter, toward the demesne gate, the walls and the wayside were lined with gaping and noisy crowds, principally composed of the younger urchins, whose scantiness of attire obliged them to make shift in this manner. One of these had clambered up a gate pier and sitting cross-legged on the back of a stone monkey, secured his seat by passing his arm around the neck of the dilapidated pug; while with the other he twirled his little hareskin cap above his head, and added his share of noisy triumph to the general voice. . . .

It is a scene quintessential to Anglo-Irish fiction, from Lever to Somerville and Ross, the dear, dirty, touching peasants and the amused, understanding landlord. But Griffin's point is entirely different. There is something sinister in the well-meaning, ineffectual Hassett being bounced along by a people whose true life is secret, violent, and conspiratorial. Griffin says it all in a felicitous and characteristic stroke: the contrasting figures of the broken but balefully potent banshee and the ludicrous, ignoble monkey.

The story reaches its climax at the Tralee Assizes. Griffin sketches the assize town and the court vigorously and with fidelity to facts:

> The generally silent and sunshiny streets were now made to echo the frequent tramp of the bespattered and reeking saddle horse, and the

lumbering rattle of the car which brought its load of corn (stacked until now, the season of scarcity), to the store of the small dealer, a sort of Lilliputian merchant, who made a new profit by shipping, or rather boating the grain to the next trading city. The fronts of the inns and *shebeens* were scowered up, and the rooms made ready for the temporary convenience of petty jurors, summoned from the furthermost limits of the county; strong farmers anxiously looking for the success of their road presentments; . . . rural practitioners demanding the legal grant for the support of a dispensary; middlemen in the commission of the peace, eager to curry favor with the mighty sojourners by the number and importance of their committals. . . .

As we follow the description along through the streets, past the inns and shebeens, into the courthouse, we realize that this is the most alert eye which had yet looked upon the Irish scene. Maria Edgeworth would never have used a court of justice to explain why ''ropemakers thrive at a certain season, why the hangman can endow his daughter so handsomely, and why the science of anatomy is so attainable, and so practically understood in Ireland.''

But **"The Aylmers"** reveals more than an accurate eye. Griffin was always to be intensely concerned with the explosive, anarchic power which lay at the center of Irish life, unchecked by social forms. The disparity between the order for which Mr. Hassett presumably stands and the violence which lies everywhere, just beyond the range of his eye, is constantly insisted upon. The effect is admirable in some of the scenes, but in others it dissolves into a lurid melodrama which was Griffin's besetting sin. It is as though his material is not amenable to control, or at least to any control within his grasp.

This is borne out more strikingly in . . . ***Tales of the Munster Festivals***. It consists of three short novels, but one, **"Suil Dhuv,"** overshadows the others. . . . [It is] a remarkable story, and yet it must be accounted a failure.

It is a sensational and quite blood-chilling re-creation of life in Munster during the Penal Days, when the mountain passes were made dangerous by bands of masterless men and when crime was as natural as breath. . . . To a stretch of road near Court Mattress Griffin brings a grotesque yet representative company of travelers—a coarse, finely dressed Limerick grazier; a glib-tongued Cork buckeen, a hedge scholar. These take shelter, when night falls, at the inn of Mark Spellacy, the *suil dhuv*, who leads a gang of Raparees. (pp. 214-17)

The halves of the story are badly joined. The figures who appear one by one, on the road or at the inn, are brilliantly sketched, and the story of Spellacy's raid has a certain cumulative force, but the two accounts do not further each other. The murderous natives and the bland, self-righteous expropriators seem involved in a common fate which lies beyond their understanding. As in [Maria Edgeworth's] *Castle Rackrent* the symbols are all of money and the money is all false. *Suil dhuv* has become a forger; the government itself has introduced debased currency into the country; a trickster named O'Neil pretends that he has found a vault filled with ''crosses and caps and rings and fine shinin' stones.'' (p. 217)

But though there are suggestions that through symbol and language we are to find unity in the story, it remains confused and shapeless. The life of the story is local, and lies in the

braggart, wonderfully rendered speech of the grazier, in the bare-boned vicious charm of Awny Farrel, the hedge scholar. *Tales of the Munster Festivals* sets out to rival not Crofton Croker, but John Banim. In **"Suil Dhuv"** Griffin turned, as Banim had done, to the garish literature of the hedges, drenching his story in blood and baleful penitential fires. It secured for him a reputation as the most promising of the young Irish writers. But that reputation was more justly earned by ***The Collegians,*** which is one of the handful of first-rate Irish novels of the period. (pp. 217-18)

[***The Collegians*** involves] the entire structure of provincial Irish society: the gentry, from the Chutes of Castle Chute to the Creaghs and Connollys and Cregans of Roaring Hall; middlemen like the Dalys, torn in their feelings between the Gaelic past and the Anglo-Irish present; the English of the Garrison: Leake, a physician, Gibson, the commandant of militia, Warner, the magistrate. Below these the peasants, the landless men, the shopkeepers of Limerick town, the horse traders of the Kerry mountains, the boatmen. (p. 220)

The Collegians is a ''social'' novel, embracing all classes and conditions. But what strikes one immediately about the culture which Griffin has created is its lack of cohesiveness. The great Norman house of the Chutes, with its pride and its kindliness, has been emasculated, peopled by women and haunted by the scheming but defeated ''ould man of all.'' It has been replaced by the gentlemanly, ineffective Garrison and the cunning and blackguardly half-sirs. The peasants, their actions shaped by their affections for a proscribed creed and a vanished order, are the followers of men who have themselves been robbed of all sense of social responsibility. The consequence is something more than mere disregard of law. ''There is scarcely a cottage in the south of Ireland,'' Griffin tells us, prosily but accurately, ''where the very circumstance of legal denunciation would not afford, even to a murderer, a certain passport to concealment and protection.'' (p. 222)

The walls [in the Daly's house] are crowded with prints—Hogarth's ''Roast Beef,'' Prince Eugene, Schomberg at the Boyne, Betterton playing Cato. There would be nothing improper in this, certainly, were it an English or an Ascendancy household. But the Dalys are Catholic and native Irish, and this makes their taste in decoration wildly inappropriate, for they have chosen to honor Hogarth's most robustly British scene, an English actor playing a Roman statesman, the ally of Marlborough, and, of all people, the Protestant mercenary who delivered Ireland to William of Orange. Perhaps the full weight of this incongruity needs, for its appreciation, some familiarity with Irish loyalties, but it borders on the grotesque.

It is as puzzling, in its way, as Charles Daly's favorite and never-answered conundrum, ''Why is that fender like Westminster Abbey?'' We are prompted to wonder why Daly has chosen to send his son to Trinity, the ferociously Protestant stronghold of the Ascendancy. It was possible for a Catholic to do so, by that time, once the student had soothed his own scruples, had overborne the disapprobation of his clergy, and had submitted to the conditions on which he would be accepted. In most instances such a course recommended itself only to families of marked social ambition. But there is no question of the Dalys' integrity, nor of the steadfastness of their religious convictions. The puzzle suggests that the novel's title may, after all, have some point.

Griffin introduces his themes in ways as oblique as this. In fact, only late in the novel does he let us know which of certain county families are Catholic and which are of "the genteel religion," although part of the action has turned upon the issue. For his point is that in religious as in cultural issues the old lines of authority and order are being blurred. (pp. 223-24)

The plot of the novel hinges upon the seduction, desertion, and at last the murder of Eily O'Connor, Mihil's daughter. Eily was the object of much sentimental interest during the novel's nineteenth-century vogue, but she is weakly drawn, and as though to compensate for this, Griffin has thrust upon her a topheavy weight of symbolic detail. Her father pursues a trade associated with death, and his ropewalk is adjacent to a gallows green; nearby stand a pesthouse, a coffinmaker's shop, and a churchyard. (pp. 224-25)

Read in the customary sentimental fashion, the novel is a study of passion and an exercise in pathos. By such standards the figure of Cregan is created with remarkable success. The springs of his actions are probed with the relentless skill of a catechist, until at last his charm and generosity are revealed as forms of self-love. (p. 225)

As a melodrama of murder and conscience *The Collegians* is remarkably effective and much of its power derives from the clarity with which Griffin has seen his central figure.

What gives the novel its richness of substance, however, is the way in which Griffin has related Cregan and his crime to the society which produced them both, and the way in which he has used secondary characters to reinforce his theme. Hardress Cregan is invested with a kind of kingliness, but beneath his graces and powers lie the terror and the ruthlessness of a child. He has come to manhood in a society in which religion has decayed into social ritual—"the genteel religion"—and law into an extension of social privilege. What matters is *code*, that emptiest of moral patterns, which had become synonymous with honor. It had carried him successfully through balls and drinking bouts, duels and hunts. But, for the moral choice which lies at the novel's core, it has left him stripped of every weapon save the knife in the hand of Danny the Lord.

For Griffin the hunt, that most cherished of Ascendancy accomplishments, is the symbol of its anarchy. The book begins with a hunt, and it ends with one. The sounds of the novel are those of horns in the morning and hoofbeats at night. From the hunt he draws his most vivid images. A peasant is hunted down for sport by hounds and their drunken masters. An old huntsman lies dying outside a cabin while his master's friends are drinking within. A duel is fought by drunken men, stumbling about in a lodge. It is during a hunt that Eily O'Connor's body is discovered. Cregan himself is run like a stag by the calmly contemptuous Gibson, to whom the gallant squires who have rallied about the murderer are a rabble of "drunken gentlemen." Their defiant bluster crumbles before the icy, resolute officer, even the physical daring of the Ascendancy failing in the last instance.

Against the Cregans of Roaring Hall stand the Dalys, Charles and Kyrle, models of exemplary feeling and deed, who live in the sober, forthright world of the Edgeworth heroes. Charles Daly, like the Scottish factor of *Ennui*, has managed by some unexhibited miracle to deal benevolently with his tenants and honorably with his neighbors; his patriotism is chastened by his sense of the practical. And Kyrle has carried this principled moderation still further.

At one point Hardress Cregan, talking to Kyrle Daly, launches forth upon a Byronic assault upon social convention. Daly, in

reproving him, says that "elegance of manner is not finesse, nor at all the opposite of simplicity; it is merely simplicity made perfect. I grant you that few, very few, are successful in acquiring it; I dislike its ape, affectation, as heartily as you do. But we find something that is conventional in all classes, and I like affectation better than vulgarity, after all." . . . Molière's Philinthe [in *The Misanthrope*] could hardly have improved upon this. How Kyrle reacts to more solemn matters may be imagined.

But it would be far from the fact to suppose that Daly is intended as a counterweight to Cregan, or as the novelist's didactic voice. He seems to be, certainly, but this is a measure of the novel's skill. The Dalys, father and son, are revealed as tragically inadequate. Cregan damns himself. But to be damned, it is necessary first to be alive. The Dalys have molded themselves to their high, hard principles in so repressive a fashion that they cannot be said to live. There is at the end of the novel a climactic moment of reversal and possibility which makes this apparent. In a manner fittingly Irish the Dalys are summoned back to life by the fact of death. (pp. 225-27)

The Dalys, with their rectitude and virtues, with a son at Trinity and the victor of the Boyne on the parlor wall, are cut off from the instinctual life of their people, yet remain, at the core, unassimilated to the culture whose manners and whose stoicism they emulate. It is a harsh, perhaps a provincial, moral which Griffin has drawn, yet alienation is one powerful theme of the novel.

His design has a flaw near its center, though. He needed a figure to incarnate what he considered the abiding worth of Irish life. He knew better than to employ some such allegorical offering as Maria Edgeworth's O'Halloran [in *The Absentee*] or one of Lady Morgan's elegant outcasts. He knew, indeed, that the Irish past lived most vividly and most fully in its peasants. And peasant types he can create well and without condescension. A reader numbed by Lover and Lever is apt to dismiss his Lowry Looby as another stage servant, but he is more than that. When Looby remembers the past, he begins singing "The Blackbird," with its echoes of another age and a gentility unknown to the half-sirs. Looby himself has an instinctive courtesy and tact. It is through his anecdotes, rambling and seemingly inconsequential, that we learn the history of the intertwined Limerick families. And, each in his way, Father O'Connor and old Mihil are effective figures. But in the third of the novel's three young men, Miles na Coppaleen, Griffin tried for something finer than he could achieve.

Miles is the figure whose kingliness is neither false nor achieved at the expense of life. Griffin places him far beyond Limerick in the rocky hills of Kerry, that proud and isolated land. The peasants honor him for his character, his skill with horses, and his fighting prowess, but the gentry, too, accord him a grudging admiration. He is an attractive character, certainly, striding through the fairs with his straight-handled whip. But he is kept too far from the events of the story, perhaps because Griffin was afraid to risk him against the chances of life which had compromised Daly and Cregan. Miles na Coppaleen was to become a darling . . . of the Dublin stage when the novel was dramatized by Dion Boucicault, but he exists in Griffin's novel as a touching failure. (pp. 229-30)

[*The Collegians* won its popularity] on merits which are unique in the nineteenth-century Irish novel. Griffin had not written a novel *about* Ireland; he had written an Irish novel. The Ireland of *The Collegians* is not presented to the reader as an object of sympathy or commiseration or indulgent humor. It simply exists. It exists in rich and exact detail; it is "picturesque" and "romantic," enchanted and accursed. But it is given to us in a work of art, not in a disguised tract. And, even when the complexities and ironies of the novel went unnoticed, its moral feeling struck a responsive chord. Griffin was an acute moralist, and one who lived within the same world of moral experience as did the majority of his countrymen. If the phrase "Catholic novelist" is at all meaningful, it may properly be applied to him. (p. 230)

> *Thomas Flanagan, "Gerald Griffin," in his* The Irish Novelists: 1800-1850, *Columbia University Press, 1959, pp. 203-51.*

FRANK O'CONNOR   (essay date 1967)

[*O'Connor is a twentieth-century Irish poet, short story writer, and critic.*]

The best Irish story-teller of the [early nineteenth century] was probably Gerald Griffin, though this is not saying much. . . . Judging by the one scene of [*Gisippus*] I have read, it might be the work of any stage-struck English parson. His best-known novel, *The Collegians,* is a different affair, and the first seventy or eighty pages is as good fiction as any Irishman has written. Though Griffin's only education had been in a hedge-school, he could, when he was working well, write excellent English, and compared with his contemporary, Carleton, he was a civilized and intelligent man. (p. 146)

[The] 'Collegians' of his title are two young Trinity College men, one a man of sense, the other of sensibility. Being as opposed to sensibility as Jane Austen herself, Griffin turns the emotional man into a murderer, which is an even greater *non sequitur* than Jane Austen's.

For close on a hundred pages Griffin describes his Ireland, and in these he is out on his own. Not only does he write excellent English; he shows that he is aware of a secret that few story-tellers master. No two human beings speak exactly alike, and each of Griffin's humbler characters speaks a language of his own. But the moment he approaches his real theme—the psychology of love and murder—Griffin simply collapses. As the old man in his novel *Tracy's Ambition* says, 'Faix, I never seen any love committed there, nor murthers aither.' Not only does he not know what a murderer is like; he has no idea what a lover is like or how a woman in a sexual relationship behaves. For a while I was tempted to believe that this was a class difference, and that Griffin, like Thomas Hardy, thought love-making an occupation better suited to the gentry since it had to be conducted in the most elegant style, but now I think that with Griffin it was more and worse than that. He is interested in men, and only in men, and the only sort of novel he could have done really well would have had to be based upon the psychology of friendship. Two fine scenes in the novel illustrate this. In one, Hardress Cregan, the man of sensibility, denounces the wickedness of duelling in a high-minded way, but a few minutes later when his friend, Kyrle Daly, has been insulted, he insists on fighting a duel with the man who had insulted him. In the second scene, Kyrle, realizing that Hardress has robbed him of his girl, is insane with rage, but later, at his mother's wake, he behaves with perfect friendliness to Hardress, and Hardress realizes that their friendship is at an end. If this were a novel about unconscious homosexuality everyone would admire those scenes, but it isn't, and what

Griffin gives us instead of a novel about love and murder is a five-act English melodrama in verse—English verse.

And not only that, but it is clear that he visualized it with English actors. . . . All Hardress Cregan's tirades tend to turn into blank verse of the English type:

> I would have saved her, but it is too late.
> Now, my good angel, be at peace with me.
> I would have saved her. I obeyed your call.
> Amid the storm, the darkness and the rain
> I flew to execute your gentle will.

No novel of Irish life could possibly have sustained an authentic note under those circumstances. More and more as the story goes on Griffin is sucked into the whirlpool of imitation. (pp. 146-48)

> *Frank O'Connor, "The Beginnings of Modern Literature," in his* A Short History of Irish Literature: A Backward Look, *G. P. Putnam's Sons, 1967, pp. 143-53.**

BENEDICT KIELY   (essay date 1972)

[*Kiely argues that the intellectual discussions between Kyrle Daly and Hardress Cregan in* The Collegians *are best understood as Griffin's attempt "to puzzle over his own problems of conscience." According to Kiely, Daly and Cregan represent conflicting aspects of Griffin's personality "in an odd, intellectual, Damon and Pythias way." In focusing on the psychological intensity with which Griffin depicts his characters, Kiely anticipates the commentary of John Cronin (1978).*]

[Most] of us are familiar with at least the bare details of the story of the murder case that Griffin used and altered when he wrote *The Collegians*: that John Scanlan, a young half-mounted gent from the County Limerick, eloped with a teenager called Ellen Hanley who took with her all the money her uncle, with whom she lived, had saved; that Scanlan went through some form of marriage with her, tired of her shortly, and with the help of his servant, Stephen Sullivan, had her brutally murdered and dumped into the Shannon. It was a sordid little crime, but the use Griffin made of it is a fine illustration of what Henry James meant when he said that the art of fiction is not in telling what happened but what should have happened. . . .

Around that sad little murder-case, transformed into something still tragic but a deal more dignified, if the murder of a hapless girl could ever be so described, Griffin painted the best picture that we have, outside William Carleton, of the Ireland of the period. In the characters of the good Kyrle Daly and of the wilful, generous, brilliant, violent, wrong-headed, ill-fated Hardress Cregan, and in the serious, sometimes pedantic talks between them, Griffin, splitting his own character into fragments, mulled over his own problems: the fear of death, his nerves and melancholia and sense of isolation, the desire for fame, the taste of ashes that went with fame if the eternal needs of the soul were left unsatisfied. (p. 243)

[Daniel O'Connell, John Scanlan's lawyer,] knew the sorts of minds that he would be likely to get on a jury in the Ireland of the time, and when he said, 'Find Sullivan (who was on the run) and you will find the murderer', he was passing the crime along to the person whom the upper and middle classes had decided was responsible for all Irish crime: to the peasant. Griffin, who had in him a streak of middleclassery as wide as the yard of Dublin Castle and who had never given much thought to the real reasons for the woeful state of the realm, was easily inclined to follow that argument, and the deplorable Scanlan became the frequently splendid Hardress. The novelist was happier with a villain like Suil Dubh the Coiner in the *Tales of the Munster Festivals,* whom he sent to an end not unlike that of Pinkie in Graham Green's *Brighton Rock,* and who didn't have to be tormented with Cregan's or Griffin's scruples and remorse, and who was, best of all, a member of the lower classes. (p. 244)

Sullivan, the servant of Scanlan, was a straight-backed man but Griffin made Danny Mann, the servant of Cregan, a hunchback and attributed the deformity to an injury inflicted in boyhood, and accidentally, by Hardress, and thus, for him, another source of guilt and remorse. That invention of the accident and the hunch as an explanation for the irrational attachment of man to master was a genuine stroke of Gothic genius: it gave visible shape to something unseen and amoral, it gave the dignity of agony to the despicable lack of status of the hanger-on. . . . A lot of decent people hopefully expected that [Sullivan's] dying confession would clear Scanlan's name. It did everything but that, and Griffin, when he came to puzzle over his own problems of conscience in the persons of Hardress Cregan and Kyrle Daly, shrank away from the reality of Scanlan.

But at any rate he did deal with Hardress in a serious novel and in the name of conscience in whose power he had a strong old-fashioned belief, for Griffin himself was as tormented as any stainless, scrupulous man with a morbid vision of the blackness of his own peccadilloes. His later adapters and vulgarizers, Dion Boucicault and Sir Jules Benedict, threw conscience to the dogs and went on blatantly and for the sake of box-office to prove that the dashing gentleman-born was, like Bonny Prince Charlie, everybody's darling; and in doing so they rescued Cregan not only from the gallows but from that sad, and clearly repentant, death on the convict ship, and rescued the Colleen Bawn from the grave. (p. 245)

Hardress is Byronic as it was the fashion of the time for popular heroes to be: there is even a suggestion of the Napoleonic. . . . Griffin introduces him in style!

> It was such a figure as would have at once awakened associations in the beholder's mind of camps and action, of states confounded in their councils and nations overrun by sudden conquest. His features were brightened by a lofty and confident enthusiasm, such as the imagination might inscribe to the Royal Adventurer of Sweden, as he drew his sword on his beleaguers at Belgrade.

Now if Griffin had anything to repent of when he turned more and more to religion he could well have added that passage to the list of his imagined sins—moral and artistic. The utter absurdity of it was that this demigod, Hardress, was completely under the thumb of his formidable mother, and that, so great was the power of conscience—as Griffin would have thought of it—or so great his fear of being found out, that he spends a lot of the last third of the book ranting and drivelling and in the jigs of nerves. (p. 246)

Griffin, grappling with his hero, half-unwilling that he should become a hero, and still haunted by that dubious ghost of Scanlan, had many varying thoughts about Hardress. Here is Hardress, the nature lover, not Scanlan, . . . talking to Kyrle. . . .

> I love a plain beefsteak before a grilled attorney, this excellent whiskey-punch before my mother's confounded currant-wine, and anything else that is pure and natural before anything else that is adulterated and artificial; so do I love the wild hedge-flower, simplicity, before the cold and sapless exotic, fashion; so do I love the voice of affection and of nature before that of finesse and affectation.

Kyrle Daly responds by telling Hardress that his terms are too hard, that elegance of manner is not finesse nor at all the opposite of simplicity. So the two friends go on, Hardress talking magnificently out of character and saying so much that should be said by Kyrle who remains mostly mute or remains at best the fall-guy; and all the time it is Griffin talking to and about himself. (pp. 246-47)

Griffin considered that Byron's failings were not so much his own as the result of his education and background. This is interesting—for the downfall of Hardress can then be more mercifully seen against the background of a graceless, drunken, spendthrift, violent society: hard-riding country gentlemen who would hunt not only animals but men, and would chase poor hunchbacked Danny Mann along the road for the gentlemanly pleasure of pricking him with their swords. Or who would demand the last hunting-cry from Dalton, the huntsman, even though the effort of uttering that cry kills the poor fellow and spatters his deathbed with diseased blood. . . . [The] gentlemen, two of whom are crazy duellists, plethoric with a drunken arrogance which is less than pride and which they miscall honour, go on drinking because, as the father of Hardress temperately says: 'I call no man dead drunk while he lies on the high road with sense enough to roll out of the way when a carriage is driving towards him.' The rough outline of those events gives Griffin some of the best pages in the Irish fiction of the time, but his range was wide, and he could be every bit as effective in describing a happy colourful day at the races, or a storm on the wide river, or in reporting a droll story from Lowry Looby or Dunat O'Leary, the barber; or again in describing the splendid, patriarchal anger of Mihil O'Connor, the ropemaker, when he knows that his daughter has been stolen; or the agony of sorrow at the wake of Kyrle Daly's mother where Lowry talks to the unknowing infant whose birth has caused the mother's death. . . . (p. 248)

Hardress reproves the drunkards and the duellists to the point of drawing down a lunatic duel on himself. But he reproves them in words that should really be used by the virtuous Kyrle Daly. Hardress uses them simply because, by the way the novel is going, he and not Daly happens to be there. Yet the truth of the matter may be a little more complicated than that. Griffin, it is said, was fond of quoting the words that Byron was supposed to have used on his deathbed: 'Perhaps I am not so unfit to die as people think.' That could have been a hint to a sensitive, over-scrupulous man, as Griffin assuredly was, that the soul and God might have things between them that society and society's two-handed engine, the Church and the law, could never understand: that there could be explanations in the case of Hardress and perhaps even mysteries in the case of Scanlan. On top of all which, Griffin had scruples within scruples that both he was, and his readers would be, giving more admiration to Hardress than to the exemplary Kyrle Daly who had nothing to recommend him except irreproachable virtue and a stock of platitudes. Kyrle, it is true, once allows himself (or is allowed) to be angry at what he thinks is the treachery of Hardress in relation to the lovely young lady, Ann Chute, to whom Hardress is affianced and with whom Kyrle is hopelessly, but not violently, in love. Apart from that anger Kyrle displays no redeeming vices and the anger is brief. Of necessity it had to be, not only because Kyrle was so virtuous but because Hardress and Kyrle were, in an odd, intellectual, Damon and Pythias way, two portions of the same person: Gerald Griffin. (pp. 248-49)

When he was struggling for fame in London Griffin said he feared failure worse than death. Another fear was to dominate him, not that of death but of eternal darkness that might follow death. The consideration of Scanlan, even under the milder mask of Hardress, must have brought that fear closer to him. With all due regard for the law of probability in storytelling, it would seem that Griffin started off to make something tolerable out of Kyrle Daly and that Kyrle was not so much outshone by as absorbed by Hardress. Kyrle, indeed, vanishes after a while like a wax figure in a furnace, and, to vary the metaphor, is only brought back to life by his mother's death at a time when, oddly enough, Hardress is upbraiding *his* mother as the cause of his misfortunes. Griffin, who was to be so virtuous in his own life, for once almost allowed evil to take over in his imagination, or could not prevent it attempting to take over. His casuistic compromise was to make Hardress a fine young fellow tormented by remorse and uncertain even about the degree of his own guilt, not an evil man but a rash impulsive one, reared in a violent society, dominated by a stern mother, dogged by the devil. For all this, there could be for Griffin, the creator, no easy solution. The wages of sin would have to be death: his strict morality combined with his artistic sense saved him from the outrages committed by the popularizers Boucicault and Benedict. . . . (p. 250)

> Benedict Kiely, ''The Two Masks of Gerald Griffin,'' in *Studies*, Vol. LXI, No. 243, Autumn, 1972, pp. 241-51.

JOHN CRONIN (essay date 1978)

[*In* Gerald Griffin (1803-1840): A Critical Biography, *the first full-length critical study of Griffin, Cronin contends that the author's works provide revealing insight into his own psychology. According to Cronin, Griffin* ''charted his personal dilemma and gave it artistic objectivity'' *in a series of morbidly sensitive characters. He singles out Hardress Cregan in* The Collegians *as the* ''most remarkable'' *of Griffin's* ''sensitives','' *and maintains that an examination of Cregan's development is essential to an understanding of Griffin's achievement and decline. While Cronin complains that many of Griffin's stories are overly melodramatic, he praises their vivid accounts of peasant life in Ireland. He concludes that* ''if a writer deserves to be judged on his best work, then Griffin may safely be accounted one of the great Irish realistic writers.'']

[Padraic Colum's comparison of *Holland-Tide* and *Tales of the Munster Festivals*] with the early Hardy is reasonably accurate [see excerpt above, 1918]. *Holland-Tide* and *Tales of the Munster Festivals* are not unlike the Hardy of, say, *Desperate Remedies,* the Hardy of melodramatic confrontations and improbable contrivances. Griffin shares Hardy's fondness for near-miss situations (for example, Dorgan's narrow escape from hanging in *Card Drawing* and Eugene Hamond's almost-marriage to Emily in *The Half-Sir*). Like Hardy's, his early stories are marred by improbabilities. Simple stereotypes in the realm of character are susceptible to manipulation only by coincidences, lost letters, thunderstorms, dreams, mysterious strangers

and magic. The stories in *Holland-Tide* abound in 'dramatic' confrontations (the scene between Katharine Fitzmaurice and her father in *The Aylmers of Bally-Aylmer,* for example) and well-known dramatic situations from Shakespeare's plays tend to loom harmfully in the background (for example, the scene in *The Aylmers of Bally-Aylmer* when William Aylmer, Hamlet-like, confronts the ghost of his father). The trial scene with which this story concludes, where Robert Aylmer, who has been thought to be dead, returns to clear his name and exonerate his old friend Fitzmaurice from a murder charge, is lurid melodrama. Indeed, Griffin seems conscious of the need to cool the atmosphere a little by making the affair the subject of jest among the lawyers in the courtroom: . . .

> [Several] admirable witticisms passed among the junior counsel on the back benches; such as that his lordship was a clever resurrection-man—that he had given a *grave* turn to the proceedings—that it was a dead-letter affair, with various inflictions of a similar nature, which we grieve to say our slippery memory will not enable us to lay before the reader.

One regrets that Griffin did not more often give way to even this kind of heavy-handed facetiousness—the melodrama is, all too often, served quite straight.

The diction employed in these early narrations is an alarmingly periphrastic one, heavily larded with pseudo-Augustan circumlocutions. . . . This distressing style is combined with the Irish regional writer's inevitable obligation to explain the oddities of regional customs and behaviour to an English public. It would be quite unfair to Griffin to suggest that he condescends to his material at any point. He does not, but at this point (and, perhaps, throughout his career) he works in two kinds of prose, the first this clumsily artificial 'grand' style which leads him into regrettable coyness and unfunny asides, and the other the homely style of his peasant characters with which he is much more successful. (pp. 37-9)

In view of his obvious pleasure in the gaieties of Anglo-Irish, it is reasonable to suggest that, had his career developed differently and had he lived longer, Griffin might have won his way to a personal narrative style of an effective kind. Occasionally the writer's compassionate involvement with his characters appears with unusual clarity, as for example when he comments on the practice of the law in Irish courts. . . . It is certainly true that Griffin's prose loses much of its clumsiness when he engages in direct description of the Irish social scene, and this is equally true of the change in his style when he applies himself to descriptions of landscapes familiar to him from childhood. We retain from his pages a memory of vividly depicted places, of wide stretches of harsh, lonely bogland, of mountains where law cannot reach and steep cliffs where smugglers ply their profitable but risky business.

The most effective story in *Holland-Tide* is probably *The Brown Man,* an effective piece of rustic Grand Guignol the brevity of which preserves it from the structural defects of the longer stories. In these the writer's control of the structure of his tales is generally poor. He frequently interrupts the line of his narrative to fill in some necessary part of the plot and he never hesitates to break off to allow a character to tell a story whether it happens to be relevant or not. The result is that it is easy to lose the thread of the main story in catching up with the clumsily inserted sub-plots. The writer frequently intrudes into the narrative with coy comments on the habits of 'the fair sex' or explanatory remarks addressed to the 'gentle London reader'. Character is never explored. It is assumed that all young ladies are virtuous, dutiful and proper and all young gentlemen gallant, faithful and industrious except when they are led astray by equally stereotyped villains. Such interest as the tales possess consists in their presentation of a convincing landscape and of glimpses of unfamiliar rural practices, such as the touching of the corpse in *The Hand and Word.* (pp. 39-40)

Two of the stories in *Tales of the Munster Festivals (Card Drawing* and *Suil Dhuv the Coiner)* are of the kind already made familiar in *Holland-Tide.* They are melodramatic, regional stories frequently spoilt by clumsily contrived plots, sometimes redeemed by vivid depictions of scenery or local conditions. Early in *Card Drawing* we are given the following hint of an aspect of the writer's practice which was to prove damaging to his style: 'But as the reader may observe throughout these tales, an ambition to render them almost as analogous to the drama as Fielding rendered his to the epic, (a circumstance in which the public taste seems, fortunately, to coincide with our inclination), we shall allow our hero to introduce himself.' This histrionic inclination in the writer, this tendency to think in terms of 'strong' scenes of a 'dramatic' kind, was to persist. (p. 43)

Card Drawing is a simple, melodramatic tale of a sailor wrongly accused of murder and rescued in the nick of time by the repentance of the real murderer, but, in the course of it, Griffin brings together a group of a kind we shall encounter in his novels again. The forces of law and respectability are represented by the Coroner, the priest and Dr Mahony. The real murderer, Kinchela, with his wild companions, earns a precarious living on the rocky shore, fishing and scavenging for 'barnocks'. In between, we have the comical Mr Madigan, an inn-keeper, a Malaprop whose affected and absurd English is richly mocked. The atmosphere of wild lawlessness is presented as the logical outcome of appalling social conditions. . . . Kinchela's mother commonly addresses him in the Irish language and has a kind of simple, uncomplicated honesty which distinguishes her from the silly and pretentious Madigan. Altogether, we are being presented with an accurate picture of a society struggling to express itself in an emergent language, struggling to come to terms with an alien code of justice—it is a world which Synge would have found familiar and enthralling. The writing, on the whole, is more direct and uncomplicated than in [*Holland-Tide*], though *Suil Dhuv the Coiner* does, perhaps, revert to the stylistic and structural clumsiness of the longer stories of *Holland-Tide.*

The story in [*Tales of the Munster Festivals*] which is of particular interest for the student of Griffin is *The Half-Sir.* The figure which should command our particular attention here is that of Eugene Hamond. What one remarks, first of all, is that the character of Eugene Hamond is depicted with an unusual depth of psychological insight. . . . He is the 'half-sir' of the title, caught between 'simplicity and refinement'. He is also a young man of morbidly sensitive temperament, quite unfitted for dealing with the snubs and gibes of the ignorant, wealthy boors like Mr O'Neil. . . . Mr O'Neil, whose family is 'one of the best in Ireland', is an effective comic creation who is depicted as a being filled with mock humility about himself and arrogance about his family, constantly protesting that he himself is but the black sheep of his line. . . . (pp. 44-5)

As always when he treats of this kind of morbid sensitive, Griffin writes with unusual penetration. Witness, for example, the effective scene in Chapter 4 when Emily Bury sets out to

entertain the company with a funny tale about Eugene's servant, Remmy O'Lone. Her narrative requires her to pronounce local names of places and objects with which she is not familiar and she appeals to Eugene for assistance:

> 'Hamond was telling me a still more curious anecdote about him. He was sent once to a fair in Munster, the fair of Hanna—Vanna—Shana—what was it, Hamond?'
>
> 'Shanagolden,' said Eugene, bowing and smiling.
>
> 'O yes, the fair of Shanagolden. His mistress wanted to purchase half a dozen mug—hog—pig—'
>
> '*Piggins,* they were,' said Hamond in reply to her puzzled look, 'p-i-g-pig, g-i-n-s-gins, piggins,' spelling the word, to show how coolly and equally he took it. 'A kind of wooden vessel used for drinking the coagulated residuum of milk, called by the peasantry thick, or skimmed milk.'

This scene, with Emily Bury's casual condescension combining with Hamond's tense restraint (vividly conveyed in his spelling of the peasant word 'piggins'), has the peculiar life which Griffin always manages to impart to this kind of encounter. Here he abandons the contrived stereotypes which normally contented him and writes with his finger firmly on the pulses of his characters. (pp. 45-6)

On the personal level, [*The Half-Sir*] gives a real insight into Griffin's own mind and many of the later passages have the ring of unwitting autobiography. . . . The writer's genuine involvement with certain aspects of his material lends him an unusual force and insight. The unhappy childhood experiences of Eugene Hamond and his subsequent social disasters engender in him a hatred of those who have scorned and condescended to him and the blighting effects of these experiences on his character are traced with real penetration. Later in the story, when Hamond is working at relieving the famine-stricken poor, his muddled motives are convincingly analysed:

> The more Hamond saw of the misery, and of the dispositions of the impoverished classes of his countrymen, the more that dislike of the wealthy and high-born, which had constituted the disease of his mind for many years, was irritated and increased—and (without seeking maliciously to detract from the merit of his benevolence) we might say, that the poor benefited nearly as much by his resentment to their superiors, as by his compassion for themselves.

There is a genuine link here between Eugene's peculiarly motivated charity and his guardian's perverted benevolence. This provides a kind of moral coherence for the narrative which has previously been absent from Griffin's stories. (pp. 47-8)

[Hardress Cregan's] glamorous and excitable character takes us to the heart of the reasons for [the success of *The Collegians*] and to the core also of Griffin's personal puzzle and paradox. Hardress is the most remarkable of a long series of Griffin 'sensitives', a group which includes Eugene Hamond of *The Half-Sir,* the Saxon Kenric in *The Invasion* and Gisippus. . . . In these figures Griffin charted his personal dilemma and gave it artistic objectivity. The contention is not that the novels and the play are merely autobiographies in thin disguise but that, in these works, Griffin is exploring minds which he desperately needed to understand, minds subject to pressures all too familiar to the writer himself. . . . [An] examination of the development of Hardress Cregan in *The Collegians* will show the relevance of the novel to any full consideration of Griffin's achievement and decline. . . . (pp. 59-60)

Padraic Colum faults the ending of the book, asserting that the narrative is strained [see excerpt above, 1918]. . . . This is not altogether fair to the book. Danny Mann is made to explain his reasons for informing. Hardress has helped him to escape on condition that he fly the country. Danny remains and encounters Hardress on the public highway in the scene where Hardress and Anne Chute meet the mummers and Hardress is forced to dance with them. It is entirely acceptable that Hardress, seeing his erstwhile servant going about in company with the mummers instead of escaping abroad as arranged, should become enraged and assault him furiously. Danny Mann's resentment is equally acceptable since, in any case, an ambivalent attitude on the part of Danny Mann to his employer has been prepared for from the beginning, where we are told that the hunchback's deformed condition was brought about by Hardress who pushed him downstairs in the course of a childish game. That the deformed servant should veer from fidelity to bitter resentment back to repentant fidelity is entirely acceptable, particularly in the feverishly heightened context of melodramatic guilt which the novelist builds so skilfully around his hero. What Gerald Griffin is depicting in Hardress Cregan, then, is a young man who espouses and acts upon a naively over-simplified social philosophy, a sensitive creature incapable of compromise, a kind of Gothic George Marvin Brush [the hero of Thornton Wilder's *Heaven's My Destination*]. (pp. 64-5)

In *The Collegians* Griffin found the perfect story for his intense and tragically narrow gift of characterisation. The book is the inevitable climax of his achievement. Hardress Cregan is certainly melodramatic. He oversimplifies life, plunges into a disastrous situation, lunges this way and that in his efforts to escape, sins dreadfully, repents passionately—it is all extremes.

But it was a similar 'simplicity' which caused his creator so much daily difficulty in his own life and brought him eventually to destroy his manuscripts and abandon at once the world and his craft. Hardress refuses to make the compromise with society which Kyrle urges on him. He will carry his Rousseau-istic *simplesse* into his practice in life—and does so, with disastrous effects. This creature of extremes, starting from a hatred of sham, transgresses his social code, reacts violently to the resultant predicament and brings ruin upon himself. It is a fictional analogue of Griffin's own predicament. Hardress's social morality is as simple, as unsophisticated as Griffin's artistic morality. They are both sensitive, warm-hearted, full of 'nature', passionate and intense. They both have an over-simplified view of life and they both murder what they love: Hardress murders Eily; Griffin tries to destroy his work. Surely Griffin's penetration of the ambiguities of the character of Hardress is made possible because of some war within himself between two sharply opposed views of life and art, views which might be described in Kyrle Daly's words as 'simplicity' and 'elegance'. Hardress is brought to ruin by acting on his 'simplicity', but when he finds that it is just as possible to love the well-born and haughty Anne Chute and be loved by her in return it is too late to profit by his new sophistication and he is reduced to a frantic impotence. His stasis parallels his creator's.

The Collegians is Griffin's greatest work because it combines a hero whose psychology paralleled the author's own with a vivid depiction of a society in decay. It is the combination of personal with social which makes this novel memorable. Hardress's predicament is made poignant though the book is not always well plotted. He is a possible person, a character whom the author understands, at least in part, and whose setting he knows very well indeed. Thrown over all this is the romantic gloom of mountains, woods and streams and the result is a memorable melodrama which at times verges on being a great psychological study. Griffin was to write other novels but never again did he achieve the kind of Macbethian, doom-laden atmosphere of his best-known work. Hardress is an amateur of life, just as Griffin is essentially an amateur of letters. The Hardress who expresses his impatience of social *politesse* is the Griffin who feels that he is wasting time on story-telling while others are doing real work like doctoring or teaching and who therefore tries to qualify himself in the law, thinks of becoming a priest, teaches young local children their catechism and finally retires from the world. *The Collegians* is not merely Gerald Griffin's masterpiece. It is also the master key to an understanding of his development and decline. (pp. 68-9)

[*The Rivals* and *Tracy's Ambition*] make clear his growing interest in and profound compassion for the wretched state of the Irish peasantry. In spite of the intrusive melodrama of *The Rivals*, both that story and [*Tracy's Ambition*] give a memorably realistic picture of the grim world inhabited by the Irish peasant of the first quarter of the nineteenth century. (p. 70)

[The absurd plot of *The Rivals*] is merely the necessary, novelistic façade for a really effective piece of rustic realism which is sometimes very funny and often disturbing. Griffin sets his story in County Wicklow, around the beautiful vale of Glendalough, and seizes the opportunity to describe the small and lively rustic world of the place. In the depiction of Mr Lenigan's hedge school he achieves some of his most celebrated comic effects. So vividly is the schoolhouse brought to life that we find ourselves bitterly regretting that Griffin did not pursue this vein of his abilities and eschew the melodramatic effects in which he so often indulges. The lesson in 'consthering' Virgil's *Aeneid*, conducted by Mr Lenigan's Classical assistant, is both hilariously comic in itself and richly relevant to the entire history of verbal acrobatics in the Anglo-Irish novel. The teacher leads his rustic scholars vigorously through a passage from the *Aeneid*, contriving on the way a marvellous, forced marriage between the sonorous splendours of the Latin and the hilarious vividness of the Anglo-Irish idiom of the south of Ireland. Here, clearly, is beginning one notable strand of Anglo-Irish literature, the flamboyant, thrasonical, vigorous line which is to include Carleton, Lever, Boucicault, Joyce, Flann O'Brien and Brendan Behan. Griffin's polymaths are the harbingers of such complex achievements as the 'Oxen of the Sun' episode in *Ulysses*.

The world of *The Rivals*, however, though productive of such hilarities as these, is essentially a grim place. The author's tone is a combination of the sombre and the sardonic. . . . As often with Griffin . . . , the highly-flavoured histrionics of the principal actors are based on a clearly observed foundation of reality. The miseries of the Irish poor are made constantly clear. (pp. 70-2)

The turbulence of Irish life is reflected in lively discussions in shebeens and at death-beds. Mr Lenigan's brother, Davy, is made the spokesman of the sort of liberal conservatism which was probably Griffin's own political faith. . . . [Griffin] effectively brings home to his readers the genuineness of the peasants' grievances while constantly managing to suggest that all would be well if the laws were decently administered. Corrupt local politicians are the villains of the piece and are, essentially, as much the enemies of all loyal, middle-class citizens as of the peasants whom they more obviously oppress. The novel constantly affords us revealing glimpses of the troubled tangle of the life of the Irish poor, living close to the breadline and subject to savage penalties for transgressions which their appalling conditions render inevitable. (pp. 72-3)

[*Tracy's Ambition*] is in every way more successful than *The Rivals,* more powerfully imagined, more forcefully and succinctly realised. . . . The work has an almost Jonsonian force, with Abel possessing the comprehensive significance of a 'humour'. In his rendering of the main character Griffin displays considerable sardonic insight into Abel's psychology and employs it to involve us both with Abel himself and the turbulent times in which he lives. (p. 73)

It is appropriate that Griffin should have woven one of his most successful stories around the idea of an obsessive ambition. Intensely ambitious himself at the outset of his career, he gradually lost his taste for worldly success and found his work as a writer becoming increasingly distasteful to him. . . . For the depiction of Abel Tracy he reached within himself and applied profound convictions and insights concerning excessive human aspirations to his keen perception of the social ills of his day. In his effectiveness as a narrator, Abel Tracy recalls Maria Edgeworth's Thady Quirke in *Castle Rackrent.* Dangerously balanced between two classes, two religions, he inhabits a moral no-man's-land which Griffin charts with instinctive skill. This short and powerful work is altogether lacking in the longueurs which affect the much better-known novel, *The Collegians. Tracy's Ambition* possesses an impressive moral coherence and offers convincing glimpses of small-town life and the day-to-day existence of the country people. Griffin's Ireland often appears as a pullulating pit of restless helots but the depiction of their miseries is made all the more convincing by the fact that the novel is far from unrelievedly sombre. Indeed, there is a generous measure of the sort of comedy which would be at home in the 'R.M.' stories of Somerville and Ross when Griffin recounts the hilarious doings of the corps of yeomanry of which Abel Tracy is a member. His eye for comic detail is nicely evidenced in the second lieutenant who brushes his eyebrows against the grain to give himself an appearance of military ferocity. At the same time, the comedy is effectively used to suggest the chaotic state of the forces of law and order. (pp. 76-7)

Maria Edgeworth had seen the peasantry through the eyes of Thady Quirke as that dangerous serf had gazed out through the cracked panes of Castle Rackrent. Griffin, through his narrator Abel Tracy, brings the people Thady saw to vivid life for us, and in this short but powerful novel we stumble with them along the muddy roads of a barbarous and bitter land, we feel them huddling their wretched rags about them, we inhabit with them their miserable cabins and feel their winter cold. Many of Griffin's personal tensions must have been generated by the clash between his powerfully realistic vision of the Irish world about him and the demands of his comfortable, middle-class background. A different sort of man would have either joined in the exploitation or perhaps undertaken an active campaign against it. Griffin, intelligent, sensitive, peace-loving, separated by birth and fortune from the mass of his countrymen but utterly unable to identify with their oppressors, worked out

the logic of the situation and came to his own conclusion, that the only hope for his country and its people lay in improving their lot by educating them. . . . [We] can see in the tragic vision he displays in *Tracy's Ambition* the reason for his eventual decision to join a teaching Order dedicated to the educational betterment of the Irish poor. (p. 78)

In both *The Rivals* and *Tracy's Ambition,* Griffin writes with a powerful realism which is undimmed by the occasional melodrama of the plots. Both stories provide the reader with an unusual insight into the daily harshness of the lives of the Irish poor. Country roads with their travelling people, small towns with their poor markets and their beggars and prostitutes, paupers' cabins and paupers' graves, informers, 'nightwalkers', all pass before us in a sombre panorama of national desperation. (p. 80)

[The stories in *The Christian Physiologist*] are generally unimpressive. *The Kelp Gatherer* is a moral tale about a patient widow who endures blindness until, as a reward for her submission to God's will, she is cured of a cataract by a surgeon. . . . It is noticeable that, although the story is set in Ireland, Griffin does not here equip his characters with a regional idiom. They are made to speak a correct, indeed formal English. *The Day of Trial* . . . is rather more elaborately constructed and more effective. . . . Some of the ornate detail of this story resembles that of the long historical novel, *The Invasion.* . . . (p. 82)

[In *The Voluptuary Cured,* mild] fun is poked throughout at the Englishman's notion of Ireland as a wild country full of brigands and thieves. Lord Ulla, like Maria Edgeworth's Lord Glenthorne [in *Ennui*], has his eyes opened to his duties and to his own best interests. Despite its heavily moralistic tone, this is one of the more effective stories in the book and, in Lord Ulla's distaste for London and in the mild satire at the expense of English ignorance of Irish life, one occasionally catches a glimpse of Griffin's own sensations and attitudes. *The Self-Consumed* is a short and improbable tale illustrative of the evils of self-indulgence and luxury. Its detail is, once again, similar to that of *The Invasion,* with considerable emphasis on items of antique ornament, weapons and dress. This type of description is even more lavishly employed in *The Selfish Crotaire.* . . . (p. 83)

The account of the intellect [in the last chapter of *The Christian Physiologist*] is interestingly premonitory of Griffin's eventual flight from the world, and *A Story of Psyche* is really an extension into the theological and moral fields of the old argument carried on between Hardress Cregan and Kyrle Daly about the conflicting claims of 'elegance and simplicity'. . . . Griffin's brief version of a pilgrim's progress [in *A Story of Psyche*] is in no way theologically startling but the whole piece is interestingly analogous to Griffin's own life and very revealing of the type of thinking which lay behind some of his major decisions. (pp. 83-4)

[The] great mass of detailed information which [Griffin compiled for *The Invasion* gives the story] an authenticity which is, in places, a great advantage to it but which is often a dead weight, particularly at the beginning of the novel where the writer grossly overindulges himself in antiquarian description at every possible opportunity. . . . [*The Invasion*] begins very tediously and one soon wearies of the writer's determination to load every rift with the results of his antiquarian researches. Once the story gets under way, however, there is a certain interest in the confident depiction of a remote period and Griffin's reading would seem to have had this beneficial result, that it enabled him to move naturally enough through the remote times he is describing. It is, of course, a sentimentalised Ireland, full of richly apparelled chieftains and exotic Druids. There is little mention of the common people who, if they appear at all, do so merely as extras in the crowd scenes of a very glamorous production. The novel is leisurely in the extreme and perhaps the most curious aspect of it is that the invasion from which it derives its title barely happens. (p. 90)

What seems to have happened is that the focus of Griffin's interest changed as he wrote the book and turned from antiquarianism into [more familiar] channels. . . . The book's strongest focus is on the character of Elim's Saxon friend, Kenric, who is yet another in [Griffin's] gallery of proud, discontented solitaries. . . . Griffin's preoccupation with this sort of character is, perhaps, nowhere more startlingly displayed than in this book where the treatment of Kenric's character is allowed to take precedence even over the carefully amassed historical detail. In the last analysis this is, in spite of all early appearances, a novel about Kenric rather than an historical novel. (p. 91)

[Though] the Vikings, their beliefs and practices are elaborately described, they barely touch the shores of Ireland and we get instead a novel about a tormented Saxon solitary. This change of direction on the writer's part also renders irrelevant his early insistence on the dangers of faction among the Irish chieftains (a theme which Griffin probably wished to relate to the factious politics of the Ireland of his own day). If the book had shown an Ireland ravaged by the Vikings from without and torn by dissensions from within, the point about the dangers of faction would have been forcefully demonstrated. Since, however, Elim successfully repels the brief Viking attack at the end, much of the earlier detail about differences among the Irish chieftains seems ultimately irrelevant and the novelist seems to be aware of this when he closes his story by glancing briefly into the future and refers to the larger and more successful Viking invasions which lie ahead. (p. 92)

[*Tales of My Neighbourhood*] is a long work, a somewhat uneasy amalgam of long and short stories with interspersed narrative poems. . . . The collection is something of a job lot and the quality of the work varies wildly from story to story. This book contains examples of Griffin's more notable virtues and defects as a writer. (p. 113)

[*The Barber of Bantry*] is in Griffin's worst manner. Excessively long, circuitous, slow to get to the point, it rambles on from anecdote to anecdote, from one pointless digression to another, before the line of the main narrative emerges. . . . The leisurely narrative is dressed in a sauce of superstition. Fiends and apparitions of a rustically Faustian kind abound. In its detail and general tone, the narrative is sometimes reminiscent of some of the more melodramatic sections of *The Collegians*. Once again one feels the ranting shade of Edmund Kean at Griffin's elbow, prompting him to 'strong' dramatic scenes flavoured with melodrama and superstition. Yet, as with the earlier and more famous novel, there is here also a solid base of closely observed and effectively rendered detail of a realistic kind. Behind all the fustian there is a lively and interesting Irish world of small tradesmen and cobblers, barbers and pedlars, shopkeepers and farmers, shading upwards into the 'half-quality' of Tipsy Castle and Castle Tobin. Melodramatic sonorities unexpectedly taper off into lively and convincing rustic humour. Structurally, however, the story is al-

together a lamentable performance for a writer of Griffin's experience. (pp. 113-14)

[*The Great House*] is an effectively controlled exposure of the cruel abuse of Peter's rustic innocence. His own voice is used for the narration of the incidents and the nastiness of the 'great' is revealed throughout. Peter remains ignorant of the cruel joke that has been played on him to the very end. His dialogue is competently devised, at once amusing and engaging. . . . The contrast between rustic naiveté and Big-House condescension is achieved with fine economy in a racy narrative notably devoid of the appalling longueurs which disfigure [*The Barber of Bantry*]. It is, perhaps, significant that Griffin achieves this kind of force and power on this particular subject, the baiting of an Irish innocent by a collection of semi-Anglicised half-gentry. (pp. 114-15)

A Night at Sea is rather a long story and, like the other longer items in this book, would have benefited from sharp pruning. In so far as it has a main theme, it could be said to concern the effects of an excessively liberal education on the young. Griffin not infrequently adverts to conflicting notions on the education of the young and is himself quite clearly sceptical of the unduly permissive approach of theorists like Rousseau who advocate giving the young their head. . . . The narrative is slack and leisurely but, along the way, we are presented with an amusing picture of Irish small-town life with its local jealousies and animosities. The moralising narrative fails to hold our attention but we are occasionally entertained by the scenery and the characters.

Touch My Honour, Touch My Life is a piously serious attack on the vogue for duelling which obtained in a slightly earlier phase of Irish history. . . . [The] narrative is excruciatingly moral but there is an entirely hilarious portrait of a rustic Irish dancing master, one Thady Houlahan, who marvellously unfits his pupils for the polite measures of the metropolis. Thady, along with the schoolmaster, Theophilus O'Gallagher, proves some compensation for the tedium of the main narrative. (pp. 115-16)

[*Mount Orient*], one of the more amusing tales, gaily pillories a vulgar family of pretentious half-gentry. . . . [Miss Mimosa M'Orient] is delightfully depicted and we rejoice in her comic overthrow in the proposal scene where she imagines that the eligible Mr Fitzpatrick is wooing her elegant self when, in fact, he has come in pursuit of her plainer, less showy relative, Miss de Courcy. The amiable satire is pleasantly and lightly handled and the serious message about Ireland's poor, which underlies the flimsy story, is, for once, ably implied rather than stressed. (pp. 118-19)

The Philanthropist is a mildly fantastic story in which Griffin achieves a comic success. . . . Once again, as in the earlier story, *A Night at Sea,* excessive liberalism in education is being attacked but the attack this time is through comedy and, accordingly, more palatable. Everard Sweetman develops, in the course of the story, into a sort of Celtic Walter Mitty who plunges his family into debt in order to pay for his experiments and runs away from home to pursue his theories. His doings are recounted in a spirit of fun and this slight and amusing story reveals in Griffin a real talent for comic absurdity. (p. 119)

Unsatisfactory as *Tales of My Neighbourhood* may be in the many respects indicated, it does, nevertheless, convey a genuine sense of the chaos of Griffin's times and, at its best, manages to do so quite entertainingly. This flawed book reflects the struggle between his fine comic gift and the moral pedantry which was its greatest foe. Artistically flawed though it is, it gives us a genuine sense of the place and its many people. The book has a modest place in a line which eventually flowers into Moore's *The Untilled Field* and Joyce's *Dubliners*. An effort is made to link the stories by allowing occasional characters to reappear from story to story. The series of tales is by no means altogether lacking in art and the range of effects is considerable. There is enough successful social satire in the book to make one regret Griffin's decline into a tragic, aesthetic *simplesse*. (p. 120)

[In *The Duke of Monmouth*] Aquila is 'married' to Kirke by a demented preacher who is forced to enact a mockery of a wedding ceremony which, clearly, could not have fooled a child, let alone the practical young woman Aquila Fullerton has shown herself to be. She has, earlier in the story, been depicted as an emancipated and ardent supporter of Monmouth who argues with her lover and his loyal sister and actually stops Monmouth in the streets of Taunton in order to present to him some new colours she has woven for him. To suggest that she could have been taken in by the absurd stratagem devised by the prudish Griffin is utter nonsense. He preserves his heroine's reputation to the detriment of his fiction and does so, in any case, quite unnecessarily by any standards one cares to apply. The incident is sadly trivial and it is embarrassingly revelatory of the dire pass to which this writer had come at this late stage of his career. (p. 122)

Griffin achieved much between the publication of *Holland-Tide* . . . and his withdrawal from the world a decade later. . . . He showed himself to be one of the most convincing users of the regional English of the province of Munster, peopling his pages with hosts of richly-spoken and memorable figures, using the emergent English of the Irish poor for all kinds of effects, both humorous and tragic. At his best he is a powerfully realistic depictor of the troubled Ireland of his time. The ragged Irish scarecrows who crowd his pages prepare us for the horrors which fell upon the country in the dreadful decade after Griffin's early death. His discerning account of their irresponsible overlords is equally accurate and prophetic. In novels such as *The Collegians* and *Tracy's Ambition* we find vividly recorded the dark Ireland which lies between the Union and the Great Famine. If a writer deserves to be judged on his best work, then Griffin may safely be accounted one of the great Irish realistic writers. When one turns to analysing the causes of his artistic decline one finds that he eventually succumbed to temptations which have visited even the greatest writers. (p. 140)

> *John Cronin, in his* Gerald Griffin (1803-1840): A Critical Biography, *Cambridge University Press, 1978, 163 p.*

ROBERT DAVIS   (essay date 1980)

[*In his* Gerald Griffin, *Davis suggests that Griffin's "propensity to preach denied him the full realization of his artistic potential." Like Padraic Colum and John Cronin (1918, 1978), he argues that* The Collegians *marks Griffin's finest artistic achievement and signals the end of his creative development. Though Davis considers most of Griffin's works overly didactic, he maintains that "by equating his characters with national purpose—unity and peace in Ireland—[Griffin] became a social evaluator, a prophet, a guardian of his people's destiny."*]

[Griffin] feared that the creation of highly believable characters, such as Hardress Cregan in his best work *The Collegians*, would be morally detrimental to himself and to his reading

public. . . . [His] propensity to preach denied him the full realization of his artistic potential. [In] the dramatic structuring of his scenes and the social verisimilitude which his peasants deliver . . . are found the value of an artist who believed that his primary function was to teach a moral. (p. 7)

Gerald Griffin wanted to write morally perfect novels. When he failed, he decided to live, as best he could, a morally perfect life. His piety, genius, and profound sense of Ireland's past led him quite naturally to the overall theme of reform. His moralism stemmed from an unalterable sense that his people, the Catholic peasants, who constituted four-fifths of the population of Ireland in the third decade of the nineteenth century, must be directed to the practice of forgiving and forgetting so that individuals could be made whole and national unity and identity achieved. (p. 8)

Griffin fits conveniently into the eighteenth century and the tradition of the didactic English novel. He is also one of the first Irish Catholic novelists to write preponderantly in a moralistic vein. (p. 9)

Art and didacticism were of one piece in the works of Gerald Griffin until a moral paralysis ended his art at a point in his career clearly marked by success and promise. . . . He was never again to create a character of such effective moral force and beauty as Hardress Cregan [in *The Collegians*], for, when Griffin refused to oppose his scruples in the creation of characters, he denied himself a deeper knowledge of himself as an artist as well as a greater verisimilitude in his art. The works which followed this resolution to resist what had become tantamount to an occasion of sin, the creative act, are mediocre; nevertheless, they indicate the potential which had been abandoned. What becomes increasingly clear to the reader of Griffin's works is that the writer's decision to avoid passion in the creation and representation of characters is also his plea to his readers to avoid passion in their lives. (p. 10)

When the moral lesson, Griffin's chief concern in writing, failed to eclipse the artistic values of dramatic structure, characterization, and tragicomedy, then Griffin's writing was at its best. Some of his early tales were beautifully balanced pieces: art and morality complemented one another. Other tales of his early work bore obvious signs of hasty construction and crude didacticism, but the latter seems in the minority. The rapidity with which Griffin wrote *Tales of the Munster Festivals* . . . , for example, and the arduous conditions under which he wrote them explain their weaknesses, but the *Tales* clearly demonstrate his genius.

Griffin's works involve his probing, moral consideration of the various social planes of Irish life filled with fragmented loyalties and ancient hatreds. As artist, moralist, and national prophet he presents the lives and destinies of Munstermen who endured Penal days, hoped for emancipation, and dreamed of freedom and sovereignty. The structural unity of this Munsterman's writings, his brilliant comedy so intrinsically a part of the social tragedy he presented, the moral force and beauty of his early characterizations all combine to render Irish character and tradition, to record a culture. . . . For the "complicated and self-contradictory society" that was Ireland in the first decades of the nineteenth century, Griffin created an identity. By equating his characters with national purpose—unity and peace in Ireland—he became a social evaluator, a prophet, a guardian of his people's destiny. (pp. 10-11)

Today *Gisippus* exists not as a work of art but as an indication of Griffin's potential. It is melodramatic and excessively sentimental; its characters are highly improbable and its themes far too many. However, in Griffin's themes and, at times, in his flashes of brilliant dialogue are the signs that this young Irishman could serve art and society. (p. 48)

Melodrama presides in ["**The Aylmers of Bally-Aylmer**"], but Griffin's use of dramatic structuring of scenes—the converging of Will's and his father's paths to the court, for example—his outlay of humor, and the vivid scenes of peasant realities make it effective entertainment. Griffin was appealing to the rising middle class who were, in the main, his readers. He believed reform should start with them. Just as Will feels instinctively a need for justice or Kate cries out against a law that "persecutes after God has forgiven," Griffin preached for charity and an end to crippling pride. (pp. 58-9)

Griffin's peasants are convincing in spite of their brief exposure. These are the people he knew best. His first "crathurs" no doubt pleased the young writer and he was soon to build on them: Sandy and Lewy become the brilliant characters Lowry Looby and Danny Mann of *The Collegians*. The middle men in "**The Aylmers**" are pale indeed: Hasset names a type and a place and Will apes unconvincingly the supposed manners and motives of a college student. (p. 59)

The characters in ["**The Hand and Word**"] are ensnared in melodramatic fits of dialogue, and moved along hurriedly to their tragic fates. However, in their brief exposure they seem sufficiently motivated and appear "real" in the sense that their lives are peculiar to the locale that Griffin describes so effectively. Taken together, "**The Aylmers**" and "**The Hand and Word**" lend validity to the claim that Griffin's conversion from drama to prose was greatly facilitated by his efforts with shorter pieces. He neglects characterization in "**The Hand and Word**" in his outlay of landscape, action, dialogue, imagery, themes, symbols, morals, and humor. However, all the ingredients of this tale are so precisely balanced and thematically linked that Griffin had little space for melodrama as a vehicle for his preachment. "**The Aylmers**" attempts more and betrays more of this flaw. (pp. 62-3)

The melodrama of "**Card Drawing**" is made more palatable by recurring motifs from *Holland-tide* (for instance, Griffin's continued use of the cliff) which tend to expand Griffin's art and didacticism through more effective characterizations. Dorgan and Kinchela, though stock contrasts, are delivered with more force and effect in the multiple viewing which Griffin brings to the story. They view a community; a community views them. They reveal their inner thoughts during moments of extreme physical and mental stress and the reader receives, in total effect, a comprehensive view of a society of peasants, priests, and middlemen, highly believable in their moral and immoral behavior. (p. 73)

From the sheep-stealers of the Kerry hills in "**The Aylmers**" of *Holland-tide* to the "tolerable faithful picture of a Munster cottage life" in the *Tales,* Griffin expands his presentation of the social turmoil he knew through personal observation. Characters [in the *Tales*] seem to be more believable. Will Aylmer, an orphan at the time he is sent to Dublin for an education, is pale in comparison to Hamond [in "**The Half Sir**"], also an orphan, whose character is more fully delineated in terms of his childhood experience with a neurotic guardian. Hamond's diffidence and pride, for example, before Emily's Dublin coterie is understandable because of his old uncle's warped view of reality. In "**Suil Dhuv**," Issac Segur's return to his adopted homeland and his search for his daughter are a continuation of

Griffin's development of the exile-return theme in which dramatic, moral structuring of scenes leads to more psychologically penetrating characterizations and a heightening of moral force. (p. 81)

The order of the *Tales* seems to suggest the growth of Griffin's powers as a novelist. The actions of characters like Duke Dorgan in "**Card Drawing**" are described—he does very little acting. Eugene Hamond is more fully realized—he speaks and acts forcefully. His inner thoughts deepen the significance of his performance. Griffin lost some of his diffidence as a writer when he began to allow his own experiences to become part of his writing. For example, Hamond's reactions to Emily's Dublin circle, the Anglo-Irish aristocracy, were also Griffin's, on those occasions when he too found himself in unfamiliar company. "**Suil Dhuv**," Griffin's best piece in the series, shows his talent for arranging scenes and juxtaposing characters for maximum exposure. A slackening in the application of melodrama, Griffin's principal weakness, is also apparent in "**Suil Dhuv**." Pryce Kinchela's remorse, arrived at while he hangs over a cliff's edge at the end of a rope, is far less effective than the chapel scene [in "**Suil Dhuv**"] in which Dinny's past becomes his present and his tortured soul is bared.

Implied Christian principles of education and psychological insight into human motivations and actions were . . . two of Griffin's most important subjects. He was a teacher in his art and an artist in his teaching. He was an artist of feelings and the times in which they occurred. He knew how to portray the dignity and failure of his people. The misfits of his stories appear as strong deterrents to the peace and unity of his nation for which he daily prayed. (pp. 88-9)

Griffin's characters in *The Collegians* are far superior to those of his earlier works. They are fully motivated figures who react to the new information which they daily encounter. However, as artistically finished as the entire book seems in its characterizations, setting, and plot, as knowledgeable as Griffin's sociological approach to this eighteenth-century Irish scene appears, the precisely balanced structure of characters and scenes produces a moral impact indicative of the fact that teaching a moral lesson in literature was inevitable for Griffin, even when he seemed most unfettered by his scruples. The moral structure of *The Collegians,* the form its movements and parts take in delivering his preachments, mark his finest artistic effort and signal the end of his artistic growth.

Griffin referred to *The Collegians* as a "domestic drama," and having used all his powers as a dramatist he structured his scenes to advance a Roman Catholic theme of duty to God and to family. He was certainly intent upon achieving a balance in the emotional response of his readers. Tension caused by the conflict which Hardress creates is evenly distributed through a logical and unified series of scenes patterning the emotions of Griffin's characters and directing the reactions and emotions of his readers. The entire structure of *The Collegians* consists of precise juxtaposings of characters and scenes for a moral impact. As Lowry Looby and Danny Mann parody Hardress Cregan and Kyrle Daly, for example, or Cregan contrasts Daly, the reader encounters[, in the words of Thomas Flanagan,] "a social novel, embracing all classes and conditions" [see excerpt above, 1959] and is directed along the moral plane of duty to God and family. (pp. 92-3)

The fates of the two collegians, Cregan's exile and death and Kyrle's final success with the chastened Anne, are amplified by the other richly dramatic, highly didactic, warmly humorous scenes involving the inheritors of Munster culture, Griffin's peasants, who possess grace, wit, and pathos. They move parallel much of the time to the fortunes of the collegians, offering objectivity, irony, and common sense compounded by a remembrance of things past and a glowing pride in their ability to endure. (p. 94)

Griffin, with all of the dramatist's bent on holding his audience, carefully allots sufficient space to advance the Dalys' high moral character. He knows they are dull and sentimental in comparison to the Cregans and hence less entertaining. However, it is Griffin's profound respect for Christian principles in the home that prompts this contrast to the Cregans. . . . (p. 97)

[*The Rivals, Tracy's Ambition, The Christian Physiologist,* and *The Invasion*] clearly indicate that Griffin abandoned the formula he had discovered in writing *The Collegians.* His writing was now a part of his daily prayers for guidance into a religious life, and from his experience with *The Collegians* he was acutely aware of the fact that one element in a book or story could completely set aside the moral purpose he had in mind for his reader. The balance of psychological realism in *Tracy's Ambition* and the dense moral tone of *The Rivals* attest to the fact that Griffin's scrupulosity would never again allow his readers to be merely entertained. (p. 104)

Resurrection is the principal theme in *The Rivals.* . . . As melodramatic and redundant as scenes from *The Rivals* become with their religious and political overtones, the tale displays Griffin as a master storyteller of his people and their times. (p. 105)

The theme of resurrection, Riordan's return from exile, Esther's role as a ghost, Lacy's durability in combat and his inclination toward repentance, are contrasted by the realism of the opening dispensary scene in which Doctor Jarvis struggles to handle a throng of ailing peasants and one of the closing scenes of the tale in which Davy Lenigan, before his cronies at the local inn, eloquently and judiciously lodges his complaint against the British government and prescribes the Irish Catholic's best stand against it—peace and endurance. However effective these scenes are in terms of social verisimilitude and thematic relevance, Griffin's serializing of the combat between Riordan and Lacy and such scenes as the lover's spell in the burial vault render the tale hopelessly melodramatic.

Undoubtedly, Griffin felt justified in such handling of the theme of "resurrection" because he knew that Abel Tracy's "rebirth" [in *Tracy's Ambition*] would more than compensate his reader for the improbabilities in *The Rivals. Tracy's Ambition* achieves distinction as an example of Griffin's ability to trace realistically a life of moral ruin and regeneration in a time of national crisis. (p. 107)

Tracy's character is among the first creations of Griffin to undergo detailed psychological change, for the most part recorded by the character himself, as he experiences two opposing worlds—the world of the Protestant landlord and magistrate, basing his idea of Ireland's worth on what service can be got from a "shiftless" peasantry, and the world of the peasants, who look on Tracy's desertion as symptomatic of the continuing failure of the Protestant ruling class to understand their position—natives of the soil they may not possess, victims of a tyranny they may not oppose. With *Tracy's Ambition* Griffin is beginning to evoke, in addition to a highly moral tone, psychological realism and strong social commentary in his presentation of the turmoil leading up to the Rebellion of 1798. And if the presence of the "yellow man," noted at

various stages of Tracy's decline, can be accepted as a literary device, representing Tracy's lust for gold and power, on the one hand, and his former charity, on the other, then Griffin was indeed showing fine artistic promise, using the essential ingredient of his art—passion in the hearts of the people he knew best. (p. 111)

[Griffin's style in *The Invasion*] is grandiose: politics, nationalism, and antiquarianism fill a story of epic proportions but one which fails to sustain such bulk because of weak characterizations; moreover, the peasants who live close to the fortresses and temples are seldom seen. Instead of characters, Griffin provides names for his several voices—political, moral, historical, personal. *The Invasion* is the "objective correlative" for Griffin's feelings about invasions which take place not only on the shores of countries throughout the world but in the hearts and minds of individuals: the invasion of pride, for example, which in crippling private conscience endangers society as a whole. (p. 118)

Griffin made his book into a treatise on solving the ills of contemporary Ireland. "Union and love," words sung by Eithne to Elim and before a Druid audience, are rather empty without some understanding of Ireland's glorious past, the author felt. Druid and Celt, in this fiction, learn to live in peace and harmony, and part of their ability to do so is through an understanding of each other's values and heritages. Griffin's attempts at placing his readers in ninth-century Ireland involve scenes depicting marriage, burial, battle, and government, but they succeed only in impeding the story's progress and deadening characterizations. (p. 120)

From the chaotic and yet interrelated rush of anecdotes delivered by characters in the first half of **"The Barber of Bantry"** to the remaining twelve tales [in *Tales of My Neighbourhood*] in which character cross-references and reappearances reinforce the theme of social and moral instability, Griffin produces for his reader a growing familiarity with the character of a neighborhood through ever-widening disclosures about its inhabitants. (p. 122)

[Griffin's] peasants, middlemen, and Protestant gentry possess the same strengths and weaknesses throughout. Problems and solutions remain the same. All that seems to matter to the author is that there is time for retribution, reconciliation, and charity in the lives of his characters once they learn the error of their ways. Social unity emerges as the central theme from folklore, realism, caricatures, and melodrama, suggesting Griffin's awareness that if he were to influence his people in matters of social reform as they were striking for religious and political freedom, then his material had to be close to home, immediately recognizable. *The Invasion*'s failure was his proof. (p. 123)

With the exception of Griffin's artful manipulation of the narrators in **"The Barber of Bantry"** and the full, dramatic play of his peasants in the tale of an Irish feud in **"The Black Birds and Yellow Hammers,"** *Tales of My Neighbourhood* adds little to the artistic credits of the Irish novelist. The remaining tales are exercises, some charming, others dull and even exasperating in their heavy inlay of melodrama and threadbare themes. (p. 127)

For the most part, [the] tales are thematically linked. They complement and reinforce one another and, generally, in a light, satiric tone Griffin conveys his message that his neighborhood is wholesome but flawed, that it holds a very special place in his heart, that it possesses in the practice of Christian charity its own power for moral regeneration. (p. 128)

[In *The Duke of Monmouth,* the] duke's party, consisting of Fletcher, his chief advisor and a devout Republican, Lord Grey, his ineffectual general but loyal supporter, and Ferguson, an equally honest but deluded follower of the profligate, would-be monarch, fails to create either suspense or dramatic tension for the reader, who is shunted from one camp to another and exposed to bits of dialogue from a class with whom Griffin had no experience. Although Griffin followed closely the actual history of Monmouth's rebellious landing and his subsequent defeat at Sedgemoor, his protrayals of Monmouth and his cohorts are complete failures. There is, for example, never a moment when they convince the reader of the magnitude of their adventure or of their ability to carry it off. (p. 130)

The note of moderation in politics Griffin wished to convey in *The Duke of Monmouth* for Ireland's immediate future would have been lost to his readers, even with a preface similar to the one he supplied for *The Invasion* in which he pompously outlined his patriotic role. *The Duke of Monmouth*'s plot is feeble and anticlimactic. Characters think and act solely in terms of their political feelings. As crucial as Monmouth's advance is to the lives of the Fullartons and the Kingslys, it simply does not generate human response in characters like Aquila Fullarton who can calmly crochet a handkerchief to present to the duke while the lives of those most dear to her are threatened. Griffin strove to show the effects of excessive patriotism, but he explained little of the human condition which caused it. What he is successful in demonstrating is the shock of war upon the people of Taunton and Bridgewater. What he conjures is the memory of what befell the Irish people after the fall of Limerick in 1691. (p. 132)

Anglo-Irish prose began with writers like Edgeworth, Banim, and Griffin, but only Griffin attempted to justify all he wrote in terms of moral instruction. Perhaps his readers were less afraid of either a spiritual or a physical death than this earnest moralist, or, perhaps, as Arland Ussher says, an ''Irishman cannot really take morality seriously, as a good in itself like religion or beauty; for him it is either the book of the rules for getting to heaven, or a matter of personal fastidiousness.'' In either case, Griffin's success and achievement ended as soon as it began. As an artist he never was able to transcend the deepest significance of the Judeo-Christian concept of man's fall.

Griffin's lasting literary contribution is *The Collegians* and the recreation of a Munster neighborhood. Inextricably a part of this creation was his commitment to the teachings of the Roman Catholic Church which he imposed upon his readers, thus making any appreciation of his work in his time and today somewhat difficult. In the fifty to one hundred years that separates Griffin from writers like Synge, Joyce, O'Faolain, and Brian Moore, Griffin appears more the priest ready with direct counseling, one eager to set problems of the soul aright rather than to shed any light upon the passions which created his character's predicament. More accessible to readers who understand his purpose in writing, Griffin enters the world of reprinted editions as a fine Irish Catholic regionalist whose life was analogous to that of his country: emerging as an artist at a time when his people were being lead to religious freedom, Griffin finally turned from art in writing to art in Christian living. . . .

That such novelists as Graham Greene, Brian Moore, Iris Murdoch, and Evelyn Waugh were influenced by Griffin's writings is not improbable. That these writers, among others, constitute a Roman Catholic tradition in the novel, a tradition of writing stories espousing the teaching of the Catholic Church, seems quite apparent to the reader. And that this tradition began in Ireland with Gerald Griffin is to his credit. (p. 139)

> *Robert Davis, in his* Gerald Griffin, *Twayne Publishers, 1980, 151 p.*

ADDITIONAL BIBLIOGRAPHY

De Vere, Aubrey. ''Youth.'' In his *Recollections of Aubrey De Vere,* pp. 27-58. New York: Edward Arnold, 1897.*
    Affectionate biographical sketch by one of Griffin's childhood friends.

Foster, Roy. ''The Young Man of Limerick.'' *Times Literary Supplement,* No. 3986 (25 August 1978): 947.
    Praises *The Rivals* and *Tracy's Ambition* for their penetrating descriptions of Irish village life and attention to the hardships of the Irish peasantry. Foster asserts, however, that these novels, unlike *The Collegians,* are marred by the ''moralizing scrupulousness'' that eventually caused Griffin to abandon his literary career.

Gill, W. S. *Gerald Griffin: Poet, Novelist, Christian Brother.* Dublin: M. H. Gill & Son, 1940, 111 p.
    A sympathetic biography, published on the centenary of Griffin's death, that includes a survey of Griffin's works. Gill, a member of the Society of the Christian Brothers, devotes an entire chapter to Griffin's activities as a Christian Brother.

Griffin, Daniel. *The Works of Gerald Griffin: The Life of Gerald Griffin, Vol. 1.* 2d ed. New York: D. & J. Sadlier & Co., 1857, 406 p.
    The chief source of biographical information concerning Griffin, written by his brother. In his tribute to Gerald, Daniel relies heavily on his brother's journals and correspondence.

Hall, S. C. ''Gerald Griffin.'' In his *A Book of Memories of Great Men and Women of the Age, from Personal Acquaintance,* 2d ed., pp. 229-30. London: J. S. Virtue and Co., 1877.
    Character sketch based on personal reminiscences. Hall considers Griffin ''a coward in the battle of life'' for his decision to forsake his literary career and join the Society of the Christian Brothers.

John, Prester. ''Gerald Griffin.'' *The Dublin University Magazine* LXXXIX, No. DXXXII (April 1877): 534-41.
    Appreciative biographical and critical sketch. John's essay focuses on *The Collegians,* which he calls the most accurate delineation of Irish character in Irish fiction.

MacCarthy, B. G. ''Irish Regional Novelists of the Early Nineteenth Century: Parts I and II.'' *The Dublin Magazine* XXI, Nos. 1, 3 (January-March 1946; July-September 1946): 26-32, 28-37.*
    Separates early nineteenth-century Irish novelists into two categories—the Ascendancy class, who depict the peasants in relation to their masters, and the native Irish class, who portray the masters in relation to the oppressed. According to MacCarthy, Griffin sympathizes with the native population, but ''never comes off his high-horse to write from their point of view.''

Mannin, Ethel. ''Gerald Griffin.'' In her *Two Studies in Integrity: Gerald Griffin and the Rev. Francis Mahony ('Father Prout'),* pp. 17-132. New York: G. P. Putnam's Sons, 1954.
    Biographical study that contains previously unpublished letters and journals. In her exploration of Griffin's personality, Mannin focuses on his relationships with John Banim and Lydia Fisher.

Monahan, Michael. ''Gerald Griffin.'' In his *Nova Hibernia: Irish Poets and Dramatists of Today and Yesterday,* pp. 168-85. 1914. Reprint. Freeport, N.Y.: Books for Libraries Press, 1967.
    Laudatory assessment of Griffin's career. Ultimately, Monahan's praise of Griffin rests on what he describes as his ''genuine cre-

ative gift,'' an ''informing faculty'' that enabled him to depict Irish peasants more accurately than any other Irish novelist.

Somerville, E. E., and Ross, Martin. ''Stage Irishmen and Others.'' In their *Stray-aways,* pp. 241-54. London: Longmans, Green and Co., 1920.*

Favorably contrasts the simple, dignified language of the peasants in *The Collegians* to the bombastic speech of the upper-class characters in the novel. Somerville and Ross argue that Griffin's peasants are ''creatures real enough to outweigh the artificiality of their masters and mistresses'' and to give *The Collegians* value as an historical document.

Wolff, Robert Lee. Introduction to *The Collegians,* by Gerald Griffin, pp. v-lxi. Ireland: From the Act of Union, 1800, to the Death of Parnell, 1891. New York: Garland Publishing, 1979.

A general critical introduction to Griffin's works that includes a brief account of his life. Wolff provides plot summaries of many of Griffin's stories and discusses other critics' interpretations of his works.

Jean Paul

1763-1825

(Pseudonym of Johann Paul Friedrich Richter) German novelist, essayist, short story and sketch writer, and autobiographer.

Although Jean Paul was one of the most popular German novelists of his day, his reputation has declined considerably and today his appeal is limited. Henry Wadsworth Longfellow aptly characterized him as "Jean Paul, the Only-One," for he does not fit into any literary movement, and his work eludes strict classification. While commentators unfailingly praise the humor, intelligence, and imagination of his writing, they differ widely in their opinions of his slight yet chaotic plots and complex style.

Jean Paul's early years were marked by financial hardship. His father, a school teacher, organist, and pastor, died in 1779 and the family quickly descended into poverty. Jean Paul attended grammar school in Hof and later studied theology at the University of Leipzig. While at the university he published a collection of satirical sketches entitled *Grönländische Prozesse; oder, satirische Skizzen*. His next collection of satires, *Auswahl aus des Teufels Papieren: Nebst einem nöthingen Aviso vom Juden Mendel*, was published six years later. Neither of these works, modeled on the writings of the eighteenth-century English satirists Jonathan Swift and Alexander Pope, met with success.

Because of financial difficulties, Jean Paul left the university after three years and returned to the family home in Hof. There, he found a position as a private tutor and later became a schoolmaster. After the death of his mother in 1797, Jean Paul lived for short periods in Leipzig, Weimar, Berlin, Meiningen, and Coburg. In 1801, he married Caroline Mayer, and three years later they settled in Bayreuth. Jean Paul was granted a pension by Prince Karl Theodor von Dalberg in 1808 that guaranteed him life-long financial security.

Jean Paul's most important works can be divided into four groups: early novels, major novels, theoretical works, and late novels. The first group, written in the 1790s, includes *Die unsichtbare Loge: Eine Biographie* (*The Invisible Lodge*), *Hesperus; oder, 45 Hundsposttage: Eine Biographie* (*Hesperus; or, Forty-Five Dog-Post-Days*), *Blumen-, Frucht- und Dornenstücke; oder, Ehestand, Tod und Hochzeit des Armen-advocaten Firmian Stanislaus Siebenkäs* (*Flower, Fruit and Thorn Pieces; or, The Married Life, Death and Wedding of the Advocate of the Poor, Firmian Stanislaus Siebenkäs*), and *Leben des Quintus Fixlein, aus funfzehn Zettelkästen gezogen: Nebst einem Mustheil und einigen Jus de Tablette* (*Life of Quintus Fixlein*). These novels reflect an abrupt change in the nature of Jean Paul's work. The deaths of two close friends and his brother's suicide in 1790 led to a hallucinatory vision of his own death; as a result, the bitter satire characterizing his first works gave way to sentiment, imagination, and gentle humor. The eighteenth-century English novelist Laurence Sterne replaced Jonathan Swift as Jean Paul's literary model.

The Invisible Lodge, written soon after his death vision, was Jean Paul's first successful work and the first for which he used the pseudonym Jean Paul, adopted in homage to the French

philosopher and novelist Jean Jacques Rousseau. With the publication of his next novel, *Hesperus*, Jean Paul became one of the most popular authors in Germany. Central to both novels is Jean Paul's concept of the *hohe Menschen*: lofty, superior human beings who must endure the trivialities and hardships of everyday life though more suited to a transcendent existence. In his essay "Von hohen Menschen" in *The Invisible Lodge*, Jean Paul described these individuals as distinguished by their "elevation above the earth, a conviction of the triviality of all earthly activities and of the lack of accord between our heart and our station . . . a wish for death and a glance that ranges above the clouds." In his next works, *Flower, Fruit and Thorn Pieces*, better known as *Siebenkäs*, and in *Life of Quintus Fixlein*, Jean Paul turned from the sublime to the prosaic. Often described as idylls, these novels affectionately portray the lives of quiet, ordinary people. While their plots are frequently termed insubstantial, critics praise their humor and sentiment.

Although *Titan* and *Flegeljahre: Eine Biographie* (*Walt and Vult; or, The Twins*) are regarded as Jean Paul's greatest novels, critics generally focus on *Titan*. Considered Jean Paul's *Bildungsroman*, or apprenticeship novel, the work traces the development of the main character, Albano, who is Jean Paul's embodiment of an ideal man. Albano is a titan, or *hohe Menschen*, whose interactions with other characters demonstrate the contrast between his striving for a harmonious existence and other, less balanced approaches to life. Hedonism, aestheticism, and extreme emotionalism are each personified by a character in the novel. In this work, in addition to developing his concept of *hohe Menschen*, Jean Paul expressed his views on the political, social, and intellectual issues of his day.

During the next few years, at the height of his career, Jean Paul devoted himself to writing essays on such topics as aesthetics, education, and politics. *Vorschule der Aesthetik: Nebst einigen Vorlesungen in Leipzig über die Parteien der Zeit* (*Horn of Oberon: Jean Paul Richter's School for Aesthetics*), an explication of his aesthetic theory, is usually considered his most important theoretical work. *School for Aesthetics* contains fifteen detailed and theoretical "Courses" followed by three more loosely-organized "Lectures" that focus on aspects of contemporary literature and criticism. The individual essays examine such diverse topics as humor, wit, imagination, style, characters, and plot. René Wellek described Jean Paul's purpose in this work as self-analysis, for he "has most to say about the kind of novel he was writing himself: the sprawling humorous romance, his own strange mixture of the fantastic, dreamy, and sentimental with the odd and grotesque." In fact, critics often look to *School for Aesthetics* to clarify and illuminate Jean Paul's creative works.

Jean Paul's late novels include *Des Feldpredigers Schmelzle Reise nach Flätz mit fortgehenden Noten: Nebst der Beichte des Teufels bey einem Staatsmanne* (*Army-Chaplain Schmelzle's Journey to Flaetz*), *Dr Katzenbergers Badereise: Nebst einer Auswahl verbesserter Werkchen, Leben Fibels, des Verfassers der Bienrodischen Fibel*, and *Der Komet; oder, Nikolaus Marggraf: Eine komische Geschichte*. Critics comment that the personal unhappiness of his last years is reflected in his late novels, which repudiate the world view of such earlier novels as *The Invisible Lodge, Hesperus,* and *Titan*. The quiet idealism and gentle sentimentality characteristic of those works give way to the cynical realism and sardonic humor of his last novels.

Jean Paul's best novels share certain themes, including the search for a harmonious existence that is crucial to his concept of *hohe Menschen*, and the conflict between the real and ideal. Dualism recurs throughout Jean Paul's works; comedy and pathos, intellect and emotion, body and soul, earthly existence and eternal paradise are continually contrasted. This dualism is also manifested in the dream passages, which critics cite when discussing Jean Paul's works as precursors of the modern psychological novel. Characterized by their free association of ideas, these passages are often praised for their lyrical beauty. Many sections address philosophical issues, including "Rede des todten Christus" in *Siebenkäs*, in which Jean Paul questions the existence of God. His novels are considered formless: many critics complain that his plots are insubstantial and frequently interrupted by digressions and interpolations. His style, too, is regarded as complex. Yet, although his writing is often described as overcrowded with allusions drawn from his extensive readings, critics also acknowledge passages of great simplicity and beauty.

Jean Paul's critical and popular reception has fluctuated since his death. Although he was one of the most popular German novelists of his day and admired and imitated long after his death, by the end of the nineteenth century his works were rarely read in Germany. Contemporary critics agree that this decline resulted largely from his sentimentality and the obscurity of his prose. Many critics find that Jean Paul's style has

discouraged translation, thus rendering his works inaccessible to an English-speaking audience. The length and complexity of his works are thought to deter readers, and many commentators contend that his novels require perseverence to be appreciated. Of all his writings, the dream passages in his novels have received the most sustained critical attention. Nineteenth-century critics, beginning with Thomas Carlyle, praised these passages, while twentieth-century interest in the role of the subconscious in the creative process has won them renewed attention. Consistently, though, critics agree that Jean Paul's varied use of humor remains his major contribution to the German novel.

PRINCIPAL WORKS

Grönländische Prozesse; oder, Satirische Skizzen (sketches) 1783
Auswahl aus des Teufels Papieren: Nebst einem nöthingen Aviso vom Juden Mendel (sketches) 1789
*Die unsichtbare Loge: Eine Biographie (unfinished novel and short story) 1793
[*The Invisible Lodge* (partial translation) 1883]
Hesperus; oder, 45 Hundsposttage: Eine Biographie (novel) 1795
[*Hesperus; or, Forty-Five Dog-Post-Days*, 1865]
Blumen-, Frucht- und Dornenstücke; oder, Ehestand, Tod und Hochzeit des Armenadvocaten Firmian Stanislaus Siebenkäs. 3 vols. (novel) 1796-97
[*Flower, Fruit and Thorn Pieces; or, The Married Life, Death and Wedding of the Advocate of the Poor, Firmian Stanislaus Siebenkäs*, 1845]
Leben des Quintus Fixlein, aus funfzehn Zettelkästen gezogen: Nebst einem Mustheil und einigen Jus de Tablette (novel) 1796
[*Life of Quintus Fixlein* published in *German Romance: Specimens of Its Chief Authors, Vol. 3*, 1827]
Titan. 4 vols. (novel and essay) 1800-03
[*Titan*, 1862]
Flegeljahre: Eine Biographie. 4 vols. (unfinished novel) 1804-05
[*Walt and Vult; or, The Twins*, 1846]
Vorschule der Aesthetik: Nebst einigen Vorlesungen in Leipzig über die Parteien der Zeit (essay) 1804
[*Horn of Oberon: Jean Paul Richter's School for Aesthetics,* 1973]
Levana; oder, Erziehungslehre (essay) 1807
[*Levana; or, The Doctrine of Education*, 1848]
Des Feldpredigers Schmelzle Reise nach Flätz mit fortgehenden Noten: Nebst der Beichte des Teufels bey einem Staatsmanne (novel) 1809
[*Army-Chaplain Schmelzle's Journey to Flaetz* published in *German Romance, Vol. 3*, 1827]
Dr Katzenbergers Badereise: Nebst einer Auswahl verbesserter Werkchen (novel) 1809
Leben Fibels, des Verfassers der Bienrodischen Fibel (novel) 1812
Der Komet; oder, Nikolaus Marggraf: Eine komische Geschichte. 3 vols. (unfinished novel) 1820-22
Jean Paul's sämmtliche Werke. 65 vols. (novels, unfinished novels, essays, short stories, sketches, and letters) 1826-38
Wahrheit aus Jean Paul's Leben. 8 vols. (unfinished autobiography) 1826-33
["The Autobiography" published in *Life of Jean Paul F. Richter*, 1842]

Werke. 6 vols. (novels, unfinished novels, essays, short stories, and sketches) 1959-66

*This work includes the short story "Leben des vergnügten Schulmeisterleins Maria Wuz in Auenthal" ("Maria Wuz" in *"Maria Wuz" and "Lorenz Stark"; or, English Prints of Two German Originals*, 1881); this work also includes the essay "Von hohen Menschen."

JEAN PAUL FRIEDRICH RICHTER (essay date 1795)

[*The following essay, dated 1795, first appeared as a preface to Jean Paul's novel* Life of Quintus Fixlein, *published in 1796. Here the author states that his reason for writing the novel is to teach the reader to enjoy life. According to Jean Paul, there are three ways to attain happiness. The first is to view life from a lofty perspective, removed from the trivialities of daily experience; the second is to lose oneself in domesticity and ignore the world. Jean Paul recommends a third approach, which is to combine both methods and entertain both philosophic and domestic concerns.*]

[*Life of Quintus Fixlein*] contains the life of a Schoolmaster, extracted and compiled from various public and private documents. With this Biography, dear Friends, it is the purpose of the Author not so much to procure you a pleasure, as to teach you how to enjoy one. In truth, King Zerxes should have offered his prize-medals not for the invention of new pleasures, but for a good mythodology and directory to use the old ones.

Of ways for becoming happier (not happy) I could never inquire out more than three. The first, rather an elevated road, is this: To soar, away so far above the clouds of life, that you see the whole external world, with its wolf-dens, charnel-houses and thunder-rods, lying far down beneath you, shrunk into a little child's garden. The second is: Simply to sink down into this little garden; and there to nestle yourself so snugly, so homewise, in some furrow, that in looking out from your warm lark-nest, you likewise can discern no wolf-dens, charnel-houses or thunder-rods, but only blades and ears, every one of which, for the nest-bird, is a tree, and a sun-screen, and rain-screen. The third, finally, which I look upon as the hardest and cunningest, is that of alternating between the other two.

This I shall now satisfactorily expound to men at large.

The Hero, the Reformer, your Brutus, your Howard, your Republican, he whom civic storm, or genius, poetic storm, impels; in short, every mortal with a great Purpose, or even a perennial Passion (were it but that of writing the largest folios), all these men fence themselves in by their internal world against the frosts and heats of the external, as the madman in a worse sense does: every *fixed* idea, such as rules every genius, every enthusiast, at least periodically, separates and elevates a man above the bed and board of this Earth, above its Dog's-grottoes, buckthorns and Devil's-walls; like the Bird of Paradise, he slumbers flying; and on his outspread pinions, oversleeps unconsciously the earthquakes and conflagrations of Life, in his long fair dream of his ideal Motherland.—Alas! to few is this dream granted; and these few are so often awakened by Flying Dogs [vampires]!

This skyward track, however, is fit only for the winged portion of the human species, for the smallest. What can it profit poor quill-driving brethren, whose souls have not even wing-shells, to say nothing of wings? Or these tethered persons with the best back, breast and neck fins, who float motionless in the wicker Fish-box of the State, and are not allowed to swim, because the Box or State, long ago tied to the shore, itself swims in the name of the fishes? To the whole standing and writing host of heavy-laden State-domestics, Purveyors, Clerks of all departments, and all the lobsters packed together heels over head into the Lobster-basket of the Government office-rooms, and for refreshment, sprinkled over with a few nettles; to these persons, what way of becoming happy *here,* can I possibly point out?

My *second* merely; and that is as follows: To take a compound microscope, and with it to discover, and convince themselves, that their drop of Burgundy is properly a Red Sea, that butterfly-dust is peacock-feathers, mouldiness a flowery field, and sand a heap of jewels. These microscopic recreations are more lasting than all costly watering-place recreations.—But I must explain these metaphors by new ones. The purpose for which I have [written] *Fixlein's Life* . . . is simply that in this same *Life,*—therefore in this Preface it is less needful,—I may show to the whole Earth that we ought to value little joys more than great ones, the nightgown more than the dresscoat; that Plutus' heaps are worth less than his handfuls, the plum than the penny for a rainy day; and that not great, but little good-haps can make us happy.—Can I accomplish this, I shall, through means of my Book, bring up for Posterity, a race of men finding refreshment in all things; in the warmth of their room and of their nightcaps; in their pillows; in the three High Festivals; in mere Apostles' days; in the Evening Moral Tales of their wives. . . . You perceive, my drift is that man must become a little Tailor-bird, which, not amid the crashing boughs of the storm-tost, roaring, immeasurable tree of Life, but on one of its leaves, sews itself a nest together, and there lies snug. The most essential sermon one could preach to our century, were a sermon on the duty of staying at home.

The *third* skyward road is the alternation between the other two. The foregoing *second* way is not good enough for man, who here on Earth should take into his hand not the Sickle only, but also the Plough. The *first* is too good for him. He has not always the force. . . . And then his *pains* are not less lasting than his *fatigues*. Still oftener is Strength denied its Arena: it is but the smallest portion of life that, to a working soul, offers Alps, Revolutions, Rhine-falls, Worms Diets, and Wars with Xerxes; and for the whole it is better so: the longer portion of life is a field beaten flat as a threshing-floor, without lofty Gothard Mountains; often it is a tedious ice-field, without a single glacier tinged with dawn.

But even by walking, a man rests and recovers himself for climbing; by little joys and duties, for great. The victorious Dictator must contrive to plough down his battle Mars-field into a flax and carrot field; to transform his theatre of war into a parlour theatre, on which his children may enact some good pieces from the *Children's Friend*. Can he accomplish this, can he turn so softly from the path of poetical happiness into that of household happiness,—then is he little different from myself, who even now, though modesty might forbid me to disclose it—who even now, I say, amid the creation of this Letter, have been enabled to reflect, that when it is done, so also will the Roses and Elder-berries of pastry be done, which a sure hand is seething in butter for the Author of this Work. (pp. 193-95)

Jean Paul Friedrich Richter, "Letter to My Friends,"
in German Romance: Hoffmann, Richter, Vol. II,

edited and translated by Thomas Carlyle, Charles Scribner's Sons, 1904, pp. 193-96.

MADAME THE BARONESS DE STAËL-HOLSTEIN (essay date 1810)

[*A French critic and novelist, Mme. de Staël wrote during the late eighteenth and early nineteenth centuries. She is credited with bringing the influence of German Romanticism to French literary and political thought. Her belief that critical judgment is relative and based on a sense of history sharply altered the French literary attitudes of her time. In her* De la littérature considerée dans ses rapports avec les institutions sociales (The Influence of Literature upon Society), *published in 1800, Mme. de Staël distinguished between the classically-influenced literature of Southern Europe and the Romantic aspects of Northern European literature. The book's thesis states that a literary work must reflect the moral and historical reality, or Zeitgeist, of the country in which it is created. In 1810, Mme. de Staël published* De l'Allemagne (Germany), *which contains the passage below on Jean Paul; this work is credited with introducing German Romanticism to France.* Germany *is a historical and critical survey of German manners, philosophy, literature, and religion—or, in René Wellek's words, "a picture of a whole nation, a sketch of national psychology and sociology." The work also includes Mme. de Staël's influential translation of the dream passage in* Siebenkäs *in which Jean Paul questions the existence of God. Critics agree that the omission of the ending in her translation intensified the impact of the passage. It was through this translation that Jean Paul became known in France; according to Byron R. Libhart (see Additional Bibliography), "a whole generation of French Romantic writers was greatly influenced by the concept of a 'dead God' as revealed in Madame de Staël's presentation of Jean Paul Richter."*]

Jean Paul Richter is possessed of powers certainly more than sufficient to compose a work that would be as interesting to foreigners as to his own countrymen, and yet nothing that he has published can ever extend beyond the limits of Germany. His admirers will say that this results from the originality even of his genius; I think that his faults are as much the cause of it as his excellencies. . . . We might beg Jean Paul never to be singular except in spite of himself; whatever is said involuntarily always hits some natural feeling; but when natural originality is spoiled by the pretension to originality, the reader has no perfect enjoyment even of what is true, from the remembrance and the dread of what is otherwise.

Some admirable beauties are to be found, nevertheless, in the works of Jean Paul; but the arrangement and frame of his pictures are so defective, that the most luminous traits of genius are lost in the general confusion. The writings of Jean Paul deserve to be considered in two points of view, the humorous and the serious, for he constantly mixes both together. His manner of observing the human heart is full of delicacy and vivacity, but his knowledge of it is merely such as may be acquired in the little towns of Germany; and in his delineation of manners, confined as it is, there is frequently something too innocent for the age in which we live. Observations so delicate, and almost minute, on the moral affections, recall a little to our recollection the personage in the fairy tales who went by the name of *Fine-Ear,* because he could hear the grass grow. (pp. 66-8)

Thoughts extracted from the writings of Jean Paul would . . . form a very remarkable work; but we perceive, in reading them, his singular custom of collecting from every quarter, from obsolete books, scientific works, etc., his metaphors and allusions. The resemblances thus produced are almost always

very ingenious; but when study and attention are required to enable us to find out a jest, scarcely any but the Germans would consent thus to laugh after a serious study, and give themselves as much trouble to understand what amuses them as what is calculated for their instruction. (p. 69)

Jean Paul Richter is often sublime in the serious parts of his works, but the continued melancholy of his language sometimes moves till it fatigues us. When the imagination is kept too long in the clouds, the colors are confused, the outlines are effaced, and we retain of all that we have read rather a reverberation of the sound than a recollection of the substance. The sensibility of Jean Paul affects the soul, but does not sufficiently strengthen it. The poetry of his style resembles the sounds of a harmonica, which delight us at first, but give us pain a few minutes afterwards, because the exaltation excited by them has no determinate object. We give too great an advantage to cold and insipid characters, when we represent sensibility to them as a disease, while, on the contrary, it is the most energetic of all our moral faculties, since it imparts both the desire and ability to devote ourselves to others. (pp. 69-70)

> *Madame the Baroness de Staël-Holstein, "On Literature and the Arts: Of Romances," in her* Germany, *Vol. II,* Houghton, Mifflin and Company, 1887, *pp. 50-76.**

GRASMERIENSIS TEUTONIZANS [PSEUDONYM OF THOMAS DE QUINCEY] (essay date 1821)

[*An English critic and essayist, De Quincey used his own life as the subject of his best-known work,* Confessions of an English Opium Eater, *in which he chronicled his addiction to opium. In addition, De Quincey contributed reviews to a number of London journals and earned a reputation as an insightful if occasionally verbose literary critic. At the time of De Quincey's death, his critical expertise was underestimated, though his prose talent had long been acknowledged. In the twentieth century, many critics still disdain the digressive qualities of De Quincey's writing, yet others find that his essays display an acute psychological awareness. The following excerpt is from one of the earliest appraisals of Jean Paul published in English. De Quincey here praises Jean Paul's use of pathos, humor, and intellect, comments on the characteristics that earned Jean Paul his reputation as a difficult author to understand, and concludes that these traits have contributed to his lack of popularity. A thorough understanding and appreciation of Jean Paul's work informs this essay, and De Quincey's explanation for Jean Paul's obscurity is frequently reiterated in subsequent criticism. Later critics have commented on the similarities in the two authors' works, particularly in their depiction of dream states.*]

[In point of originality] there cannot arise a question between the pretensions of Richter and those of any other German author whatsoever. He is no man's representative but his own: nor do I think that he will ever have a successor. Of *his* style of writing, it may be said, with an emphatic and almost exclusive propriety, that except it proceeds in a spirit of perfect freedom it cannot exist; unless moving from an impulse self-derived it cannot move at all. What then *is* his style of writing? What are its general characteristics? (p. 607)

[The] characteristic distinction of Paul Richter, amongst German authors, I will venture to add amongst modern authors generally, is the two-headed power which he possesses over the pathetic and the humorous: or, rather, let me say at once, what I have often felt to be true, and could (I think) at a fitting opportunity prove to be so, this power is *not* two-headed, but a one-headed Janus with two faces:—the pathetic and the humorous are but different phases of the same orb; they assist each other, melt indiscernibly into each other, and often shine each through each like layers of coloured chrystals placed one behind another. (pp. 607-08)

Judge as you will . . . on the comparative pretensions of Sterne and Richter to the *spolia opima* [spoils] in the fields of pathos and of humour; yet in one pretension . . . [Richter] leaves Sterne at an infinite distance in the rear. . . . John Paul's intellect—his faculty of catching at a glance all the relations of objects, both the grand, the lovely, the ludicrous, and the fantastic,—is painfully and almost morbidly active: there is no respite, no repose, allowed. . . . One of his books (*Vorschule der Aesthetik*) is absolutely so surcharged with quicksilver, that I expect to see it leap off the table as often as it is laid there. . . . [There] cannot be a more valuable endowment to a writer of inordinate sensibility, than this inordinate agility of the understanding; the active faculty balances the passive; and without such a balance, there is great risk of falling into a sickly tone of maudlin sentimentality, from which Sterne cannot be pronounced wholly free. . . . [It] is this fiery, meteoric, scintillating, corruscating power of John Paul, which is the true foundation of his frequent obscurity. You will find that he is reputed the most difficult of all German authors; and many Germans are so little aware of the true derivation of this difficulty, that it has often been said to me, as an Englishman, "What! can *you* read John Paul?" meaning to say, can you read such difficult German? Doubtless, in some small proportion, the mere language and style are responsible for his difficulty. . . . [These] verbal obscurities are but the necessary result and product of his style of thinking; the nimbleness of his transitions often makes him elliptical: the vast expansion and discursiveness in his range of notice and observation, carries him into every department and nook of human life, of science, of art, and of literature; whence comes a proportionably extensive vocabulary, and a prodigious compass of idiomatic phraseology: and finally, the fineness, and evanescent brilliancy of his oblique glances and surface-skimming allusions, often fling but half a meaning on the mind; and one is puzzled to make out its complement. *Hence* it is, that is to say, from his mode of presenting things, his lyrical style of connexion, and the prodigious fund of knowledge on which he draws for his illustrations and his images, that his obscurity arises. (pp. 609-10)

You will naturally collect from the account here given of John Paul's activity of understanding and fancy, that over and above his humour, he must have an overflowing opulence of wit.— In fact he has. . . . I am acquainted with no book of such unintermitting and brilliant wit as his *Vorschule der Aesthetik;* it glitters like the stars on a frosty night; . . . in fact, John Paul's works are the galaxy of the German literary firmament. I defy a man to lay his hand on that sentence which is not vital and ebullient with wit. (p. 611)

[John Paul] constantly reminds me of Shakespeare. Every where a spirit of kindness prevails: his satire is every where playful, delicate, and clad in smiles; never bitter, scornful, or malignant. But this is not all. I could produce many passages from Shakspeare, which show that, if his anger was ever roused, it was against the abuses of the time: not mere political abuses, but those that had a deeper root, and dishonoured human nature. Here again the resemblance holds in John Paul; and this is the point in which I . . . notice a bond of affinity between him and Schiller. Both were intolerant haters of ignoble things,

though placable towards the ignoble men. Both yearned, according to their different temperaments, for a happier state of things: I mean for human nature generally, and, in a political sense, for Germany. To his latest years, Schiller, when suffering under bodily decay and anguish, was an earnest contender for whatever promised to elevate human nature, and bore emphatic witness against the evils of the time. John Paul, who still lives, is of a gentler nature: but his aspirations tend to the same point, though expressed in a milder and more hopeful spirit. With all this, however, they give a rare lesson on the *manner* of conducting such a cause: for you will no where find that they take any indecent liberties, of a personal sort, with those princes whose governments they most abhorred. Though safe enough from their vengeance, they never forgot in their indignation, as patriots and as philosophers, the respect due to the rank of others, or to themselves as scholars, and the favourites of their country. Some other modern authors of Germany *may* be great writers: but Frederick Schiller and John Paul Richter I shall always view with the feelings due to great men. (p. 612)

> *Grasmeriensis Teutonizans* [*pseudonym of Thomas De Quincey*], "*John Paul Frederick Richter*," *in* The London Magazine, *Vol. IV, No. XXIV, December, 1821, pp. 606-12.*

[THOMAS CARLYLE]   (essay date 1827)

[*A noted nineteenth-century essayist, historian, critic, and social commentator, Carlyle was a central figure of the Victorian age in England and Scotland. In his writings, Carlyle advocated a Christian work ethic and stressed the importance of order, piety, and spiritual fulfillment. Known to his contemporaries as the "Sage of Chelsea," Carlyle exerted a powerful moral influence in an era of rapidly shifting values. Carlyle is credited with introducing Jean Paul to English readers: he wrote several essays about the German author and translated two of his novels. The following is considered the best nineteenth-century criticism of Jean Paul in English. While acknowledging such faults in Jean Paul's writings as chaotic form and obscure language, Carlyle also maintained that the works require intense concentration for the reader to realize their true beauty. By identifying Jean Paul's outstanding qualities, including his intellect, imagination, and humor, and by noting the connection between his character, style, and subject matter, Carlyle delineated the major themes of nineteenth-century criticism of Jean Paul.*]

Except by name, Jean Paul Friedrich Richter is little known out of Germany. The only thing connected with him, we think, that has reached this country, is his saying, imported by Madame de Staël, and thankfully pocketed by most newspaper critics:—"Providence has given to the French the empire of the land, to the English that of the sea, to the Germans that of—the air!" Of this last element, indeed, his own genius might easily seem to have been a denizen: so fantastic, many-coloured, far-grasping, everyway perplexed and extraordinary, is his mode of writing, that to translate him properly is next to impossible; nay, a dictionary of his works has actually been in part published for the use of German readers! These things have restricted his sphere of action, and may long restrict it, to his own country: but there, in return, he is a favourite of the first class; studied through all his intricacies with trustful admiration, and a love which tolerates much. During the last forty years, he has been continually before the public, in various capacities, and growing generally in esteem with all ranks of critics; till, at length, his gainsayers have been either silenced or convinced; and Jean Paul, at first reckoned half-mad, has long ago vindicated his singularities to nearly universal satisfaction, and now combines popularity with real depth of endowment, in perhaps a greater degree than any other writer; being second in the latter point to scarcely more than one of his contemporaries, and in the former second to none. (p. 180)

Hesperus and *Titan* [are] the largest and the best of his novels. It was the former that first . . . introduced him into decisive and universal estimation with his countrymen: the latter he himself, with the most judicious of his critics, regarded as his master-piece. But the name Novelist, as we in England must understand it, would ill describe so vast and discursive a genius: for with all his grotesque, tumultuous pleasantry, Richter is a man of a truly earnest, nay, high and solemn character; and seldom writes without a meaning far beyond the sphere of common romancers. . . . Amusement is often, in part almost always, a means with Richter; rarely or never his highest end. His thoughts, his feelings, the creations of his spirit, walk before us embodied under wondrous shapes, in motley and ever-fluctuating groups: but his essential character, however he disguises it, is that of a Philosopher and moral Poet, whose study has been human nature, whose delight and best endeavour are with all that is beautiful, and tender, and mysteriously sublime in the fate or history of man. This is the purport of his writings, whether their form be that of fiction or of truth; the spirit that pervades and ennobles his delineations of common life, his wild wayward dreams, allegories, and shadowy imaginings, no less than his disquisitions of a nature directly scientific.

But in this latter province also, Richter has accomplished much. His *Vorschule der Aesthetik (Introduction to Aesthetics)* is a work on poetic art, based on principles of no ordinary depth and compass, abounding in noble views, and, notwithstanding its frolicsome exuberance, in sound and subtle criticism; esteemed even in Germany, where Criticism has long been treated of as a science, and by such persons as Winkelmann, Kant, Herder, and the Schlegels. Of this work we could speak long. . . . We fear, it might astonish many an honest brother of our craft, were he to read it; and altogether perplex and dash his maturest counsels, if he chanced to understand it,—Richter has also written on Education, a work entitled *Levana;* distinguished by keen practical sagacity, as well as generous sentiment, and a certain sober magnificence of speculation; the whole presented in that singular style which characterizes the man. . . . Among writers on this subject, Richter holds a high place; if we look chiefly at his tendency and aims, perhaps the highest.—The *Clavis Fichtiana* is a ludicrous performance, known to us only by report; but Richter is said to possess the merit, while he laughs at Fichte, of understanding him; a merit among Fichte's critics, which seems to be one of the rarest. (pp. 182-84)

We defy the most careless or prejudiced reader to peruse these works without an impression of something splendid, wonderful, and daring. But they require to be studied as well as read, and this with no ordinary patience, if the reader, especially the foreign reader, wishes to comprehend rightly either their truth or their want of truth. Tried by many an accepted standard, Richter would be speedily enough disposed of; pronounced a mystic—a German dreamer—a rash and presumptuous innovator; and so consigned, with equanimity, perhaps with a certain jubilee, to the Limbo appointed for all such wind-bags and deceptions. (p. 184)

There are few writers with whom deliberation and careful distrust of first impressions are more necessary than with Richter.

He is a phenomenon from the very surface; he presents himself with a professed and determined singularity: his language itself is a stone of stumbling to the critic; to critics of the grammarian species, an unpardonable, often an insuperable, rock of offence. Not that he is ignorant of grammar, or disdains the sciences of spelling and parsing; but he exercises both in a certain latitudinarian spirit; deals with astonishing liberality in parentheses, dashes, and subsidiary clauses; invents hundreds of new words, alters old ones, or, by hyphen, chains, pairs, and packs them together into most jarring combination; in short, produces sentences of the most heterogeneous, lumbering, interminable kind. Figures without limit, indeed the whole is one tissue of metaphors, and similes, and allusions to all the provinces of Earth, Sea, and Air; interlaced with epigrammatic breaks, vehement bursts, or sardonic turns, interjections, quips, puns, and even oaths! A perfect Indian jungle it seems; a boundless, unparalleled imbroglio; nothing on all sides but darkness, dissonance, confusion worse confounded! Then the style of the whole corresponds, in perplexity and extravagance, with that of the parts. Every work, be it fiction or serious treatise, is embaled in some fantastic wrappage; some mad narrative accounting for its appearance, and connecting it with the author, who generally becomes a person of the drama himself, before all is over. . . . No story proceeds without the most erratic digressions, and voluminous tagrags rolling after it in many a snaky twine. Ever and anon there occurs some "Extra-leaf," with its satirical petition, program, or other wonderful intercalation, no mortal can foresee on what. It is, indeed, a mighty maze; and often the panting reader toils after him in vain, or, baffled and spent, indignantly stops short, and retires, perhaps for ever.

All this, we must admit, is true of Richter; but much more is true also. Let us not turn from him after the first cursory glance, and imagine we have settled his account by the words Rhapsody and Affectation. They are cheap words, we allow, and of sovereign potency; we should see therefore that they be not rashly applied. Many things in Richter accord ill with such a theory. There are rays of the keenest truth, nay, steady pillars of scientific light rising through this chaos: Is it in fact a chaos, or may it be that our eyes are not of infinite vision, and have only missed the plan? (pp. 184-85)

The secret of the matter, perhaps, is, that Richter requires more study than most readers care to give; for as we approach more closely, many things grow clearer. In the man's own sphere there is consistency; the farther we advance into it, we see confusion more and more unfold itself into order; till at last, viewed from its proper centre, his intellectual universe, no longer a distorted, incoherent series of air-landscapes, coalesces into compact expansion; a vast, magnificent, and variegated scene; full, indeed, of wondrous products, and rude, it may be, and irregular; but gorgeous, and varied, and ample; gay with the richest verdure and foliage, and glittering in the brightest and kindest sun.

Richter has been called an intellectual Colossus; and in truth it is still somewhat in this light that we view him. His faculties are all of gigantic mould; cumbrous, awkward in their movements; large and splendid rather than harmonious or beautiful; yet joined in living union,—and of force and compass altogether extraordinary. He has an intellect vehement, rugged, irresistible; crushing in pieces the hardest problems; piercing into the most hidden combinations of things, and grasping the most distant: an imagination vague, sombre, splendid, or appalling; brooding over the abysses of Being; wandering through

Infinitude, and summoning before us, in its dim religious light, shapes of brilliancy, solemnity, or terror: a fancy of exuberance literally unexampled; for it pours its treasures with a lavishness which knows no limit, hanging, like the sun, a jewel on every grass-blade, and sowing the earth at large with orient pearl. But deeper than all these lies Humour, the ruling quality with Richter; as it were the central fire that pervades and vivifies his whole being. He is a humourist from his inmost soul; he thinks as a humourist, he feels, imagines, acts as a humourist: Sport is the element in which his nature lives and works. A tumultuous element for such a nature, and wild work he makes in it! A Titan in his sport as in his earnestness, he oversteps all bounds, and riots without law or measure. (pp. 186-87)

[Of all German authors], there is none that, in depth, copiousness, and intensity of humour, can be compared with Jean Paul. He alone exists in humour; lives, moves, and has his being in it. With him it is not so much united to his other qualities, of intellect, fancy, imagination, moral feeling, as these are united to it; or rather unite themselves to it, and grow under its warmth, as in their proper temperature and climate. Not as if we meant to assert that his humour is in all cases perfectly natural and pure; nay, that it is not often extravagant, untrue, or even absurd: but still, on the whole, the core and life of it are genuine, subtile, spiritual. Not without reason have his panegyrists named him *Jean Paul der Einzige*—"Jean Paul the Only:" in one sense or the other, either as praise or censure, his critics also must adopt this epithet; for surely in the whole circle of literature, we look in vain for his parallel. Unite the sportfulness of Rabelais, and the best sensibility of Sterne, with the earnestness, and, even in slight portions, the sublimity of Milton; and let the mosaic brain of old Burton give forth the workings of this strange union, with the pen of Jeremy Bentham! (p. 190)

[We] imagine Richter's wild manner will be found less imperfect than many a very tame one. To the man it may not be unsuitable. In that singular form, there is a fire, a splendour, a benign energy, which persuades us into tolerance, nay into love, of much that might otherwise offend. Above all, this man, alloyed with imperfections as he may be, is consistent and coherent: he is at one with himself; he knows his aims, and pursues them in sincerity of heart, joyfully, and with undivided will. . . . Richter's worst faults are nearly allied to his best merits; being chiefly exuberance of good, irregular squandering of wealth, a dazzling with excess of true light. These things may be pardoned the more readily, as they are little likely to be imitated. (p. 191)

Regarding his novels, we may say, that, except in some few instances, and those chiefly of the shorter class, they are not what, in strict language, we can term unities: with much *callida junctura* [skillful joining] of parts, it is rare that any of them leaves on us the impression of a perfect, homogeneous, indivisible whole. A true work of art requires to be *fused* in the mind of its creator, and, as it were, poured forth (from his imagination, though not from his pen,) at one simultaneous gush. Richter's works do not always bear sufficient marks of having been in *fusion;* yet neither are they merely *rivetted* together; to say the least, they have been *welded.* A similar remark applies to many of his characters; indeed, more or less, to all of them, except such as are entirely humorous, or have a large dash of humour. In this latter province, certainly, he is at home; a true poet, a maker: his *Siebenkäs,* his *Schmelzle,* even his *Fibel* and *Fixlein* are living figures. But in heroic personages, passionate, massive, overpowering as he is, we

have scarcely ever a complete ideal: art has not attained to the concealment of itself. With his heroines again he is more successful; they are often true heroines, though perhaps with too little variety of character; bustling, buxom mothers and housewives, with all the caprices, perversities, and warm generous helpfulness of women; or white, half-angelic creatures, meek, still, long-suffering, high-minded, of tenderest affections, and hearts crushed yet uncomplaining. Supernatural figures he has not attempted; and wisely, for he cannot write without belief. Yet many times he exhibits an imagination of a singularity, nay, on the whole, of a truth and grandeur, unexampled elsewhere. In his *dreams* there is a mystic complexity, a gloom, and amid the dim, gigantic, half-ghastly shadows, gleamings of a wizard splendour. . . . (p. 192)

Time has a contracting influence on many a wide-spread fame; yet of Richter we will say, that he may survive much. There is in him that which does not die; that Beauty and Earnestness of soul, that spirit of Humanity, of Love and mild Wisdom, over which the vicissitudes of mode have no sway. This is that excellence of the inmost nature which alone confers immortality on writings. . . . To men of a right mind, there may long be in Richter much that has attraction and value. In the moral desert of vulgar Literature, with its sandy wastes, and parched, bitter, and too often poisonous shrubs, the writings of this man will rise in their irregular luxuriance, like a cluster of date-trees, with its greensward and well of water, to refresh the pilgrim, in the sultry solitude, with nourishment and shade. (p. 195)

[*Thomas Carlyle*], *"John Paul F. Richter,"* in The Edinburgh Review, *Vol. XLVI, No. XCI, June, 1827, pp. 176-95.*

THOMAS CARLYLE   (essay date 1827)

[*Carlyle's work* German Romance, *which was first published in 1827, contains an essay on Jean Paul (excerpted below) and translations of two of his works.*]

The most cursory inspection, even an external one, will satisfy us that [Richter] neither was, nor wished to be considered as, a man who wrote or thought in the track of other men, to whom common practices of law, and whose excellences and defects the common formulas of criticism will easily represent. The very titles of his works are startling. One of his earliest performances is named *Selection from the Papers of the Devil;* another is *Biographical Recreations under the Cranium of a Giantess.* His novels are almost uniformly introduced by some fantastic narrative accounting for his publication and obtainment of the story. *Hesperus,* his chief novel, bears the secondary title of *Dog-post-days,* and the chapters are named *Dog-posts,* as having been conveyed to him in a letter-bag, round the neck of a little nimble Shock, from some unknown Island in the South Sea.

The first aspect of these peculiarities cannot prepossess us in his favour; we are too forcibly reminded of theatrical clap-traps and literary quackery; nor on opening one of the works themselves is the case much mended. Piercing gleams of thought do not escape us; singular truths conveyed in a form as singular; grotesque and often truly ludicrous delineations; pathetic, magnificent, far-sounding passages; effusions full of wit, knowledge and imagination, but difficult to bring under any rubric whatever; all the elements, in short, of a glorious intellect, but dashed together in such wild arrangement, that their order seems the very ideal of confusion. The style and structure of the book appear alike incomprehensible. The narrative is every now and then suspended to make way for some "Extra-leaf," some wild digression upon any subject but the one in hand; the language groans with indescribable metaphors and allusions to all things human and divine; flowing onward, not like a river, but like an inundation; circling in complex eddies, chafing and gurgling now this way, now that, till the proper current sinks out of view amid the boundless uproar. We close the work with a mingled feeling of astonishment, oppression and perplexity; and Richter stands before us in brilliant cloudy vagueness, a giant mass of intellect, but without form, beauty or intelligible purpose.

To readers who believe that intrinsic is inseparable from superficial excellence, and that nothing can be good or beautiful which is not to be seen through in a moment, Richter can occasion little difficulty. They admit him to be a man of vast natural endowments, but he is utterly uncultivated, and without command of them; full of monstrous affectation, the very high-priest of bad taste: knows not the art of writing, scarcely that there is such an art; an insane visionary floating forever among baseless dreams, which hide the firm Earth from his view. . . . (pp. 119-20)

[There] is something in Richter that incites us to a second, to a third perusal. His works are hard to understand, but they always have a meaning, and often a true and deep one. In our closer, more comprehensive glance, their truth steps forth with new distinctness; their error dissipates and recedes, passes into venality, often even into beauty; and at last the thick haze which encircled the form of the writer melts away, and he stands revealed to us in his own steadfast features, a colossal spirit, a lofty and original thinker, a genuine poet, a high-minded, true and most amiable man.

I have called him a colossal spirit, for this impression continues with us: to the last we figure him as something gigantic; for all the elements of his structure are vast, and combined together in living and life-giving, rather than in beautiful or symmetrical order. His Intellect is keen, impetuous, far-grasping, fit to rend in pieces the stubbornest materials, and extort from them their most hidden and refractory truth. In his Humour he sports with the highest and the lowest, he can play at bowls with the sun and moon. His Imagination opens for us the Land of Dreams; we sail with him through the boundless abyss, and the secrets of Space, and Time, and Life, and Annihilation hover round us in dim cloudy forms, and darkness and immensity and dread encompass and overshadow us. Nay, in handling the smallest matter, he works it with the tools of a giant. A common truth is wrenched from its old combinations, and presented us in new, impassable, abyssmal contrast with its opposite error. . . . The treasures of his mind are of a similar description with the mind itself; his knowledge is gathered from all the kingdoms of Art and Science and Nature, and lies round him in huge unwieldy heaps. His very language is Titanian; deep, strong, tumultuous, shining with a thousand hues, fused from a thousand elements, and winding in labyrinthic mazes.

Among Richter's gifts, perhaps the first that strikes us as truly great is his Imagination; for he loves to dwell in the loftiest and most solemn provinces of thought; his works abound with mysterious allegories, visions and typical adumbrations; his Dreams, in particular, have a gloomy vastness, broken here and there by wild far-daring splendour, and shadowy forms of meaning rise dimly from the bosom of the void Infinite. Yet, if I mistake not, Humour is his ruling quality, the quality which lives most deeply in his inward nature, and most strongly in-

fluences his manner of being. In this rare gift,—for none is rarer than true humour,—he stands unrivalled in his own country; and among late writers, in every other. To describe humour is difficult at all times, and would perhaps be still more difficult in Richter's case. Like all his other qualities, it is vast, rude, irregular; often perhaps overstrained and extravagant; yet fundamentally it is genuine humour, the humour of Cervantes and Sterne, the product not of Contempt but of Love, not of superficial distortion of natural forms, but of deep though playful sympathy with all forms of Nature. It springs not less from the heart than from the head; its result is not laughter, but something far kindlier and better; as it were, the balm which a generous spirit pours over the wounds of life, and which none but a generous spirit can give forth. Such humour is compatible with tenderest and sublimest feelings, or rather, it is incompatible with the want of them. In Richter, accordingly, we find a true sensibility; a softness, sometimes a simple humble pathos, which works its way into every heart. (pp. 121-23)

It is on the strength of this and its accompanying endowments that his main success as an artist depends. His favourite characters have always a dash of the ridiculous in their circumstances or their composition, perhaps in both: they are often men of no account; vain, poor, ignorant, feeble; and we scarcely know how it is that we love them; for the author all along has been laughing no less heartily than we at their ineptitudes, yet so it is, his Fibel, his Fixlein, his Siebenkäs, even his Schmelzle, insinuate themselves into our affections; and their ultimate place is closer to our hearts than that of many more splendid heroes. This is the test of true humour; no wit, no sarcasm, no knowledge will suffice; not talent but genius will accomplish the result. It is in studying these characters that we first convince ourselves of Richter's claim to the title of a poet, of a true creator. For with all his wild vagueness, this highest intellectual honour cannot be refused him. The figures and scenes which he lays before us, distorted, entangled, indescribable as they seem, have a true poetic existence; for we not only *hear* of them, but we *see* them, afar off, by the wondrous light, which none but the Poet, in the strictest meaning of that word, can shed over them.

So long as humour will avail him, his management even of higher and stronger characters may still be pronounced successful; but whenever humour ceases to be applicable, his success is more or less imperfect. In the treatment of heroes proper he is seldom completely happy. They shoot into rugged exaggeration in his hands, their sensibility becomes too copious and tearful, their magnanimity too fierce, abrupt and thorough-going. In some few instances they verge towards absolute failure: compared with their less ambitious brethren, they are almost of a vulgar cast; with all their brilliancy and vigour, too like that positive, determinate, choleric, volcanic class of personages whom we meet with so frequently in novels; they call themselves Men, and do their utmost to prove the assertion, but they cannot make us believe it; for after all their vapouring and storming, we see well enough that they are but Engines. . . . In the general conduct of such histories and delineations, Richter seldom appears to advantage: the incidents are often startling and extravagant; the whole structure of the story has a rugged, broken, huge, artificial aspect, and will not assume the air of truth. Yet its chasms are strangely filled up with the costliest materials; a world, a universe of wit and knowledge and fancy and imagination has sent its fairest products to adorn the edifice; the rude and rent cyclopean walls are resplendent with jewels and beaten gold; rich stately foliage screens it, the balmiest odours encircle it; we stand astonished if not captivated, delighted if not charmed, by the artist and his art.

By a critic of his own country Richter has been named a Western Oriental. . . . The mildness, the warm all-comprehending love attributed to Oriental poets may in fact be discovered in Richter; not less their fantastic exaggeration, their brilliant extravagance; above all, their overflowing abundance, their lyrical diffuseness, as if writing for readers who were altogether passive, to whom no sentiment could be intelligible unless it were expounded and dissected, and presented under all its thousand aspects. In this last point Richter is too much an Oriental: his passionate outpourings would often be more effective were they far briefer. Withal, however, he is a Western Oriental: he lives in the midst of cultivated Europe in the nineteenth century; he has looked with a patient and piercing eye on its motley aspect; and it is this Europe, it is the changes of its many-coloured life, that are held up to us in his works. His subject is Life; his chosen study has been Man. Few have known the world better, or taken at once a clearer and a kindlier view of its concerns. For Richter's mind is at peace with itself: a mild, humane, beneficent spirit breathes through his works. His very contempt, of which he is by no means incapable or sparing, is placid and tolerant; his affection is warm, tender, comprehensive, not dwelling among the high places of the world, not blind to its objects when found among the poor and lowly. Nature in all her scenes and manifestations he loves with a deep, almost passionate love; from the solemn phases of the starry heaven to the simple floweret of the meadow, his eye and his heart are open for her charms and her mystic meanings. . . . It is not with the feeling of a mere painter and view-hunter that he looks on Nature: but he dwells amid her beauties and solemnities as in the mansion of a Mother; he finds peace in her majestic peace; he worships, in this boundless Temple, the great original of Peace, to whom the Earth and the fulness thereof belongs. For Richter does not hide from us that he looks to the Maker of the Universe as to his Father; that in his belief of man's Immortality lies the sanctuary of his spirit, the solace of all suffering, the solution of all that is mysterious in human destiny. The wild freedom with which he treats the dogmas of religion must not mislead us to suppose that he himself is irreligious or unbelieving. It is Religion, it is Belief, in whatever dogmas expressed, or whether expressed in any, that has reconciled for him the contradictions of existence. . . . In Richter alone, among the great (and even sometimes truly moral) writers of his day, do we find the Immortality of the Soul expressly insisted on. . . . (pp. 123-26)

> *Thomas Carlyle, "Jean Paul Friedrich Richter," in* German Romance: Hoffmann, Richter, Vol. II, *edited and translated by Thomas Carlyle, Charles Scribner's Sons, 1904, pp. 117-30.*

MARGARET FULLER OSSOLI (letter date 1833)

[*Ossoli is the married name of Sarah Margaret Fuller, but she is commonly known as Fuller. A distinguished critic and early feminist, Fuller played an important role in the developing cultural life of the United States during the first half of the nineteenth century. As a founding editor of the Transcendentalist journal the* Dial, *and later as a contributor to Horace Greeley's* New York Tribune, *she was influential in introducing European art and literature to the United States. Although the following letter reveals her early negative reaction to Jean Paul, a later poem (1850?) expressed only warm praise.*]

I brought your beloved Jean Paul with me, too. I cannot yet judge well, but think we shall not be intimate. His infinitely variegated, and certainly most exquisitely colored, web fatigues attention. I prefer, too, wit to humor, and daring imagination to the richest fancy. Besides, his philosophy and religion seem to be of the sighing sort, and, having some tendency that way myself, I want opposing force in a favorite author. Perhaps I have spoken unadvisedly; if so, I shall recant on further knowledge. (p. 147)

> *Margaret Fuller Ossoli, in an extract from a letter to an unidentified recipient in May, 1833, in her* Memoirs of Margaret Fuller Ossoli, Vol. I, *W. H. Channing, R. W. Emerson, J. F. Clarke, eds., Phillips, Sampson and Company, 1852, pp. 146-47.*

THE SELECT JOURNAL OF FOREIGN PERIODICAL LITERATURE (essay date 1834)

[In *Wahrheit aus Jean Paul's Leben*] Richter wrote, as circumstances afforded occasion, reminiscences of his life, and reflections thereupon. . . . He selected the form of academic lectures, appointing himself, *Professor of his own history,* and presenting himself in that capacity to the public. His lectures however are but three in number, they embrace only the period from his birth . . . to his confirmation, and form the first number of this work. The boy, as described herein with much humor, attracts us by his soft but intellectual character, so much so that we would gladly accompany him through his subsequent course. (pp. 76-7)

If all the parts of this book do not appear to us worthy of publication, no blame attaches to Richter (who did not prepare it with the view of giving it to the public in its present form), but only to the editor. The words of Jean Paul,—"*If I could, (what no author can) I would gladly have all my thoughts made known to the world after my death, no idea should be omitted,*"—by no means justify the editor; for Jean Paul would certainly have put some limit to the application of his strange and somewhat vain sentiment. He was certainly conscious when he wrote this, that many ideas, even of the deepest thinker, become fit to be given to the world only when brought into connexion with others and moulded into a particular form. But we have more than once thought, while reading this collection, that the editor had determined to print every syllable . . . , and that he looked upon the German public as disposed, like the followers of the Dalai-Lama, to revere and preserve the very excrements of the object of their veneration. At least he seems to have taken for granted the existence of an endemic *Jean-Paulomania,* which however has fortunately subsided. That there are some grains of wheat in the mass of chaff, we do not wish to deny; but these are all that it was desirable to have given to the public. (p. 77)

> *"Life of Jean Paul Richter," in* The Select Journal of Foreign Periodical Literature, *Vol. III, No. I, January, 1834, pp. 76-81.*

[HENRY WADSWORTH LONGFELLOW] (essay date 1839)

[*An American poet, novelist, and critic, Longfellow was considered among the most popular American writers of the nineteenth century. However, his reputation suffered a serious decline after his death. The very characteristics which made his poetry popular in his own day—gentle simplicity and a melancholy reminiscent of the German Romantics—are those that fueled the posthumous debate against his work. However, despite the continuing con-*

troversy regarding Longfellow's stature, he is credited with having been instrumental in introducing European culture to the American readers of his day. Longfellow's autobiographical novel Hyperion *recounts the experiences of its American hero, Paul Flemming, as he wanders throughout Europe after the death of his wife. During his travels he meets a German who had known Jean Paul; this character's comments are excerpted below.*]

[The] character of Richter is too marked to be easily misunderstood. Its prominent traits are tenderness and manliness,—qualities, which are seldom found united in so high a degree as in him. Over all he sees, over all he writes, are spread the sunbeams of a cheerful spirit,—the light of inexhaustible human love. Every sound of human joy and of human sorrow finds a deep-resounding echo in his bosom. In every man, he loves his humanity only, not his superiority. The avowed object of all his literary labors was to raise up again the down-sunken faith in God, virtue, and immortality; and, in an egotistical, revolutionary age, to warm again our human sympathies, which have now grown cold. And not less boundless is his love for nature,—for this outward, beautiful world. He embraces it all in his arms. (pp. 39-40)

Most undoubtedly [the prominent characteristics of Richter's genius are] his wild imagination and his playfulness. He throws over all things a strange and magic coloring. You are startled at the boldness and beauty of his figures and illustrations, which are scattered everywhere with a reckless prodigality;—multitudinous, like the blossoms of early summer,—and as fragrant and beautiful. With a thousand extravagances are mingled ten thousand beauties of thought and expression, which kindle the reader's imagination, and lead it onward in a bold flight, through the glow of sunrise and sunset, and the dewy coldness and starlight of summer nights. He is difficult to understand,—intricate,—strange,—drawing his illustrations from every by-corner of science, art, and nature,—a comet, among the bright stars of German literature. When you read his works, it is as if you were climbing a high mountain, in merry company, to see the sun rise. At times you are enveloped in mist,—the morning wind sweeps by you with a shout,—you hear the far-off muttering thunders. Wide beneath you spreads the landscape,—field, meadow, town, and winding river. The ringing of distant church-bells, or the sound of solemn village clock, reaches you;—then arises the sweet and manifold fragrance of flowers,—the birds begin to sing,—the vapors roll away,—up comes the glorious sun,—you revel like the lark in the sunshine and bright blue heaven, and all is a delirious dream of soul and sense,—when suddenly a friend at your elbow laughs aloud, and offers you a piece of Bologna sausage. As in real life, so in his writings,—the serious and the comic, the sublime and the grotesque, the pathetic and the ludicrous are mingled together. At times he is sententious, energetic, simple; then again, obscure and diffuse. His thoughts are like mummies embalmed in spices, and wrapped about with curious envelopements; but within these the thoughts themselves are kings. At times glad, beautiful images, airy forms, move by you, graceful, harmonious;—at times the glaring, wild-looking fancies, chained together by hyphens, brackets, and dashes, brave and base, high and low, all in their motley dresses, go sweeping down the dusty page, like the galley-slaves, that sweep the streets of Rome, where you may chance to see the nobleman and the peasant manacled together. (pp. 42-4)

[The] figures and ornaments of his style, wild, fantastic, and oft-times startling, like those in Gothic cathedrals, are not merely what they seem, but massive coignes and buttresses, which support the fabric. Remove them, and the roof and walls

fall in. And through these gurgoyles, these wild faces, carved upon spouts and gutters, flow out, like gathered rain, the bright, abundant thoughts, that have fallen from heaven.

And all he does, is done with a kind of serious playfulness. He is a sea-monster, disporting himself on the broad ocean; his very sport is earnest; there is something majestic and serious about it. In every thing there is strength, a rough good-nature, all sunshine overhead, and underneath the heavy moaning of the sea. Well may he be called 'Jean Paul, the Only-One.' (pp. 44-5)

[Henry Wadsworth Longfellow], "Jean Paul, the Only-One," in his Hyperion, a Romance, Samuel Colman, 1839, pp. 37-50.

THE BRITISH QUARTERLY REVIEW   (essay date 1847)

[Jean Paul's early years, before the publication of '**Hesperus,**' make up the] portion of his life that is both most interesting in itself, and which affords us the best insight into the character and genius of the man, revealing their formation and development. He has himself told us, in his own peculiar style, his reminiscences of childhood, in the unfinished production which he intended for an Autobiography, entitled '**Wahrheit aus meinem Leben.**' (Truth from my own life.) This, however, goes no farther than his thirteenth year, when he received his first communion; but such as it is, it is rich, not merely in pictures from memory of external scenes, but also in lively images of the feelings and conceptions which these awakened. Such images seem to have been cherished with a simple fondness in his soul, which remained to the last childlike and sincere; even as great nations love to dwell on the hallowed traditions of their earliest age, and to linger in recollection among its shadowy forms. The distinctness with which he retained and was able to represent those inward impressions, shows that, even as a child, the habit of self-observation was natural to him. He has thus been able to note with vividness and accuracy some of the most important traces of his mental progress, the development of his intellect, imagination, and affections. And in such simple annals of the morning hours of our being, how much of true psychological instruction may be found! It is often then as in the morning hours of the day—the brilliancy of the light and the clearness of the air invest the outward world with a beauty, and kindle emotions within us, that are afterwards unknown. To seize those perceptions, and enshrine them in the memory, is to gather some of not the least valuable of life's treasures. If Richter has done nothing more towards his biography, he has done this. (pp. 376-77)

"Jean Paul Richter," in The British Quarterly Review, Vol. VI, No. XIII, November 1, 1847, pp. 375-407.

MARGARET FULLER OSSOLI   (poem date 1850?)

[*The date of the following poem is unknown; 1850 is the year Fuller died. The warm praise recorded here for Jean Paul contrasts sharply with Fuller's earlier reaction (1833), and the third stanza responds to critics' charges that the works of Jean Paul suffered from a "want of order."*]

Poet of Nature! Gentlest of the wise,
　　Most airy of the fanciful, most keen
Of satirists!—thy thoughts, like butterflies,
　　Still near the sweetest scented flowers have been;

With Titian's colors thou canst sunset paint,
   With Raphael's dignity, celestial love;
With Hogarth's pencil, each deceit and feint
   Of meanness and hypocrisy reprove;

Canst to devotion's highest flight sublime
   Exalt the mind, by tenderest pathos' art,
   Dissolve, in purifying tears, the heart,
Or bid it, shuddering, recoil at crime;
   The fond illusions of the youth and maid,
At which so many world-formed sages sneer,
   When by thy altar-lighted torch displayed,
Our natural religion must appear.
All things in thee tend to one polar star,
Magnetic all thy influences are! . . .

A labyrinth! a flowery wilderness!
   Some in thy "slip-boxes" and "honey-moons"
Complain of—*want of order,* I confess,
   But not of *system* in its highest sense.
Who asks a guiding clue through this wide mind,
In love of Nature such will surely find.

   In tropic climes, live like the tropic bird,
Whene'er a spice-fraught grove may tempt thy stay;
   Nor be by cares of colder climes disturbed—
No frost the summer's bloom shall drive away;
Nature's wide temple and the azure dome
Have plan enough for the free spirit's home!

                       (pp. 147-48)

    Margaret Fuller Ossoli, "'Richter'," in her Memoirs of Margaret Fuller Ossoli, *Vol. I, W. H. Channing, R. W. Emerson, J. F. Clarke, eds., Phillips, Sampson and Company, 1852, pp. 147-48.*

R. H. STODDART (essay date 1857)

[Jean Paul] appeals to the thoughtful alone; nay, only to the most thoughtful—the sincere lovers and seekers after truth, who are willing to dig out an author's meaning, if it be buried in a crabbed and obscure style, under cartloads of intellectual rubbish. That there is a world of rubbish in Jean Paul, even his admirers allow; but it differs from the rubbish of dull and hackneyed authors. It is not so much the sweepings of his mind—dust, and cobwebs, and worthless odds and ends—as its natural imperfections, its magnificent towers and palaces, meanly built, or, worse still, in ruins. There is always something *in* Jean Paul, if we have the clew to it, and the patience to follow up the clew. But most of us lack patience; we read for amusement, and *pour passerle temps* [to pass the time]: consequently Jean Paul is not for us. Still we have a sort of curiosity about him, just as we have about a famous city, or a dexterous mountebank. He commands our attention because he is unlike all other authors. Even in Germany, where literary nondescripts abound, he is Jean Paul *der Einzige*—the only. (p. 405)

As a general thing the *style* of Jean Paul displeases his readers. It is too unlike the world-language of literature to be easily understood. Obscure in his own tongue, Jean Paul is still more so in English. He lacks directness and simplicity. Instead of stating his theme, and working it up in a clear and reasonable manner, he seizes it when it is but a dim and vague conception, and plays all sorts of vagaries with it, beclouding it with a crazy style, and burying it under a profusion of metaphors. Sometimes it is poetical prose; sometimes prose run mad. With all these drawbacks it is still magnificent writing, grand and stately in diction, and noble in thought. The old Titans might have talked in just such music. It is Olympian—

    The large utterance of the early gods.

Jean Paul is often puzzling because he means so much. There is no poverty of matter in his books, but an *embarras de richesse* [embarrassment of riches]. He is too lavish with his barbaric pearl and gold. . . .

He is one of the greatest humorists that ever lived, not only in his own country, but in the whole world, and in all time, worthy of a place beside Cervantes and Shakspeare. Humor is the ruling quality of his mind, the central fire that animates his being. Titanic in his humor as in his earnestness, he oversteps all bound and limit, and riots without law or measure. His humor is not in all cases natural and unalloyed. It is often unnatural, extravagant, and absurd; but take it all in all, it is genuine, subtle, and spiritual, drawn from the deepest, and purest, and sweetest recesses of his being. His good and great heart is in it, his simple and tender nature, the kindliness and friendliness of his genius. (p. 406)

    R. H. Stoddart, "Jean Paul," in The National Magazine, *New York, Vol. X, May, 1857, pp. 405-11.*

[W. R. ALGER] (essay date 1863)

[*Alger's essay, which discusses Jean Paul's works in general and then focuses on his novel* Titan, *is one of the earliest detailed studies of the author. Alger identifies the "chief qualities which give power and attraction" to Jean Paul's work: his wealth of material, discriminating wisdom, healthy and invigorating subjects, and skillful style. In an otherwise positive essay, Alger notes one important defect in Jean Paul's works: their lack of a unified and coherent form.*]

We are acquainted with no eminent literary artist who more sorely needs, or better deserves, or will more richly repay, every help to popular intelligibility and circulation than Jean Paul; for the human and the literary idiosyncrasies which his natural admirers find the most fascinating, are fatal barriers to his immediate reception into the regards of the average reader. His flooding sensibility, titanic imagination, resilient whimsicality, endless entanglement of remote allusions, bewildering superabundance of metaphor, unfailing supplies of humor and irony, require, as conditions of relishable reaction, greater resources of spirit, learning, and experience than most readers have at their command. His repulsiveness never arises from meagreness of matter, or sloth of faculty, or vulgarity of mind, or viciousness of temper, but from his extraordinary fertility, his half-chaotic exuberance,—the transcendent richness and energy of his genius presenting drafts upon the intellects and hearts of his readers which only a few have the spiritual funds to honor. (p. 2)

Notwithstanding many seeming crudenesses and many real imperfections, the chief qualities which give power and attraction to works of literary genius coexist in Jean Paul in a high degree. He has *wealth.* He teems with treasures. For his materials of statement and illustration, he ransacks heaven and earth, every province of art and learning, every department of science and experience, all varieties of natural scenery and human history. He pours forth thought, feeling, imagery, without hinderance and almost without bound. The copiousness of his spiritual riches is somewhat astonishing. He has *wisdom* in a degree only inferior to his wealth. He is not a mere omnivorous collector of facts and opinions: he is also a comprehensive and patient student of them. He surveys the matter of his information and thoughts, arranges it, criticises it, knows its relative place and value, is master of its uses. His huge and ardent imagination melts down his mental treasure, and his massive and powerful understanding recasts it into appropriate shapes. He is an amply competent critic of all kinds of philosophical and literary works, a still more competent judge of human nature and experience and their manifold diversities. His strokes of discrimination are ever penetrative and shrewd, and his abundant aphorisms rank him with the soundest and most nutritious of ethical thinkers. He has likewise *health* in a striking degree. He invigorates his reader. To peruse one of his works is to feel a fresh breeze of victorious strength and sympathy. . . . The true test of a literary work is, Does it strengthen and cheer? If so, clasp it to your breast. Does it sour, enervate, or confuse? Then fling it into the fire. Jean Paul may court this criterion, for the total influence of his writing is surprisingly wholesome. Furthermore, he has *skill* to set his thoughts in grace and beauty, to present his material in forms that delight the reader. However frequently he appears to violate, or actually violates, the canons of good taste, shocking the proprieties of fine art, and repelling the fastidious, he is familiar with the principles of aesthetics, knows thoroughly the rules for producing the choicest effects, and neglects them, not from ignorance or incapacity, but from an overbearing inward fulness and impetuosity, or for the securing of some end which he considers of superior importance. He can on occasion give his thoughts and images with a delicacy and force, a simple perfectness of finish, a lucid precision, which might awaken the envy of the greatest masters of style, even of Goethe himself. His pages sparkle with separate sentences and paragraphs, which are gems of blended wisdom and beauty scarcely susceptible of improvement. . . . The artistic accuracy of insight and taste which he shows in the parts of his works often fail him in the wholes, so that their outlines are blurred, and their filling-up confusedly crowded. This is because the misleading excess of his sympathy, or an overfondness for the teeming products of his own mind, obscures his critical perceptions, and causes him, rather than reject anything that occurs to him, to indulge in a gorgeous accumulation of ornament,—to associate with the straightforward matter an involved medley of allusion, inference, and suggestion, a swift interaction of seriousness and wit, which cannot but confound and baffle an unprepared reader. This vitiating deficiency of clearness and simplicity in the plot and conduct of his works—a formidable obstacle to popularity it must be acknowledged—has produced in many quarters an unfortunate blindness to his extraordinary merits. (pp. 4-6)

[The most distinctive trait] of Jean Paul,—that in which he stands supreme among authors,—is his unrivalled combination of serious earnestness and overpowering pathos with imaginative humor and comicality. He is at the same time a grave student and a satirist; a jocose philosopher and a devout humorist. He is as much at home in the sublime as in the ridiculous. He laughs and weeps, loves and adores, with the same rhapsodic sincerity. He is a three-headed, three-hearted giant, equipped with an equal perception of the droll and the dread, an equal feeling of the tender and the absurd, vibrating swiftly through all that lies between the extremes. This association of contradictory endowments and defects is what astonishes and repels the uninitiated as they attempt his works. Intelligent readers of Jean Paul have always recognized this double nature in him. He was fully aware of it himself, and of its value, and freely played it forth with genial consciousness in what he wrote. It is singular to notice how it expresses itself in the twin

characters which are associated and repeated in all his principal works. In **"The Invisible Lodge"** we have Ottoman and Fenk; in the **"Flower, Fruit, and Thorn Pieces,"** Siebenkäs and Leibgeber; in **"Hesperus,"** Victor and Emanuel; in **"Flegeljahre,"** Walt and Vult; in **"Titan,"** Albano and Schoppe. . . . In single qualities of genius, with the exception of human sensibility, others have surpassed Jean Paul; in the blended operation of [his] apparently incongruous powers . . . , no one has equalled him. (pp. 13-15)

When we consider Jean Paul as an artist, we find a singular limitation in his genius. He has a gigantic creative power combined with a diminutive shaping power. He can grasp and associate truth, feeling, facts, phenomena, more copiously than any except the very greatest minds; but in grouping his material into coherent relations to a general design, fashioning it into symmetrical forms, giving it proper location, perspective, and movement, many rank much above him who are incomparably inferior to him in everything else. He suffers in popularity greatly in consequence of this defect. Most persons read chiefly for the story; with him the story is the least important thing, and is buried in gorgeous masses of incidental matter. His sporadic mind and style bewilder and weary the reader who has not agile faculties and wealthy resources to follow his clews of swift and complex allusion, and to fill his swarming symbols with responsive meaning. One feels, after reading a work of Jean Paul, as if the treasury of some god had exploded, and his book had caught the scattering contents. (pp. 15-16)

But if the art of Jean Paul seems lame and weak in the conduct and total form of his work, we should not forget, or fail to see, that it is often exact and faultless in details. This is shown almost invariably in his maxims and incidental reflections, very frequently also in detached images, and in special passages of description. The *story* of the **"Titan"** is highly dramatic and intense, yet it is well nigh lost sight of in the tropical wilderness of riches by the way. So involved is it with mysteries and whimsicalities, wheels within wheels, that it is an arduous task to master its outline, and thread and carry along its incidents in any sort of collective unity. But there is hardly a paragraph of it in which there is not something rich and strange to stimulate the thoughtful, to gratify and instruct the curious, to touch or console the tender, to inspire the noble, to develop the sense of beauty, to cherish the love of virtue and humanity, and to clothe the ideas of nature and God with new attractiveness and majesty. To neglect or condemn this vast array of appetizing spiritual riches for its comparative disorder, is as foolish as it would be to despise a chamberful of gold because the ingots were not piled in regular rows. . . . It is true that most of his personages are not wholly dramatized, but partly described. He ekes out his deficiency in the perfect interior possession and enactment of his characters, by means of outward paintings and expositions of them. He makes skilful use of the artifice of a chorus of explanatory and critical remarks accompanying the action and dialogue,—an artifice of which the greatest masters have no need. In a degree, he imposes the diverse features and elements of men and experience on persons, instead of thoroughly conceiving original moulds of character, and running life and nature into them. Yet, in despite of this comparative limitation, by his wonderful psychological tact and his familiarity with the workings of human nature, especially on the side of the affections, added to his vast and acute knowledge and sympathy, he gives a surpassing interest and reality to the chief personages in his works. They are living beings to us. We can never forget them, nor the powerful lessons they insinuate into our souls. They are acquaintances whom we have actually known; and, warning, amusing, inspiring, with their wickedness, their grotesque drollery, their grand and tender nobility, they stay with us, and we are glad to have them stay. (pp. 18-20)

In the **"Titan,"** we are introduced to a world of sharply defined and well-supported [male] characters,—characters of many qualities, grades, and positions, whose contrasts of spirit and conduct are strikingly brought out by a happy management of lights and shades in the incidents of the narrative and the conversation of the actors. . . . The female characters in this romance also form a memorable group, all most distinctly defined, depicted, and sustained throughout with singular felicity. Not one of them, however often or rarely she comes upon the scene, ever loses her distinctive personality, though, with the verisimilitude of nature, it is constantly varying in its manifestations. (pp. 20-1)

On Albano [the hero of the romance] the author lavishes all his powers, and our interest is concentrated in him from first to last. . . . The purpose of the author in his **"Titan"** . . . is to depict the ideal man and woman; by means of descriptions, critical analyses, dramatic incidents, contrasts, and foils, to portray the true types of perfect manhood and womanhood. Such are Albano and Idoine. This aim runs through the whole gorgeous mass of the work, like a silver thread through a mountain of jewels. It is the highest task of the human mind, and has been a favorite subject with many great authors. But it is wrought out in the **"Titan"** with a power and wealth of moral earnestness and wisdom not equalled by any similar attempt in literature. (pp. 23-4)

> [*W. R. Alger*], *"Traits of Jean Paul and His Titan," in* The North American Review, *Vol. XCVII, No. CC, July, 1863, pp. 1-35.*

GEORGE BRANDES   (essay date 1873)

[*Brandes, a Danish literary critic and biographer, was the principal leader of the intellectual movement which helped to bring an end to Scandinavian cultural isolation. He believed that literature reflects the spirit and problems of its time, and that it must be understood within its social and aesthetic context. Brandes's major critical work,* Hovdedstrømninger i det 19de aarhundredes litteratur (Main Currents in Nineteenth-Century Literature), *won him admiration for his ability to view literary movements within the broader context of all of European literature. In the following essay, first published in 1873 in volume two of* Main Currents, *subtitled* Den romantiske Skole i Tydakland (The Romantic School in Germany), *Brandes discusses Jean Paul in relation to the German Romantic school. He considers Jean Paul "in many ways the forerunner of Romanticism."*]

Jean Paul is in many ways the forerunner of Romanticism; in the Romantic School Hoffmann recalls him to us, as Tieck recalls Goethe. He is a thorough Romanticist in the absolute arbitrariness with which, as an artist, he sets to work. As Auerbach says, he has "in readiness studies of men, moods, traits of character, psychological complications, and miscellaneous imagery, which he introduces at random, adjusting them to given characters or situations." He thrusts all kinds of irrelevant matter into the elastic framework of his story. He is, further, a Romanticist in his absorption in self—for it is himself, always himself, who speaks by the mouth of his characters, whatever they may be; in the famous humour which with him lords it over all else, respecting none of the conventions of style; and, finally, in the fact that he is the antipodes of classical culture. But, whatever he may have been in art,

in life he was not the defender of lawlessness, but the ardent champion of liberty, Fichte's equal in enthusiastic persistence. He was neither the foe of enlightenment, nor of reason, nor of the Reformation, nor of the Revolution; he was convinced of the historical value and the full validity of the ideas which it is the glory of the eighteenth century to have produced and championed. Therefore he uplifted a warning voice against the futile, demoralising fantasticality of the Romanticists.

Titan contains the most powerful of Jean Paul's ideal characters, Roquairol. His strength did not lie in the delineation of ideal characters; he was first and foremost the admirable, realistic idyll-writer.

Roquairol is a prototype of the form in which the age moulded its passion and its despair. He is burning, conscious desire, which develops into fantastic eccentricity, because circumstances have no use for it, and because it does not possess the power to take hold of reality, re-mould it and subject it to itself; it becomes a disease, which strikes inwards and leads to morbid self-contemplation and suicide. (pp. 66-7)

> *George Brandes, "Tieck and Jean Paul," in his* Main Currents in Nineteenth Century Literature: The Romantic School in Germany, *Vol. II, translated by Diana White and Mary Morison, Boni & Liveright, Inc., 1923, pp. 59-68.**

J. F. WALLACE   (essay date 1893)

[Reading Jean Paul's works is like descending] into a peaceful vale, where limpid streams flow through flowering meads, where sunshine and birds make warmth and melody, with only the shadows of far-off clouds dimming for a moment the bright serenity of the landscape, after having been on lonely mountain-tops during a storm, when the forces of Nature met in mighty conflict. Our natures were uplifted by the grandeur of the contest; the deeps of our souls were stirred; we obtained glimpses of the Infinite; the power and majesty of creation penetrated into our very being; the earth below us, with its small experiences, seemed too remote to disturb us. We revelled on the heights of great undefined thoughts, dissatisfied with the narrowness of human life, and impatient at its trivialities, while we soared into realms of the unknown.

But we are mortal. The environments of Time and Space draw us down earthward; and we return, wearied with the turmoil of a struggle with the Limitless, and yield our souls to the sweet influence of Nature made manifest in more peaceful guise. It seems to be the impulse of Richter's genius to present to us the universe in this manner. His mind turns toward light and warmth. These are the elements of growth, and certainly the genius which basks in them must develop something of perfection. He is an apostle of hope and joy. (pp. 551-52)

While Byron seems to revel in the magnificent misery of his dream of darkness, Jean Paul recoils with unspeakable horror from the unfathomable abyss of chaos his imagination pictures. We admire the one; we yield ourselves to melancholy and romance, and allow our deepest sympathy to be stirred by his pictures of woe. By the other, our hearts are uplifted. We become cheerful, and are buoyed up with patience and hope in our pilgrimage through life. We are ready to grasp all that is bright and cheery, rather than sink into apathy and despair. (p. 552)

How Richter as a writer is to be considered, depends upon the decision of the literary world as to the scope of novelist. If it be simply to present us with a narrative of human life enclosed within its web of sentiments, aspirations, and acts, then Jean Paul cannot be considered a novelist. . . . His books, considered simply as novels, are not artistic. There is no well-conceived plot, smoothly and completely worked out to a pleasing *dénouement,* with due regard paid to received rules of critics. There is an unusual admixture of elements in them which produces an incongruous whole. The man possessed the most far-reaching imagination, the most acute poetical sensibility, a keenest sense of humor, a philosophical mind, the most penetrating intellect, the softest, kindest heart, the simplest faith in God and good, the most enthusiastic love of Nature, and a thousand other traits, which are all shining in his writings.

The main incidents of the stories could be told in a hundred sentences, but the world of feeling and thought portrayed repay the reader for travelling through his voluminous works. He is never satisfied with one perusal. He will read them over and over again, finding new riches each time. . . . (p. 553)

The **'Campaner Thal,'** Richter's last writing, is perhaps the most interesting and important of his works. The characters in it stand out clearly,—real persons, without any minute pencilling of traits. Besides Jean Paul himself we have the sceptical, disputatious would-be philosopher, the poetical, melancholy lover, the happy, genial, successful man of the world, the pure, cold, meditative maiden, and the bright, tender, sparkling, sympathetic girl plainly before our mind's eye with very few words of description. . . . His descriptions of the beauty of Nature in this book are the most exquisite I have ever met with. He not only sees them with an artist's eye, and describes them with a poet's tongue, but his spirit seems to have penetrated to the very heart of Nature, and beats responsive to her throbs. . . . (p. 555)

[The] dissertation on the immortality of the soul [in **'Campaner Thal'** is] the most satisfying ever given by any philosopher. There is a charm in the picture presented to the mind's eye by the author, in his description of this day in the beautiful valley. The sunshine, the birds, the flowers, the streams, the mountains, the happy companionship, the grave discourses, the merry jests, the softening shadows of sorrow, the mellowing influence of love, the strengthening tonic of irony, while over all, in Carlyle's words, lay "a deep genial humor like warm sunshine, softening the whole, blending the whole into light sportful harmony,"—everything is there to create harmony of tone in the mind of the reader. (p. 556)

> *J. F. Wallace, "Jean Paul Richter," in* Poet Lore, *Vol. V, No. 11, November, 1893, pp. 551-57.*

GEORGE SAINTSBURY   (essay date 1904)

[*Saintsbury was an English literary historian and critic of the late nineteenth and early twentieth centuries. A prolific writer, Saintsbury composed a number of histories of English and European literature as well as several critical works on individual authors, styles, and periods. In the following excerpt, Saintsbury praises Jean Paul's theoretical work, the* School for Aesthetics, *as "one of the best of its kind."*]

There is a note to the Preface of the second edition of Jean Paul's **Vorschule der Æsthetik** which expresses my own opinions on its subject so completely that I must give it in full. "A collection of Wieland's reviews in the *Teutsche Merkur,* or, in short, any honest selection of the best æsthetic reviews from newspapers and periodicals, would be a better bargain for the artist than any newest **Æsthetic.** In every good review

there is, hidden or revealed, a good 'Æsthetic,' and, more than that, an applied one, and a free, and the shortest of all, and (by dint of the examples) the best."

No one, of course, who has the slightest knowledge of Richter will suppose that the whole book is written in such a straightforward and common-sense style as this. But it is very far indeed from being one of his thorniest or most acrobatical: and Carlyle need scarcely have feared that it might "astonish many an honest brother of our craft were he to read it, and altogether perplex and dash his maturest counsels if he chanced to understand it" [see excerpt above from *The Edinburgh Review,* 1827]. Nobody who can understand [Samuel Taylor Coleridge's] *Biographia Litteraria* could have the faintest difficulty with the **Vorschule.**

Such Richterisms as do appear are chiefly in the appendix lectures, the ***"Miserikordia-**Lecture for Stylists," the ***"Jubilate-**Lecture for Poetical Persons," and the ***"Kantate-**Lecture on Poetical Poetry,"** which, nevertheless, do contain excellent things. In the main body of the book there are only occasional flings (such as, "according to Kant, the formation of the heavenly bodies is easier to deduce than the formation of a caterpillar"), while the famous and very just description of a certain thing as "like a lighthouse, high, shining, empty," is mere justice lighted up itself by wit. The fact is, that the book is one of the best of its kind, and deserves to be reserved from that exclusion of titular Æsthetics which prevails in this part of our History, not more by the large intermixture of actual criticism in it than by the sanity, combined with inspiration, of the rest. From its separation at the beginning of the "Nihilists" of Poetry (those who generalise everything) and the Materialists (who abide wholly in the sensuous) to the fragments on Style and Language at the end, it is a really excellent book, and if it has not been translated into English it ought to have been, and to be. (pp. 384-86)

> *George Saintsbury, "Goethe and His Contemporaries," in his* A History of Criticism and Literary Taste in Europe from the Earliest Texts to the Present Day: Modern Criticism, *Vol. III, William Blackwood & Sons Ltd., 1904. pp. 352-405.**

HERMANN HESSE   (essay date 1921)

[*A German novelist and poet, Hesse is best known for his novels* Siddhartha *and* Der Steppenwolf (Steppenwolf). *In this essay, originally published in 1921 as "Ueber Jean Paul," Hesse briefly comments on Jean Paul's life, work, and reputation. Hesse praises the easy familiarity with which Jean Paul drew on the subconscious in his writings, maintaining that "he knew, cared for, and studied that many-colored bridge between the conscious and the unconscious, the dream, more than any other poet, with the possible exception of Dostoevsky."*]

If I were to be confronted in an examination with the question: in what book of modern times does the German soul express itself most forcefully and characteristically, I would answer without hesitation—Jean Paul's *Flegeljahre (Unfledged Years).* In Jean Paul that secret Germany—which continues to live on though for several decades now a different, noisier, more hectic, more soulless Germany has been standing in its light—gave birth to its most characteristic, richest, and most bewildered spirit, one of the greatest poetic talents of all time, whose work presents a native jungle of poesy. And Germany with its astounding riches and its astounding forgetfulness has once more forgotten Jean Paul. . . . (p. 113)

[The] secret of Jean Paul's wealth of vision, of his profusion, of his tropical proliferation [is that] his communication with the unconscious was accomplished easily and playfully, he needed only to penetrate a thin membrane and he stood on the primeval ground of memories, where earliest childhood and the primitive world of men and planets were recorded, in the primeval ground which contains all history, out of which all religions, all arts, have emerged and constantly re-emerged. And, to put the matter plainly at once (for naturally every poet draws on the unconscious), Jean Paul not only possessed this happy faculty, this dexterity in the play of inspiration, this constant presence of the apparently forgotten, but he was aware of it, he had apprehended the secret of this source, he expressed ideas that are in conformity with the present-day conceptions of psychoanalysis, and he knew, cared for, and studied that many-colored bridge between the conscious and the unconscious, the dream, more than any other poet, with the possible exception of Dostoevsky. Jean Paul had a profound intuition of what we of today seek under new images and with new theories as happiness, as perfection, as harmony of soul: an intuition of the balance of psychological functions, of a peaceful and fruitful coexistence of knowledge and intuition, thought and feeling. (pp. 119-20)

Jean Paul greatly loved tears and delicate feelings and he was prolific in soft, sweet, noble, fairylike, tender female figures—but above all he loved the opposite, created the opposite. He created characters that are like aeolian harps, soft, passive, perpetually melting into emotion, and beside them he placed other characters of a hardness, coldness, harsh manliness, contempt for the world, and inner loneliness such as are to be found in few poets. And so Jean Paul is not sentimental? On the contrary, of course he is sentimental, and very likely he was unacquainted with that cowardly timidity of the younger writers of today at the signs of emotion, at the appearance of sensitivity! But he is also the opposite of sentimental, he is also a thinker, a scoffer, he is also a lonely Prometheus, aware of the impossibility of true understanding between human beings, enclosed in lonely greatness, cold and crushingly severe.

For Jean Paul is not an intellectual or an emotionalist, a thinker or an intuitive or a sensitive—he is all of these. . . . Jean Paul is the perfect example of a genius who has not cultivated a single specialty but whose ideal is the free play of all the powers of the soul, who would like to say yes to everything, enjoy everything to the full, love and experience everything. So we see the poet in each of his works (aside from a few small idyls such as *Wuz* or *Fibel*) unceasingly running back and forth between hot and cold, between hard and soft, between all the hundred poles and antipoles of his existence; and the hithering and thithering, the electrical discharge between all these poles is quite literally the life of his creations. (pp. 120-21)

He to whom the thought of the polarity in all fields was so profoundly familiar has uncommon much to say to us today. [Jean Paul] will not and should not be a "leader" for us, but a confirmer and also a comforter, for no poet preaches to us so penetratingly the fact that "the most important thing for the poet, love," suffers no diminution through the recognition of the opposites, that harmony between the divergent powers of the soul is a living and life-giving goal. (p. 122)

Hermann Hesse, "About Jean Paul," translated by Denver Lindley, in My Belief: Essays on Life and Art *by Hermann Hesse, edited by Theodore Ziolkowski, translated by Denver Lindley with Ralph Manheim, Farrar, Straus and Giroux, 1974, pp. 113-22.*

H. C. DENEKE (essay date 1937)

[*The following essay, written in 1937, is an overview of Jean Paul's work. Through a consideration of the literary movements of Jean Paul's day and the similarities and differences between his writings and those of his contemporaries, Deneke explores Jean Paul's reaction to "the intellectual and moral problem of his time": the need to reconcile emotion and reason.*]

Taking Jean Paul's writings as they stand one is confronted with very individual work which defies pigeon-holing. One finds oneself in the company of a personality in the making, very complex in its impulses, and the strangest mixture of *naïveté* and self-consciousness; a disorderly mind, in its wealth, its eccentricity, its imaginative flights, its depth, its fondness for detail, its fullness. One thing emerges: Jean Paul is concerned with the human soul as poets are, that is not as an abstraction but as a living thing. His works record an impressive endeavour to hold fast his vision and then to interpret actual life in the light of it. And his chief novel, *Titan,* read as a whole, is the document both of this endeavour and of its ultimate failure, for the facts of life defy him; sustained inspiration is denied.

The rare quality in his creative gift induces speculation as to why it stops short as it does. This question has frequently engaged the attention of his critics and interpreters and it is of high interest since it brings us face to face with his mind. Jean Paul's mental attitude results from his particular response to the intellectual influences of his age, and leads him to hold a balance between an ideal world of the imagination that is revealed in dreams and visions and a material world of sense that can be coloured by, and so can support, the ideal world, but that also proves a check. . . . Jean Paul's intuition of the grandeur and the high destiny of the human spirit is his profoundest inspiration, and he has expressed it fully. With it, too, his perception of how men fall short. . . . [The] very profundity of his inspiration challenges the comparison with his greater contemporaries Goethe and Schiller and then of how they met the outstanding intellectual and moral problem of their time. Emotion, rediscovered and over-emphasized in the days of *Sturm and Drang* [storm and stress], called for reconciliation with the demands of full reason. The synthesis that was required, and that nowadays unfolds itself impressively before our eyes in the classicism of Goethe and Schiller and in the philosophy of Kant, was then in the making. Jean Paul did not attain to it, and it is arguable that, in failing to attain to it as a thinker or as a man, he also failed as an artist. Perhaps in this failure he was merely fulfilling the law of his nature. The problem of the age did not come to him as one of passion that is directed towards a great objective. It came as the need to save the belief and the high instincts which had revealed to the imaginative child Friedrich Richter his central intuition of the majesty of the human spirit. Without this, faith must die and Jean Paul's best faculty perish. He could not sacrifice the predominance of imagination. He was too intellectual and too profound to escape the influence of rationalism, which touched him first on its destructive side, and too sensitive not to respond to the age of Werther. The clash of class distinctions had entered into his soul as it did into young Schiller's. In coming to terms with the intellectual and moral problem of his time he does not fully face the difficulties but he gleans his humour. Measured by Goethe and Schiller he is seen to evade the problem by a retreat upon his own best intuition. At the hand of Kant, and upon the basis of Jacobi's philosophy, he found a foundation for his faith in God and in immortality. The way of this isolates him intellectually from Goethe, the naturalist and thinker, and from Schiller, the moralist and thinker, and from both in their artistic aim of objectivity. It associates him intimately with Herder, the thinker and theologian, and leaves him free to express universal human values on his own terms. His vision of the grandeur of man's spirit becomes in his hands the romance of poor men in the Germany that he knew best. By immortalizing its narrowness and its potential spirituality he expressed experience that both Goethe and Schiller had left aside. In this there rests his historical significance and his touch with future generations.

Whatever may be thought of Jean Paul's novels as a whole on artistic grounds, he finds adequate forms of his own for things that he has to say. Among these his power of wielding emotional tension is interesting. His imagination is strong in conceiving fruitful situations, in complicating these by packing them with associations of thought and feeling from what has gone before or premonitions of what is to come. Then he unravels and recomplicates by charging his sentences with allusions that reach out far, or by following some change of mood temperamentally through a set theme, while he writes from visual impressions that are animated by what they signify. (pp. 147-50)

Jean Paul very frequently lifts out some central event or some central theme and uses it so as to focus the reactions of different temperaments or characters. It is a favourite method. In interesting instances he subtilizes the situation by playing off emotional tension in some person or persons against unconcern in others. At the beginning of *Titan* the enthusiastic hero Albano is travelling by boat across Lago Maggiore to Isola Bella. The landscape is atmospherically pictorial and Albano's emotions are tense. He is consciously luxuriating in his sensations and concentrating on his intense longing to see his lovely birthplace and meet a mysterious and unknown father. These two *motifs* of desire are drawn out and wrought into the description of a chapter that rises to the crest of a wave. (pp. 151-52)

Another time in *Titan*, Jean Paul has a scene which grows to its climax as those concerned in it listen to music. It is at the court of a petty prince where all high instincts of the soul are quelled and we know that it is against a background of scheming elders that the young people there dream their visionary dreams of romance. We are made aware of a setting such as Wieland uses when he presents nymphs and cupids and garlands in the stylized scenery of rococo days with temples, groves, and fountains. What is decorative setting in clear outline to Wieland gives to Jean Paul nodal points for a musical description in which setting is surcharged with feeling. In the ducal pleasure gardens at Lilar, with their chestnut avenue, the stone figures, the grotto fitted with bewildering mirrors, the marvellous moving staircase and the waterworks that can be turned on to play sprays as a surprise, a group of young people are taking a walk. We know the complex cross-currents of feelings and loyalties between them, particularly for the idealistic hero Albano and his delicate lover Liane, shadowy as she is, yet articulate in music. . . . A visit to a little room by the waterworks is suggested. It holds a musical instrument made of glass, where the player can sit concealed, and there Liane takes her seat. Above, on the bridge, a fine red sunset gilds the listeners as she plays and makes the spraying water sparkle in gold. With the description of the sound, the light and the colours there are subtly conveyed the sentiments of all and of each present, Albano's love *motif*, moody and half in longing and in passionate discontent, Roquairol in cool detachment as he turns on the waterworks, Princess Julienne, anxious that all should feel com-fortable with one another, little Helena quite unperturbed, as she drops her auriculas into the rushing water for the pleasure of seeing them washed away. . . . A setting like Wieland's has been used for purposes beyond Wieland's range of clear outline, witty contrast, and good sense, for Jean Paul's description has learnt from the Werther tradition, where figures and landscape blend with mood, and it has been influenced by the luminous radiance of Wilhelm Meister. But his touch is not Goethe's nor his effects. He lacks Goethe's objectivity, the creator's gift to withdraw while his creatures pursue or seem to pursue a life of their own. (pp. 152-54)

The nearest approach to constructive character development is his presentation of Roquairol the villain in *Titan*, on whom he has bestowed care, since he intended him to typify a man who became a victim to the special temptations of that age. The novel was to be an argument against the exaggerated passions which the age of *Sturm und Drang* discovered and the young romantics cultivated, and, inasmuch as Jean Paul's experience led him to such condemnation, he was approximating to Goethe's view and was consciously marking disagreement with the romantics. Roquairol, 'mixed ethereal and mud', was possessed of qualities that in juxtaposition always intrigued Jean Paul. His imagination was seized by what is sinister in such a figure—its suavity, its unexpected violence—and by the contrast with the radiance that is showered upon Albano and the women. He can go as far as the threshold to view such a soul, can place it in relation to its opposite and point to its destructiveness. Taken as a whole this character leaves the impression of a fine sketch that degenerates into caricature. Perhaps a realist method alone could have made Roquairol convincing. Jean Paul fails to give him flesh and blood, the archangel ruined whom we hoped to know ends as a melodramatic cad. The whole of Jean Paul's plot and of his thesis carries no conviction and is, in some ways, curiously outrageous. Tragedy remains outside his range and for moral issues he is capable of using a light-hearted and perfunctory pen. (pp. 155-56)

Humour and pathos blend in him in a way that is wholly his own. Perhaps it is hardly true to say that Jean Paul develops progressively when he has once found himself. But he learns as a writer and improves in the skill with which he summons old impulses. In his last novel, *Die Flegeljahre*, the perspective is widened on the idyllic and narrowed on the romantic side by the creation of the immortal twins: Walt, the dreamer, and Vult, the man of the world, the very opposites of one another but united by close ties of affection. Again these figures must not be measured by a realist standard, again the development that he had in mind for them fails in that it was never carried out, but in their imaginative setting they are alive, for each is a side of Jean Paul himself. Their disagreements and reconciliations call forth some of his best and most characteristic moments. . . . (p. 157)

It is because of his inveterate idealism that idyllic moments, one way or another, are his best, for in these he can best wield the facts of life to suit his outlook. A Wuz [from **"Leben des vergnügten Schulmeisterleins Maria Wuz in Aventhal"**] or a Lenette [from *Blumen-, Frucht- und Dornenstükke*] are true to life and are idealists because of a besetting notion that disregards all obstacles, Wuz in his temperamental optimism, Lenette in her relentless energy for keeping her house spick and span; in them and many others humour is quite unconscious; the conscious humorists, Leibgeber and Schoppe, bring Jean Paul's own perspective and are restlessly torn between a haunting idealism that they wish almost forcibly to impose upon life, and a baffling impotence. (p. 158)

Jean Paul made the most of his gifts and his greatness stands. What there is of weakness has remarkable psychological and historical interest and it is incident to his strength. (p. 159)

> H. C. Deneke, *"Some Observations on Jean Paul,"* in German Studies Presented to Professor H. G. Fiedler, M.V.O., *Oxford at the Clarendon Press, Oxford, 1938, pp. 145-59.*

RENÉ WELLEK   (essay date 1955)

[*Wellek's* A History of Modern Criticism *is a major, comprehensive study of the literary critics of the last three centuries. Wellek's critical method, as demonstrated in* A History *and outlined in his* Theory of Literature, *is one of describing, analyzing, and evaluating a work solely in terms of the problems it poses for itself and how the writer solves them. For Wellek, biographical, historical, and psychological information are incidental. Although many of Wellek's critical methods are reflected in the work of the New Critics, he does not consider himself a member of that group and rejects their more formalistic tendencies. In the essay excerpted below, Wellek describes and analyzes Jean Paul's theory of poetics as presented in his* School for Aesthetics.]

[Jean Paul's *Vorschule der Aesthetik*] is not an aesthetics but rather a poetics or, more correctly, a series of chapters on aspects of literary theory: poetry in general, imagination, genius, Greek and romantic poetry, the comic, humor and wit, characters and plot, the novel and style. Though the book is written in a florid, highly metaphorical style, full of recondite comparisons and allusions and unending displays of pedantic wit, it propounds a sane theory of literature and adds something new and personal on questions rarely discussed at that time: the technique of the novel, characterization and motivation, and the theory of the comic, humor, and wit.

It is not easy to define Jean Paul's general position. He is very satirical about Schelling and the Schellingians, "polarization," "the indifference of the subjective and objective pole," and so on. He attacks the Schlegels for their Fichtean idealism (which to Jean Paul was pernicious solipsism and egoism), their violent partisanship, their self-conceit, and their limited, exclusive taste; he has little use for Schiller's aesthetics, which he considers formalistic and frivolous, misunderstanding the play concept. His personal and philosophical associations were with Herder and F. H. Jacobi. At times we might think that Jean Paul was simply a good 18th-century empirical psychologist: he could even say that Kames's *Elements of Criticism* is of a "higher critical school than the high one at Jena," i.e. Schiller and the Schlegels. The avowed purpose of his book is, in part at least, self-analysis and self-observation in a very concrete way. Jean Paul has most to say about the kind of novel he was writing himself: the sprawling humorous romance, his own strange mixture of the fantastic, dreamy, and sentimental with the odd and grotesque.

But while Jean Paul preserved a considerable independence among the literary parties of the time and also his ties with an earlier past, he agreed with the romantics on fundamental issues of poetics. In spite of his reservations against the Schlegels and Schelling, his main position is the same: the proclamation in the preface to the first edition that "the newer school is right in the main" must be taken as final. Not only is Jean Paul dependent on Friedrich Schlegel for a number of specific points, but their basic views of poetry are identical. Though Jean Paul tried to keep a dispassionate balance between the classical and romantic in his theory, there cannot be any doubt where his preference lay in practice. But as opposed to the Schlegels he

kept his admiration for the English humorous novel of the 18th century, for Richardson, Sterne, Fielding, and even Smollett, from whom his own art, at least in part, was derived. (pp. 100-01)

> René Wellek, *"The Early Romantics in Germany,"* in his A History of Modern Criticism, 1750-1950: The Romantic Age, *Yale University Press, 1955, pp. 74-109.**

WOLFGANG KAYSER   (essay date 1957)

[*Kayser's 1957 study* Das Groteske: Seine Gesaltung in Malerei und Dichtung (The Grotesque in Art and Literature), *published in 1957 and excerpted below, was the earliest attempt to compose a critical history of the grotesque as a distinct category of aesthetics. Kayser traces the evolution of the term "grotesque" from its first application to an ornamental style in Roman architecture through its various manifestations in the works of nineteenth and twentieth-century authors and artists, among them Edgar Allan Poe, Franz Kafka, and the Surrealist painters. Kayser defines the grotesque as "the estranged world" and sees it manifested in the artistic expression of alienation and estrangement. Surprise, confusion, and the macabre are some of its characteristic elements. The chapter in which Kayser discusses Jean Paul begins with an analysis of the grotesque in the works of the German Romantics, Jean Paul's contemporaries. It continues with an explication of Friedrich von Schlegel's theory of the grotesque as outlined in his* Gespräch über die Poesie, *in which he discusses Jean Paul. According to Kayser, Schlegel defines the grotesque as "a clashing contrast between form and content, the unstable mixture of heterogeneous elements, the explosive force of the paradoxical, which is both ridiculous and terrifying." Schlegel's concept thus embodies both the tragic and comic. While acknowledging that Schlegel's theory describes many essential elements of the grotesque, Kayser asserts that "one aspect is definitely lacking: the abysmal quality, the insecurity, the terror inspired by the disintegration of the world." Kayser finds that this quality is present in* School for Aesthetics, *discussed below. While Jean Paul does not use the term "grotesque," the concept informs his theory of humor: the grotesque, according to Kayser, is the "annihilating idea" in Jean Paul's work, revealed in the destructive capability of humor.*]

[Like Friedrich Schlegel,] I, too, would speak of Sterne and Jean Paul as writers of the grotesque, as can be shown by a wealth of illustrations from the latter's works—and by no means only those already published at that time. In Jean Paul's writings we find the clashing contrasts which seem to remove the ground from under our feet, the sinister games with wax dolls and demonized mechanisms, the constantly renewed invocation of fear in the presence of a world about to be alienated, and, most strikingly, the abysmal visions in the speech of the dead Christ, delivered from on high and postulating the nonexistence of God. . . . But is this what Friedrich Schlegel found . . .? Are the grotesque elements he discovered in the work of Jean Paul and Sterne those which we find there? (p. 51)

"Jean Paul's grotesques [are] the only romantic products of this unromantic age" [said Schlegel]—it may surprise us that Jean Paul himself neither elaborated on this statement nor used the word "grotesque" in his *Vorschule der Ästhetik.* This very omission, however, is significant. The praise of Jean Paul, the writer of grotesques, had been a little too ambiguous for him to feel tempted to give this term a central place in his esthetic, which was intended as a justification and exegesis of his own work. But even though the word itself is never used, the phenomenon is sighted and circumscribed by entire programs. It is an ingredient of humor as Jean Paul sought to define it, namely, its "annihilating idea." Reality, the terrestrial, finite world as a whole, is destroyed by humor; it is the bird Merops which soars up to heaven with raised tail and draws us after it. The laughter which humor evokes is not detached but contains a certain measure of pain. (p. 54)

[No] matter how annihilating and satanic this humor may appear, Jean Paul does not find it to be solely destructive or abysmal. . . . The annihilation of finite reality can and may take place only because humor also leads upward toward the "idea of infinity." Jean Paul's language indicates that he thought of humor as aiming at an absolute. Jean Paul's grotesque and his annihilating humor resemble Schlegel's definitions of the grotesque and arabesque in his *Gespräch über die Poesie*. . . . The true essence of humor, however, is not only intellectual (as is the case with the comic) but also religious; the *Himmel* into which the bird Merops rises is not a sky but heaven. (pp. 55-6)

[The section of *Vorschule der Ästhetik*] which deals with the annihilating idea of humor quite clearly indicates how familiar Jean Paul was with the satanic humor, which destroys and estranges without lending us wings for a flight into heaven. But is the idea of infinity, of heaven, of the divine world, of the body of light (characteristically enough, Jean Paul makes use of several diverse images) as much of a certainty in Jean Paul's poetic world as it may have been in his philosophy? I am inclined to believe that a final uncertainty is essential to Jean Paul's writings. The fervor with which he describes the spiritual flight of his exalted figures seems infused not only with grief over the transitoriness of the great moments and with pain caused by the awareness that all feelings are subjective and the heavenly gates will never open, but also with doubt whether they really are the heavenly gates and walls. The poet of seraphic and Dionysiac moods felt constantly urged to create abysmal visions, those nightmares of destruction and terror inspired by the knowledge that there is no God. These are perhaps the most poignant expressions of the grotesque in the German language. (p. 56)

> Wolfgang Kayser, "The Grotesque in the Age of Romanticism," in his The Grotesque in Art and Literature, *translated by Ulrich Weisstein, Columbia University Press, 1981, pp. 48-99.*

THE TIMES LITERARY SUPPLEMENT   (essay date 1961)

[*The following is a review of the first two volumes of the collection* Jean Paul: Werke; *the later volumes are reviewed in the next excerpt (1963).*]

In his lifetime even more famous than Goethe, after his death admired and imitated by the young men of the *Biedermeier* period, Jean Paul fell into neglect during the latter part of the nineteenth century. In England today he is scarcely known even among students of German, and in Germany the Jean Paul revival of this century has largely been confined to scholars. There are no doubt reasons for this: Jean Paul is a difficult writer and one whose sentimentality does not wear well. Yet there is much in him which would speak to the modern reader. . . .

[*Die unsichtbare Loge* and *Hesperus* are both] expressions of eighteenth-century *Empfindsamkeit* grafted more or less arbitrarily on to a fashionable framework of intrigue and hidden identities. The modern reader will hardly react to Jean Paul's ecstatic sensibility as enthusiastically as did his public in the 1790s, but there is, even in these comparatively weak early works, an imaginative grandeur and a manipulation of figurative language which seem startlingly "modern" and which make most of Jean Paul's successors in German Romanticism seem very small beer indeed. . . .

Siebenkäs, one of the most psychologically acute accounts in German literature of the urban *Kleinbürgertum*, is Jean Paul's most realistic work, and the first major novel in which he subdues his humorous virtuosity to the demands of the work as a whole. The shamdeath, by means of which Siebenkäs escapes from a stiflingly conventional milieu into a freer and more spacious world, is a typical example of Jean Paul's epic invention, at once *opera buffa* and metaphysical allegory hovering uneasily perhaps between the realistic and the symbolic, but inexhaustibly rich in its implications. In the *Flegeljahre* poetic idealism and satirical realism confront each other in the figures of the twins, Walt and Vult. The fact that Jean Paul is here facing wryly the conflict within himself gives the work its tension and ambivalence. Walt, the poetic dreamer, is involved in a series of richly comic episodes which travesty the idealistic world of the *Bildungsroman*. Throughout, however, humour is tinged with regret, for Walt's setbacks are setbacks for Jean Paul's own sentimental idealism. . . .

[These early works] show something of Jean Paul's bewildering variety: death-centred *Empfindsamkeit* rubs shoulders with the products of his "satirical vinegar-factory", idyllic and realistic passages are found side by side with some of the most bizarre flights of fancy in German literature, the cosmic vision of the *Rede des toten Christus* contrasts with the worm's-eye view of **"Schulmeisterlein Wutz"**.

> "Sentimental Idealist," *in* The Times Literary Supplement, *No. 3087, April 28, 1961, p. iii.*

THE TIMES LITERARY SUPPLEMENT   (essay date 1963)

[Jean Paul's] smaller narrative works of the mid and late 1790s to some extent prepare the ground for *Flegeljahre* and, especially, *Titan;* it is almost as if Jean Paul were getting into practice. *Titan,* when it finally appeared . . . , seemed to review the whole of Jean Paul's experience up to that time, and to define his attitude towards the cultural and political movements and social phenomena of his day. Weimar, Fichtean subjectivism, the French Revolution, the new type of emancipated woman—these are some of the elements woven into the complicated pattern of *Titan,* which is a political novel, a portrait of the age and an *Entwicklungsroman* [apprenticeship novel] combined. It represents the greatest paradox even in the work of this paradoxical author, for it is profoundly Goethean in form and spirit, and at the same time a bitter polemic against the "aristocratic" and "formalist" trends of Weimar Classicism. In its attacks on the Fichtean philosophy and in the cautionary tales of Roquairol, Schoppe and Liane, it is an attempt to cut loose, at whatever cost, from the subjectivity and *Empfindsamkeit* [sentimentality] of the earliest novels, to define a more practical approach to life.

After *Titan* and the fragmentary *Flegeljahre* there was a lull in Jean Paul's creative work. Theoretical and political writings claimed most of his time and attention until that strange group of late comic novels culminating in *der Komet.* . . . These are novels which grew out of an ever-deepening mood of disillusionment. Jean Paul was oppressed too by a growing dissatisfaction with his work, and a feeling of spiritual loneliness, of belonging to an outdated generation. In these years he found it increasingly painful to look back on the idealism of his early work, and the four comic novels which appeared between 1809 and 1822 all reflect his tendency to seek refuge from disappointment in mockery. They all revolve around the disparity between the ideal and the actual, the appearance and the reality, or between man's opinion of himself and his true worth. *Schmelzle* and *Fibel* are fairly straightforward—although highly virtuoso—examinations of this last theme, which also plays a part in *Doktor Katzenbergers Badereise.* . . . *Katzenberger* represents a complete reversal of the world of *Hesperus* and *Titan,* for it is dominated by Katzenberger's cynical realism, in which the poetic ideal cannot survive; the sentimental is always refuted in purely scientific or physiological terms.

Katzenberger is justly famous as the most brilliant sustained comic character-study in German literature; it is a pity, however, that it has been allowed to divert attention from Jean Paul's last unfinished novel, *der Komet.* This reads like a more grotesque, Teutonic *Don Quixote.* . . . [The ludicrous adventures of Nikolaus, the hero, and his entourage] are often unmistakable travesties of elements in the earlier novels, and a mood of uneasy questioning permeates the work: Is Nikolaus a prince or a madman? What is illusion and what is reality? Thus these last novels seem to repudiate the early works. Their humour is made disquieting and ambiguous by the self-questioning out of which they grew; this gives them a sardonic flavour which is not often found in German literature.

"The German Dickens," in The Times Literary Supplement, *No. 3215, October 11, 1963, p. 806.*

J. W. SMEED (essay date 1966)

[Smeed's book-length study provides a thorough analysis of the dream sequences in Jean Paul's works. Smeed describes Jean Paul's historical and literary sources, dream theory, and use of symbolism; he also provides a complete list of the dreams as they appear in Jean Paul's works. The following is taken from the discussion of the role of the dream within the novel.]

As far as I know, there was no exact precedent for Jean Paul's treatment of the *Dream* within the novel. With him it has neither a prophetic nor a moralizing nor a satirical function. It it not at all closely bound up with the action of the novel or even, as we shall see, with the character of the dreamer. . . . [It] is nearly always the least forceful and least original *Dreams* which have the most direct thematic links with the novels of which they form part. For all his insistence on the way in which the dream reveals the unconscious workings of the mind, Jean Paul is hardly concerned with using these revelations as an aid to characterization, or with showing how the unconscious blends waking experiences into the irrational texture of the dream. In Jean Paul, in fact, the dreamer is hardly important as an identifiable individual at all; rather is he a representative of mortal man, so that his dream expresses, as it were, the desires and fantasies of Everyman's soul. Where the *Dream* is linked with the action of the novel, it is usually with the inner action of moods and emotions rather than with events in the 'story'. The only major *Dream* which is related to the plot in any conventional way is '**Albanos Traum**' . . . [in *Titan*] which indicates that Albano is destined to love Idoine, but here too the metaphysical burden of the *Dream* is at least as important. The '**Flegeljahretraum**' has no link with the *action* of the novel, although it may perhaps have some bearing on the characterization of the dreamer. By this I mean that Walt, the poet, author of the romantic parts of the *Doppelroman* in which he

collaborates with his brother, is now revealed as the possessor of a key to the transcendental mysteries. For all his naïveté, his *hohes Menschentum* is further endorsed by this mystic vision. But the vision is self-sufficient and self-contained. This curious circumstance—that the identity of the dreamer is of almost negligible importance for the understanding and appreciation of the dream—puts Jean Paul's *Traumdichtungen* in a category of their own. (pp. 62-3)

[The] *Traumdichtungen* can deepen our understanding of Jean Paul's novels in a more oblique way. Where the novel expresses moods similar to those prevailing in the *Traumdichtungen*—whether terror, frustration, or ecstasy—Jean Paul shows a tendency towards a very revealing type of self-quotation, using motifs or images borrowed from the *Dreams* or introducing visionary passages reminiscent of them into 'waking' contexts, which are thus enriched by the associations set up by the *Dreams*. (p. 63)

[In *Blumen-, Frucht-, und Dornenstücke; oder, Ehestand, Tod und Hochzeit des Armenadvokaten, Firmian Stanislaus, Siebenkäs,*] Siebenkäs has a sudden surrealist vision induced by the knowledge that he and his wife Lenette are incompatible. This is a vital moment in the hero's development, for this incompatibility is not merely between two individuals but between two worlds, the materially orientated middle-class world of Lenette and a 'higher', freer existence for which Siebenkäs longs and into which he will presently escape. The whole novel is charged with revulsion against frustrating limitations and a longing for ideal freedom; it fluctuates between these contrasting moods as the *Traumdichtungen* fluctuate between distaste for mortal life, and·mystic yearning. (pp. 63-4)

Another, more direct evocation of the *Traumdichtungen* occurs in *Titan,* at the moment of Albano's estrangement from Liane. Among the features which clearly recall the hellish scenes are the spiders, the eclipse, the shadows, the greyness and darkness, and the wild beasts. . . . Liane's blindness and the eclipse of the sun are described in metaphors which play down their importance as physical events, and make them rather into symbolic events belonging to the realm of the *Dreams*. [The] account of Liane's blindness is matched by Jean Paul's description of her death, with its clear evocations of the heavenly visions. I do not of course wish to imply a comparison on the aesthetic level; the treatment of this episode, as indeed of all parts of *Titan* in which Liane figures, is extremely sentimental, resembling in tone only the weakest *Traumdichtungen*. . . . (pp. 64-5)

It is difficult to sum up the importance of the *Dreams* for, like all Jean Paul's works, they will appeal to different readers for widely differing reasons. Stylistically, they are remarkable examples of rhythmic prose in which—at the best—there is a perfect synthesis of idea and symbol, mood and dream-sequence. (p. 68)

As far as an understanding of Jean Paul himself is concerned, the *Dreams* represent the purest and most direct expression of his dualistic view of life. This is particularly true, for self-evident reasons, of the *Dreams* in binary form. His obsession with certain fundamental conflicts and polarities (thought and feeling, temporal and eternal, despair and hope) dominates his works and gives them their characteristic form and tone. Nearly all the most striking episodes in the novels spring in some way from this dualistic attitude. Yet these episodes—allegorical and metaphysical as they are in essence—can only be motivated, that is, made compatible with the demands of a plot regulated by cause and effect and eschewing *das Wunderbare,* by desperate and often highly transparent devices. Jean Paul's metaphysical concerns threaten to burst the confines of the 'realistic' novel. Only in the *Traumdichtungen* did he find a form which allowed his imagination to work freely, unhampered by the demands of real-world causality.

If we regard the *Traumdichtungen* as [a] product of Jean Paul's preoccupation with the disparity between the ideal and actual, we may be justified in seeing an implied connexion between a *Dream* and the novel in which it is incorporated, even in the cases where there is no link with the action of the novel. Where finite imperfections are regarded in the light of eternity the result is humour, in the most radical sense in which Jean Paul used that word; where man seeks to escape out of his imprisonment in space and time, the result is the mystical yearning of the *Traumdichtungen.* The longing of the *hohe Menschen* for perfection, and the scorn poured on earthly imperfection by the *Humoristen* are thus the two sides of the same coin. (pp. 68-9)

For the modern reader who has grappled with Surrealist 'automatic' writing, the *Dreams* demonstrate a style which probably carries the principle of writing at the dictation of the unconscious as far as is compatible with sense and formal coherence. Works like the **'Rede des todten Christus'** and the **'Flegeljahretraum'** are uniquely poised between the contrived (as exemplified by the *Dreams* of Jean Paul's imitators), and the anarchic. (pp. 69-70)

> *J. W. Smeed, in his* Jean Paul's "Dreams," *Oxford University Press, London, 1966, 111 p.*

J. W. SMEED   (essay date 1969)

[*The following survey focuses on the dualism in Jean Paul's works. Smeed divides the novels into two groups, the comic and the ecstatic, a division that he believes reflects "the contrasting sides of Jean Paul's character."*]

In his day one of the most idolised writers in Germany, and after his death one of the most imitated, Jean Paul has remained comparatively unknown in England, apart from a brief vogue in the nineteenth century, following Carlyle's attempts to popularise him here. The reasons are not far to seek: many of his best works are very long, they are all stylistically difficult and demand some patience and perseverance from the reader. But the rewards are correspondingly great. Jean Paul's output is very large: it includes six long novels, many shorter narrative works, comic character-studies and idylls, satires, visionary pieces, collections of aphorisms, and writings on aesthetics, politics and education. (p. 31)

Jean Paul's earliest published works were two collections of satires, *Grönländische Prozesse* . . . and *Auswahl aus des Teufels Papieren.* . . . Both subject matter and method are borrowed from the English satirists of the eighteenth century, so that we find Jean Paul writing in a curiously unconvincing and artifical way, often about matters outside his experience. Studying Swift and Pope and their German imitators, he had come to believe that the art of satire consisted of developing and varying a theme by means of metaphors, witty analogies and the like. The more difficult and abstruse the comparisons and conceits, he felt, the better. No one would read these satires for pleasure nowadays; their importance lies in the fact that they helped to establish Jean Paul's characteristic wayward manner.

In the early 1790s, however, the sentimental side of Jean Paul's character asserted itself, and he wrote the two novels which first made him famous, the unfinished *Unsichtbare Loge* . . . and *Hesperus.* . . . The key to an understanding of these novels is, I believe, to be found in an essay included as a digression (*Extrablatt*) in *Die unsichtbare Loge.* Entitled **"Von hohen Menschen"**, this essay sets forth a totally unworldly ideal of personality and behaviour. *Der hohe Mensch* is characterised by

> "die Erhebung und der Unförmlichkeit zwischen unserem Herzen und unserem Orte über die Erde, das Gefühl der Geringfügigkeit alles irdischen Tuns . . . den Wunsch des Todes und den Blick über die Wolken.
>
> Elevation above the earth, a conviction of the triviality of all earthly activities and of the lack of accord between our heart and our station . . . a wish for death and a glance that ranges above the clouds.

Possessed by an ideal of transcendental perfection, he holds the pursuit of worldly success or satisfaction in contempt. Both *Die unsichbare Loge* and *Hesperus* present groups of "hohe Menschen", who are set off against more worldly characters. Ecstatic or elegiac scenes between the "hohe Menschen" contrast with the satirical treatment of courtiers and mercantile philistines. But it was, needless to say, neither these satirical elements nor the fantastic and complex plots of the two novels which made Jean Paul popular, but rather the scenes of idealised love and friendship between "hohe Menschen". Often such scenes involved music, which was for Jean Paul, as for the Romantics after him, the most intense and the purest of the arts and the one best able to give expression to man's spiritual yearnings. It is always the most "romantic" instruments that figure, flutes and horns, violas d'amore, glass-harmonicas and Aeolian harps. . . . *Hesperus,* particularly, strikes the modern reader as almost morbidly sentimental and obsessed with death. (pp. 32-3)

The works of the middle period [*Siebenkäs, Titan,* and *Flegeljahre*] . . . curb both the luxuriant figurative style of the early satires and the excessive sentimentality of the novels just discussed. (p. 33)

Titan is Jean Paul's *Entwicklungsroman* [apprenticeship novel], his attempt to show an ideal of "harmonious" personality (in the Greek sense) and to demonstrate that the sublimity of the "hohe Menschen" was compatible with practical aptitude. As in all such novels, the ideal is contrasted with the less balanced attitudes towards life, manifested by a number of characters with whom the hero, Albano, comes into contact, and who influence his development—usually by virtue of being warning examples. Through them we can learn a great deal about Jean Paul's attitude towards various trends in the Germany of his day. In the figure of Gaspard he attacks the aristocratic coldness and the over-emphasis on purely aesthetic values which, as he thought, characterised Weimar Classicism. In Schoppe he expresses his antagonism to the Idealist philosophy of Fichte and to Romantic subjectivity in general. Fichte's philosophy said— or seemed to say—that the world of objects exists only by virtue of being posited by the Ego. Schoppe studies Fichte and gradually comes to feel himself to be living in a world of shadows, surrounded only by the projections of his own consciousness. . . . He ends in madness—the madness of extreme subjectivity which, Jean Paul held, was one of the trends which threatened balance and sanity in his age. Another aspect of Romantic subjectivity is attacked through the figure of Roquairol, described by Jean Paul as ''Kind und Opfer des Jahrhunderts'' [child of the century, and its victim]. Jean Paul felt that the cult of feeling was a disease of the day, that young men ran through the gamut of emotional experiences at too early an age, so that the sensibilities became jaded and the search for new experiences ever more frantic. All this applies to Roquairol: emotionally precocious, he deliberately whips up his feelings, anticipating events in his imagination, so that actual events disappoint him and ever-stronger emotional stimuli become necessary. At the same time, since this cult of the feelings is so deliberate and conscious, Roquairol is a witness to his own emotions and thus robs them of all spontaneity and immediacy. Jean Paul expresses all this symbolically by describing Roquairol's life as a play, and Roquairol himself as an actor playing a part. This part culminates in suicide: while acting in a play which deals with his own situation, Roquairol shoots himself.

Thus *Titan* already shows the extent to which Jean Paul was out of tune with his age. In his later years, he grew disillusioned and apathetic. . . . To this period belongs a group of remarkable comic novels, all of which joke bravely about this disillusionment [*Schmelzle, Doktor Katzenbergers Badereise, Fibel,* and *Der Komet*]. . . . (pp. 33-5)

Jean Paul's style is unmistakable. Let us listen to him for a moment on [the] point concerning the abandonment of youthful idealism:

> Die Menschen, nämlich die edleren unter ihnen, haben wie bisher fortgefahren, sich von den Insekten zu unterscheiden, welche in der jungen Zeit als Raupen nur rohes Kraut genießen, sich an Blumen aber erst entpuppt in älterer als Schmetterlinge hängen, indem ungekehrt solche Menschen schon in der Jugend nach den süssen Blumen der sittlichen Ideale durstig fliegen, und erst nach der Entpuppung im gesetzten Alter auf den Krautblättern der etwas unsittlichen Gemeinheit kriechen und kauen.

> Men—of the nobler sort, that is—continue as before to differ from the insects which as caterpillars in their early life feed on raw cabbage leaves and only later, when they have turned into butterflies, alight to feed on flowers; for on the contrary such men fly thirstily after the sweet flowers of moral ideals while still young, and only when they emerge into old age do they crawl about on, and feed off, the cabbage leaves of ordinary life—which is not specially moral.

From Sterne he had learnt to prefer a meandering and digressive way of telling a story to any sort of straight and direct narrative. He plays games with the reader, teases him. He plays too with language itself, inventing new words and compounds, often in comic analogy to existing words. . . . He composes in figures of speech (''Noch kein Autor hat so oft 'wie' oder 'gleich' hingeschrieben als ich.'') [Never has an author written ''as'' or ''like'' as often as I have.] From being a deliberately cultivated manner in the earliest works, this figurative style became natural to Jean Paul; he thought, wrote and talked in figures of speech. His pages are full of witty analogies and allusions from his encyclopedic reading. Relationships are dis-

covered between apparently quite unrelated sets of objects or phenomena:

> Das Haus von Schleunes war ein offner Buchladen, dessen Werke (die Töchter) man da lesen, aber nicht nach Hause nehmen konnte. Obgleich die fünf andern Töchter in fünf Privatbibliotheken als Weiber standen, . . . so waren doch in diesem Töchter-Handelhaus noch drei Freiexemplare für gute Freunde feil.

> Schleunes' house was a bookshop, where one could read the works (the daughters), but not take them home. Although the five other daughters stood as wives in five private libraries, there were still in this daughter-trading-house three copies going cheap for good friends. . . .

Jean Paul looks at the world with tremendous eagerness, as if constantly fascinated and elated by what he finds, but he does indeed see it as if he were from another planet and had different organs of perception, ignoring the obvious links and causal relationships that the rest of us would see, and instead bringing the most disparaging things together (through metaphor, allusion, etc.), rearranging the objects of our familiar world into new patterns which shock us out of acceptance and force us to re-examine each thing or event in the light of the comparisons, implicit or explicit, which Jean Paul makes. (pp. 37-8)

Jean Paul hoards up all the potentially comic or incongruous data which come his way. Life, he seems to say, is so funny that one hardly needs to invent. . . . [His] imaginative activity most commonly consists of presenting things from the world around him in fresh combinations. The preference is always for the out-of-the-way, the truth-is-stranger-than-fiction type of fact. It is typical that, in the short comic novel *Schmelzle,* the *sole* piece of information concerning canaries is that they could be trained to fire off tiny cannons, and that the *sole* reference to hamsters is to their ferocity in (allegedly) threatening even horses when provoked. (pp. 38-9)

Yet to concentrate on the comic and fantastic elements in Jean Paul's style is to tell only half the story. His works contain some of the most highly-charged passages of rhythmic prose in German literature. The mood may be ecstatic or elegiac. Such passages are commonest in the early novels, where, as already mentioned, friendship and love had been treated in near-mystical terms. (p. 39)

[The] two contrasting styles, the comic and the ecstatic, reflect the contrasting sides of Jean Paul's character. Seldom can a writer have been so obsessed with the dualism of thought and feeling, soul and body, temporal and eternal. . . . [The] early novels depend on such contrasts for their very construction. Work after work explores various manifestations of the dualism which, for Jean Paul, characterised mortal life. Many of his most typical and recurring images reflect this obsession. Earthly life is represented as a masked ball, a slave-ship, a ''Plato's cave''. Human activities are likened to children's games, and man's emergence after death into the *zweite Welt* to the emergence of a butterfly from the chrysalis. Music images, and motifs based on the contrast of light and darkness abound, with all their traditional metaphysical or even mystical associations. This dualistic interpretation of the world affects Jean Paul's characterisation quite radically. Man can turn his back on the world (as do the ''hohe Menschen'') or he can pursue worldly ends, extinguishing the divine spark within himself. (A few of his characters, however, have a naïve innocence and contentment which make them unaware of any conflict between the real and ideal; these can find happiness in a limited sphere, without even knowing that it *is* limited: this point is made in Jean Paul's most famous idyll, ***Leben des vergnügten Schulmeisterlein Maria Wutz.***) (pp. 39-40)

The conflicts within man are, for Jean Paul, ultimately metaphysical in nature; they are due to "die Unförmlichkeit zwischen unserem Herzen und unserem Orte". (Walt acts as he does because he still expects reality to conform to the ideal; Vult acts as *he* does because he knows that it won't.) The only thing which can reconcile us to the failings of life on earth is humour: "Der Humor . . . vernichtet . . . das Endliche durch den Kontrast mit der Idee" [Humour annihilates the finite through the contrast with the Idea]. That is to say: humour makes finite existence bearable by showing its infinite distance from transcendental perfection as something comic. (p. 41)

Jean Paul's concept of *Humor* is best illustrated by his last two novels, ***Fibel*** and ***Der Komet.*** The idea for ***Fibel*** was suggested to Jean Paul by an ABC-book with crude rhymes accompanied by equally crude woodcuts. Why not write an imaginary and satirical biography of the author? We read of Fibel's childhood and of his desire to be a writer. He attains fame through his ABC-book and is easily persuaded by a friend that he is a great author. But in old age he realises his folly and vanity, and retires from the world to live as a hermit. . . . (p. 42)

The hero of ***Der Komet,*** Nikolaus Marggraf, is brought up as the son of a chemist, but, when he presently learns that he is in fact the illegitimate son of a prince, he sets out to seek his real father. He takes to using the Royal We, raises his friends to positions of high-sounding dignity, and aspires to a form of life appropriate to his new station. But all he achieves is a grotesque travesty of princely splendour. Thus the humour of these two works does indeed "annihilate" finite pretensions. For in them Jean-Paul suggests, if only obliquely, that the proudest achievements of the human spirit are . . . no more significant than a ridiculous book of rhymes for children, and that worldly pomp is fundamentally as irrelevant to man's true nature and destiny as is Nikolaus' would-be splendour to *his* real nature. If this is so, if nothing in mortal life is other than paltry and ridiculous when compared with the ideal, the only thing left to do is to laugh.

Jean Paul is a writer of extremes. His most grotesque fancies can make the modern Theatre of the Absurd seem tame, his play with narrative form makes even Sterne seem almost straightforward. His books contain a gallery of eccentrics, comparable with those to be met with in the pages of Peacock or Dickens. (pp. 42-3)

In my opinion, it is the comic Jean Paul who has had the most lasting influence and who is likely to find most readers today. But Jean Paul's Dreams, too, have aroused great interest in a century which has seen the systematic investigation of the human unconscious and the vogue of Surrealism . . . These Dreams are attempts to express in visionary form Jean Paul's central metaphysical preoccupations: the desire for mystical union with God, the nature of the afterlife, the struggle between doubt and faith. Like the mystics, Jean Paul often resorts to paradox to express the ultimate and inexpressible. Here (from the last chapter of the ***Flegeljahre***) is his variation on the ancient mystical idea that everything finite is merely the echo of an inaudible (divine) tone:

> . . . vernimm das alte Widerhallen; noch kein
> Wesen hat den Ton gehört, den es nachspricht.

Wenn aber einst der Widerhall aufhört, so ist die Zeit vorbei, und die Ewigkeit kommt zurück und bringt den Ton; sobald alles sehr still ist, so werd' ich die drei Stummen hören, ja den Urstummen, der das älteste Märchen sich selber erzählt. . . .

Listen to the ancient echo; no being has ever heard the tone which it repeats. But when the echo ceases, time is past, and eternity returns and brings the tone with it. As soon as everything is very still, I shall hear the three silent ones, even the original silent one who recounts to himself the oldest tale of all. . . .

—Realities incomprehensible to man are expressed in terms of tones inaudible to human ears. The silence which so often settles over the mystic's attempt to describe his most ineffable experiences, and the witty chatter through which Vult and Schoppe try to keep their *Weltschmerz* at bay: these are the extremes between which Jean Paul's writings move. (pp. 43-4)

> *J. W. Smeed, "Jean Paul," in* German Men of Letters: Twelve Literary Essays, Vol. V, *edited by Alex Natan, Oswald Wolff (Publishers) Limited, 1969, pp. 31-47.*

MARGARET R. HIGONNET (HALE) (essay date 1973)

[*Higonnet's lengthy introduction to* School for Aesthetics *is both a description and analysis of Jean Paul's aesthetic theory. The excerpt below forms part of her examination of the style and structure of the work. Because* School *"is not only a work of theory about art, but also, according to its author, a work of art," it should, according to Higonnet, embody Jean Paul's literary theories; thus, in the following excerpt, she measures the* School *against the aesthetic criteria presented in the work.*]

[*The School for Aesthetics*] is not only a work of theory about art, but also, according to its author, a work of art. . . . Its form should therefore embody Jean Paul's literary theories; it should, as Jean Paul says, be the horn of Oberon which calls its listeners to the dance. A comparison of the form with the theory is of special interest to the translator, for he must decide the significance of such features as diction, imagery, and syntax. Some light can be shed on Jean Paul's artistic goals in the ***School*** by a brief survey of his mental processes in drafts and in letters; the heart of the question, however, can be settled only by cognitive examination of the structure and of the style as medium of the message.

In 1794 Jean Paul began his notebooks on aesthetic questions and by 1796 he had announced his intention to write a book of literary theory and criticism. His primary materials, the notes, are largely what we should now think of as characteristically Romantic brevities: aphoristic statements, unanswered questions, and examples requiring explication. Most concern the novel and comic modes, as one might expect from an author of comic romances, and many reflect a fascination with the anomalous, with oddities. (pp. xlviii-xlix)

One problem which delayed crystallization [of the notes] into a final order was the choice of a mood and manner of presentation. . . . [The testimony of Jean Paul's letters indicates that] he intended a mixture of moods, and therefore chose the form of lectures: "I have finally found the freest, most scholarly, most serious dress, one which also allows some jesting." . . . (p. xlix)

The phrase "serious dress" corresponds to his emphasis on enveloping his work in rhetorical or fictive wrappings. As early as May 1803, months before he began the *School,* he was considering one hundred guises for his critical work and thought he might have to end up using them all. . . . Thus he toyed with the idea of a correspondence with famous men modeled on Petrarch's letters and the idea of a dialog, which like letters would allow the presentation of opposed points of view: "In a dialog one can seem to develop a point of view one-sidedly, then completely reverse oneself." Such structures function ironically, of course.

The titles Jean Paul considered imply still other possibilities for the form: an anthology of reviews, the diary of a journey, or a novel. One title, *Waage (Scales),* reminds us of his strategic emphasis on impartiality, also echoed in the projected letters and dialog. Sometime late in January 1804, he cast the body of the work into the form of "Courses," retaining the last part in "Lectures." Among other titles, he suggested *School for Aesthetics,* whose didactic implications are reflected in certain stylistic principles Jean Paul had in mind as he wrote.

Thus his many titles and proposed rhetorical forms imply deliberate disguise. The drafts call repeatedly for hiding the meaning: "At first gnomic generalizations . . . Do not disclose, but conceal your opinion." Obscurity is a protective device for the serious: "Ultimately it is best to envelop everything great in dark words so that it cannot be parroted, but only guessed at by those who will not destroy but explore it further." The insistence on obscurity in comic as well as serious modes is explained by the fact that Jean Paul considers it not only a protective but also a didactic device: "Like children, those who are capable will learn through the incomprehensible how to understand." His goal is not mere incomprehensibility but a difficulty of comprehension which will lead to deeper understanding. The reader must be forced to reflect and read again.

With jesting seriousness Jean Paul claims in the Second Preface that the work is an educational puzzle. He says he has tried both to correct his predecessors' deliberate errors, as one corrects a false paradigm, and to create new errors to be corrected by his readers. To expand the implications: the reader who accepts the difficult task will be led by obscurity, as if through a labyrinth, to the point where he also can accept a paradox or grasp the confusing details of reality which give depth and breadth to all great principles.

Jean Paul sets up certain stylistic guidelines for creating this labyrinth. One note associates mystery, brevity, and novelty. In comic styles he recommends disrupting logical connections: "Always change—expound one thing, begin another, return to the first," as in the unresolved antitheses of the dialog form. He advises authors to use surprising details and unexpected turns, as in puns, and to avoid the mechanical empty convention in order to force the attention of the reader.

It becomes clear that Jean Paul aimed not only at a jestingly didactic structure ironically balancing points of view but at a didactically obscure style. (pp. xlix-l)

The structure supports his dualistic theory, balancing Greek against romantic, stylists against poeticists, and in the subdividing chapters materialists against nihilists. The work as a whole progresses from general Courses to the more specific ones, as well as from theoretical Courses to critical Lectures. This development through antithesis is frequently marked by rough, often ironically self-conscious transitions. We are not allowed to forget Jean Paul's distance from the materials he discusses. . . . To a great extent the general scheme is associative, as in the vague links between nihilists, poeticists, passive genius, and romantic writers.

The greatest shock in the use of structural oppositions is surely the shift from the discursive Courses to the fictive mode of the Lectures. The first two Lectures together with the two Prefaces provide a predominantly comic framework, distinguished for its subjectively complicated presentation and reflexive mockery. Here the fiction of a lecturer addressing an obstreperous audience during a trade fair suggests a satire on academic life, the bartering of souls in an age of printed paper, and the degeneration of art to mere mechanical engineering. One is impressed by the long-winded proliferation of subdivisions, whose bewildering variety is compounded and mocked by the leitmotif of the audience's stampede for the garden gate at sundown. Jean Paul takes the opportunity to explore different literary forms: serious and comic dialogs, a comic letter, and a comic nightmare as well as straight lectures. Sliding thus from one form to the next he manifests his belief in the vitality and multiplicity of poetry, at the same time that he confirms the importance of romantic irony in his theory by juggling with levels of reality. (pp. l-li)

[Lecture III, which presents a serious dialog between the lecturer and a youth who is nearly his peer,] relinquishes the parody of a preparatory schoolteacher abandoned by all but one of his students and the reader. Like the work as a whole, it moves from general poetics in the first part to discussion of an individual writer, Herder, in the second. The dialog concludes dramatically with the conversion of the youth, whose acknowledgment of Herder's importance provides a symbolic act of learning, the final step forward on completing the course of Jean Paul's *School.* Just as Herder mediates between philosophy and poetry, West and East, life and death, the youth embodies the marriage of past and future literature. (p. li)

[Here] the fictional setting is symbolic. The evening landscape suggests Herder's death: Herder is a "sunflower" gone to become one with his sun. The silence of the night brings on a crisis of doubt which can in turn be resolved when the night and death are interpreted as transition points, like the equator. This conclusion resembles the "greater Romantic lyric" in its correspondences between man and nature, reaching for integral images which will lead beyond discursive statement. We have shifted from argument to eulogy, to chains of images, to intensifying repetitions, to the logic of emotions.

The sublime conclusion is not, perhaps, the place to begin an analysis of stylistic techniques, but it is remarkable to what extent the ironic, sublime, and even fairly neutral passages consistently employ a stock of verbal techniques. Lecture III follows in its dialog first a pattern of questions and answers which turns into a hortatory vision of poetry extended through dashes associatively linking phrases, and culminating in a series of idealist images for the transcendental muse. The eulogy of Herder then is constructed almost entirely of figures: a rod in water, a loving yet stern father, swans, and later compound images such as the fortress of flowers. But it too is interrupted by questioning how to explain this complex man. In the search for an answer the lecturer uses not only similes but broader analogies and climactic redefinitions: "He was something better, namely a *poem.*" The dramatic intensification is supported by phrases like "as it were" to remind us that the search for complete expression is still underway, by antithetical constructions like "not . . . but," comparative constructions like "however . . . still," and powerfully assertive sentences beginning causally "Therefore . . ." or "Hence . . ." The descriptive attempt breaks off suddenly, plunges into doubt with questions, then resolves through the reestablishment of the dialog form, when the youth answers, providing dramatic harmony, as well as emotional harmony through his image of death as the silent equator.

Most of the same techniques can be found throughout the *School*, in part because they reflect the basic materials of the notebooks, and in part apparently because they reflect the direction of Jean Paul's mind, the mental activity which he considers necessary both to the expression and to the understanding of his poetic theory. The notebooks provided an initially argumentative structure, with their questions, examples, and aphorisms. But surprisingly, the verbal structure of the *School* generally sets up an argumentative line only to abandon it. (pp. li-lii)

The high frequency of causal sequences suggests . . . a straightforward development of the argument. Often conjunctions such as "since," or adverbs like "therefore" preface a series of instances and results, as a legitimate if tiresome rhetorical device for achieving unity. But such a word may have so broad a reference that it signifies little more than an emphatic breath, and can hardly be transferred into English. In this way Jean Paul sometimes both dilutes the meaning of causality and in passages of heavy irony even suggests arbitrary play with the rhetoric of argumentation.

The pattern of antithesis observed in the general structure of the *School* is pervasive in its syntax. The argument moves "not . . . but," or even more often follows the concessive construction "although . . . yet." These may be heightened by puns such as "staatsbürger . . . Spiessbürger" (urbane as opposed to provincial men). The comic parts of the *School* tend to be particularly rich in "perhapses," negative assertions such as "I cannot assert," and digressively antithetical asides set off by dashes. A strong sense of limits emerges from these highly qualified affirmations. The antithesis, like the dialog, tends to give equal stress to unreconciled ideas, as on a balanced scale.

All such argumentative patterns lead to and evaporate into patterns of imagery here. When Jean Paul rejects definitions it is in figurative terms: "I feel that such definitions are either only systematizations of natural history according to stamens or teeth, or inventories of chemical analyses of organic corpses." The very images he chooses melt one into another. Images represent here not only a shift to the concrete, paralleling the trend overall from theory to practical examples, but a shift to antidiscursive presentation. The practice fits neatly with the theory of chapter 1: "mere images can often express more than definitions." As in the landscapes of the Lectures, imagery can convey a correspondence between nature and man, words and life, better than "dead concepts." (pp. lii-liii)

Multiplication of figures in turn provides an effect of different perspectives. Passive geniuses are thus seen successively as feminine, primitive, or handicapped. Each image is incomplete, a distortion of the truth as well as a way of illuminating the truth. We sense the writer striving for further understanding here, as in the eulogy of Herder. When hesitation accompanies images by "as it were" or the self-translating "in short" and "namely," subtilizing of meaning begins to betray a sense of futility.

The Romantic reach for an unattainable infinity is especially evident in some of Jean Paul's best known stylistic traits: unanswered questions, subjective interjections, and disruptive punctuation. He restlessly shifts tenses or implies a new deep structure in mid-sentence. Yet the dash, which can be a breathless, intensifying link in the sublime passages on the Greeks, on wit, and on Herder, can also serve just as often as a teasing obstacle: "I shall select a few examples from among—the dead." Many qualifying clauses have this obstructive function as well. Jean Paul admonishes the reader, "Slow down!"

Even imagery and concrete details may become obstacles rather than significant tools. While elaboration is Jean Paul's stock method of reviving a cliché or drawing attention to an image, such development of details may lead the reader away from the main point of a comparison. If many of the outdated erudite notes seem burdensome and distracting, we may consider the possibility that they represent a parody of scholarship as well as Jean Paul's omnivorous reading. Similarly, his neologisms and compounds can in some cases be extraordinarily vivid. . . . While many will detain and amuse the reader, the proliferation of startling neologisms and awkward compounds may also indicate the writer is struggling against the inadequacies of language. A tension arises between the meaning and the manner of expression, which confronts the reader with the role of artifice in art and forces him to search for the meaning on his own.

Such an overall effect of colorful obscurity, . . . through the dazzling flicker of syntactic shifts, melting images, esoteric references, and witty neologisms might be called the "picturesque" in another art, making the transition away from neoclassical forms. The remnants of normal syntactic development lead the reader from logical refinement of meaning into translogical development through images or, as in the Lectures, through satiric and dramatic fiction. This process takes place at the level of individual sentences, of chapters, of single Lectures, and of the combined whole. A Romantic revolution is manifest in the defiance of serious scholarship with its elevated public language; parentheses, conversational interjections, and ironic inversions fuse into an antipedantic style. The emphasis on balanced nuances, progressive suggestion, and ineffable mystery prefigures the Symbolist aesthetics and techniques of Verlaine and Mallarmé. Barriers between animate and inanimate break down through deviance from syntactic norms: bureaucratic style becomes a parading "harlequin," Herder becomes a "poem." Linguistic forms thus serve the vision of correspondences which lies at the heart of Jean Paul's aesthetic theory.

The layered imagery, aphorisms, and paratactic or even disruptive syntax combine ultimately to create a metaphysical vision. . . . (pp. liii-lv)

If we recognize a general separation of the two types of presentation, Courses balanced against Lectures, for example, we must also recognize the significant integration of the jesting with the serious, of disrupted argument with extended imagery. The remarkable consistency of verbal techniques in the *School* stems from the fact that Jean Paul's basic dualism, his concern for correlating this world with a transcendent world or outer with inner, can be made manifest on the one hand through compounds or metaphors which unite two different levels or kinds of meaning, and on the other hand through the ironic contrasts between appearance and reality in his paradoxes and corrective, concessive clauses. As Jean Paul claims, the humorous and serious modes share one form and one concept of art, even if their materials are at opposite ends of experience. . . . (pp. lv-lvi)

[The] close correlation between the theories and the practice in this consciously constructed work warn against any simplistic dismissal of the style as a verbal tic or mere sloppiness. No one can deny the significance of Jean Paul's exemplary wit in discussing Voltaire's puns or his whimsical analysis of whimsy. Friedrich Schlegel seems to recognize the programmatic nature of the style when he celebrates it as a reflection of the age:

> If you want an example of a writer whose relationship to his age maintains a mean between flattery of its weaknesses and the rather bold attempt by Fichte wilfully to reshape it and turn it on its head, remember that humorist, favorite of the nation, who reached this mean by manifesting the entire wealth of an extremely complex age, all its dissonances and allusions, with wit and feeling in his whimsical, dissonant, mixed, piebald style—a style which though all his own reflected the age itself in its rich chaos.

By taking advantage of the Protean flexibility of the German language and by experimenting with a multitude of forms, Jean Paul has created a style and structure which mirror the "latitudinarian spirit" of his aesthetics as well as the Romantic philosophy of correspondences. The complications, the perplexity of his language are an essential part of his preparatory schooling for readers; the paradoxes and unresolved antitheses train the reader's faculties for a transcendentally balanced perspective, the true positive freedom achieved through poetry. (pp. lvi-lvii)

> *Margaret R. Higonnet (Hale), "Introduction: 'The Horn of Oberon'," in* Horn of Oberon: Jean Paul Richter's "School for Aesthetics" *by Jean Paul Richter, translated by Margaret R. Higonnet (Hale), Wayne State University Press, 1973, pp. xvii-lx.*

ADDITIONAL BIBLIOGRAPHY

Altenhein, Margarete Reckling. *Jean Paul's Reception in the Nineteenth and Twentieth Centuries.* New York: Graduate School of New York University, 1938, 26 p.
    A survey of German critical response to Jean Paul from his death in 1825 through the mid-1930s, including citations for essays in periodicals and books.

Benham, G. F. "On Some Salient Features of Jean Paul's Pedagogical Writings." *Colloquia Germanica* II, Nos. 3/4 (Summer 1978): 233-62.
    Outlines views on education that Jean Paul presented in his theoretical and critical writings.

Berger, Dorothea. *Jean Paul Friedrich Richter.* New York: Twayne Publishers, 1972, 176 p.
    An introduction to Jean Paul's life and a survey of his work.

Birznieks, Paul. "Jean Paul's Early Theory of Poetic Communication." *The Germanic Review* XLI, No. 3 (May 1966): 186-201.
    Describes Jean Paul's theory of poetic communication. According to Birznieks, Jean Paul believed that communication between poet and reader requires participation by both. The poet "writes a good and formal 'outline' that speaks not only to fancy and imagination but also to the association of ideas and sentiments." The reader "needs even more genius than the poet," for, once provided with an incomplete outline by the poet, the reader must understand and interpret it according to both the writer's original intent and the reader's experience.

Blake, Kathleen. "What the Narrator Learns in Jean Paul's *Wutz.*" *The German Quarterly* XLVIII, No. 1 (January 1975): 52-65.
    An analysis of the role of the narrator in Jean Paul's idyll *Leben des Vergnügten Schulmeisterlein Maria Wutz in Auenthal.*

Brewer, Edward V. *The New England Interest in Jean Paul Friedrich Richter.* University of California Publications in Modern Philology, edited by S. G. Morley, Rudolph Altrocchi, J. E. de La Harpe, and Archer Taylor, vol. 27, no. 1. Berkeley: University of California Press, 1943, 26 p.
    A thorough review of nineteenth-century New England interest in Jean Paul. Brewer traces the influences of Thomas Carlyle and the Transcendentalists on Jean Paul's reception in America and lists bibliographic citations for original sources.

Burwick, Frederick. "The Dream-Visions of Jean Paul and Thomas De Quincey." *Comparative Literature* XX, No. I (Winter 1968): 1-26.*
    A comparative study of "the imagistic, thematic, and structural devices" in the works of Jean Paul and Thomas De Quincey. Burwick determines that De Quincey was indebted "to Jean Paul for his literary conception of the dream-vision."

[Carlyle, Thomas]. "Jean Paul Friedrich Richter." *The Foreign Review* V, No. IX (January 1830): 1-52.
    A biographical and critical sketch. Although Carlyle repeats many of the critical assessments formulated in his earlier essays (see excerpts above, 1827), he also includes a fuller account of Jean Paul's life based on his autobiographical fragment *Wahrheit aus Jean Pauls Leben.*

Cooper, Berenice. "A Comparison of *Quintus Fixlein* and *Sartor Resartus.*" *Transactions of the Wisconsin Academy of Science, Arts and Letters* XLVII (1958): 253-72.*
    Compares the form, content, and style of Jean Paul's *Life of Quintus Fixlein* and Thomas Carlyle's *Sartor Resartus* to prove that the latter "is a distinctively original work and not an imitation of *Quintus Fixlein.*"

Fischer, William B. "German Theories of Science Fiction: Jean Paul, Kurd Lasswitz, and After." *Science Fiction Studies* 3, No. 10, Part 3 (November 1976): 254-65.*
    Assesses Jean Paul's role in the development of German science fiction.

Gooch, G. P. "The Romantic School." *Germany and the French Revolution,* pp. 230-49. New York: Longmans, Green and Co., 1927.*
    An examination of Jean Paul's political views. The aim of *Germany and the French Revolution,* according to the preface, is "to measure the repercussion of the French Revolution on the mind of Germany." To this end, Gooch discusses several works by Jean Paul, including *Greenland Trials, Selections from the Devil's Papers, The Invisible Lodge,* and *Levana,* to determine the effect of the French Revolution on the author's beliefs, and he concludes that Jean Paul was "a standard bearer in the army of literary revolt."

Hannah, Richard W. "The Tortures of the Idyll: Jean Paul's *Wutz* and the Loss of Presence." *The Germanic Review* LVI, No. 4 (Fall 1981): 121-27.
    A structuralist analysis of Jean Paul's *Leben des vergnügten Schulmeisterlein Maria Wutz in Auenthal.* Hannah's essay, based on the theories of French critic Jacques Derrida, asserts that "*Wutz* is about the impossibility of presence."

[Lee, Eliza Buckminister]. *Life of Jean Paul F. Richter.* 2d ed. London: John Chapman, 1849, 478 p.
    The earliest English-language biography of Jean Paul. The story of the first part of his life is actually Lee's translation of Jean Paul's unfinished autobiography, *Wahrheit aus Jean Pauls Leben,* which abruptly ends while describing the author's thirteenth year.

Libhart, Byron R. "Madame de Staël, Charles de Villers, and the Death of God in Jean Paul's *Songe.*" *Comparative Literature Studies* IX, No. 2 (June 1972): 141-51.*

Examines Madame de Staël's translation of a well-known passage from *Siebenkäs* in which Jean Paul questions the existence of God. Staël's rendering of the work appeared in her *De l'Allemagne* as "Un songe," and Libhart finds that "for the writers of that generation [the French Romantics], the concept of a dead God clearly originated with the novelist Jean Paul Richter." By omitting the ending in her translation, Staël intensified the impact of the work. Libhart questions whether this distortion was done by Staël or by her friend Charles de Villers, and whether it was intentional or accidental.

Morgan, Estelle. "A Note on Jean Paul." *German Quarterly* XXVIII, No. 1 (January 1955): 43-6.

Describes Jean Paul's provincial background and its effect on his life and writing. Morgan asserts that "there were two souls within Jean Paul's breast, the one inclined to Philistinism, the other of great genius."

Rowson, P. D. "The Role of the Practical Joke in Jean Paul's *Die unsichtbare Loge.*" *Neophilologus* LX, No. 3 (July 1976): 412-20.

Identifies five practical jokes in *Die unsichtbare Loge* and examines their effect on characterization and plot.

Smeed, J. W. "Thomas Carlyle and Jean Paul Richter." *Comparative Literature* XVI (Summer 1964): 226-53.*

A close analysis of Jean Paul's influence on Thomas Carlyle's works.

Walden, Helen. *Jean Paul and Swift*. n.p., 1940, 156 p.*

An examination of Jean Paul as a creative writer. Walden describes Jean Paul's theory of humor and compares passages from the writings of Jean Paul and Jonathan Swift to determine the influence of Swift upon three groups of Jean Paul's writings: his early satires, the works of his prime, and his later works.

Elizabeth Montagu

1720-1800

(Also Montague; born Elizabeth Robinson) English essayist and critic.

A literary patron of the late eighteenth century, Montagu is remembered primarily for her *An Essay on the Writings and Genius of Shakespear, Compared with the Greek and French Dramatic Poets; with Some Remarks upon the Misrepresentations of M. de Voltaire,* a work which challenges François Marie Voltaire's authority as a critic and undermines his appraisal of Shakespeare. In her own day, Montagu was renowned for her lively correspondence and enlightened conversation, and she became famous for her *salons,* known as the Bluestocking Circles, which provided an intellectual forum for upper-class English women.

The child of wealthy, educated parents, Montagu was unusually precocious. Even as an adolescent, she corresponded ably with adults and was known for her wit and candor. In 1742, she married Edward Montagu, the grandson of the first Earl of Sandwich, who encouraged her literary interests. Montagu was soon recognized as a patron of the arts, and many fledgling artists and writers sought her financial support. Most significant of Montagu's activities were her informal gatherings, or *salons,* which were created for intellectual women who wanted to discuss literature and art with men. Eventually, these parties became known as Bluestocking Clubs or Circles, because the women wore blue woolen stockings rather than black silk as an indication of their seriousness. The term "bluestocking," which refers to a woman with literary or intellectual interests, derives from these meetings. Among the participants in the Bluestocking Clubs were such literary figures as Elizabeth Carter, Edmund Burke, Samuel Johnson, Hannah More, and George, Lord Lyttleton.

Montagu's first published work was "Three Dialogues of the Dead," an anonymous contribution to Lyttleton's *Dialogues of the Dead,* a collection of fictitious conversations. She achieved recognition as a writer with the publication of *An Essay on the Writings and Genius of Shakespear.* In this work, Montagu responded to Voltaire's famed essay on Shakespeare, which censured the playwright for failing to embrace the Neoclassical precepts of drama. Voltaire maintained that Shakespeare's works were unrefined, and he championed the work of the French playwrights Jean Racine and Pierre Corneille as embodiments of the ideal elements of classical drama. Montagu's essay appeared after the publication of Samuel Johnson's famous critical preface to Shakespeare's works. Although Johnson had discussed the flaws in Voltaire's argument, Montagu believed that Voltaire's misinterpretations required a more vigorous denunciation. *An Essay on the Writings and Genius of Shakespear* was the first direct attempt to defend Shakespeare against Voltaire. Here Montagu questions Voltaire's ability as a literary critic and faults his knowledge of the English language, suggesting that his misinterpretation of Shakespeare stems from his ignorance of Elizabethan English. In turn, Montagu praises Shakespeare's characterization and his use of comic and tragic elements and the supernatural.

While Montagu's essay was widely accepted, some of her contemporaries, notably Samuel Johnson, deemed it poorly

Mary Evans Picture Library

written. Johnson criticized Montagu's style and stated publicly that her ideas were better expressed in conversation than in writing. However, another contemporary, the Shakespearean editor William Warburton, praised Montagu's essay as the "most elegant and judicious piece of criticism this age has produced." Although some later critics have concurred with Johnson that *An Essay on the Writings and Genius of Shakespear* is not particularly well written, many still consider Montagu's approach innovative and daring.

Montagu was a prolific correspondent who is praised by some for her commentary on the social issues of her day. Yet her letters have been largely ignored by both nineteenth- and twentieth-century scholars. While she continues to hold some interest for literary historians, it is as a Shakespearean critic that she is chiefly known by present-day critics.

PRINCIPAL WORKS

"Three Dialogues of the Dead" (dialogues) 1760;
    published in *Dialogues of the Dead*
An Essay on the Writings and Genius of Shakespear,
    Compared with the Greek and French Dramatic Poets;
    With Some Remarks upon the Misrepresentations of M.
    de Voltaire (essay) 1769

*The Letters of Mrs. Elizabeth Montagu, with Some of the
Letters of Her Correspondents.* 4 vols. (letters)
1809-13

ELIZABETH MONTAGU (letters date 1766)

[*In Montagu's letters to her lifelong correspondent, Elizabeth
Carter, Montagu discusses her reasons for writing* An Essay on
the Writings and Genius of Shakespear *and explains why her essay
will surpass Samuel Johnson's preface to Shakespeare's works in
both popularity and scope. She attacks Voltaire's treatment of
Shakespeare and states that "he has ruined the principles of half
our young people and to shew him superficial in everything would
be of great use."*]

I have sent only one sheet of scrawl, for Mr. Johnson having
just published his Shakespear I must see that I do not servilely
seem to imitate, or presumptuously contradict him. You will
think me perhaps conceited to go on with the work when he
has just published a preface on Shakespear, and perhaps it may
make me suppress the work, but having begun, I will finish
it. I cannot say I am convinced that Mr. Johnsons criticisms
are just, but I am afraid his talents will make the scale pre-
ponderate, as I cannot put into mine the weight of authority
or that prevailing charm of writing which he can throw into
his. The method I have persued is quite different from his; I
thought there were enough already of vague panegyricks and
general criticisms upon Shakespears works, so have taken a
larger view of the dramatick art, and a more particular consideration of his merits and faults, excellencies and defects.
(p. 144)

* * * * *

I suppose you may have seen some extracts of Mr. Johnsons
preface to Shakespear, I have got the whole edition down here.
It will appear presumption to go on with my work after Mr.
Johnson has given his preface and notes, and yet having taken
a quite different track I think I shall proceed for my amusement;
but there will be many reasons against my ever making my
performance publick. I do not agree with this critick in some
of his opinions of Shakespear, and when I do not, it will appear
presumption to oppose a name of such authority; where we
agree he will have express'd this opinion with so many more
graces of manner and style that I had better hold my tongue.
Both Mr. Pope and Johnson have written the prettiest essays
imaginable on Shakespear, but I think they have done very
little in shewing his excellencies in particular circumstances,
and either general encomium or invective, is to me not properly
criticism; both these writers aim to please rather than to teach.
I had enterd into a particular critique of his historical plays,
and a very full one of [Shakespeare's *Henry the Fourth*]. I
have shewn Mr. Voltaires injustice, and compared our Countryman with his boasted Corneille in many places where the
subjects bore any relation, and also shewn the defects of the
french Theater. Mr. Johnsons remarks at the end of *Henry the
4th* are very short and by no means such as one should expect
from a critick. When I have put Mr. Popes and Johnsons essays
together I do not mean to represent them as perfectly similar.
Mr. Popes is by far I think the best composition, but he has
only gatherd the finest flowers in the Field, Johnson has more
nearly glean'd it, but his preface is not so beautiful as the other.
His language is laboured, rather too fine for my taste, who

love the negligences of genius better than the ornaments of
study, but perhaps I judge so for want of refinement. I never
love the velvet style, an equal pile as if cut by an engine,
however in these effeminate days perhaps it will be admired
for the very thing I dislike. (pp. 145-46)

* * * * *

The attack I shall make upon Voltaire as a Critick is not the
last contest I intend to have with him. He has ruined the principles of half our young people, and to shew him superficial
in every thing would be of great use. I am sorry Mr. Johnson
has pass'd him over with supercilious contempt, it is true that
he deserves to be used so, but as he stands high in the opinion
of many, I wish Mr. Johnson had exposed him. I wish you
could get the whole of Johnson's preface, it teizes me sadly;
if he had said more upon Shakespear I should have dropt my
undertaking, if he had said less, I should have gone on with
more confidence; the more I read this preface the better I like
it, and the less I like my own. I have enter'd more into the
subject in a critical way, and I think have better exhibited the
perfections of Shakespear, as I have more minutely observed
on them, but I shall entertain and please less perhaps, a few
general observations will satisfy the generality of readers. I
was provoked to this undertaking by the flippancy of Voltaire
in a great measure, and also by thinking we had erred widely
from the true dramatick art. I have so far proceeded, and am
so warm'd by the subject, that I hardly care to drop it, and yet
I dont know whether after Mr. Johnson people will desire any
more criticisms on Shakespear. I understood he was only to
write notes upon him, and those merely to rectify the errors
of the copies, but alas! his Preface is so ingenious it terrifys
me. I want to hear what people say of it, the eyes of jealousy
admire a rival tho the tongue does not always confess his merit;
however, I assure you I have no wicked animosity against the
man, tho I wish he had not written this preface, and I shall do
it all possible honour in my way of speaking of it to his friends
and his foes; and indeed I am so afraid that where I think I
perceive it faulty, that opinion should arise from the jealousy
of an author, I shall hardly trust myself to speak of it, but with
general commendation. If I find people think he has thoroughly
discuss'd the merits of Shakespear, my work instead of going
printed under pyes to the oven, shall go in manuscript into the
fire. (pp. 147-48)

> *Elizabeth Montagu, in extracts from letters to Eliz-
> abeth Carter in 1766, in her* Mrs. Montagu, "Queen
> of the Blues," Her Letters and Friendships from 1762
> to 1800: 1777-1800, Vol. II, *edited by Reginald Blunt,
> Houghton Mifflin Company, 1923, pp. 144-48.*

THE EDINBURGH REVIEW (essay date 1809)

[A considerable portion of *The Letters of Mrs. Elizabeth Montagu, with Some of the Letters of Her Correspondents*] are published, we should suppose, rather as curiosities, than on account of their intrinsic excellence. Several of them—and by
no means the worst in the collection—were written, it seems,
while the author was under fifteen years of age; and would
certainly be considered as extraordinary performances—even
in this age of premature womanhood and infant accomplishment. The subsequent letters, indeed, scarcely keep the promise
that is held out by those early effusions. They are not at all
more lively or more natural; and are all the worse, we think,
for being more plentifully garnished with moral reflections and
morsels of elaborate flattery. If the correspondence does not

improve faster in its subsequent stages, we fear greatly that there will be no climax in the reader's admiration.

The merit of the pieces before us seems to us to consist mainly in the great gaiety and vivacity with which they are written. The wit, to be sure, is often childish, and generally strained and artificial; but still it both sparkles and abounds: and though we should admire it more if it were better selected, or even if there were less of it, we cannot witness this profuse display of spirits and ingenuity, without receiving a strong impression of the talents and ambition of the writer.

The faults of the letters, on the other hand, are more numerous. In the first place, they have, properly speaking, no subjects. They are all letters of mere idleness, friendship, and flattery. There are no events,—no reasonings,—no anecdotes of persons who are still remembered,—no literature, and scarcely any original or serious opinions. The whole staple of the correspondence consists of a very smart and lively account of every-day occurrences and every-day people,—a few common-places of reflection and friendship,—and a considerable quantity of little, playful, petulant caricatures of the writer's neighbours and acquaintances. All this has a fine familiar effect, when interspersed with more substantial matter,—or when it drops from the pen of a man of weight and authority; but whole volumes of mere prattlement from a very young lady, are apt, however gay and innocent, to produce all the symptoms of heavier reading.

A second, and perhaps a greater fault, is want of nature and simplicity; and this, in so far as we can judge, pervades the whole strain of the correspondence. There is an incessant effort to be witty or eloquent, which takes away from the grace of success, and makes failure ridiculous. There is no flow from the heart,—no repose for the imagination,—no indolent sympathy of confidence. Every thing is gilded and varnished in the most ostentatious manner, and exposed in the broadest light. It is not the learning only, or the ridicule, that is introduced for effect;—all the familiarity must be brilliant, and all the trifling picturesque. It is evident, in short, that Mrs Montagu wrote rather from the love of her own glory, than from any interest in the subjects of her correspondence; and the less we can sympathize with this feeling, the less we shall be delighted with her performance.

The last, and the most serious want we shall notice in this girlish correspondence, is the want of heart and affection. We naturally reckon upon a little romance in the confidential epistles of a damsel of eighteen; or, at any rate, upon some warmth of attachment: but, in these letters, though we have plenty of eloquent professions of friendship, we confess that we have looked in vain for this common bloom of sensibility. There is no softness,—no enthusiasm,—nothing which could, for one moment, be mistaken for the language of tenderness or emotion. Yet these are letters to chosen friends and early associates; and embrace the period in which the writer became a wife and a mother. It is not enough that the letters of a woman should be lively and witty;—female gaiety loses both its charm and its dignity, when it is not shaded with softness;—even female intellect is not quite respectable without it. . . . [Mrs. Montagu] no doubt appears very good-natured and obliging; but without any devotedness of affection, or much concern, beyond that of admiration and amusement. On the whole, we think her professions of friendship and serious morality the least attractive parts of her performance. Her ludicrous descriptions and witty remarks, except that they are always too elaborate, are often tolerably successful; but the most entertaining of all,

we think, are her lively personalities,—those half malicious, half playful delineations of common acquaintance, by which the merriment and the jealousies of polite society have been chiefly maintained, ever since the period of its first formation. (pp. 76-7)

Upon the whole, we think the vivacity of [Mrs. Montagu's] letters attractive;—though it is sometimes childish, and almost always theatrical. We think the familiar style excellent, and the eloquence abominable; and are of opinion, that they would have been infinitely more charming, if two thirds of the wit could have been exchanged for a few traits of simplicity and affection. Comparing them even with the earliest letters of [Mrs. Montagu's mother-in-law,] Lady Mary Wortley, it is impossible not to be struck with the vast superiority of the latter, in sound sense, good taste, and facility. There is, in those delightful compositions, such a mixture of just thinking and solid sagacity, as gives both dignity and relief to the wit and trifling which intervenes; and the trifling itself is far more graceful and striking, both because it is less laboured, and infinitely less verbose. Mrs Montagu certainly comes nearest that admirable model in her lighter strokes of personal satire, and the purity of such parts of her diction as she had not determined to make splendid. (p. 87)

> *A review of "The Letters of Mrs. Elizabeth Montagu with Some of the Letters of Her Correspondents," in* The Edinburgh Review, *Vol. XV, No. XXIX, October, 1809, pp. 75-87.*

THE QUARTERLY REVIEW   (essay date 1813)

[*The Letters of Mrs. Elizabeth Montagu. Part the Second*] shew very clearly that she was a superior woman, and quite as clearly that in the early part of her life (though she died within our own recollection) women were very far from having reached their present standard of taste and knowledge. Her attainments would not now be considered as very remarkable, but it is evident that they were then admitted to be so, both by herself and her friends. She was naturally gay, intelligent, and ingenious, and her style is on the whole agreeable. But she deals largely—according, we presume, to the custom of the age among those that piqued themselves upon writing good letters—in stale, pedantic, unprofitable morality; praising that which was never blamed, insisting upon that which was never denied, and condemning that which nobody ever undertook to defend. But this was not her fault, but the fault of the age. No woman of three and twenty, clever, fashionable, and well educated, would now think it right to acquaint her correspondent, even though that correspondent were an uncle or a father, a bishop or a judge, that 'every thing in the world is of a mortal nature'; that 'true and faithful affection is not a pearl to be cast before the profane'; that 'hypocrisy is an abominable vice'; that 'happiness opens the heart to benevolence, and affliction softens it to pity';—all which apophthegms may be found in the space of two pages. But they by no means prove with regard to Mrs. Montagu, what they would most undoubtedly prove with respect to any person in these days that should be guilty of uttering them. They merely shew that people still thought it very pretty and proper to transplant sentences from copy books into their familiar correspondence, and that it was a great want of respect to their elderly friends and relations not to inflict upon them a large quantity of dulness and commonplace. She has considerable comic powers, which break out agreeably enough when she is writing with less care than usual, but on great occasions, when she is desirous of shewing herself to the best advantage, to duchesses and other high persons, her pleasantry becomes forced, wire-drawn, and childish to the most melancholy excess. (pp. 35-6)

Mrs. Montagu is evidently oppressed by the load of her own superiority. She writes like a person that has a character to support, and whose correspondents would have a right to complain if she ceased one moment to be very wise or very witty. (p. 37)

There are, perhaps, five hundred women now that can write as well as Mrs. Montagu, and that too without being guilty of those sins against good taste with which she is justly chargeable. But how many of these *would have written* as well in her time, and in her circumstances, is quite another question. We are inclined to believe that the number would have been comparatively very small. On the other hand, if Mrs. Montagu had lived in our days, she would have maintained nearly the same station. Her acquirements would not have been so remarkable, which would have been attended by this advantage, that she would have thought less about them, and been free from that tinge of pedantry which is now visible in her writings. Her ethics would not have been so trite, nor her wit so laboured. But her talents would have carried her equally far in a happier direction. She would have been now, as she was then, one of the liveliest, cleverest, best-informed women of the age. . . . However, although we have derived considerable amusement from these letters, and though they have, as we have already acknowledged, inspired us with a favourable opinion as to the talents of their author, we have some doubts whether they have quite body and substance enough for publication. Mrs. Montagu did not write at one of those distant periods when a mere account of the ordinary occurrences of life, and a mere picture of the state of society as they appear in a familiar correspondence, interest one from their contrast with our own habits and manners; nor are her letters sufficiently interspersed with anecdotes of eminent persons in her own time, to gratify our curiosity in a different but equally agreeable manner. We own that we were at first a good deal disappointed at the little notice Mrs. Montagu takes of her illustrious contemporaries; and the more, because it is evident that she enjoyed the advantage of being familiarly acquainted with the greater part of them. However, upon consideration, it appears to us that though the absence of this sort of information renders her letters vastly less interesting now that they are published at an interval of two generations, it is no cause of just blame to the writer. Her correspondents were just as well acquainted with the history and character of the time as herself, and it would have been only telling stories they all knew, and delivering opinions in which they all agreed. . . . In general, we should say that the merit of her letters is in an inverse proportion to the pains she takes with them. (pp. 37-8)

A review of "The Letters of Mrs. Elizabeth Montagu. Part the Second," in The Quarterly Review, *Vol. X, No. XIX, October, 1813, pp. 31-41.*

WILLIAM HAYLEY   (poem date 1820?)

[*Hayley was an English biographer, poet, and memoirist. He is remembered as much for his friendship with such luminaries as William Blake and Robert Southey as for his writing, which is generally regarded as second-rate. The following poem, which is believed to have been written in 1820, was originally published in Hayley's* Book of the Dead, *a collection of epitaphs.*]

Thou chief of Britain's literary Fair,
Thy merits Montague let truth declare.

Radiant in Genius and refined in Taste
By Wit and Wisdom emulously graced
By each alternately empowered to please
Enlivening Dignity with graceful Ease,
Shakespear whose Powers thy Critic Page displays
Shakespear Himself is proud to speak thy Praise.

Permit no flattering Eulogist to tell
How on thy Converse 'twas my joy to dwell
Sweet was that Converse when thy Evening Hour
Drew Learning's Sons to hail its cheering Power
Yet sweeter when it pleased thee to unbend
In social Breakfast with a single Friend
That banquet treasured in Remembrance Kind
Keeps thee still present to my grateful Mind
Thy Letters, of my Breakfast-Board the Grace
Still let me hear Thee speaking, Face to Face,
They all thy various attributes impart
Delightfully unveil thy Mind and Heart
Thy fine Perception and thy forceful Nerve
That win the confidence they well deserve
Make Admiration on thy Words attend
And feeling Breasts enshrine Thee as their Friend.

William Hayley, "'On Mrs. Montague'," in The Cornhill Magazine, *n.s. Vol. XXXVII, No. 219, September, 1914, p. 405.*

REBECCA WEST   (essay date 1937)

[*West was a twentieth-century English novelist and critic. Though West finds* An Essay on the Writings and Genius of Shakespear *"pompously and diffusely written," she praises its "workmanlike exposure of Voltaire's inaccuracies and mistranslations."*]

[Though *An Essay on the Writings and Genius of Shakespeare, compared with the Greek and French dramatic poets, with some remarks upon the misrepresentations of Monsieur de Voltaire*] is not as good a book as it was said to be at the time of its publication, it is much better than a great many people have pretended since. It is important to note that it was not a mere desire to stand on the side of accepted opinion which made [Mrs. Montagu] take up the challenge for Shakespeare. She was less swayed by such considerations than one might suppose. For example, the piety which she constantly expresses in her letters sounds conventional, but it is actually proof of an independent spirit; for her husband, like her father and her stepfather, was inclined to free thought. She was as hardy in her defence of Shakespeare, since a great many of the writers with whom she would have liked to rank as an equal, such as Shaftesbury, Bolingbroke, Chesterfield, and David Hume, regarded him as either unimportant or as an inspired barbarian. Had she joined them in their shuddering rejection, it might have given her a pleasantly eclectic reputation. But she owned to her real opinions and made a very creditable show in justifying them. It is true that she makes some concessions to the legend of Shakespeare's barbarism, but it must be remembered that the Georgians were genuinely shocked by the Elizabethans, though they were certainly under a misapprehension regarding the reason for their emotions. (pp. 172-73)

But she soon got over that [misapprehension], and settled down to a treatment of her subject which, even when compared with Dr. Johnson's Preface, is not at all contemptible. It is, of course, pompously and diffusely written. . . . But it contains a very workmanlike exposure of Voltaire's inaccuracies and mistranslations. In the exegetical passages there are hardly any fatuities to match Dr. Johnson's opinion that in Shakespeare's "tragick scenes there is always something wanting", or that Catherine of Aragon's last speech is "above any other part of Shakespeare's tragedies", and his blindness to the poetic value of Ariel's songs and *Antony and Cleopatra*. Her discussion of *Macbeth* is very much more intelligent than his, and in her chapter on **"Preternatural Beings"** she actually begins to discuss what Herder was discussing in Germany, on such an infinitely higher critical level than herself and her friends that it seems extraordinary they were contemporaries: the place of myth in poetry. She is not to be despised when she points out the immense advantage enjoyed by poets who write of myths in which they and their hearers believe, and the diminution in poetic intensity caused by the change from fable to allegory which is bound to accompany an advance towards rationalism. Dr. Johnson said the worst about her book when he said that it was nearly impossible to get through it. There is certainly a nucleus of critical thought in it which makes it regrettable that Mrs. Montagu did not write on behalf of Shakespeare as lucidly and tersely as when she spoke for him. (pp. 173-74)

> Rebecca West, "Elizabeth Montagu," in From Anne to Victoria: Essays by Various Hands, *edited by Bonamy Dobrée, Cassell and Company Limited, 1937, pp. 164-87.*

J.W.H. ATKINS (essay date 1951)

[The significance of *Essay on the Writings and Genius of Shakespeare*] lies in the fact that it was a direct attempt to defend Shakespeare against Voltaire's destructive criticism. [In the preface to his edition of Shakespeare,] Johnson, it is true, had spoken of Voltaire's 'minute and slender criticism', . . . but Mrs. Montagu has throughout his delinquencies in mind, and her attack is forthright and detailed. Her work is not without many obvious defects; and among others, an inconsequent arrangement, a lack of historical knowledge, besides pretentious aims which unfulfilled give an air of superficiality to the work in general. Yet it has also definite critical interest in calling attention to an important phase of Shakespeare criticism at the time, while the remarks on Shakespeare, if rarely original, are nevertheless of no negligible kind. (p. 257)

Apart from denying Voltaire's claims to pronounce finally on the merits of Shakespeare's plays, Mrs. Montagu . . . calls attention to some of Shakespeare's positive qualities. It is true that in her ignorance of the actual conditions under which he wrote, she concedes too much to hostile critics in lamenting his many indecorums and attributing them to 'paltry tavern, unlettered audiences' and the like. Yet despite this apologetic tone, of her genuine and well-founded admiration there can be no question. 'Approved by his own age and admired by the next', she writes, 'he is revered, almost adored by the present refined age'; and while 'no great poet or critic', she adds, 'except Voltaire had disparaged him', she claims that he stood alone in characterization and expression, 'with faults true critics dare not mend'. Elsewhere again she reminds her readers that the 'boulders of Stonehenge can be admired without knowing by what law of mechanics they were raised'; and Shakespeare's art she compares with that of 'the dervish in the Arabian Nights, who could throw his soul into the body of another man and adopt his passions'.

Nor does she confine her defence to remarks of a general kind; for, regarding him notably as an explorer, she points to some of his innovations, and has besides some interesting comments to make on his dramatic art. (p. 259)

[Equally interesting] are her occasional remarks on other aspects of Shakespeare's art, as when, for instance, she describes *2 Henry IV* as that rare thing, a successful sequel, in which earlier characters are consistently maintained under changed conditions, or when she points out that Shakespeare's sententious utterances, so far from being excrescences, arise naturally out of the various situations. Nor has she failed to appreciate his skilful characterization. . . . [The *Essay* contains] more than the idle comments of a fashionable society hostess; and the work cannot fairly be dismissed as 'feeble and pretentious'. Least satisfactory is the attempted comparison with Greek and French dramatists announced on the title page; though the idea of comparing was in itself commendable, as widening the approach to Shakespeare. And, for the rest, something was doubtless owed to earlier critics, notably to Thomas Warton and Hurd. Yet the *Essay* has a positive value of its own in its timely reply to Voltaire and to neo-classical ideals generally; and despite all defects, it makes a contribution to Shakespeare criticism that cannot well be overlooked. (p. 260)

> J.W.H. Atkins, "Shakespeare Criticism: Rowe, Pope, Theobald, Johnson, Kames, Mrs. Montagu, and Morgan," in his English Literary Criticism: Seventeenth and Eighteenth Centuries, *Methuen, 1951, pp. 225-67.**

ADDITIONAL BIBLIOGRAPHY

Blunt, Reginald, ed. *Mrs. Montagu, "Queen of the Blues": Her Letters and Friendships from 1762 to 1800, Vol. I.* Boston: Houghton Mifflin Co., 1923, 369 p.
    A study of Montagu that provides thorough biographical notes, as well as pages from Montagu's correspondence.

Climenson, Emily J. *Elizabeth Montagu, the Queen of the Blue-Stockings: Her Correspondence from 1720 to 1761. 2 vols.* New York: E. P. Dutton & Co., 1906.
    An intimate portrait of the society in which Montagu lived. Climenson, the great-great-niece of Montagu, collected her aunt's social correspondence and incorporated it into an account of Montagu's private life.

Doran, John. *A Lady of the Last Century (Mrs. Elizabeth Montagu): Illustrated in Her Unpublished Letters.* London: Richard Bentley and Son, 1873, 372 p.
    An anecdotal biography of Montagu that focuses on her social relationships.

Jones, W. Powell. "The Romantic Bluestocking, Elizabeth Montagu." *The Huntington Library Quarterly* XII, No. 1 (November 1948): 85-98.
    A view of Montagu's personality that emphasizes her romantic side. Jones reprints portions of her unpublished letters that demonstrate her interest in nature, Gothic architecture, medieval literature, and physical manifestations of divinity, all of which, according to the critic, form part of eighteenth-century romanticism.

(Louis Charles) Alfred de Musset

1810-1857

French dramatist, poet, novelist, and novella and essay writer.

Musset is considered to be one of the leading figures of the French Romantic movement. Although his best dramas have been judged as more original than his poetry, he distinguished himself in both genres, and critics point to similar qualities and themes in each. He was, above all, a lyric writer, even when composing in forms other than poetry. For Musset, inspiration always came from within, rather than from the world around him. His work is often a depiction of his experiences in love, and he considered his characters to be projections of himself.

Musset's parents were both descended from cultured families, and they provided an intellectual environment for their sensitive, precocious child. A brilliant though undisciplined student, Musset pursued medicine, law, and painting at the Collège Henri IV in Paris before choosing a career in literature. This decision was influenced in part by his acquaintance with Victor Hugo, who introduced him to the Romantic *cénacle,* or literary society, that included Hugo, Alfred de Vigny, Charles Augustin Sainte-Beuve, Charles Nodier, and Prosper Merimée.

Musset's earliest literary work was a free translation and redaction of Thomas De Quincey's *Confessions of an English Opium Eater.* Published before De Quincey's work became well known, *L'anglais mangeur d'opium* received little attention from his contemporaries. Unfortunately, its choice of subject foreshadows Musset's drunken, dissipated lifestyle. His next work, *Contes d'Espagne et d'Italie (Tales of Spain and Italy),* was an immediate popular success that introduced the eighteen-year-old author to all of Paris. The work is a collection of narrative poems and verse dramas which, although set in foreign lands, were conceived entirely by Musset's imagination. The work reveals the influence of the *cénacle* and Romantic elements, such as exoticism, fantasy, and passion, predominate. Yet the collection also represents Musset's break with the members of the French Romantic movement. "Mardoche" humorously mocks Hugo in its opening lines, "Les secrètes pensées de Rafaël, gentilhomme français" ("Secret Thoughts of Raphael") praises French Classical writers shunned by Hugo's followers, and "Ballade à la lune" ("Ballad to the Moon"), the best-known piece in the collection, ridicules writers of the Romantic movement by likening the moon, their favorite and revered subject, to the dot on the letter "i."

In 1830, Musset's first drama, *La nuit vénitienne; ou, Les noces de Laurette (A Venetian Night),* was produced. Its failure prompted the author to avoid the stage, and most of his subsequent dramas were written to be read, not produced. Musset's next volume of drama, *Un spectacle dans un fauteuil (Scene in an Armchair),* lent its name to a form of drama later known as "armchair theater." The French stage of Musset's day was dominated by Eugène Scribe, who stressed the importance of dramatic technique and the need to entertain the audience, and by such Romantic writers as Hugo and Alexandre Dumas *(père),* whose works are noted for their exoticism and extravagance. By writing for the reader instead of the stage, Musset avoided these influences and followed his own taste without concern

for popular success or problems of staging. Critics agree that Musset's armchair dramas are marked by their freedom and spontaneity and note that they rely on the reader's imagination, rather than excessive use of imagery, to convey visual impressions of scenes and characters.

In 1833, Musset met the French novelist George Sand at a dinner in honor of contributors to *Revue des deux mondes.* Their ensuing affair, though brief, provided the passion that he felt his poetry lacked. After spending several months together in Paris, they went to Venice for the winter. Musset became ill, and, while nursing him back to health, Sand fell in love with his doctor, Pietro Pagello. Musset left Italy, devastated. Upon Sand's return to Paris they resumed their tempestuous love affair, which continued intermittently until early 1835.

Despite its disastrous effect on his physical and emotional health, Musset's relationship with Sand proved an unequalled inspiration. Most critics agree that his most brilliant poetry and drama, including "Les nuits" ("The Nights"), "Lettre à M. de Lamartine" ("Letter to Lamartine"), and "Souvenir," was produced during this period. "The Nights" is made up of four separate poems: "La nuit de mai" ("The Night of May"), "La nuit de décembre" ("The Night of December"), "La nuit d'août" ("The Night of August"), and "La nuit d'octobre"

("The Night of October"). These poems chronicle the author's gradual recovery from the intense suffering and bitterness caused by the end of the affair until, in "The Night of October," the poet is reconciled with his past. All but "The Night of December" take the form of a conversation between the poet and his Muse. In that work, an evocation of winter that depicts loneliness and desperation, a black-clad figure of death appears. Through the form of dialogue, Musset affirms his belief in the importance of love and its relationship to art. The works of this period, wholly focused on the theme of love, were considered solipsistic by some and earned Musset the title of "the patron of self-pity." His later poetry, collected in *Poésies complètes* and *Poésies nouvelles, 1836-1852*, differs widely from that written immediately following his relationship with Sand and is not as highly acclaimed as those earlier works. The tone of the later poems recalls that of "Ballad to the Moon." Witty, light, graceful, and detached, these poems are said to reflect the influence of Jean de La Fontaine and André Chénier. Despite the differences in tone and subject, Musset's early and late poetry share certain stylistic qualities, including striking, controlled imagery, natural speech, and varied metre, rhythm, and rhyme patterns.

Like his other writings, Musset's dramas were deeply affected by his relationship with Sand: *Lorenzaccio, Fantasio,* and *On ne badine pas avec l'amour (No Trifling with Love),* ranked among his greatest works, were all written during their brief affair. As these works demonstrate, Musset was accomplished in many dramatic forms, including historical dramas, comedies, and proverbs, written both in verse and prose. His *proverbes dramatiques,* or dramatic proverbs, are short sketches designed to illustrate the aphorism or proverb that forms the title. Although these works derive from the eighteenth-century tradition of light verse, Musset is credited with elevating the proverb from a slight entertainment to an art form. Critics praise the works for their wit, sentimentality, gaiety, lightness of touch, and psychological insight and cite *No Trifling with Love* and *Il faut qu'une porte soit ouverte ou fermée (A Door Must Be either Open or Shut)* as his best work in this form. *Lorenzaccio,* one of Musset's tragedies, provides the basis for his fame as a Romantic dramatist. This historical drama is often compared with the works of William Shakespeare because of its wide scope of characters and action. *Lorenzaccio* shows the gradual disillusionment and surrender of the hero, Lorenzo, to treachery and deceit. While many critics find *Lorenzaccio's* plot confusing and the character development insufficient, others consider the dialogue brilliant and natural and praise the drama's classically simple style. They note that Musset, unlike other Romantics, avoided the striking and picturesque in favor of straightforward language.

In 1847, Musset's comedy *Un caprice (A Caprice)* was successfully produced at the Comédie-Française, the French national theater in Paris. During the late 1840s and early 1850s, Musset revised several of his armchair dramas for the stage and wrote new works. Critics agree, however, that this period is marked by a decline in his creative powers and that he completed his most important work by 1840. In that year, he suffered the first of a series of debilitating illnesses, brought on in part by heavy drinking. Although an exceptionally gifted youth, Musset had exhausted much of his talent by age thirty, when Heinrich Heine described him as "un garçon d'un bien beau passé" (a young man with a fine past). When Musset won election to the Académie française at age forty-two after two unsuccessful nominations, his contemporaries were honoring him for the works of his youth.

Of all his writings, Musset's prose works have received the least attention. His novel *La confession d'un enfant du siècle (The Confession of a Child of the Century)* is autobiographical and chronicles the protagonist's search for pleasure following a failed love affair. The work also depicts the Romantic *mal du siècle* (unease) of the generation that was born after the fall of Napoleon, too late to take part in the glories of the Revolution and Empire. Although Musset's contemporaries praised both his novel and critical essays collected in *Lettres de Dupuis et Cotonet (Letters of Dupuis and Cotonet),* neither work is widely read today.

Musset's reputation rests on his poetry and drama. Many early critics praised his verse, agreeing with Henry James that he was "one of the first poets of our day." Discussion of his poetry largely focuses on its personal nature. While some condemn the single-minded concern with love in his early poetry, others consider his approach an effective means of presenting the theme of suffering and love in artistic creation. Recent critics, however, many of whom are concerned with style rather than content, label his poetry slipshod and careless. Response to Musset's drama has been consistently positive. Although his plays range from serious drama to light comedy, critics note certain qualities in all of them, including elegance, charm, delicacy, and power. The value of these works, critics agree, lies not in their plot and action, but in their depiction of feelings. According to current thought, Musset's characters convey psychological depth because they are projections of their author, embodying both his descent into debauchery and search for innocent, exalted love. Critics often point to the dual nature of many of his dramas, noting that their surface qualities of grace, wit, and refinement often belie their dramatic power, methodical composition, and inevitable tragic conclusion. The continuing popularity of Musset's work attests to the universality of his descriptions of love and loss.

*PRINCIPAL WORKS

L'anglais mangeur d'opium [translator; from the
      autobiography *Confessions of an English Opium Eater*
      by Thomas De Quincey] (autobiography) 1828
Contes d'Espagne et d'Italie (drama and poetry) 1830
      [*Tales of Spain and Italy,* 1905]
La nuit vénitienne; ou, Les noces de Laurette (drama)
      1830
      [*A Venetian Night,* 1905]
Un spectacle dans un fauteuil. 3 vols. (drama) 1833-34
      [*Scene in an Armchair,* 1905]
Les caprices de Marianne [first publication] (drama)
      1834; published in *Un spectacle dans un fauteuil*
      [*The Follies of Marianne,* 1905]
Fantasio [first publication] (drama) 1834; published in
      Un spectacle dans un fauteuil
      [*Fantasio: A Proverb,* 1852?]
Lorenzaccio [first publication] (drama) 1834; published in
      Un spectacle dans un fauteuil
      [*Lorenzaccio,* 1905]
On ne badine pas avec l'amour [first publication] (drama)
      1834; published in *Un spectacle dans un fauteuil*
      [*No Trifling with Love* published in *Comedies,* 1890; also
      published as *Camille and Perdican,* 1961]
La confession d'un enfant du siècle (novel) 1836
      [*The Confession of a Child of the Century,* 1892; also
      published as *A Modern Man's Confession,* 1902]

Un caprice [first publication]   (drama)   1840; published in
  Comédies et proverbes
  [*A Caprice*, 1905]
Comédies et proverbes   (drama)   1840
"Les nuits"   (poetry)   1840; published in *Poésies
  complètes*
  ["The Nights," 1905]
Poésies complètes   (poetry)   1840
**Nouvelles* (novellas)   1848
"Lettre à M. de Lamartine"   (poetry)   1852; published in
  Poésies nouvelles, 1836-1852
  ["Letter to Lamartine," 1905]
Poésies nouvelles, 1836-1852   (poetry)   1852
"Souvenir"   (poetry)   1852; published in *Poésies
  nouvelles, 1836-1852*
  ["Souvenir," 1905]
Comédies et proverbes   (drama)   1853
Il faut qu'une porte soit ouverte ou fermée [first publication]
  (drama)   1853; published in *Comédies et proverbes*
  [*A Door Must Be either Open or Shut* published in
  Comedies, 1890]
On ne saurait penser à tout [first publication]   (drama)
  1853; published in *Comédies et proverbes*
  [*One Can Not Think of Everything*, 1905]
Contes   (novellas and essays)   1854
Lettres sur la littérature   (essays)   1854; published in
  Contes; also published as *Lettres de Dupuis et Cotonet*
  (date unknown)
  [*Letters of Dupuis and Cotonet*, 1905]
Oeuvres posthumes   (drama, poetry, and letters)   1860
Oeuvres complètes de Alfred de Musset. 10 vols.   (drama,
  poetry, novel, novellas, essays, and letters)   1866
Comedies   (drama)   1890
Correspondance de George Sand et d'Alfred de Musset
  (letters)   1904
The Complete Writings of Alfred de Musset   (drama,
  poetry, novel, novellas, essays, and letters)   1905
Correspondance (1825-1857)   (letters)   1907

*Most of Musset's work was originally published in the periodical
Revue des deux mondes. Most of his works were first translated in
1905 in *The Complete Writings of Alfred de Musset.*

**This work also includes stories written by Paul de Musset.

ALFRED DE MUSSET   (poem date 1830)

[*The following verse from Musset's dedication to "La coupe et
les lèvres," first published in 1830 and considered the most
Byronic of his poems, includes his rebuttal to critics' charges that
he plagiarized Lord Byron's work.*]

> For my part, I care not for criticism;
> Fly though it may, it seldom has a sting.
> Last year they called me Byron's copyist;
> You know me, and you know it is not so.
> I loathe as death the state of plagiarist;
> My glass, though small, from it alone I drink.
>
>   (p. 208)

> *Alfred de Musset, "Dedication to 'The Cup and the
> Lip'," in his* Poems of Alfred de Musset, Vol. I,
> *translated by Marie Agathe Clarke, Hill, 1905, pp.
> 205-17.*

ALEXANDER PUSHKIN   (essay date 1830)

[*Considered the greatest poet and dramatist of nineteenth-century
Russia, Pushkin is important for his critical as well as his creative
work. His reviews of Russian writers and of European literature
in translation were particularly influential because he wrote during the nascent stages of Russia's literary development. Critics
praise Pushkin's clear-sighted critical view and consider it to be
among the most distinguished of his era. Pushkin appreciated and
kept fully abreast of contemporary French literature. In the following excerpt, originally an untitled essay written in 1830, the
first paragraph probably reflects Pushkin's longing for literary
freedom; censorship was a lifelong problem for the Russian author.*]

Musset, it seems, took upon himself the obligation of singing
only mortal sins, murders, and fornication [in *Contes d'Espagne
et d'Italie*]. In vividness, the voluptuous scenes with which his
poems are filled perhaps eclipse the most explicit descriptions
of the late Parny. He doesn't even think about morality, he
ridicules didacticism—and, unfortunately, in an extremely attractive way. He stands on as little ceremony as possible with
the solemn Alexandrine; he fractures and mangles it so that
it's a horror and pity. He sings the moon [in *Ballade à la lune*]
in verses that no one would have dared, except perhaps a poet
of the blissfully simple XVI century, when neither Boileau nor
Messrs. La Harpe, Joffman, and Colnet yet existed. And how
was the young prankster received? He should have been terrified. You would expect to see the indignation of the journals
and all the ferules raised against him. Not at all. The candid
prank of the amiable rake was so surprising, so pleasing, that
not only did the critics not abuse him, but they took it upon
themselves to justify him; they declared that the *Spanish Tales*
prove nothing, that one may describe robbers and murderers
without even having the aim of explaining how unpraiseworthy
their craft is—and still be a good and honorable man, that a
twenty-year old poet may be forgiven vivid scenes of pleasures,
that when reading his poetry his family probably would not
share the horror of the newspapers and see a monster in him,
that, in one word, poetry is fantasy and has nothing in common
with the prosaic truth of life. Glory to God! It ought to have
been thus long ago, dear sirs. (pp. 125-26)

[The *Italian and Spanish Tales*] are characterized by extraordinary vividness. Of these, I think *Porcia* has the most merit:
the night rendezvous scene, the portrait of the jealous man
whose hair has suddenly turned grey, the conversation of the
two lovers on the sea—all this is charming. The dramatic sketch
Les Marrons du feu promises France a romantic tragedian. And
in the story *Mardoche* Musset is the first of the French poets
to grasp the tone of Byron's comic verses—which is not at all
a joke. (p. 126)

> *Alexander Pushkin, "On Alfred de Musset," in his*
> The Critical Prose of Alexander Pushkin, with Crit-
> ical Essays by Four Russian Romantic Poets, *edited
> and translated by Carl R. Proffer, Indiana University
> Press, 1969, pp. 125-26.*

CHARLES AUGUSTIN SAINTE-BEUVE   (essay date 1854)

[*Sainte-Beuve is considered to be the foremost French literary
critic of the nineteenth century. Of his extensive body of critical
writings, the best known are his "lundis"—weekly newspaper
articles which appeared every Monday morning over a period of
several decades in which he displayed his knowledge of literature
and history. While Sainte-Beuve began his career as a champion
of Romanticism, he eventually formulated a psychological method
of criticism. Asserting that the critic cannot separate a work of*

literature from the artist, Sainte-Beuve considered an author's life and character integral to the comprehension of his work. The following is an appreciative review of Contes d'Espagne et d'Italie *in which Sainte-Beuve comments that Musset's poetic inspiration flows from within, not from the world around him; this observation is repeated throughout Musset criticism. Sainte-Beuve's essay was originally published in* Le moniteur *in 1854.]*

M. de Musset came before the public when scarcely twenty years old [with the publication of *Contes d'Espagne et d'Italie*], and from the very first wished to mark emphatically his unlikeness to the other poets then famous. In order that there should be no mistake he assumed from the first a mask, a fantastic costume, a manner; he disguised himself as a Spaniard and an Italian, although he had not yet seen Spain and Italy: hence ensued disadvantages which were not easily thrown off. I am certain that, endowed as he was with original power and an individual genius, even if he had begun more simply and without taking so much pains to make himself singular, he would soon have been distinguished from the poets whose society he disclaimed and whose sentimental and melancholy, solemn and serious temperaments were so different from his. He possessed a feeling for raillery which the others lacked, and a need of true passion they felt but rarely. "My first verses are those of a child, my second those of a youth," he said, criticising himself. M. de Musset wrote his juvenile poems, but with a brilliance, an insolence of animation (as Regnier says), with a more than virile audacity, with a page's charm and effrontery: he was Cherubino at a masked ball, playing the part of Don Juan. The early manner, in which we note a vein of affectation and traces of reminiscences, is crowned by two poems (if we may call poems things not composed as such), by two wondrous divagations, **"Namouna"** and **"Rolla,"** in which, under the pretext of relating a story he always forgets, the poet breathed forth his dreams and fancies, and abandoned himself to unrestrained freedom. Wit, nudities and crudities, lyrical power, a charm and refinement at times adorable, the highest poetry for no reason, debauch along with the ideal, sudden whiffs of lilac that bring back freshness, here and there a scrap of *chic* (to speak the language of the studio), all these things mingled and compounded, produced the strangest and certainly the most astonishing thing that French poetry, the virtuous girl who, already elderly, had formerly espoused M. de Malherbe, had yet furnished. It may be said that in Namouna we find the faults and fine qualities of Alfred de Musset, the poet. But the latter are so great and of such a high order that they compensate for everything. (p. 120)

[I need not] hesitate to say that in the poems of **"Rolla"** and of **"Namouna"** there is a good half that does not correspond with the other. The fine part of **"Namouna,"** the part in which the poet reveals himself with full power, is the second canto. It is there that M. de Musset unfolds his theory of Don Juan, and contrasts the two sorts of libertines who, according to him, share the stage of the world: the heartless libertine, ideal, full of egoism and vanity, finding it difficult to get pleasure out of anything, and only desirous of inspiring love without returning it, *Lovelace*, in fact; and the other type of libertine, amiable and loving, almost innocent, passing through all phases of inconstancy in order to reach an ideal that eludes him, believing he loves, the dupe of none but himself in his seductions, and changing only because he ceases to love. There, according to M. de Musset, is the real poetical Don Juan. . . . M. de Musset attempts to paint him in the brightest and most charming colours, in colours which remind me (Heaven forgive me!) of those used by Milton when painting his happy couple in

Eden. . . . From a poetical point of view nothing could be more delightful, better imagined, and better carried out. Nevertheless, in vain has the poet created, in vain has he desired to draw for us an unique Don Juan, a contradiction as he makes him, living almost innocent in the midst of his crimes; the "innocent corrupter" does not exist. He succeeded in evoking him, in giving momentary life by his magic to an impossible abstraction. It is said that words do no harm on paper. Such a combination and contrast of virtues and vices in the same being is all very well to write about, and especially to celebrate in verse, but it is true neither according to humanity nor nature. And then, why put us to the absolute alternative of choosing between the two sorts of libertines? Would poetry suffer, oh, poet! if there were no libertines? In the divine company of Virgil's Elysian Fields, in which the greatest of mortals hold a place, there is room in the first rank for the virtuous poets, for the poets who were entirely human. . . . (pp. 121-22)

So much for my reservations. There are, however, in **"Namouna"** two or three hundred consecutive lines quite beyond comparison. Be incredulous, and turn them about in every sense; apply the surgeon's knife; cavil at your pleasure; a few stains, a little loud colouring may be discovered; but if you possess true poetic feeling, and if you are sincere, you will recognise the strength and power of the inspiration; the god—or if you prefer it, the devil—has touched it. (p. 122)

[M. de Musset's love for George Sand was the great event of his] life, I mean of his poetic life. His talent was suddenly purified and ennobled; the sacred flame seemed on a sudden to reject all impure alloy. In the poems composed under that powerful star almost all the faults disappeared; his finer qualities, till then, as it were, scattered and fragmentary, were combined, assembled, and grouped in a powerful although sad harmony. The four poems M. de Musset called **"Nights"** are short, complex, meditative poems, marking the loftiest height of his lyrical genius. The **"May Night"** and the **"October Night"** are the finest for the flow and the inexhaustible vein of the poetry, for the expression of violent and unmasked passion. But the **"December Night"** and the **"August Night"** are also delightful—the latter for action and sentiment, the former for grace and flexibility of expression. The four, taken together, make one work, animated by the same sentiment, possessing harmony and skilfully contrived relations.

Parallel with De Musset's **"Nights"** I read over again the famous poems of Milton's youth, **"L'Allegro,"** and especially **"Il Penseroso."** But in those compositions of supreme and somewhat cold beauty the poet was passionless; he waited for an impulse from without. . . . Let us not displace august names from their proper sphere. All that is fine in Milton is beyond comparison; it reveals the calm habitude of high regions and a continuity of power. However, in the more terrestrial, and at the same time more human, **"Nights"** of M. de Musset, it is from within that the inspiration, the passion that paints and the breeze that makes nature fragrant, springs; or, rather, the charm consists in the combination and alliance of the two sources of impressions—that is to say, of a deep sorrow and of a soul still open to vivid impressions. The poet, wounded to the heart, shedding real tears, is conscious of a renewal of youth, and is almost intoxicated by the spring. He is more sensitive than before to the innumerable beauties of the universe, to the verdure and the flowers, to the morning sunlight, to the birds' songs, and fresh as at the age of fifteen, he brings us his posy of lilies and eglantine. M. de Musset's muse will always, even at the least happy moments, be conscious of such renewals; but in no other place will the natural freshness be so happily wedded, as in this case, to bleeding passion and sincere grief. Poetry, chaste consoler, was there treated almost with adoration and affection. (pp. 123-24)

The lyrics produced by M. de Musset since the "**Nights**" [collected in *Poésies nouvelles de M. Alfred de Musset*], contain some remarkable poems. I point out one called "**A Lost Evening**," where he charmingly mingles a motive of André Chénier with a thought of Molière, a satire "**On Idleness**," in which the poet was influenced by reading Regnier; a pretty tale, "**Simone**," savouring of Boccaccio and La Fontaine; but especially a "**Recollection**," full of charm and feeling, where the inspiration came from himself alone. (p. 126)

M. de Musset's taste has reached maturity, and it would be best henceforth for his talent to obey his taste and not to allow itself any more weaknesses. After so many varied attempts and experiences, after trying to love many things in order to discover the only and supreme one worthy of love, that is to say simple truth clothed at the same time with beauty, it is not wonderful that when we return to it and recognise it, we find ourselves less animated and more fatigued in its presence than we were in the presence of the idols. However, his genius possesses power of renewal, sources of youth of which he has more than once shown that he knew the secret, and which he has not yet exhausted. For a few years his genius has exhibited itself to the public in a new form, and the poet has triumphed in a somewhat hazardous experiment. The delicate sketches, charming proverbs that he did not intend for the stage, suddenly became delightful little comedies that arose and walked before us. The success of his *Caprice* did honour, I do not fear to say it, to the public, and proves that for him who can awaken it, it still possesses delicate literary feeling. He has seen the circle of his admirers extend as if by magic. Many minds that would never have dreamed of seeking him out for his lyrical talent learned to appreciate him in his easy and graceful proverbs. . . . M. de Musset as a dramatic poet has still much to learn. On the stage a happy situation, ingenious dialogue are not enough; invention, fertility, development, above all, action, are necessary to consummate, as it has been said, *the work of the devil*. . . . [Without] asking too much, without making more ceremony than M. de Musset himself, I shall end with a line of his own that puts a stop to argument—

What do I say? Such as he is, the world loves him still.
(pp. 126-27)

Charles Augustin Sainte-Beuve, "Alfred de Musset," in his Essays by Sainte-Beuve, *edited and translated by Elizabeth Lee, Walter Scott, Ltd., 1910, pp. 118-27.*

E. L. [ELIZA LYNN LINTON] (essay date 1857)

There is a wide difference of tone between the earlier and later poems of Alfred de Musset [which appear in *Contes d'Espagne et d'Italie*], though there is in them all that homogeneity of thought which must of necessity run through the works of a true man: that is, a man whose nature develops itself from internal force, and is not trained by outward circumstance. His early poems are essentially young in both form and subject. . . . [In the verses of his childhood] there is simply the natural impulse to poetry which exists in the hearts of the young; poetry is to him what song is to the bird—the necessity, the law, and the joy of his being, in which he finds both expression and relief, without knowing precisely how or why.

In the verses of [his adolescence], when, broken with sorrow, he merges thoughts and passions together, do we for the first time begin to see traces of the poet's conscious art; while it is only [his adult verses] that are perfect both in form and spirit, both in artistic expression and intellectual origin. But apart from their comparative artistic value, the secret of the difference between his early and his later poems consists in their relation to himself. Though the master-thought of each period is the anguish that lies for the loving in the union of truth and falsehood, of real passion and passing fancy, of earnest devotion and light intrigue, yet *Don Paez, Les Marrons du Feu,* and *La Coupe et les Lèvres,* have a very different and inferior value, as revelations of the author's own mind, from *Les Nuits, L'Espoir en Dieu,* and other smaller pieces. In the first it is a dramatist who arranges his actors—skilfully and beautifully enough; but they are none the less actors for all their velvet drapery and jewelled robes; they talk but as they are bidden, and move through the scene as expositors, not originators: in the second it is the author himself who speaks—the man—the initiated—with the brand of fire on his own brow, and the bitter cup at his own lips. In the first he discourses of human life as he sees it, as he hears of it from others, watches and analyses it for himself; in the second he speaks of passion as he has felt it, of the anguish under which he himself has writhed, of the cross beneath which he has fallen. The long sad cry for TRUTH— truth in the innermost, truth in the lightest things of humanity— which sounds through his writings, takes a far deeper significance as years go on. . . . (p. 106)

[Let] us examine his pieces individually. . . . [In *Don Paez* there] are passages of marvellous force and beauty . . . ; there is a sentiment of life, a movement, a power, a passion in it, not surpassed by any of his later works. If it has the faults of youth in its immaturity and false taste, it has also its luxuriance, its richness and its sweeping flow, its prodigality of power, and the gorgeous generosity of its genius. (p. 107)

La Coupe et les Lèvres [is a] revolting but still most pitiable page of mental history; where, through all the blue light of the false melodramatic glare flung over it, we see the same figure we have met with in de Musset's other pieces, kneeling in the desert made by his own passions, asking vainly enlightenment and guidance of the God he has denied; we hear again the same bitter mockery of humanity with the same consciousness of a higher nature within, the same abhorrence of the littleness and falseness of the world, with the same perception of the holy ultimate destinies of man. It is the old mournful drama of the soul which many a thinking mind has lived through, and which stands embodied in its distinct division of nature as Faust and Mephistopheles—the weaker man desiring good and knowledge, and the mocking fiend snatching both from his grasp. . . .

Suzon is untranslateable. Ghastly, ghostlike, unnatural, it is a blot on the pages of the book; and its only fit recognition would be, total erasure from all future editions. *La Saule* is the fragment of a romance, with pure and tender bits scattered through it. But the name of 'miss Smolen' is in unfortunate contradiction to the tragic feeling, for English readers. The gem of the first volume, however, is *Les Voeux Stériles;* a mourning gem indeed, but with the lines cut clearly and sharply. It breathes throughout that painful weariness of the present order of things, that longing for a more definite creed than the restless scepticism of the age affords, and that sentiment of disquiet which all generations have felt when the old gods are falling from their altars and the temples of the new are not yet consecrated. And in what does his knowledge of humanity end?—in contempt; in contempt of all, but chiefly of himself. (p. 109)

De Musset was saved from the worst phase of that dreary [French] school of moral scepticism by the germ of true poetry which never died within him. As a man of modern society he believed in social corruption; as a poet he felt the truth of human regeneration. He saw the evils about him clearly enough, and knew them for evils; but he believed in the possibility of man's redemption, while accepting these evils as the present and undoubted conditions of society. But this war between his spiritual perceptions and intellectual convictions did not help him to a truer knowledge of human life.

He was true, though, in some of his denunciations. In that eloquent burst, beginning 'Grèce, ô mère des arts!' [Greece, o mother of the arts!], who does not feel with him how the art and glory and poetry of the past have in truth passed away from the present, leaving us too literally an age 'where the artist is a tradesman and art a trade?' (p. 110)

[*Les Nuits*] are among the most remarkable poems he has written. (p. 111)

It is in *Les Nuits* that we first see what manner of man de Musset really was: hitherto he has been a boy, with beautiful thoughts sadly mingled with unlovely ones; now he is a man, whose chief attribute of mental manhood is knowledge of humanity, and pity for its failings. (p. 113)

> *E. L. [Eliza Lynn Linton], ''Alfred de Musset,'' in* Fraser's Magazine, *Vol. LVI, No. CCCXXXI, July, 1857, pp. 106-13.*

CHARLES BAUDELAIRE   (letter date 1860)

[*Baudelaire is considered one of France's greatest poets. Though best known for his masterpiece,* The Flowers of Evil, *Baudelaire is also considered an insightful and influential critic. His criticism reflects his belief that both poetry and art should serve only to inspire and express beauty. In the following excerpt, Baudelaire displays his displeasure with Musset's ''incapacity to understand the work through which a reverie becomes a work of art.''*]

Except at the age of one's first communion, in other words at the age when everything having to do with prostitutes and silken ladders produces a religious effect, I have never been able to endure [Musset,] that *paragon of lady-killers*, his spoiled child's impudence, invoking heaven and hell about hotel room adventures, his muddy torrent of mistakes in grammar and prosody, and finally his utter incapacity to understand the work through which a reverie becomes a work of art. Someday you will find that you are enthusiastic only about perfection and you will scorn all those effusions of ignorance. I ask your pardon for speaking so sharply about certain things; incoherence, banality and carelessness have always caused me an irritation that is perhaps too acute.

> *Charles Baudelaire, in an extract from a letter to Armand Fraisse on February 18, 1860 in his* Baudelaire As a Literary Critic, *edited and translated by Lois Boe Hyslop and Francis E. Hyslop, Jr., The Pennsylvania State University Press, University Park, 1964, p. 7.*

[J. A. SYMONDS]   (essay date 1868)

[Sometimes] there arises a true poet, a real singer, in France, uniting the force and fire of Northern passion with French subtlety and logical precision. One of these was Alfred de Musset. . . . His language exactly embodies the thoughts and feelings which he wishes to express. It is never redundant or defective, never inverted like Tennyson's, or obscure like Browning's, or melodiously meaningless like much of Swinburne's. The good and bad things of the mind are shown through its thin veil with equal clearness, and there is no conscious effort to restrain the truth. Delicate shades of meaning and subtle emotions are reflected with such fulness in his verse that we seem to come into direct contact with the living spirit of the writer. At the same time, De Musset knows when to stop,— when to rein in the steed of fancy, and to check the flow of metaphor. He is never extravagant or spasmodic in expression. While reasoning on the deep problems of humanity, he avoids becoming oracular; and while abandoning himself to anguish, he maintains a perfect equability of utterance, evincing true artistic mastery. In these respects he is essentially a French poet,—logical, precise, obedient to law. Again, he has the power of expressing what by its nature is vague in feeling. Thoughts to which music alone seems capable of giving utterance are not distorted or exaggerated in his words. These eulogies are chiefly applicable to his lyrical poetry. In his prose works and dramatic sketches we find a far greater intemperance of language, spasmodic exaggeration, improbability, and extravagance of every kind, than can be paralleled by any equally artistic productions of the English Muse. (p. 287)

[De Musset] does not lose himself in his subject, or catalogue its details with minute fidelity. He looks inward, copying the image stamped on the soul's retina, selecting the most prominent points, and representing them with reference to his own state of feeling. His picture is a piece of man, and all the man within us thrills while gazing on it. The touches are as few and delicate as possible. Emotion, and not description, predominates. Shelley's ''Lines written in Dejection at Naples'' fairly represent De Musset's mode of treating nature. He does not, as in the ''Ode to the West Wind,'' seize some passionate idea, and carry it through all its phases, building up a fugue of gorgeous images and swift-winged thoughts, eddying about the central subject, departing from it and returning, pouring in fresh lights, and leading the mind through labyrinths of suggestion and association. There is no such redundancy of imagination in De Musset. Again, in verisimilitude he falls far below the English poets. His stories are improbable. His characters are not like life. There is a want of coherency, and a flimsiness about his conceptions of human action, which betray national levity and defective dramatic power. . . . Of his other faults it would not be difficult to make a long list, prominent in which must stand vanity, flippancy, and a sentimental sort of sensuality. Against these we have to set reverence, tenderness, love, and the aspirations of a spirit seeking in vain for satisfaction. (pp. 288-89)

His style must be studied before it can be fully appreciated. Its beauty depends upon a limpid purity of language and exquisiteness of expression which cannot well be analysed. But great interest, independent of its form, attaches to his poetry, as the articulate cry of a man who suffered much during a period of transition, and who truly felt whatever he expressed in words. Like Rousseau, like George Sand, like other French writers of the highest eminence, De Musset is greatest—is indeed only truly great—when he records his own emotions. The main topics, which, viewed in this light, his works suggest, are the scepticism and the aimless want of interest in life experienced by Frenchmen during the first half of this century, the Nemesis of Faith and the Nemesis of Love which brought De Musset to despair, moral corruption resulting from social anarchy and intellectual hopelessness; in all, a sorry picture, rendered tolerable by the strength and sweetness of the poet who had fallen on such disjointed days. (p. 289)

[De Musset] had the rare gift, for a French poet, of feeling nature and of expressing it, a concrete force of imagination hitherto almost unknown in the literature of his nation. He had the rare gift, for an English poet, of expressing a subtle feeling vividly and with simplicity, and the sincerity of absolute unaffectedness. He performed the task, which all true poets ought to undertake, of representing his own age. But he had not either intellectual power or moral dignity enough to lead it and inaugurate a new period. . . .

No poet sets more nakedly side by side the clay and spirit of our double nature, filth and refinement, blasphemy and veneration. No one displays wisdom and folly, pain and pleasure, purity and foulness, in more extreme antagonism. No one wishes more and wills so little. No one is less philosophical and more anarchical than Alfred de Musset. (p. 312)

> *[J. A. Symonds], "Alfred de Musset," in* The North British Review, *Vol. XLIX, No. XCVIII, December, 1868, pp. 287-312.*

WESTMINSTER AND FOREIGN QUARTERLY REVIEW (essay date 1869)

No one can help being reminded of Shelley in reading much of De Musset's poetry, written between twenty and thirty; the opening of **"Rolla,"** and **"L'espoir en Dieu,"** for example. The poignant sympathy with human suffering and wrong, the anguish of doubt, and deep desire for faith—there is none of this in all Byron. . . . [De Musset] saw deeper than Shelley in that he did not confound the erring human conception of God with God himself, and accuse the Creator for the shortcoming of the creature. (p. 415)

De Musset's writings from the age of twenty to twenty-three have all the genius of his later ones, though they abound in crudities and excesses, which gradually disappear, until at twenty-five there is almost no trace of them. Then an influence passed over him, which may have scathed and blasted his life, but which undoubtedly brought his genius to sudden and wonderful maturity. His boyish fancies were succeeded by a real and great passion, which called out all the strength of his nature. . . . [His love's] track lies across his writings, dividing what went before from what came after; the end was disillusion and bitter disappointment. He has given us the picture of two men who attempt to sound the depths of evil, intending, when they had wallowed enough, to return to good in Lorenzaccio and the hero of **"La Coupe et les Lèvres."** The moral is to be found in Lorenzaccio's confession to the virtuous Philip Strozzi, and in these words of Frank's: . . .

> Woe, woe to him who suffers vice to write
> The earliest word upon his virgin heart!
> Man's heart is like a deeply hollowed vase,
> If the first drop that falls therein be foul,
> The sea itself could not wash out the stains,
> So deep the vase, deepest of all the stain.

This is, on the whole, the sum of De Musset's experience and the moral of his life. (pp. 416-17)

The series entitled **"Les Nuits,"** . . . with his exquisite **"Souvenir,"** most resemble Lamartine . . . ; they have more strength and simplicity than Lamartine, and if they do not quite equal his sweetness and smoothness are wholly free from his occasional mawkishness. De Musset's wit and pith sometimes cause his intense feeling to be forgotten; but we know of nothing, in French poetry at least, to equal his pathos and passion—nothing which surpasses the profound sentiments of some of his shorter pieces. (p. 417)

One involuntarily compares the sentiment of all modern French poets with Lamartine, and De Musset gains by the comparison; his sentiment is less wordy and deeper. There is a certain carelessness of rhyme and rhythm in his verses, especially the earlier ones, a relic of his youthful impatience of the mellifluous harmonies of the Romantic school; but through it all we see a real master of versification, and in his maturer productions it vanishes entirely save when used for a purpose. No poet ever had his Pegasus more thoroughly in hand; he is not afraid to give him rein and let him soar, but he can check and curb him, bring him to earth at will, throw him on his haunches, or wheel him short round, spur him through thickets and torrents, and lift him lightly over any obstacle.

De Musset's charming little comedies, called **"Proverbes,"** . . . are like bits of the lives of those delightful people who throw a veil of grace and tact over our common humanity without hiding it. . . . It is difficult to cite any portion of these **"Proverbes"** without destroying its effect; each is a pearl, perfect only as a whole. **"Fantasio"** is the most sparkling. . . . (pp. 417-18)

But **"On ne badine pas avec l'amour"** carries off the palm in our opinion; it would be an exquisite specimen of genteel comedy but for the thrilling tragic tones of the last scene, which, together with the human interest of the whole play, raise it to a higher place. De Musset's attempts at real tragedy are considered failures; . . . yet among his posthumous works there is a striking fragment on the story of "Fredegonde," called **"La Servante du Roi,"** and notwithstanding the want of dramatic unity in **"Lorenzaccio,"** a historical drama on Alexander de Medicis, and its manifest inappropriateness for the theatre, it contains passages of so much power that one cannot but believe the man who wrote them to have been capable of producing a fine tragedy. (p. 419)

[De Musset was] pre-eminently successful in adapting what one may call the atmosphere of his compositions to the subject, and producing effects by a single stroke of description like a clever painter; he always has the local colouring of his theme. Some of his poems are as breezy as a spring morning, others as languid as an Indian summer afternoon. He had a happy hand at imitation, and has followed Bocaccio in two metrical tales, **"Simone,"** and **"Sylvia,"** of which the smooth and simple diction recalls Lafontaine. This versatility seems to arise from his artistic temperament, and is to be found in his prose, which some people affect to like better than his poetry. His style is, indeed, remarkable for its ease and point, and at times for its nervous power. There is great keenness and delicacy in his art-criticisms, though they are disfigured now and then by a touch of exaggeration, sometimes almost melodramatic, which does not accord with either the style or the subject. Very few Frenchmen of the present day escape sensationalism, but it is singular that where there are so few faults of taste as in De Musset's mature writings, there should be any. However, there is but little room for fault-finding in either the manner or matter of his criticisms, and his ideas upon art are remarkably just and true. (p. 424)

The essays on modern [literary] style in the sensible and humorous **"Lettres de Dupuis Cotonet,"** scarcely apply to the literature of the last ten years. . . . Radical as he was in opinion, in questions of form he was conservative. His writings are full of reflections on the bad taste of recent times, the degeneracy of the stage, the low tone of the press, the exaggerated and unmeaning praise which has superseded criticism, the loss of elegance, refinement, and distinction in society. In some respects he belonged to a bygone age. (pp. 424-25)

De Musset's so-called novel, **"La Confession d'un Enfant du Siècle,"** is rather a monody than a story; it opens with a chapter . . . of wonderful force and effect—a sort of battle symphony, rising to sublime bursts. The whole book abounds in passages of the greatest eloquence and beauty, in pithy and pregnant sentences which condense great observation and knowledge of human nature, in chapters which are perfect poems of fancy and tenderness, and interrupt the dreary chant of the narrative like strains of soft music; but as a work of art it is incomplete and incoherent, and as the unveiling of a heart, a terrible revelation.

From time to time he published a number of short stories or sketches, which have been collected under the title of **"Contes et Nouvelles."** They all have his charm of style, and are strewn with gems of poetry; for like Midas of the golden touch, wherever his hand has passed we see the shining trace, and these are written with grace and vivacity, but as a class have less merit than any of his other productions. There is one delicious little satire, called **"Le merle blanc,"** which stands alone among them. . . . There are two striking portraits of grisettes in the collection, Mimi Penson and Bernerette, and several other pretty studies of female heads; but it is not in depicting women that we think De Musset excels. His men have more individuality, and there is more variety among them. We may detect a little of the author in them all; but he was many-sided enough to create a long procession of heroes all bearing marks of their paternity, yet all differing from each other. The women are nearly all of the same type, notwithstanding superficial differences; the outlines are graceful and characteristic, especially in his portraits of young girls, such as Laurette in **"Une nuit Venitienne,"** the self-willed heroine of **"Il ne faut jurer de rien,"** and Camille in **"On ne badine pas avec l'amour,"** who is far beyond the rest. The married women are charming creatures—refined, amiable, irrational, amusing, frivolous, bird-witted, with an irresistible perfume of high breeding about them; one could fall in love with any of them; but they are so much alike that one wanders from Madame de Léry to the Comtesse de Vernon, and on to the Marchioness in **"Il faut qu'une porte soit ouverte ou fermée,"** unable to choose. . . . De Musset has attempted to vary his type of woman in Barberine the merry and wise, the honest and true, in Bettine, and the Marchioness del Cibo in **"Lorenzaccio"**—a fine outline; but there are none of them so finished and real as his fine ladies. Throughout his works, however, especially in his poetry, there is a latent aspiration towards a different kind of ideal, a different companionship from any to which all these bear witness. (pp. 425-26)

For seven years before [De Musset's] death there is hardly a poem, play, or even fragment of prose, bearing the name of that fertile talent which for twenty years had charmed the world with such multitudinous and varied proofs of power. His inspiration deserted him; he lost the faculty of writing; and if we compare the few utterances of this gloomy era with those of former days, the change is lamentably apparent. The unfortunate poet knew better than any one that his power was gone. . . . (p. 428)

Of all the names in modern literature, there is none which wakes such melancholy echoes as that of Alfred de Musset. Keats, Chatterton, Hégesippe Moreau, Henri Mürger, and many others are quoted as tragic instances of early promise broken with the cord of life strained too far; but here is a far sadder sight—a promise more than half fulfilled, a life touching its meridian, genius which claims no indulgence on the score of immaturity. Yet what remains? Only incompleteness; a sword snapped and flung away before the fight was over; a noble temple, still unfinished, falling into ruin. (p. 429)

"Alfred de Musset," in Westminster and Foreign Quarterly Review, *n.s. Vol. XXV, No. II, April 1, 1869, pp. 410-29.*

[MARGARET OLIPHANT]   (essay date 1876)

To many a reader who has felt in all other cases the bondage of the French rhythm, with its rigid, artificial laws, to be an oppression and tedium insupportable, De Musset has been the one singer whose natural command of melodious and varied expression has made the national form of art endurable. He has triumphed over those rigours and monotonies by the force of genuine life in him, not always lofty, but yet real—by the passion, by the vitality, the quiver and thrill of feeling which moves himself in every pulse, more than and before it moves his audience. His power is not, like the gay and delightful genius of Beranger, capable of throwing itself abroad upon the world, and lighting up the whole face of the country with expression and meaning. The France, the *siècle* [century] of De Musset is within himself. What he is able to expound in verse is not the fresh and varied episodes of the national life, the loves and sorrows of his race, but only that struggle between passion and reason in his own bosom, that perpetual and conflicting ferment of wishes and thoughts—the one eager, wild, and irrestrainable, the other melancholy, fastidious, and unbelieving—of which he is always conscious, which scarcely intermits for a moment, which brings disgust close upon the heels of pleasure, and mingles the sentiment, which in his vocabulary is entitled love, with sudden loathings still more passionate than itself. It is this which gives intensity and reality to his work. . . . (p. 362)

His first boyish publication [*Contes d'Espagne et d'Italie*], brought out when he was but eighteen, contains little but tales of intrigue after the worst Byronic model—Byron diluted with Lamartine, the most sickly compound possible. But after this, the most singular change appears all at once in the young poet—a change unperceived or unappreciated by his contemporaries, but as remarkable now to the thoughtful reader as any symptom of mental convulsion could be. In the midst of those old complacent echoes of cynicism and vice, which all his audience were ready to applaud to the echo, and in which the sweetest boy, like an infant taught to blaspheme, rolling big oaths out of its rosy mouth in delightful uncomprehension, was ready to out-do all competitors,—there suddenly rang out a deeper note—a tragic tone, undreamed of before by either singer or hearers. If here and there some one who listened was startled by it, or if he himself was aware of the rare thing he was doing, who can tell? But certainly the Sainte-Beuves remained calmly unaware, not perceiving that between the brilliant verses of **"Namouna"** and the tragic, almost prophetic solemnity of **"Rolla,"** there lay a gulf wide enough to appal the observer. What produced this sudden outburst of new perception, new meaning, enlightenment so tragic and terrible, we have no way of knowing. (p. 367)

The strange crude drama called "**La Coupe et les Lèvres**" gives the first sombre sign of the rising feeling. But it is in the poem called "**Rolla**" that the poet bursts upon us in all the passion of this new and strange strength. Few efforts of genius so startling, so hideous, so beautiful, have ever been made. Another world seems suddenly to have revealed itself in which the cynic has no longer a place, but where some stern despairing angel, himself fallen yet pitiful, above the shrinkings of human feeling, ventures to combine the most hostile elements, and make a desperate sally in favour of innocence and purity from the very stronghold, and with the very arms, of vice. . . . It would seem to be only a stronger representation than usual of that hideous travesty of love which is the leading principle of debauch, at which De Musset aims; but what tragic suggestions of life made worthless, of needless and unprofitable destruction, of ruin, debasement, and despair, open up around the central idea! The poem is . . . woven through and through with the images of impurity and the agitations of vice, and the chief situation is [revolting]. . . . (pp. 367-68)

The description of [the unconscious Marie], wrapt in profound and childlike slumber, would be one of the most beautiful examples of French poetry could it be detached from its surroundings; but it is these surroundings which give it its sinister and terrible power. The contrast of the vile circumstances around with that calm, that youth, that human flower, to which still all kinds of lovely blossomings are possible, though the deepest pollution is close at hand, surround the scene with tragic and sombre shadows,—to be heightened and deepened by the entrance of the other life, breathing nothing but vigour and vitality, but with death close at hand, and ruin reigning in heart and soul. We turn with a shudder from the appalling picture, which no manipulation could make fit to be regarded by innocent eyes, but which yet is, we think, the most powerful, as it certainly is the most tragical, of all De Musset's productions. Nowhere has he struck so high yet so deep a note, and shown so profound a perception of that last sting and poignant climax of debasement, the possibility of moral salvation, the sense of what might have been. (pp. 368-69)

[Unfortunately] this deeper note, though it still echoes here and there in an undertone, found no such lasting place in De Musset's poetry as '**Rolla**' promised. (p. 369)

[Notwithstanding] an occasional gleam of genius, the prose works of De Musset are entirely unworthy of his reputation. There is nothing in them of the refined grace of his '**Proverbes**,' nor of the profound feeling which sometimes reaches a tragic depth in the higher efforts of his poetry. All the dignity of true genius, the balance which intellectual power must confer more or less, steadying the most uneven march, and giving a certain force and weight to the most fantastic imagination, is lost in the maunderings of a weak self-analysis, or in the flippant '**Contes**.' . . . The mournful poet, he who even in his youth could be caught by the stern prophet-inspiration which almost justifies the horrors of '**Rolla**'—the graceful dramatist, full of airy and delightful fancy, yet not without a capability of heroic perception—are lost in the white-gloved exquisite [dandy]. . . . (pp. 371-72)

The dramas upon which a great part of [De Musset's] reputation depends belong almost entirely to [the period of suffering and labour following his break with George Sand]. With the exception of a pretty trifle, too much applauded by his contemporaries, called, '**À quoi rêvent les jeunés filles**,' and of the tragic sketch called '**La Coupe et les Lèvres**,' already referred to, all his best dramatic works were produced in the eventful

years, traversed by so many joys and agonies, between 1833 and 1840. We may leave without notice the somewhat heavy 'Louison' and 'Carmosino,' and some of the slighter sketches; the 'Caprice,' though it became a favourite of the public; the bit of drawing-room romance called '**Il faut qu'une porte soit ouverte ou fermée**,' the '**Nuit Venetienne**,' and one or two others. But the remaining comedies are at once so graceful and full of life, and on French soil so original and independent in conception, that they are equally interesting to the critic and to the reader, to whom this '**Spectacle dans un fauteuil**' will, we promise, afford a pleasure more refined and varied than most spectacles produce. The most admirable are those which were written during the very crisis of his personal grief. . . . The ease and lightness of touch, the refined and animated dialogue, the tone of perfectly good society and manners, without exaggeration or extravagance, are apt at the first glance to conceal from the reader the real depth and dramatic power of these works. . . . De Musset has struck out for himself an independent path [in both] plot and subject. He is a daring rebel against those primary laws of the drama which require regular construction and a definite end. Those broken lights of life, those episodes that come to nothing, those breakings off so common in actual existence, which may be worked out in sentimental fiction, but are generally supposed quite unsuitable to the stage, are his favourite inspirations. He seems to take a pleasure in demonstrating exactly by that manner of art which is most opposed to such treatment, the fantastic irregularity of human affairs, the gleams of capricious meaning, the suggestions which are so often more interesting, more moving, than anything which is fully carried out. For example, what can exceed the daring which could throw into dramatic form, or present on the stage, the strange, wild scintillation of fancy called '**Fantasio**'—fantastic a thousand times, a mere sport of the imagination, a nothing leading to nothing yet full of wayward power, and that half-sad, half-mad play with the mystery of life which has so great an attraction for those who can understand it? (pp. 374-76)

['**Fantasio**" is] the slightest of sketches, not noticed even by the critics; but full of those semitones of meaning, those fleeting shades of feeling, as rapid as the shadows on the hills, and that pensive sport of the spectator with mysterious life, which are among the most subtle charms of art. More or less, this favourite strain of fancy is in everything De Musset does, even when his dramatic work is more formal and *selon les règles* [according to the rules]. The sudden chances which tantalise men, the failures of happiness with which we are all familiar—not brought about by any tragic accident or misfortune, but by the perversity of human hearts, the caprices of fancy—are the subjects which he most loves. (p. 377)

'**On ne badine pas avec l'amour**' is perhaps the most striking of the '**Proverbes**,' and it is manageable upon the stage, which is not the case with all. . . . The story is nothing but caprice all through, lightly begun, but rising in intensity till it comes to a high climax of tragic suggestion. (pp. 377-78)

Nowhere else, except in the tragic essay of '**Rolla**,' has De Musset touched so high a chord. The play is far from being faultless; and we cannot say that the mixture of fun and buffoonery, though evidently an attempt to follow Shakespearian models and relieve the more serious strain of the story, is at all a successful one. . . . But nothing could be more delicate, more subtle, and by times more powerful than the struggle between the two lovers; or rather, indeed, between love itself and all those fanciful disquiets, impatiences, quick risings of pride, jealousy, and offence, all visionary, and put in with the lightest, firmest outline—which threaten its very existence. All, or almost all, might have happened in the soberest household; and yet how dramatic, how tragic, is the tale! An art more exquisite could not be imagined; it is the quintessence of refined fancy and observation, added to a knowledge of those unsuspected depths which lie beneath the smoothest, simple surface of inexperience and ignorance which is rarer still. . . .

The most ambitious effort De Musset has made, however, is in '**Lorenzaccio.**' . . . The feebleness of an incoherent plot, and the purely literary, not dramatic, character of the work, are its great disadvantages. . . . ['**Lorenzaccio**'] contains several characters elaborately sketched out, as if intended for an important *rôle*, who drop here and there, and are seen no more—a curious fault of construction, which looks more like the lapsed memory of inexperience than the error of a well-trained workman. But the figure of Lorenzo himself is full of interest. Had the conception been fully carried out, French poetry might have been enriched with a new heroic type worthy to stand on something of the same footing as Hamlet and Faust; but the lines are faint in many places, the outline imperfectly kept; and dropping from the fatigued hand of his creator, the patriot-debauchee falls by times into the vileness he feigns, and loses his power. (p. 380)

[Margaret Oliphant], ''*Alfred de Musset*,'' in Blackwood's Edinburgh Magazine, *Vol. CXX, No. DCCXXXI, September, 1876, pp. 361-82.*

HENRY JAMES, JR. (essay date 1878)

[*James was an American-born British novelist, short story writer, critic, essayist, and playwright of the late nineteenth and early twentieth centuries who is considered to be one of the greatest novelists in the English language. Although best known for his novels, James is also admired as a lucid and insightful critic. His appreciative essay, excerpted below, is considered to be the most insightful nineteenth-century discussion of Musset's poetry. James ranks Musset as ''one of the first poets of our day.'' In James's opinion, ''Rolla,'' ''Nuit de mai,'' ''Nuit d'août,'' ''Nuit d'octobre,'' ''Lettre à Lamartine,'' and ''Stances à la Malibran'' represent the poet's best work, and most modern critics concur with this estimation. What distinguishes these works, according to James, is their youthfulness, passion, and personal tone. Although he faults Musset's carelessness with form, James asserts that the poet's ''exquisite feeling'' and ''ineffable natural grace'' overshadow his weaknesses: ''His grace is often something divine; it is in his grace that we must look for his style.''*]

During his stay in Italy [Alfred de Musset] had written nothing; but the five years which followed his return are those of his most active and brilliant productiveness. The finest of his verses, the most charming of his tales, the most original of his comedies, belong to this relatively busy period. Everything that he wrote at this time has a depth and intensity that distinguish it from the jocosely sentimental productions of his commencement and from the somewhat mannered and vapidly elegant compositions which he put forth, at wide intervals, during the last fifteen years of his life. This was the period of Musset's intellectual virility. He was very precocious, but he was at the same time, at first, very youthful. On the other hand, his decline began early; in most of his later things, especially in his verses (they become very few in number) the inspiration visibly runs thin. 'Mon verre n'est pas grand, mais je bois dans mon verre'' [My glass isn't large, but I drink from my glass], he had said, and both clauses of the sentence are true. His

glass held but a small quantity; the best of his verses—those that one knows by heart and never wearies of repeating—are very soon counted. We have named them when we have mentioned ''**Rolla**,'' the ''**Nuit de Mai**,'' the ''**Nuit d'Août**,'' and the ''**Nuit d'Octobre**''; the ''**Lettre à Lamartine**,'' and the ''**Stances à la Malibran**.'' These, however, are perfection; and if Musset had written nothing else he would have had a right to say that it was from his own glass that he drank. (pp. 21-2)

He was beyond question one of the first poets of our day. If the poetic force is measured by the *quality* of the inspiration—by its purity, intensity, and closely personal savour—Alfred de Musset's place is surely very high. He was, so to speak, a thoroughly *personal* poet. He was not the poet of nature, of the universe, of reflection, of morality, of history; he was the poet simply of a certain order of personal emotions, and his charm is in the frankness and freedom, the grace and harmony, with which he expresses these emotions. The affairs of the heart—these were his province; in no other verses has the heart spoken more characteristically. (pp. 23-4)

Half the beauty of Musset's writing is its simple suggestion of youthfulness—of something fresh and fair, slim and tremulous, with a tender epidermis. This quality, with some readers may seem to deprive him of a certain proper dignity; and it is very true that he was not a Stoic. You may even call him unmanly. He cries out when he is hurt; he resorts frequently to tears, and he talks much about his tears. . . . But his defence is that if he does not bear things like a man, he at least, according to Shakespeare's distinction, feels them like a man. What makes him valuable is just this gift for the expression of that sort of emotion which the conventions and proprieties of life, the dryness of ordinary utterance, the stiffness of most imaginations, leave quite in the vague, and yet which forms a part of human nature important enough to have its exponent. If the presumption is against the dignity of deeply lyric utterance, poor Musset is, in the vulgar phrase, nowhere—he is a mere grotesque sound of lamentation. But if in judging him you do not stint your sympathy, you will presently perceive him to have an extraordinarily precious quality—a quality equally rare in literature and in life. He has passion. There is in most poetry a great deal of reflection, of wisdom, of grace, of art, of genius; but (especially in English poetry) there is little of this peculiar property of Musset's. When it occurs we feel it to be extremely valuable; it touches us beyond anything else. It was the great gift of Byron, the quality by which he will live in spite of those weaknesses and imperfections which may be pointed out by the dozen. Alfred de Musset in this respect resembled the poet whom he appears most to have admired. . . . Musset resembles Byron in the fact that the beauty of his verse is somehow identical with the feeling of the writer—with his immediate, sensible warmth—and not dependent upon that reflective stage into which, to produce its great effects, most English poetic expression instantly passes, and which seems to chill even while it nobly beautifies. (pp. 24-6)

If people care supremely for form, Musset will merely but half satisfy them. [His poetry] is very pretty, they will say; but it is confoundedly unbusinesslike. His verse is not chiselled and pondered, and in spite of an ineffable natural grace it lacks the positive qualities of cunning workmanship—those qualities which are found in such high perfection in Théophile Gautier. To our own sense Musset's exquisite feeling more than makes up for one-half the absence of ''chiselling,'' and [his] ineffable grace . . . makes up for the other half. His sweetness of passion, of which the poets who have succeeded him have so little, is a more precious property than their superior science. His grace is often something divine; it is in his grace that we must look for his style. . . . His harmony, from the first, was often admirable; the rhythm of even some of his earliest verses makes them haunt the ear after one has murmured them aloud. (p. 28)

Musset's grace, in its suavity, freedom, and unaffectedness, is altogether peculiar; though it must be said that it is only in the poems of his middle period that it is at its best. . . . [With] his youth Musset's inspiration failed him. It failed him in his prose as well as in his verse. **"Il faut qu'une Porte soit ouverte ou fermée,"** one of the last of his dramatic proverbs, is very charming, very perfect in its way; but compared with the tone of the **"Caprices de Marianne,"** the **"Chandelier," "Fantasio,"** the sentiment is thin and the style has rather a simper. It is what the French call *marivaudage.* There can, however, be no better example of the absoluteness of the poetic sentiment, of its justifying itself as it goes, of lyrical expression being as it were not only a means, but an end, than the irresistible beauty of such effusions as the **"Lettre à Lamartine"** and the **"Nuit d'Août."**

> Poëte, je t'écris pour te dire que j'aime!
> [Poet, I write to tell you that I love!]

—that is all, literally, that Musset has to say to the "amant d'Elvire" [loving Elvire]; and it would be easy to make merry at the expense of so simply candid a piece of "gush." But the confidence is made with a transparent ardour, a sublime good faith, an audible, touching tremour of voice, which, added to the enchanting harmony of the verse, make the thing one of the most splendid poems of our day. . . . [Musset] has, in strictness, only one idea—the idea that the passion of love and the act of loving are the divinest things in a miserable world; that love has a thousand disappointments, deceptions, and pangs, but that for its sake they are all worth enduring. . . . Sometimes he expresses this idea in the simple epicurean fashion, with gaiety and with a more or less cynical indifference to the moral side of the divine passion. Then he is often pretty, picturesque, fanciful, but he remains essentially light. At other times he feels its relation to the other things that make up man's destiny, and the sense of aspiration mingles with the sense of enjoyment or of regret. Then he is at his best; then he seems an image of universally sentient youth. (pp. 29-30)

[The **"Lettre à Lamartine"** is] Musset's highest flight, but the **"Nuit de Mai"** is almost as fine a poem—full of imaginative splendour and melancholy ecstasy. The series of the **"Nuits"** is altogether superb; with an exception made, perhaps, for the **"Nuit de Décembre,"** which has a great deal of sombre beauty, but which is not, like the others, in the form of dialogue between the Muse and the poet. . . . (p. 32)

[The famous passage about the pelican in **"Nuit de Mai"**] is perhaps—unless we except the opening verses of **"Rolla"**—Musset's noblest piece of poetic writing. We must place next to it—next to the three **"Nuits"**—the admirably passionate and genuine **"Stanzas to Malibran"**—a beautiful characterization of the artistic disinterestedness of the singer who suffered her genius to consume her—who sang herself to death. The closing verses of the poem have a wonderful purity; to rise so high, and yet in form, in accent, to remain so still and temperate, belongs only to great poetry. . . . (pp. 33-4)

It is true that the drama with Musset has a decidedly lyrical element, and that though his persons always talk prose, they are constantly saying things which would need very little help

to fall into the mould of a stanza or a sonnet. In his dramas as in his verses his weakness is that he is amateurish; they lack construction; their merit is not in their plots, but in what, for want of a better term, we may call their sentimental perfume. If feeling is the great quality in his verses, the case is the same in his strange, fantastic, exquisite little *comédies;* comedies in the literal English sense of the word we can hardly call them, for they have almost always a melancholy or a tragical termination. They are thoroughly sentimental; he puts before us people who convince us that they really feel; the drama is simply the history of their feeling. . . . But the great charm is Musset's dramatic world itself, the atmosphere in which his figures move, the element they breathe.

It seems at first a reckless thing to say, but we will risk it: in the *quality* of his fancy Musset always reminds us of Shakespeare. His little dramas go forward in the country of "As You Like It" and the "Winter's Tale"; the author is at home there, like Shakespeare himself, and he moves with something of the Shakespearean lightness and freedom. His fancy loves to play with human life, and in the tiny mirror that it holds up we find something of the depth and mystery of the object. Musset's dialogue, in its mingled gaiety and melancholy, its sweetness and irony, its allusions to real things and its kinship with a romantic world, has an altogether indefinable magic. To utter it on the stage is almost to make it coarse. Once Musset attempted a larger theme than usual; in **"Lorenzaccio"** he wrote an historical drama on the scale of Shakespeare's histories; that is, with multitudes of figures, scenes, incidents, illustrations. . . . The play shows an extraordinary abundance and vivacity of imagination, and really, out of those same "histories" of Shakespeare, it is hard to see where one should find an equal spontaneity in dealing with the whole human furniture of a period. Alfred de Musset, in **"Lorenzaccio,"** has the air of being as ready to handle a hundred figures as a dozen—of having imagination enough for them all. The thing has the real creative inspiration, and if it is not the most perfect of his productions it is probably the most vigorous. (pp. 34-6)

Alfred de Musset's superfine organization, his exaltations and weaknesses, his pangs and tears, his passions and debaucheries, his intemperance and idleness, his years of unproductiveness, his innumerable mistresses (with whatever pangs and miseries it may seem proper to attribute to *them*) his quarrel with a woman of genius, and the scandals, exposures, and recriminations that are so ungracefully bound up with it—all this was necessary in order that we should have the two or three little volumes into which his *best* could be compressed. It takes certainly a great deal of life to make a little art! In this case, however, we must remember, that little is exquisite. (pp. 37-8)

> *Henry James, Jr., "Alfred de Musset," in his* French Poets and Novelists, *Macmillan and Co., London, 1878, pp. 1-38.*

JOSEPH KNIGHT   (essay date 1879)

[*The following essay originally appeared in* The Nation and The Athenaeum, *June 14, 1879.*]

[The dramatic works of Musset] stand by themselves, and have a charm which is wholly their own. Written in a spirit of cynicism which recalls Heine, they have a sadness deeper, because more human, than the gloom of the great German lyrist, while in imagination they stand before all contemporary work. **"Les Caprices de Marianne"** is a combination of qualities one might almost believe irreconcilable. In vividness of description and in colour it is like a tale of Boccaccio; in the way it blends what is real with what is fantastic it shows the influence of Shakespeare. Its action passes in Naples, and the life of mediaeval Italy is depicted with a fidelity that brings each detail before the eyes, yet the scene is in other respects as imaginary as the forest of Arden. It is possible to fancy that the whole is inspired by "Romeo and Juliet". . . . What is not fanciful is that a piece written in prose is yet the most exquisite poetry, and that a termination grim, tender, and tragic awaits scenes which are humorous or cynical, and sometimes almost playful in treatment. (p. 262)

> *Joseph Knight, in a review of "Les caprices de Marianne" and "Il faut qu'une porte soit ouverte ou fermée," in his* Theatrical Notes, *Lawrence & Bullen, 1893, pp. 261-62 .*

A. C. SWINBURNE (essay date 1881)

[*Swinburne was an English poet, dramatist, and critic. He was renowned during his lifetime for his lyric poetry, and he is remembered today for his rejection of Victorian mores. His explicitly sensual themes shocked his contemporaries; although they demanded that poetry reflect and uphold current moral standards, Swinburne's only goal, implicit in his poetry and explicit in his critical writings, was to express beauty. In the following, Swinburne compares Musset and Alfred Lord Tennyson to determine who is the better poet. While praising Tennyson's superiority in the "graver and loftier ways of work," Swinburne finds that Musset surpasses his English rival in "lightly thoughtful and gently graceful verse" and in prose. He states: "The more distinctive and typical proofs of this exquisite poet's most fine and bright intelligence, as contrasted with his pure lyric genius, are to be gathered from his tales and plays in prose. . . ."*]

[There must be an end to] the long contested question of poetic precedence between Alfred Tennyson and Alfred de Musset. Four lines of [Tennyson's] *Rizpah,* placed in one scale of the balance of judgment, would send all the loveliest verse of Musset flying up in the other, to kick the beam and vanish. Of passion such as this he knew no more than he knew of such execution. He was about as capable of either as of writing . . . [William Shakespeare's] *King Lear.*

It would seem to follow from this, if such a decision be accepted as equitable, that any comparison of claims between the two men must be unprofitable in itself, as well as unfair to the memory of the lesser poet. But it needs no great expense of argument to prove that such is by no means the case. We cannot, in any fair estimate of the two rival claimants, omit or neglect to take account of the rich legacy left by Musset in the province of imaginative prose, narrative and dramatic. And when we have thus taken account of all his various and exquisite work on those lines—so delicate, so subtle, so supple, so gaily grave and so fancifully pensive, so full of inspired ease and instinctive ability, it becomes more difficult to trim the balance with absolute security of hand; especially when we consider that all this charming work, without ever once touching on the detestable as well as debateable land of pseudo-poetic rhapsody in hermaphroditic prose after the least admirable manner of such writers as De Quincey, is always, so to speak, impregnated and permeated with something of a genuinely poetical sense or spirit. Grace and sweetness never fail him in any part of his work which any kindly reader would care to remember. (pp. 131-32)

[The] world of letters has hardly ever seen such a first book as the ***Contes d'Espagne et d'Italie.*** Its very faults were promises—unhappily too soon to be falsified—of riper and not less radiant excellence to come. Of all thin and shallow criticisms, none ever was shallower or thinner than that which would describe these firstlings of Musset's genius as mere Byronic echoes. In that case they would be tuneless as their original: whereas they are the notes of a singer who cannot but sing—though perhaps they gave no great evidence that he could do much else. But of all poems written in youth these are perhaps the likeliest or rather the surest for a season to stir the brain and sting the blood of adolescence. To do them justice, they should be first read at the age of eighteen. . . . He has more than the audacious charm and seductive impudence of Chérubin; and the graceless Grace who served his boyhood for a Muse had some half-a-dozen nightingale notes in the compass of her voice which in clear sheer quality of blithe and birdlike spontaneity were beyond the reach of Tennyson's. But when the pretty page of Thackeray's ballad grows bearded and then bald, it remains to be tried what manner of brain was ripening under the curly gold locks of his nonage. . . . [A] couplet of Sir Henry Taylor's is exactly significant of the later emotion felt towards Musset by men whom he naturally fascinated before their own minds were *hors de page* [independently formed].

> I heard the sorrowful sensualist complain,
> If with compassion, not without disdain.

To Musset, of all men, this rebuke was most applicable. For such a sufferer as the author of ***Rolla*** contempt no sooner thaws into compassion than compassion freezes back into contempt. And the next instant, as in my own case at this moment of writing, the fresh crust of curdling scorn begins again to soften and dissolve under the warm spring wind of pity. It is for Musset alone among poets that this exact shade of feeling is possible to men at once charitable and rational. . . . In the most charming and daring of all boyish poets there was less than little of the making of a man.

It is true that he could weep very musically. For sweetness and fulness and melody of feeling and thought and language it would be hard to match and harder to eclipse his ***Souvenir.*** Nor has too much praise been given, though evidently too much would have been given if it could, to those four limpid rillets from the famous *Lake* of Lamartine, his now no less famous ***Nights.*** At the same time it is natural and allowable to wonder what manner of work this magical musician's hand would have found to do if neither Byron nor Lamartine nor one far greater than both had made themselves instruments before him, which hung sometimes within reach of his delicate and skilful fingers. Starting in life as page to Victor Hugo, he never rose higher in sustained poetry than when he figured as henchman to Lamartine. Always conceding and remembering this, we can hardly overpraise either the freshest of his earlier works or the tenderest of his later. . . .At his best, Musset is representative of nothing but himself; at his worst, if the hard clear bitter truth must be spoken out—as it must—without flinching, he represents the quintessence of those qualities, the consummation of those defects, which made possible in France the infamous rise, and inevitable the not less infamous fall, of the Lower Empire. . . . He lived to produce some of the vilest verses that ever blotted paper, in praise of the very meanest of all villains that ever disgraced even a throne. (pp. 132-34)

I make no objection to the existence of such a poem as [***Namouna***], which I find, of all poems read and admired in early youth, to be the one which will least endure reperusal and reconsideration in after years: I take it as perhaps the fairest and most popular sample of Musset at the full-flowing spring-tide of his genius. It would certainly be but bare justice to call it exquisite and graceful: and perhaps it might be unjust as well as Puritanical to call it effeminate or prurient. . . . There is something in his tone which is unlike anything and alien from everything in the work, for instance, of Gautier and of Baudelaire. . . . [The] pervading note of spiritual tragedy in the brooding verse of Baudelaire dignifies and justifies at all points his treatment of his darkest and strangest subjects. This justification, this dignity, is wanting in the case of Musset. The atmosphere of his work is to the atmosphere of Gautier's as the air of a gas-lit alcove to the air of the far-flowering meadows. (pp. 136-37)

The overture to **Rolla,** down at least to the fourteenth line, is one of the very few jewels in its author's casket, or feathers in his cap, which may seem as admirable to a critic at forty as to a student at twenty. The radiance and vibration of the verse, its luminous rapture and living melody, could hardly be overpraised. . . . There is as it were a broken or fitful note of sincerity in the poem as a whole which redeems it from everlasting damnation: but it hangs by a hair over that critical abyss of most just judgment. It is exquisitely wrought in the main, and not utterly hollow or demonstrably insincere: but it is impossible to revert in thought without an inward smile to the adolescent period when despite a certain note of falsity or "pathetic fallacy," too gross to impose even on a boy, it seemed altogether the produce of such profound and tender inspiration.

No doubt, however, there are more than a few things bequeathed us by Musset for which the advance of time cannot and should not utterly change or chill the fervid imprint of our early admiration. A few of his songs are altogether of the very highest order. Nothing can be truer, sweeter, more blameless in positive and simple completeness of native beauty than such of them as Fortunio's, Barberine's, the Good-bye and again the Good-day to Suzon. All these are perfect honey. . . . And one other, if one only, has a note in it such as can be found in no song of Mr. Tennyson's—the indescribable wonderful note of a natural and irrational fascination like that of a sudden sweet cry from the joyous throat of some strange bird; I mean of course the song which so haunted Gautier [Swinburne does not identify the poem]. . . . There never were more delicious words in the world; no truer and clearer note came ever, surely, from the lips of even any Greek lyrist. It has the very sweetness of Sappho's own—though wanting of course the depth and fervour never wanting to the voice that never was matched on earth.

But if this be nearly all—and I cannot but think that indeed it is nearly all—which can possibly be advanced on behalf of Musset's claim to rank simply as a mere poet above Tennyson, I cannot but also think that few claims can be less tenable. (pp. 140-41)

If the prose work of Musset be excluded from our account, the balance between him and the Laureate would be very much easier to adjust. . . . But if it be included the question is very much more difficult to settle. The only line of poetry on which, as I think, the superiority of Musset in easy power and exquisite seduction cannot for a moment be disputed, is that of lightly thoughtful and gently graceful verse. I hope and believe that I fully appreciate the charm of such enchanting work as [Tennyson's] *The Talking Oak* and *Will Waterproof's Lyrical Monologue:* but their grace would lose half its glow, their radiance

half its light, if set beside the far brighter and more delicate loveliness of **Une Bonne Fortune** or **A quoi rêvent les jeunes filles.** On all graver and loftier ways of work the palm of power as well as of beauty has been won . . . by the more virile as well as the more careful hand of Mr. Tennyson. . . . But Musset without his prose is at best but half himself. And his prose, being either "of imagination all compact," or all composed of pure fancy, wit, and qualities all proper if not all necessary to a poet, must in bare justice be considered when we come to cast up the account of his genius. . . . [His] plays are a most important part and parcel of his necessary credentials at the court of Prince Posterity. Of **Les Marrons du Feu,** and even of **La Coupe et les Lèvres,** most of my coevals, I should conjecture, will agree with me in thinking that much the same must now be said, and remembering that much the same was thought in our salad days, as of **Rolla, Namouna,** and all their brilliant fellowship. Their splendid sheet lightning no longer seems more splendid than mere sunlight; the plunging hand-gallop of their verses no longer carries us off at such a joyous and irrational rate of rapture. Perhaps the first stage on the sober way back to some point of critical reason is reached when we come to understand that the profile of Marco in the **Confession** is a truer and more perfect piece of tragic work than all the full-faced portraits of Belcolores and Camargos; that her bloodless hands are more perfectly drawn and far more powerfully terrible than theirs yet quivering with the passion of homicide. We shall then be not far from perception of the truth that the more distinctive and typical proofs of this exquisite poet's most fine and bright intelligence, as contrasted with his pure lyric genius, are to be gathered from his tales and plays in prose; **Fantasio** and **Le Chandelier, Mimi Pinson** or **Le Fils du Titien,** so specially precious for love of two sonnets as perfect as verse can be. In both these fields, of comedy and of story, it cannot be denied that his work is equally unequal; the story of **Les Deux Maîtresses** is "as water unto wine" or water-gruel to champagne if compared with the radiance of Gautier's early study (*Celle-ci et Celle-là*) on the same moral or fanciful subject; and the least brilliant of his later comedies are almost actually flat. But even to an English audience it would now be surely an impertinence to sing the praises of his more finished comedies and dramatised "proverbs." The finest or the most jaded palate that any epicurean in letters might boast or might lament could certainly desire no daintier luxury than these. Never elsewhere in any work of Musset's has the impassioned intelligence of his genius given such proof of its active and speculative powers [as in **Lorenzaccio**]. The central figure of the man whose energies, half palsied by postponement, all vitiated by habit and satiety and weary sensual sloth, have life yet left in them to fret and fever him by fits, and conscience enough behind them to constrain or corrode him to the end, is perhaps but the fuller and darker outline of one sketched or shadowed out by the same hand again and again with a lighter and tenderer touch than here; but the bloodred background of historic action gives it a more tragic relief and dignity. Above all, there is a grandeur which is wanting to all other works of Musset supplied by the central fact that in this man's "despised and ruinous" life—this "ruined piece of nature"—the surviving spark of fire, the disinfectant grain of salt, is not, as in the wrecked lives of other such actors on the stage of Musset's fancy, mere love or mere desire for success or fame as lover or as poet, as fighter or adventurer, but the uncorrupted grain, the unextinguished fire, of a pure thought and a vital principle, the mission of a deliverer and the motive of a tyrannicide. The utter and flagrant scepticism—the flat and spiritless infidelity—of the poet himself, however visibly revealed and sorrowfully displayed, is powerless to blunt the edge or to quench the ardour of interest inherent in the central idea. No cynicism can deaden it, and no disbelief degrade. (pp. 143-45)

> A. C. Swinburne, "Tennyson and Musset," in The Fortnightly Review, n.s. Vol. XXIX, No. CLXX, February 1, 1881, pp. 129-53.*

GEORGE BRANDES (essay date 1882)

[Brandes, a Danish literary critic and biographer, was the principal leader of the intellectual movement which helped to bring an end to Scandinavian cultural isolation. He believed that literature reflects the spirit and problems of its time and that it must be understood within its social and aesthetic context. Brandes's major critical work, Main Currents in Nineteenth-Century Literature, originally published as Hovedstrømninger i det 19de aarhundredes literatur: Den romantiske Skole i Frankig in 1882, won him admiration for his ability to view literary movements within the broader context of all European literature. In this work, Brandes devotes three chapters to Musset. In the first, from which the following is drawn, Brandes discusses Musset in relation to the developing French Romantic movement. He compares Musset's works with those of Victor Hugo, the most popular and respected French Romantic writer, and he describes the reaction of Musset's contemporaries to his verses. The next two chapters, not included here, examine Musset's liaison with George Sand and his artistic development, with particular reference to the influence of Sand.]

Contes d'Espagne et d'Italie [is] a series of tales in verse abounding in situations which it would be scarcely permissible to describe. In the longer ones (*Don Paez, Portia,* & c.) treachery runs riot. . . . Shakespeare's earliest works are not more wanton than these, and these are, moreover, not naïvely, but refinedly wanton. There is . . . a constant parade of unbelief, with odd interruptions in the shape of unconscious confessions of weakness and spasmodic longings for the comforts of religion. (pp. 98-9)

This was Romanticism of an entirely new kind, much less doctrinaire than Victor Hugo's. Here was a still more direct defiance of the classic rules of metre and style; but this defiance was frolicsome and witty, not martial like Hugo's. (p. 99)

Hugo's heroic bearing and giant's stride had compelled reverence; his imposing rhetoric roused respectful admiration; but this miraculous jaunty grace, this genius for shameless drollery, had both an emancipatory and a fascinating effect. There was a diabolical irresistibility about it, a quality which women as a rule are, and in this case were, the first to appreciate. De Musset wrote of women, always of women, and not, like Hugo, with precocious maturity, with chivalrous tenderness, with romantic gallantry—no, with a passion, a hatred, a bitterness, a fury, which showed that he despised and adored them, that they could make him writhe and scream in agony, and that he took his revenge in clamorous accusation and fiery scorn.

There is here no ripeness, wholesomeness, or moral beauty, but a youthful, seething, incredible intensity of life, any description of which would be no more successful than the description of scarlet given to the blind man, which drew forth the remark: "Then it is like the sound of a trumpet." And in this poetry there is, verily, a quality which suggests scarlet and the flourish of trumpets. That beauty in art is immortal is true; but there is something still more certainly immortal, namely, life. These first poems of De Musset lived. They were followed

by his mature, beautiful works; and all men's eyes were opened to his merits. (pp. 99-100)

[As] De Musset developed and approached the years of discretion, he continued to reveal qualities which outshone Victor Hugo's. He won the hearts of the reading public by his essential humanness. He confessed his weakness and faults; Victor Hugo felt it incumbent on him to be unerring. He was not the marvellous artificer of verse, could not, like Hugo, hammer the metal of language into fashion and put word gems into a setting of gold. He wrote carelessly, rhymed anyhow, even in more slipshod fashion than Heine; but he was never the rhetorician, always the human being. In his joy and his grief there seemed to be an immortal truth. (p. 101)

> George Brandes, "Hugo and de Musset," in his Main Currents in Nineteenth Century Literature: The Romantic School in France, Vol. V, translated by Diana White and Mary Morison, William Heinemann, 1904, pp. 90-105.*

BERNARD SHAW (essay date 1897)

[Shaw's essay originally appeared in The Saturday Review (London), June 26, 1897.]

De Musset, though a drunkard, with his mind always derelict in the sea of his imagination, yet had the sacred fire. **"Lorenzaccio"** is a reckless play, broken up into scores of scenes in the Shakespearean manner, but without Shakespeare's workmanlike eye to stage business and to cumulative dramatic effect; for half these scenes lead nowhere; and the most gaily trivial of them—that in which the two children fight—is placed in the fifth act, *after* the catastrophe, which takes place in the fourth. According to all the rules, the painter Tebaldeo must have been introduced to stab somebody later on, instead of merely to make Lorenzaccio feel like a cur; Filippo Strozzi is a Virginius-Lear wasted; the Marquise was plainly intended for something very fine in the seventeenth act, if the play ever got so far; and Lorenzaccio's swoon at the sight of a sword in the first act remains a mystery to the end of the play. False starts, dropped motives, no-thoroughfares, bewilder the expert in "construction" all through; but none the less the enchanter sustains his illusion: you are always in the Renaissant Italian city of the Romanticist imagination, a murderous but fascinating place; and the characters, spectral as they are, are yet as distinct and individual as Shakespeare's, some of them—Salviati, for instance—coming out with the rudest force in a mere mouthful of lines. Only, the force never becomes realism: the romantic atmosphere veils and transfigures everything: Lorenzaccio himself, though his speeches bite with the suddenest vivacity, never emerges from the mystic twilight of which he seems to be only a fantastic cloud, and no one questions the consistency of the feet stealing through nameless infamy and the head raised to the stars. (pp. 291-92)

> Bernard Shaw, "'Lorenzaccio'," in his Dramatic Opinions and Essays with an Apology, Vol. 2, 1906. Reprint by Constable and Company, Ltd., 1910, pp. 287-95.

JEAN CARRÈRE (essay date 1904?)

[Although Carrère praises Musset as a genius, he condemns the poet's preoccupation with love. According to Carrère, Musset never experienced true sorrow, and his lamentations about a failed love affair make "a mockery of human misery, a sacrilege of *sorrow.'' Carrère contradicts the view that Musset's greatness lies in his depiction of passion and his own internal life.*]

I will not waste time in discussing the position which ought to be assigned to Musset amongst the poets of the nineteenth century. . . . Only one thing matters—was he a genius? In other words, did he create a living work, and has this work left its mark on the minds of men? It is beyond question. . . .

His genius included all the graces and all the seductive arts. Above all, he received that gift of harmonious phrase which makes his style as captivating and irresistible as the rustle of leaves or the murmur of waves. He received that gift of imagery in virtue of which each of his thoughts takes external form in a luminous reflection. He received that gift of lyricism by means of which his soul enfolds us, raises us, and bears us away with it across space, like Faust's cloak, which he invoked. He received the gift of emotion, of tenderness, and of pity, which makes his every verse groan, weep, and pour out like the little waterfalls which tremble and leap in the forest. (p. 125)

His work is one sustained groan. . . . Love has become in him so sickly and perverse an obsession that he mingles it with all the acts of his life and all the interests of his age.

I know nothing more astounding in this regard than his famous **Letter to Lamartine.** One poet writes to another, both of them distinguished. They live in the dawn of an age when the whole race is being transformed. They have been witnesses of prodigious adventures. And the only question that occupies the mind of the young poet at the height of his power is, why women push wickedness to the extent of abandoning their unhappy lovers. . . . (pp. 127-28)

What are we to expect, then, in those poems of his which were solely inspired by love, such as **The Nights,** his masterpiece? They breathe nothing, they vibrate and tremble with nothing, but love? History, nature, heaven, even the gods—everything turns in maddening appeals round this single fact that the poet has been deceived by his lover. (p. 129)

Is this a poet of sorrow? What! For thousands and thousands of years poor humanity has dragged itself over the earth in pursuit of a happiness that ever recedes before it like a mirage . . .—and you would call the man who, in the midst of all this tragedy, has suffered a little from a woman's caprice the poet of sorrow! No, no. (p. 134)

[To] speak about a great sorrow, to weep out one's soul in desperate sobs, to conjure up the most tragic figures, to call to witness all the forces of nature and all the ages of human history, to declare oneself a victim of the gods just because Dame Sand has gone off with the solid Pagello, really—I must say it, though I be disgraced for ever in the eyes of all girls in the first flush of puberty and all young men of erotic dreams— it is a mockery of human misery, a sacrilege of sorrow. (pp. 135-36)

> *Jean Carrère, ''Alfred de Musset'' (1904?), in his* Degeneration in the Great French Masters: Rousseau—Chateaubriand—Balzac—Stendhal—Sand—Musset — Baudelaire — Flaubert —Verlaine — Zola, *translated by Joseph McCabe, T. Fisher Unwin, Limited, 1922, pp. 125-36.*

MARY MOSS (essay date 1907)

After *Elle et Lui, Lui et Elle,* the first *Lettre d'Un Voyageur,* the **Confession d'Un Enfant du Siècle,** after allusions without

number in contemporary memoirs, after *his* poems, *her* novels, a less rich subject [than the George Sand—Alfred de Musset affair] might well have been exhausted. Never, except in [Samuel Richardson's] *Clarissa Harlowe* . . . have so diverse points of view been brought to bear upon any episode of passion. Nevertheless, nothing that has come before begins to compare in interest with [*Correspondance de George Sand et D'Alfred de Musset*]. . . . This slender volume holds the outpouring of two great masters of language at the most emotional period of their entire lives. . . . They even overstep the possible limits of human candour, but with such searching, relentless analysis, such gemlike beauty of utterance, that, merely as literature, the collection possesses the imperishable freshness of a classic. Beyond this, it is the tangible presentment of such hidden throes as ordinary people seldom experience, never by any chance are competent to express. (p. 136)

No description, no quotations can give the faintest idea of this extraordinary picture of their lives. It is as if their actual voices spoke, not always clearly, but with a freshness which leaves you with the sense of having been present, or at least in the next room, during the very scenes to which they allude. (p. 142)

Whatever objections may be urged against making public letters of so sacred and intimate a character, in this case unquestionably it [has enriched] . . . the world by a piece of literature which can hardly be rated too high. . . . (p. 143)

> *Mary Moss, ''The Final Touch,'' in* The Bookman, *New York, Vol. XXVI, October, 1907, pp. 136-43.*

BENEDETTO CROCE (essay date 1923)

[*Croce was an Italian philosopher, historian, editor, and literary critic whose writings span the first half of the twentieth century. He founded and edited the literary and political journal* La critica, *whose independence, objectivity, and strong stand against fascism earned him the respect of his contemporaries. According to Croce, the only proper form of literary history is the* caratteristica, *or critical characterization, of the poetic personality and work of a single artist; its goal is to demonstrate the unity of the author's intention, its expression in the creative work, and the reader's response. In the following, Croce contends that Musset attempted to make his life and art ''perfectly identical'' by imbuing both with a singular preoccupation with love. Croce differs from the many critics who describe Musset's work as personal, a direct reflection of the poet's soul. Croce calls it imitative, and he denounces ''Les nuits'' and ''Rolla,'' commonly ranked among Musset's greatest works, as contrived, pretentious, and theatrical. According to Croce, Musset succeeds only when he ''unites and tempers his erotic-dolorous with his mirthful poetry.'' Croce's essay originally appeared in his* Poesia e non poesia: Note sulla letteratura europea del secolo decimonono *in 1923.*]

If poetry could be identical with life (as some extreme romantics of all times dream), Alfred de Musset would have approached this ideal more nearly than any ever did, and should be numbered among the great poets. For he did not conceive of poetry otherwise than as an efflux from his life and his life as an efflux from his poetry, making them perfectly identical. And in order to arrive at this identity, he gave to his life for unique content what is reputed to be the content most proper to poetry: the drama of love. Not politics then, not country, not humanity, not family, not religion, not search for truth; but only love. (p. 252)

What Musset sought . . . was passionate love, with all the volubility and all the contradictions which are of its very nature: love, which is a rose rich in thorns, a rose to be plucked with loud outcry at the pricks, yet the desire that the thorns should be there. . . . Poetry should be the echo of this, echo of joy, of enthusiasm, of delirium, and then of delusion and desperation and bitterness and disdain. . . .

There is something juvenile, almost childish, in this idea both of love and of poetry. And it is for this reason that De Musset has been called the young man's poet. . . . (p. 253)

We all know what happened [to Musset's verse as a result of his love affair with Sand], that it became emphatic and rhetorical in the search for spontaneity, all exclamations, apostrophes, interrogations, comparisons made for effect broadening into pictures, the versification certainly fluent but monotonous with something . . . of the effect of a children's swing. . . . (p. 254)

Not a single intense, sculptured or profoundly musical verse ever comes out of all this; but instead, the verse very frequently dominates the thought, and sounds for sound's sake. . . .

We can pass over his youthful verses and plays, **Don Paez, Portia, La coupe et les lèvres,** literary *pastiches* where it is a question of the usual Spain, Italy and Alps as invented by English and French romanticism. . . . [The] verses are so composed as to enter immediately the memory of the ear and there to resound like the rhythmical surging of waves. But even when Musset conceives a truly poetic motive, as in **Rolla,** he translates it into a ready-made form, instead of developing and so of penetrating it deeply. Thus we hear of conventional romantic heroes (the man of noble, great, loyal and proud heart, who falls into dissoluteness), of philosophico-historical dissertations, which are intended to explain the fall of angels into the modern world, of oratorical invectives and perorations in profusion as though from a preacher in a pulpit, or rather, a lawyer addressing a jury. (p. 255)

Even the so celebrated **Nuits** fail to satisfy me altogether, because their creation does not seem to me to arise from within, but to be cheaply acquired by means of dialogues with allegorical personages (the Muse), and a variety of metres intended to supply missing gradations and minute distinctions in the representations of states of the soul, in the images, in the syntax and in the verse, by means of mechanical changes of metre. (pp. 255-56)

I feel much pretentiousness and theatricality in these famous compositions, as though of one who fulfils the duty of weeping and accusing, and tries to show himself in the right and to obtain pity for the evil that has been done to him and to draw down upon the perfidious authoress of his misfortunes reproof and reprobation. But they contain little poetry, and it could not be abundant, because the **Nuits** are the result of a practical need rather than anything else, and the querulous lover occupies too often in them the place of the poet.

De Musset, entirely captivated by his loves and lacking any other moral and mental interest, is without the vigour to raise himself above his soul sufferings, in order to contemplate and fix and represent them with that objectivity which is like poetic justice. Certainly the effusions of the heart and the living memories remain in the non-rhetorical passages, but they are rather elements and details of poetry than poetry in themselves. . . . (p. 257)

Since Musset was in the habit of treating verse as an instrument to be employed in the service of his amorous adventures and disadventures, it is not to be wondered at that he also employed it as an instrument for joking and jesting. Hence his numerous

compositions, or parts of compositions, which are capricious random epistles and narratives. . . . [This part of his work] is juvenile and appeals to young men by its impishness and lack of discipline, and by its boast of being impish and undisciplined.

Where Musset on the contrary attains to art is in the poems, or parts of poems, light in tone, amorous or tender, which are to be found among his earliest work (**Le lever, Madame la marquise,** etc.), and in greater number in the later poems (**Suzon, Mimi Pinson, Rondeau,** etc.), and among the little poems, **Mardoche, Namouna, Une bonne fortune.** (pp. 258-59)

It may be said that in this kind of lyric De Musset unites and tempers his erotic-dolorous with his mirthful poetry, in neither of which he was wholly successful when taken separately; and that in it he frees himself from the practical preoccupations of the first and the frivolity of the second, assuming a more expressly artistic attitude, looking at himself in his affections and in his defects, his illusions and delusions, his serious and his comical aspects, as though at a spectacle. Not however by any means as a spectacle seen from above, with the sense of the grandiose and vertiginous (he was not capable of that), but as a very much more placid, circumscribed, modest spectacle seen from an arm-chair in the frame-work of a pretty little stage. **Un spectacle dans un fauteuil** was indeed the title of his first collection of little comedies, little thought of when they first saw the light, but justly acquiring in the course of time that reputation which his lyrics and small poetical pieces have been gradually shedding. They are really exquisite works: **Les caprices de Marianne, Le chandelier, Fantasio, On ne badine pas avec l'amour, La nuit vénitienne,** and the others. . . . Emphasis, declamatory tone, empty and resonant verses, excesses, lack of proportion, incorrections, blandishments, altogether vanish and these little dramas unfold themselves in their lightness and grace, in their sober, acute, incisive and at the same time spontaneous prose. (pp. 260-61)

With a little reflection, we become aware that we still have before us the old heart of De Musset, that of the stories of Spain and of Italy, of the Nights, of the Confessions; but converted from subject into object, that is to say, into an object of art, and converted as the result of its own work alone in its genial moments. (p. 261)

[Since] the minor works are becoming more and more clearly revealed as the true major works of De Musset, will it not be of advantage that his stories and prose narratives should rise in general esteem? If Alfred de Musset to some extent imposed silence upon the passionate or burlesque—passionate tumult of his lyrics, and grew calm and smilingly moved again in the stories and the narratives, so limpid, simple, calm and free in treatment, we sometimes even hear him uttering (as in **Les deux maîtresses**) words of moral wisdom and noble renunciation. (pp. 265-66)

Benedetto Croce, ''de Musset,'' *in his* European Literature in the Nineteenth Century, *translated by Douglas Ainslie, Alfred A. Knopf, 1924, pp. 252-66.*

HUGH ALLISON SMITH (essay date 1925)

[*In the following discussion of Musset as a Romantic dramatist, Smith examines Musset's style, form, characters, plot, and his use of the foremost Romantic theme: love. Smith maintains that Musset's work, ''personal and original as it is, can be considered as the most characteristic product of Romantic philosophy combined with French temperament.''*]

In the theatre, Hugo is to be studied largely for the importance of his theory and Dumas for the influence of his practice, but Musset's plays can still be read for their own interest and charm. He was too young to play a rôle in the inauguration of Romantic drama, and his pieces, written to be read, were not represented until its decline, so he has hardly had an influence on dramatic evolution. With all that, his work is the most durable of the Romantic school, and, personal and original as it is, can be considered as the most characteristic product of Romantic philosophy combined with French temperament.

Musset is the perfect "enfant du siècle" [child of the century], that Romantic flower of passion and imagination grafted on the perennial plant of French realism; its fruit had the color and form of Romanticism, but the sap, savor and vitality came from a more native and hardier stock. (p. 49)

Altogether [Musset] has left some fifteen comedies worth mentioning, for the most part short plays published under the title *Comédies et Proverbes*. Most of them are written in prose but in tone all are idealistic and poetic. (p. 50)

Written as they were at the whim of the author and to fit no dramatic system, these plays represent an unusual variety of moods and categories. A few, such as *Il faut qu'une porte soit ouverte ou fermée* or *Un Caprice*, are nothing more than witty dialogues, airy trifles made of nothing. However, they are expressed in a style so beautiful, a style suggesting Marivaux but infinitely more natural and simple, and are such perfect examples of the fine art of Parisian conversation, that they have become classic French curtain-raisers and have invited frequent imitation. Others, such as *A quoi rêvent les jeunes filles* and *Il ne faut jurer de rien,* are hardly less light in tone and in the play of fancy and humor, but are, at the same time, remarkably keen psychological expositions. The two mentioned are particularly notable for their insight into the heart of the young girl, showing its romance, its innocence, and its purity. There is much of the feminine in Musset's intuitions, and in the characterization of the young woman especially, he is almost unequalled on the French stage. (pp. 50-1)

However, the plays on which rests Musset's chief dramatic fame are dramas of love, its ecstasies and tortures, its surprises and tragedies. Perhaps his masterpiece is *On ne badine pas avec l'amour.* . . . It is highly poetic, rising to tense emotion, and terminating in tragedy, and it is at the same time relieved by humorous and burlesque strokes that would furnish worthy pencil sketches to put in a Shakespearean gallery. It is hard to find anywhere, except in Shakespeare, truth and fancy blended in an atmosphere more charming, and few dramas, written in a tone of high idealism, bring nearer to us the eternally poignant problems of love. Also we have here, most pointedly expressed, Musset's own philosophy of love and life: "One is often deceived in love, often hurt and often unhappy; but one loves, and when he is on the brink of his grave and turns to look behind, he says to himself: I have often suffered, I have sometimes been deceived, but I have loved." (p. 51)

The popularity of Musset's pieces is undeniable and has been strikingly universal; even the extreme realists, violent enemies of Romanticism, have had little but praise for his work. This appreciation is easy for one who reads his plays, for they seem today as fresh as ever; the difficulty is to point out adequately the precise reasons for their durability.

In the first place, he has confined himself to the field which Romantic and subjective drama was most competent to cultivate, an intimate study and exposition of the human heart in the passion of love. To do this, his own heart was not only an instrument of remarkable delicacy and capacity for recording all the tremors of love and passion, but he had a frankness, sincerity and lucidity, perhaps unequalled, in laying bare these secret records of the soul. Racine undoubtedly made a much wider analysis of human passions and presented it in a drama of more sustained intensity, while Shakespeare's was not only wider but is translated into a variety of realistic action that is incomparable; but Musset suggests both these masters and neither is Musset's superior within his specialty.

Another merit, of which the full value can be appreciated only by reading him, is the purity and charm of Musset's style. It is Classic in its simplicity, and yet it uses all the liberty and resources won by the Romanticists. One quality is ever recurrent and always delightful; in situations where we expect to find, and where other Romanticists seek for, the word or expression that would be fine, striking, or picturesque, Musset surprises us by the revealing power of the simple, natural phrase. It is in fact a frequent touch of realism that is exceedingly important in holding his characters near to earth and maintaining our contact with them. To this extent Musset is a realist. This trait perhaps explains in part the approval he has had from realistic writers, and it certainly identifies him with the long line of French masters of the simple and precise phrase, from Pascal and Racine down to the present day.

Finally, Musset's freedom from the mold of a dramatic system has been a great factor in his durable popularity. . . . This does not mean, however, that he was without a dramatic art; it is in fact most sound, only it was not hampered by the conventions or exigencies of the acting stage. His character drawing is really superior, strikingly so for the haste with which these sketches must often be made in his short plays.

But it is in his plots especially that we find the highest art which conceals itself. At first glance, perhaps, nothing seems more capricious, more carelessly motivated, than the plots of Musset's plays. Certainly this action carries no suggestion of the exciting, tumultuous stream of Dumas, that sweeps its breathless victims to destruction. In comparison, it is rather the winding brook, that turns here and there to water a fern or flower, that murmurs gaily down the slopes, and spreads out in placid pools, but none the less it has an object and a goal, to which it tends as irresistibly and as naturally as water seeks its level; and Musset's characters also, lured by their pleasures, are sometimes, before they are aware, carried over the falls to destruction. (pp. 54-6)

> *Hugh Allison Smith, "Other Romantic Dramatists (Dumas—Delavigne—Vigny—Musset)," in his* Main Currents of Modern French Drama, *Henry Holt and Company, 1925, pp. 36-58.**

ARTHUR TILLEY (essay date 1933)

Writing definitely for the stage, Shakespeare was compelled to be dramatic. Alfred de Musset was under no such compulsion, but he had a natural instinct for drama. . . . But dramatic instinct is not enough in itself, and Musset's great admiration for Shakespeare made it natural that he should turn to this supreme master of drama in order to learn how to construct a play. Certainly the first two scenes of *Lorenzaccio* suggest that he had carefully studied the openings of Shakespeare's four great tragedies and of *Romeo and Juliet.* . . . Just as in Shakespeare, these two scenes give us the key-note of the whole play, the odious character of the debauched Duke, and the servile condition of Florence under his rule. Lorenzaccio only appears in the first scene, but the cynical libertinism of his one effective speech is profoundly revealing. In the remaining four scenes of the first act these three essential elements of the play, the condition of Florence and the characters of the Duke and his cousin, are further developed. (pp. 144-45)

After the fourth act there is a decided drop in the interest. But it must be remembered that in order to fill out the portrait of Lorenzaccio and to complete the picture of enslaved Florence it was necessary to shew the uselessness of the murder. The execution of the fifth act, however, cannot be considered satisfactory. The first scene is good, for it vividly represents the confusion caused by Alessandro's murder, ending in the election of Cosimo as the new Duke. But the other Florentine scenes, except the last, are unnecessary and add nothing to the picture. (p. 146)

There are two scenes in *Lorenzaccio* which have in a high degree [the] Shakespearian quality of life. These are the second and fifth scenes of the first act, in both of which representatives of different classes of Florentine society, coming together in a perfectly natural and life-like way, give a vivid picture of the condition of Florence previous to the Duke's assassination. (p. 147)

But it is in the character of Lorenzaccio himself that we most clearly recognise the influence of Shakespeare and particularly of *Hamlet*. There is little resemblance between the two protagonists, but they have this in common that the same task has been imposed on them, on the one by his own decision, on the other by the command of his father's ghost, namely that of killing a relative. Both being introspective—whether by nature or as the result of spiritual loneliness, it matters not— they are given to communing with themselves and to expressing their thoughts (for stage purposes) in soliloquies. But their soliloquies differ in character. While Hamlet is constantly urging himself to action, Lorenzaccio has no hesitations and is chiefly concerned with planning his attack. Again, while Hamlet with his higher intelligence and broader outlook wanders into the region of speculative philosophy, Lorenzaccio, more self-centred, is concerned only with his plan, or with self-justification, or with reminiscences of his past. (p. 148)

[Just] as Filippo Strozzi helps to bring out the character of Lorenzaccio, so Maddalena Cibo serves to shew up her brother-in-law Cardinal Cibo in his true light as an unscrupulous and Machiavellian ecclesiastic. He is an Iago with a different mask and a wider outlook, but with the same devilish ingenuity in executing his schemes. He is admirably drawn, and if it is objected that his part is episodic and that he only touches the main action when he warns the Duke against his cousin, the answer is that the play is not a tragedy but a historical drama. Lorenzaccio is not, like Hamlet, the central figure of the piece, towards whom everything converges, but he shares our interest with the city of Florence. (p. 150)

Such is *Lorenzaccio*. In spite of its faults of construction, due partly to its author's indifference to stage requirements, partly to the difficulty of giving an adequate share in the representation to the picture of decadent Florence, it is a great play. The principal character is a remarkable feat of creation, and he is well supported by several others, while various minor characters, though they only make transient appearances, reveal a rare power of creating by a few rapid strokes types that are at once real and imaginative. Moreover there is ever present a dramatic sense, which is never exaggerated into melodrama,

and a feeling for life and movement equal to that of Dumas and Hugo, but accompanied by the psychological insight in which they are so conspicuously wanting. (p. 151)

If *Lorenzaccio* is the most solid and the most ambitious product of Musset's dramatic genius, the one which shews the greatest concentration of effort, his most characteristic pieces are *Les Caprices de Marianne, Fantasio,* and *On ne badine pas avec l'amour. . . .* Though all alike are called comedies, the sole theme of the first and last is a love-story which ends in a poignant tragedy. *Fantasio* is a comedy throughout and there is no love-making in it, but like the others it gives us the expression of Musset's views on love. It is often said that he himself is the hero of all three comedies and that in *Les Caprices de Marianne* he appears under the double rôle of Claudio and Coelio. I think it would be truer to say that in all four characters, Claudio, Coelio, Fantasio, and Perdican, he has embodied his own experiences and his own meditations rather than that he has identified himself with any of the characters. (pp. 152-53)

A common feature [of these plays] is that they contain a fantastic element. In the two latest it is considerable, but it exists also in *Les Caprices de Marianne*. The dialogue, for instance, between Claudio and his servant Tibia is fantastically comic in the irrelevance of some of the remarks, and, although the atmosphere of the play is more or less Italian, the place might be any other Italian city just as well as Naples. So in *On ne badine pas avec l'amour,* though we are evidently in France, there is no attempt to localise the scene, the only place indicated being a château with its immediate surroundings. In *Fantasio* "the scene is at Munich", but Munich is [purely imaginary]. . . . (p. 153)

The great merits of [*Les Caprices de Marianne*] are its originality, its simplicity, and its tragic intensity. The characters are rapid sketches rather than searching portraits, but they are thoroughly alive, and if the psychology does not go very deep, it is true to nature. The most strongly drawn is Octave. . . . (p. 156)

It must be admitted that [*Fantasio*] is not very dramatic. . . . But it is a joy to the reader. The second scene of the first act, which culminates in the famous dialogue between Fantasio and Spark, is one of the finest and most original things that Musset ever wrote, and of all the dissipated youths in whom he has embodied and exaggerated his own experiences Fantasio is the most attractive. . . . (p. 159)

[The] last scene, short and slight though it is, is a good example of Musset's power of suggestion. Underlying his airy witticisms there is often a depth of thought, which, because it does not come to the surface, is apt to be lost on the stage. Another of his characteristics is that his leading characters generally make a more favourable impression upon us at the end of the play than at the beginning. His young rakes for instance are often "fanfarons du mal" [braggarts of evil]. They exaggerate their vices in a spirit of swagger. This repels us at first, but gradually they reveal an undercurrent of good sense and good feeling, which, added to their innate honesty, both towards themselves and towards others, attracts us to them, and we part from them with regret. . . . Elsbeth, unlike Marianne and Camille, attracts us at once, partly by her affectionate regrets for Saint-Jean, and partly by her unselfish devotion to her father and her country. But she too grows on us. At first cold and reserved towards the new fool, she gradually becomes more friendly, and when he is in prison and unmasked she is full of sympathy and understanding. We leave her, not only with admiration for her serene and smiling courage, but with the feeling that she has the makings of a great as well as a good woman. . . . (pp. 163-64)

The plot [of *On ne badine pas avec l'amour*], like that of every comedy by Musset, is at once original and very simple. It captivates us by the intensity of its psychological interest and by the unexpected tragedy of its conclusion. But if in a sense it is the most tragic of Musset's dramas, it also contains the largest and most laughable comic element. This, however, fits in naturally with the serious part of the story, and there is no more discord between the two elements than there is in *Henry IV*. The comic element is represented by four *grotesques,* to use the French term—characters of much the same type as [Shakespeare's] Shallow and Silence, or Dogberry and Verges. They consist of the Baron, Maître Blazius, his son's tutor, Maître Bridaine, the *curé* [priest] of the village, and Dame Pluche, the governess of his niece, Camille. We have a full and vivid description of the two first by the Chorus of villagers, for it is one of the original features of this play that there is a Chorus. (pp. 164-65)

Dame Pluche and the two priests are admirable as types, but the Baron is a more individual and a more subtle creation. As appears from his language to Dame Pluche, he cannot bear contradiction or opposition from those about him, but when he is obeyed, he is kindly and condescending. . . . [He] has a strong sense of his own position and importance, but he is fussy rather than pompous. He is meticulous in his love of details and of everything that conduces to order and regularity. When anything goes wrong with his carefully prepared plans, he at once loses his head. . . . In spite of his slender intelligence and his other weaknesses, we have a kindly feeling for him, such as we do not have for [Shakespeare's] Claudio or the Prince of Mantua. (p. 165)

The character of Camille is a masterpiece of fine perception and firm construction. . . . [All the] stages in her development from a cold convent-bred schoolgirl to a passionate woman are portrayed with deep psychological insight and striking dramatic power. On a first reading, the character of Perdican seems to be less firmly drawn. . . . But when we study the character more closely, we become aware of the artistic workmanship with which its finer shades are rendered. Perdican's chief characteristic is his impulsiveness. This makes him inconsistent in what he says and thoughtless in what he does. He says that he believes in nothing: yet immediately afterwards he expresses astonishment at Camille because she does not believe in love, and in the final scene he prays fervently to God. To punish Camille he tells Rosette that he loves her, and then, carried away by his feelings, he says he will marry her. . . . He is not a strong character, but he has his good qualities. (pp. 168-69)

[In *Barberine,* based on a story by Matteo Bandello,] Musset has closely followed Bandello in all essential points, but it is remarkable how out of a simple, though charmingly told, narrative he has constructed a real drama of conflicting desires and emotions, and how out of mere names, with only one or two hints to help him, he has created characters alert with life and individuality. . . . Ulric is little more than a sketch. He is the loving husband who has complete confidence in his wife; he is also modest, brave, and honourable. But Barberine, with her complete lack of self-consciousness, her naïvety, her interest in her domestic occupations, her quick insight into Rosemberg's character, her humorous punishment of his fatuous

audacity, is a perfectly delightful and satisfying portrait. (pp. 171-72)

Though *Le Chandelier* is founded on an incident in Musset's own life, it has an air about it of a tale by Boccaccio. . . . (p. 174)

The one sympathetic character is Fortunio. . . . [Because Musset] was dramatising his own story, he was able to put into the part all the pathos and the passion that distinguishes it. For Fortunio is his own portrait, inwardly as well as outwardly. Like Fortunio, he was at once a timid and an audacious lover, a Cherubino of deeper feelings; he had too Fortunio's candour, his touch of melancholy, and his poetic accent. (p. 175)

Nothing can be finer than the four speeches of Fortunio which follow Jacqueline's request to him to let her keep his song. Never has the passionate love of a youthful idealist been more delicately expressed; there is not a word to alter in any of them. But one cannot help wondering at the sudden change that they produce in Jacqueline's heart. What does it imply? Is it merely a caprice, or is she really sincere in the avowal of her love? Would it not have been more in accordance with her character, if, like the original Jacqueline, she had callously dismissed her *chandelier* when she found that he was too much in earnest? (p. 176)

[The fantastic element in *Il ne faut jurer de rien*] is as considerable as it is in any of [Musset's three-act comedies in prose]. Valentin van Buck, the would-be Lovelace, is a *fat* [fop] of the first water, but his project of seducing within a week a carefully brought-up girl of good family is perfectly fantastic. Moreover one realises, as the play proceeds, that Valentin's Lovelace airs are very much on the surface and that, when brought face to face with Cécile's naïvety and trusting innocence, he almost at once becomes a humble lover in his heart. The long scene between him and his uncle which opens the play is deservedly famous and contains some of Musset's most brilliant dialogue. (p. 177)

The second and third acts are not well constructed, and the reader has some difficulty in following the movements of the actors. For stage purposes there had to be some transposition of the scenes. (p. 178)

The last scene, the love scene under the trees between Valentin and Cécile, with its beautiful setting—the clearing in the wood, the moonlight after the storm, the pearl-drops on the leaves of the birches—is Musset at his tenderest and most charming. . . . (p. 179)

[In Musset's next drama] he made somewhat of a new departure. *Un Caprice* is in one act instead of three, and there are only three characters. Moreover, there is complete unity of place—Mathilde's bedroom—and the division into scenes is perfectly orthodox. The theme is even slighter than in the majority of Musset's comedies. The two purses are merely symbols, the red purse of Mathilde's love for her husband, and the blue purse of her husband's capricious fancy for another woman. The real theme is this caprice, which, aided by the wife's jealousy, the husband's pride, and the inexperience of both, provokes a *scène conjugale* [marital quarrel]. Neither character is more than a rapid sketch, but each has quite sufficient individuality for the purpose of the play. Mathilde is gentle and timid, but she is deeply in love with her husband and thoroughly loyal to him. Chavigny, the husband, is not attractive, nor is he meant to be. (p. 180)

In contrast to the low-toned sketches of this married couple the finished portrait of Mme de Léry stands out in a brilliant light. On the surface she is an agreeable rattle, but beneath her airy *sans gêne* [unflappability] she is a woman of intelligence, good sense, and feeling. She is fundamentally serious, especially where the heart is concerned. (p. 181)

There are only two characters [in *Il faut qu'une porte soit ouverte ou fermée*], and as neither of them leaves the stage for a moment the unities of place and time are not only completely observed but the action occupies the exact time that it takes to act the play. Not that there is any action in the sense of external action; it takes place solely within the hearts of the actors. . . . [The stages by which the Count and the Marquise reach their engagement] are indicated with such subtlety and delicacy that it requires close attention and some divination on the part of the reader to detect them. (p. 183)

Il faut qu'une porte soit ouverte ou fermée and *Un Caprice* were the two plays of Musset which shewed most strongly the influence of Marivaux. Like Marivaux he was more interested in character than plot, and like Racine and Marivaux he loved to probe its inmost recesses. In most of his comedies there is one great scene, in which two characters act and re-act upon one another through speech and argument, with the result that their relations to one another at the end of the scene are different from what they were at the beginning. . . . [The scene between Valentin and Cécile in *Il ne faut jurer de rien*] comes nearest to Marivaux, who . . . habitually used such scenes to dispel the doubts or break down the defences of hesitating lovers, but who achieved his purpose by a series of encounters and not by a single and decisive one. In Musset's *Un Caprice* the scene between the Marquise and the Count occupies nearly half the play, but it is not an encounter between equal antagonists. Rather, Mme de Léry is like a fisherman coaxing Chavigny to rise to her fly and, as soon as he has taken it, landing him without a struggle. But the solitary scene of *Il faut qu'une porte soit ouverte ou fermée* would have most rejoiced the heart of Marivaux. (pp. 185-86)

Carmosine is founded on a story of Boccaccio's. . . . This story is told by Boccaccio with all his direct simplicity, enlivened by his delicate and irresistible touches of pathos and tenderness, and Musset has kept pretty closely to his source. But he has introduced two new characters—Perillo, who has loved Carmosine (Lisa) from childhood . . . , and Ser Vespasiano, one of those conceited and uncomprehending fools whom Musset loved to ridicule, but . . . [is] a little out of place in *Carmosine*. Also two of Boccaccio's characters are greatly developed—Minuccio the troubadour, and the Queen. The scene in which the latter by her tactful sympathy administers consolation to Carmosine . . . is as beautiful as it is affecting. Equally good is the one . . . in which Minuccio, who with all his wit and gaiety is no less sympathetic and helpful, tells Carmosine's story to the Court in language as simple and as moving as Boccaccio's. The other characters are more or less sketches. . . . [On] the whole the play is inferior to the best of Musset's comedies, and it is so, I think, for two reasons. In the first place the story, at least as Musset has treated it, has not enough matter for three acts. In consequence he has been obliged to fill out his play, just as he did *Barberine,* with scenes or portions of scenes that can only be called padding. Secondly, though the chief characters are drawn with great charm and with sufficient insight to convince us of their goodness and intelligence, there is no attempt to probe deeper. We know nothing of their internal conflicts, not even of Carmosine's or Perillo's, nothing, in short, of their inner life. . . . In spite of its weak points, however, the play has much charm and should be better known than it is. Musset, indeed, regarded it as one of his two best plays, the other being *Lorenzaccio*. . . . (pp. 188-89)

[*Bettine*] is a stronger play than *Carmosine*. It shews greater insight into the human heart and the characters have more depth. . . . [In] spite of its superficial air of contemporary life, the fantastic element is just as strong as in any of Musset's comedies. The strange wedding, which is apparently about to take place in the presence of the notary as the sole official and the sole witness (except perhaps Calabre), Bettine's unreasoning and unreasonable love for "ce drôle" [this scoundrel] Steinberg, still more her philosophic acceptance of her old friend Stéfani as his substitute, are all in the highest degree fantastic. Yet, such is Musset's art that under the spell of his dialogue we ignore the improbabilities and are content to follow the inward life of his characters, as he chooses to present them to us. (pp. 190-91)

As a young man [Musset] overflowed with enthusiasm for certain writers, especially for Shakespeare and Byron. . . . He comes under the influence of writers whom he admires, but it is only a suggestive influence. He could truly say, "Je bois dans mon verre" [I drink from my glass]. And nowhere is he more original than in his dramatic work. It is true that *André del Sarto* evidently comes from the Romantic camp, but it differs considerably from the typical Romantic drama. It shews for one thing far more psychological insight, especially in the character of André. . . . [In his later plays], Musset breaks away altogether from the Romanticists, and henceforth he works entirely on lines of his own—influenced, indeed, by the lessons that he had learnt from great masters, but without a trace of imitation. And if one is asked what these lines are, one might define them as the combination of psychological realism with a fantastic setting.

If "Je bois dans mon verre" is true, so also is "Mon verre n'est pas grand" [My glass is not large]. Musset wrote no poetry and only one drama on the grand scale. His comedies never exceed three acts, and two—perhaps the most perfect— are in one act. The characters are few, and of these only two or three are of the first importance. In his three most characteristic comedies we have Octave and Marianne, Perdican and Camille, Fantasio and Elsbeth. Of these only Perdican and Camille are lovers; but love is the theme of all three plays. (pp. 191-92)

Musset's plots are extremely simple. Some are of his own invention, some are founded on personal experience, and some are taken from books. But if the plot is simple it is often very effective, especially in the two comedies, *Les Caprices de Marianne* and *On ne badine pas avec l'amour,* which have a tragic ending. There are others which, if less striking, have at any rate the merit of originality—those of *Il ne faut jurer de rien, Le Chandelier,* and *Un Caprice*. . . .

It is not in the glamour of his characters that Musset excels, but in their psychological truth. Like Racine and Marivaux he can penetrate to the recesses of the heart; he can detect its half-formed desires, its hesitations, its sudden changes—in short the whole curve of its wavering course. As a result his characters demand close attention from both spectator and reader, and all the more so because he sometimes records his observations rather by suggestion than by direct statement. (p. 197)

Musset's usual method of revealing character is by means of dialogue, and for that purpose his style is singularly well adapted.

Easy and supple, it lends itself readily to various uses, and among others to the interchange of conflicting views in such a way as to bring out the characters of the speakers. We have first-rate examples in the scenes between Octave and Marianne, between Perdican and Camille, between Mme de Léry and Chavigny, and between the Count and the Marquise. The opening dialogue of *Il ne faut jurer de rien* . . . [is] a famous example of Musset's ease and brilliance. It is not only a clear and adequate exposition of the play, but it gives us considerable insight into the characters of both uncle and nephew. (p. 198)

[Dialogue] is also a means of developing the plot, and when there is little physical action, this function may become highly important. Musset, in whose comedies physical or external action is of the slightest, is a little capricious in this use of dialogue. . . . In *Fantasio* the dialogue throughout contributes little or nothing to the development of such plot as there is, and the *dénouement* is the result of a pure caprice. It is very different with *On ne badine pas avec l'amour*. From the moment that Perdican and Camille first meet, their conversations determine the whole dramatic movement of the play. Growing love, piqued vanity, jealousy, pride, conflict between love and religion, all find expression; and thus of this play it is preeminently true that the plot is created by the characters. (pp. 200-01)

[Nowhere] is Musset's skill in making speech the mirror of the soul better displayed than in the two one-act comedies, *Un Caprice* and *Il faut qu'une porte soit ouverte ou fermée*. The dialogue between the Marquise and the Count is the longest that Musset ever wrote, which is natural, seeing that it forms the whole play, but that between Mme de Léry and M. de Chavigny is more than two-thirds as long. The miracle is that in neither case does the interest ever flag. From first to last we follow with keen intent the jealousy, the bad temper, the amorous desires, of M. de Chavigny, and the skill with which Mme de Léry plays him, and then his sudden rise to the bait and the swift blow with which she crushes him. Less thrilling and less brilliant, but even more remarkable as an example of dramatised psychology, is the encounter between the Marquise and the Count, in which, after many hesitations and misunderstandings, many advances and retreats, an ordinary afternoon call ends in a matrimonial engagement. (pp. 201-02)

[Musset's] dialogue is all the more effective because he employs it almost solely for the purpose either of portraying character or of developing his story. He never turns aside to discuss social problems or other topics of the day; he has no theories to air, no gospel to preach. For him the play is the thing.

It is very seldom that sentiments uttered by his characters can be taken as representing his own opinions, though they may be, and no doubt often are, expressions of his varying moods. . . . But the one doctrine which stands prominently out in his comedies and which certainly represents his own belief, is that the only good thing, the only reality, is love. That is the burden of *Les Caprices de Marianne*, of *Fantasio*, of *On ne badine pas avec l'amour*, of *Il ne faut jurer de rien*. . . . [Musset] lacked the patient perseverance and power of concentration necessary for the production of a really considerable work. Thus with all his great natural gifts—his dramatic instinct, his imaginative hold of his characters, his psychological insight, his transparent sincerity, his easy, vigorous, and always artistic style—he failed to write more than one great drama. But, probably because he recognised his own limitations, he confined himself, after this one more or less successful effort on the great scale, to pieces of more modest aims and dimensions; to three-act and even one-act comedies. All have merits and the majority are, within their limits, masterpieces. . . . [They] have a careless freedom carried to audacity, which reminds one of Shakespeare, an abiding charm, and a convincing originality. (pp. 205-06)

> *Arthur Tilley, "Musset," in his* Three French Dramatists: Racine, Marivaux, Musset, *1933. Reprint by Russell & Russell, 1967, pp. 137-206.*

ALBERT THIBAUDET   (essay date 1936)

[*Thibaudet was an early twentieth-century French literary critic and follower of the French philosopher Henri Bergson. He is often described as versatile, well-informed, and original, and critics cite his unfinished* Histoire de la littérature française de 1789 à nos jours, *first published in 1936 and excerpted below, as his major critical treatise. In this work, Thibaudet classified authors by the generations of 1789, 1820, 1850, 1885, and 1914-1918, rather than by literary epochs.*]

The basis of Musset's genius, his true vocation in another time, was the dramatic form, and his well-balanced verse often requires the tone of the theatrical speech. For a long time the public ear would welcome this kind of verse, which was to be, for example, that of Emile Augier's verse comedy. Beginning with Baudelaire it was wounded and exiled by the exigencies of pure poetry. . . . There is a whole doctrine of classicism in Musset. And something of it, after all, can be retained. First of all, in his character as the poet of unhappy love, the author of the most sincere, the most reserved, the most naked, the most desperate love poetry of his time, in *Le Souvenir*, in *Les Nuits*, in so many shorter poems of *Les Poésies nouvelles*, he occupies among the romantics the position of a witness to the human heart analogous to Racine's position among the classics. Further, he took little or no part in romantic illusionism; he was indeed the child of his century, not its giant or its prophet; unlike George Sand or Hugo, he did not lay his raptures to the credit of God's cause. He recognized weakness and evil in himself as weakness and evil: the poet was singly, ordinarily, classically a man. Finally, he had neither a politics nor a philosophy, he was a man of letters, a poet in the old style, like Malherbe and Boileau; the freedom of his utterance was not on God or the state but on customs and letters. He was a young-bourgeois, with the hyphen in order to make it plain that it was a question not only of age but of ideas and condition. All the same, later on and to subsequent generations he seemed more bourgeois than young. The generation of the Second Empire, Baudelaire and Flaubert, formed itself to a certain extent in opposition to him. To the question, who is the most outmoded of the four great romantic poets, the usual answer would be Musset. But, if the epithet is justified, it is not without its compensations. More or less withdrawn from fashion and trend, Musset has been carried, like a classic, toward an eternal left center of French literature. In fact he has lost readers and hearts. Between the spirit of the eighteenth century and romanticism he established a connection, a society, it might almost be said a golden mean: he was less the child of the century than the child of the July Revolution, the little Parisian who grabbed his pistols and ran out to stand before Delacroix's *Liberté*—in this case, literary liberty. This child of July is the sole great poet of the nineteenth century whom nothing, absolutely nothing, allows us to call a great man and who . . . has left nothing, absolutely nothing, of a testimony, or, as they say, of a message; and not, alas, for lack of the desire. (pp. 193-94)

Albert Thibaudet, ''Alfred de Musset,'' in his French Literature from 1795 to Our Era, *translated by Charles Lam Markmann, Funk & Wagnalls, 1968, pp. 190-94.*

GEORGES POULET (essay date 1952)

[*Poulet is a modern Belgian critic whose writings attempt to reconstruct an author's consciousness: specifically, the relation to and understanding of time and space as rendered in fiction. His early criticism demonstrates his belief that authors live in an isolated world and thus cannot be understood in terms of generalizations about the era in which they lived. The task of the critic is to enter the artist's consciousness and define it. In contrast to his early critical criteria, Poulet's later work often suggests that writers are influenced by the spirit of their time, and he studies their representation of the widespread characteristics of their age. In the following essay, originally published in his* La distance interieure, *1952, which he prefaces with a quote from Musset's* The Confessions of a Child of the Century, *Poulet discusses Musset's rendering of time and duration and its effect on the reader.*]

To the right, to the left, over there, at the horizon, everywhere voices call to him. All is desire, all is reverie . . . If one had a hundred arms, one would not hesitate to open them in the void; one has only to clasp there his mistress, *and the void is filled.*

The earliest of Musset's poetry is . . . the presentiment of a plenitude, the feeling of an imminence; it is a poetry of youthfulness and of youth, a poetry of pleasure or rather of the flight toward pleasure, which singularly recalls that of the true masters of Musset, that is to say, the petty masters of the eighteenth century. But whereas these, a Voltaire, a Bertin, a Boufflers, are fully confident of instantaneously capturing that instantaneous thing called happiness, the poetry of Musset cannot be resigned to awaiting the moment which is going to present him his object. It mounts up, it bursts forth in a kind of smarting realization of not yet being what it is going to be; it is the feeling of mad impatience and of extreme thirst. . . . [All] the thought of Musset is condensed into a sort of temporal interval in which it is possible that the duration will change and the moment transmute itself into another; and it is this anticipation, this piercing hope which gives him a life that is like the beating of a heart, like a leaping forth of being, a rapid and precipitate capturing of the consciousness of self between the time when one was not, or when one had nothing, and the time when occasion and love can bestow everything. . . . (pp. 183-84)

The first movement of thought with Musset is thus a passionate dedication of the whole being to a future that is on the point of becoming present. Like the poetry of Vigny, that of Musset is the thought of a human being ''always ready to become transfigured'' [*Lettre à Lamartine*]. But in contrast to Vignian poetry, it is by no means a pure anticipation of itself, in which one apprehends oneself as one dreams of being, as solitarily one foresees oneself. Here, on the contrary, the future is an imminent pleasure, dependent upon a precise object which has already entered the field of desire and regard. All existence feels itself dependent upon an immediate future which it must seize in flight. And the heart palpitates at the idea that its beating marks the exact instant which precedes that of happiness. (pp. 184-85)

[In] Musset's eyes, the moment of love takes on an importance beyond any other, and that by reason of its ''eternity.'' This doesn't mean, of course, that it continues forever, identical to itself, replacing the transitory duration of man by a permanent duration, like that of God; though, it is true, Musset will never explain to himself, except by the intervention of infidelity and falsehood, the abrupt termination of the lover's ecstasy and his dropping back into time. But the thing of which Musset will never entertain a doubt—save in the darkest hours when the anguish consists precisely in asking oneself if one has not lived a lie—is the revetment of eternity which these lone hours acquire when the voice of desire is silenced, and when one can forget his temporal condition. Eternal moments, in that they repudiate and erase all others, in that they do not reintegrate common duration, but stay in isolation without being linked, before or behind, to other moments which their refulgence abolishes. Hence, despite the violence of the sensual ecstasy, what Musset essentially remembers of them is the consciousness of a *pause* in time, a resting place:

[From *Le Saule:*]

It is a pause—a calm—an inexpressible ecstasy.
Time—that traveler whom an invisible hand,
From age to age, at a slow pace, leads to eternity—
Pensive, at the side of the road, pauses and stops.

But this pause, this interior silence, this peaceful dispensation from desiring, which the being who loves enjoys at the instant he loves, if it is a part of the instant, it is no longer the center, the heart, but already the end of it. This pause is no longer an ardent, actual joy; it is a joy that has been thought and is almost over. And it is striking that [*Le Saule* and *La Confession d'un enfant du siècle,*] the two places in which Musset chooses to describe at greatest length the realization of the happiness of loving, are those each time when the lover finds himself *after* the night of love ''leaving with slow steps'' the house of the loved one, and thanking God, not for possessing, but for *having* possessed his happiness. (pp. 186-87)

[For] Musset, as for all who place happiness in the erotic moment, happiness is never directly apprehended, never lived interiorly and at his center of being. It is never a present happiness, but a mysterious nonactual presence hemmed in between two moments of extraordinary distinctness: the moment in which happiness is a hope that becomes present, and the moment in which it is a present that becomes memory.

As a necessary consequence, the history of the man who wants to live in the eternal moment, becomes the history of the man who perceives himself always to be withdrawing from this moment. He is going away from his ecstatic moment. . . . (pp. 187-88)

But the pain which Musset suffers does not consist solely in the consciousness of a moving away and a tearing apart. A past from which one feels himself torn apart is an immediate occasion of great suffering at the end of which there is a hope of healing and pacification. And a past from which one is removed is a sad farewell that one says to himself, up to the moment when the being one was is effaced in the distance in order to give place to the being one is, changed and consoled. But the particularity of the eternal moment is to continue to be eternal, even when it has ceased to be a moment, ceased to be lived. And as at the moment in which it was being lived it was forgetful of all the rest, so in departing from the moment in which it ceases to be lived, it becomes impossible to be itself forgotten:

[From *Le Confession d'un enfant du siècle:*]

> Those memories, after I had lost her, pursued me
>   without respite. . . .
>
>   (p. 188)

The past is not blotted out then, nor cured. Can one even say that it is past, since it continues to exist? It is there, present, though outside of the present, distant without being blurred by distance, ineffaceable memory which never ceases to attest, to aggravate by its negative splendor, the tragic deficiency of the moment which it is not. Such is the strange dividing into two of being and time which Stendhal once called the "repining grief," and which is less the division of time between past and present, than the division of the present itself between a past always present to the mind but no longer lived, and a present which it is necessary to live but which is consumed and unbearable. . . . (pp. 188-89)

The contemplation of the past is thus the contemplation of the interior abyss into the depths of which, step by step, one has fallen down all the way to the present. How did one pass from such a height to such a depth, from such a plenitude to such a misery? Existence appears as a progressive denudation, as a rapid ageing: "It seemed to me that all my thoughts were falling like dry leaves" [*Le Poète déchu*]. And if one is carried despairingly back, on the one hand, to an anterior epoch of profusion, to a time "when Life was young," in which "Heaven walked and breathed on earth in a people of gods" [*Rolla*], on the other hand one thereby perceives, and only the more clearly, the moral and physical disgrace of the time which has now become ours. And so the phantom clothed in black, which sets about constantly to accompany Musset in existence, is neither the past nor youth, but "the ghost of youth" [*Nuit de décembre*], that is to say the image of oneself one sees appear when, in solitude, regarding oneself with the eyes of the past, one begins to understand what one has become, "a shadow of oneself" [*Lorenzaccio*] stripped of its youth, its innocence, its power, a sort of tragic caricature of the being which had once lived. . . . (pp. 190-91)

So eternal, for Musset, seemed the death of the heart, so unforeseeable its rebirth, finally so nimble, so prompt is the passage from the one to the other and from the past to the future, that it is as if it were supernatural, immediately and irresistibly efficacious, and of a grace coming not from on high but from below, lifting itself up from palpable depths. . . . Each of these resurrections is accompanied by a total rejuvenation of the old being, by a gay gesture of forgetfulness throwing off the shroud of the past.

[From *La Coupe et les lèvres:*]

> From the day when I saw thee,
> My life began; the rest was nothing;
> And my heart has ever beaten only on thine. . . .

It seems that the being awakens to life for the first time, or rather that it discovers with rapture the independence of the moment in which it is reborn, over against all preceding moments. Old promises, old hopes, old tears, and even the lot of fallen angel to which one thought himself condemned forever, all that is found, perhaps not abolished, but dropped down, left behind, like a time unloaded on the side of the road. And behold one finds oneself afresh to be desirous, happy, loving, living, carelessly participating, as if one had never lived before, in an utterly fresh time, the adventurous time of love. Doubtless this adventure is the same one which has already more than

once lived. And, one knows only too well, it can end only in suffering and death. But beyond suffering and death there are still other loves, and other deaths, and other lives; so that in this mixture of experience and heedlessness, the independence of moments becomes the independence of successive loves and lives. . . . (pp. 193-94)

The principle of the independence of the moments of time becomes for Musset a sort of creation reiterated by love. It becomes also an affirmation of the eternity of each moment of life, an eternity at which each moment arrives when, *ceasing to be, it begins to no longer cease to have been.* Each moment enters in its turn into a particular immortality which is its *truth.* It can no longer be either disavowed or denied. It is intact forever. (p. 196)

> Georges Poulet, "Musset," in his The Interior Distance, *translated by Elliott Coleman, The Johns Hopkins University Press, 1959, pp. 182-96.*

GEOFFREY BRERETON   (essay date 1956)

Two months after the final break with George Sand, Musset walked under the chestnut-trees in the Tuileries, treading on perhaps exactly the same ground that Racine had paced as he walked there over a hundred and fifty years before declaiming the still molten verse of *Mithridate.* Then he went home, called for all the available candles in the house to be lit and taken to his room, and worked among them until morning on the composition of his poem. If we did not know that *La Nuit de mai* was composed in this way, we could almost deduce it. Such a poem would be launched in an illumination and finished in a fever. Once begun, it sings itself on inevitably, and there is little that the author can afterwards do to correct or change it. In form it is a dialogue between the Muse and the Poet—as are all the *Nuits,* except *La Nuit de décembre.* It contains the master-theme of them all—that a good poet must have had experience of suffering. . . . (pp. 139-40)

The enthusiasm of the spring-drunk Muse, eager to express her rapture, is opposed to the muteness of the Poet, too broken to respond. These artificial-looking figures stand for something much deeper than a literary convention. The Muse can be taken as the Ideal Woman, the *âme soeur* [soul sister] of nearly all the Romantics, but more properly this is a debate between Musset's natural vitality, beginning to reassert itself after his emotional buffeting by George Sand, and his despair which he is beginning to realize and define. . . . In *La Nuit de décembre,* it is winter. The theme of despair has moved up into full focus. The Muse is absent, and in her place is a mysterious black-clad double who has appeared to the poet at all the critical moments of his life, particularly the saddest ones. . . . (p. 140)

La Nuit d'août is really a spring or early-summer poem, and is best appreciated when read as the counterpart of *La Nuit de mai.* . . . [It expresses the hub of Musset's dilemma: without] emotional and sensual excitement he had no sensation of living and no stimulus to write. With it, he knew that his energy and his interest in life must dwindle year by year like a *peau de chagrin* [as in Honoré de Balzac's tale of the same name, which means "the sorrowful skin"]. This inescapable dilemma—and not a spoilt-child screaming for one particular woman—forms the tragic heart of the *Nuits* poems. It explains their intensity, their impatience, their exaggerations of emotion, for—as Musset too lucidly saw—time and youth were running out, and his was not a nature capable of recollecting emotion in tranquillity. (pp. 141-42)

[*Les Nuits, Lettre à Lamartine, L'Espoir en Dieu,* and *Souvenir*] are the record of the effects of a violent emotional experience upon a highly sensitive and unstable temperament. They combine an intensity of personal feeling and an undisguised exposure of the poet's *moi* [me] with a certain artificiality in the form and idiom. . . . [Writing] when he did, in a decade of bourgeois sentimentality from which Hugo had already swept the neoclassic ornamentation, his verse was too readily accepted as the outpourings of a simple heart. . . . The artifice, the style, the distinctive stamp were lost sight of, and only the tear-provoking sentiments were seen. If Musset is considered, because of *Les Nuits,* as the poet-patron of self-pity, it was largely his own fault, yet many of his imitators and admirers overlooked the stiffening framework, the stylization of sorrow which distinguishes these poems from, say, a Dickensian death-bed scene. There is an essential distinction—though Musset does not invariably observe it—between an artist's pride in his suffering because it brings him good artistic material and an unorganized clamour of grief.

The rest of Musset's work contains little that resembles *Les Nuits* at all closely; its distinguishing marks are lightness, grace and wit. These qualities were the product of several influences, from Byron's in the early poems to La Fontaine's, Chénier's and then the spirit of the eighteenth century more generally in his later verse. But however numerous his—freely acknowledged—masters, Musset used them only as a basis for work which is quite distinctive and full of small but delightful surprises.

Much of it is written in the form of sonnets, *rondeaux* and short song-poems such as *La Chanson de Fortunio, J'ai dit à mon coeur, à mon faible coeur . . . , Fut-il jamais douceur de coeur pareille . . . , Tristesse, Mimi Pinson, A M. Victor Hugo, A Sainte-Beuve.* These poems are intentionally unsubstantial and their point must be taken at once or not at all. Only pedantry would stop to analyse it. But in such longer poems as *Mardoche, Namouna, Une bonne fortune,* the wit is more sustained. (pp. 142-43)

Much of [Musset's humour] is 'period', reflecting the assumed detachment of the dandy of the eighteen-thirties, whose motto might have been *Surtout, pas de sérieux* [throughout, not serious], but who was only half cured of [François Chateaubriand's novel] *René* and the *mal du siècle* and was ironically aware of the old dichotomy of body and spirit experienced also by Villon and by the 'baroque' Sponde. . . . (p. 145)

If Musset has dated in places, in others he remains very fresh, and in any case the reader is carried on by the rapid movement of his verse. This feature distinguishes him markedly from Hugo, and often from Vigny. It can be studied as a technical quality and related to the great variety of metres which Musset handled and his ingenuity in linking 'natural' speech with complicated rhyme-patterns, as few French poets except La Fontaine had done before him. Thus, the six-line stanzas of *Namouna* are rhymed in some ten different ways. *Les Nuits* show a mobility of metre and a variety of rhyme-changes which make them comparable to [John Milton's] *Lycidas* in their forward-moving effect. But this is not only a matter of technique—indeed Musset disclaimed all pretension to studied effects, insisting that he wrote purely as an amateur when the mood came to him. It rests on some mysterious quality inherent in the poet's mind, or his ear, or even his respiratory system. As Milton wrote most naturally not in couplets, or in quatrains, but in long soaring verse-paragraphs, Musset also, in his less

sublime way, spins out his verse in integrated paragraphs. (pp. 145-46)

The confident march of Musset's style is too easily obscured by the pathos of his subject. Here is a man who seems to be humiliating himself in language more suitable for defiance. But when it is remembered that he was proud to exhibit his suffering, the contradiction disappears.

In one other respect he equals, or sometimes excels, the . . . other great Romantics. His use of imagery is as bold as in any of them, but more varied and often more apposite. (p. 146)

But, unlike more luscious-sounding poets, [Musset] was not carried away by his imagery. His use of it was discreet, varied and controlled. He has nothing comparable to that eternal contrasting of the cradle and the tomb, the dawn and the sunset, which obsessed Hugo. Yet on the other hand, when he used metaphors he developed them to the full, drawing in all their implications, and so he cannot be thought of as a forerunner of the Symbolists. In his treatment of imagery he falls between Hugo and Verlaine and, unless it is recognized that there is a third place for him, he disappears.

That would be more than a pity. It would leave French Romantic poetry without humour. It would mean that for lightness and grace in the expression of personal passion we should have to go back to the sixteenth century, or else forward some forty years. Musset was a necessary poet in his generation. Still better, he was an unexpected one. (pp. 146-47)

> *Geoffrey Brereton, "Alfred de Musset," in his* An Introduction to the French Poets: Villon to the Present Day, *Methuen & Co. Ltd., 1956, pp. 137-47.*

MARGARET A. REES (essay date 1963)

[Asked] to predict the characteristics of [Musset's] imagery in the *Comédies et Proverbes,* scoffers at Romanticism would probably open the list with cloying sentimentality, followed by a glut of themes dear to the Romantics—such as moonlit nights, ghostly ruins, pallid lovers, the passionate South—and of their typical and often exaggerated moods—melancholy, despair, emotional fervor, and exaltation. One might certainly expect images of such a nature to prevail in Musset's plays and also, although dramatic prose is inherently less given to original metaphor than poetry, to appear more often and in brighter colors than in the works of a more sober literary age.

Yet when one turns to the *Comédies et Proverbes,* one finds images used with a surprising economy. Indeed, in many plays there are scarcely any except those which have passed into everyday life as part of the small change of conversation. The absence of striking imagery in those pieces which are chiefly comedies of polished wit set in a brilliant society—for instance, *Il faut qu'une porte soit ouverte ou fermée, Il ne faut jurer de rien,* and *Un Caprice*—points to an interesting conclusion about Musset's use of such imagery as a dramatist. It is not settings and situations in which superficial sparkle predominates that act as tinder to his flashes of poetic comparison. Brilliant and witty as some of his images may be, they do not occur primarily as demonstrations of verbal or mental agility.

At first sight it seems surprising to find imagery rare in *La Nuit vénitienne* also. Surely, since this was an early play, an attempt by a young frequenter of Hugo's group at storming the Parisian stage, the dialogue might be expected to display sparkling and colorful word-pictures. Yet practically the only metaphor to be developed at any length is the musical one. . . . *La Nuit vénitienne* indicates that in the *Comédies et Proverbes* images will not be chiefly baubles to serve as ornament any more than they are merely an opportunity for wit. This view of their function is borne out by later plays, including those where intense feeling prevails and where poetic outbursts might have been expected. (pp. 245-46)

Images which have lost their impact through frequent use, such as ''comme l'aiguille aimantée attire le fer'' . . . and ''cette fraiche aurore de jeunesse, dans cette rosée céleste de la vie'' [that fresh dawn of youth, in that dewy heaven of life] . . . occur as a matter of course throughout the *Comédies et Proverbes,* but to find more than a sparse sprinkling of original comparisons we must turn to a small number of plays—*Fantasio, Lorenzaccio, On ne badine pas avec l'amour,* and, above all, *Les Caprices de Marianne.*

Even here, every act or scene does not always yield a greater crop of images than those of, say, *Le Chandelier* or *Barberine.* Rather, there often seem to be sudden volcanic eruptions of image-making, of which one of the most striking is found in *Lorenzaccio.* The early scenes of this play have little to offer in new comparisons, bright with color though the dialogue may be. Yet in a scene which is perhaps, even more than that showing the accomplishment of Lorenzo's mission of murder, the crux of the play, images start cascading. This passage . . . [takes place] during the interview with Philippe Strozzi in which Lorenzo, an enigmatic figure until this point, drops his mask, stirred by Philippe's state of mind to reveal the secret of his life, the transformation which took an idealistic, studious young man and made him the cynical, debauched weakling of the earlier scenes. Here, as he speaks of the purpose which dominates him and for which he has already paid a high price, Lorenzaccio launches into a whole series of images. . . . (pp. 246-47)

It is worth noting that, although imagery flowers in Musset's theater at moments of intensity, these peaks do not always coincide with the climax of the plot, but rather with one in the emotions of a leading character. It is not the murder scene in *Lorenzaccio* which is especially rich in comparison, but the interview mentioned above, empty of physical action but supremely important for the light it throws on the hero's motives and mental state. In the same way, Fantasio, always ready for verbal conjuring, is particularly quick to draw imaginative parallels at times when the dialogue touches on matters which concern him deeply. . . .

Once he has entered the Court as royal jester, it is during his conversations with the princess, whose approaching marriage of convenience to a princely dolt has stirred him to indignation, that the most striking and highly developed images occur. The palace flower garden lends its tulips to provide comparison with the princess's marriage contract, and its roses as figures of the ladies of the Court. One of the most extended images equates the princess with a glittering toy which brings to mind the shop-windows of the rue Saint-Honoré. . . . (p. 248)

Musset's images are clearly not merely ornament or rhetoric. Rather their function is one which C. Day Lewis has pointed out as typical of the Romantics' use of comparison—to probe more deeply thoughts and emotions, here those of the principal characters and often, through them, those of the writer himself.

This is not the sole function of imagery in the *Comédies et Proverbes,* since Musset was too gifted a dramatist to rivet his eyes entirely on those figures in whom he could see reflections of himself and his own problems. Often images used by or of a character are effective additional touches to the picture which is being drawn of his personality. So Claudio, the humourless, stupid judge in *Les Caprices de Marianne,* describes his wife as ''un trésor de pureté'' [a treasure of purity] . . . , a conventional phrase typical of the pompous dullness Musset saw in him. . . . In the same way, Ser Vespasiano in *Carmosine* helps to ridicule himself through overblown stereotypes. (p. 249)

[Imagery] helps the patron of this ''spectacle dans un fauteuil'' [armchair theater] to form his visual impression of Blazius and Dame Pluche, and in a drama whose spectacle exists only in the imagination of the reader it is often valuable too in summoning up a picture of the setting against which the action is taking place. Musset has little of Hugo's fondness for prefacing each change of stage set with a luxuriantly detailed description, but when Fantasio has finished drawing his parallel between human beings and the flowers among which he and the princess are standing, a vision of the palace flower garden is as clear to us as though we had been given an account of its exact layout. (p. 250)

It would be a strange prose which did not make use of traditional comparisons such as ''pâle comme la neige'' [pale like the snow], but the more one reads of the *Comédies et Proverbes,* the more striking appears the high proportion of original images, which yet are never so obtrusive as to hinder or detract from the dramatic purpose of the passage where they are found. . . . Among the slightly longer images, freshness of treatment and sensitivity of perception are the rule. A dealer in trite similes, depicting a lover seeing his beloved as a huntsman catching sight of a doe, would not have spared the reader a mention of the creature's liquid eyes and grace, but [in *Les Caprices de Marianne*] Musset creates an unhackneyed and attractive picture almost exclusively in sound and silence:

> C'est ainsi qu'au fond des forêts, lorsqu'une biche avance à petits pieds sur les feuilles sèches, et que le chasseur entend les bruyères glisser sur ses flancs inquiets, comme le frôlement d'une robe légère, les battements de coeur le prennent malgré lui; il soulève son arme en silence, sans faire un pas, sans respirer. . . .

(pp. 250-51)

Whether the images have the softness of sound and delicacy of suggested colour of this last image or the warmth and splendour of *Barberine's* liveried valets, they are usually arresting in their pictorial charm. Scarcely ever could they be judged insipid and sentimental. It is also surprisingly rare to come upon an image whose material might be classified as ''typically Romantic,'' formed of the themes which were in danger of becoming clichés in the writings of the period. There are a few of this kind, such as Fantasio's vision of a girl who might have stepped from the ballet routine of *Les Sylphides* . . . ; but this type of comparison is not necessarily less appealing because it is expected.

Strangely lacking in Romantic stereotypes, Musset's imagery has a surprise in store too for those who hold the view that nature plays a far smaller part in the works of this Parisian dandy than in those of most of his contemporaries. It is true, as we have seen, that many of his metaphors and similes have their source in city life—in the circus scene to which Octave compares his life, in the vistas of streets which seem to Lorenzaccio and Fantasio to represent existence, or around the gaming tables as in the line from *Les Caprices de Marianne:* "Qu'importe comment la bille d'ivoire tombe sur le numéro que nous avons appelé . . . !'' Yet that type occurs no more frequently than others such as Octave's woodland picture of the doe, or Coelio's evocation of a boating scene which might so easily belong to the banks of the Seine. City-dweller though he might be, Musset knew too from his childhood the scenery around his grandfather's country house, apart from the landscapes with which he became familiar in later life, and the dialogue of his plays makes it clear that he had a store of mental pictures of the countryside on which he drew readily. (pp. 251-52)

[Imagery on the theme of love] probably overshadows all other subjects of his comparisons. Occasionally love is shown in the pose which one would expect of a Romantic writer—high on a pedestal and draped with an air of fatality and melodrama. To see love idealized, there is no need to look further than Perdican's famous speech in *On ne badine pas avec l'amour,* where the world is depicted as "un égout sans fond où les phoques les plus informes rampent et se tordent sur des montagnes de fange" and in which love between two human beings is the one thing of importance and beauty. . . .

[It] would be easy to foretell in these plays the presence of imagery showing the Romantic sanctification of love, as in the comparison Fantasio makes with a sacramental wafer which must be divided before an altar and both halves swallowed in a kiss. The same attitude can be seen in Cordiani's vision of love as an angel, fallen but still superb. Yet even here on this holy ground of the Romantics Musset's sense of comic reality is too strong to be prevented from breaking in. (p. 253)

[Musset's images] dealing with love seem to conform far more closely to what might generally be expected, or feared, of Romantic imagery than is typical of Musset in his theater. Certainly samples of what was prevalent at this period can be found in the *Comédies et Proverbes,* both in subject matter and in mood. Yet, among those images which are not merely a part of everyday speech, these are rare, outnumbered by imagery which is the result of an original mind. Above all, the keenness and delicacy of perception are those of a poet who couples with the powerful imagination and powerful feelings capable of conjuring up in his metaphors worlds in which the reader is completely absorbed for their duration, the restraint which never allows a passage of imagery to slow down the action of a play. Indeed, a study of the images in his dialogue intensifies admiration for Musset's workmanship as a dramatist. Never obtruding themselves for their own sake, never appearing merely as decorative tinsel, his metaphors and similes help the lines of the dialogue to delineate more firmly and vividly the background characters, and to penetrate more incisively into the mind of the main characters. Even more important for us, while delighting our ear and imagination, they reveal a little more of the mind of Musset himself. (p. 254)

Margaret A. Rees, "Imagery in the Plays of Alfred de Musset," in The French Review, Vol. XXXVI, No. 3, January, 1962-63, pp. 245-54.

HERBERT S. GOCHBERG   (essay date 1967)

[*Gochberg's study traces the development of Musset's dramatic art through the publication of* Scene in an Armchair. *The excerpt below examines the narrative and theatrical elements of the sequence of poems in* Tales of Spain and Italy, *which, according to the critic, contains Musset's initial dramatic attempts.*]

[*Don Paez*] is Musset's first really ambitious enterprise in verse. Although the poem reveals decided weaknesses of execution, it is consistent in its setting of rhymed alexandrine couplets. . . . [The] pattern is basically narrative, but it is frequently interrupted by conversational and descriptive passages. In addition, the narrator does not detach himself from the reader, whom he addresses from time to time as "frère" [brother]. The result of this familiarity is that the narrator is able to have the "listener" interrupt the tale by asking questions which the obliging narrator is only too happy to answer. Much of the narration tends therefore to be unusually colloquial, more in keeping with a tall tale than with heroic deeds of love and battle. (pp. 25-6)

[*Don Paez* represents] a significant step forward in the process of moving from narrated dialogue to dramatized dialogue. Each of the four parts is accompanied by an appropriate dialogue or scene. (p. 28)

Is *Don Paez* a drama? Certainly not, for of its 500 lines, only 160 represent dialogue, and only half of its dialogued sections are executed in the distinct dramatic form which we find in the scenes of Parts III and IV. Still, to look upon *Don Paez* only as a narrative forces the critic to chastise the author for capricious adulterations in form and genre. It is clear that Musset started out to write a *récit.* . . . The narrative mold breaks down in the last two parts in which the dialogued scenes become theatrical. In spite of this breakdown, the author succeeds in carrying out his basic plan of developing a narrative of four episodes, in each of which there is a corresponding dramatic moment. It is even possible to say that there is four-scene drama incorporated into the text: Don Paez and Juana bidding each other a fond farewell, Don Paez and Don Etur on the walls of the citadel, Don Paez and Belisa and their deadly lover's brew, and finally, Don Paez and Juana embracing in love and death. From all angles, the dramatic import and intent of *Don Paez* are perfectly clear, although it is neither a play nor a narrative poem when assessed as an artistic whole. It is built on the same narrative and topical foundations which underlie the earliest works of its architect. It looks like a narrative when viewed from the front, but in the back and on the inside the construction and decoration are those of a dramatist, even though he has yet to write his first play. (pp. 31-2)

The author's prologue tells us that [*Les Marrons du feu*] is a "comédie", and that it is his "premier pas" [first step]. The form is strictly dramatic. The speaking parts are indicated in the traditional manner and the division into scenes is quite clear. Finally, there is a literal flood of stage directions designed to transport the reader into an imaginary theater. A discussion of *Les Marrons du feu* is therefore a discussion of Musset's first play, not only in terms of the genre *drama,* but also in terms of "spectacle dans un fauteuil" [armchair theater], intended for a reader who can have his fourth-row-center seat as long as his imagination cooperates with that of the author.

Les Marrons du feu is a one-act play, divided into nine scenes. The duration and separation of the scenes are determined not so much by the entrances and exits of the characters as by the necessity of removing the action to different places in the unnamed seaside city . . . within which the play is set. In fact, the armchair spectator has to prod his geographic imagination eight times, for no two scenes are set consecutively in exactly the same place. . . .

Like *Don Paez,* it is written in alexandrines, but with a few shifts to lyric verse. It contains only a few long speeches scattered amid a great deal of rapid-fire dialogue characterized by multiply-interrupted lines. The most extreme break is in Scene VII, where two alexandrine lines are spread over nine printed lines, and shared by *four* different characters! (p. 33)

Another extravagence of *Les Marrons du feu* is that it treats a normally serious subject in a frivolous and farcical manner. The line of the story is in fact similar to that of *Don Paez,* but without a trace of the somber mood which permeates the earlier work. In spite of this absence, the play unravels threads of love, jealousy, rivalry, vengeance and death, all presided over by the laughing mask of comedy. During the play, the three main characters all participate in homicide. The male lead ends by having his throat cut, not between scenes, but on stage, so to speak, and his body is thrown into the sea. In fact, the entire cast is motivated by vicious and ignoble considerations. Violence and death, hallmarks of tragedy or melodrama, are deliberately blended with farce and parody. (p. 34)

While Musset's gallery will include many a lady whose pride has been bruised, nowhere else in his dramatic works will we encounter a distaff role so violent and so unpleasant as that of Camargo. Her type tends to become extinct in the evolution of Musset's art. The abbé is also unusual in the extent of his lust and of his capacity for violence. It is bad enough for an ecclesiastic to trespass on the domain of profane love, although behind this lies a long Gallic tradition. In the abbé's efforts to seduce Camargo, there is also a reflection of a stock comic situation, one in which the audience is encouraged to laugh at the awkward love-gestures of an unsympathetic clown. To cast Annibal in addition as an abbé is clearly unnecessary, and it is from this additional dimension of casting that the play's blasphemy derives. Rafael's violent death is enough of a jolt; its perpetration by a man of the cloth serves no other purpose than to highlight Camargo's viciousness, which is readily apparent in any event. Later ecclesiastic characters created by Musset will be assigned comic values, but they will not be developed into lovers and murderers.

On the other hand, the characterization of Rafael cannot be placed in a fossilized class. His youth, his attractiveness, his unfettered happy-go-lucky outlook, his gentility are all trademarks of the Musset hero. The curious thing about Rafael is that he does whatever he feels like doing, without introspection or rationalization, without taking anything seriously. . . . The bequeathing of his property to the family jester bolsters the idea that no matter what happens in *Les Marrons du feu,* it must not be taken too seriously. (pp. 37-8)

The suggestion that the abbé, the false man of God, may be a fiendish agent focuses our attention . . . on the blasphemous atmosphere of the play, especially as it is revealed by the profane attitudes of the abbé and by the exhortations and expletives of the main characters. The play preaches no conventional values as such, for it is in essence a vehicle of comic fantasy. The characters are all base to some degree. No one is right and no one is wrong. Even love, one of Musset's favorite life-principles, is the loser. There is no thesis to be accepted or rejected or to be taken seriously. Nevertheless, no matter how fantastic or frivolous the play may appear in its substance, it was evidently written seriously, for . . . the drowning motif [is] an unmistakable effort to master an artistic problem. The irreverent mood of the play is significant because it derives from characterization and from language, and because Musset seems to try, with partial success, to relate the irreverent elements to the action proper. (p. 45)

Comédie or *proverbe,* *Les Marrons du feu* has in it a premeditated murder and a senseless accidental killing. The seriousness of the characterization of Camago can be reduced only by reading it as parody. Moreover, the care with which the author attempts to unify his work by means of a cultivated pattern of language suggests that within the mold of sport and frivolity there is a pocket of earnestness, in outlook as well as in execution. By looking both forward and back, it is possible to see that the disquieting generic ambivalence is related to, and perhaps derived from the writer's conception of his favorite subject, love. *On ne badine pas avec l'amour* and *Les Caprices de Marianne* are also comedies in their essence, but the dénouements are tragically disastrous, leading to death and to the end of love. . . . [As in most of Musset's earliest work], love is a house of fantasy, in which pleasure and pain, dream and nightmare, and life and death sit at the same table. (pp. 48-9)

Don Paez and *Les Marrons du feu* are only two of the fifteen selections published as *Contes d'Espagne et d'Italie,* but they occupy almost as much space as the other *contes* put together. None of the remaining components is dramatic in organization, but . . . some of them yield important clues to Musset's artistic progress. (p. 51)

[*Portia*] is slightly longer than *Don Paez* and is organized as a narrative, without shifts to dramatic form. On the other hand, there are a few places where the alexandrine is broken into two printed lines in order to emphasize a change of speaker, and approximately half of the narration represents dialogue. Musset wrote many narrative poems after *Portia,* so that *Portia* must not be viewed as a reversal of dramatic tendencies. It is as much a narrative step beyond *Don Paez* as *Les Marrons du feu* is a dramatic step. In other words, *Don Paez* serves as a transitional experiment from which develops on the one hand an extensive dramatic literature, and on the other, a less extensive narrative poetry.

There is no humor in *Portia,* no trace of parody, no attempt at comic relief. There is the expected triangular situation, but its constituency and eventual disintegration are different from those of *Don Paez* and *Les Marrons du feu.* In *Don Paez,* jealousy leads to the death of all three characters, through the agency of the offended party. In *Les Marrons du feu,* jealousy brings about the death of the offender and the incapacitation of the supplanter, but the offended party remains triumphantly avenged. In *Portia,* an offended husband is killed in a duel by his younger rival. The rival supplants the husband, flees with his beloved, but will not be able to live happily ever after, partly because he has had to kill in order to possess, partly because he suspects at the end that his love has lost the divine seal of approval which it once seemed to have. (pp. 51-2)

[In *Portia*], moments of love are expressed as something human and as something godlike, but the human side is unable to retain for long its brief identity with the divine. Love needs heavenly support in order to be fulfilled, but the very realization of eternity is itself too much for profane lovers to endure. Musset's expression of the paradox of human love is clearly part of the pattern which we have seen emerging from his earlier work. Because love is both mortal and immortal, it is inextricably bound to life and death, to pleasure and pain, and to dream and nightmare. (p. 55)

[*Mardoche*] is a rambling narration of a young man's elaborate, but futile attempt to seduce an attractive neighbor. The lady of the story has a role which is virtually nil, and the only characters as such are Mardoche and his uncle. The dialogue is tied to the narration by an almost invisible fiber. (p. 56)

[As we read **Mardoche**], it becomes increasingly obvious that the dialogue is largely a variation of the central theme of **Portia**. The role of God vis-à-vis profane, adulterous lovers comes up for discussion. . . . The discussion between the two comic characters [Mardoche and his uncle] tends to polarize the attitudes toward love and God developed by the narrator of **Portia**. Mardoche represents an extravagant development of the young Dalti, who felt neither respect nor scorn in the temple of God. His uncle becomes in turn a caricaturized spokesman for the traditional religious and moral values of society. The beadle's reaction to his nephew's escapade seems at first to be merely extreme and ridiculous. To expect Mardoche to take seriously the idea that God may have attempted to smite him for his peccadilloes is to assume that nephew and uncle are actually able to communicate with each other. The absurdity of the situation, however, does not alter the fact that the treatment of the profane and divine aspects of love in **Mardoche** does not differ substantially from the viewpoints to be found in **Portia**. . . . (pp. 57-8)

There is, in sum, ample evidence that the non-dramatic works of Musset's nineteenth year . . . [form] part of an evolving dramatic art. The verse which Musset conceived in 1829 reveals . . . that the only hiatus between **Les Marrons du feu** and **La Quittance du diable** is the absence of a work wholly dramatic in form. **Portia** and **Mardoche** show that certain patterns of imagery and certain ways of looking at love, life and death,—patterns which go back to the earliest phase of Musset's artistic maturation—have continued to enjoy an existence of their own. (p. 59)

> *Herbert S. Gochberg, in his* Stage of Dreams: The Dramatic Art of Alfred de Musset (1828-1834), *Librairie Droz, 1967, 220 p.*

PAUL SAWYER (essay date 1969)

[Musset's "translation" of *Confessions of an English Opium Eater* titled **L'Anglais, Mangeur d'opium**] was one of the most weird, unfaithful, highly personalized translations ever made— it was in fact not really a translation at all, but a sort of paraphrase with extraordinary deletions, additions, and errors. . . . (p. 403)

Let us first consider what is not in the translation. Roughly twenty per cent of the text proper . . . is missing completely— not even summarized. Musset has also performed an appendectomy—not one word of the twenty-page appendix is found. The longest omission . . . deals with De Quincey's opium-taking experiences, about which he makes certain postulations. Inevitably something of the unique De Quincey personality is lost because of these omissions, but perhaps nothing essential. In general, Musset made omissions for one of three reasons. He removed much that interrupted the flow of narrative, such as De Quincey's discussions of his unhappy London memories . . . ; he excised material that presented translation difficulties, such as lines of poetry and certain prose sections. For example, he ignores . . . [several lines] from De Quincey's splendid panegyric on opium. . . . And finally, he deletes because he thought his French readers would neither understand nor be helped by De Quincey's references—thus an allusion to Oliver Cromwell . . . does not appear.

In addition to omitting much, Musset condenses greatly, sometimes skillfully, often with considerable loss. Most readers probably applaud his lightening of De Quincey's occasionally ponderous style. . . . Frequently, however, in his reductions, Musset alters the content. (pp. 404-05)

Probably the worst job of condensation is found at the very end. Much is omitted and what is not omitted is botched. Even such an important part of the *Confessions* as the moral is so hurried over that although Musset declares that he is giving it, he actually does not. . . . Almost as disturbing as the lack of a moral in Musset's translation is the lack of a hint of De Quincey's progress in his battle with opium. De Quincey writes, "I triumphed." . . . True, he hastens to qualify the triumph, but he definitely feels there has been an improvement while Musset somehow misses any optimistic note at all. . . .

Balancing the many omissions and condensations are the additions, and they are the best known parts of this little known work. There are three lengthy ones, none of them containing any indication that the insertion is not part of the De Quincey text. In the first, . . . Musset selects Spain as his favorite country. (p. 405)

[The second addition is] highly romantic, and is almost three times as long. . . . Recalling the brief and beautiful section about Ann of Oxford Street, Musset brings her back in an episode which is very badly introduced, if indeed it is introduced at all. (p. 406)

This interpolation seems to me to be one of the worst in the Musset translation. The exquisitely touching Ann story is made into adolescent melodrama with the usual paraphernalia of romance. It is clumsily introduced and lamely concluded, although straightforwardly told. As further evidence of Musset's youthful romantic nature, it perhaps has value; certainly as literature it has none. (pp. 406-07)

[Although] Musset's translation reveals a fair familiarity with the English language for an eighteen-year-old Frenchman, it betrays a gravely deficient comprehension for a translator. It shows Musset's direct, straightforward prose style with few adornments, frequently easier to understand than De Quincey's, but it conceals (probably because Musset was not able to recognize them) the poetic diction and flashes of humor of the original. It demonstrates his carelessness, haste, and at times over-confidence in his own knowledge. It evidences his readiness to alter his text whenever he wishes, but it is in those alterations, particularly the insertions, that the mature Musset as person and poet is adumbrated. (p. 408)

> *Paul Sawyer, "Musset's Translation of 'Confessions of an English Opium Eater'," in* The French Review, *Vol. XLII, No. 3, February, 1969, pp. 403-08.*

NICHOLAS OSMOND (essay date 1969)

Musset habitually referred to himself as a child, and irresponsibility is a key to his work. This can be an asset: when Musset is not taking himself seriously, the reader can. . . . Like a naughtier Chénier, he employs [in **'Mardoche'**] the alexandrine with adroit casualness. . . . This is Voiture in the manner of Byron, the form making fun of poetic respectability, the content rather self-consciously wicked about religion. Much of Musset's later work places him as a brilliant album poet, as in **'A Sainte-Beuve'** (*Poésies nouvelles*), in which he takes a quotation in prose to the effect that poetry is a young man's game and neatly makes it contradict itself by writing it out as verse. Like

Gautier, Musset is a virtuoso, treating poetry as an elaborate game, choosing the cheeky rhyme in the short line for the pleasure of exhibiting his own skill, though his occasional lapses into doggerel make him a highly gifted amateur rather than a true professional like Gautier.

Musset's playfulness is already evident in the self-consciously Romantic poems of his early manner. Dashing heroes in whom he only half believes move against a colourful but cardboard décor taken invariably from a guide-book dream of Italy or Spain. There is a set-piece on almost every page: the hero swarms up a silken ladder to embrace the Andalusian or Venetian beauty who waits voluptuously in her boudoir. These poems hover amusingly on the edge of self-parody. . . . (pp. 30-1)

But when Musset tries to reach our deeper responses, we tend to balk. **'Souvenir'**, written in the same rhythm as [Lamartine's] 'Le Lac' and invoking the same pathetic fallacy, seems deliberately to invite comparison. Despite some beautiful images, Musset's poem only occasionally matches the effortless musicality of Lamartine, and in trying to force a tone of pathos he achieves only a stiff peroration on the theme of love and time. Intimate self-revelation turns too easily into the vulgar dramatization of the poet's experience—a temptation to which Lamartine certainly succumbs in some of the poems of the *Nouvelles Méditations* and the commentaries which he appended to his poems later, but which in poems like 'Le Lac' he so effortlessly avoids. (p. 31)

The pelican in that famous passage from **'La Nuit de mai'**, which provides an archetypal image of the Romantic artist feeding the public on his own palpitating entrails, is a theatrical exhibitionist, and we notice that he waddles carefully to the top of a hill before beginning his act of self-sacrifice. The image tells us nothing about what it is like to suffer. It is designed, not to define experience, but to incite an easy reaction. This is the rhetoric of self-pity, and in the poems it is not leavened, as it is in the autobiographical novel, *La Confession d'un enfant du siècle*, by lucid self-analysis.

There is of course good rhetoric as well as bad. **'La Nuit de décembre'**, for example, has an extended sentence spanning seven stanzas, leading us in the hopeless pursuit of hope towards the predictable but splendidly withheld climax: the poet's confrontation with the personified loneliness which is his other self. The poem called **'Stances à la Malibran'** is a fine amplification of the Romantic theme that the great artist must experience the feelings he depicts; the famous singer is consumed by the flame of genius which burns within her and to which her life is given in willing sacrifice. But the fact that Musset could express a theme so much a part of the intellectual climate of the Romantic era, in a poem for whose careful construction any neo-classical poet would have been proud to be responsible, marks the degree to which his literary 'Romanticism' was incidental. Rolla fails to convince us because, just as much as Mardoche, he is a *persona* assumed in order to impress, which can be discarded when the poet finds another part to play. For at heart Musset, like Lamartine, is a conservative, a classic instance of the man whose advanced ideas are a product of youthful exuberance rather than conviction, so that they give way to a staid and, in the case of the dissolute Musset, a premature old age. (pp. 31-2)

> *Nicholas Osmond, ''Rhetoric and Self-Expression in Romantic Poetry,'' in* French Literature and Its Background, *edited by John Cruickshank, Oxford University Press, London, 1969, pp. 18-36.**

CHARLES AFFRON   (essay date 1971)

Impertinently dotting ''i's'' with moons, weeping over the tomb of la Malibran, and spinning verse tales of Italy and Spain, Musset is at once an ironic caricature of the romantic and a singularly pure example of the species. His theatre manifests this paradox, with attitudes expressive of commitment and sincerity counterbalanced by shafts of parody and sarcasm. . . . His peculiar brand of ''armchair theatre,'' designed with freedom, imagination, and disdain for the mechanics of representation, has proved eminently stageworthy. . . . [His dramatic proverbs] reveal a sure theatrical sense, a gift for *badinage* and niceties of sentiment which are still fresh. Yet these entertainments are not representative of Musset's dramatic vision, and do not reveal his projection of a poetic mode into a theatrical genre. It is only in the first moments of his creative life, from 1830 to 1835, years marked by an exhilarating variety of manner and culminating in the initiation of the *Nuits* series, that Musset finds in the dialectic of the theatre a degree of tension that allows the voicing of his artistic self-consciousness. (pp. 116-17)

La Nuit vénitienne was a fiasco that did much to deter Musset from entrusting any more of his plays to a theatrical troupe. It is admittedly an imperfect play, but its imperfections are revealing, and its positive qualities suggest the direction his theatre will eventually take. An eerie prefiguration of Musset's personal *nuit vénitienne* [Venetian night], and undoubtedly inspired by the ritualistic exoticism of the period, the play is strewn with gondolas and serenades. The suicide-bent lover, the epigraph from Shakespeare's *Othello,* and generally undistinguished prose show the extent to which Musset has yielded to cliché romanticism.

There is, however, one character who throws the play out of its predictable equilibrium: the Prince d'Eysenach, Laurette's husband by proxy. He introduces a tone that is governed by the use of highly inflected prose, and a point of view that is categorically opposed to banality. The tone and point of view are of course related. The rejection of common norms for judging reality is verbalized by the rejection of common speech patterns. The preciosity and the literary inventions of the Prince are part of his search for ideal beauty. He is not interested in Laurette the woman, but rather a presence of femininity, which can be captured only through style and art. He has purposely married Laurette in absentia to preserve the magical integrity he first encountered in a portrait.

The portrait-reality doubling is swiftly acted out as the Prince makes his entrance. Musset's [stage] directions leave no doubt of his intention: . . .

> The prince enters at the back. He has a portrait
> in his hand; he advances slowly looking now
> at the original, now at the copy. . . .

A drastic alteration of point of view is insured by the reversal of elements in the comparison. The original is in effect the portrait. What follows is a rather conventional avowal on the part of the Prince that art is inferior to nature, after all. (pp. 118-19)

[Yet his] disdain for art is fake. The Prince can barely speak without borrowing analogies from art, thereby revealing the extent to which his perception is dependent upon it. His description of love is an elaborately engineered musical metaphor, replete with variations, andante, and presto. The finale of this ''morceau d'ensemble'' is particularly rich, indicating the kind of development Musset is prepared to grant a metaphor. . . .

The feelings of the character are controlled by strong doses of imagination and irony. In order to create the distance necessary for perspective, the Prince transfers love into non-verbal domains: painting and music. To the musical analogy yeast is added in the form of ''le romanesque,'' ''la bénédiction apostolique et romaine'' and the whole series of gestures and attitudes which form a caricature. The Prince's craving for love and beauty is tempered and ironized by this measure of condescension.

In *La Nuit vénitienne* Musset attempts to resolve the dilemma inevitable in a theatre whose aim is essentially the elucidation of feeling rather than the working out of destiny. His interests are sentiment and the media of sentiment. These cannot be served through the traditional apparatus of dramatic encounter. The conflict between characters is bypassed. Musset's preoccupations with art and love, with form and personality are focused in the perception of the Prince d'Eysenach. The matter is imagination rather than incident, and the preservation of imagination's integrity is the playwright's major concern. The theatrical encounter of this play is between Laurette and portrait, love and music, and the resulting tension is sufficiently dramatic to give the impression that an action has transpired. (pp. 120-22)

The play's poetic movement is the discovery of a personal ideal of beauty, and hence the possibility of love. The portrait and the musical analogy are levels of style which lead to the ideal woman. The Prince's vision and his sensitivity to art create the form through which the real Laurette can be possessed. The analysis of this process of idealization is misleading in that it is out of proportion to the play's scope and merits. . . . The poet-dramatist has not yet found the technique which will do justice to both poetry and drama, but the Prince d'Eysenach leads us to believe that he will.

In addition to exhibiting Musset's undeveloped theatrical technique, *André del Sarto* takes up some of the motifs of *La Nuit vénitienne*. The Italian setting, the triangle and its inevitable jealousy, the linking of love and art are predictable ingredients, and their combination is no more successful here than it was in the earlier play. *André del Sarto* is a step backwards in at least one sense, for it has no character as articulate as the Prince d'Eysenach. The plot is without twist, the diction unambiguous. Musset seems victim of the prototype romantic melodrama, a model inimical to his particular ironic stamp.

The play's defects do not stem entirely from its conventionality. One senses that here Musset is inhibited by the fact that both the play's heroes are artists. . . . André and Cordiani do not successfully reveal the soul of the artist precisely because for them it is professional baggage. The evolution, the obliquity, and the revelation of perception in characters like the Prince d'Eysenach, Elsbeth, Lorenzo, and others is denied the painter and sculptor. André and Cordiani are unconvincing because they conform to a preconceived and rigid image of the artist. They do however provide insight into that image.

Musset again seeks to define the relationship between art and reality which he introduced in *La Nuit vénitienne*. (pp. 122-23)

Musset accomplishes an interesting variation on the love-art theme as André's dominance [over Cordiani] emerges. The teacher replaces the pupil, the disillusioned professional is substituted for the hopeful apprentice. André characterizes the relationship between love, inspiration, and nature in a way that prefigures the complaint of sterility expressed in *La Nuit de mai*. . . . A struggle develops between the ideal woman, muse, fairy, and the real woman, the unfaithful Lucrèce. Reality is stronger than illusion, the painter can function no more, the poet is silenced. The tenuous link between the artist's craft and his life is here responsible for the passage from love to despair. . . . The distance that separates impression and art will be bridged in various ways by the characters in Musset's theatre, but their awareness of the gap is not always a guarantee of success in closing it. Such distinctions account for the most intriguing ambiguities and the dramatic tension of the subsequent plays. (pp. 125-27)

[The] distance between *André del Sarto* and *Les Caprices de Marianne* is enormous. Musset suddenly finds the means for rendering his most pressing intentions; the characters and the diction take on the sentimental irony that is peculiar to his best work. More significant, and perhaps the key to these changes, the latter play is both theatrical and poetic.

One of the strengths of *Les Caprices de Marianne* is its consistency of tone. The isolated scene of the Prince d'Eysenach and the remarks of Cordiani and André, provocative and anticipatory, suddenly blossom into a play. Acuteness of perception is vested even in minor characters, creating a linguistic system closed to banality. Claudio, Marianne's husband, appears only briefly, yet his diction is as highly inflected as that of the heroes. Despite the fact that he represents conventionality, his speech is figurative, and he enunciates one aspect of the play's dominant motif: . . .

> Yes, there is an odor of lovers about my house;
> no one seems to pass my door naturally. There
> is a rain of guitars and procuresses. . . .

The ''odeur d'amants'' [odor of lovers] immediately ironizes the amorous activities of Célio, who is inadequate to the demands of the role he is trying to play: Harlequin yearning for Columbine. His love instead is emphatically unconventional, transcending the under-the-balcony mooning of a young Neapolitan swain. . . . For Célio, love is poetry and music, and it is his task to transform the pose into sentiment through the projection of his unique personality.

Célio's confusion and frustration are clear reminders of the poetic problem encountered in *La Nuit vénitienne* and *André del Sarto*. Ostensibly suffering because he cannot speak of love to Marianne, he is really tormented by an inability to speak of love at all. (pp. 128-29)

Octave and Célio voice a contrapuntal composition, a thorough working out of one destiny, one personality through the conjunction of two halves. It is not the reflection of one or the other, but the juxtaposition of two identities, a dramatic collaboration that gives the play movement. This is a significant advance in technique over *La Nuit vénitienne* and *André del Sarto*.

Célio is the poet of vague countries, cut off from life and unable to find an alternate existence either in art or in the realization of his dreams. Octave the rhetorician never lacks the right word, the pertinent image. The whole of life is a well of metaphors; living and talking are acts of boundless energy. During [their] first meeting the introspection of Célio is played against the activity of Octave. The characters shadow each other. . . . They share the same self-consciousness, two voices sound their dual presence, and the details of manner reinforce their antiphony. . . . The poet [Célio] finds equilibrium a prison, the rhetorician [Octave] proudly sustains it as necessary to his eloquence. The first is doomed to silence, the second is a master of style. Energy is style itself, and replaces sentiment in Octave. The extent to which Octave's existence is defined by expression is revealed in the last line of this passage. For him, the true reality is the metaphor. The personality refined by allusions and images is the seizable essence. The elaboration of metaphoric personality intensifies the distinction between Célio and Octave. (pp. 132-33)

The first encounter between Célio and Octave is subtly modulated to provide an increasingly complex set of clues. Each enthusiasm of Octave is feebly parried by Célio's pessimism, his self-deprecation. . . . [Célio's] small joys are second-hand. [The] tender reprise of the guitar motif introduced by Claudio in the first scene follows Octave's tight-rope act, and aptly defines the distinct manners of the two characters. Célio's participation in the serenade is theoretical, abstract. He provides the beat while a modest group of musicians sings the melody. Musset again exploits the rather pathetic frustrations of Célio, the incomplete artist, desirous but incapable of making his own music.

The doubling device seems to prove that Célio and Octave are but two parts of the same man, the heart and the brain, or perhaps the soul and the voice. Célio sighs and Octave sings, one providing the feeling and the other its expression. Musset is here dramatizing the symbolic process, but is careful to clothe the allegory with plot, exotica, and recognizably human characters. (pp. 133-34)

Musset does not abandon the structure of a dual hero he initiated in Act I. The voice of Octave is evoked as a response to Célio's silence. Gratuitous flourishes of style define its nature, musical but frivolous, in sharp contrast to Célio's unrelenting gravity. Octave is ever ready to engage in word games. The clever Marianne is a worthy measure of his verbal dexterity. During their first meeting they speak of nothing but love without once uttering its name. The word, unspoken yet the object of a series of metaphors, is the hinge of their imaginative and literary self-consciousness. . . . It is the presence of Marianne that inspires Octave to accumulate the metaphors in a veritable collection of love's clichés: ambrosia, a sickness, the faded rose, the song's refrain, the bee, the honey, the garden, etc. etc. These accoutrements of love are all the more artificial in that their extravagance is dissonant to the simplicity of the absent lover, Célio. The preciosity of Marianne and Octave sets off Célio's sincerity. (pp. 143-45)

In the play's final moments the confusion of identity is complete. . . . The scheme of reciprocity has been further realized. Célio learns something about words by listening to the voice of Octave. Octave gains insight into love by witnessing Célio's torment and accepting his sincerity. Both of them find ultimate satisfaction in death, in its fact and in its poetization. The shared identity is the element which rechristens the love-death commonplace.

Musset's particular irony focuses these concerns through the caprices of Marianne. The poetic stance is set in a small, in fact a diminishing frame. The disproportion between intent and manner gives an unexpected tone to love, death and poetic expression. This play's mixture of stock characters, conventional *peripéties* [sudden turns of fortune], literary self-consciousness, sincerity, and paradox is the first example of a formula Musset will use to great advantage in *Fantasio* and *On ne badine pas avec l'amour*. The poets Célio-Octave, Fantasio, and Perdican assume a variety of ironic and often ridic-

ulous poses, but neither they nor Musset can conceal an obsession with the essence of art. The caprice is the spring which holds the poet and the man in theatrical tension. (pp. 148-49)

> Charles Affron, "Analogy and Sentiment: 'La Nuit vénitienne' and 'André del Sarto'" and "From Rhetoric to Poetry: 'Les Caprices de Marianne'," in his A Stage for Poets: Studies in the Theatre of Hugo & Musset, *Princeton University Press, 1971, pp. 116-27, 128-49.*

DAVID SICES (essay date 1974)

[*On ne badine pas avec l'amour,*] which begins with an archly stylized set of apostrophes by the chorus to its comic characters and ends on a melodramatic cry of despair, is generally accepted as Musset's most typical and most popular dramatic work, despite its internal contradictions and its moments of grandiloquence. (p. 93)

[Camille is a striking example] of a psychological phenomenon which affects both of the play's protagonists: the coexistence within a single person of multiple, conflicting personalities. Camille is a passionate woman whose thirst for love and genuine tenderness are countered by her ardent idealism and her fear of disappointment: rather than settle for a temporary idyll with a Perdican who will be unfaithful to her as he has been to his mistresses, she will become the "bride of Christ." Perdican is an intelligent but headstrong young man who genuinely loves his cousin, and seeks the calm, durable values that the village and its peasants represent; yet he is too jealous of his freedom, too piqued by Camille's insistence, to be willing to give guarantees or to swear fidelity.

As in *Fantasio,* we are here in the presence of that barrier to understanding which prevents even lovers from achieving real union: individuality, vanity, the insidious claims of the body. . . . [The French critic Louis Jouvet associates] the couple's misunderstanding with the coexistence in them of two mentalities, two ages. . . . It is one of the roots of conflict in this work, as in all of Musset's major theater. The emotional ambivalence of youth here takes on a special poignancy: Perdican and Camille are capable of knowing love for each other because they are young; but their youthful egoism is the very source of their duel. Camille has some of the child about her still—her despotic idealism is proof of that, as well as her petulance—but she has been given a kind of false experience by Sister Louise which makes her refuse real experience, with its danger, and cling to the absolutes of love and religion. Perdican has returned to the country to seek a kind of simplicity and stability which he lost in Paris—he speaks of a return to childhood—but at the same time he jealously stakes out his future so that no one, not even the woman he loves, can dispute his entire claim to it.

In *On ne badine pas avec l'amour* more than in any other of Musset's comedies, we see the author's obsession with time and its treachery. Nostalgia for the past, even for a painful past, incapability of existing in the fleeting present; fear of the future, with its inevitable deceptions and betrayal of hope. . . . [If] past unhappiness is worth more, in the eyes of memory, than present tranquility, that is because tranquility has been purchased at too high a price—the ransom of youth and love demanded by time. The most painful realization of all is that, despite his lucidity and good will, Musset was condemned like all men to bear within himself the dead and dying remains of past emotions, thus of past selves, and to witness his own impotence to revitalize, to keep alive the stages of his past self, which he realized, nonetheless, were the capital moments of his existence—not only on the level of experience but on that of internal essence. (pp. 94-6)

On ne badine pas avec l'amour, straddling as it does two clearly defined periods of Musset's existence, translates this nagging obsession into striking dramatic terms; and its apparent structural duality should be understood in that frame of reference. But it is important to examine the play's thematic and dramatic structure in the light of its peculiar literary unity. . . .

The presence of bits of dialogue obviously drawn from life, fragments of correspondence, and the suggestive polemic between hero and heroine shift the focus of [critical] interest away from the play's inner structure, toward external points of reference and toward psychological analysis. The work's superficial regularity, which has no doubt facilitated its theatrical success . . . , has further discouraged examination of its construction. (pp. 96-7)

Although Musset uses grotesque characters in *Les Caprices de Marianne* and *Fantasio,* . . . he does not bring us into contact with them so quickly or so strikingly as in this play. The Chorus's half-poetic, half-satirical apostrophes draw wonderfully charged portraits of the pair of tutors which, aesthetically, go far beyond Octave's lightning darts at Claudio in their exchange of insults. . . . (p. 97)

This effective participation of grotesques in the action is nowhere to be found, however, in *On ne badine pas avec l'amour.* The Baron, though father and uncle to the protagonists, is essentially a bewildered, frustrated observer of the course of events, signifying his impotence by reiterating after each report that comes in to him, "That is impossible" or "That is unheard of!" Blazius and Bridaine, far from exerting any effect on the central dramatic progression, carry out an unrelated action, a burlesque epic subplot having to do with the gaining or losing of honors at the Baron's copious table. And Dame Pluche, a dried-out caricature of Camille's devoutness and prudery, is ironically limited in her action to the role of unwilling and ineffectual go-between. Although all of these puppet figures spend their time discussing and reporting on the extravagant actions of the protagonists, their confusion suggests to us that they live in another world, totally separate from the emotional and spiritual goings-on of the real characters.

And yet in this play (unlike *Fantasio,* where strikingly enough the hero and his grotesque "rival" never meet or even share the stage), Musset chooses to have his protagonists and his grotesques appear at the same time in a variety of combinations and circumstances . . . , or else to have them divide a scene alternately. . . . In the latter case, by making his two sets of characters share, but separately, the place and time of the action, Musset creates a simultaneous sense of division and unity which is in some ways the most typical sign of his theatrical genius. As critics of the author have pointed out, it is his need to dramatize the dialectic of his own personality and of the human soul which lies at the basis of his enduring greatness as a playwright, and the relative decline of his reputation as a poet. (pp. 98-9)

This dialogue of man with himself (with his other self) is worked out in . . . complex terms in *On ne badine pas avec l'amour.* The complication is due to the fact that Musset chooses here to embody his psychological and existential problem—unity and integrity of the personality vs. fragmentation and multiplicity—not only in two central characters, but in two sets of characters: Perdican and Camille (the "real" protag-

onists), and the grotesques. Furthermore, the problem is stated not only in terms of the dialogue between characters and sets of characters, but also in terms of each one of the main characters themselves, in time: childhood, maturity, and old age. And this time motive is further complicated by the fact that it is distributed as well between Perdican and a third group of characters, existing on yet another plane of literary reality: the Chorus.

It is the Chorus, half caricature and half real character, which makes us aware from the first scene of the play that number—unity vs. duality, and integrity vs. multiplicity—is to be one of the major themes informing the work. . . . At any rate, the Chorus seems to be both humane and anonymous. And it is the Chorus which first reveals to us, through its delightfully artificed introduction of Blazius and Pluche (as well as later on, in its mock epic account of the clerics' duel at table) that all "matched pairs" are inherently ridiculous, whether they are matched by polar opposition or by Tweedledee-Tweedledum similarity. (pp. 99-100)

[The Chorus] thus establishes a sort of parallel between the ridiculous matched pairs of the *fantoches* [puppets] and the ill-matched pair of protagonists. This parallelism, or ironic echo, is not merely incidental but essential to the structure of the play.

Nowhere else in his dramatic production does Musset make such extensive use of deliberately visible artifice as in this work. His borrowing and adaptation of the Greek chorus is only the first of many palpably "theatrical" and traditional devices in the play. Our entry into the central action—the amorous duel between Perdican and Camille, and its tragic end with the death of Rosette—comes via a series of artificial hurdles which serve as successive frames, creating through the introductory comments of the Chorus, Master Blazius, Dame Pluche, and then the Baron an effect of aesthetic distancing between the spectator/reader and the "real"—internal—action of the protagonists. Despite the intimacy of atmosphere that characterizes this play, one cannot help feeling that the author's irony required this technique of multiple aesthetic frames to reinforce the isolation of his protagonists within their existential framework, and in themselves.

Is this not the real explanation of the fact that much of the action of *On ne badine pas avec l'amour*—of its central plot as well as its subplot—is "narrated" (if we may so term the grotesques' babblings) in a caricature of the classical messenger or chorus, rather than acted? . . . It is all seen as through a glass, darkly but with a grotesque rather than a tragic darkness of the spirit. That it is Bridaine, in the first case, and Blazius, in the second, who narrates the events in question to the near-apoplectic Baron is of the utmost significance. Both narratives affect the status of the speakers themselves. . . . Both also contribute to his sense of confusion and futility in regard to the complex drama that is unfolding under his roof, despite all his plans. The narratives thus contribute to the development of the trivial subplot acted out by the grotesque characters in echo to the real drama. But at the same time, they serve an inverse function of distancing in relation to the protagonists. The audience must look at the latter more objectively, see them not only as they themselves, our hearts, and the author's evident sympathy see them, but also as the indifferent world, the inane, heartless marionettes (thus our wit), and the author's irony perceive them. This technique of multiple vision fulfills the needs of the deeper theme underlying Camille or Perdican's unrequited love: the problem of human integrity or integration. (pp. 100-02)

It is not only that the natures of Perdican and Camille do not "match" properly; there exists within the character of each a profound, irreconcilable split which acts to prevent their match. In the case of Camille, it is the "counterfeit being" or "borrowed character." . . . Like so many of Musset's young characters, she has a combination of immaturity and precocious disillusionment. . . . It is only in the final scene of the play that the two halves of her character are momentarily reintegrated.

Perdican, too, is a character in quest of his integrity, even more consciously than Camille. He has returned home not so much in search of a bride as in search of his past. Through the comforting "forgetfulness of what one knows" (not merely the material of his studies), he wishes to reintegrate his present, doctoral, and sentimentally experienced self with the innocent joy of his youth. Perdican seeks a harmonization of all the conflicting forces within him, a unity that will reconcile the contradictions of which his experience in time has made him conscious. . . . Perdican's most ardent desire is to keep for himself the flexibility, the *disponibilité* [availability] which will make it possible for all these contradictions to form a unity across time. (pp. 102-03)

Musset's play is not a polemical comparison between two kinds of life, or two manners of looking at life. The drama of Perdican and Camille is that they are indeed, obviously, the mutilated parts of one kind of human integrity: the fragile unity of the human couple, [or, in Perdican's words,] "the union of two of these imperfect, horrible creatures." Their tragedy lies in not being able to realize this integrity *in time*. I mean this latter expression in its ambiguity: the couple's ephemeral moment of knowledge and hope in Act III, scene 8, arrives just before the consequences of their badinage across the time of the action, their game of hide-and-seek with love, are realized in the death of Rosette. It is there, in the sudden cry of recognition ("She is dead. Farewell, Perdican!"), that the real force of Musset's seemingly innocent title strikes us. Not only *must* one not "play with love"; one *does* not play with love: it never turns out to be play. (pp. 104-05)

[The] *fantoches* are the deformed and deforming voice of Camille's and Perdican's destiny as suffering beings in a hostile universe, where the principal threat is that of fragmentation and destructive accumulation in the lives of those who seek continuity and unity through the endurance of human sentiment. Perdican is condemned at the end of the play to be the banal lover of the series of mistresses Camille has accused him of having—a series to which she both does and does not now belong, since she is one out of many, but not "the one." Camille, too, is left by destiny without having resolved her dilemma: she will be neither a good nun nor a woman loved, she can very well join the ambiguous group of disappointed "brides of Christ" in her convent.

Perdican and Camille thus succumb to their destiny through a double failure. Each fails to achieve a harmony of conflicting forces within his personality: love vs. pride, altruism vs. egotism, youthful passion vs. precocious cynicism. And by this failure they fail to attain that ultimate unity of Musset's romantic vision: the "union of two of these imperfect, horrible creatures" which Perdican, in his celebrated moment of lucidity at the end of Act two, sees transcending the base material reality of the physical world. In both instances the essential

fault is rigidity, the triumph of the categorical and the mechanical over the fluid and humane. At the end, the *fantoches'* distorted vision of the protagonists replaces the latter's vision of themselves, for they have been caught in a trap of their own devising. The last-minute realization expressed in Camille's "Farewell, Perdican!" marks the final, total defeat, the end of the couple's brief chance for salvation through love. (p. 107)

> *David Sices, in his* Theater of Solitude: The Drama of Alfred de Musset, *The University Press of New England, 1974, 268 p.* [*revised by the author for this publication*].

ADDITIONAL BIBLIOGRAPHY

Callen, A. "The Place of *Lorenzaccio* in Musset's Theatre." *Forum for Modern Language Studies* V, No. 3 (July 1969): 225-31.
    Argues that *Lorenzaccio* demonstrates the unity of Musset's dramatic vision.

Faguet, Émile. "Part VII, The Nineteenth Century: The Second Epoch of Romanticism." In his *A Literary History of France*, translated by F.H.L., pp. 561-71. London: T. Fisher Unwin, 1907.*
    A brief, appreciative comment on Musset as a Romantic poet.

Fredrick, Edna C. "Marivaux and Musset: *Les serments indiscrets* and *On ne badine pas avec l'amour*." *The Romantic Review* XXXI, No. 3 (October 1940): 259-64.*
    Examines Pierre Marivaux's influence on Musset's drama. Fredrick demonstrates that in *On ne badine pas avec l'amour*, "Musset renewed and transformed the classical play [*Les serments indiscrets*] of Marivaux" by updating the earlier work to conform to the spirit of his age.

Gautier, Théophile. "Alfred de Musset." In *Famous French Authors: Biographical Portraits of Distinguished French Writers*, by Théophile Gautier, Eugene de Mirecourt, and others, pp. 102-18. New York: R. Worthington, 1879.
    An account of Musset's life, his work, and the reaction of his contemporaries to his writings.

Grimsley, Ronald. "The Character of Lorenzaccio." *French Studies* XI, No. I (January 1957): 16-27.
    Asserts that the complex psychology of the main character is the crux of *Lorenzaccio*. According to Grimsley, some of the conflicting elements of Lorenzo's personality include pride, hidden idealism, debauched behavior, and an unstable temperament with widely fluctuating moods.

Grimsley, Ronald. "Romantic Emotion in Musset's *Confession d'un enfant du siècle*." *Studies in Romanticism* IX, No. II (Spring 1970): 125-42.
    Contends that Musset's novel *Confession d'un enfant du siècle* is at once an autobiographical portrait of his relationship with Sand, a historical depiction of the post-Napoleonic era and the Romantic mood of that generation, and a moral and psychological analysis of the hero Octave and his relationships with women.

Haldane, Charlotte. *Alfred: The Passionate Life of Alfred de Musset.* New York: Roy Publishers, 1961, 222 p.
    An emotional portrait that depicts Musset as a delicate and spoiled child and as a sensitive and romantic adult. Haldane describes her biography as "the story of 'The Child of the Century', of the man, the lover, and—since in his case the two are almost synonymous—the poet."

Houssaye, Arsène. "Alfred de Musset: Parts I and II." *The Fortnightly Review* n.s. XLV, Nos. CCLXVIII, CCLXIX (April 1889; May 1889): 515-28, 627-38.
    A biographical sketch in two parts by a friend of Musset who was also the manager of the Comédie-Française, which produced several of Musset's dramas.

Huxley, Aldous. "A Study in Romanticism." *The New Statesman* XIII, No. 315 (19 April 1919): 72-3.

A mocking account of the love affair of Musset and Sand. Unlike most critics, Huxley blames neither individual for the end of their affair, but instead charges both with immaturity.

James, Henry. "She and He: Recent Documents." *Yellow Book* XII (January 1897): 15-38.

A history of the relationship and correspondence between Musset and Sand.

King, Adele. "The Significance of Style in *Fantasio*." *Language and Style* IV, No. 4 (Fall 1971): 301-10.

Investigates the relationship between Musset's use of language in *Fantasio* and his attitude towards life.

Rees, Margaret A. *Alfred de Musset*. New York: Twayne Publishers, 1971, 141 p.

An exploration of Musset's personality and a survey of his career organized by genre. Rees considers Musset's drama "the summit of his achievement" and finds that the theater offered Musset the greatest opportunity for developing the whole range of his gifts.

Ridge, George Ross. "The Anti-Hero in Musset's Drama." *French Review* 32 (April 1959): 428-34.

An analysis of Fantasio as a Romantic anti-hero.

Rothschild, Suzanne Arvedon. *A Critical and Historical Study of Alfred de Musset's "Barberine."* Privately printed, n.d., 202 p.

Traces the evolution of Musset's art by comparing three versions of the story "Barberine": the sixteenth-century tale by Matteo Bandello, Musset's original version published in 1835, and his stage version published in 1853. Rothschild asserts that "by relating the meaning of the theme to his own life at these two periods, we shall see the evolution of the man as well as the artist."

Sand, George. *The Intimate Journal of George Sand*. Edited and translated by Marie Jenney Howe. New York: The John Day Co., 1929, 198 p.

Contains Sand's "Journal to Musset," a record of her thoughts and feelings as her relationship with Musset ended. As the editor Howe states in her introduction: "When George Sand was normal she did her work. Whenever she lost her poise she wrote a journal." A view of Sand emerges here that is strikingly different from the cold, ruthless woman usually portrayed by Musset's critics and biographers.

Sand, George. *She and He*. Translated by George Burnham Ives. Chicago: Cassandra Editions, Academy Press, 1978, 224 p.

Sand's fictional account of her affair with Musset. In this work, Sand portrays the autobiographical Thérèse Jacques as virtuous, loving, and patient, and depicts Laurent de Fauvel, patterned after Musset, as eccentric, egotistic, and violent. Publication of the novel in 1859 caused a sensation; although critics considered the work imprudent and indiscreet, the book was widely read.

Sayce, R. A. "'La blanche Oloossone': Some Reflections on Romanticism and Classicism." *Balzac and the Nineteenth Century: Studies in French Literature Presented to Herbert J. Hunt by Pupils, Colleagues and Friends*, edited by D. G. Charlton, J. Gaudon, and Anthony R. Pugh, pp. 283-95. Leicester, England: Leicester University Press, 1972.

An examination of the influence of the ancient Greek authors, particularly Homer, on Musset's poetry.

Sedgwick, Henry Dwight. *Alfred de Musset: 1810-1857*. Indianapolis: The Bobbs-Merrill Co., 1931, 343 p.

A sympathetic biography that focuses on Musset's social life by examining his friendships, his romances, and his dependence on alcohol.

Walter (Horatio) Pater

1839-1894

English essayist, novelist, and fictional portrait writer.

Pater is one of the most famous proponents of aestheticism in English literature. Distinguished as the first major English writer to formulate an explicitly aesthetic philosophy of life, he advocated the "love of art for art's sake" as life's greatest offering, a belief which he exemplified in the essays collected in his *Studies in the History of the Renaissance* and elucidated in his novel *Marius the Epicurean: His Sensations and Ideas* and other works. Exalting art and the artist, Pater's writings have appealed to and influenced many authors. Oscar Wilde and the young William Butler Yeats are included among his acknowledged disciples, and critics detect Pater's influence in the work of such notable modern writers as Virginia Woolf, Wallace Stevens, and James Joyce. Pater is also recognized as a master prose stylist and a leading exemplar of impressionist criticism.

Pater was born in Shadwell, East London. Raised by his widowed mother until her death in 1854, he attended King's School, Canterbury, earning a reputation for youthful piety; he won a scholarship to Oxford University in 1858. Although Pater's undergraduate work was not exceptional, the Oxford environment proved congenial to his temperament, for he left the university but briefly during his lifetime. After taking his degree in humane letters in 1862 and working for a short time as a private tutor, he accepted a fellowship at Brasenose College, Oxford, a position that he held from 1864 until his death. The only other vocation that Pater is known to have considered during his undergraduate years—clerical service in the Church of England—was denied to him when suspicions arose regarding his allegiance to Christian doctrine.

Some believe that Pater confirmed these suspicions in his first published work, an 1866 essay on Samuel Taylor Coleridge in which he condemned the poet's faith in "hard and abstract moralities" and asserted that nothing is or can be known except "relatively, and under conditions." Gradually acquiring a reputation for intellectual heterodoxy among his colleagues, he explored the ramifications of his scepticism in a series of essays which appeared in English periodicals between 1867 and 1873. Published in 1867, the essay "Winkelmann" depicts the eighteenth-century German Neoclassicist Johann Winckelmann as the model of a refined speculative individual who achieved harmony in his own life by embodying the harmony of body and soul exemplified in Greek culture and art. Displaying both temperament and values similar to Winckelmann's, Pater subsequently extolled the Hellenistic qualities of selected Renaissance artists in "Notes on Leonardo da Vinci" (1869), "A Fragment of Sandro Botticelli" (1870), and "The Poetry of Michelangelo" (1871), eschewing absolute critical standards in favor of his own personal impressions of the artists' works. "Winkelmann," the Renaissance studies, and other essays were collected and published as *Studies in the History of the Renaissance*.

The Renaissance provoked strong reactions which profoundly affected Pater's career and reputation. Many critics objected to the subjectivity of his method, labeling his Hellenistic interpretation of Renaissance art a paganized debasement of the Christian artistic tradition. Still others protested against the book's now-famous "Conclusion," in which Pater set forth his relativist-oriented views on art and life. Alarmed by his assertion that sustained intensity of experience is the highest good in a life comprising momentary sensations, angered by his dismissal of any system of thought that prohibited such experience, and alienated by his suggestion that the love of art for art's sake represented the supreme human experience, critics attacked Pater's "Conclusion" as antireligious propaganda for unrestrained hedonism. Conversely, young "aesthetes" such as Oscar Wilde, Lionel Johnson, and Arthur Symons interpreted it as a manifesto for artistic freedom and became the leading members of his coterie of literary disciples. Pater's reaction to this attention was paradoxical. Regarded by both friends and foes as a daring nonconformist, he quietly withdrew the "Conclusion" from the second edition of the *Renaissance* and assiduously cultivated the image of a retiring Oxford don. Commentators have suggested that the controversy surrounding *The Renaissance* induced a wariness—perhaps even a weariness—in Pater from which he never rebounded.

Marius the Epicurean, Pater's next major work, represents the fullest exposition of his philosophy. Written with the avowed purpose of elucidating the thoughts suggested by the "Conclusion" to the *Renaissance,* the novel follows the career of

the fictional character Marius as he searches for a satisfactory philosophy of life in Aurelian Rome. Considering but eventually rejecting a number of nondeist philosophies (including Stoicism and a form of Epicureanism which closely resembles the "hedonism" set forth in the *Renaissance*), Marius is ultimately attracted to the ritual and sense of community which he discovers in the early Christian church. The nature of Marius's attraction to Christianity and the circumstances surrounding his death—self-sacrifice for a Christian friend, followed by his burial as a Christian martyr—have provoked critical debate. While early critics tended to accept Marius's death as evidence of Pater's personal commitment to Christianity, A. C. Benson, T. S. Eliot, and others have demurred, pointing out that Pater's hero had acquiesced to the aesthetic charms of Christian ritual rather than to the precepts of Christian doctrine. Reputed to have once described Christianity as a "beautiful disease," Pater characteristically remained silent on the subject of his personal faith.

Moving from Oxford in 1885, the year of *Marius*'s publication, Pater established a quiet residence in London with his two sisters. During the next two years, he contributed "Sebastian van Storck," "A Prince of Court Painters: Extracts from an Old French Journal," "Denys l'Auxerrois," and "Duke Carl of Rosenmold" to *Macmillan's Magazine*. Published as *Imaginary Portraits* in 1887, the essays serve as fictional counterparts to the *Renaissance* studies. Much as Pater had explored the interaction of Leonardo's Hellenistic temperament with the medieval culture of the early Renaissance, he here imaginatively recreated the interaction of various intellectual, artistic, and moral temperaments with the cultures of selected periods of historical transition. Marked by frequent descriptions of death and acts of cruelty, the *Imaginary Portraits* reveal a dark side of Pater's personality which is also evident in *Marius* and *The Child in the House*, an autobiographical "imaginary portrait" first published in *Macmillan's* in 1878. Pater added "The School of Giorgione," a previously published essay which includes a critically acclaimed discussion of the relationship of form and matter in art, to the 1888 edition of *The Renaissance*, but his next significant publication, the beginning of a novel titled *Gaston de Latour*, was a disappointment. He abandoned the ambitious project, designed to resemble *Marius* in scope and format, after publishing five chapters in *Macmillan's* in 1888.

Pater subsequently published two major works, *Appreciations: With an Essay on Style* and *Plato and Platonism*, before his death. The former volume is a collection of essays in which Pater uses the method of subjective impressionism to elucidate the qualities informing the genius of Coleridge, William Wordsworth, and other English writers. Functioning as something of a companion piece to his literary "appreciations," the essay "Style" reveals Pater's thoughts on what contemporary critics had come to regard as his domain: the art of writing prose. In particular, his comments on Gustave Flaubert's painstaking measures as a *prosateur*, or prose writer, touch on a salient aspect of his own prose technique—the obsessive effort to find what Flaubert termed the "mot juste," the perfect word to convey his mood and meaning. Published shortly before he returned to Oxford for the final time in 1883, *Plato and Platonism* has a similar value as a revelation of Pater's thought. His last effort to explore the genius of a culture which seemed to him to have achieved a balance between the physical and the spiritual, it is considered a fitting final product of a lifelong effort to incorporate his abiding faith in the things of this world within a wider system of philosophy.

Pater's critical reputation reached its zenith in the twenty years following his death. Mollified by his apparent rapprochement with Christianity in *Marius*, the critics of this period generally overlooked his heterodoxy and extolled his virtuosity as a prosodist. The trial of Oscar Wilde for homosexuality and the general dissipation of other of Pater's "aesthetic" disciples eventually re-emerged as issues, however, undermining his reputation and bringing his ideas into disrepute. T. S. Eliot confirmed Pater's fall from grace in 1930 in a negative commentary including the remark that Pater's aesthetic philosophy "may not have been wholly irresponsible for some untidy lives" among his followers. But Eliot at the same time placed Pater's aestheticism within the tradition of religious humanism epitomized in the work of Matthew Arnold, thus anticipating such later critics as David J. De Laura, who have explored the philosophical dimension of Pater's works in great detail. Indeed, the recognition of the intellectual responsibility of Pater's doctrines has spurred a recent resurgence of interest in his writings. Led by Gerald Monsman, scholars published numerous studies of Pater's works during the 1960s and 1970s, most of them focused on *Marius the Epicurean*.

In his own day, the impressionist meditation on Leonardo's *Mona Lisa* published in *The Renaissance* was the best-known passage of Pater's writings. Impressionist criticism is now unpopular, as is his studied prose style, but certain aspects of Pater's thought seem likely to survive. As Yeats and others have noted, Pater's views on art and life are remarkably consonant with the spirit of alienation experienced by writers of the modern era. Yeats considered the relationship so telling as to include the *Mona Lisa* passage as *vers libre* in his edition of *The Oxford Book of Modern Verse*.

*PRINCIPAL WORKS

Studies in the History of the Renaissance (essays) 1873;
    also published as *The Renaissance: Studies in Art and
    Poetry*, 1877
Marius the Epicurean: His Sensations and Ideas (novel)
    1885
Imaginary Portraits (fictional portraits) 1887
Appreciations: With an Essay on Style (essays) 1889
Plato and Platonism (lectures) 1893
An Imaginary Portrait (fictional portrait) 1894; also
    published as *The Child in the House*, 1895
Greek Studies (essays) 1895
Miscellaneous Studies (essays) 1895
Essays from the "Guardian" (essays) 1896
Gaston de Latour (unfinished novel) 1896
Uncollected Essays (essays) 1903
New Library Edition of the Works of Walter Pater. 10 Vols.
    (essays, novel, unfinished novel, fictional portraits, and
    lectures) 1910
Walter Pater: Selected Works (essays, novel, fictional
    portraits, and lecture) 1948
Letters of Walter Pater (letters) 1970

*Most of Pater's essays and fictional portraits were originally published
 in periodicals.

[SIDNEY COLVIN]   (essay date 1873)

[In the review excerpted below, Colvin expresses qualified admiration for Pater's prose style and critical approach in The Renaissance, *but disagrees with his assertion that Michaelangelo's art is characterized by sweetness united with strength. Referring to the hedonistic principles outlined in the book's "Conclusion," he also warns that, if practiced by everyone, indulgence in "exquisite impressions" would actually result in the indulgence of gross pleasures. Colvin was a well-known English art critic. In addition to writing art criticism for the* Pall Mall Gazette, *he served as Slade Professor of Fine Art at Cambridge from 1873 to 1885 and Keeper of Prints and Drawings at the British Museum from 1884 to 1912. Colvin's essay originally appeared in the* Pall Mall Gazette *on March 1, 1873.]*

Mr Pater has gone over a wide field for episodes, both of art and literature, with which to illustrate [the Renaissance in his *Studies in the History of the Renaissance.*] (p. 49)

[Mr Pater's] choice of subjects is fragmentary, and quite incomplete for any purpose of connected history. But . . . it is a representative choice, and if it lacks completeness or the approach to it, possesses symmetry and a governing idea. Thus, although having the essay form and essay origin which prevail in contemporary literature, [*Studies in the History of the Renaissance*] is very remarkable among contemporary books, not only for the finish and care with which its essays are severally written, but for its air of deliberate and polished form upon the whole. If anything, we should say that Mr Pater was even too great a refiner and polisher of his work. . . . One feels that he has refined and melted down conscientiously, nay, fastidiously, until all that is left is matter transfused with his best powers. The consequence is that one often feels at the end of one of these essays as if too little had been said, as if one wanted more. The book is not one for any beginner to turn to in search of 'information'. The information to be found in any one of the essays as to the personage who is its subject will be accurate as far as it goes, but will only go just far enough to carry the criticism, the definition of the impression the personage has made upon the writer individually. That, as Mr Pater in his preface leads us to expect, will be the main object of the essay. His idea of the function of the aesthetic critic is a very distinct idea. . . . The analysis and discrimination of impressions, which by another phrase you may call the virtues or qualities of the things which give the impressions, whether or not it is the whole of criticism, is certainly a great part of it; and to be well done it must certainly be done by one who feels the impressions strongly. By the strength and delicacy of the impressions the present writer feels, by the pains he has taken completely to realize them to himself, above all, by the singular and poetical personality with which they are transfused, he shows himself born for the task; he seems like a congener of those Florentines of the fifteenth century in whom he delights, because he thinks it their characteristic to show

> the impress of a personal quality, a profound expressiveness, what the French call *intimité*; by which is meant a subtle sense of originality—the seal on a man's work of what is most inward and peculiar in his moods and manner of apprehension.

Of course the writer thus setting himself to convey the impression of what is most inward and peculiar in the moods of an ancient artist or poet, has a much harder task than the writer setting himself to give general information about characters and careers. The former undertaking is open to much more

contradiction than the latter, since the finest perceptions differ, and every one may find fault with his neighbour's. For ourselves, the impressions here realized with such careful meditation, and written down with so refined an art, commend themselves in considerably different degrees. The essay on Michael Angelo . . . is an essay of very great interest; but we doubt about the main point it enforces, which is this: that the true stamp of Michael Angelo, and true type of the Michael Angelesque, is sweetness together with strength, or sweetness through strength—*ex forti dulcedo.* . . . [We] should rather have said, though there were undoubtedly moments and flashes of sweetness in Michael Angelo, his true stamp, speaking generally, was one not of sweetness at all, but of an energy which has little to do with that, and much to do with indignation, menace, and sublimity; we should say that his characteristic expressions were those of a science and power above other mortals, but an imaginative ambition still transcending that science and power and chafing against their insufficiency; that is, of sentiments too Titanic, unquiet, and rebellious, to leave much place for those sentiments of love, tranquillity, and tenderness which express themselves in graceful and caressing physical conditions, such as in art are what we call sweet. Similarly, when we hear how Robbia's system of using low relief, and copying evanescent expression in his sculpture, is one means out of many that sculpture has tried for, avoiding a hard and importunate realism, and how beside it the Greek means to this end was an ideal abstractness and universality, and Michael Angelo's means a calculated technical incompletion and the mystery arising from that; when we hear this view, we are inclined to say that it is very ingenious and subtle rather than that it unreservedly commends itself. But it is the property of this kind of writing, when it is thoughtfully done, to suggest even where it does not illuminate. And on the other hand, we should say that the accounts of Botticelli and Leonardo commended themselves signally by their felicity and penetration as well as by their subtlety and poetry; and that the account of Winckelmann . . . was completely excellent from beginning to end. (pp. 49-52)

Mr Pater's style is often beautiful, always intimately his own, and always sedulously taken care of. The worst that could possibly be said against it, by a critic having no sympathy with its personal sentiment, would be that it went sometimes to the edge of fancifulness and affectation, or that the poetry of its descriptions and allusions seemed sometimes to cloy by recurrence. The best that could be said of it is something almost stronger than we like to venture. Or we should say that no English prose writer of the time had expressed difficult ideas and inward feelings with so much perfection, address, and purity, or had put more poetical thoughts or more rhythmical movement into his prose without sacrificing that composure and lenity of manner which leave it true prose nevertheless. The masterpiece of the style is the **"Conclusion"**, in which the writer expounds something like a philosophy of life. That philosophy is not ours. It is a Hedonism—a philosophy of refined pleasure—which is derived from many sources: from modern science and the doctrine of relativity; from Goethe, from Heine, Gautier, and the modern French theorists of art for art's sake; from the sense of life's flux and instability and the precious things which life may yield notwithstanding—from all these well transfused in a personal medium of temperament and reflection, well purged from technicalities, and cast into a literary language of faultless lucidity and fitness. But to go with the writer when he analyzes and discriminates exquisite impressions is not to go with him when he makes the research of exquisite impressions the true business of a wise man's life. By all means, let the people whose bent is art follow art, by all means refine the pleasures of as many people as possible; but do not tell everybody that refined pleasure is the one end of life. By refined, they will understand the most refined they know, and the most refined they know are gross; and the result will not be general refinement but general indulgence. (pp. 53-4)

> [*Sidney Colvin*], *in a review of "Studies in the History of the Renaissance," in* Walter Pater: The Critical Heritage, *edited by R. M. Seiler, Routledge & Kegan Paul, 1980, pp. 47-54.*

[MRS. PATTISON]   (essay date 1873)

> [*In the following excerpt, Pattison, a historian of French art, vigorously objects to the absence of historical considerations in* The Renaissance. *Some commentators have suggested that Pattison's contention that the book's original title,* Studies in the History of the Renaissance, *was misleading prompted Pater to retitle his work* The Renaissance: Studies in Art and Poetry *in its second edition.*]

"Studies in the History of the Renaissance" is the title of a volume of essays . . . recently published by Mr. Walter Pater, Fellow of Brasenose College, Oxford. The title is misleading. The historical element is precisely that which is wanting, and its absence makes the weak place of the whole book. . . . For instead of approaching his subject, whether in Art or Literature, by the true scientific method, through the life of the time of which it was an outcome, Mr. Pater prefers in each instance to detach it wholly from its surroundings, to suspend it isolated before him, as if it were indeed a kind of air-plant independent of the ordinary sources of nourishment. The consequence is that he loses a great deal of the meaning of the very objects which he regards most intently. This is especially noticeable when he passes from the examination of fragments to deal with the period as a whole. Take for instance the passages of general criticism with which the first essay opens. Mr. Pater writes of the Renaissance as if it were a kind of sentimental revolution having no relation to the conditions of the actual world. Whilst he discriminates or characterizes with great delicacy of touch the sentiment of the Renaissance, he does not let us know that it was precisely as the expression of vital changes in human society that this sentiment is so pregnant for us with weighty meaning. Thus we miss the sense of the connexion subsisting between art and literature and the other forms of life of which they are the outward expression, and feel as if we were wandering in a world of unsubstantial dreams. We do not feel that the writer has that intimate possession of his subject in its essence and entirety which alone can convey to us the impression of reality. The hold upon the art of the day becomes uncertain because the grasp of the life of the day is ill-assured. This it is which destroys for us much of the charm of a charming book, a book which shows a touch of real genius. Mr. Pater possesses to a remarkable degree an unusual power of recognising and finely discriminating delicate differences of sentiment. He can detect with singular subtlety the shades of tremulous variation which have been embodied in throbbing pulsations of colour, in doubtful turns of line, in veiled words; he can not only do this, but he can match them for us in words, in the choice of which he is often so brilliantly accurate that they gleam upon the paper with the radiance of jewels. In this respect these studies of the sentiment of the Renaissance have a real critical value. But they are not history, nor are they even to

be relied on for accurate statement of simple matters of fact. (pp. 639-40)

> [*Mrs. Pattison*], *in a review of "Studies in the History of the Renaissance," in* The Westminster Review, *n.s. Vol. XLIII, No. 2, April 1, 1873, pp. 639-45.*

[MARGARET WILSON OLIPHANT]   (essay date 1873)

> [*Oliphant was a prolific nineteenth-century Scottish novelist, biographer, and historian. A regular contributor to Blackwood's Mgazine, she published nearly one hundred novels, many of them popular tales of English and Scottish provincial life similar to the* Chronicles of Carlingford, *her best-known work. In the review excerpted below, Oliphant charges Pater with degrading art in* The Renaissance studies *by approaching it chiefly as a source of self-self-gratification. She finds the book a "mixture of sense and nonsense, of real discrimination and downright want of understanding."*]

["Studies in the History of the Renaissance,"] though there are bits of very pretty writing in it, and here and there a saying which is worth quoting, is full of so much "windy suspiration of forced breath," and solemn assumption of an oracular importance, that the critic scarcely knows whether to laugh or frown at the loftiness of the intention. . . . Mr. Pater sets the "aesthetic critic" at once before us, in full possession of his high office, standing, as it were, as mediator between art and the world. . . . [It] is in furtherance of the grand pursuit of self-culture that he writes, treating all the great art and artists of the past, and all the centuries of men, as chiefly important and attractive in their relations to that Me who is the centre of the *dilettante's* world. That class of pious persons who call themselves Evangelical have passionately taken up the same view, and have had to bear much abuse on account of their determined effort to save the soul of their Me at all hazards— an attempt which has been characterised as the last horror of spiritual selfishness by many an indignant critic; yet self-culture claims all the sympathy of most of these critics, and is set forth here as the highest of aims, as it is also set forth in many a finer and more important work. We do not, we fear, understand the distinction. Let us have fair-play; High Intellectualism and Low-Churchism are in this point so entirely at one, that their agreement merits full recognition. To ourselves, the idea of regarding Michael Angelo or Leonardo, or even Botticelli, a lesser name, as only interesting in so far as we can get something out of them, is as revolting as it would be to apply the same rule to our living friends, whom generally we are fond of in exactly an inverse ratio, liking those best to whom we give most, instead of receiving. The world is bad enough, we suppose, but it would be considerably worse were this highest, lofty, superior principle to be put in practical operation. Mr. Pater, however, has after all a better definition of a critic to give us. When he describes his special function as that of identifying the special excellence of each artist's work, and separating this highest soul and meaning of art from the earthly elements in which it is so often enveloped, we understand and sympathise in his view; and his application of this theory to the case of Wordsworth is very felicitous—and while magnifying, not unjustly, the critic's office, gives us a real perception of its value to all less careful and studious readers. (pp. 604-05)

Very different, however, is that fantastic criticism which, taking for its subject the works of Sandro Botticelli, . . . fixes upon this simple-minded artist of an early age, on whom the questionings of a perturbed nineteenth century had certainly never dawned, a meaning oddly characteristic of the conventional over-refinement of the present day. . . . Mr. Pater finds in the old painter's reverential, pathetic angel-faces, and wistful, thoughtful Madonnas, a sentiment of dislike and repulsion from the divine mystery placed among them, such as, we think we may venture to say, never entered into the most advanced imagination within two or three hundred years of Botticelli's time, and was as alien to the spirit of a mediaeval Italian, as it is perfectly consistent with that of a delicate Oxford Don in the latter half of the nineteenth century. Sheer determination to confer upon this primitive teacher some "unique faculty," which no one else has divined, and to find out for him a special virtue which shall act upon Mr. Pater's Me in a distinct and recognisable way, lies, it is apparent, at the bottom of this complacent suggestion. (p. 606)

The same mixture of sense and nonsense, of real discrimination and downright want of understanding, runs through the whole book. On one page we have a really fine description of Da Vinci's "Gioconda," . . . while on another our author drops into absolute obtuseness, explaining the sublime group, often repeated, to which Italian sentiment has given the name of Pieta, as an embodiment of pity, the "pity of all mothers over all dead sons,"—the still more abstract pity of philosophical observers over death in general!

On this point Mr. Pater elaborately explains to us how Italian painters must have "leant over" the "lifeless body," studying it in its first solemnity and quiet; and how, following it perhaps one stage further, and dwelling for a moment on the point where all that transitory dignity broke up, and discerning with no clearness a new body, they paused just in time, and abstained with a sentiment of profound pity." We doubt very much if any man with a human soul in him, painter or otherwise, ever contemplated a fellow-creature dead with this perfectly calm and abstract sentiment; but there is a curious dullness of apprehension which is quite startling, in the mind which can take this superficial feeling as exposing all that is to be found in Michael Angelo's Pieta. What can be said to such a conception? It seems to argue some fundamental incompetence—some impotency of the mind and imagination against which all manner of remonstrance might beat in vain.

The conclusion of this very artificial book has a curious kind of human interest in it, as showing what Greek—not the language but the tone of mind and condition of thought, taken up a thousand years or so too late, on the top of a long heritage of other thoughts and conditions—may bring Oxford to. Poor, young, too rich, too clever, too dull, too refined souls! Greekness, if we may use such a word, developed far down here in the centuries—with that uneasy consciousness of a long spell of Christianity lying between, of which the most Hellenic mind cannot divest itself—is as different a thing from the real lighthearted Greek, in its own time and generation, as is the armour of a masquerade from the rude coats of mail in which our forefathers hacked and hewed at each other. It is hard to accept as quite serious the grandiloquent description of life as set forth by the writer in the closing pages, which is half pitiful, half amusing, in its earnest self-persuasion, and attempt to look and feel as if so many fine-sounding words must be true. (p. 607)

[We] are not afraid that [Mr. Pater's] elegant materialism will strike many minds as a desirable view of life; but it evidently sounds very fine and original, as overstrained conventionality often does to the writer. The book is *rococo* from beginning to end,—in its new version of that coarse old refrain of the Epicureans' gay despair, "Let us eat and drink, for to-morrow we die"—as well as in its prettiness of phrase and graceful but far-fetched fancies. . . . To weight this purely decorative piece of work with a pompous confession of faith at the end, is about as bad taste—and rather less cognate to the matter— as the Athanasian Creed would be appended to a work on Christian art. It is just this curious mingling, however, of bad taste and conventional originality, with much that is really graceful and attractive, which gives to art the characteristics which are embodied in the term *rococo*. And we are obliged to add, that though . . . [this pretty production is exotic, it is] conceived in a limited atmosphere, comprehensible only in a narrow sphere, and, by the very peculiarities of [its] being, betraying the decay among us of all true and living art. If art were alive and vigorous in this world, its enthusiasts would have something better to do than to seek its dim altars with such ephemeral wreaths of evanescent flowers. (pp. 608-09)

> [*Margaret Wilson Oliphant*], *in a review of "Studies in the History of the Renaissance," in* Blackwood's Edinburgh Magazine, *Vol. CXIV, No. DCXCVII, November, 1873, pp. 604-09.*

[WILLIAM JOHN COURTHOPE]   (essay date 1874)

Aristotle blamed the Sophists for making prose poetical, observing acutely that those who wrote in this manner sought to conceal the poverty of their thought by the showiness of their style. Poetical prose, however, introduced by Mr. Ruskin and Mr. Carlyle, has made rapid advances in England. . . . Mr. Pater's criticism on Leonardo da Vinci's picture 'La Gioconda' [published in **'Essays on the Renaissance'**] is a good specimen of this epicene style. . . . (p. 411)

[It] is plain, downright, unmistakable poetry. The picture is made the thesis which serves to display the writer's extensive reading and the finery of his style. Of reasoning in the ordinary sense there is positively none. 'The eyelids are a little weary,' therefore it is quite plain that 'all the ends of the earth are come upon her head.' The beauty is different from the Greek type. What then can be more obvious than that this particular face expresses the whole experience of mankind between the age of Phidias and Leonardo? The lady appears to Mr. Pater to have a somewhat sensual expression. A fact which fully warrants a critical rhetorician in concluding that she is an unconscious incarnation of all the vices which he has found preserved in the literature of the Renaissance. Judgments of this kind, we are told, are the result of 'penetrative sympathy' or 'perceptive insight.' It may be so; we cannot say that the qualities Mr. Pater discovers in this picture are not to be found there. What we can say is that, as [such reasoning] assumes a knowledge in the critic of motives which are beyond the reach of evidence, there is no justification for calling that criticism which is in fact pure romance. (pp. 411-12)

> [*William John Courthope*], *"Modern Culture," in* The Quarterly Review, *Vol. CXXXVII, No. CCLXXIV, July, 1874, pp. 389-415.**

SARAH B. WISTER   (essay date 1875)

> [*Wister complains of Pater's affectations and inaccuracies in depicting the Renaissance, but praises his expressive prose. She disagrees with his analysis of Michelangelo and, concerning his discussion of Leonardo da Vinci, suggests that common sense "might have been useful."*]

We think we recognize in Mr. Pater, whose work heads this article, one of the new Mahomets, although he has not yet bared his scimitar and proclaimed himself monarch as well as prophet. He lacks two capital qualifications for such a mission,—originality and earnestness; yet he has already votaries, and, seeking for the secret of his influence, we are inclined to think that it lies primarily in the subjects of which he treats, names and themes which are incantations in themselves, whose very sound possesses a magic which nothing can dispel; secondly, in his treatment of them, and this is a snare. He has the peculiar eloquence which goes with insobriety of style, and all the charm and force which can be snatched by breaking rules. Still, the effects of this lawlessness are by no means always happy. The spell would also be more potent for many readers, if the author were not so palpably intoxicated by it himself; sometimes his ear seems to be tickled by a single word, which he repeats in every imaginable combination; thus we have "comely clerks," "comely decadence," "comely gestures," "comely divinities," "comely ways of conceiving life"; then it is "sweetness," *ad nauseam* [to a sickening degree]; sometimes a whole phrase repeated verbatim, like the burden of a ballad. Now this trick of iteration may be pardoned in an old gentleman like Mr. Carlyle, but it certainly suggests dotage. He coins like a true despot, and uses words without italics which are not English, such as "débris" and "cult,"— to whatever language that may belong,—and gives us such parts of speech as "siderealized." And why does he talk about Pico della Mirandula, whom all modern Europe knows as Mirandola? This is mere affectation; but when he speaks of the Pitti Palace and the Sistine Chapel as "the Pitti" and "the Sistine," it is a bad habit, and has a taint of vulgarity. A graver fault than these is his inaccuracy. . . . [There] is a trifling detail which strongly marks his preference for effect over exactness; he gives a minute and poetical description of Raphael's great frescos known as the Debate on the Sacrament and Parnassus, speaking of them as companion pieces designed to illustrate respectively orthodoxy of doctrine and orthodoxy of taste. Now these compositions are in no sense whatever companions; they differ in shape, size, and position; of the *Disputa* have a companion, it is the famous School of Athens.

To pass to the more agreeable task of pointing out merits, Mr. Pater has a most unusual gift of conveying half-defined emotions, modulations of feeling, shades of thought; rare fineness of perception, and aerial grace and delicacy of touch; an exquisite felicity of epithet, of description, of presenting lovely images to the mind; his prose is sometimes as fraught with the unspeakable as music itself, although never with the highest rapture; in these twin talents of calling up the seen and the unseen must lie much of his fascination. A more tangible quality, though one seldom brought into service, is his power of giving to his theories—and some few of those about art are perfectly sound—the clearness of chiselled marble. It is true that they are mainly borrowed, but he makes good use of them occasionally. An example of this is his remarks on the proper limits of sculpture . . . , or a still finer passage concerning the influence of external conditions on religion. . . . (pp. 156-58)

Having called attention to these beauties, . . . there is no help for it but to go back to fault-finding. . . . [We] have a quarrel with him at the outset, for we deny the right to wrest a term of long-established and universally accepted significance from its conventional meaning and give it a wider, perhaps a broader, but at the same time a looser and less accurate application, so that it ceases to be the aid that all such general terms are meant to be. The word Renaissance has been used technically to express an epoch, a fact, an intellectual phase, and a social condition. To use it as Mr. Pater does is as though a writer on ecclesiastical history should persist in including in the term Reformation the Albigenses, Waldenses, iconoclast emperors, or whatever resistance to hierarchical authority has arisen in Christendom from apostolic days down. . . . The review of this movement leads Mr. Pater to touch upon some of the gravest preoccupations of the human mind; he always does so with the air of one who is trifling with his subject; there is no earnestness in his manner; he never goes to the root of the question, he never sounds the soul of the inquirer; he talks about "religions," but he knows nothing of religion; fallacies bloom about his path; he never forgets that he is a *dilettante*; he shrinks from no assertion however unfounded, and has no hesitation in contradicting himself a few pages later. In his preface he says that, to the critic, "all periods, types, schools of taste, are in themselves equal. . . . 'The ages are all equal,' says William Blake, 'but genius is always above its age.'" . . . [Are] we to believe that Mr. Pater really esteems the school of taste which produced Mansard and Lemercier equal to that which brought forth Arnolfo and the Pisani? His definition of the critic's function, to discern and detach from the mass of an author's works the pure ore, the fine crystals of his genius, which make its intrinsic and distinctive value, is true and well put; but what are we to think of his own critical capacity when in that very passage he classes Byron with Goethe as artist or workman?

The first example given of that revival of classic feeling which common consent has assigned to the fifteenth and sixteenth centuries, but which Mr. Pater wishes to trace back to the dark ages, is a poetical story in Provençal of the latter half of the thirteenth century, or even later; there is no proof extant of an older derivation. . . . This date is the fact; the shadowy possibilities of an earlier origin are not sufficient to make this story serve as proof of a return towards Hellenism in the eleventh century; moreover those very possibilities indicate, not a Greek, but an Arabic source. Mr. Pater gives no complete or consecutive account of this tale or the literature of which it is a sample; we are not told the story; the selections are few and scanty, though so full of beauty, grace, and quaintness as to make us long for more; his method throughout is like humming bits of a tune to one's self. Reduce chapter first to its substance and what remains is about this: that in a certain book there is a story which Mr. Pater thinks very pretty, and which confirms, to his mind, certain notions of his own. (pp. 158-60)

[In Mr. Pater's description in **Studies in the History of the Renaissance** of several of Botticelli's most noted pictures,] we are told of the "peevish-looking Madonnas," who wish they had been let alone in their humble homes among the gypsy brood who are their true children. It is impossible to argue such a subject by pitting description against description; but let any one who has seen and studied them recall the circular picture of the Uffizi where the child guides the mother's pen, and that in the Louvre where he lays his little hand against her face with unutterable love and compassion, yet with a natural baby action which every mother knows, and let them decide whether Mr. Pater has not gone very far out of his way to find a meaning for Botticelli's painting which is foreign to it. . . . Botticelli's Madonnas may not be reciting the *Magnificat* or the *Gaude, Maria*, but they are ready to say with drooping head, "Ecce ancilla Domini; be it unto me according to thy word." (p. 162)

Before we reach the essay on Michael Angelo's poetry . . . , we have met . . . with the statement that the unfinished condition of many of Michael Angelo's greatest statues was "his way of etherealizing pure form," that "this incompleteness is Michael Angelo's equivalent for color in sculpture." . . . Even those who have never seen the original statues can judge of the value of the interpretation when they learn that the only unfinished portion of the David is a very small bit among the locks of the hair, and in the Dawn, the toes of one foot. Our next surprise is the ascription of "sweetness" to Michael Angelo as an essential element of his ascendency. Most people would, indeed, be "puzzled" . . . if asked to define wherein that sweetness resides, and equally so to point it out in Victor Hugo, to whom Mr. Pater compares Michael Angelo in this particular. . . . Of Michael Angelo's *tenderness,* the deep well whence flows all that softens his severity and makes his tremendous sublimity tolerable to weaker humanity, we hear not a word. Nor of those strange spheres, unvisited by any other mortal, where he dwelt apart among the grand beings whom he has depicted,—that mighty world with its mighty race, Titans, or demi-gods, or stupendous avatars, incorporations of great primordial and moral forces, standing, reposing, or stalking about in their own immensurate realm.

Mr. Pater closes his chapter on Michael Angelo with a sort of monody on the Medicean chapel, where are the tombs of Lorenzo and Giuliano with their slumberous guardians. . . . He who can stand in the silent precincts of those awful presences, those solemn genii of the mysterious borderland between Life and Death, the Known and the Unknown, talking of them as if they were airy sylphs or shapeless phantasms, howver full of fancy he may be, lacks imagination, enthusiasm, feeling for the power and magnitude of what is real, wholly lacks the capacity to lose himself in the genius even of the greatest.

The essay upon Leonardo da Vinci is far above any which precedes it, because the subject legitimately affords scope for speculation and paradox. The most general and ordinary reading of it must needs abound in guesses and half-expressed meanings, and Mr. Pater's fantastic pen finds here fit material for exquisite elaboration and overlaying with mystical embroidery. . . . When Mr. Pater has said that it is "by a certain mystery in his work, and something enigmatical beyond the usual measure of great men, that he fascinates, or perhaps half repels"; that "his type of beauty is so exotic that it fascinates a larger number than it delights, and seems more than that of any other artist to reflect ideas and views and some scheme of the world within"; that by the study of Nature and her occult relations "he learned the art of going deep, of tracking the sources of expression to their subtlest retreats"; and—by way of summing up—"curiosity and the desire of beauty,—these are the two elementary forces in Leonardo's genius"; he has perhaps given us as distinct a conception of Leonardo's genius as words alone can convey. Yet some common-place and common-sense might have been useful in the analysis even of this subject. (pp. 163-65)

In fine, had Mr. Pater been more occupied with his subject than himself, he would have given us, instead of *silhouettes* on cobwebs, a vivid, full-face portrait of Leonardo's personality. . . . (p. 166)

The notice of Joachim du Belley is in one way the best chapter in [*Studies in the History of the Renaissance*], giving the author opportunity for his dainty and delicate fingering, his light strokes of metaphor and suggestion, the short, airy, discursive flights, which he loves, and from which he alights for a moment on cathedral-spires, palace-pinnacles, and tree-tops, on the horizon of his subject, often just at the vanishing-point. But if one

wishes for the gist rather than the pollen-dust of the matter, it is given by Ste. Beuve in the last volume of his *Nouveaux Lundis.* (pp. 166-67)

[Mr. Pater] stands aloof, in an attitude of superfine separateness, whence he critically and dispassionately surveys the world of morals. The most striking instance of this is his way of looking at Winckelman's apostasy, confessedly the result of interested motives; he considers it the consistent act of a man who is true to the key-note of his nature, who obeys his highest instinct, which, in Winckelman was the artistic. We admit that frequent and careful reading has still left us in doubt as to Mr. Pater's meaning in certain passages, and we shrink from incurring the charge of stupidity, which we ourselves have sometimes sharply brought against critics who cannot discriminate between an author's real opinions and his temporary assumption of the opinions of others. But throughout this last essay, and the conclusion, Mr. Pater lays himself open to the charge of being a heathen, or of trying to be one; for no Englishman of the present day can become a genuine heathen, any more than he could become a Jew or a Mussulman; even Mr. Swinburne has only succeeded in being godless. . . . [Apparently, Mr. Pater argues] that the only compensation Christianity has given mankind for Greek paganism is in that the resurrection of the body immortalizes materialism. "The form in which one age of the world chose 'the better part,'"—does he really mean that men may choose "the better part"—in any form which seems good to themselves? Is there no such thing as calling the worse the better, and that bread which satisfieth not? . . . He says that "the mystical art of the Christian middle age is always struggling to express thoughts beyond itself"; and in this respect compares Fra Angelico's Coronation of the Virgin with "the many-headed gods of the East, the orientalized Ephesian Diana with its numerous breasts, . . . overcharged symbols, a means of hinting at an idea which art cannot adequately express, which still remains in the world of shadows." So the best that mediaeval genius and piety have produced is to be likened to the monstrous idols of barbarous nations! "Such forms of art are inadequate to the matter they clothe; they remain ever below its level." Ay, but how do they lift the soul and intellect to regions which cannot be expressed? *there* is the key to the language which cannot be translated into common speech; *there* dwell the truths which can only be shown in types,—but that language is not a whisper, those truths are not shadows. . . . [Mr. Pater] will have it that whatever of calm or joyousness was left in the religious life of Christendom was a remnant of paganism or a revival of art. "Even in the worship of sorrow the native blitheness of art asserted itself." . . . Why not acknowledge that, to the exalted religious perception, the eternal sun becomes visible behind the clouds, that the clear shining of the perfect day transfuses the mists of earth? He insists on the "*grayness* of the ideal or spiritual world," as compared with the rich colors of the sensuous; he has never lifted his eyes to the sun-illumined blue of the purest ideal, the highest spiritual life, nor beheld the snowy ranges of sublimest abstract thought and principle flushed with the warm feelings of humanity and benevolence, fiery with patriotism, with the martyr-spirit, with all intense enthusiasms; he has not rejoiced in the rainbow tints of hope, the glow of faith, the deep-hued ardor of adoration. (pp. 167-70)

The last two chapters [of *Studies in the History of the Renaissance*] have little in common with the rest, beyond that of being within the same covers. The preceding essays form a separate part, of which the result is inconclusive and insubstantial; the theories of art are Winckelman's, the theories of life are Goethe's;

but Mr. Pater has passed them through his own peculiar medium, and we are left with only the fine-spun sieve and a residuum of filmy impressions. Compared with the latter portion of the book, Mr. Ruskin's most incoherent utterances are worthy of respect, for he at least is always in earnest, and never talks of art with its high aspirations and profound convictions as a pastime, or of life with its solemn issues, its rapture and its anguish, as a play or a picture-gallery where the wise man lounges in cold-blooded dilettanteism, reckoning his emotions by clock and thermometer. These concluding chapters have at least this merit: they are definite and tangible as to what they attempt to express; it is for the reader to judge whether that be true, wholesome, even sensible, or false, foolish, and pernicious. (p. 171)

Sarah B. Wister, "Pater, Rio, and Burckhardt," in
The North American Review, *Vol. CXXI, No.*
CCXLVIII, July, 1875, pp. 155-90.*

W. H. MALLOCK   (essay date 1878)

[*First published serially in 1876 and revised in 1878, Mallock's novel* The New Republic, *excerpted below, is a lively satire on Victorian intellectual society. Skillfully parodying Pater's prose style and ideas through the character of Mr. Rose, Mallock depicts Pater as an abstracted dilettante and suggests that his aesthetic doctrines are morally and intellectually irresponsible. Many commentators assert that Mallock's unflattering caricature was a major factor in Pater's decision to withdraw the "Conclusion" from the second edition of the* Renaissance.]

[Lady Ambrose made] a rush at another topic, 'But what is Mr. Rose,' she exclaimed, 'saying about the Clock-tower and the Thames Embankment?'

'I was merely thinking,' said Mr. Rose, who had been murmuring to himself at intervals for some time, 'of a delicious walk I took last week, by the river side, between Charing Cross and Westminster. The great clock struck the chimes of midnight; a cool wind blew; and there went streaming on the wide wild waters with long vistas of reflected lights wavering and quivering in them; and I roamed about for hours, hoping I might see some unfortunate cast herself from the Bridge of Sighs. It was a night I thought well in harmony with despair. Fancy,' exclaimed Mr. Rose, 'the infinity of emotions which the sad sudden splash in the dark river would awaken in one's mind—and all due to that one poem of Hood's!' (pp. 159-60)

'Ah,' said Mr. Rose earnestly, 'don't despise this merely literary culture . . . or the pleasure it is to have at command a beautiful quotation. As I have been lying on the bank here, this afternoon, and looking up into the trees, and watching the blue sky, glancing between the leaves of them—as I have been listening to the hum of the insects, or looking out with half-shut eyes towards the sea across the green rustling shrubs, and the red rose-blossoms, fragments of poetry have been murmuring in my memory like a swarm of bees, and have been carrying my fancy hither and thither in all manner of swift luxurious ways. The "spreading favour," for instance, of these trees that we sit under, brought just now into my mind those magical words of Virgil's—

O qui me gelidis in vallibus Haemi
Sistat, et ingenti ramorum protegat umbrâ!

What a picture there! What a thrill it sent all through me, like a rush of enchanted wind! In another moment the verse that goes just before, also came to me—

Virginibus bacchata Lacaenis
Taygeta—

and into the delicious scene now around me—this beautiful modern garden—mixed instantly visions of Greek mountains, and ragged summits, and choirs of Laconian maidens maddened with a divine enthusiasm, and with fair white vesture wildly floating. Again, another line from the same poem, from the same passage, touched my memory, and changed, in a moment, the whole complexion of my feelings—

Felix qui potuit rerum cognoscere causas.

Think of that! The spirit is whirled away in a moment of time, and set amongst quite new images, quite other sources of excitement. But again, in an instant, the splash of the fountain caught my ear, and awoke, I scarcely know how, the memory of some lines in one of Petrarch's Epistles—

Soporifero clausam qui murmure vallem
Implet inexhausto descendens alveus amne—

and my imagination, on the wings of the verses, was borne away floating toward Vaucluse. Think, then, within the space of five minutes how many thoughts and sensations, composite and crowded, can, by the agency of mere literature, enrich the mind and make life intenser.' (pp. 161-63)

W. H. Mallock, in a chapter in his The New Republic; or, Culture, Faith, and Philosophy in an English Country House, *revised edition, 1878. Reprint by Michael Joseph Ltd., 1937, pp. 146-70.**

J. M. GRAY   (essay date 1885)

With comparatively little action, with hardly any display of the more ordinary human emotions—with, for instance, scarcely a reference in it to sexual love, ["**Marius the Epicurean**"] never fails of interest. It is attractive through the author's vivid sense of beauty, through his constant mode of throwing even the processes of thought into a concrete and pictured form. Its personalities seem not quite the historical Stoic Aurelius, hardly the possibly historical Epicurean Marius: they are raised a little, refined on a little, set on a somewhat higher plane than that of mere actuality. They come to us with a certain sense of strangeness: homely touches, here or there, make us recognise their human nearness; yet their treatment is as far removed as it could well be from the crude realism that is so commonly substituted for delicate artistry, and the cry for which is one of the most unreasoning of the cants of our time.

The exposition of Epicureanism which these "sensations and ideas" of Marius present is more complete than any the author has hitherto given; fuller, also, of "gentleness and sweet reasonableness," more fairly perceptive of the difficulties and weaknesses of a philosophy which manifestly is a scheme of things that possesses the strongest personal attractions for the writer, and the most serious claims, in his view, to be considered as a guide towards a right practice of life. He admits that a career ordered with the aim of making each moment rich, many-coloured, and full of exquisite experiences, is open to the constant dread, to the final certainty, that the last of all these moments may come, must come; and surely it can be no perfect philosophy which leaves its followers liable to be startled by each possible chance of every day, by every falling stone that grazes their heel, and which permits their whole life to be shadowed with the terror of its certain end. We have no due prominence given to the fact that this delicate Epicureanism is possible only to the few, and that even they at any moment may be prevented by disease or mischance from participation in it; nor does the author lay sufficient stress upon the dangers that beset such a life: the temptation to seclude one's self in some lovely "palace of art," regardless of surrounding misery. . . . Again, the favourite doctrines of the book—that the means, not the end, is the main thing, that life should be a jealous calculation of loss and gain, so that each moment may yield its utmost, its most refined, product—do these not smile on the very face the highest life of man? Can all this preoccupation with self have any absorbing place in a right human life? Is it not in quite another fashion that the chosen spirits of the race have lived, with a fine unconsciousness which hungered and thirsted after righteousness itself, and not after any exquisite moments that righteousness might bring either now or in the future? . . .

No, the Epicureanism which finds such calm and delicate exposition in ["**Marius the Epicurean**"] can be no permanent dwelling-place of the human spirit. It may, indeed, afford a healthful corrective to many crude and unlovely tendencies of modern thought. In a mood of wise eclecticism we may receive much from it, may linger for a while in its charmed and golden, though enervating air; but if we would preserve our spiritual health we must press onwards, and breathe the more bracing atmosphere of sterner upland places.

As we should expect from the philosophy of the book, which is so constantly occupied with the concrete, the visible, the tangible, its descriptions of men, of landscape, are especially varied and beautiful. For instance of this we may turn to the chapter which describes the feast given in honour of Apuleius: [very like the paintings of Sir Lawrence Alma-Tadema] in its perfection of finish, in its legitimate and artist-like use of archaeological knowledge for the purposes of mere present beauty; a Tadema, too, in its delighted preoccupation with the lovely details of precious objects of still-life, with . . . the "crystal cups darkened with old wine," and the "dusky fires of the rare twelve-petalled roses." (p. 198)

Before closing, a word should be said as to the style of the book—a style of perfectly finished beauty, full of an exquisite restraint, and, after all, only the fitting and adequate expression of the exactest thinking. The author's style is like that of his own Fronto, in whose lectures, he says, "subtle unexpected meanings were brought out by familiar words." It is so easy and apparently unlaboured in its flow that it seems like mere spontaneous talk—only become strangely select, as though ordered, by some happy chance, with uncommon sweetness. The wise labour that has been spent upon the book has effaced all marks of labour; but, undoubtedly, each sentence has been often touched by the file which, to use an expression that the author is fond of repeating, adds more than value for each particle of gold which it removes. As we read the pages characterised by such unfailing fitness of phrase, finished from their first to their final line with a flawless perfection which one demands in the brief lyric of a master, but hardly looks for in a prose work of extended length, we find far more than the justification of the author's long cessation from slighter literary efforts—a continued silence which has been felt, at least by some lovers of sweet and sifted English, as nothing less than a real personal loss. (pp. 198-99)

J. M. Gray, in a review of "Marius the Epicurean, His Sensations and Ideas," in The Academy, *Vol. XXVII, No. 672, March 21, 1885, pp. 197-99.*

HARPER'S NEW MONTHLY MAGAZINE (essay date 1885)

[*The following commentary on* Marius the Epicurean *was originally published in the May, 1885 issue of* Harper's New Monthly Magazine.]

Much the most important and characteristic work of pure literature published this month, indeed the most essentially literary work of recent date, is Mr W. H. Pater's '**Marius the Epicurean**'. . . . It might be, and was, objected to Mr Pater's early book ['**Studies of the Renaissance**'] that his view of life was narrow, was touched, in spite of so-called 'Hedonism' or advocacy of pleasure, with the deepest gloom, and was stated in language always carefully selected and personal, but somewhat too 'precious' and somewhat too exclamatory. We do not think that the latter accusation, at all events, can be brought against the style of '**Marius the Epicurean**'. . . . [Yet, while] far less florid than certain passages of '**Studies of the Renaissance**', the manner of '**Marius**' is not without the defects of its qualities. Certain adjectives, such as 'firm' (applied to the unbroken summer weather and morning atmosphere), such as 'bland', 'dainty', with a few others, recur frequently. They and their chosen companions among adjectives go a considerable way towards producing the effects at which Mr Pater aims, but their 'repeated air' may not improbably irritate as many readers as they charm. The length of many of Mr Pater's periods, too, may bewilder some of his audience. . . . His subject is difficult; the involutions of his sentences do not make his sense more easy to grasp by a hurrying modern generation. But it is not easy to speak too highly of the conscientious care which has presided over the production of '**Marius the Epicurean**'. As a student of the age of Marcus Aurelius, the age of the Antonines, Mr Pater shows wide and deeply attentive reading. . . . This period of human thought Mr Pater examines on all sides, we may say, except two. He writes little, if at all, about the life of the people, the cobblers and parasites, the traders, the starveling Greeks and Syrians, the untaught peasants, the idle beggar population of Rome and of rural Italy. . . . The people he cares for are all 'seekers after a city', whether the universal city of Stoicism, or the New Jerusalem of Christianity. . . . [The] humorous no less than the popular aspect of human existence is wholly neglected in this picture of old Rome. . . . Yet Mr Pater had many excellent opportunities to relieve the grave austerity of his labours. He introduces Lucian among his characters, Lucian, the most modern of the ancients, the Voltaire and the Rabelais of the classical world, the contented mocker, . . . the most diverting of all writers who have sought fun, and found it, in burlesquing an out-worn mythology. But Lucian only appears in one of his moods of gravity, to hold a serious Platonic dialogue with a young student. It is curious, too, that Mr Pater, writing about the emotional and intellectual life of a young man, says nothing about what a young man's fancy 'lightly turns to'. . . . Marius the Epicurean, in short, is never in love. . . . But we suppose that, if Marius had fallen in love, there would not have been this long tale of a subjective and contemplative life to tell. Mr Pater would have lost his topic, and Marius, in ceasing to be a prig, would have become the hero of a novel. The narrative of his brooding existence is an apologue, or a parable, or a study, or a sermon, not a romance: there is no young woman in it, and the hero does not even lose his heart to Faustina, as a French hero certainly would have done. The book is as 'inward', almost, as the letters of Senancour, but it has the advantage of containing many admirable pictures of human manners and occupations in an age little known to any one but the professional student. In these pictures of old Roman life the rapid general reader will find his pleasure and reward, for we can hardly expect him not to skip the reveries and spiritual sensations (which are not 'sensational') of Marius. He will like the studies of the ancient rural religion of Italy, the services and rites paid to ancestral ghosts, and garden gods. He will like the beautiful description, grave as sculpture, yet glowing with subdued colour, of a rustic temple of Æsculapius, in the hills. . . . The portrait of Marcus Aurelius, the admirably delicate sketch of Faustina, the enigmatic empress, are certain to allure, and there is an extraordinary contrast between a Roman dinner-party (less noisy than the supper of Petronius) and a scene in the family vault of a Christian family, or the beautiful description of the celebration of the Eucharist. Just when the loveliness of the early Christian services, and the happiness of the early Church, are winning Marius (always through his aesthetic consciousness) he dies, an unreclaimed epicurean, indeed, but in circumstances which win for him the name and fame of a Christian martyr. We are not led to think, however, that Marius would ever have left the old gods, formally, or even have stood the torments of the persecutors. He was, indeed, *felix opportunitate mortis* [happy to have a chance to die]. . . . Perhaps one cannot pretend to much sympathy with this rather too open-minded and indifferent young man. His whole view of life was the view suggested to an unimpassioned and sceptical, but not heartless, nature, by the visible aspects of the world. He hated cruelty, he loved order, intellectual and spiritual, because he naturally hated what was ugly, and liked what was beautiful. . . . But he lacked the power of losing himself in other people, he lacked spontaneity and charm, and, in a miraculous manner, and to a wonderful extent, Marius the Epicurean lacked humor. So his creator has been pleased to design him, in one of the most remarkable, and to the right reader, one of the most interesting books of the decade. (pp. 138-41)

> *A review of "Marius the Epicurean," in* Walter Pater: The Critical Heritage, *edited by R. M. Seiler, Routledge & Kegan Paul, 1980. pp. 138-41.*

M.A.W. [MARY AUGUSTA WARD] (essay date 1885)

[*Marius the Epicurean*] is a book which has long been expected with interest by a certain circle of readers. The *Studies in the History of the Renaissance,* which Mr. Pater published twelve years ago, made a distinct mark in modern literary history. They excited as much antipathy as admiration, perhaps. . . .

[What Mr. Pater asked in this work] was simply that life under whatever banner should be lived strenuously and not listlessly, with ardour and not with apathy. Still it was felt that the foundation of it all was in the true sense epicurean. (p. 132)

Mr. Pater has [subsequently] published a certain number of scattered essays, on Greek and English subjects, of which the latter at least have showed a steadily widening and developing power. The masterly essay on Wordsworth . . . must have taken some innocent Wordsworthians by surprise. The austere and yet tender feeling of the whole, the suggestiveness and pregnancy of treatment, the deep sympathy it showed for the peasant life and the peasant sorrows, and a sort of bracing mountain-breath in it, revealed new qualities in the man whose

name in certain quarters had become unreasonably synonymous with a mere effeminate philosophy of pleasure. The two English studies which followed the Wordsworth, one on *Measure for Measure,* the other on Charles Lamb, though less intrinsically weighty, perhaps, had even higher artistic merit, while in the articles on the Demeter myth, Mr. Pater employed extraordinary resources of style with results which were not wholly adequate to the delicate labour spent upon them. Then came an attempt in a totally new direction—the curious story **The Child in the House**. . . . The author never finished it; nor is the fact to be seriously regretted. The disguise furnished by the story for the autobiographical matter, of which it was obviously composed, was not a particularly happy one; above all, it was not disguise enough. Some form of presentation more impersonal, more remote from actual life was needed, before the writer's thought could allow itself fair play. Such a form has now been found in the story of **Marius the Epicurean.** (pp. 132-33)

Those who know Mr. Pater's work will hardly need to be told with what delicacy and beauty he has worked out the theme of **Marius**. . . . There are some half-dozen scenes, which in their own way are unrivalled, where both thought and expression are elaborated with a sort of loving, lingering care, while yet the general impression is one of subdued and measured charm, of a fastidious self-control in the writer, leading to a singular gentleness and purity of presentation. Then to the beauty of style, which springs from his own highly-trained faculty, Mr. Pater has added all that classical culture could supply in the way of adorning and enrichment. The translations from the literature, both Greek and Latin, of the time, in which the book abounds, are in themselves evidence of brilliant literary capacity; the version of Cupid and Psyche especially is a masterpiece. And there is also added to the charm of style, and deftly handled learning, a tenderness of feeling, a tone of reverence for human affections, and pity for the tragedy of human weakness worthy of George Eliot. . . . (pp. 133-34)

Most of those, however, who have already fallen under Mr. Pater's spell will certainly approach the book differently. They will see in such wonderfully delicate and faithful reflection of the workings of a real mind, and that a mind of the nineteenth century, and not of the second. . . .

No one can fail to catch the autobiographical note of *Marius* who will compare the present book with its predecessors. Marius, in fact, as a young man, starts in life on the principles expressed in the concluding pages of the **Studies**. While still a student at Pisa, he reads Heraclitus and Aristippus. . . . From Heraclitus, or from his school, he learns the doctrine of the "subjectivity of knowledge," according to which "the momentary sensible apprehension of the individual is the only standard of what is or is not;" while from Aristippus he learns how to cultivate and refine sensation, and how to make the philosophy of pleasure minister to the most delicate needs of the spiritual and intellectual life. (p. 134)

In this frame of mind Marius goes up to Rome, makes acquaintance with Marcus Aurelius, and is brought across the [philosophy of Stoicism]. . . . The effect of this contact with Stoicism on the flexible mind of Marius, is to lead to a certain modification of his main point of view and in the remarkable chapter called **"Second Thoughts,"** Mr. Pater describes, in the person of Marius, what is evidently the main development of the mind which produced the **Studies in the History of the Renaissance**. (p. 135)

To put it in the language of the present book,

> Marius saw that he would be but an inconsistent
> Cyrenaic—mistaken in his estimate of values,
> of loss and gain, and untrue to the well-con-
> sidered economy of life which he had brought
> to Rome with him—that some drops of the great
> cup would fall to the ground

if he did not make the concession of a "voluntary curtailment
of liberty" to the ancient and wonderful order actually in possession of the world, if he did not purchase by a willing self-
control, participation in that rich store of crystallised feeling
represented by the world's moral beliefs. (p. 136)

[Although] the fundamental argument is really the same as that
on which Mr. Pater based a general view of life twelve years
ago, the practical advance in position shown by the present
book is considerable. . . . After protesting [in the *Studies*],
against the curtailment of experience in favour of "some abstract morality we have not identified with ourselves," Mr.
Pater now presents obedience to this same morality as desirable, not because of any absolute virtue or authority inherent
in it, but because practically obedience is a source of pleasure
and quickened faculty to the individual.

There is nothing new, of course, in such an argument, though
Mr. Pater's presentation of it is full of individuality and fresh
suggestions. But what makes the great psychological interest
of [*Marius the Epicurean*], while it constitutes what seems to
us its principal intellectual weakness, is the further application
of this Epicurean principle of an æsthetic loss and gain not
only to morals, but to religion. We have [seen] the way in
which Mr. Pater handles the claim of the moral system of the
civilised world upon a mind in search of beauty. His treatment
of the claim of religion on a similar order of mind is precisely
the same in tone and general plan. Just as adhesion to the
accepted moral order enriches and beautifies the experience of
the individual, and so gives a greater savour and attractiveness
to life, so acquiescence in the religious order, which a man
finds about him, opens for him opportunities of feeling and
sensation which would otherwise be denied him, provides him
with a fresh series of "exquisite moments," and brings him
generally within the range of an influence soothing and refining, by virtue partly of its venerableness, its source in an
immemorial past, partly of the wealth of beautiful human experience which has gone, age after age, to the strengthening
of it. . . . [This] theory of religious philosophy, which is much
commoner among us than most of us think, . . . has never
been expressed so fully or so attractively as in the story of
Marius.

Submit it seems to say, to the religious order about you, accept
the common beliefs, or at least behave as if you accepted them,
and live habitually in the atmosphere of feeling and sensation
which they have engendered and still engender; surrender your
feeling, while still maintaining the intellectual citadel intact;
pray, weep, dream with the majority while you think with the
elect; only so will you obtain from life all it has to give, its
most delicate flavour, its subtlest aroma.

Such an appeal has an extraordinary force with a certain order
of minds. Probably as time goes we shall see a larger and larger
response to it on the part of modern society. But with another
order of mind in whom the religious need is not less strong,
it has not, and never will have, any chance of success, for they
regard it as involving the betrayal of a worship dearer to them
than the worship of beauty or consolation, and the surrender

of something more precious to them than any of those delicate
emotional joys, which feeling, divorced from truth, from the
sense of reality, has to offer. All existing religions have issued
from the sense of reality, from a perception of some truth;
certain facts or supposed facts of sense or spirit have lain at
the root of them. It is surely a degradation of all religion to
say to its advocates: "Your facts are no facts; our sense of
reality is opposed to them; but for the sake of the beauty, the
charm, the consolation to be got out of the intricate practical
system you have built upon this chimerical basis, we are ready
to give up to you all we can—our sympathy, our silence, our
ready co-operation in all your lovely and soothing rites and
practices, hoping thereby to cheat life of some of its pain, and
to brighten some of its darkness with dreams fairer even than
those which Aesculapius inspired in his votaries." (pp. 137-
38)

There are many other minor points in [*Marius*] which would
repay discussion. Has it done justice to the complexities either
of the Roman world or of Christianity in the second century?
In fairness to Marcus Aurelius and the pagan world, ought
there not to have been some hint of that aspect of the Christian
question which leads [the French scholar Ernest] Renan to apply
to the position of the Christian in a pagan city the analogy of
that of "a Protestant missionary in a Spanish town where Catholicism is very strong, preaching against the saints, the Virgin, and processions?" Would it not have been well, as an
accompaniment to the exquisite picture of primitive Christian
life, to have given us some glimpse into the strange excitements
and agitations of Christian thought in the second century? As
far as Marius is concerned, the different currents of Christian
speculation at the time might hardly have existed. Then again,
is there not a little humour wanting, which, according to the
facts, ought to have been there, in such a description as that
lovely one, of the temple and rites of Aesculapius? But these
questions we can only throw out for the reader of *Marius* to
ponder if he will. However they may be answered, the value
and delightfulness of the book remain. It is so full of exquisite
work, of thought fresh from heart and brain, that when the
reader has made all his reservations, and steadily refused his
adhesion to this or that appeal which it contains, he will come
back with fresh delight to the passages and descriptions and
reveries in which a poetical and meditative nature has poured
out a wealth of imaginative reflection. (pp. 138-39)

> *M.A.W. [Mary Augusta Ward], "'Marius the Epi-*
> *curean'," in* Macmillan's Magazine, *Vol. LII, No.*
> *308, June, 1885, pp. 132-39.*

[GEORGE EDWARD WOODBERRY] (essay date 1887)

That subtle appreciation and the infinite number of small touches
in the rendering of what he sees, which lie at the heart of Mr.
Pater's literary individuality and give to his style its extraordinary distinction, lift [**'Imaginary Portraits'**] out of the range
of the common, and set it apart as unique with his other work. . . .
But it does not in all respects reach the level of that stronger
and richer, though not more elaborated, work; and the four
studies, as between themselves, have very different degrees of
success. . . .

The first of these [studies] is so much the most highly finished
and clearly made out as to leave the others far behind. It is in
the main a criticism on Antony Watteau, . . . but it is directly
a criticism of Watteau's temperament rather than his works,
and indirectly a view of the whole real meaning of that age as

seen through art. It is all very simple, however. Only two lights are thrown on the painter—one, which shows him ironically indifferent to the luminous gayety in depicting which he was so easily master; the other, which reveals the impatient jealousy of genius in the presence of that talent which by industry comes so nigh to the same perfection. There is praise enough of his works—excellent, discriminating, definite praise. (p. 78)

One cannot condense Pater's work, . . . or give any impression of its structural completeness, of its endless charm of detail, by bringing the traditional brick in the shape of a paragraph. Of the minor touches, nevertheless, let us spare space to mention the beautiful old age of Monseigneur le Prince de Cambrai, seen by a sidelight of the narrative, the almost dramatic vividness of the chance introduction of the story of 'Manon Lescaut' [by Abbé Prévost], then a new book, the imaginative pathos of the incident of the bird lost among the cathedral arches where it will beat its life out helplessly, and the glimpse of the Revolution to come which he affords us when, looking on some of Watteau's designs, the writer says:

> Only as I gaze upon those windless afternoons I find myself always saying to myself involuntarily, 'The evening will be a wet one.' The storm is always brooding through the massy splendor of the trees, above those sun-dried glades or lawns where delicate children may be trusted thinly clad; and the secular trees themselves will hardly outlast another generation.

None of the remaining three studies approach measurably near this of Watteau either in power or subtlety or purity. . . . The legend [of Denys L'Auxerrois] is perhaps too obviously managed, and too much is crowded into it for a single impersonation. The opening landscape is possibly the best of it.

So, in the next study (the contrast of the Low Dutch life with Spinozism in Sebastian Van Storck . . .), the landscape is the one thing successfully treated. . . . In the personal part of the story and in the thought history of it, the author is out of his own field. The heavy grossness of the circumstances and the incongruousness of the intellectual parts with the scene are too difficult matters for his hand—in the mass at least, for there are felicities in the detail.

In the [study of Duke Carly Rosenmold], likewise, one finds lack of that substance in the midst of picturesqueness to which Pater has accustomed us, and the picturesqueness itself is of a somewhat rubbishy kind. The time was rubbishy, possibly the author would say in comment on the criticism; and it is of interest to observe that he sets up a defence for those poor people who go into raptures and enthusiasms over third-rate things:

> The higher informing capacity, if it exist within, will mould an unpromising matter to itself; will realize itself by selection and the preference of the better in what is bad or indifferent, asserting its prerogative under the most unlikely conditions.

Carl, he says, made "a really heroic effort of mind at a disadvantage," and put into his enthusiasm for Louis XIV. and the aesthetic achievements of that age what young France had felt for Francis I. and Da Vinci. This is of great comfort to the aesthetic class that has no access to the best and greatest, yet must feel strongly. To us, unfortunately, the essay in which

it occurs seems to belong to the grade of Louis XIV. rather than of Francis I., and too clearly within hailing distance of Pater's feminine disciple, Vernon Lee. When a man's best is as good as Pater's, *noblesse oblige* [rank imposes obligations]—he must keep to it. (pp. 78-9)

> [*George Edward Woodberry*], in a review of "Imaginary Portraits," in The Nation, *Vol. IX, No. 1152, July, 1887, pp. 78-9.*

ARTHUR SYMONS   (essay date 1887)

[*An English critic, poet, dramatist, short story writer, and editor, Symons initially gained notoriety as an English decadent in the 1890s and eventually established himself as one of the most important critics of the modern era. His The Symbolist Movement in Literature provided his English contemporaries with an appropriate vocabulary with which to define their new aesthetic—one that communicated their concern with dreamlike states, imagination, and a reality existing beyond the boundaries of the senses. Symons also discerned that the concept of the symbol as a vehicle by which a "hitherto unknown reality was suddenly revealed" could become the basis for the entire modern aesthetic, and therefore laid the foundation for much of modern poetic theory. As the following excerpt indicates, Symons revered Pater. Socially and philosophically, their relationship was close: the two men befriended each other in the late 1880s, and Symons became a key member of the Rhymers' Club, a late-nineteenth-century literary group which looked to Pater for its aesthetic philosophy. Edmund Wilson maintained that Pater inspired Symons's faith in the ascendancy of the imagination, thus contributing to the evolution of the Symbolist movement in England (see Additional Bibliography).*]

As a critic, in that unique volume of **"Studies in the Renaissance,"** and in the scattered essays on poets and painters, [Mr. Pater] has selected for analysis only those types of artistic character in which "delicacy," an exquisite fineness, is the prevailing feature; or if, as with Michel Angelo, he has been drawn towards some more rugged personality, some more massive, less finished art, it has been less from sympathy with these more obvious qualities of ruggedness and strength, than because he has divined the sweetness lying at the heart of the strength—*ex forti dulcedo.* Leonardo da Vinci, Charles Lamb, Joachim du Bellay, Giorgione: in every one something not merely frank and broad, a large straightforward talent, but in one direction or another a refinement upon refinement, a choice and exotic exquisiteness, a subtle and *recherché* [refined] beauty; something which it requires an effort to disengage, and which appeals for its perfect appreciation to a public within the public,—people who take their aesthetic pleasures consciously, deliberately, critically, as amateurs take their wine. And not as a critic only, judging others, but in his own person as a writer, both of critical and of imaginative work, Mr. Pater shows his preoccupation with the "delicacies of fine literature." He expends as much labour over his prose as Lord Tennyson gives to his poetry. Nothing is left to inspiration; like Baudelaire, he would better nature; and he would certainly reject a "fine careless rapture," if one came to him. It is all goldsmith's work as he has told us; . . . and he has wrought in the spirit of the craftsmen of olden days, with a laborious delight.

The development of Mr. Pater's style is interesting to observe. . . . Taken on its own formal merits, ["Studies"] is the most beautiful book of prose in our literature. It is a book to be read, as Lamb or Shelley speaks somewhere of doing, with "shouts of delight;" or perhaps rather with a delight silent and continuous, for it is all finished and perfect, and it rings everywhere flawless as a bell. From beginning to end there is not a hasty sentence, a cadence not considered, not prepared, a word thrown on the page at random. Anything like eloquence, anything of rhetoric or display, is not to be found in it. Like Baudelaire, Mr. Pater has *"rêvé le miracle d'une prose poétique, musicale sans rhythme et sans rime"* [dreamed the miracle of a poetic prose, musical without rhythm and without rhyme]; and, like Baudelaire, he has effected his miracle without any violent aids or thefts from the domain proper to poetry. An almost oppressive quiet—a quietness which seems to breathe of an atmosphere heavy with tropical flowers—broods over these pages; a subdued light shadows them; they depend for their charm on no contrasts, epigrams, paradoxes, sudden twists and turns, thunder-claps, summersaults of diction, lyric raptures. The most felicitous touches come we know not whence— "a breath, a flame in the doorway, a feather in the wind,"— effects produced by the cunning employment of the simplest words, words which take suddenly a new colour and sound, and reveal undreamt-of properties. In this book of the **"Studies,"** prose seemed to have conquered a new province. So difficult is it, however, to avoid the defects of our qualities, that it was feared lest Mr. Pater's mastery over colour and sound in words should lead him too far; lest, as it has been cruelly said, he should "swoon by the way over the subtle perfumes he has evoked." And perhaps some of the essays, wonderfully beautiful as they are, which followed the publication of that volume, might have seemed a little to confirm the fear. But when . . . Mr. Pater's second work ["**Marius the Epicurean**"] appeared, it was found, probably to the surprise of many people, that alike in style and in thought the progress had been, not in the direction of licence, of over-sumptuous richness, but towards a somewhat chill asceticism, a restraint sometimes almost painful. The goldsmith, adding more value, as he thought, for every trace of gold that he removed, might seem to some to have scraped a little too assiduously. And in this third book ["**Imaginary Portraits**"], . . . we find the same self-restraint, perhaps grown still more fastidious, and the same self-conscious artistry that has ruled from the first. (pp. 157-58)

The merit more than any other which distinguishes Mr. Pater's prose, though it is not the merit most on the surface, is the attention to, and perfection of, the *ensemble* [whole]. Under the soft and musical phrases an inexorable chain of logic hides itself, sometimes only too well. Link is added silently but faultlessly to link; the argument marches, carrying you with it, while you fancy you are only listening to the music with which it keeps step. You can take an essay to pieces, and you will find that it is constructed with mathematical precision; every piece can be taken out and replaced in order. I do not know any contemporary writer who observes the logical requirements so scrupulously, who conducts an argument so steadily from deliberate point to point towards a determined goal. And what I have said about the essays may be applied, with slight changes, to the imaginative work—to **"Marius the Epicurean,"** and to these **"Imaginary Portraits."** With the construction of **"Marius,"** when viewed as a whole, I do not know that it is possible to be quite satisfied; it is too much a mere sequence of scenes and of moods; but certainly each of these many sections has an admirable *ensemble* of its own. The **"Imaginary Portraits"** much shorter, are placed, arranged, developed with an art which of its kind is quite flawless; I am not sure that they do not show Mr. Pater's combined imaginative and artistic faculties at their point of most perfect fusion. (pp. 158-59)

The result of Mr. Pater's method [in **"Imaginary Portraits"**] is so charming that we have no right, I think, to complain that

he gives us just, and only, what he does. At the same time it is quite obvious that neither Watteau, nor Denys, nor Sebastian, nor Duke Carl really lives, in so much as a finger-tip, with actual imaginative life; they are all ghosts, names, puppets of an artist and a philosopher who has evoked or constructed them for his purpose, but has not been able, or has not wished, to endow them with flesh and blood, with the breath of life. . . . [Mr. Pater] has indeed an almost complete lack of passion, of emotion, of any directly humanising instinct; at least he admits nothing of the kind in his work, or only in so faint a form that it never gets so far as our hearts; and there can be no doubt, I suppose, that the greatest literature, other things being equal, is that which represents the most of "life immense in passion, pulse, and power." But putting aside the Shakespeares and Michel Angelos, there is exquisite delight to be obtained, no doubt on a much lower plane, from the Gautiers and Albert Moores—serene artists who seek only beauty, and to whom any emotional disturbance is a mere distraction and a trouble. I do not think we have any right to turn from these men, to be dissatisfied with what they give us; for the aim they have reached at and attained is a perfectly legitimate one, and we show ourselves narrow, *borné,* if we refuse to see it. (pp. 159-60)

[What Mr. Pater has done in these four portraits,] and what he has doubtless intended to do, is to give a concrete form to abstract ideas; to represent certain types of character, to trace certain developments, in the picturesque and attractive way of narrative. Each, also, with perhaps one exception, is the study of a soul, or rather of a consciousness; such a study as one might make, granted certain gifts and cultures, by simply looking within, and projecting now this now that side of oneself on an exterior plane. I do not mean to say that I attribute the philosophical theories of Sebastian van Storck, or the artistic ideals of Duke Carl of Rosenmold, to Mr. Pater himself. I only mean that the attitude of mind, the outlook, in the most general sense, is always limited and directed in a certain way, giving one always the picture of a delicate, subtle, aspiring, unsatisfied personality, open to all impressions, living chiefly by sensations, little anxious to reap any or much of the rich harvest of its intangible but keenly possessed gains; a personality withdrawn from action, which it despises or dreads, solitary with its ideals, in the circle of its "exquisite moments," in the Palace of Art, where it is never quite at rest. (p. 160)

Personally, for one deals here only in impressions, it seems to me that the most wonderful of the four portraits in this new book is the poem, for it is really a poem, named **"Denys l'Auxerrois."** This is not the study of a soul, it is the study of a myth—a translation, in which one hardly knows whether most to admire the learning, the ingenuity, or the real imagination, of the strangest myth of the Greeks, that "Pagan afterthought" of Dionysus Zagreus, into the conditions of mediaeval life. It is a poem in prose, and in prose so coloured, so modulated, that one can scarcely feel as if the rhythm of actual metre could add to its charm. And what a variety of every sort of poetic richness does it contain! It has even the *suggestiveness* of poetry, that most volatile and unseizable property, of which prose has so rarely been able to possess itself. And all this without any sort of approach to that rhapsodic manner which mimicks the cadences of verse without becoming verse, and is neither verse nor prose, but a hateful and impotent hermaphrodite. The style of **"Denys l'Auxerrois"** has a subdued heat and veiled richness of colour, which contrasts very strikingly with the silver-grey coolness of **"A Prince of Court-Painters,"** the chill, more leaden grey of **"Sebastian van Storck,"** though it has a certain affinity, perhaps, with the more variously-tinted canvas of **"Duke Carl of Rosenmold."** Watteau, Sebastian, Carl—unsatisfied seekers, all of them, this after an artistic ideal of impossible perfection, that after a chill and barren ideal of philosophic thinking and living, that other after yet another ideal, unattainable to him in his period, of life "im Ganzen, Guten, Schönen," a beautiful and effective culture. The story of each is a tragedy, ending in every case with an actual physical severance of bodily existence, always with some subtly ironic effect, as if Fate "struck them gracefully, cutting off their young histories with a catastrophic dash." (pp. 160-61)

Just so, it will be remembered, was Marius left at the end of the beautiful book of his sensations and ideas; dying ambiguously, half, or altogether, or not at all a Christian, and buried by humble people with Christian rites, as a martyr: "for martyrdom, as the Church had always said, was a kind of sacrament with plenary grace." Just so [in **"The Child in the House"**] we take leave of the child Florian, at the crisis of a great change, with his foot on the long road leading who knows whitherward? It is evident that to Mr. Pater there is a particular charm in this abrupt finish, this sudden displacement and descent, as through one of those *oubliettes* [trap dungeons] of the Middle Ages, of the human figure walking forward so uncertainly, yet with no suspicion of any such prompt solving of the *grand Peut-être* [grand possibilities]. . . . In truth, Mr. Pater is no moralist, and alike as an artist and as a thinker, he feels called upon to draw no moral, to deduce no consequences, from the failures or successes he has chronicled to a certain culminating point. "There is the portrait," he seems to say; "all I have been writing is but as so many touches towards that single visible outline: there is the portrait!" (pp. 161-62)

Arthur Symons, "Walter Pater: 'Imaginary Portraits'," in Time, *London, n.s. Vol. XVII, No. 32, August, 1887, pp. 157-62.*

PALL MALL GAZETTE (essay date 1889)

[*The following criticism of Pater's writing style was originally published in a review of* Appreciations *in the* Pall Mall Gazette *on December 10, 1889.*]

How comes it, one would like to know, that the act of writing about style tends to play havoc with the style of the writer? Mr Stevenson's essay on style, published some time ago in the 'Contemporary Review', was probably the worst piece of writing he ever put his name to. Mr John M. Robertson, in his 'Essays towards a Critical Method', has a paper on Science in Criticism, mainly concerned of course with style, which would be luminous—if it were not obscure. And now Mr Pater, with some excellent things to say [in his essay on **'Style'** in **'Appreciations'**] contrives to say some of them with curious infelicity. We do not, on the whole, admire Mr Pater's style so fervently as some people. It has distinction and delicacy, but it lacks vivacity, and, worse than that, it is not always absolutely clear. Mr Pater's sedateness verges upon solemnity. Urbane and even insinuating as his discourses are, one feels now and then an impish longing to play some practical joke on this bland imperturbability, in the hope of extorting from it either a smile or a frown. . . . We cannot but regard this monotony of mood, this total absence of buoyancy or sparkle, as a serious limitation in Mr Pater's style. It makes us yearn at times for the elaborate wit of Mr Lowell or even the allusive flippancy of Mr Lang. In support of our second and graver accusation let us quote the following sentence from the essay on **'Style'**:

The true distinction between prose and poetry he [Wordsworth] regarded as the almost technical or accidental one of the absence or presence of metrical beauty, or, say! metrical restraint; and for him the opposition came to be between verse and prose of course—you can't scan Wordsworth's prose: but, as the essential dichotomy in this matter, between imaginative and unimaginative writing, parallel to De Quincey's distinction between 'the literature of power and the literature of knowledge', in the former of which the composer gives us not fact, but his peculiar sense of fact, whether past or present, or prospective, it may be, as often in oratory.

Now, frankly, reader, have you more than a faint glimmer of the meaning of this wounded snake of a sentence? Don't you want to try back, to unravel it, laboriously tracing out the logical structure, the process and opposition of ideas? And this, though perhaps an extreme, is very far from being a solitary, case. Again and again, one has to re-read a sentence in order to make quite sure of its meaning. In one or two instances, we have at first suspected that the printer must have made havoc of the text. . . . Further study has in almost all cases exonerated the compositor, at Mr Pater's expense. For there is surely something amiss when a fairly attentive reader keeps on stumbling and having to try back. We happened to take up a book of Jules Lemaître's immediately after finishing this essay on **'Style',** and the sensation was that of skating on smooth ice immediately after having struggled through an obstacle-race. (pp. 199-200)

A review of "Appreciations," in Walter Pater: The Critical Heritage, *edited by R. M. Seiler, Routledge & Kegan Paul, 1980, pp. 198-200.*

OSCAR WILDE   (essay date 1890)

[*Wilde, an Anglo-Irish dramatist, novelist, poet, critic, essayist, and short story writer, was one of Pater's most flamboyant and outspoken followers. His discipleship eventually became a liability to Pater, for he included elements of Pater's thought in his sensational novel* The Picture of Dorian Gray *and testified when he was tried in 1895 for committing homosexual acts that Pater had been a formative influence in his life. Many of Pater's early supporters attempted to disassociate the two writers, insinuating that Wilde had perverted the lofty ideals of the "true Paterism" (see excerpt below by Richard Le Gallienne, 1912). Wilde's review of* Appreciations, *excerpted below, was originally published in the* Speaker *on March 22, 1890.*]

When I first had the privilege—and I count it a very high one—of meeting Mr Walter Pater, he said to me, smiling, 'Why do you always write poetry? Why do you not write prose? Prose is so much more difficult.' (p. 232)

I may frankly confess now that at the time I did not quite comprehend what Mr Pater really meant; and it was not till I had carefully studied his beautiful and suggestive essays [in **'Studies in the History of the Renaissance'**] that I fully realised what a wonderful self-conscious art the art of English prose-writing really is, or may be made to be. . . . [His] essays became to me 'the golden book of spirit and sense, the holy writ of beauty'. They are still this to me. It is possible, of course, that I may exaggerate about them. I certainly hope that I do; for where there is no exaggeration there is no love, and where there is no love there is no understanding. . . .

'Appreciations', in the fine Latin sense of the word, is the title given by Mr Pater to his [latest] book, which is an exquisite collection of exquisite essays, of delicately wrought works of art—some of them being almost Greek in their purity of outline and perfection of form, others mediaeval in their strangeness of colour and passionate suggestion, and all of them absolutely modern, in the true meaning of the term modernity. (p. 233)

Perhaps the most interesting, and certainly the least successful, of the essays contained in ['**Appreciations**'] is that on Style. It is the most interesting because it is the work of one who speaks with the high authority that comes from the noble realisation of things nobly conceived. It is the least successful, because the subject is too abstract. A true artist like Mr Pater, is most felicitous when he deals with the concrete, whose very limitations give him finer freedom, while they necessitate more intense vision. (p. 234)

As [the essay] on Wordsworth seems to be Mr Pater's last work, so that on [William Morris] . . . is certainly his earliest, or almost his earliest, and it is interesting to mark the change that has taken place in his style. . . . In 1868 we find Mr Pater writing with the same exquisite care for words, with the same studied music, with the same temper, and something of the same mode of treatment. But, as he goes on, the architecture of the style becomes richer and more complex, the epithet more precise and intellectual. Occasionally one may be inclined to think that there is, here and there, a sentence which is somewhat long, and possibly, if one may venture to say so, a little heavy and cumbersome in movement. But if this be so, it comes from those side-issues suddenly suggested by the idea in its progress, and really revealing the idea more perfectly; or from those felicitous after-thoughts that give a fuller completeness to the central scheme, and yet convey something of the charm of chance; or from a desire to suggest the secondary shades of meaning with all their accumulating effect, and to avoid, it may be, the violence and harshness of too definite and exclusive an opinion. . . . The critical pleasure, too, that we receive from tracing, through what may seem the intricacies of a sentence, the working of the constructive intelligence, must not be overlooked. As soon as we have realised the design, everything appears clear and simple. After a time, these long sentences of Mr Pater's come to have the charm of an elaborate piece of music, and the unity of such music also.

I have suggested that the essay on Wordsworth is probably the most recent bit of work contained in this volume. If one might choose between so much that is good, I should be inclined to say it is the finest also. The essay on Lamb is curiously suggestive; suggestive, indeed, of a somewhat more tragic, more sombre figure, than men have been wont to think of in connection with the author of the 'Essays of Elia'. It is an interesting aspect under which to regard Lamb, but perhaps he himself would have had some difficulty in recognising the portrait given of him. He had, undoubtedly, great sorrows, or motives for sorrow, but he could console himself at a moment's notice for the real tragedies of life by reading any one of the Elizabethan tragedies, provided it was in a folio edition. The essay on Sir Thomas Browne is delightful, and has the strange, personal, fanciful charm of the author of the 'Religio Medici'. . . . That on Coleridge, with its insistence on the necessity of the cultivation of the relative, as opposed to the absolute spirit in philosophy and in ethics, and its high appreciation of the poet's true position in our literature, is in style and substance a very blameless work. Grace of expression, and delicate subtlety of thought and phrase, characterise the essays on

Shakespeare. But the essay on Wordsworth has a spiritual beauty of its own. It appeals, not to the ordinary Wordsworthian with his uncritical temper, and his gross confusion of ethical with aesthetical problems, but rather to those who desire to separate the gold from the dross, and to reach at the true Wordsworth through the mass of tedious and prosaic work that bears his name, and that serves often to conceal him from us. The presence of an alien element in Wordsworth's art, is, of course, recognised by Mr Pater, but he touches on it merely from the psychological point of view, pointing out how this quality of higher and lower moods gives the effect in his poetry 'of a power not altogether his own, or under his control'; a power which comes and goes when it wills, 'so that the old fancy which made the poet's art an enthusiasm, a form of divine possession, seems almost true of him'. (pp. 234-36)

Certainly the real secret of Wordsworth has never been better expressed. After having read and re-read Mr Pater's essay— for it requires re-reading—one returns to the poet's work with a new sense of joy and wonder, and with something of eager and impassioned expectation. And perhaps this might be roughly taken as the test or touchstone of the finest criticism.

Finally, one cannot help noticing the delicate instinct that has gone to fashion the brief epilogue that ends this delightful volume. The difference between the classical and romantic spirits in art has often, and with much over-emphasis, been discussed. But with what a light sure touch does Mr Pater write of it! How subtle and certain are his distinctions! If imaginative prose be really the special art of this century, Mr Pater must rank amongst our century's most characteristic artists. In certain things he stands almost alone. The age has produced wonderful prose styles, turbid with individualism, and violent with rhetoric. But in Mr Pater, as in Cardinal Newman, we find the union of personality with perfection. He has no rival in his own sphere, and he has escaped disciples. And this, not because he has not been imitated, but because in art so fine as his there is something that, in its essence, is inimitable. (p. 236)

Oscar Wilde, in a review of "Appreciations," in Walter Pater: The Critical Heritage, *edited by R. M. Seiler, Routledge & Kegan Paul, 1980, pp. 232-36.*

W. J. COURTHOPE (essay date 1890)

Many critics now make it their object, not so much to judge the artist's work by their conception of the laws of art, as to expound to the world the nature of the artist's motives. The method of this school of criticism is admirably indicated in the title and illustrated by the contents of Mr. Pater's book [*Appreciations*].

It is a method with conspicuous excellences and defects. . . . The value of an artist's performance cannot be justly estimated by the critic, unless he endeavours to *appreciate* his intentions. Mr. Pater never fails to do this. His volume comprises among others essays on Wordsworth, Coleridge, Charles Lamb, Mr. William Morris, and the late Mr. Rossetti. All these writers may be described as innovators in art, yet in Mr. Pater's judgments of their work there is rarely to be found a word of depreciation. He confines himself to discovering by delicate analysis the working of each individual mind, and the external forces by which it was influenced. In this he is admirably successful, and if, in the style which he employs to communicate the results of his analysis, simplicity is somewhat painfully conspicuous by its absence, the fault—if fault it be—is due, not to the love of rhetorical display, but to a conscientious attempt to embody in words the most subtle complexities of thought. Perhaps his best essays are those on Wordsworth and Charles Lamb. With both of these writers he seems to be in special sympathy, and his 'appreciation' of their motives is marked by an exquisite refinement. (pp. 658-59)

At the same time this excellence should not blind us to the accompanying defect of Mr. Pater's method. There can in fact be no thoroughly just appreciation without a mixture of depreciation. Even the good Homer is supposed sometimes to nod; and it is surely right that the critic should judge an artist's work, not merely by the skill the latter shows in executing his own intentions, but by those ideal laws to which, if criticism is anything more than a name, every work of art must be assumed to be subject. Mr. Pater would not deny this; but his tendency is to assume first principles of taste which seem to explain the practice of his favourite authors, rather than to estimate their performances by reference to the practice of the greatest writers. For example, he says very truly:

> An intimate consciousness of the expression of natural things, which weights, listens, penetrates, where the earlier mind passed roughly by, is a large element in the complexion of modern poetry.

Later on he explains this practice on the following principle:

> That the end of life is not action but contemplation—being as distinct from doing—a certain disposition of the mind: is in some shape or other the principle of the higher morality. . . . Wordsworth, and other poets who have been like him in ancient or modern times, are the experts in this art of impassioned contemplation.

Now I think it can scarcely be denied that in the work of all the greatest poets—Homer, Virgil, the Greek dramatists, Shakespeare, Milton, even Dante—Doing, to a greater extent than Being, lies at the foundation of their art. There is therefore a sanction of between two and three thousand years in favour of the law that action, in some form or other, must be the predominant principle in every great poem. More than this. It can be shown that what are acknowledged to be defects in modern poets are due to the excessive preponderance in their work of the contemplative element. Mr. Pater accepts Wordsworth's defence of his system of poetic diction, as if it were an exposition of a sufficient law of art. He allows that a very large portion of Wordsworth's poetical compositions is artistically worthless; but he does not seem to see that the frequent flaws in his genuinely pathetic poems (such for instance as 'Simon Lee' and 'Resolution and Independence'), the mistaking of homely triviality for artistic simplicity, and of a garrulous prosiness for a *natural* manner of writing in metre, arise from his exaggerated attachment to his own conceptions, and his neglect of positive rules of art.

Mr. Pater's appreciation of Coleridge is more severe, and therefore more just; yet he pronounces Coleridge . . . to be 'the perfect flower of the *ennuyé* [mentally wearied] type;' and he even finds in 'The Ancient Mariner' 'a perfectly rounded wholeness and unity.' Surely it would be much truer to say plainly that this poem and 'Christabel' are the splendid *tours de force* [feats of skill] of a great but fragmentary genius; and that Coleridge's constant struggles as a philosopher after a conception of the Absolute were, in themselves, the cause of his infertility as a poet. (pp. 660-61)

The fallacy involved in Mr. Pater's method of judging artistic conception [also] makes itself felt in his remarks on style, which are otherwise often just and opportune. In an incidental reference to Gustave Flaubert he remarks on his painful struggles after exact precision in language. (p. 661)

Mr. Pater ascribes Flaubert's efforts (which, from his own account, amounted to agony) to the boundless love of art. But they are surely capable of another explanation. Neither Shakespeare nor Scott troubled themselves greatly to find the *one* word to express their thought, because they wrote out of full minds on subjects of general imaginative interest. Flaubert's aim, on the other hand, like that of so many modern artists, was to discover the imaginative secret underlying commonplace objects and actions, while he was obliged to use as his instrument of expression a language built up by men who judged of such objects and actions by the light of common sense. Putting aside all moral considerations, Flaubert, in an artistic sense, 'considered too curiously.' For instance, in 'Madame Bovary' he takes eight lines to describe, in the most refined words, the action of a woman drinking a glass of liqueur. No wonder that he was oppressed by a feeling of artistic impotence!

To sum up: Mr. Pater's criticism, in my opinion, suffers from . . . excess of sympathy. In his fine perception of the motives of his authors, and in his delicate description of their styles, his *Appreciations* are all that can be desired; but he seems to me to flinch from the severe application of critical law. He exhibits invariably the taste of a refined literary epicure. But the taste of an epicure is not always that of a judge. (pp. 661-62)

> *W. J. Courthope, in a review of "Appreciations,"* in The Nineteenth Century, *Vol. XXVII, No. CLVIII, April, 1890, pp. 658-62.*

LEWIS CAMPBELL (essay date 1893)

[*Plato and Platonism: A Series of Lectures* is] a brilliant critical essay of the kind which, in Mr. Pater's view, is, ever since Montaigne employed it, the best vehicle for modern philosophic thought. Readers of *Marius the Epicurean*, who remember the subtle exposition there of Cyrenaicism will be prepared for similar *tours de force*. Yet it is not without a feeling of pleased and exhilarating surprise that they will alight on such pages of the present volume as that in which the character and mind of Zeno the Eleatic are delineated . . . , or those which explain perhaps more luminously than has been done hitherto the value which Plato set on Dialectic. . . . (p. 263)

[Mr. Pater] has made a strong and earnest effort on his own account . . . to understand and realize Plato [by following the historic method of criticism]. But in setting forth his conception he has freely availed himself of the wealth of illustration readily afforded by his own full and fertile mind. His readers are insensibly drawn within a magic circle of quintessential flame that has been fed with all the choicest products of art and literature. Not one century alone is present here. Much rather, all the centuries, the bloom of every civilization, flowers culled from every soil, are intertwined to form the delicately broidered framework. Talk of . . . [variable things]! Why here are Isaiah and the children of Sion, Louis the IXth, Fra Damiano of Bergamo, the Gregorian Chant, St. Ouen and Notre Dame de Bourges (confessedly a 'far cry' from Athens), Montaigne and Thackeray, Dante and Berkeley, Wordsworth and Henry Vaughan—not to mention Marcus Aurelius, Spinoza, Descartes and Bacon (whose business in such affairs is more obvious)—contributing their several tones to the production of this symphony in prose! These cross-lights, as from 'storied windows richly dight' on forms of alabaster, shed a manifold radiance on the firm outlines of the solid central work, which is also permeated by a remote Hegelian influence and by the writer's personal idiosyncrasy, in which refined aesthetic sensitiveness is blended with a quiet intensity of religious feeling. . . .

The *matter* of the book before us has, much of it, been common property for about forty years, commencing from the time when the historic method was first seriously applied to criticism. But it is not the less a solid gain to possess this bright and genial exposition of truths which we have long potently believed. For, however he may try to veil his gift, Mr. Pater is essentially a poet. And if Goethe and [the classical philologist Gottfried] Hermann offered to discourse on Homer, who would not be tempted to exclaim 'Dear Gottfried, we will gladly listen to you . . . [again],—on some other day'? The siren voice of Mr. Pater will be heard, where that of the unkempt Heraclitean 'Sibyl' could not penetrate. (p. 264)

Mr. Pater is really charmed with Plato; but there are other and rival charms which he will not forego. . . . [Some discrepancies] may be thus accounted for. He admires Marcus Aurelius . . . , yet he is struck with a 'mortal coldness' . . . in thinking of him. 'Monotheism' has his good word upon occasion; yet he finds it 'repellent.' At one moment Form is everything and Matter nothing . . . , though by and by precipitancy of Form without Matter is shown to be a mark of Sophistry. . . . In writing on metaphysical subjects he appears like some strong-winged butterfly which now mounts into the pure azure, now flits about the tree-tops, but anon is sure to be found hovering amongst the fragrant garden-flowers. . . .

Mr. Pater appears to dwell with most complacency on the *Phaedrus, Symposium* and *Charmides*. And I venture to think that, of the eternal triad, Beauty, Goodness, Truth, the first obtains more importance with him than in the long run with Plato. . . . In saying that Beauty alone has a visible antitype, Plato did not mean to subordinate Wisdom to Beauty. It is true that under Plato's influence Mr. Pater declares himself as the upholder of a 'dry beauty,'—of severe simplicity in art and life. . . . [But] is not the Puritanism of the *Republic* (especially in Book x.) even more thoroughgoing than our author imagines, and is it quite fair to infer from isolated positions in Book i. that Art is to be for Art's sake alone, and not rather for the sake of Life? (p. 265)

Plato's attitude towards mysticism is another point where Mr. Pater's view appears hardly adequate. Not regress, but progress seems to me the distinguishing note of Platonism. . . . The *Phaedo* indeed counsels withdrawal from the world, the meditation of death. But this is not the lesson of the *Symposium,* nor the spirit of the prayers at marriage festivals in the *Republic,* nor the motto of the great victory of primaeval Athens over Atlantis.

The incidental chapter on Lacedaemon has been universally admired. It is a prose poem, in which all that is most valuable of K. O. Müller's great work has been condensed, so as to bring out the significance of Plato's reaction towards Laconism. But (1) was the actual dividing line between Ionian and Dorian so wide and deep as Pericles and Mr. Pater would have us think, or had the Dorian consciously that sense of the beauty of austerity which Mr. Pater attributes to him? (2) Granting that Pythagoreanism found a congenial habitat in Dorian cities,

is there any ground for supposing that Laconian culture 'held' in any way directly of Pythagoras? (3) Why are the Perioeci passed over almost silently? May not they as well as the Helots have contributed to relieve the monotony of Spartan discipline:—for instance by fine work in iron:—of which the 'street of the smiths' in Tripolitza reminds the traveller of to-day? (pp. 265-66)

The subject of **'Plato and Platonism'** is not yet exhausted. Mr. Pater has brought his delicate spectroscope to bear upon that 'bright particular star,' has registered its prismatic colouring, and ascertained the elementary constitution of this distant world. But if we could come nearer, should we not know more? . . . [Could the] order in which the dialogues were written [be] approximately ascertained, our conception of the evolution of this master mind might be in some ways modified; his points of contact with earlier and contemporary thought and the manner of his reaction from them might appear more evidently. The assumption, which scholars in an increasing number are beginning to accept as proved,—that the dialectical dialogues as well as the *Timaeus* are intermediate between the *Republic* and the *Laws,*—seems destined to play no inconsiderable part in future Platonic studies. (p. 266)

*Lewis Campbell, "Pater's 'Plato and Platonism',"
in* The Classical Review, *Vol. VII, No. LXI, June,
1893, pp. 263-66.*

EDMUND GOSSE　(essay date 1894)

[*A distinguished English literary historian, critic, and biographer, Gosse wrote extensively on seventeenth- and eighteenth-century English literature. His commentaries in such works as* Seventeenth-Century Studies, A History of Eighteenth Century Literature, Questions at Issue, *published respectively in 1883, 1889, and 1893, are generally regarded as sound and suggestive, and he is also credited with introducing the works of Norwegian dramatist Henrik Ibsen and other Scandinavian writers to English readers. In the following excerpt, Gosse describes Pater's laborious method of composition and suggests that it invested his prose with "a certain deadness and slipperiness of surface."*]

It may be of interest to record the manner in which [Pater,] this most self-conscious and artistic of prose-writers, proceeded. . . . He read with a box of [little squares of paper] beside him, jotting down on each, very roughly, anything in his author which struck his fancy, either giving an entire quotation, or indicating a reference, or noting a disposition. He did not begin, I think, any serious critical work without surrounding himself by dozens of these little loose notes. (p. 806)

Having prepared his box of little squares, he would begin the labour of actual composition, and so conscious was he of the modifications and additions which would supervene that he always wrote on ruled paper, leaving each alternate line blank. . . . On this broad canvas of alternate lines, then, Pater would slowly begin to draw his composition, the cartoon of what would in time be a finished essay. In the first draft the phrase would be a bald one; in the blank alternate line he would at leisure insert fresh descriptive or parenthetical clauses, other adjectives, more exquisitely related adverbs, until the space was filled. . . . Cancelling sheet by sheet, Pater then began to copy out the whole—as before, on alternate lines of copy-book pages; this revise was treated in the same way—corrected, enlarged, interleaved, as it were, with minuter shades of feeling and more elaborate apparatus of parenthesis. (pp. 806-07)

It is not possible to work in this way, with a cold hammer, and yet to avoid a certain deadness and slipperiness of surface. Pater's periods, in attaining their long-drawn harmony and fulness, were apt to lose vigour. Their polish did not quite make up for their langour, for the faintness and softness which attended their slow manipulation. Verse will bear an almost endless labour of the file; prose, as the freer and more spontaneous form, is less happy in subjection to it. "What long sentences Plato writes!" Pater says in his **"Platonism,"** and no doubt Plato might return the compliment. The sentences of the Oxford critic are often too long, and they are sometimes broken-backed with having had to bear too heavy a burden of allusion and illustration. His style, however, was his peculiarity. It had beautiful qualities, if we have to confess that it had the faults of those qualities. It was highly individual; it cannot be said that he owed it to any other writer, or that at any period of his thirty years of literary labour he faltered or swerved from his own path. . . . Pater did not study his contemporaries; last summer he told me that he had read scarcely a chapter of Mr. Stevenson and not a line of Mr. Kipling. "I feel, from what I hear about them," he said, "that they are strong; they might lead me out of my path. I want to go on writing in my own way, good or bad. I should be afraid to read Kipling, lest he should come between me and my page next time I sat down to write." It was the excess of a very native and genuine modesty. He, too, was strong, had he but known it, strong enough to have resisted the magnets of contemporary style. Perhaps his own writing might have grown a little simpler and a little more supple if he had had the fortitude to come down and fight among his fellows. (p. 807)

Edmund Gosse, "Walter Pater: A Portrait," in Contemporary Review, *Vol. LXVI, December, 1894, pp. 795-810.*

ANDREW LANG (essay date 1895)

[In Mr. Pater's **"Greek Studies,"**] I seem to be in a gallery almost hieratic in its stately repose, rather chill, full of good things, but not very interesting, somehow the words "fine," "dainty," "delicate," "strange," "subtle," eternally repeated, become as dull as modern copies of Greek decorative designs. They are good words, but staled by constant use. One has a feeling that they could be stuck on anywhere, and that it would be agreeable to take some of them away. One compares a vocabulary like Mr. Stevenson's, with its constant surprises, usually delightful, and only surprising by their unexpected aptness.

So much for style; on my head be it! As to matter, . . . I may have become pedantic. I want facts and authorities, though, to be sure, I know most of the authorities. Again, I really do not think that the Greeks (or any other people) were like Mr. Pater's Greeks. What he squeezes out of their religion and art, they did not—at least, did not consciously—pour into these vessels. . . . The inner sense of Dionysus, as the spirit of the vine, in flower and fall, the inner sense of Demeter, are finely expressed; but only a very rare Greek here and there would have thought about them as Mr. Pater thinks. Then, being a kind of "specialist" (*mea culpa* [the guilt is mine]), I cannot but see how much he omits, and how important it is. . . .

We get a prettified picture of Greek faith and custom from Mr. Pater. The comparative method he abjures. The Goddess of Theocritus at the Harvest Home is our Kirnababy, is familiar to ancient Peruvians; and this makes Greeks and other peoples much akin. . . . Oeno and the other girls who turn out wine and corn and oil are in all the fairy tales of the world. Greece merely made them classical. . . .

Is this the result of transmissions, or of coincident fancy? Such questions get the better of me, when I am brought to contemplate mythology. For Mr. Pater (if he was acquainted with the facts) such questions appear to have had no interest. Again, speaking of Mycenaean art, he seems to deny an Egyptian influence . . . "The theory which derived Greek art, with many other Greek things, from Egypt, now hardly finds supporters." The theory was sadly overworked. But there, in the Mycenaean graves, are the daggers, of which the spirit is Achaean (or early Greek), while the technique is of the age of Aah Hotep . . . ; and, in at least one case, the landscape is Egyptian, with a view of papyrus reeds. To these facts I do not observe that Mr. Pater makes any allusion. Now, all this may be brutally pedantic on my part, but in archaeology and mythology one does like facts. The real, and impossible, problem is to discover how and why Greece, working on the same savage fancies as the rest of the world, "turned all to favour and to prettiness." In that "favour" Mr. Pater is perfectly at home, and in the similar "favour" of the French and Italian Renaissance. From the works of France and Italy, in the Middle Ages and in the fifteenth century, he draws many pleasant and beautiful illustrations. Art, in fact, is his province, not this kind of science. His knowledge of art is manifold, and is informed by an exquisite sense and taste. But his intellect lived in an air infinitely refined, and peopled by the grave and beautiful Spartans of his essay on Lacedaemon [in **"Plato and Platonism"**]. The ruffianly element in these Spartans he winks at, so that he gives us a life as ideal as that lived in the "Hypnerotomachia" of Poliphile. It is magnificent, but it is not history. . . . These coarse remarks would not have been penned had Mr. Pater been here to read them. They amount to no more than this—that he was an idealist, no less, or rather more, than Plato. He does not show us (nobody does!) workaday Greece, that medley of barbarism and beauty, so lovely happy, wise, lustful, dirty, and cruel. . . . Not in Greece are we, with Mr. Pater, but in a Hellas of dreams, going delicately, as one of their own poets says, in delicate air. His work needs human beings, human interest, of which we have a little in his essay, or romance, **"The Veiled Hippolytus."** But, taking the dream as a dream, no one has seen and told it more excellently than the accomplished writer, and . . . the laborious and conscientious scholar, whose most valuable work here, probably, is in the later essays on the more accomplished Greek sculptors.

Andrew Lang, "Mr. Pater's 'Greek Studies'," in The Illustrated London News, *Vol. CVI, No. 2916, March 9, 1895, p. 299.*

A. M. [AGNES HARRISON MacDONNELL] (essay date 1895)

[Of the essays collected in Mr. Pater's **"Miscellaneous Studies,"** the] imaginative pieces, **"The Child in the House,"** **"Emerald Uthwart,"** and **"Apollo in Picardy"** may possibly make the widest appeal. But while owning their grace, their refinement, they seem to me to show Mr. Pater on his weakest side. I can conceive of several other persons writing that favourite, **"The Child in the House,"** and this is not praise when employed to so individual a writer; it hovers now and again on the merely pretty; there is a great deal of the same kind of thing, just less good, in fiction to day. . . .

It is in his criticism that his highest imaginative qualities are revealed, where he is lightest, brightest, and also most profound. . . . [In] this representative collection you not only find more robustness, more intellectual vigour in the masterly essays on Mérimée or Pascal, and on French architecture, than when he played delicately with fiction, but a greater stimulus to the imagination as well. For all his fastidious exclusiveness, it is not the severe scholar that speaks in his critical work. His first interest is always in the man that made the books he is writing of. . . . [It is Mérimée himself,] the man Raphael, the man Pascal, he is interested in; but he examines their medium of expression with great and unostentatious learning; for there are no short cuts to his desire. Mr. Pater, at least, is not impersonal. His loves and ideals are written plainly here; his delight in clearness and order, his wholesome love of beauty, his shrinking from disease in art, or religion, or thought, his reverence even for the things that clothe his spirit no longer (like Raphael's, the "scholar who never forgot a lesson,"), his gentle conscientiousness.

A. M. [Agnes Harrison MacDonnell], "Mr. Pater's 'Miscellaneous Studies'," in The Bookman, *London, Vol. IX, No. 50, November, 1895, p. 58.*

LIONEL JOHNSON   (poem date 1902)

[*Johnson, a late-nineteenth-century English poet and critic, was an enthusiastic disciple of Pater and a notorious alcoholic. His discipleship and despair were brilliantly linked by William Butler Yeats, who characterized Johnson's literary circle as the "tragic generation" of poets (see Additional Bibliography and excerpt below, 1936). Johnson's glowing tribute to Pater first appeared in the* Academy *on October 11, 1902.*]

Gracious God rest him! he who toiled so well
    Secrets of grace to tell
Graciously; as the awed rejoicing priest
    Officiates at the feast,
Knowing, how deep within the liturgies
    Lie hid the mysteries.
Half of a passionately pensive soul
    He showed us, not the whole:
Who loved him best, they best, they only, knew
    The deeps they might not view;
That which was private between God and him;
    To others, justly dim.
Calm Oxford autumns and preluding springs!
    To me your memory brings
Delight upon delight, but chiefest one:
    The thought of Oxford's son,
Who gave me of his welcome and his praise,
    When white were still my days;
Ere death had left life darkling, nor had sent
    Lament upon lament:
Ere sorrow told me, how I loved my lost,
    And bade me base love's cost. . . .
Oh, sweet grove smiling of that wisdom, brought
    From arduous ways of thought;
Oh, golden patience of that travailing soul,
    So hungered for the goal,
And vowed to keep, through subtly vigilant pain,
    From pastime on the plain,
Enamoured of the difficult mountain air
    Up beauty's Hill of Prayer!
Stern is the faith of art, right stern, and he
    Loved her severity.

Momentous things he prized, gradual and fair,
    Births of a passionate air:
Some austere setting of an ancient sun,
    Its midday glories done,
Over a silent melancholy sea
    In sad serenity:
Some delicate dawning of a new desire,
    Distilling fragrant fire
On hearts of men prophetically fain
    To feel earth young again:
Some strange rich passage of the dreaming earth,
    Fulfilled with warmth and worth.
Ended, is service: yet, albeit farewell
    Tolls the faint vesper bell,
Patient beneath his Oxford trees and towers
    He still is gently ours:
Hierarch of the spirit, pure and strong,
    Worthy Uranian song.
Gracious God keep him: and God grant to me
    By miracle to see
That unforgettably most gracious friend,
    In the never-ending end!

               (pp. 268-69)

Lionel Johnson, "Walter Pater," in his The Complete Poems of Lionel Johnson, *edited by Iain Fletcher, The Unicorn Press, 1953, pp. 268-69.*

A. C. BENSON   (essay date 1906)

[*Benson was one of the first commentators to provide a comprehensive critical survey of Pater's works. While he explores many facets of Pater's oeuvre, including some lesser-known critical essays, Benson's most telling criticism concerns Pater's approach to Christianity in* Marius the Epicurean *and other works. His contention that Marius is merely attracted to the aesthetic blandishments of Christian ritual is addressed by both T. S. Eliot (1930) and Graham Hough (1948) in their discussions of Pater's contribution to modern religious thought.*]

The only definite artistic influence under which [Pater] is known to have fallen in his school-days is the influence of Ruskin. . . . It is possible to trace this influence in Pater's mature style; there is something of the same glowing use of words, something of the same charming *naïveté* and transparency in the best passages of both; but whereas Ruskin is remarkable for prodigality, Pater is remarkable for restraint; Ruskin drew his vocabulary from a hundred sources, and sent it pouring down in a bright cascade, whereas Pater chose more and more to refine his use of words, to indicate rather than to describe. Ruskin's, in fact, is a natural style and Pater's is an artifical one; but he undoubtedly received a strong impulse from Ruskin in the direction of ornamental expression; and a still stronger impulse in the direction of turning a creative force into the criticism of beautiful things. . . . (pp. 7-8)

[In **"Diaphaneité,"** dated July 1864,] Pater traces his ideal of intellectual and moral sincerity; but the value of the paper is that, in the first place, it shows a power of acute and subtle psychological analysis, and in the second place it expresses with difficult wistfulness the ideal with which the young student meant to approach the world. To that ideal he was unfailingly true. He meant to know, to weigh, to consider; not to see things through the eyes of others, but to follow step by step the golden clue that ran for him through the darkness. It indicates a fearlessness, an independence of mind, which few achieve so early, and which fewer still have the patience to follow out. (p. 11)

The essay on Coleridge [1866] . . . reveals the beginnings of Pater's style. It is clear that he is struggling hard with the German influence; the terminology is technical, and a vague and dreamy emotion seems to be moving somewhat stiffly in the grip of metaphysical ideas; the sentences are long and involved, and there is a great lack of lucidity of construction, combined with a precision of expression, that produces a blurred and bewildering effect upon the mind. (pp. 13-14)

[In the 1867 essay **"Winckelmann,"**] the real Pater steps quietly upon the stage.

The style in which **"Winckelmann"** is written is a formed style; it contains all the characteristics which give Pater his unique distinction. . . . But it has also a passion, a glow, which is somewhat in contrast to a certain sense of weariness that creeps into some of the later work. It is youthful, ardent, indiscreet. (p. 28)

It is plain, in the **"Winckelmann,"** that the writer had been hitherto occupied in somewhat experimental researches; but here he seems to have found his own point of view in a moment, and to have suddenly apprehended his attitude to the world. (pp. 28-9)

Pater saw in Winckelmann a type of himself, of his own intellectual struggles, of his own conversion to the influence of art. After a confused and blinded youth, self-contained and meagrely nourished, Winckelmann had struck out, without hesitation or uneasy lingering, on his path among the stars. It is impossible not to feel in many passages that Pater is reading his own soul-history into that of his hero. (pp. 29-30)

[The essay on **"Aesthetic Poetry,"** written in 1868,] is a strange and somewhat dreamy composition, rather a mystical meditation upon a phase of thought than a disentangling of precise principles. . . . [Pater] compares the [Aesthetic] movement with the development of mystical religious literature, and defines the dangerous emotionalism of the monastic form of life, when adopted by persons of strongly sensuous temperament, saying that such natures learn from religion "the art of directing towards an unseen object sentiments whose natural direction is towards objects of sense."

> Here, under this strange complex of conditions, as in some medicated air, exotic flowers of sentiment expand, among people of a remote and unaccustomed beauty, somnambulistic, frail, androgynous, the light almost shining through them.

One cannot help feeling that the above sentence may be the very passage, from the air of strange passion which stirs in it, for which the essay was condemned. Or again the following sentence:

> He (Morris) has diffused through 'King Arthur's Tomb' the maddening white glare of the sun, and tyranny of the moon, not tender and far-off, but close down—the sorcerer's moon, large and feverish. The colouring is intricate and delirious, as of 'scarlet lilies.' The influence of summer is like a poison in one's blood, with a sudden bewildered sickening of life and all things.

There is indeed a certain disorder of the sense in this passage, the hint of a dangerous mood which seems to grasp after strange delights and evil secrets, in a reckless and haunted twilight. It

is a veritable *fleur du mal* [flower of evil]; and Pater, with his strong instinct for restraint and austerity of expression, probably felt that he was thus setting a perilous example of oversensuous imagery, and an exotic lusciousness of thought. (pp. 33-4)

The Studies in the History of the Renaissance deserve close attention, in the first place for themselves, because of the elaborateness of the art displayed, the critical subtlety with which typical qualities are seized and interpreted. . . . [These] essays exhibit each a characteristic savour of the art or the figure which furnished them. They are no shallow or facile impressions, but bear the marks of resolute compression and fine selection. But they are not mere forms reflected in the mirror of a perceptive mind. They are in the truest sense symbolical, charged to the brim with the personality of the writer, and thus to be ranged with creative rather than critical art. (pp. 35-6)

And in the second place they reveal, perhaps, the sincerest emotions of a mind at its freshest and strongest. No considerations of prudence or discretion influenced his thought. . . . [In] his later writings one feels that criticism and even misrepresentation had an effect upon him. He realised that . . . the frank enunciation of principles evoked impatience and even suspicion in the sturdy and breezy English mind. He held on his way indeed, though with a certain sadness. But there is no touch of that outer sadness in these first delicate and fanciful creations. . . . (pp. 36-7)

The essay on **"Leonardo da Vinci"** is certainly the most brilliant of all the essays, and contains elaborate passages which, for meditative sublimity and exquisite phrasing, Pater never surpassed. . . . The essay is a wonderful piece of constructive skill, interweaving as it does all the salient features of the "legend" of Vasari with a perfect illustrative felicity. But it is in the descriptive passages that Pater touches the extreme of skill. . . . (p. 41)

[The passage which describes "La Gioconda"] has an undeniable magic about it; though its vagueness is not wholly characteristic of Pater's ordinary manner, it is a wonderful achievement. . . . To say that Leonardo himself would have disclaimed this interpretation of his picture is not to dispel the beauty of the criticism. . . . It is possible, too, to dislike the passage for its strong and luscious fragrance, its overpowering sensuousness, to say that it is touched with decadence, in its dwelling on the beauty of evil, made fair by remoteness; but this is to take an ethical view of it, to foresee contingencies, to apprehend the ultimate force of its appeal. As in all lofty art, the beauty is inexplicable. . . . [It] must remain as perhaps the best instance of Pater's early mastery of his art, in its most elaborate and finished form. (pp. 42-3)

[In his art criticism, Pater's] concern was entirely with the artistic merits of a picture and its poetical suggestiveness. . . . [Thus] the errors which he made, of which we may quote one or two examples, do not really affect the value of his criticism very greatly.

To take his criticism of Leonardo. He was certainly wrong, for instance, in his judgment of the Medusa picture. This is a picture which shows strong traces both of classical and realistic influences. The head is classical, the serpents are realistic. It is almost certainly at least a century later than Leonardo's period. (pp. 48-9)

[But this] really affects very little the value of Pater's work. After all, the pictures which he described exist; the message which they held for his own spirit was generated by the sight of them, and the poetical suggestiveness of his criticism is full of vital force. . . . (p. 51)

"Wordsworth" (1874) is a very subtle piece of criticism. It is often taken for granted that Wordsworth valued tranquillity above ardour, and thus the essay is peculiarly felicitous in pointing out that not mere contemplation, but *impassioned* contemplation, was the underlying purpose of the poet's life. Pater shows that Wordsworth's choice of incidents and situations from common life was made "not for their tameness, but for (their) passionate sincerity." (p. 60)

It is abundantly clear that, in the case of Wordsworth, Pater felt himself drawing near to a highly congenial personality. . . . [Thus] the whole essay is redolent of a sort of trustful affection, the mood in which a man speaks simply and sincerely of a point of view which he instinctively admires, a character that is very dear to his heart. (pp. 61-2)

The essay on **"Charles Lamb"** (1878) is another instance of Pater's power of selecting and emphasising the congenial elements of a character. It is not the inconsequent, the reckless humour of Charles Lamb that Pater values most. . . . [He] is rather in love with the contrast of Lamb's life, the tragic undercurrent of fate, that ran like a dark stream below his lightness, his pathetic merriment. (p. 62)

Perhaps it may be thought that Pater's judgment of Lamb is coloured by too strong an infusion of his own personality, and that the Charles Lamb of the essay is hardly recognisable, clothed, as he appears to be, in his critic's very wardrobe; that Pater puts aside certain broad aspects of Lamb's character as being less congenial to himself; but I should rather myself feel that he has indeed passed behind the smiling mask which Lamb often wore, or has, perhaps, persuaded him to doff it; and that he has thus got nearer, in fact, to this melancholy loving spirit, with its self-condemned indulgences, its vein of mockery, its long spaces of dreariness, its acute sensibilities. . . . Pater has seen the innermost heart of the man with the insight that only affection can give, an insight which subtler and harder critics seem to miss, even though the picture they may draw is incontestably truer to detail. (pp. 63-4)

The Child in the House is the sweetest and tenderest of all Pater's fancies, the work, we may say, where his art approached most nearly to a kind of music. (p. 79)

In *The Child in the House* we see a boy deeply sensitive to beautiful impressions, to all the quiet joys, the little details of home. . . . (p. 80)

Yet in this region there falls a certain vain of what may be called macabre, which might be thought morbid were it not obviously so natural—a dwelling on the accidents of mortality, the gradations of decay.

> He would think of Julian, fallen into incurable sickness, as spoiled in the sweet blossom of his skin like pale amber, and his honey-like hair; of Cecil, early dead, as cut off from the lilies, from golden summer days, from women's voices; and then what comforted him a little was the thought of the turning of the child's flesh to violets in the turf above him.

There is very little of human emotion in the vision; little dwelling upon companionship and near affections and relationships; and this is true to nature. The child whose nature is thus sensuously perceptive is often so much taken up by mere impression, by the varied, the enchanting outsides of things, . . . that there is little leisure, little energy, to give to the simple affections of life. . . . Thus the pure art of the conception lies in the picturing the perfect isolation of the childish soul,—not a normal soul, it must be remembered,—though perhaps the haunted emphasis of the style . . . may tend to disguise from us how real and lifelike indeed, how usual an experience, is being recorded.

And for the style itself, it is a perfect example of a kind of poetical prose; there is no involution, no intricacy. The language is perfectly simple; and though some may feel a lusciousness, an over-ripeness of phrase, to predominate, yet the effect is perfectly deliberate, and it is by the intention that we must judge it. It may be set in a paradise of floating melodies in which the brisk, the joyful, the energetic may be loath to linger; yet for all who love the half-lit regions of the spirit, the meditative charm of things, *The Child in the House* must remain one of the purest pieces of word-melody in the language, and one of the most delicate characterisations of a mood that comes to many and always with a secret and wistful charm. (pp. 81-2)

[In his 1883 essay, **"Dante Gabriel Rossetti,"**] Pater seems delicately to weigh and test the author he is discussing; but one cannot help feeling that the innermost world of mystical passion in which Rossetti lived was as a locked and darkened chamber to Pater. He can look into it, he can admire the accessories of the scene, he can analyse, he can even sympathise to a degree; but it was after all to Pater an unnatural region. . . . (p. 86)

Pater chooses as the typical instance of Rossetti's work the single composition which he says he would select if he had to name one to a reader desiring to make acquaintance with him for the first time—*The King's Tragedy,* a ballad which is hardly typical of Rossetti at all, a piece of somewhat languid unemotional workmanship. . . . The reason of this is that Pater, admiring with a deep respect and regard the attitude of Rossetti to art, but yet not entering into his inner mood, found the restraint, the directness, the absence of exotic suggestiveness displayed in this poem more congenial to him; and thus the essay remains rather a *tour de force* than a sympathetic appreciation; he was surveying Rossetti from the outside, not . . . from the inside. Pater in his critical work bears always, like the angel of the Revelation, a golden reed to measure the city; but in this particular essay it is a piece of measuring and no more; and nothing could more clearly show the impersonal, the intellectual trend of Pater's temperament than his comparative failure to accompany Rossetti into the penetralia of his beauty-haunted and beauty-tortured spirit. (pp. 87-8)

[*Marius the Epicurean*] may be said to have nothing heroic about it, but to be almost purely spectatorial. It may be easily labelled introspective, even morbid; but it is of the very essence of the book that it is designed to trace the story of a soul to which the ordinary sources of happiness are denied, and to which, from temperament and instinct, the whole of life is a species of struggle, an attempt to gain serenity and liberty by facing the darkest problems candidly and courageously, rather than by trying to drown the mournful questionings of the mind in the tide of life and activity. What we have to do is, granted the type and the conception, to see how near the execution comes to the idea which inspired it.

It will be seen that the book is to a certain extent the history of a noble failure; Marius' attempt to arrive, by his own unassisted strength, by a firm and candid judgment, at a solution for life, breaks down at every point. He falls back in a kind of weariness upon the old religious intuitions that had been his joy in boyhood. He learns that not in isolation, not in self-sufficiency, does the soul draw near to the apprehension of the truth, but in enlarged sympathy, in the sense of comradeship, in the perhaps anthropomorphic instinct of the Fatherhood, the brotherhood of God. It is a passionate protest not only against materialism, but against the intellectual ideal too; it is a no less passionate pronouncement of the demand of the individual to be satisfied and convinced, within his brief span of life, of the truth that he desires and needs.

But the weakness of the case is, that instead of emphasising the power of sympathy, the Christian conception of Love, which differentiates Christianity from all other religious systems, Marius is after all converted, or brought near to the threshold of the faith, more by its sensuous appeal, its liturgical solemnities; the element, that is to say, which Christianity has in common with all religions, and which is essentially human in character. And more than that, even the very peace which Marius discerns in Christianity is the old philosophical peace over again. What attracts Marius in the Christian spirit is its serenity and its detachment, not its vision of the corporateness of humanity and the supreme tie of perfect love. This element is introduced, indeed, but fitfully, and as if by a sense of historical fidelity, rather than from any personal conviction of its supreme vitality. With all its candid effort the spirit of the writer could not disentangle itself from the sense of personal isolation, of personal independence; there is no sense of union with God: the soul and its creator, however near they draw in a species of divine sympathy, are always treated of as severely apart and separate. The mystical union of the personality with God is outside the writer's ken; the obedience of the human will to the divine, rather than the identification of the two, is the end to which he moves; and this perhaps accounts for the drawing of the line at the point which leaves Marius still outside the fold, because one feels that the author himself hardly dared to attempt to put into words what lay inside. (pp. 110-12)

The one artistic fault of the book is . . . the introduction of alien episodes, of actual documents into the imaginary fabric; and these give the effect, so to speak, of pictures hung upon a tapestry. The style is of course entirely individual; it is a style of which Pater was the inventor. . . . (pp. 112-13)

[*Marius*] remains a monument of sustained dignity and mellifluous precision. The style of it is absolutely distinctive and entirely new: the thing had never been done before; it is a revelation of the possibilities of poetical prose which the English language contains. (p. 115)

[Following the publication of *Marius* Pater] began to contribute reviews to the *Guardian,* the *Athenaeum,* the *Pall Mall Gazette.* (p. 118)

What strikes one most in reading them is, in the first place, a marked tenderness for the feelings of the author whom he is reviewing, and a great and princely generosity of praise. There seems to be no severity about Pater; and he enters into the intentions of the writer with a great catholicity of sympathy. There is also visible a certain irresponsible enjoyment about the tone of the reviews, as if with anonymity he had put on a certain gaiety to which in his public appearances he felt bound to be a stranger. (p. 119)

[In] the *Imaginary Portraits* Pater gave himself up to the luxurious pleasure of evolving fantasies arising from some bio-

graphical hint, some piece of unnamed art; some type of character that he conceived. They are true creations, worked out in a sober pictorial manner. But they make it abundantly clear that he had not the dramatic gift; there is no attempt at devising the play of situations, no contrast of character. . . . [The] interest in each concentrates upon a single figure, and they are told in a species of dreamy recitative. (pp. 123-24)

In **"Denys l'Auxerrois"** we have one of the most fantastic of all Pater's writings; indeed, in this strange combination of the horrible and the beautiful, there is something almost unbalanced, something that reminds one of the rich madness of Blake; as if the mind, though kept in artistic check, had flung itself riotously over the line that divides imagination from insanity. . . . (p. 126)

[This imbalance manifests itself when Pater describes Denys's public appearance] at a pageant. The haircloth he wears scratches his lips and makes them bleed, and at the sight, an unholy fury fills the crowd. He is literally torn in pieces.

> The soul of Denys was already at rest, as his body, now borne along in front of the crowd, was tossed hither and thither, torn at last limb from limb. The men stuck little shreds of his flesh, or, failing that, of his torn raiment, into their caps; the women lending their long hairpins for the purpose.

In such a passage as this the horror passes beyond the range of perfect art; and the shadow is heightened by the natural tranquillity and austerity of the writer. One cannot help feeling that Pater was here overpowered by his conception, and that he allowed to escape him, for almost the only time in his writings, a kind of almost animal zest in blood and carnage. (p. 127)

"Sebastian van Storck" is an astonishing contrast to the last. (p. 128)

Pater seems in this essay to have endeavoured . . . to depict in neutral tints the natural course of the quest of pure reason. It is a melancholy essay. Sebastian seems to suffocate under warmth and light; and the whole sketch has something of the frozen silence, the mute impassivity, of the stiffened leafless earth. It is more like a piece of cold and colourless sculpture than a picture; and the contrast of the stainless icy figure of the victim of thought thrown into relief by the warm, fire-lit, comfortable indoor world, peopled with types of indolent and contented materialists, is skilfully enough wrought. But the subtle beauty of the treatment does not remove a certain inner dreariness of thought, and the central figure seems to shiver underneath the rich robe draped about it. (pp. 129-30)

[The whole volume] is based on an idea of intellectual and artistic revolt; each of the four types depicted, Watteau, Denys, Sebastian, and Duke Carl, is a creature born out of due time, and suffering from the isolation that necessarily comes from the consciousness of being out of sympathy with one's environment. In all four there is a vein of physical malady. Watteau and Sebastian are phthisical, and Denys and Duke Carl are of unbalanced mind. This tendency to dwell on what is diseased and abnormal has a curious psychological interest; and it will be observed, too, that all the four figures depicted are youthful heroes, endowed with charm and beauty, but all overshadowed by a presage of death. There is thus something of the macabre, the decadent element, about the book. (p. 131)

[Pater] seems for some cause to have abandoned [*Gaston de Latour*] in dissatisfaction. . . . I am myself disposed to think that he found the historical setting too complicated and the canvas too much crowded. As the story advances the personality seems to ebb out of the figure of the hero, and he becomes a mere mirror of events and other personalities. The influences, too, that are brought to bear on him are of so complicated a nature that his development seems hampered rather than enlarged. No doubt Pater felt that the book was not exhibiting his own best qualities of workmanship; and there is a growing weariness visible, as if he felt that he was failing to cope with the pressure of historical experience that was closing in upon the central figure. (pp. 140-41)

[Gaston's] is a case of a soul the very breath of whose life was the arriving at canons of some kind, whose most sacred duty appeared to be to select from the immense mass of experience and material flung so prodigally down in the world, the things that belonged to his peace. The difficulty is to comprehend what was to be the issue. In the theory of Montaigne and Bruno alike, Gaston is brought into contact with types essentially uncritical, and one would suppose that they were intended to have an enlarging effect. But the hint seems rather to be that they were to act in the opposite direction, and to throw Gaston back upon the critical attitude, as the one safeguard in the bewildering world.

One feels as though Pater had here essayed too large a task; that he was, so to speak, preaching to himself the doctrine of robust tolerance, of good-humoured sympathy with a more vivid and generous life; and that he could not to his satisfaction depict the next steps in the development because it was precisely the very type of development of which he had had no personal experience.

Thus the book, from its very incompleteness, has the interest of being again an intimate self-revelation. (pp. 146-47)

[Dated 1888, the essay on **"Style"**] is the summary of Pater's artistic creed. (p. 151)

[The] concluding paragraphs of the essay, the frank confession of his belief . . . in the ultimate mission of art, have an intense and vital significance; the increase of sympathy, the amelioration of suffering, the service of humanity—these . . . were in his deliberate view the ends of art. The very use, in the very crucial passage of the summary, of the vague and trite phrase "the glory of God" as a motive for high art, has a poignant emphasis: it reveals the very depth of the writer's soul. He of all men, at the very crisis of the enunciation of his creed, could never have used such an expression unless it contained for him an essential truth; and this single phrase bears eloquent testimony to the fact that, below the aesthetic doctrine which he enunciated, lay an ethical base of temperament, a moral foundation of duty and obedience to the Creator and Father of men. (pp. 152-53)

[Written in 1892 as a lecture, the essay on **"Raphael"** is] a careful and sympathetic attempt to give a learners a lucid introduction to the art of Raphael. But it differs from his own chosen subjects, and is therefore less characteristic of Pater as a writer than much of his work—in that there is no attempt at tracing the recondite, the suggestive element, in the work of Raphael. He intermingles little of his own preference, his own personality, with the verdict; but it is still deeply characteristic of Pater in another region of his mind, of the patient sympathy which he was always ready to give, of his desire to meet others halfway, not to mystify or to bewilder the half-cultivated learner,

whose zeal perhaps may outrun his critical knowledge. . . . Here, then, at least, we see Pater in the light of the educator, the scribe, the expounder of mysteries, rather than as the hieratic presenter of the deeper symbol. . . .

[*Plato and Platonism*] was the main and serious occupation of Pater's last years. He placed the book at the head of his own writings. A friend once asked him whether he thought that *The Renaissance* or *Marius* was his best book. "Oh, no," he said, "neither. If there is anything of mine that has a chance of surviving, I should say it was my *Plato*." (p. 162)

The whole book cannot be held to be exactly characteristic of Pater's deliberate style. It is composed not so much to embody his own dreams as to make a personality, an age, a spirit, clear to younger minds; but there is a sense of a delighted zest, a blithe freedom about it, as though it were the work of a mind which had escaped from tyrannical impulses and uneasy questionings into a gentle tranquillity of thought. One feels that not only is the subject dear to him, but that those whom he would address are also dear; there is thus an affectionate solicitude, a buoyant easiness, about the book, as of a master speaking simply and unconstrainedly among a band of eager and friendly pupils. The book is full of echoes out of a well-filled mind, of Augustine and Dante, of Shakespeare and Wordsworth. Not only Plato himself, but the other incidental figures are brilliantly touched. (pp. 166-67)

[His last work, the] essay on **"Pascal"** has a deep significance among the writings of Pater; it contains, thinly veiled under the guise of criticism, some of his deepest thoughts on the great mystery of life—freewill and necessity—and his views of orthodox theology. It is true that he is nominally justifying Pascal and confuting the Jesuits; but there is a passionate earnestness about his line of argument which shows only too clearly that he was doing what it suited his natural reticence to do—fighting like Teucer under the shield of Ajax, and taking a part, an eager part, in the controversy between Liberalism and Authority. (pp. 169-70)

In [this essay] breathes the accent of the liberal spirit, the spirit which dares to look close into great questions; declines to admit more than it can prove, or at least infer; refuses, at whatever loss of serenity, to formulate its hopes and desires as certainties. (p. 171)

[Nowhere] else in the whole of his writings does [Pater] touch on the great dilemma, namely, that our consciousness tells us we are free, our reason that we are bound. He only surveys it from the spectatorial point of view. "Who", he says, "on a survey of life from outside would willingly lose the dramatic contrasts, the alternating interests, for which the opposed ideas of freedom and necessity are our respective points of view?"

But Pater leaves us in little doubt as to the side on which his own heart was engaged. It is clear that he felt that we are not, when our humanity is sifted to the very bottom, independent beings; we are deeply involved and hampered; something outside of us and anterior to us determines our bent, our very path. (pp. 171-72)

[In] a secret chamber of thought, which in his writings at all events he did not often visit, lay that consciousness of the hard, dark, bare truth which, if a man once truly apprehends, prevents him from figuring as a partisan, except through a certain sophistry, on the side of authoritative religion. (p. 172)

[There] must lie, in all reasoning men's hearts, a streak of agnosticism. The triumph of faith can never, until faith melts into certainty, be of the same quality as the triumph of reason; and it is upon the proportion of doubt to faith in any man's mind that his religious attitude depends. There is little question as to which way Pater's sympathies and hopes inclined; but this essay clearly reveals that the doubt was there. (p. 173)

[His last work] reveals him, I think, as a deep though unwilling sceptic; it shows a soul athirst yet unsatisfied; it shows that the region of beauty, both in art and religion, in which he strove to live, was but an outer paradise in which he found what peace he could; but in the innermost shrine all is dark and still. (p. 174)

> *A. C. Benson, in his* Walter Pater, *Macmillan, 1906, 226 p.*

P.E.M. [PAUL ELMER MORE]   (essay date 1911)

[*More was an American critic who, along with Irving Babbitt, formulated the doctrines of New Humanism, an early-twentieth-century philosophical and critical movement which espoused traditional, conservative values in reaction to the prevailing individualism of the age. The New Humanists were strict moralists, maintaining, for example, that the aesthetic qualities of a work of art should be subordinate to its moral purpose. More was particularly opposed to Naturalism, which he believed accentuated the animal nature of humans, and to any literary movement, such as Romanticism, that broke with established classical tradition. His rigid ideology, expounded with great erudition in his* Shelburne Essays *and other works, polarized American critics into hostile opponents—Van Wyck Brooks, Edmund Wilson, H. L. Mencken—and devoted supporters—Norman Foerster, Stuart Sherman, and, to a lesser extent, T. S. Eliot. In the following essay, More denies that Pater was a true critic, arguing that "history was only an extension of his own ego, and he saw himself withersoever he turned his eyes."*]

Whatever else one may say of Pater, however one may like or dislike him, he stands in the complex, elusive nineteenth century as a clear sign of something fixed and known. But he performs this office not as a critic, as he is commonly reckoned; indeed, of the critical mind, exactly speaking, he had little, being at once something more and something less than this. It is, of course, legitimate to take the expression of life as it comes to the critic in literature, and from this to develop a philosophy and vision of the critic's own; and this rather than any weighing of relative values was the intention of Pater. Such an aim is entirely justifiable, but it is not justifiable to misunderstand or falsify the basis on which the critic's own fabric is to be reared. If he is true critic his first concern must be the right interpretation of the documents before him, and whatever else he may have to offer must proceed from primary veracity of intention or vision. Just here Pater faulted, or defaulted. He has much to say that is interesting, even persuasive, about the great leaders and movements of the past, but too often his interpretation, when the spell of his manner is broken, will be found essentially perverted. (p. 365)

In his three greatest works—**"Plato and Platonism," "Marius the Epicurean,"** and **"The Renaissance"**—Pater has dealt with three crises of history; and in each case he has gravely, though in varying degrees, falsified the reality.

"Plato and Platonism" is a book that every student of Greek and of life should read; it is in itself a beautifully wrought work of art in which each detail is fitted into its place as part of a total designed effect; but that effect, presented as an interpretation of Plato, is of a kind, it can scarcely be said too emphatically, that differs *toto cœlo* [as the whole sky] from what Plato himself meant to convey in his dialogues, and is gained by a wilful distortion of the facts of history. In one of his chapters, Pater gives a picture, based largely on Karl Otfried Müller, of the Doric life in Lacedaemon as the actuality which Plato had in mind when he conceived his ideal city-state. . . . This city, as [Pater's] picture finally arranges itself, is simply not the cold, hard Sparta that stood on the banks of the Eurotas, but some idyllic Auburn wafted into some Arcadia of the imagination. At the end of the chapter, after giving a noble account of the training . . . by which the Lacedaemonian youth were drilled for life, Pater represents an Athenian visitor as asking: "Why this strenuous taskwork day after day; why this loyalty to a system, so costly to you individually, though it may be thought to have survived its original purpose; this laborious, endless education, which does not propose to give you anything very useful or enjoyable in itself?" The question is apt, and Pater puts the answer into the mouth of a Spartan youth: "To the end that I myself may be a perfect work of art, issuing thus into the eyes of all Greece." The discipline of Lycurgus, that is to say, was to the end that the young men of Sparta might be "a spectacle, aesthetically, at least, very interesting" (the words are Pater's) to the rest of Greece! Really, a more complete perversion of history has not often been conceived. The institutions of Sparta, as the Lacedaemonian in Plato's "Laws" admits without hesitation, were ordered to the end "that Sparta might conquer the other states in war." Not the indulgence of vanity, however chastely controlled, but the law of self-preservation and the terrible survival of the fittest made the Lacedaemonians the most comely of the people of Hellas; they were warriors and the mothers of warriors, not aesthetes.

And this same misrepresentation extends through much of Pater's analysis of Platonism. Pater saw, as all who study Plato are forced to see, that the heart of Plato's doctrine lay in his conception of ideas, in his use and enforcement of dialectic or the process of passing from particulars to generals. But Pater saw also something in this process that militated against his particular notion of aesthetics, and he was bound, if he accepted Platonism, as it was his desire to accept all the great movements of history, to interpret Platonic ideas in his own way. . . . Doubtless to represent Plato as an enemy of the decent and comely things of life, as an iconoclast of art and poetry and music in themselves, would be to forget some of the great passages in his "Republic" and other dialogues, in which the practical effect of beautiful things upon conduct is largely recognized and in which beauty in the abstract is placed by the side of the True and the Good in the supreme trinity of ideas. I would even admit that much of what Pater says in regard to Plato's conception of beauty is sound and worthy of emphasis. He has done well in drawing out the element of discipline in the Platonic aesthetics—the value of the capacity for correction, of patience, of crafty reserve, of intellectual astringency, which Plato demanded of the poet and the musician and of every true citizen of the ideal republic. Plato, as Pater rightly observes, was of all men faithful to the old Greek saying, *beauty is hard to attain.* But Pater's interpretation of Plato ends in a creed which Plato would have rejected with utter indignation. To recommend the pursuit of ideas for the sake of lending piquancy to the phenomenal, to use the intellectual apparatus in order to enhance the significance of the particular object, to undergo philosophical discipline for the sake of adding zest to sensuous pleasure; in a word, to make truth the servant of beauty, and goodness the servant of pleasure, is to uphold a doctrine essentially and uncompromisingly the contrary of everything that Plato believed and held sacred. To follow such a course, however purely and austerely beauty may be conceived, is, as Plato says, to be . . . the subject of beautiful things and not their master. Plato taught that the perception of beauty in the particular object was one of the means by which a man might rise to contemplation of the idea of beauty in the intellectual world, and wherever he saw the danger of inverting this order, as Pater and many other self-styled Platonists have inverted it, he could speak of art with all the austerity of a Puritan. There is no sentence in the dialogues that cuts more deeply into the heart of his philosophy than the foreboding exclamation: ''When any one prefers beauty to virtue, what is this but the real and utter dishonor of the soul?''

From the study of **''Plato and Platonism''** we turn naturally to the greatest of Pater's works, **''Marius the Epicurean,''** and here again we are confronted by a false interpretation of one of the critical moments of history. . . . In the choice of Epicureanism instead of the harsher Stoic creed as a preparation for Christian faith, Pater, I think, shows a true knowledge of the human heart. . . . [Fifteen centuries later] Pascal, too, saw that the step from Epicureanism to Christianity was easier than from Stoicism. So far Pater in his account of the relation of the Pagan philosophies and Christianity was psychologically right, but his portrayal of Christianity itself one is compelled to condemn in the same terms as his portrayal of Platonism. Read the story of Marius at the home of the Christian Cecilia and at the service of the mass, and you will feel that here is no picture of a militant faith in training for the conquest of the world, of a sect looking for struggle and moral regeneration, but the report of a pleasant scene where the eye is charmed and the ear soothed by the same subdued and languid loveliness that seemed to Pater to rule in Sparta and the ideal city of Plato. No doubt it would be wrong, as Pater asserts, to set over ''against that divine urbanity and moderation the old error of Montanus'' . . .—to set up as the complete Christian ideal the ''fanatical revolt'' of Montanus, ''sour, falsely anti-mundane, ever with an air of ascetic affectation, and a bigoted distaste in particular for all the peculiar graces of womanhood.'' It is well to avoid extremes in either direction. Yet if choice had to be made between the dainty voluptuousness of religion as it appeared to Marius, and the moral rigor of Tertullian, the great Montanist preacher who was contemporary with Marius, it would not be hard to say on which side lay the real Christianity of the second century. (pp. 365-66)

The simple fact is that in Marius we have no real conversion from Epicureanism to religion, no Christianity at all as it would have been recognized by St. Paul or St. Augustine, but that peculiarly languid aestheticism which Pater sucked from the romantic school of his century and disguised in the phraseology of an ancient faith. To write thus was to betray Christianity with a kiss.

In the third of Pater's major works, **''The Renaissance,''** there is again a reading of Paterism into the past, but without the offensiveness that is felt in his treatment of Platonism and Christianity. Not a little of the romanticism from which Pater drew his philosophy may be traced to the Italy of Botticelli and Leonardo da Vinci; but the tone, the energy, the *êthos* [distinguishing character or spirit], are changed. The nature of the change cannot be better displayed than in the famous description of the La Gioconda in the essay on **''Leonardo da Vinci.''** . . . [Pater's description is] subtly perversive of the truth. It may be true in a way that the genius of Leonardo, as Goethe said, had ''thought itself weary'' . . . ; but the deadly and deliberate languor that trails through the lines of Pater— not, I admit, without its own ambiguous and troubling beauty—

has no correspondence in the virile art of Leonardo. And whatever may have been the sins of Leonardo in the flesh, and whatever may have been his intellectual doubts or indifferences, he would not have understood that strange and frequent identification among the modern romantics of the soul and disease. Into the face of Mona Lisa, says Pater, ''the soul with all its maladies has passed!'' as if health were incompatible with the possession of a soul.

The simple truth is that Pater was in no proper sense of the word a critic at all. History was only an extension of his own ego, and he saw himself whithersoever he turned his eyes. To form any just estimate of Pater's work, we must forget the critical form in which so much of his writing is couched, and regard the substance of his own philosophy apart from any apparent relation to the period or person to which it is transferred. (p. 366)

The motto of [the concluding chapter of **''The Renaissance''**] is the famous saying of Heraclitus, ''All things are in a state of flux and nothing abides''; and the chapter itself is but a brief exhortation to make the most of our human life amidst this endless and ceaseless mutation of which we are ourselves an ever-changing element. That is the sum of Pater's philosophy as it is everywhere implicitly expressed in critical essay and fiction: the admonition to train our body and mind to the highest point of acuteness so as to catch, as it were, each fleeting glimpse of beauty on the wing, and by the intensity of our perception and participation to compensate for the brevity of the world's gifts; in a word, the admonition to make of life itself an art. Now, we ought, I think, to be grateful first of all to anyone who recalls to us and utters in manifold ways this lesson of the immediate perception of lovely things, of grace within answering to grace without. Perhaps no other philosophy to-day has so completely passed out of our range of vision as this doctrine of the art of living which has been one of the guiding principles of the great ages of the past. . . . And there is much also to commend in the method Pater proposes for attaining this ideal. If he teaches that the art of life is to train our emotions, like a well-trimmed lamp, ''to burn always with a hard, gemlike flame,'' he also endlessly reiterates the lesson that this joy of eager observation and swift response can be made habitual in us only by a severe self-discipline and moderation. (p. 367)

Yet withal, the account with Pater cannot stop here, nor, if we consider the fruit of his teaching in such men as Oscar Wilde, can we admit that his teaching was altogether without offence. His error was not that he inculcated the art of life at all seasons, but that his sense of values was finally wrong; his philosophy from beginning to end might be called by a rhetorician a kind of hysteron-proteron. . . . This exaltation of beauty above truth, and aesthetic grace above duty, and refined perception above action, this insinuating hedonism which would so bravely embrace the joy of the moment, forgets to stay itself on any fixed and unselfish principle, and forgetting this, it somehow misses the enduring joy of the world and empties life of its true values. It is for such reasons as this that we cannot finally accept Pater's philosophy of the art of life, notwithstanding all that may be said in its favor; that even his lesson of moderation and self-restraint, much as that lesson is needed to-day and always, seems at last to proceed from some deep-seated taint of decaying powers rather than from conscious strength. So intimately are good and evil mingled together in human ideals. (pp. 367-68)

P.E.M. [Paul Elmer More], "Walter Pater," in The Nation, *London, Vol. XCII, No. 2389, April 13, 1911, pp. 365-68.*

RICHARD LE GALLIENNE   (essay date 1912)

[Le Gallienne was an English poet, critic, essayist, and novelist. Best known for his literary activities in the 1890s, he was closely associated with such fin de siècle *artists as Aubrey Beardsley and Oscar Wilde. Le Gallienne may well be referring to Wilde when he observes that Pater's "elevation of the doctrine of the moment" had been misinterpreted, prompting "certain natures to unbridled sensuality." Originally published in the February, 1912, issue of the* North American Review, *Le Gallienne's essay serves to elucidate the qualities which attracted numerous late-nineteenth-century writers to Pater's works.]*

The acceptance of Walter Pater is not merely widening all the time, but it is more and more becoming an acceptance such as he himself would have most valued, an acceptance in accordance with the full significance of his work rather than a one-sided appreciation of some of its Corinthian characteristics. The Doric qualities of his work are becoming recognized also, and he is being read, as he has always been read by his true disciples . . . not merely as a *prosateur* [prose writer] of purple patches, or a sophist of honeyed counsels tragically easy to misapply, but as an artist of the interpretative imagination of rare insight and magic, a writer of deep humanity as well as aesthetic beauty, and the teacher of a way of life at once ennobling and exquisite. (pp. 257-58)

For those of us, perhaps more than a few, who have no assurance of the leisure of an eternity for idleness or experiment, [Pater's] expansion and elevation of the doctrine of the moment, carrying a merely sensual and trivial moral in the Horatian maxim of *carpe diem* [seize the day], is one thrillingly charged with exhilaration and sounding a solemn and yet seductive challenge to us to make the most indeed, but also to make the best, of our little day. To make the most, and to make the best of life! Those who misinterpret or misapply Pater forget his constant insistence on the second half of that precept. . . . There is surely a great gulf fixed between [the] lofty preoccupation with great human emotions and high spiritual and intellectual excitements [favored by Pater], and a vulgar gospel of "eat, drink, for tomorrow we die," whether or not both counsels start out from a realization of "the awful brevity" of our mortal day. That realization may prompt certain natures to unbridled sensuality. . . . [But for] such it can hardly be claimed that they have translated into action the aspiration of this tenderly religious passage:

> Given the hardest terms, supposing our days are indeed but a shadow, even so we may well adorn and beautify, in scrupulous self-respect, our souls and whatever our souls touch upon— these wonderful bodies, these material dwelling-places through which the shadows pass together for a while, the very raiment we wear, our very pastimes, and the intercourse of society.

Here in this passage from *Marius* we find, to use Pater's own words once more, "the spectacle of one of the happiest temperaments coming, so to speak, to an understanding with the most depressing of theories." That theory, of course, was the doctrine of the perpetual flux of things as taught by Aristippus of Cyrene, . . . his influence depending on this, "that in him

an abstract doctrine, originally somewhat acrid, had fallen upon a rich and genial nature well fitted to transform it into a theory of practice of considerable stimulative power toward a fair life." Such, too, was Pater's nature, and such his practical usefulness as what one might call a philosophical artist. Meredith, Emerson, Browning, and even Carlyle were artists so far related to him and each other in that each of them wrought a certain optimism, or, at all events, a courageous and even blithe working theory of life and conduct, out of the unrelenting facts of existence unflinchingly faced, rather than ecclesiastically smoothed over—the facts of death and pain and struggle, and even the cruel mystery that surrounds with darkness and terror our mortal lot. Each one of them deliberately faced the worst, and with each, after his own nature, the worst returned to laughter. . . . It is no longer necessary . . . to fight the battle of [Pater's] prose. Whether it appeal to one or not, no critic worth attention any longer disparages it as mere ornate and perfumed verbiage, the elaborate mannerism of a writer hiding the poverty of his thought beneath a pretentious raiment of decorated expression. It is understood to be the organic utterance of one with a vision of the world all his own striving through words, as he best can, to make that vision visible to others as nearly as possible as he himself sees it. (pp. 264-68)

This striving to express the truth that is in him has resulted in a beauty of prose which for individual quality must be ranked with the prose of such masters as De Quincey and Lamb, and, to make a not irrelevant comparison, above the very fine prose of his contemporary Stevenson, by virtue of its greater personal sincerity. (pp. 268-69)

Those who judge of Pater's writing by a few purple passages such as the famous rhapsody on the *Mona Lisa* [in his essay **"Leonardo da Vinci"**], conceiving it as always thus heavy with narcotic perfume, know but one side of him, and miss his gift for conveying freshness, his constant happiness in light and air and particularly running water, "green fields—or children's faces." His lovely chapter [in **Marius**] on the temple of Aesculapius seems to be made entirely of morning light, bubbling springs, and pure mountain air; and the religious influence of these lustral elements is his constant theme. (pp. 270-71)

[There is] no limit to the variety of method and manner a creative artist is at liberty to employ in his imaginative treatment of human life. All one asks is that the work should live, the characters and scenes appear real to us, and the story be told. And Pater's **Marius** entirely satisfies this demand for those to whom such a pilgrimage of the soul will alone appeal. It is a real story, no mere German scholar's attempt to animate the dry bones of his erudition; and the personages and the scenes do actually live for us, as by some delicate magic of hint and suggestion; and, though at first they may seem shadowy, they have a curious way of persisting, and, as it were, growing more and more alive in our memories. The figure of Marcus Aurelius, for example, though so delicately sketched, is a masterpiece of historical portraiture, as the pictures of Roman life, done with so little, seem to me far more convincing than the like over-elaborated pictures of antiquity, so choked with learned detail, of Flaubert and of Gautier. Swinburne's famous praise of Gautier's *Mademoiselle de Maupin* applies with far greater fitness to Pater's masterpiece; for, if ever a book deserved to be described as

> The golden book of spirit and sense,
> The holy writ of beauty,

it is **Marius the Epicurean.** (pp. 271-72)

[Although Pater's various gifts are concentrated in *Marius*,] some one or other of these gifts is to be found employed with greater mastery in other of his writings. . . . It is only necessary to recall the exquisitely austere **"Sebastian Van Storck"** and the strangely contrasting Dionysiac **"Denys L'Auxerrois"** [in *Imaginary Portraits*] to justify one's claim for Pater as a creative artist of a rare kind, with a singular and fascinating power of incarnating a philosophic formula, a formula no less dry than Spinoza's, or a mood of the human spirit, in living, breathing types and persuasive tragic fables.

This genius for creative interpretation is the soul and significance of all his criticism. It gives their value to the studies of *The Renaissance,* but perhaps its finest flower is to be found in the later *Greek Studies*. . . . This same creative interpretation gives a like value to his studies of Plato; and so by virtue of this gift, active throughout the ten volumes which constitute his collected work, Pater proved himself to be of the company of the great humanists.

Along with all the other constituents of his work, its sacerdotalism, its subtle reverie, its sensuous colour and perfume, its marmoreal austerity, its honeyed music, its frequent preoccupation with the haunted recesses of thought, there go an endearing homeliness and simplicity, a deep human tenderness, a gentle friendliness, a something childlike. He has written of her, "the presence that rose thus so strangely beside the waters," to whom all experience had been "but as the sound of lyres and flutes," and he has written of **"The Child in the House."** Among all "the strange dyes, strange colours, and curious odours, and work of the artist's hands," one never misses "the face of one's friend"; and, in all its wanderings, the soul never strays far from the white temples of the gods and the sound of running water.

It is by virtue of this combination of humanity, edification, and aesthetic delight that Walter Pater is unique among the great teachers and artists of our time. (pp. 272-74)

> *Richard Le Gallienne, "On Re-Reading Walter Pater," in his* Vanishing Roads and Other Essays, *G. P. Putnam's Sons, 1915, pp. 257-74.*

EDWARD THOMAS (essay date 1913)

[After Pater presented the essay **"Diaphaneité"** in an address delivered to Oxford's *Old Morality* society in 1864, contemporary] gossip credited him with a 'wonderful style.' It was obviously a style which aimed consciously at accuracy and a kind of perfection; unconsciously, perhaps, at a hard purity and dignity. It abhorred paraphrase, anything like padding even for the purpose of connection, all looseness, repetition, emphasis and personal accent. It had not attained to being a 'wonderful style' except by causing wonder. It was obscure and almost without grace. It was wonderful particularly in its detachment. For it retained no sign of an original impulse in it. If there had been a strong impulse the after elaboration had worn it completely away. This detachment made language seem to be as hard and inhuman a material as marble, and like marble to have had no original connection with the artist's idea. It was shy but decided, as well as stiff. It suggested the desire of a narrow, intense perfection both in language and in life.

The essay on Coleridge of a year later is less noticeable in style because less obscure. Such obscurity as there is, or rather uncertainty, is due to the lack of continuity; for here again detachment and elaboration have checked the flow which the original impulse might have given to the thought. . . . The writing is still stiff, progressing with many pauses and much difficulty. . . . It is aiming at a naked perfection, disencumbered of all clothes, colour, and even flesh. The reader has to pause again and again . . . to make sure that he has put the right accents on the sentence:—

> His 'spirits,' at once more delicate, and so much more real, than any ghost—the burden, as they were the privilege, of his *temperament*—like it, were an integral element in his everyday life.

It is an uncomfortable, reticent style. Sentences like the following are shorn of all human quality except *naïveté* and pedantry:—

> Fancies of the strange things which may very well happen, even in broad daylight, to men shut up alone in ships far off on the sea, seem to have occurred to the human mind in all ages with a peculiar readiness, and often have about them, from the story of the stealing of Dionysus downwards, the fascination of a certain dreamy grace, which distinguishes them from other kinds of marvellous inventions.

'May very well happen' is *naïve*: 'in all ages' must be the inadvertence of pedantry. Did he expect his readers to be ready with instances from all ages? If not, the value of 'a certain dreamy grace' is doubtful. (pp. 100-02)

Speaking of Coleridge's *Aids to Reflection, The Friend* and *Biographia Literaria,* [Pater] calls them 'bundles of notes,' the 'mere preparation for an artistic effect which the finished literary artist would be careful one day to destroy,' 'efforts to propagate the volatile spirit of conversation into the less ethereal fabric of a written book.' That kind of weakness was impossible to Pater: fear of it carried him to an opposite weakness that might prove as dangerous. He avoided obscurity more and more, by dealing chiefly with the concrete and with the ideas and images of other men. The stiffness, the lack of an emotional rhythm in separate phrases, and of progress in the whole, the repellent preoccupation with an impersonal and abstract kind of perfection, did not disappear. The rarity of blank verse in his prose is the chief mark of its unnaturalness. When his prose sounds well it is with a pure sonority of words that is seldom related to the sense. He expresses himself not by sounds, but by images, ideas, and colours. (p. 103)

[He] came to repeat words expressing what was pleasant or in some way fascinating. 'Strange' begins in **"Diaphaneité."** Words expressing refinement followed in large numbers, so that one page contains *'finesse,'* 'nicety' twice, 'daintiness,' 'light aerial delicacy,' 'simple elegance,' 'gracious,' 'graceful and refined,' and 'fair, priestly'; they continually remind us of the author's delight in delicacy, elegance, etc., and his always obviously conscious use of language does the same. When he has to say that Leonardo was illegitimate, he uses eight words: 'The dishonour of illegitimacy hangs over his birth.' He at once makes the 'dishonour' a distinction with some grandeur: he almost makes it a visible ornament. Whenever he can, he seeks the visible, insisting, for example, that Pico della Mirandola was buried 'in the hood and white frock of the Dominican order.' Even his ideas appeal as much as possible to the eye. Thus, in **"Winckelmann,"** alluding to the growth and modification of religions, he says that they 'brighten under a bright sky' and 'grow intense and shrill in the clefts of human life, where the spirit is narrow and confined, and the stars are visible at noonday.' His very words are to be seen, not read aloud; for if read aloud they betray their artificiality by a lack of natural expressive rhythm. (pp. 103-04)

Some of his sentences, complicated and not merely long, suggest an ideal essay that should consist of one perfect sentence. Pater could have arranged any biography in *Who's Who* in one sentence. But it would not be worth while. Some of these long sentences are admirable, some difficult; some make a footnote unnecessary. In nearly all the length seems to be arbitrary, or dictated by the need of variety in the paragraph. Neither in long nor in short sentences has he any fear of misinterpretation. He will say, for example, in **"Pico della Mirandola"**:—

> It was after many wanderings . . . that Pico came to rest in Florence. Born in 1463, he was then twenty years old.

Which at first seems to say that Pico was already twenty on entering this world. His way of pausing to qualify, or to corroborate, sometimes leads him actually to slip, as, in **"The School of Giorgione,"** when he says:—

> It is noticeable that . . . each art may be observed to pass . . .

He allows himself a few colloquial forms by way simply of variety, now and then an exclamatory phrase, now and then a phrase that is attached as if it were an after-thought, as here:—

> He is initiated into those differences of personal type, manner, and even of dress, which are best understood there—that 'distinction' of the *Concert* of the *Pitti* Palace.

Such devices—for they are used too often to be accidents—do not give any ease to the writing. (pp. 105-06)

Nearly every one of the essays in *The Renaissance* opens abruptly. Pater cannot wind into our confidence. He is a shy man, full of 'it may be' and 'we may think,' and he has the awkward abruptness of a shy man. But this sudden entry is due also to his disdain of mere connections and of any words that are under weight. He will have nothing 'common or mean.' If he has to mention the pleasure of a cold plunge in summer, he speaks of 'the moment of delicious recoil from the flood of water in summer heat.' 'The flood of water' is very foreign. His sentences must not only be essential and perfectly fitting parts of a whole, but they must be somehow exquisite of themselves, certainly in form, if possible in content.

As he says that not the fruit of experience, but experience itself, is the end of life, so he would wish to have every sentence, every clause, every word, conspicuously worthy, apart from the sum and effect of all. . . . Every inch has the qualities of the whole. Open any essay at any page: it will yield some beautiful object or strange thought presented in the words of a learned and ceremonious lover. . . . He loves the spectacle of 'brilliant sins and exquisite amusements.' The strong, the magnificent, the saintly, the beautiful, the cruel, the versatile, the intense, the gay, the brilliant, the weary, the sad-coloured, everything but the dull, delights him. From religion, philosophy, poetry, art, Nature, human life, he summons what is rich and strange. He delivers it in choicest language because it has to be worthy of his own choicest moments of enjoyment. For . . . he is an eclectic, ignoring the ordinary, the dull, the trite.

Thus his prose embalms choice things, as seen at choice moments, in choice words. . . . How far he escaped dulness in

real life at Oxford, in Kensington, or on the Continent, we do not certainly know, though we do know that his French travels tired him, that he had an air of fatigue, that his writing often is languid. But in *The Renaissance* all save the best is hidden away. We do not see the grey working day, the cap and gown, the note-books, the feet burning from the pavements of picture galleries, but things 'that set the spirit free for a moment,' 'stirring of the senses,' 'strange dyes,' 'strange colours and curious odours,' 'work of the artist's hands,' 'passionate attitudes.' It is not the style of ecstasy such as can be seen in Jefferies' *Story of My Heart,* or Sterne's *Journal to Eliza,* or Keats' last letter to Fanny Brawne. Hardly does it appear to be the style of remembered ecstasy as in Traherne's *Centuries of Meditation* or Wordsworth's "Tintern Abbey." It is free from traces of experience. All is subtilised, intellectualised, 'casting off all debris.' It is a polished cabinet of collections from history, nature, and art; objects detached from their settings but almost never without being integrated afresh by Pater's careful arrangement, whether they are pictures, books, landscapes or personalities. It fulfils Pater's own condition of art by putting its own 'happy world' in place of 'the meaner world of our common days.' (pp. 106-09)

> *Edward Thomas, in his* Walter Pater: A Critical Study, *Mitchell Kennerley, 1913, 232 p.*

T. S. ELIOT (essay date 1930)

[*Eliot, an American-born English poet, essayist, and critic, is regarded as one of the most influential literary figures of the first half of the twentieth century. As a poet, he is closely identified with many of the qualities denoted by the term Modernism, such as experimentation, formal complexity, artistic and intellectual eclecticism, and a classicist view of the artist working at an emotional distance from his or her creation. As a critic, he introduced a number of terms and concepts that strongly affected critical thought in his lifetime: his concept of the "objective correlative," which he defined in his* Selected Essays *as "a set of objects, a situation, a chain of events which shall be the formula of [a] particular emotion" and which have the ability to evoke that emotion in the reader is considered a major contribution to literary analysis, and his overall emphasis on imagery, symbolism, and meaning helped to establish the theories of New Criticism. Eliot, who converted to Christianity in 1928, stressed the importance of tradition, religion, and morality in literature. These values are evident in the following essay, in which Eliot characterizes Pater's "aesthetic religion" as a minor, but equally subversive, continuation of Matthew Arnold's attempt to "set up Culture in the place of Religion." While David J. De Laura (1969) recast Eliot's comparison into a sympathetic study of Pater's relationship with Arnold, Graham Hough (1948) protested that Eliot's comparison of the two writers' religious philosophies was misleading. Eliot's essay was originally published in the September, 1930, issue of the* Bookman *(New York).*]

The total effect of Arnold's philosophy is to set up Culture in the place of Religion, and to leave Religion to be laid waste by the anarchy of feeling. And Culture is a term which each man not only may interpret as he pleases, but must indeed interpret as he can. So the gospel of Pater follows naturally upon the prophecy of Arnold.

Even before the [1870s] began Pater seems to have written, though not published, the words:

> The theory, or idea, or system, which requires of us the sacrifice of any part of this experience, in consideration of some interest into which we cannot enter, or some abstract morality we have

not identified with ourselves, or what is only conventional, has no real claim upon us.

Although more outspoken in repudiating any measure than man for all things, Pater is not really uttering anything more subversive than the following words of Arnold:

> Culture, disinterestedly seeking in its aim at perfection to see things as they really are, shows us how worthy and divine a thing is the religious side in man, though it is not the whole of man. But while recognizing the grandeur of the religious side in man, culture yet makes us eschew an inadequate conception of man's totality.

Religion, accordingly, is merely a '"side" in (sic) man'; a side which so to speak must be kept in its place. But when we go to Arnold to enquire what is 'man's totality', that we may ourselves aim at so attractive a consummation, we learn nothing. . . . (p. 387)

The degradation of philosophy and religion, skilfully initiated by Arnold, is competently continued by Pater. 'The service of philosophy, and of religion and culture as well, to the human spirit', he says in the 1873 conclusion to *The Renaissance*, 'is to startle it into a sharp and eager observation.' 'We shall hardly have time', he says, 'to make theories about the things we see and touch.' Yet we have to be 'curiously testing new opinions'; so it must be—if opinions have anything to do with theories, and unless wholly capricious and unreasoning they must have— that the opinions we test can only be those provided for our enjoyment by an inferior sort of drudges who are incapable of enjoying our own free life, because all their time is spent (and '*we* hardly have time') in making theories. (p. 388)

Had Pater not had one gift denied to Arnold, his permutation of Arnold's view of life would have little interest. He had a taste for painting and the plastic arts, and particularly for Italian painting, a subject to which Ruskin had introduced the nation. He had a visual imagination; he had also come into contact with another generation of French writers than that which Arnold knew; the zealous Puritanism of Arnold was in him considerably mitigated, but the zeal for culture was equally virulent. So his peculiar appropriation of religion into culture was from another side: that of emotion, and indeed of sensation; but in making this appropriation, he was only doing what Arnold had given licence to do.

Marius the Epicurean marks indeed one of the phases of the fluctuating relations between religion and culture in England since the Reformation; and for this reason the year 1885 is an important one. Newman, in leaving the Anglican Church, had turned his back upon Oxford. Ruskin, with a genuine sensibility for certain types of art and architecture, succeeded in satisfying his nature by translating everything immediately into terms of morals. The vague religious vapourings of Carlyle, and the sharper, more literate social fury of Ruskin yield before the persuasive sweetness of Arnold. Pater is a new variation.

We are liable to confusion if we call this new variation the 'aesthete'. Pater was, like the other writers I have just mentioned (except Newman), a moralist. . . . His famous dictum: 'Of this wisdom, the poetic passion, the desire of beauty, the love of art for art's sake has most; for art comes to you professing frankly to give nothing but the highest quality to your moments as they pass, and simply for those moments' sake', is itself a theory of ethics; it is concerned not with art but with

life. The second half of the sentence is of course demonstrably untrue, or else being true of everything else besides art is meaningless; but it is a serious statement of morals. And the disapproval which greeted this first version of the "Conclusion" to *The Renaissance* is implicitly a just recognition of that fact. 'Art for art's sake' is the offspring of Arnold's Culture; and we can hardly venture to say that it is even a perversion of Arnold's doctrine, considering how very vague and ambiguous that doctrine is. (pp. 388-90)

Only when religion has been partly retired and confined, when an Arnold can sternly remind us that Culture is wider than Religion, do we get 'religious art' and in due course 'aesthetic religion'. Pater undoubtedly had from childhood a religious bent, naturally to all that was liturgical and ceremonious. Certainly this is a real and important part of religion; and Pater cannot thereby be accused of insincerity and 'aestheticism'. His attitude must be considered both in relation to his own mental powers and to his moment of time. There were other men like him, but without his gift of style, and such men were among his friends. . . . [Yet] Pater, more than most of his devout friends, appears a little absurd. His High Churchmanship is undoubtedly very different from that of Newman, Pusey and the Tractarians, who, passionate about dogmatic essentials, were singularly indifferent to the sensuous expressions of orthodoxy. It was also dissimilar to that of the priest working in a slum parish. He was 'naturally Christian'—but within very narrow limitations: the rest of him was just the cultivated Oxford don and disciple of Arnold, for whom religion was a matter of feeling, and metaphysics not much more. Being incapable of sustained reasoning, he could not take philosophy or theology seriously; just as, being primarily a moralist, he was incapable of seeing any work of art simply as it is.

Marius the Epicurean represents the point of English history at which the repudiation of revealed religion by men of culture and intellectual leadership coincides with a renewed interest in the visual arts. It is Pater's most arduous attempt at a work of literature. . . . *Marius* itself is incoherent; its method is a number of fresh starts; its content is a hodge-podge of the learning of the classical don, the impressions of the sensitive holiday visitor to Italy, and a prolonged flirtation with the liturgy. Even A. C. Benson, who makes as much of the book as anyone can, observes in a passage of excellent criticism [see excerpt above, 1911]:

> But the weakness of the case is, that instead of emphasizing the power of sympathy, the Christian conception of Love, which differentiates Christianity from all other religious systems, Marius is after all converted, or brought near to the threshold of the faith, more by its sensuous appeal, its liturgical solemnities; the element, that is to say, which Christianity has in common with all religions, and which is essentially human in character. And more than that, even the very peace which Marius discerns in Christianity is the old philosophical peace over again.

This is sound criticism. But . . . it is surely a merit, on the part of Pater, and one which deserves recognition, to have clarified the issues. Matthew Arnold's religion is the more confused, because he conceals, under the smoke of strong and irrational moral prejudice, just the same, or no better, Stoicism and Cyrenaicism of the amateur classical scholar. Arnold Hellenizes and Hebraicizes in turns; it is something to Pater's credit to have Hellenized purely.

Of the essence of the Christian faith . . . Pater knew almost nothing. One might say also that his intellect was not powerful enough to grasp—I mean, to grasp as firmly as many classical scholars whose names will never be so renowned as that of Pater—the essence of Platonism or Aristotelianism or Neo-Platonism. He therefore, or his Marius, moves quite unconcerned with the intellectual activity which was then amalgamating Greek metaphysics with the tradition of Christ; just as he is equally unconcerned with the realities of Roman life as we catch a glimpse of them in Petronius, or even in such a book as Dill's on the reign of Marcus Aurelius. Marius merely *drifts* towards the Christian Church, if he can be said to have any motion at all; nor does he or his author seem to have any realization of the chasm to be leapt between the meditations of Aurelius and the Gospel. To the end, Marius remains only a half-awakened soul. Even at his death, in the midst of the ceremonies of which he is given the benefit, his author reflects 'often had he fancied of old that not to die on a dark or rainy day might itself have a little alleviating grace or favour about it', recalling to our minds the 'springing of violets from the grave' in the **"Conclusion"** to *The Renaissance,* and the death of Flavian.

I have spoken of the book as of some importance. I do not mean that its importance is due to any influence it may have exerted. I do not believe that Pater, in this book, has influenced a single first-rate mind of a later generation. His view of art, as expressed in *The Renaissance,* impressed itself upon a number of writers in the [1890s], and propagated some confusion between life and art which is not wholly irresponsible for some untidy lives. The theory (if it can be called a theory) of 'art for art's sake' is still valid in so far as it can be taken as an exhortation to the artist to stick to his job; it never was and never can be valid for the spectator, reader or auditor. How far *Marius the Epicurean* may have assisted a few 'conversions' in the following decade I do not know: I only feel sure that with the direct current of religious development it has had nothing to do at all. So far as that current—or one important current—is concerned, *Marius* is much nearer to being merely due to Pater's contact—a contact no more intimate than that of Marius himself—with something which was happening and would have happened without him.

The true importance of the book, I think, is as a document of one moment in the history of thought and sensibility in the nineteenth century. The dissolution of thought in that age, the isolation of art, philosophy, religion, ethics and literature, is interrupted by various chimerical attempts to effect imperfect syntheses. Religion became morals, religion became art, religion became science or philosophy; various blundering attempts were made at alliances between various branches of thought. Each half-prophet believed that he had the whole truth. The alliances were as detrimental all round as the separations. The right practice of 'art for art's sake' was the devotion of Flaubert or Henry James; Pater is not with these men, but rather with Carlyle and Ruskin and Arnold, if some distance below them. *Marius* is significant chiefly as a reminder that the religion of Carlyle or that of Ruskin or that of Arnold or that of Tennyson or that of Browning, is not enough. It represents, and Pater represents more positively than Coleridge of whom he wrote the words, 'that inexhaustible discontent, languor, and home-sickness . . . the chords of which ring all through our modern literature'. (pp. 390-93)

T. S. Eliot, "Arnold and Pater," in his Selected Essays, *Harcourt Brace Jovanovich, Inc., 1950, pp. 382-93.* *

W. B. YEATS (essay date 1936)

[*Yeats, an Irishman, is regarded as one of the most influential and accomplished poets of the twentieth century. As a critic, he often judged the works of others according to his own poetic values of sincerity, passion, and vital imagination. Yeats was influenced by Pater early in his career and in 1891 founded the Rhymers' Club, a literary group inspired by Pater's aesthetic philosophy. In 1936 he chronicled the birth and dramatic decline of that group in his introduction to* The Oxford Book of Modern Verse, *excerpted below, and acknowledged Pater as an important forerunner of modern poets such as Ezra Pound and Walter James Turner, who seemed to him to have followed Pater in owning fluctuation and change as properties of the individual's—and the poet's—mind.*]

[Among the new generation of poets who were in revolt against Victorianism, one writer had that generation's] entire uncritical admiration, Walter Pater. That is why I begin this book with the famous passage from his essay on Leonardo da Vinci. Only by printing it in *vers libre* [free verse] can one show its revolutionary importance. Pater was accustomed to give each sentence a separate page of manuscript, isolating and analysing its rhythm; Henley wrote certain 'hospital poems' [in *vers libre*], . . . but did not permit a poem to arise out of its own rhythm as do Turner and Pound at their best and as, I contend, Pater did. I shall presently discuss the meaning of this passage which dominated a generation, a domination so great that all over Europe from that day to this men shrink from Leonardo's masterpiece as from an over-flattered woman. For the moment I am content to recall one later writer:

> O wha's been here afore me, lass,
> And hoo did he get in?

The revolt against Victorianism meant to the young poet a revolt against irrelevant descriptions of nature, the scientific and moral discursiveness of [Tennyson's] *In Memoriam* . . . the political eloquence of Swinburne, the psychological curiosity of Browning, and the poetical diction of everybody. Poets said to one another over their black coffee—a recently imported fashion—'We must purify poetry of all that is not poetry', and by poetry they meant poetry as it had been written by Catullus, a great name at that time, by the Jacobean writers, by Verlaine, by Baudelaire. Poetry was a tradition like religion and liable to corruption, and it seemed that they could best restore it by writing lyrics technically perfect, their emotion pitched high, and as Pater offered instead of moral earnestness life lived as 'a pure gem-like flame' all accepted him for master.

But every light has its shadow, we tumble out of one pickle into another, the 'pure gem-like flame' was an insuffient motive; the sons of men who had admired Garibaldi or applauded the speeches of John Bright, picked Ophelias out of the gutter, who knew exactly what they wanted and had no intention of committing suicide. My father gave these young men their right name. When I had described a supper with Count Stenbock, scholar, connoisseur, drunkard, poet, pervert, most charming of men, he said 'they are the Hamlets of our age'. Some of these Hamlets went mad, some drank, drinking not as happy men drink but in solitude, all had courage, all suffered public opprobrium—generally for their virtues or for sins they did not commit—all had good manners. Good manners in written and spoken word were an essential part of their tradition—'Life', said Lionel Johnson, 'must be a ritual'; all in the presence of women or even with one another put aside their perplexities; all had gaiety, some had wit:

> Unto us they belong,
> To us the bitter and gay,
> Wine and woman and song.

Some turned Catholic—that too was a tradition. . . . Lionel Johnson was the first convert; Dowson adopted a Catholic point of view without, I think, joining that church, an act requiring energy and decision.

Occasionally at some evening party some young woman asked a poet what he thought of strikes, or declared that to paint pictures or write poetry at such a moment was to resemble the fiddler Nero, for great meetings of revolutionary Socialists were disturbing Trafalgar Square on Sunday afternoons. . . . We poets continued to write verse and read it out at 'The Cheshire Cheese', convinced that to take part in such movements would be only less disgraceful than to write for the newspapers.

Then in 1900 everybody got down off his stilts; henceforth nobody drank absinthe with his black coffee; nobody went mad; nobody committed suicide; nobody joined the Catholic church; or if they did I have forgotten.

Victorianism had been defeated. . . . (pp. viii-xii)

When my generation denounced scientific humanitarian preoccupation, psychological curiosity, rhetoric, we had not found what ailed Victorian literature. The Elizabethans had all these things, especially rhetoric. . . . There are only two long poems in Victorian literature that caught public attention; [Robert Browning's] *The Ring and the Book* where great intellect analyses the suffering of one passive soul, weighs the persecutor's guilt, and [Tennyson's] *The Idylls of the King* where a poetry in itself an exquisite passivity is built about an allegory where a characterless king represents the soul. I read few modern novels, but I think I am right in saying that in every novel that has created an intellectual fashion from Huysmans's *La Cathédrale* to Ernest Hemingway's *Farewell to Arms,* the chief character is a mirror. It has sometimes seemed of late years . . . as if the poet could at any moment write a poem by recording the fortuitous scene or thought, perhaps it might be enough to put into some fashionable rhythm—'I am sitting in a chair, there are three dead flies on a corner of the ceiling.'

Change has come suddenly, the despair of my friends in the 'nineties part of its preparation. Nature, steel-bound or stone-built in the nineteenth century, became a flux where man drowned or swam; the moment had come for some poet to cry 'the flux is in my own mind'.

It was Turner who raised that cry, to gain upon the instant a control of plastic material, a power of emotional construction, Pound has always lacked. . . . [But generations] must pass before man recovers control of event and circumstance; mind has recognized its responsibility, that is all; Turner himself seems the symbol of an incomplete discovery. . . . I think of him as the first poet to read a mathematical equation, a musical score, a book of verse, with an equal understanding; he seems to ride in an observation balloon, blue heaven above, earth beneath an abstract pattern.

We know nothing but abstract patterns, generalizations, mathematical equations, though such the havoc wrought by newspaper articles and government statistics, two abstractions may

sit down to lunch. But what about the imagery we call nature, the sensual scene? . . . In [Turner's] *The Seven Days of the Sun,* where there is much exciting thought, I find:

> But to me the landscape is like a sea
> The waves of the hills
> And the bubbles of bush and flower
> And the springtide breaking into white foam!
>
> It is a slow sea,
> *Mare tranquillum,*
> And a thousand years of wind
> Cannot raise a dwarf billow to the moonlight.
>
> But the bosom of the landscape lifts and falls
> With its own leaden tide,
> That tide whose sparkles are the lilliputian stars.
>
> It is that slow sea
> That sea of adamantine languor,
> Sleep!

I recall Pater's description of the Mona Lisa; had the individual soul of da Vinci's sitter gone down with the pearl divers or trafficked for strange webs? or did Pater foreshadow a poetry, a philosophy, where the individual is nothing, the flux of *The Cantos* of Ezra Pound, objects without contour as in *Le Chef-d'oeuvre Inconnu* [of Honoré de Balzac], human experience no longer shut into brief lives, cut off into this place and that place, the flux of Turner's poetry that within our minds enriches itself, re-dreams itself, yet only in seeming—for time cannot be divided? Yet one theme perplexes Turner, whether in comedy, dialogue, poem. Somewhere in the middle of it all da Vinci's sitter had private reality like that of the Dark Lady among the women Shakespeare had imagined, but because that private soul is always behind our knowledge, though always hidden it must be the sole source of pain, stupefaction, evil. A musician, he imagines Heaven as a musical composition, a mathematician, as a relation of curves, a poet, as a dark, inhuman sea. (pp. xxvii-xxxi)

> *W. B. Yeats, in an introduction to* The Oxford Book of Modern Verse: 1892-1935, *edited by W. B. Yeats, Oxford University Press, New York, 1936, pp. v-xlii.*

GRAHAM HOUGH (essay date 1948)

[*Hough maintains that in placing Pater alongside Matthew Arnold as a proponent of a "religion of culture," T. S. Eliot (1930) had underestimated the profound moral subversiveness of Pater's doctrines. Taking exception to A. C. Benson (1906), he also minimizes Pater's "liturgical preoccupations" with Christianity. In his opinion, Pater was attracted to Christian ideals, but refused to make the necessary sacrifice of renouncing his Epicurean values. Hough's essay was originally published in 1948.*]

[Mr. Eliot's essay on Arnold and Pater] has the peculiarity of being largely about Matthew Arnold; but that is because its purpose is "to trace a direction from Arnold, through Pater, to the nineties, with, of course, the solitary figure of Newman in the background". . . . His concern is with Pater as a moralist and writer on religious themes, and the most significant point about the essay is the close association of Pater with Arnold; or rather the reason given for this collocation—that they are members of a joint conspiracy whose object is to usurp the throne of religion and put culture in its place. (p. 134)

But what, one feels disposed to ask, is Pater doing in this company? For the whole emotional tone of his writing is strikingly different from Arnold's. If the road from Arnold to the nineties lies through Pater, it takes a remarkably sharp bend on the way. Pater has none of Arnold's nostalgia for the age of faith; on the contrary, he quite complacently identifies himself with modernity; he has none of Arnold's longing for certitude; instead, he shows considerable willingness to involve himself in the flux.

> Modern thought is distinguished from ancient by its cultivation of the "relative" spirit in place of the "absolute". . . . The relative spirit has invaded moral philosophy from the ground of the inductive sciences. There it has started a new analysis of the relations of body and mind, good and evil, freedom and necessity. Hard and abstract moralities are yielding to a more exact estimate of the subtlety and complexity of our life.

We find here a quite contented recognition of the relative spirit of modern thought, and an obvious approval of the disintegration of accepted moral codes that has been its result. Throughout his work we find the same tendency to hail the deliquescence of all rigid forms of belief. (pp. 137-38)

The desire for metaphysical security, central in Arnold's life, is to Pater something a little unworthy; and the further we read in his work, the more evident it becomes that his kind of culture is not intended as a support for traditional certainties, but as a solvent. Pater's aim is not to defend a threatened set of moral values, but to release the sensibilities, to set them free to form new ones.

That Pater himself feared that his ethic might be a subversive one is evident from the fate of the conclusion to *The Renaissance*. This . . . is probably the frankest and certainly the extremest version of his creed. . . . (p. 138)

[The succeeding passage] is the crux of the essay.

> Every moment some form grows perfect in hand or face; some tone on the hills of the sea is choicer than the rest; some mood of passion or insight or intellectual excitement is irresistibly real and attractive to us,—for that moment only. Not the fruit of experience, but experience itself, is the end. A counted number of pulses only is given to us of a variegated dramatic life. How may we see in them all that is to be seen in them by the finest senses? How shall we pass most swiftly from point to point, and be present always at the focus where the greatest number of vital forces unite in their purest energy?
>
> To burn always with this hard gemlike flame is success in life.

> (pp. 142-43)

[The] most striking thing about this creed is the obscurity of its practical consequences. The object of life is to be present always at the focus where the greatest number of vital forces unite in their purest energy; but obviously the focus is continually shifting, and will be found in different regions by different people. There is hardly any kind of conduct which could not be sanctioned by this doctrine, including the conduct of the philosophic or religious ascetic. The heroine of [D. H. Lawrence's] *Lady Chatterley's Lover* and the Platonist in contemplation of the eternal verities equally feel themselves to be at the focus where the greatest number of vital forces unite in

their purest energy. And this is precisely what Pater intends. Though its expression is suppressed by donnishness, timidity, and probably lack of physical vitality, Pater has an immense appreciation of the variety and multitudinousness of the world, and what is peculiar to his creed is not its sensationalism, but its unwillingness to sacrifice any of this variety. (p. 143)

[*Marius the Epicurean*] is the record of a religious development, and in its own day was widely taken as a contribution to the religious problems of the time. But fashions in religious development change, as in other matters; Pater's attitude is far outside the stream of current religious feeling, and it is now common to dismiss this aspect of the book as a mere aesthetic flirtation with the Church. It is as well, therefore, to recall at the start Pater's own statement of his purpose in writing *Marius*. In a letter to Vernon Lee . . . he says, "I regard this matter as a sort of duty. For you know I think that there is a . . . sort of religious phase possible for the modern mind, the condition of which phase it is the main object of my design to convey." . . . Pater is perfectly clear about [the work's] intended application to his own day. The religious development of a cultivated agnostic in the time of Marcus Aurelius is meant to indicate a possible development for a cultivated agnostic in the time of Queen Victoria. (p. 145)

He came to feel that the physical sciences, with their concentration on empirical knowledge, had rendered necessary the abandonment of all "high priori" doctrines in ethics and metaphysics also. (pp. 146-47)

With this attitude of mind there naturally goes a strong tendency to rely on immediate sensuous apprehension, and to be extremely suspicious of abstractions. (p. 147)

This aspect of his thought is indicated . . . in *The Child in the House*:

> In later years he came upon philosophies which occupied him much in the estimate of the proportion of the sensuous and the ideal elements in human knowledge, the relative parts they bear in it; and, in his intellectual scheme, was led to assign very little to the abstract thought, and much to its sensible vehicle or occasion.

It is natural, indeed inevitable, that with this temper of mind religion should appear as a matter of feeling, of sensible forms and practices, rather than a matter of abstract theological speculation. He describes such a religion in the first chapter of *Marius*—"A religion of usages and sentiment rather than of facts and belief, and attached to very definite things and places". . . . [This] is of course what religion has generally been to the great majority of the human race. To the greater part of the faithful in all cultures, religion has commonly meant customary ways of behaving, customary ways of feeling, rather than formal theological belief. But in the nature of things, such religion usually remains unanalysed and unexpounded. What perhaps is found shocking and repellent in Pater's position is that he attempts a sophisticated defence of an attitude which would pass without comment in an inarticulate peasant. To see what kind of religious sentiment can grow from this modest root we have to follow the development of *Marius*.

The first chapter, **"The Religion of Numa",** describes beautifully the traditional "paganism" of the Roman countryside, formal, serious, unspeculative, and rich in the pieties of the home. (pp. 147-48)

I can find no "aesthetic" triviality here: only a singularly candid and sensitive account of the effect of a gracious inherited religion on an impressionable boy whose speculative faculties are just beginning to awaken. The stage to which this speculative activity conducted him is described in the chapter on the New Cyrenaicism, which corresponds closely enough to the doctrine of the conclusion to *The Renaissance*. (p. 149)

But the limitations [of this doctrine] are here seen pretty clearly. The Cyrenaicism of *Marius* . . . implies the possibility of development as the attitude of *The Renaissance* did not.

The development begins with the lecture on ethics delivered at court by Cornelius Fronto. . . . [He] puts his finger at once on the weakness of Pater's position up to now. He puts the case of a Cyrenaic or Epicurean who feels after all the lack of a central principle of conduct, something to give unity of motive to behaviour which, if it has been conventionally moral, has hitherto been so for no particular reason. He finds it in the idea of a commonwealth of humanity, in which the highest ethical apprehensions of men would be as the laws of a single city. . . . But as Marius listens to this discourse on the purely ideal City of God, his own thoughts take a different turn,

> not in the direction of any clearer theoretic or abstract definition of that ideal Commonwealth, but rather in search of its visible locality and abiding place, the walls and towers of which, so to speak, he might really trace and tell, according to his own old natural habit of mind. . . . At moments, Marius even asked himself with surprise, whether it might be some vast secret society the speaker had in view: that august community, to be an outlaw from which, to be foreign to the manners of which, was a loss so much greater than to be excluded, into the ends of the earth, from the sovereign Roman commonwealth.

The intention of this is hardly ambiguous. Does it not mean that Pater . . . is becoming dissatisfied with the position of the isolated Epicurean, alone with his own sensations; that he feels the need of belonging to a society; that the need is not met by existing political societies, or by the notion of a purely ideal commonwealth, and that he is beginning to consider the claims of the historic Church?

But the Church after all is a society founded upon a belief: it is not a society formed for the purpose of being sociable, and one cannot properly belong to it merely because of the need to belong to something. Pater sometimes seems to be perilously near to that attitude. It is easy to laugh at those who admire the Church but unfortunately do not believe in God: but it is an unintelligent failure of the historical imagination not to see how real the dilemma was to many in Pater's age. (pp. 149-51)

[For] Marius-Pater religious conviction could never come in the form of abstract theological doctrine; his scepticism is too radical: nor in the form of some supernatural fantasy: he is too determined to rely on the testimony of sense. It must come as an actual experience, the experience of a society which he can see, whose atmosphere he can feel, in which he has some hope of participating. So that the effect of Marius's first experience of a Christian society is felt as a series of impressions—impressions of sense, or feelings very closely connected with impressions of sense. He hears the singing in the church:

> It was the expression not altogether of mirth, yet of some wonderful sort of happiness—the blithe self-expansion of a joyful soul in people upon whom some all-subduing experience had wrought heroically, and who still remembered, on this bland afternoon, the hour of a great deliverance.
>
> (p. 151)

He observes the funeral ornament in the catacomb.

> Yet these imageries after all, it must be confessed, formed but a slight contribution to the dominant effect of tranquil hope there—a kind of heroic cheerfulness and grateful expansion of heart, as with the sense, again, of some real deliverance, which seemed to deepen the longer one lingered through these strange and awful passages.

Nor is Pater in any doubt about the nature of these physical impressions, and their relation to a possible moral or spiritual world.

> It was still, indeed, according to the unchanging law of his temperament, to the eye, to the visual faculty of mind, that those experiences appealed—the peaceful light and shade, the boys whose very faces seemed to sing, the virginal beauty of the mother and her children. But, in his case, what was thus visible constituted a moral or spiritual influence, of a somewhat exigent and controlling character, added anew to life, a new element therein, with which, consistently with his own chosen maxim, he must make terms.
>
> Might this new vision, like the malignant beauty of pagan Medusa, be exclusive of any admiring gaze upon anything but itself? At least he suspected that, after the beholding of it, he could never again be altogether as he had been before.
>
> (pp. 151-52)

Later, he attends the mass at Cecilia's house. . . .

He hears the cry *Adoremus te Christe, puia per crucem tuam redemisti mundum* [praise to Christ, because through his crucifixion mankind is redeemed]; and it seems to him at moments as if the very object of the cry was actually drawing near. (p. 152)

But the experience of the Eucharist at Cecilia's house is the farthest limit of Marius's approach to Christianity. He dies uncertain, in the company of Christians, and comforted by their rites, but with no formal admission to their society, and no inward assurance of the truth of their beliefs.

A. C. Benson has written, in a passage which has been commended by T. S. Eliot:

> But the weakness of the case is, that instead of emphasising the power of sympathy, the Christian conception of love, which differentiates Christianity from all other religious systems, Marius is after all converted, or brought near the threshold of the faith, more by its sensuous appeal, its liturgical solemnities; the element, that is to say, which Christianity has in common with all religions, and which is essentially hu-

man in character. And more than that, even the very peace which Marius discerns in Christianity is the old philosophical peace over again.

What Benson wrote and Eliot approved of course demands reverent consideration: but is this really true? It has become the fashion for some reason vastly to exaggerate the extent of Pater's liturgical preoccupations. It is perhaps inevitable, since the turn of the century, that Pater should be looked at through the distorting medium of the nineties, and the result is a composite picture of the ecclesiastically minded aesthete: we remember how "Johnson [Lionel] died by falling from a high stool in a pub"; and perhaps the final comic vulgarisation of the type in the Carling of Mr. Huxley's *Point Counter Point*. Eliot credits Pater with a few "conversions" in the generation after his own, and with the responsibility for a few untidy lives. These may indeed be accidental consequences of some of Pater's attitudes, but they have not a great deal to do with Pater himself, and they should not be allowed to get in the way of fair consideration of what Pater really said. I have tried to show that Marius, far from being drawn to Christianity by ceremony (he had found that as a boy in the religion of Numa) was drawn to it precisely by the sense of a community bound together in charity. It was the need for this that took him beyond his early Cyrenaicism; and it was in the society of Cecilia's house that he found the possibility of satisfying the need. Experience of a Christian society is not a disreputable motive for being attracted to Christianity; and if the peace Marius finds there appears only as the philosophical peace over again, how could it have done otherwise, since he never makes the final submission to Christian supernaturalism? (pp. 153-54)

However, we began by saying that Pater's ethos was genuinely subversive, and it is now time to substantiate it. . . . This can be done quite easily by . . . [following A. C. Benson's example and examining Pater's] *Robert Elsmere* review. Stopping at the point where Benson does we get the impression that . . . [Pater] is associating himself with those who in spite of an obstinate scepticism are in some degree believers, that the only question for him is how much or how finally one is to believe. Pater goes on to say, however, that . . . it is not there that the really vital question of the day will be found to lie. The real opposition—he quotes the formulation of it from the book he is reviewing—is between "Two estimates of life—the estimate which is the offspring of the scientific spirit, and which is for ever making the visible world fairer and more desirable in mortal eyes; and the estimate of Saint Augustine". Between these two estimates, he seems to imply, there is no possibility of reconciliation, there is only the necessity of choice. And he thus reopens the whole question, for it is this choice which Marius never made. Marius realises dimly that the new vision of the Christian life "might be exclusive of any admiring gaze upon anything but itself". But he never accepts the full implication of this; and that is why he does not die a Christian.

This is also why we cannot fit Pater into the pattern of even the broadest of Broad Churchmanship. The Augustinian element is not the whole of Christianity, but there is not Christianity without it.

The soul hath, through the same senses of the body, a certain vain and curious desire, veiled under the title of knowledge and learning, not of delighting in the flesh. The seat whereof being in the appetite of knowledge, and sight being the sense chiefly used for attaining

knowledge, it is in Divine language called, The lust of the eyes.

Thou art the Truth who presidest over all, but I through my covetousness, would not indeed forgo thee, but would with thee possess a lie. . . . So then I lost thee, because Thou vouchsafest not to be possessed with a lie.

A renunciation is required, and to this Pater never commits himself; the whole development described in *Marius* after all takes place within the framework of the ethic of the Renaissance.

While all melts under our feet, we may well grasp at any exquisite passion, or any contribution to knowledge that seems by a lifted horizon to set the spirit free for a moment.

The Christian ethos is one of these exquisite passions, and one on which Pater's mind happens to have dwelt for long: but it has as its possible rivals "any stirring of the senses, strange dyes, strange colours, and curious odours, or work of the artist's hand, or the face of one's friend". Pater feels so exquisitely for a time the beauty of a Christian society that one almost fancies he is on his way to becoming a believer. But you have only to confront him for a moment with a real believer to see where his destination lies. Dante would have placed him unhesitatingly, just inside the gates of Hell, among the trimmers; and he has delivered his verdict on such; *Non ragioniam di lor, ma guarda e passa* [let us not speak of him, but look and pass]; a verdict in which Mr. Eliot seems to concur, as he passes on his way from Arnold to the nineties.

However, let us turn this scandal to the ends of edification if we may. As much as many more decisive characters, the trimmer has a contribution to make to our culture; he is one who is genuinely in suspense, and he serves to remind us that suspense is a not dishonourable attitude. However undramatic a figure he may be himself, he exhibits in a peculiarly dramatic form the tension of a conflict between two powerful and equally balanced forces. The position is an exhausting one; and the weariness of Pater's style is not wholly constitutional; it is partly due to the continued presence of this conflict. His writing represents the slight and hardly won successes, now of one side and now of the other, in a contest which, however little we like to be reminded of it, is no nearer decision now than it was in Pater's day. (pp. 155-57)

Graham Hough, "Pater: Marius the Latitudinarian," in his The Last Romantics, *1949. Reprint by Methuen, 1961, pp. 134-57.*

RICHARD ALDINGTON   (essay date 1948)

[*Aldington, an English poet, novelist, biographer, and critic, was associated early in his career with the Imagists, a group of early-twentieth-century poets who sought to free poetry from excessive verbiage and vague generalities and to utilize precise imagery. He concentrated primarily on writing prose after suffering from shell shock in World War I, achieving some success as a novelist with his angry yet honest attacks on war and on his native England. Informed by his poetic skills, his perceptiveness as an extremely sensitive reader, and his personal reminiscences, Aldington's criticism is considered both creative and well-informed. In the following essay, originally published in 1948, Aldington depicts Pater as an exemplar of moderation and cultural refinement and commends him as a "civilizing influence" in the modern world. Herbert Read (1948) charged that Aldington had misrepresented Pater by thus placing him in the "camp of reaction."*]

Pater had laid down the principle that: "To regard all things and principles of things as inconstant modes or fashions has more and more become the tendency of modern thought."

And again: "'What we have to do is to be forever curiously testing new opinions and courting new impressions, never acquiescing in a facile orthodoxy."

Now, it would seem as if the intellectuals of this century had set out to burlesque Pater's ideas by applying them too literally. This "regarding all things as fashions" and "ever courting new impressions" has turned the palace of art into a giant Aesthetic Fun Fair, where newer and wilder exhibits vie with one another, and a jaded if impecunious public calls incessantly for bigger thrills and cleverer titters. Among the exhibits and side shows have been Russian novelists and American poets, Muscovite ballets and Studio 28 films, African idols and Mexican mosaic masks, Japanese novels and Chinese poems, "Les Chants de Maldoror" and "Frankie and Johnny," Brancusi's sea-shore eggs and Henry Moore's calamitous excrescences. Painting has been a vertiginous harlequinade of Impressionists, Post-Impressionists, Fauves, Futurists, Cubists, Vorticists, Expressionists, Abstractionists, Surrealists, and music has ranged from the tortured pigs of Stravinski's "Sacre" to the jig-a-jig of Jellyroll Morton's Red Hot Peppers, while the whole Fun Fair shakes and stamps to the inescapable crescendos of Ravel's "Boléro." (p. 92)

After decades of this *fracas* [brawl], it will do none of us any harm to turn aside and enter a quiet lecture room and listen to a gentle voice speaking of the European tradition. As long as our aircraft-carrier island remains (unfortunately) anchored off the misty north-western shores of Europe, and any breathing space is granted for the living of life and not a mere scramble to survive, the study of the influences which have built civilization as we know it or aspire to it will lie chiefly within the areas marked out by Pater's interests. Pater certainly did not wish (as the quotations just made show) that these should remain static, a body of orthodoxy to which no additions or alterations must be made, a republic of letters which is forbidden to annex new territory. But the prudent use he made of his own principles of "fashions" and "courting new impressions" is a testimony to his good sense and good taste, his "divine moderation." (pp. 92-3)

If we believe that there is a genuine difference between a "culture-complex" (which means any group functioning as gregarious tool-making animals) and "civilization" (which means humanely-ordered men seeking finer ways of feeling and living), then the world of Walter Pater has much to offer us. (p. 93)

It is probably wise to admit that Pater's work is the work of a *dilettante*—and we need not recoil from the word if we recollect that its real meaning is "one who delights in the arts and the things of the mind for their own sake." Pater wrote because writing enabled him to enjoy more fully and intelligently what he loved in the world and the creations of men's minds and hands. He was also a graceful and tactful revealer of these things to others who were willing to listen. He never scolds, never preaches, never pontificates, never sneers, never splits hairs, never patronizes, never browbeats, never wrangles. No English prose writer has better manners. He does not affect wit, and the pedantries which afflict learning and ignorance alike are alien to him. The life of the mind and of "the senses

purged" was his theme, which he presents with rare gentleness and persuasion.

All Pater's books were occasionally used by him to express his own highly personal views and "philosophy." . . . [It is Pater's dangerous] view of "all things and principles of things as inconstant modes and fashions" which has dominated aesthetic taste for so long. . . . [It] was also Pater who held the equally dangerous view that poetry is all the better for not being lucid (when did great poets write nonsense?) and that "all art tends to the condition of music," which is abstractionism. He held that:

> In its primary aspect, a great picture has no more definite message for us than an accidental play of sunlight and shadow for a few moments on the wall or floor: is itself, in truth, a space of such fallen light, caught as the colours are in an Eastern carpet, but refined upon, and dealt with more subtly than by nature itself.

Dear me! How we have been crushed these thirty years and more with that "Eastern carpet" by noisy enthusiasts who certainly had no notion that they were quoting the abhorred Walter Pater. And how willing after these years of putting those ideas into practice we would treat the resulting pictures as carpets. But Pater is hardly to be blamed for this, as his shade hovers in the background murmuring in agitation, "divine moderation," "ascêsis" [self-discipline], "burn with a clear gemlike flame." (pp. 99-101)

We lack a word to express the idea of complete education, or civilized training of mind, muscles and senses, which was Pater's ideal. It was a rare gift which enabled him to show so vividly the charm, life, and vigor in the classics of Antiquity, when they had been made trite and worn by more than four centuries of intensive or conventional study. To take subjects which the vulgar consider "dry" and the highbrows vote "academic," and to invest them with new glamour, a wistful attractiveness, is part of Pater's achievement. . . . No one who comes under his influence before the age of twenty will ever be content to remain gross and ignorant.

Every age is an age of transition, but it may be that ours is much more than this, that it is becoming one of those violent breaks with the past, with tradition, which put men into a hateful attitude of hostility and destruction to all that they have inherited. . . . [If] now certain world trends and pseudo-philosophies should indeed result in the ultimate violences and destructions, any surviving fragment of humanity will be too much preoccupied with the mere animal urge of survival to care or even know about "the things of the mind" which across the millennia have alike interested a Plato and a Pater. . . . Until and unless that evil time comes, Pater will hold, and under favorable circumstances greatly increase, his civilizing influence, particularly over sensitive and studious youth. (pp. 101-02)

Richard Aldington, "Walter Pater," in his Richard Aldington: Selected Critical Writings, 1928-1960, *edited by Alister Kershaw, Southern Illinois University Press, 1970, pp. 71-102.*

HERBERT READ   (essay date 1948)

[*In the course of aligning Pater with the forces of tradition, Richard Aldington (1948) offended the sensibilities of Read, a distinguished English critic who championed "organic" artistic ex-*

pression and who was deeply concerned with the role of art in furthering human development. Read's reply to Aldington, which was originally published in the November, 1948, issue of the World Review, *places Pater in the vanguard of artistic progressivism.*]

Instead of trying to show the relevance of Pater's philosophy to our present needs, [Mr. Richard Aldington] accuses the ''intellectuals of this century'' of setting out ''to burlesque Pater's ideas by applying them too literally''. Pater had said that we should ''regard all things and principles of things as inconstant modes or fashions'', and that we should be ''for ever curiously testing new opinions and courting new impressions, never acquiescing in a facile orthodoxy''. I believe that Pater meant what he said in such passages, and practised what he preached. But acting on these principles, says Mr. Aldington, we have ''turned the palace of art into a giant Aesthetic Fun Fair, where newer and wilder exhibits vie with one another, and a jaded if impecunious public calls incessantly for bigger thrills and cleverer titters''. Mr. Aldington then enjoys himself in giving us a long list of such thrills and titters, and while it includes items of a kind that would hardly have come within the range of Pater's observation, such as ''Jellyroll Morton's Red Hot Peppers'', there are others, not only ''Japanese novels and Chinese poems'', but even ''Henry Moore's calamitous excrescences'' and ''the tortured pigs of Stravinsky's 'Sacre''', that would not, in my opinion, have been outside the range of Pater's sensibility. Pater had two qualities that Mr. Aldington seems to lack: an instinctive sympathy for the struggles and aspirations of the artists of his own time, and a readiness to listen to ''the note of revolt'', as he called it, whenever and wherever sounded. There is a passage in the essay on ''**Coleridge**'' which well expresses his attitude . . . . :

> Modern thought is distinguished from ancient by its cultivation of the ''relative'' spirit in place of the ''absolute''. Ancient philosophy sought to arrest every object in an eternal outline, to fix thought in a necessary formula, and the varieties of life in a classification by ''kinds'', or *genera*. To the modern spirit nothing is, or can be rightly known, except relatively and under conditions. The philosophical conception of the relative has been developed in modern times through the influence of the sciences of observation. Those sciences reveal types of life evanescing into each other by inexpressible refinements of change. . . . Always, as an organism increases in perfection, the conditions of its life become more complex. Man is the most complex of the products of nature. Character merges into temperament: the nervous system refines itself into intellect. Man's physical organism is played upon not only by the physical conditions about it, but by remote laws of inheritance, the vibration of long-past acts reaching him in the midst of the new order of things in which he lives. When we have estimated these conditions he is still not yet simple and isolated; for the mind of the race, the character of the age, sway him this way or that through the medium of language and current ideas. It seems as if the most opposite statements about him were alike true: he is so receptive, all the influences of nature and of society ceaselessly playing upon him, so that every

hour in his lfie is unique, changed altogether by a stray word, or glance, or touch. It is the truth of these relations that experience gives us, not the truth of eternal outlines ascertained once for all, but a world of fine gradations and subtly linked conditions, shifting intricately as we ourselves change—and bids us, by a constant clearing of the organs of observation and perfecting of analysis, to make what we can of these. To the intellect, the critical spirit, just these subtleties of effect are more precious than anything else. What is lost in precision of form is gained in intricacy of expression.

Is it likely that a critic who could write in these terms *in 1865* would have been blind, as Mr. Aldington assumes, to the characteristic art of the period that followed—to Impressionism and Post-Impressionism, to Expressionism and Abstraction, to Proust and Kafka, to Bartok and Stravinsky, to Picasso and Moore. Mr. Aldington is entitled to his own opinion, but I would submit that a critic who could write with such prophetic foresight more than ninety years ago . . . , and who could at the same time give Goethe as a true illustration of ''the speculative temper''—as one ''to whom every moment of life brought its contribution of experimental, individual knowledge; by whom no touch of the world of form, colour, and passion was disregarded''—such a spirit would not today be in the camp of reaction. (pp. 60-2)

[The] ''relative spirit'' has been somewhat crushed in these days of dogmatic politics and totalitarian states. All the more reason for returning to Pater, his wisdom, his poetry, his subtlety, his gentle humour. Humour is perhaps an unexpected word to apply to him, but he himself said that ''a kind of humour is one of the conditions of the just mental attitude, in the criticism of by-past stages of thought''; and he charged Coleridge with ''an excess of seriousness, a seriousness arising not from any moral principle, but from a misconception of the perfect manner. There is a certain shade of unconcern, the perfect manner of the eighteenth century, which may be thought to mark complete culture in the handling of abstract questions.'' Pater himself had this ''shade of unconcern'', and that is perhaps why he was not popular in Oxford, and why a suggestion that he was ''superficial'' still persists. It is a gross error. It is a common assumption that in order to be ''profound'' a writer must be pessimistic about nature and humanity—that a Pascal, therefore, is necessarily more profound than a Montaigne, a Kierkegaard than a Goethe. This is to confuse wisdom with metaphysics or mysticism. Pater quoted Montaigne with approval: ''I love a gay and civil philosophy. There is nothing more *cheerful* than wisdom: I had like to have said more wanton.'' . . . The governing method [of Pater's philosophy] is ignorance—an ignorance ''strong and generous, and that yields nothing in honour and courage to knowledge; an ignorance which to conceive requires no less knowledge than to conceive knowledge itself''—a sapient, instructed, shrewdly ascertained ignorance, suspended judgment, doubt, everywhere. Pater is speaking for Gaston (in **Gaston de Latour**): Gaston who is the final exponent of his philosophy and the pupil of Montaigne:

> Balances, very delicate balances; he was partial to that image of equilibrium, or preponderance, in things. But was there, after all, so much as preponderance anywhere? To Gaston there was a kind of fascination, an actual aesthetic beauty, in the spectacle of that keen-edged intelligence,

dividing evidence so finely, like some exquisite steel instrument with impeccable sufficiency, always leaving the last word loyally to the central intellectual faculty, in an entire disinterestedness.

Mr. Aldington is right in regarding Pater as a bulwark resisting those world tendencies and pseudo-philosophies which "must result in a contemptuous repudiation of all that has for so many centuries formed the material of 'culture'". But the image is too negative, too static, for there is in Pater a positive philosophy, a philosophy which inspires and vitalizes the creative mind. He appreciated, none better, "the old, immemorial, well-recognized types in art and literature", but he was not so stupid as "to entertain no matter which will not go easily and flexibly into them". He was on the side of the progressive element in his own generation, one of those

> born romanticists, who start with an original, untried *matter,* still in fusion; who conceive this vividly, and hold by it as the essence of their work; who, by the very vividness and heat of their conception, purge away, sooner or later, all that is not organically appropriate to it, till the whole effect adjusts itself in clear, orderly, proportionate form; which form, after a very little time, becomes classical in its turn.

(pp. 64-5)

Herbert Read, "Walter Pater," in his The Tenth Muse: Essays in Criticism, *Routledge & Kegan Paul, 1957, pp. 58-66.*

KENNETH BURKE (essay date 1953)

[*Burke, an American critic, philosopher, translator, poet, and short story writer, is considered one of the major literary theorists of the twentieth century. He has been associated with many of the New Critics because of his advocacy of a close reading of the text and his strong interest in the theories of I. A. Richards. However, believing that the "main idea of criticism . . . is to use all that there is to use," Burke has also drawn upon his knowledge of linguistics, psychology, theology, and sociology to produce a diverse body of literary criticism. In the following essay, Burke discusses the innovative nature of Pater's approach to prose writing and enlarges on his belief that "ideology in Pater was used for its flavor of beauty, rather than of argument."*]

Whatever our reservations as to Walter Pater, we must recognize his superior adjustment of technique to aesthetic interests. An unenterprising thinker, an inveterate borrower of other men's ideas, concerned with a probably non-existent past, he was more of an "innovator" than many of his outstanding contemporaries who gave great thought to innovation. Without the slightest element of "rebellion," he shaped prose fiction to his purposes. (p. 9)

A subject was valuable to him in that it offered possibilities for a show of deftness. In *Marius the Epicurean* he has a scene of the somewhat godless court listening to an address by Fronto, an effulgent oratory in praise of the rigid Stoic doctrine; they sit about with their tablets ready to write down some especially happy phrasing, arranged comfortably among the images and flowers, and "ready to give themselves wholly to the intellectual treat prepared for them; applauding, blowing loud kisses through the air sometimes, at the speaker's triumphant exit from one of his long, skilfully modulated sentences." Pater's audience is expected to bring somewhat the same critical ap-

preciation to bear, watching with keen pleasure as the artist extricates himself from the labyrinths of his material—a process which Pater loves so greatly that he often seems to make his labyrinths of his extrications. Art to Pater was "not the conveyance of an abstract body of truths," but "the critical tracing of . . . conscious artistic structure." He thought of a sentence as a happening—he prized particularly "the resolution of an obscure and complex idea into its component parts." He wrote fiction as though he were writing essays. Other men have sought the values of power and directness; Pater was interested, rather, in laying numerous angles of approach. Consequently, he wrote, to use his own term, as a scholar, interested vitally in the mechanism of his sentences, using words with an almost philological emphasis, "prescribing the rejection of many a neology, many a license, many a gipsy phrase which might present itself as actually expressive." His preference for artifice was consistent: "We shall not wish our boys to sing like mere birds," he says in the best *fin de siècle* accent. And he decides that the *Phædo* [of Plato] gives the true death of Socrates since "in the details of what there happened, the somewhat prosaic account of the way in which the work of death was done, we find what there could have been no literary satisfaction in inventing." It is harder to understand his complaint that "to Browne the whole world is a museum," or his untroubled aspersions upon "those lengthy leisurely terminations which busy posterity will abbreviate," for it is only by enjoying such qualities in Browne that we can forgive them in Pater. (pp. 12-13)

Poets, deciding that the world needs or does not need woman suffrage, or the forty-four-hour week, or being interested in how someone starts a traction company in Idaho, write accordingly. But Pater must take only such subjects as are "categorically" dignified, subjects in his case concerned with the culture and traditions of whole peoples. He manifested that philosophic—or perhaps, in the truest sense, cultured—turn of mind which finds the specific interesting only through its correlations with the general (the general with him usually bearing on the Mediterranean and its traditions, Hellenism, the growth of the Gothic, humanism, and the like). (p. 13)

Having become saturated with his humanism, he carried it back as far as he could, which was to the earth. This attitude is seen at its finest in the opening chapters of *Marius the Epicurean,* where the hero starts with a dignity, a "sweetness," that is, so far as I know, unique in literature. The peculiar literary value lies in this early stabilization which is given to Marius, so that at the very beginning he is an entity, to be subtly dispersed later by the intricate conflicts of his times. His grave bewilderment in this mosaic work of ethics has a purer balance, superimposed as it is upon the soberness and placidity of the pastoral.

Ideology in Pater was used for its flavor of beauty, rather than of argument. He treated ideas not for their value as statements, but as horizons, situations, developments of plot, in short, as any other element of fiction. The reader who looks into *Marius the Epicurean* for an addition to Stoicism or Epicureanism will find nothing of value there; for the disclosures arise solely from the interplay of these two moralities, as they follow upon the spontaneous gods and are followed by Christianity.

Any number of people have been interested in the contemporary "transvaluation of values," and have written of it in some minutely particular application; it is perhaps the favored theme of the last half-century's novelists. But whereas many writers who sought the brightly new attained the mere superficialities of such transvaluing, Pater caught some of its deepest elements even while "prescribing the rejection of many a neology" and choosing subjects remote in history. In this one respect he may be linked with Nietzsche: both kept the theme of transvaluation well within the sphere of ceremony.

As Pater observes in his study of Plato, however, even Heraclitus, the philosopher of eternal change, the inventor of the dictum that "everything flows," seems in the end to have been searching for those changeless principles which might govern perpetual change. Similarly Pater follows to its conclusion his predilection for the fluctuant, and dwells in the vicinity of the . . . Immutable, the Absolute. But as an artist rather than a metaphysician, he was content to retain this Immutable solely for its contribution to his vocabulary of flux. The contemplation of permanent things served primarily to strengthen his depiction of the evanescent. Having thus a balance of thesis and antithesis, the issue demanded no further penetration on his part. He could content himself with drawing out the effects of his subject, aware that there was at least the indubitable and immediate certainty of his craft. And if, by the doctrines of his century, the dignity of man in nature had been prejudiced atrociously, the predicament meant hardly more to Pater than an added incentive to proclaim the dignity of man in art. (pp. 14-15)

> Kenneth Burke, "Three Adepts of 'Pure' Literature," in his Counter-Statement, second edition, Hermes Publications, 1953, pp. 1-28.*

LORD DAVID CECIL   (lecture date 1955)

[*Cecil, a modern British literary critic who has written extensively on eighteenth- and nineteenth-century authors, is highly acclaimed for his work on the Victorian era. Cecil does not follow any school of criticism; instead, his literary method has been described as appreciative and impressionistic. His essays are characterized by their lucid style, profound understanding, and conscientious scholarship. In the following essay, which was originally delivered as the Rede Lecture at Cambridge University in 1955, Cecil depicts Pater as a scholar-artist who, "as no one else before or since, . . . has put into words . . . the aesthetic emotion as it is experienced by learned, refined, and meditative spirits." At the same time, he observes that Pater's aestheticism was occasionally uncontrolled, and detects a fundamental incongruity in Pater's donnish, "low-spirited" advocacy of hedonism.*]

[Walter Pater] was that rare hybrid, the scholar-artist. We can easily see why it is rare. The scholarly spirit is intellectual and impersonal, and refers its judgments to standards of reason and fact; the artistic is sensuous and personal, and refers its judgments to standards of feeling and imagination. It is unlikely that the two strains should appear in the same man. If they do, he generally takes care to keep them apart. Lewis Carroll's mathematical works are very different from *Alice in Wonderland;* A. E. Housman, the professor of Latin, is not at all the same person as A. E. Housman, the Shropshire lad. But Pater the lecturer on Plato is recognizably the same man as Pater the creator of *Marius the Epicurean.* In him the two strains are twined together. (pp. 259-60)

The vision of beauty he wished to express was largely an intellectual vision, an intellectual vision of aesthetic experience. He was a creative critic and his subject was art. (p. 260)

[The forms that Pater] employed were his own, freshly devised to suit his dual purpose, aesthetic and intellectual. They must give him opportunity to state his views precisely, but also in a manner that would stir the reader's imagination and delight

his aesthetic sense. Pater made use of two modes for this purpose: *The Renaissance* and *Appreciations, Greek Studies* and *Plato and Platonism* are critical essays; *Marius the Epicurean, Gaston de Latour* and *Imaginary Portraits* are fictitious biographies or biographical sketches. In the critical essay the basic pattern is intellectual; Pater expounds his views and the reasons for them openly and directly. But he transfigures his statement of them by expressing them in a style deliberately designed to stir emotion and imagination as poetry does; heightened, melodious, thickly embroidered with imagery. In his fictitious biographies, on the other hand, the basic pattern is aesthetic. Picturesquely he tells the story of a personage, real like Watteau, or imaginary like Sebastian van Storck; human like Marius or half-supernatural like Denys L'Auxerrois. But—and here Pater's intellectual bias shows itself—the story is concerned less with his hero's character, and with the drama of his life, than with the ideas he holds or stands for. (p. 268)

The dual strain in Pater equipped him to make a success of such books. *The Renaissance,* in particular, is the outstanding example in English of a book about works of art which is also itself a work of art. It is admirably designed. In the **"Prefatory Note"** Pater sets out his principles of criticism in general, and of their application to the Renaissance in particular. He then proceeds to illustrate these in a series of studies of artists and personalities, each of which starts with a passage of generalization and then modulates into an eloquent re-creation of his subject's personality and the sentiment it stirs in him. Finally, in the **"Epilogue,"** he broadens the scope of his vision and displays all that has gone before in relation to the fundamental problem of how to live as it presented itself to him. The book is thus at once the expression of Pater's critical judgment, of his moral personality, and of his aesthetic impulse. Yet it is not heterogeneous or disparate. It has unity, the intellectual unity of an orderly logical structure, and the aesthetic unity that comes from the fact that every sentence of it is steeped in the colour of Pater's imaginative temperament.

The two sides combine with equal profit when he comes to make particular critical judgments. Unlike most critics, he is equally distinguished by his sense and his sensibility. This sensibility was subtle, passionate, and various. He loved the principle of beauty in all things, in practice as well as in theory: and he can discern it in the most diverse manifestations. Equally he delights in Greek and Gothic, Dutch painting and Italian painting, the homely and the exotic, the grave and the frivolous, Flaubert and Scott, the statues of Michelangelo and the operettas of Gilbert and Sullivan. With an exquisite discrimination he savours the particular flavour of each. But he does more than savour. His intellect is always at work to analyze each flavour into its component ingredients. Deftly he isolates that sense of wild terror and darkness that shadows and makes poignant the flights of Charles Lamb's playful, homely fancy. Subtly he discerns that mysterious, preternatural streak in Wordsworth's imagination, that sense of "unknown modes of being," whose unearthly light transfigures his pictures of simple peasant life and makes them sublime and disturbing. (pp. 268-70)

Pater does not confine his intellectual activity to analyzing the individual work. Since he sees it always as the expression of a period and phase of culture, he goes on to relate it to these. He is the most expert of time travelers, equally able to take himself back in imagination to Plato's Sparta and Montaigne's France and Spinoza's Holland, and as sharp to discriminate and analyze the quality of a period as he is of an individual.

Finally, he allowed himself now and again to speculate from his experience of particular works of art as to the laws governing art in general. He does this tentatively, for . . . he deeply distrusted aesthetic lawgiving. But when he does touch on it he goes straight to the point, as in his **"Essay on Style."** How true is the distinction he draws between truth to fact which is the quality of good writing, and truth to the author's "sense of fact" which is the quality of fine writing! How clearly and justly he defines in art the relation of form to matter! (p. 271)

It is the paradoxical triumph of his intellect that it teaches him never to take art too intellectually. He was clear-minded enough to see that because poetry is first of all an art like music, it has therefore more in common with music than with ethics or philosophy. He can appreciate both Flaubert and Scott because he had the wits to see that the important thing about both was not their ideas, in which they differed, but their common gift of expressing their inspiration in an artistic form. No English critic is at once so sensitive and so hard-headed as Pater; so catholic and so acute. It was the two strains in him that made him so. His artist's sensibility made him responsive; his academic intellect made him understand his responses. (p. 272)

[But] when Pater stops confining himself to appreciation and sets up as a creator in his own right, the two strains combine less easily. For creative writing involves, in a way that critical writing does not, the expression of the artist's whole personality with all its attendant idiosyncrasies and limitations: and Pater's personality and his purpose do not always harmonize. Like his mind, his personality was an odd mixture. . . . Imaginatively he was a child of his age; a native of the nineties, a typical contemporary of Rossetti and Burne-Jones, delighting in the subtle, the voluptuous, the refined, the exotic; an amateur of rare and curious flavours, enamoured, like his own Mona Lisa, of "strange thoughts and fantastic reveries and exquisite passions." . . . But he enjoyed these things only in imagination. His temperament, as it showed itself in life, was very different. He was a decorous, low-spirited don, celibate and solitary, fastidiously shrinking alike from intimacy and from adventure, detesting conflict and controversy, clinging affectionately to established forms and traditions, and ill at ease, for long, anywhere but in England. "Between you and me and the post," he once said, "I hate a foreigner." (pp. 272-73)

The two strains in Pater's personality were comically incongruous, both with each other and with his opinions. It is absurd to rhapsodize about Leonardo da Vinci to the extent that Pater does, when in life one would have avoided him as just another dreadful foreigner: there is something ludicrous in the contrast between the life of passionate experience which Pater advises us to embrace and the tone of refined languor in which he proffers his advice. The low-spirited hedonist cannot fail to be something of a figure of fun.

Did Pater realize this? I doubt it. For, though his friends tell us he was humorous, there is precious little sign of it in his writings. Here is another element in his composition which did not harmonize with his theory of the good life. We need the help of the comic spirit, if we are to view life in the same way as we view art. Life is so full of inconsistency and discord and anticlimax that, more often than not, the only sort of aesthetic satisfaction it can provide is that given by comedy or farce. Pater could not take it like this. . . . Pater's lack of humour did make him thus liable to some of the more laughable extravagancies of the aesthetic movement. There are moments when his taste for the exquisite gets out of control of his good sense, and he becomes all too like Bunthorne. Emerald and

Florian are pretty names; but I cannot think them probable or appropriate Christian names for a couple of Victorian English schoolboys (in **"The Child in the House"** and **"Emerald Uthwart"**). Nor can I believe that such a schoolboy would be consoled for the death of a playfellow by the thought that this playfellow's flesh would turn into violets in the following spring. (pp. 274-75)

[The] quirks and limitations in Pater's personality could not be kept out of his work. . . . [*The Renaissance* and *Greek Studies*] are tinged all too strongly with the colour of Pater's creative personality. He means to identify himself with his subjects; but more often he identifies his subject with himself. Botticelli, Leonardo, Michelangelo, present themselves before us, unexpectedly and improbably, as shrinking, shy, highly cultured souls, oscillating languidly between faith and belief and with marked Oxford accents. Even when they are not like Pater himself, his personages do seem in some sort to belong to his period. The Pre-Raphaelites of Florence in 1460 appeared miraculously changed into the Pre-Raphaelites of London in 1870; in Pater's *Greek Studies,* Dionysus, Demeter, and the other classic deities emerge for all the world like figures in a picture by Burne-Jones, with nerveless limbs and fragile, pensive faces. . . . To see Olympus and fifteenth-century Florence through the eyes of a Victorian Oxonian and irradiated by the ideal light of his romantic enthusiasm for them, is to see something odd and new and delightful. But it is not the same thing as seeing them as they really were.

These limitations show up even more flagrantly in his imaginative biographies. For these are stories; and to make stories convincing needs dramatic power. The author must be able to exhibit his characters in speech and action. Pater, stiff, solitary and contemplative, could no more do this than fly. Listen to Emerald Uthwart the schoolboy, addressing his form master just after he has had a beating from him: "And now, sir, that I have taken my punishment," he remarks in a submissive tone, "I hope that you will forgive my fault." I refuse to believe that any English schoolboy in the nineteenth or any other century, even if he were called Emerald Uthwart, ever spoke like this. Pater is no more successful when, in **"A Prince of Court Painters,"** he sets up as a female impersonator and attempts to write an appreciation of Watteau in the form of a diary kept by the young daughter of a provincial bourgeois French family. The appreciation is exquisite but the diary is as much like a real girl's diary as Lord Fancourt Babberley was like Charlie's Aunt. As a matter of fact such gross lapses are rare in Pater's work. Aware perhaps that he had no dramatic gift, he generally tries to avoid the occasion for its use. Such dramatic incidents as his plot involves are related briefly and, as it were, in parenthesis, after they have taken place; conversations are related in reported speech, so that Pater has no need to try to simulate his character's tone of voice and colloquial idiosyncrasies. These devices save him from bathos, but at the cost of making his stories remote and lifeless. (pp. 275-77)

The style is the man. This is eminently true of Pater. . . . No style is more fully expressive of its author. This means that, in spite of the pains he spent on it, it is not a faultless style. Like himself, Pater's sentences are a touch languid and spiritless, and they mirror all too accurately his nervous shrinking from conflict. Rather than commit himself in any way that might seem aggressive, he will hesitate, qualify, intersperse his statements with 'perhaps," "almost," "somewhat," till the reader sometimes loses the thread of the argument altogether. Pater's determination to avoid ugliness at all costs leads him still further to perplex the reader. For the sake of euphony he sometimes twists and inverts the order of his sentences, so that we have to plough through two or three qualifying parentheses before we come to the main clause. Such a style is unsuitable for exposition, and still more for storytelling, for stories and arguments have to be kept moving. Pater's choice of words too can exhibit his streak of aesthete's silliness. . . . For example, in the famous passage on Mona Lisa [from his essay on Leonardo da Vinci], he represents her in the course of her mysterious peregrinations through the ages as having "trafficked in strange webs with eastern merchants." No doubt he chose the epithet "strange" because he wanted to suggest the exotic romance involved in such a transaction. But the word "strange" also means "odd." Though Pater may not remember this, the reader does, and experiences a jar. "What *is* an odd web?" he asks himself. The picture which arises in his mind is not a romantic one. The fact is that in his choice of words, as in his construction of sentences, Pater was liable to fall into the besetting sin of the conscious stylist. Like Henry James, like James Joyce, he was so anxious to write in accordance with his own ideal of the perfect style that he forgot it is a writer's first obligation to communicate his meaning to his readers.

All the same his style does cast its spell. His intelligence appears in the winnowed concentration of his phrasing, his sensibility in the refinement of his sense of language, and in the slow, intricate melody of his cadences, which, even at his most impassioned, never, as in so much fine writing, slip into a recurrent rhythm so as to become a sort of uneasy verse, but always retain the specific music of prose. Pater's writing is never ugly or slipshod or diffuse. Or undistinguished; his every sentence exhales a perfume as strong and unmistakable as the scent of a gardenia flower; and with some of the same languorous, compelling sweetness. (pp. 277-79)

[Though Pater] was no storyteller, there is a strain in his work which reveals him as a creative writer, in the strictest, fullest meaning of the word. Not only did he appreciate the principle of beauty as manifested in the work of others, he added to theirs a manifestation of his own. As no one else before or since, he has put into words the scholar's distinctive sense of the beautiful, the aesthetic emotion as it is experienced by learned, refined, and meditative spirits: and he has done this not in mere arid, intellectual statement, but distilled by the intensity with which his imagination apprehended it, into a phase of feeling, a pervading mood—the Paterian mood we may fairly call it—which saturates his most memorable passages and leaves its perfume on every page he writes. It is a mood of reverie—intent, trancèd reverie—attainable it would seem only in tranquil and immemorial surroundings, where the spirit feels itself cloistered and sealed off from the din and flux and pressure of the active world. But though it is a cloistered mood there is nothing ascetic about it. It is relaxed, receptive; and the senses, so far from being suppressed, are tremblingly awake to respond, as they could not except in tranquillity, to the subtlest and most fleeting impressions; to the play of light and shadow on running water, the flutter of a rose petal to the grass, a snatch of song heard faintly in the distance, a waft of scent from the lime trees borne on the warm windless air of a summer afternoon. Nor is Pater's response to these things a mere movement of light, indifferent pleasure. They come to him murmurous with imaginative overtones, heavy with evocative memories—of pictures, books, bygone ages, his own

past—all mingling dreamily together to flood the soul, if only for a moment, with a sense of timeless beauty. (pp. 281-82)

> *Lord David Cecil, "Walter Pater," in his* The Fine Art of Reading and Other Literary Studies, *The Bobbs-Merrill Company, Inc., 1957, pp. 259-82.*

IAIN FLETCHER   (essay date 1959)

[Pater's essay *Style*] from its unusual firmness of statement may constitute something of an aesthetic *credo* [creed]. (pp. 31-2)

[According to Pater, all of the requisites of style] are subdued to the architectonic quality that reveals the shaping presence of *Mind.* . . . All the laws of good writing aim . . . at an identity almost of word with object, so that word, phrase, sentence, sequence of cadences seems almost to *become* what it presents. (p. 33)

[But even] if the architectonic ideal of Mind in style is satisfied, this does not imply that *great* as opposed to *good* literature will result. For Pater concludes his essay by telling us that greatness in literature depends not on form but matter, not on handling, but substance; on the range and depth of the human interest of its theme.

> Given the conditions I have tried to explain as constituting good art;—then, if it be devoted further to the increase of men's happiness, to the redemption of the oppressed, or the enlargement of our sympathies with each other, or to such presentment of new or old truth about ourselves and our relation to the world as may ennoble and fortify us in our sojourn here, or immediately, as with Dante, to the glory of God, it will be also great art . . . it (will have) something of the soul of humanity . . . and find its logical, its architectural place, in the great structure of human life.

This argument undercuts not merely the ideal of unified matter and form, but the whole of Pater's earlier insights into the nature of literary art. . . . If the quotation above is to be taken as his final position, then Pater has renounced Aestheticism and submitted to a simple Christian humanitarianism. However, the issue is not so plain. In his writings after *Style* we find little practical outcome, and in *Style* itself, the architectonic ideal itself is not observed. The aesthetic unit, for Pater, remains fixed at the sentence, if necessary, a sentence extended by parenthesis, distinction and qualification to paragraph length. That style is a matter of *perception*, not of cadence or euphony, is the principle laid down in the essay; but one finds everywhere in Pater the isolated cadence or sentence making its impact by itself; one must pause after every sentence to adjust oneself to a new rhythm (not a new turn of argument). In *Style* itself, the plea for a flexible prose and the rejection of Flaubert are only loosely connected. We must read *Style,* with its jagged transitions, as a set of related perceptions, or set, even, of ultimately isolated perceptions, held together only by their occurrence within a common periphery. . . . Pater's ideal vocabulary is purged and ranging, scholarly but adventurous; but his actual vocabulary, even at its most mature and discriminating in the finally revised *Marius* . . . consists of many words that are either precious, intensive or cloudy. His vocabulary is purged and scholarly, but very narrow; that of a special, even an intensely private personality. And though Pater asserts that literature is great through the dignity of its broad human interests, what, as Mr. Chandler asks [see Additional Bibliography] are we to make [of] this passage:

> . . . not only scholars, but all disinterested lovers of books, will always look to (literature), as to all other fine art, for . . . a sort of cloistral refuge, from a certain vulgarity in the actual world. A perfect poem like *Lycidas,* a perfect fiction like *Esmond,* the perfect handling of a theory like Newman's *Idea of a University,* has for them something of the uses of a religious 'retreat'.

The assumption here still seems to be that art is closed, finished, perfect, while life has an indefinitely open texture. Art is the moral object, intrinsically superior to everyday reality, not a means of encountering experience with greater openness and alertness. So Pater's actual criticism remains fixed always upon the work of art as a thing in itself, and does not move beyond the work of art to its wider or deeper human relevance. He comes back always to his private sensibility, and the immediate modifications a work of art has produced in that; all wider ranges of interest are left out of consideration. *Style* represents an honest awareness of the limitations of his own attitudes to art and life, and his own inability at a late stage of development to transcend these. (pp. 33-6)

> *Iain Fletcher, in his* Walter Pater, *British Council, 1959, 44 p.*

SOLOMON FISHMAN   (essay date 1963)

Ideally, Pater should have developed the principal idea of **"The School of Giorgione"** concerning the importance of medium in determining the formal constitution of the work of art into a conception of pictorial style, in which the formal elements are seen as the embodiment of the painter's inner vision. But to perceive Giorgione's achievement in terms of style would have required the kind of connoisseurship and technical and historical knowledge that Pater simply did not possess. He would have had to place Giorgione's individual style in relation to the Venetian school in particular, to Italian Renaissance painting in general, and ultimately to the whole history of art conceived of in terms of the evaluation and transmission of styles.

Nevertheless **"The School of Giorgione,"** as far as it goes, is a notable document in art criticism, providing the rationale, if not the means, for the formal analysis of style. It is a carefully reasoned work, the major part of which is devoted to relatively abstract critical theory, and not at all characteristic of the impressionist approach announced in the **"Preface."** Pater begins in the vein of Lessing's *Laocöon* by enforcing the distinction between the visual arts and literature and by protesting the traditional kind of literary treatment of painting. Unlike Lessing, who makes the mimetic capability the distinguishing factor, Pater concentrates on the sensuous appeal of the medium, on aesthetic surface. . . . (pp. 66-7)

This may appear to be rudimentary to us, but we must recall that in Pater's earlier writing on art and most of Ruskin's, pictures were interpreted in terms of their illustrative values. Ruskin was not entirely consistent on this point, but he often assumed the substance of painting and poetry to be identical, and the difference in medium a minor difference in "language." Pater is now very explicit in ruling out a literary approach. (p. 68)

In designating the essential pictorial quality to lie midway between technique of execution and literary interest, Pater has defined the area which was to absorb the attention of the formalist critics of the present century—the area of "significant form," perhaps the most problematic question in modern art criticism. Pater specifies both the creative and the essential aspects of pictorial form, but he does not actually succeed in linking form and expression. A lacuna exists between the formalist approach implicit in the Giorgione essay and the idea of style he formulated later in connection with literary art. . . .

[He then] proceeds to what is actually propaganda for an art of pure form, in which the pictorial qualities are primary in the sense of principal. Pater's rationale is based on the analogy of music, an idea which was widespread in nineteenth-century Symbolist aesthetics, and recurs in certain twentieth-century theories of nonfigurative art. Pater's remains the classic statement of the case. . . . (p. 69)

The idea of "form as an end in itself" is much more important both historically and critically than that of art for art's sake, with which Pater is usually associated. For though one may regard the doctrine of pure poetry as a minor or negligible literary phenomenon, one cannot take a comparable attitude toward the parallel movement in the visual arts. It is possible to take issue with the statement that all art constantly aspires toward the condition of music. . . . [Pater] is voicing an hypothesis which, though not eccentric, does not adequately account for the historical development of the visual arts. Furthermore, analogy with music is ambiguous, in that the status of musical form and content remains a baffling problem in aesthetics. If one regards music as an art of pure form devoid of content, Pater's statement looks forward to the nonobjective art of our time. But it is more likely . . . that Pater thinks of music as embodying fusion of form and content so complete that neither can be extricated from the other. While the notion of an organic fusion of form and content is one of the most fruitful discoveries of modern critical theory and one that is almost universally accepted, it is a difficult hypothesis to demonstrate. An obvious example is the interaction of meter and meaning in a poem. We may be intuitively convinced of a unified effect, but, as I. A. Richards has observed, the metrical and the semantic analysis must proceed on planes which never actually converge. The interaction of matter and form in representational art may be more intimate than in poetry, but it still presents great difficulties for critical analysis. (pp. 70-1)

Pater's version of formalism is handled with considerable discretion and tact. Far from arguing the irrelevance of subject matter, he demonstrated that in the case of Giorgione, the formal aim, which is the principal or even exclusive aim, is achieved by the control of subject matter. Giorgione's distinction is his discovery of *genre,* a special kind of subject matter wholly amenable to the formal ends of the artist, since it makes no historical, theological, literary, or naturalistic claims on his fantasy. (p. 71)

Pater's criticism of the visual arts encompasses both of the dominant aesthetic approaches of our own time—the expressionist and the formalist—but does not really succeed in achieving a synthesis. His idea of expressiveness is primarily the product of his literary experience, his idea of form that of his visual sensibility. He does not find Giorgione's work to be less expressive than that of the Florentines: the difference lies in the degree to which formal and expressive elements are fused. For him, Giorgione's pictures constitute "painted poems," in which the literary element is so refined, so idealized (so remote from actuality) that it is no longer felt to be an intrusion upon the purely visual, or "decorative," element. Pater appears to be on the verge of "significant form," but it is doubtful that without the example of Post-Impressionist art he could have arrived at the absolute formalism of Clive Bell and Roger Fry, or without a knowledge of nonobjective art at the synthesis of formalism and expressionism which is the singular achievement of Sir Herbert Read. (p. 72)

> *Solomon Fishman, "Walter Pater," in his* The Interpretation of Art: Essays on the Art Criticism of John Ruskin, Walter Pater, Clive Bell, Roger Fry, and Herbert Read, *University of California Press, 1963, pp. 43-72.*

RENÉ WELLEK   (essay date 1965)

[*Wellek's* A History of Modern Criticism, *from which the following excerpt is taken, is a major, comprehensive study of the literary critics of the last three centuries. Wellek's critical method, as demonstrated in the* History *and outlined in his* Theory of Literature, *is largely one of describing, analyzing, and evaluating a work solely in terms of the problems it poses for itself and how the writer solves them. Except for what he perceives as a major breach in the essay "Style," Wellek discerns a remarkable consistency in Pater's critical philosophy and method, noting at the beginning of his essay that Pater seldom allowed his personal impressions to usurp his larger critical aims.*]

Today Pater is under a cloud. He is no longer widely read, and he is dismissed as an "impressionistic" critic. T. S. Eliot gives him as the example of a type of criticism which he calls "etiolated." "This is not worth much consideration, because it only appeals to minds so enfeebled or lazy as to be afraid of approaching a genuine work of art face to face." Eliot must be thinking of the famous passage on Mona Lisa, which has become the stock warning against "creative" criticism. The young smiling woman with a widow's veil is transformed into a *femme fatale*, "older than the rocks among which she sits; like the vampire, she has been dead many times." In addition a passage from the **Conclusion** to **The Renaissance** is remembered: "To burn always with this hard, gemlike flame, to maintain this ecstacy, is success in life." It is often quoted as the summary of Pater's philosophy, an aesthetic hedonism or hedonistic aestheticism. Today few want to burn with such a gemlike flame, and those few are usually very young indeed.

But these two passages—too well known for the good of Pater's reputation—are not really representative either of his method or his philosophy. The Mona Lisa passage is quite isolated in Pater's work. . . . If we look for other examples of a metaphorical method of criticism, even on a small scale, we are hard put to find many in Pater's writings. I have noticed only four which are at all conspicuous. Morris' poem "The Defense of Guenevere" is described in an early essay, **"Aesthetic Poetry"** . . . as "a thing tormented and awry with passion, like the body of Guenevere defending herself from the charge of adultery." In the sonnets of Michelangelo, we are told, there is "a cry of distress," "but as a mere residue, a trace of the bracing chalybeate salt, just discernible, in the song which rises like a clear, sweet spring from a charmed space in his life." The concluding paragraph of the essay on Lamb . . . compares him elaborately to the London of sixty-five years before. The *Bacchae* of Euripides is described as "excited,

troubled, disturbing—a spotted or dappled thing, like the oddly dappled fawn-skins of its own masquerade." These are little marginal fancies or rhetorical flourishes, but one would give an entirely false impression of Pater's mind and method if one advanced them as typical.

Rather, Pater's theory of criticism stresses not only personal impression but the duty of the critic to grasp the individuality, the unique quality of a work of art. . . . He paraphrases Goethe when he asks, "What is this song or picture, this engaging personality in life or in a book to *me?* Does it give me pleasure?" But this personal pleasure is merely the first step, the prerequisite of criticism. The critic must go beyond it: penetrate "through the given literary or artistic product, into the mental and inner condition of the producer, shaping his work." . . . In practice, Pater looks for the "formula," the "virtue," the "active principle," the "motive" in a work—terms substantially the same as Taine's "master-faculty" or Croce's "dominant sentiment." . . . [For example, in his essay on Wordsworth, he maintains that the] "virtue," the "active principle" in Wordsworth is "that strange, mystical sense of a life in natural things, and of man's life as a part of nature."

The whole essay . . . circles around this one problem: how to define this "intimate consciousness of the expression of natural things," his sense for "particular spots of time," his "recognition of local sanctities." . . . Pater puts Wordsworth in a framework of intellectual history: he speaks of the survival of ancient animism; he draws the parallel with pantheism in France which from Rousseau to Hugo sought the "expressiveness of outward things." When he writes on the *Intimations Ode*, he alludes to the Platonic doctrine of reminiscence and elsewhere quotes the anticipation of mood and doctrine in Henry Vaughan's "The Retreat." He speaks of Wordsworth's drawing on old speculations about the *anima mundi*, the one universal spirit. He is certain that Wordsworth felt, as Pater probably did too, that "the actual world would, as it were, dissolve and detach itself, flake by flake," that "he himself seemed to be the creator, and when he would the destroyer, of the world in which he lived—that old isolating thought of many a brain-sick mystic of ancient and modern times." Pater, in short, attempts to define the mood, the temper, the dominant quality of Wordsworth's personality and work, what he once calls "the fine mountain atmosphere of mind." He uses the traditional methods of 19th-century criticism: historical, when he suggests the intellectual affinities; descriptive, evocative, when he recalls "the biblical depth and solemnity which hangs over this strange, new, passionate, pastoral world"; and evaluative, when he discriminates between the good and the inferior in Wordsworth. As to method, there is nothing new except insight and finesse, nor is there anything subjective in it except sympathy. It is a "portrait" as good as anything in Sainte-Beuve.

Pater's essays vary greatly in quality. . . . But if we make the necessary discriminations, we are left with a handful of subtle studies, models of the art of the essayist and portraitist. (pp. 381-84)

In *Marius* Pater tells us that hedonism means "Be perfect in regard to what is here and now," and not "let us eat and drink, for tomorrow we die." It is culture, *paideia*, "an expansion and refinement of the power of reception," "not pleasure, but fulness of life, and insight as conducting to that fulness." The association with the Epicurean style . . . is a gross libel. I find no difficulty in recognizing the high-mindedness of Pater's ideal and in admitting that the pleasures he recommended are intellectual and aesthetic. . . . The point important for criticism is Pater's central experience of time. To him "our existence is but the sharp apex of the present moment between two hypothetical eternities." "All that is actual is a single moment, gone while we try to apprehend it." Such a feeling for "the perpetual flux" . . . is the corollary of Pater's almost solipsistic sense of man's confinement within "the narrow chamber of the individual mind," "that thick wall of personality through which no real voice has ever pierced on its way to us." Man is a "solitary prisoner" with his own "dream of a world." This basic conception—no doubt a psychological *datum* of the retiring, shy, and unloving man—must lead him to a theory that sees the highest possible value in the individual moment of aesthetic experience. "Art comes proposing to us frankly to give nothing but the highest quality to your moments as they pass, and simply for those moments' sake." This highest quality concentrated in a moment, is, however, inconsistently interpreted as oriented toward an outward reality. Art, in these moments, presents us with the concrete variety of the world. This hedonism is a form of empiricism and sensationalism. Pater condemns philosophical and aesthetic abstractions and the world of Platonic ideas. "Who would change the colour or curve of a rose leaf . . . for that colourless, formless, intangible being—Plato put so high?" . . . Poetry should be as "veritable, as intimately near, as corporeal, as the new faces of the hour, the flowers of the actual season." Poetry is thus concrete and sensuous, almost imagistically so. But poetry in this moment must be also intense and hence charged with emotion, with personal emotion. Pater thus values—side by side with a poetry of images—the personal lyric. As emphatically as Leopardi, John Stuart Mill, and Poe, Pater declares lyrical poetry to be "the highest and most complete form of poetry." . . . Unity of impression follows from lyrical intensity as a criterion of good art. Pater can praise a poem of Browning for the "clear ring of a central motive. We receive from it the impression of one imaginative tone, of a single creative act." *Measure for Measure* is even considered as having "almost the unity of a single scene." (pp. 389-90)

If art is lyrical, emotional, intense, it must be "sincere." Pater often uses this term, as do other English critics, as a vague term of praise for successful art, for the tone of conviction in Browne, or even for "the grandeur of literary workmanship," the great style of Rossetti. But often sincerity means something more concrete to him, "that perfect fidelity to one's own inward presentation, to the precise features of the picture within, without which any profound poetry is impossible." . . . Often it is another term for personality, the "impress of a personal quality, a profound expressiveness, what the French call *intimité*, by which is meant some subtler sense of originality. . . . It is what we call *expression*, carried to its highest intensity of degree. . . . It is the quality which alone makes work in the imaginative order really worth having at all." Pater finds such personality even in the pale terra-cotta reliefs of Luca della Robbia, and he "longs to penetrate into the lives" of the Florentine sculptors of the 15th century "who have given expression to so much power and sweetness." But in spite of this statement and although the life of Winckelmann attracts him, Pater is not primarily interested in biography. He has to make some defense for the "loss of absolute sincerity" which Winckelmann suffered when he became a convert to Roman Catholicism in order to go to Rome. But his guess that there is "something of self-portraiture" in Shakespeare's Mercutio and Biron is a quite isolated remark in Pater's work. (pp. 390-91)

Pater's preference for concrete, intense, sincere, personal poetry manages to include the criterion of unity, and unity . . .

is the fusion of matter and form. "The ideal of all art is . . . the point where it is impossible to distinguish form from the substance or matter." . . . This is also the meaning of Pater's much misinterpreted dictum that "all art constantly aspires towards the condition of music." This does not mean that all art should become music, or even like music. Music is the "typically perfect art . . . precisely because in music it is impossible to distinguish the form from the substance or matter." Good poetry should aspire to such an identity, but with its own means, and the arts should and will remain separate, since "each art has its peculiar beauty, untranslatable into the forms of any other." (pp. 391-92)

So far Pater's concept of poetry and art is consistently romantic, lyrical, pastoral. Romantic also is the great role Pater ascribes to imagination. The office of imagination is "to condense the impressions of natural things into human form," to achieve "the complete infusion of the figure into the thought," to be as it is in Coleridge, a "unifying or identifying power." . . . Romantic also (though hardly reconcilable with his emphasis on the intense moment) is Pater's acceptance of the idea of an ideal world of poetry, "a new order of phenomena, a creation of a new ideal" which we are to contemplate (and not merely enjoy), "behold for the mere joy of beholding." This ideal world is often thought of as a "refuge," "a sort of cloistral refuge from a certain vulgarity in the actual world," and even compared, in its uses, to a religious "retreat," or called "a refuge into a world slightly better—better conceived, or better finished—than the real one." The ivory tower—the dream world of the poet, the theme of escape—is prominent in Pater.

But these romantic motifs are crossed and modified or even contradicted by Pater's intellectualistic strain: by his sense of art as craft and labor. He thought of "severe intellectual meditation" as the "salt of poetry" and argued that "without a precise acquaintance with the creative intelligence itself, its structure and capacities . . . no poetry can be masterly." He can even say that "the philosophical critic" (and here Pater himself is the philosophical critic) "will value, even in works of imagination seemingly the most intuitive, the power of understanding in them, their logical process of construction, the spectacle of a supreme intellectual dexterity which they afford." . . . Only in the case of Wordsworth would he grant that the "old fancy which made the poet's art an enthusiasm, a form of divine possession, seems almost literally true." But just this feeling that "the larger part was *given* passively" explains the unevenness, the fitfulness, of Wordsworth's achievement. (pp. 392-93)

[Pater concludes his essay **"On Style"** by drawing] a distinction between good and great art not according to form but according to matter . . . :

> It is on the quality of the matter it informs or controls, its compass, its variety, its alliance to great ends, or the depth of the note of revolt, or the largeness of hope in it, that the greatness of literary art depends, as the *Divine Comedy, Paradise Lost, Les Misérables, The English Bible,* are great art. Given the conditions I have tried to explain as constituting good art;—then, if it be devoted further to the increase of men's happiness, to the redemption of the oppressed, or the enlargement of our sympathies with each other, or to such presentment of new or old truth about ourselves and our relation to the world as may ennoble and fortify us in our

sojourn here, or immediately, as with Dante, to the glory of God, it will be also great art; if, over and above those qualities I summed up as mind and soul—that colour and mystic perfume, and that reasonable structure, it has something of the soul of humanity in it, and finds its logical, its architectural place, in the great structure of human life.

There could not be a fuller and more explicit revocation of Pater's earlier aestheticism. It is a recantation at the expense of any unified, coherent view of art. It gives up the earlier insight into the unity of matter and form, divides and distinguishes them again, and either introduces a double standard of judgment or shifts the burden of criticism to the subject matter. Pater ends in a dichotomy destructive of his own insights into the nature of art. . . . [Pater's] phrases about "the increase of men's happiness, the redemption of the oppressed, the enlargement of our sympathies with each other, the soul of humanity" imply that he has now accepted art as an agency of sympathy and even of humanitarianism. He had returned to the Church. In his last days he wrote an essay on Pascal, who interested him "as precisely an inversion of what is called the aesthetic life."

It is true, however, that even in his last stage Pater preserved the fundamental critical insight of his time, the historical sense. (pp. 395-96)

In his very first essay, he had criticized Coleridge for "the dulness of his historical sense," for getting involved in difficulties "which fade away before the modern or relative spirit, which, in the moral world as in the physical traces everywhere change, growth, development." . . . Relativism applies also to art. "All beauty is relative." Everything changes and passes, develops and progresses. Pater was pleased with the Darwinian theory.

> The idea of development [he says approvingly] is at last invading . . . all the products of mind, the very mind itself, the abstract reason; our certainty, for instance, that two and two make four. Gradually, we have come to think, or to feel, that primary certitude. Political constitutions, again, as we now see so clearly, are 'not made,' cannot be made, but 'grow.' Races, laws, arts, have their origins and end, are themselves ripples only on the great river of organic life; and language is changing on our very lips.

The evolutionary theory—Hegelian and Darwinian—confirms the old Heracliteanism, the *panta rhei*, Pater's fundamental experience of the flux of time. What to him personally was a tragic experience of the transience of all things he accepts as part of a cosmic scheme in which he, as a good Victorian, still sees "the dominant undercurrent of progress in things." (p. 396)

In the early essay on Winckelmann, Pater had still accepted "a standard of taste, an element of permanence, fixed in Greece." . . . But the view that the classical tradition is "the orthodoxy of taste" did not last. Pater's later Hellenism is a historical Hellenism, which sees Greece as a past stage of human culture that cannot be revived today. . . . [In] his theorizing Pater accepts the full consequence of historicism. "All periods, types, schools of taste are in themselves equal." He proclaims for his own time the role of "eclecticism," as he had, in *The Renaissance,* admired the syncretism of Christianity and paganism propounded by Pico della Mirandola. What Pater wants

for himself and his time is humanism, "the belief that nothing which has ever interested living men and women can wholly lose its vitality," a feeling for the totality of the past, which is still alive in us. . . . (pp. 397-98)

[Pater found an] image in Bunyan's *Pilgrim's Progress* for this living past. He speaks of the *House Beautiful* "which the creative minds of all generations—the artists and those who have treated life in the spirit of art—are always building together." In it the oppositions between styles and types, classical and romantic, cease. "The Interpreter of the *House Beautiful,* the true aesthetic critic, uses these divisions, only so far as they enable him to enter into the peculiarities of the objects with which he has to do." In our age "we must try to unite as many diverse elements as may be." "The individual writer or artist, certainly, is to be estimated by the number of graces he combines, and his power of interpenetrating them in a given work. . . . The legitimate contention is, not of one age or school of literary art against another, but of all successive schools alike, against the stupidity which is dead to the substance, and the vulgarity which is dead to form." (pp. 398-99)

[It] seems to me that Pater's House Beautiful has not escaped, and none of Pater's work has escaped the limitations of 19th-century aestheticism, its hectic cult of Beauty (a very narrow and exclusive type of beauty), its Alexandrian eclecticism, which made it impossible for the age to create a style of its own and which encouraged a historical masquerade. Historicism had to be transcended, as it has been during more recent years in Eliot's concept of tradition or in Malraux's imaginary museum. (p. 399)

> René Wellek, "The English Aesthetic Movement: Walter Pater," in his A History of Modern Criticism, 1750-1950: The Later Nineteenth Century, Vol. 4, Yale University Press, 1965, pp. 381-99.

GERALD CORNELIUS MONSMAN (essay date 1967)

[*Monsman argues that Pater's belief in the relativity of all phenomena was but one element of a larger philosophical scheme in which Pater recognized the existence of order and continuity in the human experience. Monsman is also the author of a psychological interpretation of Pater's work (see excerpt below, 1980).*]

[The readers of Pater] have somewhat too hastily concluded that Pater taught all knowledge to be relative because he could "make no sincere claim to have apprehended anything beyond the veil of immediate experience." . . . Pater, differing from Coleridge, certainly did not look for some static and absolute pattern above and beyond the world of relative, finite entities; rather, he held that within the shifting fabric of the sensuous veil itself—for those eyes and ears delicately attuned to the changes of the material world—there can be discerned the eternal outline of the Absolute.

Time and again Pater protests that the uncritical acceptance of a scientific empiricism plunges one into the yielding sands of skepticism. In *Plato* he asserts the same ideas he did in *Marius,* using the same metaphor of music to describe the divine life within the shimmering flux of phenomena. Pater writes:

> Yet from certain fragments in which the *Logos* [rational principle] is already named we may understand that there had been another side to the doctrine of Heraclitus; an attempt on his part, after all, to reduce that world of chaotic

mutation to *cosmos,* to the unity of a reasonable order, by the search for and the notation, if there be such, of an antiphonal rhythm, or logic, which, proceeding uniformly from movement to movement, as in some intricate musical theme, might link together in one those contending, infinitely diverse impulses. It was an act of recognition, even on the part of a philosophy of the inconsecutive, the incoherent, the insane, of that Wisdom which "reacheth from end to end, sweetly and strongly ordering all things."
. . .

All change is contained within a framework, a harmony of the whole. Something akin to the "intelligible relationships" of an Absolute Reason unites all diverse psychic and material entities; the world of Eternal Ideas is not lost, only immersed within the flowing stream of phenomena. Paradoxically, then, both the Absolute idealist and the empiricist could subscribe to Heraclitus and his flux:

> It is the burden of Hegel on the one hand, to whom nature, and art, and polity, aye, and religion too, each in its long historic series, are but so many conscious movements in the secular process of the eternal mind; and on the other hand of Darwin and Darwinism, for which "type" itself properly *is* not but is only always *becoming.* . . .

Whatever one does choose to say about the discontinuous and subjective entities in flux, one need not deny the existence of that eternal and objective order which unites them. This relation between the subjective and objective worlds was fundamental to Pater's philosophy and recurs in his thoughts in a variety of ways. (pp. 6-7)

[In his *History and Antiquities of the Doric Race,* Karl Ottfried Müller] treated the psychology, politics, and art of the Greeks in terms of a systematic subject-object conflict, the opposed tendencies labeled "Ionian" and "Dorian" by him. Pater accepted the distinction, and in **"The Marbles of Aegina,"** in the *Greek Studies,* he creates his own terms for the Ionian-Dorian opposition—"the centrifugal and centripetal tendencies, as we may perhaps not too fancifully call them." . . . On the one side, says Pater,

> there is the centrifugal, the Ionian, the Asiatic tendency, flying from the centre, working with little forethought straight before it, in the development of every thought and fancy; throwing itself forth in endless play of undirected imagination; delighting in brightness and colour, in beautiful material, in changeful form everywhere, in poetry, in philosophy, even in architecture and its subordinate crafts. In the social and political order it rejoices in the freest action of local and personal influences; its restless versatility drives it towards the assertion of the principles of separatism, of individualism,—the separation of state from state, the maintenance of local religions, the development of the individual in that which is most peculiar and individual in him. Its claim is in its grace, its freedom and happiness, its lively interest, the variety of its gifts to civilisation;

its weakness is self-evident, and was what made the unity of Greece impossible. . . .

One could compile a list of a dozen or more qualities, each of which Pater somewhere employs to describe the centrifugal. It is Ionian, Asiatic, colorful, undirected, restless, individual, variegated, subjective, myriad-minded, and releasing, among other things. For Pater, the centrifugal was best expressed in the philosophy of Heraclitus. It revels in the rich variety and flux of the phenomenal world, emancipating the individual from the weary weight of custom and external authority; but its trap lies in its individuality, which eventually becomes solipsistic—"each mind keeping as a solitary prisoner its own dream of a world."

Pater continues his discussion with a description of the centripetal, or Dorian, aspect of existence which served as a counterbalance to the centrifugal. Plato, in particular, saw the need to invoke the centripetal as a corrective:

> It is this centrifugal tendency which Plato is desirous to cure, by maintaining, over against it, the Dorian influence of a severe simplification everywhere, in society, in culture, in the very physical nature of man. An enemy everywhere to *variegation,* to what is cunning or "myriad-minded," he sets himself, in mythology, in music, in poetry, in every kind of art, to enforce the ideal of a sort of Parmenidean abstractness and calm. . . .

Perhaps, writes Pater, Plato carried his battle against the disintegrative forces too far, but he was nevertheless essentially right:

> This exaggerated ideal of Plato's is, however, only the exaggeration of that salutary European tendency, which, finding human mind the most absolutely real and precious thing in the world, enforces everywhere the impress of its sanity, its profound reflexions upon things as they really are, its sense of proportion. It is the centripetal tendency, which links individuals to each other, states to states, one period of organic growth to another, under the reign of a composed, rational, self-conscious order, in the universal light of the understanding. . . .

While other races may also reflect such qualities, the Dorian race, says Pater, has historically best manifested the centripetal tendency "in its love of order, of that severe *composition* everywhere, of which the Dorian style of architecture is, as it were, a material symbol—in its constant aspiration after what is earnest and dignified, as exemplified most evidently in the religion of its predilection, the religion of Apollo.". . . A list of the qualities of the centripetal tendency would be, in effect, a list of opposites to the centrifugal tendency: the centripetal is Dorian, European, colorless, limiting, calm, unifying, simple, objective, universal, and ordered.

The whole of Pater's world view is structured around this tension between the Heraclitean centrifugal tendency and the Parmenidean centripetal tendency. It is a relation which is described again in Pater's interesting **Postscript** to *Appreciations,* in which the political ideas of the *Greek Studies* are translated into aesthetic theory. The terms *romantic* and *classic,* says Pater, are "but one variation of an old opposition, which may be traced from the very beginning of the formation of

European art and literature.''. . . Romanticism, we are told, is characterized by strength, energy, liberty, strangeness, and curiosity, and it seeks, as an illustration of these qualities, the medieval world "because, in the overcharged atmosphere of the Middle Age, there are unworked sources of romantic effect, of a strange beauty, to be won, by strong imagination, out of things unlikely or remote.''. . . Romanticism, says Pater, represents the addition of these qualities to the underlying classical objective of beauty: ''the desire of beauty being a fixed element in every artistic organisation, it is the addition of curiosity to this desire of beauty, that constitutes the romantic temper.''. . . (pp. 7-10)

''There are,'' says Pater,

> the born classicists who start with *form,* to whose mind the comeliness of the old, immemorial, well-recognised types in art and literature, have revealed themselves impressively; who will entertain no matter which will not go easily and flexibly into them. . . . On the other hand, there are the born romanticists, who start with an original, untried *matter,* still in fusion; who conceive this vividly, and hold by it as the essence of their work; who, by the very vividness and heat of their conception, purge away, sooner or later, all that is not organically appropriate to it, till the whole effect adjusts itself in clear, orderly, proportionate form; which form, after a very little time, becomes classical in its turn. . . .

For Pater, *form* designates the fixed outline or type which belongs to the objective centripetal world, whereas *matter* is the fluid or individual ingredient belonging to the subjective centrifugal realm. The Dorian world of the centripetal is truly the classic tendency, and the Ionian centrifugal is the romantic tendency; for romanticism derives its energy and strength from some inward source and is subjective in nature, whereas classicism, on the other hand, is not related to the revolutionary, individualistic world of romanticism, but belongs to the fixed world of the type and tends instead to be authoritative.

Pater takes great care to point out that the extremes of both the centrifugal romanticism and centripetal classicism are destructive of true art: ''When one's curiosity is deficient . . . one is liable to value mere academical proprieties too highly, to be satisfied with worn-out or conventional types, with the insipid ornament of Racine, or the prettiness of that later Greek sculpture, which passed so long for true Hellenic work.''. . . Also, the opposite extreme, romanticism, is equally faulty: ''When one's curiosity is in excess, when it overbalances the desire of beauty, then one is liable to value in works of art what is inartistic in them; to be satisfied with what is exaggerated in art.''. . . Thus, in romantic works of art ''a certain distortion is sometimes noticeable, . . . something of a terrible grotesque, of the macabre.''. . . (pp. 10-11)

Toward the end of his **Postscript,** Pater quite clearly defines what he feels the highest art must be:

> But explain the terms as we may, in application to particular epochs, there are these two elements always recognisable; united in perfect art—in Sophocles, in Dante, in the highest work of Goethe, though not always absolutely balanced there; and these two elements may be

not inappropriately termed the classical and romantic tendencies.

> (pp. 11-12)

The balance which Pater seeks to strike is that between the highly stylized and the painfully grotesque, and the achievement of this balance is the mutual accommodation of the centripetal and the centrifugal tendencies within the work of art. (p. 12)

Perhaps one of the most famous of Pater's dicta is also one of his most succinct statements on this theme of artistic balance: ''All art constantly aspires towards the condition of music,'' he writes in his essay on Giorgione. Pater, following certain Symbolist writers, held that music most perfectly fuses matter and form:

> While in all other kinds of art it is possible to distinguish the matter from the form, and the understanding can always make this distinction, yet it is the constant effort of art to obliterate it. That the mere matter of a poem, for instance, its subject, namely, its given incidents or situation—that the mere matter of a picture, the actual circumstances of an event, the actual topography of a landscape—should be nothing without the form, the spirit, of the handling, that this form, this mode of handling, should become an end in itself, should penetrate every part of the matter: this is what all art constantly strives after, and achieves in different degrees. . . .

In great art, then, the distinction between objective form and subjective matter no longer exists—as Hegel had said, the aesthetic object presents the universal incorporated in the particular. . . .

Hence, for Pater, as well as for Hegel and the Symbolists, the creation of a work of art is inextricably bound up with the perfecting of a balance between the centripetal and the centrifugal tendencies. But what for the French or German thinkers is only a philosophy of aesthetics becomes with Pater the basis for a broader theory of cultural rebirth. Quite simply, Pater sees the Italian Renaissance as a bringing to the classical heritage of Greece a romanticism derived from the Middle Ages. It was, we might say, a rediscovery by the old Dorian tradition of what the Many contribute to the One. But while the Renaissance, the ''enchanted'' balance, lasted only momentarily, the reality of a great cultural flowering can be renewed repeatedly. The Age of Pericles, as well as the Age of Lorenzo, reflected the centripetal and centrifugal in perfect tension. Moreover, this rebirth belongs not merely to national awakenings: it occurs continuously on a more limited scale—in villages, in families, and in individuals—whenever the opposite ends of experience are momentarily fused. (p. 15)

Consonant with his belief that abstract ideas must have concrete expression, Pater incarnates his centrifugal-centripetal romantic-classic dialectic in human personality. In clothing the bones of his abstract subject-object opposition in concrete and individual form, in personality, Pater moves out of philosophy altogether and into the realm of [the myths of Dionysus and Apollo]. (p. 16)

As Pater tells us in the ***Greek Studies,*** Dionysus is ''the vinegrowers' god, the *spiritual form* of fire and dew.'' The image of Dionysus, says Pater, carries us back to a ''world of vision unchecked by positive knowledge, in which the myth is be-gotten among a primitive people, as they wondered over the life of the thing their hands helped forward, till it became for them a kind of spirit, and their culture of it a kind of worship.''. . . [The] later forms of Greek sculpture are especially successful in portraying Dionysus, since in Greek art the office of the imagination, when it treats of the gods, is ''to condense the impressions of natural things into human form; to retain that early mystical sense of water, or wind, or light, in the moulding of eye and brow; to arrest it, or rather, perhaps, to set it free, there, as human expression.''. . . Of course, says Pater, ''the human form is a limiting influence also; and in proportion as art impressed human form, in sculpture or in the drama, on the vaguer conceptions of the Greek mind, there was danger of an escape from them of the free spirit of air, and light, and sky. . . . The artistic embodiment, then, of the old wine-god reflects a dynamic tension between ''the teeming, still fluid world, of old beliefs, as we see it reflected in the somewhat formless *theogony* of Hesiod'' and ''the spirit of a severe and wholly self-conscious intelligence; bent on impressing everywhere, in the products of the imagination, the definite, perfectly conceivable human form, as the only worthy subject of art; less in sympathy with the mystical genealogies of Hesiod, than with the heroes of Homer, ending in the entirely humanised religion of Apollo.''. . . (pp. 17-18)

[In his *Geburt der Tragödie,* Friedrich Nietzsche also] speaks of ''the Apollonian appearances, in which Dionysus objectifies himself,'' the Apollonian art form being ''the objectification of a Dionysian state.'' Whereas the purpose of the Apollonian plastic art, according to Nietzsche, is to arouse within us ''a delight in beautiful forms,'' Dionysus endows these forms with ''a convincing metaphysical significance, which the unsup-ported word and image could never achieve.'' Nietzsche conceives of Dionysus as subjective and centrifugal and of Apollo as objective and centripetal. Pater, likewise, identifies the subjective or Ionian tendency with Dionysus—words like *teeming, fluid,* and *formless* describe his world—while asserting that the ''Dorian or European influence embodied itself in the religion of Apollo.''. . . Moreover, both Nietzsche and Pater agree that Apollo, in opposition to Dionysus, is the god of order and rationality. Contrasting Apollo and his religion to their opposites, Pater says that such centrifugal deities as the summer-time goddess

> Demeter, the spirit of life in grass,—and Dio-nysus, the ''spiritual form'' of life in the green sap,—remain, to the end of men's thoughts and fancies about them, almost wholly physical. But Apollo, the ''spiritual form'' of sunbeams, early becomes (the merely physical element in his constitution being almost wholly sup-pressed) exclusively ethical,—the ''spiritual form'' of inward or intellectual light, in all its manifestations. He represents all those spe-cially European ideas, of a reasonable, personal freedom, as understood in Greece; of a reason-able polity; of the sanity of soul and body, through the cure of disease and of the sense of sin; of the perfecting of both by reasonable exercise or *ascésis* [self-discipline]; his religion is a sort of embodied equity, its aim the real-isation of fair reason and just consideration of the truth of things everywhere.
>
> (pp. 18-19)

[It] is necessary to note that for Pater the personality of Dio-nysus is somewhat more complex than it was for Nietzsche. Although Pater's Dionysus is certainly the god of the narrow, subjective world and its fear of death, he has, says Pater, ''his alternations of joy and sorrow.''. . . Pater devotes a consid-erable amount of space in his first essay in the *Greek Studies* to an examination of the double nature of the god:

> The whole compass of the idea of Dionysus, a dual god of both summer and winter, became ultimately . . . almost identical with that of Demeter. The Phrygians believed that the god slept in winter and awoke in summer, and cel-ebrated his waking and sleeping; or that he was bound and imprisoned in winter, and unbound in spring; . . . and a beautiful ceremony in the temple at Delphi, which, as we know, he shares with Apollo, described by Plutarch, represents his mystical resurrection. . . . He is twofold then—a *Doppelgänger* [double]; like Perse-phone, he belongs to two worlds, and has much in common with her, and a full share of those dark possibilities which, even apart from the story of the rape, belong to her. He is a *Chthon-ian* [earth] god, and, like all the children of the earth, has an element of sadness; like Hades himself, he is hollow and devouring, an eater of man's flesh—*sarcophagus.* . . .

For Nietzsche, Dionysus was merely a personification of a component in an abstract philosophical scheme. Pater's han-dling of the god, on the other hand, is poetically far superior, for he introduces him as a protagonist not merely in an ideo-logical pattern but in a truly mythic pattern. Dionysus' alter-nations between summer and winter mark him as a vegetative god, a representative of the seasonal cycle, and his relation to Apollo resembles that of Persephone to Demeter. As Pater has described it at length in the *Greek Studies,* Demeter is the *Magna Mater* [great mother], the goddess of the eternal earth itself, and Persephone is the cyclic, vegetative deity of summer and winter. Pater has taken this Demeter-Persephone pattern and, with the figures of Apollo and Dionysus, transposed it to the context of cultural history. Apollo . . . represents humanity itself, Pater's equivalent for the *Magna Mater* of the old fertility myth. The Paterian Dionysus is the consort or priest of hu-manity; his sacrificial death, by renewing the creative powers of humanity, makes way for the cultural awakening, for the ''renaissance'' which is the Apollonian phase of civilization.

The mythic pattern of Dionysus and Apollo is definitely related to the theory of art expressed in the **''Conclusion''** to *The Renaissance,* where the summer and winter phases of Dionysus are treated in the first and second paragraphs, respectively. In the former Pater considers ''physical life.''. . . and in the latter he takes up ''the inward world.''. . . Because there is a kind of resistance to change in nature, the summer side of Dionysus, which corresponds to the bloom of sensuous things, exhibits only a ''gradual fading.''. . . In the antique world of the Greeks and in the world of childhood, the soul can find release from its own subjectivity in the sensuousness of nature. For the young there is always a classic quality in the world of the summer Dionysus. But precisely because the world of the sum-mer Dionysus is finite, the soul can expand beyond it, its inner visions becoming too great to find their counterpart merely in nature. Suddenly, what had been the objective world becomes subjective. There is no external outlet; the bloom of nature has become a trap; the dreaming soul is imprisoned; it descends to the delirium of the winter god. The ''sleeping'' or ''imprisoned'' Dionysus corresponds to the psychic realm, with its vastly heightened awareness of the shortness of life and the sense of death—the mind imprisoned in its own dreams, as the **''Conclusion''** describes this winter world. (pp. 19-20)

In one of his early essays, **''Aesthetic Poetry,''** Pater discusses the youth of civilization and how this Greek world of the summer Dionysus became the wintry world of the Middle Ages. Writing of monastic religion, Pater tells us that it was, ''in many of its bearings, like a beautiful disease or disorder of the senses: and a religion which is a disorder of the senses must always be subject to illusions. Reverie, illusion, delirium: they are the three stages of a fatal descent both in the religion and the loves of the Middle Age.''. . . And Pater continues, describing the way in which the trapped soul poisons all that it touches:

> A passion of which the outlets are sealed, begets a tension of nerve, in which the sensible world comes to one with a reinforced brilliancy and relief—all redness is turned into blood, all water into tears. Hence a wild, convulsed sensuousness in the poetry of the Middle Age, in which the things of nature begin to play a strange delirious part. Of the things of nature the medieval mind had a deep sense; but its sense of them was not objective, no real escape to the world without us. The aspects and motions of nature only reinforced its prevailing mood, and were in conspiracy with one's own brain against one. A single sentiment invaded the world: everything was infused with a motive drawn from the soul. . . .

Obviously, the summer Dionysus is inadequate for the service of the expanding soul. He is finite, bound by the restrictions of time and space—the present moment, the particular place—for he embodies the discontinuity of the flux. The mature soul, which dreams of an immortality stretching from past to future, cannot be happy in this narrow world of the present, this simple life of sensations enjoyed from moment to moment.

But we recall that, for Pater, the flux of Dionysus is contained within an eternal framework, a harmony, which unites all diverse mental and material entities. The significance of art for the **''Conclusion''** lies precisely here. Art represents, in sensuous form, that larger order of the Absolute. Art is as concrete and real as the world of the summer Dionysus, but its form mirrors the eternal world of the ideal, and the soul cannot outgrow it. The mature mind, the expanded soul with larger vision, can relieve itself of the burden of its subjective dreams in this greater world of Apollonian art. All art is indeed dream, the dream of the romantic Dionysus objectified. (pp. 20-1)

The hero of the historical and imaginary portraits has a very natural relation to Pater's theory of art. He is the Dionysian priest of Apollo, and his function is the awakening of art in a barren world. . . . Certainly Pater's heroes, by their great love of the natural world, bring a new appreciation of physical nature to the dead world of the winter Dionysus. But they do more than that. They help humanity grow beyond its childhood to the maturity of artistic creation. By their mediation the first Golden Age of the summer Dionysus is replaced by that truer and greater Golden Age, the Age of Apollo. Tha Paterian hero, the bringer of art to humanity, possesses the Apollonian purity

of the eternal type while simultaneously displaying true Dionysian selfhood; that is, living incarnated in time and space and enduring the pangs of death.

One of the most revealing studies of the character of the hero is found in the paper **''Diaphaneitè.''**. . . One cannot doubt that the ''diaphanous'' character-type here being defined is truly Apollonian. According to K. O. Müller, Apollo, or Phoebus, is a name from which the words *bright, clear, pure,* and *unstained* can be derived etymologically, and again and again Pater returns to the metaphor of light in describing his ideal Apollonian personality. The Apollonian individual has a transparency of nature which allows the light of the Absolute to shine through him:

> The artist and he who has treated life in the spirit of art desires only to be shown to the world as he really is; as he comes nearer and nearer to perfection, the veil of an outer life not simply expressive of the inward becomes thinner and thinner. . . . It is just this sort of entire transparency of nature that lets through unconsciously all that is really lifegiving in the established order of things; it detects without difficulty all sorts of affinities between its own elements, and the nobler elements in that order. . . .

In Pater's fiction, as in ancient statuary, it is the form of the god which, by its lack of nonessential characteristics, gives expression to the eternal world of the type. For this reason the artist-heroes of Pater's imaginary portraits have a certain Apollonian neutrality about them and display all the attributes of the gods of Greek statuary, sharing with them that ''colourless, unclassified purity of life, with its blending and interpenetration of intellectual, spiritual, and physical elements, still folded together, pregnant with the possibilities of a whole world closed within it, [which] is the highest expression of the indifference which lies beyond all that is relative or partial.'' . . . This neutrality, the most striking aspect of the Apollonian personality, is not, however, a reflection of the ''colourless uninteresting existence'' of the man who has been neutralized ''by suppression of gifts''; rather, it is the colorless all-color of those individuals among whose talents there is a ''just equipoise.'' ''In these,'' says Pater, ''no single gift, or virtue, or idea, has an unmusical predominance.''. . . (pp. 21-3)

[In *The Renaissance,* we] are not left merely to deduce that Pater's bringers of the Renaissance are related to the gods of myth. Very often Pater specifically identifies the individual who, for example, brings a Greek love of nature into the rigid medieval Christian world as an ancient god exiled by the coming of Christianity. Pater borrowed this idea of the gods in exile from Heinrich Heine and made it one of the major themes in *The Renaissance,* a fact which indicates that the god-like nature is associated in Pater's thought with the rebirth of the arts. Heine's idea was fundamental to Pater's world view, and because Pater's writings always describe artistic creativity, it is the constant subject of his portraits. (p. 24)

[For example, there is] Leonardo da Vinci, a sort of magician, not dissimilar to his own Mona Lisa, who ''has been dead many times, and learned the secrets of the grave.''. . . And, of course, there is Botticelli, whose beautiful figures, ''in a certain sense like angels, but with a sense of displacement or loss about them—the wistfulness of exiles, conscious of a passion and energy greater than any known issue of them explains,''. . . remind us once again of the wandering gods. And, finally, there is Winckelmann, whose Apollonian nature was ''like a relic of classic antiquity, laid open by accident to our alien, modern atmosphere; . . . and he seems to realise that fancy of the reminiscence of a forgotten knowledge hidden for a time in the mind itself; as if the mind of one, lover and philosopher at once in some phase of pre-existence, . . . fallen into a new cycle, were beginning its intellectual career over again, yet with a certain power of anticipating its results.''. . . (pp. 25-6)

Pater relates this theme, the reappearance of the god-like hero, to the old mythic pattern of Dionysus. . . . [Leonardo and his Mona Lisa], Botticelli's comely figures, Winckelmann—all are in some sense, like Dionysus, gods of renewal. But just as Christianity surpassed Mithraicism, so the Paterian hero surpasses the primitive Dionysus. He is not merely a god of the renewal of spring: like Christ Himself, he becomes an instrument of fertility in the cosmic pattern, the regenerative agent on all levels of life—religious, aesthetic, intellectual—as well as physical. (p. 26)

Just as the original myth of Dionysus saw the birth of the new year already implicit in the destruction of the summer Dionysus, so in Pater's thought it is specifically the sacrificial death of the hero which quickens humanity. ''Poetry and poetical history,'' says Pater in **''Diaphaneitè,''** ''have dreamed of a crisis, where it must needs be that some human victim be sent down into the grave.'' It is the Dionysian hero ''whom in its profound emotion humanity might choose to send.''. . . Certainly this sacrifice is not an unalleviated tragedy, for his death is his final awakening from mortality, and the blaze of cultural renewal that follows is an echo within the human community of the renewal which has taken place within the soul itself. The dying hero, as the highest expression and representative of humanity, becomes the means by which civilization is purified of its mortality and initiated into the dawning light of Apollo. It is not difficult to see why the image of the mother plays such a large part in the lives of all of Pater's heroes, for, as the *Magna Mater* of the modern god, she is none other than humanity itself, and the love between hero and humanity is, for Pater, the most perfect love possible. This also explains why all of Pater's heroes are celibate. As gods, they have ritually consecrated their virility to their Great Mother, and the violent death of the hero comes as the ultimate expression of his love, for it is a giving, after the manner of the sexual act itself, of the very blood and members of his body to fructify the *Magna Mater*. Appropriately, Pater often presents the death of his hero as the consummation of marriage; as, for example, with Marius, Watteau, Denys, Sebastian, Carl, and Hippolytus. And because this self-sacrificial ''marriage'' is consummated by blood, it becomes also a kind of eucharist, a sacred communion of which humanity partakes. (pp. 26-7)

No doubt because so much of the Dionysian pattern pervades his fiction, Pater has often been accused of being morbid, of being a high priest of decadence, who views existence as incompatible with engagement in the world. In a sense, a somberness does pervade Pater's world view, for the romantic element is certainly present. (p. 27)

But the gods will be reborn, for in their death we see the destruction of death. Pater had written in his essay on **''The Bacchanals of Euripides''** that in the hunting by the winter Dionysus of the innocent summer Dionysus, we must see the winter god of death as his own victim ''if we are to catch, in its fulness, that deep undercurrent of horror which runs below,

all through this masque of spring, and realise the spectacle of that wild chase, in which Dionysus is ultimately both the hunter and the spoil.''. . . (p. 28)

Death comes, it is true, but while the body is a victim, the soul need never be. As Pater wrote of Pico, early dead, ''while his actual work has passed away, yet his own qualities are still active, and himself remains, as one alive in the grave . . . and with that sanguine, clear skin . . . as with the light of morning upon it.''. . .

[Pater's] early apprenticeship at writing *The Renaissance* proved a fine prelude to the art of imaginary portraiture, and by a natural and almost imperceptible progress [he] moves from a fictionalized criticism to a critical fiction, from the historical portrait to the imaginary portrait. The subject matter and technique remain essentially identical, for Pater's concern in the fiction is the same as it was in *The Renaissance*—culture, its birth and flowering—and all of his Dionysian heroes are represented as bringers of artistic and cultural enlightenment to their ages. In the writing of his essays for *The Renaissance*, in asking himself what cultural rebirth means, Pater seems to have found the materials of fiction; and one may say that the title of his first slim volume will serve as the metaphor of his future thought, for it involves an attitude toward life fundamental to his art, and each of his portraits will recount anew the myth of renaissance. (p. 29)

Gerald Cornelius Monsman, in his Pater's Portraits: Mythic Pattern in the Fiction of Walter Pater, *The Johns Hopkins University Press, 1967, 225 p.*

DAVID J. DE LAURA   (essay date 1969)

[*In his* Hebrew and Hellene in Victorian England, *excerpted below, De Laura examines the efforts of Pater and Matthew Arnold to adapt traditional religious culture to the needs of the later nineteenth century. According to De Laura, this effort principally involved an attempt by both men to formulate a new spiritual basis for European civilization founded on a synthesis of Christian and Hellenistic values. In describing Pater's treatment of these ideas, De Laura links many of Pater's pronouncements directly to the career and philosophy of Arnold. For additional discussions of Arnold and Pater see T. S. Eliot (1930) and Graham Hough (1948).*]

A complex and highly dialetical process, worked out in the thought of the major German [Hellenists] and everywhere related to the cult and ''myth'' of Greece first effectively formulated by Winckelmann, enjoys an extraordinary recrudescence in the careers of Arnold and Pater. Put simply, the problem is that of the transcendence, whether through rejection or synthesis, of the dualisms with which the Western tradition, especially in Platonism and Christianity, was seen to have burdened man. In Goethe's time as in Arnold's there is a search for a new basis of life compatible with the exigencies of modern thought and experience, and yet ensuring fullness of consciousness, ''fulness of being.'' In ethics, in human psychology, and especially in artistic production, the attempt to provide what Arnold, looking to Goethe, called in 1866 a new interpretation of human life and ''a new spiritual basis'' for European civilization . . . involved as its major counters a special version of ''Hellenic'' values and a radical revaluation of the Christian tradition. (pp. 166-67)

Arnold's and Pater's own relations with Christianity varied significantly through the years, and the precise relationship in their work between the classical deposit and ''Christianity'' fluctuates in important ways. However, three crucial themes provide much of the unity of each career and link the men indissolubly: the persistent merging of religious and aesthetic categories; the concern for the transcendence of human duality at the psychological and ethical levels; and culturally, the pitting of a "Greek" ideal of life, derived in large part from the German Hellenists, against a rejected "medieval" Christianity. (p. 169)

Their relationship is a curious combination of open, implied, and perhaps concealed borrowing; and of modification and correction, often through amplification. Whether as a stimulus or sometimes as an irritant, Arnold is surprisingly often at the base of Pater's most important statements concerning art, religion, and the problems of modern life. (pp. 169-70)

The decisive issues for both Arnold and Pater, as for the Germans, were the authority and viability of religion and religious experience, the split old wine of the past, in the modern synthesis, and the relation of religion to other aspects of life. That sustained critical effort entailed, as a result, a redefinition of human nature, the attempt to strike a new balance among the components of the human totality. . . . Their varying responses to "ascetic," "medieval," otherworldly Christianity become a touchstone of their own development. The responses vary from a virtual rejection of Christianity in favor of a classical ideal to the positing of two Christianities, one life-destroying and illegitimate, the other life-bestowing and humane. (p. 170)

[*Marius the Epicurean*] is not only the supreme intellectual and artistic effort of Pater's career, but it represents the ultimate reach of the dialectical impulse that had governed so much of his earlier career. Moreover, the ethical and intellectual thrust of Pater's dialectic is closely parallel to the central line of Matthew Arnold's development in the sixties and seventies. (p. 263)

The basic opposition of the book between Hellenic culture and a "visionary" religion informs each stage of the dialetic. The early contrast between the childhood religion and the young man's new Epicureanism is presented in terms of Arnold's dichotomy between "culture" and traditional Christianity, Hellenism and Hebraism. The second dichotomy, that marked out between Marcus Aurelius' Stoicism and early Christianity, is drawn . . . from Arnold's disparagement of Aurelius' melancholy in contrast to Christian "joy," in [Arnold's 1863 essay on Marcus Aurelius] and elsewhere. The final reach of Pater's dichotomizing impulse is achieved when he introduced a new disjunction within Christianity, one between the "humanistic" Christianity of the second century and the unsatisfactory "ascetic" Christianity of the Middle Ages. The rejected ascetic Christianity plays the role assigned to English Puritanism in the interplay of Hebraism and Hellenism in *Culture and Anarchy.* His favored version of Christianity hovers between two related ideals: one, a Christianized version of Arnold's culture or Hellenism, with several dashes of the religion of *Literature and Dogma;* the other, a naturalistic, nondogmatic Christianity not unlike that moralized secular Christianity of Arnold's religious writings of the seventies, though Pater pointedly eschews the heavily *moral* emphasis Arnold imparts to his reading of religious history and psychology.

The point of especial importance here is that *Marius* recapitulates not only a number of stages in Pater's own development but also, with significant changes of tone and emphasis, the crucial struggles of Arnold's career. . . . [Pater had] borrowed from Arnold's works the essential structure of his dilemmas,

[and] he now more systematically responds to a number of the very pressures that impelled Arnold continually to reshape the dilemmas and disjunctions of his own intellectual career. (pp. 266-67)

A review of Marius' career reveals that [the] ethical direction in Arnold's thought provides a pattern for the stages of Marius' spiritual progress. In tracing this movement, Pater not only revises a number of his earlier views but also subjects his own and Arnold's conception of culture to the kind of scrutiny given it by their critics; in this way, *Marius* becomes almost an epitome of the successive attempts by Arnold and Pater to shore up the assailable basis of culture. In the formation of Marius' Cyrenaicism, there are many echoes from *Culture and Anarchy* concerning mankind's deep yearning "towards ideal perfection," "completeness of life," "insight through culture," and culture as "a wide, a complete, education" and "the expansion and refinement of the power of reception." . . . Not only does Marius himself have a "poetic and inward temper," but he senses that his culture and "intellectual discipline" (referred to in Schiller's phrase as "an 'aesthetic' education") "might come even to seem a kind of religion—an inward, visionary, mystic piety, or religion." . . . Similarly, "the true aesthetic culture would be realisable as a new form of the contemplative life, founding its claim on the intrinsic 'blessedness' of 'vision,'" in a "world of perfected sensation, intelligence, emotion.". . . The first challenge to this ideal comes with the admission that culture may become "antinomian" by the standards of the received morality. . . . Pater's first answer to criticism is that the charge of immoralism and hedonism is not applicable to Marius' form of Cyrenaic reflection: "Not pleasure, but fulness of life," was his goal. . . . This phase of Marius' career even ends with a saving "inconsistency" in Marius, a note of limited selflessness. . . . The furthest reach of Marius' selfless feelings at this period is shown by his determination, not unconnected with the conscientious religion of his childhood, "to add nothing, not so much as a transient sigh, to the great total of men's unhappiness" . . .—which is a negative version of Arnold's "desire for . . . diminishing human misery," the "noble aspiration to leave the world better and happier than we found it.". . . (pp. 271-72)

Much of volume II is preoccupied with the possibility, under the new Stoical influence, of an "adjustment" between "the old morality" and the Epicurean view of things. The old morality had been allowed no place in Marius' intellectual scheme because he feared its first principles might stand in the way of his goal of "a complete, many-sided existence." Now he fears that this dismissal reveals a "graceless 'antinomianism.'" Aware of "a strong tendency to moral assents," his concern becomes "to find a place for duty and righteousness in his house of thought.". . . In this "search after some principle of conduct," for some "theoretic equivalent to so large a proportion of the facts of life," Marius finds a temporary clue in Cornelius Fronto's defense of "the purely aesthetic beauty of the old morality.". . . Pater has now arrived almost exactly at the stage of culture indicated late in "Sweetness and Light," where Arnold speaks of the "best art and poetry of the Greeks, in which religion and poetry are one, in which the idea of beauty and of a human nature perfect on all sides adds to itself a religious and devout energy, and works in the strength of that.". . . Pater's "adjustment" of morality and culture is precisely the point of a key passage in "Hebraism and Hellenism" which describes the Greek "idea of a comprehensive adjustment of the claims of both the sides in man, the moral as well as the intellectual, of a full estimate of both, and of a reconciliation of both." . . . (pp. 272-73)

Chapter XVI, **"Second Thoughts,"** is at once Pater's most poignant defense of his aestheticism and the most telling critique of its limitations. The argument breaks neatly in the middle, and each half implicitly acknowledges different kinds of critical challenges. The framework is the "isolating narrowness" that Marius now sees in his scheme of life, by contrast with the "wide prospect over the human, the spiritual, horizon" revealed in the discourse of the Stoic Fronto. Marius applies his own aesthetic criterion of "loss and gain," or the "economy" of life, to determine whether his Epicureanism "missed something in the commerce of life, which some other theory of practice was able to include," and whether it "made a needless sacrifice.". . . This fear of "sacrificing" some part of consciousness, pervasive in *Marius,* seems clearly derived from Arnold's definition of the bent of Hellenism, "to follow, with flexible activity, the whole play of the universal order, to be apprehensive of missing any part of it, of sacrificing one part to another, to slip away from resting in this or that intimation of it, however capital." . . . At any rate, Pater's limited defense of Cyrenaicism takes the line that it is simply the philosophy of youth, ardent and sincere, but one-sided and even fanatical, the "vivid, because limited, apprehension of the truth of one aspect of experience.". . . (pp. 273-74)

In short, the doctrine is that of the idealistic young man and not of "the 'jaded Epicurean'.". . . The very intensity of his self-development makes him especially open to the appeal of religion: "he has, beyond all others, an inward need of something permanent in its character, to hold by.". . . Although truth admittedly resides "'in the whole'—in harmonisings and adjustments" (almost Arnold's very prescription of the "comprehensive adjustment" and harmonious "reconciliation" of the two sides of man's nature), the "nobler form of Cyrenaicism—Cyrenaicism cured of its faults" paradoxically merges with the religious temper:

> If it starts with considerations opposed to the religious temper, which the religious temper holds it a duty to repress, it is like it, nevertheless, and very unlike any lower development of temper, in its stress and earnestness, its serious application to the pursuit of a very unworldly type of perfection. The saint, and the Cyrenaic lover of beauty, it may be thought, would at least understand each other better than either would understand the mere man of the world. Carry their respective positions a point further, shift the terms a little, and they might actually touch. . . .

In this ultimate defense of a purified aestheticism, Pater can list the qualities of the nobler Cyrenaicism which approach those of the nobler phases of the traditional morality: "In the gravity of its conception of life, in its pursuit after nothing less than a perfection, in its apprehension of the value of time . . . it may be conceived, as regards its main drift, to be not so much opposed to the old morality, as an exaggeration of one special motive in it." . . . This rather strained performance, one of the most "synthesizing" in Pater, parallels Arnold's listing of the qualities in which culture is like religion—with the significant difference that Arnold's culture went *beyond* religion in inclusiveness, while Pater's aestheticism is somehow the extreme development of one aspect of religion itself.

Thus Pater refutes the charges of hedonism and antinomianism directed against the view of life expressed in the *Renaissance* by offering a purified and elevated aestheticism not only compatible with religion but actually especially conducive to religious vision. He goes on, in the second part of the argument, so far to acknowledge the charges of self-centeredness and narrowness as to shake the self-sufficiency of culture to its foundations. This new strategy takes the form of admitting that the older masters of Cyrenaic philosophy, though they experienced moments of almost "beatific" pleasure and knowledge, paid too high a price, "in the sacrifice of a thousand possible sympathies, of things only to be enjoyed through sympathy, from which they detached themselves, in intellectual pride." . . . By rejecting even the "higher view" of Greek religion available to the philosopher, these thinkers rejected a "whole comely system of manners or morals" which gracefully enveloped the whole of life and which would satisfy even the "merely aesthetic sense." . . . The failure of this Cyrenaic culture to profit by attention to Greek religion and Greek morality shows, Pater concludes, "their fierce, exclusive, tenacious hold on their own narrow apprehension." . . .—which is, by an amusing shift in rhetoric, the very terminology Arnold habitually employed to abuse English Puritans for their "rigidness and contentiousness" and for their "narrow and mechanical conception" of salvation. . . . But Marius, it is clear, must be carefully preserved from these harsher strictures: for it was perfection he had sought all along, even if a narrow perfection centered in "his capacities of feeling, of exquisite physical impressions, of an imaginative sympathy." . . . (pp. 274-76)

Chapter XIX, **"The Will as Vision,"** is crucial in presenting the growth of Marius' conscience and religious sense. His apprehensions of divinity are presented in some detail, and seem clearly to reflect Arnold's struggles with the idea of the transcendent in his writings of the seventies. Marius' speculation on a providential hand in his life and affairs, "an unfailing companion," brought him in the first place "an impulse of lively gratitude." . . . Under the direct influence of natural beauty, "he passed from mere fantasy of a self not himself, beside him in his coming and going, to those divinations of a living and companionable spirit at work in all things, of which he had become aware from time to time in his old philosophic readings," a "reasonable Ideal" known to the Greeks and to the Old and New Testaments. . . . He saw that

> his bodily frame . . . Nay! actually his very self—was yet determined by a far-reaching system of material forces external to it, a thousand combining currents from earth and sky. Its seemingly active powers of apprehension were, in fact, but susceptibilities to influence. The perfection of its capacity might be said to depend on its passive surrender, as a leaf on the wind, to the motions of the great stream of physical energy without it. And might not the intellectual frame also, still more intimately himself as in truth it was, after the analogy of the bodily life, be a moment only, an impulse or series of impulses, a single process, in an intellectual or spiritual system external to it, diffused through all time and place—that great stream of spiritual energy, of which his own imperfect thoughts, yesterday or to-day, would be but the remote, and therefore imperfect pulsations? . . .

Gratitude, a self not himself, the currents from earth and sky, susceptibilities to influence, passive surrender, the great stream of physical energy, the great stream of spiritual energy: these are some of the key terms and ideas of Arnold's theodicy and cosmology. Agnostic as to the "personality" of the transcendent element in things, Arnold prefers in *St. Paul and Protestantism* to define God as the *"stream of tendency by which all things strive to fulfil the law of their being."* . . . This sense of God as "the source of life and breath and all thngs" is the "infinite element," the "element in which we live and move and have our being, which stretches around and beyond the strictly moral element in us, around and beyond the finite sphere of what is originated, measured, and controlled by our own understanding and will." . . . "By this element," says Arnold, "we are receptive and influenced, not originative and influencing." . . . In *Literature and Dogma,* in discussing the origin of the religious impulse, Arnold again brings in those "facilities and felicities . . . suggestions and stimulations," to which visitations, he concludes, "we may well give ourselves, in grateful and devout self-surrender." . . . When Pater says that [the] sense of companionship with a transcendent force "evoked the faculty of conscience, . . . in the form . . . of a certain lively gratitude" . . . , he echoes the Arnold who speaks of "gratitude for righteousness," or put differently, who says that with the happiness brought by morality, comes a "sense of gratitude." . . . (pp. 276-78)

[Not until **"The Minor Peace of the Church"**] does Pater present his ultimate dialectical effort. Here Pater reasserts his Hellenic humanism, but now as one of the two traditions *within* historic Christianity and superior to Greek religion. The effect is to confound critics of the allegedly antireligious tone regarding culture in the ***Renaissance*** by showing it to be somehow the highest Christian ideal. Moreover, the poles of Pater's dialectic—the familiar ones of culture and a puritan Christianity: in a word, Hellenism and Hebraism—are taken bodily from Arnold. (p. 278)

[The] genius and power of Christianity, says Pater, are shown in the hope nurtured by Christian chastity. This chastity issued "in a certain debonair grace, and a certain mystic attractiveness, a courtesy, which made Marius doubt whether that famed Greek "blitheness," or gaiety, or grace, in the handling of life, had been, after all, an unrivalled success." . . . Again he adopts Arnold's previously rejected view that the Greek religion of gaiety and pleasure . . . was a "manifest failure" as a religion for men to live by. . . . (p. 279)

This view of Christianity as a more successful sponsor of grace and courtesy than pagan culture is the clue to Pater's remarkable development of what amounts to the idea of "two Christianities." Christian belief had inspired chastity, which in turn rehabilitated "peaceful labour" after the pattern of Christ, "another of the natural instincts of the catholic church, as being indeed the long-desired initiator of a religion of cheerfulness." . . . In Marius' mind, the favored version of "Christianity in its humanity, or even its humanism, in its generous hopes for man, its common sense and alacrity of cheerful service, its sympathy with all creatures, its appreciation of beauty and daylight," is sharply contrasted with Marcus Aurelius' burden of "unrelieved melancholy." . . . The clue to the nature of this humanistic Christianity lies in Pater's remark that "so much of what Marius had valued most in the old world seemed to be under renewal and further promotion." . . . At this stage of its exposition, this Christianity is simply Pater's Arnoldian culture and Hellenism taking to itself certain religious graces. . . .

[Pater then explains that the] major part of Christian history, before and after this brief episode under the Antonines, was the reign of the Christianity of "the dark ages," of an "austere *ascêsis,*" of "exclusiveness, . . . puritanism, . . . ascetic gloom" and "tasteless controversy." But this "gracious spirit" of the second century marked a Christianity true to the "profound serenity" in the soul of Christ and thus "conformable to the original tendency of its genius." It was the spirit of this better Christianity—"Amiable, in its own nature, and full of a reasonable gaiety"—which reasserted itself centuries later in St. Francis, Dante, and Giotto. . . . (pp. 279-81)

This theory of the two Christianities is only the prelude to an even more ambitious universal theory of ethical history:

> In the history of the church, as throughout the moral history of mankind, there are two distinct ideals, either of which it is possible to maintain—two conceptions, under one or the other of which we may represent to ourselves men's efforts towards a better life—corresponding to those two contrasted aspects . . . discernible in the picture afforded by the New Testament itself of the character of Christ. The ideal of asceticism represents moral effort as essentially a sacrifice, the sacrifice of one part of human nature to another, that it may live the more completely in what survives of it; while the ideal of culture represents it as a harmonious development of all parts of human nature, in just proportion to each other. . . .

There can be little doubt that this contrast between asceticism with its "sacrifice" and culture with its "harmonious development" is precisely that which Arnold makes the center of his discussion of Hebraism and Hellenism. There, intelligence and morality are two "forces," "in some sense rivals, . . . as exhibited in man and his history," which the world is attracted to in alternation. . . . The passage that probably comes closest to Pater's words is one in which Arnold says of Hellenism that "it opposes itself to the notion of cutting our being in two, of attributing to one part the dignity of dealing with the one thing needful, and leaving the other part to take its chance." . . . Pater had turned to Arnold's ethical and historical theory to explain the relations between Marius' Cyrenaicism and his broadening Stoic vision; here again, he draws on Arnold's definitions of Hebraism and Hellenism, but with a strikingly different balance of values. For it is evident that Pater's rather factitious Christianity as described in this chapter is in fact a blend of his own "comely" aestheticism and Arnold's Hellenism and culture, while the contentious kind of Christianity, militant, puritan, ascetic, exclusive, is parallel to Arnold's Hebraic English Protestantism. That the favored Christianity is indeed what "Marius had valued most in the old world" is confirmed by the characteristic vocabulary used concerning Christianity in this chapter—serene, blithe, debonair, sweetness, humanism, appreciation of beauty, freshness, grave and wholesome beauty, gracious spirit, amiable, reasonable gaiety, the grace of graciousness, tact, good sense, urbanity and moderation, cheerful liberty of heart, aesthetic charm, comely order, the graces of pagan feeling and pagan custom: the whole panoply of the Paterian rhetoric which had adorned, and given the characteristic resonance to, the often aggressively "pagan" Renaissance and Greek studies. The only potentially moral or mystical notions contained in the chapter are those of a cheerful service, a sympathy with all creatures, and the "priesthood and kingship'' of the soul—all undeveloped at this stage. Pater cannot of course be accused of deception; certainly his emphasis on ''the naturalness of Christianity'' . . . , Arnold's characteristic phrase in his later years, indicates both some of the source of this religion, as well as its metaphysical status. (pp. 281-82)

Fairness demands, of course, that this crucial chapter on the ''Minor Peace'' be seen as only a stage, not the ultimate reach, of Marius' pilgrimage. There is more to the religion of this chapter than Winckelmannian or Goethean Hellenism in blasphemous disguise for this is not merely Arnold's culture in its more religious mood. I believe that when Pater makes ''a cheerful temper'' the special quality of Christian character . . . , he is reflecting Arnold's more deeply moral conviction, in the religious writings, that ''Christianity is, first and above all, a temper, a disposition.'' . . . In one of his most conciliatory moods, in *St. Paul and Protestantism,* Arnold insists that both Hebraism and Hellenism are ''beauty and charm''; if Hellenism is ''amiable grace and artless winning good-nature, born out of lucidity, simplicity, and natural truth,'' Christianity . . . is ''grace and peace by the annulment of our ordinary self through the mildness and sweet reasonableness of Christ.'' Both, then, are ''eminently *humane.*'' . . . *Literature and Dogma* repeatedly stresses that authentic Christianity—as opposed to the strange ''aberrations'' of medieval asceticism—consists in a spirit of ''mercy and humbleness,'' ''meekness, inwardness, patience, and self-denial,'' and ''the exquisite, mild, winning felicity'' of Jesus. . . . Now Pater's Christ and his ''amiable'' Christianity are of the very same spiritual quality: Christ is ''the Good Shepherd, serene, blithe and debonair,'' who announces ''a reign of peace—peace of heart''; this ''spirit of a pastoral security and happiness'' reflects the ''profound serenity,'' ''the peaceful soul,'' of Jesus; and the Church is ''a power of sweetness and patience.'' . . . (pp. 282-83)

[But] Pater parts company with Arnold precisely . . . at the moment of Marius' rather abortive beautifying vision. Marius' point of view is curiously double: he retains the essential norm, and the phrases, of the **''Wordsworth''** essay, insisting on ''vision'' or *seeing* as the end of life, above *having* or *doing.* This vision of ''beauty and energy'' in things implies using life, ''not as the means to some problematic end, but, as far as might be . . . an end in itself.'' . . . On the other hand, it is just this ''elaborate and lifelong education of his receptive powers'' which enables Marius to open himself, however tentatively, ''towards possible further revelation some day—towards some ampler vision.'' Marius remains forever poised, the house of his soul ''ready for the possible guest,'' buoyed up by ''the great hope.'' . . . Both halves of this double vision fall outside the purview of Arnold's agnostic Christian moralism. The intense ethical strain in Arnold's religious writings strives for an active engagement with the world beyond even the highly qualified aesthetic views of *Essays in Criticism* and *Culture and Anarchy;* at the same time, despite certain hints of companionship with Christ and of a ''mystical'' self-surrender to the not ourselves, there emphatically will be no further revelation, no possible guest, in the cleanswept house of Arnold's religion of *joy in righteousness.* (pp. 284-85)

> *David J. De Laura, in his* Hebrew and Hellene in Victorian England: Newman, Arnold, and Pater, *University of Texas Press, 1969, 370 p.*

RICHARD L. STEIN (essay date 1975)

The tendency of *The Renaissance* is to simplify its material, to reduce the Renaissance itself to a few major figures, and to reduce their own significance to the meaning of a few central episodes or works. Pater's object is to merge the roles of historian and aesthetic critic, presenting history as a series of intense sensations, until it is impossible to distinguish the form from the content of the past. Far more than Ruskin, Pater self-consciously develops an art of history, which involves new techniques for the analysis of the past and new standards for the sort of materials that characterize an epoch. The revolutionary quality of *The Renaissance* depends not merely on a reinterpretation of the meaning of a particular historic period but also on a reassessment of the nature of history itself. (p. 224)

[The] doctrine of Heraclitean flux enunciated in the **''Conclusion''** to *The Renaissance* provides a philosophic justification for the aestheticism of Pater's historic method. A successful account of history must . . . impose its own order on the randomness of human events. Indeed, as implied in the Biblical epigraph to *The Renaissance,* . . . only the metaphoric captures the essence of events or human relations: ''Yet shall ye be as the wings of a dove.'' The emphasis on metaphor is repeated in the opening of the first historical study in the book, **''Two Early French Stories,''** with a rhythmic evocation of the past in the language of a fairy tale: ''The history of the Renaissance ends in France, and carries us away from Italy to the beautiful cities of the country of the Loire.'' This wistfully contemplative tone persists throughout the book, as does the image of time as a flowing stream. Rivers reappear as metaphors for time and history in the essays on Leonardo and Giorgione, as well as in the language of the **''Conclusion,''** where Pater describes the ''whirlpool'' of thought, the endless ''drift'' of experience, and the ''flood of external objects'' which constitutes our impression of the world. . . . The force of these metaphors, as of the entire **''Conclusion,''** suggests that experience is a rich, mysterious, elusive process, which art alone can arrest into significant moments. The artists and art works Pater chooses as subjects form a series of such beautiful historic moments through which the vague phenomenon called ''Renaissance'' makes itself known and gains its only real existence.

Thus . . . the meaning of the past is made convincing by its potential to be treated as fiction. Indeed, *The Renaissance* reads like a novel. Despite the seeming limits of history and actual artifacts, Pater creates the illusion we demand from any successful fictional work—that it engross us in a self-contained, orderly world entirely of the author's making. In *The Renaissance,* history becomes a delightful fable, narrated with soothing precision, a prose poem formed out of the materials of biography, literature, and art. Fact is transformed consistently by a fictional impulse; and it is finally to the fiction, a unified collection of interpretations of the past, that Pater assigns the label ''history.'' (p. 225)

One of the central fictional themes of the book is the narration of an historic evolution of temperament, culminating in Pater's ideal modern type. The essays written expressly for *The Renaissance*—the **''Preface,'' ''Two Early French Stories,'' ''Luca della Robbia,''** and **''Joachim Du Bellay''**—form conspicuous links in an effort to arrange the rest of the volume into a gradual but distinct progress toward this terminal point. Luca della Robbia, for example, who is not particularly colorful in and for himself, appears as a transitional sculptor in the progress leading to Michelangelo. The essay on Joachim Du Bellay is laced with the themes of the essays on Leonardo and Winckelmann, and serves as a bridge between them. Pater himself remarks in the **''Preface''** (also appearing for the first time) that the newly published essay on **''Two Early French Stories''** and the essay on Du Bellay help define "the unity of the series." . . . His description of this unity makes clear that it is not merely chronological but a personal harmony as well, as if *The Renaissance* will define a perfect, universal type of life: "The Renaissance, in truth, put forth in France an aftermath, a wonderful later growth, the products of which have to the full that subtle and delicate sweetness which belongs to a refined and comely decadence, just as its earliest phases have the freshness which belongs to all periods of growth in art, the charm of *ascesis,* of the austere and serious girding of the loins in youth." . . . (pp. 226-27)

Pater's biographies outline the characteristics of a general Renaissance type, dressed in assorted historical costumes, defining the most vital possibilities of human personality as they have been expressed from the twelfth century to the present day. The **"Conclusion"** only solidifies the impression which should have grown since the **"Preface"** that the book defines an ideal form of selfhood. There is, in this sense, a "hero" of Pater's *Renaissance,* a disembodied sensibility whose identity is gradually characterized over time. This form of being, which is most prominent in the lives of great artists and thinkers, is to be recovered in the nineteenth century not only through the creation of great art but through the study of great art and artists in the past. Thus, in the **"Conclusion"** the modern form of an ideal past existence merges with the role of Pater's "aesthetic critic"—"How shall we pass most swiftly from point to point, and be present always at the focus where the greatest number of vital forces unite in their purest energy?" . . .

Before that final "success in life" when he will "burn always with this hard, gemlike flame," Pater's disembodied "hero" passes through a gradual cultural development. He enjoys his infancy and youth in the guises of the naïve characters of the "early French stories" and in Pico della Mirandola's "childish" ideal of a simple, "limited" world, still as lovely and manageable as "a painted toy." . . . The middle of the book describes a kind of historical summer, in which minor advances in the progress of the human spirit are stored up for the use of greater men. With Michelangelo this growth attains "immense, partiarchal age," . . . until in the person of Leonardo da Vinci, "Italian art dies away as a French exotic." . . . As Leonardo retires to the court at Amboise, one of "the beautiful cities of the country of the Loire," the cycle projected in the first pages of the volume is complete. Returning to the homeland of Abelard, also discussed in the first essay, Pater introduces in Leonardo's dying place the locale in which Du Bellay and the Pleiad wrote. Thus, the themes of decay and death link the aging Renaissance figure . . . to the tragic condition of modern life depicted at the end of the essay on Winckelmann and in the **"Conclusion."** (p. 227)

Du Bellay's modern ennui and tragic early death link him to Winckelmann, whose murder is a symbol within *The Renaissance* for the fate of the modern aesthetic consciousness. The point of the parallel is partly that the ideal Renaissance man cannot survive long in the contemporary world—but his is still a possible condition to which the modern mind can aspire. By ending with an eighteenth-century art critic, a figure sharply resembling himself, as well as with the modern references of the **"Conclusion"** itself, Pater insists that his Renaissance "hero" has a role in the nineteenth century, that as he suggests in **"Winckelmann,"** such "culture" is not "a lost art." . . . (p. 228)

The only illustration in the book [the frontispiece by Leonardo] confirms this sense that Pater's object is to define a single, consummate Renaissance type. . . . Pater describes the drawing as "a face of doubtful sex," which suggests that he also found in it a more personal significance and appeal. As the first image to be encountered on opening the book, it stands as a concrete if slightly ambiguous illustration that life itself can become symbolic and gain aesthetic unity. In his chapter on Leonardo, Pater compares the drawing to another series of bizarre bisexual images by the artist, which Pater calls "Daughters of Herodias." Pater's language suggests the almost magical ambiance of these figures:

> They are the clairvoyants, through whom, as through delicate instruments, one becomes aware of the subtler forces of nature, and the modes of their action, all that is magnetic in it, all those finer conditions wherein material things rise to that subtlety of operation which constitutes them spiritual, where only the final nerve and the keener touch can follow. It is as if in certain significant examples we actually saw those forces at their work on human flesh. Nervous, electric, faint always with some inexplicable faintness, these people seem to be subject to exceptional conditions, to feel powers at work in the common air unfelt by others, to become, as it were, the receptacle of them, and pass them on to us in a chain of secret influences. . . .

Such images not only reveal life being transformed into higher and subtler forms; they possess the power, as apparently does the frontispiece itself, to lure us under the spell of the same magic. And *The Renaissance* as a whole implies that such an experience reveals to us the essence of the past.

As history for Pater is subsumed within the history of the fine arts, art history in turn is contained within the history of its masterpieces. In tracing the history of this "many-sided movement," he passes "swiftly from point to point" in order to focus on the essential, formative moments in the past, to contemplate the intense creations through which history is made. Pater's history thus divides into a series of essays on individual geniuses, and he selects artists whose work lends itself to a masterpiece approach. . . . [In Pater's work,] the masterpiece serves as a kind of prism to history, refracting all its varied forms of light onto a brilliant, unified image of crystalline beauty. Similarly, the greatest artists are those who manage to express forces larger than themselves; aesthetic, social, and historical "centrality" represents the very quintessence of genius for Pater. It is precisely this quality that fifteen years later in the essay on **"Style"** he defines as the keynote of "great art"—the condition of art when "it has something of the soul of humanity in it, and finds its logical, its architectural place, in the great structure of human life." . . . (pp. 228-30)

The Renaissance concentrates on masterpieces of the fine arts (in which Pater seems to include philosophy) in order to locate them within a larger "structure" of culture and history. In every work subject to close examination one can discover the resonance of associations from the memory of the individual and, indeed, of the entire race; history is concentrated and recapitulated in every decisive aesthetic moment. . . . [The masterpiece, then,] is not merely a vehicle of a wide range of intense "impressions" but the medium in which one can enjoy the distilled experience of other epochs. Very much as does Ruskin, he implies that we actually enter history through our sympathetic appreciation of the arts. Contemplating artistic masterpieces . . . we participate in the essential energies of the past. (pp. 230-31)

The Renaissance as a whole sacrifices comprehensive chronology and sociological accuracy for the vague but powerful flavor of certain significant moments. Its structure imitates the progress of history, the flowering of its energies, by moving from masterpiece to masterpiece in a series of deliberate crescendo effects. We are forced to view events and personalities through the isolated but pregnant images of the arts. The structure of the book makes an understanding of history dependent on a full response to its central aesthetic creations. Graham Hough has complained that the essays "tend to split up in the mind of the reader into a few famous purple passages" [see excerpt above, 1948]. But this is an intentional consequence of the expressive form of the book. History for Pater is a series of dramatic flowerings and realizations. Great personalities, significant events, consummate works of art all embody the potential of vital human impulses to find new and exciting forms of expression. *The Renaissance* demonstrates that history becomes meaningful only when it fuses with art—when, as in Ruskin's Venice, reality and the imagination wholly interpenetrate one another. The body of each separate essay forms a background of distinct events, personalities, and artistic traditions that Pater will draw together at a few central moments, usually moments of artistic creation. In this way the chief works of art celebrated in *The Renaissance* sum up all the varied contexts defined in the rest of the book, and give the rest of history a kind of fictional unity. (p. 231)

Pater traces the history of civilization through its chief artifacts in much the same way as Ruskin did with architecture in *The Stones of Venice*. But the distinction between their subject matter immediately underscores the extent of Pater's achievement, for unlike Ruskin, he is not dealing with public arts. Ruskin deliberately excluded painting from the chronology of the Venetian mind that he established by the evidence of Gothic. He argued that painting lags slightly behind the public consciousness, that as a personal creation, it can be secluded and even anachronistic. Pater not only traces the history of the Renaissance mind through private creations but offers as examples relatively minor artists, who stood out of the cultural mainstream and probably exerted only a small influence on it. Della Robbia is the most obvious example, but the interest in minor achievements is observed elsewhere. Pater limits his discussion of Michelangelo to his poetry, as if to concentrate on the least public aspect of his genius. The "early French stories" are chosen precisely for their quiet uniqueness. Botticelli was a minor, almost unknown artist for the audience of the 1870s. Even Giorgione, by virtue of the reattribution of most of the famous pictures once ascribed to him, becomes an increasingly shadowy figure. . . . We find ourselves in a tenuous, "perishable" realm of history. Pater establishes an intentionally personal tradition, so that questions of influence become ambiguous and subtle. For him the progress of civilization is as complex and "many-sided" as for Ruskin it was simple, direct, and morally explicit. Pater's almost eccentric choice of Renaissance subjects enables him to keep his version of history from becoming a Ruskinian moral chronology, and indeed, the ethical status of many of the figures he treats is kept deliberately uncertain. (p. 232)

To distinguish between "major" and "minor" figures in history implies an assessment of the individual in terms of his culture; Pater's technique is precisely the reverse. He defines the period in terms of its most suggestive figures. There is an implicit equation between the personalities that yield the most "impressions" to an aesthetic historian and those that, like artistic masterpieces, sum up within themselves major currents of history. To depict the spirit of the Renaissance as a whole, then, Pater needs only to assemble a series of suggestive individual portraits, creating a composite portrait of the complete, ideal Renaissance type. The volume as a whole narrates the development of this disembodied figure. Each study adds another contour to the outline; each new personality discussed supplies another element of the richness of mind to which the period as a whole aspired. Including subjects of so many different sorts, "major" as well as seemingly "minor" artists and works, illustrates the scope of aesthetic interests and human accomplishments contained within the age. Pater implies through the very breadth of figures under consideration that no human impulse is excluded from his concept of the harmonious, complete Renaissance type. (p. 233)

> *Richard L. Stein, "History As Fiction in 'The Renaissance',' " in his* The Ritual of Interpretation: The Fine Arts As Literature in Ruskin, Rossetti, and Pater, *Cambridge, Mass.: Harvard University Press, 1975, pp. 213-59.*

GERALD MONSMAN (essay date 1980)

[*Monsman provides a psychological interpretation of Pater's works based on the theory that writers exorcise fundamental psychological conflicts by reclaiming their identities or "parenting" themselves in the act of literary creation.*]

About 1887-88 [Pater] seems to have faced a creative crisis that caused him to abandon at midpoint the autobiographical "trilogy" he had begun with *Marius the Epicurean* . . . and was continuing in *Gaston de Latour*. . . . The origin of this crisis lay in the childhood loss of both Pater's father and mother, a dreaded yet desired separation from parental dominance that left an indelible sense of guilt and remorse for having somehow caused or willed their deaths. Pater dealt with this guilt by a textual sublimation or displacement, exorcising his conflicting emotions through the act of autobiography. There, in the text, the paternal figure, reembodied as any preexisting work or critically conservative dogma, is slain so that the younger, as the autobiographical author of his life, might endow himself with that paternity for which as a child he had insatiably yearned. But when in 1887 the death of his elder brother William had summoned that old sense of triumph and remorse for the third time in Pater's life, the public autobiographical assumption of paternity could no longer appease the private guilt. Owing to the hostility of critics who irrevocably linked him with those errant sons, his decadent disciples, Pater balked at taking upon himself the role of father. Because there could be no satisfactory public exchange of roles, there could be no private discharge of the burden of blood-guilt, and "the hand collapses."

The relation between Pater's private psychological drama and the form or structure of his fiction is a shared reflexiveness: the turning of the child back upon the parent is echoed in the multiple levels of the reflexive text turning back perpetually upon each other. . . . [More] than any other Victorian Pater succeeded, by heroic force of intellect spurred on by the most painful of psychological urgencies, in giving a new emphasis to the point of view involved in the act of artistic creation; that is, to the processes and problems of consciousness and to the activities of reading and composition as themselves the subjects of fiction. In this, Pater inevitably seems something of an anomaly as a Victorian, a transitional figure who was in, but no longer of, the nineteenth century. But against whom, then, should he be scaled if not his contemporaries? The immediate answer—the "old masters" of twentieth-century fiction, Conrad, Joyce, Woolf—is certainly not wrong; but it would be more exciting to see Pater as a figure impressively bridging the gap between romanticism and postmodernism, between nineteenth-century fictional models and those ultrareflexive writers whose fictional worlds invariably lead back to the generative activity of art itself: Borges, Beckett, Robbe-Grillet, Leiris, Nabokov, Fowles, Barth, Barthelme, to name several. What these writers openly proclaim (a bit shrilly at times) Pater had whispered elegantly but urgently: language does not merely imitate reality but creates it. (pp. 3-5)

Pater neither knew his father (Richard Glode Pater died prematurely—significantly, the males in the family all died early—and afterward Walter could scarcely remember him) nor, being "all powerful in written word, impotent in life," had he a child—except the text.

To understand this motif of paternity as it relates to Pater's life and art, one must begin with the relation of father and son in his earliest and most explicitly autobiographical portrait. . . . Reflecting as it does the paternal-filial relationship, **"The Child in the House"** is . . . the source of Pater's imaginative, autobiographical work. In the portrait, Pater's deceased father, depicted as a soldier dead in India, becomes a ghostly presence the child "hated." . . . This antagonism that Florian-Pater initially feels toward the absent father is, typically, that sense of a broken wholeness, the absent godhead, halves disjoined. Although the connection is not overtly stated, certain militaristic-biblical figures (Joshua, Jacob, Aaron, Moses) assume the paternal role and develop the idea of the recovered father as the "sacred double" who is "at once the reflex and the pattern" . . . of the child's nobler self. In this recovery of his father within "sacred history," . . . Florian anticipates Gaston's perception of the Latour family record as "a second sacred history." . . . (pp. 79-80)

"The Child in the House" closes with a symbolic death in which the house appears to the child who has left it to be "like the face of one dead." . . . [The house] is expressive of an outworn, "dead" classical form which must be paternally rejuvenated. [In *Marius the Epicurean,* the] generations of ancestors laid away in the dusty family mausoleum at White-nights represent Marius's own dead heritage, but a heritage which the recovery of the father will be able to revitalize. There in the mausoleum Marius the son is symbolically buried with his mother ("this boy of his own age had taken filial place beside her there, in his stead"), and he becomes identified with his father:

> That hard feeling, again, which had always lingered in his mind with the thought of the father he had scarcely known, melted wholly away, as he read the precise number of his years, and reflected suddenly—He was of my own present age. . . . And with that came a blinding rush of kindness, as if two alienated friends had come to understand each other at last. . . .
>
> (pp. 80-1)

The textual nature of the recovery of this paternal figure is significant. . . . [In **"The Child in the House,"**] the centrality of the text is affirmed through the recovery of the father in the holy pictures of the sacred book. . . . So too, in Marius's ritual of death and rebirth, the discovery of identity with his father

comes through the act of *reading* the inscription on his tomb. Fulfilling paternity in his act of sacrifice, Marius discovers Cornelius to be " 'More than brother!' . . .—'like a son also!' " through whom he can possess the future "even as happy parents reach out, and take possession of it, in and through the survival of their children." . . . Further, Marius's paternity and Cornelius's possession of futurity refer back to Pater's role as autobiographer; for in the year *Marius* was published, . . . Pater himself was, like Marius, "the precise number of years" that his own father had been when, at age forty-five, he had died. As Marius and Pater attain the age at which their respective fathers died, each in turn enacts a ritual designed to father himself anew, Pater's act of writing the novel becoming thereby, on the deepest level, the subject of the autobiographical narrative itself. In producing his autobiography, re-creating his life textually, Pater becomes both a father and a son. He fathers the text, and yet that text is his own life, himself. Pater thereby becomes his own *pater* [father], compensating for the actual father he could scarcely remember.

Pater's loss of his father at the age of two and a half and his lifelong effort to regain the absent paternal presence belong to a larger pattern of psychological trauma. At the age of fourteen, Pater also unexpectedly lost his mother. . . . Although Maria Pater died at a moment when her son, not happy at school, must have especially needed her comfort, his dependence would have been balanced also by a desire for freedom. One recalls Marius's relief in the liberty afforded him by the death of his father whom he perceived as hard and stern; Pater as a very young child, but not so young as not to have felt an oedipal rivalry with the father for his mother's favors, may have perceived the sudden death of his father as a consequence of his own will. Of course, an ambiguity of feeling results: the removal of the rival is achieved, but guilt and an insatiable yearning for the absent father's love arise. Afterward, the mother's death suddenly constitutes this paradoxical condition of loss and gain as a pattern. . . . [It is likely that, for Pater,] the traumatic occurrence of a dreaded yet desired separation from parental dominance, exacerbated by a sense of power misused for destruction, created an indelible sense of guilt and remorse for having caused or willed [his mother's] sudden death. Such an inference can be supported by an analysis of the overdetermined passages in Pater's writings which reveal his autobiographical fears and desires. (pp. 81-3)

[The] most transparently autobiographical projection may well be given by Pater in his essay on Botticelli. There he writes that Botticelli's Madonnas "shrink from the pressure of the divine child, and plead in unmistakable undertones for a warmer, lower humanity," . . . a mother-son relationship which seems undeniably a reflection of Pater's own sense of maternal experience. (p. 84)

The central passage, a description of the Uffizi *Madonna del Magnificat,* is as follows:

> Her trouble is in the very caress of the mysterious child, whose gaze is always far from her, and who has already that sweet look of devotion which men have never been able altogether to love, and which still makes the born saint an object almost of suspicion to his earthly brethren. Once, indeed, he guides her hand to transcribe in a book the words of her exaltation, the *Ave,* and the *Magnificat,* and the *Gaude Maria,* and the young angels, glad to rouse her for a moment from her dejection, are eager to

hold the inkhorn and to support the book. But the pen almost drops from her hand, and the high cold words have no meaning for her, and her true children are those others, among whom, in her rude home, the intolerable honour came to her, with that look of wistful inquiry on their irregular faces which you see in startled animals—gipsy children, such as those who, in Apennine villages, still hold out their long brown arms to beg of you, but on Sundays become *enfants du choeur* [choirboys], with their thick black hair nicely combed, and fair white linen on their sunburnt throats. . . .

Pater has read into Botticelli's painting the predicament of a commonplace mother, able neither to love her gifted child (whose otherworldly look of devotion perhaps was duplicated in the pietistic young Pater) nor even to fathom his destiny. Although, significantly, the child himself encourages the transcription of those words—the composition of the scriptural text—which testify to the mother's supposed beatific vision, feelings of inferiority threaten him in her clear preference for that "warmer, lower humanity" of his more active siblings. Whereas in *Marius* the idealized fantasy omitted the rival brother(s) and allowed the mother's attention to be focused wholly on Marius himself, here in the description of Botticelli's Madonna the psychic overtones of Pater's rivalry with William for the mother's affection come to the fore. Indeed, the concluding lines of the description, having forsaken Botticelli entirely, are located squarely within the precincts of Pater's own sphere of adult experience, on those irresistible beggars of money—or of love. In competition with this sensuous reality, even the Christ child loses. (pp. 84-5)

[One] must note that Pater's mother's name was also Mary— . . . in the Latin form of Botticelli's Madonna: *Maria* Pater. . . . [Not] only does her married name invoke the holy family (mother Maria and the fathering presence, Pater), but the close equivalence of Maria-Marius (similar to Amis-Amile, Denys-Dionysus, Apollo-Apollyon, or such veiled *doppelgängers* [doubles] as Florian-Flavian, Cecil-Cecilia, Apuleius-Aurelius, Gaston-Gabrielle, or even the alliterative Walter Pater) hints that the feminine has been elided with the masculine to create a figure that for Pater is a projection of both the maternal and paternal, as Marius's eventual identification with both mother and father at White-nights affirmed, Pater, orphaned child longing for the love of an absent father and a remote mother, and his mirrored opposite, Marius, the parental figure he himself has created, together dramatize that lost familial wholeness which only the textual dialectic between inner and outer levels of character and author can restore. As Marius lies dying, "the tablet of the mind white and smooth, for whatsoever divine fingers might choose to write there," . . . he waits for Pater in the next frame out to reconstitute his wholeness and is thus turned back upon the divine child of the Uffizi *Magnificat* who himself will write those words in a book that will bestow lasting glory upon the parent. The dying parent is replaced by the child who, through the power of the autobiographical text to recreate himself, has assumed the parental role. In this, the character within the work of fiction has become the author of the fiction he is in, the inner frame swallowing the outer, the work turning itself inside out.

The metamorphosis of the mother who seems first to destroy the child with a threatening sense of inferiority but who ultimately is herself totally subordinated to his reputation is akin to the dialectical transformations of Dionysus who is ultimately "both the hunter and the spoil." . . . That this vindication of the son involves an almost mythic measure of hostility and violence, as well as an enormous guilt, seems clear from a number of considerations. For example, Pater was drawn to Charles Lamb not only because he was the closest writer in temperament and style that Pater had read; not only because Lamb, living with his sister, was an inescapable double of Pater and his sister(s); but most darkly because Mary Lamb actually killed her mother as Pater feared he himself had had the power to do as a child. Charles's sister Mary was both a reflection of Pater's mother (Mary-Maria) and a component of his own nature: she is that murderous double which slays the mother and yet as Mary (gentle as a lamb) *is* the mother herself. Pater, I think, was struck by the same conflict of impulse and restraint in the Lambs' lives as in his; and toward the end of his essay he explains Lamb's very Paterian languor as shock at discovering himself to have survived a Greek tragedy. . . . [In the] final paragraph of the essay, Pater recalls that at his childhood home of Enfield, which the Lambs had left barely a decade earlier, beneath the tame and humdrum "surface of things" lie violent alternations of atmosphere—"nowhere is there so much difference between rain and sunshine"—perpetually transforming the place and the individual with its "portent of storm in the rapid light on dome and bleached stone steeples." . . . This atmospheric alternation has its counterpart in the landscape of Denys's Auxerre, attractive for its mixtures of mood "when the tide of light and distant cloud is travelling quickly over it, when rain is not far off, and every touch of art or of time on its old building is defined in clear grey." . . . Foreshadowing in Denys's portrait the ceaselessly interacting antinomies which destroy and renew, this alternation of rain and sun in the essay on Lamb, in the only directly personal recollection in the whole range of Pater's writings, implies that Lamb's memories have become Pater's fantasies, not of place alone but also of murderous circumstance.

Significantly, parricide occurs at the structural center of *Marius the Epicurean* in the chapter **"Manly Amusement."** And, within this chapter, at its exact center lies the sentence narrating the beginning of the amusing games: "The arena, decked and in order for the first scene, looked delightfully fresh," . . . Finally, at the center of the arena . . . and bespeaking that middle moment of destruction and renewal spread "certain great red patches." . . . There in the central chapter of *Marius* at the center of the arena is the blood on the sand, indicative of that terrifying, cruel, mystical moment in which one life is given for another. In Pater's first translated story in *The Renaissance* . . . , he provides a variation on the myth of the Dioscuri in which the blood of the slain elder is given to "heal" the younger. This, the strongest image of blood in Pater's writings, occurs in the barbaric tale of Amis and Amile. . . . Amis, the leper with the wife who would strangle him, correlates with the figure of Castor, the mortal subject to death, whereas Amile, together his his wife who weeps over Amis and yearns to heal him, correlates with the elder Polydeuces who can bestow the gift of life. Or, to shift from the fraternal to the parental and read the tale in terms of another mythic paradigm, the wives embody the opposing traits of Demeter's daughters or of Artemis who is not only "the assiduous nurse of children, and patroness of the young," but also the goddess of death. . . . Amile beheads his children to obtain blood for a ritual washing so that Amis might be restored to health. But the would-be destruction of the child by the parent turns out to be a vicarious sacrifice of the parent for the sake of his offspring. Echoing the returns of Polydeuces and Persephone, the culminating restoration of Amis to health is thus paralleled by the return of the children to life, he being an equivalent for them.

So too, in the amusing games, Artemis is present in the arena as

> the symbolical expression of two allied yet contrasted elements of human temper and experience—man's amity, and also his enmity, towards the wild creatures, when they were still, in a certain sense, his brothers. She is the complete, and therefore highly complex, representative of a state, in which man was still much occupied with animals . . . as his equals, on friendly terms or the reverse,—a state full of primeval sympathies and antipathies, of rivalries and common wants . . .

The love-hate relationship of the arena with its slaughter of the pregnant animals can be seen to correspond to Pater's fantasy of slaying the mother in the place of the child. In this, Pater the orphaned son numbers himself among the newborn creatures who escape "from their mother's torn bosoms." . . . This same image occurs later in a slightly altered guise in the martyr Blandina whose "'whole body was torn asunder'." . . . Her symbolic maternity is attested to:

> 'Last of all, the blessed Blandina herself, as a mother that had given life to her children, and sent them like conquerors to the great King, hastened to them, with joy at the end, as to a marriage-feast; the enemy himself confessing that no woman had ever borne pain so manifold and great as hers' . . .

That the young may be enfranchised—albeit themselves sent to death but as the conquerors of death—the mother must be rent. (pp. 85-90)

In the chapter entitled **"Euphuism,"** Pater speaks of "the burden of precedent, laid upon every artist," . . . a theme connected with Marius's earlier yearning to be free from the gods' and his father's control. Yet the desire to break free of the burden of precedent leaves the writer with a sense of guilt for "a sympathy and understanding broken, . . . the thought of those averted or saddened faces grown suddenly strange to us." The way to "make it new" (as Ezra Pound later exhorted) without suffering the constraint of having alienated the past is simply to become the elder, the parent, by reweaving in one's own art the elements of the past. . . . As the alienation of Botticelli's Christ child is resolved by fathering the words in the book, so also the birth of Pater as an artist corresponds to his liberation from the past, from parental threats of inferiority or from literary precedent, by the assertion of his own paternity through writing. The ostensible "aim at an actual theatrical illusion" . . . in the games of the arena provides Pater with the perfect paradigm for the undermining of all those distinctions between parent and child, origin and repetition, subject and object, author and reader, center and margin. Thus, in contrast to the undeniable reality of the spectators in the grandstands, the "scene" in the ring seems illusory; but . . . the playacting turns out to be real. Pater perhaps had witnessed spectacles at Covent Garden or elsewhere; there the purpose would have been to create an illusion of reality, whereas at Rome the actual was made to seem merely staged. In the interplay between Rome and London, the opposition between center and margin becomes a perpetual turning back of the one upon the other so that in the world of the arena the question is perpetually open: which is the origin, the real? and which the repetition, the illusion? So, too, within the arena of the text there are no primordial, first parental figures to which the child need be subordinate. Pater becomes his own *pater* through a logic which prohibits the ontological determination of any one entity at the expense of the other. (pp. 91-3)

> *Gerald Monsman, in his* Walter Pater's Art of Autobiography, *Yale University Press, 1980, 174 p.*

ADDITIONAL BIBLIOGRAPHY

Beerbohm, Max. "Diminuendo." In his *The Works of Max Beerbohm,* pp. 163-75. New York: Dodd, Mead and Co., 1922.
> A reprint of Beerbohm's satirical account of his youthful disillusionment with Pater's epicurean philosophy.

Bowra, C. M. "Walter Pater." *The Sewanee Review* LVII, No. 3 (July-September 1949): 378-400.
> A thoughtful consideration of Pater's achievement as a critic, novelist, prose writer, and philosopher. In Bowra's estimation, Pater served as an "apostle of beauty" in fulfilling these functions, and helped to correct the Victorian tendency to compartmentalize beauty and goodness.

Buckler, William E. "*Marius the Epicurean*: Beyond Victorianism." In his *The Victorian Imagination: Essays in Aesthetic Exploration*, pp. 260-85. New York: New York University Press, 1980.
> Designates *Marius the Epicurean* as a "mythic modern classic" deserving to be ranked among the "apex-documents" of the nineteenth century.

Child, Ruth C. *The Aesthetic of Walter Pater*. New York: Macmillan Co., 1940, 157 p.
> An analysis of Pater's aesthetic theory. Child enlarges on Pater's recognition of the ethical value of art and underscores the accessibility and objectivity of his criticism.

Court, Franklin E. *Walter Pater: An Annotated Bibliography of Writings About Him*. An Annotated Secondary Bibliography Series on English Literature in Transition, 1880-1920, edited by Helmut E. Gerber. De Kalb: Northern Illinois University Press, 1980, 411 p.
> A comprehensive annotated bibliography of commentary published from 1871 through 1973 on Pater's life and works.

Crinkley, Richmond. *Walter Pater: Humanist*. Lexington: University Press of Kentucky, 1970, 186 p.
> A study designed to elucidate the humanistic principles upon which Pater founded his aesthetic philosophy and his art.

Downes, David Anthony. *Victorian Portraits: Hopkins and Pater*. New York: Bookman Associates, 1965, 176 p.*
> An exploration of the artistic affinities shared by Pater and Gerard Manley Hopkins, who became acquainted at Oxford.

Ellmann, Richard. "Overtures to 'Salome'." In his *Golden Codgers: Biographical Speculations*, pp. 39-59. London: Oxford University Press, 1973.*
> An inquiry into the sources and significance of Oscar Wilde's drama "Salome." Ellmann speculates that the work is an expression of Wilde's dual attraction to the opposing moralities presented to him through his association with Pater and John Ruskin.

Evans, Lawrence. Introduction to *Letters of Walter Pater*, by Walter Pater, edited by Lawrence Evans, pp. xv-xliv. Oxford: Oxford at the Clarendon Press, 1970.
> Enlightening commentary on Pater's personality and literary career, as revealed in his letters. Contrasting the man and his image, Evans writes: "This is not the correspondence of Mr. Rose [see excerpt above by William Hurrell Mallock]—there is nothing here of his 'aesthetic' silliness or leering immodesty—but one of whom

Vernon Lee saw in 1882 as a 'very simple, amiable man, avowedly afraid of almost everything.'''

Harris, Frank. "Walter Pater." In his *Contemporary Portraits, second series,* pp. 203-26. New York: Privately printed, 1919.
> A personal portrait drawn from Harris's recollections of his acquaintance with Pater.

Johnson, Lionel. "A Note Upon Mr. Pater." *The Academy* LI, No. 1289 (16 January 1897): 78-9.
> A notice of Pater's *Essays from "The Guardian".* Johnson urges Pater's readers to recognize his mentor's instinctive humanity and quiet mirth.

──────. "For a Little Clan." *The Academy* LVIII, No. 1484 (13 October 1900): 314-15.
> An appreciation inspired by the publication of the first edition of Pater's collected works. Johnson maintains that Pater's "little clan" of admirers will increase, and he predicts that he will continue to "live" by virtue of the "lovableness, the winning personality, of his gracious writings."

Kermode, Frank. *Romantic Image.* New York: Macmillan Co., 1957, 171 p.*
> An important study of the Romantic concept of the artist as a socially isolated visionary and its impact on twentieth-century literature and criticism. According to Kermode, Pater was a major influence in transmitting the doctrine of the artist's "separateness" to the twentieth century.

Knoepflmacher, U. C. "Walter Pater: The Search for a Religious Atmosphere" and "The 'Atmospheres' of *Marius the Epicurean.*" In his *Religious Humanism and the Victorian Novel: George Eliot, Walter Pater, and Samuel Butler,* pp. 149-88, pp. 189-223. Princeton: Princeton University Press, 1965.
> Analyzes Pater's fictional works as expressions of the Victorian attempt to satisfy religious yearning without benefit of a religious object. Knoepflmacher uses *Plato and Platonism* and *Marius the Epicurean* as his primary texts.

Lee, Vernon [pseudonym of Violet Paget]. "Valedictory." In her *Renaissance Fancies & Studies,* 2d ed., pp. 233-60. London: John Lane, The Bodley Head, 1909.*
> Includes a tribute to Pater as moral exemplar. Lee asserts that Pater's "spiritual evolution" from the perception of visible beauty to the knowledge of spiritual beauty teaches a harmonious approach to art and life.

Le Gallienne, Richard. "Walter Pater: *Marius the Epicurean*—Third Edition Revised." In his *Retrospective Reviews: A Literary Log, Vol. I,* pp. 174-81. London: John Lane, The Bodley Head; New York: Dodd Mead and Co., 1896.
> A reprinted review of the 1892 edition of *Marius the Epicurean.* An admirer of the original edition of *Marius,* Le Gallienne ascribes the numerous grammatical changes made in the 1892 edition to Pater's "morbid desire of punctuation."

Levey, Michael. *The Case of Walter Pater.* London: Thames and Hudson, 1978, 232 p.
> A reassessment of the nature of Pater's personality. Levey challenges Pater's reputation for donnish drabness by offering evidence of his vital—and sometimes courageous—commitment to religious, social, and intellectual heterodoxies.

Meisel, Perry. *The Absent Father: Virginia Woolf and Walter Pater.* New Haven: Yale University Press, 1980, 249 p.*
> A discussion of Pater's influence on Virginia Woolf as an essayist and novelist. Meisel hypothesizes that, just as Woolf was originally attracted to Pater's aesthetics as a means of escaping the intellectual domination of her father, the English critic Leslie Stephen, so she denied her manifest indebtedness to him for the same reason.

Monsman, Gerald. *Walter Pater.* Twayne's English Authors Series, edited by Sylvia E. Bowman, no. 207. Boston: Twayne Publishers, 1977, 213 p.
> A sound introduction to Pater's life and work.

[Oliphant, Margaret]. "The Old Saloon." *Blackwood's Edinburgh Magazine* CXLVII, No. DCCCXCI (January 1890): 131-51.*
> An unfavorable review of Pater's *Appreciations.* Oliphant is especially critical of the "Essay on Style."

Praz, Mario. "Byzantium." In his *The Romantic Agony,* 2d ed., translated by Angus Davidson, pp. 303-434. London: Oxford University Press, 1970.*
> Pages 422-23 include a lengthy note on Pater's decadent tendencies. Praz's remarks focus on Pater's alliance of beauty with death and decay.

Richards, I. A. "Adumbrations." In his *Coleridge on Imagination,* pp. 23-43. Bloomington: Indiana University Press, 1960.*
> Includes a stinging criticism of a passage in the "Essay on Wordsworth" in which Pater somewhat casually dismisses the distinction that Coleridge makes between the faculties of fancy and imagination. According to Richards, Pater's tone is patronizing, and his own contribution to the subject "amateur's work, mere nugatory verbiage—empty, rootless and backgroundless postulation—unless we put into it just that very piece of patient laborious analysis that it pretends so airily to dismiss or surpass."

Saintsbury, George. "Modern English Prose." *The Fortnightly Review* n.s. XIX, No. CX (1 February 1876): 243-59.*
> A discourse on the general decline of style in modern English prose. Saintsbury regards Pater's prose style in *Studies in the History of the Renaissance* as an exception to this trend and recommends that it be studied and imitated.

──────. "The Later Nineteenth Century, English Criticism from 1860-1900: Pater." In his *A History of Criticism and Literary Taste in Europe from the Earliest Texts to the Present Day: Modern Criticism,* Vol. III, pp. 544-51. Edinburgh: William Blackwood & Sons, 1904.
> Discusses Pater's importance as a literary critic. Saintsbury observes that Pater lacked "definite four-square originality" as a literary theorist, but credits him with formulating and consistently practicing modern critical methods.

──────. "Walter Pater." *The Bookman,* London XXX, No. 179 (August 1906): 165-70.
> An exposition of the "true Paterism." Saintsbury stresses the intellectual respectability and attractiveness of Pater's critical doctrines and condemns the notion that they are sanctions for irresponsible hedonism.

Seiler, R. M., ed. *Walter Pater: The Critical Heritage.* The Critical Heritage Series, edited by B. C. Southam. London: Routledge & Kegan Paul, 1980, 449 p.
> An extensive collection of commentary, including reviews, notices, tributes, and extracts from letters, journals, and books, which provides a profile of Pater's critical reputation between 1873 and 1911.

Symons, Arthur. *A Study of Walter Pater.* 1932. Reprint. Folcroft, Pa.: Folcroft Press, 1969, 112 p.
> A rather discursive work in which Symons reveals his personal impressions of Pater's thought, achievement, and personality.

Tillotson, Geoffrey. "Arnold and Pater: Critics Historical, Aesthetic and Unlabelled." In his *Criticism and the Nineteenth Century,* pp. 92-123. London: Athlone Press, 1951.*
> Compares Pater's critical theories and practices with those of Matthew Arnold, and discusses Pater's vagarious habits as a self-proclaimed "aesthetic" critic.

Ward, Anthony. *Walter Pater: The Idea in Nature.* London: Macgibbon & Kee, 1966, 202 p.
> An in-depth intellectual biography. Ward identifies the insecurities arising from modern theories of relativism as Pater's central intellectual preoccupation, and he maintains that Pater failed in his attempt to resolve his insecurities by adopting an Hegelian approach to nature wherein the relative principle would be subsumed under the stabilizing influence of the principle of *Geist.*

Wilson, Edmund. *Axel's Castle: A Study in the Imaginative Literature of 1870-1930.* New York: Charles Scribner's Sons, 1948, 319 p.*

An important study of the development of Symbolism in modern literature. According to Wilson, Pater contributed to the evolution of Symbolism in English letters by insisting on the subjectivity of experience and by transmitting the Symbolist faith in the sovereignty of the imagination to such writers as William Butler Yeats and Arthur Symons.

Wright, Samuel. *A Bibliography of the Writings of Walter H. Pater*. New York: Garland Publishing, 1975, 190 p.
> Provides a chronological record of all original periodical and book publications of Pater's writings as well as a bibliographical description of the collected and selected editions of his works.

Wright, Thomas. *The Life of Walter Pater*. 2 vols. New York: G. P. Putnam's Sons; London: Everett & Co., 1907.
> The earliest full-length Pater biography. Wright's account is held in disrepute by most scholars, but bibliographer Franklin E. Court concedes that the book is "indispensable" because it is the sole source for most of what is known of Pater's life.

Yeats, W. B. "The Tragic Generation." In his *Autobiographies,* pp. 277-349. London: Macmillan & Co., 1955.*
> A chapter from Yeats's autobiographical work *The Trembling of the Veil* which includes his reminiscences of The Rhymers' Club, a late nineteenth-century literary group whose chief members included Yeats, Ernest Dowson, Lionel Johnson, and Arthur Symons. Yeats suggests that the Paterian "attitude of mind" that the group adopted may have undermined the lives of his friends.

Henry David Thoreau

1817-1862

(Born David Henry Thoreau) American essayist, poet, and translator.

Thoreau is considered one of the key figures of the American Transcendental movement, and his *Walden; or, Life in the Woods,* a record of two years that he spent living alone in the woods near Concord, Massachusetts, is viewed as one of the finest prose works in American literature. Part autobiography, part fiction, part social criticism, *Walden* is a highly individual work. In it, Thoreau advocates a simple, self-sufficient way of life in order to free the individual from self-imposed social and financial obligations. He also pleads for a more intimate relationship between human beings and nature as an antidote to the deadening influence of an increasingly industrialized society. Though considered a nature book by many, *Walden* is not so much about nature as it is about Thoreau's response to nature, and it represents an experiment in Transcendentalism despite its attention to mundane detail and practical advice about everyday living. Although critics observe that Thoreau's ideas do not form a unified system of philosophy, his very way of life, marked by individualism and closeness to nature, embodied the tenets of American Transcendentalism as articulated by Ralph Waldo Emerson and others. His aphoristic yet lyrical prose style and intense moral and political convictions have secured his place beside Emerson as the most representative and influential of the New England Transcendentalists. He is considered along with such figures as Emerson, Nathaniel Hawthorne, and Herman Melville as a major nineteenth-century American author.

Born in Concord, Thoreau grew up in an atmosphere of genteel poverty. Although his father, a businessman with a history of failure, ultimately succeeded in pencil manufacturing, Thoreau's mother kept a boarding house to supplement the family's income. The only child in the family to receive a college education, Thoreau graduated in 1837 from Harvard, where he became interested in natural history, religious studies, the classics, and English, French, and German literature. Two important influences at Harvard were the famous naturalist Louis Agassiz and the rhetorics professor Edward Tyrel Channing. Following his commencement, Thoreau taught at the Concord Academy but was soon dismissed because of his opposition to corporal punishment. He and his brother John founded their own school in 1838 and became renowned for utilizing the progressive educational methods of the American Transcendentalist Amos Bronson Alcott. Yet Thoreau wanted to be a poet and when Emerson invited him in 1841 to live with him and his family in Concord, where he could write and earn his keep by acting as a general handyman, he accepted. The Concord community, already scandalized by Thoreau's unconventional way of life, ridiculed his lack of ambition and material success. However, Thoreau flourished with Emerson as his mentor. He kept an extensive journal and became an avid reader of Hindu scripture. He had ample time after his chores to write and think, and in Emerson's home he met many of the greatest figures of American Transcendentalism, including Sarah Margaret Fuller and George Ripley. Emerson and Fuller had recently founded a journal, the *Dial,* as the literary organ

of the New England Transcendentalists, and there they published Thoreau's first efforts in prose and poetry. Thoreau also worked as an assistant on the *Dial* and regularly lectured at the Concord Lyceum during this period. He briefly lived in New York during 1843 and 1844 as a tutor to Emerson's brother's children. When he returned to Concord, he supported himself by working as a surveyor, managing his father's pencil factory, and securing odd jobs around town. But Thoreau and Emerson had grown distant due to differences of opinion and temperament and were no longer on close terms.

On July 4, 1845, Thoreau moved to Walden Pond, located on Emerson's property, where he remained for almost two years. Though he was actually near Concord and had many visitors daily, Thoreau was regarded as a hermit, mystic, and eccentric, an image that was enhanced by a night he spent in jail in Concord in 1846. Thoreau was incarcerated for refusing to pay taxes to the commonwealth of Massachusetts because of its endorsements of slavery and the Mexican War; Thoreau was morally opposed to both. He explored the individual's right to dissent from a government's policies in accordance with his or her own conscience in his later political essays, where he also treated the issue of slavery. An active abolitionist in later years, Thoreau lectured widely and publically spoke against the Fugitive Slave Law of 1850. In keeping with his interest in naturalism, much of his writing and lecturing in the 1850s also concerned the conservation of natural resources. Thoreau had suffered from poor health most of his life and was stricken in 1860 with tuberculosis, from which he never recovered. Although Thoreau was considered cold, misanthropic, and disagreeable by some, he was much respected and admired by his circle of friends.

While some of Thoreau's poems, essays, and translations appeared in periodicals during his lifetime, most were not published until after his death. His two longer works, *A Week on the Concord and Merrimack Rivers* and *Walden*, both appeared during his lifetime. *A Week on the Concord and Merrimack Rivers*, a travel narrative interspersed with meditative essays, recounts a boating trip Thoreau took with his brother John in 1839. A leisurely, meandering book, it has been praised for its excellent nature descriptions, its joyous mood, and its union of the active and contemplative life. *Walden*, regarded by most critics as Thoreau's masterpiece, comprises a group of loosely connected essays which are organized in a seasonal sequence so that the narrative concludes in spring, a time of spiritual as well as natural rebirth. Thoreau telescoped his two years' experience at Walden Pond into the span of one year in order to fit his essays into his chosen time frame. Contemporary critics who had greeted *A Week on the Concord and Merrimack Rivers* with mixed reviews reacted to *Walden* with measured praise and also some cries of "humbug." Modern critics especially praise his playful, witty prose style in *Walden*, as well as the sense of humor manifested in his use of paradox, puns, and satire. Yet, whimsical and lyrical as Thoreau appears in *Walden*, he never loses sight of his philosophical intent—to insist on every person's right to independent thinking.

Thoreau's remaining writings can be generally divided into two groups—travel essays and political essays. *The Maine Woods, Cape Code, Excursions*, and the title piece of *A Yankee in Canada, with Anti-Slavery and Reform Papers*, are travel narratives. They combine perceptive observations about flora and fauna with Thoreau's philosophical musings. The political essays—"Resistance to Civil Government," later published as "Civil Disobedience," "Slavery in Massachusetts," "A Plea for Captain John Brown," and "Life without Principle" are impassioned rhetorical statements of Thoreau's belief in individual choice and responsibility. Thoreau's poems, mostly celebrations of nature, are most often considered banal, whereas his prose is usually seen by critics to be especially poetic. His *Journal*, because of its completeness and intensity, is sometimes named as his greatest literary achievement.

Though Thoreau was not well known during his lifetime outside the circle of New England Transcendentalists, his reputation has gradually grown. Assessment of his literary merits was long hampered by James Russell Lowell's disparagement of his early work. An extremely influential critic, Lowell accused Thoreau of being an imitator of Emerson and attacked what he saw as his egocentrism and lack of humor. Robert Louis Stevenson deemed Thoreau a "prig," a "skulker," and an idler, but valued his "singularly eccentric and independent mind." Ironically, Emerson's funeral elegy on Thoreau served to reinforce the image of Thoreau as a cold, reclusive man. Thoreau's admirers, however, came to his defense: John Burroughs praised his dedication as a naturalist and Amos Bronson Alcott and Ellery Channing offered testimonials to his personal warmth and charm. There had been a Thoreau critical revival at the centenary of his birth, but Thoreau's critical reputation did not really blossom until the 1930s when the depressed American economy imposed a radically frugal, Thoreauvian

life style on many people, and when Thoreau's ideas about individual freedom and responsibility stood out in stark relief against the growing threat of fascism. In the 1940s, encouraged by F. O. Matthiessen's landmark study of sense imagery in *Walden*, scholars turned their attention to more particular matters of Thoreau's style and diction. Critics now almost universally admire Thoreau's prose style for its directness, pithiness, and variety. Though Lowell termed his poetry "worsification," modern critics praise Thoreau's vivid use of imagery and irregular rhythms and suggest that his poetry anticipated the experimental verse of the twentieth century. Many of the most recent studies of Thoreau, aided by closer examination of his journals and letters, are psychological in approach.

During the nineteenth century, Thoreau was generally considered an obscure, second-rate imitator of Emerson. Twentieth century critics, however, rank him as one of the greatest figures in American literature. "Civil Disobedience" has influenced such diverse writers and leaders as Leo Tolstoy, Martin Luther King, Jr., Jack Kerouac, Mohandas Gandhi, and Allen Ginsberg. *Walden*, the work of a man who spent almost his entire life in his native town of Concord, has been translated into virtually every modern language and is today known all over the world.

(See also *Dictionary of Literary Biography*, Vol. I: *The American Renaissance in New England*.)

PRINCIPAL WORKS

"Resistance to Civil Government" (essay) 1849;
    published in journal *Aesthetic Papers*; also published as
    "Civil Disobedience" in *The Writings of Henry David
    Thoreau*, 1894-95
A Week on the Concord and Merrimack Rivers (essays)
    1849
"Slavery in Massachusetts" (essay) 1854; published in
    newspaper *The Liberator*
Walden; or, Life in the Woods (essays) 1854
"A Plea for Captain John Brown" (essay) 1860;
    published in journal *Echoes of Harper's Ferry*
"Walking" (essay) 1862; published in journal *The
    Atlantic Monthly*
Excursions (essays) 1863
"Life without Principle" (essay) 1863; published in
    journal *The Atlantic Monthly*
The Maine Woods (essays) 1864
Cape Cod (essays) 1865
A Yankee in Canada, with Anti-Slavery and Reform Papers
    (essays) 1866
Early Spring in Massachusetts (essay) 1881
Summer (essay) 1884
Winter (essay) 1888
Autumn (essay) 1892
The Writings of Henry David Thoreau. 20 vols. (essays,
    journal, letters, and poetry) 1906
Journal. 14 vols. (journal) 1949
*Consciousness in Concord: The Text of Thoreau's "Lost
    Journal" (1840-1841)* (journal) 1958
The Correspondence of Henry David Thoreau (letters)
    1958
Collected Poems (poetry) 1964

[JAMES RUSSELL LOWELL]   (essay date 1848)

[*Lowell was a celebrated nineteenth-century American poet, critic, essayist, and editor. He is noted today for his satirical and critical writings, including* A Fable for Critics, *a book-length poem featuring witty critical portraits of his contemporaries. Often awkwardly phrased, and occasionally vicious, the* Fable *is distinguished by the enduring value of its literary assessments. Commentators generally agree that Lowell displayed a judicious critical sense, despite the fact that he sometimes relied upon mere impressions rather than critical precepts in his writings. Most literary historians rank him with the major nineteenth-century American critics. Lowell's sentiments in the following excerpt from the* Fable *are representative of many contemporaries who viewed Thoreau as merely an imitator of Ralph Waldo Emerson. In his later review of* A Week on the Concord and Merrimack Rivers *(see excerpt below, 1865), however, Lowell offers a more positive view of Thoreau's work.*]

There comes ——, for instance; to see him's rare sport,
Tread in Emerson's tracks with legs painfully short;
How he jumps, how he strains, and gets red in the face,
To keep step with the mystagogue's natural pace!
He follows as close as a stick to a rocket,
His fingers exploring the prophet's each pocket.
Fie, for shame, brother bard; with good fruit of your own,
Can't you let neighbor Emerson's orchards alone?
Besides, 'tis no use, you'll not find e'en a core,—
—— has picked up all the windfalls before.

(p. 32)

[James Russell Lowell], in his A Fable for Critics: A Glance at a Few of Our Literary Progenies, *G. P. Putnam, 1848, 80 p.*

GEORGE RIPLEY   (essay date 1849)

[*In this essay, which first appeared in the* New York Tribune *in 1849, Ripley praises Thoreau's nature descriptions in* A Week on the Concord and Merrimack Rivers, *but criticizes his Transcendentalist philosophy. In doing so, he sounds a note which pervades later criticism of Thoreau's writings.*]

A really new book—a fresh, original, thoughtful work—is sadly rare in this age of omniferous publication. Mr. Thoreau's [*A Week on the Concord and Merrimack Rivers*], if not entirely this, is very near it. Its observations of Nature are as genial as Nature herself, and the tones of his harp have an Aeolian sweetness. His reflections are always striking, often profoundly truthful, and his scholastic treasures, though a little too ostentatiously displayed, are such as the best instructed reader will enjoy and thank him for. His philosophy, which is the Pantheistic egotism vaguely characterized as Transcendental, does *not* delight us. It seems second-hand, imitative, often exaggerated—a bad specimen of a dubious and dangerous school. (p. 1)

Mr. Thoreau is a native and resident of Concord, Massachusetts—a scholar, a laborer, and in some sort a hermit. He traveled somewhat in his earlier years (he is still young) generally trusting to his own thoughts for company and his walking-cane for motive power. It would seem a main purpose of his life to demonstrate how slender an impediment is poverty to a man who pampers no superfluous wants, and how truly independent and self-sufficing is he who is in no manner the slave of his own appetites. (pp. 1-2)

Half the book is [good]. . . .—Nearly every page is instinct with genuine Poetry except those wherein verse is haltingly attempted, which are for the most part sorry prose. Then there is a misplaced Pantheistic attack on the Christian Faith. (p. 6)

[Thoreau] directly asserts that he considers the Sacred Books of the Brahmins in nothing inferior to the Christian Bible. It was hardly necessary to say in addition that he is not well acquainted with the latter—the point worth considering is rather—*ought not* an author to *make himself* thoroughly acquainted with a book, which, if true, is of such transcendent importance, before uttering opinions concerning it calculated to shock and pain many readers, not to speak of those who will be utterly repelled by them? Can that which Milton and Newton so profoundly reverenced (and they *had* studied it thoroughly) be wisely turned off by a youth as unworthy of even consideration? Mr. Thoreau's treatment of this subject seems revolting alike to good sense and good taste. (p. 8)

We would have preferred to pass the theme [of religion] in silence, but our admiration of his book and our reprehension of its Pantheism forbade that course. May we not hope that he will reconsider his too rashly expressed notions on this head? (p. 10)

George Ripley, "H. D. Thoreau's Book," in Pertaining to Thoreau, *edited by S. A. Jones, The Folcroft Press, Inc., 1969, pp. 1-10.*

[JAMES RUSSELL LOWELL]   (essay date 1849)

The great charm of Mr. Thoreau's [*A Week on the Concord and Merrimack Rivers*] seems to be, that its being a book at all is a happy fortuity. The door of the portfolio-cage has been left open, and the thoughts have flown out of themselves. The paper and types are only accidents. The page is confidential like a diary. Pepys is not more minute, more pleasantly unconscious. It is like a book dug up, that has no date to assign it a special contemporaneousness, and no name of author. It has been written with no uncomfortable sense of a public looking over the shoulder. And the author is the least ingredient in it, too. All which I saw and part of which I was, would be an apt motto for the better portions of the volume: a part, moreover, just as the river, the trees, and the fishes are. Generally he holds a very smooth mirror up to nature, and if, now and then, he shows us his own features in the glass, when we had rather look at something else, it is as a piece of nature, and we must forgive him if he allow it a too usurping position in the landscape. He looks at the country sometimes (as painters advise) through the triumphal arch of his own legs, and, though the upsidedownness of the prospect has its own charm of unassuetude, the arch itself is not the most graceful.

So far of the manner of the book, now of the book itself. It professes to be the journal of a week on Concord and Merrimack Rivers. We must have our libraries enlarged, if Mr. Thoreau intend to complete his autobiography on this scale—four hundred and thirteen pages to a sennight! He begins honestly enough as the Boswell of Musketaquid and Merrimack. It was a fine subject and a new one. We are curious to know somewhat of the private and interior life of two such prominent and oldest inhabitants. (pp. 46-7)

Much information and entertainment were to be pumped out of individuals like these, and the pump does not *suck* in Mr. Thoreau's hands. As long as he continues an honest Boswell, his book is delightful, but sometimes he serves his two rivers as Hazlitt did Northcote, and makes them run Thoreau or Emerson, or, indeed, anything but their own transparent element.

What, for instance, have Concord and Merrimack to do with Boodh, themselves professors of an elder and to them wholly sufficient religion, namely, the willing subjects of watery laws, to seek their ocean? We have digressions on Boodh, on Anacreon, (with translations hardly so good as Cowley,) on Persius, on Friendship, and we know not what. We come upon them like-snags, jolting us headforemost out of our places as we are rowing placidly up stream or drifting down. Mr. Thoreau becomes so absorbed in these discussions, that he seems, as it were, to *catch a crab,* and disappears uncomfortably from his seat at the bow-oar. We could forgive them all, especially that on Books, and that on Friendship, (which is worthy of one who has so long commerced with Nature and with Emerson,) we could welcome them all, were they put by themselves at the end of the book. But as it is, they are out of proportion and out of place, and mar our Merrimacking dreadfully. We were bid to a river-party, not to be preached at. They thrust themselves obtrusively out of the narrative, like those quarries of red glass which the Bowery dandies (emulous of Sisyphus) push laboriously before them as breastpins.

Before we get through the book, we begin to feel as if the author had used the term week, as the Jews did the number *forty,* for an indefinite measure of time. It is quite evident that we have something more than a transcript of his fluviatile experiences. The leaves of his portfolio and river-journal seem to have been shuffled together with a trustful dependence on some overruling printer-providence. We trace the lines of successive deposits as plainly as on the sides of a deep cut, or rather on those of a trench carried through made-land in the city, where choiceness of material has been of less import than suitableness to fill up, and where plaster and broken bricks from old buildings, oyster-shells, and dock mud have been shot pellmell together. Yet we must allow that Mr. Thoreau's materials are precious, too. His plaster has bits of ancient symbols painted on it, his bricks are stamped with mystic sentences, his shells are of pearl-oysters, and his mud from the Sacramento.

"Give me a sentence," prays Mr. Thoreau bravely, "which no intelligence can understand!"—and we think that the kind gods have nodded. There are some of his utterances which have foiled us, and we belong to that class of beings which he thus reproachfully stigmatizes as intelligences. We think it must be this taste that makes him so fond of the Hindoo philosophy, which would seem admirably suited to men, if men were only oysters. Or is it merely because, as he naïvely confesses in another place, "his soul is of a bright invisible *green*"? We would recommend to Mr. Thoreau some of the Welsh sacred poetry. Many of the Triads hold an infinite deal of nothing, especially after the bottoms have been knocked out of them by translation. But it seems ungrateful to find fault with a book which has given us so much pleasure. We have eaten salt (Attic, too,) with Mr. Thoreau. It is the hospitality and not the fare which carries a benediction with it, and it is a sort of ill breeding to report any oddity in the viands. His feast is here and there a little savage, (indeed, he professes himself a kind of volunteer Redman,) and we must make out with the fruits, merely giving a sidelong glance at the baked dog and pickled missionary, and leaving them in grateful silence.

We wish the General Court had been wise enough to have appointed our author to make the report on the Ichthyology of Massachusetts. Then, indeed, would the people of the state have known something of their aquicolal fellow-citizens.

Mr. Thoreau handles them as if he loved them, as old Izaak recommends us to do with a worm in impaling it. He is the very Asmodeus of their private life. He unroofs their dwellings and makes us familiar with their loves and sorrows. He seems to suffer a sea-change, like the Scotch peasant who was carried down among the seals in the capacity of family physician. He balances himself with them under the domestic lily-pad, takes a family-bite with them, is made the confidant of their courtships, and is an honored guest at the wedding-feast. He has doubtless seen a pickerel crossed in love, a perch Othello, a bream the victim of an unappreciated idiosyncrasy, or a minnow with a mission. He goes far to convince us of what we have before suspected, that fishes are the highest of organizations. . . . We wish Mr. Thoreau would undertake a report upon them as a private enterprise. It would be the most delightful book of natural history extant.

Mr. Thoreau's volume is the more pleasant that with all its fresh smell of the woods, it is yet the work of a bookish man. We not only hear the laugh of the flicker, and the watchman's rattle of the red squirrel, but the voices of poets and philosophers, old and new. There is no more reason why an author should reflect trees and mountains than books, which, if they are in any sense real, are as good parts of nature as any other kind of growth. . . . But we think that Mr. Thoreau sometimes makes a bad use of his books. Better things can be got out of Herbert and Vaughan and Donne than the art of making bad verses. There is no harm in good writing, nor do wisdom and philosophy prefer crambo. Mr. Thoreau never learned bad rhyming of the river and the sky. He is the more culpable as he has shown that he can write poetry at once melodious and distinct, with rare delicacy of thought and feeling. (pp. 47-50)

If Mr. Emerson choose to leave some hard nuts for posterity to crack, he can perhaps afford it as well as any. We counsel Mr. Thoreau, in his own words, to take his hat and come out of that. If he prefer to put peas in his shoes when he makes private poetical excursions, it is nobody's affair. But if the public are to go along with him, they will find some way to boil theirs.

We think that Mr. Thoreau, like most solitary men, exaggerates the importance of his own thoughts. The "I" occasionally stretches up tall as Pompey's pillar over a somewhat flat and sandy expanse. But this has its counterbalancing advantage, that it leads him to secure many a fancy and feeling which would flit by most men unnoticed. The little confidences of nature which pass his neighbours as the news slip through the grasp of birds perched upon the telegraphic wires, he received as they were personal messages from a mistress. Yet the book is not solely excellent as a Talbotype of natural scenery. It abounds in fine thoughts, and there is many a critical *obiter dictum* which is good law. . . . (p. 50)

Since we have found fault with some of what we may be allowed to call the worsification, we should say that the prose work is done conscientiously and neatly. The style is compact and the language has an antique purity like wine grown colorless with age. (p. 51)

[*James Russell Lowell*], *in a review of "A Week on the Concord and Merrimack Rivers," in* Massachusetts Quarterly Review, *Vol. III, No. IX, December, 1849, pp. 40-51.*

GRAHAM'S MAGAZINE (essay date 1854)

Whatever may be thought or said of [*Walden: or Life in the Woods*], nobody can deny its claims to individuality of opinion, sentiment, and expression. Sometimes strikingly original, sometimes merely eccentric and odd, it is always racy and stimulating. . . . Mr. Thoreau, it is well known, belongs to the class of transcendentalists who lay the greatest stress on the "I," and knows no limitation on the exercise of the rights of that important pronoun. The customs, manners, occupations, religion, of society, he "goes out" from, and brings them before his own inward tribunal for judgment. He differs from all mankind with wonderful composure; and, without any of the fuss of the come-outers, goes beyond them in asserting the autocracy of the individual. Making himself the measure of truth, he is apt to think that "difference from me is the measure of absurdity;" and occasionally he obtains a startling paradox, by the simple inversion of a stagnant truism. He likes to say that four and four make nine, in order to assert his independence of the contemptible trammels of the world's arithmetic. He has a philosophical fleer and gibe for most axioms, and snaps his fingers in the face of the most accredited proprieties and "do-me-*goodisms*" of conventional life. But if he has the wildness of the woods about him, he has their sweetness also. Through all the audacities of his eccentric protests, a careful eye can easily discern the movement of a powerful and accomplished mind. He has evidently read the best books, and talked with the best people. His love for nature, and his eye for nature, are altogether beyond the ordinary love and insight of nature's priests; and his descriptions have a kind of De Foe-like accuracy and reality in their eloquence, peculiar to himself among all American writers. We feel, in reading him, that such a man has earned the right to speak of nature, for he has taken her in all moods, and given the same "froile welcome" to her "thunder and her sunshine." (p. 298)

We might easily fill a page with short, sharp, quotable sentences, embodying some flash of wit or humor, some scrap of quaint or elevated wisdom, or some odd or beautiful image. Every chapter in the book is stamped with sincerity. It is genuine and genial throughout. Even its freaks of though are full of suggestions. When the author turns his eye seriously on an object, no matter how remote from the sphere of ordinary observation, he commonly sees into it and through it. He has a good deal of Mr. Emerson's piercing quality of mind, which he exercises on the more elusive and flitting phenomena of consciousness, with a metaphysician's subtilty, and a poet's expressiveness. And as regards the somewhat presumptuous manner in which he dogmatizes, the reader will soon learn to pardon it for the real wealth of individual thinking by which it is accompanied, always remembering that Mr. Thoreau, in the words of his own motto, does not intend to write an "ode to dejection, but to brag as lusily as chanticleer in the morning, standing on his roost, if only to wake his neighbors up." (p. 300)

A review of "Walden; or, Life in the Woods," in Graham's Magazine, *Vol. VLX, No. 3, September, 1854, pp. 298-300.*

[C. F. BRIGGS]   (essay date 1854)

[*Briggs's essay is typical of many early reviews which treated Thoreau as an eccentric, if thoughtful, hermit. Briggs questions the sincerity of Thoreau's dedication to his way of life at Walden.*]

The New England character is essentially anti-Diogenic; the Yankee is too shrewd not to comprehend the advantages of living in what we call the world; there are no bargains to be made in the desert, nobody to be taken advantage of in the woods, while the dwellers in tubs and shanties have slender opportunities of bettering their condition by barter. When the New Englander leaves his home, it is not for the pleasure of living by himself; if he is migratory in his habits, it is not from his fondness for solitude, nor from any impatience he feels at living in a crowd. Where there are most men, there is, generally, most money, and there is where the strongest attractions exist for the genuine New Englander. A Yankee Diogenes is a *lusus* [an amusing object], and we feel a peculiar interest in reading the account which an oddity of that kind gives of himself. The name of Thoreau has not a New England sound; but we believe that the author of ***Walden*** is a genuine New Englander, and of New England antecedents and education. Although he plainly gives the reasons for publishing his book, at the outset, he does not clearly state the causes that led him to live the life of a hermit on the shore of Walden Pond. But we infer from his volume that his aim was the very remarkable one of trying to be something, while he lived upon nothing; in opposition to the general rule of striving to live upon something, while doing nothing. Mr. Thoreau probably tried the experiment long enough to test its success, and then fell back again into his normal condition. But he does not tell us that such was the case. He was happy enough to get back among the good people of Concord, we have no doubt; for although he paints his shanty-life in rose-colored tints, we do not believe he liked it, else why not stick to it. We have a mistrust of the sincerity of the St. Simon Sylites', and suspect that they come down from their pillars in the night-time, when nobody is looking at them. Diogenes placed his tub where Alexander would be sure of seeing it, and Mr. Thoreau ingenuously confesses that he occasionally went out to dine, and when the society of woodchucks and chipping-squirrels were insufficient for his amusement, he liked to go into Concord and listen to the village gossips in the stores and taverns. Mr. Thoreau informs us that he lived alone in the woods, by the shore of Walden Pond, in a shanty built by his own hands, a mile from any neighbor, two years and a half. What he did there besides writing the book before us, cultivating beans, sounding Walden Pond, reading Homer, baking johnny-cakes, studying Brahminical theology, listening to chipping-squirrels, receiving visits, and having high imaginations, we do not know. He gives us the results of his bean cultivation with great particularity, and the cost of his shanty; but the actual results of his two years and a half of hermit life he does not give. (p. 443)

[It] strikes us that all the knowledge which the "Hermit of Walden" gained by his singular experiment in living might have been done just as well, and as satisfactorily, without any experiment at all. We know what it costs to feed prisoners, paupers and soldiers; we know what the cheapest and most nutritious food costs, and how little it requires to keep up the bodily health of a full-grown man. A very simple calculation will enable any one to satisfy himself in regard to such points, and those who wish to live upon twenty-seven cents a week, may indulge in that pleasure. The great Abernethy's prescription for the attainment of perfect bodily health was, "live on sixpence a day and earn it." But that would be Sybaritic indulgence compared with Mr. Thoreau's experience, whose daily expenditure hardly amounted to a quarter of that sum. And he lived happily, too, though it don't exactly speak volumes in favor of his system to announce that he only continued his economical mode of life two years. If it was "the thing," why did he not continue it? (p. 444)

There is nothing of the mean or sordid in the economy of Mr. Thoreau, though to some his simplicity and abstemiousness may appear trivial and affected; he does not live cheaply for the sake of saving, nor idly to avoid labor; but, that he may live independently and enjoy his great thoughts; that he may read the Hindoo scriptures and commune with the visible forms of nature. We must do him the credit to admit that there is no mock sentiment, nor simulation of piety or philanthropy in his volume. He is not much of a cynic, and though we have called him a Yankee Diogenes, the only personage to whom he bears a decided resemblance is that good humored creation of Dickens, Mark Tapley [in *Martin Chuzzlewit*], whose delight was in being jolly under difficulties. (p. 445)

There is a true vagabondish disposition manifested now and then by Mr. Thoreau which, we imagine, was more powerful in leading him to his eremite way of life, than his love of eastern poetry, and his fondness for observing the ways of snakes and shiners. If there had been a camp of gipsies in the neighborhood of Concord, he would have become a king among them. . . . (p. 446)

There is much excellent good sense delivered in a very comprehensive and by no means unpleasant style in Mr. Thoreau's book, and let people think as they may of the wisdom or propriety of living after his fashion, denying oneself all the luxuries which the earth can afford, for the sake of leading a life of lawless vagabondage, and freedom from starched collars, there are but few readers who will fail to find profit and refreshment in his pages. Perhaps some practical people will think that a philosopher like Mr. Thoreau might have done the world a better service by purchasing a piece of land, and showing how much it might be made to produce, instead of squatting on another man's premises, and proving how little will suffice to keep body and soul together. But we must allow philosophers, and all other men, to fulfil their missions in their own way. If Mr. Thoreau had been a practical farmer, we should not have been favored with his volume; his corn and cabbage would have done but little towards profiting us, and we might never have been the better for his labors. As it is, we see how much more valuable to mankind is our philosophical vagabond than a hundred sturdy agriculturists; any plodder may raise beans, but it is only one in a million who can write a readable volume. (p. 447)

> [*C. F. Briggs*], *"A Yankee Diogenes," in* Putnam's Monthly, *Vol. IV, No. XXII, October, 1854, pp. 443-48.*

NATHANIEL HAWTHORNE (letter date 1854)

[*Hawthorne is considered one of the greatest American fiction writers. His novel* The Scarlet Letter, *with its balanced structure, simple, expressive language, and superb use of symbols, is a recognized classic of American literature. In the following letter to Monckton Miles, dated 1854, Hawthorne harshly refers to Thoreau as "an intolerable bore." Yet, Hawthorne was a fellow Transcendentalist and was generally supportive of Thoreau's endeavors.*]

[Thoreau] despises the world, and all that it has to offer, and, like other humorists, is an intolerable bore. . . . [He] is not an agreeable person, and in his presence one feels ashamed of having any money, or a house to live in, or so much as two coats to wear, or having written a book that the public will read—his own mode of life being so unsparing a criticism on all other modes, such as the world approves.

> *Nathaniel Hawthorne, in an extract from a letter to Monckton Miles, November 13-18, 1854, in* Thoreau:

Man of Concord, *edited by Walter Harding, Holt, Rinehart and Winston, 1960, p. 175.*

[LYDIA MARIA CHILD?]   (essay date 1854)

[*Scholars have suggested that this essay, originally published in the* Anti-Slavery Standard *in 1854, was written by Lydia Maria Child, an American abolitionist, editor, and writer.*]

[Thoreau's] books spring from a depth of thought which will not suffer them to be put by, and are written in a spirit in striking contrast with that which is uppermost in our time and country. Out of the heart of practical, hard-working, progressive New England come these Oriental utterances. The life exhibited in them teaches us, much more impressively than any number of sermons could, that this Western activity of which we are so proud, these material improvements, this commercial enterprise, this rapid accumulation of wealth, even our external, associated philanthropic action, are very easily overrated. The true glory of the human soul is not to be reached by the most rapid travelling in car or steamboat, by the instant transmission of intelligence however far, by the most speedy accumulation of a fortune, and however efficient measures we may adopt for the reform of the intemperate, the emancipation of the enslaved, &c., it will avail little unless we are ourselves essentially noble enough to inspire those whom we would so benefit with nobleness. External bondage is trifling compared with the bondage of an ignoble soul. Such things are often said, doubtless, in pulpits and elsewhere, but the men who say them are too apt to live just with the crowd, and so their words come more and more to ring with a hollow sound.

It is refreshing to find in these books the sentiments of one man whose aim manifestly is to *live*, and not to waste his time upon the externals of living. Educated at Cambridge, in the way called liberal, he seems determined to make a liberal life of it, and not to become the slave of any calling, for the sake of earning a reputable livelihood or of being regarded as a useful member of society. He evidently considers it his first business to become more and more a living, advancing soul, knowing that thus alone (though he desires to think as little as possible about that) can he be, in any proper sense, useful to others. Mr. Thoreau's view of life has been called selfish. His own words, under the head of **"Philanthropy"** in **Walden,** are the amplest defense against this charge, to those who can appreciate them. In a deeper sense than we commonly think, charity begins at home. The man who, with any fidelity, obeys his own genius, serves men infinitely more by so doing, becoming an encouragement, a strengthener, a fountain of inspiration to them, than if he were to turn aside from his path and exhaust his energies in striving to meet their superficial needs. As a thing by the way, aside from our proper work, we may seek to remove external obstacles from the path of our neighbours, but no man can help them much who makes that his main business, instead of seeking evermore, with all his energies, to reach the loftiest point which his imagination sets before him, thus adding to the stock of true nobleness in the world.

But suppose all men should pursue Mr. Thoreau's course, it is asked triumphantly, as though, then, we should be sure to go back to barbarism. . . . If men were to follow in Mr. Thoreau's steps, by being more obedient to their loftiest instincts, there would, indeed, be a falling off in the splendor of our houses, in the richness of our furniture and dress, in the luxury of our tables, but how poor are these things in comparison with the new grandeur and beauty which would appear in the souls of men. What fresh and inspiring conversation should we have, instead of the wearisome gossip, which now meets us at every turn. Men toil on, wearing out body or soul, or both, that they may accumulate a needless amount of the externals of living; that they may win the regard of those no wiser than themselves; their natures become warped and hardened to their pursuits; they get fainter and fainter glimpses of the glory of the world, and, by and by, comes into their richly-adorned parlours some wise and beautiful soul, like the writer of these books, who, speaking from the fullness of his inward life, makes their luxuries appear vulgar, showing that, in a direct way, he has obtained the essence of that which his entertainers have been vainly seeking for at such a terrible expense.

It seems remarkable that these books have received no more adequate notice in our Literary Journals. But the class of scholars are often as blind as others to any new elevation of soul. In *Putnam's Magazine* [see excerpt above by C. F. Briggs, 1854], Mr. Thoreau is spoken of as an oddity, as the Yankee Diogenes, as though the really ridiculous oddity were not in us of the "starched shirt-collar" rather than in this devotee of Nature and Thought. Some have praised the originality and profound sympathy with which he views natural objects. We might as well stop with praising Jesus for the happy use he has made of the lilies of the field. The fact of surpassing interest for us is the simple grandeur of Mr. Thoreau's position—a position open to us all, and of which this sympathy with Nature is but a single result. This is seen in the less descriptive, more purely thoughtful passages, such as that upon Friendship in the **"Wednesday"** of the *Week*, and in those upon **"Solitude,"** **"What I Lived for,"** and **"Higher Laws,"** in *Walden*, as well as in many others in both books. We do not believe that, in the whole course of literature, ancient and modern, so noble a discourse upon Friendship can be produced as that which Mr. Thoreau has given us. It points to a relation, to be sure, which, from the ordinary level of our lives, may seem remote and dreamy. But it is our thirst for, and glimpses of, such things which indicate the greatness of our nature, which give the purest charm and colouring to our lives. The striking peculiarity of Mr. Thoreau's attitude is, that while he is no religionist, and while he is eminently practical in regard to the material economics of life, he yet manifestly feels, through and through, that the loftiest dreams of the imagination are the solidest realities, and so the only foundation for us to build upon, while the affairs in which men are everywhere busying themselves so intensely are comparatively the merest froth and foam. (pp. 8-11)

> [*Lydia Maria Child?*], *"Thoreau's 'Walden',"* in Thoreau: A Century of Criticism, *edited by Walter Harding, Southern Methodist University Press, 1954, pp. 8-11.*

THE KNICKERBOCKER   (essay date 1855)

[*Like many of Thoreau's contemporaries, the author of the following humorous essay finds the experiment at Walden absurd.*]

[Henry David Thoreau, a] Concord philosopher, or modern Diogenes, who has an eye of acute penetration in looking out upon the world, discovered so much aimless and foolish bustle, such a disproportion of shams to realities, that his inclination or self-respect would not permit him to participate in them; so he built himself in the woods, on the banks of a pond of pure water—deep enough for drowning purposes if the bean-crop failed—a tub of unambitious proportions, into which he crawled. In this retreat, where he supported animal and intellectual life for more than two years, at a cost of about thirteen (!) dollars per annum, he wrote a book full of interest, containing the most pithy, sharp, and original remarks. (p. 235)

Beyond all question, ['**Walden**' is one of the] most remarkable books that [has] been published the last year. . . . (p. 236)

It was pretty well understood by physiologists, before the recent experiment of Mr. Thoreau, how little farinaceous food would suffice for the human stomach; and Chatham-street clothiers have a tolerably accurate knowledge of how little poor and cheap raiment will suffice to cover the back, so that his 'life in the woods' adds but little to the stock of information scientific men already possessed. (p. 237)

If we were obliged to choose between being shut up in 'conventionalism's air-tight stove,' (even if the said stove had all the surroundings of elegance and comforts that wealth could buy,) and a twenty-eight dollar tub in the woods, with a boundless range of freedom in the daily *walks* of life, we should not hesitate a moment in taking the tub, if it were not for a recollection of those horrid beans, and that melancholy mixture of meal and water. Aye, there's the rub; for from that vegetable diet what dreams might come, when we had shuffled off the wherewith to purchase other food, must give us pause. There's the consideration that makes the sorry conventionalisms of society of so long life. We rather bear those ills we have, than fly to others that we know not of. A very reasonable dread of something unpleasant resulting to us from eating beans in great quantities, would be likely to be a consequence of our experience alone, if we happened to be deficient in physiological knowledge. Whatever effects, however, different kinds of diet may have upon different persons, mentally or physically, nothing is more clear than the fact that the diet of Mr. Thoreau did not make him mentally windy. (pp. 237-38)

There is a good deal more virtue in beans than we supposed there was, if they are sufficient to sustain a man in such cheerful spirits as Thoreau appears to have been in when he wrote that book. The spirit oftentimes may be strong when the flesh is weak; but there does not appear to be any evidence of weakness of the flesh in the author of '**Walden**.' (p. 238)

We do not believe there is any danger of proselytes to Mr. Thoreau's mode of life becoming too numerous. . . . We ask the reader to look around among his acquaintances, and see if the number of those whose resources of mind are sufficient to enable them to dispense with much intercourse with others, is not exceedingly small. We know of some such, though they are very few; but their fondness for solitude unfortunately is not associated with any particular admiration for a vegetable diet. It is a melancholy circumstance, and one that has been very bitterly deplored, ever since that indefinite period when 'the memory of man runneth not to the contrary,' that the accompaniments of poverty should go hand-in-hand with a taste for a solitary life. A hearty appreciation of and love for humble fare, plain clothes, and poor surroundings generally, are what men of genius need to cultivate. '**Walden**' tends to encourage this cultivation. (p. 239)

Mr. Thoreau gives a description of a battle fought upon his wood-pile between two armies of ants, that is exceedingly graphic and spirited. We think it surpasses in interest the description of battles fought about Sebastopol, written by the famous correspondent of the London *Times*. Perhaps, however, we are somewhat prejudiced in the matter. The truth is, we have read so much about the war in Europe, that the whole subject has become somewhat tiresome; and this account of the battle of the ants in Concord has so much freshness about it—so much novelty, dignity, and importance, which the battles in Europe cease to possess for us—that we have read it over three or four times with increased interest each time. (p. 240)

[The French poet François de Malherbe,] once upon hearing a prose work of great merit extolled, dryly asked if it would *reduce the price of bread!* If '**Walden**' should be extensively read, we think it would have the effect to reduce somewhat the price of meat, if it did not of bread. At all events it encourages the belief, which in this utilitarian age enough needs encouragement, that there is some other object to live for except 'to make money.'

In the New-England philosophy of life, which so extensively prevails where the moral or intellectual character of a man is more or less determined by his habits of *thrift,* such a book as '**Walden**'' was needed. Extravagant as it is in the notions it promulgates, we think it is nevertheless calculated to do a good deal of good, and we hope it will be widely read. (p. 241)

"Town and Rural Humbugs," in The Knickerbocker, *Vol. XLV, No. 1, January, 1855, pp. 235-41.*

GEORGE ELIOT   (essay date 1856)

[*Eliot is considered one of the foremost English novelists of the nineteenth century. Her novels, including* Middlemarch *and* The Mill on the Floss, *explore psychological and moral issues and provide intimate pictures of everyday life informed by a profound insight into human character. Unlike most of her contemporaries, Eliot took Thoreau and* Walden *seriously. In this review, originally published in the* Westminster Review *in 1856, she praises Thoreau's independence of spirit and "sturdy sense."*]

[In *Walden; or, Life in the Woods*] we have a bit of pure American life (not the 'go a-head' species, but its opposite pole), animated by that energetic, yet calm spirit of innovation, that practical as well as theoretic independence of formulae, which is peculiar to some of the finer American minds. The writer tells us how he chose, for some years, to be a stoic of the woods; how he built his house; how he earned the necessaries of his simple life by cultivating a bit of ground. He tells his system of diet, his studies, his reflections, and his observations of natural phenomena. These last are not only made by a keen eye, but have their interest enhanced by passing through the medium of a deep poetic sensibility; and, indeed, we feel throughout the book the presence of a refined as well as a hardy mind. People—very wise in their own eyes—who would have every man's life ordered according to a particular pattern, and who are intolerant of every existence the utility of which is not palpable to them, may pooh-pooh Mr. Thoreau and this episode in his history, as unpractical and dreamy. Instead of contesting their opinion ourselves, we will let Mr. Thoreau speak for himself. There is plenty of sturdy sense mingled with his unworldliness. . . . (pp. 12-13)

George Eliot, *"Review of 'Walden',"* in The Recognition of Henry David Thoreau: Selected Criticism Since 1848, *edited by Wendell Glick, The University of Michigan Press, 1969, pp. 12-13.*

[AMOS BRONSON ALCOTT]   (essay date 1862)

[*Alcott, a close friend of Thoreau and fellow Transcendentalist, was an American poet, essayist, philosopher, and educator. In the following adulatory essay, written shortly before Thoreau's death, Alcott argues that Thoreau "has come nearer the antique spirit" than any other American poet, though he remains "our best sample of an indigenous American." Praising his wholesomeness as a moralist, Alcott also mentions Thoreau's erudition and originality.*]

I had never thought of knowing a man so thoroughly of the country as this friend of mine, and so purely a son of Nature. Perhaps he has the profoundest passion for it of any one living; and had the human sentiment been as tender from the first, and as pervading, we might have had pastorals of which Virgil and Theocritus would have envied him the authorship, had they chanced to be his contemporaries. As it is, he has come nearer the antique spirit than any of our native poets, and touched the fields and groves and streams of his native town with a classic interest that shall not fade. Some of his verses are suffused with an elegiac tenderness, as if the woods and fields bewailed the absence of their forester, and murmured their griefs meanwhile to one another,—responsive like idyls. Living in close companionship with Nature, his Muse breathes the spirit and voice of poetry; his excellence lying herein: for when the heart is once divorced from the senses and all sympathy with common things, then poetry has fled, and the love that sings.

The most welcome of companions, this plain countryman. One shall not meet with thoughts invigorating like his often: coming so scented of mountain and field breezes and rippling springs, so like a luxuriant clod from under forest-leaves, moist and mossy with earth-spirits. His presence is tonic, like ice-water in dog-days to the parched citizen pent in chambers and under brazen ceilings. Welcome as the gurgle of brooks, the dripping of pitchers,—then drink and be cool! He seems one with things, of Nature's essence and core, knit of strong timbers, most like a wood and its inhabitants. There are in him sod and shade, woods and waters manifold, the mould and mist of earth and sky. Self-poised and sagacious as any denizen of the elements, he has the key to every animal's brain, every plant, every shrub; and were an Indian to flower forth, and reveal the secrets hidden in his cranium, it would not be more surprising than the speech of our Sylvanus. He must belong to the Homeric age,—is older than pastures and gardens, as if he were of the race of heroes, and one with the elements. He, of all men, seems to be the native New-Englander, as much so as the oak, the granite ledge, our best sample of an indigenous American, untouched by the Old Country, unless he came down from Thor, the Northman; as yet unfathered by any, and a nondescript in the books of natural history.

A peripatetic philosopher, and out of doors for the best parts of his days and nights, he has manifold weather and seasons in him, and the manners of an animal of probity and virtues unstained. Of our moralists he seems the wholesomest; and the best republican citizen in the world,—always at home, and minding his own affairs. Perhaps a little over-confident sometimes, and stiffly individual, dropping society clean out of his theories, while standing friendly in his strict sense of friendship, there is in him an integrity and sense of justice that make possible and actual the virtues of Sparta and the Stoics, and all the more welcome to us in these times of shuffling and of pusillanimity. Plutarch would have made him immortal in his pages, had he lived before his day. Nor have we any so modern as he,—his own and ours; too purely so to be appreciated at once. A scholar by birthright, and an author, his fame has not yet travelled far from the banks of the rivers he has described in his books; but I hazard only the truth in affirming of his prose, that in substance and sense it surpasses that of any naturalist of his time, and that he is sure of a reading in the future. There are fairer fishes in his pages than any now swimming in our streams, and some sleep of his on the banks of the Merrimack by moonlight that Egypt never rivalled; a morning of which Memnon might have envied the music, and a greyhound that was meant for Adonis; some frogs, too, better than any of Aristophanes. Perhaps we have had no eyes like his since Pliny's time. His senses seem double, giving him access to secrets not easily read by other men: his sagacity resembling that of the beaver and the bee, the dog and the deer; an instinct for seeing and judging, as by some other or seventh sense, dealing with objects as if they were shooting forth from his own mind mythologically, thus completing Nature all round to his senses, and a creation of his at the moment. I am sure he knows the animals, one by one, and everything else knowable in our town, and has named them rightly as Adam did in Paradise, if he be not that ancestor himself. His works are pieces of exquisite sense, celebrations of Nature's virginity, exemplified by rare learning and original observations. Persistently independent and manly, he criticizes men and times largely, urging and defending his opinions with the spirit and pertinacity befitting a descendant of him of the Hammer. . . . Seldom has a head circumscribed so much of the sense of Cosmos as this footed intelligence,—nothing less than all out-of-doors sufficing his genius and scopes, and, day by day, through all weeks and seasons, the year round.

If one would find the wealth of wit there is in this plain man, the information, the sagacity, the poetry, the piety, let him take a walk with him, say of a winter's afternoon, to the Blue Water, or anywhere about the outskirts of his village-residence. Pagan as he shall outwardly appear, yet he soon shall be seen to be the hearty worshipper of whatsoever is sound and wholesome in Nature,—a piece of russet probity and sound sense that she delights to own and honor. His talk shall be suggestive, subtile, and sincere, under as many masks and mimicries as the shows he passes, and as significant,—Nature choosing to speak through her chosen mouth-piece,—cynically, perhaps, sometimes, and searching into the marrows of men and times he chances to speak of, to his discomfort mostly, and avoidance. Nature, poetry, life,—not politics, not strict science, not society as it is,—are his preferred themes: the new Pantheon, probably, before he gets far, to the naming of the gods some coming Angelo, some Pliny, is to paint and describe. The world is holy, the things seen symbolizing the Unseen, and worthy of worship so, the Zoroastrian rites most becoming a nature so fine as ours in this thin newness, this worship being so sensible, so promotive of possible pieties,—calling us out of doors and under the firmament, where health and wholesomeness are finely insinuated into our souls,—not as idolaters, but as idealists, the seekers of the Unseen through images of the Invisible.

I think his religion of the most primitive type, and inclusive of all natural creatures and things, even to "the sparrow that falls to the ground,"—though never by shot of his,—and, for whatsoever is manly in man, his worship may compare with that of the priests and heroes of pagan times. Nor is he false to these traits under any guise,—worshipping at unbloody altars, a favorite of the Unseen, Wisest, and Best. Certainly he is better poised and more nearly self-reliant than other men.

Perhaps he deals best with matter, properly, though very adroitly with mind, with persons, as he knows them best, and sees them from nature's circle, wherein he dwells habitually. I should say he inspired the sentiment of love, if, indeed, the sentiment he awakens did not seem to partake of a yet purer sentiment, were that possible,—but nameless from its excellency. Friendly he is, and holds his friends by bearings as strict in their tenderness and consideration as are the laws of his thinking,—as prompt and kindly equitable,—neighborly always, and as apt for occasions as he is strenuous against meddling with others in things not his. (pp. 443-45)

We have been accustomed to consider him the salt of things so long that they must lose their savor without his to season them. And when he goes hence, then Pan is dead, and Nature ailing throughout. (p. 445)

> [*Amos Bronson Alcott*], "*The Forester*," *in* The Atlantic Monthly, *Vol. IX, No. LIV, April, 1862, pp. 443-45.*

[RALPH WALDO EMERSON]   (essay date 1862)

[*Emerson was an American essayist and poet, who, as founder of the Transcendental movement, shaped a distinctly American philosophy which embraced optimism, individuality, and mysticism. His philosophy stresses the presence of ongoing creation and revelation by a god who exists in everyone, as well as the essential unity of all thoughts, persons, and things in the divine whole. Emerson is considered one of the most influential figures of the nineteenth century. He was Thoreau's earliest mentor and the chief influence on his life and works, but the two men became estranged as Thoreau established his own views. Though Emerson is largely positive in the following eulogistic tribute, he is critical of Thoreau when he states that "his genius was better than his talent," that he was often paradoxical, and that it was perhaps to Thoreau's detriment that he lacked ambition.*]

[Thoreau] was equally interested in every natural fact. The depth of his perception found likeness of law throughout Nature, and I know not any genius who so swiftly inferred universal law from the single fact. He was no pedant of a department. His eye was open to beauty, and his ear to music. He found these, not in rare conditions, but wheresoever he went. He thought the best of music was in single strains; and he found poetic suggestion in the humming of the telegraph-wire.

His poetry might be bad or good; he no doubt wanted a lyric facility and technical skill; but he had the source of poetry in his spiritual perception. He was a good reader and critic, and his judgment on poetry was to the ground of it. He could not be deceived as to the presence or absence of the poetic element in any composition, and his thirst for this made him negligent and perhaps scornful of superficial graces. He would pass by many delicate rhythms, but he would have detected every live stanza or line in a volume, and knew very well where to find an equal poetic charm in prose. He was so enamored of the spiritual beauty that he held all actual written poems in very light esteem in the comparison. . . . His own verses are often rude and defective. The gold does not yet run pure, is drossy and crude. The thyme and marjoram are not yet honey. But if he want lyric fineness and technical merits, if he have not the poetic temperament, he never lacks the causal thought, showing that his genius was better than his talent. He knew the worth of the Imagination for the uplifting and consolation of human life, and liked to throw every thought into a symbol. The fact you tell is of no value, but only the impression. For this reason his presence was poetic, always piqued the curiosity to know more deeply the secrets of his mind. He had many reserves, an unwillingness to exhibit to profane eyes what was still sacred in his own, and knew well how to throw a poetic veil over his experience. (p. 246)

His riddles were worth the reading, and I confide, that, if at any time I do not understand the expression, it is yet just. Such was the wealth of his truth that it was not worth his while to use words in vain. His poem entitled **"Sympathy"** reveals the tenderness under that triple steel of stoicism, and the intellectual subtilty it could animate. His classic poem on **"Smoke"** suggests Simonides, but is better than any poem of Simonides. His biography is in his verses. His habitual thought makes all his poetry a hymm to the Cause of causes, the Spirit which vivifies and controls his own.

> I hearing get, who had but ears,
> And sight, who had but eyes before;
> I moments live, who lived but years,
> And truth discern, who knew but learning's lore.

And still more in these religious lines:—

> Now chiefly is my natal hour,
> And only now my prime of life;
> I will not doubt the love untold,
> Which not my worth or want hath bought,
> Which wooed me young, and wooes me old,
> And to this evening hath me brought.
>
> (pp. 246-47)

His virtues, of course, sometimes ran into extremes. It was easy to trace to the inexorable demand on all for exact truth that austerity which made this willing hermit more solitary even than he wished. Himself of a perfect probity, he required not less of others. . . .

The habit of a realist to find things the reverse of their appearance inclined him to put every statement in a paradox. A certain habit of antagonism defaced his earlier writings,—a trick of rhetoric not quite outgrown in his later, of substituting for the obvious word and thought its diametrical opposite. He praised wild mountains and winter forests for their domestic air, in snow and ice he would find sultriness, and commended the wilderness for resembling Rome and Paris. "It was so dry, that you might call it wet."

The tendency to magnify the moment, to read all the laws of Nature in the one object or one combination under your eye, is of course comic to those who do not share the philosopher's perception of identity. To him there was no such thing as size. The pond was a small ocean; the Atlantic, a large Walden Pond. He referred every minute fact to cosmical laws. Though he meant to be just, he seemed haunted by a certain chronic assumption that the science of the day pretended completeness, and he had just found out that the *savans* had neglected to discriminate a particular botanical variety, had failed to describe the seeds or count the sepals. (p. 247)

Had his genius been only contemplative, he had been fitted to his life, but with his energy and practical ability he seemed born for great enterprise and for command; and I so much regret the loss of his rare powers of action, that I cannot help counting it a fault in him that he had no ambition. Wanting this, instead of engineering for all America, he was the captain of a huckleberry-party. Pounding beans is good to the end of

pounding empires one of these days; but if, at the end of years, it is still only beans! (p. 248)

The scale on which his studies proceeded was so large as to require longevity, and we were the less prepared for his sudden disappearance. The country knows not yet, or in the least part, how great a son it has lost. It seems an injury that he should leave in the midst his broken task, which none else can finish,—a kind of indignity to so noble a soul, that it should depart out of Nature before yet he has been really shown to his peers for what he is. But he, at least, is content. His soul was made for the noblest society; he had in a short life exhausted the capabilities of this world; wherever there is knowledge, wherever there is virtue, wherever there is beauty, he will find a home. (p. 249)

> [*Ralph Waldo Emerson*], *"Thoreau," in* The Atlantic Monthly, *Vol. X, No. LVIII, August, 1862, pp. 239-49.*

[THOMAS WENTWORTH HIGGINSON]   (essay date 1865)

Cape Cod is photographed at last, for Thoreau has been there. Day by day, with his stout pedestrian shoes, he plodded along that level beach,—the eternal ocean on one side, and human existence reduced to its simplest elements on the other,—and he pitilessly weighing each. [In *Cape Cod,* his] mental processes never impress one with opulence and luxuriance, but rather with a certain sublime tenacity, which extracts nutriment from the most barren soil. He is therefore admirably matched against Cape Cod; and though his books on softer aspects of Nature may have a mellower charm, there is none in which the very absence of mellowness can so well pass for an added merit.

No doubt there are passages which err upon the side of bareness. Cape Cod itself certainly errs that way, and so often does our author; and when they are combined, the result of desiccation is sometimes astounding. But so much the truer the picture. . . . No one ever dared to exhibit Cape Cod "long, and lank, and brown" enough before, and hence the value of the book. . . . If the dear public will tolerate neither the presence of color in a picture, nor its absence, it is hard to suit.

Yet it is worth remembering, that Thoreau's one perfect poem,—and one of the most perfect in American literature,—**"My life is like a stroll upon the beach,"** must have been suggested by Cape Cod or some kindred locality. And it is not the savage grandeur of the sea alone, but its delicate loveliness and its ever-budding life, which will be found recorded forever in some of these wondrous pages, intermixed with the statistics of fish-flakes and the annals of old men's diseases.

But in his stern realism, the author employs what he himself calls "Panurgic" plainness of speech, and deals with the horrors of the sea-shore as composedly as with its pearls. His descriptions of the memorials of shipwrecks, for instance, would be simply repulsive, but that his very dryness has a sort of disinfectant quality, like the air of California, where things the most loathsome may lie around us without making the air impure.

He shows his wonted formidable accuracy all through these pages, and the critic feels a sense of bewildered exultation in detecting him even in a slip of the pen,—as when . . . he gives to the town of Rockport, on Cape Ann, the erroneous name of Rockland. After this discovery, one may dare to wonder at his finding a novelty in the "Upland Plover," and naming it among the birds not heard in the interior of the State, when he might be supposed to have observed it, in summer, near Mount Wachusett, where its wail adds so much, by day or night, to the wildness of the scenery. Yet by the triviality of these our criticisms one may measure the astonishing excellence of his books.

This wondrous eye and hand have passed away, and left no equal and no second. Everything which Thoreau wrote has this peculiar value, that no other observing powers were like his; no one else so laboriously verified and exhausted the facts; and no other mind rose from them, at will, into so subtile an air of meditation,—mediation too daring to be called devout, by church or world, yet too pure and lofty to merit any lower name. Lycidas has died once more, and has not left his peer.

Cape Cod does not change in its traits, but only in its boundaries, and this book will stand for it, a century hence, as it now does. It is the Cape Odyssey. Near the end, moreover, there is a remarkable chapter on previous explorers, which shows, by its patient thoroughness, and by the fearless way in which the author establishes facts . . . that, had he chosen history for his vocation, he could have extracted its marrow as faithfully as that of his more customary themes.

> [*Thomas Wentworth Higginson*], *in a review of "Cape Cod," in* The Atlantic Monthly, *Vol. XV, No. LXXXIX, March, 1865, p. 381.*

[REV. JOHN WEISS] (essay date 1865)

"Cape Cod" shows [Thoreau's] sensibility for human moods and emotions, and sometimes surprises the reader with a wealth which he had not credited to this sturdy refuser of all ordinary taxes. The more minute and satisfactory his observation of Nature became, the more gently his spirit learned to share the yearnings in each of us "of some natural kind." How solemn and tender is the figure of the sunken anchors! . . .—notwithstanding its slight rust of irony, and the homely close. And throughout this volume, wherever he comes into contact with fragments of shipwrecks, whether by the seas or fates; with peculiar isolations of life; with the odd, stunted, and grotesque specimens which the tide itself seems to deposit and nourish upon that long spit of sand,—his humor is just touched with tenderness "beyond the reach of art," and he betrays that the great undertow sweeps outward from his spirit also to the deep. This is the most human of all his writings. And, at the same time, his own humanity becomes identified with the scene in a way that cannot be mistaken for conceit. The beach becomes the wave-rolled floor of his privacy to walk upon: the lighthouse is enflamed at evening with his sympathetic thought. He pleases himself, as he lies awake underneath the lamp-chamber of the Highland light, with spinning the yarns of all seaward vessels towards a centre, which was his temporary couch; may we not say rather, his unperturbed and friendly heart? (pp. 112-13)

Of all his books, "Cape Cod" has the most finished and sustained style. With the exception of some papers in "Excursions," the reader will find that here the pages bear him best, without consciousness of effort. The chapters were probably written in different years, some earlier, some later; but they make us regret that he did not visit sea-side localities more often,—for the ocean lifts his pen better than the forest,—though he doubtless felt more at home in the latter, and more

in harmony with the broad complacent meadow and the placid lapse of streams. He went into the woods, because he "wished to live deliberately, to front only the essential facts of life." Pan's mysterious piping drew him still deeper into solitude, by the paths of streams and the tracks of the fox and partridge, where the beach-sounds in the pine-tree might remind him of Glaucus without swelling into envy for his enterprise. But it is plain, that, after salt water had once run up and lapped his feet, not all the epithets in Homer could pacify the hunger of this new sensation. He was powerfully attracted: the movement and unbounded freedom, the contrasts of strength and gentleness in the horizon filled with the downright sincerity that he prized, braced him like the high living of camps and explorations, and gave to his pulse an activity which he refused to derive from towns and business. But his observation is as sympathetic here as on the shore of Walden Pond; dealing, that is, not with general description of objects, or careful arrangement of their traits, but seizing their individuality, and transferring it with a touch of the precisest color into a sentence. Thus objects, instead of mutely falling into their natural place, aspire to interest us through something in the imagination that is kindred; and the whole scene becomes peopled instead of classified. . . . All the local history and topography is well interwoven with great skill to enhance the human and personal impression of [Thoreau's] scenes. (pp. 114-16)

> [*Rev. John Weiss*], *"Thoreau," in* The Christian Examiner, *Vol. LXXIX, No. 1, July, 1865, pp. 96-117.*

JAMES RUSSELL LOWELL (essay date 1865)

> [*Published in the* North American Review *in 1865, Lowell's essay was highly influential in shaping Thoreau's critical reputation in the United States. He attacks what he describes as Thoreau's egocentrism, limited critical powers, lack of "artistic mastery," and his "intellectual selfishness." In addition, Lowell berates Thoreau for his insincerity, "unhealthy mind," and humorlessness. Lowell concludes, however, by referring to Thoreau as a "master," and ranking him with John Donne and Novalis.*]

Among the pistillate plants kindled to fruitage by the Emersonian pollen, Thoreau is thus far the most remarkable; and it is something eminently fitting that his posthumous works should be offered us by Emerson, for they are strawberries from his own garden. A singular mixture of varieties, indeed, there is;—alpine, some of them, with the flavor of rare mountain air; others wood, tasting of sunny roadside banks or shy openings in the forest; and not a few seedlings swollen hugely by culture, but lacking the fine natural aroma of the more modest kinds. Strange books these are of his, and interesting in many ways,—instructive chiefly as showing how considerable a crop may be raised on a comparatively narrow close of mind, and how much a man may make of his life if he will assiduously follow it, though perhaps never truly finding it at last. (p. 368)

[Thoreau] seems to me to have been a man with so high a conceit of himself that he accepted without questioning, and insisted on our accepting, his defects and weaknesses of character as virtues and powers peculiar to himself. Was he indolent, he finds none of the activities which attract or employ the rest of mankind worthy of him. Was he wanting in the qualities that make success, it is success that is contemptible, and not himself that lacks persistency and purpose. Was he poor, money was an unmixed evil. Did his life seem a selfish one, he condemns doing good as one of the weakest of superstitions. To be of use was with him the most killing bait of the wily tempter Uselessness. He had no faculty of generalization from outside of himself, or at least no experience which would supply the material of such, and he makes his own whim the law, his own range the horizon of the universe. He condemns a world, the hollowness of whose satisfactions he had never had the means of testing, and we recognize Apemantus behind the mask of Timon. He had little active imagination; of the receptive he had much. His appreciation is of the highest quality; his critical power, from want of continuity of mind, very limited and inadequate. He somewhere cites a simile from Ossian, as an example of the superiority of the old poetry to the new, though, even were the historic evidence less convincing, the sentimental melancholy of those poems should be conclusive of their modernness. He had none of the artistic mastery which controls a great work to the serene balance of completeness, but exquisite mechanical skill in the shaping of sentences and paragraphs, or (more rarely) short bits of verse for the expression of a detached thought, sentiment, or image. His works give one the feeling of a sky full of stars,—something impressive and exhilarating certainly, something high overhead and freckled thickly with spots of isolated brightness; but whether these have any mutual relation with each other, or have any concern with our mundane matters, is for the most part matter of conjecture,—astrology as yet, and not astronomy.

It is curious, considering what Thoreau afterwards became, that he was not by nature an observer. He only saw the things he looked for, and was less poet than naturalist. Till he built his Walden shanty, he did not know that the hickory grew in Concord. Till he went to Maine, he had never seen phosphorescent wood, a phenomenon early familiar to most country boys. At forty he speaks of the seeding of the pine as a new discovery, though one should have thought that its golddust of blowing pollen might have earlier drawn his eye. Neither his attention nor his genius was of the spontaneous kind. He discovered nothing. He thought everything a discovery of his own, from moonlight to the planting of acorns and nuts by squirrels. This is a defect in his character, but one of his chief charms as a writer. Everything grows fresh under his hand. He delved in his mind and nature; he planted them with all manner of native and foreign seeds, and reaped assiduously. He was not merely solitary, he would be isolated, and succeeded at last in almost persuading himself that he was autochthonous. He valued everything in proportion as he fancied it to be exclusively his own. He complains in **"Walden"** that there is no one in Concord with whom he could talk of Oriental literature, though the man was living within two miles of his hut who had introduced him to it. This intellectual selfishness becomes sometimes almost painful in reading him. He lacked that generosity of "communication" which Johnson admired in Burke. . . . But Thoreau seems to have prized a lofty way of thinking (often we should be inclined to call it a remote one) not so much because it was good in itself as because he wished few to share it with him. It seems now and then as if he did not seek to lure others up "above our lower region of turmoil," but to leave his own name cut on the mountain peak as the first climber. This itch of originality infects his thought and style. To be misty is not to be mystic. He turns commonplaces end for end, and fancies it makes something new of them. . . . [Thoreau] seeks, at all risks, for perversity of thought, and revives the age of *concetti* [the wit] while he fancies himself going back to a pre-classical nature. . . . It is not so much the True that he loves as the Out-of-the-Way. As the Brazen Age shows itself in other men by exaggeration of phrase, so in him

by extravagance of statement. He wishes always to trump your suit and to *ruff* when you least expect it. Do you love Nature because she is beautiful? He will find a better argument in her ugliness. Are you tired of the artificial man? He instantly dresses you up an ideal in a Penobscot Indian, and attributes to this creature of his otherwise-mindedness as peculiarities things that are common to all woodsmen, white or red, and this simply because he has not studied the pale-faced variety.

This notion of an absolute originality, as if one could have a patent-right in it, is an absurdity. A man cannot escape in thought, any more than he can in language, from the past and the present. As no one ever invents a word, and yet language somehow grows by general contribution and necessity, so it is with thought. Mr. Thoreau seems to me to insist in public on going back to flint and steel, when there is a match-box in his pocket which he knows very well how to use at a pinch. Originality consists in power of digesting and assimilating thought, so that they become part of our life and substance. . . . In Thoreau much seems yet to be foreign and unassimilated, showing itself in symptoms of indigestion. A preacher-up of Nature, we now and then detect under the surly and stoic garb something of the sophist and the sentimentalizer. I am far from implying that this was conscious on his part. But it is much easier for a man to impose on himself when he measures only with himself. A greater familiarity with ordinary men would have done Thoreau good, by showing him how many fine qualities are common to the race. The radical vice of his theory of life was that he confounded physical with spiritual remoteness from men. A man is far enough withdrawn from his fellows if he keep himself clear of their weaknesses. He is not so truly withdrawn as exiled, if he refuse to share in their strength. . . . It is a morbid self-consciousness that pronounces the world of men empty and worthless before trying it, the instinctive evasion of one who is sensible of some innate weakness, and retorts the accusation of it before any has made it but himself. To a healthy mind, the world is a constant challenge of opportunity. Mr. Thoreau had not a healthy mind, or he would not have been so fond of prescribing. His whole life was a search for the doctor. (pp. 369-74)

Thoreau had no humor, and this implies that he was a sorry logician. Himself an artist in rhetoric, he confounds thought with style when he undertakes to speak of the latter. He was forever talking of getting away from the world, but he must be always near enough to it, nay, to the Concord corner of it, to feel the impression he makes there. . . . This egotism of his is a Stylites pillar after all, a seclusion which keeps him in the public eye. The dignity of man is an excellent thing, but therefore to hold one's self too sacred and precious is the reverse of excellent. There is something delightfully absurd in six volumes addressed to a world of such "vulgar fellows" as Thoreau affirmed his fellowmen to be. (pp. 374-75)

Solitary communion with Nature does not seem to have been sanitary or sweetening in its influence on Thoreau's character. On the contrary, his letters show him more cynical as he grew older. While he studied with respectful attention the minks and woodchucks, his neighbors, he looked with utter contempt on the august drama of destiny of which his country was the scene, and on which the curtain had already risen. He was converting us back to a state of nature "so eloquently," as Voltaire said of Rousseau, "that he almost persuaded us to go on all fours," while the wiser fates were making it possible for us to walk erect for the first time. Had he conversed more with his fellows, his sympathies would have widened with the assurance that his peculiar genius had more appreciation, and his writings a larger circle of readers, or at least a warmer one, than he dreamed of. . . . [Thoreau] was not a strong thinker, but a sensitive feeler. Yet his mind strikes us as cold and wintry in its purity. A light snow has fallen everywhere in which he seems to come on the track of the shier sensations that would elsewhere leave no trace. We think greater compression would have done more for his fame. A feeling of sameness comes over us as we read so much. Trifles are recorded with an over-minute punctuality and conscientiousness of detail. He registers the state of his personal thermometer thirteen times a day. . . [There] is no writing comparable with Thoreau's in kind, that is comparable with it in degree where it is best; where it disengages itself, that is, from the tangled roots and dead leaves of a second-hand Orientalism, and runs limpid and smooth and broadening as it runs, a mirror for whatever is grand and lovely in both worlds.

George Sand says neatly, that "Art is not a study of positive reality," (*actuality* were the fitter words,) "but seeking after ideal truth." It would be doing very inadequate justice to Thoreau if we left it to be inferred that this ideal element did not exist in him, and that too in larger proportion, if less obtrusive, than his nature-worship. He took nature as the mountain-path to an ideal world. If the path wind a good deal, if he record too faithfully every trip over a root, if he botanize somewhat wearisomely, he gives us now and then superb outlooks from some jutting crag, and brings us out at last into an illimitable ether, where the breathing is not difficult for those who have any true touch of the climbing spirit. His shanty-life was a mere impossibility, so far as his own conception of it goes, as an entire independency of mankind. The tub of Diogenes had a sounder bottom. Thoreau's experiment actually presupposed all that complicated civilization which it theoretically abjured. He squatted on another man's land; he borrows an axe; his boards, his nails, his bricks, his mortar, his books, his lamp, his fish-hooks, his plough, his hoe, all turn state's evidence against him as an accomplice in the sin of that artificial civilization which rendered it possible that such a person as Henry D. Thoreau should exist at all. . . . His aim was a noble and a useful one, in the direction of "plain living and high thinking." It was a practical sermon on Emerson's text that "things are in the saddle and ride mankind," an attempt to solve Carlyle's problem (condensed from Johnson) of "lessening your denominator." His whole life was a rebuke of the waste and aimlessness of our American luxury, which is an abject enslavement to tawdry upholstery. He had "fine translunary things" in him. His better style as a writer is in keeping with the simplicity and purity of his life. We have said that his range was narrow, but to be a master is to be a master. He had caught his English at its living source, among the poets and prose-writers of its best days; his literature was extensive and recondite; his quotations are always nuggets of the purest ore: there are sentences of his as perfect as anything in the language, and thoughts as clearly crystallized; his metaphors and images are always fresh from the soil; he had watched Nature like a detective who is to go upon the stand; as we read him, it seems as if all-out-of-doors had kept a diary and become its own Montaigne; we look at the landscape as in a Claude Lorraine glass; compared with his, all other books of similar aim, even White's "Selborne," seem dry as a country clergyman's meteorological journal in an old almanac. He belongs with Donne and Browne and Novalis; if not with the originally creative men, with the scarcely smaller class who are peculiar, and whose leaves shed their invisible thought-seed like ferns. (pp. 377-81)

James Russell Lowell, "Thoreau," in his Literary Essays, *Vol. I,* Houghton, Mifflin and Company, *1893, pp. 361-81.*

LITTELL'S LIVING AGE   (essay date 1874)

[It] is a vital error to lead in any way to the idea that Thoreau was a hermit, or that he permanently banished himself to Walden Wood to study trees, and beasts, and fishes, and to map out the land like a surveyor. He built a hut, it is true, with his own hands, and lived there for a time—fully two years it was—but the escapade, as some would call it, of Walden, was never meant by Thoreau to be other than an interlude. And yet with us in England he is too much conceived of in this light, as a sort of semi-wild man of the woods, and, in our idea, is saved from being a wild man altogether only by a dash of finer *instinct*, which made him influential with the lower creatures, but divorced him totally from human society. (p. 643)

Hawthorne's works are, in essence, a protest against every kind of republican levelling down. He sought, in the Puritan sentiment which was supplied to American history, with its relations to old English life, for traditions that recalled the inherited mysteries and dooms of life—breeding distinctions—and from that root what a tree grew up in the atmosphere of his quaint genius! Emerson, again, found compensating forces in the solitude and the occupations possible only in a country which is new, and not yet pressed for breathing space; and Thoreau, perhaps, more than either in the testimony which a real retirement from society could render to the highest idea of individuality, as the foundation-stone of a truly cultured society. Goethe said that when he needed to recruit himself for serious thought, he must retire into solitude; and so it was with Thoreau. But it was the opposite idea to that of Rousseau, for instance, which led Thoreau to Walden. He went there not to escape men, but to prepare himself for them; not to brood, but to act—only to act in lines that would enable him to stand forever after—free, vigorous, independent. There is a strange, close-packed realism in his writing, thoroughly symptomatic of the man and his character, as though he specially followed Nature in her economy of seed-packing; and it should be observed that you never get hint of the recluse, who speedily falls to dreaming and vain pitying of himself. There is no self-pity in Thoreau, rather a robust self-sufficiency that could claim the privilege of rendering manly help, though never seeking or accepting any, and that loves to administer readily what Emerson calls "shocks of effort." But there was in him nothing of the rebel proper; he delighted above all things to be at home, and to reverence, only you must allow him something of his own way. (pp. 643-44)

Thoreau was a naturalist, because he was primarily a poet. . . . He held things by inner affinities, rather than by hard classification. Instincts and habits were ever of more account with him than the mere organs and functions, whose expressions he held that these were, and nothing more. Yet he was observant of these also, and was seldom out in a matter of fact or calculation. Correctness in details, surprising patience, and a will that nothing could defeat or embarrass, held in closest union with fine imagination, without sense of contradiction—this was his first characteristic. His grand quality was sympathy. He came to everything with the poet's feeling, the poet's heart, the poet's eye. To observe was his joy. What pictures he can draw of wholly uninteresting places and things! What loving rapture he falls into over the commonest appearances! What new metaphors he finds lurking in ordinary sylvan occurrences! The common on-goings of nature were to him a mighty parable, and he set some part of it to adequate music, to which we may listen with delight, and learn wisdom. And as he brought sympathy with him towards every person he met and every object he examined, so he demanded it in those he encountered, though he had an utter horror of false professions of it. . . . He makes a poem out of the most ordinary object, event, or incident; but he will be the last to celebrate it as such; and, while some men seek a climax, he despised rhetoric and all conscious aims at effect. (pp. 647-48)

With Thoreau, in one word, everything is seen in relation to human sentiment and fitness. He is a reconciler. His great aim is to recommend Nature to Man—to prove her worthy of the recommendation, and so induce and enhance the idea of individuality—which, in midst of all her masses and mighty generalities, she everywhere faithfully celebrates. Thoreau went to Nature an individualist, and came back the prophet of society, as truly reconstructed, with liberty for its groundwork—but liberty which would give no quarter to licence of any kind. Sobriety, severity, and self-respect, foundation of all true sociality, are his motto. (p. 649)

Of fine saying his books are full. No more dainty fancy, or power of exactly presenting the image of what lay in his own mind, has any recent writer possessed in greater measure. And a sudden humour, like summer lightning, plays over his pages. . . .

And in his poems there is often a rarity and chastity of expression, and a quality such as we seldom meet with. . . .

His character was like those seaside flowers which smell the sweeter and grow the purer in that they are touched by the rough sea-salt. (p. 650)

> " *Henry Thoreau, the Poet-Naturalist* ," *in* Littell's Living Age, *Vol. CXX, No. 1552, March 7, 1874, pp. 643-50.*

R.L.S. [ROBERT LOUIS STEVENSON]   (essay date 1880)

[*A famed Scottish novelist and essayist, Stevenson wrote some of the nineteenth century's most beloved novels, including* Treasure Island, Doctor Jekyll and Mr. Hyde, *and* Kidnapped. *His novels are considered classics and are noted for their fast-paced action, strong plots, and well-drawn characters. In the following influential essay, Stevenson criticizes Thoreau for his coldness and self-centeredness. Terming Thoreau's way of life at Walden a "state of artificial training," Stevenson adds that Thoreau's choice to avoid humor worked against him. However, the critic also expresses admiration for Thoreau's willingness to be jailed for his "calm but radical opposition" to slavery. Stevenson recanted some of his criticism in a later essay (see excerpt below, 1886).*]

Thoreau's thin, penetrating, big-nosed face, even in a bad woodcut, conveys some hint of the limitations of his mind and character. With his almost acid sharpness of insight, with his almost animal dexterity in act, there went none of that large, unconscious geniality of the world's heroes. He was not easy, not ample, not urbane, not even kind; his enjoyment was hardly smiling, or the smile was not broad enough to be convincing; he had no waste lands nor kitchen-midden in his nature, but was all improved and sharpened to a point. . . . [His] many negative superiorities begin to smack a little of the prig. From

his later works he was in the habit of cutting out the humorous passages, under the impression that they were beneath the dignity of his moral muse; and there we see the prig stand public and confessed. It was "much easier," says Emerson acutely, much easier for Thoreau to say *no* than *yes;* and that is a characteristic which depicts the man. It is a useful accomplishment to be able to say *no,* but surely it is the essence of amiability to prefer to say *yes* where it is possible. There is something wanting in the man who does not hate himself whenever he is constrained to say no. And there was a great deal wanting in this born dissenter. He was almost shockingly devoid of weaknesses; he had not enough of them to be truly polar with humanity; whether you call him demi-god or demi-man, he was at least not altogether one of us, for he was not touched with a feeling of our infirmities. The world's heroes have room for all positive qualities, even those which are disreputable, in the capacious theatre of their dispositions. Such can live many lives; while a Thoreau can live but one, and that only with perpetual foresight.

He was no ascetic, rather an Epicurean of the nobler sort; and he had this one great merit, that he succeeded so far as to be happy. (p. 665)

Now Thoreau's content and ecstasy in living was, we may say, like a plant that he had watered and tended with womanish solicitude; for there is apt to be something unmanly, something almost dastardly, in a life that does not move with dash and freedom, and that fears the bracing contact of the world. In one word, Thoreau was a skulker. He did not wish virtue to go out of him among his fellow-men, but slunk into a corner to hoard it for himself. He left all for the sake of certain virtuous self-indulgences. It is true that his tastes were noble; that his ruling passion was to keep himself unspotted from the world; and that his luxuries were all of the same healthy order as cold tubs and early rising. But a man may be both coldly cruel in the pursuit of goodness, and morbid even in the pursuit of health. . . . We need have no respect for a state of artificial training. True health is to be able to do without it. Shakespeare, we can imagine, might begin the day upon a quart of ale, and yet enjoy the sunrise to the full as much as Thoreau, and commemorate his enjoyment in vastly better verses. A man who must separate himself from his neighbours' habits in order to be happy, is in much the same case with one who requires to take opium for the same purpose. What we want to see is one who can breast into the world, do a man's work, and still preserve his first and pure enjoyment of existence. (p. 666)

Thoreau had decided, it would seem, from the very first to lead a life of self-improvement: the needle did not tremble as with richer natures, but pointed steadily north; and as he saw duty and inclination in one, he turned all his strength in that direction. He was met upon the threshold by a common difficulty. In this world, in spite of its many agreeable features, even the most sensitive must undergo some drudgery to live. It is not possible to devote your time to study and meditation without what are quaintly but happily denominated private means; these absent, a man must contrive to earn his bread by some service to the public such as the public cares to pay him for; or, as Thoreau loved to put it, Apollo must serve Admetus. This was to Thoreau even a sourer necessity than it is to most; there was a love of freedom, a strain of the wild man, in his nature, that rebelled with violence against the yoke of custom; and he was so eager to cultivate himself and to be happy in his own society, that he could consent with difficulty even to the interruptions of friendship. "*Such are my engagements to myself* that I dare not promise,'' he once wrote in answer to an invitation; and the italics are his own. Marcus Aurelius found time to study virtue, and between whiles to conduct the imperial affairs of Rome; but Thoreau is so busy improving himself, that he must think twice about a morning call. And now imagine him condemned for eight hours a day to some uncongenial and unmeaning business! He shrank from the very look of the mechanical in life; all should, if possible, be sweetly spontaneous and swimmingly progressive. (p. 667)

It was his ambition to be an oriental philosopher; but he was always a very Yankee sort of oriental. Even in the peculiar attitude in which he stood to money, his system of personal economics, as we may call it, he displayed a vast amount of truly down-east calculation, and he adopted poverty like a piece of business. Yet his system is based on one or two ideas which, I believe, come naturally to all thoughtful youths, and are only pounded out of them by city uncles. Indeed, something essentially youthful distinguishes all Thoreau's knock-down blows at current opinion. Like the posers of a child, they leave the orthodox in a kind of speechless agony. These know the thing is nonsense. They are sure there must be an answer, yet somehow cannot find it. So it is with his system of economy. He cuts through the subject on so new a plane that the accepted arguments apply no longer; he attacks it in a new dialect where there are no catchwords ready made for the defender; after you have been boxing or years on a polite, gladiatorial convention, here is an assailant who does not scruple to hit below the belt. (p. 668)

Prudence, which bids us all go to the ant for sluggards and hoard against the day of sickness, was not a favourite with Thoreau. He preferred that other, whose name is so much misappropriated: Faith. When he had secured the necessaries of the moment, he would not reckon up possible accidents or torment himself with trouble for the future. He had no toleration for the man ''who ventures to live only by the aid of the mutual insurance company, which has promised to bury him decently.'' He would trust himself a little to the world. ''We may safely trust a good deal more than we do,'' says he. ''How much is not done by us! or what if we had been taken sick?'' And then, with a stab of satire, he describes contemporary mankind in a phrase: ''All the day long on the alert, at night we unwillingly say our prayers and commit ourselves to uncertainties.'' It is not likely that the public will be much affected by Thoreau, when they blink the direct injunctions of the religion they profess; and yet, whether we will or no, we make the same hazardous ventures; we back our own health and the honesty of our neighbours for all that we are worth; and it is chilling to think how many must lose their wager. (pp. 669-70)

[When he decided to leave Walden,] he showed the same simplicity in giving it up as in beginning it. There are some who could have done the one, but, vanity forbidding, not the other; and that is perhaps the story of the hermits; but Thoreau made no fetish of his own example, and did what he wanted squarely. And five years is long enough for an experiment and to prove the success of transcendental Yankeeism. It is not his frugality which is worthy of note; for, to begin with, that was inborn, and therefore inimitable by others who are differently constituted; and again, it was no new thing, but has often been equalled by poor Scotch students at the universities. The point is the sanity of his view of life, and the insight with which he recognised the position of money, and thought out for himself the problem of riches and a livelihood. Apart from his eccen-

tricities, he had perceived, and was acting on, a truth of universal application. For money enters in two different characters into the scheme of life. A certain amount, varying with the number and empire of our desires, is a true necessary to each one of us in the present order of society; but beyond that amount, money is a commodity to be bought or not to be bought, a luxury in which we may either indulge or stint ourselves, like any other. (pp. 670-71)

If Thoreau had simply dwelt in his house at Walden, a lover of trees, birds, and fishes, and the open air and virtue, a reader of wise books, an idle, selfish self-improver, he would have managed to cheat Admetus, but, to cling to metaphor, the devil would have had him in the end. Those who can avoid toil altogether and dwell in the Arcadia of private means, and even those who can, by abstinence, reduce the necessary amount of it to some six weeks a year, having the more liberty, have only the higher moral obligation to be up and doing in the interest of man. (p. 671)

Thoreau composed seemingly while he walked, or at least exercise and composition were with him intimately connected; for we are told that ''the length of his walk uniformly made the length of his writing.'' He speaks in one place of ''plainness and vigour, the ornaments of style,'' which is rather too paradoxical to be comprehensively true. In another he remarks: ''As for style of writing, if one has anything to say it drops from him simply as a stone falls to the ground.'' We must conjecture a very large sense indeed for the phrase ''if one has anything to say.'' When truth flows from a man, fittingly clothed in style and without conscious effort, it is because the effort has been made and the work practically completed before he sat down to write. It is only out of fulness of thinking that expression drops perfect like a ripe fruit; and when Thoreau wrote so nonchalantly at his desk, it was because he had been vigorously active during his walk. For neither clearness, compression, nor beauty of language come to any living creature till after a busy and a prolonged acquaintance with the subject on hand. . . . Thoreau was an exaggerative and a parabolical writer, not because he loved the literature of the East, but from a desire that people should understand and realise what he was writing. He was near the truth upon the general question; but in his own particular method, it appears to me, he wandered. Literature is not less a conventional art than painting or sculpture; and it is the least striking, as it is the most comprehensive, of the three. To hear a strain of music, to see a beautiful woman, a river, a great city, or a starry night, is to make a man despair of his Lilliputian arts in language. Now, to gain that emphasis which seems denied to us by the very nature of the medium, the proper method of literature is by selection, which is a kind of negative exaggeration. It is the right of the literary artist, as Thoreau was on the point of seeing, to leave out whatever does not suit his purpose. Thus we extract the pure gold; and thus the well-written story of a noble life becomes, by its very omissions, more thrilling to the reader. But to go beyond this, like Thoreau, and to exaggerate directly, is to leave the saner classical tradition, and to put the reader on his guard. And when you write the whole for the half, you do not express your thought more forcibly, but only express a different thought which is not yours.

Thoreau's true subject was the pursuit of self-improvement combined with an unfriendly criticism of life as it goes on in our societies; it is there that he best displays the freshness and surprising trenchancy of his intellect; it is there that his style becomes plain and vigorous, and therefore, according to his own formula, ornamental. Yet he did not care to follow this vein singly, but must drop into it by the way in books of a different purport. *Walden, or Life in the Woods, A Week on the Concord and Merrimack Rivers, The Maine Woods,* such are the titles he affects. He was probably reminded by his delicate critical perception that the true business of literature is with narrative; in reasoned narrative, and there alone, that art enjoys all its advantages, and suffers least from its defects. Dry precept and disembodied disquisition, as they can only be read with an effort of abstraction, can never convey a perfectly complete or a perfectly natural impression. Truth, even in literature, must be clothed with flesh and blood, or it cannot tell its whole story to the reader. Hence the effect of anecdote on simple minds; and hence good biographies and works of high, imaginative art, are not only far more entertaining, but far more edifying, than books of theory or precept. Now Thoreau could not clothe his opinions in the garment of art, for that was not his talent; but he sought to gain the same elbow-room for himself, and to afford a similar relief to his readers, by mingling his thoughts with a record of experience.

Again, he was a lover of nature. The quality which we should call mystery in a painting, and which belongs so particularly to the aspect of the external world and to its influence upon our feelings, was one which he was never weary of attempting to reproduce in his books. The seeming significance of nature's appearances, their unchanging strangeness to the senses, and the thrilling response which they waken in the mind of man, continued to surprise and stimulate his spirits. It appeared to him, I think, that if we could only write near enough to the facts, and yet with no pedestrian calm, but ardently, we might transfer the glamour of reality direct upon our pages; and that, if it were once thus captured and expressed, a new and instructive relation might appear between mens thoughts and the phenomena of nature. This was the eagle that he pursued all his life long, like a schoolboy with a butterfly net. . . . Perhaps the most successful work that Thoreau ever accomplished in this direction is to be found in the passages relating to fish in the *Week.* These are remarkable for a vivid truth of impression and a happy suitability of language, not frequently surpassed.

Whatever Thoreau tried to do was tried in fair, square prose, with sentences solidly built, and no help from bastard rhythms. Moreover, there is a progression—I cannot call it a progress—in his work towards a more and more strictly prosaic level, until at last he sinks into the bathos of the prosy. . . . He began to fall more and more into a detailed materialistic treatment; he went into the business doggedly, as who should make a guide-book; he not only chronicled what had been important in his own experience, but whatever might have been important in the experience of anybody else; not only what had affected him, but all that he saw or heard. His ardour had grown less, or perhaps it was inconsistent with a right materialistic treatment to display such emotions as he felt; and, to complete the eventful change, he chose, from a sense of moral dignity, to gut these later works of the saving quality of humour. He was not one of those authors who have learned, in his own words, "to leave out their dulness." He inflicts his full quantity upon the reader in such books as *Cape Cod,* or *The Yankee in Canada.* Of the latter he confessed that he had not managed to get much of himself into it. God knows he had not, nor yet much of Canada, we may hope. "Nothing," he says somewhere, "can shock a brave man but dulness." Well, there are few spots more shocking to the brave than the pages of *The Yankee in Canada.*

There are but three books of his that will be read with much pleasure; the *Week, Walden,* and the collected letters. . . . [As to his poetry,] he relied greatly on the goodwill of the reader, and wrote throughout in faith. It was an exercise of faith to suppose that many would understand the sense of his best work, or that any could be exhilarated by the dreary chronicling of his worst. (pp. 673-76)

"What means the fact," he cries, "that a soul which has lost all hope for itself can inspire in another listening soul such an infinite confidence in it, even while it is expressing its despair?" The question . . . forms the keynote of his thoughts on friendship. No one else, to my knowledge, has spoken in so high and just a spirit of the kindly relations; and I doubt if it be a drawback that these lessons should come from one in many ways so unfitted to be a teacher in this branch. The very coldness and egoism of his own intercourse gave him a clearer insight into the intellectual basis of our warm, mutual tolerations; and testimony to their worth comes with added force from one who was solitary and disobliging, and of whom a friend remarked, with equal wit and wisdom, "I love Henry, but I cannot like him."

He can hardly be persuaded to make any distinction between love and friendship; in such rarefied and freezing air, upon the mountain-tops of meditation, had he taught himself to breathe. (p. 676)

[Thoreau] has no illusions; he does not give way to love any more than to hatred; but preserves them both with care like valuable curiosities. A more bald-headed picture of life, if I may so express myself, or a more selfish, has seldom been presented. He is an egoist; he does not remember, or does not think it worth while to remark, that, in these near intimacies, we are ninety-nine times disappointed in our beggarly selves for once that we are disappointed in our friend; that it is we who seem most frequently undeserving of the love that unites us; and that it is by our friend's conduct that we are continually rebuked and yet strengthened for a fresh endeavour. Thoreau is dry, priggish, and selfish. It is profit he is after in these intimacies; moral profit, certainly, but still profit to himself. If you will be the sort of friend I want, he remarks naïvely, "my education cannot dispense with your society." His education! as though a friend were a dictionary. And with all this, not one word about pleasure, or laughter, or kisses, or any quality of flesh and blood. It was not inappropriate, surely, that he had such close relations with the fish. We can understand the friend already quoted, when he cried: "As for taking his arm, I would as soon think of taking the arm of an elm-tree!" (pp. 677-78)

The secret of his retirement lies not in misanthropy, of which he had no tincture, but part in his engrossing design of self-improvement and part in the real deficiencies of social intercourse. He was not so much difficult about his fellow human beings as he could not tolerate the terms of their association. . . . It seemed to him, I think, that society is precisely the reverse of friendship, in that it takes place on a lower level than the characters of any of the parties would warrant us to expect. The society talk of even the most brilliant man is of greatly less account than what you will get from him in (as the French say) a little committee. And Thoreau wanted geniality; he had not enough of the superficial, even at command; he could not swoop into a parlour and, in the naval phrase, "cut out" a human being from that dreary port; nor had he inclination for the task. I suspect he loved books and nature as well and near as warmly as he loved his fellow-creatures:

a melancholy, lean degeneration of the human character. (pp.678-79)

In the case of Thoreau, so great a show of doctrine demands some outcome in the field of action. If nothing were to be done but build a shanty beside Walden Pond, we have heard altogether too much of these declarations of independence. That the man wrote some books is nothing to the purpose, for the same has been done in a suburban villa. That he kept himself happy is perhaps a sufficient excuse, but it is disappointing to the reader. We may be unjust, but when a man despises commerce and philanthropy alike, and has views of good so soaring that he must take himself apart from mankind for their cultivation, we will not be content without some striking act. It was not Thoreau's fault if he were not martyred; had the occasion come, he would have made a noble ending. As it is, he did once seek to interfere in the world's course; he made one practical appearance on the stage of affairs; and a strange one it was, and strangely characteristic of the nobility and the eccentricity of the man. It was forced on him by his calm but radical opposition to negro slavery. . . . [In] 1843 he ceased to pay the poll-tax. The highway-tax he paid, for he said he was as desirous to be a good neighbour as to be a bad subject; but no more poll-tax to the State of Massachusetts [because the state supported the Fugitive Slave Law]. (p. 681)

And the upshot? A friend paid the tax for him; continued year by year to pay it in the sequel; and Thoreau was free to walk the woods unmolested. It was a *fiasco,* but to me it does not seem laughable; even those who joined in the laughter at the moment would be insensibly affected by this quaint instance of a good man's horror for injustice. We may compute the worth of that one night's imprisonment as outweighing half a hundred voters at some subsequent election; and if Thoreau had possessed as great a power of persuasion as (let us say) Falstaff, if he had counted a party however small, if his example had been followed by a hundred or by thirty of his fellows, I cannot but believe it would have greatly precipitated the era of freedom and justice. We feel the misdeeds of our country with so little fervour, for we are not witnesses to the suffering they cause; but when we see them wake an active horror in our fellow-man, when we see a neighbour prefer to lie in prison rather than be so much as passively implicated in their perpetration, even the dullest of us will begin to realise them with a quicker pulse. (p. 682)

> *R.L.S. [Robert Louis Stevenson], "Henry David Thoreau: His Character and Opinions," in* The Cornhill Magazine, *Vol. XLI, No. 246, June, 1880, pp. 665-82.*

JOHN BURROUGHS (essay date 1882)

[*Burroughs, an American naturalist, generally extols Thoreau's life and works. His essay in part disputes Robert Louis Stevenson's evaluation of Thoreau (1880).*]

[Thoreau's] journal was probably written with an eye to its future publication. It does not consist of mere scraps, hasty memoranda, and jottings-down, like Hawthorne's note-book, and like the blotter most literary men keep, but of finished work—blocks carefully quarried, and trimmed, and faced, at least with a plumb spot upon each, to be used or rejected in the construction of future works. When he wrote a book, or a lecture, or an essay, he probably went to his journal for the greater share of the material. The amount of this manuscript matter he left behind him at his death was, perhaps, equal to

all the matter he had printed, and, though it had doubtless been sorted over more or less, yet a large per cent. of it seems to be quite as good as any of his work and quite as characteristic. He revised, and corrected, and supplemented his record from day to day and from year to year, till it reflects truly his life and mind. Every scrap he ever wrote carries his flavor and quality unmistakably, as much as a leaf or twig of a sassafras-tree carries its quality and flavor. He was a man so thoroughly devoted to principle and to his own aims in life that he seems never to have allowed himself one indifferent or careless moment. He was always making the highest demands upon himself and upon others.

In his private letters his bow is strung just as taut as in his printed works, and he uses arrows from the same quiver, and send them just as high and far as he can. In his journal it is the same. (pp. 368-69)

In writing of Thoreau, I am not conscious of having any criticism to make of him. I would fain accept him just as he was, and make the most of him, defining and discriminating him as I would a flower or a bird or any other product of nature—perhaps exaggerating some features the better to bring them out. I suppose there were greater men among his contemporaries, but I doubt if there were any more genuine and sincere, or more devoted to ideal ends. If he was not this, that, or the other great man, he was Thoreau, and he fills his own niche well, and has left a positive and distinct impression upon the literature of his country. He did his work thoroughly; he touched bottom; he made the most of his life. He was, perhaps, a little too near his friend and master, Emerson, and brought too directly under his influence. If he had lived farther from him, he would have felt his attraction less. But he was just as positive a fact as Emerson. The contour of his moral nature was just as firm and resisting. He was no more a soft-shelled egg, to be dented by every straw in the nest, than was his distinguished neighbor.

An English reviewer [Robert Louis Stevenson] has summed up his estimate of Thoreau by calling him a "skulker." . . . Thoreau was a skulker if it appears that he ran away from a noble part to perform an ignoble, or one less noble. The world has a right to the best there is in a man, both in word and deed: from the scholar, knowledge; from the soldier, courage; from the statesman, wisdom; from the farmer, good husbandry, etc.; and from all, virtue; but has it a right to say arbitrarily who shall be soldiers and who poets? Is there no virtue but virtue? no religion but in the creeds? no salt but what is crystallized? Who shall presume to say the world did not get the best there was in Thoreau—high and much needed service from him?—albeit there appear in the account more kicks than compliments. Would you have had him stick to his lead-pencils, or to school-teaching, and let Walden Pond and the rest go? We should have lost some of the raciest and most antiseptic books in English literature, and an example of devotion to principle that provokes and stimulates like a winter morning. I am not aware that Thoreau shirked any responsibility or dodged any duty proper to him, and he could look the world as square in the face as any man that ever lived. (p. 369)

As a writer, Thoreau shows all he is, and more. Nothing is kept back; greater men have had far less power of statement. His thoughts do not merely crop out, but lie upon the surface of his pages. They are fragments; there is no more than you see. It is not the edge or crown of the native rock, but a drift bowlder. He sees clearly, thinks swiftly, and the sharp emphasis and decision of his mind strew his pages with definite and striking images and ideas. His expression is never sod-bound, and you get its full force at once.

One of his chief weapons is a kind of restrained extravagance of statement, a compressed exaggeration of metaphor. The hyperbole is big, but it is gritty and is firmly held. Sometimes it takes the form of paradox, as when he tells his friend that he needs his hate as much as his love:

> Indeed, indeed, I cannot tell,
> Though I ponder on it well,
> Which were easier to state,
> All my love or all my hate.

Or when he says, in **"Walden":** "Our manners have been corrupted by communication with the saints," and the like. Sometimes it becomes downright brag, as when he says, emphasizing his own preoccupation and indifference to events: "I would not run around the corner to see the world blow up"; or again: "Methinks I would hear with indifference if a trustworthy messenger were to inform me that the sun drowned himself last night." Again it takes an impish, ironical form, as when he says: "In heaven I hope to bake my own bread and clean my own linen." Another time it assumes a half-quizzical, half-humorous turn, as when he tells one of his correspondents that he was so warmed up in getting his winter's wood that he considered, after he got it housed, whether he should not dispose of it to the ash-man, as if he had extracted all its heat. Often it gives only an added emphasis to his expression, as when he says: "A little thought is sexton to all the world"; or, "Some circumstantial evidence is very strong, as when you find a trout in the milk"; but its best and most constant office is to act as a kind of fermenting, expanding gas that lightens, if it sometimes inflates, his page. His exaggeration is saved by its wit, its unexpectedness. It gives a wholesome jostle and shock to the mind.

Thoreau was not a racy writer, but a trenchant; not nourishing so much as stimulating; not convincing, but wholesomely exasperating and arousing, which, in some respects, is better. There is no heat in him, and yet in reading him one understands what he means when he says that, sitting by his stove at night, he sometimes had thoughts that kept the fire warm. I think the mind of his reader always reacts healthfully and vigorously from his most rash and extreme statements. The blood comes to the surface and to the extremities with a bound. He is the best of counter-irritants when he is nothing else. There is nothing to reduce the tone of your moral and intellectual systems in Thoreau. Such heat as there is in refrigeration, as he himself might say,—you are always sure of that in his books.

His literary art, like that of Emerson's, is in the unexpected turn of his sentences. Shakspere says:

> It is the witness still of excellency
> To put a strange face on his own perfection.

This "strange face" Thoreau would have at all hazards, even if it was a false face. If he could not state a truth he would state a paradox, which, however, is not always a false face. He must make the commonest facts and occurrences wear a strange and unfamiliar look. The commonplace he would give a new dress, even if he set it masquerading. But the reader is always the gainer by this tendency in him. It gives a fresh and novel coloring to what in other writers would prove flat and wearisome. He made the whole world interested in his private experiment at Walden Pond by the strange and, on the whole, beaming face he put upon it. Of course, this is always more

or less the art of genius, but it was preëminently the art of Thoreau. We are not buoyed up by great power, we do not swim lightly as in deep water, but we are amused and stimulated, and now and then positively electrified.

To make an extreme statement, and so be sure that he made an emphatic one, that was his aim. Exaggeration is less to be feared than dullness and tameness. The far-fetched is good if you fetch it swift enough; you must make its heels crack—jerk it out of its boots, in fact. Cushions are good provided they are well stuck with pins; you will be sure not to go to sleep in that case. Warm your benumbed hands in the snow; that is a more wholesome warmth than that of the kitchen stove. This is the way he underscored his teachings. Sometimes he racked his bones to say the unsayable. His mind had a strong gripe, and he often brings a great pressure to bear upon the most vague and subtle problems, or shadows of problems, but he never quite succeeds to my satisfaction in condensing bluing from the air or from the Indian summer haze, any more than he succeeded in extracting health and longevity from water-gruel and rye-meal.

He knew what an exaggeration he was, and he went about it deliberately. He says to one of his correspondents, a Mr. B——, whom he seems to have delighted to pummel with these huge boxing-gloves; "I trust that you realize what an exaggerator I am,—that I lay myself out to exaggerate whenever I have an opportunity,—pile Pelion upon Ossa to reach heaven so. Expect no trivial truth from me, unless I am on the witness-stand. I will come as near to lying as you can drive a coach-and-four."

We have every reason to be thankful that he was not always or commonly on the witness-stand. The record would have been much duller. Eliminate from him all his exaggerations, all his magnifying of the little, all his inflation of bubbles, etc., and you make sad havoc in his pages—as you would, in fact, in any man's. Of course it is one thing to bring the distant near, and thus magnify as does the telescope, and it is quite another thing to inflate a pigmy to the stature of a giant with a gas-pipe. But Thoreau brings the stars as near as any writer I know of, and if he sometimes magnifies a will-o'-the-wisp, too, what matters it? He had a hard commonsense, as well as an uncommon sense, and he knows well when he is conducting you to the brink of one of his astonishing hyperboles, and inviting you to take the leap with him, and what is more, he knows that you know it. Nobody is deceived and the game is well played. (pp. 375-76)

The bird Thoreau most admired was Chanticleer, crowing from his perch in the morning. . . .

Thoreau pitched his **"Walden"** in this key; he claps his wings and gives forth a clear, saucy, cheery, triumphant note—if only to wake his neighbors up. And the book is certainly the most delicious piece of brag in literature. There is nothing else like it; nothing so good, certainly. It is a challenge and a triumph, and has a morning freshness and *élan*. Read the chapter on his "beanfield." One wants to go forthwith and plant a field with beans, and hoe them barefoot. It is a kind of celestial agriculture. (p. 376)

Emerson says Thoreau's determination on natural history was organic, but it was his determination on supernatural history that was organic. Natural history was but one of the doors through which he sought to gain admittance to this inner and finer heaven of things. He hesitated to call himself a naturalist;

probably even poet-naturalist would not have suited him. He says in his journal: "The truth is, I am a mystic, a transcendentalist, and a natural philosopher to boot," and the least of these is the natural philosopher. He says: "Man cannot afford to be a naturalist, to look at Nature directly, but only with the side of his eye. He must look through and beyond her. To look at her is as fatal as to look at the head of Medusa. It turns the man of science to stone." It is not looking at Nature that turns the man of science to stone, but looking at his dried and labeled specimens, and his dried and labeled theories of her. Thoreau always sought to look through and beyond her, and he missed seeing much there was in her; the jealous goddess had her revenge. I do not make this remark as a criticism, but to account for his failure to make any new or valuable contribution to natural history. He did not love Nature for her own sake, or the bird and the flower for their own sakes or with an unmixed and disinterested love, as Gilbert White did, for instance, but for what he could make out of them. (p. 377)

Hence, when we regard Thoreau simply as an observer or as a natural historian, there have been better, though few so industrious and persistent. He was up and out at all hours of the day and night, and in all seasons and weathers, year in and year out, and yet he saw and recorded nothing new. I cannot say that there was any felicitous and happy seeing; there was no inspiration of the eye, certainly not in the direction of natural history. He has added no new line or touch to the portrait of bird or beast that I can recall—no important or significant fact to their lives. What he saw in this field everybody may see who looks; it is patent. He had not the detective eye of the great naturalist; he did not catch the clews and hints dropped here and there, the quick, flashing movements, the shy but significant gestures by which new facts are disclosed, mainly because he was not looking for them. His eye was not penetrating and interpretive. It was full of speculation; it was sophisticated with literature, sophisticated with Concord, sophisticated with himself. His mood was subjective rather than objective. He was more intent on the natural history of his own thought than on that of the bird. To the last his ornithology was not quite sure, not quite trustworthy. In his published journal he sometimes names the wrong bird, and what short work a naturalist would have made of his night-warbler, which Emerson reports Thoreau had been twelve years trying to identify. (pp. 377-78)

Thoreau was a man eminently "preoccupied of his own soul." He had no self-abandonment, no self-forgetfulness; he could not give himself to the birds or animals: they must surrender to him. He says to one of his correspondents: "Whether he sleeps or wakes, whether he runs or walks, whether he uses a microscope or a telescope, or his naked eye, a man never discovers anything, never overtakes anything, or leaves anything behind, but himself." This is half true of some; it is wholly true of others. It is wholly true of Thoreau. Nature was the glass in which he saw himself. He says the partridge loves peas, but not those that go into the pot with her! All the peas Thoreau loved had been in the pot with him and were seasoned by him.

I trust I do not in the least undervalue Thoreau's natural history notes; I only wish there were more of them. What makes them so valuable and charming in his rare descriptive powers. He could give the simple fact with the freshest and finest poetic bloom upon it. (pp. 378-79)

John Burroughs, "Henry D. Thoreau," in The Century, *Vol. 24, No. 3, July, 1882, pp. 368-79.*

ROBERT LOUIS STEVENSON   (essay date 1886)

[*This essay, which originally appeared in Stevenson's* Familiar Studies of Men and Books *in 1886, is somewhat of an apology for his earlier criticism of Thoreau (see excerpt above, 1880). He attributes his reconsideration of Thoreau largely to H. A. Page's biography, which discussed details of Thoreau's life that compelled Stevenson to reconsider his appraisal of Thoreau's life at Walden.*]

[My criticism of Thoreau] is an admirable instance of the "point of view" forced throughout, and of too earnest reflection on imperfect facts. Upon me this pure, narrow, sunnily-ascetic Thoreau had exercised a great charm. I have scarce written ten sentences since I was introduced to him, but his influence might be somewhere detected by a close observer. Still it was as a writer that I had made his acquaintance; I took him on his own explicit terms; and when I learned details of his life, they were, by the nature of the case and my own *parti-pris*, read even with a certain violence in terms of his writings. There could scarce be a perversion more justifiable than that; yet it was still a perversion. (p. 84)

On two most important points, Dr. Japp [pseudonym of H. A. Page, Thoreau's English biographer,] added to my knowledge, and with the same blow fairly demolished that part of my criticism. First, if Thoreau were content to dwell by Walden Pond, it was not merely with designs of self-improvement, but to serve mankind in the highest sense. Hither came the fleeing slave; thence was he despatched along the road to freedom. That shanty in the woods was a station in the great Underground Railroad; that adroit and philosophic solitary was an ardent worker, soul and body, in that so much more than honorable movement, which, if atonement were possible for nations, should have gone far to wipe away the guilt of slavery. But in history sin always meets with condign punishment; the generation passes, the offence remains, and the innocent must suffer. (pp. 84-5)

Second, if appears, and the point is capital, that Thoreau was once fairly and manfully in love, and, with perhaps too much aping of the angel, relinquished the woman to his brother. Even though the brother were like to die of it, we have not yet heard the last opinion of the woman. But be that as it may, we have here the explanation of the "rarefied and freezing air" in which I complained that he had taught himself to breathe. Reading the man through the books, I took his professions in good faith. He made a dupe of me, even as he was seeking to make a dupe of himself, wrestling philosophy to the needs of his own sorrow. But in the light of this new fact, those pages, seemingly so cold, are seen to be alive with feeling. What appeared to be a lack of interest in the philosopher turns out to have been a touching insincerity of the man to his own heart; and that fine-spun airy theory of friendship, so devoid, as I complained, of any quality of flesh and blood, a mere anodyne to lull his pains. The most temperate of living critics once marked a passage of my own with a cross and the words, "'This is nonsense." It not only seemed; it was so. It was a private bravado of my own, which I had so often repeated to keep up my spirits, that I had grown at last wholly to believe it, and had ended by setting it down as a contribution to the theory of life. So with the more icy parts of this philosophy of Thoreau's. He was affecting the Spartanism he had not; and the old sentimental wound still bled afresh, while he deceived himself with reasons.

Thoreau's theory, in short, was one thing and himself another: of the first, the reader will find what I believe to be a pretty faithful statement and a fairly just criticism in the study; of the second he will find but a contorted shadow. So much of the man as fitted nicely with his doctrines, in the photographer's phrase came out. But that large part which lay outside and beyond, for which he had found or sought no formula, on which perhaps his philosophy even looked askance, is wanting in my study, as it was wanting in the guide I followed. In some ways a less serious writer, in all ways a nobler man, the true Thoreau still remains to be depicted. (pp. 85-6)

> *Robert Louis Stevenson, ''Stevenson's Recantation,'' in* Thoreau: A Century of Criticism, *edited by Walter Harding, Southern Methodist University Press, 1954, pp. 84-6.*

WALT WHITMAN [AS REPORTED BY HORACE TRAUBEL] (conversation date 1888)

[*American poet, essayist, novelist, short story writer, journalist, and editor, Whitman is regarded as one of America's finest poets, and a great literary innovator. His* Leaves of Grass, *a collection of poems which celebrates the ''divine average,'' democracy, and sexuality, was a major influence on modern free verse. In the following conversation with Horace Traubel, which took place in 1888, Whitman states that ''Thoreau's great fault was disdain . . . for men.''*]

Thoreau's great fault was disdain—disdain for men (for Tom, Dick and Harry): inability to appreciate the average life—even the exceptional life: it seemed to me a want of imagination. He couldn't put his life into any other life—realize why one man was so and another man was not so: was impatient with other people on the street and so forth. We had a hot discussion about it—it was a bitter difference: it was rather a surprise to me to meet in Thoreau such a very aggravated case of superciliousness. It was egotistic—not taking that word in its worst sense. . . . We could not agree at all in our estimate of men—of the men we meet here, there, everywhere—the concrete man. Thoreau had an abstraction about man—a right abstraction: there we agreed. We had our quarrel only on this ground. Yet he was a man you would have to like—an interesting man, simple, conclusive. . . .

> *Walt Whitman [as reported by Horace Traubel in 1888], in* Thoreau: Man of Concord, *edited by Walter Harding, Holt, Rinehart and Winston, 1960, p. 116.*

HAVELOCK ELLIS   (essay date 1890)

[*Ellis was a pioneering sex-psychologist and often controversial English man of letters. His most famous work, the seven-volume* The Psychology of Sex (1897-1928) *is a study containing frankly stated case histories of sex-related psychological abnormalities which was greatly responsible for changing British and American attitudes toward the hitherto forbidden subject of sexuality. Ellis argues that Thoreau was an artist and a moralist rather than a naturalist. Yet his knowledge of nature, Ellis adds, was at the expense of ''ignorance of his fellows. The chief part of life he left untouched.''*]

It has been claimed for Thoreau by some of his admirers, never by himself, that he was a man of science, a naturalist. Certainly, in some respects, he had in him the material for an almost ideal naturalist. . . . [But] he seems to have been absolutely deficient in scientific sense. His bare, impersonal records of observations are always dull and unprofitable reading; occasionally he stumbles on a good observation, but, not realizing its significance, he never verifies it or follows it up.

His science is that of a fairly intelligent schoolboy—a counting of birds' eggs and a running after squirrels. Of the vital and organic relationships of facts, or even of the existence of such relationships, he seems to have no perception. . . . He was not a naturalist: he was an artist and a moralist.

He was born into an atmosphere of literary culture, and the great art he cultivated was that of framing sentences. . . . Undoubtedly he succeeded; his sentences frequently have all the massive and elemental qualities that he desired. They have more; if he knew little of the architectonic qualities of style, there is a keen exhilarating breeze blowing about these bowlders, and when we look at them they have the grace and audacity, the happy, natural extravagance of fragments of the finest Decorated Gothic on the site of a fourteenth century abbey. He was in love with the things that are wildest and most untamable in Nature, and of these his sentences often seem to be a solid artistic embodiment, the mountain side, ''its sublime gray mass, that antique, brownish-gray, Ararat color,'' or the ''ancient, familiar, immortal cricket sound,'' the thrush's song, his *ranz des vâches,* or the song that of all seemed to rejoice him most, the clear, exhilarating, braggart, clarion-crow of the cock. (pp. 90-2)

Thoreau was a piece; he was at harmony with himself, though it may be that the elements that went to make up the harmony were few. The austerity and exhilaration and simple paganism of his art were at one with his morality. He was, at the very core, a preacher; the morality that he preached, interesting in itself, is, for us, the most significant thing about him. Thoreau was, in the noblest sense of the word, a cynic. The school of Antisthenes is not the least interesting of the Socratic schools, and Thoreau is perhaps the finest flower that that school has ever yielded. . . . A life in harmony with Nature, the culture of joyous simplicity, the subordination of science to ethics— these were the principles of cynicism, and to these Thoreau was always true. (pp. 92-3)

Every true Cynic is, above all, a moralist and a preacher. Thoreau could never be anything else; that was, in the end, his greatest weakness. This unfailing ethereality, this perpetual challenge of the acridity and simplicity of Nature, becomes at least hypernatural. . . . He had learnt something of the mystery of Nature, but the price of his knowledge was ignorance of his fellows. The chief part of life he left untouched.

Yet all that he had to give he gave fully and ungrudgingly; and it was of the best and rarest. We shall not easily exhaust the exhilaration of it. ''We need the tonic of wildness.'' Thoreau has heightened for us the wildness of Nature, and his work— all written, as we need not be told, in the open air—is full of this tonicity; it is a sort of moral quinine, and, like quinine under certain circumstances, it leaves a sweet taste behind. (pp. 94-5)

> *Havelock Ellis, ''Whitman,'' in his* The New Spirit, *Boni and Liveright, 1890, pp. 86-127.**

PAUL ELMER MORE   (essay date 1901)

[*More was an American critic who is especially esteemed for the philosophical and literary erudition of his multi-volume series,* Shelburne Essays (1904-21). *Here he asserts that Thoreau's work is marked by his sense of awe and wonder of nature. His ''New World inheritance,'' moreover, distinguishes his attitude toward nature from that of the great poets who preceeded him. The most notable divergence in Thoreau's thinking from his English models, More concludes, is Thoreau's "lack of pantheistic reverie."*]

Thoreau was the creator of a new manner of writing about Nature. In its deeper essence his work is inimitable, as it is the voice of a unique personality; but in its superficial aspects it has been taken up by a host of living writers, who have caught something of his method, even if they lack his genius and singleness of heart. (p. 860)

Thoreau's work was distinguished from that of his American predecessors and imitators by . . . [the] qualities of awe and wonder which we, in our communings with Nature, so often cast away. Mere description, though it may at times have a scientific value, is after all a very cheap form of literature; and . . . too much curiosity of detail is likely to exert a deadening influence on the philosophic and poetic contemplation of Nature. Such an influence is, as I believe, specially noticeable at the present time, and even Thoreau was not entirely free from its baneful effect. Much of his writing, perhaps the greater part, is the mere record of observation and classification, and has not the slightest claim on our remembrance,—unless, indeed, it possesses some scientific value, which I doubt. Certainly the parts of his work having permanent interest are just those chapters where he is less the minute observer, and more the contemplative philosopher. Despite the width and exactness of his information, he was far from having the truly scientific spirit; the acquisition of knowledge, with him, was in the end quite subordinate to his interest in the moral significance of Nature, and the words he read in her obscure scroll were a language of strange mysteries, oftentimes of awe. It is a constant reproach to the prying, self-satisfied habits of small minds to see the reverence of this great-hearted observer before the supreme goddess he so loved and studied.

Much of this contemplative spirit of Thoreau is due to the soul of the man himself, to that personal force which no analysis of character can explain. But, besides this, it has always seemed to me that, more than any other descriptive writer of the country, his mind is the natural outgrowth, and his essays the natural expression, of a feeling deep-rooted in the historical beginnings of New England; and this foundation in the past gives a strength and convincing force to his words that lesser writers utterly lack. (pp. 860-61)

[The] dryness of detailed description in the New World was from the first modified and lighted up by the wondering awe of men set down in the midst of the strange and often threatening forces of an untried wilderness; and this sense of awful aloofness, which to a certain extent lay dormant in the earlier writers, did nevertheless sink deep into the heart of New England, and when, in the lapse of time, the country entered into its intellectual renaissance, and the genius came who was destined to give full expression to the thoughts of his people before the face of Nature, it was inevitable that his works should be dominated by just this sense of poetic mystery.

It is this New World inheritance, moreover,—joined, of course, with his own inexplicable personality, which must not be left out of account,—that makes Thoreau's attitude toward Nature something quite distinct from that of the great poets who just preceded him. There was in him none of the fiery spirit of the revolution which caused Byron to mingle hatred of men with enthusiasm for the Alpine solitudes. There was none of the passion for beauty and voluptuous self-abandonment of Keats; these were not in the atmosphere he breathed at Concord. He was not touched with Shelley's unearthly mysticism, nor had he ever fed

> on the aerial kisses
> Of shapes that haunt thought's wildernesses;

his moral sinews were too stark and strong for that form of mental dissipation. Least of all did he, after the manner of Wordsworth, hear in the voice of Nature any compassionate plea for the weakness and sorrow of the downtrodden. Philanthropy and humanitarian sympathies were to him a desolation and a woe. (pp. 861-62)

But the deepest and most essential difference is the lack of pantheistic reverie in Thoreau. It is this brooding over the universal spirit embodied in the material world which almost always marks the return of sympathy with Nature, and which is particularly noticeable in the poets of the present century. . . . If Nature smiled upon Thoreau at times, she was still an alien creature who only succumbed to his force and tenderness, as she had before given her bounty, though reluctantly, to the Pilgrim Fathers. A certain companionship he had with the plants and wild beasts of the field, a certain intimacy with the dumb earth; but he did not seek to merge his personality in their impersonal life, or look to them for a response to his own inner moods; he associated with them as the soul associates with the body.

More characteristic is his sense of awe, even of dread, toward the great unsubdued forces of the world. The loneliness of the mountains as they appeared to the early adventurers in a strange, unexplored country; the repellent loneliness of the barren heights frowning down inhospitably upon the pioneer who scratched the soil at their base; the loneliness and terror of the dark, untrodden forests, where the wanderer might stray away and be lost forever, where savage men were more feared than the wild animals, and where superstition saw the haunt of the Black Man and of all uncleanness,—all this tradition of sombre solitude made Nature to Thoreau something very different from the hills and valleys of Old England. (pp. 862-63)

I do not mean to present the work of Thoreau as equal in value to the achievement of the great poets with whom I have compared him, but wish merely in this way to bring out more definitely his characteristic traits. Yet if his creative genius is less than theirs, I cannot but think his attitude toward Nature is in many respects truer and more wholesome. Pantheism, whether on the banks of the Ganges or of the Thames, seems to bring with it a spreading taint of effeminacy; and from this the mental attitude of our Concord naturalist was eminently free. There is something tonic and bracing in his intercourse with the rude forces of the forest. . . . Nature was to him a discipline of the will as much as a stimulant to the imagination. (p. 863)

And withal his stoic virtues never dulled his sense of awe, and his long years of observation never lessened his feeling of strangeness in the presence of solitary Nature. If at times his writing descends into the cataloguing style of the ordinary naturalist, yet the old tradition of wonder was too strong in him to be more than temporarily obscured. Unfortunately, his occasional faults have become in some of his recent imitators the staple of their talent; but Thoreau was preëminently the poet and philosopher of his school. . . . (p. 864)

Paul Elmer More, "A Hermit's Notes on Thoreau," in The Atlantic Monthly, *Vol. LXXXVII, No. DXXIV, June, 1901, pp. 857-64.*

BRADFORD TORREY (essay date 1905)

Thoreau was a man of his own kind. Many things may be said of him, favorable and unfavorable, but this must surely be said first,—that, taken for all in all, he was like nobody else. . . .

By good fortune he left [his journal] behind him, and, to complete the good fortune, it is at last to be printed, no longer in selections, but as a whole; and if a man is curious to know what such an original, plain-spoken, perfection-seeking, convention-despising, dogma-disbelieving, wisdom-loving, sham-hating, nature-worshiping, poverty-proud genius was in the habit of confiding to so patient a listener at the close of the day, he has only to read the book. (p. 5)

[If] a man wishes to know Thoreau as he was, let him read [his journal]. He will find himself in clean, self-respecting company, with no call to blush, as if he were playing the eavesdropper. Of confessions, indeed, in the spicy sense of the word, Thoreau had none to make. He was no Montaigne, no Rousseau, no Samuel Pepys. How should he be? He was a Puritan of Massachusetts, though he kept no Sabbath, was seen in no church,—being very different from Mr. Pepys in more ways than one,—and esteemed the Hebrew scriptures as a good book like any other. (p. 6)

His fellow mortals, as a rule, did not recommend themselves to him. His thoughts were none the better for their company, as they almost always were for the company of the pine tree and the meadow. Inspiration, a refreshing of the spiritual faculties, as indispensable to him as daily bread, his fellow mortals did not furnish. For this state of things he sometimes (once or twice at least) mildly reproaches himself. It may be that he is to blame for so commonly skipping humanity and its affairs; he will seek to amend the fault, he promises. (p. 7)

With all his passion for "that glorious society called solitude," and with all his feeling that mankind, as a "past phenomenon," thought far too highly of itself, it is abundantly in evidence that Thoreau, in his own time and on his own terms, was capable of a really human delight in familiar intercourse with his fellows. . . . What is very constant and emphatic [in his journal]—emphatic sometimes to the point of painfulness—is the hermit's hunger and thirst after friendship; a friendship the sweets of which, so far as appears, he was very sparingly to enjoy. For if he was at home in the family group and in huckleberry excursions with children, if he relished to the full a talk with a stray fisherman, a racy-tongued wood-chopper, or a good Indian, something very different seems to have been habitual with him when it came to intercourse with equals and friends.

Here, even more than elsewhere, he was an uncompromising idealist. His craving was for a friendship more than human, friendship such as it was beyond any one about him to furnish, if it was not, as may fairly be suspected, beyond his own capacity to receive. (p. 9)

His life, the quality of his life, that for Thoreau was the paramount concern. To the furthering of that end all things must be held subservient. Nature, man, books, music, all for him had the same use. This one thing he did,—he cultivated himself. If any, because of his so doing, accused him of selfishness, preaching to him of philanthropy, alms-giving, and what not, his answer was not to wait for. (p. 12)

Yes, he was undoubtedly peculiar. As to that there could never be anything but agreement among practical people. In a world where shiftiness and hesitation are the rule, nothing looks so eccentric as a straight course. . . .

He was constitutionally earnest. There are pages of the journal, indeed, which make one feel that perhaps he was in danger of being too much so for his own profit. Possibly it is not quite wholesome, possibly, if one dares to say it, it begets a something like priggishness, for the soul to be keyed up continually to so strenuous a pitch. In Thoreau's case, at all events, one is glad for every sign of a slackening of the tension. "Set the red hen to-day;" "Got green grapes to stew;" trivialities like these, too far apart (one is tempted to colloquialize, and call them "precious few," finding them so infrequent and so welcome), strike the reader with a sudden sensation of relief, as if he had been wading to the chin, and all at once his feet had touched a shallow. (p. 13)

More refreshing still are entries describing hours of serene communion with nature, hours in which, as in an instance already cited, the Spirit of the Lord blessed him, and he forgot even to be good. These entries, likewise, are less numerous than could be wished, though perhaps as frequent as could fairly be expected; since ecstasies, like feasts, must in the nature of things be somewhat broadly spaced; and it is interesting, not to say surprising, to see how frankly he looks upon them afterward as subjects on which to try his pen. In these "seasons when our genius reigns we may be powerless for expression," he remarks; but in calmer hours, when talent is again active, "the memory of those rarer moods comes to color our picture, and is the permanent paint-pot, as it were, into which we dip our brush." But, in truth, the whole journal, some volumes of which are carefully indexed in his own hand, is quite undisguisedly a collection of thoughts, feelings, and observations, out of which copy is to be extracted. (p. 14)

Thoreau the naturalist appears in the journal, not as a master, but as a learner. It could hardly be otherwise, of course, a journal being what it is. There we see him conning by himself his daily lesson, correcting yesterday by to-day, and to-day by to-morrow, progressing, like every scholar, over the stepping-stones of his own mistakes. (p. 15)

He maintained stoutly, from beginning to end, that he was not of the ordinary school of naturalists, but "a mystic, a transcendentalist, and a natural philosopher in one;" though he believed himself, in his own words, "by constitution as good an observer as most." He will not be one of those who seek facts as facts, studying nature as a dead language. He studies her for purposes of his own, in search of the "raw material of tropes and figures." "I pray for such experience as will make nature significant," he declares; and then, with the same penful of ink, he asks: "Is that the swamp gooseberry of Gray now just beginning to blossom at Saw-Mill Brook? It has a divided style and stamens, etc., as yet not longer than the calyx, though my slip has no thorns nor prickles," and so on, and so on. Pages on pages of the journal are choke-full, literally, of this kind of botanical interrogation, till the unsympathetic reader will be in danger of surmising that the mystical searcher after tropes and symbols is sometimes not so utterly unlike the student of the dead language of fact. But then, it is one of the virtues of a journal that it is not a work of art, that it has no form, no fashion (and so does not go *out* of fashion), and is always at liberty to contradict itself. As Thoreau said, he tumbled his goods upon the counter; no single customer is bound to be pleased with them all; different men, different tastes; let each select from the pile the things that suit his fancy. (pp. 16-17)

[There] are better things than flowers and jewels to be found in Thoreau's stock. There are cordials and tonics there, to brace a man when he is weary; eye-washes, to cleanse his vision till he sees the heights above him and repents the lowness of his aims and the vulgarity of his satisfactions; blisters and irritant plasters in large variety and of warranted strength; but little or nothing, so far as the present customer has noticed, in the line of anodynes and sleeping-powders. There we may buy moral wisdom, which is not only the "foundation and source of good writing," as one of the ancients said, but of the arts in general, especially the art of life. If the world is too much with us, if wealth attracts and the "rust of copper" has begun to eat into the soul, if we are in danger of selling our years for things that perish with the using, here we may find correctives, and go away thankful, rejoicing henceforth to be rich in a better coinage than any that bears the world's stamp. The very exaggerations of the master—if we call them such—may do us good like a medicine; for there are diseased conditions which yield to nothing so quickly as to a shock.

As for Thoreau himself, life might have been smoother for him had he been less exacting in his idealism, more tolerant of imperfection in others and in himself; had he taken his studies, and even his spiritual aspirations, a grain or two less seriously. A bit of boyish play now and then, the bow quite unbent, or a dose of novel-reading of the love-making, humanizing (Trollopean) sort, could one imagine it, with a more temperate cherishing of his moodiness, might have done him no harm. It would have been for his comfort, so much may confidently be said, whether for his happiness is another question, had he been one of those gentler humorists who can sometimes see themselves, as all humorists have the gift of seeing other people, funny side out. But then, had these things been so, had his natural scope been wider, his genius, so to say, more tropical, richer, freer, more expansive, more various and flexible, more like the spreading banyan and less like the soaring, sky-pointing spruce,—why, then he would no longer have been Thoreau; for better or worse, his speech would have lost its distinctive tang; and in the long run the world, which likes a touch of bitter and a touch of sour, would almost certainly have found the man himself less interesting, and his books less rememberable. And made as he was, "born to his own affairs," what else could he do but stick to himself? "We are constantly invited to be what we are," he said. The words might fittingly have been cut upon his gravestone. (pp. 17-18)

Bradford Torrey, "Thoreau As a Diarist," in The Atlantic Monthly, *Vol. 95, No. 1, January, 1905, pp. 5-18.*

FANNY HARDY ECKSTORM (essay date 1908)

It must be admitted in the beginning that [Thoreau's] *The Maine Woods* is not a masterpiece. . . . *The Maine Woods* is of another world. Literature it may not be, nor one of "the three books of his that will be read with much pleasure;" but it is—the Maine woods. Since Thoreau's day, whoever has looked at these woods to advantage has to some extent seen them through Thoreau's eyes. Certain it is that no other man has ever put the coniferous forest between the leaves of a book. (p. 243)

Thoreau's abilities have been overrated. *The Maine Woods* contains errors in the estimates of distance, area, speed, and the like, too numerous to mention in detail. (p. 245)

[Yet, it] was not as an observer that Thoreau surpassed other men, but as an interpreter. He had the art—and how much of an art it is no one can realize until he has seated himself before an oak or a pine tree and has tried by the hour to write out its equation in terms of humanity—he had the art to see the human values of natural objects, to perceive the ideal elements of unreasoning nature and the service of those ideals to the soul of man. "The greatest delight which the fields and woods minister, is the suggestion of an occult relation between man and the vegetable," wrote Emerson; and it became Thoreau's chief text. It is the philosophy behind Thoreau's words, his attempt to reveal the Me through the Not Me, reversing the ordinary method, which makes his observations of such interest and value.

> Flower in the crannied wall,
> I pluck you out of the crannies;—
> Hold you here, root and all, in my hand,
> Little flower—but *if* I could understand
> What you are, root and all, and all in all,
> I should know what God and man is.

This power to see is rare; but mere good observation is not supernormal. We must not attribute to Thoreau's eyes what was wrought in his brain; to call him uniquely gifted in matters wherein a thousand men might equal him is not to increase his fame. (p. 246)

[The] whole description of Katahdin is unequaled. **"Chesuncook"** is the best paper of the three, taken as a whole, but [the] few pages on Katahdin are incomparable. Happily he knew the traditions of the place, the awe and veneration with which the Indians regarded it as the dwelling-place of Pamola, their god of thunder, who was angry at any invasion of his home and resented it in fogs and sudden storms. ("He very angry when you gone up there; you heard him gone *oo-oo-oo* over top of gun-barrel," they used to say.) Thoreau's Katahdin was a realm of his own, in which for a few hours he lived in primeval solitude above the clouds, invading the throne of Pamola the Thunderer, as Prometheus harried Zeus of his lightnings. The gloomy grandeur of Aeschylus rises before him to give him countenance, and he speaks himself as if he wore the buskin. But it is not windy declamation. He does not explode into exclamation points. Katahdin is a strange, lone, savage hill, unlike all others,—a very Indian among mountains. It does not need superlatives to set it off. Better by far is Thoreau's grim humor, his calling it a "cloud factory," where they made their bed "in the nest of a young whirlwind," and lined it with "feathers plucked from the live tree." Had he been one of the Stonish men, those giants with flinty eyebrows, fabled to dwell within the granite vitals of Katahdin, he could not have dealt more stout-heartedly by the home of the Thunder-God.

The best of Thoreau's utterances in this volume are like these, tuned to the rapid and high vibration of the poetic string, but not resolved into rhythm. It is poetry, but not verse. Thoreau's prose stands in a class by itself. There is an honest hardness about it. We may accept or deny Buffon's dictum that the style is the man; but the man of soft and slippery make-up would strive in vain to acquire the granitic integrity of structure which marks Thoreau's writing. It is not poetical prose in the ordinary scope of that flowery term; but, as the granite rock is rifted and threaded with veins of glistening quartz, this prose is fused at white heat with poetical insights and interpretations. Judged by ordinary standards, he was a poet who failed. He had no grace at metres; he had no aesthetic softness; his sense always overruled the sound of his stanzas. The fragments of verse which litter his workshop remind one of the chips of flint about an Indian encampment. They might have been the heads of arrows, flying high and singing in their flight, but that the stone was obdurate or the maker's hand was unequal to the shaping of it. But the waste is nothing; there is behind them the Kineo that they came from, this prose of his, a whole mountain of the same stuff, every bit capable of being wrought to ideal uses. (pp. 249-50)

Fanny Hardy Eckstorm, "Thoreau's 'Maine Woods'," in The Atlantic Monthly, *Vol. 102, No. 2, August, 1908, pp. 242-50.*

MARK VAN DOREN (essay date 1916)

Thoreau's permanent, best qualities—his sly and edged excellence, his leavening power—come into fuller recognition as his less essential qualities are subtracted and retreat. He is properly discounted only as his readers grow civilized and distrust the exposition of the elementary; he will come fully into his own when there is no one left who takes him literally and recommends his audacity as either profound or ultimate. The by-products of his living and his thinking—the excellences of the **"Week"** and **"Walden,"** and whatever he prepared for print—are more essential than their central product, the extravagances of the **"Journal."** His theory of life, so neatly conceived, so skillfully and variously expressed, so pointedly reinforced by reading and quotation, comes ultimately to seem futile and somewhat less than adequate; while the very neatness of conception, the very skill and variety and flavor of expression, the very quotations, endure. That Thoreau's main product was nothing, and his main effort vain, his own **"Journal"** best betrays. Emerson thought "he had exhausted all the capabilities of life in this world." The many pages of the **"Journal"** which uncover his private sense of bewilderment and pain when friends disappeared and confess his growing impotence in expansion, are the flattest denial that Thoreau died with any such conviction in his heart.

Yet the **"Journal"** is also the best witness that it was indeed Thoreau's ambition to exhaust all the capabilities of life in this world. Better still, the **"Journal"** reveals why he had to fail. It is the **"Journal"** which gives the best clue to the character of Thoreau's thinking, which gives to understand that Thoreau's whole philosophical significance is involved in the fact that he thought in a vacuum. (pp. 109-10)

Thoreau deluded himself, not because he was introspective, but because he was introspective in a certain mistaken, fruitless way. His speculations and experiences, intellectual, moral, aesthetic, yielded no important results, not because they were private, but because their privacy was their sole end and aim. Plato and Shakespeare were introspective, and learned to know the world in private; but the world they learned to know was large and important, the "great and common world." They studied themselves along with the rest of the world—Plato his opinions with the opinions of other men, Shakespeare his impressions with the impressions of other men; Thoreau studied himself alone—his opinions and his impressions by themselves. Shakespeare and Plato, like all men who are versed in the arts of comparison or dialectic, studied themselves as members of the universe; Thoreau studied himself as the universe. Shakespeare and Plato sought to learn their bearings in the world; Thoreau lost sight of bearings, and sought to be the world itself. Thoreau deluded himself precisely in proportion

as he refused to keep the very delicate balance which it is necessary for a great and good man to keep between his private and his public lives, between his own personality and the whole outside universe of personalities. Thoreau's introspection was sterile in so far as it was a brooding reverie of self-contemplation rather than an effort to measure and correct and check himself by reference to things beyond himself. His counsel of perfection is meaningless to others in so far as it is intended to be realized in a vacuum, apart from contacts or comparisons; it was useless to him in that it did not permit of friction with other perfections, did not provide for that jostling and settling into place which the seasoned philosophy of life has undergone. (pp. 115-17)

If it is asked what led Thoreau into his error, what led him to believe he could find out all things by and in himself, perhaps Matthew Arnold gives the keenest answer: "The blundering to be found in the world," says Arnold, "comes from some people fancying that some idea is a definite and ascertained thing, like the idea of a triangle, when it is not." The difficulty with Thoreau, as with many a philosopher during the nineteenth century, was that he had hypostatized an abstraction and seen his own reflection in it. (p. 118)

Thoreau is one of the most deliberate of all hypostatizers. Born into a philosophical school whose ideas were already well formed, younger by ten years than most of its adherents, and with a craftman's mind for visualizing details, it is no wonder that he, most scrupulously of all men in America or Europe, should have assumed to be real, and attempted to live, the generalizations of Goethe and the abstractions of the transcendental philosophy. . . . Thoreau's whole life was a search for embodied Reality, and his whole contention on paper is that Reality is accessible. (pp. 119-21)

Philosophically considered, the best of Thoreau is not his extreme transcendental gospel, the darkest corner of his little private darkness; is not his urging of the elementary; is not his association with a very provincial school which did not know enough in general. If read as scripture, as some of his friends read him, or as madman, as Lowell read him [see excerpt above, 1865], he will yield nothing. He cannot be taken literally any more than a wild odor can be seized and kept. "I am permitted to be rash," he said in the **"Week."** It is his temper which is needed and felt, and not his vagaries that need be worshiped or excused. He is a good hater and refuser, and the world likes that now and then. Men like to be pricked; men demand to be made mad on occasions. Men like Thoreau's temper in the atmosphere as much as they like the flavor of his wild apples in their memories. (p. 124)

If Thoreau loses in the broadest sense by being terribly single-minded, he is valuable in a narrower sense by virtue of his very singleness—valuable as a protestant, valuable as an antidotal flavor.

Thoreau, finally, is an American classic. He will always appeal to the "confirmed city-men" he affected to pity. For the same reason that [Daniel Defoe's novel] "Robinson Crusoe" appeals most to land folk, **"Walden"** will appeal more and more to the men and women of "institutions," to men in studies and clubs, to boys by the fireside in winter. Thoreau is eminently a citizen in the republic of letters, and continues some excellent traditions. (pp. 126-27)

"No truer American existed than Thoreau," said Emerson. At least no more plain-spoken representative of transcendental

New England could be asked for, it seems safe to say. There can be little doubt that the spirit of **"Walden"** has pervaded the American consciousness, stiffened the American lip, steadied the American nerve, in a ponderable degree. By creating a classic image of the cynic hermit in ideal solitude Thoreau has demonstrated some of the meannesses of the demands of Time and Matter, and furnished the spirit and will for social criticism; he has made men acute critics, if not sensible shepherds, of their own sentiments. (p. 128)

> *Mark Van Doren, in his* Henry David Thoreau: A Critical Study, *Houghton Mifflin Company, 1916, 138 p.*

THE OUTLOOK   (essay date 1917)

[*This essay commemorates the centenary of Thoreau's birth by reevaluating his works.*]

No American writer has had a greater influence [than Thoreau] in helping his countrymen to an appreciation of the proper relation between man and nature, a relationship which since the eighteenth century has had many curious developments.

From the urban civilization of the eighteenth century, through the romantic sentimentalism of those who imagined that they were protesting against the artificialities of the age in which they lived, to the vital friendship between Thoreau and the wild life of Walden Pond is a long journey indeed. The artificial grotto of Pope, the sentimentality of Rousseau, or the mawkish enthusiasm for the simplicity of savage life of Bernardin de Saint-Pierre—even perhaps Thomson's love of nature or Gray's appreciation of the wild beauty of the Alps—belong in a very different world from that which has been made familiar to us and a part of our daily lives through the message of Thoreau. The dividing line between these two worlds is not a difficult one to draw.

On the one hand there is imitation, insincerity, sentimentality, and, at the best, little more than the appreciation of an outsider who observes with pleasure a phenomenon apart from his own life. On the other side of the line there is originality, sincerity, sentiment, and an appreciation of the fundamental unity of man and nature—a unity which demands neither the renunciation of nature for the sake of civilization nor a renunciation of civilization for the sake of nature.

Thoreau was never guilty of proclaiming a savage state better than a state of civilization, but he harbored a clear understanding of the deficiencies of the civilization of his time and a tremendous longing to bring within its limits the boundless advantages which come to those who free themselves from the dictates of materialism and who place a true value upon the cultivation of the imagination.

Thoreau played a part in the warfare against low public ideals, and a still more important part in proving by his private life the possibility of putting those ideals within the reach of the average conscience.

As the inevitable charges of "peculiarity" which always attend the progress of a man of genius have died out of the public discussion of the message of Thoreau, he stands forth as one of the greatest and most inviting figures in our literary history. It is not too much to say of Thoreau, as did Emerson: "Here is a Damascus blade of a man such as you may search through nature in vain to parallel."

> *"The Centenary of Thoreau," in* The Outlook, *Vol. 117, No. 2, September 12, 1917, p. 44.*

NORMAN FOERSTER   (essay date 1921)

[*Foerster, one of the first critics to evaluate Thoreau apart from his personality, argues that, though he had many talents, Thoreau was not "a man of letters." His poetry was not successful but, Foerster continues, "his poetic feeling . . . is worthily embalmed in his prose." Foerster considers Thoreau a great prose writer whose writing rings sincere and true, with much of its charm residing in its "lurking humor."*]

Inveterate observer and recorder that he was, at heart Thoreau was assuredly not a naturalist, but rather—what? A literary artist? . . . Yet it must be remembered that in his lifetime he published only two books, the **Week** and **Walden;** that the creative impulse in him was neither vehement nor persistent, most of his **Journal** being a bare record of facts; and that he wanted both the spur of fame and the desire to serve men, at least as these aims are usually conceived by writers. If writing was his work, it was his work in much the same sense in which surveying and pencil-making were his work: he was not a surveyor or manufacturer of pencils, nor was he a man of letters.

Poet, at all events, he was not, for a man can scarcely be a poet without achieving a certain bulk of successful verse, and the total bulk of Thoreau's verse, most of it unsuccessful, would fill less than an ordinary volume. That he wrote it at all is to be explained less in terms of his artistic powers, since he lived in a time of renaissance when the homespun of prose was disparaged in favor of purple singing-robes, in a time when, it has been said, one could not throw a stone in the city of Boston without hitting a poet. So Thoreau versified; his prose works abound in interjected poems or poetic fragments, many of which have the odd effect of serving, not to lift the reader aloft on the wings of sudden inspiration, but to make him halt in consternation before a veritable New England glacial boulder, shapeless and inert. There is little in him of the lyrical poet's instinct to burst into song at every provocation of nature. Although he tells us repeatedly that he is inspired, he also tells us that the mood is gone before he can versify it; the best poetry, he says broadly, is never expressed—an assertion not without its measure of truth. Indeed, it was fatally true of his own practice. Delicately perceptive of the concrete world, eagerly responsive to beauty, inwardly living the life of the poet, he was so intent on understanding and appropriating his visions that when the time came for singing them he was dumb. (pp. 2-3)

In natural metrical skill he was more deficient even than Emerson. Most of his verses are benumbed, and crawl along, with an occasional spurt, like a grasshopper in the autumn. For example:—

> Let such pure hate still underprop
> Our love, that we may be
> Each other's conscience,
> And have our sympathy
> Mainly from thence. . . .

[If] Emerson's judgment is right, he could . . . be a successor and improver of Simonides, as in the best of all his poems, the **Walden** verses on **"Smoke"**:—

> Light-winged Smoke, Icarian bird,
> Melting thy pinions in thy upward flight;
> Lark without song, and messenger of dawn,
> Circling above the hamlets as thy nest;

A view of Walden. A small glacial pond, Walden is located about two miles south of Concord Village. The Bettmann Archive, Inc.

Or else, departing dream and shadowy form
Of midnight vision, gathering up thy skirts;
By night star-veiling, and by day
Darkening the light and blotting out the sun;—
Go thou, my incense, upward from this hearth,
And ask the gods to pardon this clear flame.

Virtually blank verse, this delicate yet classically firm little poem suggests the possibilities of that form for lyrical use. Had Thoreau lived in the England of Elizabeth, he might well have been a builder of lofty rhyme; like Whitman, although for other reasons, he was a great poet *in posse* [potentially].

His poetic feeling, however, is worthily embalmed in his prose. Moments of inspiration, as he remarks, are not lost merely because they fail to leave a deposit in verse; the impression abides, and in due time is expressed in a form equally genuine if less ardent: when time has emphasized the essential truth in these ecstatic states,—

> In cooler moments we can use them as paint to gild and adorn our prose . . . They are like a pot of pure ether. They lend the writer when the moment comes a certain superfluity of wealth, making his expression to overrun and float itself.

Without this superfluity of wealth, Thoreau's prose would be shorn of most of its beauty and power. If not a great poet, Thoreau is a great prose writer.

The first and last impression produced by Thoreau's prose is its sincerity, its unflinching truth. It is faithfully idiosyncratic, the mirror of his sincerity of character. "I would rather sit on a pumpkin and have it all to myself than be crowded on a velvet cushion"—who but Thoreau could have written that? Speaking of the art of writing, Thoreau leans upon that universally applicable maxim of the transcendentalists: "Be faithful to your genius!" This is for him the central precept. . . . He was instinctively and somewhat bitterly suspicious of "the *belles-lettres* and the *beaux arts* and their *professors,* which we can do without". He would simply say, with Buonaparte: "Speak plain; the rest will follow", with his eye on the truth and not on the ornaments. He would not seek expressions, but thoughts to be expressed—and even this did not satisfy him, for best of all, he says somewhere, is "the theme that seeks me, not I it". He is only to report, to obey, to serve as agent, to lend himself to an utterance "free and lawless as a lamb's bleat": an account true enough of his habit if one bears in mind that he was a somewhat wolfish lamb bred in a highly civilized tradition. His distinction in this matter, however, is not in his theory of style, which is the common property of the romantic school, but in his practice, which is all but unequalled in its resoluteness. . . . So rigorously does Thoreau follow his ideal that he demands of every sentence that it be "the result of a long probation", expressing in words what had already been expressed in action. . . . It may well be that the idiosyncratic quality of Thoreau's prose style springs more from the Puritan in him than from the romanticist, more from the voice of conscience then from the "lamb's bleat".

The charm of Thoreau's prose rests, then, on its complete sincerity, and his prose is to be enjoyed to the full only by readers who find his personality attractive. Yet it has definite qualities that win the approval of any discriminating reader. His sentences, for one thing, are alive. Living in his way, an intense life constantly alert to what was going on in his inner being and in nature, he could not well write a page devoid of life, like the flaccid writing of the ordinary journalist. A writer without a full experience, as he says, used "torpid words, wooden or lifeless words, such words as 'humanitary', which have a paralysis in their tails". His own diction is fresh, dewy, an early morning diction. It has the enormous advantage of unusual concreteness—to be expected of a writer whose perceptions were so highly trained, and whose aversion was metaphysics. And his store of concrete words and images he used with gusto, if not abandon, responding to his theme, seeking to penetrate, by sympathy, to its heart or essence, as in this perfect account of the nighthawk's antic swoop and boom:—

> The night-hawk circled overhead in the sunny afternoons—for I sometimes made a day of it— like a mote in the eye, or in heaven's eye, falling from time to time with a swoop and a sound as if the heavens were rent, torn at last to very rags and tatters, and yet a seamless cope remained.

That slight turn, "or in heaven's eye", with its unexpected shifting of the image, is typical of his restrained animation. . . . Figures of speech abound in such passages, as in all his writing—his concreteness is largely a figurativeness. His acquaintance with nature is, of course, reflected in his metaphors and similes, as in that perfect comparison of the big guns with a puff-ball; or in his comparison of the weeping of Ossian's heroes with the perspiration of stone in the heat of summer; or in his comparison of the man of intellect with a barren, staminiferous flower, and of the poet with a fertile and perfect flower; or in that graphic comparison, mentioned by Channing, of the branches of Darby's oak with gray lightning stereotyped on the sky.

His love of paradox, his fondness for puns (in which he rivals his favorite poets of the great period of English literature), and the ever-present element of surprise in his style, are additional manifestations of his desire fully to rouse himself and his reader to the inner nature of his theme, whether it be night-hawks, or celebrations by the rude bridge that spanned the river, or the sense of time and space. A penetrating impression must be made, at all costs. He is never, or almost never, languid, but holds his stilus firmly, as in this sentence, which illustrates its own meaning:—

> A sentence should read as if the author, had he held a plow instead of a pen, could have drawn a furrow deep and straight to the end.

Here the emphasis falls distinctly and precisely where it should fall. . . . He would not spread himself thin, either in his life or in his writing. Everything must be deliberate and concen-

trated. . . . And indeed, as a stylist, Thoreau is something of a marksman; now his sentences crack close at hand, now they sound as from a remoter station, reverberating solemnly, as if nature had taken them unto herself and charged them with a meaning of her own.

Such command is invaluable in satire and wit. Humor, that "indispensable pledge of sanity", he had, but a good-natured spontaneous wit, with a trace of sharpness, was more characteristic. . . . Instances are everywhere, even in the sober *Journal*, as when he tells of a party, warm and noisy, where he suffered himself to be introduced to two young women, one of whom "was as lively and loquacious as a chickadee; had been accustomed to the society of watering-places, and therefore could get no refreshment out of such a dry fellow as I", while the other, said to be pretty, could not make herself heard, "there was such a clacking", and he sagely concludes that parties are social machinery designed for matrimonial connections, and prefers to eat crackers and cheese in the silent woods with old Joseph Hosmer. (pp. 4-9)

Much of the charm of Thoreau's best pages resides in this lurking humor, this dry wit always ready to kindle. Without them, he might have been an intolerably disagreeable social critic, though he might still have written pleasantly of nature,— a possibility not so remote when we learn that in his last years he blotted the humorous parts of his essays, saying: "I cannot bear the levity I find". (p. 9)

With Carlyle and Ruskin and other typical writers of his century, Thoreau obviously excelled in the expressive side of art; but what of form? His sense of form has been placed with Emerson's (Emerson, to speak brusquely, having none). It is true that both Transcendentalists had the same weaknesses, even preparing their essays in the same manner by extorting them, so to say, out of their jewel-laden diaries. There is, however, a difference of degree. Thoreau's sentences and paragraphs cohere better than do Emerson's: he generally leaves the impression of continuity even when he lacks the reality, while Emerson often has the reality without leaving the impression. Thoreau, that is, writes from Parnassus, Emerson from Delphi. Thoreau, again, if less noble, is more luminous—not only because his subjects are different, but also because his mode of thinking is more concrete. Although wanting a true sense of the value of architectonics in literature, he loved shapeliness, fine carving, beauty of form, "elegance", as he termed it—the informing quality that is simply the flowering of a nature well-tempered and wisely civilized, a humane nature. Much of this love of beauty he must have derived from his intimate studies in Greek and Latin literatures. . . . In his own work he attained in large measure his ideal of elegance, partly through revision (a facile writer, he resorted constantly to the use of the file), and partly through his realizing in his character something of the classical decorum. He believed that beauty is the final excellence, that whereas a first inspection of good writing should reveal its common-sense, a second should reveal its severe truth, and a third beauty.

He was well fitted to see beauty in external nature. Coming back to nature from the ancient classics, he perceived with added force the meaning of the third of "those celestial thrins",— Truth, Goodness, Beauty,—in the loveliness of line, and light and shade, and color. Despite his provincial ignorance of the plastic arts—an ignorance emulating Emerson's—he succeeded in some degree in acquiring the point of view of the plastic arts through training his eye for landscape. Again and again in his writings he dominates the natural scene, composing it with the craftsman's sense of design, displaying a feeling for balance, repetition, emphasis, harmony, quite apart from his feeling for spiritual significance lurking behind or expressed by outer beauty. He could enjoy beauty as such. His layman's interest in aesthetic principles is indicated by his careful reading of William Gilpin on landscape, and of Ruskin's *Modern Painters*. (pp. 9-11)

The result of all this study was the inimitable charm, the intimate mastery, of all of his descriptions of nature, whether an individual leaf or the whole of a vast prospect. That sensuous equipment that served him as an observer of natural fact, served him equally as an observer of natural beauty, giving him a high degree of truth in both spheres. What other writer of our time has perceived so subtly and expressed his vision with so delicate a truth? Ruskin, beside Thoreau, seems theatrical, melodramatic, entranced by his own powers, giving nature the stamp of his expansive personality: Thoreau's self-restraint steadies his insight, lets him penetrate closer to the heart of nature as to his own heart. His magical truth has won him many a devoted reader who finds himself indifferent to, or exasperated by, Thoreau's personal piquancy and his paradoxical satire of human society. Who that knows *Walden* can forget those glorious white pines of **"Baker Farm"**?—

> Sometimes I ramble to pine groves, standing like temples, or like fleets at sea, full-rigged, with wavy boughs, and rippling with light, so soft and green and shady that the Druids would have forsaken their oaks to worship in them.

One sentence could scarcely do more. (p. 12)

> Norman Foerster, "Thoreau As Artist," in The Sewanee Review, *Vol. XXIX, No. 1, January, 1921, pp. 2-13.*

LEWIS MUMFORD (essay date 1926)

[*Mumford is an American sociologist, historian, philosopher, and critic whose primary interest is in the relationship between the modern individual and his or her environment. Here he postulates that in his writings Thoreau gave a report of the true pioneer movement in America—one which sought culture rather than material goods.*]

The pioneer who broke the trail westward left scarcely a trace of his adventure in the mind: what remains are the tags of pioneer customs, and mere souvenirs of the past, like the Pittsburg stogy, which is our living connection to-day with the Conestoga wagon, whose drivers used to roll cigars as the first covered wagons plodded over the Alleghenies. (p. 107)

Henry David Thoreau was perhaps the only man who paused to give a report of the full experience. In a period when men were on the move, he remained still; when men were on the make, he remained poor; when civil disobedience broke out in the lawlessness of the cattle thief and the mining town rowdy, by sheer neglect, Thoreau practiced civil disobedience as a principle, in protest against the Mexican War, the Fugitive Slave Law, and slavery itself. Thoreau in his life and letters shows what the pioneer movement might have come to if this great migration had sought culture rather than material conquest, and an intensity of life, rather than mere extension over the continent. (p. 108)

Thoreau seized the opportunity to consider what in its essentials a truly human life was; he sought, in Walden, to find out what

degree of food, clothing, shelter, labor was necessary to sustain it. It was not animal hardihood or a merely tough physical regimen he was after; nor did he fancy, for all that he wrote in contempt of current civilization, that the condition of the woodcutter, the hunter, or the American Indian was in itself to be preferred. What he discovered was that people are so eager to get the ostentatious "necessaries" of a civil life that they lose the opportunity to profit by civilization itself: while their physical wants are complicated, their lives, culturally, are not enriched in proportion, but are rather pauperized and bleached.

Thoreau was completely oblivious to the dominant myths that had been bequeathed by the Seventeenth Century. Indifferent to the illusion of magnitude, he felt that Walden Pond, rightly viewed, was as vast as the ocean, and the woods and fields and swamps of Concord were as inexhaustible as the Dark Continent. . . . Thoreau sought in nature all the manifold qualities of being; he was not merely in search of those likenesses or distinctions which help to create classified indexes and build up a system. The aesthetic qualities of a fern were as important for his mode of apprehension as the number of spores on a frond; it was not that he disdained science, but that, like the old herbalists and naturalists he admired, he would not let the practical offices of science, its classification, its measurements, its numerations, take precedence over other forms of understanding. Science, practiced in this fashion, is truly part of a humane life, and a Darwin dancing for joy over a slide in his microscope, or a Pupin, finding the path to physics through his contemplation of the stars he watched as a herdboy through the night, are not poorer scientists but richer ones for these joys and delights: they merely bow to the bias of utilitarianism when they leave these things out of their reports. In his attitude toward scientific truth Thoreau was perhaps a prophetic figure; and a new age may do honor to his metaphysics as well as to his humanity. (pp. 109-12)

Thoreau's attitude toward the State, one must note, was just the opposite to that of the progressive pioneer. The latter did not care what sort of landscape he "located" in, so long as he could salute the flag of his country and cast his vote: Thoreau, on the contrary, was far too religious a man to commit the idolatry of saluting a symbol of secular power; and he realized that the affairs controlled by the vote represented only a small fraction of an interesting life, while so far from being indifferent to the land itself, he absorbed it, as men have absorbed legends, and guarded it, as men preserve ceremonies. The things which his contemporaries took for the supreme realities of life, matter, money, and political rights, had only an instrumental use for Thoreau: they might contribute a little to the arrangement of a good life, but the good life itself was not contained, was not even implied in them. One might spend one's life pursuing them without having lived. (p. 113)

What drove Thoreau to the solitude of the woods was no cynical contempt for the things beyond his reach. (p. 114)

What the aboriginal Indian had absorbed from the young earth, Thoreau absorbed; what the new settlers had given her, the combing of the plow, the cincture of the stone fence or the row of planted elms, these things he absorbed too; for Thoreau, having tasted the settled life of Concord, knew that the wilderness was not a permanent home for man: one might go there for fortification, for a quickening of the senses, for a tightening of all the muscles; but that, like any retreat, is a special exercise and wants a special occasion: one returned to Nature in order to become, in a deeper sense, more cultivated and civilized, not in order to return to crudities that men had already discarded. Looking ahead, Thoreau saw what was needed to preserve the valuable heritage of the American wilderness. (pp. 116-17)

The individualism of an Emerson or a Thoreau was the necessary complement of the thoroughly socialized existence of the New England town; it was what prevented these towns from becoming collections of yes men, with never an opinion or an emotion that differed from their neighbors. He wrote for his fellowtownsmen; and his notion of the good life was one that should carry to a higher pitch the existing polity and culture of Concord itself. (p. 117)

Just as Thoreau sought Nature, in order to arrive at a higher state of culture, so he practiced individualism, in order to create a better order of society. Taking America as it was, Thoreau conceived a form, a habitat, which would retain what was unique in the American contact with the virgin forest, the cultivated soil, and the renewed institutions of the New England town. He understood the precise thing that the pioneer lacked. The pioneer had exhausted himself in a senseless external activity, which answered no inner demands except those for oblivion. In his experiment at Walden Pond, Thoreau "learned this, at least . . . that if one advances confidently in the direction of his dreams, and endeavors to live the life which he has imagined, he will meet with success unexpected in the common hours. . . . In proportion as he simplifies his life, the laws of the universe will appear less complex, and solitude will not be solitude, nor poverty poverty, nor weakness weakness. If you have built castles in the air, your work need not be lost; that is where they should be. Now put foundations under them."

In short, Thoreau lived in his desires; in rational and beautiful things that he imagined worth doing, and did. The pioneer lived only in extraneous necessities; and he vanished with their satisfaction: filling all the conditions of his environment, he never fulfilled himself. With the same common ground between them in their feeling towards Nature, Thoreau and the pioneer stood at opposite corners of the field. What Thoreau left behind is still precious; men may still go out and make over America in the image of Thoreau. What the pioneer left behind, alas! was only the burden of a vacant life. (pp. 118-20)

> Lewis Mumford, "The Golden Day," in his The Golden Day: A Study in American Experience and Culture, *Boni & Liveright Publishers, 1926, pp. 85-156.**

VERNON LOUIS PARRINGTON (essay date 1927)

[*An American historian, biographer, and critic, Parrington is best known for his unfinished literary history of the United States,* Main Currents in American Thought. *Though modern scholars now disagree with many of his conclusions, they view Parrington's work as a significant first attempt at fashioning an intellectual history of America based on a broad interpretive thesis. Written from the point of view of a Jeffersonian liberal,* Main Currents in American Thought *has proven a widely influential work in American criticism. Declaring that Thoreau's is "one of the great names in American literature," Parrington stresses that "the eighteenth-century philosophy of individualism . . . came to fullest expression in New England" in Thoreau.*]

The single business of Henry Thoreau, during forty-odd years of eager activity, was to discover an economy calculated to provide a satisfying life. His one concern, that gave to his ramblings in Concord fields a value as of high adventure, was to explore the true meaning of wealth. Honest, fearless, curiously inquisitive—a masterless man who would give no hostages to fortune—he proved his right to be called a philosopher by seeking wisdom as a daily counselor and friend, and following such paths only as wisdom suggested. Out of his own experience, tested in the clear light of the Greeks, he wrote a transcendental declaration of independence that may be taken as the final word of the Concord school touching the great issues of practical living. *Walden* is the handbook of an economy that endeavors to refute Adam Smith and transform the round of daily life into something nobler than a mean gospel of plus and minus.

It was the common opinion of his neighbors that Henry Thoreau was a queer fellow who had somehow got all his values topsy-turvy. And yet the more thoughtfully one considers him, the more doubtful it appears whether the queerness lay with him or with his critics. . . . To the Concord farmers Thoreau appeared strange only because he applied in his daily life a truth they assented to on the Sabbath. The principle that life is more than the meat and the body than raiment was familiar enough to the Sunday doctrines of Concord; but that a man should seriously apply it on week-days; that he should propose to regulate his mid-week activities by the economy of the Sermon on the Mount, passed the comprehension of practical Yankees who followed quite another economy. It was Thoreau's conduct that perplexed them, rather than his philosophy.

From first to last that conduct was serenely logical. To this disciple of the ancient wisdom, Sabbath and week-day were one, and in seeking to square his daily life with the ancient precept, Thoreau became the arch-rebel of his group, the most individual amongst the "lunatic fringe" of the transcendental movement, the one who escapes elusively from the grip of an adjective. He slips out of all phrases devised to imprison him. "A bachelor of nature," Emerson, with his gift for cryptic phrase, called him; "poet-naturalist," Ellery Channing, who knew him intimately, chose to call him. "I am a poet, a mystic, and a transcendentalist," Thoreau said of himself, disregarding his nature writings. Yet none of these phrases, true as they are, quite adequately sums him up. At the risk of committing a fresh futility, one may perhaps suggest that he was a Greek turned transcendental economist. His life seems to have been a persistent experiment in values. A philosopher of the open air who kept his mind clear and his nerves robust by daily contact with wind and weather; a mystic who pried curiously into the meaning of nature and was familiar with Hellenic and Oriental systems of thought; a Yankee, skilled in various homely crafts, yet rather interested in proving for himself what things were excellent and taking nothing on hearsay—Thoreau's chief business would seem to have been with life itself, and how it might best be lived by Henry Thoreau; how a rational being, in short, might enjoy the faculties God has given him, following the higher economy and not enslaving himself to the lower, so that when he came to die he might honestly say, I have lived. (pp. 392-94)

To save one's soul has always been accounted in New England a matter worthy of a man's best effort, and Thoreau's days were given over to it with a single-heartedness without parallel even in New England. The Puritan, he believed, had suffered his high spiritual mission to be sacrificed to the economic; he would recover that mission by sacrificing the economic to the spiritual; but he would interpret the spiritual as a Hellenist rather than a Hebraist. The Christian other-worldliness seemed to him unduly regardless of the loveliness of this world. "Christianity," he says in the *Week,* "only hopes. It has hung its harp on the willows, and cannot sing a song in a strange land. It has dreamed a sad dream, and does not yet welcome the morning with joy." (p. 396)

His extraordinarily frank evaluation of the New Testament, and of Calvinistic New England that had too long chewed the cud of conscience—"they did not know when to swallow their cud, and their lives of course yielded no milk"—is the work of a pagan from whom all creeds slip easily. Few more searching sermons have been preached in Massachusetts than the sermon that composed itself as Thoreau's boat floated down the Concord River, past the Billerica meeting-house where the honest villagers were worshiping the God of New England— a sermon that with fine irony summons minister and congregation to consider the deeper teachings of their sacred book. (pp. 396-97)

As Thoreau understood the problem of economics there were three possible solutions open to him: to exploit himself, to exploit his fellows, or to reduce the problem to its lowest denominator. The first was quite impossible—to imprison oneself in a treadmill when the morning called to great adventure, to burden oneself with useless fardels when the pack must be kept light, was the folly of a slave mind. He had observed his neighbors closely and found little good in their way of self-exploitation. . . . Freedom with abstinence seemed to him better than serfdom with material well-being, for he was only giving up the lesser to enjoy the greater, as was the privilege of the philosopher. (pp. 397-98)

It was the reply of the arch-individualist to the tyrannous complexities of society, and it set him apart even in the world of transcendentalism. (p. 398)

The story of Thoreau's emancipation from the lower economics is the one romance of his life, and *Walden* is his great book. More restrained than the *Week* and lacking the exuberant beauty of the latter—its noble talk and scathing criticism—it is "informed by a more explicit unifying philosophy." It is a book in praise of life rather than of Nature, a record of calculating economies that studied saving in order to spend more largely. But it is a book of social criticism as well, in spite of its explicit denial of such a purpose, and in its speculations much of Carlyle and Ruskin and William Morris crops out. In considering the true nature of economy he concluded, with Ruskin, that "the cost of a thing is the amount of what I will call life which is required to be exchanged for it, immediately or in the long run." Conceive of life as cheap, a poor thing to be exploited, and the factory system becomes the logical economic order; but conceive of it as dear, and the common happiness the great objective of society, and quite another sort of industrialism will emerge. Thoreau did not look with approval on the rising city of Lowell, with its multiplying spindles and increasing proletariat, and he did not understand why Americans should boast of a system that provided vulgar leisure for the masters at the cost of serfdom for the workers. (p. 399)

In other bits *Walden* is curiously like *Hopes and Fears for Art,* and the drift of the whole is one with the revolutionary teachings of Morris, that the abiding satisfactions are those which spring from free creative work. This Yankee Greek had learned that it is a beautiful life back of the tool that creates beauty, and that if the work of our hands is ugly, it is because our lives are mean and sordid, affording no outlet for the free creative spirit. In New England, Puritan and Yankee alike had conspired

against beauty, and the gods had taken revenge by clothing life in drab. (pp. 399-400)

Thoreau needed only to have lived in a world that honored craftsmanship to have opened fully the vein of gold that Morris dug his philosophy from; he had the instinct of the craftsman but not his training. His turning from the workshop to the fields, hearing no call in the humdrum village economy to develop a beautiful craftsmanship, was an implied criticism of the common sterility of labor in everyday Concord. . . . (p. 400)

[*Civil Disobedience*] is a somewhat astonishing performance. This Yankee transcendentalist quite evidently has turned philosophical anarchist. But read in the light of Emerson's *Journals,* or in the light of Godwin's *Political Justice,* it is easily comprehensible. It is no more than transcendental individualism translated into politics, with all comfortable compromises swept away. Its sources run straight back to eighteenth-century liberalism with its doctrine of the minimized state—a state that must lose its coercive sovereignty in the measure that the laws of society function freely. Very likely Thoreau had never read Godwin, yet his political philosophy was implicit in *Political Justice.* In Godwin's thinking the problem of man in society is the problem of a voluntary adjustment of the individual to the state; and it is only by establishing economics and politics on morality, the political justice is possible. The moral law is the fundamental law, superior to statutes and constitutions; and to it the citizen is bound to render allegiance. (p. 402)

By his own path Thoreau came to identical conclusions. There is little in *Civil Disobedience* that is not in *Political Justice.* To neither thinker is there an abstract state, society or nation— only individuals; and to both, the fundamental law is the law of morality. Political expediency and the law of morality frequently clash, and in such event it is the duty of the individual citizen to follow the higher law. Thoreau went even further, and asserted the doctrine of individual compact, which in turn implied the doctrine of individual nullification; no government, he said, can have any "pure right over my person or property but what I concede to it." (pp. 402-03)

"Let your life be a counter friction to stop the machine"—in this doctrine of individual syndicalism Thoreau's conception of the relation of the citizen to the state is tersely summed up. In so far as he was a democrat it was of the transcendental school, rather than the Jacksonian. He would be governed by the majority no more than by the minority. The scorn of a fine ethical mind for practical government by politicians could scarcely be more tellingly phrased than in the bit of verse he tucks into *Civil Disobedience*:

> A drab of state, a cloth-o'-silver slut,
> To have her train borne up, and her soul trail in the
> dirt.

Such a man quite evidently would go for Nullification as fiercely as Garrison. Even though he might wash his hands of society, the cries of those who suffered injustice followed him, and when the Fugitive Slave Law passed, it robbed him of his peace, destroying his pleasure in wonted things. (p. 404)

In Thoreau the eighteenth-century philosophy of individualism, the potent liberalisms let loose on the world by Jean Jacques [Rousseau], came to fullest expression in New England. He was the completest embodiment of the *laissez-faire* reaction against a regimented social order, the severest critic of the lower economics that frustrate the dreams of human freedom. . . . He and his deeds are looked down upon in our time—"It is obvious that none yet speaks to his condition, for the speaker is not yet in his condition." . . . One of the great names in American literature is the name of Henry Thoreau. Yet only after sixty years is he slowly coming into his own. (pp. 405-06)

> *Vernon Louis Parrington, "Henry Thoreau—Transcendental Economist," in his* Main Currents in American Thought, an Interpretation of American Literature from the Beginnings to 1920: The Romantic Revolution in America, 1800-1860, Vol. 2, *Harcourt Brace Jovanovich, 1927, pp. 392-406.*

LLEWELLYN POWYS (essay date 1929)

Thoreau is cried up as being one of the greatest American writers. In reality, he was an awkward, nervous, self-conscious New Englander who, together with an authentic taste for oriental and classical literature, developed a singular liking for his own home woods. He does not strike me as an original thinker, bolstered up as his thoughts always are by the wisdom of the past. Mysticism, that obstinately recurring form of human self-deception, is, in his case, even more unsatisfactory than usual, while his descriptions of nature that have won such applause are seldom out of the ordinary. I am inclined to think that his reputation owes much to his close association with Emerson, that truly great man, who under so kindly and sedate an exterior possessed so mighty a spirit.

The naïveté of Thoreau's mind is incredible. At his best, he is second best. He is too cultured and not cultured enough. It is, in truth, amazing that this provincial pedant, who so strained to be original, should enjoy the distinction he does. . . . As I read this dilettante of the bluebird and the bobolink, I constantly find myself becoming impatient. He is too bookish, too literary. To draw direct power out of the ground, out of the smelling, fecund, sweet soil of the earth, it is necessary to lose oneself, it is necessary to lose one's soul to find it. Thoreau never is able to do this. He is always there, the transcendental original of Concord with a lesson to impart. It is impossible for him to feel nature in his lungs, in his navel, in the marrow of his bones. He must always have his journal-book within reach and must be fussing to enter on its pages some apothegm or apt description which he knows will later be commended by Emerson or by his less discerning lyceum audiences.

Thoreau plays at loving nature but his authentic background is not really in the cold woods as, for example, was the background of Thomas Bewick or even John Burroughs. We learn that he was extremely deft at making lead pencils. . . . Thoreau certainly used these dainty productions to some purpose, for what a murmur he made about his retreat at Walden Pond!

When we look into the matter there was really little enough "to it". At best, it was but a dramatic gesture. (pp. 163-64)

Much of his writing is sheer affectation. He was asked whether he was not lonely and answered, "no more lonely than the loon on the pond that laughs so loud, or the Walden Pond itself. What company has that lovely lake, I pray. And yet it has not the blue devils, but the blue angels in it, in the azure tint of its waters". He goes for an excursion into Canada. "We styled ourselves Knights of the Umbrella and the Bundle". He was, in truth, a woodsman of the umbrella!

He is never weary of girding at the rich and conventional. "Simplicity, simplicity, simplicity," he exhorts and, then, the next moment can pen a sentence that has upon it the very stamp of finical banality. "The luxuriously rich are not simply kept comfortably warm but unnaturally hot; as I implied before, they are cooked, of course, *à la mode*." Sometimes it is as though he has no conception of what dignity of style means. (p. 164)

This back-door hermit has in his mouth all those convenient utterances that are in their very essence contrary to nature. He should have given more attention to the song of the hermit thrush! . . .

And yet one must not be too captious. One must not depreciate unfairly this bookish philosopher. . . .

It is possible from his pages to cull certain passages of wisdom. . . . He can also give us glimpses of his life in the woods that have a true beauty, as, for example, when paddling about Walden Pond after dark he would see "perch and shiners, dimpling the surface with their tails in the moonlight". To those of us who love the American countryside, there is a magic in the mere enumeration of the familiar flora, the goldenrod, the St. John's wort, the sumach! And yet, even here, one can be jarred by his method of expression. In his journal we come upon this passage about skunk cabbages. And how discouraging its jocular tone seems when one remembers the sturdy growth of this swamp vegetation which heralds the coming of the spring by thrusting up through the chilled ground mottled, red, curling horns that smell of the arm pits of Pan! . . .

Thoreau was a great reader of books of the ancient tradition, but he was neither a profound thinker nor a great writer, and that is the truth. (p. 165)

> *Llewellyn Powys, "Thoreau: A Disparagement," in* The Bookman, *New York, Vol. LXIX, No. 2, April, 1929, pp. 163-65.*

HENRY SEIDEL CANBY (essay date 1931)

There are two Thoreaus, the Thoreau of want and the Thoreau of ought. What he consistently wanted, was to follow his own bent and belief and live in terms of closest intimacy with wild nature. *Not* because nature contained implications of the Deity and ultimate truth, although this he believed. *Not* because he was a Transcendentalist, although he observed transcendentally. But because to live in such intimacy was what he instinctively loved ("There is in my nature, methinks, a singular yearning toward all wildness") and, still more, because, in the Emersonian sense, he felt himself in tune with the universe when he was in the fields and the woods.

The very interesting chapter on **"Higher Laws"** in **"Walden"** may be readily translated into psychological language. Thoreau began, like most New England boys, with a gun and a fishing rod. He loved, as he says, the wild not less than the good, and his savage nature like his spiritual grew stronger in the woods. He had a taste for violence. But the wild thing captivated his imagination and stirred his mind. He sublimated his savagery into observation and comment. He sublimated his passions also into this single passion. As we find him in his **"Journal,"** he had apparently no amorous emotions which could not be satisfied by friendship, and indeed friendship with him seems to be synonymous with love, and is regarded as something to be won rather than enjoyed. He had dreamed of sexual intercourse as "incredibly beautiful, too fair to be remembered.". . . (pp. 193-94)

[Yet, the] ferocity of sex pursuit bent away in him from sex to nature. He was clearly a lover in his walks, with a lover's jealousy for his solitude, and a lover's reticence as to his ends. I do not think this either morbid or pathological. The rather rarefied purity of his Concord circle made such a course easier than it would have been, say, in Italy, and it is more than probable that his rule of non-intercourse with mere society kept temptation away. But there is nothing surprising in his shift of love. It is a phase of the merging of the carnal into the divine familiar in other civilizations. There was nothing inhuman in Thoreau. With children he was delightful, and his fierce intolerance of polite conversation was unsocial perhaps, but certainly not true misanthropy.

He was, if you please, a "case" of the romantic movement, where nature becomes an obsession and loving observation a passion so satisfying as to engross the best energies. With Thoreau it was a permanent obsession. It is White of Selborne getting his love and his religion from the fruit of his sight. The "bliss of solitude" to such men is a passionate joy because the endless variety, movement, mystery, and beauty of nature satisfy every one of their emotions, absorbing their energies as fast as produced. Men in war and great adventure are so engrossed, and we take it with them as a matter of course. With Thoreau, it was doubly engrossing because his critical, philosophic mind hovered, like his favorite marsh hawk, above the sly coverts of his instincts, viewing each minute experience from on high as possible game for the soul—an ultimate secret slipping through the world's wild bush.

I emphasize this passion for the wild, because this is Thoreau's will and in a true sense himself. He is primarily a lover of life; and it is necessary to take his wilderness delights seriously, understanding that not Raleigh in the voyage to Cadiz, or Mohammed returning from the desert, was more urgently engaged in business of highest personal moment. (pp. 194-96)

But there are negative Thoreaus also: a protestant Thoreau, radical, rebel, economist, Puritan—an unwilling Thoreau who turned aside from his proper business with nature to protest against a society that bent a man toward its own misdirected aims; and again, a puzzled Thoreau, whose conscience would not let him escape a duty to the minds of his fellow men although he so readily shrugged off their companionship. Conscience also, he said, has its diseases.

The positive Thoreau is all rugged tenderness and shrewd and happy contemplation. He is not a mystic, and yet would have lived happily with his philosophy, fishing with Walton in "a wide halo of ease and leisure." But the negative Thoreau is either a seeker, eager to justify his idea of truth, or a fighter against a society that will not let him alone. . . . Both the negative Thoreaus are Puritan. It was his innate Puritanism as much as the moralism of his environment that made him try to moralize nature. The two million words of his **"Journals"** are a tribute to duty. It was no essential part of his scheme of independent and individual living that he should set it all down and try to rationalize it for others. The positive Thoreau would have been content with poetry and essays, the Puritan Thoreau must prepare a vast storehouse of ammunition by which the world might eventually be driven toward truth. It was the Puritan Thoreau that turned, like an angry woodchuck, on an interfering world, gnashed at it with invective, scorned its idleness, and then prepared at Walden a thoughtful answer to the argument of industrialism that you must produce or be barbarous. (pp. 197-98)

It was not nature but himself that he was defending. If his zest had been for textual criticism, or contemplating his navel, his cause would have been the same, his indignation equal, his argument as sound. Of the two Thoreaus, the one belongs to Concord, and with . . . . the true discoverers of America, but the other is an individualist citizen of the universe, who will not endure interference with his idea of living. He is a belated perfectionist set in sudden opposition to the new industrial slant of Western civilization, a Milton attacking not despots, but machines. This Thoreau belongs definitely and without reference to aesthetic values in the world movements of our time, and has a place in intellectual history that only the ignorant will belittle because his stance was merely Walden Pond and the village life of Concord. (p. 199)

Thoreau went to Walden Pond to make a book from his **"Journals,"** to live under such circumstances as would permit him, the individualist, seer, and nature-lover, to be useful and happy in a high sense, but most of all to prove that in an acquisitive society based upon production and proceeding by competition, a man could do what he most wanted, even if there were no cash profits in it, and still subsist.

Stevenson's idea that Thoreau was dodging life and its responsibilities [see excerpt above, 1880] is nonsense from a romanticist whose sacrifices were all capitalized. When Thoreau went to Walden, he walked toward the problem, not away from it. His answer was not an Oriental renunciation of all worldly things, whose logical conclusion is a seat in the dust and scraps of food from the faithful. His answer was renunciation of whatever does not primarily concern *you*—a sifting and threshing of desire until the chaff of imposed wants flies upward and the good grain of essential need remains. For Henry Thoreau, the woods, books, enough solitude, and the simplest food and clothing were prerequisites for successful leisure. **"Walden"** records the results of the experiment—and note that an equal emphasis in that well-digested book falls upon the fruits of happy contemplation and the means by which it was secured. The actual cash account of Thoreau's living is there, carefully set down. It is not your living, your wants—but he asked neither you nor anyone to come to Walden, and if he implores the generality to bind themselves like Ulysses to the mast of higher pleasure until the wasteful meridian of the dinner hour is past, that is his little joke upon hungry Transcendentalists who had to eat at a table. His is a type solution of which the principle is applicable in a thousand fashions. When he had enough of solitude (one factor only in his need) and another way of beating foolish labor around the bush offered itself, he left Walden and came to live with Emerson. Walden had served its purpose. (pp. 203-04)

I do not wish to write of Thoreau as if he were a Force, although a latent force in his own mid-century of many fanatics and a boundless optimism of opportunity he undoubtedly was, and an active force of slow-gathering momentum in ours. Both man and books are very human. He was a failure in the world's eye, or rather in the eyes of the little Concord world that knew him, and by no means a success in his own. His lack of fame has not been without reason and his success with a few devoted readers has been a success almost by accident. A tip of the scale and **"Walden"** would never have been published, or, if published, would have come home to make another private library, like the unsold copies of his **"Week."** The strength of his program is that he actually lived and had faith in it. There are limitations in his ideas fatal to general acceptance, even as there are shortcomings in his writings most prejudicial to art.

I believe him a great writer as well as a great man, a critic of the first rank as well as a sincere and candid individualist, but he never found the hound, the bay horse, and the turtledove that he pursued through life. These symbolized, said Emerson, his disappointments. (p. 209)

[Thoreau was not,] like Emerson, a pure Transcendentalist in nature. He accepted Emerson's belief that facts alone were valueless, but he was never content to stop with Emerson's generalities. He went on collecting while he speculated. He set down and reiterated the same observations year after year. Emerson observed with passion and his very passion carries him instantly up into metaphysics. But Thoreau is not satisfied. He sees the purple grasses waving and below them the tiny star of a new flower, which must be identified. He lies for hours in his boat watching the waving meadow grass of the river bottom. He notes how the woodchuck carries his tail, records the variant colors of Walden ice, sees all that eye can see. His measurements are surveyor's measurements, infinitely crude beside the exact and minute methods of science. And yet he will neither take his evidence into the laboratory (and would not if he had the best of laboratories today) nor give up collecting it. He is like a scholar bogged in a morass of texts.

Hence a confusion that went deep into his life and from whose perplexities he never escaped. Nature was for him an intense and continuous experience. But his faith, one might well say his self-respect, required that he should make something of it beyond the pure fabric of happy episodes that are so lovingly recorded in his **"Journals."** He could not generalize, like Emerson, from second-hand information. He was too scientific for that. But neither could he stop to dissect a leaf when the secret of being was in all nature. In a world of which he was the only inhabitant he would have been a happy observer, content with his intuitions and constantly excited by discoveries that needed no words. But in a culture already electric with science, and in a New England vibrant with the desire to learn and teach, he was tensely indeterminate between research and philosophy. He knew too little to generalize; his intuitions were too deep to be sounded by a millimetre scale. (pp. 213-14)

The more I read Thoreau, the more I feel that with all his faults of discontinuity, and occasional rhetoric, as of a solitary trying to write in the accent of a sophisticated society, he is one of the masters of English prose, purer, stronger, racier, closer to a genuine life rhythm, than any one of his contemporaries, in England or America. A perfectionist in philosophy, he can claim no perfection here—for in suavity and organization and the organ roll of phrase there are a hundred better than he. But his style is like a hill of sumachs and wild apples which has a natural subtlety of expression that partakes of the secret of nature itself, although man has been there, has cut if not planted, and perhaps made the harmony from his own imagination. The hill slope merges into woods, it is a moment only between the cornfield and the forest, and Thoreau is his best self only by paragraphs, but there a master.

Of his verse I say little, because even more than with Emerson, who rose occasionally to poetry, it is a function of his prose. Poetry, he said in the **"Week,"** is an irruption, great prose of equal elevation commands more respect than great verse, it reaches "a more permanent and level height." It did with him. His best verse contains lines of point and power exactly equivalent to the epigrams that dot his prose. He had no rhythmic flow in poetry, but a recurrent rise and fall like the hum of his favorite telegraph wires. Poetry, he thought, was a subsidence, "drawn from under the feet of the poet," a vital function like

breathing; the poet was more than the poem. In short, like Emerson, he would not constrain his nature to be beat up into a regular rhythm. There was too much raw material in his philosophy for sonnet forms. A journal, like his, is best kept in prose and indeed, as his translations from the Greek show, his ear was not set to literary cadences. It took nature to move him to poetry, but it was only by the poetry of prose that he could speak. Metre bound his tongue. (pp. 217-18)

I do not intend for an instant to depreciate Thoreau as a master in the literature of nature. When it comes to mere information there are, it is true, many who can beat him at his own game,—which, however, Hudson, perhaps excepted, they learned from him. Burroughs is more consecutive in his descriptions, as well as more accurate. Muir is often more picturesque. Even Audubon, with his quaint stilted style, can better suggest the vast diversity of an American wilderness.

But Thoreau lifts far above the latitudes in which these nature-lovers work. They are draughtsmen, he is the artist who sees the part in its relation to a whole. Nor are the achievements of **"Winter Visitors"** or **"Wild Apples"** or the river scenes in the **"Week"** or the literary geography of Walden, merely transcendentalized description. For Thoreau in his rôle of a relater and interpreter was attempting a feat beside which these other nature sketches were just literary games. He has a self-appointed task to adjust himself and his race with him to New England, with the full consciousness that, as a nature-lover, he is a pioneer on a new continent, which is known but not humanized [as environment, whose airs, waters, flowers, birds, and stones are still alien to Europeans, who themselves are still squatters in its woods. See how carefully in all his descriptive writings he searches the records of the centuries of settlement, to find what Maine, or Cape Cod, or Concord was like in the seventeenth, in the eighteenth, century. How lovingly he lingers over the history of his river, letting his imagination drift down the history of its slow adjustment to the urgencies of civilized man.

This is the true explanation of his fervid and never-waning interest in the Indian. It was not Cooper's romantic attachment to a "nature man." Read **"The Maine Woods"** carefully and you will see that it was knowledge that Thoreau sought, that intimate knowledge of environment which every English poet has by inheritance, and even yet, few Americans. A most striking characteristic of American imaginative literature is its lack of roots in the soil. Even with Whitman, who belongs to the school of Thoreau, the relationship is indicated in broad terms, by strings of American things and names. Compare him in this respect with Masefield or with Tennyson. The Indian knew his forest as a cockney knows his street, and as no American knows even his wood lot. It was the reticence of the savage, not his romance, that piqued Thoreau into his Maine journeys. He wished to unseal the aboriginal lore of America. (pp. 220-22)

The battle between the city and the country reaches one of its climaxes in Thoreau. The conflict between two ways of life, which is a deeper and longer conflict than any merely economic struggle, was sharply visible from Walden. He did not make the mistake of thinking that a man was a countryman because he lived in the country, nor commit the fallacy of praising labor with the plough in contrast to labor at the machine. He was free from this kind of sentimentalism, spared perhaps because the horrid results of factory life were less visible in New than in Old England. He was concerned rather with the deeper difference between accord with nature and its exploitation. (p. 223)

Henry Seidel Canby, "Henry David Thoreau," in his Classic Americans: A Study of Eminent American Writers from Irving to Whitman, with an Introductory Survey of the Colonial Background of Our National Literature, *1931. Reprint by Russell & Russell, Inc., 1959, pp. 184-225.*

SINCLAIR LEWIS (essay date 1937)

[*Lewis was a prominent American novelist best known for* Main Street, Babbitt, *and other fiction critical of American middle-class values.*]

Once upon a time in America there was a scholar who conducted a one-man revolution and won it. He died 75 years ago, and we aren't within 75 years of catching up with him. He was Henry Thoreau, who helped to make Concord, Mass., as vast as London. He wanted, more than anything else, to buy his own time, and not to "buy time" on the radio—that cosmic feat—but to buy it from life; and out of that time he wanted leisure, not to sleep or shout or show off to the neighbors, but to enjoy the fruits of his growing brains and the delights of his ever-sharpening eyes, that took in not the clumsy hewings of the Acropolis or the Taj Mahal, but the divine delicacies of twigs and bird wings and morning ripples on Walden Pond.

He did not merely want it. He did it. Devoting a shrewd Yankee brain to the accurate measuring of his own wants, he saw just how few things he needed to wear and eat and own in order to be comfortable. No half-jeering questions of his neighbors could induce him to toil—as surveyor, as pencil maker—for one pennyworth more. He built his own warm shack, and in it he lived with a dignity vaster than any harassed emperor. He was popular in his social set, though it was not composed of the humble Bedauxes of his day, but of swallows and chipmunks and sunfish, and other swift, elegant, and shining notabilities.

All this, with gaiety and warmth, he wrote out in **"Walden,"** one of the three or four unquestionable classics of American literature; published in 1854 and more modern than Dos Passos. The greater noises of his human circle, such as Emerson and Hawthorne and Louisa May Alcott's powerfully argumentative papa, considered him amiable but idiotic, and he is outlasting all of them. . . .

I am burning a candle in the hope that 100,000 copies [of **"Walden"**] will be given as Christmas presents this year, to all young persons who are, and very reasonably, worrying about their economic futures, all married couples envious of their friends' automobiles, all Communists, all reactionaries, and all who have been affected by . . . [the phenomenon of] Dale Carnegie, the Bard of Babbittry. . . .

I would not set Andrew Carnegie and Heywood Broun as the captains of our freedom, now that it is menaced by Italy, by Germany, by Japan—and by the United States of America. But Henry Thoreau I would set, and this man, to whom the very notion of dictatorship would be inconceivable, I would make the supreme Duce.

Sinclair Lewis, "One Man Revolution," in The Saturday Review of Literature, *Vol. XVII, No. 7, December 11, 1937, p. 19.*

F. O. MATTHIESSEN (essay date 1941)

[*Matthiessen, a literary critic and historian, was chiefly interested in the concepts of cultural and literary tradition and is considered one of the foremost critics of American literature. Matthiessen discusses Thoreau's criticism of the materialism of his day and expands on "The Service" as Thoreau's starting point for his interest in the use of rhythm and imagery. Thoreau's emphasis on imagery of the senses, Matthiessen contends, became crucial because he came to understand the "material world as a symbol of the spiritual" and used external nature imagery to project his inner life.*]

[Thoreau's] contribution to our social thought lies in his thoroughgoing criticism of the narrow materialism of his day. It is important to remember that when he objected to the division of labor, he was writing from an agrarian and craft economy where the forces of industrialism were still an encroaching minority. But his human values were so clear that they remain substantially unaltered by our changed conditions.

He objected to the division of labor since it divided the worker, not merely the work, reduced him from a man to an operative, and enriched the few at the expense of the many. As a critic of society he had the advantage of being close to its primary levels. The son of a man who had failed as a small merchant and had then set up as a pencil-maker, sign-painter, and jack-of-all-trades, Thoreau came about as close to the status of proletarian writer as was possible in his simple environment. (pp. 77-8)

The social standards that Thoreau knew and protested against were those dominated by New England mercantilism. He granted that the life of a civilized people is '*an institution, in which the life of the individual is to a great extent absorbed, in order to preserve and perfect that of the race.*' But he insisted that it was essential to re-examine the terms under which that absorption was being made, to see whether the individual was not being ruthlessly sacrificed to the dictates of a mean-spirited commercialism. (pp. 78-9)

['**The Service,**' an essay by Thoreau which was rejected by *The Dial,*] is of cardinal value since it lets us follow the very process by which Thoreau found what he wanted to do with language. It has been suggested that the title, underscored by those of its first and last sections, 'Qualities of the Recruit' and 'Not how Many, but where the Enemy are,' was the product of Thoreau's private reaction to current discourses on pacifism. The repeated imagery of a crusade seems borrowed from Tasso's *Jerusalem Delivered,* which had been one of his favorites in college, and whose hero Godfrey is cited here. However, the campaign that Thoreau urges is quite other. The first section sounds the theme, 'For an impenetrable shield, stand inside yourself.' The final pages are a trumpet blast to rouse the soul hovering on the verge of life, to call man not to action against others, but to the realization of his submerged potentialities. All such passages are what Emerson found in Thoreau at this time, simply Emerson's own thoughts originally dressed. But the middle section, 'What Music shall we have?' hints, if somewhat obscurely, at Thoreau's special qualities, and at the way by which he was to arrive at them. One of its sentences, 'A man's life should be a stately march to unheard music,' may seem a vague enough acceptance of the romantic belief in such melodies. But it meant something compelling to Thoreau, since it became a recurrent image throughout his work. He varied it a decade later in his journal: 'It is not so much the music as the marching to the music that I feel.' He picked it up again in the conclusion to **Walden**: 'Let him step to the music which he hears, however measured or far away.' He obviously did not mean merely the disembodied harmony of thought, and it is worth trying to see upon what he grounded his image since it came to epitomize for him the relation between his life and his writing.

In **'The Service'** Thoreau seems groping to convey his recognition, which was to grow increasingly acute, that a deep response to rhythm was his primary experience. He tried to develop it in this fashion: 'To the sensitive soul the Universe has her own fixed measure, which is its measure also, and as this, expressed in the regularity of its pulse, is inseparable from a healthy body, so is its healthiness dependent on the regularity of its rhythm.' The first statement is the usual transcendental doctrine of the merging of the individual with the Over-Soul; the remainder of the sentence, blurred as it is by its loose pronouns, still adumbrates what is going to be Thoreau's particular forte, his grasp of the close correspondence, the organic harmony between body and spirit. Emerson perceived this trenchantly when he said: 'The length of his walk uniformly made the length of his writing. If shut up in the house he did not write at all.' The context of the demand that Lowell mocked is nearly always forgotten: 'Give me a sentence which no intelligence can understand. There must be a kind of life and palpitation to it, and under its words a kind of blood must circulate forever.' Thoreau's first conviction about the artist was that his words should speak not to the mind alone but to the whole being. (pp. 83-5)

Thoreau's emergence from the cloud-land of **'The Service'** onto similar solid earth was due in large part to his having clung fast to his perception that both language and rhythm have a physical basis. His theory of language, in so far as he recorded one, seems at first glance to approximate Emersons's. He held that the origin of words is in nature ('Is it not as language that all natural objects affect the poet?') and that they are symbols of the spiritual. He spoke of the difficulty in finding the word that will exactly name and so release the thing. But he had a more dogged respect for the thing than any of his companions, and limitless tenacity in waiting to find the word. (pp. 85-6)

Thus far nothing has really differentiated his position from what Emerson developed with much greater wealth of detail. But while discussing the primitive sense of words he made a remark that suggests what carried his practice such a considerable distance from his master's: 'We reason from our hands to our head.' Thoreau was not inclined to rate language as superior to other mediums of expression on the ground that it was produced solely by the mind and thence could share more directly in the ideal. On the contrary, he insisted upon its double parentage: 'A word which may be translated into every dialect, and suggests a truth to every mind, is the most perfect work of human art; and as it may be breathed and taken on our lips, and, as it were, become the product of our physical organs, as its sense is of our intellectual, it is the nearest to life itself.' (p. 87)

What separates Thoreau most from Emerson is his interest in the varied play of all of his senses, not merely of the eye, a rare enough attribute in New England and important to dwell on since it is the crucial factor in accounting for the greater density of Thoreau's style. You think first, to be sure, of his Indian accuracy of sight that could measure distances like the surveyor's instrument and tell time almost to the minute by the opening of the flowers. This alertness remained constant. . . . But usually he felt that sight alone was too remote for the kind of knowledge he wanted, that 'we do not learn with the eyes;

they introduce us, and we learn after by converse with things.' He held that scent was 'a more primitive inquisition,' 'more oracular and trustworthy.' It showed what was concealed from the other senses: by it he detected earthiness. Taste meant less to him, though eating became a kind of sacrament and out in the berry field he could be thrilled to think that he owed a perception to this 'commonly gross sense,' that he had been inspired through the palate. (pp. 87-8)

He became ecstatic as he talked about touch: 'My body is all sentient. As I go here or there, I am tickled by this or that I come in contact with, as if I touched the wires of a battery.' He knew, like Anteus, that his strength derived from ever renewed contact with the earth. . . . But as his preoccupation in **'The Service'** has told us, he gave his most rapt attention to sounds. These alone among his sense impressions were to have a chapter devoted to them in *Walden*. He can hardly find enough verbs of action to describe what they do to him. They melt and flow, and he feels himself bathed in their surge. . . . The most exquisite flavor is not to be compared to the sweetness of the note of the wood thrush. As he listens, it seems to take him out of himself: he leaves his body in a trance and has the freedom of all nature. After such an experience he can say, measuring his words, 'The contact of sound with a human ear whose hearing is pure and unimpaired is coincident with an ecstasy.' (pp. 88-9)

He was therefore intent to study the exact evidence of his senses, since he believed that only only through their concrete reports could he project his inner life. Sometimes he felt a danger involved in forming too exact habits of observation, for they could run to excess and yield him, instead of fresh knowledge, merely a flat repetition of what he already knew. His remedy for this was what he called a free 'sauntering of the eye.' The poetic knowledge he wanted would come only through something like Wordsworth's 'relaxed attention,' only if he was not a scientific naturalist, 'not prying, nor inquisitive, nor bent upon seeing things.' He described his desired attitude towards nature by calling it one of indirection, by repeating frequently that the most fruitful perception was 'with the unworn sides of your eye.' We remember Keats' delight in 'the sidelong glance,' and his feeling that his ripest intuitions came through indolence. Thus nonchalantly, almost unconsciously, Thoreau could catch the most familiar scene in new perspective, with possibilities hitherto untold to his direct scrutiny, and with a wholeness of impression that could give it composition in writing. (pp. 89-90)

[To] the end, even in his most sterile moods, he could respond to such never stale melodies as those of the wood thrush, though he could not recapture quite this earlier pitch: 'Where was that strain mixed into which this world was dropped but as a lump of sugar to sweeten the draught? I would be drunk, drunk, drunk, dead drunk to this world with it forever.'

In that moment Thoreau approached Keats, but, in the act of making the comparison, you recall that Thoreau's idea of luxury was to stand up to his chin in a retired swamp and be saturated with its summer juices. This man, who, unlike Whitman, hated to lie with the sun on his back, was constant in his dislike of sensuality. His desire was for 'no higher heaven than the pure senses can furnish, a *purely* sensuous life.' The double suggestion here of the need for clarified perception and of the vision into which it could lead him brings out the mystical element that always remained part of his experience. Yet even when he was swept beyond his moments of physical sensation he did not forget his debt to them. The triumphal strains to which he was set marching in **'The Service'** were not a nebulous fancy. They were the imaginative transformation of a rhythm he had actually heard and which he was trying to symbolize in words: 'In our lonely chambers at night we are thrilled by some far-off serenade within the mind, and seem to hear the clarion sound and clang of corselet and buckler from many a silent hamlet of the soul, though actually it may be but the rattling of some farmer's waggon rolling to market against the morrow.'

The checkrein of his senses was what held even such a passage from gliding away into a romantic reverie of escape. Their vigilance constituted his chief asset as an artist. It brought his pages out of the fog into the sunlight in which he wanted them to be read. (pp. 90-1)

In spite of his keenness in scrutinizing the reports of his senses, Thoreau remained wholly the child of his age in regarding the material world as a symbol of the spiritual. He who held that 'the poet writes the history of his body' declared in another mood that 'poetry is the mysticism of mankind.' He could even contradict his enunciation that it was not the subject but the roundness of treatment that mattered, by saying that 'a higher truth, though only dimly hinted at, thrills us more than a lower expressed.' He stated early and kept repeating that he was ever in pursuit of the ineffable: 'The other world is all my art; my pencils will draw no other; my jack-knife will cut nothing else; I do not use it as a means.'

Yet even in that affirmation of faith Thoreau does not disappear into the usual transcendental vapor. He gives us the sense that he is a man whose grip remains firm on this world as well, whose hand can manage both his knife and his pencil. In fact, Thoreau's success as an artist is exactly in proportion to such balance between means and end. On the occasions when he attempts a direct approach to his end, when, that is to say, he voices his bare thoughts, as in his pages on ideal friendship, his mind is revealed as much less capacious and less elastic than Emerson's. On the other hand, when he simply heaps up facts, as in the later volumes of his journal, he himself recognizes that facts so stated are parched, that they 'must be the vehicle of some humanity in order to interest us,' that they 'must be warm, moist, incarnated—have been breathed on at least. A man has not seen a thing who has not felt it.' This is to remark again that Thoreau was not specially equipped either for abstract theorizing or for strictly scientific observation. But when he could base theory on his own sturdy practice, as in **'Life Without Principle'** or **'Civil Disobedience,'** the impact of his humanity was dynamic. And when, as a writer, he could fuse his thought and his observation by means of a symbol, which was not just suggested but designed in sharp detail, he was able, in Coleridge's phrase, to 'elicit truth as at a flash.'

Thoreau's own description of his most fertile process, in the chapter **'What I lived for,'** is that 'we are able to apprehend at all what is sublime and noble only by the perpetual instilling and drenching of the reality that surrounds us.' The gerunds are characteristic, drawn from verbs of touch that penetrate to his inner being. They show the kind of fusion he could make by training into his writing the alertness of his senses. (pp. 93-4)

The rhythm [in the passage about the Concord fisherman in *A Week*] is a clear instance of what Thoreau meant by saying that it was not so much the music as the marching to the music that he felt. For here, as in many other typical passages, his eye is reinforced not by varied sounds so much as by impres-

sions of movement and of muscular pressure. He catches the step of the fisher in unison with the sweep of his scythe, though the word 'undulatory' blends too with the flow of the river, merging the old man as closely as possible with the source of his former pleasures. In that fashion Thoreau projected his conception of the harmonious interaction between man and nature, without which he did not believe that man could be adequately described.

But the river in which so many things have gone down stream is also that of the fisherman's throat, of his drunken life, the disintegration of which Thoreau conveys entirely in concrete terms, each suggesting a significance beyond itself. The snake that the old man might encounter while mowing is likewise that of his temptation; and his own figure with its scythe calls up that of Time. The final metaphor may seem too literary, the romantic stock-in-trade. Along with Thoreau's fondness for his whimsical pun on 'fluid,' it may be the kind of thing Carlyle objected to when he called the *Week* 'too Jean Paulish.' However, 'the Great Mower' saves itself, at least to a degree that most of Richter's self-conscious fancies do not, by the fact that it has not been lugged in arbitrarily. It has grown integrally out of the context, and that lends some freshness to it.

The organic structure of Thoreau's symbols became more marked in *Walden,* as in the laconic: 'Having each some shingles of thought well dried, we sat and whittled them, trying our knives, and admiring the clear yellowish grain of the pumpkin pine.' The deft telescoping of sense impression and thought allows full play to both. We can share in the relish of what he has seen, since his delicate skill has evoked the very look of the wood at the moment of being cut into. But the desultory act of whittling becomes also the appropriate image for conversation between Alcott and Thoreau around the winter hearth in Thoreau's hut. The single sentence gives a condensed dramatic scene, the very way these two friends appeared while trying their minds on thoughts 'well dried' by use; and, in this case, Thoreau's double meaning is pungent, since it frees the air of the suspicion of solemness that might be there without it. (pp. 94-5)

By [his] method of presenting an experience instead of stating an abstraction, Thoreau himself has elucidated both the meaning and the value of his long preoccupation with 'wholeness.' From the time he announced in **'The Service'** that 'the exploit of a brave life consists in its momentary completeness,' he continued to make brief definitions of that quality, and of how it might be gained. . . . The year after **'The Service'** he developed his sentence further: 'The best and bravest deed is that which the whole man—heart, lungs, hands, fingers, and toes—at any time prompts . . . This is the meaning of integrity; this is to be an integer, and not a fraction.' He subsequently shifted his symbols to correspond to his own mode of existence, and grouped them not around the warrior hero but around the scholar, who, if he is wise, 'will confine the observations of his mind as closely as possible to the experience or life of his senses. His thought must live with and be inspired with the life of the body . . . Dwell as near as possible to the channel in which your life flows.' In this respect more than in any other was the practice of Thoreau's scholar more thoroughgoing than Emerson's. (p. 96)

In desiring to push as near as possible to the boundaries between the visible and the invisible, to reassert the primitive quality of wonder, Thoreau . . . approached Browne. . . . Attention to the objects around him, not intricate speculation, furnished him with his best analogies. . . . He was nearest the practice of the seventeenth-century poets when he insisted on the use of *all* materials that experience affords; but his experience was less complex if no less concentrated than Donne's. It approximated that of the explorers in its excited immediacy of discovery, though what he wanted to discover was himself. His ability to do whatever he did with his whole being was the product of an awakened scrutiny, not, as for them, an unconscious response of minds that had never conceived any arbitrary gap between thought and feeling and so reacted with equal directness to physical and spiritual adventures. So Thoreau's pages are inevitably more literary, a mixture of the cultivated and the wild. Indeed, one of his chief distinctions—and again he shares this with Browne—is the infusion of his reading into his perception. . . . (p. 117)

The structural wholeness of *Walden* makes it stand as the firmest product in our literature of . . . life-giving analogies between the processes of art and daily work. Moreover, Thoreau's very lack of invention brings him closer to the essential attributes of craftsmanship, if by that term we mean the strict, even spare, almost impersonal 'revelation of the object,' in contrast to the 'elaborated skill,' the combinations of more variegated resources that we describe as technique. (p. 173)

He had understood that in the act of expression a man's whole being, and his natural and social background as well, function organically together. He had mastered a definition of art akin to what Maritain has extracted from scholasticism: *Recta ratio factibilium*, the right ordering of the thing to be made, the right revelation of the material. (p. 175)

> *F. O. Matthiessen, in his* American Renaissance: Art and Expression in the Age of Emerson and Whitman, *Oxford University Press, New York, 1941, 678 p.*

HENRY W. WELLS (essay date 1944)

[*In this essay, the first serious, in-depth consideration of Thoreau's poetry, Wells explores the influences that affected Thoreau's verse. Though Wells recognizes Thoreau's familiarity with Greek, medieval, and Romantic poetry, he denies that Thoreau was imitative or overly derivative, and he praises Thoreau's scholarship.*]

Almost all Thoreau's poetry may be regarded as the achievement of a conspicuously independent young man who resolutely declined to ape the popular fashions of his age. While Emily Dickinson quietly discarded much of the specious writing of her times and country, Thoreau displayed a more vigorous opposition. To a remarkable degree he turned away from the main streams of contemporary taste in poetry as directed by Wordsworth, Byron, and the younger British writers of his own day. To be sure, he loved Wordsworth, and his poetry betrays this love; but in its rugged, terse, and abrupt expression it shows an art fundamentally unlike Wordsworth's. Scarcely a single poem from his hand can be associated with American fashions soon to be securely established by Longfellow, Whittier, and Lowell. In short, he is unregenerately unorthodox so far as midnineteenth-century America is concerned. It is well known that his reading was very little in his contemporary fellow countrymen and widely disseminated among the English classics and the literatures of the world. His unusual grasp of Greek and Latin poetry and his exercises in the translation of classical verse, notably Pindar, at least indicate his scope. It is true that whatever he writes springs from his heart—the clearest evidence of his genuine poetic faculty. Yet one of the outstanding features of his work is this evidence of the fruits

of his reading and prophetic insight. Of his major poems not a single specimen adheres narrowly to the norm of romantic verse at the time of its composition, although, as we shall see, some extraordinary variations on romantic themes are to be found. The American environment itself is clearly indicated by his art in only half a dozen pieces, which at least resemble though they do not entirely agree with Emerson's rugged, didactic manner. At least an equal number strongly suggest Horace and the pure classical vein itself. A few stand in a surprising relation to medieval thought, feeling, or verse patterns. Slightly more are in much the same style as the manly verse of the founder of British neoclassicism, Ben Jonson. The more mannered and pseudo-heroic eloquence of the English Augustans, as in James Thomson, is occasionally turned by Thoreau to his own purpose. A larger group of lyrics share the spiritual inwardness, lively imagination, and chaste exterior of the English seventeenth-century metaphysical poets, whom Thoreau read and grasped uncommonly well. The nervous vigor and high excitement of some of the spiritual or didactic poetry of the Revolutionary period, notably William Blake's, has striking analogues in the New England radical. Where his nature poetry and his expressions of exaggerated idealism, optimism, and enthusiasm most approximate the high romantic style, he still shows his characteristic independence in thought and feeling. Finally, the largest group of his most memorable poems, nearly a third of them, belongs when historically considered not so much with the past as with the future. Thoreau, like Emily Dickinson or Baudelaire, anticipates the bold symbolism, airy impressionism, stringent realism, and restless inconsistencies of twentieth-century poetry. In the art of poetry no less than in his metaphysics, the recluse of Walden made the world and its epochs his province. . . . Moreover, he is a spiritual cosmopolitan by virtue of his intuitive grasp of the poetic imagination of other periods than his own and not by any mere wealth of allusions which he plunders from abroad. None of Poe's exotic bric-a-brac glitters from his pages. He makes no display of his internationalism, for it is the most natural and instinctive thing about him. His allusions and images are drawn from common nature and from life as seen in the neighborhood of Concord. It is with the eye of the soul and not of the body that his art looks toward past, future, and the ultramontane world.

His classical studies left him, while still in his teens, with a sense of form sufficiently rare in the comparatively formless nineteenth century. His insight is suggested by a few quatrains with a shapeliness resembling the Greek Anthology. In speaking of Thoreau's epigrams Emerson not unnaturally referred to Simonides. A less derivative and more creative poet than Landor, Thoreau transports the classical form to the New England scene; the form is revitalized, the scene reinterpreted. . . . The long and impressive ode entitled **"Let such pure hate still underprop"** is clearly fashioned with the strict Horatian sense of proportion. One of his more romantic nature poems ends with an obvious recollection of Horace; the bare New England trees are pictured thus:

> Poor knights they are which bravely wait
>   The charge of Winter's cavalry,
> Keeping a simple Roman state,
>   Disencumbered of their Persian luxury.

It is worth notice that he refers to several of his poems as odes. Moreover, his lyrics are often classical in content as well as in form. He appropriately expresses Platonic doctrine in a poem of strict classical outline, **"Rumors from an Aeolian Harp."**

Much of the classical morality of life appealed to him, especially in his later years when the extremes of his naturalistic romanticism wore thin. In **"Manhood"** he sees man and not nature as master of human fate. Man guides nature to do his will, as he might guide a horse. Experience teaches him a doctrine of ripe humanism. . . . (pp. 100-02)

Traces of thought and art more or less deliberately derived from medieval sources may at first seem incongruous in a lover of the Maine woods, but they are present in no negligible degree. Thus a surprising poem entitled **"The Virgin"** reveals her place in the Catholic system midway between Heaven and Earth, the Old Law and the New. This paradoxical account of Mary resembles her praise as put into the mouth of Saint Bernard by Dante, yet Thoreau follows the spirit rather than the letter of medieval sources:

> With her calm, aspiring eyes
> She doth tempt the earth to rise,
> With humility over all,
> She doth tempt the sky to fall.
>
> In her place she still doth stand
> A pattern unto the firm land
> While revolving spheres come round
> To embrace her stable ground.

If this poem does not consciously refer to the Virgin Mary, it affords at least a remarkable coincidence. Much more usual in his poetry than theological reminiscences are inheritances, conscious or unconscious, from medieval verse patterns, possibly with aid from the German lyric tradition. Thoreau is a keen metrical experimenter, seeking exotic devices, both in rhyme and a free blank verse, to express his highly various moods. He revives Skeltonic measures, dimeter in general, and a dipodic verse typical of medieval poetry no less than of nursery rhymes. Metrically, and to some degree verbally, such a stanza as the following carries us back to the inspired doggerel of medieval mystery plays:

> The axe resounds,
> And bay of hounds
> And tinkling sounds
> Of wintry fame;
> The hunter's horn
> Awakes the dawn
> On field forlorn,
> And frights the game.

But to Thoreau the poetry and culture of the Middle Ages must indeed have seemed an interlude. To his ear as an English-speaking poet the classical manner which he loved was to be heard most forcibly rendered in English by Ben Jonson, father of English neoclassicism, and by Jonson's most intimate followers. Their simple and disciplined style leaves an unmistakable mark upon the wholly unaffected elegy, **"Brother Where Dost Thou Dwell."** The balanced and severely controlled style is crystalized in **"Inspiration"**:

> I hearing get who had but ears,
>   And sight, who had but eyes before,
> I moments live who lived but years,
>   And truth discern who knew but learning's lore.

Also from the English seventeenth century Thoreau drew a poetic heritage still more congenial to him. Such lucidity and formality as are illustrated in the foregoing quotation, drawn ultimately from ancient models, were transformed by the "metaphysical" poets following Donne into a more sensitive and indigenous English verse, thus bestowing upon our poetry in general and upon Thoreau in particular the most charming of octosyllabic verse and a similarly fluid and controlled stanzaic structure. Marvell or some other poet of his times may be regarded as godfather to such a passage as the conclusion of **"The River Swelleth More and More"**:

> Here Nature taught from year to year,
> When only red men came to hear;
> Methinks 'twas in this school of art
> Venice and Naples learned their part;
> But still their mistress, to my mind,
> Her young disciples leaves behind.

Marvell's school, with its metaphysical and subjective insight, also contributed an important part to the transcendental vision and lusty imagination of the New Englander. His inwardness appears notably in such a poem as **"The Inward Morning."** A highly fanciful symbolism ingeniously employed to express the mysteries of consciousness appears very much after the pattern of the "metaphysicals" in **"Farewell," "Poverty,"** and **"On Ponkawtasset, Since, We Took Our Way."** The New Englander, with a realism exceeding Vaughan's, uses in **"Upon This Bank at Early Dawn"** the same bold and spiritualized image of the cock which Vaughan employs in his memorable "Cock-Crowing." The rigid architecture of the typical metaphysical poem also leaves an imprint on Thoreau's art, as may be seen in **"I Knew a Man by Sight,"** with its stanzas in the most logical sequence possible. In one of the most nearly imitative of all his truly successful pieces, **"I Am a Parcel of Vain Strivings Tied,"** he comes strikingly close to the verse forms of Herbert. . . . (pp. 103-05)

He became sensible to the charms of the baroque neoclassical rhetoric of the age and school of James Thomson and William Cowper. The poet who in one lyric employs the simplest and most colloquial manner, in another assumes for gravity's sake the full panoply of Augustan artifice and eloquence. He uses a heroic or an epic diction in treating subjects where such a diction seems far from inevitable. Yet here his warmth of feeling proves his salvation. There is something genuinely poetic and instinctively noble in his style, so that his poetry is seldom frozen into the rhetorical frigidities which occasionally deface not only Lowell but Emerson. **"The Sluggish Smoke Curls up from Some Deep Dell"** is a piece by Thoreau in this pseudo-epic manner. Augustan robes, though worn lightly, are still perceptible. (pp. 105-06)

Thoreau was kindled from the spiritual fires struck by the violence of the French Revolution upon the sterner and more masculine of English minds, such as Blake's. The revolutionary temper, so strong in Thoreau, found in the language of these earlier revolutionaries an inspiration for his own poetic speech. There are revolutionary explosives in the defiant poem which begins:

> The Good how can we trust?
> Only the Wise are just.

Several of his more reflective quatrains strike with an energy very similar to that of Blake. Again, in their faith and enthusiasm some of his most vigorous transcendental verses, as the superb lyric **"All Things Are Current Found,"** bear the accent of spiritual assertion belonging to the more spiritual discoveries of the pioneers of the romantic movement.

Although Thoreau is never a strictly representative figure of either the earlier or later phases of romanticism, he naturally participates to a considerable degree in some of its major trends. An imagery finely descriptive of nature, a power in this imagery to beget a mood rich in emotion and vague in intellectual definition, as well as an audacious idealism show him a cousin, though not quite a brother, to the leading popular romantic poets in America and Europe. Thus while his remarkable poems on smoke and clouds bear the strongest marks of his own genius, they obviously stem from the main body of romantic nature verse. Notable in the same connection is his romantic fondness for autumn, almost as marked as in Corot. (p. 106)

Thoreau also participated in the rugged but somewhat strident didacticism which entered American poetry with Emerson and his immediate associates; and once more he reflected a movement without in any way losing his own individuality. Since he most nearly resembles Emerson yet differs from him notably, it becomes a nice test of Thoreau's art to place beside his own pieces Emerson's poems on like themes. Each poet, for example, wrote a fairly long ode on Mount Monadnock, alike not only in much of their imagery but in their ideas, language and, to a rather less degree, in rhythm. Yet the differences afford an excellent measurement of the general distinction between the two poets. Emerson's poem is clearer in meaning and nearer to the usual practices of the times in metre, symbol, texture, and total effect. A Yankee practicality in his verse withholds it from the more catholic and liberated imagination conspicuous in all Thoreau's best lyrics. To his contemporaries Thoreau's poem must certainly have appeared rough and raw. To us it seems less regular in its beauty, subtler, more meditative and, in the very delicacy and elusiveness of its symbolism, so much the more poetic. Thoreau's picture of mountains as ships pioneering on strange seas possesses a poetic scope and a richness of imagination of which Emerson proved incapable.

Thoreau as a poet flourished more in spiritual contact with past and future than with his own present. Hence the largest single group into which his chief poems fall, when considered historically, is that showing him in various ways anticipating the mind of the twentieth century. He touches the poetry of our own times closely largely in terms of its acute tensions. His verse, for example, often directly expresses the abrupt and vivid experience of the moment. Monuments to such sharp and intense experience appear in such pieces as **"Music,"** **"The Cliffs and Springs,"** and that unique poem on the imaginative import of unmusical sounds:

> They who prepare my evening meal below
> Carelessly hit the kettle as they go
> With tongs or shovel,
> And ringing round and round,
> Out of this hovel
> It makes an eastern temple by the sound.

A typical abruptness of phrase and boldness in sound connotative imagery may be seen in the first line of one of his lyrics, **"Dong, sounds the brass in the East."** The close and astringent conjunction of the concrete and the elusive, so much sought after in the poetry of the present age, may be seen in a poem comprised of six short lines:

> The waves slowly beat,
> Just to keep the noon sweet,
> And no sound is floated o'er,
> Save the mallet on shore,
> Which echoing on high
> Seems a-calking the sky.

As in much twentieth-century verse, nature imagery is first used to produce a mood and then suddenly surprises us by unveiling an imaginative idea, as when, in the lyric **"Where Gleaming Fields of Haze,"** the "ancient" sound of the name "Souhegan" abruptly leads to thoughts of the Xanthus and Meander. The nervous heightening in subjectivity so keenly felt in much poetry of the twentieth century appears foreshadowed in the startling couplet at the end of **"I Am the Autumnal Sun"**:

> And the rustling of the withered leaf
> Is the constant music of my grief.

Some less drastic features of modern verse making it appear more rugged than its nineteenth-century predecessor also give nerve and vigor to Thoreau's lines. These may be seen in bits of light but effective verse where humor comes to the support of idealism, or a homely realism to the aid of a lofty transcendentalism. **"My Boots"** and **"Tall Ambrosia"** offer instances. Finally, Thoreau's drastic and startling realistic satire in such highly acid poems as **"For Though the Caves Were Rabitted"** and **"I Am the Little Irish Boy"** resembles in a broad way the forthright manner of the brilliant satires of Yeats.

These powerful projections into the poetic mood of a restless age still almost a century in advance should free the scholar poet from any suspicion that he is merely imitative, overderivative, or immature. It is obviously true that as a young man he revolted from most contemporary fashions in letters as well as in life and gave himself to a devoted study of our heritage from Greece and Rome and from all the periods of the English literary record. But his scholarly habits were vitalizing habits, which happily added strength to his strongly creative mind and in no way fettered his creative faculties in chains of pedantic imitation. His scholarship is merely the outward sign of his universality as poet. His occasional lapses owing to bad taste may generally be ascribed to the limitations of his age, from which even so pronounced an individualist as he could not entirely escape. The refinements of his art, on the contrary, may best be discerned in his highly varied and modulated rhythms, his uncommonly flexible vocabulary and his many unclassifiable nuances. His strength is most intimately associated with his breadth. Thoreau found all schools of poetry his teachers, none his master. . . . Thoreau's breadth of vision is precisely what our own age, tragically seeking a new consolidation of mankind, most of all requires. (pp. 107-09)

> *Henry W. Wells, "An Evaluation of Thoreau's Poetry," in* American Literature, *Vol. 16, No. 1, March, 1944, pp. 99-109.*

STANLEY EDGAR HYMAN   (essay date 1946)

[*Hyman was an American critic who is best known for his theory that modern literary criticism would be determined by the use of knowledge outside the field of literature. Terming Thoreau the "most ringing and magnificent polemicist America has ever produced," Hyman suggests that Thoreau was at worst a "nut reformer," and at best "the clearest voice for social ethics that ever spoke out in America." Hyman discusses* Walden *as "a vast rebirth ritual," which moves thematically from "individual isolation to collective identification." In addition, Hyman writes that Thoreau was more engaged in the question of literary craft than any American writer except Henry James.*]

[Why celebrate the centenary of Thoreau's night in jail?] For only one reason. As a political warrior, Thoreau was a comic little figure with a receding chin, and not enough high style to carry off a gesture. As a political writer, he was the most ringing and magnificent polemicist America has ever produced. Three years later he made an essay called **Civil Disobedience** out of his prison experience, fusing the soft coal of his night in jail into solid diamond. **Civil Disobedience** has all the power and dignity that Thoreau's political act so signally lacked. (p. 137)

In the relative futility of Thoreau's political act and the real importance of his political essay based on it, we have an allegory for our time on the artist as politician: the artist as strong and serviceable in the earnest practice of his art as he is weak and faintly comic in direct political action. In a day when the pressure on the artist to forsake his art for his duties as a citizen is almost irresistible, when every painter is making posters on nutrition, when every composer is founding a society devoted to doing something about the atom bomb, when every writer is spending more time on committees than on the typewriter, we can use Henry Thoreau's example.

In the past century we have had various cockeyed and contradictory readings of Thoreau's "essence." But from them we can reach two conclusions. One is that he is probably a subtler and more ambiguous character than anyone seems to have noticed. The other is that he must somehow still retain a powerful magic or there would not be such a need to capture or destroy him, to canonize the shade or weight it down in the earth under a cairn of rocks. It is obvious that we shall have to create a Thoreau for ourselves.

The first thing we should insist on is that Thoreau was a writer, not a man who lived in the woods or didn't pay taxes or went to jail. At his best he wrote the only really first-rate prose ever written by an American, with the possible exception of Abraham Lincoln. The **Plea for Captain John Brown,** his most sustained lyric work, rings like [John Milton's] *Areopagitica,* and like *Areopagitica* it is the product of passion combined with complete technical mastery. . . .

Thoreau was not only a writer, but a writer in the great stream of the American tradition, the mythic and non-realist writers, Hawthorne and Melville, Mark Twain and Henry James, and, in our own day, as Malcolm Cowley has been most insistent in pointing out, Hemingway and Faulkner. In pointing out Hemingway's kinship, not to our relatively barren realists and naturalists, but to our "haunted and nocturnal writers, the men who dealt in images that were symbols of an inner world," Cowley demonstrates that the idyllic fishing landscape of such a story as [Hemingway's] "Big Two-Hearted River" is not a real landscape setting for a real fishing trip, but an enchanted landscape full of rituals and taboos, a metaphor or projection of an inner state.

It would not be hard to demonstrate the same thing for the landscape in **Walden.** One defender of such a view would be Henry Thoreau, who writes in his **Journals,** along with innumerable tributes to the power of mythology, that the richest function of nature is to symbolize human life, to become fable and myth for man's inward experience. (p. 138)

At Walden, Thoreau reports the experience of awakening one morning with the sense that some question had been put to him, which he had been endeavoring in vain to answer in his sleep. In his terms, that question would be the problem with which he begins *Life Without Principle:* "Let us consider the way in which we spend our lives." His obsessive image, running through everything he ever wrote, is the myth of Apollo,

glorious god of the sun, forced to labor on earth tending the flocks of King Admetus. In one sense, of course, the picture of Henry Thoreau forced to tend anyone's flocks is ironic, and Stevenson is right when he notes sarcastically: "Admetus never got less work out of any servant since the world began" [see excerpt above, 1880]. In another sense the myth has a basic rightness, and is, like the Pied Piper of Hamelin, an archetypal allegory of the artist in a society that gives him no worthy function and no commensurate reward.

The sun is Thoreau's key symbol, and all of **Walden** is a development in the ambiguities of sun imagery. The book begins with the theme: "But alert and healthy natures remember that the sun rose clear," and ends: "There is more day to dawn. The sun is but a morning star." Thoreau's movement from an egocentric to a sociocentric view is the movement from "I have, as it were, my own sun, and moon, and stars, and a little world all to myself" to "The same sun which ripens my beans illumines at once a system of earths like ours." The sun is an old Platonist like Emerson that must set before Thoreau's true sun can rise; it is menaced by every variety of mist, haze, smoke, and darkness; it is Thoreau's brother; it is both his own cold affection and the threat of sensuality that would corrupt goodness as it taints meat; it is himself in a pun on s-o-n, s-u-n.

When Abolitionism becomes a nagging demand Thoreau can no longer resist, a Negro woman is a dusky orb rising on Concord, and when John Brown finally strikes his blow for Thoreau the sun shines on him, and he works "in the clearest light that shines on the land." The final announcement of Thoreau's triumphant rebirth at Walden is the sun breaking through mists. It is not to our purpose here to explore the deep and complex ambiguities of Thoreau's sun symbol, or in fact to do more than note a few of many contexts, but no one can study the sun references in **Walden** without realizing that Thoreau is a deeper and more complicated writer than we have been told, and that the book is essentially dynamic rather than static, a movement *from* something *to* something, rather than simple reporting of an experience.

Walden is, in fact, a vast rebirth ritual, the purest and most complete in our literature. We know rebirth rituals to operate characteristically by means of fire, ice or decay, mountains and pits, but we are staggered by the amount and variety of these in the book. We see Thoreau build his shanty of boards he has first purified in the sun, record approvingly an Indian purification ritual of burning all the tribe's old belongings and provisions, and later go off into a description of the way he is cleansed and renewed by his own fireplace. We see him note the magic purity of the ice on Walden Pond, the fact that frozen water never turns stale, and the rebirth involved when the ice breaks up, all sins are forgiven, and "Walden was dead and is alive again." We see him exploring every phase and type of decay: rotting ice, decaying trees, moldy pitch pine and rotten wood, excrement, maggots, a vulture feeding on a dead horse, carrion, tainted meat, and putrid water.

The whole of **Walden** runs to symbols of graves and coffins, with consequent rising from them, to wombs and emergence from them, and ends on the fable of a live insect resurrected from an egg long buried in wood. Each day at Walden Thoreau was reborn by his bath in the pond, a religious exercise he says he took for purification and renewal, and the whole two years and two months he compresses into the cycle of a year, to frame the book on the basic rebirth pattern of the death and renewal of vegetation, ending it with the magical emergence of spring.

On the thread of decay and rebirth Thoreau strings all his preoccupations. Meat is a symbol of evil, sensuality; its tainting symbolizes goodness and affection corrupted; the shameful defilement of chastity smells like carrion (in which he agreed with Shakespeare); the eating of meat causes slavery and unjust war. (pp. 138, 140)

But even slavery and injustice are a decaying and a death, and Thoreau concludes *Slavery in Massachusetts* with: "We do not complain that they *live*, but that they do not *get buried*. Let the living bury them; even they are good for manure." Always, in Thoreau's imagery, what this rotting meat will fertilize is fruit, ripe fruit. It is his chief good. He wanted "the flower and fruit of man," the "ripeness." The perfect and glorious state he foresees will bear men as fruit, suffering them to drop off as they ripen; John Brown's heroism is a good seed that will bear good fruit, a future crop of heroes. Just as Brown, in one of the most terrifying puns ever written, was "ripe" for the gallows, Thoreau reports after writing *Civil Disobedience*, as he dwells on action and wildness, that he feels ripe, fertile: "It is seedtime with me. I have lain fallow long enough." On the metaphor of the organic process of birth, growth, decay, and rebirth out of decay, Thoreau organizes his whole life and experience.

I have maintained that *Walden* is a dynamic process, a job of symbolic action, a moving *from* something *to* something. From what to what? On an abstract level, from individual isolation to collective identification—from, in Macaulay's terms, a Platonic philosophy of pure truth to a Baconian philosophy of use. It is interesting to note that the term Bacon used for the utilitarian ends of knowledge, for the relief of man's estate, is "fruit." The Thoreau who went to Walden was a pure Platonist, a man who could review a Utopian book and announce that it was too practical, that its chief fault was aiming "to secure the greatest degree of gross comfort and pleasure merely." The man who left Walden was the man who thought it was less important for John Brown to right a Greek accent slanting the wrong way than to right a falling slave.

Early in the book Thoreau gives us his famous Platonic myth of having long ago lost a hound, a bay horse, and a turtle dove. Before he is through, his symbolic quest is for a human being, and near the end of the book he reports of a hunter: "He had lost a dog but found a man." All through *Walden* he weighs Platonic and Baconian values. . . . By the end of the book he has brought Transcendentalism down to earth, has taken Emerson's castles in the air, to use his own figure, and built foundations under them.

Thoreau's political value, for us, is largely in terms of this transition from philosophic aloofness. We see in him the honest artist struggling for terms on which he can adjust to society *in his capacity as artist*. As might be expected from such a process, Thoreau's social statements are full of contradictions, and quotations can be amputated from the context of his work to bolster any position from absolute anarchism to ultimate toryism, if indeed they are very far apart. At his worst, he is simply a nut reformer, one of the horde in his period, attempting to "improve" an Irish neighbor by lecturing him on abstinence from tea, coffee, and meat as the solution to all his problems, and the passage in *Walden* describing his experience is the most condescending and offensive in a sometimes infuriating book.

At his best, he is the clearest voice for social ethics that ever spoke out in America.

One of the inevitable consequences of Emersonian idealism was the ease with which it could be used to sugar-coat social injustice, as a later generation was to discover when it saw robber barons piling up fortunes while intoning Emersonian slogans of Self-Reliance and Compensation. If the Lowell factory owner was more enslaved than one of his child laborers, there was little point in seeking to improve the lot of the child laborer, and frequently Emerson seemed to be preaching a principle that would forbid both the rich and the poor to sleep under bridges. Thoreau begins *Walden* in these terms, remarking that it is frivolous to attend to "the gross but somewhat foreign form of servitude called Negro Slavery when there are so many keen and subtle masters that enslave"; that the rich are a "seemingly wealthy, but most terribly impoverished class of all," since they are fettered by their gold and silver; that the day laborer is more independent than his employer, since his day ends with sundown, while his employer has no respite from one year to another; even that if you give a ragged man money he will perhaps buy more rags with it, since he is frequently gross, with a taste for rags.

Against this ingenious and certainly unintentional social palliation, *Walden* works through to sharp social criticism: of the New England textile factory system, whose object is, "not that mankind may be well and honestly clad, but, unquestionably, that the corporations may be enriched"; of the degradation of the laboring class of his time, "living in sties," shrunken in mind and body; of the worse condition of the Southern slaves; of the lack of dignity and privacy in the lives of factory girls, "never alone, hardly in their dreams"; of the human consequences of commerce and technology; of the greed and corruption of the money-mad New England of his day, seeing the whole world in the bright reflecting surface of a dollar.

As his bitterness and awareness increased, Thoreau's direct action became transmuted. He had always, like his friends and family, helped the Underground Railway run escaped slaves to Canada. He devotes a sentence to one such experience in *Walden*, and amplifies it in his *Journal*, turning a quiet and terrible irony on the man's attempt to buy his freedom from his master, who was his father, and exercised paternal love by holding out for more than the slave could pay. These actions, however, in a man who disliked Abolitionism, seem to have been simple reflexes of common decency, against his principles, which would free the slave first by striking off his spiritual chains.

From this view, Thoreau works tortuously through to his final identification of John Brown, the quintessence of direct social action, with all beauty, music, poetry, philosophy, and Christianity. Finally Brown becomes Christ, an indignant militant who cleansed the temple, preached radical doctrines, and was crucified by the slaveowners. In what amounts almost to worship of Brown, Thoreau both deifies the action he had tried to avoid and transcends it in passion. Brown died for him, thus he need free no more slaves.

At the same time, Thoreau fought his way through the Emersonian doctrine that a man might wash his hands of wrong, providing he did not himself commit it. He writes in *Civil Disobedience:*—

> It is not a man's duty, as a matter of course,
> to devote himself to the eradication of any, even

the most enormous wrong; he may still properly
have other concerns to engage him; but it is his
duty, at least, to wash his hands of it, and, if
he gives it no thought longer, not to give it
practically his support. If I devote myself to
other pursuits and contemplations, I must first
see, at least, that I do not pursue them sitting
upon another man's shoulders. I must get off
him first, that he may pursue his contemplations too.

Here he has recognized the fallacy of the Greek philosopher,
free because he is supported by the labor of slaves, and the
logic of this realization was to drive him, through the superiority and smugness of "God does not sympathize with the
popular movements," and "I came into this world, not chiefly
to make this a good place to live in, but to live in it, be it
good or bad," to the militant fury of "My thoughts are murder
to the State, and involuntarily go plotting against her."

Thoreau's progress also involved transcending his economics.
The first chapter of *Walden*, entitled **"Economy,"** is an elaborate attempt to justify his life and views in the money terms
of New England commerce. He speaks of going to the woods
as "going into business" on "slender capital," of his "enterprise"; gives the reader his "accounts," even to the halfpenny,
of what he spends and what he takes in; talks of "buying dear,"
of "paying compound interest." He accepts the ledger principle, though he sneaks into the Credit category such unusual
profits on his investment as "leisure and independence and
health." His money metaphor begins to break down when he
writes of the Massachusetts citizens who read of the unjust war
against Mexico as sleepily as they read the prices-current, and
he cries out: "What is the price-current of an honest man and
patriot today?" By the time of the John Brown affair he has
evolved two absolutely independent economies, a money economy and a moral economy. He writes:—

> "But he won't gain anything by it." Well, no,
> I don't suppose he could get four-and-sixpence
> a day for being hung, take the year round; but
> then he stands a chance to save a considerable
> part of his soul,—and *such* a soul!—when *you*
> do not. No doubt you can get more in your
> market for a quart of milk than for a quart of
> blood, but that is not the market that heroes
> carry their blood to.

What, then, can we make of this complicated social pattern?
Following Emerson's doctrine and example, Thoreau was frequently freely inconsistent. One of his chief contradictions was
on the matter of reforming the world through his example. He
could disclaim hoping to influence anyone with "I do not mean
to prescribe rules to strong and valiant natures" and then take
it back immediately with "I foresee that all men will at length
establish their lives on that basis." Certainly to us his hatred
of technological progress, of the division of labor, even of
farming with draft animals and fertilizer, is backward-looking
and reactionary. Certainly he distrusted coöperative action and
all organization. But the example of Jefferson reminds us that
a man may be economically backward-looking and still be our
noblest spokesman, just as Hamilton reminds us that a man
may bring us reaction and injustice tied up in the bright tissue
of economic progress.

To the doctrine of naked expediency so tempting to our time,
the worship of power and success for which the James Burn-

hams among us speak so plausibly, Thoreau opposes only one
weapon—principle. Not policy or expediency must be the test,
but justice and principle. "Read not the Times, read the Eternities." *Walden* has been a bible for the British labor movement
since the days of William Morris. We might wonder what the
British Labor Party, now that it is in power, or the rest of us,
in and out of power, who claim to speak for principle, would
make of Thoreau's doctrine: "If I have unjustly wrested a plank
from a drowning man, I must restore it to him though I drown
myself."

All of this takes us far afield from what must be Thoreau's
chief importance to us, his writing. The resources of his craft
warrant our study. One of his most eloquent devices, typified
by the crack about the Times and the Eternities, is a root use
of words, resulting from his lifelong interest in language and
etymology, fresh, shocking, and very close to the pun. We
can see the etymological passion developing in the *Journal*
notes that a "wild" man is actually a "willed" man, that our
"fields" are "felled" woods. His early writings keep reminding us that a "saunterer" is going to a "Sainte Terre,"
a Holy Land; that three roads can make a village "trivial";
that when our center is outside us we are "eccentric"; that a
"landlord" is literally a "lord of the land"; that he has been
"breaking" silence for years and has hardly made a "rent"
in it.

By the time he wrote *Walden* this habit had developed into one
of his most characteristic ironic devices: the insistence that
telling his townsmen about his life is not "impertinent" but
"pertinent," that professors of philosophy are not philosophers, but people who "profess" it, that the "bent" of his
genius is a very "crooked" one. In the *Plea for Captain John
Brown* the device rises to a whiplash power. He says that
Brown's "humanities" were the freeing of slaves, not the study
of grammar; that a Board of Commissions is lumber of which
he had only lately heard; of the Governor of Massachusetts:
"He was no Governor of mine. He did not govern me." Sometimes these puns double and triple to permit him to pack a
number of complex meanings into a single word, like the "dear"
in "Living is so dear." The discord of goose-honk and owl-
cry he hears by the pond becomes a "concord" that is at once
musical harmony, his native town, and concord as "peace."

Closely related to these serious puns in Thoreau is a serious
epigrammatic humor—wry, quotable lines which contain a good
deal of meaning and tend to make their point by shifting linguistic levels. (pp. 140, 142, 144)

Thoreau was perhaps more precise about his own style and
more preoccupied generally with literary craft than any American writer except Henry James. He rewrote endlessly, not
only, like James, for greater precision, but unlike James, for
greater simplicity. "Simplify, Simplify, Simplify," he gave
as the three cardinal principles of both life and art. Emerson
had said of Montaigne: "Cut these words and they would
bleed," and Thoreau's is perhaps the only American style in
his century of which this is true. . . .

[Thoreau] notes that writing must be done with gusto, must be
vascular. A sense of Thoreau's preoccupation with craft comes
with noting that when he lists "My faults" in the *Journal,* all
seven of them turn out to be of his prose style. Writing for
Thoreau was so obsessive, so vital a physical process, that at
various times he describes it in the imagery of eating, pro-
creation, excretion, mystic trance, and even his old favorite,
the tree bearing ripe fruit. An anthology of Thoreau's passages

on the art of writing would be as worth compiling as Henry James's prefaces and certainly as useful to both the writer and the reader. . . .

"This unlettered man's speaking and writing are standard English," he writes in another paper on Brown. "It suggests that the one great rule of composition—and if I were a professor of rhetoric I should insist on this—is, to *speak the truth*." It was certainly Thoreau's great rule of composition. "He was a speaker and actor of the truth," Emerson said in his obituary of Thoreau. We have never had too many of those. He was also, perhaps as a consequence, a very great writer. We have never had too many of those, either. (p. 146)

Stanley Edgar Hyman, "Henry Thoreau in Our Time,"
in The Atlantic Monthly, *Vol. 178, No. 5, November,
1946, pp. 137-38, 140, 142, 144, 146.*

JOSEPH WOOD KRUTCH   (essay date 1948)

[*Krutch's* Henry David Thoreau *was first published in 1948. In his treatment of Thoreau, Krutch emphasizes the author's elusiveness, argumentativeness, and scornfulness. He points out that Thoreau's most memorable passages are characterized by "powerful extravagance " and suggests that his power lies in his ability "to unite without incongruity things ordinarily thought of as incongruous."*]

A Week on the Concord and Merrimack Rivers had been the account of a vacation, which is to say of an interlude, a truancy, or an escape. *Walden* was an account of a way of life, even of a permanent way of life if one considers that what it describes is not merely a way of living by a pond but a general attitude capable of making life so simple that there is, as Thoreau put it, no need for the brow to sweat. The finder can be, as the seeker seldom is, gay; and *Walden* is, among many other things, a gay book. In the *Journal* Thoreau speaks often of joy and even of ecstasy. He may at most periods of his life have known a good deal of both, although it is also evident that he had moments, especially as he grew older, when the transcendental voices remained stubbornly silent and even nature awoke only feeble response. But neither joy nor ecstasy is the same as gaiety, and in *Walden* there is much that can hardly be called by any other name. He is gay when he describes the routine

A replica of Thoreau's cabin at Walden. The exact site of the original cabin is marked by a pile of stones. Photograph courtesy of Dennis Poupard.

of daily living, gay when he reports his interviews with visitors human or animal, and gay when he flings into the face of his fellow citizens his account of their preposterous, self-imposed labors—Herculean in their magnitude, Sisyphean in their endless futility. And he is gayest of all, perhaps, when he goads them with some blasphemy, some gently insinuated renunciation of stern duty. (p. 105)

Walden is divided into eighteen chapters, each devoted to a topic. Some of them, like **"The Bean-field," "The Ponds," "Brute Neighbours,"** etc., are largely descriptive. Others, like **"Economy,"** which is the first, and **"Higher Laws,"** which is the eleventh, are expository or argumentative, and nowhere is there an orderly presentation of the thesis from first things to last. In other words the over-all shape of the book preserves the main outlines of the thing it professes to be: not an argument, but an account of the somewhat eccentric experiment concerning which Thoreau's neighbors had expressed a curiosity. The theses and the adjurations which actually constitute a considerable part of its bulk are, formally, to be considered as obiter dicta [incidental remarks or observations] or, at most, digressions, which the author permits himself in the course of his report on life at Walden. Actually, however, there are four related but distinct "matters" with which the book concerns itself, and they might be enumerated as follows: (1) The life of quiet desperation which most men lead. (2) The economic fallacy which is responsible for the situation in which they find themselves. (3) What the life close to nature is and what rewards it offers. (4) The "higher laws" which man begins, through some transcendental process, to perceive if he faithfully climbs the stepladder of nature whose first rung is "wildness," whose second is some such gentle and austere but not artificial life as Thoreau himself was leading, and whose third is the transcendental insight he only occasionally reached.

The elements of an inclusive system are present, scattered here and there through the logically (though not artistically) fragmentary discourse. Thoreau has, for instance, a theory of wages and costs ("the cost of a thing is the amount of what I will call life which is required to be exchanged for it, immediately or in the long run") and a somewhat Marxian—and Carlylesque—conception of production for use ("I cannot believe that our factory system is the best mode by which men get clothing . . . since, as far as I have heard or observed, the principal object is, not that mankind may be well and honestly clad, but, unquestionably, that the corporations may be enriched"). He has also, however, a theory of ultimate value which is metaphysical rather than economic. That theory of ultimate value, together with the distrust of mass action which goes with it, leads him away from any concern with social reforms other than those which every man can achieve for himself. It also leads him in the direction of a solitary life in nature to which he was temperamentally inclined and which can be justified on mystical grounds. It is a bridge across which he may go toward those ultimate ends the Transcendentalists and the wise Orientals are seeking.

The fact that he never attempts to schematize these various convictions has, moreover, the effect of making *Walden* more persuasive, or at least more difficult to controvert, than would otherwise be the case, because it makes it less easy for the reader to get hold of any link in a chain of reasoning which he is tempted to try to break. Thoreau does not so much argue that it is possible and desirable to live in a certain way as tell us how he lived and what rewards he discovered. He presents us, as it were, with a *fait accompli* [an accomplished and presumably irreversible thing], and, like Captain Shotover in Shaw's *Heartbreak House,* he will not abide our question. He discharges a shaft, and is gone again before we can object or challenge.

For all his seeming directness he is extremely difficult to corner. No writer was ever, at dangerous moments, more elusive, and no proponent of fundamental paradoxes ever more skillfully provided himself with avenues of escape. His residence at Walden is, when he wishes to make it so, an experiment whose results have universal significance; but it can, on convenient occasion, shrink to the status of a merely personal expedient. It is alternately, as a point is to be made or an objection to be met, a universal nostrum or the whim of an individual eccentric. . . . He did not come into the world, he had previously protested, to make it better; and yet, until you catch him at it, this is exactly what he is trying to do. When you do catch him at it, he retreats again into the extremest possible individualism. In some sense he is certainly suggesting that others imitate him; but he also protests that he would like to have as many different kinds of men in the world as possible. If you ask him what would happen if all tried to find a pond to live beside, he answers that he never suggested they should; that in fact he himself lived there for only two years; and that he left, perhaps, because he had some other lives to lead. (pp. 108-11)

In *A Week on the Concord and Merrimack Rivers* there is a minor element of burlesque. The setting sail is described in deliberately grandiose terms, as though the author had in mind at the moment the classical genre which Pope illustrated in *The Rape of the Lock.* An even fainter suggestion of the same thing is present in the scheme of *Walden.* Thoreau was not unaware of the comic element involved in a flight from civilization which took him only a mile from the edge of his native village, only one field away from the highroad, and only half a mile from his nearest neighbor. Indeed, as he himself tells us in the *Journal,* at least one reader thought the whole book a joke and relished the map of the pond as a caricature of the Coast Surveys. But Thoreau's jokes are almost always serious—*i.e.,* revelations of truths which are commonly overlooked, and that form of burlesque which consists in finding *multum* in *parvo* [much in little] is not for him merely burlesque. As he himself said, any place is as wild as the wildness one can bring to it, and Walden pond was a solitude for the simple reason that he could be alone there. (p. 116)

Different classes of readers inevitably find different portions of *Walden* the most meaningful. Comparatively few are, as Thoreau himself was, almost equally interested in the aspects of external nature, in mystical intimations, and in sociological deductions. But if one leaves aside the question which sections are the most engaging and the most valuable, there can be little doubt that the first chapter and the last are the most unforgettably vigorous pieces of writing, the most astonishing demonstrations of virtuosity. In the sections which lie between, Thoreau is often discursive, picturesque, and engaging, often humorous, persuasive, and charming; but he is also relaxed and almost conversational. It is chiefly in the first chapter and the last that he undertakes to hit hard and speak with the fiery earnestness of the man formally assuming the prophet's robe and determined that, willy-nilly, he will be heard.

Yet these two sections are too unlike in both substance and style to compete with one another or even to be compared. The first, called **"Economics,"** concerns itself with the most practical and homely aspects of his subject and hits hard with

prose, earnestly describing the "penances" which drive men to quiet desperation and suggesting immediate, concrete remedies. The other is spoken from the tripod by a prophet whom the divine fumes have intoxicated and who, in his vision, sees things not quite utterable. Emerson would never have wished to be so down-to-earth as Thoreau was in the chapter on Economy; it is doubtful, on the other hand, if he ever succeeded in sustaining through an equal number of connected pages so original an Orphic strain as that which makes the chapter called merely **"Conclusion"** a succession of lightning flashes. (pp. 117-18)

Throughout whole paragraphs almost every sentence is a metaphor and the metaphors range all the way from those readily translatable into prose to those genuinely Orphic in their tantalizingly elusive implications. At the same time almost every sentence is illuminated by a grotesque humor which juxtaposes the homely to the ineffable, and is pointed by scorn for those who tamely prefer what is to what might be. Thoreau's mind seems to leap from subject to subject as though, in a moment of insight, truth had been revealed and the only danger was that no utterance could be found sufficiently elliptic to communicate it all before the moment passed. (pp. 118-19)

The brilliance of that final chapter is pyrotechnic in its effect; one seems to be present at the birth of a whole galaxy of dancing stars. How, the reader is likely to find himself asking, can any writer have been at any given time so sustainedly incandescent? And the answer—which is of course that Thoreau was not, and that perhaps no writer could be—is an answer which helps to explain why no other such masterpiece as *Walden* was ever to come from its author. The book as a whole was a crystallization and the last chapter was a mosaic of crystals. The moment of sustained and inclusive illumination never existed, and the Orphic profundities never fell as they seem to fall, one after another, from the lips of a prophet in the grip of a divine seizure. They had been written down as fragments, neither successive nor connected, and they were then, sometimes years later, carefully selected and carefully fitted together in such a way that what looks like explosive brilliance was actually the result of a patient craftsmanship carefully matching and arranging brilliants which had been hoarded one by one over the years. The reader of the *Journal* comes across them here and there, imbedded, often, in a matrix not in itself gleaming, and they leap out at his eye as they evidently leaped out at their author when he went searching through his own pages. In *Walden* we pass in a few minutes from the sentence about the wild goose who is more cosmopolite than we to the sentence about the necessity of speaking extravagantly. (pp. 119-20)

To the tidy mind of a technical philosopher, Thoreau's thought must seem hopelessly confused. Puritanism, New England Transcendentalism, and Hindu mysticism made some sort of peace with one another because all were to some degree dualistic, but they were also all at war with both an objective, quasi-scientific curiosity and a tendency to deduce from the results of that curiosity a religion of nature in which the worshiper is tempted on beyond good and evil as either can be defined in humanistic terms. But Thoreau was well served by this constant balancing of possibilities, by his very inability to hold firm to a doctrine. Because of the doubts, his relentless persistence in what appeared to outsiders a mere routine actually took on the character of a ceaseless quest, and the moments of empathy were all the more eagerly sought because Thoreau himself could never be sure what they meant. His "nature writings" have a quality which immediately distinguishes them not only from the almost trivial tranquillity of Gilbert White but also from a John Burroughs or a W. H. Hudson. To some readers, at least, they are more varied, and they have, besides, a certain tenseness, a certain excitement which is unique. Thoreau is an observer without the mere observer's coldness, and he is a lover of wisdom without the mere teacher's monotonous dogmatism. The quest remains exciting because he himself does not know what he is going to find. No doubt he was, as he himself insisted, a happy man; but he was not settled or certain. A hunger and a thirst are elements in his happiness and make it something other than mere content. And it is the hunger and thirst which are responsible for the excitement of his writing. (pp. 214-15)

Sometimes—more frequently perhaps than one would suspect if one did not take pains to note the occasions—Thoreau can employ an almost Gothically intricate ornamentation when he summons to his aid a splendor of bookish rhetoric obviously caught from Sir Thomas Browne; as, for example, in the passage that concludes the sixteenth chapter of *Walden*, or, to take a less hackneyed one, the paragraph from *A Week on the Concord and Merrimack Rivers* which begins, "It is remarkable that the dead lie everywhere under stones" and ends: "Fame itself is but an epitaph; as late, as false, as true. But they only are the true epitaphs which Old Mortality retouches." Perhaps the most remarkable thing about these bookish passages is the completeness with which they have been assimilated into the texture of a prose which is elsewhere so seemingly direct and simple. And that is, of course, an indication of the fact that Thoreau had, in his own consciousness, assimilated Concord into the universe so that he not only said but felt that the local and the temporal were indistinguishably a part of the universal and the eternal. The grand style and the homely were not appropriate respectively to ancient and to contemporary, but indiscriminately to both; so that Therien, the woodchopper, could on occasion be seen as Homeric, and on other occasions Agamemnon could be treated like a Yankee.

These elaborately ornamented passages are, however, most likely to be reserved for Thoreau's more serenely elevated moments. For his hortatory and vituperative outbursts he is more likely to employ that strong, direct, hard-hitting, more austerely functional prose which, unjustly perhaps, we are more likely to think of as characteristic of him. (pp. 273-74)

"Powerful extravagance" would, indeed, serve as well as any mere pair of words could serve to describe the general effect of his most often remembered paragraphs, and the effect of power usually is produced by bold tropes which employ a reference to some familiar object or situation to drive home a point or make clear an attitude. Moreover, the individual sentences are frequently both deliberately extravagant in themselves and arranged, one after another, to create a mounting climax of what calmer writers would call overstatement. "I fear chiefly," he wrote in *Walden,* "lest my expression may not be *extra-vagant* enough," and it is clear that though extravagance was sometimes a rhetorical device, it was also, and perhaps more frequently, the inevitable result of his conviction that the truth about neither man's potentialities nor his failure to realize them could possibly be overstated. When he wrote to a friend the advice not to worry about his health because "you may be dead already," that was both a deliberately shocking statement and an expression of Thoreau's sincere conviction that most men were actually, in the realest possible sense, not alive.

These most often remembered passages of powerful extravagance are, it should be observed, usually argumentative or scornful. In intention they are almost always, directly or indirectly, didactic or hortatory. They are concerned with what Thoreau did not approve of rather than with what he did; with what he blamed others for "living for," not with what he lived for himself. And there is another whole body of writing markedly different in style and purpose which is considerably less well known—partly because readers have, on the whole, tended to understand and sympathize with his criticism of life as it is commonly lived rather more than they have with the positive aspects of his philosophy, partly because his protestant writing is more adequately represented outside the little-read *Journal* than the other kind is.

Probably he himself would have been distressed to think that he might be remembered chiefly as a satirist or a critic; as a man who had managed to convey only his dissatisfaction with the world and not the happiness which he believed to have been his. (pp. 275-76)

Certain of the intermediate chapters of *Walden* are devoted to the life he loved rather than the life he hated, and so too are a good many pages of *A Week on the Concord and Merrimack Rivers*. But much of the second is juvenile, and the *Walden* chapters do not seem to contain the best of his writing of the sort they attempt—perhaps because they actually do not, or perhaps only because their gentler tone cannot successfully compete for our attention against the powerful urgency of the sermonizing in the first chapter and the last. The posthumous *The Maine Woods* and *Cape Cod* are too nearly mere travel books, too deliberately directed at a relatively vulgar audience, to represent him at his best, though they contain some very fine passages; and so it is to the unquarried *Journal* itself that one must go for any adequate idea of the bulk or importance of a kind of writing which will contribute more to Thoreau's fame than it yet has, if it should ever be collected, as it easily might, into volumes selected to illustrate its own special intention and quality.

Much the largest part of the *Journal* is, it must be remembered, devoted not to Thoreau's criticism of his neighbors and their society but to a vast record of his intercourse with trees and flowers, with animals, wild and domestic, and with inanimate nature as well. The record of this intercourse varies in manner from the barest quasi-scientific, or sometimes merely perfunctory, jotting down of facts and observations to the most elaborately worked-up set pieces—many of which exhibit unmistakable evidence of having been carefully composed and suggest that they were probably several times rewritten. (pp. 277-78)

Most interesting, because most nearly unique, are those of the set pieces where the working up consists in a process for which dramatization rather than poetizing might be an appropriate word. Here the attempt is to keep the attention fixed on the object itself; to return again and again to its own various aspects rather than merely to use the object as something from which the mind can take off. It is not the meaning of the hieroglyph but the thing itself which the writer is trying to grasp and which he wishes the reader to grasp also, so that experience itself rather than any explanation or interpretation of it is what he is trying to communicate. (pp. 278-79)

The intermingling without incongruity of Thoreau's humor with his seriousness is a phenomenon essentially similar to the intermingling of his homely style with his bookishly elaborate one, and of his delight in simple physical things with his mystical exaltation. Indeed it might be maintained that to unite without incongruity things ordinarily thought of as incongruous *is* the phenomenon called Thoreau, whether one is thinking of a personality or of a body of literary work. This is what constitutes his oneness, and the oneness of a man is the most important thing about him; is perhaps the man himself. (p. 286)

Joseph Wood Krutch, in his Henry David Thoreau, *William Morrow & Company, Inc., 1974, 298 p.*

ALFRED KAZIN   (essay date 1951)

[*A highly respected American literary critic, Kazin is best known for his essay collections* The Inmost Leaf *(1955),* Contemporaries *(1962), and particularly* On Native Grounds *(1942), a study of American prose writing since the era of William Dean Howells. Kazin's review of Thoreau's* Journal *originally appeared in the* New York Herald Tribune *in 1951.*]

Many writers have kept journals—the habit is almost an occupational necessity. (p. 187)

But even among writers' journals—and usually, with the exception of dry business-like records like Benjamin Constant's and Arnold Bennett's, each is as interesting as the man who kept it—Thoreau's must stand in a special place. For his journal . . . is not merely the record of a life lived almost entirely within. It is the life itself. Thoreau's **"Journal"** was not a hide-out for his lacerated soul, not altogether what he and others have most used it for—the storehouse out of which his published books would come. It was the thing he lived in, the containment of his love—and therefore had to be as well-written as a prayer or a love letter. . . . This is where he sang, sentence by sentence; the journal took its "shape" from the manner of his love.

Actually, the **"Journal"** bogs down after the middle volumes into disjointed nature notes of whose barrenness even as scientific information he was well aware. But it is the unflagging beauty of the writing, day after day, that confirms its greatness among writers' journals. It is not natural for a man to write this well every day. Only a man who had no other life but to practice a particularly intense and truthful kind of prose could have done it—a man for whom all walks finally came to end in the hard athletic sentence that would recover all their excitement. Other writers have been lonely, and have learned to accept their loneliness; have felt yearnings toward God that their distrust of churches could not explain; have dissected their solitary characters down to the last bearable foundation in human self-analysis; have, at least in the privacy of a journal, scored off at last the obtuseness of their neighbors, the insipidity of their contemporaries and the unfeelingness of the age. And of course all writers of memorable journals have made characters out of themselves; you have to be thoroughly suffused in yourself before you can break away and take a good look back. Thoreau did all this, and something more. For in and through his **"Journal"** he finally made himself a prose that would fully evoke in its resonant tension and wildness the life he lived in himself every day. (pp. 187-88)

But by and large the **"Journal"** is the attempt to shape into words the vision he took back from his walks, a testing-ground for his art, and a commentary on the journal itself—that is, on the necessities of his character. What he sought from those walks he very consciously defined to himself in 1857, after twenty years of the **"Journal,"** in one of those sentences which are so heartbreaking in their truthfulness, for when you read it you realize not only that he has said everything he means, but that he has put his whole life into that sentence. "I come to my solitary woodland walk as the homesick go home."

In this same passage, however, he added with his usual canny awareness of the type he represents in history, "I suppose that this value, in my case, is equivalent to what others get by churchgoing and prayers." As a statement of the facts this is altogether more deft than accurate. Though Thoreau was genuinely and even profoundly mystical, God did not occupy his mind to that extent; it was writing he cared about first, not a belief. But what such nimble and all too often repetitive analyses of his character point up so sharply is that he spent much more time painting himself as Concord's leading crank than on following to the depths the stunning originality of his nature. (p. 190)

[Had Thoreau not been aware of what other people thought of him] he could never have written **"Walden,"** which is exhilarating precisely because of its defiance and far more self-dramatizing than even [Walt Whitman's] "Leaves of Grass." But Thoreau had an even more deeply original quality to him than **"Walden"** reveals; you see it in the **"Journal"** over and over again—a quality that was perhaps best described by the French mystical writer Simone Weil when she said that "attentiveness without an object is prayer in its supreme form." Only the very purest and most solitary writers have had the gift of such attentiveness; to be alive entirely to the creation itself. But for many reasons, not least of which was the fact that Thoreau was so much the end of a tradition that he had to retrace it for himself, he went to nature as his formal vocation, a background to his quest, something that would support his picture of himself. "Nature" itself was not his chief interest; he was so entirely subjective that he distrusted scientific method even when used by others. But he was looking for a subject; that is, for an opportunity. And of course he could always find a subject in himself. But by constantly dwelling on how different he was, he tended to become uncharacteristically smug about who he was.

Still, without these excited daily inroads into the fields, Thoreau could never have found the measure for his prose. It is a prose, like Hemingway's and Faulkner's, that most characteristically defines the American in literature. We have had greater or at least more comprehensive writers, but none who with such deep intuition grasped in their solitariness the secret of the wilderness, of the legendary unoccupied Western lands, the very tone of man's battle in America against empty space. Emerson had given the call. It was Thoreau who went out and tried it: who wrote as if a sentence were not even true unless you heard it first ring against the ground. (p. 191)

Alfred Kazin, "Thoreau's Journals," in Thoreau: A Century of Criticism, *edited by Walter Harding, Southern Methodist University Press, 1954, pp. 187-91.*

R.W.B. LEWIS   (essay date 1955)

[*Lewis, an American literary critic and historian of ideas, discusses* Walden *in terms of Thoreau's "personal purification rite" and his attempts to achieve a life determined by nature. He concludes that Thoreau's "account of the recovery of nature . . . [is] the noblest expression, in fact and in language," of the strivings of the Transcendentalists.*]

Probably nobody of [Thoreau's] generation had a richer sense of the potentiality for a fresh, free, and uncluttered existence; certainly no one projected the need for the ritual burning of the past in more varied and captivating metaphors. This is what *Walden* is about; it is the most searching contemporary account of the desire for a new kind of life. But Thoreau's announcement of a spiritual molting season (one of his favorite images) did not arise from a belief that the building of railroads was proof of the irrelevance of too-well-remembered doctrines. Long before Whitman, himself a devotee of the dazzling sum, attacked the extremes of commercialism in *Democratic Vistas,* Thoreau was insisting that the obsession with railroads did not demonstrate the hope for humanity, but tended to smother it. (p. 20)

The narrator of *Walden* is a witness to a truly new world which the speaker alone has visited, from which he has just returned, and which he is sure every individual ought to visit at least once—not the visible world around Walden Pond, but an inner world which the Walden experience allowed him to explore. Thoreau liked to pretend that his book was a purely personal act of private communion. But that was part of his rhetoric, and *Walden* is a profoundly rhetorical book, emerging unmistakably from the long New England preaching tradition; though here the trumpet call announces the best imaginable news rather than apocalyptic warnings. Thoreau, in *Walden,* is a man who has come back down into the cave to tell the residents there that they are really in chains, suffering fantastic punishments they have imposed on themselves, seeing by a light that is reflected and derivative. A major test of the visionary hero must always be the way he can put his experience to work for the benefit of mankind; he demonstrates his freedom in the liberation of others. Thoreau prescribes the following cure: the total renunciation of the traditional, the conventional, the socially acceptable, the well-worn paths of conduct, and the total immersion in nature.

Everything associated with the past should be burned away. The past should be cast off like dead skin. . . . Thoreau recorded with approval and some envy a Mexican purification rite practiced every fifty-two years; and he added, "I have scarcely heard of a truer sacrament." These periodic symbolic acts of refreshment, which whole societies ought to perform in each generation ("One generation abandons the enterprises of another like stranded vessels"), were valid exactly because they were images of fundamental reality itself. Individuals and groups should enact the rhythmic death and rebirth reflected in the change of season from winter to spring, in the sequence of night and day. "The phenomena of the year take place every day in a pond on a small scale." These were some of the essential facts discovered by Thoreau when he fronted them at Walden; and the experience to which he was to become a witness took its shape, in act and in description, from a desire to live in accordance with these facts. (pp. 21-2)

The language tells us everything, as Thoreau meant it to. He had his own sacramental system, his own rite of baptism. But his use of the word "nature" indicates that the function of sacraments was to expose the individual again to the currents flowing through nature, rather than to the grace flowing down from supernature. The ritual of purification was no less for Thoreau than for St. Paul a dying into life; but Thoreau marched to the music he heard; it was the music of the age; and he marched in a direction *opposite* to St. Paul. (p. 22)

It is not surprising that transcendentalism was Puritanism turned upside down, as a number of critics have pointed out; histor-

ically, it could hardly have been anything else. Transcendentalism drew on the vocabularies of European romanticism and Oriental mysticism; but the only available local vocabulary was the one that the hopeful were so anxious to escape from, and a very effective way to discredit its inherited meaning was to serve it up in an unfamiliar context. There was something gratifyingly shocking in such a use of words: "What demon possessed me that I behaved so well?" Thoreau spoke as frequently as he could, therefore, about a *sacrament,* a sacred mystery, such as baptism: in order to define the cleansing, not of St. Paul's natural man, but of the conventional or traditional man; in order, precisely, to bring into being the natural man. For the new tensions out of which insights were drawn and moral choices provoked were no longer the relation of nature and grace, of man and God, but of the natural and the artificial, the new and the old, the individual and the social or conventional. Thoreau had, as he remarked in his . . . deathbed witticism, no quarrel with God; his concern was simply other.

His concern was with the strangulation of nature by convention. The trouble with conventions and traditions in the New World was that they had come first; they had come from abroad and from a very long way back; and they had been superimposed upon nature. They had to be washed away, like sin, so that the natural could reveal itself again and could be permitted to create its own organic conventions. They had to be renounced, as the first phase of the ritual; and if renunciation was, as Emily Dickinson thought, a piercing virtue, it was not because it made possible an experience of God in an infusion of grace, but because it made possible an experience of self in a bath of nature. (p. 23)

Thoreau's personal purification rite began with the renunciation of old hats and old spoons and went forward to the moment—as he describes himself in the opening paragraph of **"Higher Laws"**—when the initiate stood fully alive in the midst of nature, eating a woodchuck with his fingers, and supremely aware, at the same instant, of the higher law of virtue. "I love the wild not less than the good," Thoreau admitted, announcing duplicity in his own peculiar accent. The structure of *Walden* has a similar beginning and a similar motion forward. The book starts amid the punishing conventions of Concord, departs from them to the pond and the forest, explores the natural surroundings, and exposes the natural myth of the yearly cycle, to conclude with the arrival of spring, the full possession of life, and a representative anecdote about the sudden bursting into life of a winged insect long buried in an old table of apple-tree wood.

Individual chapters are sometimes carried along to the same rhythm. **"Sounds,"** for example, starts with conventional signs and then looks to nature for more authentic ones; it picks up the cycle of the day, as Thoreau listens to sounds around the clock; and it concludes with a total surrender to the vitalizing power of unbounded nature. (pp. 24-5)

It was with the ultimate aim of making such an experience possible—a life determined by nature and enriched by a total awareness—that Thoreau insisted so eloquently upon the baptismal or rebirth rite. What he was demanding was that individuals start life all over again, and that in the new world a fresh start was literally and immediately possible to anyone wide enough awake to attempt it. It was in this way that the experience could also appear as a return to childhood, to the scenes and the wonder of that time. In a particularly revealing moment, Thoreau reflected, while adrift on the lake in the moonlight and playing the flute for the fishes, on a boyhood adventure at that very place. "But now," he said, "I made my home by the shore." Thoreau reflected the curious but logical reverence of his age for children: "Children, who play life, discern its true law and relations more clearly than men, who fail to live it worthily." Children seemed for Thoreau to possess some secret which had been lost in the deadening process of growing up, some intimation (like Wordsworth's child) which had faded under the routine pressure of everyday life. Emerson found the new attitude of adults toward children the appropriate symbol with which to introduce his retrospective summary of the times (1867): "Children had been repressed and kept in the background; now they were considered, cosseted and pampered." Thoreau thought he knew why: because "every child begins the world again"; every child managed to achieve without conscious effort what the adult could achieve only by the strenuous, periodic act of refreshment. In this sense, the renewal of life was a kind of homecoming; the busks and the burnings were preparatory to recapturing the outlook of children.

Psychologists who have followed Jung's poetic elaboration and doctrinaire schematizing of the guarded suggestions of Freud could make a good deal of the impulse. They might describe it as an impulse to return to the womb; and some support could doubtless be found in the image-clusters of Walden: water, caves, shipwrecks, and the like. This approach might persuasively maintain that the end of the experience narrated by Thoreau was the reintegration of the personality. And since, according to Jung, "the lake in the valley is the unconscious," it is possible to hold that **Walden** enacts and urges the escape from the convention-ridden conscious and the release of the spontaneous energies of personality lying beneath the surface, toward a reuniting of the psychic "old double." An analysis of this sort can be helpful and even illuminating, and it could be applied to the entire program of the party of Hope [Lewis's classification for a group of nineteenth-century American writers, including Thoreau, Emerson, and Whitman, whose work is characterized by optimism about the past and future], substituting terms associated with the unconscious for all the terms associated with Emerson's "Reason." A certain warrant for the psychological interpretation can be found in the novels of Dr. Holmes, and the methodological issue arises more sharply in that discussion. But we may also remind ourselves that the psychological vocabulary simply manipulates a set of metaphors other than those we normally use. Probably we do not need to go so far afield to grasp what Thoreau was seeking to explain; we may even suspect that he meant what he said. And what he said was that he went to the woods in order to live deliberately, "to front only the essential facts of life"; because human life and human expression were so burdened with unexamined habits, the voice of experience so muffled by an uninvestigated inheritance, that only by a total rejection of those habits and that inheritance and by a recovery of a childlike wonder and directness could anyone find out whether life were worth living at all.

Thoreau, like most other members of the hopeful party, understood dawn and birth better than he did night and death. He responded at once to the cockerel in the morning; the screech owls at night made him bookish and sentimental. And though their wailing spoke to him about "the low spirits and melancholy forebodings of fallen souls," the whole dark side of the world was no more than another guaranty of the inexhaustible variety of nature. Thoreau knew not evil; his American busk would have fallen short, like the bonfire in Hawthorne's fantasy ["Earth's Holocaust"], of the profounder need for the puri-

fication of the human heart. He would have burned away the past as the accumulation of artifice, in the name of the natural and the essential. But if the natural looked to him so much more wholesome and so much more dependable than others have since thought it, his account of the recovery of nature was never less than noble: the noblest expression, in fact and in language, of the first great aspiration of the age. (pp. 25-7)

> *R.W.B. Lewis, "The Case against the Past," in his*
> The American Adam: Innocence, Tragedy and Tradition in the Nineteenth Century, *The University of Chicago Press, 1955, pp. 13-27.**

GEORGES POULET (essay date 1956)

[*Poulet is a modern Belgian critic whose writings attempt to reconstruct an author's consciousness, specifically the relation to and understanding of time and space as rendered in fiction. His early criticism demonstrates his belief that authors live in an isolated world and thus cannot be understood in terms of generalizations about the era in which they lived. The task of the critic is to enter the artist's consciousness and define it. In contrast to his early critical criteria, Poulet's later work often suggests that writers are influenced by the spirit of their time, and he studies their representation of the widespread characteristics of their age.*]

In contrast to Hawthorne, Thoreau does not see the moment as something that passes and disappears. For him it is something that *appears*, "an incessant influx of novelty into the world." Hence of all the points of time the one that matters most to him is the moment when this novelty is immediately perceptible, that is to say the present moment: "I am simply what I am. . . . I live in the present." "We cannot afford not to live in the present." The present is the moment in which one exists. It is also—what is even better—the moment in which the world exists. Infinitely narrow in the order of duration, it is infinitely vast in the order of extent. It is the place in which all places are together present, the hour in which our being coincides with nature. . . . (p. 334)

To the incessant flow of novelty into the world . . . there must correspond in me an equivalent perception of that novelty. In order to achieve this I must "transcend my daily routine . . . have my immortality now, in the *quality* of my daily life." To perceive with fresh senses is to be inspired. But what would one become if he were no longer inspired? "I am stranded at each reflux of the tide, and I, who sailed as buoyantly on the middle deep as a ship, am as helpless as a mussel on the rock. . . ." What can one do when he has appended his whole spiritual life to the hour and to nature, and when nature stops speaking and the hour becomes neutral and mute? The moment of union is inevitably followed by a moment of dryness and disunion. Then the present is "without halo," the hour owns its insufficiency.

Thus it is with all Quietist thought. Passive, it depends upon a grace which, given for the moment, will perhaps not be given in the moment following. Spiritless moments often replace moments of communication and grace. It seems then as if everything were already over and the universe congealed. The eye now discerns only conventional forms. It is not only the actual world, that is to say nature, that appears to us thus, when we regard it with the eyes of common sense and the rational intelligence, but also the corresponding extent of the past, when we wish to understand it in its historical significance. . . . (pp. 334-35)

History is a fixation, an arbitrary intellectualization of life. Life, on the contrary, exists only in fluctuation. It is a sudden fire, a ceaseless emergence, a coloration always new. . . . (p. 335)

Under the antihistorical eye of Thoreau, history decomposes. It is dissolved in the multiplicity of its parts. Contrary to what Hawthorne maintains, the past, as past, has neither secret nor treasure. It hides nothing besides moments which, each in its time, have been present moments.

Thus, history is not time, it is not even simply time past. For time past existed before being transformed into history; it had its peculiar tints, a future, a motion of its own, a novelty. Long before Bergson, Thoreau insists on the anterior *actuality* of the past. But has this past which was then living now lost its life? Are we forever condemned to seeing what no longer is as no longer being? Should we reject all our memories as turning us away from the only thing that counts, the present and living hour? . . . Thoreau also knows—better than most—that memory is not necessarily historical. Memory is not content simply to put us in rapport with the past; it restores it to us, it brings it alive once more in the actuality of our thought. Let us not renounce memory, therefore. Like nature it makes up an integral part of the present moment. Let us not even renounce regret. On the contrary, let us intensify it: "To regret deeply is to live afresh. By so doing you will find yourself restored to all your emoluments."

From the time of our earliest infancy, each of our lived moments can thus be replaced in its own actuality: "My imagination, my love and reverence and admiration, my sense of the miraculous, is not so excited by any event as by the remembrance of my youth." "As I come over the hill, I hear a woodthrush singing his evening lay. . . . It reinstates me in my dominion. . . ." "The summer's eternity is reestablished by this note." Here memory is no longer the retrograde motion by which thought quits the present and plunges itself into anterior regions; it is, on the contrary, the prospective motion which, leaving the past, goes toward the present in order to transmit an eternal richness to it. Like Kierkegaardian repetition, Thoreau's reinstitution is not directed backwards but ahead. It makes the present the future of the past. If the past has accumulated in the depths of the mind, it is not in order to constitute history or predetermine the future, but to transmit to the present an impulse which is that of life itself: "All the past plays into this moment."

But this *play* of the past into the present is that of streaming waters that never stop and which, of themselves, perpetually flow from the present to the future as well. Of the three dimensions of duration, the one that is finally established for Thoreau as the most important is that of the future: "My future deeds bestir themselves within me and move grandly towards a consummation, as ships go down the Thames. A steady onward motion I feel in me. . . ." "We anticipate the future with transcendental senses."

Now these senses, transcendental as they may be, remain senses nevertheless. Recovering the past, disclosing the future, they continue to be nonetheless attached to the eternally perceptible actuality of nature. What the mind foreshadows in its future is the perpetually renewed play of a nature that is refreshed simply by beginning the round of its seasons again. . . . (pp. 335-37)

But this perennial life, as we have seen, is as much that of past nature as of future nature. Thus in situating ourselves upon the present, we situate ourselves "on the meeting of two eternities, the past and the future, which is precisely the present moment." In this present moment God culminates. He culminates by the motion of the seasons. Each "gives a tone and hue to my thought." All together, at one and the same time recollected, prefigured, and lived, they form "an annual phenomenon which is a reminiscence and a prompting." Time itself is "a shallow stream," "cheap and rather insignificant." But the seasons are not in time; they are in eternity; they are eternity. An eternity of changing colors, a perpetual cycle. He who apprehends it lives in another time, a time that has nothing to do with chronology or clocks; he lives in a *seasonal* time, where, to the phases of nature, the phases of human life exactly correspond: "The seasons and all their changes are in me. . . . My moods are thus periodical." (p. 337)

> *Georges Poulet, "Thoreau," in his* Studies in Human Time, *translated by Elliott Coleman, The Johns Hopkins University Press, 1956, pp. 334-37.*

PERRY MILLER (lecture date 1958)

[*An American historian, Miller is considered a pioneer in recording and interpreting the literature and culture of seventeenth-century New England. In this essay, originally delivered as a lecture in 1958, Miller asserts that* Walden *is "a continuation . . . of the Puritan determination to speak plainly." Though most critics consider Thoreau's actions and writing style a reaction against Puritanism, Miller focuses on the evidence for Thoreau's Puritan intentions in* Walden, *and claims that Thoreau actually "outdid" the Puritans in regard to directness of writing style. For Miller's later consideration of Thoreau and Romanticism, see excerpt below, 1960.*]

[Thoreau wrote in **"Walking,"**] "I believe in the forest, and in the meadow, and in the night in which the corn grows." . . . [Let] me call attention to Thoreau's sentence as constituting an indubitable triumph of [the Puritan plain style]. What indeed could be plainer, and yet what phrasing could more effectively employ the impact of surprise, the arresting of vulgar attention, which in the Puritan aesthetic had ever been the aim of the manner? (pp. 216-17)

We should commence by noticing in Thoreau's sentence the barely disguised blasphemy: it is a parody of confession of belief in the Trinity: the "forest" (God the father), the "meadow" (Christ the Savior), and a "night in which the corn grows" (assuredly this, if anything, is the Holy Ghost). Something curious had happened to the concept of the use of the word between the time of [the Puritan clergyman Thomas] Hooker and of young Henry Thoreau—or at least in Thoreau's brain something had happened to the concept. (p. 218)

Thoreau's **Walden** is essentially a continuation, into a radically altered universe, of the Puritan determination to speak plainly, using art to conceal art, and metaphor suited to the common understanding. Almost any sentence of Thoreau's will stand as the essence of the style, and some of them, by their brusqueness, have become famous: "I never dreamed of any enormity greater than I have committed. I never knew, and never shall know, a worse man than myself." This, you will perceive, was the confession toward which the plain style was always driving. In Puritan congregations, the ministers never quite asked candidates to venture upon so positive or sweeping a self-condemnation; they trusted that some more "hopeful," some modest signs of election might be disclosed. Of course, they expected a repentant sinner to confess the enormity of his unregeneracy, but they never quite envisioned confession, full confession, by a recalcitrant child of the covenant who would glory in his participation in the community of sin. Hence, would they not be doubly confused, while recognizing him as a grandson of their loins, that he outdid them all, outdid even Benjamin Franklin, in an ascetic way of life, eschewing meat and alcohol, spurning marriage, molding himself to the implacable rules of a Divinity in whom he no longer believed? And would they not then be trebly bewildered to find in him, amid the calculated efforts of his Puritan contemporaries, the one writer in whom the ideals of strict conformity to the injunction of plainness were most energetically followed? (p. 226)

There is, for example, Thoreau's arabesque upon the first answer in the Westminster Catechism: "What is the end of man?" the interrogation runs, and the reply follows, "To glorify God and enjoy him forever." Thoreau was haunted by this dialogue; he comes back to it repeatedly, always wringing some ironic scandal out of it, nowhere more pointedly than in the second chapter of **Walden**. He quotes the Catechism with a bit of preface, noting that men are in a strange uncertainty about whether life be of the devil or of God, and so have (italics his) "*somewhat hastily* concluded" that man's end is to glorify the Creator and enjoy Him. To Thoreau, after two centuries of ritual reiteration, it was high time that a Puritan conscience should arouse itself against this "hasty" Puritan tenet. There was no other instrument for him but the plain style, the only disruptive implement the Puritans had left to generations after them.

Thus armed, both in authority and in rebellion, Thoreau stated the purpose of his book, and again we perceive the links with Hooker:

> I went to the woods because I wished to live deliberately, to front only the essential facts of life, and see if I could not learn what it had to teach, and not, when I came to die, discover that I had not lived. I did not wish to live what was not life, living is so dear; nor did I wish to practise resignation, unless it was quite necessary. I wanted to live deep and suck out all the marrow of life, to live so sturdily and Spartanlike as to put to rout all that was not life, to cut a broad swath and shave close, to drive life into a corner, and reduce it to its lowest terms, and, if it proved to be mean, why then to get the whole and genuine meanness of it, and publish its meanness to the world; or if it were sublime, to know it by experience, and be able to give a true account of it in my next excursion.

Leaving aside for the moment the fact that **Walden** does seem to assert at the end that life is sublime, the point we have to confront is the sincerity of Thoreau's invitation to life to prove itself mean, and his readiness thereupon to publish that meanness "to the world." Egocentric as he was, he still thought he should address "the world." This was ever the Puritan intention; where are we if the world pays no heed? (p. 227)

Renouncing all recourse to the utilitarian purposes that had brought success to the Puritan preacher, [Thoreau and Melville] strove to invest the pure word with full power to expound both the "marrow of life" and "right worship." Belatedly, we pay a sort of homage to them; but these master-Puritans come down

to us as cryptic geniuses. We placate them endlessly, but we have yet fully to realize, if indeed we ever shall, how they beseech us to consider the way in America that words, the beautiful and terrible words, must serve us, all by themselves, without any adventitious assistance from generalized profession, to comprehend our peculiar position in history. We have every reason, in the inheritance of Benjamin Franklin and of the Revolutionary documents, to insist that our words mean only what they say; however, as long as we have also in our memory the sentences of Thoreau and Melville, we have the task of realizing how our words signify more than they say. We have no choice but to drive life into a corner, we have no option but to greet omnipotence with defiance. This in reality is the true literature of America. (p. 228)

> *Perry Miller, "An American Language," in his* Nature's Nation, *Cambridge, Mass.: Belknap Press, 1967, pp. 208-40.**

WRIGHT MORRIS (essay date 1958)

> I went to the woods because I wished to live deliberately, to front only the essential facts of life, and see if I could not learn what it had to teach, and not, when I came to die, discover that I had not lived.

This statement, by one of the world's free men, has captivated and enslaved millions. It is a classic utterance, made with such art that what is not said seems nonexistent, civilization and its ways a mere web of *ine*ssentials, distracting man from the essential facts of life. The texture of this language and the grain of this thought are one and the same. To fall under its spell is to be in possession of *one* essential self. A sympathetic mind may find the call irresistible. The essential facts of life will seem to be these facts, all others but stratagems, snares, and delusions, although the facts to support such a conclusion are not self-evident. They are implied, but implied with such persuasion they seem facts. That is Thoreau's intention. But his art is greater than his argument. Although he sought to persuade through *facts*, through the testimony of the raw material, it is his craft as a writer that gives his facts conviction, and his example such power. It is his art, not his facts, that sent his readers to the woods. . . . (pp. 39-40)

The American mind, the Yankee imagination, had sap and substance before this man spoke, but I believe we can say it had no grain until Thoreau. It is the natural grain of this mind that still shapes our own. The self-induced captivity of the American mind to some concept of Nature—NATURE writ large—can be traced, it would seem, to the shores of Walden Pond. Here is the first contour map of what we might call our *natural* state of mind. (p. 40)

Nature—even Nature tooth and claw—is child's play when confronted with *human* nature. The problem, reduced to its essentials, is NATURE v. Human Nature. It was this problem that led Thoreau to take to the woods. But he would not have been led there—he more or less tells us—if he had not believed that taking to the woods was the prevailing tendency of his countrymen.

In **Walden** that prevailing tendency received its classical form. Back to Nature was not new with Thoreau—it had, in fact, lost the gloss Crèvecoeur gave it—but Thoreau endowed it with a civilized respectability. The romantic wash of color is replaced with the essential facts. But the result—since he was an artist—was to heighten the romantic effect. Through the sharp eyes of this capital realist, NATURE, writ large, looked even more inviting, and the realistic myth took precedence over the romantic one. It remains, to this day, a characteristic quality of the American wilderness.

Flight from something, we can say without quibbling, was foreign to Thoreau's mind, and we know that when he turned his back on the city it was *toward* the facts—not away from them. In his own mind he was facing the very facts that his friends and neighbors turned away from, and it is this sentiment, not a romanticized Nature, that gives *Walden* its power. But in a culture of cities, as the country was then becoming, this sentiment went against the very grain of culture, and became, in time, a deliberate rejection of the essential facts of this culture.

In 1845, when Thoreau went to Walden, he had a continental wilderness lying *before* him, and he was hardly in a position to see that he had actually turned his back on the future. Or that the prevailing tendency of Americans was *flight*. Flight, not from what they had found, but from what they had created—the very culture of cities they had labored to establish.

Each of these cultural centers, each of these established towns, became a fragment of Europe and a past to get away from—the prevailing tendency of Americans being what it was. Thoreau did not expose this tendency to examination—he accepted it. It satisfied, after all, the drift and grain of his own mind. H *began* at that point—in a language and a tone similar to that which informed the Declaration of Independence. He established, as that document sought to, certain inalienable human rights. One of them being to take to the woods, if and when you felt the need.

The principle of turning one's back on unpleasant facts—unpleasant because they were so deeply inessential, so foreign, in a way, to our essential Nature—is one *naturally* congenial to the American mind. Thoreau gave this principle its classic utterance. In his spirit, if not in his name, we still take to such woods as we can find. If his genius had been of another kind he might have scrutinized this principle, rather than Nature, but it was his destiny to be the archetypal American. To put, that is, the prevailing tendency to a rigorous test. That he did; that he did and found it wanting, since he both went to the woods and then left them, is an instructive example of how a necessary myth will survive the conflicting facts. The wilderness is now gone, a culture of cities now surrounds us, but the prevailing tendency of Thoreau's countrymen—his more gifted countrymen—is still to withdraw into a private wilderness. William Faulkner is the latest, but he will not be the last, to pitch his wigwam in the pine-scented woods.

If other American classics have been more widely read—and as a rule they would be children's classics—none has left such an impression where it counts the most: on impressionable men. In Thoreau they see the archetypal *man* as well as the American. He is our first provincial with this universal mind. Under the spell of his style his raw material, that little piece of it around Walden Pond, was processed into a universal fact. There it stands, like an act of Nature, having little to do with the man who made it, and, as so often happens, we henceforth have little to do with him. (pp. 41-3)

> *Wright Morris, "To the Woods: Henry Thoreau,"*
> *in his* The Territory Ahead, *1958. Reprint by Atheneum, 1963, pp. 39-50.*

PERRY MILLER   (essay date 1960)

[*This essay first appeared in the* Thoreau Society Bulletin *in 1960.*]

Thoreau does not often mention Wordsworth, but the very opening segments of the *Journal* show that he hardly needed to. He was already a Wordsworthian, and in that sense a child of the Romantic era. (p. 149)

Even more revealing is a praise of Goethe . . . which approves of his being satisfied "with giving an exact description of objects as they appear to him." This, Thoreau pontificates, is the trait to be prized, and its skill consists in the device whereby "even the reflections of the author do not interfere with his descriptions." For Thoreau had thus already completely comprehended one of the major problems of the Romantic movement—for that portion of Romanticism preoccupied with the new interpretation of Nature it was the major problem—of striking and maintaining the delicate balance between object and reflection, of fact and truth, of minute observation and generalized concept. There can be no doubt that Thoreau was made aware of the problem at least in part by Emerson's *Nature,* which with its Platonic ascent from the lowly level of **"Commodity"** into the intellectual vistas of **"Prospects"** sought to offer an original method for combining the two poles of the Romantic dilemma. But it does seem to me that from the beginning Henry possessed an insight which, though it too must be located within the larger framework of Romantic Naturalism, is very different from Emerson's. The contrast becomes vivid if you put Emerson's famous sentences about becoming a transparent eyeball and about the currents of universal being circulating through him alongside this entry of Thoreau's, on March 3, 1839, on **"The Poet"**:

> He must be something more than natural—even supernatural. Nature will not speak through but along with him. His voice will not proceed from her midst, but, breathing on her, will make her the expression of his thought. He then poetizes when he takes a fact out of nature into spirit. He speaks without reference to time or place. His thought is one world, hers another. He is another Nature,—Nature's brother. Kindly offices do they perform for one another. Each publishes the other's truth.

It was from this duality of vision—what in *Walden* he would call "doubleness" and which, he would say, often made its possessor a bad neighbor—that he was able to extract from the *Journal* and put into **"The Natural History"** such contradictory assertations as, on the one hand, "Nature will bear the closest inspection; she invites us to lay our eye level with the smallest leaf, and take an insect view of its plain," and then, on the other, invoking in full awareness of its intellectualized nature one of the grand conceptual techniques of Biblical scholarship, this remark, "When I walk in the woods, I am reminded that a wise purveyor has been there before me; my most delicate experience is typified there." If at one and the same time Nature is closely inspected in microscopic detail and yet through the ancient system of typology makes experience intelligible, then Thoreau will have solved the Romantic riddle, have mastered the destructive Romantic Irony. Seen in such a context, his life was an unrelenting exertion to hold this precarious stance. In the end, the impossibility of sustaining it killed him. But not until, at least in *Walden,* he had for a breathless moment, held the two in solution, fused and yet still kept separate, he and Nature publishing each other's truth. Surely, it was a demoniacal enterprise from start to finish. This is why, it seems to me, that Thoreau can at long last be seen as a major writer of his century, not because he also happened to know boatcraft and fishcraft. (pp. 150-51)

Walden is one of the supreme achievements of the Romantic Movement—or to speak accurately, of Romantic Naturalism. . . . [It] was not and is not some spontaneous impulse from the vernal wood, although unfortunately many of its modern champions pretend that it was. No, it is truly emotion, but emotion ostensibly recollected in tranquility. Yet it is assuredly emotion, passion. There is no substitution for the original experience, there are no excellencies of diction contrived so as to suggest an inferiority of the original to the narration. Still, it is not a mere recital, item by item, atomic moment after moment, of two years beside the pond. It is a magnificent autobiography, faithful in every detail to the setting, arising to the level of a treatise on imagination and taste, and all this without ever becoming didactic. When seen in such a perspective, it can be placed beside [William Wordsworth's] *The Prelude*. It is the "growth of a poet's mind," and despite all its wealth of concrete imagery it is centered not upon Nature, but upon Nature's brother, the intelligence of the artist.

I need hardly observe that in this century the entire philosophy of what I call Romantic Naturalism has been attacked from innumerable sides and is generally thought to be completely discredited. (pp. 156-57)

If the twentieth-century judgment of the Romantic aesthetic is correct, then Henry Thoreau is one of its monumental failures and martyrs, along with Shelley and Novalis. Neither he nor they were able to answer the terrible question of whether, once they committed themselves to the proposition that their most delicate experience was typified in Nature, they were thereafter actually writing about Nature—about Walden Pond, for instance—or about nothing more than their delicious experiences. If in reality they were only projecting their emotions onto the Natural setting, if the phoebes do not weep for human miseries, then their effort to find someone additional to themselves was doomed to ghastly defeat. In this view, the career of Henry Thoreau is as tragic as that of [William Shakespeare's] King Lear. He too sacrificed himself needlessly to a delusion.

In his first organized statement, Thoreau could say, with all the confidence that a Lear had in the love of his daughters, that when he detects a beauty in any recess of Nature he is reminded of the inexpressible privacy of a life, that he may rest content with nothing more than the sight and the sound. On the premise of that doctrine, he may properly say no more than "I am affected by the sight of the cabins of muskrats," or than "I am the wiser in respect to all knowledges, and better qualified for all fortunes, for knowing that there is a minnow in the brook." In the glowing confidence of these aphorisms lurks the assumption that moral law and natural law contain analogies, and that for this reason the writer may safely record facts without metaphors, since truths are bound to sprout from them. The later portions of Thoreau's *Journal,* those after 1854, with their tedious recordings of mere observations, of measurements, of statistics, seem to attest not only the dwindling of his vitality but the exhaustion of the theory upon which he commenced to be an author in the first place. He immolated himself on the pyre of an untenable concept of literary creation.

And yet, he refuses to be consumed. Expound *Walden*, if you will, as a temporary and so an empty triumph of the Romantic

dream, as a work doomed to diminish with the recession of that dream, yet the book refuses to go into the archeological oblivion of, shall I say? Shelley's *The Revolt of Islam*. Robert Frost, while objecting with all his Yankee soul to Thoreau's epistemology, still proclaims that with him Thoreau is a "passion." The obvious answer, or rather the easy one, is that Thoreau was a great writer, and so his pages survive in spite of changes in metaphysical fashions. But that is truly an easy, a luxurious way of salvaging our poet. The more difficult, but I believe the more honest and, in the final accounting, the more laudatory way is to say that the Romantic balance, or its "Idea" of combination, of fusing the fact and the idea, the specific and the general, is still a challenge to the mind and to the artist. Thoreau was *both* a Transcendentalist and a Natural Historian. He never surrendered on either front, though the last years of the *Journal* show how desperate was the effort to keep both standards aloft. He said, in the central conceptual passage of *Walden,* that he wanted to drive life into a corner, to publish its meanness if it proved to be mean, but that if it should turn out to be sublime, then to give a true account of its sublimity. "The universe constantly and obediently answers to our conceptions" was his resolute determination. For what more sublime a cause, even though it be a questionable thesis, can a man expend himself? (pp. 158-59)

Perry Miller, "Thoreau in the Context of International Romanticism," in The New England Quarterly, *Vol. XXXLV, No. 2, June, 1961, pp. 147-59.*

JOSEPH J. MOLDENHAUER (lecture date 1962)

[*This essay was delivered as a lecture in 1962.*]

The idiosyncrasies of Thoreau's personality and opinions are so absorbing that "paradox" has always been a key term in Thoreau scholarship. Critic of government and relentless reporter of tortoises, Platonic dreamer and statistician of tree rings, Transcendental friend who calls for "pure hate" to underprop his love, Thoreau invites description as paradoxical, enigmatic, or even perverse. . . . In *Walden* this propensity toward the resolved contradiction may be observed in full flower. Here Thoreau talks only of himself yet "brag[s] for humanity." Self-isolated in a spot as remote, he says, as Cassiopeia's Chair, he strolls to the village "every day or two." Renouncing materialism for a poetic and mystic life, he proudly reports his own prudential efficiency, and documents his "economic" success with balance sheets. Bewailing the limitations of science, he painstakingly measures the depth of the pond and counts the bubbles in its ice.

Verbal paradox is to my mind the dominant stylistic feature of *Walden.* The persistent intellectual movement through incongruities, antitheses, and contradictions is strikingly reminiscent of the seventeenth century writers, including Donne and Sir Thomas Browne, who influenced this later metaphysical. Thoreau's paradoxical assertion—for instance, "Much is published, but little printed"—seems self-contradictory and opposed to reason. As a poetic device it has intimate connections with metaphor, because it remains an absurdity, a nonsense, only so long as the terms are taken exclusively at their discursive values. The stumbling block disappears, however, as soon as the reader sees that Thoreau has shifted a meaning, has made a metaphor or a play on words. The pun, that highly compressed form of analogy in which two logically disparate meanings are forced to share the same phonemic unit, lends itself admirably to Thoreau's purpose: to dramatize his statement by giving it the superficial appearance of a contradiction. The special sense of the understood or resolved paradox results from forcing a casual and expected meaning to the side and somewhat out of focus.

The user of paradox thus defines or asserts by indirection, frustrating conventional expectations about language. . . . In *Walden,* where Thoreau wants to communicate very unconventional truths, the rhetorical figure affords him great precision as well as polemical effectiveness.

As one might almost expect, Thoreau deprecated this source of stylistic power. When he set down in the *Journal* a list of his "faults," the first was "Paradoxes,—saying just the opposite,—a style which may be imitated." On another occasion he complained that "My companion tempts me to certain licenses of speech. . . . He asks for a paradox, an eccentric statement, and too often I give it to him." . . . [But] Thoreau wisely followed the crooked bent of his genius and employed a rhetoric suitable for his needs.

These needs were in part dictated by the nature of Transcendental thinking, with its emphasis upon the perception of a spiritual reality behind the surfaces of things. Nature for the Transcendentalist is an expression of the divine mind; its phenomena, when rightly seen, reveal moral truths. By means of proper perception, said Emerson, "man has access to the entire mind of the Creator," and "is himself the creator" of his own world. . . . Idealism is the Transcendentalist's necessary premise: it assures him that things conform to thoughts. . . . Thoreau was sufficiently tough-minded, and sufficiently interested in the details of natural phenomena, to resist the systematic translation of nature into ideas which Emersonian theory implied. He placed as much emphasis upon the "shams and delusions" which hinder men from "seeing" nature as upon the spiritual meanings of individual natural objects. But he always believed that to recognize one's relations with nature is the basis of moral insight; and he was convinced that the obstacles to this wisdom were removed by the simplification of life. Strip away the artificial, Thoreau tells the "desperate" man, and you will be able to read nature's language. Reality, the "secret of things," lurks under appearances, waiting to be seen.

While Emerson's is a strategy of revelation or illumination, Thoreau's is a practical strategy of persuasion. Describing his conversations with the French-Canadian woodchopper, Thoreau says he tried to "maneuver" him "to take the spiritual view of things." This polemical approach underlies the verbal strategies of *Walden.* The problem Thoreau faced there—to some extent, indeed, in all his writings—was to create in his audience the "waking moments" in which they could appreciate "the truth of which [he had] been convinced." In other words, he tries to wrench into line with his own the reader's attitudes toward the self, toward society, toward nature, and toward God. He "translates" the reader, raising him out of his conventional frame of reference into a higher one, in which extreme truths become intelligible. To these ends Thoreau employs a rhetoric of powerful exaggeration and antithesis. Habitually aware of the "common sense," the dulled perception that desperate life produces, he could turn the world of his audience upside-down by rhetorical means. He explores new resources of meaning in their "rotten diction" and challenges ingrained habits of thought and action with ennobling alternatives: "Read not the Times," he says in *Life Without Principle.* "Read the Eternities." With all the features of his characteristic extravagance—hyperbole, wordplay, paradox, mock-

heroics, loaded questions, and the ironic manipulation of cliché, proverb, and allusion—Thoreau urges new perspectives upon his reader. (pp. 132-35)

Walden is not, of course, merely a sophisticated sermon. It is the story of an experiment; a narrative; a fable. (p. 135)

The "I" of *Walden,* Thoreau as its narrator and hero, is a deliberately created verbal personality. The dramatized Thoreau must not be confused in critical analysis with the surveyor and pencil-maker of Concord: the *persona* stands in the same relation to the man as *Walden*—the symbolic gesture, the imaginative re-creation—stands to the literal fact of the Walden adventure. The narrator is a man of various moods and rhetorical poses. He represents himself by turns as a severe moralist, a genial companion, a bemused "hermit," and a whimsical trickster who regards the experiment as a sly joke on solid citizens. The mellowest of all his moods is the one we find, for instance, in **"Baker Farm," "Brute Neighbors,"** and **"House-Warming,"** where he pokes fun at his own zeal as an idealist and reformer. In all his roles he conveys a sense of his uniqueness, the separateness of his vision from that of his townsmen.

The "fictional audience" of *Walden* likewise requires our attention. . . . I would distinguish in *Walden* a range of response *within* the dramatic context from a much broader external response. The reader in part projects himself into the role of a hypothetical "listener," whom the narrator addresses directly; and in part he stands at a remove, overhearing this address. Psychologically, we are "beside ourselves in a sane sense," both spectators who respond to *Walden* as an aesthetic entity and projected participants in the verbal action. As spectators, or what I will call "readers," we are sympathetic toward the witty and engaging narrator. As vicarious participants, or what I will term "audience," we must imagine ourselves committed to the prejudices and shortsightedness which the narrator reproves, and subject to the full tone of the address.

The rhetoric of *Walden,* reflecting in some measure the lecture origins of the early drafts, assumes an initially hostile audience. Thoreau sets up this role for us. In the first third of **"Economy"** he characterizes a mixed group of silent listeners who are suspicious of the speaking voice. He would address "poor students," "the mass of men who are discontented," and "that seemingly wealthy, but most terribly impoverished class of all, who have accumulated dross." In addition Thoreau creates individual characters who express attitudes to be refuted by the narrator, and who serve as foils for his wit. These are stylized figures, briefly but deftly sketched, who heckle or complain or interrogate. Their function is to localize and articulate the implicit doubts of the audience. "A certain class of unbelievers," "some inveterate cavillers," "housewives . . . and elderly people," "the hard-featured farmer," "a factory-owner"—such lightly delineated characters register their protests against Thoreau's farming techniques, his lack of charity, his conclusions about the pond's depth, his manner of making bread, and even the cleanliness of his bed linen. Their objections tend to be "impertinent," despite Thoreau's disclaimer early in **"Economy,"** to the lower as well as the higher aspects of the experiment. He answers these animadversions with every form of wit: puns, irony, redefinition, paradoxes, twisted proverbs, overstatements, Biblical allusions (cited by a "heathen" to shame the Christian audience), and gymnastic leaps between the figurative and the literal. It is in this context of debate, of challenge and rejoinder, of provocation and rebuttal and exhortation, that the language of *Walden* must be understood.

Thoreau's rhetoric is a direct consequence of the way he locates himself as narrator with respect to a hostile fictional audience. The dramatic status of the speaker and his hearers accounts for the extraordinary "audibility" of *Walden* as well as for the aesthetic distance between author and reader.

Our bifurcation into spectator and vicarious participant is most intense in the hortatory and satirical passages. As participant, we are incredulous, shocked, and subject to the direct persuasive techniques of the argument. As spectator, on the other hand, we applaud Thoreau's rhetorical devastation of the premises of his fictional audience. We can certainly find the instructive and polemical statements in *Walden* meaningful. But they are contained by the literary structure, and must, as statements about life, be understood first within that context. Even the reader who conforms to the type of the fictional audience, and who brings to *Walden* a full-blown set of prejudices against Thoreauvian "economy," does not stay long to quarrel with the narrator. The force of Thoreau's ridicule encourages him to quit the stage. For the participant, *Walden* is "an invitation to life's dance"; the sympathetic reader dances with Thoreau from the start.

Thoreau's paradoxes are also congenial to the plot and themes of *Walden*. The term "comedy," which I will apply to its narrative movement, need not be rejected as a misnomer on generic grounds. (pp. 135-37)

Following a traditional comic pattern, Thoreau represents in *Walden* two worlds: the narrator's private paradise and the social wasteland he has abandoned. Each of these polar worlds, the desirable and the objectionable, has its basic character type and body of symbols. The narrator is the *Eiron,* the virtuous or witty character whose actions are directed toward the establishment of an ideal order. The audience and hecklers, who take for granted "what are deemed 'the most sacred laws of society,'" serve as the *Alazon* or imposter. This comic type is a braggart, misanthrope, or other mean-spirited figure, usually an older man, who resists the hero's efforts to establish harmony but who is often welcomed into the ideal order when the hero succeeds. The narrator of *Walden,* both virtuous and witty, withdraws from a society of "skinflint[s]" to a greenwood world at the pond. His pastoral sanctuary is represented in images of moisture, freedom, health, the waking state, fertility, and birth. The society he leaves behind is described in images of dust, imprisonment, disease, blindness, lethargy, and death. Upon these symbolic materials Thoreau builds many of his paradoxes. In his verbal attacks upon the old society, whose "idle and musty virtues" he finds as ridiculous as its vices, the narrator assumes an ironic or denunciatory pose. When he records his simple *vita nuova* [new life], that is, in the idyllic passages, his tone becomes meditative or ecstatic.

But it is, after all, to the dusty world or wasteland that *Walden*'s fictional audience belongs. Despite their dissatisfactions, they are committed to this life and its values, and are thus in effect blind to the practical as well as the spiritual advantages of the experiment. The narrator, far from being a misanthropic skulker, wishes to communicate his experience of a more harmonious and noble life. His language serves this end: the first rhetorical function of paradox is to make the audience entertain a crucial doubt. . . . These paradoxes, often executed with brilliant humor, jostle and tumble the listener's perspective. To be sure, the narrator is a self-acknowledged eccentric—but he is not a lunatic. Thoreau makes sense in his own terms, and the fictional audience no longer can in theirs.

At the same time as he makes nonsense of the audience's vocabulary with satirical paradoxes, Thoreau appropriates some of its key terms to describe the special values of his experiment. For example, though he despises commerce he would conduct a profitable "trade" with the "Celestial Empire." In this second body of rhetorical devices Thoreau again exploits polarities of symbol and idea, and not without some irony. But these paradoxes differ sharply in their function from the satirical ones. They attach to the Transcendentalist's world, to nature and simplicity, the deep connotations of worth which social values and material comforts evoke for the desperate man. Thoreau astounds and disarms the audience when he calls his experiment a "business" and renders his accounts to the half- and quarter-penny. By means of this appropriately inappropriate language he announces the incompatibility of his livelihood and his neighbor's, and simultaneously suggests interesting resemblances. Thoreau's enterprise, like the businessman's, requires risks, demands perseverance, and holds out the lure of rewards. The statistical passages of **"Economy"** and **"The Bean-Field"** are equivocal. On the one hand, they prove the narrator's ability to beat the thrifty Yankee at his own game; on the other they parody the Yankee's obsession with finance. Thoreau's argument that one is successful in proportion as he reduces his worldly needs is likewise paradoxical, a queer analogue to the commercial theory of increasing profits by lowering costs. (pp. 138-40)

By nature a dialectical instrument, the paradox is thus stylistically integral to this severely dialectical work. Viewed generally, the two large groups of paradoxes reflect the comic structure of *Walden* and its two major themes: the futility of the desperate life and the rewards of enlightened simplicity. With the paradoxes of the first or satirical group, Thoreau declares that his listener's goods are evils, his freedom slavery, and his life a death. Those of the second group, corresponding rhetorically to the recurrent images of metamorphosis, proclaim that the values of the natural and Transcendental life arise from what the audience would deprecate as valueless. In these paradoxes, the beautiful is contained in the ugly, the truly precious in the seemingly trivial, and the springs of life in the apparently dead.

As *Walden* progresses the proportion of the first to the second kind gradually changes. The rhetoric of the early chapters is very largely one of trenchant denunciation, directed against the desperate life. That of the later chapters is predominantly serene, playful, and rapturous. Thoreau creates the impression of a growing concord between himself and his audience by allowing the caustic ironies and repudiations of **"Economy"** to shift by degrees to the affirmations of **"Spring"** and **"Conclusion."** Thoreau the outsider becomes Thoreau the magnanimous insider, around whom reasonable men and those who love life may gather. Rhetorically and thematically, as the book proceeds, the attack becomes the dance. (pp. 140-41)

Joseph J. Moldenhauer, "The Extra-vagant Maneuver: Paradox in 'Walden',"in The Graduate Journal, *Vol. VI, No. 1, Winter, 1964, pp. 132-46.*

CARL F. HOVDE (lecture date 1962)

[*The following essay was originally a lecture delivered in 1962.*]

The movement from particular fact, to that fact's general significance, and back again, is . . . a very common movement in Thoreau's prose. But how solidly are we back at the level of autobiographical detail when he is describing the voyage [in *A Week on the Concord and Merrimack Rivers*]? Every reader of *A Week* notices that Henry's brother John is never closely identified: he is never named; we are never told of his individual actions or thoughts; he simply does not exist in the work as a personality. He is a presence only, whose literary function is to provide that sense of companionship and joint enterprise creatable by the first person plural pronoun. He is, then, a representative companion, whose individual identity is of minimal significance.

There are, of course, many particular people mentioned in the work, and we do learn a good deal about some of them, but almost all of them are present to stand for certain qualities and attributes in a representative way; Thoreau often takes pleasure in their particularity, but is at pains to use them to show something about the general possibilities of man's spirit. And in *A Week* these possibilities are almost always positive—are good; this is a contrast with the vivid awareness of evil characteristic of the early part of *Walden*. *Walden* opens with perhaps the most brilliantly surgical scorn in American literature. It begins with a portrait of the worst of man's habits, which are even more frightening than profound evil because so much more common, and the work moves on to a presentation of what the best life must involve, wherever it may be lived. But *A Week* has neither the scorn, nor the deep penetration into the single self that is the purpose of *Walden*. In the earlier work many people are mentioned, but none of them is dwelled on very long, and while we are constantly hearing the sound of Thoreau's own voice, there is not the same deep delving into the biographical springs of personality.

The reason for this is reflected in the different evocations of Nature in the two works, for Nature is, of course, where Thoreau saw the roots of a man's proper character finding nourishment. In *Walden*, after the initial dissection of man's folly, we see Thoreau investigating himself, and at length, within the life of Nature as it existed at and around the pond. It is a confrontation of the individual with the ground of his very existence; he is much alone, though never lonely, because his enterprise is one that demands solitude for observation and for thought. This is one of the reasons for the great solitudes and silences of *Walden;* they are there so that a man may think about what he essentially is. Nature in *Walden* is never empty, but for Thoreau's imaginative purpose it must be largely uninhabited.

About *A Week*, on the other hand, one wishes to use not so much the word "nature" as the word "landscape." *Walden* does not present a panoramic view of the surroundings because there is too intense an investigation into the local particularities. But in *A Week* there are many visual sweeps, covering much territory; Thoreau moves down reaches of the river, and we have a sense of long lawns and prospects, but not of profound retreats or of vast silences—despite a passage on silence at the end of the work.

We do not have these because the enterprise is different; Thoreau is here not searching for the springs of individual identity in all its complexity, but is, on the level of the physical voyage, surveying the bright, ideal surface of much human experience—an experience achieved by men living together in the communities of towns and villages. Nature is here not the setting for the transformation of one man's soul, but is the background for a frieze of figures, whose particular members are mentioned briefly in order to exemplify, rapidly and without

travail, some of the many ways in which men may be identified as worthy. (pp. 7-9)

This drive toward the positive and exemplary is reflected in the relative scarcity of unfavorable, or negative, comment and criticism in *A Week,* something already mentioned as a contrast to the early parts of *Walden.* Take the matter of slavery, for example. It is very likely that at one time Thoreau intended to include in *A Week*—in the chapter called "Thursday"—a version of an essay he had written about Nathaniel P. Rogers, the abolitionist who published a paper called *The Herald of Freedom.* The essay had been printed in the *Dial* in 1844, and manuscript evidence suggests that Thoreau tried to rework it for *A Week.* But he rejected it because it was so much concerned with social criticism. Rogers' paper was founded to oppose slavery, a particular social abuse, and the little social criticism to be found in *A Week* is very carefully stated in general terms. Often, of course, Thoreau strikes out against those things in public life to which he objects, but he almost never does this with reference to particular evils. He mentions slavery only once in the book, but does not dwell on it, and the tone of the sentence where it appears is one of criticism in the abstract. The paper on Rogers drops out because *A Week* is not meant to be a social document in the sense that "**Civil Disobedience**" is one, or even in the subtle fashion of parts of *Walden.* There are other passages in the manuscript which were omitted for similar reasons. Thus one sees him cutting out entirely not only passages which seemed to be morally unprofitable, like that on his grandmother, but also others which seemed too moral, so to say—passages which were out of harmony with the generally affirmative tone of his work.

Thoreau often "revised by omission" in this way, but his craftsmanship is more subtly demonstrated in those reworkings of earlier material which actually changed the report of what he saw in order to make reality better serve his own ends. (pp. 11-12)

[Such reworkings] point in the direction of change from the merely amusing to the morally instructive, from the specifically individual and particular to those particulars best made generally representative and symbolic, and from the strongly negative tone or fact to the more moderate or positive attitude. No one character in *A Week* is given much space; even Thoreau himself is less biographically alive than in *Walden.* A great many people are mentioned—people met on this trip, people Thoreau had met on earlier excursions, and historical personages memorialized as the worthies of the local scene through which they were passing.

Together, these personages form an important part of the book—they serve always to inhabit the landscape, taking their place in a tradition which is created partially by memories of men like John Stark, whom Thoreau uses to build the sense of a high past which the people of his time must emulate. (p. 14)

The trip along these two New England rivers is, then, in no sense a movement away from civilization, though it is certainly a move away from habit and the familiarity that can lead to staleness. It is, among other things, the measure of the difference between this book and *Walden* that Thoreau's second book takes us so deeply into the life of Nature that we have left the village far behind—though physically it was never so far away. *A Week,* on the other hand, takes us from Concord only to take us to a long series of towns; the trip is an actual and imaginative pageant of the relationships between one man's mind and the New England both of, and before his time, and this New England is inhabited by the memories of generosity and courage and high deeds. The conception of character is idealistic; the encounters are usually with figures about whom we learn nothing but good; and the simplicity of this as a psychological view is more than balanced by the fact that heroes, including those of Massachusetts and New Hampshire towns, may be excused from our faults in exchange for their willingness to stand up like monuments on a hilltop, so that we may measure our height against them. (pp. 14-15)

> Carl F. Hovde, "The Conception of Character in 'A Week on the Concord and Merrimack Rivers'," in The Thoreau Centennial, edited by Walter Harding, State University of New York Press, 1964, pp. 5-15.

REV. MARTIN LUTHER KING, JR.   (essay date 1962)

[*King, the American civil rights leader and humanitarian, here credits Thoreau with inspiring his dedication to "non-cooperation with evil."*]

During my early college days I read Thoreau's essay on civil disobedience for the first time. Fascinated by the idea of refusing to cooperate with an evil system, I was so deeply moved that I re-read the work several times. I became convinced then that non-cooperation with evil is as much a moral obligation as is cooperation with good. No other person has been more eloquent and passionate in getting this idea across than Henry David Thoreau. As a result of his writings and personal witness we are the heirs of a legacy of creative protest. It goes without saying that the teachings of Thoreau are alive today, indeed, they are more alive today than ever before. Whether expressed in a sit-in at lunch counters, a freedom ride into Mississippi, a peaceful protest in Albany, Georgia, a bus boycott in Montgomery, Alabama, it is an outgrowth of Thoreau's insistence that evil must be resisted and no moral man can patiently adjust to injustice.

> Rev. Martin Luther King, Jr., "A Legacy of Creative Protest," in Thoreau in Our Season, edited by John H. Hicks, The University of Massachusetts Press, 1962, p. 13.

LEO MARX   (essay date 1964)

[*Marx discusses* Walden *as "an experiment in transcendental pastoralism," a distinctively American version of romantic pastoral. Using the example of Thoreau's railroad imagery to explore his treatment of the ambiguities of relationship between the machine and nature, Marx argues that Thoreau drew on "technological imagery" to represent a new "mode of perception" and culture.*]

[Thoreau's *Walden*] may be read as the report of an experiment in transcendental pastoralism. The organizing design is like that of many American fables: *Walden* begins with the hero's withdrawal from society in the direction of nature. The main portion of the book is given over to a yearlong trial of Emerson's prescription for achieving a new life. When Thoreau tells of his return to Concord, in the end, he seems to have satisfied himself about the efficacy of this method of redemption. It may be difficult to say exactly what is being claimed, but the triumphant tone of the concluding chapters leaves little doubt that he is announcing positive results. His most telling piece of evidence is *Walden*—the book itself. Recognizing the clarity, coherence, and power of the writing, we can only conclude—or so transcendental doctrine would have it—that the

The Maxham daguerreotype of Thoreau. It was taken in 1856, when Thoreau was thirty-nine years old. The Granger Collection, New York.

experiment has been a success. The vision of unity that had made the aesthetic order of *Walden* possible had in turn been made possible by the retreat to the pond. The pastoral impulse somehow had provided access to the order latent in the cosmos.

But the meaning of *Walden* is more complicated than this affirmation. Because Thoreau takes seriously what Emerson calls the "method of nature"—more seriously than the master himself —the book has a strong contrapuntal theme. Assuming that natural facts properly perceived and accurately transcribed must yield the truth, Thoreau adopts the tone of a hard-headed empiricist. At the outset he makes it clear that he will tell exactly what happened. He claims to have a craving for reality (be it life or death), and he would have us believe him capable of reporting the negative evidence. Again and again he allows the facts to play against his desire, so that his prose at its best acquires a distinctively firm, cross-grained texture. Though the dominant tone is affirmative, the undertone is skeptical, and it qualifies the import of episode after episode. For this reason *Walden* belongs among the first in a long series of American books which, taken together, have had the effect of circumscribing the pastoral hope, much as Virgil circumscribes it in his eclogues. In form and feeling, indeed, Thoreau's book has much in common with the classic Virgilian mode.

Although the evidence is abundant, it is easy to miss the conventional aspect of *Walden*. In the second chapter Thoreau describes the site as an ideal pasture, a real place which he transforms into an unbounded, timeless landscape of the mind.

And he identifies himself with Damodara (Krishna) in his rôle as shepherd, and with a shepherd in a Jacobean song:

> There was a shepherd that did live,
> And held his thoughts as high
> As were the mounts whereon his flocks
> Did hourly feed him by.

Nevertheless, the serious affinity between *Walden* and the convention is disguised by certain peculiarities of American pastoralism, the most obvious being the literalness with which Thoreau approaches the ideal of the simple life. For centuries writers working in the mode had been playing with the theme, suggesting that men might enrich their contemplative experience by simplifying their housekeeping. (The shepherd's ability to reduce his material needs to a minimum had been one of his endearing traits.) Yet it generally had been assumed that the simple life was a poetic theme, not to be confused with the way poets did in fact live. In the main, writers who took the felicity of shepherds in green pastures as their subject had been careful to situate themselves near wealth and power. The effect of the American environment, however, was to break down common-sense distinctions between art and life. No one understood this more clearly than Henry Thoreau; skilled in the national art of disguising art, in *Walden* he succeeds in obscuring the traditional, literary character of the pastoral withdrawal. Instead of writing about it—or *merely* writing about it—he tries it. By telling his tale in the first person, he endows the mode with a credibility it had seldom, if ever, possessed. Because the "I" who addresses us in *Walden* is describing the way he had lived, taking pains to supply plenty of hard facts ("Yes, I did eat $8.74, all told. . . ."), we scarcely notice that all the while he had been playing the shepherd's venerable rôle. He refuses to say whether the book is an explicit guide for living or an exercise in imaginative perception. We are invited to take it as either or both. Convinced that effective symbols can be derived only from natural facts, Thoreau had moved to the pond so that he might make a symbol of his life. If we miss the affinity with the Virgilian mode, then, it is partly because we are dealing with a distinctively American version of romantic pastoral.

No feature of *Walden* makes this truth more apparent than its topography. The seemingly realistic setting may not be a land of fantasy like Arcadia, yet neither is it Massachusetts. On inspection it proves to be another embodiment of the American moral geography—a native blend of myth and reality. The hut beside the pond stands at the center of a symbolic landscape in which the village of Concord appears on one side and a vast reach of unmodified nature on the other. As if no organized society existed to the west, the mysterious, untrammeled, primal world seems to begin at the village limits. As in most American fables, the wilderness is an indispensable feature of this terrain, and the hero's initial recoil from everyday life carries him to the verge of anarchic primitivism. . . . But Thoreau is not a primitivist. True, he implies that he would have no difficulty choosing between Concord and the wilderness. What really engages him, however, is the possibility of avoiding that choice. (Jefferson had taken the same position.) In *Walden,* accordingly, he keeps our attention focused upon the middle ground where he builds a house, raises beans, reads [Homer's] *Iliad,* and searches the depths of the pond. Like the "navel of the earth" in the archaic myths studied by Mircea Eliade, the pond is the absolute center—the *axis mundi*—of Thoreau's cosmos. If an alternative to the ways of Concord is to be found anywhere, it will be found on the shore of Walden Pond—near the mystic center.

And it had best be found quickly. The drama of *Walden* is intensified by Thoreau's acute sense of having been born in the nick of time. Though the book resembles the classic pastoral in form and feeling, its facts and images are drawn from the circumstances of life in nineteenth-century America. By 1845, according to Thoreau, a depressing state of mind—he calls it "quiet desperation"—has seized the people of Concord. . . . He locates it, above all, in their economy—a system within which they work endlessly, not to reach a goal of their own choosing but to satisfy the demands of the market mechanism. The moral, in short, is that here "men have become the tools of their tools."

The omnipresence of tools, gadgets, instruments is symptomatic of the Concord way. Like Carlyle, Thoreau uses technological imagery to represent more than industrialization in the narrow, economic sense. It accompanies a mode of perception, an emergent system of meaning and value—a culture. In fact his overdrawn indictment of the Concord "economy" might have been written to document Carlyle's dark view of industrialism. Thoreau feels no simple-minded Luddite hostility toward the new inventions; they are, he says, "but improved means to an unimproved end. . . ." What he is attacking is the popular illusion that improving the means is enough, that if the machinery of society is put in good order (as Carlyle had said) "all were well with us; the rest would care for itself!" He is contending against a culture pervaded by this mechanistic outlook. It may well be conducive to material progress, but it also engenders deadly fatalism and despair. At the outset, then, Thoreau invokes the image of the machine to represent the whole tone and quality of Concord life or, to be more precise, anti-life. . . . The clock, favorite "machine" of the Enlightenment, is a master machine in Thoreau's model of the capitalist economy. Its function is decisive because it links the industrial apparatus with consciousness. The laboring man becomes a machine in the sense that his life becomes more closely geared to an impersonal and seemingly autonomous system. If the advent of power technology is alarming, it is because it occurs within this cultural context. When Thoreau depicts the machine as it functions within the Concord environment, accordingly, it is an instrument of oppression: "We do not ride upon the railroad; it rides upon us." But later, when seen from the Walden perspective, the railroad's significance becomes quite different.

Thoreau's denunciation of the Concord "economy" [in the opening chapter, **"Economy,"**] prefigures the complex version of the Sleepy Hollow episode in the fourth chapter, **"Sounds."** The previous chapter is about **"Reading,"** or what he calls the language of metaphor. Now he shifts to sounds, "the language which all things and events speak without metaphor, which alone is copious and standard." The implication is that he is turning from the conventional language of art to the spontaneous language of nature. What concerns him is the hope of making the word one with the thing, the notion that the naked fact of sensation, if described with sufficient precision, can be made to yield its secret—its absolute meaning. This is another way of talking about the capacity of nature to "produce delight"—to supply value and meaning. It is the crux of transcendental pastoralism. Hence Thoreau begins with an account of magnificent summer days when, like Hawthorne at the Hollow, he does nothing but sit "rapt in a revery, amidst the pines and . . . sumachs, in undisturbed solitude and stillness." These days, unlike days in Concord, are not "minced into hours and fretted by the ticking of a clock." Here is another pastoral interlude, a celebration of idleness and that sense of relaxed solidarity with the universe that presumably comes with close attention to the language of nature. For a moment Thoreau allows us to imagine that he has escaped the clock, the Concord definition of time and, indeed, the dominion of the machine. But then, without raising his voice, he reports the "rattle of railroad cars" in the woods.

At first the sound is scarcely audible. Thoreau casually mentions it at the end of a long sentence in which he describes a series of sights and sounds: hawks circling the clearing, a tantivy of wild pigeons, a mink stealing out of the marsh, the sedge bending under the weight of reedbirds, and then, as if belonging to the very tissue of nature: "and for the last half-hour I have heard the rattle of railroad cars, now dying away and then reviving like the beat of a partridge, conveying travellers from Boston to the country." It would have been difficult to contrive a quieter entrance, which may seem curious in view of the fact that Thoreau then devotes nine long paragraphs to the subject. Besides, he insists upon the importance of the Fitchburg Railroad in the Walden scene; it "touches the pond" near his house, and since he usually goes to the village along its causeway, he says, "I . . . am, as it were, related to society by this link." And then, what may at first seem even more curious, he introduces the auditory image of the train a second time, and with a markedly different emphasis:

> The whistle of the locomotive penetrates my woods summer and winter, sounding like the scream of a hawk sailing over some farmer's yard, informing me that many restless city merchants are arriving within the circle of the town. . . .

Now the sound is more like a hawk than a partridge, and Thoreau playfully associates the hawk's rapacity with the train's distinctive mechanical cadence:

> All the Indian huckleberry hills are stripped, all the cranberry meadows are raked into the city. Up comes the cotton, down goes the woven cloth; up comes the silk, down goes the woollen; up come the books, but down goes the wit that writes them.

What are we to make of this double image of the railroad? First it is like a partridge, then a hawk; first it blends into the landscape like the industrial images in the Inness painting, but then, a moment later, it becomes the discordant machine of the Sleepy Hollow notes. (pp. 242-51)

The image of the railroad on the shore of the pond figures an ambiguity at the heart of *Walden*. Man-made power, the machine with its fire, smoke, and thunder, is juxtaposed to the waters of Walden, remarkable for their depth and purity and a matchless, indescribable color—now light blue, now green, almost always pellucid. The iron horse moves across the surface of the earth; the pond invites the eye below the surface. The contrast embodies both the hope and the fear aroused by the impending climax of America's encounter with wild nature. As Thoreau describes the event, both responses are plausible, and there is no way of knowing which of them history is more likely to confirm. Earlier he had made plain the danger of technological progress, and here at the pond it again distracts his attention from other, presumably more important, concerns.

Yet he is elated by the presence of this wonderful invention. In Concord, within the dominion of the mechanistic philosophy, the machine rode upon men, but when seen undistorted from Walden, the promise of the new power seems to offset the danger. (pp. 251-52)

If the interrupted idyll represents a crucial ambiguity, it also represents at least one certainty. The certainty is change itself—the kind of accelerating change, or "progress," that Americans identify with their new inventions, especially the railroad. For Thoreau, like Melville's Ahab [in *Moby Dick*], this machine is the type and agent of an irreversible process: not mere scientific or technological development in the narrow sense, but the implacable advance of history. "We have constructed a fate," he writes, "an *Atropos*, that never turns aside. (Let that be the name of your engine.)" The episode demonstrates that the Walden site cannot provide a refuge, in any literal sense, from the forces of change. Indeed, the presence of the machine in the woods casts a shadow of doubt (the smoke of the locomotive puts Thoreau's field in the shade) upon the Emersonian hope of extracting an answer from nature. The doubt is implicit in the elaborately contrived language used to compose this little event. Recall that Thoreau had introduced the chapter on **"Sounds"** as an effort to wrest an extra-literary meaning from natural facts; his alleged aim had been to render sense perceptions with perfect precision in "the language which all things and events speak without metaphor." What he actually had done, however, was quite the reverse. To convey his response to the sound of the railroad he had resorted to an unmistakably figurative, literary language. Few passages in *Walden* are more transparently contrived or artful; it is as if the subject had compelled Thoreau to admit a debt to Art as great, if not greater, than his debt to Nature. (pp. 252-53)

The need for defense against the forces of history does not tempt Thoreau to a nostalgic embrace of the "pastoral life" that is being whirled away. Quite the contrary. In **"The Bean-Field"** he turns his wit against the popular American version of pastoral. The Walden experiment, as described in **"Economy,"** had included a venture in commercial farming. (p. 255)

As he describes himself at work among his beans, Thoreau is the American husbandman. Like the central figure of the Jeffersonian idyll, his vocation has a moral and spiritual as well as economic significance. . . . Like Emerson's Young American, he blends Jeffersonian and romantic attitudes toward nature. When Thoreau describes the purpose of his bean-raising activity, accordingly, he falls into a comic idiom—a strange compound of practical, Yankee vernacular and transcendental philosophizing. . . . The better he had come to "know beans," the less seriously he had been able to take the rôle of noble husbandman. As the writer's account of that "singular experience" develops, he moves further and further from the reverential, solemn tone of popular pastoralism, until he finally adopts a mock-heroic attitude. . . . (pp. 255-56)

In part Thoreau's irony can be attributed to the outcome of his bean venture. Although he does not call it a failure, the fact is clear enough. . . . His own experience comports with what he observes of American farmers throughout the book. So far from representing a "pastoral life," a desirable alternative to the ways of Concord and the market economy, the typical farmer in *Walden* is narrow-minded and greedy. The description of the ice crews stripping the pond in winter, as if they were hooking up "the virgin mould itself," is a bitter comment on the methods of capitalist "husbandmen." Thoreau has no use for the cant about the nobility of the farmer. (pp. 257-58)

The result of the venture in husbandry prefigures the result of the Walden experiment as a whole. Judged by a conventional (economic) standard, it is true, the enterprise had been a failure. But that judgment is irrelevant to Thoreau's purpose, as his dominant tone, the tone of success, plainly indicates. It is irrelevant because his aim had been to *know* beans: to get at the essential *meaning* of labor in the bean-field. And "meaning," as he conceives it, has nothing to do with the alleged virtue of the American husbandman or the merits of any institution or "way of life"; nor can it be located in the material or economic facts, where Concord, operating on the plane of the Understanding, locates meaning and value. Thoreau has quite another sort of meaning in view, as he admits when he says that he raised beans, not because he wanted beans to eat, "but, perchance, as some must work in fields if only for the sake of tropes and expression, to serve a parable-maker one day."

This idea, which contains the gist of Thoreau's ultimate argument, also is implicit in the outcome of other episodes. It is implied by his account of fishing at night—a tantalizing effort to get at the "dull uncertain blundering purpose" he detects at the end of his line beneath the pond's opaque surface; and by that incomparable satire on the transcendental quest, the chase of the loon who "laughed in derision" at his efforts; and by his painstaking investigation of the pond's supposed "bottomlessness": ". . . I can assure my readers that Walden has a reasonably tight bottom at a not unreasonable . . . depth." In each case, as in **"The Bean-Field,"** the bare, empirical evidence proves inadequate to his purpose. Of themselves the facts do not, cannot, flower into truth; they do not show forth a meaning, which is to say, the kind of meaning the experiment had been designed to establish. If the promise of romantic pastoralism is to be fulfilled, nothing less than an alternative to the Concord way will suffice. Although his tone generally is confident, Thoreau cunningly keeps the issue in doubt until the end. By cheerfully, enigmatically reiterating his failure to extract an "answer"—a coherent world-view—from the facts, he moves the drama toward a climax. Not until the penultimate chapter, **"Spring,"** does he disclose a way of coping with the forces represented by the encroaching machine power.

At the same time, however, he carefully nurtures an awareness of the railroad's presence in the Concord woods. (The account of the interrupted idyll in **"Sounds"** is only the most dramatic of its many appearances.) . . . And Thoreau takes special pains to impress us with the "cut" in the landscape made by the embankment. . . . The Deep Cut is a wound inflicted upon the land by man's meddling, aggressive, rational intellect, and it is not healed until the book's climax, the resurgence of life in **"Spring."** By that point the organizing design of **Walden** has been made to conform to the design of nature itself; like Spenser's arrangement of his eclogues in *The Shepheards Calendar,* the sequence of Thoreau's final chapters follows the sequence of months and seasons. This device affirms the possibility of redemption from time, the movement away from Concord time, defined by the clock, toward nature's time, the daily and seasonal life cycle. It is also the movement that redeems machine power. In the spring the ice, sand, and clay of the railroad causeway thaws. The wet stuff flows down the banks, assumes myriad forms, and arouses in Thoreau a delight approaching religious ecstasy. The event provides this parable-maker with his climactic trope: a visual image that figures the realization of the pastoral ideal in the age of machines.

The description of the melting railroad bank is an intricately orchestrated paean to the power of the imagination. Although the sand remains mere sand, the warming influence of the sun causes it to assume forms like lava, leaves, vines, coral, leopards' paws, birds' feet, stalactites, blood vessels, brains, bowels, and excrement. It is a pageant evoking the birth of life out of inorganic matter. Watching the sandy rupture exhilarates Thoreau, affecting him as if, he says, "I stood in the laboratory of the Artist who made the world and me,—had come to where he was still at work, sporting on this bank, and with excess of energy strewing his fresh designs about." The scene illustrates the principle in all the operations of Nature: an urge toward organization, form, design. . . . The sight inspires Thoreau with a sense of infinite possibility. "The very globe continually transcends and translates itself. . . ." And not only the earth, he says, "but the institutions upon it are plastic like clay in the hands of the potter."

Thoreau's study of the melting bank is a figurative restoration of the form and unity severed by the mechanized forces of history. Out of the ugly "cut" in the landscape he fashions an image of a new beginning. Order, form, and meaning are restored, but it is a blatantly, unequivocally figurative restoration. The whole force of the passage arises from its extravagantly metaphoric, poetic, literary character. At no point does Thoreau impute material reality to the notion of sand being transformed into, say, leopards' paws. It assumes a form that looks like leopards' paws, but the form exists only so far as it is perceived. The same may be said of his alternative to the Concord way. Shortly after the episode of the thawing sand, the account of the coming of spring reaches a moment of "seemingly instantaneous" change. A sudden influx of light fills his house; he looks out of the window, and where the day before there had been cold gray ice there lies the calm transparent pond; he hears a robin singing in the distance and honking geese flying low over the woods. It is spring. Its coming, says Thoreau, is "like the creation of Cosmos out of Chaos and the realization of the Golden Age."

This reaffirmation of the pastoral ideal is not at all like Emerson's prophecy, in "The Young American," of a time "when the whole land is a garden, and the people have grown up in the bowers of a paradise." By comparison, the findings of the Walden experiment seem the work of a tough, unillusioned empiricist. They are consistent with Thoreau's unsparing analysis of the Concord "economy" and with the knowledge that industrial progress is making nonsense of the popular notion of a "pastoral life." The melting of the bank and the coming of spring is only "like" a realization of the golden age. It is a poetic figure. In *Walden* Thoreau is clear, as Emerson seldom was, about the location of meaning and value. He is saying that it does not reside in the natural facts or in social institutions or in anything "out there," but in consciousness. It is a product of imaginative perception, of the analogy-perceiving, metaphor-making, mythopoeic power of the human mind. For Thoreau the realization of the golden age is, finally, a matter of private and, in fact, literary experience. Since it has nothing to do with the environment, with social institutions or material reality (any facts will melt if the heat of imaginative passion is sufficient), then the writer's physical location is of no great moment. At the end of the chapter on **"Spring,"** accordingly, Thoreau suddenly drops the language of metaphor and reverts to a direct, matter-of-fact, referential idiom: "Thus was my first year's life in the woods completed; and the second year was similar to it. I finally left Walden September 6th, 1847."

There is a world of meaning in the casual tone. If the book ended here, indeed, one might conclude that Thoreau, like

Prospero at the end of [William Shakespeare's] *The Tempest,* was absolutely confident about his impending return to society. (Concord is the Milan of *Walden.*) But the book does not end with **"Spring."** Thoreau finds it necessary to add a didactic conclusion, as if he did not fully trust the power of metaphor after all. And he betrays his uneasiness, finally, in the arrogance with which he announces his disdain for the common life:

> I delight . . . not to live in this restless, nervous, bustling, trivial Nineteenth Century, but stand or sit thoughtfully while it goes by. What are men celebrating? They are all on a committee of arrangements, and hourly expect a speech from somebody. God is only the president of the day, and Webster is his orator.

In the end Thoreau restores the pastoral hope to its traditional location. He removes it from history, where it is manifestly unrealizable, and relocates it in literature, which is to say, in his own consciousness, in his craft, in *Walden.* (pp. 258-65)

> Leo Marx, "Two Kingdoms of Force," in his The Machine in the Garden: Technology and the Pastoral Ideal in America, *Oxford University Press, New York, 1964, pp. 227-353.**

LEON EDEL (essay date 1970)

[*Edel, a highly respected American biographer and critic, discusses Walden as a "work of art pretending to be a documentary." According to Edel, this "lively fable" of Thoreau's idealized version of himself and his life is often poetic, and its language reminds the critic of James Joyce's novel* Finnegans Wake. *Thoreau, Edel concludes, was capable of both eccentricity and art.*]

Of the creative spirits that flourished in Concord, Massachusetts, during the middle of the nineteenth century, it might be said that Hawthorne loved men but felt estranged from them, Emerson loved ideas even more than men, and Thoreau loved himself. Less of an artist than Hawthorne, less of a thinker than Emerson, Thoreau made of his life a sylvan legend, that of man alone, in communion with nature. He was a strange presence in American letters—we have so few of them—an eccentric. The English tend to tolerate their eccentrics to the enrichment of their national life. In America, where democracy and conformity are often confused, the nonconforming Thoreau was frowned upon, and for good reason. He had a disagreeable and often bellicose nature. He lacked geniality. And then he had once set fire to the Concord woods—a curious episode, too lightly dismissed in the Thoreau biographies. He was, in the fullest sense of the word, a "curmudgeon," and literary history has never sufficiently studied the difficulties his neighbors had in adjusting themselves to certain of his childish ways. But in other ways he was a man of genius—even if it was a "crooked genius" as he himself acknowledged. (p. 5)

All of Thoreau's writings represent a continuous and carefully documented projection of the self. *Walden* announces itself autobiography—"I should not talk so much about myself if there were anybody else whom I knew as well." The book is an idealized and romantic account of Thoreau's sojourn in the woods. Even its beautiful digressions are a series of masks. In both of his works, *Walden* and *A Week on the Concord and Merrimack Rivers,* as in his miscellaneous essays, we find an ideal self rather than the Thoreau Concord knew. The artist in

Thoreau improved on nature in the interest of defending himself against some of nature's more painful truths. (p. 6)

There is in all of Thoreau's writings an enforced calm; strange tensions run below the surface, deep obsessions. He is so preoccupied with self-assertion as to suggest that this was a profound necessity rather than an experience of serenity.

His struggle for identity gave him great powers of concentration and diligence. He was not a born writer, but he taught himself by imitation to carpenter solid verbal structures and give them rhythm and proportion. He went to school to Emerson, to Carlyle, to the Greeks, to the philosophers of India. He was first and foremost a reader of books—and only after them of nature. He read like a bee clinging to a flower, for all that he could extract from the printed page. He wrote poems, many of them banal; yet he poured a great deal of poetry into the more relaxed passages of his prose. This prose is seldom spontaneous; behind its emulation of the measure and moderation of the ancients one feels strain and subterranean violence. (pp. 8-9)

Walden is not a document, nor even the record of a calculated experiment. It is a work of art pretending to be a documentary. Thoreau talked as if he lived in the wilderness but he lived in the suburbs. He furnished his home with pieces retrieved from Concord attics. We have seen that he plastered and shingled the cabin when cold weather came. We know that he took his shoes to the Concord cobbler; that he baked bread using purchased rye and Indian meal; that he slept not in rough blankets but between sheets. He gave himself the creature comforts few Americans in the log cabins of the West could enjoy. . . . But the author of *Walden* discovered that his whim of living in the woods caught the fancy of audiences. Men and women were willing to listen to the fiction of his rude economy as if he were Robinson Crusoe [from the novel *Robinson Crusoe* by Daniel Defoe]. It is perhaps to Daniel Defoe that we may turn for a significant literary predecessor. The writer who had pretended he was keeping a journal of the plague year in London, long after the plague, who could invent a story of a man confronting the loneliness of life on a desert island, may be regarded as the forefather of Thoreau's book. The narrative of *Walden* is a composite of Thoreau's experiences in and around Concord. The little facts are so assembled as to constitute a lively fable. Thoreau blended his wide reading and his purposeful observations to the need of a thesis: and in his mind he had proved his "experiment" long before he began it. In the process of ordering, assembling, imagining, and interpreting, the artist often took possession of his data in a robust, humorous, whimsical, paradoxical, hammered style.

Walden has moments of exquisite beauty when the disciplined verbal power finds a tone and a mood expressing Thoreau's deepest artistry. . . . (pp. 29-30)

So too Thoreau can endow his narrative with the cadence of a child's storybook. . . . (p. 30)

Walden belongs with the literature of imaginary voyages which yet possess, within the imagined, a great reality of their own. It contains a rustic charm, a tender lyricism in the pages devoted to the seasons and to animal life around the pond and in the neighboring woods. (p. 31)

He is at his most imaginative—that is, his ear is perhaps truest to poetry—in the playful chapter in which he tells of his "brute neighbors" beginning with a sylvan dialogue between a Hermit and a Poet. One feels in the writing of these pages echoes of the playfulness of Carlyle; but in terms of posthumous influence this passage may have importance in its striking resemblance to the recurrent rhythms of James Joyce's *Finnegans Wake*. It was inevitable that Joyce, early in his "Anna Livia Plurabelle" section, should pun on "Concord and the Merrimake," for that chapter is compounded of river names and water imagery and associations. Thoreau's "Was that a farmer's noon horn which sounded from beyond the woods just now?" and Joyce's "Is that the Poolbeg flasher beyant, pharphar, or a fireboat coasting nyar the Kishna?" seem to have common stylistic origins and the entire Thoreauvian passage finds strong echoes— in an Irish accent—in passages in *Finnegans Wake*. Thoreau writes: "Hark! I hear a rustling of the leaves. Is it some ill-fed village hound yielding to the instinct of the chase? or the lost pig which is said to be in these woods, whose tracks I saw after the rain? It comes on apace; my sumachs and sweetbriers tremble." This has a singular rhythmic charm and one can find its parallel in Joyce. Did Thoreau and Joyce (who had much in common in their alienated temperaments) derive the rhythms and cadences from some common source? or did the Irish writer, in his exploration of rivers and water music, latch onto the peculiar Thoreauvian trouvaille of this chapter. In the strange world of letters in which songs sung in one country become new songs in another, the words of Thoreau by the Concord River have a powerful kinship with those of Joyce by the Liffey. (p. 33)

"Civil Disobedience" is an unusually cogent statement for Thoreau, who was a man of sentiment rather than of profound thought and who tended often to contradict himself. It remains a remarkable statement on behalf of individualism, as well as man's right to oppose and dissent. In the frame of Thoreau's life, however, it reveals the arbitrary nature of his philosophy. His defense of John Brown, with his espousal of violence in that instance, is hardly the voice of the same man. In both lectures, to be sure, Thoreau condemns government; but the preacher of nonviolence suddenly forgets his preachings. Brown had been wantonly destructive; he had staged a brutal massacre in Kansas and killed innocents. He was a man whose fanaticism might have made him in other circumstances a brutal Inquisitor. Thoreau's involvement in his cause has in it strong elements of hysteria. The passive countenance closes its eyes to truth; it sees only Brown's cause and Brown's hatred of authority. It does not see his cruelty or his counter-imposition of authority. The world has wisely chosen to remember **"Civil Disobedience"** rather than the three John Brown lectures—**"A Plea for Captain Brown,"** **"The Last Days of John Brown,"** and **"After the Death of John Brown."** Whether the personal anarchism Thoreau preached is possible in every age remains to be seen. In his philosophy Thoreau saw only his own dissent; he seems not to have thought of the dangers of tyranny by a minority, as of a majority. (pp. 38-9)

[Thoreau's] journal was the mirror of his days; but it is not an autobiographical record in the usual sense. It is one of the more impersonal journals of literary history. Thoreau made it the account book of his days. There are notes on his readings, his observations of nature, his record of walks, scraps of talk, observations of neighbors; on occasion the journal becomes a log, a statistical record. . . . One finds in it much matter-of-factness and little feeling. "The poet must keep himself unstained and aloof," said Thoreau and his journal is distinctly "aloof." One discerns in it a continuing note of melancholy; there is little humor; the vein is always one of high seriousness. Mankind is regarded in the mass; the generalizations are large; there is not much leaning toward the precisions of science. Nor

can one find any record of growth in these pages, some of them turgid and dull, others lucid and fascinating. From 1837 to 1861 we see the same man writing; he has learned little. If one notes a difference it is that he begins by being philosophical and in the end is more committed to observation.

The journal suggests that Thoreau was incapable of a large effort as a writer. He learned to be a master of the short, the familiar essay; he made it lively and humanized it with his whimsicalities. The method of the journal was carried over into his principal works, the journal providing the raw data, filed always for later use. . . . The assiduity with which he applied himself to his writing ultimately bore fruit. If Thoreau never forged a style and filled his work with the echoes of other styles, he nevertheless in the end learned his trade. Possessing no marked ego at the beginning of his adult life, he created a composite ego; and he learned to write by using a series of rhetorical tricks. (pp. 39-40)

Men will continue to discover these strange ambiguities in the author of **Walden**. If we are to dress a literary portrait of him, we must place him among those writers in whom the human will is organized to a fine pitch in the interest of mental and emotional survival. We must rank him with the "disinherited" and the alienated, with the writers who find themselves possessed of unconquerable demons and who then harness them in the service of self-preservation. Out of this quest sometimes mere eccentricity emerges; at other times art. There are distinct pathological traits in Thoreau, a constant sense—a few have discerned it—of inner disintegration which leads Thoreau in his **Walden** imagery to a terrible vision of human decay. One may venture a guess that this little observed Poesque streak in Thoreau testified to a crisis of identity so fundamental that Thoreau rescued himself only by an almost superhuman self-organization to keep himself, as it were, from falling apart. In doing this he clung obsessively to nature. A much deeper history of Thoreau's psyche may have to be written to explain his tenuous hold on existence in spite of the vigor of his outdoor life: his own quiet desperation, his endless need to keep a journal ("as if he had no moment to waste," said his friend Channing), and his early death of tuberculosis at forty-five in Concord during the spring of 1862. His works were the anchor of his days. He overcame dissolution during his abbreviated life by a constant struggle to assert himself in words. Some such strivings shaped his own recognition of his "crooked genius." (pp. 42-3)

> *Leon Edel, in his* Henry D. Thoreau, *University of Minnesota Press, Minneapolis, 1970, 47 p.*

JAMES McINTOSH (essay date 1974)

[McIntosh focuses on the conflicts, inconsistencies, and polarities inherent in Thoreau's consciousness and his interpretation of nature. His struggle to express proper balance between himself and nature, McIntosh suggests, is reminiscent of the German and English Romantic nature poets. Moreover, Thoreau's quest and his use of "a rhetoric of 'programmed inconsistency',"have lent "the romantic interpretation of nature a new experimental validity."]

Thoreau evades generalization. He packs his thoughts close to one another and gives each thought such immediacy that it cannot be fitted neatly into an argument. This concentration demands unusual reading. It is one reason for examining his conflicting wishes alongside his ideas. One often needs to take moving pictures of his mind as it emerges from sentence to sentence within a given episode or essay.

As we read Thoreau closely, we discover that his work is shot through with what one might call a philosophical contrary-mindedness. He had a tendency to push ideas to extremes, and another tendency to take opposed positions on a given question if he felt the truth was not simple. These two tendencies often occur together. He pits one extreme statement against another in a rhetoric of "programmed inconsistency." This means that his writings on nature are full of consciously designed anti-thetical fragments for which he provides no obvious resolution. But though his fragments often pull against each other, and though Thoreau faces their awkward conjunctions honestly, the general thrust of his work is to make them subservient to a consistent larger purpose. He struggled not to get lost in frag-ments and to express, both subtly and simply, his own affirming vision of the life in nature and his relation to it. (p. 11)

The nature which Thoreau found around him was chaotic, various and ever changing, but was nevertheless also a single organic world, ever the same. In order to love it accurately, he learned to perceive its changes by adopting continually dif-ferent stances toward it; he worked in his writing to express his shifting responses to a single, yet mutable reality. "I have travelled a good deal in Concord," he wrote in the third para-graph of *Walden*. This means in part that he reflectively ex-plored a good deal in nature; and he developed a variety of modes of thought to do justice to the variety he found. If there is a moral lesson implicit in such tactics, it is a lesson in flexibility and faithfulness toward what one loves. (p. 17)

One of his central purposes is to keep in touch with the things of nature, with its temporal rhythms and its gifts to the senses, in order to apprehend more and more deeply the significance of nature as a whole. Nature writ large is Thoreau's chief article of faith and doubt, and writ small is the world he loved and expressed. (Some have argued that Thoreau was primarily an artist or a social thinker, not a writer concerned with nature, but we need not restrict his interest in nature to his skill in botany and surveying, or his talent for conversing with chip-munks.) Ultimately, nature with all its incoherency is one for Thoreau, one subject and one source for his being. Yet in the process of living with it, Thoreau maneuvers to accommodate his writing to its shifting appearances. Obviously, he feels more than one way about nature. He is by turns braced and gentled by it; he loves and occasionally fears it. His relation with it is not so easy or automatic as we sometimes lazily think.

In his view of the promise and difficulty of nature, Thoreau resembles the great English and German romantic poets of nature from Goethe to Keats, especially Goethe and Words-worth. . . . [The] more thoughtful romantic naturalists, in-cluding Thoreau, found it by no means easy to live in nature; their complex engagement with its mystery is an eminent fea-ture of their work.

A paramount reason for this complexity and difficulty for Tho-reau is that as a self-conscious romantic he is always aware, with varying degrees of awareness depending on the occasion, that he cannot achieve identity or perfect sharing with nature, that indeed his spiritual concerns and his imagination tend to propel him away from nature toward higher—or more ephem-eral—worlds. Like Goethe and Wordsworth he combines a powerful wish to love nature and even to merge with it, with a consciousness, sometimes explicit, sometimes concealed, of separation. (pp. 18-20)

This consciousness has to be understood to include both his awareness of separation and his desire to overcome it. Often Thoreau is trying to get part way out of his own isolated mind and closer to nature, to exist in a border area between that mind and nature. He often conceives of the mental faculty of imagination not as separating him from nature but as relating him to it. He imagined his bean field and cabin as his own personal space between the town and the forest, and he pre-sented himself as a mediator between the civilized and the wild. Similarly, he made it his business to think his way back and forth between the civilizations of Europe and Asia and the wilderness of America. In parallel maneuvers, he was con-cerned to bring spirit and body, intellectual consciousness and unconsciousness into harmonious relations. (p. 21)

The basic conflicts in Thoreau, between the desire for a sep-arated self and the desire for nature, between the aspiration for a higher law and the aspiration to live naturally in his own body, appear as formal elements, patterns of consciousness in his work. Indeed, he often attains form and coherence by a display of consciousness, rather than by a systematic argument or an arrangement of images or symbols. . . . Thoreau makes literary use of his own conflicts and exploits his own incon-sistencies. The patterns that we observe in his work are thus often patterns of consciousness: opposed attitudes vibrating against each other in the crucible of an essay, a poem, or a day's journal. Some of these patterns are intended; they are clear examples of Thoreau's conscious art. For example, in the chapter **"Higher Laws"** from *Walden* he is intentionally playing off his own opposed propensities toward "the wild" and "the good" against each other. Other patterns are gen-erated less intentionally but are sometimes equally interesting. In such cases, his desires, as they are juxtaposed, reconciled, or left unreconciled, create their own patterns. For example, his account of his excursion up Mt. Wachusett is animated by two conflicting desires that are vivid in his mind as long as the episode lasts, but as he presents his narrative it seems that he is not aware of the conflict. In both these examples, whether the patterns we see are planned or unplanned, the play of conflict in Thoreau's attitude toward nature makes for intensity. Because they are full of intellectual and emotional excitement, his patterns solicit our attention, sometimes our affection, as readers. We are provoked and beguiled by them. They help us to make sense out of what we read as we take it in. Part of Thoreau's general aim is to work on us in this way. He is an artist who lets shapes happen within his writing.

Conflicts in Thoreau's consciousness create form and intensity in his work. . . . The conflicts I discuss are seldom directly psychological, but are conflicts felt in an epistemological pre-dicament: they result from his being a separated romantic ob-server trying to represent the truth and feel of nature, the facts as he sees them and his feelings about them. Though he is trying to sort out his attitudes as he writes, it would be a mistake to imagine that he wants his conflicts perfectly resolved. If nature is many-sided and his attitudes towards it diverse, he will seek to express that many-sided diversity. As he himself thought, his work in relation to nature is not dramatic (he does not cast out possibilities), but epic (he entertains them in a wavering and mixed and eternal dialectic). He achieves his amplitude of perspective by indulging in what one might call his contrary-mindedness: his specifically Thoreauvian tendency to contradict or qualify himself or write in paradoxes or pose a problem in several different ways. (pp. 22-4)

One purpose of Thoreau's programmed inconsistency is to make sense of nature as a whole, to comprehend the multiplicity of the entire natural world he lived in. The diverse meanings of "nature" shade into each other. . . . Taken together, they are to be regarded not as an array of concepts, to be separated from each other in the manner of Lovejoy, but as comprising a single beloved realm, a theatre of operation for Thoreau's psyche. Provisionally, I will define that realm: His "nature" is the nonhuman, external world of rocks, trees and plants, oceans and rivers, animals and insects. It is felt by him as interrelated, as one; and it is for him sometimes not only the aggregate of things but also the single, surging life force that animates and organizes these things. When he uses "nature" to refer to human beings, he means by it that part of man that is external to the human mind and not altered by it—thus nature may include a man's body, his unschooled impulses, his wildness, and his unconscious. Both the wildness of the landscape and his own sensual wildness, then, are nature. Both are outside of the more conscious self, part of a separate life that he would earnestly explore.

When Thoreau thinks of nature he does not jumble in confusion the disparate meanings of the word which he draws from the history of ideas. Rather, he takes the natural world as he concretely experiences it and calls that nature; for Thoreau, existence precedes essence, except that he is enough of a romantic holist and a nineteenth-century American to assume from the start that nature is one large realm to be identified with one large name. This implies, among other things, that when Thoreau experiences hostility in the natural world, he is still experiencing nature. Despite all his efforts to love and explore it, a residue of nature remains alien to him. "We live within her and are strangers to her." It is natural to feel alienated in nature as well as to feel at home in it. Nature in its very being fosters in the romantic writer the desire to feel his connection with it; but it also fosters at times a different consciousness, a recognition of its difference from man.

Thoreau's changing feelings toward nature as he experiences it inform the dynamic texture of his writing. His attitude frequently shifts almost from sentence to sentence as the scene emerges before him. Indeed, his scenes are sometimes constituted and imagined from a series of changing perspectives. Nor does he shift his stance only by changing his abstract mind. Rather, he sometimes shifts with his whole knowing-body, changes the way he senses nature as well as the way he conceives it. Thus the texture of his descriptions and narratives is volatile and dramatic from moment to moment, even if his larger perspective remains epic and constant. The excitement of some of his work is created by this potential for flickering drama; yet we should recognize that this drama dissipates in a repeated experience of reassurance, that his volatile side is balanced by a contrary ability to rest in loving descriptions of the body of nature. (pp. 26-7)

Polarity is also embedded in the texture of Thoreau's writing. Though he found it in Emerson, it is a conscious device and doctrine entirely congenial to his native contrary-mindedness. He is a man of strong, antithetical tendencies, all of which he would represent justly rather than disavow. Polarity is a useful means for leaving open such a conflict as that between his philosophical or puritanical asceticism and his romantic love of sensation. We have already seen him take diametrically opposed positions on nature, without trying to reconcile the differences. Some of his conscious oppositions are specifically Emersonian. The juxtaposition of chapter titles in **Walden** (**"Solitude"** and **"Visitors,"** for example) recalls Emerson's juggling of abstractions in his own titles. Especially in the

Week, Thoreau employs some of the same juxtapositions of values that one finds in Emerson—masculine and feminine, action and contemplation, East and West, Hindu and Yankee. (pp. 38-9)

Necessary to Thoreau's practice of exaggeration is his willingness to give himself up to the impression of the moment, on which he focuses only temporarily, and to allow each differing moment its own importance. The preference given to "this hour over all other hours" . . . is consonant with Thoreau's preference for living in the present, from moment to moment. If the truth of one moment contradicts the truth of the next—which frequently happens for him—he will exaggerate the expression of each, creating a polarity. He will not be bothered by the contradiction, but will exhibit it as a sign of his many-sidedness.

Thoreau's notion of extra-vagance is one feature of what amounts to a private theory of expression, which he developed over the years in his scattered comments on the process of writing. A central tenet of this theory is that a writer has a duty to the moment as it happens; it is his business to record the thoughts that occur to him in response to each moment, accurately, vigorously and expressively. By accumulating a store of such records, he will have honest materials with which to build his "true expression." (pp. 41-2)

But this emphasis on half-unconscious responsiveness is only one pole of Thoreau's theory. A central problem for him was how to become a "poet," a collector of beautiful moments and a bard of regeneration, without becoming what he sometimes called an "artist," an artificial writer, a poet encumbered with too much European form, too much inherited structure of any kind. Despite his disclaimers, Thoreau was an insistent artist of his own sort; his work is full of rare efforts. He is happy to collect and display "each smoother pebble and each shell more rare," as he wrote in **"The Fisher's Son,"** his 1840 verse testament to his vocation. Thoreau was thus well aware that he was a careful writer; but at the same time the metaphor of the shell-collector is characteristic of him in its small-scale image of art and the artist. He generally describes the artistic process as one of selecting exquisite specimens or of refining rough materials into small, separable objects. (p. 42)

The problem remained for Thoreau of finding an esthetic conception for works longer than single sentences or paragraphs. If his "compositions" were to be only accumulations of disparate transcripts, how could they appear as perspicuous wholes for his readers, even if each transcript were thoroughly reworked as a separate unit? Like his contemporaries, Hawthorne, Emerson and Dickinson, Thoreau felt a Puritan's reticence in exercising his shaping spirit of Imagination openly and obviously on a large scale. Large artistic structures, like pyramids and temples, were likely to be violations of nature as well as monuments of human pride. How was he as a New England poet to devise structures that would be both natural and shapely?

Thoreau found no easy answers to this question, but his work everywhere bears the indications of his efforts to achieve a thorough yet natural craftsmanship. (p. 43)

One reason for Thoreau's use of polarities is that he seems to have felt that they provided a structure for his self-presentations without the simple-mindedness of straightforward argument or the factual distortion of fiction. By exhibiting his random responses in opposition to one another, he was being true to the conflicts and inconsistencies in his own mind, and also giving form to them. If he does not always use his polarities as features of his conscious designs, they certainly find their way into the underlying patterns which give coherence as well as dramatic and intellectual tension to his writing. (p. 45)

The device of polarity specifically helps Thoreau to write in depth about his chief epistemological concern, the separation he felt between mind and nature. If he presents one point of view toward nature in one paragraph and the opposite point of view in another, he may circumvent the demand of his readers that he say everything he has to say about the subject at once. Thoreau simply has too many diverse ideas and feelings about nature to fit them into a single sustained argument or description. His polarities then become part of a larger strategy of persistent self-qualification. By returning to nature over and over in separate compositions with a new perspective and a qualified attitude, he achieves a multiple perspective on a multifarious subject; he can thus reassess, correct and improve his account of his relation to nature. Thoreau never reaches final conclusions about nature, never attempts to define it, as Emerson rightly remarked in the Graveside address [see excerpt above, 1862]; instead he presents us with a rich and varied collection of fragmentary attitudes. His relation to nature changes continually—his stance shifts. As he bends and turns he is always trying to discover or recover that perfect stance that will express a proper balance between himself and nature. (p. 46)

Thoreau's willingness to be open to the anarchic possibilities of perception could make him feel a nothingness in himself, as if he were ''a spiritual football'' or ''a dandelion down that never alights.'' But, on the other hand, it is one of his achievements in **Walden** that he projects himself as a perceptive mind-body, an unsettled, meditative, richly inconsistent egotistical sensibility. He presents no single self-image that we can grasp and label. He narrates no straightforward cause-and-effect autobiography. He does not gratify us with a set of interrelated typical attributes. He asks us instead to go beyond these forms that we usually focus on and observe within a man thinking and feeling.

The idea of symbolic wholeness of personality is breaking down in all the great followers of Emerson. For better and for worse, Thoreau, Whitman, Hawthorne, Melville, and Dickinson—as well as Emerson himself—present us with a new conception of human identity as unsettled and protean. (p. 300)

Since Thoreau makes Concord and its wilder rural surroundings reflect him, his effort to understand and describe this landscape from many standpoints and even in contradictory ways is a peculiar, Thoreauvian method of being more fully, more comprehensively human. He is not content to express a fixed personality, but wants all the personal variety his perceptions will bring him. His version of nature is at once broad and subtle enough to provide a theatre for the varied tendencies of his mind. He has the courage and the intelligence to acknowledge both the natural man and the antinaturalist in himself. He cannot be the bittern or the fox, but he knows that something in him would be, and he is willing to experiment with that impulse. By refusing to deny the idea of nature, or any aspect of his sensuous experience of it, or any part of himself that would come in contact with it, he has given the romantic interpretation of nature a new experimental validity. (pp. 301-02)

> *James McIntosh, in his* Thoreau As Romantic Naturalist: His Shifting Stance toward Nature, *Cornell University Press, 1974, 310 p.*

FREDERICK GARBER   (essay date 1977)

The actions through which we organize our relations to the world are graphically imaged on the map which shows where Americans have cleared spaces for themselves in the continental wilderness. Pioneering in America, opening up either a piece of Concord's woods or the unclaimed wilderness in Maine, is therefore an extension of an essential, elemental enterprise, proper to all men as functioning beings. (p. 10)

Each space taken away (''reclaimed'') from nature is a point of human reference within it, something that a man has made out of the undeveloped, the unencumbered, the unenclosed. (In certain of his moods Thoreau spoke of it as the unredeemed.) The act of clearing, then, is a distinctively human one: insofar as it is an act of consciousness, it is what all men do when they seek to make their worlds; insofar as it is a pioneer act in the literal wilderness it is what men do best when they are fully themselves, pitting their creative energies against the unredeemed vastness outside their private enclosures. . . . The act [for Thoreau] is both a discovery about what the world is like (or ought to be) and what he himself is like. In the same act he organizes his perception of himself and of his world. A clearing in the forest is therefore not only an instance of what consciousness can do, redeeming a piece of nature; it is also an image of the redeeming consciousness itself, the cleared place within which one stands and does one's relating to experience. Furthermore, whatever consciousness gains through these creative acts leads to an increase in the content of the mind. (p. 11)

Redemption, then, can be subjective, an enrichment and cultivation of the world within as well as a reclamation of the world without. Those activities are counterparts and can have a considerable effect on each other, as . . . Thoreau affirmed when he was hoeing his bean field or surveying. Despite the poet's frequent uneasiness, transforming a bog into a garden means that one may clear a garden within oneself, a bit of subjective paradise that is enclosed and fruitful and civil. Thoreau's faith in the subjective potential of the farmer's business was based on the possibility of the collocation of inner and outer landscapes, and therefore he could not look upon the effort to civilize as being entirely negative, whatever his discomfort with the draining of bogs. Of course the subjective reclamation was no more than a possibility, something that could happen but most often did not because the inner materials were either reticent or simply not there. . . . Thoreau held on to the possibility of collocation, preferring to think that field work should be able to effect an increase in the capacities of consciousness, that civility could be fostered by clearing a piece of the wild. In fact, he contributed to the process of cultivation with his own business as a surveyor. One suspects more design than chance in Thoreau's choice of surveying as a mode of making a living: the job fit in too neatly with the kinds of patterning through which he regulated his reading of the world. The surveyor is the harbinger of the wild's redemption, the first sign of civility to reach the uncharted wilderness. The surveyor's tools are civilizing instruments, and his acts are efforts at reclamation. Thoreau took full advantage of the imaginative potential of the characteristics of the job, turning them into tools for his interpretation of American experience. (pp. 13-14)

Outside Concord's perimeter is the wild, or at least the natural. Outside Thoreau's own circumference is not only the wild but Concord and the rest of the world, which includes all other men. Concord, the place of harmonious civility, had men within it with whom he would sometimes have things to do; and what the wild had within itself was both strange (other) and familiar (alike) but with a capacity for surprise that, at several points in Thoreau's experience, startled him into a profound uneasiness. Inside Thoreau's private configuration there was only himself, a fact that created a considerable ambivalence with which he could not always come to terms. He learned very quickly that the shape of the structure through which his consciousness functioned was that of a prison as well as a paradise. It kept other men out while it kept part of him in, however much he wanted to make that part available now and then. These complications in his relations with others revealed limitations in what he could do with consciousness, and those restrictions were to find their parallels in his work with everything else outside his private perimeter. Thoreau discovered more enforced separateness, and at more levels, than the conventional pieties of Concord would recognize or accept. He came to see that the desires of the redemptive imagination had to take all of these paradoxes into consideration, and he found it necessary to organize the work of his consciousness accordingly.

One of the most persistent activities in Thoreau's life was the putting of spaces between himself and other men, making those "suitable broad and natural boundaries" that seemed necessary for the best kinds of relationship. . . . The visual, spatial configurations with which he patterned his understanding of the self were therefore embodiments of desire, that is, exact specifications of the way he wanted experience to be. It was good that the places men carved out of the surrounding bogs had both a cleared area around their center and also a boundary around the clearing, because in that way other men could be kept distant, within their own proper spheres. (pp. 16-17)

The fluctuations and uneasiness which emerge through the flood of facts in the later journals show that half-wildness, a "chastened primitivism," could not finally be a sufficient resting place for Thoreau. Even at the time he was writing **Walden** he had begun to feel that the imagination was a more fertile and daring creator than nature itself. On the other hand—and this point is not quite contradictory—nature had offered him several resounding defeats, in part because it was always struggling to go on being itself. . . . When Thoreau began to mull over the insufficiencies of nature there were a great many pressures compelling him, some from long past in his experience and observable as early as the ending of the **Week**. He had long suspected—and the suspicion grew with time—that the clearing in the forest, man's life in the woods of this world, was not the best that the imagination could envision for him. The radical cadences of his thought, the advance and sidestep through which a position is promoted and then qualified, work here as well. The structures of consciousness which gave form to Thoreau's worldly experience were lovely in themselves and useful for him, the fruitful discoveries of an extraordinarily flexible imagination. The structures were formative and cohesive because they participated in all aspects of his life in this world and served to give unity to the complex diversity of his explorations. But their inseparability from his earthly business, as it turned out, could be a drawback as well as a positive factor for his shaping spirit: for if nature was seen, at times, to be less than he could conceive it to be, insufficient for the fullest reach of his imagination, then the forms so closely involved with nature might themselves be less than he finally needed, sufficient though they were for his life in this world. He had to go one step further and find forms which would give due acknowledgment to the pull of nature and yet realize that it was not enough. That was the ultimate dilemma for the adequacy of his imagination. (p. 178)

[There] is a community of parallel forms in Thoreau's perception, a set of enclosed shapes through which he organized his interpretation of the world and the relation of his self to experience. In each case the enclosure has the same function for Thoreau: it signifies an act of terrestrial redemption, an act which is not concluded until the enclosure is completed. One realizes that an enclosure is an image of wholeness and completion because one can start anywhere on its circumference and return eventually to where one began: spring leads again to spring; a point at the edge of the clearing is met again after a full perambulation of the edge. The relation of these forms to the circle and sphere, the basic Transcendental images of unity and perfection, is clear and, for Thoreau, quite comforting. Further, each form is opposed to the unformed, to the wild in each instance of human endeavor, to the chaos before Genesis in the instance of the regularity of the seasons. (Thoreau spoke of pure wildness as chaos when he was up on Ktaadn.) Nearly all have to do with the economy of the imagination because they are instances of the imagination's ability to make profitable use out of the materials it receives from the experience of America. With the exception of the round of nature and its diurnal equivalent, which man does not create but discovers, the forms are the product of man's capacity to clean up a piece of experience and make it fully his own, won from the world around him. Skillfully ordered through the energy of consciousness, each form is a gesture of the mind, confirming the imagination's adequacy in its perpetual encounter with the wilderness that reaches up to the edge of its confines. Each, then, is a record of success, an achieved terrestrial redemption. (p. 181)

The round of nature which Thoreau says he became aware of in 1852 is, in its shape and completeness, a grand echo of all the other redemptive forms through which he conducted the deepest business of his life. But it is an echo with a difference because some of those forms are more nearly equivalent than others. The round of nature was technically as redemptive as any other in the set, but what it redeemed him to was essentially just more of the same; and we have now seen so much evidence of Thoreau's mature dissatisfaction with the cyclical that we can specify one basic reason for his discernible uneasiness: a redemption within the round of nature was finally no real redemption at all. At best it would be as incomplete as nature itself had come to seem. His recognition of the insufficiency of natural redemption necessarily followed after his recognition of the ultimate insufficiency of nature. Nature never ceased to be lovely, a prime source for immense satisfactions. No man or creed ever matched what it could do for Thoreau, and though he sometimes wavered he continued to be intensely attracted to it up to the end of his life. To be redeemed back into nature would be a guarantee of certain future satisfactions. Yet nature would still seem incomplete, still be incommensurate with the capacities of the mind, still be the place of transient springs; and *those* facts grew to be more and more significant in the last eight years of Thoreau's life. If he managed to outlive the annuals and the winter chill that killed them, he was still locked within the round of nature which enfolded every creature. All of the enclosed forms which determine so much of the shape of Thoreau's world are redemptive because they are enclosed. To be redeemed within nature was therefore to be a lucky prisoner of the world, both beneficiary and victim at once. Thoreau's need to discover or create enclosures was countered by his concern over their potential for confinement. Nothing defines his uneasiness more precisely than his ambivalence over the effects of the redeeming round of nature. (p. 182)

[Nature] is demonstrably adequate, but it is only naturally so, and the imagination which turned the skunk cabbage into an image of terrestrial redemption had been recognizing for some time that there were vast areas of the mind's desire which even such paradoxical weeds could not fully satisfy. Thoreau's serious play with the cabbage was amusing, consoling, and challenging to the efficacy of his imagination; but when he won out in these and similar contests there was still very much to hope for beyond the promises in weeds.

Thoreau never ceased looking for compromises, but it was clear that he had to find something else because the compromises he did achieve were never sufficiently in his own favor. When he came to terms with nature in his later years—whether through delight or necessity, the pleasures of the woods or the compulsions of the cycle—the compromise was usually in favor of his natural self, and that was fine but not enough. There had been a time when nature could satisfy the spirit more than sufficiently, but there came a time when the satisfactions of the spirit began to separate more and more from nature because the spirit had other needs which grew severe in their urgency. Yet those demands could be only partly appeased, at best. Very often it seemed as though the pure forms that his spirit sought were out beyond the edge of the enclosure which enfolded him and offered him natural satisfactions. Thus, the cyclical repetition of natural processes made a closed circle whose limits would contain Thoreau so long as, and to the degree that, he was natural. . . . [There] is a perceptible sense of frustration which sometimes intensifies into a feeling of entrapment, of being ensnared inside an enclosure whose boundaries were absolutely binding and inflexible. The passage [in *Walden*] which evolves into the myth of the morning paradise is a prime instance of that feeling. Nature's enclosure was in part paradisiacal, often exceptionally so, but it could never be the morning paradise whose atemporal bliss is forever new and unchanging. Because Thoreau was not the kind of mystic who craves dissolution of all contact with palpable experience, the desire for compromise and the occasional feeling of entrapment could only continue.

The round of nature was not the only enclosure within which Thoreau could feel uncomfortably constricted. Several repeated patterns in his perception, and in the imagined wholes he made out of it, indicate that Thoreau had often been somewhat uneasy over confinement within boundaries, even as he was busily making or discovering clearings in the wilderness of the world. (pp. 188-90)

> *Frederick Garber, in his* Thoreau's Redemptive Imagination, *New York University Press, 1977, 229 p.*

JOHN HILDEBIDLE (essay date 1983)

Thoreau as historian follows his own prescription; he does not attempt to present the past. . . . He continually cites his sources, not out of a sense of scholarly protocol, but to remind the reader of the ineradicable distance between the past and present, between the authority and the careful reader. That distance is essential; but the awareness of it does not constitute a full repudiation of history or of the accumulation of second-hand knowledge generally.

History is to Thoreau useful if not presentable—a phrase which fits, as well, the character of the crotchety surveyor he adopts

as his own in **"The Succession of Forest Trees"** and elsewhere. History is a source of context and corroboration, a standard of measurement as useful, in its own way, as a notched stick or a plumbline. What is most effectively measured by history is the degree to which man has fallen, the distance which he must traverse to reach Transcendental sainthood. The nearer one approaches that blessed state, the nearer one comes, that is, to the end of the rainbow or to the bottom of Walden Pond, the less important this standard of measurement becomes—as indeed is true of all of the world's standards and disciplines. This is why the prevalence of historical matter is greater in those works, particularly *A Week* and *Cape Cod,* in which Thoreau is away from his holy place. Going over the ground in Purgatory, Thoreau takes a historical guidebook; he needs no books but his Homer in the shack by the pond.

Thoreau uses history . . . in the ways and with the wariness that characterize the methods of more traditional natural historians like Gilbert White. By insisting on the identification of true history and natural history, and by calling himself, explicitly and implicitly, a natural historian, Thoreau places himself firmly within a methodology and a literary tradition. In Thoreau's time, both the method and the genre were undergoing revision and at times outright attack by a newly professionalizing scientific community. Thoreau's hope seems to have been to maintain the old, and as it turned out dying, synthesis of literature, thought, and scientific inquiry which the naturalists represented. He sets this older, more loose and wide-ranging science against the new professionals; he is, he insists, no scientist but a true scientist. All science, he argues, evaporates at the Transcendental moment; yet even at the rainbow's end—or at least when, later, he tries to render an account of his moment of translation to purer air—the habits of the naturalist stay with him. The single fact will redeem man, the single moment will transform him; but in the evangelizing of the fallen, even the redemptive moment may gain from corroboration.

Thoreau's history is natural not only methodologically; it is natural also in its localism. Emerson had set a biographical model for the new Transcendental history; the result was a history of sorts (and especially of the new, reformed sort) called *Representative Men.* Thoreau's longer works bear the titles not of individuals or of mankind *in toto,* but of places—a river, a pond, a peninsula, a forest, a country. This is, in part, the result of editorial decisions made after Thoreau's death; but it is nonetheless true in an important way to the nature of the works. Thoreau can comprehend Man only by comprehending himself; and, like any naturalist, he can comprehend himself or any other being only in a place. His historical disquisitions and researches, his use of the old authorities, arise most commonly from his consideration of a place—the Concord River, for instance, or a Cape Cod town, or the city of Quebec. His histories are, in their origins at least, more geographical or topographical than biographical. Of course those histories are populated, and often quite memorably so, by the famous (Champlain, for instance) and by the nearly (or even altogether) forgotten, like Hannah Dustan in *A Week* or the Reverend Osborn and the Indian Lieutenant of Eastham. But no matter how colorful or exemplary, these figures are significant only in relation to a landscape, and in relation to Thoreau himself. Emerson established the equation of history with biography and autobiography; Thoreau adds geography to the formula but holds true to the fundamental Emersonian point. The only history of real importance is that history which the self can somehow re-experience, by walking, in an image much admired by both Emerson and Thoreau, over the ground personally. *Cape Cod* is, in part, the literary record of just such an effort—a personal excursion through history by way of the terrain.

This insistence on place—a characteristic element of the genre of natural history—is the consistent note in Thoreau's work which serves to make him the most *grounded*, the most settled and topographical of Transcendentalists. It provides too a workable method of using history as a sort of guidebook to the all-important present, to be employed skeptically, as any seasoned traveler does any guidebook. And it allows Thoreau to be true both to his love of antiquarian lore and to his firm belief that only by using all the senses to comprehend the immediate experience can one proceed in the radical and (in his case) unrelenting task of obeying the very old injunction: Know Thyself. (pp. 147-49)

Thoreau's eye for the limitations of science, his awareness of those states of being where science is simply of no interest, and his readiness to see the error in any authority, scientific or historical, are always strong and always the final measure in his estimation of the usefulness of the accounts which he consults. And . . . this habitual wariness is a fundamental element in the method of the naturalist. It is important to remember, too, that it is *wariness*, and not, as some critics have said, something more absolutely dismissive. Even as Thoreau remarks on the barrenness and error of science, he makes science and sympathy equally important and repeats his wish to ''go a little further'' in the direction of the world's science.

The desire to be inclusive, eclectic, and (in intention, at least) synthetic informs all of Thoreau's work and helps to explain its apparent disorder at many points. Thoreau rejects disciplines and titles insofar as they are restrictive and absolute; he will not be a scientist by the world's standards because, even in his day, to be a scientist seemed to mean one could be nothing else. This again is a part of the appeal of the older tradition of the naturalist, which did not draw firm lines of limitation and which presented models of men who at least attempted to be scientists, philosophers, and writers at very nearly the same moment. The world's conjunction is *or*—be scientist *or* writer. Thoreau's is, repeatedly, *and*—he will, he insists, be a scholar *and* Adam, be a mystic, a Transcendentalist, *and* a natural philosopher to boot. (pp. 151-52)

> *John Hildebidle, in his* Thoreau: A Naturalist's Liberty, *Cambridge, Mass.: Harvard University Press, 1983, 174 p.*

ADDITIONAL BIBLIOGRAPHY

Anderson, Charles R. *The Magic Circle of Walden*. New York: Holt, Rinehart and Winston, 1968, 306 p.
　　A reading of *Walden* ''as if it were a poem.'' Anderson emphasizes the structure, imagery, and diction of *Walden* and incorporates information from Thoreau's collected works to show the lyricism of Thoreau's style even in his journals and letters.

Atkinson, J. Brooks. *Henry Thoreau: The Cosmic Yankee*. New York: Alfred A. Knopf, 1927, 158 p.
　　A critical biography which presents Thoreau in a rather negative light. Though he praises his prose, Atkinson deems Thoreau's verse ''execrable.'' He attributes to Thoreau's misanthropy his slow development as reflected in his writings.

Bazalgette, Léon. *Henry Thoreau: Bachelor of Nature*. Translated by Van Wyck Brooks. New York: Harcourt, Brace and Co., 1924, 357 p.

A French biography without ''any claim to erudition.'' Bazalgette weaves together a narrative of Thoreau's life using the testimonies of some of his contemporaries.

Brooks, Van Wyck. ''Thoreau'' and ''Thoreau at Walden.'' In his *The Flowering of New England: 1815-1865*, pp. 286-302, pp. 359-73. New York: E. P. Dutton & Co., 1936.
　　Two affectionate and anecdotal biographical sketches of Thoreau. Brooks discusses Thoreau's life and ideas as they were influenced by the social and intellectual community of Concord.

Canby, Henry Seidel. ''The Modern Thoreau.'' *The Dail* LIX, No. 698 (15 July 1915): 54-5.
　　Canby suggests that Thoreau's nature studies link him with his pioneer ancestors because they explore the connection between man and his environment. Thoreau's success as a nature writer, Canby concludes, is due to the fact that he was interested both in scientific minutae and in philosophical issues inherent in the study of nature.

———. *Thoreau*. Boston: Houghton Mifflin Co., 1939, 508 p.
　　One of the first important critical biographies of Thoreau. Canby stresses Thoreau's importance as a creative thinker, social critic, and stylist. He also suggests, however, that Thoreau ''was too maladjusted psychologically'' to reach his full potential in any one area.

Cavell, Stanley. *The Senses of ''Walden.''* 1972. Reprint. San Francisco: North Point Press, 1981, 160 p.
　　An exploration of the philosophical bases of *Walden*. Cavell views Thoreau as a writer who wished to fulfill his prophetic calling, yet also felt the need to guard his words from his culture's ''demented wish to damage and deny them.''

Channing, William Ellery. *Thoreau the Poet-Naturalist*. 1902. Reprint. New York: Biblo and Tannen, 1966, 397 p.
　　A biography written by one of Thoreau's best friends. Generally considered overly complimentary to Thoreau, Channing's work is significant because it was the first to use excerpts from Thoreau's journals. To Channing, Thoreau's most outstanding characteristics were his ''wondrous'' imagination, his humor, his love of nature, and his moral conviction.

Christy, Arthur. ''Part Three: Thoreau and Oriental Asceticism.'' In his *The Orient in American Transcendentalism*, pp. 185-233. New York: Columbia University Press, 1932.
　　An analysis of the influence of oriental literature on Thoreau's work. Christy discusses Thoreau's reading of sacred Hindu literature and his translations from the Hindu, and he suggests that Thoreau's Walden experiment can be viewed as a Yogi retreat.

Cook, Reginald Lansing. *The Concord Saunterer*. Middlebury, Vt.: Middlebury College Press, 1940, 91 p.
　　A study of Thoreau as a naturalist. Cook suggests that Thoreau's attitude was that of a poet rather than that of a scientist. Though Thoreau aimed for an intimate relationship with nature, according to Cook, he ''did not make the mistake of intellectualizing nature into an abstraction.''

———. *Passage to Walden*. New York: Russell & Russell, 1966, 253 p.
　　An account of Thoreau's relationship with nature, from his early days as a ''saunterer'' to his later attempts to link in his writing style the vitality of nature with ''the cultivation of the human spirit.'' Cook's aim is to convey ''the essential quality and evoke the richness of his correspondence with nature.''

Fiedler, Leslie A. ''The Basic Myths, III: Two Mothers of Us All.'' In his *The Vanishing American*, pp. 84-108. New York: Stein and Day, 1968.*
　　An analysis of Thoreau's impulse to create a new American mythology which would present the conflict between the white settler and the Indian. Examining Thoreau's lifelong preoccupation with the Indian, Fiedler concludes that, for Thoreau, prelapsarian America was characterized by maleness, primitiveness, and wildness.

Floan, Howard R. "Emerson and Thoreau." In his *The South in Northern Eyes: 1831 to 1861*, pp. 51-70. Austin: University of Texas Press, 1958.*

A brief examination of Thoreau's attitude toward slavery. Floan maintains that Thoreau was an unusual abolitionist because he did not dwell on the polarities of North and South, freedom and slavery, but instead focused on the issue of human rights.

Glick, Wendell, ed. *The Recognition of Henry David Thoreau: Selected Criticism Since 1848*. Ann Arbor: The University of Michigan Press, 1969, 381 p.

A collection of key critical essays on Thoreau's works, dating from 1848 to the late 1960s, that includes essays by James Russell Lowell, Robert Louis Stevenson, Mark Van Doren, Raymond Adams, and others.

Harding, Walter, ed. *Thoreau: A Century of Criticism*. Dallas: Southern Methodist University Press, 1954, 205 p.

A collection of the essays that were essential to the shaping of Thoreau's critical reputation. Included are essays by A. Bronson Alcott, Henry S. Salt, Alfred Kazin, and others.

———, ed. *Henry David Thoreau: A Profile*. American Century Series: American Profiles, edited by Aïda DiPace Donald. New York: Hill and Wang, 1971, 260 p.

A collection of scholarly and critical essays, chronologically arranged from the 1860s to the 1960s. Included are essays by Edward Waldo Emerson, Charles Ives, and Raymond D. Gozzi, among others. Harding also provides a brief biography of Thoreau and a selected bibliography of Thoreau criticism.

———, and Meyer, Michael. *The New Thoreau Handbook*. New York: New York University Press, 1980, 238 p.

A brief overview of Thoreau's life and works. The authors include sections on Thoreau's sources, ideas, art, and reputation.

Hawthorne, Julian. "Henry David Thoreau" and "Studying Nature with Thoreau." In his *The Memoirs of Julian Hawthorne*, edited by Edith Garrigues Hawthorne, pp. 108-14, pp. 114-16. New York: Macmillan Co., 1938.

A memoir of Thoreau by Nathaniel Hawthorne's son. Hawthorne suggests that Thoreau was encouraged yet overly influenced by Ralph Waldo Emerson. In addition, Hawthorne states that Thoreau was largely a "fanatic," and "hampered and prevented by a brain poisoned by philosophy."

Jones, S. A., ed. *Pertaining to Thoreau*. 1901. Reprint. Folcroft, Pa.: Folcroft Press, 1969, 171 p.

A collection of the earliest reviews of Thoreau's works.

Kazin, Alfred. "Relevance of the American Past: Thoreau's Lost Journal." In his *Contemporaries*, pp. 47-50. Boston: Little, Brown and Co., 1962.

A discussion of the tone of Thoreau's "lost journal" of 1840-41. Kazin argues that, like other famous Romantic journals, Thoreau's journals "show the meeting of the inner and the external worlds." But Kazin suggests that Thoreau's straining "for an 'objectivity' that he could only simulate" actually reduced his observations to mere facts instead of imaginative musings.

Leary, Lewis. "Thoreau." In *Eight American Authors: A Review of Research and Criticism*, edited by Floyd Stovall, pp. 153-206. New York: W. W. Norton & Co., 1963.

A bibliographical essay which summarizes and evaluates Thoreau criticism from the 1840s to the 1960s. Leary includes biographical information, as well as sections of criticism on specific subjects in Thoreau's work.

Lebeaux, Richard. *Young Man Thoreau*. Amherst: University of Massachusetts Press, 1977, 262 p.

An analysis of the development of Thoreau's personality based on psychologist Erik Erikson's 'life cycle' model. Lebeaux delves into the circumstances of Thoreau's family and childhood experiences in order to account for his "identity crisis" as an adult.

Metzger, Charles R. *Thoreau and Whitman: A Study of Their Esthetics*. Seattle: University of Washington Press, 1961, 113 p.*

A comparative study of Thoreau's and Whitman's views of art. The two men possessed a transcendental frame of mind, Metzger concludes, yet "persisted in thinking of themselves as practical men rather than theorists." Metzger also states that both men's views of art were influenced by their religious beliefs.

Meyer, Michael. *Several More Lives to Live: Thoreau's Political Reputation in America*. Contributions in American Studies, edited by Robert H. Walker, no. 29. Westport, Conn.: Greenwood Press, 1977, 216 p.

Traces reaction to Thoreau's political ideas from the 1920s to 1970s. Meyer presents "the historical context which influenced the criticism" in each era, and concludes that, ultimately, Thoreau's political ideas do not form a coherent system.

Moldenhauer, Joseph J. "Images of Circularity in Thoreau's Prose." *Texas Studies in Literature and Language* (Summer 1959): 245-63.

A close textual analysis of "the circle as a shaping metaphor" in Thoreau's works. Moldenhauer asserts that the circle "was a basic unit of [Thoreau's] perception," and that it determined the symbolic structure of everything from his smallest images to the overall organization of *A Week on the Concord and Merrimack Rivers* and *Walden*.

Paul, Sherman. *The Shores of America: Thoreau's Inward Exploration*. Urbana: University of Illinois Press, 1958, 433 p.

A discussion of *Walden* as a "spiritual biography or a biography of vocation." Paul traces Thoreau's intellectual development by exploring the origin and growth of his thinking as revealed through his writings.

Poirier, Richard. "Is There an I for an Eye?: The Visionary Possession of America." In his *A World Elsewhere: The Place of Style in American Literature*, pp. 50-92. New York: Oxford University Press, 1966.*

An interpretation of Thoreau's style in *Walden*. Poirier describes *Walden* as "a fantasia of punning," and compares Thoreau's style with those of John Donne and James Joyce. To all three writers, Poirier asserts, ordinary experience is inextricable from visionary experience.

Porte, Joel. *Emerson and Thoreau: Transcendentalists in Conflict*. Middletown, Conn.: Wesleyan University Press, 1966, 226 p.*

Explores the relationship between Emerson and Thoreau in terms of their attitudes toward nature, aesthetics, morality, and Transcendentalism. Porte concludes that for Thoreau "only the body exists," while for Emerson "only spirit exists."

Ruland, Richard, ed. *Twentieth Century Interpretations of "Walden"*. Englewood Cliffs, N.J.: Prentice-Hall, Inc., 118 p.

A collection of critical essays on *Walden*, ranging from short excerpts to lengthy evaluations. Ruland also includes an introduction, chronological chart of Thoreau's life, and a brief bibliography.

Salt, Henry S. *Life of Henry David Thoreau*. Great Writers, edited by Eric Robertson and Frank T. Marzials. London: Walter Scott, 1896, 208 p.

Considered the first scholarly biography of Thoreau. Though Salt implicitly criticizes Thoreau for his inability to grasp the scope of the social problem which slavery presented, he praises him for sparking the revival of interest in "the poetry of natural history."

Seybold, Ethel. *Thoreau: The Quest and the Classics*. Yale Studies in English, edited by Benjamin Christie Nangle, vol. 116. New Haven: Yale University Press, 1951, 148 p.

An examination of the influence of classical literature on Thoreau's work. Charting Thoreau's reactions to classical literature, Seybold presents an interpretation of Thoreau's journals as "spiritual biography." Included are appendices listing classical books Thoreau read and classical quotations extracted from Thoreau's works.

Shanley, J. Lyndon. *The Making of "Walden": With the Text of the First Version*. Chicago: University of Chicago Press, 1957, 208 p.

A textual analysis of the various drafts of the *Walden* manuscript. According to Shanley, the first version was written at Walden in

1846-47, but Thoreau "rewrote it, doubled its length, and re-shaped it" during 1848-54. His revisions, Shanley asserts, provide "insight into his craft and art."

Sherwin, J. Stephen, and Reynolds, Richard C. *A Word Index to Walden with Textual Notes*. Charlottesville: University of Virginia Press, 1960, 165 p.
A listing of the frequency of appearance of all words in *Walden*, intended to aid in "investigations of style and usage," and in locating particular words or passages in *Walden*.

Stewart, Randall. "The Growth of Thoreau's Reputation." *College English* 7, No. 4 (January 1946): 208-14.
A brief analysis of the reasons for the revival of critical interest in Thoreau. Stewart cites the demand for clear prose, as well as reaction to the "urbanization of American life," economic difficulty, and the autonomy of the state.

Stoller, Leo. *After "Walden": Thoreau's Changing Views on Economic Man*. Stanford: Stanford University Press, 1957, 163 p.
Examines the evolution of Thoreau's economic views after *Walden*. Stoller suggests that Thoreau continued to search "for ways by which the ideas of the Walden experiment might be attained in the industrial society it had been opposed to." In particular, according to Stoller, Thoreau revised his thinking about political action and about private property.

Taylor, J. Golden. *Neighbor Thoreau's Critical Humor*. Utah State University Monograph Series, vol. VI, no. 1. Logan: Utah State University Press, 1958, 91 p.
A discussion of the style and function of Thoreau's humor. Taylor concludes that humor was an essential part of Thoreau's self-expression, and that it served to balance his didacticism and sentimentality. Like Mark Twain and Abraham Lincoln, according to Taylor, Thoreau used humor as a vehicle for social criticism, particularly of the church and state.

Thoreau, Henry David. *Consciousness in Concord*. Edited by Perry Miller. Boston: Houghton Mifflin Co., 1958, 243 p.
Presents for the first time the text of Thoreau's "lost" journal, which dates from July 30, 1840 to January 22, 1841. Miller also provides extensive introductory material outlining the history of the lost journal and textual notes.

———. *The Variorum "Walden"*. Edited by Walter Harding. New York: Twayne Publishers, 1962, 320 p.
A compilation of all textual variants of *Walden*, amply annotated, with an introduction and a secondary bibliography.

Whicher, George F. *"Walden" Revisited*. Chicago: Packard and Co., 1945, 93 p.
A centennial revaluation of *Walden* focusing both on biography and style. Whicher perceives a gradual shift in Thoreau's emphasis "from the poetic to the factual," from "homeliness to barrenness." He further asserts that *Walden* is especially successful because Thoreau was able to strike a perfect balance between poetry and fact.

Wolf, William J. *Thoreau: Mystic, Prophet, Ecologist*. Philadelphia: United Church Press, 1974, 218 p.
An interpretation of Thoreau's various guises in his writings. Wolf terms him "the theologian of creation, the apostle of wildness, and the prophet of social action."

Alexis (Charles Henri Maurice Clérel, Comte) de Tocqueville

1805-1859

French essayist, historian, and memoir and travel writer.

Tocqueville's *De la démocratie en Amérique (Democracy in America)* ranks as one of the greatest political, social, and cultural investigations ever written. Generally regarded as the first systematic and thorough analysis of American society and its institutions, *Democracy* was immediately recognized as an important philosophical treatise and is today considered a classic interpretation of the nature and tendencies of democratic governments.

Tocqueville was born into an aristocratic family in Paris. Although he never completely abandoned the values of the aristocratic tradition, he absorbed liberal ideas from childhood. At age fifteen he was sent to the college at Metz, where he studied the writings of several eighteenth-century French philosophers who taught the importance of freedom of inquiry. After completing his courses at Metz, he returned to Paris to study law and in 1827 was appointed an assistant magistrate at the law court in Versailles. There Tocqueville became acquainted with Gustave de Beaumont, a fellow assistant magistrate who shared his liberal interests. When the July Revolution of 1830 established the Orléanist regime of King Louis Phillipe, Tocqueville and Beaumont, whose families were closely identified with the Bourbon cause, were demoted to apprentice magistrates. Having little sympathy with the new government, they applied for and received a leave of absence to study the controversial new prison system in America. Tocqueville and Beaumont's actual motive in going to America, however, was their wish to study its democratic institutions with reference to their bearing upon the political and social questions that underlay the history of violent governmental changes in France.

Tocqueville and Beaumont arrived in Manhattan in May, 1831. During their nine-month stay in America, they toured the country, traveling as far east as Boston, as far west as Green Bay, as far north as Sault Sainte Marie, and as far south as New Orleans. Before Tocqueville left the United States, he had filled several travel notebooks with observations on American democracy and records of his conversations with over two hundred prominent American citizens. When Tocqueville and Beaumont returned to France, they published the result of their official investigations in *Du système pénitentiaire aux États-Unis, et de son application en France (On the Penitentiary System in the United States and Its Application in France)*. This completed, Tocqueville began writing his masterpiece, *Democracy*.

Tocqueville was not enthusiastic about democracy, but he recognized it as an inevitable development. He sought, by analyzing its advantages and disadvantages in the United States, to help France avoid the excesses and emulate the successes of the system. In one of his notes to *Democracy,* he revealed his political position: "Intellectually I have an inclination for democratic institutions, but I am an aristocrat by instinct—that is to say, I despise and fear the mob. I have a passionate love for liberty, law, and respect for rights—but not for democracy." The first part of *Democracy* is a description of specific aspects of American government and politics, such as the Fed-

eral Constitution, the judicial system, and majority rule. In the second part, which is more abstract and philosophical than the first, the advantages and disadvantages of democracy are treated according to their influence on American manners, morals, religion, science, literature, and art. Throughout, Tocqueville predicted the future of many American institutions and suggested antidotes for the negative effects of democracy. According to Tocqueville, the most striking feature of American democracy is the "equality of conditions" among the people. He regarded the gradual development of the principle of equality as a "providential fact" but stressed that the movement toward equality of conditions need not necessarily lead to democratic forms of government. Repeatedly, Tocqueville expressed his fear that the elimination of class distinctions and the banishing of disparities between individuals would result in a loss of personal freedom and initiative, thus rendering individuals in democratic societies particularly susceptible to the "tyranny of the majority."

During the years after the publication of *Democracy* until his death, Tocqueville held a number of official positions in the French government. In 1839, he won a seat in the Chamber of Deputies and was regularly reelected until the downfall of King Louis Phillipe in 1848. After the revolution of February, 1848, he was selected to participate in the drafting of the constitution of the Second Republic. His recollections of the

February Revolution and of his brief service in 1849 as Minister of Foreign Affairs to Louis Napoleon, President of the Republic, are preserved in *Souvenirs de Alexis de Tocqueville (The Recollections of Alexis de Tocqueville)*. Following Louis Napoleon's *coup d'etat* of 1851, Tocqueville retired from politics. For the remainder of his life, he devoted himself to an undertaking that he had long contemplated: a three-part history of the French Revolution and the First Empire. Poor health prevented Tocqueville from finishing the project and at the time of his death in 1859 he had completed only the first part, *L'ancien régime et la révolution (The Old Regime and the Revolution)*, a study of the social and political atmosphere of pre-Revolutionary France, and a portion of the second part, which was intended to be a history of the events of the Revolution. Two chapters of the unfinished second part were published in *Oeuvres et correspondance inédites (Memoir, Letters, and Remains of Alexis de Tocqueville)* but it was not until 1865, in the first collected edition of Tocqueville's writings, that the fragment appeared in its entirety. In *The Old Regime*, which is considered one of the most original interpretations of the Revolution and a landmark of historical scholarship, Tocqueville traced France's passage from a monarchic to a democratic state and seeks to explain why the Revolution occurred in France rather than in any other European country. As in *Democracy*, he explored the mutual relations of liberty and equality; rejecting the commonly held opinion that the Revolution marked a complete break with the past, he attempted to show how the association of democratic aspirations with revolutionary practices had increased the possibility of despotism in France.

Although some commentators, notably A. V. Dicey and J. P. Mayer, maintain that *The Old Regime* is superior to *Democracy*, most agree that the latter represents Tocqueville's finest achievement. *Democracy*'s early and extraordinary success secured Tocqueville's admission to the French Academy and established his fame throughout Europe and America. Critics frequently credit the work's widespread appeal to Tocqueville's impartiality, the acuteness of his observations, and the lucidity of his style. In one of the most famous contemporary reviews of *Democracy*, John Stuart Mill proclaimed the work "the first philosophical book ever written on democracy, as it manifests itself in modern society; a book, the essential doctrines of which it is not likely that any future speculations will subvert. . . ." Mill complained, however, that Tocqueville erred in ascribing certain features of American society to democracy, a criticism that is repeated by such commentators as Emile Faguet, Henry Commager, and George Wilson Pierson. Negative response to *Democracy* focuses primarily on Tocqueville's methods of research and analysis. While some critics argue that Tocqueville presented only those facts that supported his theories, others maintain that he relied too heavily on deductive reasoning, particularly in the second part of *Democracy*. Still others fault Tocqueville for his failure to consult other works on the subject of democracy.

Tocqueville's popularity began to decline during the late 1800s but the twentieth century has seen a renewal of interest in his work. He is alternately approached by modern scholars as a sociologist, historian, moralist, political philosopher, prophet, and pioneer of democratic liberalism. While Faguet, Phillips Bradley, and Robert A. Nisbet maintain that *Democracy* is a sociological examination of the implications of democratic government, other critics share Commager's opinion that *Democracy* primarily displays Tocqueville's "instinct for the jugular vein in history." On the basis of Tocqueville's insistence on

personal freedom in *Democracy*, Harold J. Laski classifies him as one of the foremost exponents of liberalism in the nineteenth century. Although commentators criticize *Democracy* for some errors and omissions, many point out that Tocqueville saw further into the future than any of his contemporaries. Critics marvel at the accuracy of many of his predictions, such as his anticipation of the technological revolution, and praise him for his ability to draw from his American experience principles of universal application. In spite of major transformations in American society since Tocqueville's time, *Democracy* remains significant as a study of the structural aspects and effects of democratic government. The wide variety of critical interpretation of the work attests to the breadth of Tocqueville's analysis and demonstrates the extent of his influence.

PRINCIPAL WORKS

Du système pénitentiaire aux États-Unis, et de son application en France [with Gustave de Beaumont] (essay) 1833
   [*On the Penitentiary System in the United States and Its Application in France*, 1833]
De la démocratie en Amérique (essay) 1835
   [*Democracy in America*, 1838]
De la démocratie en Amérique: Seconde partie (essay) 1840
   [*Democracy in America: Part the Second*, 1840]
L'ancien régime et la révolution (history) 1856
   [*The Old Regime and the Revolution*, 1856]
**Oeuvres et correspondance inédites* (memoir, letters, travel sketches, history, and essay) 1861
   [*Memoir, Letters, and Remains of Alexis de Tocqueville*, 1861]
Souvenirs de Alexis de Tocqueville (memoirs) 1893
   [*The Recollections of Alexis de Tocqueville*, 1896]
Oeuvres, papiers et correspondances (essays, history, memoirs, letters, lectures, and travel sketches) 1951-
"*The European Revolution*" & *Correspondence with Gobineau* (history and letters) 1959

*This work includes a memoir written by Gustave de Beaumont.

ALEXIS DE TOCQUEVILLE   (letter date 1835)

[*In the following excerpt, which is drawn from a letter that Tocqueville wrote to his lifelong friend Eugène Stoffels, Tocqueville delineates his reasons for writing* Democracy. *He explains that in his work he sought primarily to show how society could "march on peaceably towards the fulfillment of its destiny." He states that he took care to bring out the faults of democracy as well as its virtues in an effort to moderate the extravagant hopes of those who regarded democracy as a "brilliant and easily realized dream" and to allay the fears of those who equated democracy with "destruction, anarchy, spoliation, and murder."*]

This is the political object of [*Democracy in America*]:

I wished to show what in our days a democratic people really was; and by a rigorously accurate picture, to produce a double effect on the men of my day. To those who have fancied an ideal democracy, a brilliant and easily realized dream, I endeavoured to show that they had clothed the picture in false colours; that the republican government which they extol, even though it may bestow substantial benefits on a people that can bear it, has none of the elevated features with which their imagination would endow it, and moreover, that such a government cannot be maintained without certain conditions of intelligence, of private morality, and of religious belief, that we, as a nation, have not reached, and that we must labour to attain before grasping their political results.

To those for whom the word democracy is synonymous with destruction, anarchy, spoliation, and murder, I have tried to show that under a democratic government the fortunes and the rights of society may be respected, liberty preserved, and religion honoured; that though a republic may develop less than other governments some of the noblest powers of the human mind, it yet has a nobility of its own; and that after all it may be God's will to spread a moderate amount of happiness over all men, instead of heaping a large sum upon a few by allowing only a small minority to approach perfection. I attempted to prove to them that whatever their opinions might be, deliberation was no longer in their power; that society was tending every day more and more towards equality, and dragging them and every one else along with it; that the only choice lay between two inevitable evils; that the question had ceased to be whether they would have an aristocracy or a democracy, and now lay between a democracy without poetry or elevation indeed, but with order and morality; and an undisciplined and depraved democracy, subject to sudden frenzies, or to a yoke heavier than any that has galled mankind since the fall of the Roman Empire.

I wished to diminish the ardour of the republican party, and, without disheartening them, to point out their only wise course.

I have endeavoured to abate the claims of the aristocrats, and to make them bend to an irresistible future; so that the impulse in one quarter and resistance in the other being less violent, society may march on peaceably towards the fulfilment of its destiny. This is the dominant idea in the book—an idea which embraces all the others. . . . [However, few] have discovered it. I please many persons of opposite opinions, not because they penetrate my meaning, but because, looking at only one side of my work, they think that they find in it arguments in favour of their own convictions. But I have faith in the future, and I hope that the day will come when all will see clearly what now only a few suspect. (pp. 397-98)

> Alexis de Tocqueville, in a letter to Eugène Stoffels on February 21, 1835, in his Memoir, Letters, and Remains of Alexis de Tocqueville, Vol. I, edited by M.C.M. Simpson, translated by Gustave de Beaumont, revised edition, Macmillan and Co., 1861, pp. 397-99.

JOHN STUART MILL   (essay date 1835)

[An English essayist and critic, Mill is regarded as one of the greatest philosophers and political economists of the nineteenth century. At an early age, Mill was recognized as a leading advocate of the utilitarian philosophy of Jeremy Bentham, and he was a principal contributor to the Westminster Review, an English periodical founded by Bentham that later merged with the London Review. During the 1830s, under the influence of William Wordsworth, Samuel Taylor Coleridge, and Auguste Comte, he gradually diverged from Bentham's utilitarianism. As part owner of the London and Westminster Review from 1835-40, Mill was instrumental in modifying the periodical's utilitarian stance. He is considered a key figure in the transition from the rationalism of the Enlightenment to the renewed emphasis on mysticism and

the emotions of the Romantic era. Mill was Tocqueville's greatest champion among English reviewers. His favorable assessment of the first part of Democracy originally appeared in the Westminster Review in October, 1835. Mill summarizes Tocqueville's conclusions in the first part of Democracy and hails the work as the first unbiased and analytic study of its subject. In focusing on Tocqueville's impartiality and analytic ability, Mill sounds critical points that will be repeated throughout the criticism. In a later essay, Mill reviewed the second part of Democracy (1840).]

To depict accurately, and to estimate justly, the institutions of the United States, have been . . . but secondary aims with the original and profound author of [**Democracy in America**]— secondary, we mean, in themselves, but indispensable to his main object. This object was, to inquire, what light is thrown, by the example of America, upon the question of democracy; which he considers as the great and paramount question of our age. (p. 188)

America is usually cited by the two great parties which divide Europe, as an argument for or against democracy. Democrats have sought to prove by it that we ought to be democrats; aristocrats, that we should cleave to aristocracy, and withstand the democratic spirit.

It is not towards deciding this question, that M. de Tocqueville has sought to contribute, by laying before the European world the results of his study of America. He considers it as already irrevocably decided.

The crowd of English politicians, whether public men or public writers, who live in a truly insular ignorance of the great movement of European ideas, will be astonished to find, that a conclusion which but few among them, in their most far-reaching speculations, have yet arrived at, is the point from which the foremost continental thinkers *begin* theirs; and that a philosopher, whose impartiality as between aristocracy and democracy is unparalleled in our time, considers it an established truth, on the proof of which it is no longer necessary to insist, that the progress of democracy neither can nor ought to be stopped. Not to determine whether democracy shall come, but how to make the best of it when it does come, is the scope of M. de Tocqueville's speculations. (pp. 188-89)

There is a country, says he, where the great change, progressively taking place throughout the civilized world, is consummated. In the United States, democracy reigns with undisputed empire; and equality of condition among mankind has reached what seems its ultimate limit. The place in which to study democracy, must be that where its natural tendencies have the freest scope; where all its peculiarities are most fully developed and most visible. In America, therefore, if anywhere, we may expect to learn—first, what portion of human well-being is compatible with democracy in any form; and, next, what are the good and what the bad properties of democracy, and by what means the former may be strengthened, the latter controlled. We have it not in our power to choose between democracy and aristocracy; necessity and Providence have decided that for us. But the choice we are still called upon to make is between a well and an ill-regulated democracy; and on that depends the future well-being of the human race.

When M. de Tocqueville says, that he studied America, not in order to disparage or to vindicate democracy, but in order to understand it, he makes no false claim to impartiality. Not a trace of a prejudice, or so much as a previous leaning either to the side of democracy or aristocracy, shows itself in his work. He is indeed anything but indifferent to the ends, to which all forms of government profess to be means. He manifests the deepest and steadiest concern for all the great interests, material and spiritual, of the human race. But between aristocracy and democracy he holds the balance straight, with all the impassibility of a mere scientific observer. (pp. 196-97)

The bad tendencies of democracy, in his opinion, admit of being mitigated; its good tendencies of being so strengthened as to be more than a compensation for the bad. It is his belief that a government, substantially a democracy, but constructed with the necessary precautions, may subsist in Europe, may be stable and durable, and may secure to the aggregate of the human beings living under it, a greater sum of happiness than has ever yet been enjoyed by any people. The universal aim, therefore, should be, so to prepare the way for democracy, that when it comes, it may come in this beneficial shape; not only for the sake of the good we have to expect from it, but because it is literally our only refuge from a despotism resembling not the tempered and regulated absolutism of modern times, but the tyranny of the Caesars. For when the equality of conditions shall have reached the point which in America it has already attained, and there shall be no power intermediate between the monarch and the multitude; when there remains no individual and no class capable of separately offering any serious obstacle to the will of the government; then, unless the people are fit to rule, the monarch will be as perfectly autocratic as amidst the equality of an Asiatic despotism. Where all are equal, all must be alike free, or alike slaves.

The book, of which we have now described the plan and purpose, has been executed in a manner worthy of so noble a scheme. It has at once taken its rank among the most remarkable productions of our time; and is a book with which, both for its facts and its speculations, all who would understand, or who are called upon to exercise influence over their age, are bound to be familiar. It will contribute to give to the political speculations of our time a new character. Hitherto, aristocracy and democracy have been looked at chiefly in the mass, and applauded as good, or censured as bad, on the whole. But the time is now come for a narrower inspection, and a more discriminating judgment. M. de Tocqueville, among the first, has set the example of analysing democracy; of distinguishing one of its features, one of its tendencies, from another; of showing which of these tendencies is good, and which bad, in itself; how far each is necessarily connected with the rest, and to what extent any of them may be counteracted or modified, either by accident or foresight. He does this, with so noble a field as a great nation to demonstrate upon; which field he has commenced by minutely examining; selecting, with a discernment of which we have had no previous example, the material facts, and surveying these by the light of principles, drawn from no ordinary knowledge of human nature. We do not think his conclusions always just, but we think them always entitled to the most respectful attention, and never destitute of at least a large foundation of truth. The author's mind, except that it is of a soberer character, seems to us to resemble Montesquieu most among the great French writers. The book is such as Montesquieu might have written, if to his genius he had superadded good sense, and the lights which mankind have since gained from the experiences of a period in which they may be said to have lived centuries in fifty years. (pp. 197-99)

M. de Tocqueville's ideas do not float thinly upon a sea of words; none of his propositions are unmeaning, none of his meanings superfluous; not a paragraph could have been omitted without diminishing the value of the work. . . .

[In] no one point has M. de Tocqueville rendered a greater service to the European public, than by actually giving them their first information of the very existence of some of the most important parts of the American constitution. We allude particularly to the municipal institutions; which, as our author shows, and as might have been expected, are the very fountainhead of American democracy, and one principal cause of all that is valuable in its influences. (p. 199)

In this system of municipal self-government, coeval with the first settlement of the American colonies . . . , our author beholds the principal instrument of that political education of the people, which alone enables a popular government to maintain itself, or renders it desirable that it should. It is a fundamental principle in his political philosophy, as it has long been in ours, that only by the habit of superintending their local interests can that diffusion of intelligence and mental activity, as applied to their joint concerns, take place among the mass of a people, which can qualify them to superintend with steadiness or consistency the proceedings of their government, or to exercise any power in national affairs except by fits, and as tools in the hands of others.

These considerations are of the highest importance. It is not without reason that M. de Tocqueville considers local democracy to be the school as well as the safety-valve of democracy in the state,—the means of training the people to the good use of that power, which, whether prepared for it or not, they will assuredly in a short time be in the full exercise of. There has been much said of late—and truly not a word too much—on the necessity, now that the people are acquiring power, of giving them education, meaning school instruction, to qualify them for its exercise. The importance of school instruction is doubtless great; but it should also be recollected, that what really constitutes education is the formation of habits; and as we do not learn to read or write, to ride or swim, by being merely told how to do it, but by doing it, so it is only by practising popular government on a limited scale, that the people will ever learn how to exercise it on a larger. (pp. 200-01)

On the favourable side [of the tendencies of democracy, M. de Tocqueville] holds, that alone among all governments its systematic and perpetual end is the good of the immense majority. Were this its only merit, it is one, the absence of which could ill be compensated by all other merits put together. Secondly, no other government can reckon upon so willing an obedience, and so warm an attachment to it, on the part of the people at large. And, lastly, as it works not only *for* the people, but, much more extensively than any other government, *by means* of the people, it has a tendency which no other government has in the same degree, to call forth and sharpen the intelligence of the mass.

The disadvantages which our author ascribes to democracy are chiefly two:—First, that its policy is much more hasty and short-sighted than that of aristocracy. In compensation, however, he adds, that it is more ready to correct its errors, when experience has made them apparent. The second is, that the interest of the majority is not always identical with the interest of all; and hence the sovereignty of the majority creates a tendency on their part to abuse their power over all minorities. . . .

[We] may remark, that the evils which M. de Tocqueville represents as incident to democracy, can only exist in so far as the people entertain an erroneous idea of what democracy ought to be. If the people entertained the right idea of democracy, the mischief of hasty and unskilful legislation would not exist; and the omnipotence of the majority would not be attended with any evils. (p. 209)

In attributing, as general characteristics, prudence and steadiness to aristocratic governments, our author has, we think, generalized on an insufficient examination of the facts on which his conclusion is founded. The only steadiness which aristocracy *never* fails to manifest, is tenacity in clinging to its own privileges. Democracy is equally tenacious of the fundamental maxims of its own government. In all other matters, the opinion of a ruling class is as fluctuating, as liable to be wholly given up to immediate impulses, as the opinion of the people. . . . (p. 219)

[While] we see in democracy, as in every other state of society or form of government, possibilities of evil, which it would ill serve the cause of democracy itself to dissemble or overlook; while we think that the world owes a deep debt to M. de Tocqueville for having warned it of these, for having studied the failings and weaknesses of democracy with the anxious attention with which a parent watches the faults of a child, or a careful seaman those of the vessel in which he embarks his property and his life; we see nothing in any of these tendencies, from which any serious evil need be apprehended, if the superior spirits would but join with each other in considering the instruction of the democracy, and not the patching of the old worn-out machinery of aristocracy, the proper object henceforth of all rational exertion. (p. 226)

> *John Stuart Mill, "Tocqueville on 'Democracy in America, Vol. I'," in his* Essays on Politics and Culture, *edited by Gertrude Himmelfarb, Doubleday & Company, Inc., 1962, pp. 187-229.*

[BASIL HALL] (essay date 1836)

It is our opinion that M. de Tocqueville has approached the working of the American institutions [in *De la Démocratie en Amérique*] in a better temper, and treated it in a far more philosophical manner than any preceding writer. . . . He has opened our eyes to the perception of numberless things which we had either entirely overlooked or entirely misconceived, or to which we had attached either too much or too little importance; and he has clearly explained to us a thousand anomalies which had perplexed our judgment or disturbed our temper. In truth, nothing has surprised us so much in reading this work, as the uniform composure with which the author engages in those discussions, the slightest touch of which has been sufficient to set other writers in a flame. (pp. 133-34)

[M. de Tocqueville] has not only shown us the country, but explained to us the reasons why it exists in its present state; and for the first time, so far as we are aware of, not only the true situation of that extraordinary people, but the true causes of their social and political situation, are clearly developed. . . . Persons, indeed, who seek in these pages for materials to advance any merely party, or other selfish purpose, will certainly be disappointed, for they are entirely free from 'envy, hatred, and malice, and from all uncharitableness.' Neither is there any satire contained in them, expressed or understood; all is grave, and plain, and above-board, and withal so temperate, that even where we do not agree with his deductions, our confidence in his good faith and singleness of purpose remains unbroken. (p. 135)

M. de Tocqueville, in his Introduction, opens at once the subject of democracy, and by positions equally startling and convincing, satisfies us of the importance of giving it the very gravest attention. Nothing, he says, struck him so forcibly during his stay in the United States, as the equality of condition; and he readily discovered the prodigious influence which this primary fact exercises on the whole affairs of the State, by giving peculiar impulses to the laws, and peculiar maxims to the governing powers. He soon discovered, likewise, what may be called its re-acting influence over the whole mass of civil society, not only in the creation of opinions and of sentiments, but in modifying what it does not actually produce. And he ended by seeing clearly, in this equality of conditions, the fundamental fact . . . from which every other appeared to flow; or, at all events, towards which, as a central point, his observations might constantly be traced.

From the New World he naturally turned with redoubled attention to the Old; and he presently satisfied himself, by means of the new lights reflected from America, that the equality of conditions amongst the nations of Europe was daily *progressing* . . . to those extreme limits which it seems to have reached in the United States. From the moment he conceived this notion, he dates the origin of his book; and we must do him the justice to say that, although in the treatment of a subject so extensive and complicated, the generating idea may often be hid, it is never lost. Like the original air, or, as it is technically called, the *theme,* in a piece of music, this reference to the politics of Europe, and the sure advance of democracy, are felt through all the variations of his topic. At times, indeed, scarcely a note reaches the ear of which we can recognise the application, but sooner or later the whole is wrought into harmony; and the judgment of every candid observer must acknowledge the fidelity with which so difficult a task has been performed. (pp. 136-37)

[M. de Tocqueville] holds that the democratic revolution has either been already brought about, or is on the eve of accomplishment, and therefore it is high time to study this overwhelming principle, in order to discern its natural consequences, and to distinguish the means by which it may be rendered profitable—to eliminate, as the mathematicians say, the elements which are mischievous, and lead to vice, misery, and national degradation, and to appropriate those which conduce to virtue, genuine freedom, and national prosperity. He, therefore, selects for description and for analysis—not as an example for imitation—that country in which, of all those which have witnessed this great change, the development of the democratic principle has been the most complete and the most peaceable. (p. 142)

> *[Basil Hall], "Tocqueville on the State of America," in* The Quarterly Review, *Vol. LVII, No. CXIII, September, 1836, pp. 132-62.*

[HORACE GREELEY] (essay date 1840)

> [*A prominent nineteenth-century American journalist, Greeley founded the* New York Tribune *in 1841 and was the newspaper's editor for thirty years. With his trenchant editorials in the* Tribune, *in which he advocated both conservative and liberal causes, Greeley exerted wide influence in both political and literary spheres. His laudatory review of the first part of* Democracy *typifies contemporary American response to the work. Although he objects to Tocqueville's assertion that literature produced in a democracy must necessarily be inferior to that produced in an aristocracy, Greeley concludes that the first part of* Democracy *is "by far the*

most important work that has been written on the Nature and Influence of Democracy.'']

M. de Tocqueville made the discovery that we have in this country no poetry, and but very little literature of any description. He expresses a belief that the literature of a democracy must necessarily be of an inferior description to that produced in aristocracies, and he argues at length in support of this proposition; but we think his reasons will not be deemed conclusive by those who are intimate with the facts which bear upon his theory. So far as the history and condition of letters in this country are concerned, we see nothing to justify a belief that we shall not have, before the close of a century, a national literature as rich as any of our aristocratic contemporaries have now. We may not, indeed, have a Shakspeare, but America is quite as likely hereafter to produce an author of his rank as England; and the prospect is much fairer of our having a Petrarch than 'aristocratic' Italy enjoys. (p. 145)

[The First Part of **'Democracy in America'**] is by far the most important work that has been written on the Nature and Influence of Democracy, and it should be studied by every one who aims at exerting an influence in the direction of public affairs in the United States. Although it contains some isolated passages that will not much gratify our national vanity, it is written with the utmost candor. The author advances no proposition which he does not support with reasons, and he arrives at no conclusions in haste or prejudice. (p. 146)

> [Horace Greeley], ''Social Influence of Democracy,'' in The New-Yorker, *Vol. 9, No. 10, May 23, 1840, pp. 145-46.*

JOHN STUART MILL   (essay date 1840)

[*Mill's appreciative assessment of the second part of* Democracy, *which was originally published in the* Edinburgh Review, *Vol. LXXII, No. CXLV, October, 1840, is the most notable contemporary English review of the work. As in his earlier review of the first part of* Democracy *(1835), Mill comments on Tocqueville's impartiality, which provided both liberals and conservatives of the time with material for substantiating their views, and he applauds Tocqueville for his scientific approach. He cautions, however, against attaching ''a character of scientific certainty'' to Tocqueville's speculations, arguing that* Democracy's *value ''is less in the conclusions than in the mode of arriving at them.'' He considers* Democracy's *greatest flaw to be its occasional ''air of over-subtlety and false refinement.'' Mill attributes this defect to Tocqueville's failure to distinguish between the effects of democracy and the effects of civilization; he complains that Tocqueville ascribed to democracy ''several of the effects naturally arising from the mere progress of national prosperity,'' a criticism that is repeated by Emile Faguet, George Wilson Pierson, and Henry Commager (1900, 1938, and 1947).*]

[When **'Democracy in America'** made its appearance], it was not likely to be overlooked, or to escape an attempt to convert it to party purposes. If ever political writer had reason to believe that he had laboured successfully to render his book incapable of such a use, M. de Tocqueville was entitled to think so. But though his theories are of an impartiality without example, and his practical conclusions lean towards Radicalism, some of his phrases are susceptible of a Tory application. One of these is 'the tyranny of the majority.' This phrase was forthwith adopted into the Conservative dialect. . . . (p. 231)

[**'Democracy in America'** is] the first philosophical book ever written on Democracy, as it manifests itself in modern society; a book, the essential doctrines of which it is not likely that any future speculations will subvert, to whatever degree they may modify them; while its spirit, and the general mode in which it treats its subject, constitute it the beginning of a new era in the scientific study of politics.

The importance of M. de Tocqueville's speculations is not to be estimated by the opinions which he has adopted, be these true or false. The value of his work is less in the conclusions, than in the mode of arriving at them. He has applied to the greatest question in the art and science of government, those principles and methods of philosophizing to which mankind are indebted for all the advances made by modern times in the other branches of the study of nature. It is not risking too much to affirm of these volumes, that they contain the first analytical inquiry into the influence of democracy. For the first time, that phenomenon is treated of as something which, being a reality in nature, and no mere mathematical or metaphysical abstraction, manifests itself by innumerable properties, not by some one only; and must be looked at in many aspects before it can be made the subject even of that modest and conjectural judgment, which is alone attainable respecting a fact at once so great and so new. (p. 232)

M. de Tocqueville has endeavoured to ascertain and discriminate the various properties and tendencies of Democracy; the separate relations in which it stands towards the different interests of society, and the different moral and social requisites of human nature. In the investigation he has left much undone, as who could possibly avoid? and much which will be better done by those who come after him, and build upon his foundations. But he has earned the double honour of being the first to make the attempt; and of having done more towards the success of it than probably will ever again be done by any one individual. His method is, as that of a philosopher on such a subject must be—a combination of deduction with induction: his evidences are laws of human nature, on the one hand; the example of America and France, and other modern nations, so far as applicable, on the other. His conclusions never rest on either species of evidence alone; whatever he classes as an effect of Democracy, he has both ascertained to exist in those countries in which the state of society is democratic, and has also succeeded in connecting with Democracy by deductions *à priori*, showing that such would naturally be its influences upon beings constituted as mankind are, and placed in a world such as we know ours to be. If this be not the true Baconian and Newtonian method applied to society and government; if any better, or even any other be possible, M. de Tocqueville would be the first to say. . . . (pp. 232-33)

That part of **'Democracy in America'** which was first published, professes to treat of the political effects of Democracy; the second . . . is devoted to its influence upon society in the widest sense; upon the relations of private life, upon intellect, morals, and the habits and modes of feeling which constitute national character. The last is both a newer and a more difficult subject of enquiry than the first; there are fewer who are competent, or who will even think themselves competent, to judge M. de Tocqueville's conclusions. But, we believe, no one, in the least entitled to an opinion, will refuse to him the praise of having probed the subject to a depth which had never before been sounded; of having carried forward the controversy into a wider and loftier region of thought; and pointed out many questions essential to the subject which had not been before attended to;—questions which he may or may not have solved, but of which, in any case, he has greatly facilitated the solution.

The comprehensiveness of M. de Tocqueville's views, and the impartiality of his feelings, have not led him into the common infirmity of those who see too many sides to a question, that of thinking them all equally important. He is able to arrive at a decided opinion. Nor has the more extensive range of considerations embraced in his Second Part, affected practically the general conclusions which resulted from his First. (pp. 233-34)

It is necessary to observe that, by Democracy, M. de Tocqueville does not, in general, mean any particular form of government. He can conceive a Democracy under an absolute monarch. Nay, he entertains no small dread, lest, in some countries, it should actually appear in that form. By Democracy M. de Tocqueville understands equality of conditions; the absence of all aristocracy, whether constituted by political privileges, or by superiority in individual importance and social power. It is towards Democracy in this sense, towards equality between man and man, that he conceives society to be irresistibly tending. Toward Democracy in the other, and more common sense, it may or may not be travelling. Equality of conditions tends naturally to produce a popular government, but not necessarily. Equality may be equal freedom or equal servitude. America is the type of the first; France, he thinks, is in danger of falling into the second. (pp. 234-35)

The opinion, that there is this irresistible tendency to equality of conditions, is perhaps, of all the leading doctrines of the book, that which most stands in need of confirmation to English readers. M. de Tocqueville devotes but little space to the elucidation of it. To French readers the historical retrospect upon which it rests is familiar; and facts known to every one establish its truth so far as relates to that country. But to the English public, who have less faith in irresistible tendencies, and who, while they require for every political theory a historical basis, are far less accustomed to link together the events of history in a connected chain, the proposition will hardly seem to be sufficiently made out. (pp. 235-36)

In estimating the effects of Democratic Government as distinguished from a Democratic State of Society, M. de Tocqueville assumes the state of circumstances which exists in America;—a popular government in the state, combined with popular local institutions. In such a government he sees great advantages, balanced by no inconsiderable evils.

Among the advantages, one which figures in the foremost rank is . . . the diffusion of intelligence; the remarkable impulse given by democratic institutions to the active faculties of that portion of the community, who in other circumstances are the most ignorant, passive, and apathetic. These are characteristics of America which strike all travellers. Activity, enterprise, and a respectable amount of information, are not the qualities of a few among the American citizens, nor even of many, but of all. There is no class of persons who are the slaves of habit and routine. Every American will carry on his manufacture, or cultivate his farm, by the newest and best methods applicable to the circumstances of the case. The poorest American understands and can explain the most intricate parts of his country's institutions; can discuss her interests, internal and foreign. Much of this may justly be attributed to the universality of easy circumstances, and to the education and habits which the first settlers in America brought with them; but our author is certainly not wrong in ascribing a certain portion of it to the perpetual exercise of the faculties of every man among the people, through the universal practice of submitting all public questions to his judgment. (p. 249)

[The other great political advantage which M. de Tocqueville ascribes to Democracy is] that the course of legislation and administration tends always in the direction of the interest of the greater number. Although M. de Tocqueville is far from considering this quality of Democracy as the *panacea* in politics which it has sometimes been supposed to be, he expresses his sense of its importance, if in measured, in no undecided terms. (p. 251)

It is perhaps the greatest defect of M. de Tocqueville's book, that from the scarcity of examples, his propositions, even when derived from observation, have the air of mere abstract speculations. He speaks of the tyranny of the majority in general phrases, but gives hardly any instances of it, nor much information as to the mode in which it is practically exemplified. The omission was in the [First Part of **'Democracy in America'**] the more excusable, as the despotism complained of was, at that time, politically at least, an evil in apprehension more than in sufferance; and he was uneasy rather at the total absence of security against the tyranny of the majority, than at the frequency of its actual exertion. (p. 256)

[The despotism] of the majority within the limits of civil life, though a real evil, does not appear to us to be a formidable one. The tyranny which we fear, and which M. de Tocqueville principally dreads, is of another kind—a tyranny not over the body but over the mind.

It is the complaint of M. de Tocqueville, as well as of other travellers in America, that in no country does there exist less independence of thought. In religion, indeed, the varieties of opinion which fortunately prevailed among those by whom the colonies were settled, has produced a toleration in law and in fact extending to the limits of Christianity. If by ill fortune there had happened to be a religion of the majority, the case would probably have been different. On every other subject, when the opinion of the majority is made up, hardly any one, it is affirmed, dares to be of any other opinion, or at least to profess it. The statements are not clear as to the nature or amount of the inconvenience that would be suffered by any one who presumed to question a received opinion. It seems certain, however, that scarcely any person has that courage; that when public opinion considers a question as settled, no further discussion of it takes place; and that not only nobody dares (what every body may venture upon in Europe) to say any thing disrespectful to the public, or derogatory to its opinions, but that its wisdom and virtue are perpetually celebrated with the most servile adulation and sycophancy. (p. 259)

To sum up our author's opinion of the dangers to which mankind are liable as they advance towards equality of condition; his fear, both in government and in intellect and morals, is not of too great liberty, but of too ready submission; not of anarchy, but of servility; not of too rapid change, but of Chinese stationariness. As democracy advances, the opinions of mankind on most subjects of general interest will become, he believes, as compared with any former period, more rooted and more difficult to change; and mankind are more and more in danger of losing the moral courage and pride of independence which make them deviate from the beaten path either in speculation or in conduct. Even in politics, it is to be apprehended that, feeling their personal insignificance, and conceiving a proportionally vast idea of the importance of society at large; being jealous, moreover, of one another, but not jealous of the central power which derives its origin from the majority, or which at least is the faithful representative of its desire to annihilate every intermediate power; they should allow that central government to assume more and more control, engross more and more of the business of society; and, on condition of making itself the organ of the general mode of feeling and thinking, should suffer it to relieve mankind from the care of their own interests, and keep them under a kind of tutelage;—trampling meanwhile with considerable recklessness, as often as convenient, upon the rights of individuals, in the name of society and the public good.

Against these political evils the corrective to which our author looks is popular education, and, above all, the spirit of liberty, fostered by the extension and dissemination of political rights. Democratic institutions, therefore, are his remedy for the worst mischiefs to which a democratic state of society is exposed. As for those to which democratic institutions are themselves liable, these, he holds, society must struggle with, and bear with so much of them as it cannot find the means of conquering. For M. de Tocqueville is no believer in the reality of mixed governments. There is, he says, always and every where, a strongest power: in every government either the king, the aristocracy, or the people, have an effective predominance, and can carry any point on which they set their heart. 'When a community really comes to have a mixed government, that is, to be equally divided between two adverse principles, it is either falling into a revolutionary state or into dissolution.' M. de Tocqueville believes that the preponderant power which must exist every where, is most rightly placed in the body of the people. But he thinks it most pernicious that this power, whether residing in the people or elsewhere, should be 'checked by no obstacles which may retard its course, and force it to moderate its own vehemence.' The difference, in his eyes, is great between one sort of democratic institutions and another. That form of democracy should be sought out and devised, and in every way endeavoured to be carried into practice, which, on the one hand, most exercises and cultivates the intelligence and mental activity of the majority; and, on the other, breaks the headlong impulses of popular opinion, by delay, rigour of forms, and adverse discussion. 'The organization and the establishment of democracy,' on these principles, 'is the great political problem of our time.'

And when this problem is solved, there remains an equally serious one; to make head against the tendency of democracy towards bearing down individuality, and circumscribing the exercise of the human faculties within narrow limits. To sustain the higher pursuits of philosophy and art; to vindicate and protect the unfettered exercise of reason, and the moral freedom of the individual—these are purposes to which, under a democracy, the superior spirits, and the government so far as it is permitted, should devote their utmost energies. (pp. 272-73)

That nothing on the whole comparable in profundity to [M. de Tocqueville's speculations has] yet been written on democracy, will scarcely be disputed by any one. . . . We must guard, at the same time, against attaching to these conclusions, or to any others that can result from such enquiries, a character of scientific certainty that can never belong to them. Democracy is too recent a phenomenon, and of too great magnitude, for any one who now lives to comprehend its consequences. A few of its more immediate tendencies may be perceived or surmised; what other tendencies, destined to overrule or to combine with these, lie behind, there are not grounds even to conjecture. (p. 275)

[Without] pretending to judge confidently of remote tendencies, those immediate ones which are already developing themselves require to be dealt with as we treat any of the other circumstances in which we are placed;—by encouraging those which are salutary, and working out the means by which such as are hurtful may be counteracted. To exhort men to this, and to aid them in doing it, is the end for which M. de Tocqueville has written: and in the same spirit we will now venture to make one criticism upon him;—to point out one correction, of which we think his views stand in need; and for want of which they have occasionally an air of over-subtlety and false refinement, exciting the distrust of common readers, and making the opinions themselves appear less true, and less practically important, than, it seems to us, they really are.

M. de Tocqueville then has, at least apparently, confounded the effects of Democracy with the effects of Civilization. He has bound up in one abstract idea the whole of the tendencies of modern commercial society, and given them one name— Democracy; thereby letting it be supposed that he ascribes to equality of conditions, several of the effects naturally arising from the mere progress of national prosperity, in the form in which that progress manifests itself in modern times.

It is no doubt true, that among the tendencies of commercial civilization, a tendency to the equalization of conditions is one, and not the least conspicuous. When a nation is advancing in prosperity—when its industry is expanding, and its capital rapidly augmenting—the number also of those who possess capital increases in at least as great a proportion; and though the distance between the two extremes of society may not be much diminished, there is a rapid multiplication of those who occupy the intermediate positions. There may be princes at one end of the scale and paupers at the other; but between them there will be a respectable and well-paid class of artisans, and a middle class who combine property and industry. This may be called, and is, a tendency to equalization. But this growing equality is only one of the features of progressive civilization; one of the incidental effects of the progress of industry and wealth: a most important effect, and one which, as our author shows, re-acts in a hundred ways upon the other effects, but not, therefore, to be confounded with the cause.

> *John Stuart Mill, "Tocqueville on 'Democracy in America, Vol. II'," in his* Essays on Politics and Culture, *edited by Gertrude Himmelfarb, Doubleday & Company, Inc., 1962, pp. 230-87.*

GUSTAVE DE BEAUMONT   (essay date 1861)

[*Beaumont, Tocqueville's traveling companion in America and collaborator on* On the Penitentiary System in the United States and Its Application in France, *was one of Tocqueville's closest friends. In his discussion of Tocqueville's life and works, Beaumont identifies what has become a focal point of Tocqueville criticism: his interest in the relationship between liberty and equality.*]

No surprise need be excited by the fact that [the success of **Democracy in America**] made all parties desirous of appropriating the book and its author. Some declared Tocqueville to be a democrat; others said that he was an aristocrat. He was neither. Born in the ranks of the aristocracy, but with a love for liberty, Tocqueville had found modern society in the hands of the democracy; and, considering this to be an established fact, which it was no longer possible to question, he thought that to the absolute equality thus produced it was essential to add liberty; for without liberty equality has no check to its impulses, no counterpoise to its oppressions; and he judged this union so necessary, that he saw no aim in the present time more important to pursue, and to it he therefore devoted his whole life. This is the leading idea of the book; and, we may add, of those which followed it.

All great political writers have written with some such object in view. That of Tocqueville was to unite liberty to the already existing equality; and he not only searched eagerly in a democratic country for the fundamental conditions of liberty, but it may even be said that he discovered and pointed them out. In the lowest order a municipal power firmly rooted, between the commonalty and the ruling order, trial by jury, and a judiciary power strong enough to arbitrate with steady impartiality between the rulers and the people; local privileges placed out of the reach of the perils which always threaten the general political freedom, so that in case of its overthrow these shall not perish with it. He was the first to understand and point out the protection afforded to liberty by judicial institutions, and the peculiar importance of these institutions to a democracy. All this is prominent in every page of his *Democracy in America*. (pp. 34-5)

One characteristic of Tocqueville's book, which belongs to all great intellectual works, is, to take a place above the narrow views of party, the accidents of the day, and the passions of the moment. For this reason, it was from the beginning, and will long continue to be, quoted as an authority by the holders of the most opposite opinions; and this explains the success obtained by it in the country where aristocracy has the ascendant, as well as in that where democracy rules. (pp. 36-7)

[The second two volumes of *Democracy in America*] cost their author much more time and much more exertion than [the first two volumes]. He felt the obligations imposed by success. He resolved not merely not to sink, but to rise. He used to say that a writer ought to aim, not at making a good book, but an excellent book—a maxim, not of vanity, but of severe self-exaction, which he applied as much to his lightest as to his most important compositions. In preparing these volumes, he gave still deeper meditation to his matter, and still more exquisite polish to his style. He had written admirably before he had reflected deeply on the secrets of the art of writing. Glimpses of them he got while he was working. He was convinced that they must be thoroughly mastered by the writer whose works are to live. He felt that every creation of the mind, great or small, is a work of art, and that the force and the effect of a thought depend on the words in which it is clothed. In the first two volumes, Tocqueville had frequently been a great artist without appearing to be one. In the last two he is always one, but not without a visible effort. If the effort, however, be visible, so is the fruit. The style approaches nearer to perfection. In his earnest ambition to attain that object, he reperused the masters of style, especially the great men of the seventeenth century. He tried to discover the rules by which each of them was guided; but there was no one whom he studied with more perseverance and more interest than Pascal. The two minds were made for one another. The duty of constant thought imposed on his reader by Pascal was a charm to Tocqueville. He perhaps owes to this predilection the only blame to which he has exposed himself, that of giving his reader no rest. In some parts of the last two volumes of [*Democracy in America*], thought is linked to thought without an interval for repose or relaxation. In the first two volumes, Tocqueville was not open to this charge. In his animated description of American institutions, facts are inseparably mixed with speculations. An Englishman . . . , was complimenting him on this part of the work; "What

I especially admire," he said, "is, that while treating so great a subject, you have so thoroughly avoided general ideas."

There could not be a greater mistake; but Tocqueville was delighted. It showed to him that the abstractions with which his book is filled, had been so skilfully presented in a concrete form, that an acute, though certainly not a profound, reader did not perceive that the particular facts were only illustrations of general principles. No one can rise from the perusal of the second part of the work with such an impression. In describing the intellectual activity, the feelings, and the manners of the Americans, it was no longer possible to conceal the presence of general ideas, and by introducing them in the form of facts to render them more effective though less obvious. The book is full of reflections upon reflections. A reader incapable of rising to their source, and of feeling in himself the subtlety of their truth, must be fatigued by what may have appeared to him a collection of ingenious propositions, capable, perhaps, of proof, but also, perhaps, of refutation. Vigorous intellects, and only those, understand and admire the power which renders clear and precise, subjects which, to most minds, are vague and obscure. To them these volumes, suggested by no model, appear like a masterpiece of skill, and they rank them even above their forerunners. (pp. 41-4)

If it be true that a literary life is a bad preparation for a political life, it is no less true that politics are an excellent introduction to literary composition; especially to that of a book in which recent facts are mingled with history, and the statesman's experience is of as much importance as the talent of the writer. A retrospective glance thrown over the long interval between 1840 and 1852, during which political action suspended [Tocqueville's] intellectual creations, would, perhaps, lead us to infer that what Tocqueville gained most from those years, was a greater fitness for the production of [*L'ancien Régime et la Révolution*]. (p. 71)

In reading [*L'ancien Régime et la Révolution*] we feel more than the pleasure of contemplating a beautiful work of art, for our minds become filled with the great interests which occupy the thoughts of the author. We see that he is not merely presenting us with a series of remarkable anecdotes, but that he studies the past with the object of exploring the secrets and unravelling the mysteries of the future. We are aware that our own destinies and the lot of our children are concerned. We read with a solemn feeling, like that of the ancients consulting their oracle. It is more than admiration; it is emotion. The reader thinks as much of himself as of the book; and such is his faith in the penetration of the writer, that while reading the premises he longs to reach the conclusion. (p. 72)

Gustave de Beaumont, in Memoir, Letters, and Remains of Alexis de Tocqueville, Vol. I *by Alexis de Tocqueville, edited by M.C.M. Simpson, translated by Gustave de Beaumont, revised edition, Macmillan and Co., 1861, 455 p.*

HENRY SIDGWICK (essay date 1861)

[*An English writer on philosophy, political economy, and economics, Sidgwick is considered one of the leading ethical philosophers of the nineteenth century. His review of* Memoir, Letters, and Remains of Alexis de Tocqueville *originally appeared in* Macmillan's Magazine *in November, 1861. Sidgwick shares Gustave de Beaumont's conviction (see excerpt above, 1861) that all of Tocqueville's writings focus on one problem: the reconciliation of liberty and equality. Unlike the majority of critics, who maintain that Tocqueville relied too heavily on deductive reasoning in the second part of* Democracy, *Sidgwick faults Tocqueville for his dependence on the inductive method.*]

[Tocqueville's letters in *Memoir, Letters, and Remains of Alexis de Tocqueville*] bear testimony to the truth of the old saying, "that politeness is but the best expression of true feeling." The warm affection that breathes in them shows beautifully through the dress of delicate compliment, varied by most genial humour, in which it is clothed. [In his own memoir] M. de Beaumont observes on "the immense space that friendship occupied in his life." The same fact will strike every reader of the letters. Tocqueville's heart and mind shared the same restless activity. He could not, therefore, be happy without a wide field of personal relations. It was as impossible for him to rest satisfied with that abstract philanthropy, which, absorbed in plans for the general good, neglects individual ties, as it was to assent to the "modern realism" (as he called it), which ignores all individual rights in behalf of the general utility of society. His hatred of this tendency seems to spring from a one-sided experience, and one may feel it exaggerated; but he calls it himself one of his "central opinions," and it was curiously in harmony with many others of his ways of feeling and thinking. Another thing that strikes one in the correspondence is the perfection with which he adapts both matter and style, apparently without effort, to suit correspondents of the most various opinions, and the most various degrees of intellectual culture. A comparison of the two first series of letters in the book, those to his two oldest friends, Louis de Kergorlay and Alexis Stoffels, will afford an excellent example of this. At the same time this happy versatility never involves the sacrifice of the smallest tittle of his individual convictions. A sensitive hatred of insincerity is one of the most marked features of his character. . . . [Sincerity] was not merely a principle with Tocqueville: it was a necessity. Without it, correspondence would have lost its whole charm for him. . . . In compositions of all kinds, description as well as dissertation, this love of truth is paramount with him. He complains that "people say the ruins of Pæstum stand in the midst of a desert; whereas their site is nothing more than a miserable, badly-cultivated country, decaying like the temples themselves! Men always insist on adorning truth instead of describing it. Even M. de Chateaubriand has painted the real wilderness in false colours." His own *Fortnight in the Wilderness* will interest even those who are sated with pictures of wild life. The fire and vivacity, the susceptible imagination and the keen observation, may be met with elsewhere; but hardly ever controlled by a reason so sober and truthful, or enlightened by such breadth of view. (pp. 364-65)

If any lack of interest should be felt in these letters, it will be, I think, from a cause which is not altogether a defect. There are no shadows, in one sense, in the picture. It is all clear sunshine in Tocqueville's life, both inner and outer. The perfect healthiness of his nature excludes the charm that is sometimes derived from an element of morbidity. But one may also say with truth, that there is a want of depth. Perhaps the most interesting element in the lives of great thinkers is their imperfect utterance of deep truths only half-grasped; their consciousness of enveloping mystery and darkness, into which the light that shines from them throws only dim suggestive rays. We find nothing of this in Tocqueville. "Shallow" and "superficial" are the last epithets that could be applied; and yet we cannot call him profound, either in character or intellect. Earnest as he was in the search after truth, he was destitute of one power, necessary in the pursuit of the highest truth; he could not endure to doubt. . . . He was devoutly attached to

Romanism; but rather from the felt necessity of having a religion, than from a deliberate conviction in favour of the particular creed. He had acutely observed some of the more particular mutual influences of religions and forms of government; but his remarks on the more general relations of religion to humanity seem to me to constitute the weakest part of his writings. To metaphysics he had a dislike which he frequently shows. . . . [In] the second part of his *Democracy in America* we can detect, here and there, that his acquaintance with philosophy is somewhat superficial. It is no contradiction to this, that Tocqueville displays considerable skill in psychological analysis. He shows the same superiority in everything that depends only or chiefly on individual observation and reflection. His insight was always both keen and wide, his analysis both ingenious and sound; but systematic abstract thought was not to his taste, and he never pursued it with his full energy. We may sum up much by saying that Tocqueville applied to the study of politics a mind that, both in its merits and in its defects, was of the scientific rather than the philosophic kind. We notice in him many traits peculiar to students of physics. Thus, he early chose and always adhered to a special and definite subject of study; his method was purely inductive; he always went straight to the original documents, which formed, as it were, the matter whose laws he was investigating; he wrote down only the results of long and laborious observation; and these results were again rigorously winnowed before they saw the light. . . . While taxing thus the resources of his observation to the utmost, he depended upon it too entirely; his avoidance of other writers on his own subject caused him, as he allows, great waste of power; his treatment of economical questions strikes one often as too empirical and tentative; political economy, when he first wrote, had not taken rank as a true science, and his was not the mind to labour at systematising and correcting a mass of alien generalisations. But, while this diminishes occasionally the intrinsic value of his speculations, it adds to the harmonious freshness of his writings; and, his observation being unerring, his most hasty generalisations are always partially true. (pp. 366-68)

Tocqueville has outstripped his age, and his works will long remain models both in style and matter. They are not made to strike or startle, but they powerfully absorb the attention and convince the reason. Their excellence often conceals their originality; the perfect arrangement of facts makes the conclusions drawn from them appear to lie on the surface; the ideas are so carefully explained, defined, and disentangled, the arguments are strained so clear, that we are cheated into the belief that we should have thought the same ourselves if we had happened to develop our views on the subject. Thus conviction steals in unawares, and it is only by carefully comparing our views before and after perusal that we find how much we have gained. (p. 369)

The bent of Tocqueville's mind was eminently practical and patriotic: he did not enter into study so much for the sake of abstract truth as for the sake of his country. He was an aristocrat by birth and sentiment, whose education and experience had enabled him to get rid of aristocratic prejudices without contracting opposite ones. His impressible mind had early conceived a strong enthusiasm for liberty; and his common sense accepted social equality as inevitable. His unique position is due to his clear discrimination between the two—liberty and equality; between the motives for which they are sought, and the results that follow their attainment. He was one of the first to tear the sophism that the tyranny of the majority is freedom, and the sophism that popular election of an omnipotent government constitutes the government of the people. (p. 370)

Henry Sidgwick, "Alexis de Tocqueville," in his Miscellaneous Essays and Addresses, *Macmillan and Co., Limited*, 1904, pp. 361-74.

THE NORTH AMERICAN REVIEW   (essay date 1866)

Democracy in America! Who in the year 1832 could have foretold the meaning these words would have in this year 1866? If it were given to any human being then living to foresee the condition and prospects of our country at this moment, that person was certainly not M. de Tocqueville. Much as he studied and well as he understood our institutions,—and he studied them deeply and with great fairness,—he signally failed, as late events have shown, to discover the real secret of their nature, or to fathom the character of our people. [*La Democratie en Amérique*] has been so much read, and has had, as we think, so considerable an influence in Europe, and particularly in England, as to have led to great misunderstanding in relation to the late Rebellion [the Civil War]. (p. 321)

[It is] very important, in forming a judgment of the value of M. de Tocqueville's work, to keep in mind the state in which he found things among us at the time of his visit in 1832. It was, as we all know, most critical. The prologue was then being recited of the great drama on which the curtain has just fallen. John C. Calhoun was then at the acme of his doleful career; the cry of nullification was then at its loudest, to be succeeded in no long time by the more appalling watchword of Secession. State rights, the true construction of the Constitution, the Virginia Resolutions of 1798, tariffs, and the "forty-bale" theory were the standing topics of angry discussion in all parts of the Union. While the controversy was carried on at the North with quite enough of eagerness and warmth, it was raging south of Mason and Dixon's line with a degree of bitterness which might well cause astonishment to a foreigner newly come among us, and tend to mislead him in his estimate of the people and government. It was at such a period that M. de Tocqueville set foot on our shores, with a sincere desire to form an impartial judgment of the nature of our institutions, and of the probable destiny of our country. (p. 323)

So long as he discusses the origin and history of our government, which he gets at by consulting historical and other documents, nothing can be more fair or more trustworthy than what he has to say. Not only are his facts indisputable, but his manner of stating and elucidating them is all that could be wished. Not so when he comes to deal with the questions of the day, and the future of the United States. That section of his tenth chapter which is headed, "What are the Chances of the Duration of the American Union, and what are the Dangers which threaten it," is a standing example of reasoning refuted by events, as well as a warning to authors, however able, who undertake to pronounce upon the institutions of a country on the strength of a few months' acquaintance. M. de Tocqueville fell into the mistake of attempting to decide, by a process of reasoning *a priori*, a question not to be settled but by the crucial test, which might never be applied. He assumes at the outset that the United States are a mere confederation of sovereignties. In this section, he says:—

> If a contest should arise to-day between the States and the Union, it is easy to perceive that the latter must succumb. I question even whether the struggle could ever be brought to a serious

issue. Whenever an obstinate resistance shall be made to the Federal government, it will give in. . . . Experience has proved thus far, that, whenever a state has obstinately insisted upon anything, and was resolved to obtain what it asked, it has never failed to succeed; and when it has refused point-blank to act, it has been let alone.

This statement he undertakes to prove by a course of reasoning which, though now quite worthless otherwise, is not without its use in showing how the wisest men may deceive themselves when arguing in support of a foregone conclusion. He lays down with great minuteness the distinction between the prerogatives which belong to the national government and those which belong to the separate States, and concludes that the latter must needs prevail over the former; that the local sovereignties are constantly gaining ground, so that the national government, growing daily more and more weak, must finally die of inanition. He follows up the argument with a cogency of logic which defies all refutation, winding up the whole with an axiom from which, he ventures to affirm, there is no escape.

> It seems then certain to me, that if one portion of the Union wished seriously to separate from the other, not only would it be impossible to prevent it, but that prevention would not even be attempted. The existing government will therefore last only so long as every one of the States composing it shall continue to wish to form a part of it.

So confident is M. de Tocqueville that this position is impregnable, that he goes on in the following complacent strain:—

> This point settled, we see our way more clearly. . . . We need no longer trouble ourselves to inquire whether the confederate States actually *can* separate, but whether or not they will desire to remain united.

He then goes into a minute examination of the inducements the States have to remain together; which, in the existing state of things, is, to say the least, amusing. A favorite notion of M. de Tocqueville was, that the State governments, being more immediately connected with the domestic interests and everyday concerns of men, would in time become the great objects of ambition, and would eventually gain the ascendency over the national Congress. Now, nothing is more notorious than that the fact is just the other way. As the concerns of the nation become more vast, and the offices, diplomatic and domestic, more important and desirable, a seat in Congress is the constant aim of every aspirant for political distinction; the local legislatures being, for such men, merely stepping-stones to that object. (pp. 324-25)

With his hereditary prejudices, it is perhaps unfortunate that [M. de Tocqueville's] visit to this country took place just at the moment when the great convulsion, whose heavings have not yet subsided, was beginning to stir the minds of men. Assailed on all sides by the clashing doctrines of contending parties; misled, or bewildered, by the specious fallacies of Calhoun and his adherents; alarmed at the growth of levelling ideas which had, not long before, rent his native country,—he was but too ready to seek, in the probable preponderance of State rights, a last hope for the old conservative doctrines which were struggling at home against the two extremes of popular license and the despotism of a single ruler. He accordingly misunderstood the vacillation of the Executive when the State of South Carolina boldly put forward pretensions to a right to nullify the decrees of Congress, and asserted the sovereignty she claimed never to have parted with. He attributed the unwillingness of Congress to deal summarily with such a case to a consciousness of weakness, whereas it grew out of love of the Union, and the desire to stave off as long as possible, by temporizing and compromise, the dreaded moment when the question of nationality must be met. All men felt a dread of what many saw to be inevitable, and hoped to pass the bitter draught to another generation. The gifted author had hardly closed his eyes on earthly things, when the momentous problem he had pondered with such anxious solicitude was solved. (p. 327)

On the subject of slavery M. de Tocqueville was more fortunate. He foretold that it must come to an end, but was mistaken as to the means by which its abolition was to be brought about. But let him speak for himself.

> Whatever, then, may be the efforts of the South to preserve slavery, they will eventually fail. Slavery, pent up in a single spot on the earth's surface, attacked by Christianity as unjust, by political economy as disastrous,—slavery, in the midst of democratic liberty, and of the intelligence of our age,—is not an institution that can last. It must come to an end by the act of the slave himself or by that of his master. In either case great misery must be the consequence.

It has come to an end, and that by neither of the agencies predicted by M. de Tocqueville, unless it be in a very indirect manner, and there is reason to hope without any of the dismal results predicted by him. (pp. 329-30)

> > *"The Error of De Tocqueville,"* in The North American Review, *Vol. CII, No. CCXI, April, 1866, pp. 321-34.*

ACTON [JOHN EMERICH EDWARD DALBERG-ACTON] (essay date 1893)

[*Acton was a nineteenth-century English historian, essayist, and editor. An ardent liberal who was influenced by Tocqueville's works, Acton saw liberty threatened by both democracy and socialism. In his discussion of* The Recollections of Alexis de Tocqueville, *he argues that Tocqueville was a "Liberal without qualification" who "cherished no special, exclusive liking for Monarchy or Democracy. . . ." According to Acton, Tocqueville's impartiality is displayed in* Recollections *by his "wholesale" condemnation of his contemporaries.*]

Tocqueville's recollections of the years 1848 and 1849 [in *Souvenirs de Alexis de Tocqueville*] contain little that is absolutely new to history, and yet they are a revelation and a surprise. They disclose, for the first time, the real Tocqueville, and show how assiduously, in his writings, and even in his well-considered correspondence, he restrained the manifestation of personal opinion and temper. The love for sententious moralising is the same, and words of wisdom flow complacently, and almost too easily, whilst he is writing without a thought of the future public. His saying, that the cheapest bargain is that which is negotiated with the vanity of mankind, because it procures something in exchange for nothing, betrays a secret which was already some centuries old. But there are passages of higher quality. Much of the historian's craft is

hidden in the remark that posterity remembers crimes better than vices. (p. 883)

In two or three places he exhibits his own belief, or rather his doctrinal negation. He is persuaded that the infirmities of old societies are beyond recovery; the symptoms may change, but not the disease, and the ancient powers will be transformed or perish. He is inclined to think that what we call necessary institutions are nothing but those we are accustomed to, and that, in the constitution of society, the margin of possible variation is almost infinite. In other words, political principles are little better than optical illusions—an instantaneous glimpse of the perpetual motion of life. This dogma of continuous change, which never rose to a distinct belief in development, progress, or divine government, and was closely akin to pessimism, released Tocqueville from attachment to party; and it was thus that one who may reasonably be called the ablest Frenchman of his generation achieved so little in public life.

He displays his impartiality in the disposition to condemn all round. He thinks ill of his countrymen both in the present and the past. The thoughtless impatience, the disregard for law, the facile yielding to example, the temerity in peril, are inherited defects; but the passionate desire to live on public money is a recent growth of middle-class institutions. On the party leaders of his time he delivers this judgment—that all were about equally unworthy to govern, some by the want of superior merit, more by the absence of all merit of any kind. As to military men, he has observed that they are the first to lose their heads in a crisis.

Whenever he has to say a good word for any public man, he is quick to qualify his praise with sneers. Living in a world of selfishness and ambition, he has met no man more indifferent to the notion of the public good than Lamartine, none more insincere or more contemptuous of truth. Ledru Rollin possesses neither principles nor ideas; he has not even enough malice to cut off the head of an adversary—unless, indeed, under stress of historical reminiscences or to please a friend. Odilon Barrot is accustomed to mingle a certain foolishness with his weaknesses as well as with his virtues, and compels the masses by his intrepidity, his loud voice, and his pompous declamation. Thiers is a poltroon; and Rémusat, at once a friend of Thiers and a man of honour (which is unusual), discerns clearly what can be done, and obscurely what ought to be done. (pp. 883-84)

These are the judgments pronounced on his contemporaries by the most thoughtful, the most moderate, the most high-minded of men, in an age prodigiously rich in talent. Swift could hardly have excelled him in his bitter and comprehensive irony. It is obvious to explain such strange vituperation in one so dignified and so impersonal by disappointment and disgust at the men whose conduct, under Monarchy and Republic, brought in the Empire. For Tocqueville was simply a Liberal, a Liberal without qualification. He cherished no special, exclusive liking for Monarchy or Democracy, for the influences of religion, or the prerogative of France. (p. 885)

[Perhaps] there is something in the wholesale verdicts of Tocqueville more significant than any personal character or experience. We have passed through the phase of vindications. Every cause that has early ancestors, long traditions, or remote allies has striven to retrieve their fame; and environment, heredity, continuity, have yielded what was in them to sustain a theory dear to retrospective man. Judas Iscariot has been singled out as the one virtuous apostle; Elphinstone devoted himself to the defence of Pilate; and Proudhon yearned to clasp Satan in his arms, as a fellow-sufferer from the malignity of priests. Probably, on this line of argument, we are near the turning. We cannot form a judgment until we know the worst of the cause to be tried. From the time when the biographical element becomes distinct, for the last five hundred years, there is this constant result, that fewer characters bear the search-light; and it may generally be affirmed of ruling and leading spirits that, the better we know them, the worse they appear. Tocqueville was not known hitherto, by his books, his letters, or his conversations, as a hanging judge. What he was is now shown; and he has joined the disparaging choir, that declares the reign of sin and folly, and contributes to the Iconoclasm of History. (pp. 885-86)

> Acton [*John Emerich Edward Dalberg-Acton*], *"Tocqueville's 'Souvenirs',"* in The Nineteenth Century, *Vol. 33, No. 195, May, 1893, pp. 883-86.*

A. V. DICEY (essay date 1893)

[*In his survey of Tocqueville's works, Dicey argues that Tocqueville "is certain to be misunderstood, and in the end to be underrated" if he is judged as a historian rather than as a political philosopher. Like J. P. Mayer (1939), he maintains that* The Old Regime *is the fullest expression of Tocqueville's genius. Dicey shares Lord Acton's belief (see excerpt above, 1893) that* The Recollections of Alexis de Tocqueville *provides revealing insight into Tocqueville's personality, but he contends that the work is of interest primarily because it displays Tocqueville's "unrivalled" powers as a satirist of human nature. Dicey also praises the* Recollections *for its uninhibited style, which he finds an appealing contrast to the succinct and correct language of his other writings.*]

[*Souvenirs de Alexis de Tocqueville*] is a fragment of autobiography written with absolute sincerity by a thinker who made it his sole aim to discover and to express the truth. The perfection of Tocqueville's style and the pungency of his epigrams suggest to English readers that the Recollections were intended for publication. The idea is natural, but mistaken. It is of the very essence of Tocqueville's character, it is part of his aristocratic turn of mind, that he never wrote a sentence which was not a model of expression. Moreover, careful students will discover that [*Souvenirs*] is composed with what Tocqueville would have considered a certain laxity and freedom of language. The book gains thereby in interest. In his well-known writings Tocqueville was too careful about his style; for the sake of succinctness and correctness he sometimes sacrificed force. It would have been well had *L'Ancien Régime et la Révolution* been written off with the same recklessness as the *Souvenirs*. More of the treatise would have been completed, and what was completed would have gained in interest. We may take it, then, as certain that the *Recollections* give us Tocqueville's true impressions of [the Revolution of 1848]. But they give us something which is much more important than any addition to our knowledge of French history. They present such a portrait of Tocqueville as could have been drawn by no one but himself. They set before us his whole way of thinking and feeling. They enable us to perceive the nature and the limits of his genius; they tell us the secrets of his character. (pp. 771-72)

His whole life was a ceaseless and successful effort to understand and explain the motives which govern the action of men as members of a civilized society. It is a mistake to consider him as, in the ordinary sense, an historian, though the error is one into which readers may not unreasonably fall. For *L'Ancien Régime et la Révolution* does in fact throw a flood of light on the annals of France, and, if it had been completed, would have been an historical account of the revolutionary movement. *L'Ancien Régime,* moreover, will be the permanent monument of Tocqueville's reputation. *La Démocratie en Amérique* is the achievement—the marvellous achievement—of youthful originality and vigour; but it displays the faults of youth; it is marked by immaturity. A critic of the treatise must never forget that it is not an account of American democracy, but a very different thing, though the distinction has been often overlooked—a picture, or rather an analysis, of democracy in America. Still, Tocqueville's most ardent admirers must admit that his acquaintance with the United States was imperfect, and that his speculations on the intellectual and social conditions and results of democracy, especially those contained in his third volume, are as rash as they are brilliant. *L'Ancien Régime,* on the other hand, was produced in the full maturity of his powers. It cast a perfectly new light on the development of French institutions; it established past contradiction that the old France of the Bourbons lived on in many ways into the new France of the Revolution of Napoleon and of the Republic. It has influenced every book which since its appearance has dealt with the French Revolution. *L'Ancien Régime,* nevertheless, is not in reality a history; it is an historical essay on the nature and tendencies of modern democracy; it constitutes, paradoxical though the assertion sound, the complement to the *Democracy in America.* [*Democracy in America*] is an attempt, and not always a satisfactory one, to explain the characteristics of democratic society in France by a comparison with the fully-developed democracy of the United States. [*L'Ancien Régime*] approaches the same subject from another side: it explains the democratic society of France by tracing out the true relation between the *ancien régime* and the institutions which are the offspring of monarchical despotism, and bear, as Tocqueville proves, the marks of their lineage. And as *L'Ancien Régime* is a treatise and not a history, so Tocqueville is in reality not an historian but a master in political philosophy. If this be not realized, he is certain to be misunderstood, and in the end to be underrated. He lacks several of the gifts necessary to place a man in the first rank of historical writers. He was not a great narrator. He could depict, or rather analyze, with unrivalled skill, scenes and events which passed before his eyes. The description, for example, of the attack on the National Assembly on the 15th of May, 1848, is in its way an unequalled account of a revolutionary crisis. But there is nothing in his works to show that he could have told the great tale of the past with the lucidity and the splendour with which Macaulay narrates the annals of England. Nor was he possessed by that passion for research which (whether rightly or not) is now regarded as the chief among the virtues of an historian. He shows a competent knowledge of French history; towards the end of his life he was on the way to acquiring a mastery of that multitude of details which must be studied by any investigator who tries to explain the condition of France under the ancient monarchy. But erudition was never his strong point. His reputation does not rest upon his learning. Of the United States he knew more than one could have believed it possible for a young Frenchman to learn in not much more than two years. But his acquaintance with American institutions when he wrote the book which gave him a European reputation was superficial, and (what is characteristic) he does not seem to have increased his knowledge of America in later life. As a repertory of information about the United States *La Démocratie en Amérique* cannot stand comparison for a moment with Bryce's

American Commonwealth. In mere knowledge, again, of France before the Revolution he has been surpassed by men of far less intellectual power. Taine has accumulated a far greater number of facts about the *ancien régime* than were known to Tocqueville. Even then, when dealing with his own subjects, Tocqueville was not a great historian. This consideration does not detract from his fame; it only shows that he must be judged not as a narrator, but as a critic. His aim was to discover the tendencies which guide the destinies of modern society. For any ready-made scheme of historical philosophy he entertained a well-merited contempt. (pp. 772-73)

Slight, we may be sure, was his respect for systematizers such as Buckle and Comte. His method was the analysis of human nature as he observed it around him. His fame rests on his unrivalled gift for this kind of criticism. The interest of the **Recollections** is mainly this: They show that Tocqueville's critical faculty was always and in all circumstances at work. The past and the present, things small no less than things great, present themselves to him as problems. . . . Why Louis Philippe gave up the throne in '48, when he might have retained it by using half the vigour he displayed in 1832? . . . How it was that many of Tocqueville's friends welcomed the Revolution of February? . . . What was the course of policy by which the democratic leaders might have attained their end? What was likely to be the future of Socialism? These questions, and a hundred more, occupied the thoughts and received an answer from the genius of Tocqueville. He was possessed, one might almost say haunted, by the desire to know the causes of events and the sources of human action. In society, in the Assembly, in his study, he was in reality one and the same man. His genius was all of a piece; his superiority lay in the truthfulness no less than in the acuteness which he brought to the analysis of human nature. (p. 774)

[In **Souvenirs** the greatest proof] of Tocqueville's sagacity is his attitude towards Socialism. No man ever existed who entertained less sympathy with communistic ideals. In common with the best men of his age, he adored personal freedom; so keen was his abhorrence of tyranny that in the very midst of an insurrection he refused to vote in favour of proclaiming a state of siege. . . . It was not in his nature to observe a fact without seeking to understand it. He asks at once whether Socialism may not have a future before it. (p. 776)

At the date when he wrote down his thoughts Socialism was hated for its wickedness and derided for its absurdity. . . . The foresight of a thinker who, without any sympathy with the end of Socialism, saw that the ridiculous *fiasco* of 1848 [the revolution in France that began on February 24, 1848] did not forbid the future triumph of socialistic ideas cannot be over-rated. (pp. 776-77)

The subtlety and wisdom of Tocqueville's reflections or maxims is known to all readers of his works. But the Recollections place him in a new light. In them we see that his habitual mode of thought and feeling was characterized by a touch of irony. Criticism, when he can express himself freely, passes into satire. In virtue, further, of his supreme analytical power, he becomes more than a humourist; he turns into an historic painter of unrivalled brilliancy, and exhibits himself as the satirist of every man, friend or foe, who for a moment plays his part in the shifting scenes of the revolutionary drama. Consider Tocqueville for a moment as an historic painter. There are few things in literature which can rival his sketch of Louis Philippe's Parliament when it unexpectedly reached its last day. The rage of the Conservatives deserted by Guizot, the tem-

porary exultation of Liberals who thought they were destined to become Ministers, the dramatic effect of the appearance of the Duchess of Orleans and her children on the benches of the Chamber, the one moment at which it was possible that a happy *mot* [word], or a telling action, might have saved the crown for the Count of Paris, the effective silence and the effective rhetoric of Lamartine, all are placed before our eyes as they have never before been brought before the world. Note, too, that the humour of the scene is never absent from Tocqueville's mind. The last President of the Orleanist House of Commons, with his pompous dignity, reminding one of the verger of a cathedral . . . with his utter incapacity, with his absurd habit of showing his fears by flapping his hands, would have delighted Carlyle, who would have roared over the final blunder by which Sauzet deprived his last official act of all dignity: he adjourned the sitting by putting on a hat too big for him and then letting it fall over his face. Take, again, the picture of the National Assembly when invaded by the mob of Paris. The stolid endurance of the representatives, the shouts of the populace, the stifling heat of the room, the cracking of the benches as one ruffian after another leaped upon them, the intense anxiety with which the victims of the mob listened, and during three hours listened in vain, for the drums of the National Guard, the mixed horror and grotesqueness of the situation, are absolutely forced upon the imagination of the reader. But to a student of human nature the strangest part of the whole scene is the attitude of the observer who reports it. Any chance might have caused the massacre of Tocqueville and his friends; but he is perfectly calm, he is absolutely himself: he criticizes, he reflects, he explains how the violence of the mob overreached itself, how the populace failed to triumph because they could not for a moment keep silence; above all, he never loses sight of the absurdities of the scene. He remembers that it is, after all, a piece of acting, and reflects that the men of '48 were, in everything they did, second-rate actors bent on imitating the tragedies of the great Revolution. . . . (pp. 777-78)

Whoever wishes for another specimen of Tocqueville's satiric rendering of historic events should read his account of the Feast of Concord which men expected to turn into a massacre; the representatives of the people attended with pistols and life-preservers in their pockets. Never were pages written which so completely unveiled the hollowness of revolutionary pageants. Tocqueville, even here, whilst impressed with the absurdity, does not fail to analyze the situation; he does not for a moment let us forget that the Feast of Concord had its serious side. While we smile at Lamartine, compelled by the shouts of the mob to embrace the young washerwoman who presents him with a garland and a poem, we are made to realize that at the Feast of Concord all Paris appeared in arms: it was the review of hostile forces preparatory to the death-struggle of June [of 1848].

Tocqueville's genius for the description or analysis of historic scenes, remarkable though it be, sinks into nothing when compared with his power as a painter of character. In the **Recollections** are to be found at least a score of portraits. Louis Philippe, Derfaure, General Bedeau, Cremieux, Ampere, Ledru-Rollin, Lamartine, and many others, are described in words which it is not easy to forget. It is here that Tocqueville's full satirical force comes into play. His portraits are excellent; but they are few or none of them flattering, whilst some are more remarkable by their severity than, it may be, by their justice. (p. 778)

That Tocqueville should judge Lamartine sternly is not wonderful. His faults were exactly the faults certain to offend

Tocqueville's taste and shock his conscience. What has excited surprise is that all Tocqueville's judgments are marked by severity. He spares his friends no more than his opponents. The references even to Gustave de Beaumont do not raise our opinion of the man who (we had hitherto supposed) shared all Tocqueville's thoughts and commanded his warmest affection. The surprise felt at Tocqueville's tone is natural. Everyone knows that Tocqueville was the most devoted of friends, no less than one of the most lovable and beloved of men; and severity of judgment seems at first sight inconsistent with a lovable character. Tocqueville, again, is a philosophic thinker, and there is a commonly-received, though absurd, opinion that a philosopher's judgments ought to be marked not only by calmness but by leniency. Yet astonishment at Tocqueville's sarcastic sternness is, after all, unreasonable. It overlooks the private character of the **Recollections**: they were written for Tocqueville alone; his language must be compared not with the words but with the thoughts of other men. Whoever will reflect upon the way in which we all think about the faults of the persons we love best will conclude that we all of us judge our neighbours as severely, and few of us as justly, as Tocqueville. Surprise, again, at the pungency of Tocqueville's humour implies ignorance of his character; it ignores the vein of satire which is almost inseparable from a genius for the analysis of motives. It is, of course, a fair question whether this gift for satirical portraiture is not of itself inconsistent with sound judgment of men. But in truth every page of the **Recollections** raises curious questions of the very kind which Tocqueville himself would have delighted to examine. (pp. 779-80)

What were the causes of Tocqueville's failure as a politician? (p. 780)

Tocqueville, who had no claim to a seat either in Parliament or in the Cabinet, except his reputation as a thinker and as a writer, stood high in the esteem both of the country and of the Parliament. If he did not become a leader of men, the main cause of his want of success was to be found in his own nature. His **Recollections** prove that Tocqueville understood Man better than men. The constant analysis of motives may reveal to us the principles of human nature; it does not make us understand the feelings of the human beings among whom we live. "Men may be read, as well as books, too much." The knowledge of mankind depends far more upon acute observation than upon critical reflection. Tocqueville had the gifts and the defects of a satirist. He saw with painful clearness the difference between men's actual motives of action and the moral ideals or principles which we all profess to pursue. Hence a certain unsoundness in his judgments of individuals. That French politicians were not all as wanting in virtue as Tocqueville imagines is really proved, if proof were needed, by the respect commanded by Tocqueville himself. We may admit, again, the general truth of Tocqueville's censures on Lamartine; but it is impossible to believe that intellectual inanity and moral egotism were the sole characteristics of the poet and statesman who for a time was the hero of France. Tocqueville himself admits, though grudgingly, that his estimate of Lamartine's policy needs modification. . . . [In] spite of his rare intelligence, Tocqueville hardly entered into the spirit of his age. A certain aloofness of mind kept him apart from his contemporaries; it made him an excellent critic of the facts which he perceived; but it hid from him many facts which are grasped only by sympathy. (pp. 780-81)

Will Alexis de Tocqueville take his place among the writers whose works are true classics. Will he stand in the records of French literature near, or by the side of, Montesquieu? (p. 782)

Tocqueville in 1860 was the spokesman of educated thought; in 1893 he represents a past state of opinion. What, therefore, we may ask, will be his permanent repute? In such matters nothing is decisive but the judgment of time. What that judgment will be no one dare dogmatically predict. . . . Still, it is possible to give reasons for the belief that Tocqueville's fame will be permanent. No recent writer on the philosophy of politics who is read by Englishmen can stand comparison with him for a moment. **La Démocratie en Amérique,** as a picture of modern America, would in any case be out of date. . . . But Tocqueville's work, as I have intimated, was in reality a treatise, not on the government of the United States, but on the characteristics of modern democracy. Looked at in this light, it contains stores of wisdom which even yet the world has not fully appropriated. Taine's knowledge, again, of the *ancien régime* exceeds that of his master; but Taine's writings, as regards France before the Revolution, are nothing but studies in the school of Tocqueville. They are admirable studies; they abound in information confirmatory of Tocqueville's speculations; but Tocqueville, after all, is the teacher. Taine supplies an inventory (so to speak) of the facts which, taken together, make up the *ancien régime*. Tocqueville shows what the facts mean. There is not a thought in Taine's account of society before the outbreak of the Revolution which is not suggested by Tocqueville. When, of necessity, Taine in his later volumes parts from his teacher, he has visibly lost his intellectual guide. The number of the facts collected by the industry of Taine impresses the imagination; but, for want of Tocqueville's lucid criticism, we do not feel assured that we understand their true significance.

With each of two distinguished English writers Tocqueville has some points in common. In dignity and lucidity of style there is a marked resemblance between Tocqueville and Maine. Maine's *Popular Government* reproduces something of the literary effect of Tocqueville's writings. No fair critic, however, can assert that Maine's political generalizations have anything like the merit of the reflections to be found in every page of Tocqueville. . . . The English thinker with whom Tocqueville can be most profitably compared is Bagehot. They have much in common. Both are born critics; both are supremely interested in political speculations; each by force of a genius for analysis could attain, at moments, to a sort of prophetic foresight; Bagehot's letters on the *coup d'etat* are quite as astonishing for extraordinary discernment as is Tocqueville's anticipation of revolution in the early days of '48. Both writers are governed by that passionate love for truth which makes prejudice almost impossible. But their differences are as marked as the similarities. Bagehot, with all his gift for drawing inferences, dreads generalizations with a fear which could hardly be known to a Frenchman. . . . Tocqueville, though fearing systems, certainly likes general statements. Part of the difference between the men at once resulted from and led to a difference of style. Bagehot always seems to be saying to himself, "Though I admire literary grace, though I am an accomplished man of letters, I will never let myself be the slave of style. I will use any word or expression which comes handiest, and which most exactly drives home the point I want to enforce." Tocqueville, even in the privacy of his journal, never forgets the grand style. There is nothing pompous or affected in his language any more than in his thought; but he never lays aside his air of distinction; Lamartine's avoidance of vulgarity was the only point, except his personal courage, which enlisted Tocqueville's sympathy. Tocqueville was in one sense the advocate of democracy: he bid statesmen accept it as a providential fact. But he was at bottom a scion of the old *magistrature* [magistracy] of France;

he was the last of the aristocratic writers; and this, though it may for a time deprive him of one kind of popularity, is a literary virtue. With him fine thoughts are expressed in the best language; the style, no less than the profundity, of his Reflections will make them live; he will always remain the writer who, with more success than any other man of his time, has known how to investigate, with perfect sincerity, what are the motives which have governed the actions both of himself and of his neighbours, and, having understood them, to explain them to others. (pp. 783-84)

> *A. V. Dicey, "Alexis De Tocqueville," in* The National Review, *London, Vol. XXI, No. 126, August, 1893, pp. 771-84.*

JOHN EMERICH EDWARD DALBERG-ACTON (lecture date 1895-99)

[Tocqueville] was the first to establish, if not to discover, that the [French] Revolution was not simply a break, a reversal, a surprise, but in part a development of tendencies at work in the old monarchy. He brought it into closer connection with French history, and believed that it had become inevitable, when Lewis XVI ascended the throne, that the success and also the failure of the movement came from causes that were at work before. The desire for political freedom was sincere but adulterated. It was crossed and baffled by other aims. The secondary and subordinate liberties embarrassed the approach to the supreme goal of self-government. For Tocqueville was a Liberal of the purest breed—a Liberal and nothing else, deeply suspicious of democracy and its kindred, equality, centralisation and utilitarianism. Of all writers [on the Revolution] he is the most widely acceptable, and the hardest to find fault with. He is always wise, always right, and as just as Aristides. His intellect is without a flaw, but it is limited and constrained. He knows political literature and history less well than political life; his originality is not creative, and he does not stimulate with gleams of new light or unfathomed suggestiveness. (pp. 356-57)

> *John Emerich Edward Dalberg-Acton, in a lecture delivered between 1895-99, in his* Lectures on the French Revolution, *edited by John Neville Figgis and Reginald Vere Laurence, Macmillan and Co., Limited, 1910, pp. 356-58.*

EMILE FAGUET (essay date 1900)

[*Faguet, a French literary historian and critic, was influential during the late nineteenth and early twentieth centuries. Although his favorite period was the seventeenth century, he was interested in and wrote extensively on many areas of French literature, from the Pléiade poets to the Romantics. Faguet's discussion of Tocqueville's works, which begins with his brief summary of Tocqueville's character, originally appeared in 1900 in the third volume of his* Politiques et moralistes du dix-neuvième siècle. *One of the first critics to categorize Tocqueville as a sociologist, Faguet argues that "the task which he set himself was to penetrate . . . beneath history to the physiology of peoples." While Faguet praises the originality and prescience of* Democracy *and* The Old Regime, *he contends that both works are flawed by Tocqueville's "rather limited" etiology; in his assertion that Tocqueville "thinks of Democracy as a big force* in itself *and by itself, which drives and drags modern peoples along towards an unknown or obscure goal, and he scarcely ever rises above this conception," Faguet echoes John Stuart Mill (1840) and anticipates George Wilson Pierson and Henry Steele Commager (1938 and 1947). Faguet's inter-*]

pretation of Tocqueville as a sociologist is challenged by John Lukacs (1959).]

[Tocqueville: a] Liberal patrician, with a passionate fondness for liberty and a fairly precise sense of the meaning of that word; on the other hand, so convinced of the inevitability of Democracy in modern times that he accepts it absolutely and is only concerned to reconcile it with the amount of liberty it will bear; very intelligent; conscientious in his work beyond all words; a good historian, a good observer, and not far from being a great writer; here is a very interesting character. (p. 73)

A certain solemnity which he put into his writings, but which is not noticeable in his letters, has done him some harm. It came to him from the days of his magistracy, and from his nervousness, and was a mark of respect for his public which others too often fail to pay. He disgusted those downright idiots who think themselves wits; it is a double success which only serves to flatter him.

His methods were loyal and scrupulous as his soul. He detested the sort of work which comes easily and, consequently, such things as facilitate work—that is to say, thoughts at second hand and general ideas.

He had both fear and hatred of documents at second hand: "When I want to treat of a certain subject, I find it practically impossible to read any of the books which have been written on the same question. Contact with the ideas of others disturbs and troubles me so much that reading their works is painful to me." Here is to be seen the conscientious police magistrate who went to live in America in order to study Democracy; and also the man who all his life was upset and somewhat paralysed by discussion. Some writers like books which others have written on the subjects with which they themselves deal, because they get ideas from the discussion to which such books give rise. But such discussion hinders Tocqueville in his ideas: it disturbs them without inspiring them. He is a man of personal reflections and patient deductions.

It must be admitted that herein was a fault, which accounts for the relative coldness of his books. In a work by Voltaire or Diderot, or even Montesquieu, the author is the centre of a group of thinkers, or people who believe they think, with whom he argues, discusses, yields, replies, comes to terms, and struggles. . . . Thus the book becomes a dispute, well regulated by him who writes, which means that without being necessarily well composed, it is alive. To take into account the ideas of others is a courtesy, if you like, or, if you prefer, a sacrifice; but, above all, it is a resource and an art, and is one way of preventing a book from becoming a monologue.

As for general ideas, they are so inevitable and so dangerous, so necessary and so formidable, it is so evident that the object of work is to acquire them, and that they are adopted in order to shorten labour, and it is so clearly a mark of mediocrity not to have them and a mark of intellectual laziness to be too easily content with them, that it has always been impossible to tell whether they should be more a cause for rejoicing than complaint, whether they should be rather encouraged or discouraged. Tocqueville, like all other people, adopted them towards the end of his investigations, and committed no crime, by any means, in establishing for some of them a very honourable place in the world; but, be it said in his praise, it was after having been extremely mistrustful of them. It would not be too much to say that he was afraid of them. He lived, too, at a time when both in France and in Germany they were being terribly misused. They were for him . . . both fascinating and deceptive. He saw in them particularly temptations too easily inducive to laziness. (pp. 77-8)

Tocqueville has not and does not want to have any historical philosophy. He sees general causes, he sees particular ones, he sees accidents—that is to say, facts—which, by reason of the circumstances in the midst of which they are produced, from the moment of their birth, give rise to consequences much bigger than themselves; he sees other accidents, which are called men, who might easily not have existed, who were, or who became, by reason of their genius, tremendous causative forces with extraordinary consequences, and who thus produced series of events which might not have happened and which owe their existence indisputably to chance—in a word, he sees in history necessity, probability, unexpectedness, the impossibility of anticipation, and accident, things which make the construction of a historical philosophy risky; and he always refused to take this risk.

Finally, then, what was Tocqueville? A very cautious sociologist, much more a sociologist than a historian, and a man who, although he knew history very well, almost eliminated the purely historical element from his sociology. By this I mean that the accidental and semi-accidental, the casual element in human facts, what can hardly be foreseen and cannot possibly be gauged beforehand, are precisely what he called history, and hence comes his desire not to investigate laws and not to believe that laws exist or can be drawn up. But beneath history, counteracted no doubt or favoured by it—more fixed however, and stable—does there not exist something permanent, the customs of a people, the institutions (such as are modelled on these customs), customs which in their turn have been influenced by institutions of very long standing; and this permanent basis, very slow in evolution, has it not also its history, which pursues its course beneath that of the more variable and varied history proper, more calmly, more smoothly, more surely and, consequently, in a way more capable of being foreseen and written about in advance? This seemed probable to Tocqueville, and the task which he set himself was to penetrate beneath accidental history to solid history, or beneath history to the physiology of peoples. (pp. 79-80)

One single big sociological fact struck Tocqueville: the establishment of Democracy in the whole civilized world. In the light of this fact he studied characters, sought causes, foresaw consequences. (p. 81)

Tocqueville never defined Democracy, but he made it everywhere apparent what he meant by the word. To him it is the need which man feels, not by any means to suppress government, but to suppress hierarchy. What annoys man is not the fact of being governed but of being dominated, so to speak, menaced; not of having to obey but of having to respect; not of being restrained but of having to bow down; not of being a slave but of being inferior. This sentiment is neither good nor bad; it is natural and it is eternal. Human society never entirely complies with it but, precisely for this reason, man's efforts in this direction are continuous. Institutions have so much power that they create sentiments; societies are always hierarchical, and when they have been vigorously so, it has happened that the idea of hierarchy became a sentiment with man, counterbalancing the democratic sentiment, and at such a time, social hierarchy, urged on first by its necessity and then by an unnatural, though traditional, inherited and sound sentiment, was never so strong. But all the same the anti-hierarchical sentiment has always existed and the chief social contradiction is precisely the contrast between the necessity for hierarchy and the sentiment for equality. Men then experience the need, not to destroy government . . . , but to destroy and weaken, as far as lies in their power, all the deputy governments, all the authorities, castes, classes, corporations, which come in layers between them and the central government. What they commonly call Liberty is no other than this thing. (pp. 81-2)

Men, if they had (but they had not) the intention, by establishing Democracy, of founding Liberty, would be very much mistaken. The essence of Democracy is not at all to abolish despotism, but, on the contrary, to be attracted to it. Democracy does not establish Liberty, but, as Tocqueville admirably expresses it, "It immaterializes despotism." Under Democracy, despotism is everywhere, but is not perceptible anywhere. It is not in a particular man, a particular temple, a particular senate, a particular caste, it is in the very body of the nation as a whole. It is the nation, represented by its majority, which binds you and imprisons you according to its will. . . . One is tied down by all one's neighbours. Without any joking it must be said that this is a great consolation; for despotism, by force of being impersonal, comes at least to be anonymous. To be oppressed is to be oppressed; but to be conscious of oppression is, above all, to be able to name one's oppressor. When this name is pronounced, by specifying one's affliction, one becomes conscious of it. It is not widespread suffering which is hard but localized suffering. By the suppression of hierarchies, democracies increase the amount of government but diminish the pain of being governed.

They have other advantages. In general they are very conservative. Born out of a relative equality of fortunes, they maintain and increase this equality, which they like, by all the means within their power. . . . [They] create a middle class which is so large as to form a half of the nation. They diminish the rich class and the poor. The class which they thus create is an extremely conservative one, with a horror of revolution and even of any change, which, incidentally, gives added strength to despotism, but decreases the strength of the revolutionary army which all nations possess. Democracy will always be so far conservative as to retain quite patiently things remaining from old régimes which are against its principles. This view, which has received since the establishment of universal suffrage in France a confirmation so striking that it can boast of having become common, was as original as possible when Tocqueville expressed it. (pp. 82-4)

Democracies are also and for the same reasons very pacific. First, they do not like changes, and a big war is a vast change throughout the social state; then, they do not like war because they like neither victory nor defeat. Defeat is fatal to their interests and victory to their prejudices. Defeat is ruinous and disturbing to all the interests of the middle class for one or two generations. Victory creates not only a chief, a state of things to which Democracy can adapt itself, but a hierarchy, which is its contrary. It militarizes a nation and disposes it from top to bottom, according to the military hierarchy; it even creates for a time, maybe quite long, a caste, the warrior caste, which is a thing insupportable to a democratic nation. Democracy, then, is just as pacific as conservative. (p. 84)

Finally, according to Tocqueville, democracies permit and develop a certain gentleness of manners. When a nation is divided into classes, each develops solidarity within its ranks and thus prevents the nation from becoming a united whole. These classes create within the country so many camps which regard each other angrily, or at least with animosity. The suppression of classes, relative equality of conditions, make man sympathetic to his fellows, because they are in like position to himself. Since sympathy for others is, first of all, a matter of self-examination and then of consideration that other people are beings like oneself, it can exist only if other people are visibly similar in nature to oneself. It is just this consciousness of likeness which disappears or is forgotten when a people is divided into classes. Democracy is thus favourable to good will among men. (pp. 84-5)

Here Tocqueville seems quite simply to make a mistake through a strange oversight. He thinks of classes and not of parties. In the change from aristocracy to a democratic state, parties replace classes, and there is not less violent hate between the former than the latter. Indeed, it is more violent. Classes despise each other or envy each other—they do not exactly fight against each other, or at least not all the time. But parties are constantly at war for power. Hatred is endemic in democratic states. This is so true that, on the one hand, politics become in the middle and lower classes under Democracy the art of mutual hatred; while, on the other hand, abstention from politics, even feigned, becomes a sign of good-heartedness. (p. 85)

This flattering section of Tocqueville's picture of Democracy is, all the same, very interesting, and quite true as a whole. At the time of its appearance it had especially the piquancy of paradox in the light of recent events. To characterize Democracy as pacific, as conservative, as gentle-mannered, to men to whom the word Democracy meant unquestionably the Revolution and who could hardly visualize Democracy under any other form than the Revolution, was to arouse interest by provoking contradiction. A certain courage was needed to do this. Paradox is just a game for ordinary men of letters; but in M. de Tocqueville's world it has a bad effect and is not permitted.

Herein must be recognized Tocqueville's principal virtue, that he had the courage of his ideas. When he returned from America, where he had seen Democracy characterized by certain things which it had never had in France, he risked being accused of exaggerating to attract attention by reporting quite frankly what he had seen, and even added that Democracy would have these same characteristics anywhere where it should be solidly established. Except for a few details he was so far right as to be, even for France, a very good prophet. (pp. 85-6)

Tocqueville did not conceal the inconveniences which he believed he discovered in Democracy any more than he did its advantages. I believe he is quite the first person who said that Democracy lowers the intellectual level of governing bodies. Very generally accepted nowadays, this idea was absolutely unheard of in Tocqueville's time. Montesquieu, not really very democratic, had said: "The people is admirable at choosing its magistrates"; and it was fairly natural that his opinion should be general. It is so evidently to a group's interest to choose only its devoted servants, and also so evidently to a whole people's interest to choose only the most intelligent men, that it seemed merely a question of common sense that Democracy should return to power only the chosen intellects of the country. Tocqueville saw in America that this is not at all the case and that practically the contrary is true: "I was astounded to discover how common talent is among the governed and how often it is lacking in those who govern." (pp. 86-7)

[*Democracy in America*] has the single fault of being too full and too comprehensive. Tocqueville is so concerned, and really so obsessed, with the idea of Democracy that he records in this book all that he saw in the United States of America, and attributes to the existence of Democracy in American soil any-

thing characteristic or striking, or even ordinary, that he finds from Boston to New Orleans. The turn of mind, the way of speaking, education, family habits, characters, artistic tastes, many other less important things, all these are considered by Tocqueville as so many effects of democratic government, and as phenomena which must be reproduced, or are almost necessary, wherever democratic government is established. He took into account only one cause, and treated all that he saw as an effect of it. He ought to have overcome his horror of theories of race and climate a little, and especially to have considered the national character independently of institutions and customs, and the traditions preceding the democratic constitution, foreign to it without being hostile, and existing beside it without having to owe their lives to it. It is surprising and rather amusing to find in this book, destined to show what Democracy makes of a people, chapters on: "General ideas and why the Americans show more aptitude for them than the English"; "Americans' susceptibility, small in their own country and big in ours"; "Democracy modifying the relations between master and servant"; "Democratic institutions tending to shorten the duration of leases," etc. Truly there is but little connexion between these various things and democratic government. Tocqueville had many notes and he wanted to put them all within the framework of a study of Democracy. In his notes he had material for two works, one on American life and the other on American Democracy. He ought to have written both separately. . . . [*Democracy in America*] really is, however, a very powerful work, very acute, full of views which were new to his time, and have since been almost all verified with an exactitude which leaves room for reflection.

The Old Régime is the counterpart, and, one might say, the counter-proof, of *Democracy in America*. The latter is an analysis of the democratic state, and the former is an inquiry into the way by which the French passed from the monarchic to the democratic state. *The Old Régime* was made by Tocqueville, like *Democracy,* by direct observation. He had travelled in America; he travelled through the old régime. He restricted his reading to archives only. He pictured to himself Normandy, Touraine and Languedoc as they were in the eighteenth century, and observed their way of living.

He had a surprise. All people set out with preconceived ideas; only those whose minds are small stick to them, whereas those whose minds are vigorous and honest either retain them or renounce them according to the discoveries they make. Tocqueville set out with this idea, very general—I must not say in his party because he never belonged to any party, but in his class— about 1830, that the French Revolution, by centralizing France, had founded, or made easy, despotism in this country; that before the Revolution there was on the surface of the nation a crowd of liberties, localized as well as corporate, which limited and obstructed the central will, and that the only work of the Revolution was to destroy all these franchises. In the presence of well-studied facts he very soon rectified these opinions, in which there was both truth and falsehood, and he made the truest and most precise rough sketch of the work of the Revolution that I know, though he did not have time to enter into the history, properly speaking, of the Revolution.

Before the Revolution there had been three governments in France: (1) a central government—the king and his council, directing France through ministers and commissioners, administering the country down to the tiniest detail, regulating it, making it serve and pay—in short, a modern government, centralizing, attracting and absorbing; (2) a feudal government, making itself felt more or less strongly here and there, imposing local slavery, taxes and particular obligations—tortures and humiliations rather than subjections—not very strong, but embarrassing, cumbersome and irritating; (3) free provincial institutions, surviving in a certain number of places, but common only in Brittany and Languedoc.

These three governments—the one at once a product and an agent of modern centralization, the two others remains from the past—inconvenienced and hindered each other; but the first was incomparably the most powerful. French centralization had been in existence for two centuries, more solidly than in any other country in the world, when the Revolution, which is accused of having made it, came about. (pp. 90-2)

The Revolution came along and, in the presence of the three governments, set to work to destroy the two which had no force and to strengthen the one which was already almost all-powerful. It took pains to overthrow the feudal government and the provincial institutions and to constitute a central government decidedly unhampered and unlimited. These were so certainly its tendencies that its first dream was "royal Democracy," its second, government by one house, and its third, the Empire.

Its conception of Liberty went no further than to place beside the all-powerful central authority an elected house which superintended and controlled it. This was an excellent precaution from the point of view of the administration of finances, and as a guarantee of liberty for the citizens; but it was bad from the point of view of personal, municipal and provincial initiative. It was no guarantee for the rights and interests of minorities, which is the essence of Liberty; indeed, almost it was the contrary, for the parliamentary majority, the country's only representative, gave a legal sanction and apparent authority to the violences committed by the executive against minorities. In a purely political way, the Revolution did nothing more than this: of three governments, of which only one was oppressive, it destroyed the two which were not so.

Here is the theory invented by Tocqueville to explain this peculiar Liberalism; it is ingenious, plausible, perhaps a bit too shrewd, but fairly correct. The lighter a yoke, the more it seems insupportable; what exasperates is not the crushing burden but the impediment; what inspires to revolt is not oppression but humiliation. The French of 1789 were incensed against the nobles because they were *almost* the equals of the nobles; it is the slight difference that can be appreciated, and what can be appreciated that counts. The eighteenth-century middle class was rich, in a position to fill *almost* any employment, *almost* as powerful as the nobility. It was exasperated by this *"almost"* and stimulated by the proximity of its goal; impatience is always provoked by the final strides.

With all respect to this point of view, it must be observed that the Revolution was not Liberal because it is easier to go downhill than to climb up, and to make a state worse than better. France had been becoming more and more centralized for two centuries, and the chances were that any shock would turn this tendency into an accomplished fact. It was easier to continue the work of the monarchy than to try to reform it. The Revolution was based more on Equality than on Liberty because, whereas the levelling process was three parts accomplished, the application of Liberal principles had not begun. Furthermore, Liberal principles are always applied from below upwards, while the Revolution, itself centralized in its assembly and its capital, worked from above downwards: finally, Liberal

principles are applied sensibly and gradually, never by revolution. (pp. 92-3)

Tocqueville paid too little attention to the causes which have involved modern peoples in the democratic state, and this is the chief defect of both [*Democracy in American* and *The Old Régime*]. In general, he thinks of Democracy as a big force *in itself* and by itself, which drives and drags modern peoples along towards an unknown or obscure goal, and he scarcely ever rises above this conception. He can say, surely enough, that the development of wealth derived from real estate, produced as a result of improvements in communication, created among European peoples a middle class which found itself one day the equal of the nobility, seeing that, moreover, especially in France, the nobility did nothing but impoverish and diminish itself. He can say that in America there has recently been implanted on virgin soil a race of equals, not containing in it any germ of aristocracy, and, moreover, maintained by its religion in sentiments of fraternal equality. But I do not see that he goes much farther in his etiology. As a matter of fact, Tocqueville's etiology in general is cautious—for which he should be praised—but rather limited. (pp. 96-7)

[Tocqueville bestowed his ideas upon the public] with great clearness, in good and charming style, with perfect intellectual honesty, and with occasional tediousness and some digressions. He was a good observer; above all, he was a very penetrating and very deft *analyst*. Although he is a good logician, he does not argue from the dialectical point of view, nor is he fond of using the instrument of logic. To him an institution is a living being, whose mind and disposition he discerns by observations of its intrigues and its proceedings; so to speak, its aspect. He is right; for institutions are only men who have disposed themselves in a certain state, united by certain sentiments which were common to the great majority of them. By very energetic application, Tocqueville became fairly familiar with those collective beings which are called nations, and fairly skilled at discerning the chief sentiments which move them. He had more than anybody else an intuition of the modern world, of what it was and what it was going to become, and he is one of those men whose prophecies have been the least belied by subsequent facts. His was a very fine intellect, not very vast, but very alive, which travelled far along the path which it had once for all chosen, and was especially as much as possible sheltered from the danger of being obscured or diverted by the passions. He gave some excellent lessons on the progress of Democracy in modern times and some good advice on the precautions to be taken in the course of this great change. He is a professor of politics, very exact, very enlightening, very well informed and very sharp. (p. 109)

Emile Faguet, "Tocqueville," in his Politicians & Moralists of the Nineteenth Century, *Vol. 3, translated by Dorothy Galton, Ernest Benn Limited, 1929, pp. 71-109.*

HAROLD J. LASKI (lecture date 1931-32)

[*An English political scientist and economist, Laski was a Marxist critic who wrote extensively on American government, politics, and history. Laski's essay, in which he summarizes "what Tocqueville considered the moral ethics of democracy," was originally one of a series of lectures delivered at King's College, University of London, during 1931-32. According to Laski, Tocqueville yielded to the inevitability of democracy with a "sad indignation" at some of its consequences, particularly its subordination of the individual to the masses. Arguing that Tocque-*

ville was one of the foremost exponents of liberalism in the nineteenth century, Laski contends that the dominant theme of both Democracy *and* The Old Regime *is Tocqueville's "insistence on the right of the individual at all costs to affirm his own essence." His opinion that Tocqueville's observations on nineteenth-century economic trends are similar to those of Karl Marx in* The Communist Manifesto *is shared by Albert Salomon and Phillips Bradley (1935 and 1944). Like Salomon and Salwyn Schapiro (1942), Laski acknowledges Tocqueville's recognition of the incompatibility of a capitalist economy and a political democracy.*]

Who does not know Tocqueville cannot understand liberalism. A case of unanswerable power could, I think, be made out for the view that he and Lord Acton were the essential liberals of the nineteenth century. For liberalism is the expression less of a creed than of a temperament. It implies a passion for liberty; and that the passion may be compelling it requires a power to be tolerant, even sceptical, about opinions and tendencies you hold to be dangerous, which is one of the rarest of human qualities. To be conscientious about facts which tell against your desire, to be calm and detached in the presence of events by which, within yourself, you are deeply moved, to admit the inevitability of change and, as a consequence, the impermanence of all matters of social constitution, to recognise that history gives no sanction to any dogmas which claim an absolute value—these, I venture to think, are of the very heart of the liberal temper. Acton and Tocqueville seem to me to have embodied these qualities with a fullness to which no other thinkers of that age can pretend.

The significance of Tocqueville as an observer, indeed, is likely to seem greater rather than less as the years go by. His calm and reflective insight saw with remarkable profundity into the secret of his time. He was the first writer of the nineteenth century able to survey the phenomena of democracy, not, indeed, without passion—beneath the gravity of his sentences any careful reader can detect his depth of emotion—but with something of the detachment that a physicist brings to the study of atomic structure. Compare the inferences he drew from his American voyage with those of any contemporary traveller; set his *Ancien Régime* alongside the narratives of Thiers or Mignet, Quinet or Louis Blanc, and the penetrating quality of his vision becomes at once apparent. With the single exception of Marx, he seems to me to have seen more profoundly the inevitable consequences of the French Revolution as they met the results of industrialisation than any other thinker of the period.

To understand his work, even more, to appreciate its quality, we must grasp for a moment the character of the man himself. He was an aristocrat who recognised that the day of his order was done. He was an aristocrat who realised that the new forces threatened at every turn the qualities in life he most deeply cherished. Sensitive, timid, indifferent to public applause, proud, but unwilling to stoop to conquer the objects of his ambition, made for reflective solitude, yet with a constant yearning to play his part on the theatre of great events, a man of the study who longed to be the leader of a party, yet wholly devoid of all the qualities by which a man can grow into political leadership, it was his fate to watch, with a full understanding, events he did not know how to control. He could see their import; he could not communicate his insight nor lead men to act upon it in the world of affairs. He who longed to be an actor in the drama was given only those qualities which make the supreme commentator upon the play. . . . His temperament drove him to reflection instead of action, to the obligation to analyse instead of the capacity to convince. (pp. 100-01)

I cannot explain a certain remote disdain in Tocqueville except by the assumption that the recognition he received, great though it was, was not the recognition he wanted; that the career upon which his heart was set was the career for which, within himself, he knew himself to be unfitted. It would not be true to say that he regarded himself as a failure, for he knew—how could he help knowing?—the significance of his books. But it is, I think, true to say that he would have forgone gladly the glory they achieved for Guizot's chance, or Thiers', of adjusting principle to action. The political philosopher yearned to play the statesman; and something of the melancholy realisation that the part of each is different accounts for not a little of the temper in which his books are written. He never reconciled himself to the recognition that the value of the thinker depends upon his ability to take long-term views. Though he looked upon humanity from an eminence, it is clear that his heart was always in the dusty conflict of the arena, whose fortunes he yearned to control. (p. 101)

[The] first thing one is tempted to say is that [*Democracy in America*] is not really about America at all. The New World has merely served to provide Tocqueville with materials through which to emphasise the truth of a message he had seen already in the experience of the Old. The book itself, his own journals and correspondence, show us that, in fact, his acquaintance with the United States in general was rather superficial, with its governmental system particularly so. What he saw there, what interested him in its life, was the spectacle of a society freed from the control of an aristocracy. He sought, in terms of a profound observation of the French scene, to deduce from the American condition the lessons of the French Revolution.

The abrogation of privilege, he argued, means an inevitable trend to an equal society. The consequences of this change are momentous. They mean rapid innovation, because the barriers of status are withdrawn. They mean a constant instability of social structure, since the absence of privilege will mean a decreased authority for established families. A democratic society will not, like its predecessors, have natural leaders to whom a public career will remain the highest obligation. Men will have to battle for political position; their power will be built upon the interests they can persuade to support them rather than the principles they seek to fulfil. The abrogation of privilege, indeed, may make it difficult for superior men to emerge, for the passion for equality tends to make men look for identity rather than difference of outlook. They are jealous of difference because it destroys equality; they desire to see the society made in terms of the greatest common measure. The leaders most likely to emerge are those who can best interpret the common mind to itself, rather than the older type who will seek, from the very elevation of their position, to draw ordinary men to their own level. (pp. 102-03)

An equal society tends, from its very nature, to discover a plane of behaviour upon which identity of outlook is at its maximum. This plane is that of material welfare. That standard of progress is immediately and widely intelligible. Its appeal to a democracy is profound. Higher wages, better housing, shorter hours of labour—these are objects of ambition which every one can understand. They bring with them their own scheme of values. They make of material success a goddess. They abandon simplicity because ostentation, being the proof of success, is also the proof of virtue. And material welfare, as an ideal, transforms all social institutions into its own image; their development is conditioned by its demands. In a democratic society religion, for instance, loses its unworldliness, and ceases to be a critic of material standards. It renounces that interference with the daily life of men which was its medieval habit, and becomes, instead, a way of escape from the hard facts of the practical world about it. (p. 104)

Much the same is true of the arts and sciences. It is untrue, Tocqueville argues, to say that democracy is the enemy of either. What it does is to change their direction for its own purposes. Science in an aristocracy is a search for the abstract principles of the universe; the arts are an attempt to discover ultimate principles of beauty which a small and wealthy class has the leisure to contemplate. But a democracy is not interested in abstractions. Aiming at material welfare, its effort is necessarily to extract from human ingenuity the maximum service it can render to this end. The observer will find, accordingly, that its emphasis is laid upon their practical character. Men seek for principle only as it issues into application. It is science as it gives the mastery of nature; science as it leads to invention which increases comfort; science as it minimises the cost of heavy toil, which is revered. Democracy is unlikely to produce men like Newton; but it will produce a hundred inventors who shape principle to useful ends.

So, also, with the arts. There is a greater audience for them, but the range of their understanding is smaller. More artists appear, but the merit of their production is diminished. The handicraftsman can rarely live in an equal society, as he could live in an aristocratic, by supplying the lofty taste of a few; he searches for means which will enable him to make more things more quickly. Inevitably, he becomes the ally of the machine; and the unique products of a past age are replaced by commodities which satisfy a general rather than a particular taste. Where an aristocracy demands the diamonds and pearls of nature, a democracy manufactures them. The rare becomes the commonplace; and it is the characteristic of the commonplace in art to replace what is profound by what is elegant and pretty. . . . So, too, with literature. In a democratic society it will, in general, be the object of authors to attract rather than to convince. "Authors," wrote Tocqueville,

> will aim at rapidity of execution rather than perfection of detail. . . . There will be more wit than erudition, more imagination than profundity; and literary performances will bear marks of an untutored and rude vigour of thought, frequently of great variety and singular fecundity. The objects of authors will be to astonish rather than to please, to stir the passions more than to charm the taste.

A democracy, in a word, wants a literature suited to its leisure hours; and because that is where material success is to be secured the bent of the writer will be turned in that direction.

This is, I hope, a fair summary of what Tocqueville considered the moral ethics of democracy. Clearly enough, its inherent principle is the setting of standards in terms of the wants of the mass. It is clear enough that not a little of his view is shaped by a half-conscious nostalgia for an aristocratic system. He yields to the inevitability of a democracy without comfort in the values it will create. And this hesitation is apparent even more decisively when he discusses the economic and political aspects of its future. Because a democracy is built upon the elevation of material welfare it naturally tends to an emphasis upon the importance of commerce. In a society where the barriers of privilege have been broken down the manufacturer is king; and because equality, on the horizons he can foresee,

is limited to the political sphere its consequences are of a character which fill him with grim foreboding.

In the political sphere it leads to centralisation. The people is sovereign, and the more power it possesses in its organised expression the more sense it has that its sovereignty is real. The tendency, therefore, of every democracy is a concentration of authority in the central government. Men come to regard it as a Providence to the capacities of which they set no limits. The more it does on their behalf the greater the material welfare each believes himself to possess; the wider the scope of its activities the less the distance between citizen and citizen. The tendency is a dangerous one. It enervates the society by making men look rather to the exertions of Government than to their own for their improvement. It weakens the sense of civic responsibility by persuading them that a Government's interests are naturally coincident with their own. It diminishes the interest in public affairs by a continual diminution in the numbers of those who participate in public business. The result is an *étatisme* [state socialism] fatal to the spirit of liberty and independence. From a citizen the individual is transformed into the mere recipient of orders from the administration. His way of life is increasingly regulated for him. The range of pressure and restraint to which he is subjected becomes so wide and so profound that he is deprived of the chance to experiment with himself. The variety of life is stifled; his will is softened and bent; he and his fellows are so compressed and stupefied that they are "reduced to be nothing better than a flock of timid and industrious animals, of which the Government is the shepherd." Liberty, in a word, is sacrificed to the demand for equality; and it is the tragedy of a democratic society that the masses are persuaded to accept the erosion of individuality by the administration as a benefit for which they should be grateful.

Nor is this all. In the establishment of political democracy there is a contingent contradiction which men too rarely perceive. The field is open to the talents; the barriers of privilege have been withdrawn. But because democracy makes material comfort its ideal the field in which talent finds the main outlet for its energy is commerce; and the opportunities afforded there lead rapidly to great inequalities of fortune. (pp. 104-07)

[Manufacturers] develop an aristocracy of wealth without social or political function. The worker has been taught that in the political field he is his master's equal; in the industrial his patent inferiority is brought home to him every day. And, since he learns from the effect of centralisation that he should use his political power to increase his material welfare, it is inevitable that he should ask himself why the equality of political life should not be paralleled by an equality in the economic field. The contrast of his position as a citizen with his subordination as a worker arouses in him a sense of indignation and envy. He begins to demand that legislation shall equalise the results of the industrial process; and when he is told that the rights of property stand in the way he sees no reason why the rights of property, also, should not be the subject of control by popular sovereignty.

Tocqueville's foresight in this regard seems to me one of the major prophecies of the nineteenth century. His sense that an individualistic economy and a political democracy are incompatible has been justified by all subsequent history. (pp. 107-08)

On the basis of a fairly wide study of provincial archives he sought [in *Ancien Régime*] to trace the transformation of the *ancien régime* into the Revolution. What he demonstrated was the gradual character of the transition. Ideas, principles, hopes, institutions, underwent no startling change. One arbitrary system was exchanged for another. The aristocracy deserved to lose its privileges, because, by misusing them, it made a revolution inevitable. But the root of the change was less the depth of the oppression than the fact that improvement made its burden seem less tolerable. Its tragedy was the acceptance by the new epoch of all the centralising tendencies of the old. Thereby, like its predecessor, it chose equality in subjection instead of liberty. But to establish equality by the abrogation of privilege it had to pass through a period of anarchy; and, like its predecessor, it found that only despotism can stem those forces of disorder which anarchy lets loose. . . . It made the laws equal, the administration uniform, the power centripetal; but to attain these things it sacrificed local liberty and civic individuality. . . . (p. 110)

For Tocqueville, therefore, the Revolution did no more than complete the structure of the *ancien régime*. The latter had sought to destroy feudalism by making the Crown the equal master of all its subjects; it succeeded, but only at the price of maintaining the feudal privileges of nobility and clergy. To do so it destroyed local independence—that intermediate power in society which Tocqueville held to be the key of freedom—and transformed the aristocracy from an order which enjoyed privilege in return for function into a leisured and idle caste. The Revolution abolished the privilege, and replaced the Crown by the nation itself. But so much had the privilege been hated that men mistook the attainment of equality for the victory of freedom. Feudalism was destroyed, but its place was taken by a new system of authority more powerful and more brutal than the old.

It was said by Scherer of Tocqueville that his history did for the Revolution what Lyell had done for geology; he substituted evolution for catastrophe. In a sense that is true; and this aspect of his work has marvellously stood the test of time. Indeed, it may be doubted whether any great historical work, Gibbon apart, has been less materially altered by subsequent research. But what remains outstanding in Tocqueville as an historian is the intensity of feeling his work displays. Behind the assumption of calm objectivity it is not difficult to discover the real passion by which it is informed. It is not that he condemns the Revolution even while he understands it; no one has ever written of the Revolution, one way or another, in the way in which a naturalist can describe his specimens. It is rather that, perhaps despite himself, he could not avoid what he intended to be dispassionate science transforming itself into an exalted defence of liberalism. The real clue to his book is its sadness. There, as always, he is an aristocrat driven to accept defeat because he recognised that his order had proved unworthy of its principles. There, as always also, he recognises the inevitability of a new social system even while he is convinced that its results are bound to be disastrous. The history, as it were, is really the prelude to the *Democracy in America,* even though the latter is earlier in date. Like all true liberals, the essence of his creed is unchanging. It is an insistence on the right of the individual at all costs to affirm his own essence, a sad indignation at those implications of social life which, by their nature, subordinate the individual to the mass. It was, I think, John Stuart Mill who said of him that he mistook the consequences of civilisation for the principles of democracy [see excerpt above, 1840]. I should not express the difficulty quite in that way. But I should argue that, both as observer and as historian, Tocqueville is so essentially the aristocrat that

he is unable to accept without pain the collectivist discipline involved in societies of the modern scale. He wanted a degree of uniqueness for men of generous ability, such as himself, that is only capable of purchase upon terms which demand the sacrifice of ordinary humanity to a privileged order. He wanted it; but he knew it to be impossible. Hence, as I think, the pervasive and sombre warning that is the constant undercurrent of all his speculation. (pp. 110-11)

[I] take the essence of Tocqueville's teaching to be even more vital for our day than it was for his own. He was right in his perception that the union of political equality and economic inequality is an unhappy one. It enthrones, as he saw, material well-being as the ideal; it shapes all principles to that single end. Out of it, as he insisted, there emerges a conflict certainly as profound, and probably more decisive, than that which enthroned the middle class in power in 1789. The real lesson of [*Democracy in America*] is the argument that once a people has set its foot on the path of equality in the realm of material well-being there is no logical end to its journey until it has abolished significant differences within that realm. He saw that the privileges of property are an inherent contradiction of popular sovereignty, and that they involve either surrender by their possessors or challenge by those excluded from them. He realised that the natural conclusion of popular sovereignty is the deliberate use of the legislative power to mitigate the sharp differences between men's economic position. A democratic and centralised society comes, sooner or later, to mean the social service State.

But, with a foresight that seems to me remarkable, he saw also that there is a point in the history of that State where its development is either halted or slows down. Some failure in the continuity of economic expansion makes taxation of the rich for the benefit of the poor a more difficult, perhaps even an impossible, adventure. At that point, as he argued, the very progress of the poor in well-being makes them, as in 1789, more resentful of the privileges of the rich than they were in an earlier period when their own advantages were smaller. Before they were prepared to accept privilege on the condition that their own position was consistently improved; now they are led to challenge the very basis of privilege itself. (pp. 112-13)

If I had to find a pedigree for the ideas Tocqueville represents the line of his intellectual ancestry would, I think, be fairly clear. His roots are in Royer-Collard and the Doctrinaires of the Restoration, and, through them, he goes back to Burke, and particularly to that side of Burke which Montesquieu so profoundly shaped. It is, I believe, curious that few of the commentators on Tocqueville have noticed the relation between [Burke's] *Reflections on the French Revolution* and . . . *Democracy in America.* The one, no doubt, is conceived in passion, the other in gravity; the one, also, is a pamphlet fighting for victory while there is still time, the other a pamphlet registering with sadness a defeat. But, at bottom, different as they were in temperament, I think Burke and Tocqueville would have agreed in basic desires. A disposition to preserve and an ability to improve would have been, with each, the essential standard of a statesman.

There is another element in Tocqueville to which it is worth while to draw attention. Few men have seen more clearly how economic systems produce their own schemes of values, or how profoundly these control the thoughts and ideals of men. However different their ways of expression, however antagonistic the purposes they served, Tocqueville would, I suspect, have subscribed to a good deal of what we call the Marxian interpretation of history. Many of his conclusions bear a striking resemblance to those of *The Communist Manifesto;* with, of course, the important difference that what for Marx represented victory for Tocqueville represented defeat. But Tocqueville saw hardly less clearly than Marx the disharmony of interest between masters and men in a capitalist democracy. He underlined hardly less emphatically its probable issue in revolution. He lacked, indeed, that positive—dare I say Utopian?—element in Marx which made the latter welcome the advent of that revolution as the maker of a society in which freedom and equality were reconciled; he was insistent that revolution can never be the parent of freedom. He was too sceptical to believe that a change in the system of production can effect a final improvement in the relations of men. Like Burke, there is, at the foundations of his being, an element of religious mysticism which made him find in a supernatural ideology the only ultimately effective canons of right conduct in men. And there is, of course, the final difference between them, that Marx's interest was in the massed legions of humanity, where Tocqueville's passion is always for a solitary figure, incapable of assimilation by the herd, devoted to high thoughts upon a lonely eminence. There is a fascinating sense in which the whole effort of his thought was to discover the secret of a social order in which there was scope for the manner of man he himself was. Yet that difference must not be allowed to conceal an important resemblance between thinkers so wholly alien in objective. (pp. 113-14)

As a young man [Tocqueville] had written: "I do not know any way of life more honourable or more attractive than to write with such honesty about the great truths that one's name becomes known to the civilised world. I would wish, if only in a small degree, to serve the great cause."

He may claim to have realised it. None of those who inherited directly the results of 1789 saw more clearly the stregnth and weakness of its implications; none, certainly, strove more earnestly or more disinterestedly to make them of service to his contemporaries. He was always loyal, and invariably scrupulous. He put into the work he did all the energies of a remarkable mind and a generous heart. The quality of his effort dignified the great intellectual tradition whose boundaries he so notably enlarged. (pp. 114-15)

> *Harold J. Laski, "Alexis de Tocqueville and Democracy," in* The Social & Political Ideas of Some Representative Thinkers of the Victorian Age, *edited by F.J.C. Hearnshaw, 1933. Reprint by Barnes & Noble, Inc., 1950, pp. 100-15.*

ALBERT SALOMON   (essay date 1935)

[*Salomon contends that critics such as Lord Acton and Harold J. Laski (1893 and 1931-32) who classify Tocqueville as one of the leading liberals of the nineteenth century neglect the "philosophical temper" of his thought. He argues that Tocqueville's "intellectual endeavor essentially transcends any political purpose" and maintains that he was a moralist whose works display "a new mode of thought: the historical and sociological consciousness." In his assertion that Tocqueville's works are distinguished by their sociological approach, Salomon echoes Emile Faguet (1900) and anticipates Phillips Bradley and Robert A. Nisbet (1944 and 1966).*]

We may question the usual interpretation of Tocqueville as a foremost exponent of liberalism, in view of the fact that [*Democracy in America*] was praised by conservatives as well as

liberals. . . . It appears rather that Tocqueville's thinking does not represent merely the concrete intellectual expression of a definite political tendency of the nineteenth century. Although he sought to effect a compromise between the divergent political groups of his time, his intellectual endeavor essentially transcends any immediate political purpose.

To designate Tocqueville as a moralist means two different things. First it indicates that it was a purely personal need that drove him, the thinking man, liberated from scientific and academic traditions, to seek an understanding of the social and political situation and his own place in it. Second, it suggests that in following out the consequences of his researches, Tocqueville came inevitably upon the problem of human nature, and his own distinct idea of man became the presupposition and goal of his work, as in the cases of Montaigne, Pascal, Hobbes and Shaftesbury. Because he assumed this philosophical attitude, which the seventeenth and eighteenth centuries dubbed that of moralist, Tocqueville's work breaks through the narrow boundaries of political actuality. It was not only that he felt grief over the political and social decline of the nobility, but much more that he was affected by the problematic situation of the forms of personal perfection in moral, intellectual and spiritual life under the new social order. Hence the changing of the old society of estates into a democratic order and the resulting transformations of man and his social relations became the center of his thinking. As the spiritual hero or great man was the most intense concern of his life, Tocqueville's historical experience led him to perceive the profound connection of the forms of social and personal life with the totality of the social structure. These are the reasons why we designate Tocqueville as moralist and sociologist. In his experience there were the elements, preformed, of a new mode of thought: the historical and sociological consciousness. . . . [The] existential and intellectual presuppositions of Tocqueville's work indicate that a summary interpretation of it as liberal in the sense of the nineteenth century neglects the philosophical temper of his thinking.

It would not have been surprising if . . . Tocqueville, as a representative of the politically vanquished nobility, had espoused a traditionalist or counter-revolutionary political theory. On the other hand, he might have followed the example of many men of his class who followed enthusiastically the new political movement. But Tocqueville never became a political partisan, even when he accepted the new social and political order and strove to make the best of it. His intellectual perspicacity and moral sensitiveness lifted him above the plane of the political thinkers of his epoch. He was able to understand the unity of the historical process and the inner continuity of the revolutionary movement, begun in 1789 and not yet finished in 1848. He was one of the first to see that the social revolution was the inner consequence of the political democratic revolution. The same intellectual and moral vision enabled him to understand that the decline of the nobility was an inexorable historical process begun seven hundred years earlier. (pp. 405-07)

Tocqueville possessed all the personal qualities necessary for envisaging the crisis of his epoch. He was intellectually and morally so detached that he understood in its logical development the historical process and the final defeat of his class, and therefore he regarded the outcome as providential. Moreover he was so deeply dominated by social morality and the feeling of social justice that he proclaimed the process of economic leveling as a presupposition of the decent existence of the great masses. Nevertheless, in spite of his strong opposition to the nobility as a social class, his family life and personal experience enabled him to perceive that freedom could exist as a form of personal perfection even within the rigid structure and conventions of that order. Quite independently of the political commonplaces of his period, he was aware of liberty as a permanent element in social structure, changing its content with varying historical and social conditions, and remaining correlative to institutional forms and order. His thinking brought him inevitably to a realistic, positivistic and historical interpretation of political institutions, since he felt the need of observing the practical application of political ideas and their functioning under social and historical conditions. (pp. 407-08)

[The first section of *Democracy in America*] is a realistic empirical analysis of the political institutions of the United States. But in [Tocqueville's] interpretation he looks upon American democracy only as an example of the general form of modern social and political structure. From the observation of a specific historical form as found in the constitution of the United States, he had therefore to pass on to general sociological concepts, which comprehend the typical events and movements of modern democracy. Even in the first part of his work Tocqueville goes beyond mere empirical analysis and attempts to derive some general concepts from his realistic observations and the inner logic of democratic principles. A result of the combination of deductive and inductive methods is that the sociological character of his concepts is not always plainly evident.

The second part of his book is far from being an analysis of American democracy, and presents only a few and fairly unimportant American illustrations. In this section of his work it becomes clear how heavily the transformations in the political and social structure of the Western world weighed upon Tocqueville, and how they cast their shadow upon his interpretation of American democracy. Yet this volume reveals Tocqueville at his profoundest. Here he attempts to show the potency of the social structure in fashioning human types; and to demonstrate what transformation in types of thought, forms of emotional response, and moral and intellectual attitudes have been brought about by democratic society, as contrasted with a world of estates and aristocracy. Just as in practical life he accepts the trends toward democracy, so in theory he recognizes the interconnection of all the spheres of human existence. He sees that different social structures aim at different forms of realization. Thus one age will strive for fame and military glory in the social sphere, and for the contemplative life in the intellectual sphere, while another will glorify the civil virtues, human welfare and peace, practical morality, and social sympathy. But whatever the historical transformation of men, the structure of the permanent social functions is always realized even though in varying historical constellations.

Tocqueville entered upon his new approach to reality through history and the sociological consciousness, in response to the obligation imposed upon him by the situation of crisis. His work therefore stands beside the works of Comte, Burke, Marx and Jacob Burkhardt as among the first great attempts at a criticism of western culture on the basis of a new intellectual method, deeply influenced by the political and social situation. (pp. 409-10)

[The] concepts in the *Democracy in America* involve many difficulties of interpretation, which root in the discrepancy between the content of ideas and their concrete literary formulation. Tocqueville was of course intimately acquainted with the great French political and social philosophers of the eighteenth century. The influence of Montesquieu, in particular, is evident in Tocqueville's terminology. Nevertheless the inner content of the book and its place within the framework of his complete works, including his correspondence and conversations, afford the means for a proper interpretation of Tocqueville's rational and formal categories. For example, when at the beginning of *Democracy in America* he remarks that he considers the equality of conditions a characteristic mark of the new world he is referring not only to the political equality of all citizens, but rather to the entire social structure of capitalist democratic society. So also he often uses the political concept democracy, when he means the bourgeois social structure of the post-revolutionary world. In other words the methodological difficulty in interpreting the *Democracy in America* consists in the fact that while the outward form of his concepts is political, their content nearly always refers to a sociological structure or relation. Only in his later work did Tocqueville acquire an adequate conceptual form for the content of his ideas. (pp. 410-11)

The presuppositions and the direction of Tocqueville's thought come to . . . clearer expression in the second part of *Democracy in America* [than in the first part]. Here for the first time in the nineteenth century the attempt is made to show the change in forms of human existence in and through the process of social development. In three great chapters Tocqueville treats of the change in forms of intellectual, emotional and ethical life. It is very significant that in this context he once remarked that he could not imagine anything more barren for the human mind than an abstract idea. Just as Hegel sought the concrete concept, whereby to comprehend the totality of things, so also Tocqueville aimed at comprehending the totality of the social *via* an interpretation of political and social reality.

He achieves new insights into that transformation of the emotions of man which has taken place since the abolition of feudal society: under feudalism personal relationships within a family were determined by social norms, the heir of an estate being considered by his relatives as belonging to a higher social stratum, but in modern society the personal relationships among members of a family are shaped by the subjective power of sentiment. With equal clearness Tocqueville recognizes how the problem of form in poetry is changed by the new psychological interests, and how the close attention to the study of individual souls is a result of the change in the social structure. He declares—a contention which the sociological analysis of literature has since proved—that the pure tale and story is supplanted by the psychological novel, which becomes the typical literary form of the new society. Similarly Tocqueville notices certain striking changes in the realm of intellectual life. Thus he believes that the interest in general and abstract concepts in the political and moral sciences and also in history may be regarded as a result of modern democracy, in which not individuality and personal effort but general social movements are the forces determining the course of history. Equally astonishing is the following insight which is in the general direction of the thinking of Hegel and Comte, although there is no trace of direct influence. Tocqueville contends that in times of a static and feudal structure of society religious thinking runs parallel to the forms of social life, and the absolute is thought of as transcendent, as a supreme creative God and director of the world, but that with the rise of modern democratic mass movements a new metaphysical tendency begins, which tends to set this absolute into the process of history itself. Thus Tocqueville binds a philosophy of immanence into the sociological structure. The second part of *Democracy in America* moves in the direction of a sociology of culture. (pp. 414-15)

[Tocqueville saw clearly] the antagonism between the political and economic form of democracy. He noted that the state was in a position to make all classes of the population dependent on it as a result of the development of financial economy. By state loans and state organization of savings banks the state was able to bring the upper and middle classes into such an immediately interested relationship to itself as to guarantee an effective dependence and participation of the citizen in a definite political form of the state. Ten years before the *Communist Manifesto* [by Karl Marx and Friedrich Engels,] Tocqueville recognized the deep opposition between capitalist economy and political democracy and the tendency of the state to regulate economic affairs. (pp. 417-18)

Tocqueville sees particularly the antinomy between the general norms of democracy, which formally guarantee to every citizen the right and opportunity of advancement, and the social development of the new industry, especially of large scale industry. He observes that the economic and technical opportunities for large scale industries will bring about new agglomerations of capital and create a new industrial aristocracy. This aristocracy, however, will have in common with the old aristocracy only economic power, and in contrast to the latter will be interested only in economic profit. Tocqueville clearly foresees the dangers presented to the social order by such a concentration and collectivization of economic interests, even though he is inclined to underestimate it. On the other hand he sees very clearly that the position of the working class in large scale industries is in insoluble contradiction to the idea of democracy. These workers will constitute the only class or estate—but a negatively privileged one—in this society, which prides itself so much on having abolished the estates. Without savings, without land, the workers are dependent upon the economic situation of the market and upon the wage offers of the entrepreneur. A crisis will bring them unemployment and throw them upon public charity. It is at this point that the state *qua* state will become interested in economic problems and will intervene in the economic order from the viewpoint of social policy. In this way the control and regulation of industry in general becomes one of the most important problems in the tendency toward a new absolutism. (pp. 418-19)

Tocqueville's idea of freedom leads us to the profoundest part of his thought in which, on the basis of sociological and historical knowledge, he undertakes to venture into the realm of general and permanent forms of human existence. Like Kierkegaard and Feuerbach the ultimate aim of his knowledge is a doctrine of man and a theory of social and political existence. It is not by chance that this was the inner tendency of his thinking. Ever since the Sophists we can observe that a time of social change produces a particular type of philosophizing. The conditions of human existence and the general forms of life become the central problem of thinking and the concrete concept the most important need in this intellectual situation. Only in this light can we understand how it is possible to find in Tocqueville's empirical analysis judgments concerning the value of social tendencies and relations for human existence. He was fearful of the stunting of mankind through occupational specialization and increased technical organization. He foresaw the dissolution and the dehumanizing technization of the forms of the economic process under a system of rational direction and administration, and the devitalization and degradation of

labor to merely a dull mechanical exertion of force. He envisaged the approach of a time when the state will not only assume the responsibility for social welfare, but will also take over the schools and churches, converting them into political institutions and the clergy into state officials. Since the state will intervene in and fashion the innermost character of man, it will limit, stultify and destroy the general character of human life. It was this danger, that in the modern democratic world man will come to exert a more or less mechanical function in an enormous abstract state machine, which determined Tocqueville's idea of freedom. (pp. 422-23)

Tocqueville knew that every historical and social structure produces its own form and specific concept of freedom. From his own experience he knew the very spiritualized form of aristocratic freedom, through which personal courage, moral responsibility and spiritual definiteness were realized. But this historical form made transparent for him the eternal task of freedom. It is the everlasting function of freedom to make possible and guarantee the spiritual, moral and intellectual realization of personal perfection. Freedom therefore stands in the service of the highest and ultimate values. It is that form of life by and through which the historical man breaks through the conditions of his existence and participates in an eternal order. In contrast to the negative concept of freedom of political liberalism, Tocqueville's concept may be designated as one of existential freedom. That is, whereas the political idea of freedom merely sets up a relationship between the state and the individual citizen, Tocqueville undertakes the task of showing in a positive way what is the function and meaning of freedom in the totality of man's social existence, no matter how various its historical forms may be. His gravest concern is that every kind of freedom will be eliminated or destroyed in the modern democracy as a result of the growing omnipotence of the state. If social justice is a social goal of the modern democratic world, the corresponding existential concepts must be personal dignity, responsibility and virtue as forms of the individual realization of the social ideal. Will these ideas, however, be able to assert themselves, find their place and preserve their function in a world which organizes human existence under the rational and inexorable direction of the state? One hundred years before the despairing attitude of Max Weber, Tocqueville raised the identical question which was the basis of Weber's work: How will it be possible in this world to preserve those forms of life in which personal, intellectual and spiritual realization are possible? For Tocqueville the future of democracy is dependent on the balance between these forms of intellectual freedom and the institutions of a social democratic order. Because he is fearful that the weight of order will overbalance that of freedom in the modern world, he clings all the more passionately to his idea of freedom as a permanent form of human realization. His optimism concerning democracy is to be explained only as a pedagogic and didactic attempt. The actual content of all his work is deeply pessimistic as to the future of political and social development. (pp. 423-24)

Albert Salomon, "Tocqueville, Moralist and Sociologist," in Social Research, *Vol. 2, No. 4, November, 1935, pp. 405-27.*

GEORGE WILSON PIERSON   (essay date 1938)

[*Pierson is regarded as one of the leading experts on the life and works of Tocqueville. His* Tocqueville in America, *from which the following discussion of* Democracy *is drawn, is considered a skillful reconstruction of Tocqueville and Beaumont's journey through America. Pierson argues that the unscientific quality of Tocqueville's philosophical method "gave birth to errors in his thinking and injected into his classic the strong dose of mortality that it undoubtedly contains." He criticizes Tocqueville for his failure to consult other works on the subject of democracy, his reliance on deductive reasoning, and his tendency to ascribe "all visible forces and phenomena" in America to democracy. Despite these reservations, Pierson concludes that* Democracy *"has merited its immortality."*]

[What Tocqueville was aiming at in *De la Démocratie en Amérique*] was clarity, brevity, and dignity of style. . . . Perhaps his ear also passed judgment on the product, for his best passages attained a cadence and a musical balance that were to haunt his readers. Primarily, however, he tried to say what he had to say exactly, and in the fewest possible words. He was not an accomplished stylist, unless the possession of a distinctly individual manner and an almost classic simplicity earned him the title. Certainly he wrote in a fashion that had become almost outmoded in his day. For all around him seethed and bubbled the heady wine of the new Romanticism. Chateaubriand and Victor Hugo, with their titanic tragedies, their unbridled imaginations, their purple passages, were the acknowledged literary demigods of the period. But Tocqueville wrote as if Romanticism had never even been born. (p. 743)

Perhaps the first 'quality' of his writing . . . was that same intense and almost mournful seriousness that ruled his own life. Few writers, as few men, have been so passionate, so devoted to the truth, and yet so entirely modest and forgetful of self in that exacting pursuit. When he had an unpalatable discovery to announce, he did not flinch. Yet he took no pleasure in criticism. He wrote what he had to, often reluctantly and as if under some outside compulsion. There was a flavour of fatalistic abnegation, of warning and of prophecy, of sadness mixed with the most sympathetic concern for the suffering humanity for whom he wrote.

Again there was another peculiarity about his style. His exposition was 'logical' and 'philosophic' to a degree. He used the inductive and deductive methods both, and never let whimsy obstruct the rigorous development of the argument. For like the classicists . . . , he instinctively believed in reason and in the sovereign capacity of man's intelligence. His own experience seemed to justify this faith; for when he sat down to develop a given topic, he never finished the chapter without, through the strait exercise of thought, seeing it grow in importance and in implications.

The immediate effect of such ratiocination was, of course, synthesis and the development of general ideas. And these ultimate generalizations, when they emerged, often came clothed with a deeper meaning and a wider application than the author himself had at first thought possible. The whole process of composition, certainly, reposed on a rigorous method, under the severest self-discipline. For the French people Tocqueville reported not only what he had found, but what he was forced—after the longest and most conscientious meditation—to conclude about his findings. (pp. 745-46)

If he was an observer of extraordinary perseverance and intelligence, a scholar of good judgment, and a philosopher with a meditative turn of mind, nevertheless his outstanding distinction lay elsewhere. At least it seems clear that part of his genius was a matter of faith and of purpose, rather than of literary performance. Specifically he held a certain belief as to the destination of mankind. And, because he held that striking and pessimistic belief, he was driven first to find and then to

advocate a special program of social insurance. Together, this foreboding conviction and these precautionary warnings constituted what might be called the *doctrine* of Alexis de Tocqueville. Without that doctrine he would never have written, and but for it he would hardly to-day be remembered in France.

The pessimistic faith or conviction, underlying Tocqueville's whole performance, was of course that famous—and by now familiar—belief of his about the foredestined levelling down of conditions that was to overtake all the peoples of the civilized world. It was his specific creed that the progressive elimination of privilege and inequality had been the unperceived but fundamental law of the past, as it would continue to be the great gravitational principle of the future, for at least another century to come. The momentum, certainly, was too strong to be resisted. All societies of which he had any knowledge were now going toward, and would sooner or later arrive at, an almost complete equality. The word that he used was *démocratie,* but by *démocratie* he did not mean what the English-speaking world sometimes supposed. The distinction is important. For when they translated his word into *Democracy,* they failed to note that what he really was predicting was *equality;* equality in social and economic conditions as well as in political: equal privileges in government, equal civil rights before the law, equal economic benefits, equal intellectual training, no classes of any kind, even the disappearance of distinctions in fashion and 'society.' (pp. 746-47)

It will not escape the student that Tocqueville . . . reversed the sequence of his perceptions. For literary purposes he implied that he had discovered his great natural law of modern societies in America. Actually, this idea had been the product of his youthful experiences at home. The sad history of the old aristocracy, the fate of the Restoration Monarchy, the suggestive lectures of Professor Guizot, the pronouncements of certain statesmen of France: all had seemed to Tocqueville to indicate that the process of levelling down had been going on for a long time and could not now be stopped. His discoveries abroad, therefore, had but confirmed a conviction that he had already begun to entertain—with the further result that now he felt justified in applying his law to the whole modern world. Such was the article of faith, the fatalistic belief, the *idée-mère* which ruled his thinking. (p. 747)

Tocqueville took no pleasure in prophesying for its own sake. The role of Cassandra held too little appeal for him. As a matter of fact, even if he had been able to paint an exact likeness of the society that was to come, he would never have undertaken the task, unless he had felt that some use could be made of the picture once it had been presented. In a word, it was only because some thread of optimism was mingled with Tocqueville's pessimism that he bothered to write. Despite his fatalistic premonitions, perhaps something *could* be done about the future. In addition to a conviction and a pat illustration, then, it should be recognized that he had an ulterior incentive, a third purpose. *De la Démocratie en Amérique* was composed, partly because he foresaw, partly because he wanted to foretell, but partly also because he wanted to forewarn, and to forewarn in time. (p. 748)

[*De la Démocratie en Amérique* contains] some really serious faults. On thoughtful analysis, for example, it will be clear that the doctrine of his commentary was tendencious, and in certain respects pretty thoroughly misleading. Again, the description of the United States that it supplied left much to be desired, both as a piece of contemporary observation and as a vision of world conditions to come. Finally, Tocqueville's *method* itself—his style of writing, his way of research, his prevailing habit of thought—was vulnerability itself. In fact it was his philosophical method that, more than any other factor, gave birth to errors in his thinking and injected into his classic the strong dose of mortality that it undoubtedly contains. . . .

It has been pointed out again and again—and with justice—that Tocqueville was neither a historian nor a scientist but a philosopher, and a philosopher whose concepts and whose habits of thought were not well calculated, if he wanted, rigorously, to find the truth.

Certainly Tocqueville was not, in practice or in intention, a real historian. For an untrained amateur—or even in comparison with some of the acknowledged historians of that day—he made an exceptionally intelligent use of original documents and of secondary works. But he was not interested in recording the past; and he so thoroughly slighted the backgrounds of his subject that in seeking explanations he came to mislead himself. (p. 756)

[It] has been said that Tocqueville was unscientific. Both as a student of politics and as a reasoner on his observations, he has been accused of being decidedly inaccurate. Certainly he was not precise in his use of terms, despite his conviction that such precision was necessary. One word alone was enough to convict him on this charge. As a matter of fact, how he ever allowed himself to use *démocratie* in seven or eight different senses is still something of a mystery. It was his key word. To *démocratie,* if to anything in his book, he should have given a precise meaning. Yet he did not. The result was that it held out false promises to men of all parties and beliefs. To Americans the word might mean representative self-government; to the French Republicans, manhood suffrage and the destruction of privilege; to the conservatives, the violences and aberrations of the populace; to the socialists the charms of a regulated commonwealth. And each of these antagonistic groups would be able to cite chapter and verse in the new gospel for proof. Perhaps Tocqueville was persuaded that the levelling tendency or law embraced all these possibilities, as special manifestations. If so, however, he was forgetting the mutual incompatibilities of the variant readings. So vague and general a term was indefensible. If generously used, it could only lead to multitudinous contradictions, as indeed it did.

Once more, Tocqueville was unscientific in his use of, or rather in his failure to use, contemporary literature. For not only did he deliberately avoid other books immediately on his own subject, but he never did do enough scattered, general, careless, miscellaneous reading. As a result, he sometimes seemed to come to subjects as to an undiscovered country. Not having the guidance of other explorers, he found it hard to start in; and in the end he often had the air of announcing a new discovery, when actually he had but restated conclusions already reached by others. In one or two instances, he slighted, or even missed altogether, what others considered a salient feature of his subject. The method had this to recommend it, that it enabled Tocqueville to dodge the ruts and that it gave his writing a tone of originality and appealing sincerity. But it was hardly scientific.

The same was true of his choice of subject, which was far too large for any exact analysis. To describe the political institutions of a foreign people—as in his first two volumes—was quite hard enough. But when he elected to compare America to France, a known to an unknown, the difficulty was immensely increased. Tocqueville himself was essentially 'binocular'; he seemed to have the power to bring two widely separated objects into one field of vision. Even when he was most successful in making this comparison clear, however, the reader found the constant switching back and forth a fatiguing business. And when he then proceeded to include in his field the even larger topic of equality in Europe—as he tried to do in volumes three and four—the strain on the reader, and on his own extraordinary powers of condensation, was visibly too great. In effect, he was analysing the whole of modern civilization, yet trying to explain it all by the development of one great idea. Obviously, such an effort could be scientific neither in method nor in result.

Yet Tocqueville personally believed that he was using a scientific method, and the most rigorous accuracy. For he had a clearly developed approach, and he governed his thinking by a most exacting law. On any given topic, his research was painstakingly pushed through the same pre-determined—and to him scientific—series of steps. He would begin, as in New York, by a conscientious search for document and information; his first step was always—eliminating prejudice—to establish the ordinary and visible facts. To Tocqueville, however, mere fact meant nothing. It did not explain. His second step was therefore inductive and interpretative. He would study the phenomena he had noted, analyse them for points of similarity, ponder their probable origins, and thus seek to read into them a message. In a word, he would *induce* into his materials their real character: find the basic idea or ideas of which they were all an expression: squeeze from them their hidden meaning. That done, he had the key. And rigorous, logical thought would *deduce* from the fundamental force that he had now discovered all the consequences that it held for the given society. By linking observation, induction, and deduction, in that order, Tocqueville made bold to think that a scientific explanation could be produced.

The trouble was that Tocqueville overreached himself on the second and third steps. He was too logical, too mathematical, too intellectual—and not sufficiently inquisitive. He relied too much on induction, and then too much on deduction. Once he had found the 'true explanation,' for example, he ceased to be interested in gathering facts, or, rather, he tended to gather only those facts that fitted his theory. And once his theory or thesis was fairly stated, then his preoccupation became the discovery of all its myriad consequences. On these he would ponder and ponder until he was satisfied; and he was rarely satisfied before he had somehow and in some fashion related almost every observable phenomenon to his great central Law or primary cause. Sometimes the intensive meditation that Tocqueville practised led him to the most unexpected and illuminating discoveries. On other occasions, however, he could be detected drawing from the same origin the most contradictory conclusions. And in any case, the tendency was to over-simplify, to explain too much by too little, to substitute a universal man for particular men, to fuse all causes and all origins into the single law.

The vice of Tocqueville's method, therefore, was precisely its *unscientific* quality. And the vice grew on him. In his first two volumes he showed himself an observer of precision and amazing insight. As his American experiences receded, however, his dependence on his reasoning powers and his dialectic increased proportionately. He became an exponent of the *a priori* method. He did not check his thesis—which had now assumed the status of an inveterate prejudice—against fresh observation. His reasonings became more and more abstract. He began to write sections on the influence of *démocratie* on American intellectual life, or on American morals; and chapters on the sources of poetry, or the proclivities of standing armies in equalitarian societies. The tendency of the eighteenth century classicists, or even of writers of his own day, to express themselves in sounding generalizations, Tocqueville unaffectedly denounced. Yet he himself came to resort more and more to sweeping statements and all-inclusive final phrases. He happened to be a master at the art of condensing thought; and some of his pages were so closely packed with ideas as to require the slowest, most painstaking digestion. Generally, the reward for the reader was proportionately great: it was as if Tocqueville had lifted himself onto some high mountain, and thence in one swift glance comprehended a majestic countryside. Yet all too often, on the other hand, his thoughts seemed to have spun out into pure theory. The process of deduction from deduction had been carried so far that all connection with fact and reality had been left behind; and in effect a rational process had wound up in purest nonsense. (pp. 757-61)

Essentially, Tocqueville's whole personal philosophy revolved around four very simple ideas. The first was a belief in *necessity* or inevitability: the concept of predestination translated into the field of social evolution. He shared this faith in natural law with Guizot and Mignet and many of his contemporaries. In his second idea, however, he was more original. Where some believed in divine law, and others in the law of economic progress, Tocqueville felt sure that the *levelling tendency*—the progressive equalization of conditions—was what was fundamental and in the long run unavoidable. His third idea was an immediate product of this assumption. If progress was toward equality, it must be away from inequality: that is, away from privileges, class divisions, and distinction of all kinds. In his mind, therefore, Tocqueville created a stuffed image of the past and labelled it *aristocratie,* just as he had already made a dummy model of the future with the cognomen of *démocratie.* Finally, his fourth idea was a belief in the superior desirability and effectiveness of moral forces, as distinguished from forces of a military or an economic or a mechanical order.

This last predilection led Tocqueville to emphasize, in fact to exaggerate, the role of religion and of personal morality and of law in the maintenance of good government. It led him also to champion the individual—or man as a moral entity—against both the claims of the State and the destructive regimentation of some mass Utopia. What he wanted to preserve was freedom and human dignity. If equality had to come, let there at least remain some opportunity for free thought and free action: in a word, for the realization of the highest capacities of man. Comfort? Physical comfort, and wealth, and economic happiness? Tocqueville hardly considered such alternatives. On any comparative basis they stood beneath his contempt. In fact, the weakness of Tocqueville's fourth belief lay exactly on its negative side. He was not interested in material progress. He was so little interested, indeed, that he had never seriously considered the industrial revolution! In England he had been struck by what had seemed a feverish commercialism. But in the United States he had neglected entirely the one great factor that was going to transform his chosen civilization almost overnight. . . . Tocqueville had spent nine months in America, and now ventured to predict the future of many American institutions, without once giving any adequate consideration to what was already becoming the most potent factor in nineteenth century American development: the industrial exploitation of the continent, with the transformation of an agrarian population into an entirely different order of economic society. The penalty

for so one-sided an assumption would of course have to be paid some day. (pp. 761-63)

Without real question, of course, it was his second idea—his belief in an inevitable *démocratie*—that constituted his most debatable proposition and the weakest link in the chain of his philosophy. For, aside from his questionable definition of the word, he tended . . . to assimilate all visible forces and phenomena under the one master head. What Tocqueville attributed to the operation of *démocratie* in England, for example, John Stuart Mill believed to be due to the normal activities of a commercial middle class [see excerpt above, 1840]. . . . Americans were to find Tocqueville transforming their representative democracy into an example of pure equalitarianism. . . . In a word, even granting that Tocqueville had divined the most important influence that was to operate on the civilization of the western world, he made his explanation too narrow and too simple. In neglecting (or misinterpreting) the other, almost equally important, influences, he falsified his interpretation. (pp. 763-64)

In the field of political science . . . Tocqueville made two considerable errors of omission. He failed to notice the growth of a two-party system, based upon patronage and spoils. And . . . he neglected the intermediate unit in American government, the State, with its significant possibilities as a balancing force and an experimental laboratory. (pp. 765-66)

Tocqueville never allowed to education the beneficent possibilities that the American people still see in it. He missed the rising abolitionist movement. He failed to give adequate credit to American enthusiasm for liberty and freedom, as distinguished from jealousy of privilege. . . . [He] underestimated the power of the executive branch in American government. And he perhaps overestimated the tendency of democracy, at least as practised in the United States, to degenerate into tyranny by the majority.

As to this last pronouncement or warning, Tocqueville's American readers were once almost unanimously of one mind. The conscientious Frenchman was entirely wrong. Majorities changed too rapidly; and, anyhow, there could be no tyranny in the United States. (p. 766)

To-day, with the Civil War, the World War, the 'Red Scare,' and the 'Depression' in retrospect, one cannot afford to be quite so complacent. Perhaps a suppression of individual or minority rights *is* possible, and even in times of peace. Perhaps, therefore, before many more years have passed, what was once a grievous error may have to be listed instead as one more example of Tocqueville's uncanny perspicacity.

Yet meanwhile a very curious omission on Tocqueville's part requires notice. In all his talk of tyranny, in all his warnings as to the dangers inherent in equalitarian government, Tocqueville never pointed to the one kind of tyranny that nineteenth century Americans actually did come to experience, to their hurt and later regret.

For where did he mention *tyranny by a minority*? . . . Might not the minority of wealth or industrial control perhaps misuse their power, even to the point of securing legal sanctions for oppression? And what, for example, was to stand in the way of unscrupulous 'machines'? Might not some ring of venal politicians so twist the democratic processes as almost openly to cheat the voting millions? In short, was not the innocence and carelessness of the masses even more to be feared in a democracy than their malevolence or positive tyranny?

Somehow—and it is to be regretted—Tocqueville never adequately grasped this possibility. With his fears of the mob, and his concern for the atom individual, he did not enough allow for the ingenuity of the designing few, the potential indifference of the many. Whatever the justice of his remarks about tyranny by the majority, therefore, the emphasis of this prophecy was hardly warranted. (pp. 766-67)

If it be granted that Tocqueville's philosophic method was too scholastic and theoretical, his interpretation of the nineteenth century too narrow, his portrait of the United States defective, and even his style too condensed and old-fashioned—if we recognize, in a word, that his commentary left so much to be desired—wherein, then, did his distinction as an author lie? (p. 768)

Tocqueville did not owe his greatness to any Olympian disinterestedness, still less to an adroit inspiration and a beguiling humour. As an observer he was able enough, but he could not remain aloof. Rather, his own commentary was solid, passionate, a little prejudiced, and very humble. One could not read a single page without being impressed with his sincerity and utter unselfishness. His every paragraph breathed a transparent honesty and an overwhelming desire to be right. . . . And when he criticized, one could not feel resentment. For it was clear that he had tried to put his 'whole dose of intelligence' into his work, and had begun by purging himself of wilful prejudice under the most austere and ascetic self-discipline. Other writers might lay claim to honourable intentions. But with Tocqueville morality and high principle were an absorbing cult. His very anxiety made an impression on his readers. And by his humility, his concern for humanity, and his devotion to the truth, he won their undying respect.

Furthermore, Tocqueville startled and interested his readers by his peculiar approach. For if he was no true historian of the past, and if his technique of observation and analysis did not in fact measure up to that employed in the physical sciences, he did possess a novel and extraordinary virtue. He was a *sociologist*—and very nearly the first sociologist in French experience. Not until many years later would it become common for men to examine into the basic laws of human association, in order to find out—as one might study the gravitational movements of the stars—what makes societies act the way they do. If Tocqueville was not interested in the 'events' of history, the unpredictable accidents, the military victories or the casual revolutions, it was precisely because he thought such 'history' superficial. What he was looking for were the underlying and enduring influences, the forces perpetually at work, the customs, moral habits and basic institutions guiding the evolution of human groups, over long stretches of years. From the point of view of society, that kind of history alone seemed real. . . . To use a modern term, he was a psychologist, and a psychologist whose subject was not the individual human but all humankind, not the people of Paris but the societies of the contemporary world, not even civilization as it was but civilization as it was becoming. Like some observant mariner who, beneath the meaningless swells of a boundless and storm-tossed waste, discovers a steadily moving tide, some great Gulf Stream irresistibly bearing him on, Tocqueville was sounding for subterranean currents. If he could find them, he would know in what direction society was moving, and how fast. Meanwhile, he could afford to ignore the contradictory winds and the accidental lurches of 'history,' for he intended to make himself the historian of institutions and of long-range societal development. And that was *fort nouveau* at the time when he undertook the task.

Tocqueville's third quality—or appeal to the readers of the nineteenth century—arose directly out of this ambition. For in his self-imposed role of pioneer he managed to make a number of real discoveries, both about the present and about the future. Despite a faulty technique and a series of errors in observation and in judgment, he proved himself an able and intelligent explorer. What he reported about the always present characteristics of human societies arrested the attention of his contemporaries; and what he ventured to offer in the way of prediction opened new vistas to their startled gaze.

It was Tocqueville more than any one else, for example, who persuaded the liberals of the nineteenth century that aristocracy could not be revived, and that a greater equality of conditions was the destiny of Europe.

Again it was Tocqueville who pointed out that democratic self-government was not necessarily the perfect government, or even perhaps a desirable state of affairs. For he never let his readers forget that the raising of the underprivileged to a share in power and responsibility would bring dangers as well as opportunities. It would mean a jealous levelling down as well as an idealistic grading up. And once classes and privileged groups were gone, the obstacles to anarchy or to despotism would also be removed. (pp. 769-70)

It was Tocqueville . . . who first made the intelligent politicians realize the benefits that, ideally, could be drawn from localism or decentralization. Surprisingly enough, he even had a suggestion as to how some of those benefits could actually be achieved without sacrificing the national strength and unity so vital to France, surrounded as she was by a hostile Europe. Let the laws continue to be national, but let the administration of those laws be decentralized. If citizens could be encouraged, and locally trained, to take a larger share in their own communal government and its affairs, the result would be, not a loss of unity, but a tremendous increase in energy, satisfaction and stability. In the same fashion, let group institutions be encouraged. In fact, let everything possible be done to encourage and bolster the individual and the small local group against the crushing weight, and the annihilating philosophy, of a superior State. (p. 771)

[When it was realized] that Tocqueville's book was essentially not one of abstract philosophical speculations but one of the most immediate and practical politics, the surprise and interest and enthusiasm of the European reading public could not be contained. And with the years a popularity that had been captured overnight matured into an enduring reputation.

Whatever his shortcomings or deficiencies, the simple fact was this: Alexis de Tocqueville had taken one of the great enthusiasms of the century, and given it a magistral analysis. (p. 772)

[A] large part of what Tocqueville wrote is still valid. As a sociologist he was sometimes primitive, and as a political scientist inexperienced, so that he made numerous mistakes. Yet more than any other writer . . . he had the gift, the extraordinary faculty, of understanding the essential problems of self-government. What the tendencies of democracy were, what its risks and dangers might be, what steps should be taken to exorcise the evils and preserve the good, he saw and carefully set down. (p. 774)

De la Démocratie en Amérique, it may reasonably be concluded, has merited its immortality. For, in the pages of this humble commentary, Tocqueville treated a great topic with the grasp of a master and a prophetic instinct hardly short of providential. . . .

[He] had written well, and on the mind of the world he had left his enduring mark. Not for his scorn, not for a towering personality would he be remembered. But because he was humble, because he was wise, because he had tried to be, so far as his frail tortured nature would alow, as just as Aristides.

His was a mind that fell just short of genius. But he had used it to pioneer. And as a pioneer he would be followed and long honoured. And this would be true despite his foreboding anxiety and his failure to comprehend the whole thought of his time.

He had 'performed the task with the air of a half-awakened man marching in the insufficient light of the first dawn.' But he had gone ahead. (p. 777)

> *George Wilson Pierson, in his* Tocqueville and Beaumont in America, *Oxford University Press, New York, 1938, 852 p.**

J. P. MAYER (essay date 1939)

[*Mayer is considered the foremost Tocqueville scholar of the twentieth century. The following discussion of* Democracy *and* The Old Regime, *which originally appeared in 1939 in Mayer's* Prophet of the Mass Age: A Study of Alexis de Tocqueville, *focuses on Tocqueville's efforts to insure the coordination of freedom and equality. While Mayer praises* Democracy *as an unparalleled description of the structural aspects of a democratic society, he argues, like A. V. Dicey (1893), that* The Old Regime *is Tocqueville's most important work. In Mayer's opinion,* The Old Regime *is a "monumental contribution" to political and philosophical thought "which will retain its validity as long as there are Europeans who seek to understand the meaning of their history."*]

De Tocqueville had been made aware, by the particular dynamic of French social development, that freedom and equality, which had been raised by the great French Revolution to be mankind's basic demands, are by no means inalienable the one from the other. Plainly the Revolution of 1789, though restoring civic equality, did nothing to bring liberty to individual man. The principle in political life of equality without freedom seems to de Tocqueville to be as untenable as that of freedom without equality. How can the co-ordination of freedom with equality be assured? De Tocqueville felt the essential importance of such a co-ordination, and sought to extract the norms of it from the nature and operation of the North American political institutions: independent administration of municipalities, freedom of religious belief and of the press, security of judicial independence; above all, centralization of government (necessary within certain bounds) without over-emphasis. At this point de Tocqueville's analysis reaches a depth which will establish for all time his place among the great masters of Western political thought. In *Democracy in America* . . . he writes:

> A general law has been made and sanctioned, not only by a majority of this or that people, but by a majority of mankind. This law bears the name of Justice. . . . The rights of every people are consequently confined within the limits of what is just. A nation may be considered in the light of a jury which is empowered to represent society at large, and to apply the great and general law of Justice. Ought such a

jury, which represents society, to have more power than the society in which the laws it applies originate? When I refuse to obey an unjust law I do not contest the right which the majority has of commanding, but I simply appeal from the sovereignty of the people to the sovereignty of mankind. It has been asserted that a people can never entirely outstep the boundaries of justice and of reason in those affairs which are more peculiarly its own; and that consequently full power may fearlessly be given to the majority by which it is represented. But this language is that of a slave. . . . I am, therefore, of opinion that some one social power must always be made to predominate over the others; but I think that liberty is endangered when this power is checked by no obstacle which may retard its course and force it to moderate its own vehemence.

(pp. 43-5)

Some have considered de Tocqueville's conception of sovereignty, as he formulates it in the preceding sentences, to be, logically speaking, not conclusive enough—an objection which seems to me entirely baseless. The abatement, by means of political devices, of undivided sovereignty—political despotism as he calls it—is in no way de Tocqueville's intention. His desire is to guarantee the freedom of the individual by creating an equilibrium in the State. He conceives of the State as being subject to a higher norm, the idea of Justice, against which idea the State is ever, in the last instance, to be measured. Thus the State is not in itself, as Hegel would have it, the realization of the ethical idea, but possesses the capacity of attaining this ultimate ethical norm only in a supreme instance, namely, by non-violation of the idea of justice. For de Tocqueville the actuality and the idea of the State constitute a tension. The State is interpreted by him as an approximation to the "Law of Justice." (pp. 46-7)

De Tocqueville cherished a profound belief in the essential freedom and equality of man, and held that only under a political regime which succeeded in establishing these two indispensable conditions could the dignity of man be inviolably assured. These presuppositions alone make possible any understanding of the doctrines of state and society for which Western thought is indebted to de Tocqueville. (p. 47)

[We] think it unjust to measure *Democracy in America* by the yard-stick of knowledge not available till the present day. Since de Tocqueville wrote his book, America has long been entirely colonized, a capitalistic structure has spanned its length and breadth, and the number of its inhabitants has increased tenfold.

The abiding importance of de Tocqueville's book in face of these major transformations is due to one determining cause, namely, that its main accent does not lie on generalizations drawn from any one particular historical situation, de Tocqueville's whole concern having been the presentation of the structural features of a democratic order of society. His purpose was to gain comprehension of the institutions and philosophy of a democratic society, of which America appeared to him to be the example *par excellence.* This designation of America is still valid up to the present time, since the basic elements of democracy have by no means disappeared, but have become welded into the traditions of American life. (pp. 49-50)

A comparison of [the last volume of *Democracy in America*] with the first two shows its undoubted superiority; the line of thought is more concise and more profound, the style maturer and more polished; the range of view has become more universal. It cannot, however, be said that the book shared the enthusiastic reception of the first two volumes. It was, according to Gustave de Beaumont, not less purchased but less read. This is easily explained, for subject and method were too novel. Who indeed before de Tocqueville would have undertaken to show, in addition to its influence on political affairs, the interconnexion of the democratic order of society with the intellectual, emotional, and moral substance of a nation? Machiavelli, Bodin, Rousseau, and Montesquieu undoubtedly initiated such an enterprise, but none of these four great modern predecessors of de Tocqueville had at his disposal so extensive and sure a knowlege of that "logic of the heart" . . . whose precepts had been rediscovered by the acute mind of Pascal, and by the deeply religious feeling of the Jansenists. Only Aristotle's *Politica,* based as it was securely on the inherent political sense of the Greek, was able to harmonize the moral forces of mankind with the nature of political institutions. None of the newer political philosophers equalled de Tocqueville in his appreciation of the idea of the totality of political man in the Greek sense, enriched now by the dawning modern mass state. A possible exception is Thomas Hobbes, whose naturalistic-mechanistic psychology, however, obscured for him phenomena which de Tocqueville found brilliantly portrayed in such great French moralists as La Rochefoucauld, La Bruyère, Vauvenargues, and, last, but not least, in Pascal.

Analysis is profitable only when things have first been seen and experienced in their living totality. Herein lay the unique greatness of Pascal, whom de Tocqueville followed in applying to the political existence of man Pascal's own method of viewing moral phenomena in connexion with their appropriate categories.

De Tocqueville, however, was not only without true predecessors, he was without true successors. The method and substantial content of the third volume of **Democracy in America** are today still completely unknown, although John Stuart Mill has described the book, with profound truth, in his review of the complete work, as "the first philosophical book ever written on Democracy as it manifests itself in modern society; a book, the essential doctrines of which it is not likely that any future speculations will subvert, to whatever degree they may modify them; while its spirit, and the general mode in which it treats its subject, constitute it the beginning of a new era in the scientific study of politics" [see excerpt above, 1840]. The validity of Mill's judgment remains unimpaired to the present day. (pp. 55-7)

[For de Tocqueville, it] is manifestly a very peculiar dialectic which is moving modern society. De Tocqueville defines its laws as follows: "As long as the democratic revolution was glowing with heat the men who were bent upon the destruction of old aristocratic powers hostile to that revolution displayed a strong spirit of independence; but as the victory of the principle of equality became more complete, they gradually surrendered themselves to the propensities natural to that condition of equality, and they strengthened and centralized their governments. They had sought to be free in order to make themselves equal; but in proportion as equality was more established by the aid of freedom, freedom itself was thereby rendered more difficult of attainment." (p. 61)

I believe that de Tocqueville has revealed the very structure of the modern mass society in this dialectical exposition. It might certainly be said that he has merely condensed into an abstract formula the historical dynamic of the French Revolution. Undoubtedly he regarded the French Revolution as the classical example of this historical dialectic. He traced the stages of this process in the period of development from July 14, 1789, to the Caesarism of Napoleon I. . . . [He] by no means regarded the French Revolution of 1789-1815 as finally concluded then, but only as the first unitary stage of a revolutionary cycle destined to repeat itself with growing intensity in accordance with the growing industrialization of the modern world.

Most earnestly and in varying terms de Tocqueville reiterates his conviction that the species of despotism by which democratic nations are menaced is a *new* phenomenon for which there is no historical analogy. "The thing itself is new; and since I cannot name it, I must attempt to define it."

He envisages a multitude of men, all equal and alike, working in order to procure for themselves petty and paltry pleasures. The age of "facilities," which Goethe apprehensively prophesied, has set in. Above the race of mankind rises a monstrous tutelary power which "provides for their security, foresees and supplies their necessities, facilitates their pleasures, directs their industry, regulates the transfer of property, and subdivides their inheritance—what remains but to spare them all the care of thinking and all the trouble of living?" Thus each nation is reduced to the condition of a flock of timid and industrious animals, of which the Government is the shepherd. Aldous Huxley's *Brave New World* stands before us! Today, perhaps, de Tocqueville would call such a democracy a "plebiscitary dictatorship," and would recognize its living image in the Fascist States! The grandeur of his prophetic gift is impressed upon one by the fact that after the passage of a hundred years his words have proved an exact description of a present-day reality. (pp. 61-3)

De Tocqueville's sociology of eighteenth-century French intellectualism as treated in [*The Ancien Régime and the Revolution*] did not confine itself, like our fashionable sociology today, to an exposition of special class relationships and the sociological significance of the contrasts they present in some given social situation, but rather comprised in its analysis the norm of a definite political and philosophical attitude of the kind that contemporary discipline poor-spiritedly rejects under the plea of scientific objectivity. The fact, its interpretation, and a deliberate political standpoint are as inseparable as inspiration and respiration—such is the very meaning of the philosophical approach to history, and such is the lesson which may be learned again and again in reading *The Ancien Régime and the Revolution.* (p. 122)

The Ancien Régime and the Revolution is one of the rare and few European books which accompany history with a philosophic commentary. . . . [In my view de Tocqueville's] book on the ancient France and the new is his most important work. The style, the articulation of ideas, show an incomparable precision: with controlled and practised hand the master hews out a monumental contribution to political thought which will retain its validity as long as there are Europeans who seek to understand the meaning of their history. (p. 126)

> *J. P. Mayer, in his* Alexis de Tocqueville: A Biographical Essay in Political Science, *translated by M. M. Bozman and C. Hahn, The Viking Press, 1940, 233 p.*

J. SALWYN SCHAPIRO (essay date 1942)

[*Schapiro regards Tocqueville as a sociologist, historian, philosopher, and pioneer of democratic liberalism. He argues that*

Tocqueville occupies a unique position in the history of nineteenth-century liberalism because unlike most of the representative French liberals of his era, who favored a government that was controlled by the bourgeoisie, he was convinced that liberalism should be democratized through mass suffrage.]

De Tocqueville's life was short, and the number of the books that he wrote was small, really only three. For all that he has an important place in the intellectual history of Europe during the nineteenth century. It would not be correct to place him in the rank of original and creative thinkers such as Montesquieu and Rousseau; his gifts were rather those of the keen observer and master analyst of the socio-intellectual situation in his day. De Tocqueville had the style, the temperament and the scholarship of a detached and discriminating analyst. In addition he had a sympathetic social imagination that gave to his analysis of a period, of a party, of a government the power of luminous suggestion of the historic forces and trends that were shaping civilization. . . . De Tocqueville's convictions were clear, strong and steadfast, without being heightened by passion or riveted by dogma. His style is elegant and cold, but not hard. In his analysis of political and social phenomena he exhibits a capacity for cool lucidity that gives an impression of "frozen logic". But this impression is dissipated by observations that reveal the author as a highly sensitive individual with generous sympathies and with an abiding love of mankind. As a writer de Tocqueville may be compared with an artist whose painting of a landscape gives the effect of softness, even of tenderness, by depicting the sun's rays breaking through a cold, gray atmosphere.

If de Tocqueville was not original in thought he was original in method. All his books bear the imprint of original ways of dealing with a subject. His *De la Démocratie en Amérique* was the first comprehensive analysis of the only great democracy of that period in action. His method was novel in his day: a first-hand study of the institutions of a country that embodied an idea. His analysis of democratic practices and methods, blended with philosophic observation, made *Democracy in America* the unique work on America until the appearance of Bryce's *American Commonwealth*, more than half a century later. (pp. 548-49)

In [*Souvenirs*] may be found a luminous exposition of the social forces that clashed in the Revolution of 1848. The author appears as the spectator of historic scenes in which the contending parties are struggling for mastery over issues that have been philosophically projected on the screen of world history since the French Revolution. His observations on the first attempt to overthrow the social order by a socialist revolution, the "June Days" of 1848, read as though they were written yesterday. No student of modern history can afford to neglect this little volume.

Equally remarkable is de Tocqueville's historic study, *L'Ancien régime et la révolution*. . . . It is the unobtrusive result of careful research without much display of the apparatus of scholarship. No compiler of facts in the manner of his contemporary, the German historian, Leopold von Ranke, de Tocqueville viewed the study of history as *problems* in human relationships throughout the ages. He was, however, strongly averse to absolutist, dogmatic interpretations "which represent all events of history as depending upon great first causes linked by the chain of fatality, and which, as it were, suppress men from the history of the human race. They seem narrow to my mind, under their pretense of broadness, and false beneath their air of mathematical exactness." His method was to arrange his-

torical events in a pattern with a central theme, but pattern and theme varied with time, place and circumstances. His interpretation of the French Revolution, for example, was that it was not a sudden break with the past but the last stage of a long process of transformation of the political and economic institutions of France. Centralization, peasant proprietorship, and the power of the bourgeoisie were forces that had been in train for centuries, but were accelerated and dramatized by the events of the French Revolution. Even now, de Tocqueville's *Old Regime* is considered a notable contribution to the study of the subject by students of the French Revolution.

Apart from his work as an historian and political philosopher, de Tocqueville has a unique position in the history of nineteenth-century liberalism. Like John Stuart Mill in England, he was, in France, the outstanding pioneer of democratic liberalism. In France after the Revolution of 1830, as in England after the Reform Bill of 1832, the bourgeois elements were in control of the government. The aristocrats were reduced to a subordinate position; and the workers were eliminated from the suffrage by a high property qualification for voting. This period in both England and France was the golden age of bourgeois liberalism. (pp. 549-50)

Endowed with a social imagination and having wide sympathies de Tocqueville clearly realized the limitations of bourgeois liberalism. . . . To de Tocqueville the rule of a capitalist oligarchy was the most revolting of all governments, since it was class despotism without class responsibility, a system offensive both to his aristocratic instincts and to his democratic sympathies. Moreover, bourgeois liberalism in France after 1830 exhibited a spirit of class selfishness and of class materialism that was in conflict with the generous ideals of the nation. With much misgiving and with great hesitation, often in spite of his aristocratic inclinations, de Tocqueville was finally convinced that the solution of the problem would be to widen the outlook of liberalism by giving it a broader base. In other words, liberalism was to cease to be bourgeois and become democratic by admitting the masses to the suffrage.

De Tocqueville's study of history and his reflections on the political situation in France convinced him that democracy was "inevitable" and, in the long run, beneficent. Democracy was, in his view, a "providential fact", having "all the characteristics of a divine decree": it was universal; it was lasting; it overcame all obstacles; and the course of events steadily flowed toward its realization. . . . This attitude toward democracy was a highly unusual one among the liberals of the bourgeois monarchy of Louis Philippe. Representative liberals of the period, like Guizot and Thiers, dreaded popular rule even more than they dreaded the reactionary Bourbons, and with good reason. They regarded popular rule as a direct challenge to the control of the government by the bourgeoisie, and, because of the Jacobin heritage of French democracy, as a menace to established property interests. In de Tocqueville's long-range view, however, the political struggles and class divisions of his day were not danger signals of universal chaos as they were to his contemporaries. To him they were the part of the never-ending efforts to establish "equality", the supreme and persistent passion of mankind throughout the ages, a passion that was "ardent, insatiable, incessant, invincible." It could best be satisfied by equality in freedom, and if that were impossible, equality in slavery would be preferred by the people to inequality in a system of aristocratic privilege. . . . At one time equality had meant that between bourgeois and aristocrat; now, concluded de Tocqueville, it meant that between poor and rich. (pp. 550-52)

The rich blend of the historian, the sociologist and the philosopher, which was so distinctively de Tocqueville, is seen in his explanations of the success of the American experiment. It was due, he explains, to the presence of fortunate circumstances, to the absence of historical obstacles, and to the national origin of most of the settlers in the Thirteen Colonies. The fact that America was a virgin continent, rich in natural resources with land free for the asking, prevented bitter class conflicts from arising that, in Europe, had proved so inimical to the progress of democracy. Discontent could be drained off in the many channels of opportunity that America offered to acquire property, as a consequence of which there was an approach to economic equality consonant with the legal and political equality enjoyed by the citizens. America was "virgin soil" in a social as well as in a physical sense. Unlike Europe, America had no such obstacle to equality as a landed aristocracy; no such obstacle to freedom as military caste; and no such obstacle to religious toleration as a national church. To cap America's historic good fortune most of its inhabitants were of English origin who had brought with them the traditions of liberty and self-government of England.

De Tocqueville was acutely sensitive to the dangers to individual liberty in a democracy unless great care was taken to avoid them. . . . To de Tocqueville the despotism of the many would be as great an evil as the despotism of an absolute monarch, and perhaps even a greater one. (pp. 554-55)

Apart from constitutional provisions de Tocqueville saw in the right of association "a necessary guarantee against the tyranny of the majority"; it was "an inalienable as individual liberty". In no other aspect of his analysis of democracy was he so perspicacious as in his wholehearted advocacy of the right of association. Unlike many liberals in France, who saw only the individual on one side and the state on the other, and who regarded associations as "conspiracies" against the state, de Tocqueville considered associations as the very bulwarks of liberty to which he was so deeply attached. In a democracy, he reasoned, the weakness of isolated individuals might encourage the government to commit acts of tyranny, but once the citizens formed associations they were "no longer isolated men, but a power seen from afar, whose activities serve as an example and whose language is listened to." The very existence of powerful associations, such as political parties, trade unions, business corporations, and cultural organizations, weakened "the moral power of the majority", and therefore deterred it from committing acts of tyranny. (pp. 555-56)

[Why] was de Tocqueville so much concerned over the possible "tyranny of the majority"? Over and over again he expressed fear of such a possibility, a fear that was shared by John Stuart Mill, his fellow pioneer of democratic liberalism. These fears had their origin in the revolutionary excesses associated with the French Revolution. . . . But the history of democratic government has proved their fears to have been groundless. . . . Scrupulous regard for the rights of property, for individual liberty, and for the protection of minorities were the outstanding features of democratic government in England and in France. With the advent of communism and fascism, in recent years, the great danger has been the tyranny of the minority, a danger all too real which was not at all foreseen by the pioneers of democratic liberalism. Let it be noted that neither to de Tocqueville nor to Mill was democracy a radiant vision; rather was it a generous hope. They were pioneers, not prophets. Hence they were very much alive to possible dangers and pitfalls that might lie in their path. De Tocqueville, even more than Mill,

feared these dangers and pitfalls, and with good reason. Had not the radiant vision of popular sovereignty in the France of 1789 become the hideous nightmare of the Reign of Terror? It was to the very great credit of de Tocqueville that he set out for America, there to behold the true face of democracy which, he was convinced, was neither a vision nor a nightmare.

Reverence for religion, in the opinion of de Tocqueville, was one of the pillars of the democratic order in America. This view is indeed surprising in a Frenchman, and especially in one who lived during the first half of the nineteenth century. Catholic Frenchmen, during this period, were almost unanimous in believing that reverence for religion was the one sure foundation of authoritarian royalism. On the other hand, freethinking Frenchmen, liberals, radicals and socialists, were almost unanimous in believing that the church in France was the one uncompromising enemy of democracy. De Tocqueville was a liberal with a reverent attitude toward the church, a rare phenomenon in the France of his day. (pp. 556-57)

[De Tocqueville's] reverence for religion was really reverence for the moral nature of man. Translated into political terms it meant respect for his rights, for his opinions, for his goods, which is "liberalism". In France de Tocqueville had seen anticlericalism quickly translated into anti-Christianity, in other words from hostility to clerical intervention in politics to hostility to religious views as such. And he keenly realized that neither tolerance nor intolerance can be kept within the bounds of one field; persecution for religious opinions would spread to persecution for political and economic opinions, thereby endangering what he had most at heart, liberty for all. The reverence for religious opinion, that de Tocqueville saw in America, was to him the acid test of freedom of opinion in any field. In this he was not far from the truth. (p. 559)

In no aspect of his thinking did he show a greater power of analysis and a keener insight into the problem of the liberal state than in his views on property. In a pregnant passage he described the position of property under modern conditions.

> The French Revolution which abolished all privileges and destroyed all exclusive right has, however, allowed one to remain and that is the right of property. However, property owners would delude themselves if they entertained an idea that the right of property is a barrier that can not be crossed because, up to the present, no part of this barrier has been crossed. When the right of property was considered as the origin and the foundation of many other rights it defended itself without difficulty, or more correctly, it was not attacked. . . . But today when the right of property, however sacred, is regarded as the last relic of a ruined world, it has lost, for a time at least, the position that made it impregnable. Daily it has to meet direct and incessant assaults of democratic opinions.

Though a strong upholder of the rights of property de Tocqueville, nevertheless, did see the contradiction involved between legal and political equality on the one hand and economic inequality on the other. He was convinced that the people would not be content to be at the same time "miserable and sovereign", and that the future would see a social conflict far more serious than any in the past. "Is it credible", he asks, "that the democracy which has annihilated the feudal system and vanquished kings will respect the citizen and the capitalist?"

His view that political democracy would sooner or later clash with laissez faire capitalism has been justified by all subsequent history.

Although he did not live to be a "socialist" like John Stuart Mill, de Tocqueville realized even more keenly than did Mill the new dangers to freedom that came with the Industrial Revolution. It is nothing less than astonishing that he visualized the problems raised by modern industrialism as far back as the thirties of the nineteenth century, when it was in its infancy in both France and America, the only two countries that he studied. In cogent language he described the effect of the machine process on the worker and of the competitive system on the capitalist. (pp. 559-60)

De Tocqueville was himself an example of the tragedy of French liberalism which, since the French Revolution, has waged unceasing war on two fronts, against a reactionary right and against a revolutionary left. His aristocratic temperament, that caused him to despise the bourgeois and to fear the mob, was in conflict with his intellectual conviction that democracy was both inevitable and desirable. In a sense his *Democracy in America* was a providential solution of the problems raised by this conflict in France. Far away in the New World was a land with no Old Régime to restore, no mob of desperately poor to fear, no ambitious dictators to foil; hence democracy, which was inevitable in Europe in the course of history, had been providential from the very outset in America. (p. 562)

> *J. Salwyn Schapiro, "Alexis de Tocqueville, Pioneer of Democratic Liberalism in France," in* Political Science Quarterly, *Vol. LVII, No. 4, December, 1942, pp. 545-63.*

PHILLIPS BRADLEY (essay date 1944)

[*In his 1944 introduction to* Democracy, *Bradley praises Tocqueville for his recognition of the interrelation of the political, social, and economic aspects of democracy and contends that his "development of sociological principles was a pioneering intellectual enterprise." Although Bradley criticizes* Democracy *for some omissions and anachronisms, he points out that much of what Tocqueville wrote is still valid. He expresses particular admiration for Tocqueville's prophetic insight into American economic trends and notes, like Harold J. Laski and Albert Salomon (1931-32 and 1935), that Tocqueville's interpretation of industrial evolution is "almost Marxian."*]

Tocqueville had come to America primarily to discover the inner meaning and the actual functioning of democracy in action, in a country which had never known aristocracy. What he found tempered some of his original enthusiasm for the universal applicability of American democratic ideas and practices. If he went home to write the *Democracy* with a more sober view of our institutions than he had had before his visit to America, he did not allow his experiences here to distort his perspective, or to make him less careful in his observations, analyses, and judgments. He found much that was missed altogether or entirely ignored by others of his contemporaries who visited America with the same curiosity about democracy, but often with very different motives in studying it. Even though his criticisms and appraisals, which cumulative observation and wide travel inspired, were not always favorable, Tocqueville never lost sight of his original purpose or deviated from his objective approach.

Tocqueville's intellectual standards and methods of research were stricter than those of most of his contemporaries. His references and citations . . . are evidence of his wide search in original sources. The range and variety of the printed sources which he used indicate how much care he took to obtain the most authentic books and documents. The extent of his travels suggests that he was not satisfied with second-hand information about the places, the conditions, or the institutions of which he wrote. . . . Altogether, Tocqueville adhered to far more scholarly standards than many of his successors, to say nothing of those who were writing of America or of political, social, and economic institutions a century ago. (pp. xii-xiv)

The first part [of the *Democracy*] as a whole is as comprehensively descriptive as it is critically analytical. There are frequent references to statutes, legislative reports, statistical data, and commentaries on their own institutions by Americans, as well as to many direct observations of his own. It is a treatise on government by the people—in America in the 1830's. There are, however, presages of the more general approach that Tocqueville was to adopt in the second part.

The second part is essentially a philosophical examination of social and economic as well as political change, traced more through the application of universal generalizations than of American data or experience. Although America is its focus and many references to American phenomena are utilized by Tocqueville, he is here less an observer than a prophet of change at home. Many of his particular forecasts of social, economic, and political change in America have been vindicated by events; others have not. His observations are not less interesting or significant to us today because not all have proved true for ourselves, or for other countries. We catch shrewd glimpses of life in America as it was a century ago from Tocqueville's observations of our society and economy as well as of our polity. Even more, we discover some of the permanent factors and conditions affecting the working of democracy as idea as well as practice.

The position of women, our aptitude for "association," the influence of the frontier on manners and morals, the diffusion of knowledge and culture (without the high attainment of the older European, aristocratic societies), the armed services in a democracy, the conditions likely to create an "aristocracy of manufactures"—these are only a few of the topics in the second part on which Tocqueville offers acute descriptions and judgments. One is impressed throughout by his search for the principles underlying action, principles susceptible of universal, not merely American, application. Here Tocqueville seems to be fulfilling the original purpose of his trip to America, to provide for every people a guide by which it can achieve the advantages of democracy without accepting its potential defects. The permanent—and perennial—quality of his observations and insights is evident even when the data on which they are based are no longer relevant. The second part ranks even among the greatest of social philosophies from Aristotle to Pareto; as a reasoned and objective appraisal of the democratic way of life it is unsurpassed. (pp. xix-xx)

In extending his definition of democracy to include [economic and social] aspects, Tocqueville was a pioneer of the first importance. What has become a commonplace for us, that democracy means more than a certain catalogue of political principles and practices, was in his day a new if not an unprecedented idea. There had been, of course, in Montesquieu and other of Tocqueville's predecessors in a long line back to Aristotle, a recognition that there is more to life than politics. Many of the seventeenth- and eighteenth-century political reformers, in seeking changes in the structure of the authoritarian governments of their time, had not been motivated only by abstract ideas about justice. The desire to achieve economic and social reforms, often with precise democratic—even equalitarian—implications, was in the air of Tocqueville's intellectual inheritance and contemporary experience.

None before him, however, had so clearly presented or so cogently demonstrated the interrelations of the political, the economic, and the social aspects of democracy. None had so thoroughly understood their connection or drawn into a single pattern of ideas their manifold and often conflicting phases. The writings of practically all of his contemporaries, whether European travelers to America or publicists, polemic and academic, when compared with the *Democracy,* are narrow in scope, biased in judgment, steeped in immediate comments and controversies. Beside them the *Democracy* stands out as a landmark in our progress towards an emergent liberal spirit and democratic thought, at once catholic in range, balanced in interpretation, and detached in the examination of every issue.

A landmark in the progress of liberal and democratic thought, it provides us also with a benchmark by which to measure our advance. Not alone on one front, the political, but on the economic and the social fronts as well, Tocqueville bequeathed us a unique and permanent record of our national evolution in the 1830's. In a period when we were on the threshold of great changes on all these fronts, he wove the strands of divergent trends into a clear and consistent design. From the details of that earlier design we can compute the distance we have traveled, appraise the character of the changes through which we have lived, and are living today.

Tocqueville gave to the world of his day a new conception of the meaning and the nature of democracy. That conception has been and remains an inescapable challenge to the aspiration and the effort of each succeeding generation. Were this all, the *Democracy* would still speak to our time and condition. It contains, however, many specific elements—descriptions, appraisals, analyses, prophecies—of great practical import for us today. (pp. lix-lx)

[No] recording of a particular period in the nation's life will always remain accurate in all its generalizations. Changes in our material position over a century have, of course, altered the working of many institutions and the relevance of more than one idea. . . . The technological revolution—which, in its social implications, Tocqueville in fact foresaw—has shifted the balance in economics and politics from the rural and the agrarian to the urban and the industrial. The growth of cities has altered the character of political as well as of economic and social organization as Tocqueville saw and described them. The catalogue of change can be extended in many other directions by the contemporary reader. That these changes should have required modification of some of Tocqueville's descriptions, appraisals, and prophecies is not remarkable. That so much of the *Democracy* remains still pertinent and timely suggests rather that it is to be cherished not merely as a brilliant record of the past but also as a more certain guide for the future. (p. lx)

[We] may note some of Tocqueville's comments and interpretations, as well as omissions, which are of only historical or transitory interest. For instance, he discussed in considerable detail the New England township and found its structure and administration a major source of democratic practice and so vitality. A century of increasing urbanization, of expanding functional responsibilities, and of multiplying political controls

has transformed town government into something quite different from his enthusiastic account of its outlines and operation. In some of the smaller and more isolated towns of the New England frontier, and in similar regions where the New England pattern or its counterpart has been reproduced, the early vitality survives. The disappearance of institutions he described has done much, however, to weaken the democratic impulse in local government which he believed these institutions promoted. (pp. lx-lxi)

Again, Tocqueville's description of the nature and operation of judicial review has been altered by time. He could hardly have envisaged the effects of the immense political power that Americans have entrusted to their courts when the major questions before the Supreme Court shifted from the political to the economic-social arena. Indeed, he was even then clearly wrong in stating that a single decision of unconstitutionality did not "abolish" a law, that "its final destruction [could] only be accomplished by reiterated attacks of judicial functionaries." He believed that legislation would be protected from "wanton assault" by linking the private interests of individuals with the attack upon its constitutionality. That assault he looked for in "the daily aggressions of party spirit . . . the tyranny of political assemblies." If it has come from sources quite different from those he foresaw, it is because of forces in our national life that were not yet strong—some not yet born. He did, none the less, underrate the influence of the judiciary as a Third Estate in the legislative process.

A third matter on which Tocqueville's description and appraisal would seem anachronistic today is the "political institution" of the jury. He believed the jury, especially the civil jury, to be "the most energetic means of making the people rule, the most efficacious means of teaching it to rule well." He rejected the idea that, because many jurors may be ignorant, the jury system is not a most efficient means of educating all ranks in society in a respect for law. Experience has not borne out his enthusiasm in this respect. Few would hold today that a judge "continues to influence the habits of thought, and even the characters, of those who acted with him in his official capacity"—at least, of any broad cross-section of the community. The widespread desire to avoid jury duty and the development of blue-ribbon juries suggest the decline of the jury as a political institution with a permeating civil influence.

Tocqueville discusses the future of the federal system in considerable detail. He makes some shrewd observations on its operation, but does not altogether foresee the shifting balance of power between the states and the Federal government which was even then impending. He anticipated that the strength of the Federal government was likely to decrease, that of the state governments to increase. . . . The interests of the citizen have not, over the last century, proved to be more closely allied to his state than to the national government. This shift, perhaps already nascent but not yet clearly evident in the 1830's, has resulted from economic and social forces that were then only emergent in our national life.

On the other hand, Tocqueville has proved fundamentally correct in his forecast of the primary forces holding the Union together. One, he thought, was the common commercial interest among the people of all the states—the advantages of a continental free-trade area. The other was their fundamental identity in political principle—the democratic faith of the people. That these influences have increased rather than decreased the relative strength of the Federal government, despite, perhaps because of, armed conflict between the states, suggests that Tocqueville's analysis was essentially correct. Whatever differences in detail may have eventuated from the impact of new forces, economic and social, the enhancement of Federal power has continued to rest on these foundations.

Among the few omissions from Tocqueville's searching analysis of the American scene, perhaps the most curious is his lack of attention to the structure and operation of state government. He devotes a scant four pages to a detailed discussion of the state and only scattered and incidental descriptions and appraisals elsehwere to its political or administrative aspects. Compared with his analyses of local government and of various aspects of the character and working of the Federal government, his inattention to state government is almost startling. Although he utilized the states tangentially in many of his generalizations, he nowhere provides a comprehensive account or a critical scrutiny of their origins or organization. (pp. lxi-lxii)

[If we look] at Tocqueville's political observations, several strike the reader at once as if they came from the best of today's editorial or political commentary. It is easy, for instance, to select such items as his discussion of the re-election of the President as having a direct bearing on the 1940's. Written long before the third-term issue was raised as a matter of practical politics, it has a very modern ring. "When the chief magistrate enters the lists [for re-election], he borrows the strength of the government for his purposes. . . . The cares of government dwindle for him into second-rate importance, and the success of his election is his first concern." . . . By not making the President ineligible for re-election, the framers "partly destroyed" one great merit of the Constitution, an executive enjoying a degree of independence in its sphere. That independence is important as a means of making the executive "able to resist [the] caprices, and refuse [the] most dangerous demands," of the majority, while its permanent determinations "must be complied with." Similarly, the executive, by its independence, would be able "to resist the encroachments of the legislature." . . . (pp. lxiii-lxiv)

Or take the current attitudes in America as to the quality of our office-holders under our present system of elections inherited from the 1830's. Tocqueville discusses the question incidentally at many points. "It is a constant fact that, at the present day, the ablest men . . . are rarely placed at the head of the affairs. . . . The democracy [people] not only lack that soundness of judgment which is necessary to select men really deserving of their confidence, but often have not the desire or the inclination to find them out. . . . An instinct not less strong induces able men to retire from the political arena, in which it is so difficult to retain their independence, or to advance without becoming servile. . . . Those who engage in the perplexities of political life are persons of very moderate pretensions." (p. lxiv)

These comments might have been written yesterday. They are among the most aristocratic in temper and outlook in the *Democracy.* Tocqueville goes so far as to advocate the extension of the system of indirect selection then in use for the choice of senators, "or run the risk of perishing miserably among the shoals of democracy." The complaint Tocqueville voices here has been perennial in writings on American political life. . . .

[It] is not altogether true that first-rate talent had not, before Tocqueville's day, entered politics, or does not today. It may be true that there have been fewer classically educated politicians at any time since the days of and after the Philadelphia Convention of 1787. Certainly the great political writers of the

past, whether in the original or in translation, are not cited in legislative halls or in administrative documents, in debate or correspondence, as often as they once were. The real "governors" of our political system are not, however, always the office-holders. There have been and still are many examples of men of first-rate ability in actual control of our political machines, openly or behind the scenes. (p. lxv)

[Tocqueville] devotes relatively little attention to the [nature and degree of corruption in American political life]. He did not hear of vote-purchasing, but often heard "the probity of public officers questioned; still more frequently have I heard their successes attributed to low intrigues and immoral practices. If, then, the men who conduct an aristocracy sometimes endeavor to corrupt the people, the heads of a democracy are themselves corrupt." Here, again, although the comment is as fresh as it was in the 1830's, its focus is blurred. Most of those who write about the corruption of American politics forget that it takes two to make a bargain. They ignore the fact that a politician who promotes a private interest in a political "deal" is merely following current business practices and ethics. Indeed, it is generally true that the initiative for corruption in this sense comes to, not from, the politician; the interests seek his favors, not he theirs. (p. lxvi)

Among Tocqueville's observations on economic conditions in the America of the 1830's several are of unique interest. In a chapter entitled: "What Causes Almost All Americans to Follow Industrial Callings," he suggests that democracy "diverts [men] from agriculture, it encourages their taste for commerce and manufactures." He attributes this encouragement to the desire for "physical gratifications" which can be more quickly secured from industrial than from agricultural callings. He notes, however, a second desire (or "drive," we might call it), "the love of constant excitement occasioned by that pursuit." Since democracy obliterates ranks in society and throws all callings open to all men on a basis of complete equality, these universal human desires find their most frequent outlets in economic, not in political activity. Rich and poor alike are animated by the same desires. Since the rich can obtain no special place or honors in democratic politics, they find satisfaction in "the excitement occasioned by [the] pursuit" of industrial success. Since the poor do not now possess the means for satisfying their desire for "physical gratifications," they enter these callings to obtain them.

Had Tocqueville written half a century or more later than he did, his observations would have seemed an accurate reflection of nineteenth-century economic trends. Written before industry had become significant, before there were many cities, and while many of the people with whom he talked were frontiersmen or political rather than business leaders, Tocqueville's analysis was prophetic in its insight into the American character.

The next chapter deals with the question of "How an Aristocracy May be Created by Manufactures." Here Tocqueville gives an almost Marxian interpretation of industrial evolution—a decade before the *Communist Manifesto* [by Karl Marx and Friedrich Engels], a quarter-century before [Marx's] *Das Kapital.* "The manufacturing aristocracy of our age first impoverishes and debases the men who serve it, and then abandons them to be supported by the charity of the public." His analysis of the relations of employers and workers in an industrial society is one of the most searching, even searing, ever written. The fact that it was written by one who had been himself an aristocrat, and before many of the most inhuman results of the

Industrial Revolution had been exposed by public inquiry or private accusation, makes Tocqueville's clear and inexorable judgments all the more prescient.

Another of Tocqueville's most far-reaching economic insights, closely related to that just noted, concerns the relations of government and industry. "Will the administration of the country ultimately assume the management of all the manufactures which no single citizen is able to carry on? . . . [And] will it be necessary that the head of the government should leave the helm of state to follow the plow?"

Tocqueville discussed the problem in terms of the capacity of the Americans he observed to form associations, including commercial and industrial firms, for every conceivable purpose. He thought this capacity an admirable one, but he wondered whether it would not be enervated by increasing governmental intervention in the economy. He noted that several states were already engaged in large-scale business enterprises; it was the period of canal- and railroad-building. He doubted whether government was suited to "carry on the vast multitude of lesser undertakings which the American citizen performs every day, with the assistance of the principle of association." He considered his countrymen mistaken when they thought the more "enfeebled and incompetent the citizens become, the more able and active the government ought to be rendered, in order that society at large may execute what individuals can no longer accomplish."

Tocqueville would be claimed by the "free enterprisers" of our own day. Here he justifies both the superiority of an economy animated by individual initiative rather than by government operation and the virtue of Small Business functioning through the enterprise of its owners.

As to the first question, a century of experience has vindicated Tocqueville's insight that the issue was to be a central one in Western capitalistic society. The argument over governmental intervention in the economy has not diminished; its focus has changed as the economy itself has been transformed by technology and management-organization. It is no longer merely a question of whether governmental or private enterprise is more efficient in enlisting the initiative and co-operation of individuals, although that debate has not been definitively settled by experience. It is also a problem in the balance of power between government and free enterprise in a society nationalized in outlook and motivated by forces inherent in the new factors of concentrated finance, mass production, and integrated communication facilities.

The free play of these factors in a privately organized and managed economy during the nineteenth and twentieth centuries made inevitable the recurrence of the debate—in terms very much like those which Tocqueville suggested. That he foresaw the issue a half-century before the results of free enterprise had made the struggle between government and a powerful private economy a continuing political problem is another indication of his prescience. (pp. lxxxviii-xc)

As to the second question, the virtue of Small Business, technological change has inexorably imposed new patterns within free enterprise. The debate is not less acute today than a century ago; the balance between small and large enterprise has greatly shifted, however, especially since the turn of the century. . . . Small Business has for half a century steadily lost ground to Big Business in the basic industries, in communications, in distribution, even in some of the service trades and professions.

Were Tocqueville writing today, what would he say of this development? What new trends would he discover in the America of the 1940's? Certainly he would find his reflections on "an aristocracy of manufactures" and its impact on American society buttressed in many ways by the evolution of business practices over a century. The struggle for power between government and private economy has in large part resulted from the shift from small to large enterprise. . . . The position of the individual, whether entrepreneur or worker, in the economic pattern we have carved out of the continent has been continuously and profoundly modified by the trends that Tocqueville foresaw. The intervention of government in economic affairs, directly through its own enterprises or indirectly by regulation, has, moreover, steadily increased. (pp. xc-xci)

The second part of the **Democracy** is primarily a sociological inquiry into the implications of democracy. As has been frequently pointed out, Tocqueville is less concerned with an analytical description of American social institutions than with a search for those universal principles which govern equalitarian societies. Even the economic ideas . . . are treated primarily in terms of their bearing on society as the living expression of mutual interests among men. All other aspects of American culture that Tocqueville described—religion, science, literature and the arts, manners and morals, the position of women, the influence of the military in a democracy, among others—are related to this central objective of his search. . . .

Tocqueville's development of sociological principles was a pioneering intellectual enterprise. He was the first, as [Albert] Salomon has pointed out, "to show the change in forms of human existence in and through the process of social development" [see excerpt above, 1935]. Tocqueville charted not only new fields of inquiry but hitherto unexplored approaches to an understanding of the process. Many of his successors have developed more scientific techniques of analysis. None has provided us with more fertile insights into the conditions of social development or with a surer guide for their appraisal. (p. xciv)

Tocqueville recognized that faith is an integral element in human action and its most powerful dynamic. He commented at a number of points on the influence of religion on American society, but he was more concerned to analyze the relation between religious faith and democratic practice. . . . "Most religions are only general, simple, and practical means of teaching men the doctrine of the immortality of the soul. That is the greatest benefit which a democratic nation derives from its belief, and hence belief is more necessary to such a people than all others. When, therefore, any religion has struck its roots deep into a democracy beware that you do not disturb it; but rather watch it carefully, as the most precious bequest of aristocratic ages."

Have we not had ample—and tragic—evidence in our time of the validity of Tocqueville's insight into the ultimate foundation of a democratic society as religious? We can observe the recognition of this insight and its prostitution by those who deny human equality and erect Leviathan as the Baal of the masses. The techniques as well as the doctrines of the totalitarian societies are founded on worship of the State and ritualistic obeisance to the Leaders. The new religion may not be overtly materialistic; its uses, in the hands of those who repudiate equality in human or theological terms, are more frightening than even Tocqueville envisaged. (pp. xcvii-xcviii)

His observations on two areas of paramount concern to us today deserve our thoughtful, and sober, consideration. The most immediate is his appraisal of the capacity of a democratic people to wage war, and of the relations between the military and the civilian hierarchy. His discussion of these questions has the clear ring of contemporaneity. As to the first, his incisive estimate of the inherent nature of problems seems almost a summary of our experience in the intervening century rather than a forecast of the ability of a democratic people to stick together and to fight. As to the second, the warnings he sounded on the effects of military influence on civilian life and public policy are not without relevance for the future. Here, too, our experience has validated much of Tocqueville's prophetic insight. If many of the details he portrayed are incorrect, the broad outlines he traced can be discovered in the record of a century.

The other area of contemporary concern which Tocqueville analyzed is that of race relations. What he had to say a hundred years ago about the psychological and the material factors implicit in these relations is as pertinent as when he wrote. Here again the specific data which he analyzed and the particular influences that he drew from them are no longer exact. But the broader implications he presented of the problems we confront in making democracy effective in the relations of the races in our great society are as profoundly true today as they were a century ago. (p. xcix)

> *Phillips Bradley, in an introduction to* Democracy in America, *Vol. 1 by Alexis de Tocqueville, translated by Henry Reeve, edited by Francis Bowen and Phillips Bradley, Alfred A. Knopf, 1945, pp. viii-c.*

HENRY STEELE COMMAGER (essay date 1947)

[*Commager is an American historian and editor who specializes in United States history. In his introduction to* Democracy, *from which the following excerpt is drawn, Commager delineates the merits and defects of the work. Among the defects he cites are Tocqueville's overindulgence in deductive reasoning and his tendency to force facts to fit his preconceived theories. Agreeing with John Stuart Mill, Emile Faguet, and George Wilson Pierson (1840, 1900, and 1938), he maintains that Tocqueville mistakenly ascribed certain features of American society to democracy. However, according to Commager, these defects are superficial and are overshadowed by* Democracy's *"shining merits": its objectivity, its dignified treatment of a "great and noble theme," its "luminous clarity," and its attention to "fundamental causes and ultimate consequences." Like Edward T. Gargan and John Lukacs (1955 and 1959), Commager stresses Tocqueville's importance as a historian.*]

What explains the fame, the longevity, of *Democracy in America*? No other book of its kind has weathered so well. . . . The book, certainly, is not without faults. It is, for all its sharpness and spareness, over-long. . . . It makes no concessions to the reader, either in analysis or in interpretation, it has no narrative quality, it is devoid of humor. It includes much that is merely descriptive; it omits much that is important.

It is, indeed, no difficult task to draw up a general indictment and itemize a bill of particulars. Tocqueville came not to observe America as a whole, but to observe the operations of democracy; and democracy, rather than America, it must never be forgotten, was his primary concern. He tended to substitute his own reflections for facts, or, where the facts were stubborn, to force them into his own preconceived pattern. When he wrote the second—and best—part of *Democracy in America* the sharp impact of personal experience was fading, the pressure of France was strong, and Tocqueville indulged himself more readily in rationalization, yielded increasingly to the

temptations of *a priori* reasoning. He did not sufficiently check what he felt was bound to happen with what actually was happening, and where history ran counter to his predictions he was inclined to give the impression that history was somehow at fault. Thus he could write at length, and ominously, of the tyranny of the majority without once citing a convincing example of such tyranny; thus he could insist upon the inherent weakness of the executive authority at a time when the strongest of American Presidents occupied the White House. His acquaintance with America was limited; he knew the East better than the West, the North better than the South. His investigations were haphazard rather than systematic, his sources of information inadequate and often misleading. He made it a point to meet the best people, and the best people, then as now, were inclined to deprecate democracy. . . . An aristocrat, Tocqueville exaggerated the importance of manners, and was capable of the observation that 'nothing is more prejudicial to democracy than its outward forms of behavior; many men would willingly endure its vices who cannot support its manners.' He was not sufficiently familiar with the English background of American institutions, and frequently mistook for peculiarly American or peculiarly democratic what was merely Anglo-American. He missed many things that less perspicacious observers saw, possibly because the obvious did not always accommodate itself to his philosophical pattern; in his anxiety to get below the surface he failed to appreciate things that were on the surface. Thus he could argue the ultimate disintegration of the Union because he failed to notice economic developments or to comprehend the nationalizing effect of the industrial revolution. He missed the abolition movement, and transcendentalism, and his interest in penal and prison reform—the ostensible ground for his visit to America—did not persuade him to study the reform movement in general. For all his concern with democracy, he seemed singularly uninterested in its immediate political manifestations, and the casual reader of his book would scarcely realize that while Tocqueville was traversing America, Andrew Jackson was President.

These are serious defects, defects that would guarantee oblivion to most volumes of description or interpretation. Yet *Democracy in America* has not only survived oblivion; it has earned for itself a place as a classic. For the faults of the book are, after all, superficial rather than fundamental; they are grievous only with reference to the standards Tocqueville himself set, and those standards were incomparably high. The omissions, the inadequacies, the misconceptions of the book can easily be supplied or corrected by other books; for its shining merits there is no substitute.

What are these merits? First, it can be said, Tocqueville chose a great and noble theme and handled it with dignity. That theme was the adjustment of the civilizations of Western Christendom to democracy. Others had written about America; Tocqueville undertook to relate America to world history, to fix the significance of America in history. His subject, he wrote in all humility, 'is interesting . . . to the whole world; it concerns not a nation, but all mankind.' His purpose was to prepare men everywhere for the 'providential fact' of equality; to dissipate fears, quiet excessive hopes, encourage accommodation; to lift men above narrow and selfish and persuade them to broad and generous views. (pp. xiv-xvi)

Tocqueville chose a great subject, and he measured up to its greatness. He was the first philosophical historian to write of the American experiment; the first political scientist to make democracy the primary object of realistic investigation. And it must be accounted a capital merit in Tocqueville that he had not only a philosophy, but the right philosophy. He saw that the significance of America in history was to be found in the opportunity it afforded as a laboratory of social, economic, and political democracy, and he fastened his attention on that aspect of America to the exclusion of the merely picturesque or sensational. He had an instinct for the jugular vein in history.

Other observers had lost themselves in the trivial, the irrelevant, the inconsequential; they maundered on about hotel service, the litter on the streets of cities, the hardships of railroad travel, the table manners of their hosts. Tocqueville, too, noted these things, but he did not suppose they were important in themselves or permit them to distract his attention from the object of his investigation—the effect of democracy on manners and morals, politics and religion, business and labor, literature and art, family and social relations. He was concerned, throughout, with fundamental causes and ultimate consequences.

And on almost every page of his book we discern the play of an alert, inquisitive, and critical mind. It is a tribute to the triumph of Tocqueville's method that we are, throughout, more interested in what he has to say about a subject than we are in the subject itself. He had, that is, not only a philosophical but an eminently reflective mind; he had not only a philosophy of history, in the grand manner, but perspicacity and penetration; he was as illuminating in his particular as in his general observations. We are constantly gratified by his shrewd insights and his happy prophecies. Who, after all, has better comprehended the American character than this French stranger who arrived at his understanding almost as by a mathematical formula, so rigorous was his analysis, so logical his conclusions? In his day our literature was still strongly colonial, but Tocqueville foresaw with astonishing perspicuity the effect democracy would have upon it in the future. He saw, too, that democracy must have its own History, one in which the individual was subordinate to the mass, fortuity to great sweeping movements; and from George Bancroft to Henry Adams and Charles Beard, American historical literature has conformed to Tocqueville's formula. He penetrated to the gnawing uncertainty of many Americans about social democracy, the pretentiousness and insincerity of much of the talk about the common man by men who invariably made it clear that they themselves were uncommon men. He understood, as have few foreigners and not many Americans, the combination—peculiarly prominent in the realm of politics—of extravagance of language and prudence of conduct. He noted, as had others, the American passion for change, and found it the natural consequence of the restless search for the ideal and the opportunities afforded all Americans to achieve that ideal. He grasped the fact, as yet concealed from many of our agitated Bourbons, that democracy makes for conservatism and that the surest guaranty of stability is the wide distribution of property. He was the first foreign observer to appreciate the significance of the dominance of the American political scene by men trained to the law, and described in terms still relevant that aristocracy of the robe which Americans take for granted but which other democratic peoples look upon with astonishment. He saw the significance of the interaction of democracy and religion and emphasized throughout his study the place of the church in American life. He discerned the natural hostility to the military in a democracy, but foresaw with startling accuracy the effect of prolonged war on American society and economy and psychology. There was little, indeed, in the American character that his penetrating eye did not see, his luminous mind comprehend.

And Tocqueville's interpretation, for all his aristocratic and alien background, was almost unfailingly judicious. He was misled, at times, by the men he consulted, the books he read, but his errors were never malicious. His view of democracy was often pessimistic, but never jaundiced, and it is gratifying that America has confounded its most astute critic where he was pessimistic rather than where he was optimistic. No other interpreter of America . . . has achieved the aloofness, the objectivity, the serene impersonality, that came naturally to Tocqueville. The explanation is, largely, in Tocqueville's own character; it is, in part, that Tocqueville was concerned to instruct his own people rather than to edify the Americans, and that patriotism and morality inexorably required the most scrupulous objectivity.

And, finally, it must be counted among the great merits of *Democracy in America* that its style is felicitous and even brilliant. There are no purple patches, there are few epigrams, but there is, throughout, a luminous clarity, a resiliency, a masculine toughness, that contrasts sharply with the rhetoric of Trollope or Martineau, the verbosity of Bryce, the strained brilliance of Siegfried or Maurois. Tocqueville has, above all others who have written about America, the magisterial style.

It is this happy combination of a great theme with a philosophy profound enough to comprehend it, a temperament judicious enough to interpret it, an intelligence acute enough to master it, a style adequate to its demands, that makes *Democracy in America* one of the great and enduring works of political literature. (pp. xvii-xx)

> *Henry Steele Commager, in an introduction to* Democracy in America *by Alexis de Tocqueville, translated by Henry Reeve, Oxford University Press, New York, 1947, pp. vii-xx.*

EDWARD T. GARGAN (essay date 1955)

[*In his full-length study of* The Recollections of Alexis de Tocqueville, *from which the following is drawn, Gargan argues that Tocqueville's experiences as a witness of the revolution of February, 1848 and as a participant in the Second Republic were central to the development of his thought. In addition, he maintains that* Recollections *must be studied alongside Karl Marx's histories of the February Revolution,* The Class Struggles in France *and* The Eighteenth Brumaire of Louis Bonaparte. *According to Gargan, both Tocqueville and Marx "saw in this Revolution their basic convictions concerning the secular trends of Western history become concrete and permanent." Gargan attributes the pessimistic tone of Tocqueville's works to his conviction that the fate of Christianity was involved in the political destiny of Western civilization. He places Tocqueville in the tradition of such philosophers and writers as Sören Kierkegaard, Friedrich Nietzsche, Charles Baudelaire, and Fedor Dostoevski as one who foresaw the decline of Western civilization.*]

In the concluding sections of volume I of the *Democracy* Tocqueville expertly heightened and celebrated the achievements of America in order to prepare his readers for the pressure he would place them under when he turned his attention to Europe. In assessing the significance of America's experience for Europe, Tocqueville subjected his European, and especially his French, readers to an unrelieved series of shocks and dire prophecies. To read these few pages more than a hundred years after they were written is still a disturbing and depressing experience. The atmosphere becomes so stark, so heavy that the reader is able to go on only because he has been exposed to the author's findings that the creation of a free democratic society is not the historical monopoly of any single people.

It has often been suggested that Tocqueville's acceptance of the democratic movement was a very noble but realistic bowing to an inevitable force. It is true that Tocqueville was greatly impressed by the pervasive character of the democratic revolution, but his reaction to it must be seen alongside of his estimation of the nondemocratic tradition which in the main made up the body of Europe's history. It is Tocqueville's assessment of the strength of this tradition which introduces the pessimistic vein which runs through all of his thought. In looking so apprehensively at the Western world in his own time, Tocqueville was one of the first to join a congregation of critics and prophets who saw the West facing an impending catastrophe. If Tocqueville was not fully a member of the circle who foretold the absolute decline of Western civilization, he yet belongs in the company of Kierkegaard, Proudhon, and Burckhardt and shares the forebodings which in the hands of Baudelaire, Nietzsche, Dostoevski and Spengler were to bear a message of irrevocable doom for the West.

To understand Tocqueville's own dark picture of the West, one must consistently bear in mind that for him the temporal order, and especially the political order, was intimately responsible for the present condition of Christendom. He could write that ''the organization and the establishment of democracy in Christendom is the great political problem of our times'' because he saw Western Christendom as owing its special difficulties to the historical fact that: ''In Europe, Christianity has permitted itself to be intimately united to the temporal powers. Today these powers are falling and Christianity is as though buried under the debris. But it is a living body that some wish to inter with these corpses: cut the bonds which are holding it and it will rise again.'' While Tocqueville's own intellectual vocation was directed to understanding the temporal order, the analysis which he achieved carries always with it his consciousness of the interconnections between the two orders. It is because Tocqueville believed that the fate of Christendom was involved in the political destiny of the West that his description of his age takes on its weight and solemn character. It is from this viewpoint that his dark examination of Europe's situation in the third decade of the nineteenth century is to be approached. (pp. 16-17)

The significance of Tocqueville's prescription for the ''present ills'' of society lies not so much in the trust which he placed at this time in the promises of democratic political reforms but in his diagnosis of those ''ills.'' His view of the times being out of joint is the source of much of his insight and prescience; it is also the source of the disquietude which accompanied all of his life's labors. The aspect of modern society which most frightened Tocqueville was the absence of corporate and communal unity. He saw the individual as inhabiting a world in which the institutions of government had multiplied at the cost of destroying the opportunity of human communication between man and man. The muteness of modern society pressed in nightmare fashion on Tocqueville's consciousness. Accepted in its most complete sense, Tocqueville's description of Western society exposes a psychological malaise of such proportions that the solution which he offers, however qualified, seems inadequate before it has had its chance to work. Here is the source of much of Tocqueville's future tension and disappointment, for the political remedies which he advised had not in themselves the means to eradicate the subtle disorders which he described. (pp. 19-20)

The *Souvenirs,* Tocqueville's basic reflection on the causes, character and significance of the Revolution of 1848, must be seen as framed in Tocqueville's own experience of the maneuvering necessary to grasp and hold power. . . . . The composition of the *Souvenirs* was begun in the summer of 1850, at a time when Tocqueville believed that he was only temporarily withdrawing from the world of practical politics. It was finished in the fall of 1851, a few months before the *coup d'état* of Louis Napoleon drove Tocqueville forever from the field of action. Tocqueville wrote sensing that the Second Republic had a brief future. He was, however, pledged to support it, and his memoir served not only as a record of its troubled history but as an opportunity to rethink his course of action as he searched for a means to keep it alive and free. This concern for the decisive months which lay ahead accounts for the tension and partisan spirit of some of the *Souvenirs.*

The experience of the historian and the politician do not clash in the *Souvenirs,* but they do bargain for priority of position in Tocqueville's mind. And, from time to time, the prejudices of the politician bid also for his attention and employment. The absence of that impartiality regularly attributed to the historian is evident in Tocqueville's harsh judgments of his opponents and even of his close friends. These were the men he had tried to persuade or frighten, to win over or defeat, and he had grown impatient with their intractability. This impatience swelled the suspicions which underlay his probings of their actions. (pp. 60-1)

Without any original departure from the traditional working premises of the historian, he divided the causes leading to the Revolution of 1848 into general and particular or accidental factors. These categories were not rich enough to satisfy the imagination of the historian, but they did identify the limits of his material. Given these, the act of creative understanding was then imperative to the fulfillment of the historian's art. (p. 63)

Subsequent histories have documented and added details, facts and additional causal factors to Tocqueville's picture, which in its barest presentation is not remarkably different from either that of other contemporary accounts or those of later historians. Those who have followed Tocqueville have not, however, as seriously evaluated the effect of historical precedent on the actors of the Revolution. Perhaps Marx alone gave this comparable attention. Tocqueville's thought about the Revolution truly separated itself from the average account when the need to decide his position, immediately after the February Revolution, prompted him to ask the meaning of 1848 within the long history of the French Revolution. Having raised this question, he was led to ask the significance of 1848 for the entire history of his race. Such a quick expansion in the breadth of his investigation was typical of the operation of his mind. When walking in the foothills of analysis, his progress was usually that of the good climber. The prospect of the view from higher hills, however, quickened his pace, and he was then often found outstripping his companions in his haste to reach the greater heights from which one could imagine that the horizon showed a faint trace of the globe's curvature. (pp. 65-6)

The full import of Tocqueville's education in the Revolution of 1848 to 1851 is best understood when it is recognized how closely many of his reflections and observations on the course and meaning of the developments of the Revolution coincide with the observations which Marx was making of these years in his *The Class Struggles in France* and *The Eighteenth Brumaire of Louis Bonaparte.* The similarity of their judgments is an unusual commentary on the separate avenues which historians and politicians can take even when they agree in many instances. A comparison of their evaluations of this history, while it reaffirms the historical validity of many of the decisions which they reached separately, is of particular importance because it exhibits in high light the significance of the decision which separated them in their pursuit of historical reality. In the final issue, the French historian remained pledged to the spiritual movement of history, while Marx, who was not unaware of this force, turned consciously to the mastering of the material forces in history. On this point they diverged irrevocably. (p. 249)

The conclusion to be drawn from any consideration of Tocqueville's and Marx's response to the Revolution of 1848 is that this experience was central to the development of their life and thought. Its importance lies not primarily in any violent changes which the Revolution imposed on them as thinkers but rather in the manner in which the Revolution served as the proving ground for the ideas of their formative years. Though they were in many ways different men as a result of their experiences from 1848 to 1852, they each saw in this Revolution their basic convictions concerning the secular trends of Western history become concrete and permanent.

It is significant that, though Marx and Tocqueville were in no sense kindred spirits, their observations on the Revolution, their judgments of its origins, its development and its denouement support, in a thorough manner, each other's validity as a witness of this important historical event. For the historian who would study the history of this Revolution, this is the relevant question. It is hard to imagine a more sensitive witness of and participant in the making of the history of the Revolution of 1848 than Alexis de Tocqueville. Similarly, it is hard to imagine a man of tougher constitution or more single-minded drive than Marx as he prepared for the Revolution and then watched it collapse. Yet despite their separate spiritual orientation and goals, their accounts of the Revolution and their assessment of its meaning confirm the value and importance of their individual histories. (pp. 303-04)

The extent to which Tocqueville had an interest in the problems of the sociologist cannot be denied. An examination of the interaction of his public and scholarly careers as they culminated during the Revolution of 1848 reveals graphically, however, that it is Tocqueville's perspective as an historian which established the framework and binds together his life work. Again and again at crucial moments it is to history that Tocqueville turned for an answer to the practical and theoretical problems he faced. Few men have ever demonstrated such faith in the wisdom to be derived from an understanding of the unity of historical experience. When first presented with the literature of social reform, Tocqueville studied it in its historical significance, using as his pivotal point the rise of Christianity conceived as the central movement in Western history. Again, when forced to an altered view of the social movement, believing during the crisis of the Second Republic that such ideas of social reform would destroy the existing civilization, he turned for a balanced view to the experience of the Western world in the fifth century after Christ, when the ancient world was suffering its last great crisis. Finally, his conception of his own period was framed within the historical dimensions of the French Revolution, which he saw issuing from the democratic movement having its rise in the period following the waning of the Middle Ages. His approach to his own time was further defined within the range of forces emerging from the

history of the Great Revolution itself, in which a plebiscitarian democratic order and a plebiscitarian despotic order were given their initial historical statement. Tocqueville's own intellectual work must be seen as crisis-oriented to specific decisive moments of modern history. Thus the *Democracy* issues from his experiences in the Revolution of 1830. . . . The heart of the *Souvenirs* can only be interpreted and understood when it is recalled that the pages making up his analysis of the Revolution of 1848 were written after a period of great trial in Tocqueville's personal life. He wrote the major portion of the *Souvenirs,* his assessment of 1848, after he had experienced the responsibilities which had carried him as close as he ever was to history-making decisions and after he had been humiliatingly dismissed from office by Louis Napoleon. Of equal significance the *Ancien Régime* was conceived and projected under the same climate of crisis. In December, 1850, Tocqueville expressed in his correspondence his plans to return to the writing of history. As he outlined what that history would be, he was making a desperate effort to repair the injuries which his body and soul had received while serving the Republic and the President who destroyed it. Even while he planned this work, however, he was waiting in anguish in Sorrento for each message from Paris carrying news of the approaching death struggle of the Republic. It was only after he had returned to sit at the bedside of the dying Republic and to watch its violent interment that he finally became free to take up his writing. That history, which now exists in the *Ancien Régime* and further fragments is Tocqueville's testimony to his convictions and to his trust in the historian's vocation. This vocation was undeniably pragmatic, but it is a golden pragmatism which gives it splendor. (pp. 309-10)

> *Edward T. Gargan, in his* Alexis de Tocqueville: The Critical Years, 1848-1851, *The Catholic University of America Press, 1955, 324 p.*

JOHN LUKACS   (essay date 1959)

[*Lukacs's* "The European Revolution" & Correspondence with Gobineau, *which was originally published in 1959, is the first English translation of the completed portion of the second part of Tocqueville's study of the French Revolution and the First Empire as well as the first English publication of the letters exchanged between Tocqueville and the French diplomat and historian Arthur de Gobineau between 1843 and 1859. In the following excerpt, which is drawn from Lukacs's introduction to* "The European Revolution" & Correspondence with Gobineau, *Lukacs challenges Emile Faguet's promotion of Tocqueville as a sociologist (1900) and cautions against classifying Tocqueville as a* "moderate," "'conservative' democrat," *or* "'liberal' aristocrat." *He contends that Tocqueville was a* "modern historian" *who always wrote with* "some moral purpose in mind." *According to Lukacs, Tocqueville's correspondence with Gobineau reveals that his* "main concern was with the future of Western Christendom."]

Everything Tocqueville wrote he wrote with some moral purpose in mind. It is, therefore, important to group and sum up his writings with their corresponding moral concerns. (p. 5)

First, Tocqueville believed that a new age of social democracy was about inevitable; that the principle of social equality had triumphed over the traditional aristocratic order of Europe; that this democratic future was full of hitherto unseen dangers but that, on the other hand, through the proper exercise of self-government, liberty and an orderly social democracy were not irreconcilable. To a broad illustration, and to an exposition of these principles, he devoted *Democracy in America.* Here his purpose was less a book about America than a book about democracy, written for the sake of France.

Second, Tocqueville came to conclude that the origins of the great European revolution which broke out in 1789 ought to be traced less to aristocratic misrule than to an ideological revolution. This was a revolution which, paradoxically, the European aristocracy itself had embraced and furthered; its overwhelming political condition had been the thoughtless and continued extension of the central powers of the State, which process, in France, had preceded the Revolution by at least a hundred and fifty years and which was still going on. To these propositions he devoted the two volumes of *The Old Regime and the Revolution.* Here his purpose was less a book about France than a book about the great Revolution, written for the sake of Europe.

Third, Tocqueville was convinced that the nineteenth century was wrong in believing that liberty and Christianity were irreconcilable. He saw that the new forces of social democracy, unlike the transitory bourgeois forces, might not be opposed to religion at all. His prophetic conclusions about the potential harmony between democracy and religion (and especially the Roman Catholic religion) appeared in *Democracy in America;* his judicious criticism of the false eighteenth-century optimism about human nature appears in *The Old Regime* and also in his *Souvenirs* . . . ; even more, these concerns appear in his letters, in his American correspondence, and in the letters written during his last decade of life, especially to Corcelle, Mme. Swetchine, De Broglie, and Freslon. But above all these is his monumental defense of Catholic Christianity and of liberty in his debate with Gobineau—written, I shall add, for the sake of Western Christendom.

It is the second and the third of these grand concerns which the contents of [*"The European Revolution" & Correspondence with Gobineau*] should illuminate. Yet, confronted as we are with the extraordinarily coherent and consistent nature of Tocqueville's philosophy, it is evident that these great concerns cannot be academically separated. He considered the French Revolution of 1789 but part and parcel of a greater, European Revolution which, sixty years after the storming of the Bastille, may have been still in its first phase. The European Revolution, in turn, was but a manifestation of a great global movement toward social democracy, at the core of which remained the fundamental problem of liberty and Christianity; and the problem of their compatibility was, to Tocqueville, inseparable from the prospects of what we now call "Western civilization." (pp. 5-7)

[Tocqueville's unique interpretation of the French Revolution in *The European Revolution*] is, of course, a history; and its writer a historian. . . . To the singular quality of Tocqueville as a historian his otherwise ungenerous critic, Émile Faguet, paid unwitting tribute when he wrote that the task which Tocqueville "set for himself was to penetrate beneath accidental history to solid history, or beneath history to the physiology of peoples" [see excerpt above, 1900]. From this correct analysis Faguet had, however, already deduced the wrong conclusion: that Tocqueville was, really, a cautious sociologist rather than a bold historian. Yet the whole key to Tocqueville's singular historical talents lies here. When Faguet wrote sixty years ago, the texture of history had not yet changed. At that time it seemed still reasonable to keep concentrating on "surface" history, on the history of the politically conscious classes. . . . Since then, however, it has become more and more obvious that, with the social and democratic character of

our age, the requirements of historiography have changed, that it is no longer possible to concentrate exclusively on the actions of leading protagonists of the politically active classes, that it is less and less possible to separate what Faguet called "surface" history from what lies "beneath" it. And this Tocqueville already knew. The importance of *The Revolution,* therefore, is not only that it is an extraordinarily instructive interpretation of the French Revolution; it is, also, an extraordinarily instructive *new type* of history.

Within it Tocqueville implicitly and, at times, explicitly refutes many of the propositions of modern "professional" historiography. He is among the earliest observers who note that political history is no longer enough. He sees that the politically active classes may frequently become powerless and that their abdication of leadership is a development often more decisive than are the alleged "demands and decisions" of the people. Revolutions are seldom made by the conscious "dynamism" of the people, yet Tocqueville rejects the fatalistic notion that accidents govern history and also the deterministic notion that people are moved by predetermined economic motives.

History is made by men, to whom God has given free will. Tocqueville refutes the notion that history is a methodological "science." He conceives his historian's duties as primarily moral ones; but, then, he is also an artist at the same time. . . . He wished to be a true painter and not a methodical chronicler; he sought to find the great latent tendencies of the human heart rather than to be an academic accountant of the obvious. His literary and historical purposes were not narration, entertainment, information but description, proposition, comprehension. This novel conception of historiography with its nobly instructive purpose was immeasurably furthered by the lucidity and the almost Cartesian symmetry of his style: unlike Descartes, however, he was not willing to substitute clarity for charity.

Tocqueville was neither an academic sociologist nor a professional chronicler but a modern historian. And yet, because of the deplorable habit of this modern age to think in terms of intellectual categories, it is seldom that he is so recognized. It is not only that he was not a "professional" historian, but he and his principles hardly fit into any of those modern preconceived categories. (pp. 10-12)

[While] Tocqueville did not believe that the voice of the people is the voice of God, neither did he believe that it was that of the devil. He was not one of those who believed that a nation has the right to go beyond her natural interests to propagate ideas and to arrogate to herself the singular role of impressing them on the world, yet he did not believe in narrow concepts of national interests either. He was not a French nationalist or a European imperialist, yet he did not believe that the achievements and the ideals of every nation and of every civilization are of the same worth. And he condemned the old regime as well as the Revolution.

Yet it is not possible to try to find a solution along liberal lines, as so many have done: to say that Tocqueville was the classic moderate, that his greatness consists of his having trodden a cautious narrow path between opposite categories. For Tocqueville was not between them. He was *above* them. He transcends these categories. No man with such absolute principles as that of Tocqueville would be a consummate compromiser, a trimmer, a mere moderate. He did not believe that the voice of the people was divine, yet he believed that it *could* echo the divine. He did not wish to steer a middle way between ideological and strategic concepts of national destiny, nor was he a moderate cosmopolitan, midway between being an internationalist or a nationalist: instead of cocking his liberal ear to ideological platitudes about one classless world or to sentimental invocations of nation or race, he fixed his patriotic eye on the providential limits of human and national ambitions. And if he condemned both old regime and Revolution for their vices, he also found virtues of lasting inspiration in both.

The Revolution, therefore, is exhortatory history. As in his letters to Gobineau, not only the occasional tone but the essential purpose is exhortatory. I have already said that it is hardly possible to comprehend the writings of Tocqueville without considering the moral purpose of their author. In turn, it is only with these moral purposes in mind that we will be able to correct some of the mistaken conceptions about him. If the main concern of *Democracy in America* was the future of democracy, that book also reveals that Tocqueville was more than a ''conservative'' democrat or a ''liberal'' aristocrat. If the main concern of *The Revolution* was the future of France and of Europe, it also reveals that Tocqueville was more than a late-comer to the historical academy or an early forerunner of sociology. And his main concern was with the future of Western Christendom; reflected in his correspondence with Gobineau, this reveals that Tocqueville was neither a ''progressive'' Catholic nor an aristocratic agnostic, but that he was a great Christian thinker with a noble heart. (pp. 12-14)

[Tocqueville's correspondence with Gobineau] is a correspondence which ranks in importance with the great dialogues of modern history, with the dialogues between Machiavelli and Guicciardini, between Proudhon and Marx, between Burckhardt and Nietzsche. It is a co-respondence in the literal sense of that word. What does it represent?

It represents not only the aristocratic and the conservative and the sensitively pessimistic but the much less known Christian and democratic and contemplatively optimistic side of Tocqueville. His letters express the truth that the gloomy and Germanic twentieth-century notion of the ''decline of the West'' has been, in reality, a sentimental and bourgeois notion. Despite his frequent personal pessimism, Tocqueville manfully rejects the argument suggested by Gobineau (and later proclaimed by so many others) about the inevitability of the decline of Europe. Which is, perhaps, the highest and most exhilarating point reached in this correspondence.

Nor it is not only that Tocqueville's predictions have proved almost always right and Gobineau's almost always wrong, that Gobineau (as did almost every nineteenth-century prophet) failed to recognize what may well be the two most astonishing developments of the twentieth century: the rise of American power and the reascendance of Catholicism all over the world. More than any other great dialogue of the nineteenth century, the Tocqueville-Gobineau correspondence is a crystalline, microcosmic representation of the great divisions of the twentieth.

It is evident that, by now, a general reaction has set in everywhere in the West against the basic assumptions of the French Revolution, against the enlightened illusions of the eighteenth century about perfectible human nature, against the inorganic optimism about the potential creation of an efficient Garden of Eden in this world, against utilitarianism, against individualism. There were many who foresaw that a reaction against these so often insubstantial and godless illusions had to come. Yet few foresaw the violent forms this reaction would take, for instance, in the form of a Hitler. That what Tocqueville

had to say is very relevant to the twentieth century is obvious to the point of a platitude. But what is not so obvious is that Tocqueville, who was so justly critical of the illusions of the eighteenth century, had already begun to worry about the potential spiritual disasters of this reaction against them. He, who so often extolled the virtues of Faith and the follies of Reason when pushed to extremes, already foresaw the dangers of that new sort of political fideism which characterizes the mass movements of the twentieth century. And today when the Communist appeal in the West has shrunk to a minority of warped minions, we should recall that Tocqueville predicted that shrinking a century ago. (pp. 16-18)

Tocqueville foresaw that in the Western world the greatest dangers to the free human spirit may no longer come from the entrenched rule of aristocratic minorities but from the emancipated majorities themselves. To him it was always evident that such democratic institutions as universal suffrage, popular education, and the advancement of social equality were not automatic guarantees of freedom. So far there is little disagreement between Gobineau and Tocqueville or between Tocqueville and the great nineteenth-century conservative or even liberal thinkers. The quality of Tocqueville's aristocratic heart and mind, however, was such that it made him rise above despair, self-pity, or sentimental rationalization: he refused to despair of democracy or to reject it. Again, this is not the position of a ''moderate''; it is the attitude of a generous man. Nor is it expressible within the nineteenth-century parliamentary categories of ''Right'' and ''Left.'' (p. 20)

Tocqueville knew that complex mystery of the human soul and will which makes it impossible to capture the difference of human beings and of their desires within fixed methodological categories or to illustrate them on mathematical scales. Mathematical logic, for instance, would compel us to say that every anti-anti-Communist is, by necessity, a pro-Communist. But this is nonsense.

This, too, Tocqueville knew. He despised communism or, indeed, all ''Leftist'' radicalism; but he would not overestimate their prospects. He saw that with the rise of social democracy the radical proletarian elements would gradually become property owners and adopt petty bourgeois ideals of spiritual and material security, but that during this pursuit of security they might thoughtlessly surrender whatever slight appetite for personal liberty they might originally have had. (p. 21)

From some of his letters we can glimpse an astonishing insight into Russia. He considered Russia, notwithstanding all of her European veneer, essentially outside of and inimical to Western civilization. He would not have been surprised to see Russia turn Communist one day. But he saw the dangers of European civilization coming not from without but from within. And our now so natural concern with the deadly power of Bolshevik Russia should not obscure this truth. We should always remember that it was from Western Europe that Marxism traveled to Russia; that there the Bolshevik Revolution succeeded only because of the awful European War of 1914-18, when the European nations tore each other apart; that Lenin was sent back to Russia by nationalist Germany; that the rulers of the same Germany helped the Communist Russia regime survive; that it was Hitler, the revolutionary leader of the ''New Europe,'' who twenty years later invited Stalin to advance into Poland; that nationalist revolutionary Germany and not Communist Russia was primarily responsible for the Second World War, from which the latter so naturally profited; that, unlike other and more spontaneous totalitarian movements ever since then, no Bolshevik regime has ever succeeded in Europe without the assistance of external, Russian, arms.

In this sense I do not hesitate to say that Tocqueville was an anti-anti-Communist. "The insane fear of socialism," he wrote in 1852, "throws the bourgeois headlong into the arms of despotism. As in Prussia, Hungary, Austria, Italy, in France the democrats have served the cause of the absolutists. But now that the weakness of the Red party has been proved, people will regret the price at which their enemy has been put down." (p. 22)

[By] now, social democracy has triumphed almost all over the world. That this is no time for nostalgic evocations of the order of the past, Tocqueville knew more than a hundred years ago. While so many pre-eminent minds were still struggling against democracy, Tocqueville concluded that democracy was here to stay and that the question was this: What kind of democracy? He foresaw that neither bourgeois society nor the bourgeois mode of thought, nor bourgeois liberalism, nor a neo-medieval romanticism would by itself prevent the devolution of democracies into national, and later continental, socialist tyrannies. But Christianity could. His chief dream remained to reconcile modern democracy with the Church. He believed "that the faults of the clergy are far less dangerous to liberty than their subjection to the State." And he said—and here he remained, until now, frequently misunderstood—that to hate democracy is, therefore, not merely impractical: it is also immoral. But he was not only ahead of Marx in a moral sense; he was ahead of him by a hundred years. (pp. 24-5)

In the end his letters to Gobineau represent the Catholic Christian Tocqueville. If *The Revolution* gives evidence of the genius of Tocqueville the historian, his letters to Gobineau especially after 1852 indicate that he was then a believing Christian. This is important, since he has seldom been so classified by his commentators. (pp. 24-5)

> *John Lukacs, in an introduction to* "The European Revolution" & Correspondence with Gobineau *by Alexis de Tocqueville, edited and translated by John Lukacs, 1959. Reprint by Greenwood Press, Publishers, 1974, pp. 1-28.*

ROBERT A. NISBET   (essay date 1966)

[*Nisbet's* The Sociological Tradition, *from which the following excerpt is drawn, is, according to the author, "an effort to set forth what is conceptually fundamental and historically distinctive in the sociological tradition." In his preface to the work, Nisbet states that "the sociological tradition may . . . be seen as a kind of magnetic field with Tocqueville and Karl Marx as the two poles of attraction." According to Nisbet, "in the long run the influence of Tocqueville on the sociological tradition has been the greater." Here, Nisbet analyzes Tocqueville's vision of democratic society and contrasts his views on capitalism and class structure with those of Marx. Nisbet also focuses on Tocqueville's concept of political power in a democracy.*]

Tocqueville's *Democracy in America* is the first systematic and empirical study of the effects of political power on modern society. This work is much else also, but at bottom it is a study, and a remarkably dispassionate one, of the impact of democracy upon the traditions, values, and social structures descended from medieval society. In his second major work, *The Old Regime and the French Revolution,* Tocqueville explored the sources of modern political power, with its twin aspects of centralization and bureaucratization. Logically one

might say that it precedes the earlier work. And no one reading *Democracy in America* will have any difficulty in seeing, between the lines, the thesis of the later work. Both studies have to be understood in the light of Tocqueville's obsession with the Revolution and its impact upon the social order.

Tocqueville's central thesis can be stated simply. All that alienates man in modern society from traditional authority—from class, guild, church, and so on—tends to drive him ever more forcefully into the haven of power, power conceived not as something remote and fearful but as close, sealing, intimate, and providential: the power, that is, of modern democracy with its roots in public opinion. This is Tocqueville's dominant theme. The decline of the aristocratic community and the release of men from old authorities were historically required, he repeatedly emphasizes, for modern power to make its appearance in the democratic-national state.

Unlike most of his contemporaries, Tocqueville saw democracy not primarily as a system of freedom but of power. Democracy with its emphasis upon equality, liberation from traditional authority, and its sense of the centralized, unified nation, is but the logical and inevitable outcome of forces that had begun centuries earlier in monarchical centralization which had, over several centuries, reduced medieval diversity and localism in favor of widening national aggregates based upon administrative power at the center. Whereas freedom is, for Tocqueville, *immunity* from power, democracy is, by its nature, a *form* of power, potentially greater in intensity and reach than any prior form of political government. (pp. 120-21)

[Individualization, sterilization, and rationalization] are the processes that Tocqueville sees operating in the long run toward a magnification of political power in a democracy. Such power, he tells us, in one of the most celebrated chapters of *Democracy in America,* may in time come to seem not power but freedom. The democratic multitudes, separated from hierarchy, isolated from traditional communities, confined to the recesses of their individual minds and hearts, may come to regard the sole remaining power of the state, not as tyranny but as a form of higher and more benevolent community.

"Above this race of men stands an immense and tutelary power, which takes upon itself alone to secure their gratifications and to watch over their fate. That power is absolute, minute, regular, provident, and mild. It would be like the authority of a parent if, like that authority, its object was to prepare men for manhood; but it seeks, on the contrary, to keep them in perpetual childhood. . . . After having thus successively taken each member of the community in its powerful grasp and fashioned him at will, the supreme power then extends its arm over the whole community. It covers the surface of society with a network of small complicated rules, minute and uniform, through which the more original minds and the most energetic characters cannot penetrate, to rise above the crowd. . . . Such power does not destroy, but it prevents existence; it does not tyrannize, but it compresses, enervates, extinguishes, and stupefies a people, till each nation is reduced to nothing better than a flock of timid and industrious animals, of which the government is the shepherd.

"I have always thought that servitude of the regular, quiet, and gentle kind which I have just described might be combined more easily than is commonly believed with some of the outward forms of freedom, and that it might even establish itself under the wing of the sovereignty of the people."

Such is Tocqueville's preview of totalitarianism: one born not of the patently evil in society but of forces and states which men everywhere were regarding as blessed by progress. What makes Tocqueville's analysis of modern totalitarianism superior to others is that he seeks to relate it to political values (rather, to corruption of values) that men prize, rather than those that are abhorred in a population. The grim vision that Weber later gives us of a Western society ground down into the robots produced by a humanitarian bureaucracy, one bereft of creative vitality, is not different from what we find in Tocqueville.

Yet it must not be thought that Tocqueville saw democracy only in the dark terms of necessary future transformation into plebiscitarian tyranny. That his vision became, before he died, a more and more governing one in his imagination is clear, but we should miss much of the sociological as well as the liberal essence of *Democracy in America* if we did not see the social checks and counter-forces to centralized power that Tocqueville found in the United States. There are many: the independence of the judiciary, the separation of religion and state, the autonomy and high status in which professions (particularly the legal profession) exist, the still intact authority of local community, the regional diversity, and the open frontier; all of these, Tocqueville emphasizes, stand as controls upon the type of political power that tends to emerge from politically dominant majorities and from the unrestrained sway of public opinion.

Even more important, he thought, is freedom of association. Few things that he observed in America struck Tocqueville more forcibly and favorably than the profusion of associations that, in innumerable spheres, discharged functions which in Europe were vested either in an aristocracy or in political bureaucracy. All societies require some degree of freedom of association, Tocqueville writes, but nowhere is the need for "intermediate associations" so great as in a democracy. For in a democracy it is only too easy to suppose that by virtue of sovereignty's locus in the people as a whole, the need for autonomous, non-political, functional associations is lessened. Associations serve the twin purposes, Tocqueville tells us, of providing a haven for the individual, thus freeing him of the desire to seek absorption in the mass, and of limiting the extent of governmental participation and centralization in society. (pp. 130-31)

Tocqueville is the first and, throughout the nineteenth century, the major exponent of the view that the modern regime is characterized not by the solidification but by the fragmentation of social class, with the key elements dispersed: power to the masses and to centralized bureaucracy, wealth to an ever-enlarging middle class, and status to the varied and shifting sectors of society which, in the absence of true class, become the theaters of the unending and agonizing competition among individuals for the attainment of the marks of status.

The clue to the modern order lies for Tocqueville in the relentless leveling of classes that has characterized the history of the West since the end of the Middle Ages. "In running over the pages of our history, we shall scarcely find a single great event of the last seven hundred years that has not promoted equality of condition." Given this formidable background of history, is it likely, he asks, that capitalism or any other feature of modern society will arrest a tendency now so deeply embedded in historical reality?

"The gradual development of the principle of equality is a providential fact. It has all the chief characteristics of such a fact: it is universal, it is durable, it constantly eludes all human interference, and all events as well as all men contribute to its progress. Would it be wise to imagine that a social movement, the causes of which lie so far back, can be checked by the efforts of one generation? Can it be believed that the democracy which has overthrown the feudal system and vanquished kings will retreat before tradesmen and capitalists? Will it stop now that it has grown so strong and its adversaries so weak?"

Tocqueville's answer to these questions forms the theme of his sociology of stratification. The dissolution of social class that began in the late Middle Ages under the twin impacts of political centralization and social individualism can only complete itself in the modern order. The dispersion of power among the democratic mass, the ever more prominent place occupied by political bureaucracy, the virtual enshrinement of the norm of equality, the incessant competition for wealth in the fluid forms that capitalism has brought, and the profound urge to status achievement in a society where each man regards himself as the equal of all—these and other forces make true social class impossible. There are, of course, economic strata, even extremes of wealth. But these do not promote a sense of belonging to a class.

"I am aware that among a great democratic people there will always be some members of the community in great poverty and others in great opulence; but the poor, instead of forming the great majority of the nation, as is always the case in aristocratic communities, are comparatively few in number, and the laws do not bind them together by ties of irremediable and hereditary penury. . . . As there is no longer a race of poor men, so there is no longer a race of rich men; the latter spring up daily from the multitude and relapse into it again. Hence, they do not form a distinct class which may be easily marked out and plundered; and, moreover, as they are connected with the mass of their fellow citizens by a thousand secret ties, the people cannot assail them without inflicting an injury upon themselves.

"Between these two extremes of democratic communities stands an innumerable multitude of men almost alike, who, without being exactly either rich or poor, possess sufficient property to desire the maintenance of order, yet not enough to excite envy."

It is in these terms exactly that Tocqueville's view of class, class consciousness, and class conflict may be seen as the obverse of Marx's. The tensions of democratic-commercial society, far from promoting revolution, constantly diminish the possibility of revolution. "Such men," Tocqueville writes of the great democratic middle, "are the natural enemies of violent commotions; their lack of agitation keeps all beneath them and above them still and secures the balance of the fabric of society." (pp. 183-84)

[The] gathering tides of democracy after the American Revolution sterilized the role of the quasi-aristocracy, and there are left, Tocqueville emphasizes, only the shifting categories of rich and poor, categories not likely to produce classes in the true sense; and so far as political power is concerned, it is more likely, in a democracy, Tocqueville argues, to lie with the masses of the poor than with the rich. "Among civilized nations, only those who have nothing to lose ever revolt," and while "the natural anxiety of the rich may produce a secret dissatisfaction," their sheer devotion to wealth and property will ensure almost any degree of political compliance.

The character of wealth in a democracy tends to make true class impossible. It is typically commercial, trading, and manufacturing wealth, not landed. Democracy not only "swells the number of workingmen, but leads men to prefer one kind of labor to another; and while it diverts them from agriculture, it encourages their taste for commerce and manufactures." Commerce does not stimulate the democratic passion for well-being; the reverse is true. (p. 185)

It is, in short, a political interpretation of capitalism that Tocqueville gives us and, characteristically, he places the interpretation in the context of democracy's difference from aristocracy. Under aristocracy, the rich are at the same time the governing power; they do not have time for the responsibilities of trade and commerce, and where an aristocrat does attempt, now and then, to enter trade, the counteractive opinion of his peers is sudden and compelling.

In democratic countries, on the other hand, "where money does not lead those who possess it to political power, but often removes them from it, the rich do not know how to spend their leisure. They are driven into active life by the disquietude and the greatness of their desires, by the extent of their resources, and by the taste for what is extraordinary, which is always felt by those who rise, by whatever means, above the crowd. Trade is the only road open to them."

In one respect only does Tocqueville see the outlines—though only the outlines—of a class, a new mode of aristocracy forming within capitalism. This is the manufacturing class. Tocqueville did not regard the system of division of labor in the optimistic light of his liberal contemporaries. It is one of the marks of his alienated view of modern society that he sees, not improvement, but degradation in the specialization of the worker. Such degradation he thought a permanent aspect of the system and one that would only heighten the superiority and influence of the manufacturing class in democracy. The latter becomes more powerful and, as a *category*, more intrenched, as the working class becomes more degraded. "Men grow more alike in the one, more different in the other; and inequality increases in the less numerous class in the same ratio in which it decreases in the community. Hence it would appear, on searching to the bottom, that aristocracy would naturally spring out of the bosom of democracy."

So it might seem. But what Tocqueville sees as the perpetual mobility of commerical democracy makes such an aristocracy impossible, in fact. There is too much circulation of the members of the classes—especially of the rich class, which is constantly losing its members, to be replaced by others. Thus, and here is the essence of Tocqueville's view of class in capitalism, the very converse of Marx's: "though there are rich men, the class of rich men does not exist; for these rich individuals have no feeling or purposes, no traditions or hopes, in common; there are individuals, therefore, but no definite class.

"Not only are the rich not compactly united among themselves, but there is no real bond between them and the poor. Their relative position is not a permanent one; they are constantly drawn together or separated by their interests. . . . The one contracts no obligation to protect nor the other to defend, and they are not permanently connected either by habit or by duty. . . . An aristocracy thus constituted can have no great hold upon those whom it employs, and even if it succeeds in retaining them at one moment, they escape the next; it knows not how to will, and it cannot act."

The differences here between Marx and Tocqueville are engaging. It is precisely *because* of the lack of reciprocal obligation between the manufacturers and workers, *because* of the dissolution of uniting bonds of protection and defense, that Marx sees the two classes becoming ever more distinct, each ever more inclusive of habits, ideas, and beliefs. But for Tocqueville true class can exist *only* in the presence of reciprocality, co-operation, and mutual dependence, and where these are gone, there can remain only levels, abstract strata, not true classes. (pp. 185-86)

Tocqueville was deeply struck—and appalled—by the position of the Negro in the United States. He was horrified by the paradox of educated and morally cultivated Southern whites able to inflict awful punishments and deprivations upon their Negro slaves without remorse. It was proof, in Tocqueville's mind, of the dependence of modern Western humanitarianism upon equality rather than upon level of education or civilization. No nation, he thought, approached the United States in the humaneness of its penal institutions and the relative gentleness of its criminal laws. But all of this was within the context of white society alone, where equalitarian sentiment dominated. (p. 193)

From this, however, it does not follow in Tocqueville's mind that the only requisite for establishment of an equalitarian temper between white and Negro is legal emancipation. Abolitionists often wrote as though simple emancipation would solve everything, but Tocqueville could see in a liberation that was *only* legal the seed of bitterness and hostility that could eventually erupt into revolution. The one possibility indeed that he could see of revolution in the United States was that engendered by the Negro *after* he had been formally freed by law. The following words are prescient:

"I am obliged to confess that I do not regard the abolition of slavery as a means of warding off the struggle of the two races in the Southern states. The Negroes may long remain slaves without complaining; but if they are once raised to the level of freemen, they will soon revolt at being deprived of almost all their civil rights; and as they cannot become the equals of the whites, they will speedily show themselves as enemies." (pp. 193-94)

Tocqueville saw that the essence of the Negro-white relationship was social, not racial, not economic, not political. He was perhaps the first to be aware of the paradox that political democracy, far from facilitating the intermingling of the two races that would be ultimately required for their peaceful equality, was in fact a mighty barrier. For democracy rests upon public opinion and it is the heavy weight of public opinion in a democracy that, above all else, tends to defeat assimilation. (p. 194)

The merit of Tocqueville's analysis of the Negro problem in the United States rests upon his conversion of the problem from the perspective of race or of simple minority group to the perspective of status and status relationships. He correctly places the problem in the turbulent arena of American democracy's quest for status and status identity. Had there been a social scene in which the dominant white majority was not itself preoccupied by status, by mobility, and by status anxiety, the problem for the Negro would have been a simpler one. But this, as Tocqueville emphasizes, is not the case in American democracy—or in democracy anywhere. The tragic consequence is that the Negro can only appear as threat to a white status already made fragile and uncertain by currents of history that have nothing to do with the Negro. (p. 195)

[Optimism is not] the word we would use today for the spirit of Tocqueville's picture [of culture and human character in *Democracy in America*]. Lights there may be in it, but there are also shadows that reflect a somberness of mood that grows steadily in his *Democracy in America*. Nearly a decade intervened between his visit to the United States and the publication of the second volume, and in that time, it is plain, a good deal happened to his assessment of democracy. And, taking the work as a whole, it is hard to resist the conclusion that Tocqueville reserved his greatest interpretive skill for the shadows. Try as he might, he could not conquer the feeling that in the achievement of equalitarian justice, American democracy . . . had run the risk of eroding away the social and cultural bases of human greatness: that is, the diversity, the variety, the hierarchy of society and culture on which individual greatness must rest. He is frank about his troubled indecision, and is willing, he says in a concluding passage, to defer to the view that perhaps only God is privileged to take.

"When I survey this countless multitude of beings, shaped in each other's likeness, amid whom nothing rises and nothing falls, the sight of such universal uniformity saddens and chills me and I am tempted to regret that state of society which has ceased to be. . . . Such is not the case with that Almighty and Eternal Being whose gaze necessarily includes the whole of created things and who surveys distinctly, though all at once, mankind and man. . . . What appears to me to be man's decline is, to His eye, advancement; what afflicts me is acceptable to Him. A state of equality is perhaps less elevated but it is more just: and its justice constitutes its greatness and its beauty." (pp. 274-75)

But if God may take comfort in equalitarian justice at the expense of men great in mind and character, Tocqueville cannot. Nothing is more vivid in his pages, read today, than the sense of the deterioration of the nobility and greatness of man: man in his relation to the universe and man in his relation to his fellows. Amid mild and humane laws there is little energy of character. Violence and cruelty are checked, but there are few instances of exalted heroism and of virtues of the highest, brightest, and purest temper. Ignorance is banished, information diffused, but men of great learning are not found and genius becomes rare. There is abundance in the arts but little perfection. The bond of humanity is strengthened, but the ties of race, rank, and country are weakened. (p. 275)

Crucial to Tocqueville's envisagement of democratic individualism is his conviction that the meaning of the individual has paradoxically and tragically diminished. First, by secularization, itself the result of the application of abstract reason to values formerly sanctified by religion. Second, by the immense sway of public opinion, the tyranny of the invisible majority. Third, by the effects of division of labor which have made man the mere creature of the machine. Fourth, by separation from the ties of community. Added to these, there is, he believes, a loosening of moral values. Such values as honor and loyalty, having lost their social roots, tend to lose their historic importance in the social order. (p. 276)

[For Tocqueville] democracy, with all its triumphs and all its inevitability as a historical force, has an inescapable tide of cultural desolation in it, a tendency toward desiccation of the values on which both personal character and legitimate government must ultimately rest. Democracy and individualism are in relentless conflict with their own premises; each threatens to destroy what it most needs—institutional and moral props that originated in pre-democratic, pre-individualistic society.

In democracy "man is exalted by precept but degraded in practice." The success of democracy rests upon preservation somehow of the image of man born of aristocratic society, but a whole host of forces are at work to make this impossible. (p. 284)

> *Robert A. Nisbet, in his* The Sociological Tradition, *Basic Books, Inc., Publishers, 1966, 349 p.**

ADDITIONAL BIBLIOGRAPHY

Adams, Herbert B. *Jared Sparks and Alexis de Tocqueville*. Johns Hopkins University Studies in Historical and Political Science, edited by Herbert B. Adams, series XVI, no. 12. Baltimore: Johns Hopkins Press, 1898, 49 p.
　　Offers a selection of Tocqueville's correspondence with Jared Sparks, a New England historian who assisted him in his investigation of American political institutions.

Review of *On the Penitentiary System in the United States and its Application in France*, by Alexis de Tocqueville and Gustave de Beaumont. *American Quarterly Review* XVI (September 1833): 228-54.*
　　Questions the verity of Tocqueville and Beaumont's account of American penal institutions. While the critic considers many of Tocqueville and Beaumont's opinions "strange," he terms *On the Penitentiary System in the United States and its Application in France* "as fair a summary of American penitentiary systems as could have been expected" from two Frenchmen.

Aron, Raymond. "Alexis de Tocqueville." In his *Main Currents in Sociological Thought: Montesquieu/Comte/Marx/Tocqueville/The Sociologists and the Revolution of 1848, Vol. I,* translated by Richard Howard and Helen Weaver, pp. 181-231. New York: Basic Books, 1965.*
　　Includes Tocqueville among the founders of sociology. Aron compares Tocqueville's sociological methods with those of Montesquieu, Auguste Comte, and Karl Marx and concludes that "Tocqueville the sociologist belonged to the lineage of Montesquieu." According to Aron, Tocqueville, like Montesquieu, was a comparative sociologist who rejected the Comtian and Marxian belief that past history and future events are governed by inexorable laws.

Bathory, Peter Dennis. "The Science of Politics and the Art of Ruling: James Madison and Alexis de Tocqueville." In *Leadership in America: Consensus, Corruption, and Charisma*, edited by Peter Dennis Bathory, pp. 11-37. New York: Longman, 1978.*
　　Contrasts the analyses of James Madison and Tocqueville regarding American democratic politics. Bathory's primary purpose is to familiarize readers with the rhetoric of both authors; in his own words, the essay is an "ateempt to recapture the spirit of inquiry—the elegance and force of style, the precision and simplicity of argument—characteristic of early American public discourse and debate."

[Bledsoe, A. T.] "De Tocqueville on the Sovereignty of the People." *The Southern Review* I, No. 2 (April 1867): 302-53.
　　A discussion of Tocqueville's methods of analysis in *Democracy*. Bledsoe disputes John Stuart Mill's interpretation of the work (see excerpt above, 1840).

Brogan, D. W. "Tocqueville." In his *French Personalities and Problems*, pp. 214-24. New York: Alfred A. Knopf, 1947.
　　General overview of Tocqueville's social and political thought. Brogan portrays Tocqueville as a nineteenth-century Aristides, arguing that his principal lesson is that "even liberty and equality are inadequate aims for a society which, if it forgets justice, forgets its greatest end."

Brogan, Hugh. "Tocqueville and the American Presidency." *Journal of American Studies* 15, No. 3 (December 1981): 357-75.

Points out errors and omissions in Tocqueville's discussion of the American presidency in *Democracy*. While Brogan regards Tocqueville's "sins of commission," such as his conclusion that the American presidency is a weak institution, as "at worst venial," he maintains that his "sins of omission," particularly his failure to recognize the significance of the president's role in party politics, indicate "a defect . . . in his understanding of democracy."

Brunius, Teddy. *Alexis de Tocqueville: The Sociological Aesthetician*. Swedish Studies in Aesthetics, edited by Teddy Brunius, vol. I. Uppsala, Sweden: Ab Lundequistska Bokhandeln, 1960, 63 p.

Asserts that Tocqueville was a cultural relativist whose works, particularly *Democracy*, are an important contribution to sociological aesthetics. Brunius contends that Tocqueville's analysis of the influences of democracy on American philosophy, religion, science, education, and literature in the second part of *Democracy* "is one of the most important sociological theories in aesthetics earlier than Hippolyte Taine's."

Bryce, James. "The Constitution of the United States As Seen in the Past: The Predictions of Hamilton and Tocqueville." In his *Studies in History and Jurisprudence*, pp. 301-58. New York: Oxford University Press, 1901.*

A delineation of the defects of *Democracy* by the author of *The American Commonwealth,* a highly regarded study of government in the United States that is frequently compared with Tocqueville's work on America.

Drescher, Seymour. *Dilemmas of Democracy: Tocqueville and Modernization*. Pittsburgh: University of Pittsburgh Press, 1968, 302 p.

Examines Tocqueville's answers to several contemporary social questions. Drescher's stated purpose is to reveal Tocqueville's response to the "problems of modernization or, perhaps more accurately, the problems created by those whose social conditions did not fit well into the nineteenth-century scheme of providential equality as denoted in its classic study of democracy."

Everett, Edward. "De Beaumont and de Tocqueville on the Penitentiary System." *North American Review* XXXVII (July 1833): 117-38.*

Synopsis of *On the Penitentiary System in the United States and its Application in France.*

Feuer, Kathryn B. "Alexis de Tocqueville and the Genesis of *War and Peace*." *California Slavic Studies* 4 (1967): 92-118.*

Relates the ideological conception of Leo Tolstoy's *War and Peace* to the influence of *The Old Regime.*

Gargan, Edward T. *De Tocqueville*. Studies in Modern European Literature and Thought, edited by Erich Heller and Anthony Thorlby. London: Bowes and Bowes, 1965, 94 p.

Critical biography that traces the origins of Tocqueville's belief in the inevitability of the spread of democracy. Gargan insists that Tocqueville cannot be easily classified as a sociologist, moralist, historian, or philosopher. Rather, Gargan argues, "everything he did and wrote flowed from his devotion to France, and it is this first influence that must be acknowledged as decisive in the formation of his character and his work."

Goldstein, Doris S. *Trial of Faith: Religion and Politics in Tocqueville's Thought*. New York: Elsevier, 1975, 144 p.

An explication of Tocqueville's religious beliefs rooted in both his personal life and nineteenth-century French politics and history.

Herr, Richard. *Tocqueville and the Old Regime*. Princeton: Princeton University Press, 1962, 142 p.

Comprehensive analysis of *The Old Regime*. Herr maintains that "fatalism is the main ingredient of *L'ancien régime*": he argues that Tocqueville's primary objective in writing the book was to show how class hatred bred by the old regime had permanently destroyed France's ability to become a liberal democracy.

Higonnet, Patrice. "Alexis de Tocqueville." In *Abroad in America: Visitors to the New Nation, 1776-1914,* edited by Marc Pachter, pp. 52-61. Reading, Mass.: Addison-Wesley Publishing Co., 1976.

Presents a selection of Tocqueville's observations on American society that exemplify what Higonnet describes as Tocqueville's "aristocratic perspective of America as an egalitarian society." Higonnet, who considers *Democracy* a "perspicacious description" of America rather than an explanation of its social and political institutions, argues that Tocqueville's talents as a critic and moralist outweigh his deficiencies as a social scientist.

Kirwan, A. W. "Alexis de Tocqueville: In Memoriam." *Fraser's Magazine* LIX, No. CCCLIII (May 1859): 610-15.

Obituary that details Tocqueville's political career.

Lively, Jack. *The Social and Political Thought of Alexis de Tocqueville*. Oxford: Clarendon Press, 1962, 263 p.

Argues that Tocqueville's political and social attitudes were founded on a complex and sustained theoretical basis. In tracing this theoretical basis throughout Tocqueville's writings, Lively stresses that Tocqueville viewed political theory as a means of informing political action.

Mayer, J. P. Introduction to *The Recollections of Alexis de Tocqueville,* by Alexis de Tocqueville, edited by J. P. Mayer, translated by Alexander Teixeira de Mattos, pp. xi-xxii. Morningside Heights, N.Y.: Columbia University Press, 1949.

Extols Tocqueville as a prophetic sociologist with "unsurpassed" powers of historical and sociological analysis.

McCarthy, Eugene J. *America Revisited: 150 Years after Tocqueville*. Garden City, N.Y.: Doubleday & Co., 1978, 256 p.

Compares Tocqueville's observations on American democracy as recorded in his travel notebooks and *Democracy* with American democracy as it existed in 1978. The American politician McCarthy devotes particular attention to Tocqueville's comments on American legal, political, and business practices.

Milnes, R. M. Review of *Memoir, Letters, and Remains of Alexis de Tocqueville,* by Alexis de Tocqueville. *The Quarterly Review* 110, No. 220 (October 1861): 517-44.

Character sketch based on *Memoir, Letters, and Remains of Alexis de Tocqueville* that focuses on Tocqueville's political opinions. Milnes examines Tocqueville's pronouncements on various French political issues and concludes that as a statesman, Tocqueville "unswervingly" insisted upon "the application, in its fullest sense, of the doctrine of Free Will to the communities of mankind."

Nicholas, H. G. "The Relevance of Tocqueville." In *Lessons from America: An Exploration,* edited by Richard Rose, pp. 46-66. New York: Halsted Press, 1974.

Delineates the characteristics of American society that Tocqueville believed favored the establishment and maintenance of democracy.

Reeve, Henry. Review of *Oeuvres complètes d'Alexis de Tocqueville, Vols. 7 and 8,* by Alexis de Tocqueville. *The Edinburgh Review* CXXII, No. CCL (October 1865): 456-81.

Provides extracts from Tocqueville's correspondence in which he outlines his position on several contemporary political issues. A friend of Tocqueville and editor of *The Edinburgh Review* from 1855-95, Reeve prepared the first English translation of *Democracy.*

Reeves, Richard. *American Journey: Traveling with Tocqueville in Search of "Democracy in America"*. New York: Simon and Schuster, 1982, 399 p.

A modern analogue to *Democracy*. Between 1979 and 1981 Reeves, a prominent American political writer, retraced Tocqueville and Beaumont's travels across America, visiting the same places and conversing with the modern counterparts of the people they interviewed during their stay in the United States. In *American Journey,* Reeves records his impressions of American democracy in the 1980s and compares his findings with those of Tocqueville.

Simpson, M.C.M., ed. *Correspondence and Conversations of Alexis de Tocqueville with Nassau William Senior from 1834 to 1859.* 2 vols. 2d ed. London: Henry S. King & Co., 1872.

A complete collection of Tocqueville's correspondence with his longtime friend Nassau William Senior, a noted English economist he met in 1833. Also included is a record of Tocqueville's conversations with Senior from 1848 to 1959 that was drawn from Senior's journal entires. This collection of Tocqueville's correspondence and conversations provides valuable biographical information as well as commentary on Tocqueville's writings by both Tocqueville and Senior.

Spender, Harold. "America Now and in the 'Thirties: In the Steps of De Tocqueville." *The Fortnightly Review* n.s. CX, No. DCLV (1 July 1921): 1-13.
    Reviews Tocqueville's predictions in *Democracy*. Spender, who considers Tocqueville a political thinker rather than a social observer, maintains that in declaring the weakness of the federal government, Tocqueville "uttered the one false judgment of his political life."

Whitridge, Arnold. "Chateaubriand and Tocqueville: Impressions of the American Scene." *History Today* XIII, No. 8 (August 1963): 530-38.*

Compares Tocqueville's writings on America with those of Francois René de Chateaubriand.

Woodruff, Douglas. "De Tocqueville on the United States." *Dublin Review* 182, No. 365 (April-June 1928): 275-85.
    Judges the accuracy of Tocqueville's predictions in *Democracy*. In addition, Woodruff delineates the reasons for the decline of the work's popularity during the latter half of the nineteenth century and the early decades of the twentieth century.

Zetterbaum, Marvin. *Tocqueville and the Problem of Democracy.* Stanford: Stanford University Press, 1967, 185 p.
    Maintains that *Democracy* is best understood as an attempt to resolve the dichotomy between justice and excellence in a society where equality of conditions prevails. For Tocqueville, Zetterbaum writes, "resolving the problem of democracy requires finding a place within democracy for liberty, for human excellence, for a renaissance of public virtue, and for the possibility of greatness."

Alfred (Victor) de Vigny

1797-1863

French poet, short story writer, dramatist, and novelist.

Vigny, a pioneer of the French Romantic movement, is considered one of the greatest French poets of the nineteenth century. He is best known today for his philosophical poems and stories, and his *Chatterton* is hailed as one of the most important and influential Romantic dramas. Critics agree that his creative use of form, command of technique, philosophical seriousness, and innovative use of symbols comprise the attributes for which Vigny is most admired.

Vigny was born at Loches in the Touraine region of France to aristocratic parents who, though once wealthy, had lost their fortune during the French Revolution. The family moved to Paris where Vigny was raised among the nostalgic survivors of the *ancien régime* of pre-Revolutionary France. In 1814, he followed family tradition by joining the Royal Guard, where he served for thirteen years. Near the end of his military service, he married Lydia Bunbury, the daughter of a rich and eccentric Englishman who disapproved of Vigny and promptly disinherited her. She became a chronic invalid shortly thereafter, and the marriage rapidly disintegrated. Vigny became involved with several other women, including the great Romantic actress Marie Dorval. Disillusioned by politics, failed love affairs, and his lack of recognition as a writer, Vigny withdrew from Parisian society after 1840. In 1845, he was elected to the prestigious literary Académie française after several unsuccessful attempts. Three years later, Vigny retreated to the family home at Charente, for which the French critic Charles Augustin Sainte-Beuve coined the famous phrase "tour d'ivoire," or ivory tower, where he lived quietly until his death.

Vigny began his literary career by writing poetry. *Poèmes antiques et modernes,* which includes the ten works published in *Poëmes* and *Éloa; ou, La soeur des anges, mystère,* contains twenty-one poems which are divided into three groups according to their sources of inspiration: "Livre mystique," "Livre antique," and "Livre moderne," or mystical, ancient, and modern poems. The "Livre antique" is further divided in "Antiquité biblique" and "Antiquité homérique," or biblical and Homeric poems. With this collection Vigny championed the *poème,* which he defined as "compositions in which a philosophic thought is staged under an epic or dramatic form." Critics praise the intense concentration of this form and its detailed exposition of a single idea. Vigny's *poèmes* are characterized by their stoical pessimism, compact form, and visual imagery. Their principal themes include God's indifference to humanity, women's deceit, inexorable fate, and the poet's alienation from a mediocre world. "Le cor," based on the medieval legend of Roland, is acclaimed for its evocation of atmosphere, particularly the description of the sound of the hero's horn in the woods. According to many critics, "Moïse" is one of the finest works in *Poèmes antiques et modernes* and an outstanding example of Vigny's use of the *poème* to dramatize a single idea through symbols. "Moïse" has been described as his pronouncement on the nineteenth-century Romantic poet's position in society. Vigny uses the biblical prophet as a symbol for genius. Like the prophet, the poet is chosen

by God for his artistic gift but must pay for his talent by becoming an outcast.

Cinq-Mars; ou, Une conjuration sous Louis XIII (Cinq-Mars; or, A Conspiracy under Louis XIII), Vigny's first prose work, is based on history, depicting the court of Louis XIII. However, the novel has a didactic purpose; in *Cinq-Mars,* Vigny intended to prove that Duc Armand du Richelieu contributed to the downfall of the French monarchy by weakening the aristocracy. Many critics consider it the first significant French historical novel. Clearly, Vigny was influenced by the fiction of Sir Walter Scott, and much of the early interest in *Cinq-Mars* can be attributed to the popularity of Scott's novels. Yet critics state that Vigny's work lacks the warmth and energy of the Scottish novelist. While critics praise Vigny's evocation of the age, they also describe the characters as flat and contend that he overemphasized the historical element. Unlike Scott, Vigny placed historical figures in the foreground and relegated the fictional scenes to a secondary role.

Vigny developed an interest in the theater when, in 1827, he saw the performances of an English Shakespearean troupe in Paris. He translated several of Shakespeare's plays into French, including *Othello,* which was produced as *Le more de Venise* at the Comédie-Française. His preface to the published version, along with Victor Hugo's preface to *Cromwell,* is regarded as

464

one of the most important manifestos of Romantic French drama. In both his translation and preface, Vigny attempted to redirect the tastes of French audiences and critics, who favored classicism, and introduce them to new forms of drama. The directness of its language ideally suited Shakespeare's work to this purpose. In addition, Vigny approached his translation as an experiment in form and, because the story of *Othello* was well known, he was able to focus attention on his alterations and thus on the style of work. Critics agree that the success of this work had a tremendous impact on Romantic drama. *Chatterton*, Vigny's next play, is regarded as his best play and one of the most influential French Romantic dramas. An adaptation of a short story published earlier in his *Stello*, *Chatterton* is the tragic love story of the English poet Thomas Chatterton. The drama depicts the fate of the poet who is eventually driven to suicide by a materialistic society that neither appreciates his talent or offers him love. The play is classical in its taut construction, simple plot, and restrained emotion. Yet the attack on society, moral examination of the hero's soul, and impassioned defense of emotion over reason all contribute to its success as a Romantic drama.

Vigny's collections of short prose works, *Les consultations du Docteur Noir: Stello; ou, Les diables bleus, Première consultation (Stello: A Session with Doctor Noir)*, *Servitude et grandeur militaires (The Military Necessity)*, and *Daphné (Deuxième consultation du Docteur Noir)*, represent his attempts to combine philosophy with storytelling. In these works, he consistently defended what he considered to be the outcasts of society: the poet, soldier, and visionary. The first, *Stello*, takes the form of a dialogue between Stello, a poet who symbolizes the imagination and generous spirit of the creative artist, and Docteur Noir, the Black Doctor, whom the poet has consulted. Docteur Noir, who speaks for rational intellect, recounts the stories of three poets—Chatterton, Nicolas Gilbert, and André Chénier—and examines the poet's relationship to authority. The work testifies to Vigny's bitterness toward a society that, in his view, despises genius. *The Military Necessity*, similar in form and thought to *Stello*, consists of three stories unified by the author's personal comments on the role of the soldier who is also a victim of society. Vigny depicted the struggle between the requirements of the soldier's conscience and the dictates of war; he contended that the soldier's greatness lies in his dignified and passive obedience to authority. Vigny began a third collection on the suffering of the religious prophet, but he only completed one story, entitled *Daphné*. Like *Stello*, *Daphné* includes a discussion between the poet Stello and Docteur Noir. In comparing these stories with his earlier prose work *Cinq-Mars*, critics commend Vigny's improved literary technique. They praise the effective combination of fiction with historical characters in *Stello* and the vivid depiction of atmosphere in *The Military Necessity*. Both collections of stories are admired for their simple plots, and the first and third stories of *The Military Necessity*, "Laurette; ou, Le cachet rouge" and "La vie et la mort du capitaine Renaud; ou, La canne de jonc," are often cited as Vigny's best works of fiction. But critics also state that by combining didactic intent with storytelling, Vigny often sacrificed coherent narrative by arranging fictional elements to further his thesis rather than the plot.

Most critics agree that Vigny conveyed his philosophic thought most successfully in his late poetry. The poems of *Les destinées: Poèmes philosophiques* are generally considered his greatest poetic achievement, though some scholars have termed them uneven in quality. Commentators agree that his technical skill is responsible for the purity of his greatest poems: "La maison du berger," "La mort du loup," "Le mont des oliviers," "La bouteille à la mer," and "L'esprit pur." Vigny's poetry has also been described as awkward, prosaic, and obscure; however, for many critics his intellect and insight outweigh these defects. His goal was to rework and condense the themes and images of his poetry until he achieved a "hard, brilliant diamond". Critics agree that Vigny used visual imagery because of its ability to both evoke a distinct mood and convey philosophical ideas. In *Les destinées*, Vigny refined and developed the ideas already presented in earlier works, including his ambivalent feelings toward women and nature, the role of the poet in an increasingly mechanized world, and the ruptured relationship between humanity and its creator, which is the governing idea of the collection. The eleven poems of *Les destinées* were composed between 1839 and 1863. While the early pieces are characterized by an attitude of stoical resignation, the later poems, particularly "L'esprit pur," Vigny's last work before his death, reflect his rejection of an earlier Christian interpretation of fate and his renewed confidence in the human spirit. Although *Les destinées* confirmed his reputation as the philosopher of Romantic poetry, Vigny is remembered now for his efforts to develop a coherent doctrine composed of pre-existing ideas rather than the introduction of any original or complex thought.

Vigny's work has received significant critical acclaim but little popular support. Only *Cinq-Mars* was an immediate popular success, yet it is ignored today. While *Chatterton* had a profound influence on the course of French drama, it, too, has fallen into neglect. Of Vigny's collections of stories *Stello* and *The Military Necessity* have enjoyed both popular and critical acclaim since their publication. *Daphné*, however, was not published until the twentieth century and has been of interest primarily to critics. It is Vigny's poetry that forms the basis of his reputation today. Although he was regarded as an innovator and leader during the early years of the Romantic movement, his small output caused his contemporaries to overlook him. His work was ignored until the beginning of the twentieth century and has undergone a steady critical revaluation since. His current position rests on *Les destinées;* Albert Thibaudet called its tercets "the most lastingly luminous poems, the fixed stars of French poetry." Though he is rarely accorded the acclaim granted to many of his better known contemporaries, Vigny is praised for the form, philosophic content, and imagery of his poetry and his work is unexcelled in the history of French literature.

PRINCIPAL WORKS

Poëmes (poetry) 1822
Éloa; ou, La soeur des anges, mystère (poetry) 1824
Cinq-Mars; ou, Une conjuration sous Louis XIII (novel) 1826
    [*Cinq-Mars; or, A Conspiracy under Louis XIII*, 1847; also published as *The Spider and the Fly*, 1925]
Poèmes antiques et modernes (poetry) 1826
Le more de Venise [translator; from the drama *Othello* by William Shakespeare] (drama) 1829
La maréchale d'Ancre (drama) 1831
Les consultations du Docteur Noir: Stello; ou, Les diables bleus, Première consultation (short stories) 1832
    [*Stello: A Session with Doctor Noir*, 1963]
Quitte pour la peur (drama) 1833
Chatterton (drama) 1835

Servitude et grandeur militaires (short stories) 1835
[*The Military Necessity,* 1953; also published as *The Military Condition,* 1964]
Oeuvres complètes. 7 vols. (poetry, short stories, novel, and drama) 1837-39
Théâtre complet du comte Alfred de Vigny (drama) 1848
**Les destinées: Poèmes philosophiques* (poetry) 1864
Alfred de Vigny: Journal d'un poète (journal) 1867
Oeuvres complètes. 8 vols. (poetry, short stories, novel, and drama) 1883-85
Correspondance de Alfred de Vigny, 1816-1863 (letters) 1905
**Shylock [translator; from the drama *The Merchant of Venice* by William Shakespeare] 1905
Daphné (Deuxième consultation du Docteur Noir) (unfinished novel) 1913

*Many of these poems were originally published in the journal *Revue des deux mondes* between 1843 and 1854.

**This work was written in 1830.

JOHN STUART MILL (essay date 1838)

[*An English essayist and critic, Mill is regarded as one of the greatest philosophers and political economists of the nineteenth century. At an early age, Mill was recognized as a leading advocate of the utilitarian philosophy of Jeremy Bentham, and he was a principal contributor to the* Westminster Review, *an English periodical founded by Bentham that later merged with the* London Review. *During the 1830s, after reading the works of William Wordsworth, Samuel Taylor Coleridge, and Auguste Comte, he gradually diverged from Bentham's utilitarianism by acknowledging the importance of intuition and feelings and attempting to reconcile them with his rational philosophy. He is considered a key figure in the transition from the rationalism of the Enlightenment to the renewed emphasis on mysticism and the emotions of the Romantic era. The following essay illustrates Mill's belief that poetry reflects the age in which it is written and that it should deal with factual, easily verified matters. Mill discusses* Cinq-Mars, The Military Necessity, *and* Stello, *all works with historical bases. The essay begins with a brief comment on the Royalist society in which Vigny was raised and how it changed after the Revolution of 1830. Mill proposes that just as this dichotomy inspired the philosophy of Alexis de Tocqueville, so it inspired Vigny's art, providing an elegiac yet deeply sympathetic tone. This essay was originally published in the* London and Westminster Review, *Vol. XXIX, No. LX, in April 1838.*]

Alfred de Vigny [is] one of the earliest in date, and one of the most genuine, true-hearted and irreproachable in tendency and spirit, of the new school of French literature, termed the Romantic. It would in fact be impossible to understand M. de Vigny's writings, especially the later and the better portion, or to enter sympathisingly into the peculiar feelings which pervade them, without this clue. M. de Vigny is, in poetry and art, as a greater man, M. de Toqueville, in his philosopy, a result of the influences of the age upon the mind and character trained upon opinions and feelings opposed to those of the age. Both these writers, educated in one set of views of life and society, found, when they attained manhood, another set predominant in the world they lived in, and, at length, after 1830, enthroned in its high places. The contradictions they had thus to reconcile—the doubts, and perplexities, and misgivings which they had to find the means of overcoming before they could

see clearly between these cross-lights—were to them that, for want of which so many otherwise well-educated and naturally-gifted persons grow up hopelessly commonplace. To go through life with a set of opinions ready made and provided for saving them the trouble of thought, was a destiny that could not be theirs. (pp. 77-8)

That this conflict between a Royalist education, and the spirit of the modern world, triumphant in July 1830, must have gone for something in giving to the speculations of a philosopher like M. de Tocqueville the catholic spirit and comprehensive range which distinguish them, most people will readily admit. But that the same causes must have exerted an analogous influence over a poet and artist, such as Alfred de Vigny is in his degree; that a political revolution can have given to the genius of a poet what principally distinguishes it, may not appear so obvious. . . . (pp. 78-9)

[Suppose] a poet of conservative sympathies, surprised by the shock of a revolution, which sweeps away the surviving symbols of what was great in the Past, and decides irrevocably the triumph of new things over the old: what will be the influence of this event on his imagination and feelings? To us it seems that they will become both sadder and wiser. He will lose that blind faith in the Past, which previously might have tempted him to fight for it with a mistaken ardour, against what is generous and worthy in the new doctrines. The fall of the objects of his reverence, will naturally, if he has an eye, open it to the perception of that in them whereby they deserved to fall. But while he is thus disenchanted of the old things, he will not have acquired that faith in the new, which animated the Radical poet. . . . The destiny of mankind, therefore, will naturally appear to him in rather sombre colours; gloomy he may not be, for to be gloomy is to be morbid, but there will be everywhere a tendency to the elegiac, to the contemplative and melancholy rather than to the epic and active: his song will be a subdued and plaintive symphony, more or less melodious according to the measure of his genius, on the old theme of blasted hopes and defeated aspirations. Yet there will now be nothing partial or one-sided in his sympathies: no sense of conflict to be maintained, of a position to be defended against assailants, will warp the impartiality of his pity. . . . His heart will open itself freely and largely to the love of all that is loveable, to pity of all that is pitiable: every cry of suffering humanity will strike a responsive chord in his breast; whoever carries nobly his own share of the general burthen of human life, or generously helps to lighten that of another, is sure of his homage; while he has a deep fraternal charity for the erring and disappointed—for those who have aspired and fallen—who have fallen because they have aspired, because they too have felt these infinite longings for something greater than merely to live and die, which he as a poet has felt. . . . (pp. 83-4)

In this ideal portraiture may be seen the genuine lineaments of Alfred de Vigny. The same features may, indeed, be traced, more or less, in the greater part of the Royalist literature of young France. . . . But M. de Vigny is the most perfect type, because he, more entirely than most others, writes from his real feelings, and not from mere play of fancy. . . . [When] we would see the true character of a Royalist poet we must seek for it in one like M. de Vigny, a conservative in feeling, and not in mere fancy, and a man (as it seems to us) of a rare simplicity of heart, and freedom from egotism and self-display. The most complete exemplification of the feelings and views of things which . . . [naturally belong] to the Royalist poet of young France will be found in his writings, subsequent to the Revolution of 1830. (pp. 85-6)

['**Cinq-Mars, or a Conspiracy under Louis XIII**' is] not free from the fault, so far as it is a fault, most common in the romantic literature of young France; it partakes somewhat of the "Literature of Despair;" it too much resembles M. Eugene Sue's novels, in which every villain dies honoured and prosperous at a good old age, after every innocent person in the tale has been crushed and exterminated by him without pity or remorse—through which the mocking laugh of a chorus of demons seems to ring in our ears that the world is delivered over to the evil spirit, and that man is his creature and his prey. But such is not the character of M. de Vigny's writings, and the resemblance in this single instance is only casual. Still, as a mere work of art, if the end of art be, as conceived by the ancients and by the German writers, the production of the intrinsically beautiful, '**Cinq-Mars**' cannot be recommended. A story in which the odious and the contemptible in man and life act so predominant a part, which excites our scorn or our hatred so much more than our pity—comes within a far other category than that of the Beautiful, and can be justified on no canons of taste of which that is the end. (pp. 114-15)

[Among] the ideas with which French literature has been *possessed* for the last ten years, is that of realizing, and bringing home to the imagination, the history and spirit of past ages. Sir Walter Scott, having no object but to please, and having readers who only sought to be pleased, would not have told the story of Richlieu and of Cinq-Mars without greatly softening the colouring; and the picture would have been more agreeable than M. de Vigny's, but it would not have been so true to the age. M. de Vigny preferred the truer to the more pleasing, and *his* readers have sanctioned the preference.

Even according to this view of its object the work has obvious defects. The characters of some of the subordinate personages, Friar Joseph, for instance, are even more revolting than the truth of history requires. De Thou, the pious and studious man of retirement, cast out into storms for which he was never meant—the only character of principle in the tale, yet who sacrifices principle as well as life to romantic friendship—is but coldly represented; his goodness is too simple, his attachment too instinctive, too doglike, and so much intensity of friendship is not sufficiently accounted for; Balzac would have managed these things better. The author also crowds his story too much with characters; he cannot bear that any celebrated personage whom the age affords should be passed over, and consequently introduces many who ought not to be drawn at all unless they could be drawn truly, and on whom he has not been able to employ the same accurate study as he has on his principal characters. His Richelieu and his Louis the XIIIth are admirable, for these are historical figures which he has taken the trouble to understand. . . . As a specimen of Art employed in embodying the character of an age, there are few works superior to '**Cinq-Mars:**' the spirit of the age penetrates every nook and corner of it; the same atmosphere which hangs over the personages of the story hangs over us; we feel the eye of the omnipresent Richelieu upon us, and the influences of France in its Catholic and aristocratic days, of ardent pleasure-loving, laughter-loving, and danger-loving France, all around us. To this merit is to be added . . . that the representations of feelings are always simple and graceful; the author has not, like so many inferior writers, supplied by the easy resource of mere exaggeration of colouring, the incapacity to show us anything subtle or profound, any trait we knew not before, in the work-

ings of passion in the human heart. On the whole, '**Cinq-Mars**' is admirable as a first production of its kind, but altogether of an inferior order to its successors, ['**Servitude et Grandeur Militaires,**'] and '**Stello**' to which we proceed.

Of M. de Vigny's prose works, '**Cinq-Mars**' alone was written previous to the revolution of 1830; and although the Carlist tendency of the author's political opinions is manifest throughout—indeed the book is one long protest against the levelling of the feudal aristocracy—it does not, nor does any part of the Carlist literature of the last twenty years, entirely answer to our description of the Conservative school of poetry and romance. To find a real Conservative literature in France one must look earlier than the first revolution, as, to study the final transformation of that literature, one must descend below the last. One must distinguish three periods, Conservatism triumphant, Conservatism militant, Conservatism vanquished. The first is represented by Racine, Fenelon, and Voltaire in his tragedies, before he quitted the paths of his predecessors. Jean Jacques Rousseau is the father and founder of the Movement literature of France, and Madame de Stael its second great apostle. . . . At the head of the literature of Conservatism in its second or militant period, stands Chateaubriand—a man whose name marks one of the turning points in the literary history of his country: a conservative poet to the inmost core. . . . To this literature of Conservatism discouraged but not yet disenchanted, still hopeful and striving to set up again its old idols, '**Cinq-Mars**' belongs. From the final and hopeless overthrow of the old order of society in July 1830, begins the era of Conservatism disenchanted—Conservatism which is already in the past tense—which for practical purposes is abandoned—and only contributes its share as all past associations and experiences do, toward shaping and colouring the individual's impressions of the present.

This is the character which pervades the two principal of M. de Vigny's more recent works, the '**Servitude et Grandeur Militaires,**' and '**Stello.**' He has lost his faith in Royalism, and in the system of opinions connected with it. His eyes are opened to all the iniquities and hypocrisies of the state of society which is passing away. But he cannot take up with any of the systems of politics, and of either irreligious or religious philosophy, which profess to lay open the mystery of what is to follow, and to guarantee that the new order of society will not have its own iniquities and hypocrisies of as dark a kind. He has no faith in any systems, none in man's power of prophecy; nor is he sure that the new tendencies of society, take them for all in all, have more to satisfy the wants of a thoughtful and loving spirit, than the old had; at all events not so much more, as to make the condition of human nature a cheerful subject to him. He looks upon life and sees most things crooked. . . . This is not a happy state of mind, but it is not an unfavourable one to poetry. If the worst forms of it produce a "Literature of Despair," the better are seen in a writer like M. de Vigny—who having now no formulas to save the credit of, looks life steadily in the face—applies himself to understanding whatever of evil, and of heroic struggle with evil, it presents to his individual experience—and gives forth his pictures of both, with deep feeling, but with the calmness of one who has no point to carry, no quarrel to maintain over and above the "general one of every son of Adam with his lot here below."

M. de Vigny has been a soldier, and he has been, and is, a poet: the situation and feelings of a soldier (especially a soldier not in active service), and, so far as the measure of his genius admits, those of a poet, are what he is best acquainted with, and what, therefore, as a man of earnest mind, not now taking anything upon trust, it was most natural he should attempt to delineate. ['**Servitude et Grandeur Militaires**' is] the embodiment of the author's experience in the one capacity, '**Stello**' in the other. Each consists of three touching and beautifully told stories, founded on fact—in which the life and position of a soldier in modern times, and of a poet at all times, in their relation to society, are shadowed out. (pp. 116-20)

The soldier, and the poet, appear to M. de Vigny alike misplaced, alike ill at ease, in the present condition of human life. In the soldier he sees a human being set apart for a profession doomed to extinction and doomed consequently, in the interval, to a continual decrease of dignity and of the sympathies of mankind. . . . Those alone, says M. de Vigny, who have been soldiers, know what servitude is. To the soldier alone is obedience, passive and active, the law of his life, the law of every day and of every moment; obedience, not stopping at sacrifice, nor even at crime. In him alone is the abnegation of his self-will, of his liberty of independent action, absolute and unreserved; the grand distinction of humanity, the responsibility of the individual as a moral agent, being made over, once for all, to superior authority. The type of human nature which these circumstances create well deserves the study of the artist and the philosopher. M. de Vigny has deeply meditated upon it. He has drawn with delicacy and profundity that mixture of Spartan and stoical impassibility with child-like *insouciance* [inconcern] and *bonhomie* [good-heartedness], which is the result, on the one hand, of a life of painful and difficult obedience to discipline—on the other, of a conscience freed from concern or accountability for the quality of the actions of which that life is made up. . . . His stories, full of melancholy beauty, will carry into thousands of minds and hearts which would otherwise have been unvisited by it, a conception of a soldier's trials and a soldier's virtues in times which, like ours, are not those of martial glory. (pp. 120-21)

Among the writings of our day we know not one which breathes a nobler spirit [than '**Servitude et Grandeur Militaires**,'] or in which every detail is conceived and wrought out in a manner more worthy of that spirit. . . . No *résumé* can convey any idea of it; the impression it makes is not the sum of the impressions of particular incidents or particular sayings, it is the effect of the tone and coloring of the whole. We do not seem to be listening to the author, to be receiving a "moral" from any of his stories, or from his characters an "example" prepense; the poem of human life is opened before us, and M. de Vigny does but chaunt from it, in a voice of subdued sadness, a few strains telling of obscure wisdom and unrewarded virtue; of those antique characters which, without self-glorification or hope of being appreciated, "carry out," as he expresses it, "the sentiment of duty to its extremest consequences," and whom he avers, as a matter of personal experience, that he has never met with in any walk of life but the profession of arms.

'**Stello**' is a work of similar merit to . . . ['**Servitude et Grandeur Militaires**,'] though, we think, somewhat inferior. (pp. 127-28)

[In '**Stello**,'] M. de Vigny has so genuine a feeling of the true greatness of a poet, of the spirit which has dwelt in all poets deserving the name of great—that he may be pardoned for what there is in his picture of a poet's position and destiny in the actual world, somewhat morbid and overcharged, though with a large foundation of universal truth. (p. 130)

John Stuart Mill, "Poems and Romances of Alfred de Vigny," in his Essays on Poetry, *edited by F.*

Parvin Sharpless, University of South Carolina Press, 1976, pp. 75-137.

WALTER BESANT   (essay date 1872)

By dint of hard work De Vigny became a writer. As a poet he is an imitator of every style which strikes him. This he cannot help, because originality does not belong to a second-class poet. Still, he is very far from those mediocre poetasters whom Horace . . . will not suffer to live. His conceptions and manner of treatment show an elevation of thought alone sufficient to raise him above the level of ordinary verse-writers, while the inflation of his style is a fault due to the efforts made to sustain his lofty flight. Thus, in his poem on Moses ["**Moïse**"], he supposes the lawgiver and leader of the Israelites laden down and crushed beneath the burden of his task and the loneliness of his station, and praying for death as a deliverance. (p. 540)

The work by which De Vigny is principally known to English readers is his romance of '**Cinq Mars.**' It is so well known that nothing need be said of it, except to call attention to the entire incapacity of the writer to understand history. He constructs his own history without the smallest care as to whether the facts bear out his theory or not, and then bases his work upon it. He does the same thing in his '**Vie Militaire**' ['**Servitude et Grandeur Militaires**'], a work of much greater power, as I venture to think, than the '**Cinq Mars**,' though its popularity is so much less. (p. 543)

De Vigny's estimate of Napoleon's character, put into Napoleon's own mouth—[is] a masterpiece of writing, but, unfortunately, without a word of truth in it. Had this scene been true there would be nothing like it in history. (p. 544)

Walter Besant, "Alfred de Vigny," in Temple Bar, *Vol. XXXIV, March, 1872, pp. 533-45.*

GEORGE BRANDES   (essay date 1882)

[*Brandes, a Danish literary critic and biographer, was the principal leader of the intellectual movement which helped to bring an end to Scandinavian cultural isolation. His major critical work,* Hovedstrømninger i det 19de aarhundredes litteratur (Main Currents in Nineteenth Century Literature), *won him admiration for his ability to view literary movements within the broader context of all of European literature. The following excerpt was originally published in 1882 in* Den romantiske Skole i Frankrig (The Romantic School in France), *Volume V of* Main Currents. *After recognizing André de Chénier's influence on Vigny, Brandes claims that what distinguishes the latter poet "is his cult of pure intellect and his proud, stoic feeling of solitude."*]

The first author to show the influence of Chénier was one of the most artistically audacious of the [Romantic] school, one of its original leaders—Alfred de Vigny—who as lyric poet was at times very faulty, at times an immaculate master. Chaste, lucid, pure, and austere, there is a quality in his best verse which has led all the critics who have attempted to describe it to employ such figures as the sheen of ivory, the whiteness of ermine, the sailing of the swan. It has the artistic severity, the sober colouring, the conciseness and the fastidiousness which also characterise Chénier's. . . . Chénier's influence upon De Vigny is . . . indisputable. The latter assimilated many of the characteristics of the rediscovered master, though he emancipated himself from the old-fashioned Hellenism of style which hampered Chénier's flight. The poem *La Dryade,* to which he gives the additional title of "**Idyll in the manner of Theocri-**

tus,'' is in reality an idyll in the manner of André Chénier. What distinguishes De Vigny most markedly from Chénier as a lyric poet is his cult of pure intellect and his proud, stoic feeling of solitude. He has painted his own ideal portrait in such poems as *Moïse, La colère de Samson,* and *La mort du loup.* He is very present in Moses' sad cry. . . . (pp. 81-2)

I feel his stoicism, and at the same time read an apology for his unproductiveness, in [*La mort du loup*]. . . . Granted that there is a little affected rigidity in this attitude of his, still it is his pride, his spiritual nobility, his desire to perpetuate in his poetry the purity and austerity of his spirit, which impel him to assume it. (p. 82)

> George Brandes, ''De Vigny's Poetry and Hugo's 'Orientales','' in his Main Currents in Nineteenth Century Literature: The Romantic School in France, Vol. V, *translated by Diana White and Mary Morison, William Heinemann, 1904, pp. 81-9.**

C. G. COMPTON (essay date 1903)

[*The following is an overview of Vigny's writings and artistic temperament. Compton stresses the relationship between Vigny's character and his art, pointing to his* Journal d'un poète *as evidence that nearly all of Vigny's work was the result of internal rather than external stimuli.*]

Vigny, like all poets, had his masters, and shows their influence. Some of his early poems have traces of the eighteenth-century spirit, others show that he had read Châteaubriand and Homer and the Bible. But he preserves his independence and looks at man and the world in his own way. He has the individual touch, the new vision, and a distinctive note of imagination which constitute originality. French critics admit his claim to be a precursor and to have done what had not been done before in French literature.

Eloa and *Moïse* first gave him this reputation. There are few more poetic figures than Vigny's *Eloa,* the angel sprung from a tear of Jesus that fell on the tomb of Lazarus. Few stories are more touching than that of the spirit of compassion who shared the misery of the fallen angel because he was unhappy. Alfred de Vigny's men and women want solidity, but his angels are essential; grave, retired and perfected spirits, they wonder at Eloa's warmth and at her sacrifice. She seems a stranger among them and has a human pathos and sweetness, for she has not long left the earth. Vigny tells the story of her fall with so much sympathy and conviction that we feel its necessity. The Eloa we love must fall or she is not Eloa. She expresses in its highest form the sympathy and the compassion which were at the root of Vigny's best work. (pp. 64-5)

Moïse has the sombre beauty and profound sadness of the greatest poetry. The *Elévation sur Paris* and the *Poèmes Philosophiques* have those qualities and attain a greater majesty and an unquestionable sublimity, with a breadth of conception and a truth of insight which justify their title. There are only eleven and it is hard to determine their rank, and it is not necessary. *Les Destinées, La Maison du Berger, La Mort du Loup* and *Le Mont des Oliviers* are of the same rank, the first. (p. 65)

Vigny's prose works cannot be classed with his poetry. The *Grandeurs et Servitudes Militaires* is the most likely to survive, *Stello* has no central interest and its best parts were used in other forms. *Cinq-Mars,* which Vigny wrote to make people read his poetry, is his only mediocre work and was greatly appreciated by the public which has not yet read his poetry. It

is not likely that they ever will nor is it desirable. No one was further from being a popular poet than Alfred de Vigny, but he is always sure of his own public, the only one for which he wrote. . . .

In Vigny there is no separation between the poet and the man. . . . *Journal d'un Poète* is the complement and confirmation of all his other work. All that is implicit in the poetry is revealed in the **Journal**. . . . His best and distinctive work was self-inspired, and, except at the beginning, he did not re-act to external stimuli. He was one of the most self-centred of poets, unimpressionable, unreceptive, and irresponsive to the sensuous suggestions which so much affected the poetry of the Romantics. (pp. 66-7)

In Vigny's **Journal** the unity of his character and temperament comes out with convincing clearness. We see that he transcribed himself faithfully in the poems. There is no trace of pose or impersonation. Never was there a temperament more of a piece. He was one thing entirely and barely anything else. His apparent range is small and the actual range is smaller. He pays for this limitation, but he gains the strength of concentration. He cannot give us human beings, but he is at home with abstractions and he can vitalise with essential truth such ideal figures as his **Eloa.** He is an idealist of the idealists, a literal absolutist who demands the kingdom of heaven upon earth. . . . He has a vision of an ideal world where truth and justice and other abstractions prevail. With absolutist logic he requires that they shall prevail here and now. The religion founded on the Bible he knew so well declared that this world is the work of an all-wise and all-just God. Gravely, not irreverently, but with courage Vigny presents the picture of the world of men. . . . [In *Le Mont des Olivers* he] asks the Creator to justify himself before the conscience of mankind. . . . There is no answer. Vigny accepts the silence. He does not accept the sentimental platitudes about the mysterious designs of a power that gives its creatures the faculty of criticism and forbids it to be exercised on the subject that most concerns them. It is not the complaint of an unbeliever, it is the exceeding bitter cry of the man who longs to believe and cannot believe in face of the injustice that is the worst of blasphemies. (p. 67)

Vigny had lost the illusions of glory, of caste and of love. Finally he lost the illusion of the divine ordinance of the world, which, to the idealist, is the irreparable disillusionment. He saw things as they are and he did not deny them because they were not as he wished them to be. His later poems show that he faced a world inevitably materialistic. Perhaps they show, too, that this acceptance was unwilling, that it represented the victory of a proud intellectual honesty over the predispositions of his imagination and emotions. If there can be a pessimistic idealist Alfred de Vigny surely was one. But the disillusioned idealist bore himself with a stoical dignity impossible to the sentimentalist of romance. (pp. 67-8)

> C. G. Compton, ''Alfred de Vigny,'' in The Fortnightly Review, *n.s. Vol. 79, No. 433, January 1, 1903, pp. 60-9.*

GEORGE SAINTSBURY (essay date 1917)

[*Saintsbury was an English literary historian and critic of the late nineteenth and early twentieth centuries. A prolific writer, Saintsbury composed a number of histories of English and European literature as well as several critical works on individual authors, styles, and periods. In the following, Saintsbury evaluates Vigny's prose works. After describing the preface to* Cinq-Mars, *Saints-*

bury faults Vigny's contention that historical novels should feature historical persons as their principal characters and that they can successfully integrate a treatise on politics and society. The result in Cinq-Mars, *according to* Saintsbury, *is flat characters and a dull story. Although* Saintsbury *allows that Vigny was more successful in* Stello *and* The Military Necessity, *he considers Vigny's poetry to be his greatest achievement.*]

For Vigny as a poet my admiration has always been profound. He appears to me to have completed, with Agrippa d'Aubigné, Corneille, and Victor Hugo, the *quatuor* [quartet] of French poets who have the secret of magnificence; and, scanty as the amount of his poetical work is, *Eloa, Dolorida, Le Cor,* and the finest passages in *Les Destinées* have a definite variety of excellence and essence which it would not be easy to surpass in kind, though it might be in number, with the very greatest masters of poetry. But I have never been able, frankly and fully, to enjoy his novels, especially *Cinq-Mars.* In my last reading of the chief of them I came upon an edition which contains what I had never seen before—the somewhat triumphant and strongly defiant tract, *Réflexions sur la Vérité dans l'Art,* which the author prefixed to his book after its success. This tractate is indeed not quite consistent with itself, for it ends in confession that truth in art is truth in observation of human nature, not mere authenticity of fact, and that such authenticity is of merely secondary importance at best. But in the opening he had taken lines—or at any rate had said things—which, if not absolutely inconsistent with, certainly do not lead to, this sound conclusion. In writing historical novels (he tells us) he thought it better not to imitate the foreigners (it is clear that this is a polite way of indicating Scott), who in their pictures put the historical dominators of them in the background; he has himself made such persons principal actors. And though he admits that "a treatise on the decline and fall of feudalism in France; on the internal conditions and external relations of that country; on the question of military alliances with foreigners; on justice as administered by parliaments, and by secret commissions on charges of sorcery," might not have been read while the novel *was;* the sentence suggests, with hardly a possibility of rebuttal, that a treatise of this kind was pretty constantly in his own mind while he was writing the novel itself. And the earlier sentence about putting the more important historical characters in the foreground remains "firm," without any necessity for argument or suggestion.

Now I have more than once . . . contended, rightly or wrongly, that this "practice of the foreigners," in *not* making dominant historical characters their own dominant personages, is *the* secret of success in historical novel-writing, and the very feather (and something more) in the cap of Scott himself which shows his chieftainship. And, again rightly or wrongly, I have also contended that the hand of purpose deadens and mummifies [history]. Vigny's own remarks, despite subsequent—if not recantation—qualification of them, show that the lie of his land, the tendency of his exertion, *was* in these two, as I think, wrong directions. And I own that this explained to me what I had chiefly before noticed as merely a fact, without enquiring into it, that *Cinq-Mars,* admirably written as it is; possessing as it does, with a hero who might have been made interesting, a great person like Richelieu to make due and not undue use of; plenty of thrilling incidents at hand, and some actually brought in; love interest [and fighting] . . . ; a tragic finish from history, and opportunity for plenty of lighter contrast from Tallemant and the Memoirs—that, I say, *Cinq-Mars,* with all this and the greatness of its author in other work, has always been to me not a live book, and hardly one which I can even praise as statuesque.

It is no doubt a misfortune for the book with its later readers—the earlier for nearly twenty years were free from this—that it comes into closest comparison with [the best work of Alexandre Dumas, père]. . . . (pp. 262-63)

Now of course Dumas could not write like Vigny; and though . . . to regard him as a vulgar fellow is the grossest of blunders as well as a great injustice, Vigny, in thought and taste . . . generally, was as far above him as in style. But that is not the question. . . . I do not quite *know* D'Artagnan, though I think I know Athos, as a man; but as a novel-hero the Gascon seems to me to "fill all numbers." Cinq-Mars may be a succession or chain of type-personages—generous but headlong youth, spoilt favourite, conspirator and something like traitor, finally victim; but these are the "flat" characters (if one may so speak) of the treatise, not the "round" ones of the novel. And I cannot *unite* them. His love-affair with Marie de Gonzague leaves me cold. His friend, the younger De Thou, is hardly more than "an excellent person." The persecution of Urbain Grandier and the sufferings of the Ursuline Abbess seem to me—to use the old schoolboy word—to be hopelessly "muffed"; and if any one will compare the accounts of the taking of the "Spanish bastion" at Perpignan with the exploit at that other bastion—Saint-Gervais at Rochelle—he will see what I mean as well as in any single instance. The second part, where we come to the actual conspiracy, is rather better than the first, if not much; and I think Vigny's presentment of Richelieu has been too much censured. (p. 264)

[Vigny] has written the novel not as he ought and as he ought not. The political and historical interests overshadow, confuse, and hamper the purely "fictional" (as people say now), and when he has got hold of a scene which *is* either purely "fictional," or historical with fictitious possibilities, he does not seem (to me) to know how to deal with it. . . . [He] has a well-conceived interview, in which Richelieu, for almost the last time, shows "the power of a strong mind over a weak one," and brings the King to abject submission and surrender of Cinq-Mars, by the simple process of leaving his Majesty to settle by himself the problems that drop in from France, England, and where or whence not, during the time of the Cardinal's absence. . . . [It] is impossible not to remember several scenes—not one only—in *Quentin Durward,* and think how much better Scott would have done it; several in [Dumas's] Musketeer-trilogy, if not also in [his] Margot-Chicot series, and make a parallel reflection. (pp. 265-66)

But if any one be of taste sufficiently like mine to find disappointment of the unpleasant kind in *Cinq-Mars,* I think I can promise him an agreeable, if somewhat chequered, surprise when, remembering *Cinq-Mars* and basing his expectations upon it, he turns to *Stello.* It is true that the book is, as a whole, even less "precisely a novel" than Sainte-Beuve's *Volupté.* But for that very reason it escapes the display of the disabilities which *Cinq-Mars,* being, or incurring obligation to be, precisely a novel, suffers. It is true also that it exhibits that fancy for putting historical persons in the first "plan" which he had avowed, and over which heads have been shaken. The bulk of it, indeed, consists of romanticised *histoires* or historiettes (the narrator calls them "anecdotes") of the sad and famous fates of two French poets, Gilbert and André Chénier, and of our English Chatterton. But, then, no one of these can be called "a dominant historical personage," and the known facts permit themselves to be, and are, "romanticised" effectively enough. So the flower is in each case plucked from the nettle. And there is another flower of more positive and less compensatory kind which blooms here, which is particularly welcome to some readers, and which, from **Cinq-Mars** alone, they could hardly have expected to find in any garden of Alfred de Vigny's. For this springs from a root of ironic wit which almost approaches humour, which, though never merry, is not seldom merciful, and is very seldom actually savage, though often sad. (pp. 266-67)

Servitude et Grandeur Militaires, is no more of a regular novel than **Stello;** but, though perhaps in an inferior degree, it shares the superiority of **Stello** itself over **Cinq-Mars** in power of telling a story. Like **Stello,** too, it is a frame of short tales, not a continuous narrative; and like that, and even to a greater degree, it exhibits the intense melancholy (almost unique in its particular shade, though I suppose it comes nearer to Leopardi's than to that of any other great man of letters) which characterises Alfred de Vigny. (p. 273)

[**Stello** and **Servitude et Grandeur Militaires**] save Vigny himself to some extent from the condemnation, or at any rate the exceedingly faint praise, which his principal novel may bring upon him as a novelist. But they do so to some extent only. It is clear even from them, though not so clear as it is from their more famous companion, that he was not to the manner born. The riddles of the painful earth were far too much with him to permit him to be an unembarrassed master or creator of pastime—not necessarily horse-collar pastime by any means, but pastime pure and simple. His preoccupations with philosophy, politics, world-sorrow, and other things were constantly cropping up and getting in the way of his narrative faculty. I do not know that . . . [any scene except one in **Stello**] goes off with complete "currency," and this is an episode rather than a whole tale, though it gives itself the half-title of *Histoire d'une Puce Enragée.* He could never, I think, have done anything but short stories; and even as a short-story teller he ranks with the other Alfred, Musset, rather than with Mérimée or Gautier. But, like Musset, he presents us, as neither of the other two did (for Mérimée was not a poet, and Gautier was hardly a dramatist), with a writer, of mark all but the greatest, in verse and prose and drama; while in prose and verse at least he shows that quality of melancholy magnificence which has been noted, as hardly any one else does in all three forms, except Hugo himself. (pp. 276-77)

> George Saintsbury, "The Novel of Style: Gautier, Mérimée, Gérard de Nerval, Musset, Vigny," in his A History of the French Novel (to the Close of the 19th Century): From 1800 to 1900, Vol. II, *1917. Reprint by Russell & Russell, Inc., 1964, pp. 208-79.**

HUGH ALLISON SMITH (essay date 1925)

[Vigny] has left only three original plays, and of these only one, **Chatterton,** . . . is of such outstanding merit and significance as to demand consideration today. (p. 46)

In its style, its lack of color, its simplicity of plot and practical conformity with the unities, and above all in its very conception as a subject, **Chatterton** is almost entirely Classic. On this latter point, the author's own words, which seem not only to approve the Classic point of view but to criticize the Romantic conception, are especially interesting as written by one who, a few years before, had proclaimed with Hugo the necessity of a drama that would present "a vast spectacle of life":

> I believe, above all, in the future and in serious things; now that the amusement of the eyes

through childish surprises makes everyone laugh in the midst of serious action, it is time, it seems to me, for the drama of thought.

> An idea which is the examination of a wounded soul should have, in its form, the most complete unity and the most severe simplicity. . . . The material action is of little importance. This is the story of a man who has written a letter in the morning and waits for the answer until evening; it arrives and kills him. But the moral action here is everything. The action is in this soul given over to black despair.

Here is a moral and mental drama, written in general conformity with the Classic rules. It would seem, then, to be an example of pure Classic tragedy; it is, in fact, a typical product of Romantic philosophy and, because of this, a thoroughly Romantic play.

Chatterton is really a thesis play of which the purpose is to uphold the rights of imagination and feeling in life as against the dominance of reason and good sense, and the appeal is imaginative and emotional, and very little rationalistic. Chatterton asks for a pension, gets a position, and kills himself. His action is as little justified by reason and good sense, by the ordinary rules of life, as is the fatalistic pessimism of [Hugo's] Hernani. . . . (pp. 46-8)

The success of the play would seem due to two factors, the Romantic vogue of such heroes and the absolute conviction in Vigny's appeal. Vigny, in his sensitiveness, pessimism and suffering, is strikingly like Chatterton. Here was the one play above all others he could write. Like Dumas in *Antony,* he could put himself into the character, and this note of sincerity was recognized. Any other explanation seems impossible, for the play lacks the usual Romantic color, has a minimum of action, and is frequently awkward in its dramatic technique.

What **Chatterton** seems to prove, then, is that the essence of the Romantic drama is a conception of life, or a state of mind: or better perhaps, considering its pathological character and brief duration, we could call it a state of nerves. (p. 48)

> Hugh Allison Smith, "Other Romantic Dramatists (Dumas—Delavigne—Vigny—Musset)," in his Main Currents of Modern French Drama, *Henry Holt and Company, 1925, pp. 36-58.**

ALBERT THIBAUDET (essay date 1936)

[*Thibaudet was an early twentieth-century French literary critic and follower of the French philosopher Henri Bergson. He is often described as versatile, well-informed, and original, and critics cite his unfinished* Histoire de la littérature française de 1789 à nos jours, *first published in 1936 and excerpted below, as his major critical treatise. In this work, Thibaudet classified authors by generations—1789, 1820 (which includes Vigny), 1850, 1885, and 1914-1918—rather than by literary epochs. In his essay he discusses Vigny's reputation, his romantic ballads, use of myth, sentiments and ideas, depiction of love, and, briefly, his philosophical poetry. The following is taken from the section on sentiments and ideas.*]

Vigny's poetry is governed by one idea, which is confirmed by *Le Journal d'un poète:* the rapture between man and the creator, the refusal to admit that the world, nature, God himself are as they are. *Eloa* may at first seem a tale inspired by Thomas Moore's *Loves of the Angels,* with its reputation derived from the richness of its poetry, the beauty of its images, the rhythm and the flow of its passages, the fluidity and the spirituality of some immortal lines. But beyond these poetic assets there is something else: the fact that Vigny's poetry is on Eloa's side, that this poetry is an eternal Eloa. *Le Déluge* and *La Fille de Jephté* tell of the same sacrifice of innocence. Above all, the poems in *Destinées* . . . take up the eternal theme again with a maturity, a concentration, a force and a seriousness that are even stronger. The tercets of *Destinées—La Maison du berger, La Mort du loup, Le Mont des oliviers*—are a quadrupled rejection of need, of nature, of complaint, of God.

They have become the most lastingly luminous poems, the fixed stars of French poetry. This they owe not to the purity of their language, which is often questionable, but to that of remarkable lines that hang here and there like grapes of Canaan; and then to their deep roots in a man's heart: the two apologias for silence, *La Mort du loup* and *Le Mont des oliviers*, are truly a testament of the poet, who himself knew when to be silent, to preserve behind walls of granite that inner life attested to by his *Journal*. And finally they owe it to their transmission from man to man along the royal road of myth and symbol.

La Maison du berger, whose stanzas thicken like a forest, is not only a symbol but an architecture of symbols. Its three parts set up three pairs of contrasts: the railroad of society and the shepherd's cottage of the individual; politics and poetry; nature and woman. Confronted with society, politics and nature, silence. But for living things, for poetry, for woman, tenderness. The machine vulgarizes the spirit, politics stultifies man, nature ignores the heart; against them the poet is the wolf, keeping the silence by which, in *Le Mont des oliviers,* he replies to the silence of God. But the shepherd's cottage is freedom, poetry is the pearl of thought, woman is Eloa's pity, of which Eve kept the greater part, that very part that the poet restores to her when he turns away from inhuman, too divine nature:

> Plus que tout votre règne et que ses splendeurs vaines
> J'aime la majesté des souffrances humaines
>
> (More than the empty splendors of your state
> I love man's majesty before his fate).

But admiration for this architecture of symbols can cause us to misunderstand the purer beauty of the poem: here and there, and especially in the last stanzas, a wholly pure disinterestedness, a presence not of the eternal feminine but, on the contrary, of the fleeting feminine, of the moment for love because she will not be seen twice, of love silent and always threatened. That imponderable disinterestedness would later become the highest quality of poetry—precisely because of its fusion with symbolism; and throughout the course of oratorical romantic poetry Vigny seems, with Gérard de Nerval, alone in his ability to sustain its hidden life.

Vigny's world is a world without God, Vigny's conscience is the tragic conscience of a world without God. It leads him to despair, but to an active despair, in this silent man the very despair of the silent: one has no need for hope in order to undertake. The enterprise survives beyond hope, and a part of *Destinées* puts the human enterprise into symbols.

The poems of the human undertaking are *La Sauvage, La Flûte, La Bouteille à la mer,* and *L'Esprit pur. La Sauvage,* which is somewhat lacking in resonance, was no digression for Vigny. Alone among the romantics, he hated nature in all its aspects. In every conflict between man and nature, he stood with man. He stood with man against God. When the problem of Rousseau

arose, he was against Rousseau; he was for the civilized man against the natural man, for the white man against the savage. It was inevitable that one of his poems should be dedicated to civilization, to effort, to effort for the sake of effort, even if, as in *La Flûte,* it does not succeed.

La Bouteille à la mer and *L'Esprit pur* go back to that seven-line stanza of *La Maison du berger* that is Vigny's most beautiful lyric achievement, as well as his first. *La Bouteille à la mer* is a poem of the human enterprise in that it is connected to what is most insubstantial and that it lives and dies for ideas. Let us not mistake Vigny's idealism for a banal word. It resembled not that of the poets but that of the philosopher. The twenty-sixth and last stanza of *La Bouteille à la mer* begins with this line:

> Le vrai Dieu, le Dieu fort est le Dieu des idées
>
> (The true, strong God is the deity of ideas).

The poetry, the work, and the life of Alfred de Vigny are strung on the heroic dialectic thanks to which this enemy of an imposed god, of a god neither sought nor wished, arrives at the platonic idea of a true, strong god, the realm of ideas, as space is the realm of bodies. The poet of *L'Esprit pur* is the man of ideas—better yet, the knight of ideas. Vigny's ideas retain the mark of the inner implement and the painful tension that created them. But it was his vocation to create them as a poet. (pp. 125-27)

> *Albert Thibaudet, "The Generation of 1820: Alfred de Vigny," in his* French Literature from 1795 to Our Era, *translated by Charles Lam Markmann, Funk & Wagnalls, 1968, pp. 122-28.*

EDWARD SACKVILLE-WEST   (essay date 1949)

Ignoring the advice of those who, in the first weeks of war, rushed in to tell us what we had best read, I returned at once to a classic of military life—Alfred de Vigny's *Servitude et Grandeur de la Vie Militaire.* The form of this book is arresting: it consists of three stories, laced together by the author's meditations on the soldier's life as he had lived it. The idea illustrated by the stories is that war is a machine, in essence anti-human, and that the soldier's greatness and pathos arise from the willing submission to it of his humanity and reason. The statement that war is the continuation of diplomacy by other means may be true, but it slurs over the fact that war is as different from any other kind of violent action—a revolution, for instance—as absolute monarchy is from the constitutional kind.

Vigny was the first poet clearly to state this distinction, which his mind was peculiarly adapted to perceive; for his naturally strong romantic feelings were held in iron control by a brilliant, jewel-hard intelligence and an exact sense of responsibility. Hence his cold hatred for all forms of vulgarity, self-deception and mendacity; for all theatrical posturing. . . . He had seen too much of both sides of the medal ever to lapse into self-dramatisation—the last refuge of those who cannot face the truth about themselves. Whether he is recounting the grief of the naval captain whose duty it was to shoot the young man in whom he had become affectionately interested; or the hideous fate of the adjutant who was guarding the powder-magazine of Vincennes on the night of the great explosion; or the grandeur of "Canne de Jonc" who gave his life to a child in return for the life of one he had killed: in all it is the tragedy of the Unjust Necessity he is celebrating. (pp. 176-77)

At least one of Vigny's points in *Servitude et Grandeur* is implicit: that what is done under pressure of the Unjust Necessity need not impair the soul. This requires to be repeated at every crisis of history. Nobility of character, generosity, forgiveness, love: these things do not depend on the State—on political systems—on war. They are unconquerably private. . . . It is not the possession of those qualities which makes Vigny's soldiers so pathetic and so grand: it is their ability to lay them aside at the call of the monster. That is their laurel crown—the sad knowledge of a necessity peculiar to their estate and one which isolates them; for even in these days of citizen armies, the true soldier is as rare as he was one hundred and twenty years ago. It is Vigny's distinction to have perceived the nature of his tragedy—his solitude, his horror, his silent face guarding the intolerably necessity. It is a tragedy in which the plaited skein of thought and act has been unravelled, and the threads lie side by side. (p. 180)

Servitude et Grandeur de la Vie Militaire is a classical book, for the terrible griefs and exaltations of its characters are seen as though from a great way off, from the marmoreal repose of an achieved perspective. No writer's tone—not Emerson's, not Matthew Arnold's—was ever higher than Vigny's, in this unique and beautiful book. Here speaks the voice of a completely distinguished nature, of a man who had learnt that few things are really worth saying, but that what must be said had better be said like this. (p. 181)

> Edward Sackville-West, "The Soldier," in his In-
> clinations, 1949. Reprint by Kennikat Press, Inc.,
> 1967, pp. 176-81.

ALBERT GUÉRARD (essay date 1957)

[*Guérard provides an assessment of Vigny's achievement in prose, drama, and poetry. He attributes much of Vigny's success to his technical skill: "Everything he wrote—poetry, drama, novel—showed a creditable, a conscientious command of technique." At times, according to Guérard, he relied too heavily on technique, as in some of his poems that expose "the tricks of the trade," yet this same technical facility enabled Vigny to create his masterpieces,* Chatterton *and* Les destinées.]

In poetry, romance, and drama, [Vigny] was a blazer of trails. He was the long-forgotten herald of our own times: we find in him our struggles, our anguish, our hopes. He anticipated Freud, Kafka, Camus, by several generations. I might have pilfered a phrase from André Maurois: "The Silences of Captain de Vigny." For in *The Deluge*, in *The Death of the Wolf*, in *The Garden of Olives*, even in *Wanda*, a poem of slight importance with a Russian setting, the theme of silence is constantly audible. I was tempted to use "Vigny and His Ivory Tower." It was for him that Sainte-Beuve, his equivocal friend, borrowed from Holy Writ and from the Litanies of the Virgin that lovely metaphor, *turris eburnea*. It is singularly apt in his case: for it denotes, not the refuge of the selfish and the irresponsible, but the strength that purity alone can impart. . . . Vigny is with us: our elder brother, not a numbered and labeled specimen in a dusty museum, not a fading demigod in a classical heaven. He is . . . a Presence in the solemn, almost mystic sense that the Quaker, in his *Chatterton*, attaches to the term: a figure of secret power, radiating an inner glow. "Vigny, My Master?" Yes, I have just acknowledged his leadership, with pride. A leader: a guide to freedom, not a taskmaster. He denounced *séidism*, the blind acceptance of an idol such as Napoleon. Vigny is not the pontiff of an orthodoxy: his example teaches us the vanity of all cliques and sects. (pp. 136-37)

Vigny, in his Preface to *Chatterton*, established a hierarchy among the makers of books: the man of letters, the writer, the poet. He spurned the petty ambitions of the mere man of letters, a Grub Street drudge even when he attains celebrity and fortune. But if he wanted to be first of all a poet, he was compelled to be also a writer, a professional, a craftsman. The nobleman had to master his trade: he knew how to wield his tool, the "iron quill." Everything he wrote—poetry, drama, novel—showed a creditable, a conscientious command of technique. He cannot be regarded as a great lord condescending to scribble when it amuses him; nor as an awkward genius, waddling ludicrously, like Baudelaire's Albatross, because his giant wings impede his walk. Vigny's "know-how," which is well above the average, is for us a cause of embarrassment. . . . In Dante or Milton, sheer talent is manifest, but it is the modest and efficient servant of genius; in Vigny, good, run-of-the-mill talent, short of supreme mastery, often constitutes a severe handicap.

Vigny's work, apart from its rare moments of unique excellence, offers at any rate two qualities which are not to be despised. It was original at the time, and it covers a very wide range. Vigny wrote Romantic stuff like many others, but ahead of all others. He wrote pleasing Greek idyls and elegies before André Chénier's posthumous works had reached the general public. He wrote a *Fall of an Angel* (his *Eloa*) before Lamartine; a *Legend of the Centuries*—in miniature before Hugo. . . . On the stage, his translation of *Othello* was the first decisive victory won by the new school, and his *Chatterton* is the high-water mark of the Romantic flood.

It is a delicate task to pass judgment on Vigny merely as a writer. In prose, he keeps up a steady level, and a high one, whether he tells a story or discusses a philosophical problem. *Cinq-Mars*, avidly read for two or three generations, does not thrill us any more; but it still commands our respect. The three narratives in *Stello*, the three in *Servitude et grandeur militaire* (especially *La Canne de jonc*), the only episode in *Daphné* that was completed, are masterly: the suspense is keen and sustained, enhanced rather than blurred by the undercurrent of vigorous thought. Even the drama *Quitte pour la peur* ("Let Off with a Scare") has the period sprightliness of a Marivaux, with an undertone of modern gravity. *La Maréchale d'Ancre* is far from tedious, and *Chatterton* is a marvel of robust construction and restrained emotion: Vigny reaches pathos through reticence more surely than Hugo or Dumas through melodrama.

It is in verse, where the tricks of the trade are more apparent, that we might complain he knew his craft too well. In the slang of French artists, *il a de la patte:* he is sure-handed, but the hand is too visible. His poems of classical antiquity (those of Biblical origin are far superior) are good exercises in versification: they fully deserve a B grade. In *Dolorida*, the tragic Spanish story is wreathed in incredible periphrases which would have enchanted Abbé Delille himself. Even in *Eloa*, with its profound central thought and its many passages of pure beauty, lengthy comparisons are reminiscent of pseudo-classicism at its last gasp, and of that Ossianism which has justly been called a *mal de siècle* [world-weariness], a literary disease for over half a century. *Madame de Soubise, La Frégate la Sérieuse,* are finger exercises, not much worse than some of Hugo's early ballads. *La Sauvage, La Flûte,* written when he had reached full maturity, are well-intentioned sermons in rhyme. All this is almost worthy of Vigny, but not quite. (pp. 142-45)

However, among those poems which are well-made, and of no great significance, there are two which possess perennial appeal: one is *La Neige* (**Snowfall**), and the other *Le Cor* (**The Horn**). Seek in them no philosophical intent: they are nothing but lovely tales, "tales of olden times." Both evoke the Carolingian cycle of legends; one is smiling and tender, the other a stark epic of heroic death. Both open with stanzas which create an atmosphere of sentiment and dream: the snow gently falling, the sound of the horn at night in the depths of the woods. It is the same formula as in Heine's *Lorelei:* a mood taking susbstance as an ancient folktale, then, before it hardens, melting again into a note of music. For generations, many readers knew nothing of Vigny except *The Horn,* and *The Horn* is perfection. But the great Vigny lies far beyond. (p. 145)

[Vigny's technical skill] enabled him to express himself with the purity, the plenitude we find in his few masterpieces. Such flawless achievements as *The Destinies* (with its slow implacable *terze rime* [a rhyme scheme that uses three-line stanzas] borrowed from the *Divine Comedy*), *Moses, The Mount of Olives, The Wrath of Samson, The Bottle in the Sea,* and above all *The Shepherd's Hut,* are not the products of chance. Awed by their depths, we forget art; but it was art that enabled the poet to reach the depths. If *The Shepherd's Hut* ranks supreme, it is because there is no poem at the same time so instinct with beauty and so indiffernt to mere beauty; so laden with thought, yet so able, with sudden effortless flight, to soar beyond thought, into the sphere of music and dream. (p. 146)

[Vigny reached] in the drama, the artistic perfection he had achieved in pure poetry, in *The Horn* and in a few strophes of *The Shepherd's Hut.* From the formal point of view, *Chatterton* is flawless. In its rigorous simplicity, it observes all the classical rules: it is as firmly knit, as precisely centered as a tragedy of Racine. It is solidly and skillfully constructed, but the technique is not obtrusive, as in the "well-made" plays of Scribe and Sardou. In book form or on the stage, it holds our breathless interest.The thesis it presents, which Vigny borrowed from his own book *Stello* is that society cannot do justice to the poet, who soars above its petty concerns. A stranger, a rebel, the poet is bound to be sacrificed. . . . Vigny discussing ideas on the stage was the forerunner of Dumas *fils;* and it was the achievement of Dumas *fils,* we are apt to forget it, that paved the way for Ibsen and Bernard Shaw. (pp. 148-49)

Pensée and *idée* [Thought and idea] are [Vigny's] key words. What did he mean by thought and idea? The terms are not coextensive, but they are inseparable: for Vigny, thought is the crucible of the idea. He subtitled his finest work, *The Destinies:* "**Philosophical Poems,**" and without excessive strain, it would be possible to enroll him in some school and elaborate from his writings a system. But to impose upon him a pattern would lower him: he is a man first of all, and a poet, not an "abstractor of quintessence." His philosophy is organic, the sum total of his sufferings, of his passions, of his character, of his will. To his mind, poetry and thought are one. They are the consciousness of life purified and concentrated to such a degree that it reaches the hard transparency, the virgin splendor, of a diamond. In poetry so conceived, verse is a mere contingency: it is to be regretted that in *Chatterton* Vigny did not draw the line more sharply. For the self-styled "poetry" whose aims are to dazzle, or to entertain, or to serve petty interests, Vigny felt the uttermost contempt, which he expressed in *The Shepherd's Hut.* The poetry that he elects as his lodestar cannot be separated from personal dignity, civic duty, science, religion. This is Art for Art's sake in its most uncompromising form, the haughtiest of all ivory towers: poetry refuses to be used for anything beneath its own lofty plane.

But it is also the abdication of mere art, art as a plaything, the most refined of vanities: art, love, and religion must be absorbed into a more profound synthesis. (p. 151)

> Albert Guérard, "Alfred de Vigny," in his Fossils and Presences, Stanford University Press, 1957, pp. 135-63.

IRVING MASSEY (essay date 1963)

Stello marks the watershed in Vigny's development as a writer, from the Romantic lyrist to the philosophical poet, from the fabricator of historical fiction to the novelist of ideas. In this book Vigny faces the necessity of defining his own character, and emerges with the full consciousness of his identity. After 1831 he gives up the quest for elusive inspiration and recognizes his mission as the spokesman for the intellect in fiction and poetry. His later prose works, *Stello, Servitude et Grandeur militaires,* and *Daphné* are philosophical novels. . . . *Stello* itself, he tells us, is "an idea in three acts."

After *Stello,* Vigny's journal becomes steadily richer in philosophical commentary. After *Stello,* too, Vigny's flirtation with the Romantic lyric peters out, and his published poems become more and more intellectual and abstract. Unlike *Chatterton* (a dramatization of one episode from his novel), *Stello* was not a great contemporary success. . . . Nevertheless, it is Vigny's most important prose work. For its author, it provided the self-analysis he needed to help him shift his efforts from contemporary stereotypes into his own literary forms. (p. xiv)

If we go beyond the plot material to the main idea of [*Stello*], we recognize that, at a glance, to be the familiar opposition between the poet and society. Absolute monarchs fear the revolutionary implications of poetry; bourgeois governments declare the poet useless; egalitarian republics fear and resent the natural superiority of artists. The poet is the mouthpiece of immediate truth, the oracle whom no society based on fictions and conventions can tolerate. . . .

Imagination, the organ of poetry, raises its possessor above all possible confusion with the inferior types of human being, the common man, the philosopher, or the statesman, all of whom are involved in the unclean world of action or circumscribed by the die of reason. Stello must remain in holy isolation; he must never concern himself with the application of his ideas or even with their relevance for social situations, if he is to accomplish his special mission successfully. Poetry simply does not mix with political reality. As the unadulterated expression of an ideal, it can keep no covenant with the shifting standards of social compromise.

Thus far, the theme of *Stello* as we have described it seems entirely conventional. But such a summary is misleading. In our précis we have chosen to ignore Vigny's ambiguities, and if we ignore these ambiguities we are sure to miss the point of the book. . . . [It] might be concluded that Stello, the Romantic poet, is both the ideal type and the spokesman for the ideal, while the doctor is the butt of the author's satire. In fact, the opposite statement would be much nearer to the truth. Stello is the patient, sick with romantic sentiment, whose cure must be effected by the acrid Doctor Noir. (p. xviii)

Stello, far from being the ideal incarnate, is a rather fatuous young man. He is not the portrait of the perfect poet; he is the portrait of Vigny's own weaknesses. Doctor Noir accuses him of the very sins of which the politicians themselves are guilty: the lust for power, which Louis XV, in the first anecdote, also attributes to poets; and the demand that his careless words should guide the multitude. . . . Stello is guilty of a more profound crime than any of these. He is a sentimentalist. He believes that the ideal can be achieved on earth. By making the impossible demand that political reality express the ideal, he betrays both the ideal and himself, both poetry and his own mind. Utterly confused, he has sunk into a state of morbid depression, and the cautery of cynicism is needed to extirpate the proud flesh of illusion.

This is the real meaning of the political theme in *Stello*. . . . In the *Première Consultation,* political utopianism is merely a symbol of the misguided search for earthly happiness. It expresses Stello's readiness to ignore the nature of the real world and to assume that we can override its requirements. Such assumptions lead inevitably to disappointment. . . . (pp. xviii-xix)

Every possible means of counteracting Stello's penchant for sentimentality is invoked. At the very beginning of the book, the claims of physiological psychology to an exhaustive description of mental functions are advanced; Stello, like Gilbert, is assaulted by the demons of rationalism, and Doctor Noir is there to help them press the attack. . . . Doctor Noir joins forces with the enemy in the onslaught upon Stello's false ideals. Stello must undergo a primary purification to prepare him for deeper understanding; he must abandon the hope for a paradise on earth before he can know the true idealism that expects no favours from this world. Living by the assumption that life harbours the possibility of perfection, Stello has fallen into apathy because his philosophy bears no relation to experience. Aimless and confused, he can know neither the external world nor himself; for the refusal to admit the refractoriness of external reality to idealistic desires is founded on an unwillingness to acknowledge the unideal elements in oneself. (pp. xix-xx)

It is not that Doctor Noir (the intellectual Vigny) rejects poetry, but that he rejects sentimentality masquerading as poetry. Himself impervious to all forms of sentiment, the Doctor stands prepared with psychiatric means to bring Stello's logos back to the realms of dispassionate understanding. By accepting such illusions as happiness and hope Stello has fallen into the contradictions that quickly make life unendurable, and he must be set back on the road to the only viable concept of existence; if he cannot become a principled pessimist like Doctor Noir, he will certainly end by committing suicide like Chatterton.

Noir's cheerful pessimism, or macabre cheerfulness, is the chief diapason of the book. The Doctor seems to enjoy hunting down Stello's illusions step by step and dispatching them. His techniques consist of an unremitting intellectual scepticism, a disconcerting readiness to satirize the most sympathetic characters in his stories, and an attitude of icy indifference toward the suffering he describes. No opportunity to insult and undermine Stello's sensibilities is overlooked, for this book is no Romantic rhapsody, but the psychoanalysis of illusion, leading to a philosophy of doubt. What we emerge with at the end of the Consultations is neither a positivistic dogma nor a doctrine of transcendence, but a grim recognition of human limitations. The two words 'Why?' and 'Alas!,' the author finally declares, comprehend the meaning of every book. 'Why?' expresses the eternal doubt which is the intellectual destiny of man; 'Alas!' is the summary of life itself. The novel culminates in these two interjections.

Enough has been said to clarify the theme *Stello* and to correct the impression which may be created by its melodramatic de-

vices: that the book is merely a prolonged effusion of sentiment. (pp. xx-xxi)

What was to be the ultimate state of mind of someone whom Doctor Noir had cured? Freed from illusion, how was he to live? What, in a word, is the moral of *Stello?* The only lesson we can be sure it teaches is the inferiority of the active to the contemplative life. "Epictetus understood," Vigny writes in his *Journal:* "independence is only in the mind. All thought and no action: that is the nature and the virtue of the philosophic genius." Within the framework of this generalization Vigny was able to construct a theory for the artist's function in society. . . .

Vigny saw that the artist's relationship to society had changed in such a way that is was impossible for creative people to serve, whether voluntarily or by prescription, the purposes of any state. . . . The days of royal patronage were over; but what was much more serious, the days of social myth, when the artist could share in the mass convictions of his group, were gone. With the death of myth the artist becomes the spokesman for a private truth; to serve the state means only to peddle slogans. And that private truth, that cherished splinter of a shattered ideal, becomes more and more difficult to preserve. . . .

In *Stello* we are witnesses to the defeat of public idealism; we watch it take up its final position for a last-ditch fight, in the silent redoubt of the poet's heart. With official slogans the creative writer can have nothing to do. God is gone from the outside world; the poet will lose the fragment of divinity that remains by collaborating with the political machine. (p. xxii)

In the private consciousness of the isolated individual, illusion fades and turns to scepticism; and the only ideal man can still hope for is what he may discover along the pathways of uncertainty. In his doubts he must find peace, in the certitude of death his security, in his abject helplessness his self-respect. The total independence recommended to the poet in *Stello* is an allegory for the total independence man himself must achieve, emancipated from the hope for assurances in any form. He must learn to do without knowledge, intellectual, spiritual, or aesthetic; then, in the pathos of his ignorance, he may begin to aspire to the peculiar dignity of the human being.

The courage required for Stello to abandon at once his hopes for knowledge and his idealism is to be gained only at great cost; but to complete his cure, Stello must espouse the philosophy of doubt, reserving the remnant of his trust for the plumb-line of analysis. Comprehensive philosophical syntheses with claims to intellectual certainty are of the same order of unreliability as apocalyptic delusions. Because its subject throughout is uncertainty incarnate, and because its form is appropriate to its theme, *Stello* continues to bewilder the critics. Yet into its very epigraph is decanted the essence of its meaning. *Stello* offers its contemporaries the wafer of doubt as the only nourishment for its author's peculiar faith:

> Analysis is a ship's lead. Sounding the depths,
> it brings terror and despair upon the weak; but
> it reassures and guides the Brave, who grasp it
> firmly.

(p. xxiii)

Irving Massey, in an introduction to Stello: A Session with Doctor Noir *by Alfred de Vigny, edited and translated by Irving Massey, McGill University Press, 1963, pp. xi-xxiii.*

STIRLING HAIG (essay date 1964)

The intent of Vigny's translation [of Shakespeare's *Othello*] was to emphasize purely formal innovations: life painted with broad strokes, in which tragic and comic elements would mingle, each scene and character having a style appropriate to the moment. It was for this reason that Vigny chose *Othello*. . . . [It] was probably the best known Shakespearean play in France. If the plot had been loosely adapted or even distorted, its outline was at least familiar to the literate public. Thus Vigny could fix the audience's attention on questions of style, for *Le More de Venise* was an *exercice de style*, an experiment in form: "Had I known of a story more told, read, performed, sung, danced, cut, embellished, spoiled than that of *Othello*, I would have chosen it, precisely so that attention would have been centered, without distraction, on a single point, the *execution*." (pp. 56-7)

Vigny was fully aware that translations rarely satisfy everyone, and pointed out that his intention was to render the spirit, and not the letter of the play. *Le More de Venise* (as Sainte Beuve clearly saw) was an instrument designed to broach the wall of classical resistance and introduce a new style. His translation was adapted to win over refractory spirits, at the price of "some concessions in their favor."

The concessions were sometimes considerable, as we shall see upon examining the translation itself. In spite of his disclaimer, Vigny did not avoid classical periphrases, and often suppressed the *pittoresque* [vividness] of Shakespeare's language. He reduced the play's length by about one-third. In the stage version at least, he cut the roles of Gratiano, the clown, and Bianca, as well as all references to them; and as [critic] Annie Sessely remarked, Othello thus killed Desdemona without ever having any proof of her guilt, for he never saw Cassio giving the handkerchief to Bianca. Iago's murder of Emilia was also suppressed, and a good number of Othello's mentions of "Honest Iago." . . . Almost everything that might be considered improper or trivial from the French standpoint was toned down or simply eliminated. . . . (pp. 57-8)

A nagging respect for the *bienséances* [decorum], the attenuation of improprieties and "extravagance," a general reduction of *Othello*'s many accents: all of these characteristics of Vigny's translation are best seen in his treatment of Iago. The character fascinated Vigny. . . . He suscribed to Young's characterization of Iago: *"une grande âme et un coeur corrompu,"* a phrase that clearly applies to *mal du siècle* [world-weariness] and a certain type of French Romantic "hero," from [Chateaubriand's] René and [Constant's] Adolphe to [Musset's] Lorenzaccio. (p. 58)

Shakespeare's first act abounds in contrasts between two moral qualities, candor and dissimulation, respectively seen in the characters of Othello and Iago. This opposition is conveyed by a pattern of related images or suggestions that cleave to one of the foregoing qualities. . . . [The] thematic antithesis of *Othello*, appearance and reality, is rapidly established as the play's concern, and it is buttressed by other elements of the first act, which are grouped in patterns of contrast, or rather, contraries. The dark of night, propitious to Iago's scheming and trouble-making . . . dominates the act, but is soon to give way to daybreak. (pp. 58-9)

How did Vigny transpose this "tone" of the play? In Shakespeare . . . there is a delicate balance of discordant qualities in each character. On the one hand we see double-edged virtues, and on the other, vice with redeeming aspects. Othello

is *rather* admirable, Iago *rather* detestable, and a good deal of the play's profundity rests upon this precarious equilibrium. But Vigny has tipped the scales in Iago's case, with the result that the black-white opposition, a human relationship in Shakespeare that is effected on the human plane, becomes a vertical, moral one in *Le More de Venise*. Shakespeare views the relationship of good and evil as ambiguous; Vigny throws them into stark contrast, with base vice sapping lofty virtue from the outset. Naturally enough, it is therefore Iago who best reveals the drift in meaning from Shakespeare's play to Vigny's copy.

In his *Lettre à Lord* *** [Vigny's preface to his translation, he] rather stridently proclaimed his right to a style befitting each character's station, thereby multiplying the play's registers by individualizing the personages. He was considerably less bold in practice. The first point where Vigny recoiled before the barbarities of the *sauvage ivre* was Iago's highly sexual imagination. In Vigny's early poems, one can find much that is mildly sensual, but nothing openly erotic, for in literature at least, Vigny was continent and discreet. . . . [Vigny expurgated] many of Iago's difficult remarks. . . . (pp. 59-60)

Nor does Vigny (a rather humorless man himself) always fully convey Iago's sardonic sense of humor; it is only half-suggested. . . . [Deprived] of the wit that redeems his rascality, Vigny's Iago is only clever and not amusing. . . . (p. 60)

And what of the *mélange des genres*? [mixture of genres] Here too, Vigny's practice is disappointingly reserved: Iago's impromptu punning and rhyming at the expense of women is cut. In this instance, one can only guess that they tend, or so Vigny thought, to spoil the effect of Othello's ensuing salute to Desdemona—"O my fair warrior!"—a line that Vigny greatly admired; one can also note that Iago's badinage contains an unseemly reference to clyster pipes. But it is clearly the indelible impress of French Classicism that is at work here. To that influence many of the qualities, as well as the shortcomings of Vigny's translation can be ascribed. Thus he excels in passages of tragic grandeur, as in his rendering of Othello's "Farewell to tranquil mind! farewell content!" (p. 62)

Stirling Haig, "Vigny and 'Othello'," in Yale French Studies, *No. 33, December, 1964, pp. 53-64.**

V. S. PRITCHETT (essay date 1964)

[*Pritchett is a highly esteemed English novelist, short story writer, and critic. Considered one of the modern masters of the short story, he is also considered one of the world's most respected and well-read literary critics. Pritchett writes in the conversational tone of the familiar essay, a method by which he approaches literature from the viewpoint of a lettered but not overly scholarly reader. A twentieth-century successor to such early nineteenth-century essayist-critics as William Hazlitt and Charles Lamb, Pritchett employs much the same critical method: his own experience, judgment, and sense of literary art are emphasized, rather than a codified critical doctrine derived from a school of psychological or philosophical speculation. His criticism is often described as fair, reliable, and insightful. In the following excerpt, he expresses his admiration for Vigny's narrative ability in* The Military Necessity.]

As a personal document, in which the self is disciplined to the point of anonymity, *The Military Necessity* is a classically clear and direct piece of writing. It is originally conceived. Vigny is an artist-philosopher. He sets out his theme a little at a time and then breaks off to tell at leisure a story that illustrates it.

The military argument is a frame (as Turgenev's after-dinner conversations were or Mérimée's reflections on travel and custom) for three dramatic stories of character and action. This method of writing a short story will always attract the aspirant because it seems to be the easiest, for it gives the writer points of rest and provides him with the easy opportunity of stating an argument or a moral. The reader is deceived: for the requirement of this art is that one shall state a case without appearing to do so. . . . Vigny is always concrete. He is various and resilient in feeling and in portraiture. The poor quartermaster is blown up at Vincennes but the tragic irony of this perfunctory death is effective because we had seen the old man in his youth, in his fairy tale love affair, his love of homely music, in his fussing care and his fantastic life-long luck. Vigny has taken care to move us; his very arguments about the military life are feelings purged of personal rancor. His second virtue is that of surprise. When we meet the broken officer who is trailing through the mud of Flanders, with a mad girl in the cart behind him, we expect some tale of the misery of war, but it turns out to be far worse, an affair of political execution and the sea. The soldier has been ordered to shoot the girl's lover and he has saddled himself with his guilt. The officer with the malacca cane in the next story is similarly engaged in expiation. By doing their duty all his soldiers isolate themselves from humanity and accept a guilt which they cannot forget, and which is not "their fault." They are the martyrs of society. The event which causes this, in every case, is always astonishing, sudden and fearful.

Vigny has an exquisite sensibility to atmosphere and place. One will not easily forget the Flanders road, the attack on the Château at Reims, the simple barrack scenes at Vincennes or the long, dull, noiseless night in Paris deserted on the eve of the Revolution; such scenes have the supreme deceptive and allaying effect found only in the great storytellers. . . . [At] the critical moment of action, this quiet and reflective writer breaks into unforgettable physical detail. It is detail, uniquely of the occasion, which a writer of stories must always seek. . . . These crises are burned in all their special detail upon the reader's mind, as the outline of the quartermaster's body was printed by blast on the wall. One never forgets the physical scene which has been exactly caught from the chaos of feeling by a cool artist.

The admirable thing in *The Military Necessity* is the novel and unobtrusive interweaving of story and argument. Again and again, when we think we are about to be fobbed off with an anecdote or a memory, we find Vigny going much further. Though the story of the malacca cane culminates in the episode at the Château, it has taken us through the life of Admiral Collingwood, through a consideration of the character of Bonaparte and the seductions and errors of the idea of glory. It has discussed whether we shall serve men or principles; it has discussed the dehumanization of man; the acceptance of retribution; the fact that ultimately life will deny us justice. We are always in deeper than we expect; we retrieve the idea of "the military necessity," just at the moment when it seemed forgotten and when false freedom seemed to be breaking in. The book does set up against the amorphous literature of our day, the dramatic blessings of an original and ingenious sense of form, the value of a decisive sense not merely of material but of fundamental subject. The latter is what we lack today. Vigny's life suggests that subjects are best found by writers who submit themselves to an intolerable spiritual pressure. (pp. 379-82)

V. S. Pritchett, "The Military Necessity," in his The Living Novel & Later Appreciations, *revised edition, Random House, 1964, pp. 376-82.*

ALBERT J. GEORGE (essay date 1964)

[*The following study of Vigny's short narratives* Stello *and* The Military Necessity *focuses on format, tone, content, and exposition of ideas. George concludes that Vigny relied too heavily on his polemical intent to the detriment of the narrative, maintaining that "his constant interruptions and persistent didacticism almost destroyed his fictional world."*]

Although Alfred de Vigny cherished his reputation as a poet as much as Lamartine or Hugo, he paid closer attention to the short prose forms. He had tried his hand at the historical novel in *Cinq-Mars,* but its lack of success induced him to try more fertile fields [in *Stello; ou Les Consultations du Docteur Noir* and *Servitude et Grandeur militaire*]. Despite the fact that his stories run a good hundred pages each, the plots are simple, the number of incidents restricted, and the cast of characters limited. And whereas history had entangled him in *Cinq-Mars,* now he created a completely fictional world. The brief narratives still betrayed a passion for philosophical theses but the ideas gained force, not through the ponderous majesty of the historical romance, but by repetition in thrice-told tales.

The trilogy of *Les Consultations du Docteur Noir* stemmed from an idea that obsessed Vigny. In *Cinq-Mars* he had dreamed of the poet as ruler in a coming age of intelligence, but this expectation died of blight during the July Revolution. From high optimism Vigny swung to dejected pessimism. Using the case histories of Gilbert, a contemporary of Louis XV, Chatterton, an English poet of the late eighteenth century, and André Chénier, he portrayed three victims of social injustice to underscore the thesis that poetry stood to lose under any form of government. (p. 141)

[The trilogy consists of] conversations between Stello, a poet, and Doctor Noir, a mysterious physician with the ageless experience of the Wandering Jew. Both characters symbolize aspects of Vigny at war with each other in a dialogue over the author's problems. Stello represents the heart, the "divine" side; Doctor Noir stands for "life," the rational approach. The latter's reasoning always reduces Stello to silence; he is sad and cynical about human behavior, the antithesis of the sulking poet. Vigny polarized the pair to reveal the ambivalence of his own attitudes and to describe the rise and fall of a romantic dream.

The entire work concerns a call the doctor made to cure Stello of the "blue devils." . . . Surprisingly, since the subject indicated serious treatment, Vigny adopted a light touch. The poet and his mentor showed a whimsical illogicality, emphasizing the unsuspected importance to human events of the infinitely small.

Vigny, in effect, tried to marry the traditional French manner of storytelling to Sterne's techniques. The three tales were told in a straightforward fashion, with interjections by Stello, followed by the doctor's explanations. In contrast to his manner in *Cinq-Mars,* Vigny adopted a bantering tone when introducing the major characters. Stello was sketched vaguely as a child favored by destiny, happy and lucky, whose spells of dejection were cured by Doctor Noir, Vigny's version of a psychiatrist. The grave and cold physician, whom Vigny never delineated, guaranteed to cure Stello's migraines by making him understand his mental condition. (pp. 141-42)

Vigny's other short narratives, incorporated in *Servitude et Grandeur militaire,* closely resemble Doctor Noir's first consultation. Three tales concern another set of social outcasts, this time the military. Remembering the dreary futility of his own service, Vigny prefaced the trilogy with a disquisition on the fate of the modern soldier, lionized in war, a pariah in peace. . . . Writing from the bitterness of personal tragedy, he broadened his own experience into that of everyman by seeking the general in the particular.

Once again he attacked the false gods of contemporary society, although, in direct contrast to Lamartine and Hugo, he ridiculed the practice of creating a public personality. No such "singerie littéraire" [literary antics] could make him hide his essential beliefs, so he proposed to defend his position by exposing the ingratitude of a whole nation. (pp. 145-46)

By the time Vigny came to write [the three stories in *Servitude et Grandeur militaire,*] *Laurette, ou le Cachet rouge, La Veillée de Vincennes,* and *La Canne de jonc* . . . , his conception of short fiction had stabilized. The tales move chronologically as in *Stello,* but this time they concern the period from the Directory to the second emigration. Doctor Noir and Stello were gone, replaced by the omniscient *I* in three illustrations of military abnegation, the theme of the struggle between blind obedience and personal conscience. (p. 146)

[In the second story, *La Veillée de Vincennes,*] Vigny used a structure based on Doctor Noir's first consultation: an introduction in which two men discussed the main point of the tale and related it to the general argument, an anecdote interspersed with reminders of the main theme, and an epilogue that stressed the principal points. The technique had worked well in *Stello,* but here Vigny seemed only to be following a pattern. He and Timoléon might well argue for the rights of the military, but the old soldier seems unbelievable. (p. 148)

The old recipe failed because the plot had little connection with the principal thesis. Neither Mathurin's love story nor his neglect can be associated with responsibility or love of danger. Moreover, Vigny and Timoléon substituted poorly for Stello and his strange doctor. Timoléon, about to leave the service to please his fiancée, contributed only his presence, his dilemma remaining extraneous to the argument. Instead of considering the difficulties of the professional soldier, Vigny approached the sentimentality of a Lamartine. . . . Stuffed with emotional recollections of the author's military career, the tale has little unity; even the interruptions meander. Timoléon interrupted the adjutant's anecdote to poke fun at contemporary literary fads, unaware of the unconscious irony of his remarks. Vigny attempted to pull the plot together by using a symbol, a hen and her chicks living under a cannon, but even the picture of a belligerent chicken that disliked the pacifist bourgeois could not rescue a badly planned narrative.

In the third episode, *La Vie et la Mort du Capitaine Renaud ou la Canne de jonc,* Vigny abandoned the device of the two friends to repeat "word for word" a story told him by its hero. (pp. 148-49)

The real hero of [this] narrative is Napoleon, even though legitimist Vigny tried to depict the imperial epic as the work of a power-mad general. The key scene occurred when Napoleon browbeat the Pope, performing like a spoiled adolescent. Collingwood was used antithetically as a modern Bayard while Renaud moved from blind adoration of ruthlessness incarnate to comprehension of devoted service to country and, finally, to the paradoxical position of soldier-pacifist. In the

end, the legendary Napoleon won over both the captain and Vigny. . . .

In his effort to communicate to even the dullest, Vigny created a black and white story in which the major characters assumed allegorical proportions at the cost of verisimilitude. Napoleon was a petty, egotistical tyrant, Collingwood a maritime Washington. While establishing this antithesis, Vigny . . . overlooked the problem of historical accuracy. . . . (p. 149)

Because Vigny understood the brief narrative as an instrument for philosophizing, his thesis often dictated the arrangement of the fictional elements. He tended to overload simple anecdotes, and his constant interruptions and persistent didacticism almost destroyed his fictional world. In the *Canne de jonc* the villain overshadowed characters who supposedly portrayed the correct attitudes. Renaud became only an observer who, after the skirmish, faced the dilemma of the soldier who refuses to kill. The major symbol referred not to his struggle to attain Collingwood's concept of honor, but to the irrationality of war. The good people emerged only as pale shadows in a world dominated by the gigantic man of action. Since Vigny sought in brief fiction only a vehicle for ideas, his work suffered from a kind of bifocalism of thesis and narrative, to the detriment of the latter. He left the possibility of subtleties in prose fiction, the use of implication rather than exposition, unrecognized. In effect, he preferred the more congenial medium of poetry. (p. 150)

> *Albert J. George, "The Major Romantics," in his* Short Fiction in France: 1800-1850, *Syracuse University Press, 1964, pp. 135-65.**

FRANK PAUL BOWMAN (essay date 1965)

[*In his explication of* Les destinées, *Bowman turns to other works by Vigny, including* Chatterton, Stello, *"Moïse," and his journals and letters, to illuminate Vigny's conception of the purpose of poetry. Bowman finds that many of the poetic qualities that critics consider faults, including confusing metaphors, historical inaccuracies, unrealistic details, and didactic elements, were intentional on Vigny's part. In describing Vigny's theory of the role of the poet, Bowman summarizes the arguments of modern critics with his contention that "Vigny differs from other Romantics in insisting that the poet is seer but not total seer; that he is also a craftsman; that his goal is didactic, not expressive; that his audience is a future rather than present one; that a fable is needed to express an idea."*]

[*Destinées,* or *Poèmes philosophiques*] was the work to which Vigny gave his greatest care and highest hopes, but the poems seem to be falling into oblivion, and are open to many criticisms. They often make contradictory points. One attacks woman, another terms her man's only salvation. One attacks material progress, another praises scientific advances. The reader suspects Vigny was either dishonest or inconsistent. Some tell a moving story—as in '**La Mort du loup**'—but Vigny ruins it by adding bombastic lines which draw out the moral lesson. Others seem disparate collections of topical material. '**La Maison du berger**' offers ideas on railroads, politics, women, nature, city vs. solitude and the values of poetry. . . . Is this what Vigny meant when he spoke of poetry as an immortal diamond, forever shedding light on humanity? Some at least have the diamond's coldness; '**L'Esprit pur**' lacks lyricism, colour, warmth—the qualities usually associated with Romantic poetry. Vigny is blithely indifferent to historical accuracy. '**Wanda**' misdates a battle and the death of a Czar; providing the dates is bad enough, but they are wilfully wrong. Others cannot be reconciled with realism. Vigny was familiar with hunting, but no hunt ever resembled the one described in '**La Mort du loup**'. Important details are beyond belief. . . . Vigny's confusing metaphors occur not in emotional out-pourings but in didactic, philosophical poems. The reader is tempted to conclude that by any standards this is very bad poetry indeed. (p. 359)

In *Chatterton* and *Stello*, in '**Moïse**' and other poems, in journals and letters, Vigny discusses extensively the poet's role in society, his notion of poetry, his poems and the poems of others. These remarks provide certain postulates for looking at *Les Poèmes philosophiques;* they show that what may seem involuntary blemishes were what he wanted to write. Several descriptions of how he wrote poems date from his later life. In the most detailed, from 1860, he states that he received an idea which moved him deeply and meditated on it lengthily as it circled through his mind, greeting and perfecting it each time. Then he chose its setting, a historical period, and studied that period for the material which would best manifest the idea, until he found the point where idea and setting united in 'la vérité de l'art', where the reality of detail rose to the ideal of thought. . . . [He] is as concerned with consonance of setting and ideas as he is with fable. The fable comes almost inevitably at a certain point in the poem's maturation, whereas he chooses the setting almost rationally. (p. 360)

[Why] write philosophical *poems*? Could not philosophy or the essay serve as well to present ideas? And if they could not because they lacked a fable, could not the novel or the theatre? Vigny would first answer yes, and in his novels and plays saw something similar to his poems. But he always maintained the superiority of poetry. In *Chatterton*, the *poète* is distinguished from *l'homme de lettres* [man of letters] and particularly from *le grand écrivain* [the great writer] by his reveries and ecstasies, by his contact with Empyrean. Philosophy and history aim at a systematic statement of total truth which Vigny, reflecting Cousin, felt could not be attained; poetry aimed at a beautiful statement of partial truth. Image, fable and prosody serve to create that beauty. . . . He thought prose was usually *more* moving than poetry—because it could encompass wider aspects of existence—but that really superior poetry, by its beauty and its contact with 'le Ciel', produced a 'ravissement extatique' [ecstatic rapture] prose could never know. . . . (p. 362)

[Vigny] differs from other Romantics in insisting that the poet is seer but not total seer; that he is also a craftsman; that his goal is didactic, not expressive; that his audience is a future rather than present one; that a fable is needed to express an idea, which fable is discovered only in conjunction with or after the discovery of an appropriate image-field. We reserve some conjectures about the significance of these theses for the history of poetry for our conclusion, and shall now see how they help read *Les Poèmes philosophiques*.

Because of his didactic intent, Vigny wanted to give the *Poèmes philosophiques* a structure, and they possess more architecture than most Romantic collections, though less than, say, [Heredia's] *Les Trophées* or [Baudelaire's] *Les Fleurs du Mal*. He often contemplated various orderings of the poems and planned a prose 'recitatif' [rhythmically free narrative passage] for each one which would explain its content and function in the series. After '**Le Mont des Oliviers**' there was to be a 'revery' on despair, after '**La Colère**' on force, after '**La Sauvage**' on civilization. The resumés are cast in didactic form. . . . Another project added to the volume a resumé of all the poems . . . , followed by a hymm to poetry. These projects were never completed; we may be grateful, for they would have made the didacticism overwhelming. But probably they were not finished because the collection's architecture was never sufficiently clear to Vigny. The *Poèmes philosophiques* do move from pessimism to optimism—which is the major objection to giving the whole collection the title of the pessimistic first poem, though even its conclusion is interrogative, not pessimistic. But this move toward hope hardly fulfills his ambitions for the collection. (p. 363)

One reason the collection could never be 'la synthèse de tout' [synthesis of everything] . . . was that Vigny was caught up in antitheses. Toward women, for instance, the hatred of '**La Colère**' exists with the adoration of '**La Maison**', to which one must add lubricity and an inhibiting timidity. This '*mari tendre et infidèle*' could hardly offer a synthetic statement about the battle of the sexes. Toward nature, his attitude varies from admiration to its malediction as cruel and indifferent. He differs from Hugo, as Saulnier observed, in seeing opposite values inhering *in* a given state of affairs—servitude *et* grandeur militaires. (pp. 363-64).

'*L'art est la vérité choisie*' [Art is a select truth.] is a common thesis of all Romantic esthetics. . . . Art presents certain truths in all their intensity rather than striving for a meaningless panorama. The poet-seer perceives *certain* ideas and develops them. He cannot perceive all ideas, or offer a synthesis. The *Poèmes philosophiques* possess unity of form, but not of content; if they did, they would lose all poetic value. Their very excellence demands that they be contradictory with one another.

This intense development of certain elements occurs within each poem. In studying these poetic procedures, we shall pay special attention to '**La Colère de Samson**,' for its source is easily available, and we can see what changes Vigny made and why.

His didactic purpose is evident. He introduces maxims which succinctly state his message at central points and at the end of the poem. 'La Femme est toujours Dalila.' 'La femme est un être impur de corps et d'âme.' 'L'homme a toujours besoin d'amour,' [Woman is always a Dalila. Woman is a corporally and spiritually impure being. Man always needs love.] etc. These examples illustrate how the maxims depend on context. They state only partial truths, and categorize from the particular statement the poem makes. Vigny always refers to an anecdote as an *exemple* [example]; individuals are symbolic of a class or of an historic force, and become capitalized abstractions. Dalila becomes the symbol of Woman, Samson of Man. . . . But if, for Vigny, the particular is only significant as a symbol of the general, this does not mean that Dalila is all women— only that she has general validity since she illustrates an idea. There must be a relation between particular and general if the poem is to have meaning; but the general has poetic, not scientific, validity. (pp. 364-65)

[Vigny's] 'philosophical' purpose is balanced by an immense concern with creating proper tone. The first ten lines of '**La Colère**' are uniquely devoted to this end. The next twenty-four, instead of beginning the action, describe Samson and Dalila physically and psychologically, and thus still serve primarily to create tone. The links between these descriptive passages and the didactic elements of the poem are numerous. . . . The elements of the setting are selected not for their own sake or for their historical accuracy, but in order to create a tone consonant with the major thesis of the poem. Each, by some particular aspect, contributes to the general impression. If the reader is willing to see in them only that particular aspect, they help create a vivid poetic experience. If he is not willing to delimit their connotations, the poem goes off in all directions. If he wonders how Samson can be in the midst of a vast, hot, dry desert, full of wild beasts, and yet be surrounded by conspiring Philistines, he will find the poem hopeless. He must sense why solitude, silence, the struggle for survival in a menacing world should be evoked at the beginning of the poem.

Many of Vigny's betrayals of the canons of poetic taste can be explained by this willingness to use words for the value of some connotations and indifference to other connotations. This is why:

He is very willing to introduce elements which in all ways except one seem dissonant. Vv. 66-7, whose precise physical detail offers an effective anti-masculine argument, might seem out of place; but they validly show the animal nature of women, and that is sufficient justification for them. Their other implications are to be neglected. (pp. 365-66)

A metaphor is often justified only because it amplifies one quality; its other qualities are irrelevant and should be disregarded. Take vv. 51-2: 'Plus fort il sera né, mieux il sera vaincu, / Car plus le fleuve est grand et plus il est ému.' We should not seek here the elements of a water image structure; water imagery is out of place in this fiery desert. Nor does Samson in any way resemble a river. The metaphor's point is the more of A, the more of B; the greater the strength, the greater the violence. . . . Again and again what matters is the action involved in the metaphor, not the connotations of the objects evoked. We might term this a *verbal* (as opposed to *substantive*) metaphor; by setting side by side two essentially unlike things, Vigny underlines the one action they have in common. This insistence on a common action explains why Vigny often personifies nature—so that it can act. . . . His most successfully developed images describe violent motion. His comparisons, in nineteen cases out of twenty, establish equivalences and only rarely degrees of comparison. But the equivalence is attached to the action involved, not to other qualities. (pp. 366-67)

[Vigny] willingly disrupts style-levels and connotational fields. In ['La Sauvage'] he associates the tritest of imagery with brazen modern inventions. Many of his metaphors refer to classical literature; others treat of railroads. 'Les Oracles' combines its obscure topical allusions to Louis-Philippe, the Divan, the 'bascule' of Garnier-Pagès, etc., some of which cannot even be identified with certainty, with references to the Bible, Ulysses, Hamlet or Cromwell. Vigny here enlarges the scope of poetic language. . . . Vigny is carrying out the Romantic programme of breaking down style-levels. But he is not simply trying to introduce handkerchiefs into tragedy; he is suggesting that diverse levels of experience, put side by side, can be mutually meaningful. (p. 367)

Vigny, whose form is no form traditional and who is no more didactic than Mallarmé, never achieves the density of the later poet; the difficulties which in Vigny seem bad poetry, when compounded force on us a new way of reading the poem. . . . One is tempted to conclude, in Hegelian terms, that Vigny, instead of creating a Symbolist synthesis, was caught in a limbo between Romantic thesis and Parnassian antithesis, but this is a view of nineteenth-century French poetry no one could take seriously. But it is helpful to remember that Vigny was working on *Les Poèmes philosophiques* while Nerval was writing *Les*

Chimères, Baudelaire *Les Fleurs du Mal* (hardly less peppered with Platonic abstractions); that they were finally published when Mallarmé was twenty-two years old, and should perhaps be read in terms of what came after rather than what came before. (pp. 368)

> Frank Paul Bowman, "The Poetic Practices of Vigny's 'Poèmes philosophiques'," *in* The Modern Language Review, *Vol. LX, No. 3, July, 1965, pp. 359-68.*

ROBERT T. DENOMMÉ (essay date 1969)

[*The following is a close study of the symbols, sources, style, form, and themes of many of the most important poems in* Poèmes antiques et modernes *and* Les destinées. *Denommé contends that Vigny's poetry is "little more than the symbolic manifestations of his ideas," and he examines the poet's representation of himself through symbol.*]

The outer reserve or discretion that characterizes the poetry of Alfred de Vigny stands in sharp contrast to the more facile and effusive lyricism of such notable counterparts as Lamartine, Hugo, and Musset. A heavy reliance upon epic, dramatic, and narrative devices strips Vigny's verse of the type of directness of expression and confessional tone that are so readily identifiable in the work of most French Romanticists. A conscious artist and technician, Vigny sought out the philosophical implications in his personal experience before transposing it into his poetry. Many of his poems unveil the effort of quiet and painstaking discernment; some poems may strike us, at first, as impersonal and generalized reflections on the human predicament. If Vigny is usually referred to as the "philosopher" of Romantic poetry, it is more in recognition of the coherence of his doctrine than for any real profundity of thought. To a great extent, Vigny went to considerable lengths to camouflage his personal ideas and emotions in his poetry. Indeed, his poems are little more than the symbolic manifestations of his ideas. Recurrent use is made of symbols in order to endow his thought with a sense of concreteness of expression and of dramatic form. Yet the symbols utilized by Vigny contain the clue to his identity as a Romantic poet. As concretizations of his ideas, the symbols resorted to in the collections, *Poèmes antiques et modernes (Old and Modern Poems)* and *Les Destinées (The Fates)*, do not always suggest easy and ready identifications with the ideas that are expressed. . . . An examination of Vigny's symbols demonstates that, by and large, they serve as paper-thin disguises for the poet himself. (pp. 63-4)

The cautious yet firm optimism that the poet voiced in the posthumously-published *Les Destinées* . . . was, to a degree, fashioned from the pessimistic stance of his earlier years. His pessimism was rooted in his own interpretation of history and in his observations of reality. . . . It cannot be denied that his poetical works do translate his disenchantment with life: his principal themes underscore man's inexorable fate and destiny, the treachery of women, the indifference of God and nature and the abject loneliness which the poet or the superior man experiences. Yet as early as 1823, Vigny reveals in his poem, **"Le Déluge" ("The Flood")**, a certain oscillation between doubt and faith in God and man that ultimately resulted in the mitigated optimism decreed in his last and most important collection, *Les Destinées*. The expression of confidence arrived at in *Les Destinées* is inspired by his constructive stoicism or resignation to his fate. Bequeathed Voltaire's practical philosophy of human progress, Vigny preaches from a distance on the necessity of man's adjustment to his condition: we must act as if we hoped. . . . Vigny's conception of a human brotherhood stems in part from his systematic rejection of any theoretical or metaphysical explanation of the human condition. Confronted by a silent God and an indifferent nature, man must learn to grope courageously and stoically toward his own betterment. Therein lies the potential greatness of man in Vigny's estimation. His religion is the religion of ideas that preaches a limited faith in human progress. The priests and guides of such a religion—the poets—must entrust their fame and appreciation to posterity.

The *Poèmes antiques et modernes* of 1826 comprise twenty-one poems which are divided, according to inspiration, into three groups: the mystical poems, the ancient poems, and the modern poems. The first group contains such notable pieces as "**Moïse**," "**Le Déluge**," and "**Eloa ou la soeur des anges**" ("**Eloa or Sister or the Angels**"), all of which assert Vigny's growing sense of pessimism through his adaptation of biblical figures as symbols of modern man's predicament. The Book of Antiquity includes the poem, "**La Fille de Jephté**" ("**Jephthah's Daughter**"), which translates Vigny's protest against unjust chastisement, but the greater number of poems in the Homeric cycle are little more than pale adaptations of André Chénier's pagan poems of the preceding century. The unevenness of the Modern Poems is somewhat offset by the memorable "**Le Cor**" ("**The Horn**"), a successful reverie evoking the heroic medieval legend of Roland and Charlemagne at the pass of Roncevaux in the Pyrenees. In all, the four or five distinguished poems contains in the *Poèmes antiques et modernes* point to the generally significant verse of *Les Destinées*. (pp. 64-6)

[Inserted] into the so-called "mystical" cycle of the *Poèmes antiques et modernes*, "**Moïse**" remains Vigny's most elaborate pronouncement on the function and position of the nineteenth-century Romantic poet. . . . As he himself so readily acknowledged, the Moses of the *Poèmes antiques et modernes* is not precisely the Moses of the Old Testament; he is rather the poet's convenient symbol of the genius or the superior man. . . . The parallelism between the prophet and the poet is the major theme elicited in "**Moïse**." Like the prophet, the poet is elected by God to share in his comprehensive vision of creation. Just as the prophet's special powers are derived from an inner force—his collaboration with God, so too are the poet's vision and articulateness derived from the inner forces of an inspiration that is not always corroborated by exterior reality. The prophet-poet, however, must pay an awful price for his special powers: his superiority denies him membership in the fraternity of men. (pp. 66-7)

Like the type of Romantic hero later to be evolved by Vigny in such poems as "**La Mort du loup**" ("**The Death of the Wolf**") and "**La Maison du berger**," the Moses of the *Poèmes antiques et modernes* is a stoical Moses, willing to accept the responsibilities of such an attitude. He is conscious that his position and the nature of his mission alienate him from the people he wishes to help; they are unable to understand and appreciate the enormity of his sacrifice in their behalf. Vigny's Moses offers psychological resistance to the accomplishment of the will of God; consequently, he is made to appear more human than the Moses of the Old Testament. As a kind of allegory of the genius and the superior man, the Moses described in the poem emerges as a Romantic character so readily identifiable with the poet himself. (pp. 67-8)

[In "**Le Déluge**"] Vigny asserts his metaphysical pessimism basing himself upon a biblical episode to underscore the tragic undertones of man's predicament. . . . "**Le Déluge**" bespeaks the poet's defiant expression of protest against the kind of God who would so indifferently punish the innocent and the just along with the wicked. The poem's conclusion is punctuated with religious skepticism; at the very least, it states the poet's waivering between doubt and faith. . . . Vigny manipulates biblical material in such a way so as to make it conform to the particular theme that he wishes to project. The last line, for example, betrays a distortion of the Old Testament account. The biblical reference to the rainbow at the end of the deluge was meant to symbolize God's reconciliation with man; Vigny's transposition of the account underscores his cynical view of the matter. (p. 68)

The poem, "**Le Mont des Oliviers**," demonstrates a greater indebtedness to the poet's own inspiration . . . than to the scriptural accounts of Matthew, Mark, Luke, and John. Vigny's Christ of the Mount of Olives emerges as a strikingly vivid incarnation of the poet himself with his sense of frustration and helplessness. Vigny's intention is made explicit in the section ending the poem, "**Le Silence**." The calm and almost emotionless language of the final admonition strikes out against traditional belief in Divine Providence. Vigny's implied thesis is singularly reminiscent of the conclusion in Voltaire's *Candide*: man is meant to live in metaphysical anguish; he must rather try to work out his own destiny, courageously and stoically, by his advocacy of human progress and fellowship with men. (p. 70)

["**Le Mont des Oliviers**"] underscores the dramatic confrontation between humanity and the implacable will of God. Unlike the Christ of the New Testament, Vigny's Christ is incapable of resigning himself to divine decree. He has evolved into an essentially more humanized Messiah; he implores God the Father to endow humanity with the happy certitude and the confident hope necessary for the endurance of pain and suffering. In "**Le Mont des Oliviers**," Christ's entreaties to his father go unanswered: "the evening sky remains dark, and God does not reply." Vigny's Christ leaves the world in sadness, knowing that he has failed to accomplish his primary mission: to rid humanity of its doubt and anguish. The poet's Romanticism is fused with the religious pessimism that is so discernible. "**Le Mont des Oliviers**" is first of all Vigny's own interpretation of the mission and message of Christ. The poet has transformed the Christ of Scripture into the type of social humanitarian that asserted himself in the France of the 1830's and 1840's. The poem emphasizes his humanity more than his claim to divinity; rather than the son of God, he is the son of Man who suffers and commiserates with humanity and seeks to better man's plight through the abolition of violence. By his frequently effective use of melodramatic devices—such as the startling antitheses between the white of hope and the black of despair—Vigny has succeeded in unifying the events of the biblical account with the theme that he meant to convey. (pp. 71-2)

In Vigny's estimation, it is evident that Christianity has failed in its social and humanitarian mission. However masked and restrained its language may appear, the second part of "**Le Mont des Oliviers**" points an accusing finger at God for all the evil and injustice in the world. Vigny's adroit manipulation of antithesis between the terms that suggest hope and despair accounts for much of the poignancy of the section. The increased use of words connoting despair anticipates the final message reserved for the last part of the poem. Man, with the departure of the Messiah that failed, is ultimately left to his own resources to achieve his destiny. . . . Both the tone and the content of **"Le Mont des Oliviers"** show the evolution undergone by the Romanticists in their handling of religious subjects. Whatever liberties in style and interpretation may be discernible in Lamartine's "Le Crucifix," for example, the kind of religiosity of sentiment prompted by the death of Madame Charles still retains a basic identification with traditional Christian belief. Vigny's **"Le Mont des Oliviers"** consciously avoids any such identification. The poet's negative attitude toward the effectiveness of religious institutions in meeting the needs of modern man explains his reluctance to share the enthusiasm of such writers as Lamartine, Lamennais, and Montalembert who hoped to refashion and modernize the social framework of Christianity.

Considered by some critics as the most important single poem in the collection, *Les Destinées*, **"La Maison du berger"** . . . was meant to serve as the prologue for a projected series of philosophical poems which failed to materialize. . . . [The] poem impresses us as a cross between an imagined and real experience recorded from the vantage point of the poet's later years. On the surface, **"La Maison du berger"** may strike the reader as an inordinately long and confused piece whose principal themes seem more disjointed than linked together by any kind of unity. Roughly divided into six major sections, the poem is written in strophes of seven alexandrine lines each. The heaviness of form that results, including several notable instances of embarrassing awkwardness, conforms, in a sense, to the weightiness of the subject matter in **"La Maison du berger."** Indeed, most of the major themes developed in the eleven poems that constitute the posthumous collection of *Les Destinées* are touched upon in this long and somewhat rambling poem. The first part of **"La Maison du berger"** is an invitation extended to Eva, the poet's companion and a composite of the qualities of the ideal woman, to flee the city with him and seek out in nature the kind of "austere silence" conducive to reverie and meditation. The tenth strophe suddenly bursts forth with a diatribe against railroads . . . that continues with breathless pace until the twentieth strophe. Then, Vigny begins a meditation on the function of poetry in a world grown more mechanized. His fourth theme praises woman for the influence that she exerts upon the poet and his poetry; her love for him prevents him from growing insensitive to the needs of his fellow man in the comfortable isolation of his retreat in nature. The last two sections, comprising Part Three, voice the poet's refusal to see in nature a benevolent mother and reassert in exalted language the love of man for woman. (pp. 72-5)

Despite Vigny's exalted praise of nature as the source of reverie and meditation for man in a world complicated by ugly and dangerous mechanization, the final strophes of **"La Maison du berger"** underscore its indifference and its insensitivity to man. Nature offers man but temporary refuge from the distraction and turmoil of the city; the poet must delve within himself to extract the resources that will assure his well-being. Contrary to Lamartine who saw in nature a source of consolation for man, Vigny views nature with distrust and caution. . . . On the philosophical level, **"La Maison du berger"** resists the establishment of the kind of association between nature and poet that is generally understood by Ruskin's conception of the pathetic fallacy. Vigny's ultimate refusal to identify so closely with nature endows most of his lyricism with an appearance of aloofness or cold detachment that offers itself in sharp contrast to the more effusive nature poetry of Lamartine, Hugo, and Musset. For Vigny, nature does not supply the unifying principle that assures man of his desired equilibrium.

Nature is revealed to be little more than the convenient receptacle wherein the poet is allowed to reflect and meditate in relative peace and isolation, and where he may attempt to solve the problems that prevent him from achieving self-definition.

As the symbolic portrait of stoical resignation, **"La Mort du loup"** (**"The Death of the Wolf"**) lays bare, once again, Vigny's habit of deliberately distorting fact and reality in order to make the imagery of his poems conform more readily to his interpretation of certain attitudes. The wolf in his poem, for example, possesses great dignity, beauty, and an urgent sense of purpose, qualities that are hardly associated with wolves in everyday contexts. Vigny reverses the usual order of supposition in **"La Mort du loup:"** instead of representing the enemy of man and civilization, man and civilization are represented as the enemies of the innocent and noble wolf. . . . Any sense of irony that could have been achieved by so focusing the main theme on the wolf family is, to a large extent, cancelled by Vigny's frequent insistence upon details that are too pointedly realistic in a poem containing such philosophical pretentions. The *faire voir* realism of **"La Mort du loup"** detracts from the basic credibility of the theme because of the falseness of the situation. The exalted language of the conclusion (Part Three) provides a striking antithesis to the two preceding sections that relate the hunt and the death of the wolf in terms that wreak of heavy realism. While the vividness of these two sections contribute undeniably to the elucidation of the final thesis, their formal relationship to the third part produces such a jarring effect as to destroy the unity of the poem. Although not a souvenir poem in the manner of Hugo's "Tristesse d'Olympio," ("Olympio's Lament"), Vigny's poem in treatment of language and in total emtional effect, bears a distinct kinship to it. Both poems rely so heavily upon concrete details that are pointedly realistic that they are unable to extract any universalized response from the reader. **"La Mort du loup"** is far from being the idealized expression of the attitude of stoical resignation that is implied in the last section. (pp. 75-8)

Stylistically, the whole poem unfolds in the form of a triangle with the setting, the *paysage* [landscape], representing the world as it appears to the poet: dark, gloomy, sinister, and filled with all types of traps and deceits. The wolf symbolizes the poet's noble reaction to this situation. Man, the hunter, represents the despicable, negative attitude of a thoughtless "civilization." The final conclusion that we are asked to accept is that the wolf's stance, in the poem, is more sensibly attuned to conditions as they really are. Thus, the wolf emerges as the easy personification of the kind of stoical resignation which vigny has been suggesting throughout **"La Mort du loup."** The final admonition, stripped of any religious allusion, "To complain, to cry out, to pray—all are equally cowardly," fits more neatly into the secular program of intellectual progress implied in the title poem of *Les Destinées* than a poem like **"Le Mont des Oliviers."** (p. 79)

[**"La Flûte"**] is a reworking of the theme presented in **"La Mort du loup,"** but this time within the more recognizable framework of the well-known myth of Sisyphus. Despite the working of the poet's imagination in this poem, the effect is largely one of a narration somewhat more objectively related. . . . In **"La Flùte"** Vigny equates idealism with the ultimate achievement of some more perfect afterlife, and the attendant limitations and failures of man with this life. . . . [The poem] is also a statement of the poet's sense of frustration when confronted by the inadequacy of his expression. The beggar's flute emerges as the personification of the written poem that is achieved in anxiety by the poet. Like the mendicant who kisses his flute so lovingly in the poem, the poet too comes to acknowledge his gift to communicate with his fellow man, however imperfect his talent may manifest itself in his work. (pp. 79-81)

"La Bouteille à la mer" ("Bottle in the Sea") is a reinforcement of the two themes which Vigny had suggested in **"La Flûte."** Bearing the subtitle, **"Counsel to an Unknown Young Man,"** the poem was initially written as the final piece in *Les Destinées*. The didactic intention of **"La Bouteille à la mer"** comes close to making it a program poem. In it, Vigny likens the position of the poet to that of the captain of a sinking vessel at sea; fated to die in the distressed ship, the seaman carefully records crucial information which he inserts into a small bottle that is flung into the sea in the hope that it will eventually be retrieved. Thus, his death is not in vain if future generations obtain and understand the ideas that he has bequeathed them. **"La Bouteille à la mer"** is Vigny's expression of hope and confidence for the future of mankind. The poet, like the sea captain, gives generously of himself to benefit posterity. The concerted efforts of poets and scientists will bring aobut the eventual reign of reason and enlightenment to the world. In a sense, the poem is an affirmation of the poet's faith in ideas as a benevolent force.

Vigny's belief in the progress and enlightenment of humanity through reason is patently buoyed by an intuitively-felt knowledge of the presence of a final benevolent Providence that accepts and encourages such efforts at the attainment of human perfection. It is the assurance behind the poet's asserted belief that distinguishes his messge from that of his more rationalistic counterparts of the eighteenth century and that imprints his verse with the indelible mark of inspiration and imagination that has become associated with French Romanticism. (pp. 81-2)

"L'Esprit pur" ("The Pure Spirit"), written six months before Vigny's death, may be considered as a legacy which the poet bequeaths to posterity. Addressed to Eva, the ten strophes of the poem define with pommeling thrusts his confidence in the forthcoming reign of mind over matter. **"L'Esprit pur"** also reaffirms Vigny's philosophical independence. If the opening poem of *Les Destinées* confirmed the pre-Christian interpretation of fate and destiny, the final poem of the collection, **"L'Esprit pur"** is a clear rejection of positivistic currents as the new force in man's life. As [the French critic] Verdun Saulnier so adroitly interprets the message, **"L'Esprit pur"** is Vigny's clever transposition of the religious significance of the dove of the Holy Spirit in Catholic dogma to secularized victory of mind over matter as effected through the ideas of the enlightened poet. The religion of ideas alluded to in **"La Bouteille à la mer"** graduates to a level of personal mysticism in **"L'Esprit pur."** Vigny's God of ideas reveals himself in sharp antithesis to the kind of knowledge that is sensuous and concrete. . . . **"L'Esprit pur"** is in a sense, also, the reaffirmation of belief in the genius of the poet. To an extent at least, Vigny's initial pessimism concerning Creation as a work badly botched is reverted into an expression of quiet confidnece and hope. Thus, the eleven poems that constitute the collection, *Les Destinées*, when seen in their relationship to one another, translate attitudes of cautious optimism. Vigny's poetry consciously shuns expressions of sweeping enthusiasm that characterize the verse of such social Romanticists as Lamartine and Hugo. Yet the mystical fervor that punctuates the messages of his counterparts finds its way into his work

in more subtle and gentle doses. . . . The symbols to which Vigny reverts to convey his personal feelings in such collections as the *Poèmes antiques et modernes* and *Les Destinées* frequently produce a steadying and sobering effect on his lyricism. . . . The symbol, in fact, betrays his attempt to avoid the kind of embarrassing indiscretion concomitant with the confessional tone underlying the lyricism that is more exclusively personal. For Vigny, the symbol served as the convenient detour from such effusiveness. It provided the necessary junction between his inspiration and the philosophical attitudes that he insisted on conveying in his verse. At the same time, the symbol acted as veil or a camouflage for whatever personal elements might have been present, allowing him to unfold his ideas with considerably more clarity and objectivity. As a covering agent for the principal theme, the symbol deters the reader from such evidence and prevents the poem from disintegrating into merely an emotionally impassioned plea. A close scrutiny of Vigny's poetry reveals his efforts to endow his inspiration and his thoughts with a poetic form and language that would ensure its survival against the ravages and prejudices of time and place. If the symbol to which he has recourse succeeds in masking the more obvious expressions of his personality, it does not purport to rescue the poem completely from its inherent subjectivity. The symbol merely allows the poem to convey its basic theme with more directness by relegating the subjective elements to the background. (pp. 82-5)

In the *Journal d'un poète*, Vigny defines the creative process as a search for the point at which the meaningful experiences of life can be elevated in order to cross the path of thought. To project his ideas with the kind of forcefulness that he sought, Vigny selected fables that were generally both moving and evocative. The frequently subtle and effective handling of a wide variety of imagery complicated the symbolism of his poems with definite subjective colorations. His insistence upon qualifying certain images to convey such contrasting attitudes as hope and despair, good and evil, doubt and knowledge, for example, bequeaths to such concepts the intimacy of his poet's imagination and inspiration. Vigny relies considerably upon the evocative power of his images to impart the major themes of his poems. By juxtaposition and transposition of many of the auditory and visual images that he employs, he often manages to suggest varying shades and degrees of intensity in his settings. The mood and the tone that emerge from the poetry appear directly but unobtrusively linked to the imagery that is linked or interrelated with the symbolism. Despite the outward form of narrative that the great majority of his poems possess, the *Poèmes antiques et modernes* and *Les Destinées,* for the most part, shun the kind of rhetorical enlargement or embellishment that characterizes some of the more typical Romantic verse in the nineteenth century.

The two major sources of imagery that are found in Vigny's poetry could conceivably have stamped it with the mark of neo-Classicism. Yet Vigny eschews employing the images that he borrows from ancient mythology and Holy Scriptures in any traditional sense. Such learned allusions are instead usually stripped of their more orthodox connotations and are used principally to endow that which is common or prosaic in the human predicatment with the indelible stamp of dignity and authority. (pp. 85-6)

With similar effectiveness, Vigny uses such obvious imagery as the desert sands and the ocean's waters not only to convey the idea of vastness and expansiveness in his poetry, but more especially to suggest with poignancy the situation of the poet in isolation. More intriguing, however, is the author's dual conception of fire imagery; it is described at times as a beneficial force and as a destructive element. In **"La Maison du berger,"** for example, the railroad is equipped with the fiery teeth of destruction as it proceeds in its opposition to man and its eradication of the shepherd's hut. In another section of the same poem, however, fire serves to inflame the enthusiasm and ecstasy that enable the poet to produce his verses. The fact that Vigny is able to ascribe different levels of meaning to his imagery invites the view that, unlike such congeners as Hugo, he possessed no logical, comprehensive view of the world. As Frank P. Bowman has suggested, Vigny's verse is to a degree "a beautified statement of partial truth." (pp. 86-7)

To convey the idea of servility—the great depths to which man has sunk in Vigny's estimation, the familiar imagery of the wild animal and of the beast of burden is employed to good effect in the eleven poems that constitute **Les Destinées.** Somewhat reminiscent of La Fontaine's animals in the *Fables,* Vigny's beasts also serve to delineate particular characteristics of humanity. It should be noted that animals appear only in the most pessimistic sections of poems. By so degrading the portrait of man to the animal level, much of the pessimism of Vigny's personal views announce themselves in an indelible fashion. (p. 87)

The auditory and visual imagery utilized by Vigny in his more philosophical poems convey the sense of the poet's personal identification with often surprising subtlety. The silence of isolation in **"La Maison du berger"** is contrasted with the streamlined, efficient silence of "progress," and the poem issues a moving description of the cries of an oppressed humanity heard above the calm and implacable silence of an indifferent nature. Vigny employs visual images, references to such colors as black and white and red, in those poems that treat of death. . . . If Vigny relies upon the use of black to suggest the complete desolation of man, such colors as green, gold, and azure blue are referred to in order to suggest optimism in the victory of reason and enlightenment over matter. (pp. 88-9)

Vigny chose the voluptuous beauty of poetry to crystallize his philosophy. He selected his imagery for its ability to convey and reinforce his thought and for its beauty, weaving metaphor, color, and symbol together to give expression to the Idea. The metaphors in his poetry, drawn from literature, from nature, and from living creatures, attain a level of highly evocative power. At times, his images may have too strong an effect, as in the case of the dying wolf. It is true that much in his verse lacks the delicacy of charm usually associated with less serious lyricism. Yet, there is great beauty to be found in such descriptive scenes as the desert in **"La Colère de Samson"** and the travel sequence in **"La Maison du berger."** The drama of the metaphorical situation of Vigny's Christ in **"Le Mont des Oliviers"** and that of Samson in **"La Colère de Samson"** captures the reader in the reality of its psychological study. (pp. 89-90)

> *Robert T. Denommé, "Alfred de Vigny, Preacher in an Ivory Tower," in his* Nineteenth Century French Romantic Poets, *Southern Illinois University Press, 1969, pp. 63-90.*

GEOFFREY BRERETON (essay date 1973)

[*Brereton begins with a general discussion of Vigny as a philosophical poet and then divides his poems into two groups, those*

published in Poèmes antiques et modernes *and the later poems of* Les destinées. *Brereton's comments are representative of modern critics' often mixed evaluation of Vigny's style.*]

[Since] Vigny has been called—by himself first and by most critics since—a philosophical poet, we must look at this 'philosophy' briefly before passing on to other aspects of his poems.

At best it is not a doctrine, but only a groping for one. It starts from the fairly constant assumption that mankind are the victims of an inescapable fatality, that unhappiness is their normal lot, and that the nobler they are the more they will suffer. The angel Éloa is damned for her divine pity in Vigny's first considerable poem, the Russian princess in **Wanda** is spiritually destroyed through the same cause in one of his last. The only answer that man can worthily return to the malignity or indifference of the powers which oppress him—whether their name is Fate, God or Nature—is a contemptuous silence. This sterile and static assumption—entirely understandable in Vigny's case— is not of course a philosophy. It barely amounts even to a philosophical approach. It has no reasoned basis, as with Schopenhauer, nor is it fertile as in Leopardi—who in his convulsions of unhappiness opens up perhaps accidentally new perspectives of thought as well as of emotion.

Distinguishing him from the pessimists of his own age, Vigny's pessimism, one might think, should carry him into the twentieth century. But he is not modern either. His disillusionments are not our disillusionments. And when, as occasionally happens, he sheds his pessimism and searches for relief, it is along roads which are no longer open. He thinks he sees daylight in the hope of progress through human intelligence (**Wanda, La Bouteille à la mer**). . . . He also had in him, profoundly ingrained, a religious faith which still insisted that the Deity was benign in spite of all the evidence. (p. 114)

More generally, the religious terminology which he uses and his habit of centering his chief problems upon biblical figures make it difficult to accept him today as a contemporary. The language he speaks is too noble and remote.

The most that can be said of this side of him is that he is a reflective poet—reflecting with the utmost earnestness on much the same overriding question throughout his life. Impersonally though he words his protests, he is basically akin to those other Romantics who openly used the *moi* [self]: he merely gives cosmic form to a personal reaction.

But this does not for a moment diminish the poet. Because his thought was stiff, his verse was too. Rather than a merit or a defect, this is a characteristic. It makes Vigny an odd poet, but only the most prudent anthologist could present him otherwise. And then he would not be Vigny.

Vigny's poems fall roughly into two groups, with a long interval between. The early group is represented by the first edition of the **Poèmes antiques et modernes,** and belongs to his twenties. Published in 1826, it included such poems as **Moïse, Le Déluge** and **Le Cor,** as well as **Éloa** and ten poems reprinted from his first slim volume of 1822 [**Poèmes**]. These latter have a certain historical interest since they originally appeared only two years after Lamartine's **Méditations** and they also announce the picturesque-narrative character of Vigny's later productions. In style, and sometimes in matter, they recall Chénier. . . . (p. 115)

Such poems would not in themselves make any great mark. It was not until he moved from classical to biblical and 'modern' themes—evoking the sombre figure of Moses isolated by Jehovah's choice, or the haunting story of Roland at Roncevaux—Vigny could be seen as an important poet.

From then until his middle forties, he published a mere half-dozen poems. Among them was *La Frégate 'La Sérieuse'* (1829), a sea-poem which, without descending to the colloquial, manages realistic description in a way that the eighteenth-century odes on sea-fights never encompassed. Vigny solved, seemingly without difficulty, the neoclassic dilemma so obtrusive in Chénier and the early Lamartine. On this ground at least his sense of language values is much surer than theirs. Here he succeeds in recapturing, through the mouth of an old sea-captain, something of the atmosphere of the days of Nelson. . . . (p. 116)

Such a poem [as *La Colère de Samson*], and the several others like it [published in *Les Destinées,* which contains the poems of his second main group], is a product less of the intellect than of an imagination soaked in the atmosphere of the Bible. It is perfectly true that Vigny expresses his ideas through descriptions and symbols. It is also true that his work is rich in various textbook Romantic qualities—Orientalism, local colour (the sand and the lions) pushed sometimes as far as the grotesque (the ostrich-egg). But these features are incidental. With him, the visual image came first, coloured, solid, almost palpable. The rest was subservient to it. Summing up his own work in *L'Esprit pur,* he calls his poems *tableaux,* and in *La Maison du berger* he promises to the ideal companion whom he never found a kind of lantern-show of all the conceptions which pass through his mind. . . . (p. 118)

Vigny's *esprits purs,* his angels, his antique characters, seem to have been creatures of his own mind which, to his despair, he recognized as such. He knew that nothing had reached him from outside, but having willed these beings into some sort of existence, he worked on to make them as real as possible. Sometimes, as in an early poem like *Le Cor,* he worked too little and the poem as a whole was clumsy, but the charm of faery remained in isolated passges. . . . (p. 119)

More often, he worked too hard—like a sculptor, as he described himself—hewing with chisel and hammer those ephemeral conceptions which most writers approach with an almost fearful delicacy. And the strangest part is that, with Vigny, they did not evaporate but remained—by the time he had finished with them—with their leaden wings, their bronze feet and their granite attitudes. Awkward, grotesque, unnatural as well as unspiritual, they stand unique in French poetry as a monument to an indomitable will.

Vigny's laborious methods of composition give to his verse, and particularly to his images, a firmness in welcome contrast to the facile vagueness into which Lamartine can degenerate at times. Occasionally, without losing this firmness, Vigny manages to maintain a flow of rhythm which combines the best features of the two extremes. This happened notably in *La Maison du berger,* which, from whatever angle it is considered, is one of the loveliest poems ever produced by a Romantic poet. Part of its attraction springs from technical causes. It is written in seven-line stanzas, rhyming *ababccb.* This well-integrated form, with its flowing feminine rhymes and its final masculine rhyme which seems to clinch rather than close the strophe, seems to have been invented by Vigny. He used it here for the first time, and increasingly in his later poems. (pp. 119-20)

But even in this outstanding poem there is a section . . . of invective against railway-trains, then a modern invention which

Vigny regarded as dangerous. Intellectually, he was perhaps right in condemning the new craze for speed. From a sentimental point of view, the section is almost worth having for the sake of one nostalgic verse in which the poet regrets the old coach journeys, with their slow and keenly tasted sensations. Yet it is very difficult to understand how a writer usually so in tune with his material could have failed to notice that his topical insertion mars the aesthetic unity of his poem as a whole. (pp. 120-21)

[In Vigny's work,] the nineteenth-century doubt (or 'anguish', to use the language of Vigny's contemporary Kierkegaard) can be seen hardening into despair. The characteristic of Vigny is that he was man enough to experience and state it without breaking down into the self-pity of the more feminine and certainly more superficial Musset; but, on the other hand, without the superhuman clairvoyance of Baudelaire, who could see round corners in his own and other people's natures. Vigny's vision, in comparision, is a fixed beam meeting an immovable object. He may he classed as basically Romantic because that object is himself. (p. 121)

> *Geoffrey Brereton, "Alfred de Vigny," in his* An Introduction to the French Poets: Villion to the Present Day, *revised edition, Methuen & Co. Ltd., 1973, pp. 112-21.*

HENRY F. MAJEWSKI   (essay date 1981)

[*The following discussion of Vigny's unfinished novel* Daphné *explores its stylistic and thematic parallels in* Stello, The Military Necessity, *and* Les destinées.]

[Vigny's novel *Daphné* is] an essential work to know for a profound comprehension of his intellectual and artistic development. An historical novel about the Emperor Julian . . . , it merits analysis as another example of the romantic use of history to illuminate contemporary events. Although it is primarily a novel of ideas, it offers a rich tapestry of characters and voices, scenes of nineteenth-century Paris juxtaposed with fourth-century Antioch, and a complex symbolic network which prefigures Vigny's use of myth and symbol in the *Poèmes Philosophiques*. In addition to consideration of the metaphysical questions raised by Julian the Apostate's renunciation of Christianity, the novel develops the theme of the artist and his role in society, and focuses specifically on the power of sign and symbol, the "crystal prèservateur" in relationship to the idea it contains.

Daphné must be read as a preamble to *Les Destinées,* for it is the culmination of Vigny's study of the possibility of action in society by the poet; Julian the Apostate, who is a poet, soldier and nobleman, unites in one figure the three victims of society's contempt. . . . [*Stello*], which concludes that action is impossible for the poet, *Grandeur et servitude militaire* . . . with its portrait of the immorality of blind obedience to society's rules, and *Daphné,* portraying the error of action through religious reform, constitute a trilogy of novels united thematically and structurally. After the completion of *Daphné,* Vigny, officially at least, accepted the advice of his Docteur Noir, devoting himself exclusively to poetry and definitively renouncing the temptation of becoming directly involved in political or social action.

The novel of *Daphné* has a frame which links it formally to *Stello.* The introductory chapters and conclusion contain a dialogue between Stello, the poet "enthousiaste," and his enemy/

friend the Docteur Noir. Stello is once again tempted to act in society; he dreams of influencing the masses of men through his religious spirit, his purified moral vision. The main body of the text was originally designed to contain three "récits" offered by the doctor to dissuade the poet from any social commitment. . . . Vigny finally chose to concentrate the doctor's lesson in only one récit, the story of Julian, which offers the conclusion that religious action is impossible and indeed destructive when undertaken by a man of poetry, or artistic sensibility. The multitude is incapable of understanding the elevated spiritual vision of the artist, deforms his truth once it is translated into concrete forms, and makes of him its scapegoat. The two consultations thus answer negatively and conclusively to the desire for action; the récits they contain illustrate its inevitable failure.

Vigny's own *Poèmes Philosophiques* therefore, are, in a very literal fashion, the poems of his fictional *Daphné,* written under the influence of the platonist and stoic Philosopher Libanius, who counsels Julian and doubles for the Docteur Noir. These are "poésie pure," the purest possible expression of the moral and religious spirit or conscience of the poet, through diamond-hard and crystal-like images and symbols, uncontaminated by sensuous matter, materialistic values and degraded language, i.e. the sophistry and opportunism of political and social discourse. A mandate to write the poetry of the "esprit pur" is the therapeutical result of the two consultations, an almost liturgical and certainly cathartic function of the "confessions" of Stello. (pp. 461-62)

Julian's legend is [one in a] series of historical fables or myths which Vigny uses to symbolize a complex, contradictory and paradoxical truth, a spiritual meaning which could not be expressed discursively; it requires the clarity, richness and durability of the crystal image to illuminate and preserve it. Like Moses, the poets of *Stello* (Gilbert, Chatterton, Chénier) and the figures of *Les Destinées,* (Christ, Samson, and the sea captain of **"La Bouteille à la mer"**), Julian belongs to the aristocracy of intelligence and spirit who are sacrificed in the name of an idea. His sacrifice, as is the case with the others, signifies the loss of an ideal, but concomitantly the affirmation of a new value. . . . The fable of Julian's life is structured on a series of binary oppositions, a thesis and antithesis whose conflict does not produce the synthesis of the optimistic poems in *Les Destinées,* in which positive change seems to result from the victory of man's creative spirit over the "fatalities" of the world (**"La Maison du Berger," "La Bouteille à la mer," "L'Esprit pur"**). (pp. 465-66)

Although *Daphné* is a short novel it offers a singular richness and density surpassing even *Stello.* On the level of narrative discourse the points of view are multiple, giving expression to the complexity of conflicting ideologies. The omniscient, impersonal narrator introduces the frame and concludes the novel with a vision of history and a lesson on human thought, the dangers of incarnating pure ideas in action or false symbols. Dialogue between the Docteur Noir and Stello dominates the frame. Each one in turn becomes the narrator of several "récits"; Stello relates the story of Abailard and Héloise and characters like the lovesick student Trivulce (an ironic double of Stello) relate their own stories. (pp. 468-69)

The multiplicity of narrative voices and "récits" corresponds to a pattern of figures and characters who symbolize a variety of philosophical and moral attitudes, united by their reactions to religious "enthousiasme." Those who express a direct emotional, even mystical perception of the divine or of the eternal

ideas, the enthusiasts, include first of all Stello himself, the pure poet. He is mirrored by Abailard the theologian and lover [and the anguished student Trivulce] . . . Contrasted with these figures in the frame are the nun (who leads Stello to the room of the sick student in the "pays latin") suggesting simple faith and charity without "pensée" or idealism, and the rationalist Docteur Noir. Once again, as in the novel *Stello,* he is the realist, the pragmatic ego, conscience or animus to the sensitive anima of his poetic counterpart.

In the main part of the novel the same oppositions define the actors: Julian is the poet and mystic who chooses to embody his ideas in political action; his friend and disciple Paul de Larissa dies a martyr's death due to his total devotion to polytheism (he is lapidated by the Christian barbarians). (pp. 469-70)

Thus the actors and the actions in the text are all a function of the opposition between idea and action which is a structuring principle in many of Vigny's works. When the poet or enthusiast acts, he transgresses the law of pure expression in art with negative or tragic consequences. . . .

The actions in the text are determined not only by the simple opposition between paganism and Christianity, or the barbarian menace to an aristocratic spirituality . . . , but between action and contemplation. The real protagonist of the novel is Libanius, who does not act, but contemplates the eternal essences of Daphné, combining in one person the enthusiasm of Stello and the stoic resignation of the Docteur Noir. (p. 470)

The essential idea for Vigny is that the life of the "esprit pur," the integrity of the spiritual and intellectual heritage which is man's greatest value msut be preserved; man's definition as a creative thinker, whose essence is spiritual, must be perpetuated even if it can be done only through the support of an ideology he cannot accept, but whose symbols still have the power to foster belief. . . .

[*Daphné*] is finally a text about ideas and how to write them. Ideas, the half-gods of our dreams, as Vigny's narrator claims, must be molded, sculpted in forms of language and art which do not betray their original purity, rendering them durable, compelling and capable of communicating their unique illumination. (p. 474)

Henry F. Majewski, "The Second Consultation of the 'Docteur Noir': Alfred de Vigny's 'Daphné' and the Power of Symbols," in Studies in Romanticism, *Vol. 20, No. 4, Winter, 1981, pp. 461-74.*

ADDITIONAL BIBLIOGRAPHY

Aldington, Richard. *"Cinq-Mars."* In his *French Studies and Reviews,* pp. 180-85. London: George Allen & Unwin, 1926.
    A brief study of *Cinq-Mars* that describes its reception by critics and its faults as a historical novel. Aldington concludes that although Vigny was a genius as a poet, "he was not a novelist by instinct."

Bird, C. Wesley. *Alfred de Vigny's "Chatterton": A Contribution to the Study of Its Genesis and Sources.* Los Angeles: Lymanhouse, 1941, 183 p.
    A study of *Chatterton,* which Bird ranks with Victor Hugo's *Hernani* as the two most popular plays of the Romantic period. Bird discusses the history of the legend of the English poet Thomas Chatterton and the themes and sources of Vigny's play.

Croce, Benedetto. "Alfred de Vigny." In his *European Literature in the Nineteenth Century,* translated by Douglas Ainslie, pp. 131-44. New York: Alfred A. Knopf, 1923.
Touches briefly on Vigny's best-known works and examines his poetry in some detail. Croce discusses Vigny's conception of the role of the poet and outlines the manner in which his philosophical poetry is pessimistic. Despite what he considers an often maladroit style, Croce extends high praise to the profundity and intensity of Vigny's poetry, concluding that as he "is among the greatest poetical writers that have ever appeared in France, so he is probably the greatest French poet of the nineteenth century."

Dale, R. C. "*Chatterton* Is the Essential Romantic Drama." *L'esprit créateur* V, No. 3 (Fall 1965): 131-37.
Summarizes Victor Hugo's and Stendhal's theories of Romantic drama and cites *Chatterton* as the outstanding example of this form. Dale concludes that this drama "is the realization of the two distinctive non-formal goals established by Stendhal and Hugo: a play written for contemporary (read Romantic) audiences dealing in contemporary problems, and one exploiting the distinguishing characteristic of the 'epoch of drama,' the grotesque."

Denommé, Robert T. "French Theater Reform and Vigny's Translation of *Othello* in 1829." In *Symbolism and Modern Literature: Studies in Honor of Wallace Fowlie,* edited by Marcel Tetel, pp. 81-102. Durham, N.C.: Duke University Press, 1978.
A historical appraisal of early nineteenth-century French drama that discusses the influence of Vigny's translation of *Othello* in liberating French theater from classical strictures.

Dey, William Morton. "The Pessimism and Optimism of Alfred de Vigny." *Studies in Philology* XXXIII, No. 3 (July 1936): 405-16.
Identifies the reasons for and manifestations of optimism and pessimism in Vigny's poetry. Dey first reviews the circumstances of the poet's life and asserts that "the main causes of Vigny's pessimism are solitude, disillusion, disappointment, and the treachery of women." Yet, Dey finds in Vigny's later work evidence of growing optimism and a newfound faith in God.

Doolittle, James. "The Function of 'La colère de Samson' in *Les destinées.*" *The Modern Language Quarterly* 18, No. 1 (March 1957): 63-8.
Discusses the themes and structure of the collection *Les destinées* and the role of the poem "La colère de Samson." Doolittle describes this poem, with its portrayal of Samson as weak and Delilah as vacuous, as incongruous in a collection that depicts man's successful struggle against Nature, Destiny, and God.

———. *Alfred de Vigny.* New York: Twayne Publishers, 1967, 154 p.
A critical biography. Doolittle discusses Vigny's works in the context of his era and the events of his life.

Evans, David O. "Vigny and the *Doctrine de Saint-Simon.*" *The Romantic Review* XXXIX, No. 1 (February 1948): 22-9.
An introduction to the principles of the French social philosopher Claude Henri de Rouvroy de Saint-Simon and an examination of his influence on Vigny.

Faguet, Émile. "Part VII, The Nineteenth Century: The Second Epoch of Romanticism." In his *A Literary History of France,* translated by F.H.L., pp. 561-71. London: T. Fisher Unwin, 1907.*
A survey of Vigny's works that briefly summarizes his position in French literature.

Gerothwohl, Maurice A. "Alfred de Vigny on Genius and Women." *The Fortnightly Review* XCIII, No. DLIII (1 January 1913): 94-111.
Examines the depictions of genius and women in Vigny's poetry. Gerothwohl focuses on "Moïse," "L'esprit pur," "Eloa," and "La colère de Samson."

Gosse, Edmund. "Alfred de Vigny." *The International Quarterly* VII, No. I (March-June 1903): 151-70.

A biographical sketch that links Vigny's works to circumstances in his life.

Grimsley, Ronald. "Kierkegaard, Vigny, and 'the Poet'." In his *Søren Kierkegaard and French Literature: Eight Comparative Studies,* pp. 130-58. Cardiff: University of Wales Press, 1966.*
Compares the conception of the poet in the work of Vigny and the Danish philosopher and theologian Søren Kierkegaard. Such a comparison, according to Grimsley, discloses "the fundamental values implicit in their whole activity as men and writers."

Higgins, D. "Social Pessimism in Alfred de Vigny." *Modern Language Review* XLIV, No. 3 (July 1949): 351-59.
A brief study of Vigny's beliefs emphasizing his social background as a key to understanding his pessimism. Unlike many critics who assert that Vigny's world view is consistently either optimistic or pessimistic, Higgins stresses the conflict in his thought, "the vacillation between hope and despair."

Hill, Charles G. "Vigny and Pascal." *PMLA* LXXII, No. 5 (December 1958): 533-37.*
Examines Vigny's works, particularly his *Journal d'un poète,* to determine the extent of the French philosopher Blaise Pascal's influence on Vigny's thought.

Porter, Laurence M. "Symbolic Gesture in Vigny's *Poëme.*" In his *The Renaissance of the Lyric in French Romanticism: Elegy, "Poëme" and Ode,* pp. 47-74. Lexington, Ky.: French Forum, 1978.
A structural analysis of Vigny's poetry. In the introduction to his book, Porter identifies the three main French Romantic lyric genres as the elegy, *poëme,* and ode, and he claims that these forms correspond to the works of Alphonse Marie Louis de Lamartine, Vigny, and Victor Hugo, respectively. In his chapter on Vigny, Porter uses specific examples from the poet's work to trace his development in form and structure.

Raitt, A. W. "Alfred de Vigny: *Chatterton.*" In his *The Nineteenth Century,* pp. 27-35. Life and Letters in France, edited by Austin Gill, vol. 3. New York: Charles Scribner's Sons, 1965.
Outlines the historical and cultural background of Vigny's drama *Chatterton.* Raitt discusses this drama as an illustration of the French Romantic interest in the role of the artist in society.

Reagan, William Francis. "The Poetry of Alfred de Vigny: A Century of Literary Criticism, 1864-1964." Ph.D. diss., The University of North Carolina, Chapel Hill, 1964, 234 p.
A survey of French and English criticism of Vigny published in journals.

Rooker, J. K. "The Optimism of Alfred de Vigny." *Modern Language Review* IX, No. 1 (January 1914): 1-11.
Traces the evolution of Vigny's world view from despair to optimism.

Ullmann, Stephen. "Some Romantic Experiments in Local Colour." In his *Style in the French Novel,* pp. 40-93. New York: Barnes & Noble, 1964.*
Describes the stylistic devices Vigny employed in *Stello, Cinq-Mars,* and *The Military Necessity.*

West, Anthony. "Alfred de Vigny." In his *Principles and Persuasions: The Literary Essays of Anthony West,* pp. 52-60. New York: Harcourt, Brace and Co., 1957.
A brief history of Vigny's life and career. West differs from mainstream critical opinion in his negative appraisal of Vigny, whom he calls "an essentially minor French writer whose reputation has been inflated by generation after generation of critics until he now occupies a position of considerable importance as a forerunner of the modern literary movement."

Whitridge, Arnold. *Alfred de Vigny.* London: Oxford University Press, 1933, 232 p.
A biography.

Appendix

The following is a listing of all sources used in Volume 7 of *Nineteenth-Century Literature Criticism*. Included in this list are all copyright and reprint rights and acknowledgements for those essays for which permission was obtained. Every effort has been made to trace copyright, but if omissions have been made, please let us know.

The Century, v. 24, July, 1882.

The Chimera, v. I, Winter, 1943.

The Christian Examiner, v. LXXVII, May, 1865; v. LXXIX, July, 1865.

CLA Journal, v. XVII, December, 1973. Copyright, 1973 by The College Language Association. Used by permission of The College Language Association.

The Classical Review, v. VII, June, 1893.

Cleveland Gazette, May 11 and June 8, 1889.

College English, v. 17, December, 1955.

Commonweal, v. LXXVII, October 26, 1962. Copyright © 1962 Commonweal Publishing Co., Inc. Reprinted by permission of Commonweal Foundation.

Contemporary Review, v. LXVI, December, 1894.

The Cornhill Magazine, v. XLI, June, 1880; n.s. v. XXXVII, September, 1914.

The Dublin Magazine, v. XXVIII, April-June, 1953. Reprinted by permission.

Dublin Review, v. XVI, June, 1844.

The Dublin University Magazine, v. XLV, May, 1855; v. XLVI, November, 1855.

Early American Literature, v. VIII, Fall, 1973. Copyrighted, 1973, by the University of Massachusetts. Reprinted by permission.

The Edinburgh Review, v. XV, October, 1809; v. XLVI, June, 1927.

Eighteenth-Century Studies, v. 4, Spring, 1971. © 1971 by The American Society for Eighteenth-Century Studies. Reprinted by permission.

Encounter, v. VII, November, 1956; v. XXVI, June, 1966. © 1956, 1966 by Encounter Ltd. Both reprinted by permission.

The Fortnightly Review, n.s. v. XXIX, February 1, 1881; n.s. v. XLIV, October 1, 1888; n.s. v. LX, September, 1896./ n.s. v. 79, January 1, 1903. Reprinted by permission of Contemporary Review Company Limited.

Forum, v. XXII, October, 1896.

Fraser's Magazine, v. LVI, July, 1857.

The French Review, v. XXXVI, January, 1962-63; v. XLII, February, 1969. Copyright 1963, 1969 by the American Association of Teachers of French. Reprinted by permission.

The Galaxy, v. XXI, February, 1876.

The Georgia Review, v. XXXVI, Summer, 1982. Copyright, 1982, by the University of Georgia. Reprinted by permission.

The Graduate Journal, v. VI, Winter, 1964 for ''The Extra-vagant Maneuver: Paradox in Walden'' by Joseph J. Moldenhauer. Copyrighted © 1964 by The Board of Regents of The University of Texas. Reprinted by permission of the publisher and the author.

Graham's Magazine, v. XXX, June, 1847; v. XLV, September, 1854.

Harper's New Monthly Magazine, v. LXXX, May, 1885; v. LXXIII, September, 1886.

Harvard Library Bulletin, v. VII, Autumn, 1953.

The Illustrated London News, v. CVI, March 9, 1895.

The International Quarterly, v. VII, June-September, 1903.

The Irish Quarterly Review, v. V, December, 1855.

The Journal of Afro-American Issues, v. V, Spring, 1977. Copyright © 1977 by Educational and Community Counselors Associates, Washington, D.C. Reprinted by permission.

The Knickerbocker, v. XLV, January, 1855.

The Liberator, v. XVIII, January 28, 1848; v. XIX, April 20, 1849; v. XXII, October 29, 1852.

Literary World, v. I, April 17, 1847.

Littell's Living Age, v. CXX, March 7, 1874.

The London Magazine, v. IV, December, 1821.

Macmillan's Magazine, v. V, November, 1861; v. LII, June, 1885.

Massachusetts Quarterly Review, v. III, December, 1849.

Midcontinent American Studies Journal, v. 9, Spring, 1968 for ''Fiction in the Age of Jefferson: The Early American Novel As Intellectual Document'' by Robert Hemenway. Copyright, Midcontinent American Studies Association, 1968. Reprinted by permission of the publisher and the author.

The Modern Language Journal, v. LIV, December, 1970. Reprinted by permission.

The Modern Language Review, v. LX, July, 1965 for ''The Poetic Practices of Vigny's 'Poèmes philosophiques''' by Frank Paul Bowman. © Modern Humanities Research Association 1965. Reprinted by permission of the publisher and the author.

Modern Philology, v. LIV, November, 1956 for ''Dostoevski and the Dream'' by Ruth Mortimer. © 1956 by The University of Chicago. Reprinted by permission of the author.

The Nation, v. XXIV, May 10, 1877; v. XLVI, January 12, 1888; v. IX, July, 1887; v. LXIII, July 9, 1896.

The Nation, London, v. XCII, April 13, 1911 for ''Walter Pater'' by Paul Elmer More. Reprinted by permission of the Literary Estate of Paul Elmer More.

The Nation and The Athenaeum, n. 2694, June 14, 1879.

National Anti-Slavery Standard, v. XV, December 16, 1854.

The National Magazine, New York, v. X, May, 1857.

The National Review, London, v. XXI, August, 1893.

The New England Quarterly, v. XXXLV, June, 1961. Copyright 1961 by *The New England Quarterly.* Reprinted by permission of the publisher.

Newsweek, v. X, November 22, 1937.

New York Herald Tribune Book Review, May 20, 1951 for ''Henry Thoreau's Journals Stand in a Special Place'' by Alfred Kazin. © 1951 by I.H.T. Corporation. And renewed 1979 by Alfred Kazin. Reprinted by permission of the author.

The New York Times Book Review, April 28, 1974. Copyright © 1974 by The New York Times Company. Reprinted by permission.

The New-Yorker, v. 9, May 23, 1840.

The Nineteenth Century, v. XXVII, April, 1890; v. 33, May, 1893.

The North American Review, v. XCVII, July, 1863; v. CII, April, 1866; v. CXXI, July, 1875.

The North British Review, v. XLIX, December, 1868.

The Outlook, v. 117, September 12, 1917.

Pall Mall Gazette, March, 1873; v. XLIX, December 10, 1889.

Partisan Review, v. XXVII, Summer, 1960 for "Dostoevsky in 'Crime and Punishment'" by Philip Rahv. Copyright © 1960 by *Partisan Review.* Reprinted by permission of *Partisan Review* and the Literary Estate of Philip Rahv.

PMLA, v. LXX, December, 1955./ n.s. v. XXIV, March, 1916. Copyright © 1916 by the Modern Language Association of America. Reprinted by permission of the Modern Language Association of America.

Poet Lore, v. V, November, 1893. Copyright, 1893 by Poet Lore, Inc. Reprinted by permission of Heldref Publications, a publication of the Helen Dwight Reid Educational Foundation.

Political Science Quarterly, v. LVII, December, 1942. Reprinted with permission.

Putnam's Monthly, v. IV, October, 1854.

The Quarterly Review, v. X, October, 1813; v. LVII, September, 1836; v. CXXXVII, July, 1874.

Scandinavian Studies, v. 50, Autumn, 1978 for "H. C. Andersen's 'Tin Soldier' in a Freudian Perspective" by William Mishler. Reprinted by permission of the publisher and the author.

The Select Journal of Foreign Periodical Literature, v. III, January, 1834.

The Sewanee Review, v. XXIX, January, 1921. Published 1921 by The University of the South. Reprinted by permission of the editor.

Social Research, v. 2, November, 1935.

The Southern Literary Messenger, v. VIII, January, 1842.

Speaker, v. I, March 22, 1890.

The Spectator, v. 68, February 6, 1892; v. 77, July 25, 1896./ v. 224, April 4, 1970. © 1970 by *The Spectator.* Reprinted by permission of *The Spectator.*

Studies, v. LXI, Autumn, 1972. © copyright 1972. Reprinted by permission.

Studies in Romanticism, v. 20, Winter, 1981. Copyright 1981 by the Trustees of Boston University. Reprinted by permission.

Studies in the Novel, v. XII, Winter, 1980. Copyright 1980 by North Texas State University. Reprinted by permission.

Temple Bar, v. XXXIV, March, 1872.

Texas Studies in Literature and Language, v. IX, Autumn, 1967. Copyright © 1967 by the University of Texas Press. Reprinted by permission of the publisher.

Time, London, n.s. v. XVII, August, 1887 for "Walter Pater: 'Imaginary Portraits'" by Arthur Symons. Reprinted by permission of the Literary Estate of Arthur Symons.

The Times Literary Supplement, n. 998, March 3, 1921, n. 2496, July 15, 1949; n. 3087, April 28, 1961; n. 3215, October 11, 1963. © Times Newspapers Ltd. (London) 1921, 1949, 1961, 1963. Reproduced from *The Times Literary Supplement* by permission.

The Universal Asylum and Columbian Magazine, v. 11, August, 1792.

Westminster and Foreign Quarterly Review, n.s. v. XXV, April 1, 1869.

The Westminster Review, v. LXV, January 1, 1856; n.s. v. XLIII, April 1, 1873; n.s. v. LXX, July, 1886.

Yale French Studies, n. 33, December, 1964. Copyright © *Yale French Studies* 1964. Reprinted by permission.

THE EXCERPTS IN NCLC, VOLUME 7, WERE REPRINTED FROM THE FOLLOWING BOOKS:

Adams, Henry. From *History of the United States of America during the First Administration of Thomas Jefferson, Vol. I*. Charles Scribner's Sons, 1889.

Affron, Charles. From *A Stage for Poets: Studies in the Theatre of Hugo & Musset*. Princeton University Press, 1971. Copyright © 1971 by Princeton University Press. Excerpts reprinted by permission of Princeton University Press.

Aldington, Richard. From an introduction to *Selected Works*. By Walter Pater, edited by Richard Aldington. Duell, Sloan and Pearce, 1948. Reprinted by permission of Rosica Colin Limited, as agents for the author's estate.

Andersen, Hans Christian. From *The Story of My Life*. Hurd and Houghton, 1871.

Atkins, J.W.H. From *English Literary Criticism: Seventeenth and Eighteenth Centuries*. Methuen, 1951. Reprinted by permission of Methuen & Co. Ltd.

Auerbach, Erich. From *Mimeses: The Representation of Reality in Western Literature*. Translated by Willard Trask. Princeton University Press, 1953. Copyright 1953 by Princeton University Press; copyright © renewed 1981 by Princeton University Press. Excerpts reprinted by permission of Princeton University Press.

Bain, R. Nisbet. From *Hans Christian Andersen: A Biography*. Dodd, Mead & Company, 1895.

Baker, Houston A., Jr. From *The Journey Back: Issues in Black Literature and Criticism*. University of Chicago Press, 1980. © 1980 by The University of Chicago. Reprinted by permission of The University of Chicago Press.

Baldick, Robert. From *The Goncourts*. Bowes & Bowes, 1960. © Robert Baldick 1960. Reprinted by permission of The Bodley Head Ltd. for Bowes & Bowes.

Bartlett, David W. From *Modern Agitators; or, Pen Portraits of Living American Reformers*. Miller, Orton & Mulligan, 1856.

Baudelaire, Charles. From a letter to Armand Fraisse on February 18, 1860, in *Baudelaire As a Literary Critic*. Edited and translated by Lois Boe Hyslop, Jr. The Pennsylvania State University Press, University Park, 1964. Copyright © 1964 by The Pennsylvania State University. Reprinted by permission.

Bell, Michael Davitt. From an introduction to *Father Bombo's Pilgrimage to Mecca: 1770*. By Hugh Henry Brackenridge and Philip Freneau, edited by Michael Davitt Bell. Princeton University Library, 1975. Copyright © 1975 by Princeton University Library. Reprinted by permission.

Benson, A. C. From *Walter Pater*. The Macmillan Company, 1906.

Berdyaev, Nicholas. From *Dostoievsky: An Interpretation*. Translated by Donald Attwater. Sheed and Ward, Inc., 1934. All rights reserved. Reprinted with permission from Andrews, McMeel & Parker.

Böök, Fredrik. From *Hans Christian Andersen: A Biography*. Translated by George C. Schoolfield. University of Oklahoma Press, 1962. Copyright 1962 by the University of Oklahoma Press. Reprinted by permission.

Boyd, Ernest. From an introduction to *Germinie Lacerteux*. By Edmond de Goncourt and Jules de Goncourt, translated by Ernest Boyd. Knopf, 1922. Copyright 1922; copyright renewed © 1949, by Alfred A. Knopf, Inc. Reprinted by permission of the publisher.

Bradley, Phillips. From an introduction to *Democracy in America, Vol. I*. By Alexis de Tocqueville, edited by Francis Bowen and Phillips Bradley, translated by Henry Reeve. Knopf, 1945. Copyright 1945 and renewed 1973 by Alfred A. Knopf, Inc. All rights reserved. Reprinted by permission of the publisher.

Brandes, Georg. From *Eminent Authors of the Nineteenth Century: Literary Portraits*. Translated by Rasmus B. Anderson. Crowell, 1886. Copyright © 1886 by Thomas Y. Crowell & Co.

Brandes, George. From *Impressions of Russia*. Translated by Samuel C. Eastman. Thomas Y. Crowell & Co., 1889.

Brandes, George. From *Main Currents in Nineteenth Century Literature: The Romantic School in Germany, Vol. II*. Translated by Diana White and Mary Morison. William Heinemann, 1902.

Brandes, George. From *Main Currents in Nineteenth Century Literature: The Romantic School in France, Vol. V*. Translated by Diana White and Mary Morison. William Heinemann, 1904.

Brawley, Benjamin. From *Negro Builders and Heroes*. University of North Carolina Press, 1937. Copyright, 1937, by the University of North Carolina Press. And renewed 1965 by the Literary Estate of Benjamin Brawley. Reprinted by permission.

Brennecke, Ernest, Jr. From an introduction to *Modern Chivalry: Containing the Adventures of Captain Farrago and Teague O'Regan*. By Hugh Henry Brackenridge. Greenberg, Publisher, Inc., 1926.

Brereton, Geoffrey. From *An Introduction to the French Poets: Villon to the Present Day*. Methuen, 1956. Reprinted by permission of Methuen & Co. Ltd.

Brereton, Geoffrey. From *An Introduction to the French Poets: Villon to the Present Day*. Revised edition. Methuen, 1973. © 1973 by Geoffrey Brereton. Reprinted by permission of Methuen & Co. Ltd.

Brown, William Wells. From *The Rising Son; or, The Antecedents and Advancement of the Colored Race*. A. G. Brown & Co., Publishers, 1874.

Browning, Elizabeth Barrett. From *Last Poems*. James Miller, 1863.

Burke, Kenneth. From *Counter-Statement*. Second edition. Hermes Publications, 1953.

Canby, Henry Seidel. From *Classic Americans: A Study of Eminent American Writers from Irving to Whitman, with an Introductory Survey of the Colonial Background of Our National Literature*. Harcourt, Brace & Company, 1931. Copyright 1931, 1958 by Henry Seidel Canby. Reprinted by permission of the Literary Estate of Henry Seidel Canby.

Carlyle, Thomas. From "Jean Paul Friedrich Richter," in *German Romance: Hoffmann, Richter, Vol. II*. Edited and translated by Thomas Carlyle. n.p., 1827.

Carrère, Jean. From *Degeneration in the Great French Masters: Rousseau—Chateubriand—Balzac—Stendhal—Sand—Musset—Baudelaire—Flaubert—Verlaine—Zola*. Translated by Joseph McCabe. T. Fisher Unwin, Limited, 1922.

Cecil, Lord David. From *Walter Pater: The Scholar-Artist*. Cambridge at the University Press, 1955. *Reprinted by permission*.

Chesterton, Gilbert K. From *The Crimes of England*. Lane, 1916. Copyright, 1916, by John Lane Company. And renewed 1943 by Oliver Chesterton. Reprinted by permission of Miss D. E. Collins.

Chirkov, Nicholas M. From "A Great Philosophical Novel," translated by Cerylle A. Fritts, in *Twentieth-Century Interpretations of "Crime and Punishment:" A Collection of Critical Essays*. Edited by Robert Louis Jackson. Prentice-Hall, 1974. © 1974 by Prentice-Hall, Inc. All rights reserved. Reprinted by permission of Prentice-Hall, Inc. Englewood Cliffs, NJ 07632.

Chulkov, Georgy. From "Dostoevsky's Technique of Writing," translated by George Gibian, in *"Crime and Punishment" by Feodor Dostoevsky, A Norton Critical Edition: The Coulson Translation, Backgrounds and Sources, Essays in Criticism*. Edited by George Gibian. Revised edition. Norton, 1975. Copyright © 1975, 1964 by W. W. Norton & Company, Inc. Reprinted by permission of W. W. Norton & Company, Inc.

Colum, Padraic. From an introduction to *The Collegians*. By Gerald Griffin. The Phoenix Publishing Company Limited, 1918. Reprinted by permission of the Literary Estate of Padraic Colum.

Colum, Padraic. From *A Half-Day's Ride; or, Estates in Corsica*. The Macmillan Company, 1932.

Commager, Henry Steele. From an introduction to *Democracy in America*. By Alexis de Tocqueville, translated by Henry Reeve. Oxford University Press, New York, 1947. Copyright © 1946 by Oxford University Press, New York, Inc. And renewed 1974 by Henry Steele Commager. Reprinted by permission of Oxford University Press, Inc.

Couser, G. Thomas. From *American Autobiography: The Prophetic Mode*. University of Massachusetts Press, 1979. Copyright © 1979 by The University of Massachusetts Press. Reprinted by permission.

Cowie, Alexander. From *The Rise of the American Novel*. American Book Company, 1948.

Cox, Rev. Samuel Hanson. From an extract from an account of Frederick Douglass' address at the World's Temperance Convention at Covent Garden on August 7, 1846, in *Frederick Douglass*. By Booker T. Washington. G. W. Jacobs & Company, 1907.

Cronin, John. From *Gerald Griffin (1803-1840): A Critical Biography*. Cambridge University Press, 1978. © Cambridge University Press 1978. Reprinted by permission.

Dalberg-Acton, John Emerich Edward. From a lecture delivered between 1895-99, in *Lectures on the French Revolution*. Edited by John Neville Figgis and Reginald Vere Laurence. Macmillan and Co., Limited, 1910.

Davis, Robert. From *Gerald Griffin*. Twayne, 1980. Copyright 1980 by Twayne Publishers. Reprinted with the permission of Twayne Publishers, a Division of G. K. Hall & Co., Boston.

De Beaumont, Gustave. From *Memoir, Letters and Remains of Alexis de Tocqueville, Vol. I*. By Alexis de Tocqueville, edited by M.C.M. Simpson, translated by Gustave de Beaumont. Revised edition. Macmillan and Co., 1861.

De Laura, David J. From *Hebrew and Hellene in Victorian England: Newman, Arnold, and Pater*. University of Texas Press, 1969. Copyright © 1969 by David J. De Laura. All rights reserved. Reprinted by permission of the publisher and the author.

Deneke, H. C. From ''Some Observations on Jean Paul,'' in *German Studies Presented to Professor H. G. Fiedler, M.V.O.* Oxford at the Clarendon Press, Oxford, 1938. Reprinted by permission of Oxford University Press.

Denommé, Robert T. From *Nineteenth-Century French Romantic Poets*. Southern Illinois University Press, 1969. Copyright © 1969 by Southern Illinois University Press. All rights reserved. Reprinted by permission of Southern Illinois University Press.

Dostoevsky, Fedor. From a letter to M. N. Katkov in September-October, 1865 in *New Dostoevsky Letters*. Translated by S. S. Koteliansky. Mandrake Press, 1929. Reprinted by permission of the Literary Estate of S. S. Koteliansky.

Douglass, Frederick. From a letter to an unidentified recipient on July 2, 1855, in *My Bondage and My Freedom*. By Frederick Douglass. Miller, Orton & Mulligan, 1855.

Dunbar, Paul Laurence. From *Lyrics of Lowly Life*. Dodd, Mead & Company, 1896.

Edel, Leon. From *Henry D. Thoreau*. University of Minnesota Press, Minneapolis, 1970. American Writers Pamphlet No. 90. © 1970, Leon Edel. Reprinted by permission.

Eliot, T. S. From *Selected Essays*. Harcourt Brace Jovanovich, 1950.

Ellis, Havelock. From *The New Spirit*. Boni and Liveright, 1890. Reprinted by permission of Francois Lafitte for the Literary Estate of Havelock Ellis.

Evnin, F. I. From ''Plot Structure and Raskolnikov's Oscillations,'' translated by Natalie Bienstock, in *''Crime and Punishment'' by Feodor Dostoevsky, A Norton Critical Edition: The Coulson Translation, Backgrounds and Sources, Essays in Criticism*. Edited by George Gibian. Revised edition. Norton, 1975. Copyright © 1975, 1964 by W. W. Norton & Company, Inc. Reprinted by permission of W. W. Norton & Company, Inc.

Faguet, Emile. From *Politicians & Moralists of the Nineteenth Century, Vol. 3*. Translated by Dorothy Galton. Ernest Benn Limited, 1928.

Fishman, Solomon. From *The Interpretation of Art: Essays on the Art Criticism of John Ruskin, Walter Pater, Clive Bell, Roger Fry, and Herbert Read*. University of California Press, 1963. Copyright © 1963 by The Regents of the University of California. Reprinted by permission.

Fitzmaurice-Kelly, James. From "Edmond and Jules de Goncourt," in *Renee Mauperin*. By Edmond de Goncourt and Jules de Goncourt, translated by Alys Hallard. Appleton & Company, 1902.

Flanagan, Thomas. From *The Irish Novelists: 1800-1850*. Columbia University Press, 1959. Copyright © 1958 Columbia University Press, New York. Reprinted by permission of the publisher.

Fletcher, Iain. From *Walter Pater*. British Council, 1959. © Profile Books Ltd. 1959. Reprinted by permission.

France, Anatole. From *On Life & Letters, first series*. Translated by A. W. Evans. John Lane/ The Bodley Head, 1924.

Galantière, Lewis. From an introduction to *The Goncourt Journals: 1851-1870*. By Edmond de Goncourt and Jules de Goncourt, edited and translated by Lewis Galantière. Doubleday, 1937. Copyright 1937 by Doubleday & Company, Inc. Copyright renewed © 1964 by Lewis Galantière. Reprinted by permission of the publisher.

Garber, Frederick. From *Thoreau's Redemptive Imagination*. New York University Press, 1977. Copyright © 1977 by New York University. Reprinted by permission of New York University Press.

Gargan, Edward T. From *Alexis de Tocqueville: The Critical Years, 1848-1851*. The Catholic University of America Press, Inc., 1955.

Garrison, William Lloyd. From a preface to *Narrative of the Life of Frederick Douglass, an American Slave*. By Frederick Douglass, edited by Benjamin Quarles. n.p., 1845.

George, Albert J. From *Short Fiction in France: 1800-1850*. Syracuse University Press, 1964. Copyright © 1964 by Syracuse University Press, Syracuse, New York. All rights reserved. Reprinted by permission.

Gochberg, Herbert S. From *Stage of Dreams: The Dramatic Art of Alfred de Musset (1828-1834)*. Librarie Droz, 1967. Reprinted by permission of the author.

Goncourt, Edmond de. From a journal entry on December 26, 1895, in *Paris and the Arts, 1851-1896: From the Goncourt Journal*. By Edmond de Goncourt and Jules de Goncourt, translated by George J. Becker and Edith Philips. Cornell University Press, 1971. Copyright © 1971 by Cornell University. Used by permission of Cornell University Press.

Grant, Richard B. From *The Goncourt Brothers*. Twayne, 1972. Copyright © 1972 by Twayne Publishers. Reprinted with the permission of Twayne Publishers, a Division of G. K. Hall & Co., Boston.

Gregory, James M. From *Frederick Douglass: The Orator*. Willey & Co., 1893.

Griffin, Gerald. From an extract from a conversation with Daniel Griffin in 1829? in *The Works of Gerald Griffin, Vol. 1*. By Daniel Griffin. Second edition. D. & J. Sadlier & Co., 1857.

Grossman, Leonid P. From ''The Construction of the Novel,'' translated by Natalie Bienstock, in *''Crime and Punishment'' by Feodor Dostoevsky, A Norton Critical Edition: The Coulson Translation, Backgrounds and Sources, Essays in Criticism*. Edited by George Gibian. Revised edition. Norton, 1975. Copyright © 1975, 1964 by W. W. Norton & Company, Inc. Reprinted by permission of W. W. Norton & Company, Inc.

Guérard, Albert. From *Fossils and Presences*. Stanford University Press, 1957. © 1957. by the Board of Trustees of the Leland Stanford Junior University. All rights reserved. Excerpted with the permission of the publishers, Stanford University Press.

Hackett, Francis. From *Horizons: A Book of Criticism*. B. W. Huebsch, 1918. Copyright 1918 by B. W. Huebsch. Copyright renewed 1946 by Francis Hackett. Reprinted by permission of Viking Penguin Inc.

Harris, Frank. From *Latest Contemporary Portraits*. The Macaulay Company, 1927.

Haugaard, Erik. From *Portrait of a Poet: Hans Christian Andersen and His Fairytales*. Library of Congress, 1973. Reprinted by permission of the author.

Hawthorne, Nathaniel. From an extract of a letter to Monckton Miles, November 13-18, 1854, in *Nathaniel Hawthorne: A Modest Man*. By Edward Mather. Crowell, 1940. Copyright © 1940 by Thomas Y. Crowell Company. All rights reserved. Reprinted by permission of Harper & Row, Publishers, Inc.

Hesse, Hermann. From "About Jean Paul," translated by Denver Lindley, in *My Belief: Essays on Life and Art*. By Hermann Hesse, edited by Theodore Ziolkowski, translated by Denver Lindley with Ralph Manheim. Farrar, Straus and Giroux, 1974. Translation copyright © 1974 by Farrar, Straus and Giroux, Inc. Reprinted by permission of Farrar, Straus and Giroux, Inc.

(Hale), Margaret R. Higonnet. From ''Introduction: 'The Horn of Oberon','' in *Horn of Oberon: Jean Paul Richter's ''School for Aesthetics.''* By Jean Paul Richter, translated by Margaret R. Hale. Wayne State University Press, 1973. English translation copyright © 1973 by Wayne State University Press, Detroit, Michigan 48202. Reprinted by permission of the Wayne State University Press.

Hildebidle, John. From *Thoreau: A Naturalist's Liberty*. Cambridge, Mass.: Harvard University Press, 1983. Copyright © 1983 by the President and Fellows of Harvard College. All rights reserved. Excerpted by permission.

Holquist, Michael. From *Dostoevsky and the Novel*. Princeton University Press, 1977. Copyright © 1977 by Princeton University Press. All rights reserved. Excerpts reprinted by permission of Princeton University Press.

Hovde, Carl. F. From ''The Conception of Character in 'A Week on the Concord and Merrimack Rivers','' in *The Thoreau Centennial*. Edited by Walter Harding. State University of New York Press, 1964. Copyright © 1964 by State University of New York. All rights reserved. Reprinted by permission of the State University of New York Press.

Huneker, James. From *Iconoclasts, a Book of Dramatists: Ibsen, Strindberg, Becque, Hauptmann, Sudermann, Hervieu, Gorky, Duse and D'Annunzio, Maeterlinck and Bernard Shaw*. Charles Scribner's Sons, 1905.

Hürlimann, Bettina. From *Three Centuries of Children's Books in Europe*. Edited and translated by Brian W. Alderson. Oxford University Press, Oxford, 1967. © Oxford University Press 1967. Reprinted by permission of Oxford University Press.

Ironside, Robin. From an introduction to *French XVIII Century Painters: Watteau, Boucher, Chardin, LaTour, Greuze, Fragonard.* By Edmond de Goncourt and Jules de Goncourt, translated by Robin Ironside. Phaidon Publishers, Inc., 1948. Reprinted by permission.

Ivanov, Vyacheslav. From *Freedom and the Tragic Life: A Study in Dostoevsky.* Edited by S. Konovalov, translated by Norman Cameron. Noonday Press, 1957. All rights reserved. Reprinted by permission of Farrar, Straus and Giroux, Inc.

Jackson, Robert Louis. From *The Art of Dostoevsky: Deliriums and Nocturnes.* Princeton University Press, 1981. Copyright © 1981 by Princeton University Press. All rights reserved. Excerpts reprinted by permission of Princeton University Press.

James, Henry, Jr. From *French Poets and Novelists.* Macmillan and Co., London, 1878.

Johnson, Lionel. From *Poetical Works of Lionel Johnson.* E. Mathews, 1915.

Karyakin, Yury F. From ''Toward Regeneration,'' translated by Robert Louis Jackson, in *Twentieth-Century Interpretations of ''Crime and Punishment:'' A Collection of Critical Essays.* Edited by Robert Louis Jackson. Prentice-Hall, 1974. © 1974 by Prentice-Hall, Inc. All rights reserved. Reprinted by permission of Prentice-Hall, Inc., Englewood Cliffs, NJ 07632.

Kayser, Wolfgang. From *The Grotesque in Art and Literature.* Translated by Ulrich Weisstein. Indiana University Press, 1963. Translation copyright © 1963 by Indiana University Press. Reprinted by permission.

King, Rev. Martin Luther, Jr. From ''A Legacy of Creative Protest,'' in *Thoreau in Our Season.* Edited by John H. Hicks. University of Massachusetts Press, 1962. Copyright © 1962, 1966 by The University of Massachusetts Press. Reprinted by permission.

Krans, Horatio Sheafe. From *Irish Life in Irish Fiction,* Columbia University Studies in Comparative Literature. Columbia University Press, 1903. © 1903 Columbia University Press. Reprinted by permission of the publisher.

Krutch, Joseph Wood. From *Henry David Thoreau.* William Sloane Associates, Inc., 1948. Copyright © 1948 by William Sloane Associates, Inc. And renewed 1975 by the Literary Estate of Joseph Wood Krutch. All rights reserved. Abridged by permission of William Morrow & Company, Inc.

Laski, Harold J. From ''Alexis de Tocqueville and Democracy,'' in *The Social & Political Ideas of Some Representative Thinkers of the Victorian Age.* Edited by F.J.C. Hearnshaw. G. G. Harrap & Company Ltd., 1933. Reprinted by permission.

Lavrin, Janko. From *Dostoevsky: A Study.* The Macmillan Company, 1947.

Leary, Lewis. From an introduction to *Modern Chivalry: Containing the Adventures of Captain John Farrago and Teague O'Regan, His Servant.* By Hugh Henry Brackenridge, edited by Lewis Leary. College & University Press, Publishers, 1965. Copyright © 1965 by College and University Press Services, Inc. All rights reserved. Reprinted by permission of The New College and University Press, Inc., New Haven, CT.

Le Gallienne, Richard. From *Vanishing Roads and Other Essays.* Putnam's, 1915. Copyright, 1915 by Richard Le Gallienne. Reprinted by permission of G. P. Putnam's Sons.

Lewis, R.W.B. From *The American Adam: Innocence, Tragedy and Tradition in the Nineteenth Century.* University of Chicago Press, 1955. © The University of Chicago, 1955. Copyright under the International Copyright Union, 1955. And renewed 1983 by R.W.B. Lewis. Reprinted by permission of The University of Chicago Press.

Locke, Alain. From a foreword to *Life and Times of Frederick Douglass.* By Frederick Douglass. Pathway Press, 1941.

Loggins, Vernon. From *The Negro Author: His Development in America.* Columbia University Press, 1931. Copyright 1931, 1959; Columbia University Press. Reprinted by permission of the Literary Estate of Vernon Loggins.

Longfellow, Henry Wadsworth. From *Hyperion, a Romance.* Samuel Colman, 1839.

Loshe, Lillie Deming. From *The Early American Novel.* Columbia University Press, 1907. Copyright, 1907 by Columbia University Press. Reprinted by permission of the publisher.

Lowell, James Russell. From *A Fable for Critics: A Glance at a Few of Our Literary Progenies.* G. P. Putnam, 1848.

Lowell, James Russell. From *Literary Essays,* Vol. I. Houghton Mifflin and Company, 1893.

Lucas, E. V. From *Adventures and Enthusiasms.* Doran, 1920. Copyright, 1920, by George H. Doran Company. Reprinted by permission of the Literary Estate of E. V. Lucas and Methuen & Co.

Lukacs, John. From an introduction to *"The European Revolution" & Correspondence with Gobineau*. By Alexis de Tocqueville, edited and translated by John Lukacs. Doubleday, 1959. Copyright © 1959 by John Lukacs. All rights reserved. Reprinted by permission of Doubleday & Company, Inc.

Lynd, Robert. From *Books and Authors*. R. Cobden-Sanderson, 1922. Reprinted by permission of the Bodley Head Ltd for R. Cobden-Sanderson.

Madaule, Jacques. From "Raskolnikov," translated by Robert Louis Jackson, in *Twentieth-Century Interpretations of "Crime and Punishment": A Collection of Critical Essays*. Edited by Robert Louis Jackson. Prentice-Hall, 1974. © 1974 by Prentice-Hall, Inc. All rights reserved. Used by permission of Robert Louis Jackson.

Mallock, W. H. From *The New Republic; or, Culture, Faith, and Philosophy in an English Country House*. Revised edition. Chatto and Windus, 1878.

Marder, Daniel. From *Hugh Henry Brackenridge*. Twayne, 1967. Copyright 1967 by Twayne Publishers. Reprinted with the permission of Twayne Publishers, a Division of G. K. Hall & Co., Boston.

Marx, Leo. From *The Machine in the Garden: Technology and the Pastoral Ideal in America*. Oxford University Press, New York, 1964. Copyright © 1964 by Oxford University Press, Inc. Reprinted by permission of Oxford University Press, Inc.

Massey, Irving. From an introduction to *Stello: A Session with Doctor Noir*. By Alfred de Vigny, edited and translated by Irving Massey. McGill University Press, 1963. Reprinted by permission.

Matthiessen, F. O. From *American Renaissance: Art and Expression in the Age of Emerson and Whitman*. Oxford University Press, New York, 1941.

Maugham, W. Somerset. From *Points of View*. Heinemann, 1958. © by William Somerset Maugham 1958. Reprinted by permission of the Executors of the Estate of W. Somerset Maugham.

Mayer, J. P. From *Alexis de Tocqueville: A Biographical Essay in Political Science*. Translated by M. M. Bozman and C. Hahn. The Viking Press, 1940. Copyright © 1940 by J. P. Mayer. All rights reserved. Reprinted by permission of the author.

McIntosh, James. From *Thoreau As Romantic Naturalist: His Shifting Stance toward Nature*. Cornell University Press, 1974. Copyright © 1974 by Cornell University. All rights reserved. Used by permission of the publisher, Cornell University Press.

Mill, John Stuart. From *Essays on Poetry*. Edited by F. Parvin Sharpless. University of South Carolina Press, 1976.

Mill, John Stuart. From *Essays on Politics and Culture*. Edited by Gertrude Himmelfarb. Doubleday & Company, Inc., 1962.

Miller, Perry. From *Nature's Nation*. Cambridge, Mass.: Belknap Press, 1967. Copyright © 1967 by the President and Fellows of Harvard College. All rights reserved. Excerpted by permission.

Mitford, Mary Russell. From *Recollections of a Literary Life; or, Books, Places, and People*. Harper & Brothers, Publishers, 1852.

Mochulsky, Konstantin. From *Dostoevsky: His Life and Work*. Translated by Michael A. Minihan. Princeton University Press, 1967. Copyright © 1967 by Princeton University Press. All rights reserved. Excerpts reprinted by permission of Princeton University Press.

Monsman, Gerald. From *Walter Pater's Art of Autobiography*. Yale University Press, 1980. Copyright © 1980 by Yale University. All rights reserved. Reprinted by permission.

Monsman, Gerald Cornelius. From *Pater's Portraits: Mythic Pattern in the Fiction of Walter Pater*. Johns Hopkins University Press, 1967. Copyright © 1967 by The Johns Hopkins Press, Baltimore, MD 21218. Reprinted by permission.

Montagu, Elizabeth. From extracts from letters to Elizabeth Carter in 1779, in *Mrs. Montagu, "Queen of the Blues," Her Letters and Friendships from 1762 to 1880: 1777-1800, Vol. II*. By Elizabeth Montagu, edited by Reginald Blunt. Houghton Mifflin Company, 1923.

Morris, Wright. From *The Territory Ahead*. Harcourt Brace Jovanovich, 1958. Copyright © 1957, © 1958, © 1961 by Wright Morris. All rights reserved. Reprinted by permission of the author.

Mumford, Lewis. From *The Golden Day: A Study in American Experience and Culture*. Boni & Liveright Publishers, 1926. Copyright © 1926, 1953 by Lewis Mumford. Reprinted by permission of the author.

Murry, J. Middleton. From *Fyodor Dostoevsky: A Critical Study*. Martin Secker, 1916. Reprinted by permission of The Society of Authors as the literary representative of the Estate of John Middleton Murry.

Musset, Alfred de. From *Poems of Alfred de Musset, Vol. I*. Translated by Marie Agathe Clarke. Edwin C. Hill Company, 1905.

Nelson, John Herbert. From *The Negro Character in American Literature*. Department of Journalism Press, 1926.

Newlin, Claude Milton. From *The Life and Writings of Hugh Henry Brackenridge*. Princeton University Press, 1932.

Nisbet, Robert A. From *The Sociological Tradition*. Basic Books, 1966. © 1966 by Basic Books, Inc., Publishers. Reprinted by permission of the publishers.

O'Connor, Frank. From *A Short History of Irish Literature: A Backward Look*. G. P. Putnams's Sons, 1967. Copyright © 1967 Harriet R. O'Donovan. All rights reserved. Reprinted by permission of Joan Daves.

Oliphant, Mrs. From *The Literary History of England in the End of the Eighteenth and Beginning of the Nineteenth Century, Vol. III*. Macmillan and Co., 1886.

Onasch, Konrad. From "The Death of Marmeladov," translated by Robert Louis Jackson, in *Twentieth Century Interpretations of "Crime and Punishment:" A Collection of Critical Essays*. Edited by Robert Louis Jackson. Prentice-Hall, 1974. © 1974 by Prentice-Hall, Inc. All rights reserved. Reprinted by permission of Prentice-Hall, Inc., Englewood Cliffs, NJ 07632.

Osmond, Nicholas. From "Rhetoric and Self-Expression in Romantic Poetry," in *French Literature and Its Background*. Edited by John Cruickshank. Oxford University Press, London, 1969. © Oxford University Press 1969. Reprinted by permission of Oxford University Press.

Ossoli, Margaret Fuller. From *Memoirs of Margaret Fuller Ossoli, Vol. I*. W. H. Channing, R. W. Emerson, J. F. Clarke, eds. Phillips, Sampson and Company, 1852.

Parrington, Vernon Louis. From *The Colonial Mind: 1620-1800*. Harcourt Brace and Company, 1927.

Parrington, Vernon Louis. From *Main Currents in American Thought, an Interpretation of American Literature from the Beginnings to 1920: The Romantic Revolution in America, 1800-1860, Vol. 2*. Harcourt Brace Jovanovich, 1927. Copyright 1927 by Harcourt Brace Jovanovich, Inc. Copyright 1955 by Vernon L. Parrington, Jr., Louise P. Tucker, Elizabeth P. Thomas. All rights reserved. Reprinted by permission of the publisher.

Phillips, Wendell. From a letter to Frederick Douglass on April 22, 1845, in *Narrative of the Life of Frederick Douglass, an American Slave*. By Frederick Douglass. n.p., 1845.

Pierson, George Wilson. From *Tocqueville and Beaumont in America*. Oxford University Press, 1938. Copyright by George Wilson Pierson. Reprinted by permission of the author.

Poulet, Georges. From *Studies in Human Time*. Translated by Elliott Coleman. Johns Hopkins University Press, 1956. © 1956, The Johns Hopkins Press, Baltimore 18, MD. Reprinted by permission.

Pritchett, V. S. From *The Living Novel & Later Appreciations*. Revised edition. Random House, 1964. Copyright © 1975 by V. S. Pritchett. All rights reserved. Reprinted by permission of Literistic, Ltd.

Pushkin, Alexander. From "On Alfred de Musset," in *The Critical Prose of Alexander Pushkin, with Critical Essays by Four Russian Romantic Poets*. Edited and translated by Carl R. Proffer. Indiana University Press, 1969. Copyright © 1969 by Indiana University Press. Reprinted by permission.

Quarles, Benjamin. From an introduction to *Narrative of the Life and Times of Frederick Douglass, an American Slave*. By Frederick Douglass, edited by Benjamin Quarles. Cambridge, Mass.: Belknap Press, 1960. Copyright © 1960 by the President and Fellows of Harvard College. Excerpted by permission.

Quinn, Arthur Hobson. From *A History of the American Drama: From the Beginning to the Civil War*. Second edition. F. S. Crofts & Co., 1943. Copyright 1923, 1943, 1951 by Arthur Hobson Quinn. And renewed 1971 by Arthur Hobson Quinn, Jr. Reprinted by permission of the Estate of Helen McKee Quinn.

Read, Herbert. From *The Tenth Muse: Essays in Criticism*. Routledge & Kegan Paul, 1957. © by Herbert Read. Reprinted by permission of Routledge & Kegan Paul PLC.

Redding, J. Saunders. From *To Make a Poet Black*. University of North Carolina Press, 1939.

Rexroth, Kenneth. From *The Elastic Retort: Essays in Literature and Ideas*. The Continuum Publishing Company, 1973. Copyright © 1973 by Kenneth Rexroth. Used by permission of Bradford Morrow for The Kenneth Rexroth Trust.

Richter, Jean Paul Friedrich. From "Letter to My Friends," in *German Romance: Hoffmann, Richter, Vol. II*. Edited and translated by Thomas Carlyle. n.p., 1827.

Ripley, George. From *Pertaining to Thoreau*. Edited by S. A. Jones. E. B. Hill, 1901.

Robb, Nesca A. From *Four in Exile*. Hutchinson & Co. (Publishers) Ltd., 1948. Reprinted by permission.

Rogers, Nathaniel Peabody. From *A Collection from the Newspaper Writings of Nathaniel Peabody Rogers*. John R. French, 1847.

Rubow, Paul V. From "Idea and Form in Hans Christian Andersen's Fairy Tales," in *A Book on the Danish Writer, Hans Christian Andersen: His Life and Work*. Edited by Svend Dahl and H. G. Topsøe-Jensen, translated by W. Glyn Jones. Det Berlingske Bogtrykkeri, 1955. Reprinted by permission.

Ruffin, George L. From an introduction to *Life and Times of Frederick Douglass*. By Frederick Douglass. Revised edition. De Wolfe, Fiske & Co., 1892.

Sackville-West, Edward. From *Inclinations*. Martin Secker & Warburg Ltd., 1949. Reprinted by permission.

Sainte-Beuve, Charles Augustine. From *Essays by Sainte-Beuve*. Edited and translated by Elizabeth Lee. Walter Scott, Ltd., 1910. Reprinted by permission.

Saintsbury, George. From *A History of Criticism and Literary Taste in Europe from the Earliest Texts to the Present Day: Modern Criticism, Vol. III*. William Blackwood & Sons Ltd., 1904.

Saintsbury, George. From *A History of the French Novel (to the Close of the 19th Century): From 1800 to 1900, Vol. II*. Macmillan and Co., Limited, 1917.

Scott, Sir Walter. From a journal entry on March 13, 1828, in *The Journal of Sir Walter Scott*. Edited by John Guthrie Tait. Revised edition. Oliver and Boyd, 1950. Reprinted by permission of the Literary Estate of John Guthrie Tait.

Scudder, Horace E. From *Childhood in Literature and Art*. Houghton, Mifflin Company, 1894.

Shaw, Bernard. From *Dramatic Opinions and Essays with an Apology, Vol. 2*. Brentano's, 1906. Copyright in United States of America by Brentano's 1906, 1907. Reprinted by permission of The Society of Authors on behalf of the Bernard Shaw Estate.

Sices, David. From *The Theater of Solitude: The Drama of Alfred de Musset*. The University Press of New England, 1974. Copyright © 1974 by David Sices. Reprinted by permission.

Simmons, Ernest J. From *Dostoevsky: The Making of a Novelist*. Vintage Books, 1940.

Smeed, J. W. From *Jean Paul's "Dreams"*. Oxford University Press, London, 1966. © University of Durham 1966. Reprinted by permission of Oxford University Press.

Smeed, J. W. From "Jean Paul," in *German Men of Letters: Twelve Literary Essays, Vol. V*. Edited by Alex Natan. Wolff, 1969. © 1969 Oswald Wolff (Publishers) Limited, London. Reprinted by permission.

Smith, Hugh Allison. From *Main Currents of Modern French Drama*. Henry Holt and Company, 1925.

Smith, James M'Cune. From an introduction to *My Bondage and My Freedom*. By Frederick Douglass. Miller, Orton & Mulligan, 1855.

Staël-Holstein, Madame the Baroness de. From *Germany, Vol. II*. Houghton Mifflin and Company, 1887.

Stein, Richard L. From *The Ritual of Interpretation: The Fine Arts As Literature in Ruskin, Rossetti, and Pater*. Cambridge, Mass.: Harvard University Press, 1975. Copyright © 1975 by the President and Fellows of Harvard College. All rights reserved. Excerpted by permission.

Stepto, Robert B. From *From Behind the Veil: A Study of Afro-American Narrative*. University of Illinois Press, 1979. © 1979 by the Board of Trustees of the University of Illinois. Reprinted by permission of the author and the University of Illinois Press.

Stevenson, Robert Louis. From *Familiar Studies of Men and Books*. Second edition. Chatto & Windus, 1886.

Stevenson, Robert Louis. From a letter to John Addington Symonds in Spring, 1886, in *The Letters of Robert Louis Stevenson: 1880-1887, Alps and Highlands—Hyères—Bournemouth, Vol. II*. Edited by Sidney Colvin. Revised edition. Charles Scribner's Sons, 1911.

Strakhov, N. From an extract of "The Nihilists and Raskolnikov's New Idea," translated by George Gibian, in *"Crime and Punishment" by Feodor Dostoevsky, A Norton Critical Edition: The Coulson Translation, Backgrounds and Sources, Essays in Criticism*. Edited by George Gibian. Revised edition. Norton, 1975. Copyright © 1975, 1964 by W. W. Norton & Company, Inc. Reprinted by permission of W. W. Norton & Company, Inc.

Symons, Arthur. From *Figures of Several Centuries*. Constable and Company Ltd., 1916. Reprinted by permission of the Literary Estate of Arthur Symons.

Thibaudet, Albert. From *French Literature from 1795 to Our Era*. Translated by Charles Lam Markmann. Funk & Wagnalls Company, 1968. English translation copyright © 1967 by Harper & Row, Publishers, Inc. All rights reserved. By permission of Harper & Row, Publishers, Inc.

Thomas, Edward. From *Walter Pater: A Critical Study*. Mitchell Kennerley, 1913.

Tilley, Arthur. From *Three French Dramatists: Racine, Marivaux, Musset*. Cambridge at the University Press, 1933. Reprinted by permission of the Cambridge University Press.

Tocqueville, Alexis de. From a letter to Eugène Stoffels on February 21, 1835, in *Memoir, Letters, and Remains of Alexis de Tocqueville, Vol. 1*. Edited by M.C.M. Simpson, translated by Gustave de Beaumont. Revised edition. Macmillan and Co., 1861.

Turnell, Martin. From an introduction to *Germinie*. By Edmond de Goncourt and Jules de Goncourt. Grove Press, 1955. Reprinted by permission of Grove Press, Inc.

Tyler, Moses Coit. From *The Literary History of the American Revolution, 1763-1783: 1776-1783, Vol. II*. G. P. Putnam's Sons, 1897.

Van Doren, Carl. From *The American Novel*. Macmillan, 1921. Copyright 1921 by Macmillan Publishing Co., Inc. Copyright renewed 1949 by Carl Van Doren. Reprinted with permission of Macmillan Publishing Company.

Van Doren, Mark. From *Henry David Thoreau: A Critical Study*. Houghton Mifflin, 1916. Copyright, 1916, by Mark Van Doren. All rights reserved. Reprinted by permission of Dorothy Van Doren.

Wasiolek, Edward. From *Dostoevsky: The Major Fiction*. The M.I.T. Press, 1964. Copyright © 1964 by The Massachusetts Institute of Technology. All rights reserved. Reprinted by permission.

Wellek, René. From *A History of Modern Criticism, 1750-1950: The Romantic Age, Vol. 2*. Yale University Press, 1955. All rights reserved. Copyright, 1955, by Yale University Press. Reprinted by permission.

Wellek, René. From *A History of Modern Criticism, 1750-1950: The Later Nineteenth Century, Vol. 4*. Yale University Press, 1965. Copyright © 1965 by Yale University. All rights reserved. Reprinted by permission.

West, Rebecca. From "Elizabeth Montagu," in *From Anne to Victoria: Essays By Various Hands*. Edited by Bonamy Dobrée. Cassell and Company Limited, 1937. Reprinted by permission.

Whitman, Walt. From *With Walt Whitman in Camden, Vol. I*. By Horace Traubel. Small, Maynard & Company, 1906.

Yeats, W. B. From an introduction to *The Oxford Book of Modern Verse: 1892-1935*. Edited by W. B. Yeats. Oxford at the Claredon Press, Oxford, 1936. Copyright © 1936 by Oxford University Press, New York, Inc. And renewed 1964 by Bertha Georgie Yeats. Reprinted by permission of Oxford University Press, Oxford, England.

Yeats, W. B. From *Representative Irish Tales*. Edited by W. B. Yeats. Humanities Press, Inc., 1979. Reprinted by permission of Anne Yeats, Michael B. Yeats and Macmillan London, Ltd.

Zola, Émile. From *The Experimental Novel and Other Essays*. Translated by Belle M. Sherman. Cassell, 1894. Copyright, 1893, by Cassell Publishing Company. Reprinted with permission of Macmillan Publishing Company.